Environmental Ethics
Readings in Theory and Application

Second Edition

Louis P. Pojman

United States Military Academy

Wadsworth Publishing Company

I(T)P® An International Thomson Publishing Company

Belmont, CA • Albany, NY • Bonn • Boston • Cincinnati • Detroit
Johannesburg • London • Madrid • Melbourne • Mexico City
New York • Paris • Singapore • Tokyo • Toronto • Washington

Philosophy Editor: *Peter Adams*
Assistant Editor: *Kerri Abdinoor*
Editorial Assistant: *Kelly Bush*
Marketing Manager: *Dave Garrison*
Project Editor: *John Walker*
Production: *Ruth Cottrell*
Print Buyer: *Stacey Weinberger*
Permissions Editor: *Robert Kauser*
Designer: *Ellen Pettengell*
Copy Editor: *Betty Duncan*
Cover Designer: *Margarite Reynolds*
Cover Image: *PhotoDisc*
Compositor: *Key West Publication Services*
Printer: *Maple-Vail Book Manufacturing Group*

Printed in the United States of America
1 2 3 4 5 6 7 8 9 10

For more information, contact Wadsworth Publishing Company, 10 Davis Drive, Belmont, CA 94002,
or electronically at http://www.thomson.com/wadsworth.html

International Thomson Publishing Europe
Berkshire House 168-173
High Holborn
London, WC1V 7AA, England

Thomas Nelson Australia
102 Dodds Street
South Melbourne
Victoria, Australia

Nelson Canada
1120 Birchmount Road
Scarborough, Ontario
Canada M1K 5G4

International Thomson Publishing GmbH
Königswinterer Strasse 418
53227 Bonn, Germany

International Thomson Editores
Campos Eliseos 385, Piso 7
Col. Polanco
11560 México D.F. México

International Thomson Publishing Asia
221 Henderson Road
#05-10 Henderson Building
Singapore 0315

International Thomson Publishing Japan
Hirakawacho Kyowa Building, 3F
2-2-1 Hirakawacho
Chiyoda-ku, Tokyo 102, Japan

International Thomson Publishing
Southern Africa
Building 18, Constantia Park
240 Old Pretoria Road
Halfway House, 1685 South Africa

Library of Congress Cataloging-in-Publication Data

Pojman, Louis P.
    Environmental ethics : readings in theory and application / Louis
P. Pojman — 2nd ed.
        p.   cm.
    ISBN 0-534-54469-X
    1. Environmental ethics. I. Title
GE42.E58   1997   97-43410
179'.1—dc21

 This book is printed on acid-free recycled paper.

Dedicated to Ruth and Brian

Contents

Preface

When I became interested in environmental ethics in the late 1970s, few articles and books existed in that area. I remember searching through journals for relevant articles, usually without much success. Not many environmental ethics courses (I knew of none) were being offered in the late 1970s when I requested permission from my university to offer such a course. My colleagues questioned whether there was a need for such a "soft," non-traditional course and whether enough material existed to put a syllabus together. Eventually, it was approved on an experimental basis. In my first courses, I relied heavily on Aldo Leopold's *Sand County Almanac*, Ian Barbour's *Western Man and Environmental Ethics*, and John Passmore's *Man's Responsibility to Nature*. The rest of my course was made up from texts in ecology, such as Charles and Penelope Revelle's *The Environment* and G. Tyler Miller's *Living in the Environment*.

Today, some 20 years later, environmental ethics is a burgeoning field. Courses in this subject are taught in most universities in the United States, and books and articles appear almost weekly. The journal *Environmental Ethics* was started by Eugene Hargrove in 1979 and has widespread circulation. Virtually every meeting of the American Philosophical Association has a whole series of papers and programs devoted to the subject. Keeping up with the literature is difficult.

When I put together the first edition of this work some four years ago, no comprehensive anthology existed. Although that has changed and other fine anthologies have appeared, I think this one combines theory and practical concerns in a particularly balanced and comprehensive manner. Theory and practice cannot be separated. To paraphrase Immanuel Kant: Theory without practice is sterile; practice without theory is blind.

Environmental Ethics: Readings in Theory and Application is intended as a comprehensive, balanced introduction to the field of environmental ethics for undergraduate students. It covers both environmental theory and practical application. Here is a list of the subjects covered.

Part One: Theory
1. Western Philosophy of Nature: The Roots of Our Ecological Crisis
2. Animal Rights
3. Does Nature Have Intrinsic Value? Biocentric and Ecocentric Ethics and Deep Ecology
4. Ecofeminism
5. The Gaia Hypothesis and Biospheric Ethics
6. Preservation of Species, Nature, and Natural Objects
7. Non-Western Perspectives on Environmental Ethics
8. Obligations to Future Generations

Part Two: Application
9. Population: General Considerations
10. Population and World Hunger
11. Pollution: General Considerations
12. Pesticides
13. Atmospheric Conditions: The Greenhouse Effect and the Ozone Layer
14. Are We Conquering Hazardous Waste?
15. Should We Revive Nuclear Power?
16. Economics and the Environment
17. From Dysfunctional to Sustainable Society

Epilogue: The Rio Declaration (1992)

The instructor need not follow my format. Different instructors will want to emphasize different aspects. I've varied course outlines from semester to semester, sometimes emphasizing the theoretical, sometimes the applied part of environmental ethics. There is enough material in this work for three or four semesters.

This anthology includes subjects not usually offered in environmental books, such as the Gaia hypothesis, non-Western perspectives, and immigration. World hunger is not usually put into an environmental ethics book, but I consider it part of the population and resource problems. What is our responsibility to distant people? Should we share our surplus resources with them even when it appears that they have gone beyond the carrying capacity of their environment? The world hunger problem also illustrates my belief that environmental ethics is a global issue, not merely a state or national problem. A growing interdependence is emerging in the world. For example, air pollution from a distant nation can affect us, by causing global warming, the depletion of the ozone layer, or the spread of radiation.

This second edition has an introduction to ethics ("What Is Ethics?") and thirteen more articles than the first edition. I have added a section to Chapter 3 entitled "Does Nature Have Intrinsic Value?" and have included a lively debate by Holmes Rolston, III, and Ernest Partridge, including two responses written for this edition. I have included Kenneth Goodpaster's article "On Being Morally Considerable" in the section "Biocentric Ethics" and Murray Bookchin's essay "Social Ecology Versus Deep Ecology" and a new essay by James Sterba, "Environmental Justice," in the section "Deep Ecology." In Chapter 6, "Preservation of Species, Nature, and Natural Objects," I have added Martin Krieger's "What's Wrong with Plastic Trees?" together with Eric Katz's response to it, "The Call of the Wild." In Chapter 8, "Obligations to Future Generations," Derek Parfit's seminal "Energy Policy and the Further Future" is now included.

In Part Two, "Application," I have commissioned Lindsey Grant to write an essay on the ethics of immigration. This will balance Jacqueline Kasun's opposing article. In Chapter 10, "Population and World Hunger," I have added an essay from the *Washington Spectator* on the ecological damage done by cattle. In Chapter 12, "Pesticides," I have included Michael Fumento's revealing essay that argues against what he sees as extremism in the environmental movement. In Chapter 16, "Economics and the Environment," Kristin Shrader-Frechette has been commissioned to write an important essay on risk assessment. In the final chapter, "From Dysfunctional to Sustainable Society," I have added "Environmental Risks, Rights, and the Failure of Liberal Democracy" by Laura Westra and "Environmental Ethics and Democracy" by Eugene Hargrove.

Using a dialogic format (pro and con), I have endeavored to present different and conflicting views on each major issue in this book. Each of the seventeen chapters has a general introduction to the subject debated therein, and each article has an introductory abstract. Study questions follow each reading, and sug-gested further readings follow each chapter. Of the eighty-four readings, eleven have been commissioned for this work (five for the first edition and six more for this second edition). I have chosen the best argued, clearest, and most accessible articles on each issue that I could find.

Several people helped me in this endeavor. For the first edition: Eugene Hargrove, Baird Callicott, John Jagger, Garret Hardin, Art Bartlett, Lynn Margulis, Andrea Donlon, Leslie Francis, and Robert Ginsberg offered helpful advice along the way. For the second edition: Kendall D'Andrade, Eric Katz, Bill Throop, Laura Westra, and Art and Nancy Bartlett provided excellent advice for improving this work.

Students in various environmental ethics classes provided a testing ground for many of these readings. Of special note are David Brown, David Ley, Scott McAuley, Catherine Parrish, Michael Tobin, Marshall Smith, and Fred Wallace. Ruth Cottrell did a splendid job taking this work through production. Most of all, my wife Trudy argued with me about many of the ideas in this work and forced me to change my views on a number of issues. She read through the whole manuscript, making cogent comments and constructive criticisms. This edition is dedicated to my daughter Ruth Freedom and her husband Brian Kemple, two young people whose dedication to global peace and justice exemplify the spirit of this work. Most of the royalties of this work have been donated to environmental organizations.

Louis P. Pojman
United States Military Academy
June 17, 1997

On Ethics and Environmental Concerns

Human beings have lived on Earth for about 100,000 years, a very short time in relation to the age of the universe (15 billion years) or even to the life of our planet (4.6 billion years). Civilization developed only 10,000 years ago, and the wheel was invented 4,000 years ago. If we compact the history of Earth into a movie lasting 1 year, running 146 years per second, life would not appear until March, multicellular organisms not until November, dinosaurs not until December 13 (lasting until the 26th), mammals not until December 15, *Homo sapiens* (our species) not until eleven minutes to midnight, and civilization one minute ago. Yet in a very short time, say less than 200 years, a mere .000002% of Earth's life, humans have become capable of seriously altering the entire biosphere. In some respects, we have already altered it more profoundly than it has changed in the past *billion* years. Paraphrasing Winston Churchill's remark about the British air force during World War II, we may say, "Never have so few done so much in so short a time." In the last 100 years or so, we have invented electricity, the light bulb, the telephone, cinema, radio, television, the automobile, the airplane, the spaceship, the refrigerator, the air conditioner, the skyscraper, antibiotics, heart transplant machines, the birth control pill, the microwave oven, the atom bomb, nuclear energy, and the digital computer Through the wonders of science and technology, we have enabled millions of people over the face of Earth to live with more freedom, power, and knowledge than our ancestors could dream of. Only in science fiction were the wonders of modern life even hinted at.

Yet with this new freedom, power, and knowledge has come a dark side. The automobile kills hundreds of thousands of people throughout the world each year (more Americans have died in automobile accidents than on all the battlefields in all the wars our nation has fought). It produces chemical pollution that degrades the atmosphere, causing cancer, and is bringing on dangerous global warming, the greenhouse effect. Refrigerators and air conditioners enable us to preserve food and live comfortably in hot seasons and climates, but they also use chlorofluorocarbons (CFCs), which rise into the stratosphere and deplete the thin ozone layer that protects us from harmful ultraviolet radiation. The result is an increase in skin cancer, especially melanoma, and harmful effects on plankton, which forms the base of much of the food chain of marine animals. Nuclear power could provide safe, inexpensive energy to the world, but instead it has been used to exterminate cities and threaten a global holocaust. Disasters like the nuclear plant steam explosion at Chernobyl in the former Soviet Union have spread harmful radiation over thousands of square miles and cause public distrust of the nuclear power industry. Nuclear waste piles up with no solution in sight. But our modern way of life does require energy, lots of it. So we burn fossil fuels, especially coal, which, unbeknownst to the public at large, is probably more dangerous than nuclear energy, causing more cancer, polluting the air with sulfur dioxide, and producing acid rain, which is destroying our rivers and lakes and killing trees. Medical science found cures for tuberculosis and syphilis and has aided in greatly lowering infant mortality, but in the process we have allowed an exponential growth of the population to produce crowded cities and put a strain on our resources. The more people, the more energy needed; the more energy produced, the more pollution; the more pollution, the more our lives are threatened by disease.

And so the story goes. For each blessing of modern technology, a corresponding risk comes into being, as the tail of the same coin. With each new invention comes frightful responsibility. It is hard to get it right. It's hard to live moderately, wisely, and frugally; it's hard to conserve our resources so that posterity will get a fair share.

Environmental ethics concerns itself with these global concerns: humanity's relationship to the environment, its understanding of and responsibility to nature, and its obligations to leave some of nature's resources to posterity. Pollution, population control, resource use, food production and distribution, energy production and consumption, the preservation of the wilderness and of species diversity—all fall under its purview. It asks comprehensive, global questions, develops metaphysical theories, and applies its principles to the daily lives of men and women everywhere on Earth.

In this work we consider readings in both environmental theory and practice. Treating "Theory" first (Part 1), we'll focus on the debate over the causes of our environmental crisis. To what extent has our Judeo-Christian religious tradition contributed to the present crisis? Has our religious heritage created a dangerous sense of alienation by emphasizing the domination of nature by humanity? Or is Western technology the primary culprit? We begin our first chapter with the first three chapters from the Book of Genesis, the source of Judeo-Christian attitudes toward creation. Then we enter the controversy as to whether our religious tradition or technology is the cause of our environmental malaise.

Next, in Chapter 2 we examine rival theories on the locus of intrinsic value, especially in regard to the wider animal kingdom What makes something valuable or morally considerable? Is it being human or rationally self-conscious, as Kant and most Western "anthropocentric" philosophers have held, or is it *sentience*, the ability to have experiences and, specifically, to suffer? What are our duties to animals, who are sentient, but (for the most part) not rationally self-conscious?

In Chapter 3 we go beyond rationality and sentience and inquire whether nature itself has intrinsic value. Do we need a broader environmental ethic that incorporates nature as a good in itself? Several theories are treated here: biocentric ethics, ecocentric ethics, and deep ecology.

In Chapter 4 we examine ecofeminism, the theory that joins feminism with radical eccentric ethics, claiming that the model of patriarchal dominance is the main source of the oppression of both nature and women.

In Chapter 5 we consider the Gaia (pronounced GUY-uh) hypothesis, the theory that Earth is a single, interactive, self-regulating, organism.

In Chapter 6 we examine the value of endangered species, the wilderness, and natural objects and consider both the moral, aesthetic, and institutional recognition of these objects (e.g., granting trees and ecosystems legal rights).

In Chapter 7 we go beyond Western horizons and view environmental ethics through non-Western eyes and theories. Environmental concerns are global concerns, so we must learn to see issues from various cultural and national perspectives. Our readings present viewpoints from Nigeria, Kenya, Ceylon, India, and the Arab world.

In Chapter 8 we take up the difficult philosophical issue of responsibility to future generations. Do we, and if so, on what basis do we have responsibilities to those not yet born? Most moral theory holds that obligations only hold toward concrete individuals, so how can we have duties to nonexistent entities?

In Part 2, "Applications," we turn to practical concerns. First (Chapter 9) to population growth: How serious is the rapidly growing global population?

Doomsdayers claim it is the number one problem. The more people we produce, the more resources we will use up, and hence the more pollution that will be produced. Doomsdayers predict that decreasing resources and increasing pollution will make life unbearable for future generations. On the other hand, the optimistic Cornucopians argue that population is nowhere near a serious problem. They say that we have the resources to accommodate reasonable needs if only we all live morally. If we distribute our resources justly, there will be enough for all and plenty more.

The debate over population comes to a head in Chapter 10 where we discuss whether we should feed the world's poor. Doomsdayers like Garrett Hardin argue that feeding the poor in an overcrowded world is like feeding a cancer. If we are to survive, we must use tough love, however hard it may be. Others disagree and argue that we can both help the starving and solve our demographic problems.

After a short debate on the relationship between population and pollution in Chapter 11, we turn to the problem of pollution itself, to its causes, effects, and types. The next three chapters deal with issues related to pollution. Should we use pesticides, herbicides, and chemical fertilizers? On the one hand, by doing so, we have been able to increase food production enormously. On the other hand, such practices have created life-threatening pollution. We also consider the debate over acid rain and the greenhouse effect.

In Chapter 15 we consider the troubling matter of disposing of hazardous waste, which is piling up at an alarming rate and threatening our soil and water and the people who use them.

In Chapter 16 we examine the debate over nuclear energy. No one seriously questions that coal-burning power plants emit dangerous pollutants (sulfur dioxide, carbon dioxide, methane, nitrogen oxide, and particulates), but what is the alternative? Although the disaster of Chernobyl has dampened the debate over nuclear power, many scientists contend that it can be made safe and play a vital role in future energy policies. Other scientists and ecologists argue that nuclear power is a dangerous Faustian bargain, which we should reject.

In Chapter 17 we examine the relationship between economics and the environment. Can the entire panoply of our value assessments be reduced to economic cost–benefit analysis? Is the classical free-market view of economics an adequate guide for protecting the environment? Or, do we need a new more socialist or nature-centered approach?

In the last chapter, we look at some practical ways we can work to maintain a sustainable, ecologically responsible society. For instance, what should we do about the powerful tool of advertising, which helps fuel the consumer society, a society that is environmentally harmful? Should we de-emphasize automobile transport and instead support mass transport and bicycle use? How can we get beyond a throwaway, nationalistic society to a recycling, sustainable, global society?

We cannot cover every environmental theory or issue in this anthology, but you will have many vital intellectual and practical issues to keep you thinking and acting for a long time. I hope the challenging readings will provoke you to be more informed, to think more deeply, and to act morally in the quest for a better environment.

It's your world—to save or lose.

What Is Ethics?

We are discussing no small matter, but how we ought to live.

SOCRATES IN PLATO'S *REPUBLIC*

What is it to be a moral person? What is the nature of morality, and why do we need it? What is the good, and how will I know it? Are moral principles absolute or simply relative to social groups or individual decision? Is it in my interest to be moral? Is it sometimes in my best interest to act immorally? What is the relationship between morality and religion? What is the relationship between morality and law? What is the relationship between morality and etiquette?

These are some of the questions that we will be looking at in this introductory essay. We want to understand the foundation and structure of morality. We want to know how we should live. The terms *moral* and *ethics* come from Latin and Greek, respectively (*mores* and *ethos*), deriving their meaning from the idea of custom. Although philosophers sometimes distinguish between these terms, I use these terms interchangeably, permitting the context to show various meanings.

Ethics, or moral philosophy, refers to the systematic endeavor to understand moral concepts and justify moral principles and theories. It undertakes to analyze such concepts as "right," "wrong," "permissible," "ought," "good," and "evil" in their moral contexts. Ethics seeks to establish principles of right behavior that may serve as action guides for individuals and groups. It investigates which values and virtues are paramount to the worthwhile life or society. It builds and scrutinizes arguments in ethical theories, and it seeks to discover valid principles (e.g., "Never kill innocent human beings") and the relationship between those principles (e.g., "Does saving a life in some situations constitute a valid reason for breaking a promise?").

ETHICS AS COMPARED WITH OTHER NORMATIVE SUBJECTS

Moral precepts are concerned with norms; roughly speaking they are concerned not with what is but with what *ought* to be. How should I live my life? What is the right thing to do in this situation? Should one always tell the truth? Do I have a duty to report a fellow student whom I have seen cheating in class? Should I tell my friend that his spouse is having an affair? Is premarital sex morally permissible? Ought a woman ever to have an abortion? Ethics has a distinct action guiding or *normative* aspect,[1] an aspect it shares with other practical institutions such as religion, law, and etiquette.

Moral behavior, as defined by a given religion, is often held to be essential to the practice of that religion. But neither the practices nor precepts of morality should be identified with religion. The practice of morality need not be motivated by religious considerations. And moral precepts need not be grounded in revelation or divine authority—as religious teachings invariably are. The most salient characteristic of ethics is that it is grounded in reason and human experience.

To use a spatial metaphor, secular ethics are horizontal, omitting a vertical or transcendental dimension. Religious ethics has a vertical dimension, being grounded in revelation or divine authority, though generally using reason to supplement or complement revelation. These two differing orientations will often generate different moral principles and standards of evaluation, but they need not. Some versions of religious ethics, which posit God's revelation of the moral law in nature or conscience, hold that reason can discover what is right or wrong even apart from divine revelation.

Morality is also closely related to law, and some people equate the two practices. Many laws are instituted in order to promote well-being, resolve conflicts of interest and/or social harmony, just as morality does, but ethics may judge that some laws are immoral without denying that they are valid laws. For example, laws may permit slavery or irrelevant discrimination against people on the basis of race or sex. A Catholic or antiabortionist may believe that the laws permitting abortion are immoral.

In the television series *Ethics in America* (PBS, 1989), James Neal, a trial lawyer, was asked what he would do if he discovered that his client had committed a murder some years back for which another man had been convicted and would soon be executed.

Mr. Neal said that he had a legal obligation to keep this information confidential and that if he divulged it, he would be disbarred. It is arguable that he has a moral obligation that overrides his legal obligation and that demands he take action to protect the innocent man from being executed.

Furthermore, some aspects of morality are not covered by law. For example, though it is generally agreed that lying is usually immoral, there is no general law against it (except under special conditions, such as in cases of perjury or falsifying income tax returns). Sometimes college newspapers publish advertisements for "research assistance," where it is known in advance that the companies will aid and abet plagiarism. The publishing of such research paper ads is legal, but it is doubtful whether it is morally correct. In 1963, thirty-nine people in Queens, New York, watched from their apartments for some forty-five minutes as a man beat up a woman, Kitty Genovese, and did nothing to intervene, not even call the police. These people broke no law, but they were very likely morally culpable for not calling the police or shouting at the assailant.

One other major difference exists between law and morality. In 1351 King Edward of England promulgated a law against treason that made it a crime merely to think homicidal thoughts about the king. But, alas, the law could not be enforced, for not even a tribunal can search the heart and fathom the intentions of the mind. It is true that *intention*, such as malice aforethought, plays a role in the legal process in determining the legal character of the act, once the act has been committed. But preemptive punishment for people presumed to have bad intentions is illegal. If malicious intentions (called in law *mens rea*) were criminally illegal, would we not all deserve imprisonment? Even if it were possible to detect intentions, when should the punishment be administered? As soon as the subject has the intention? But how do we know that he will not change his mind? Furthermore, is there not a continuum between imagining some harm to X, wishing a harm to X, desiring a harm to X, and intending a harm to X?

Though it is impractical to have laws against bad intentions, these intentions are still bad, still morally wrong. Suppose I buy a gun with the intention of killing Uncle Charlie in order to inherit his wealth, but I never get a chance to fire it (e.g., Uncle Charlie moves to Australia). I have not committed a crime, but I have committed a moral wrong.

Finally, law differs from morality in that physical and financial sanctions[2] (e.g., imprisonment and fines) enforce the law but only the sanction of conscience and reputation enforces morality.

Morality also differs from etiquette, which concerns form and style rather than the essence of social existence. Etiquette determines what is polite behavior rather than what is *right* behavior in a deeper sense. It represents society's decision about how we are to dress, greet one another, eat, celebrate festivals, dispose of the dead, express gratitude and appreciation, and, in general, carry out social transactions. Whether we greet each other with a handshake, a bow, a hug, or a kiss on the cheek will differ in different social systems, uncover our heads in holy places (as males do in Christian churches) or cover them (as females do in Catholic churches and males do in synagogues), none of these rituals has any moral superiority.

People in Russia wear their wedding rings on the third finger of their right hand, whereas we wear them on our left hands. People in England hold their fork in their left hand when they eat, people in other countries hold it in either their right or left hand, while people in India typically eat without a fork at all, using the forefingers of their right hand for conveying food from their plate to their mouth.

Polite manners grace our social existence, but they are not what social existence is about. They help social transactions to flow smoothly but are not the substance of those transactions.

At the same time, it can be immoral to disregard or flout etiquette. The decision whether to shake hands when greeting a person for the first time or putting one's hands together and forward as one bows, as people in India do, is a matter of cultural decision. Once the custom is adopted, however, the practice takes on the importance of a moral rule, subsumed under the wider principle of Show Respect to People. Similarly, there is no moral necessity of wearing clothes, but we have adopted the custom partly to keep us warm in colder climates and partly out of modesty. But there is nothing wrong with nudists who decide to live together naked in nudist colonies. But, it may well be the case that people running nude outside nudist colonies—say, in classrooms, stores, and along the road—would constitute such offensive behavior as to count as morally insensitive. Recently, there was a scandal on the beaches of South India where American tourists swam in bikinis, shocking the more modest Indians. There was nothing immoral in itself about wearing bikinis, but given the cultural context, the Americans, in willfully violating etiquette, were guilty of moral impropriety.

Although Americans pride themselves on tolerance, pluralism, and awareness of other cultures, custom and etiquette can be—even among people from similar backgrounds—a bone of contention. A friend of mine, John, tells of an experience early in his marriage. He and his wife, Gwen, were hosting their first Thanksgiving meal. He had been used to small celebrations with his immediate family, whereas his wife had been used to grand celebrations. He writes, "I had been asked to carve, something I had never done before, but I was willing. I put on an apron, entered the kitchen, and attacked the bird with as much artistry as I could muster. And what reward did I get? [My wife] burst into tears. In *her* family the turkey is brought to the *table*, laid before the [father], grace is said, and *then* he carves! 'So I fail patriarchy,' I hollered later. 'What do you expect?'"[3]

Law, etiquette, and religion are all important institutions, but each has limitations. The limitation of the law is that you can't have a law against every social malady nor can you enforce every desirable rule. The limitation of etiquette is that it doesn't get to the heart of what is of vital importance for personal and social existence. Whether or not one eats with one's fingers pales in significance compared with the importance of being honest or trustworthy or just. Etiquette is a cultural invention, but morality claims to be a discovery.

The limitation of the religious injunction is that it rests on authority, and we are not always sure of or in agreement about the credentials of the authority, nor on how the authority would rule in ambiguous or new cases. Since religion is not founded on reason but on revelation, you cannot use reason to convince someone who does not share your religious views that your view is the right one. I hasten to add that, when moral differences are caused by fundamental moral principles, it is unlikely that philosophical reasoning will settle the matter. Often, however, our moral differences turn out to be rooted in worldviews, not moral principles. For example, the antiabortionist and pro-choicer often agree that it is wrong to kill innocent persons but differ on the facts. The antiabortionist may hold a religious view stating that the fetus has an eternal soul and thus possesses a right to life, whereas the pro-choicer may deny that anyone has a soul and hold that only self-conscious, rational beings have rights to life.

Table 1 characterizes the relationship between ethics, religion, etiquette, and law.

In summary, morality distinguishes itself from law and etiquette by going deeper into the essence of rational existence. It distinguishes itself from religion in that it seeks reasons, rather than authority, to justify its principles. The central purpose of moral philosophy is to secure valid principles of conduct and values that can be instrumental in guiding human actions and producing good character. As such, it is the most important activity known to humans, for it has to do with how we are to live.

DOMAINS OF ETHICAL ASSESSMENT

It might seem at this point that ethics concerns itself entirely with rules of conduct based solely on an evaluation of acts. However, the situation is more complicated than this. There are four domains of ethical assessment:

DOMAIN	EVALUATIVE Terms
1. Action, the act	Right, wrong, obligatory, permissible
2. Consequences	Good, bad, indifferent
3. Character	Virtuous, vicious, neutral
4. Motive	Good will, evil will, neutral

Let's examine each of these domains.

Types of Action. The most common distinction may be the classification of actions as right and wrong, but the term *right* is ambiguous. Sometimes it means "obligatory" (as in "*the* right act"), but sometimes it means permissible (as in "*a* right act"). Usually, philosophers define *right* as permissible, including under that category what is obligatory.

1. A "right act" is an act that it is permissible for you to do. It may be either (a) optional or (b) obligatory.
   a. An *optional act* is neither obligatory nor wrong to do. It is not your duty to do it, nor is it your duty not to do it. Neither doing it nor not doing it would be wrong.
   b. An *obligatory act* is one that morality requires you to do; it is not permissible for you to refrain from doing it. That is, it would be wrong not to do it.
2. A "wrong act" is an act that you have an obligation, or a duty, to refrain from doing. It is an act you ought not to do. It is not permissible to do it.

Let's briefly illustrate these concepts. The act of lying is generally seen as a wrong type of act (prohibited), whereas telling the truth is generally seen as obligatory. But some acts do not seem to be either obligatory or wrong. Whether you decide to take a course in art history or English literature or whether you write your friend a letter with a pencil or a pen seems morally neutral. Either is permissible. Whether you listen to pop music or classical music is not usually considered morally significant. Listening to both is allowed, and neither is obligatory. A decision to marry or remain sin-

TABLE 1 *The Relationship Between Ethics, Religion, Etiquette, and Law*

SUBJECT	NORMATIVE DISJUNCTS	SANCTIONS
Ethics	Right, wrong, or permissible —as defined by conscience or reason	Conscience: praise and blame Reputation
Religion	Right, wrong (sin), or permissible—as defined by religious authority	Conscience: eternal Reward and punishment caused by a supernatural agent or force
Law	Legal and illegal—as defined by a judicial body	Punishments determined by the legislative body
Etiquette	Proper and improper— as defined by culture	Social disapprobation and approbation

gle is of great moral significance (it is, after all, an important decision about how to live one's life). The decision reached, however, is usually considered to be morally neutral or optional. Under most circumstances, to marry (or not to marry) is thought to be neither obligatory nor wrong but permissible. Within the range of permissible acts is the notion of *supererogatory,* or highly altruistic, *acts.* These acts are not required or obligatory but are acts that exceed what morality requires, going "beyond the call of duty." You may have an obligation to give a donation to help people in dire need, but you are probably not obliged to sell your car, let alone become destitute, in order to help them.

Theories that place the emphasis on the nature of the act are called *deontological* (from the Greek word for "duty"). These theories hold that something is inherently right or good about such acts as truth telling and promise keeping and something is inherently wrong or bad about such acts as lying and promise breaking. Illustrations of deontological ethics include the ten commandments, found in the Bible (Exodus 20); natural law ethics, such as is found in the Roman Catholic Church, and Immanuel Kant's theory of the categorical imperative.

Immanuel Kant (1724–1804) argued that two kinds of commands or imperatives existed: hypothetical and categorical. *Hypothetical imperatives* are conditional, having the form "If you want *X*, do act *A*!" For example, if you want to pass this course, do your homework and study this book! *Categorical imperatives,* on the other hand, are not conditional but universal and rationally necessary. Kant's primary version of the categorical imperative (he actually offered three versions that he thought were equivalent) states: "Act only on that maxim whereby you can at the same time will that it would become a universal law." Examples were "Never break your promise" and "Never commit suicide." Contemporary Kantians often interpret the categorical imperative as yielding objective though not absolute principles. That is, in general it is wrong to break promises or commit suicide, but sometimes other moral principles may override them. Here is where consequences enter the picture.

Kant gave a second formulation of the categorical imperative, referred to as the *principle of ends*: "So act as to treat humanity, whether in your own person or in that of any other, in every case as an end and never as merely a means." Each person as a rational agent has dignity and profound worth, which entails that he or she must never be exploited or manipulated or merely used as a means to our idea of what is for the general good—or to any other end. The individual is sacred, and our acts must reflect as much.

Consequences. We said that lying is generally seen as wrong and telling the truth is generally seen as right. But consider this situation. You are hiding in your home an innocent woman named Laura, who is fleeing gangsters. Gangland Gus knocks on your door and when you open it, he asks if Laura is in your house. What should you do? Should you tell the truth or lie? Those who say that morality has something to do with consequences of actions would prescribe lying as the morally right thing to do. Those who deny that we should look at the consequences when considering what to do when there is a clear and absolute rule of action will say that we should either keep silent or tell the truth. When no other rule is at stake, of course, the rule-oriented ethicist will allow the foreseeable consequences to determine a course of action. Theories that focus primarily on consequences in determining moral rightness and wrongness are called *teleological ethical theories* (from the Greek *telos,* meaning "goal directed"). The most famous of these theories is utilitarianism, set forth by Jeremy Bentham (1748–1832) and John Stuart Mill (1806–1873), which enjoins us to do the act that is most likely to have the best consequences: Do the act that will produce the greatest happiness for the greatest number.

Character. While some ethical theories emphasize principles of action in themselves and some emphasize principles involving consequences of action, other theories, such as Aristotle's ethics, emphasize character or virtue. According to Aristotle, developing virtuous character is most important, for if and only if we have good people can we ensure habitual right action. Although it may be helpful to have action-guiding rules, what is vital is the empowerment of character to do good. Many people know that cheating or gossiping or overindulging in eating or imbibing too much alcohol is wrong, but they are incapable of doing what is right. The virtuous person may not be consciously following the moral law when he or she does what is right and good. Though the virtues are not central to other types of moral theories, most moral theories include the virtues as important. Most reasonable people, whatever their notions about ethics, would judge that the people who watched Kitty Genovese get assaulted lacked good character. Different moral systems emphasize different virtues and emphasize them to different degrees.

Motive. Finally, virtually all ethical systems, but especially Kant's system, accept the relevance of motive. It is important to the full assessment of any action that the intention of the agent be taken into account. Two acts may be identical, but one be judged morally culpable and the other excusable. Consider John's pushing Joan off a ledge, causing her to break her leg. In situation (A), he is angry and intends to harm her; but in situation (B) he sees a knife flying in her direction and intends to save her life. In (A) what he did was clearly wrong, whereas in (B), he did the right thing. On the other hand, two acts may have opposite results, but the action may be equally good judged on the basis of intention. For example, two soldiers may try to cross enemy lines to communicate with an allied force, but one gets captured through no fault of his own and the other succeeds. In a full moral description of any act, motive will be taken into consideration as a relevant factor.

The Purposes of Morality

What is the role of morality in human existence? I believe that morality is necessary to stave off social chaos, what Hobbes called a "state of nature" wherein life becomes "solitary, poor, nasty, brutish and short." It is a set of rules that if followed by nearly everyone, will promote the flourishing of nearly everyone. These rules restrict our freedom but only in order to promote greater freedom and well-being. More specifically, morality seems to have these five purposes:

1. To keep society from falling apart
2. To ameliorate human suffering
3. To promote human flourishing
4. To resolve conflicts of interest in just and orderly ways
5. To assign praise and blame, reward and punishment, and guilt

Let's elaborate these purposes. Imagine what society would be if everyone or nearly everyone did whatever he or she pleased without obeying moral rules. I would make a promise to you to help you with your philosophy homework tomorrow if you fix my car today. You believe me. So you fix my car, but you are deeply angry when I laugh at you on the morrow when I drive away to the beach instead of helping you with your homework. Or you loan me money, but I run off with it. Or I lie to you or harm you when it is in my interest, or even kill you when I feel the urge.

Parents would abandon children and spouses betray each other whenever it was convenient. Under such circumstances, society would break down. No one would have an incentive to help anyone else because reciprocity (a moral principle) was not recognized. Great gratuitous suffering would go largely unameliorated, and people certainly would not be very happy. We would not flourish or reach our highest potential.

I have just returned from Kazakhstan and Russia, which are undergoing a difficult transition from communism to democracy. In this transition (hopefully it will be resolved favorably), with the state's power considerably withdrawn, crime is on the increase and distrust is prevalent. At night when trying to navigate my way up the staircases to apartments throughout one city, I had to do so in complete darkness. I inquired about why there were no light bulbs in the stairwells, only to be told that the residents stole them, believing that if they did not take them, their neighbors would. Absent a dominant authority, the social contract has been eroded, and everyone must struggle alone in the darkness.

We need moral rules to guide our actions in ways that light up our paths and prevent and reduce *unnecessary* suffering (some suffering is a necessary means to a good end—e.g., the pain that is incurred in practicing a sport), that enhance human (and animal, for that matter) well-being, that allow us to resolve our conflicts of interests according to recognizably fair rules and to assign responsibility for actions, so that we can praise and blame, reward and punish people according to how their actions reflect moral principles.

Even though these five purposes are related, they are not identical, and different moral theories emphasize different purposes and in different ways. Utilitarianism fastens on human flourishing and the amelioration of suffering, whereas contractual systems rooted in rational self-interest accent the role of resolving conflicts of interest. A complete moral theory would include a place for each of these purposes. Such a system has the goal of internalizing the rules that promote these principles in each moral person's life, producing the virtuous person, someone who is "a jewel that shines in [morality's] own light," to paraphrase Kant. The goal of morality is to create happy and virtuous people, the kind who create flourishing communities. That's why ethics is the most important subject on Earth.

Let's return to the questions asked at the beginning of this essay. You should be able to answer each of them.

1. What is the nature of morality, and why do we need it? It has to do with discovering the rules that will promote the human good, elaborated in the five purposes just discussed. Without morality we cannot promote that good.

2. What is the good, and how will I know it? The good in question is the human good, specified by happiness, reaching one's potential, and so forth. Whatever we decide that meets human needs and helps us develop our deepest potential is the good morality promotes.

3. Are moral principles absolute or simply relative to social groups or individual decision? It would seem that moral principles have universal and objective validity, since similar rules are needed in all cultures to promote human flourishing. So moral rules are not justified by cultural acceptance and are not relative. But neither are they absolute, if absolute means that they can never be broken or overridden. Most moral rules can be overridden by other moral rules in different contexts. For example, it is sometimes justified to lie in order to save an innocent life.

4. Is it in my interest to be moral? In general and in the long run, it is in my interest to be moral for morality is exactly the set of rules that are most likely to help (nearly) all of us if nearly all of us follow them nearly all of the time. The good is good for you—at least most of the time. Furthermore, if we believe in the superior importance of morality, we will bring up children who

will not be happy when they break the moral code. Instead, they will feel guilt. In this sense, the commitment to morality and its internalization nearly guarantee that if you break the moral rules, you will suffer—both because of external sanctions and internal sanctions—moral guilt.

5. What is the relationship between morality and religion? We have seen that religion relies more on revelation, whereas morality relies more on reason, on rational reflection. But religion can provide added incentive for the moral life, offering the individual a relationship with God, who sees and will judge all our actions.

6. What is the relationship between morality and law? Morality and law should be very close, and morality should be the basis of the law, but there can be both unjust laws and immoral acts that cannot be legally enforced. The law is not as deep as morality and has a harder time judging human motives and intentions. You can be morally evil, intending to do evil things, but as long as you don't get the opportunity to do them, you are legally innocent.

7. What is the relationship between morality and etiquette? Etiquette consists in the customs of a culture, but it is typically morally neutral in that a culture could flourish with a different set of customs. In our culture, we eat with knives and forks, but a culture that cannot afford silverware but eats with chopsticks or its fingers is no less moral because of that fact.

In this book, you will be considering questions about the environment from an ethical perspective. What should we do regarding population, pollution, our limited resources, and nature itself? How will we live?

Notes

1. The term *normative* means seeking to make certain types of behavior a norm, or standard, in a society. *Webster's Collegiate Dictionary* defines it as "of, or relating or conforming to or prescribing norms or standards."
2. A *sanction* is a mechanism for social control, used to enforce society's standards. It may consist of reward or punishment, praise or blame, and approbation or disapprobation.
3. John Buehrens, *Our Chosen Faith* (Boston: Beacon Press, 1989), 140.

PART ONE

Theory

CHAPTER ONE

Western Philosophy of Nature: The Roots of Our Ecological Situation

In 1967 Lynn White, professor of history at the University of California at Los Angeles, wrote an article contending that our current ecological crisis was primarily due to "the orthodox Christian arrogance towards nature." This arrogance, he argued, was rooted in a domineering, anthropocentric attitude that could be traced back to Genesis (reprinted as our first reading), especially Chapter 1:28, "God blessed [Adam and Eve], saying to them, Be fruitful and multiply, fill the earth and conquer it. Be masters of [*dominate*] the fish of the sea, the birds of the heaven and all living animals on earth.'" White contrasted the pagan panpsychicism (i.e., seeing spirits in natural objects) with the anthropocentricism of Christianity. In the pagan worldview, animals, trees, and streams are seen as endowed with the sacred, so it is evil to harm them without good cause and after going through proper rituals. Sometimes forgiveness is asked from the animal. In the Christian worldview, according to White, "Man shares, in great measure, God's transcendence of nature. . . . By destroying pagan animism, Christianity made it possible to exploit nature in a mood of indifference to the feelings of natural objects."

At the end of his article, White, himself a Christian, recommended that Christians follow the medieval monk St. Francis of Assisi (1181–1226), who preached to the birds and fellowshipped with the foxes, whose view of "nature and man rested on a unique sort of panpsychicism of all things animate and inanimate, designed for the glorification of their transcendent Creator." By embracing this more holistic and symbiotic view of the relation of humanity to nature, we might be better armed to save our world.

White's article immediately created an uproar. White was denounced and even called "a junior anti-Christ." Radical and even some moderate environmentalists wholeheartedly embraced his position. Some Christians were awakened by his essay and resolved to take more notice of a theology of nature. Others, like Patrick Dobel in our readings, agreed that there was much insight in White's analysis but that the biblical picture was not as crudely domineering as White claimed. Human beings were to serve as *stewards* of Earth, which

was God's gift for our careful use. Still others, like sociologist Lewis Moncrief in our third reading, argued that White's analysis was too simple and that a complex web of forces—including democracy, technology, urbanization, and an aggressive attitude toward nature—accounted for the ecological mess in which we now find ourselves. To suppose, as White does, that Christianity is the sole cause for our crisis is to support a thesis that lacks evidence.

The theme of the underlying causes of our ecological crisis will reappear in subsequent chapters of this work. The next four chapters debate which is the correct theory of nature and our relationship with it. We will look at the views of other religions and cultures in Chapter 7 of our work. Some of the sections in Part 2 (especially Chapter 17 on economics and politics) will deal with the correct way to regard our relationship to nature. Hopefully, they will help you come to your own considered judgment on the matter.

At this point let us pause to consider the central questions that are raised in this theoretical part of our work.

1. What is the correct attitude toward nature? Should we regard nature as spiritually empowered? As inherently valuable or only instrumentally valuable? As god indwelt or as simply a wild force to be subdued?

2. How can we *know* which attitude is the correct one? Suppose we conclude that it were better for us all if almost everyone believed in animism (the view that spirits indwell natural objects), but concluded that animism was in fact false? Should we try to get ourselves to believe something we have no evidence for simply to save ourselves and nature? What if we discover that the best way to save the environment is to draw up a new myth or invent a new religion (or change the one we believe in order to get the same result). Should we do it?

3. Can an anthropocentric philosophy, which values only humans, ever be sufficient to save the environment? Is enlightened self-interest adequate to resolve our environmental needs?

4. What is our obligation to animals, especially higher animals? Should we be as concerned about their welfare as about human welfare? Do animals have

rights—not to be unnecessarily harmed, experimented on, hunted, or eaten?

5. What is our obligation for preserving other species? Is there a sacred holism that suffers as species are forever destroyed? Is there a hierarchy of being that is preserved in the variety of species? How do we measure the economic benefits to humans of cutting down the rain forests versus eliminating rare species?

6. What is our obligation to future and distant people with regard to the environment? Do future people have rights so that we must be frugal (and even sacrifice) with regard to natural resources and prevent large-scale pollution? Or is the notion of rights an unwarranted moral view? Or do we at most have duties to the succeeding generation—to leave it enough resources to live on.

These are some of the central questions that we will examine in this part of this work. We will represent divergent points of view with the *best* arguments available. Your own position cannot be secure until you have critically considered all sides of an issue. And unless you have undermined the best case your opponent can make, you can never be sure it has been defeated. Philosophy is the quest for truth and the best position that reason can arrive at. Use your reason. The world needs your judgment!

We turn now to our first reading from the Book of Genesis in the Hebrew Bible (Old Testament), followed by Lynn White's important essay on the historical roots of our ecological crisis.

1

Genesis 1–3

According to ancient Hebrew tradition, Moses (ca. 1450 BC) wrote this account of the creation of the heavens, Earth, and all that dwells therein. While scholars dispute the authorship and date, they agree that it is a very old account and sets forth the Hebrew-Christian view of a divine Creator who creates the world as good and man and woman in his own image. These chapters form the basis for the Western religious view of the relationship of humanity to nature.

I. THE ORIGIN OF THE WORLD AND OF MANKIND

1. The Creation and the Fall

The First Account of the Creation. 1 ¹In the beginning God created the heavens and the earth. ²Now the earth was a formless void, there was darkness over the deep, and God's spirit hovered over the water.

³God said, "Let there be light," and there was light. ⁴God saw that light was good, and God divided light from darkness. ⁵God called light "day," and darkness he called "night." Evening came and morning came: the first day.

⁶God said, "Let there be a vault in the waters to divide the waters in two." And so it was. ⁷God made the vault, and it divided the waters above the vault from the waters under the vault. ⁸God called the vault "heaven." Evening came and morning came: the second day.

⁹God said, "Let the waters under heaven come together into a single mass, and let dry land appear." And so it was. ¹⁰God called the dry land "earth" and

the mass of waters "seas," and God saw that it was good.

¹¹God said, "Let the earth produce vegetation: seed-bearing plants, and fruit trees bearing fruit with their seed inside, on the earth." And so it was. ¹²The earth produced vegetation: plants bearing seed in their several kinds, and trees bearing fruit with their seed inside in their several kinds. God saw that it was good. ¹³Evening came and morning came: the third day.

¹⁴God said, "Let there be lights in the vault of heaven to divide day from night, and let them indicate festivals, days and years. ¹⁵Let them be lights in the vault of heaven to shine on the earth." And so it was. ¹⁶God made the two great lights: the greater light to govern the day, the smaller light to govern the night, and the stars. ¹⁷God set them in the vault of heaven to shine on the earth, ¹⁸to govern the day and the night and to divide light from darkness. God saw that it was good. ¹⁹Evening came and morning came: the fourth day.

²⁰God said, "Let the waters teem with living creatures, and let birds fly above the earth within the vault of heaven." And so it was. ²¹God created great sea-serpents and every kind of living creature with which the waters teem, and every kind of winged creature. God saw that it was good. ²²God blessed them, saying, "Be fruitful and multiply, and fill the waters of the seas; and let the birds multiply upon the earth." ²³Evening came and morning came: the fifth day.

²⁴God said, "Let the earth produce every kind of living creature: cattle, reptiles, and every kind of wild beast." And so it was. ²⁵God made every kind of wild beast, every kind of cattle, and every kind of land reptile. God saw that it was good.

26God said, "Let us make man in our own image, in the likeness of ourselves, and let them be masters of the fish of the sea, the birds of heaven, the cattle, all the wild beasts and all the reptiles that crawl upon the earth."

27God created man in the image of himself,
in the image of God he created him,
male and female he created them.

28God blessed them, saying to them, "Be fruitful, multiply, fill the earth and conquer it. Be masters of the fish of the sea, the birds of heaven and all living animals on the earth." 29God said, "See, I give you all the seed-bearing plants that are upon the whole earth, and all the trees with seed-bearing fruit; this shall be your food. 30To all wild beasts, all birds of heaven and all living reptiles on the earth I give all the foliage of plants for food." And so it was. 31God saw all he had made, and indeed it was very good. Evening came and morning came: the sixth day.

2. 1Thus heaven and earth were completed with all their array. 2On the seventh day God completed the work he had been doing. He rested on the seventh day after all the work he had been doing. 3God blessed the seventh day and made it holy, because on that day he had rested after all his work of creating.

4Such were the origins of heavens and earth when they were created.

The Second Account of the Creation: Paradise. 5At the time when Yahweh God made earth and heaven there was as yet no wild bush on the earth nor had any wild plant yet sprung up, for Yahweh God had not sent rain on the earth, nor was there any man to till the soil. 6However, a flood was rising from the earth and watering all the surface of the soil. 7Yahweh God fashioned man of dust from the soil. Then he breathed into his nostrils a breath of life, and thus man became a living being.

8Yahweh God planted a garden in Eden which is in the east, and there he put the man he had fashioned. 9Yahweh God caused to spring up from the soil every kind of tree, enticing to look at and good to eat, with the tree of life and the tree of the knowledge of good and evil in the middle of the garden. 10A river flowed from Eden to water the garden, and from there it divided to make four streams. 11The first is named the Pishon, and this encircles the whole land of Havilah where there is gold. 12The gold of this land is pure; bdellium and onyx stone are found there. 13The second river is named the Gihon, and this encircles the whole land of Cush. 14The third river is named the Tigris, and this flows to the east of Ashur. The fourth river is the Euphrates. 15Yahweh God took the man and settled him in the garden of Eden to cultivate and take care of it. 16Then Yahweh God gave the man this admonition, "You may eat indeed of all the trees in the garden. 17Nevertheless of the tree of the knowledge of good and

evil you are not to eat, for on the day you eat of it you shall most surely die."

18Yahweh God said, "It is not good that the man should be alone. I will make him a helpmate." 19So from the soil Yahweh God fashioned all the wild beasts and all the birds of heaven. These he brought to the man to see what he would call them; each one was to bear the name the man would give it. 20The man gave names to all the cattle, all the birds of heaven and all the wild beasts. But no helpmate suitable for man was found for him. 21So Yahweh God made the man fall into a deep sleep. And while he slept, he took one of his ribs and enclosed it in flesh. 22Yahweh God built the rib he had taken from the man into a woman, and brought her to the man. 25The man exclaimed:

"This at last is bone from my bones,
and flesh from my flesh!
This is to be called woman,
for this was taken from man."

24This is why a man leaves his father and mother and joins himself to his wife, and they become one body.

25Now both of them were naked, the man and his wife, but they felt no shame in front of each other.

The Fall 3. 1The serpent was the most subtle of all the wild beasts that Yahweh God had made. It asked the woman, "Did God really say you were not to eat from any of the trees in the garden?" 2The woman answered the serpent, "We may eat the fruit of the trees in the garden. 3But of the fruit of the tree in the middle of the garden God said, 'You must not eat it, nor touch it, under pain of death.'" 4Then the serpent said to the woman, "No! you will not die! 5God knows in fact that on the day you eat it your eyes will be opened and you will be like gods, knowing good and evil." 6The woman saw that the tree was good to eat and pleasing to the eye, and that it was desirable for the knowledge that it could give. So she took some of its fruit and ate it. She gave some also to her husband who was with her, and he ate it. 7Then the eyes of both of them were opened and they realized that they were naked. So they sewed fig leaves together to make themselves loincloths.

8The man and his wife heard the sound of Yahweh God walking in the garden in the cool of the day, and they hid from Yahweh God among the trees of the garden. 9But Yahweh God called to the man. "Where are you?" he asked. 10"I heard the sound of you in the garden," he replied. "I was afraid because I was naked, so I hid." 11 "Who told you that you were naked?" he asked. "Have you been eating of the tree I forbade you to eat?" 12The man replied, "It was the woman you put with me; she gave me the fruit, and I ate it." 13Then Yahweh God asked the woman, "What is this you have done?" The woman replied, "The serpent tempted me and I ate."

14Then Yahweh God said to the serpent, "Because you have done this,

"Be accursed beyond all cattle,
all wild beasts.
You shall crawl on your belly and eat dust
every day of your life.
15I will make you enemies of each other:
you and the woman,
your offspring and her offspring.
It will crush your head
and you will strike its heel."

16To the woman he said:

"I will multiply your pains in childbearing,
you shall give birth to your children in pain.
Your yearning shall be for your husband,
yet he will lord it over you."

17To the man he said, "Because you listened to the voice of your wife and ate from the tree of which I had forbidden you to eat,

"Accursed be the soil because of you.
With suffering shall you get your food from it
every day of your life.
18It shall yield you brambles and thistles,
and you shall eat wild plants.
19With sweat on your brow
shall you eat your bread,
until you return to the soil,
as you were taken from it.
For dust you are
and to dust you shall return.

20The man named his wife "Eve" because she was the mother of all those who live. 21Yahweh God made clothes out of skins for the man and his wife, and they put them on. 22Then Yahweh God said, "See, the man has become like one of us, with his knowledge of good and evil. He must not be allowed to stretch his hand out next and pick from the tree of life also, and eat some and live for ever." 23So Yahweh God expelled him from the garden of Eden, to till the soil from which he had been taken. 24He banished the man, and in front of the garden of Eden he posted the cherubs, and the flame of a flashing sword, to guard the way to the tree of life.

Study Questions

1. What is the proper relationship between humanity and nature according to the Genesis account? Go over Genesis 1:26–29. Then compare it with Chapter 2:15.
2. Genesis 1:29 commands us to subdue Earth and fill it with our species. How literally should we take these commands?
3. For a more explicit statement on the high value of human beings, consider Psalm 8. Does it confirm the picture of human dominance conveyed in the Genesis account?

Psalm 8

O Lord, our Lord, how majestic is thy name in all the
    earth!
Thou whose glory above the heavens is chanted
    by the babes and infants,
    thou has founded a bulwark because of thy foes,
    to still the enemy and the avenger.
When I look at thy heavens, the work of thy fingers,
    the moon and the stars which thou hast established;
    what is man that thou art mindful of him,
    and the son of man that thou dost care for him?
Yet thou hast made him little less than God,
    and dost crown him with glory and honor.
Thou has given him dominion over the works of thy
    hands;
    thou has put all things under his feet,
    all sheep and oxen,
    and also the beasts of the field,
    the birds of the air, and the fish of the sea,
    whatever passes along the path of the sea.
O Lord, our Lord,
    how majestic is thy name in all the earth.

2

The Historical Roots of Our Ecological Crisis

Lynn White

Lynn White (1907–1987), internationally known medieval scholar, taught history at Princeton University, Stanford University, and the University of California at Los Angeles.

White set forth the thesis that the roots of our ecological crisis lie in our Judeo-Christian idea that humanity is to dominate nature. By seeing nature as alien, as a mere resource to be exploited, we have wreaked havoc on Earth and are reaping the consequences. Either a new religion or a revision of our old one is called for to

This article, which has become something of a classic already, appeared originally in *Science*, Vol. 155, pp. 1203–1207 (10 March 1967). Copyright 1967 by the American Association for the Advancement of Science *get us out of this mess. He suggests the Italian medieval saint St. Francis of Assisi (1182–1226) as a proper example of a suitable attitude toward nature.*

A conversation with Aldous Huxley not infrequently put one at the receiving end of an unforgettable monologue. About a year before his lamented death he was discoursing on a favorite topic: Man's unnatural treatment of nature and its sad results. To illustrate his point he told how, during the previous summer, he had returned to a little valley in England where he had spent many happy months as a child. Once it had been composed of delightful grassy glades; now it was becoming overgrown with unsightly brush because the rabbits that formerly kept such growth under control had largely succumbed to a disease, myxomatosis, that was deliberately introduced by the local farmers to reduce the rabbits' destruction of crops. Being something of a Philistine, I could be silent no longer, even in the interests of great rhetoric. I interrupted to point out that the rabbit itself had been brought as a domestic animal to England in 1176, presumably to improve the protein diet of the peasantry.

All forms of life modify their contexts. The most spectacular and benign instance is doubtless the coral polyp. By serving its own ends, it has created a vast undersea world favorable to thousands of other kinds of animals and plants. Ever since man became a numerous species he has affected his environment notably. The hypothesis that his fire-drive method of hunting created the world's great grasslands and helped to exterminate the monster mammals of the Pleistocene from much of the globe is plausible, if not proved. For 6 millennia at least, the banks of the lower Nile have been a human artifact rather than the swampy African jungle which nature, apart from man, would have made it. The Aswan Dam, flooding 5000 square miles, is only the latest stage in a long process. In many regions terracing or irrigation, overgrazing, the cutting of forests by Romans to build ships to fight Carthaginians or by Crusaders to solve the logistics problems of their expeditions, have profoundly changed some ecologies. Observation that the French landscape falls into two basic types, the open fields of the north and the *bocage* of the south and west, inspired Marc Bloch to undertake his classic study of medieval agricultural methods. Quite unintentionally, changes in human ways often affect nonhuman nature. It has been noted, for example, that the advent of the automobile eliminated huge flocks of sparrows that once fed on the horse manure littering every street.

The history of ecologic change is still so rudimentary that we know little about what really happened, or what the results were. The extinction of the European aurochs as late as 1627 would seem to have been a simple case of overenthusiastic hunting. On more intricate matters it often is impossible to find solid information. For a thousand years or more the Frisians and Hollanders have been pushing back the North Sea, and the process is culminating in our own time in the reclamation of the Zuider Zee. What, if any, species of animals, birds, fish, shore life, or plants have died out in the process? In their epic combat with Neptune, have the Netherlanders overlooked ecological values in such a way that the quality of human life in the Netherlands has suffered? I cannot discover that the questions have ever been asked, much less answered.

People, then, have often been a dynamic element in their own environment, but in the present state of historical scholarship we usually do not know exactly when, where, or with what effects man-induced changes came. As we enter the last third of the 20th century, however, concern for the problem of ecologic backlash is mounting feverishly. Natural science, conceived as the effort to understand the nature of things, had flourished in several eras and among several peoples. Similarly there had been an age-old accumulation of technological skills, sometimes growing rapidly, sometimes slowly. But it was not until about four generations ago that Western Europe and North America arranged a marriage between science and technology, a union of the theoretical and the empirical approaches to our natural environment. The emergence in widespread practice of the Baconian creed that scientific knowledge means technological power over nature can scarcely be dated before about 1850, save in the chemical industries, where it is anticipated in the 18th century. Its acceptance as a normal pattern of action may mark the greatest event in human history since the invention of agriculture, and perhaps in nonhuman terrestrial history as well.

Almost at once the new situation forced the crystallization of the novel concept of ecology; indeed, the word *ecology* first appeared in the English language in 1873. Today, less than a century later, the impact of our race upon the environment has so increased in force that it has changed in essence. When the first cannons were fired, in the early 14th century, they affected ecology by sending workers scrambling to the forests and mountains for more potash, sulfur, iron ore, and charcoal, with some resulting erosion and deforestation. Hydrogen bombs are of a different order: a war fought with them might alter the genetics of all life on this planet. By 1285 London had a smog problem arising from the burning of soft coal, but our present combustion of fossil fuels threatens to change the chemistry of the globe's atmosphere as a whole, with consequences which we are only beginning to guess. With the population explosion, the carcinoma of planless urbanism, the now geological deposits of sewage and garbage, surely no creature other than man has ever managed to foul its nest in such short order.

There are many calls to action, but specific proposals, however worthy as individual items, seem too partial, palliative, negative: ban the bomb, tear down the billboards, give the Hindus contraceptives and tell them to eat their sacred cows. The simplest solution to any suspect change is, of course, to stop it, or, better yet, to revert to a romanticized past: make those ugly gasoline stations look like Anne Hathaway's cottage or (in the Far West) like ghost-town saloons. The "wilderness area" mentality invariably advocates deep-freezing an ecology, whether San Gimignano or the High Sierra, as it was before the first Kleenex was dropped. But neither atavism nor prettification will cope with the ecologic crisis of our time.

What shall we do? No one yet knows. Unless we think about fundamentals, our specific measures may produce new backlashes more serious than those they are designed to remedy.

As a beginning we should try to clarify our thinking by looking, in some historical depth, at the presuppositions that underlie modern technology and science. Science was traditionally aristocratic, speculative, intellectual in intent; technology was lower-class, empirical, action-oriented. The quite sudden fusion of these two, towards the middle of the 19th century, is surely related to the slightly prior and contemporary democratic revolutions which, by reducing social barriers, tended to assert a functional unity of brain and hand. Our ecologic crisis is the product of an emerging, entirely novel, democratic culture. The issue is whether a democratized world can survive its own implications. Presumably we cannot, unless we rethink our axioms.

THE WESTERN TRADITIONS OF TECHNOLOGY AND SCIENCE

One thing is so certain that it seems stupid to verbalize it: both modern technology and modern science are distinctively *Occidental*. Our technology has absorbed elements from all over the world, notably from China; yet everywhere today, whether in Japan or in Nigeria, successful technology is Western. Our science is the heir to all the sciences of the past, especially perhaps to the work of the great Islamic scientists of the Middle Ages, who so often outdid the ancient Greeks in skill and perspicacity: al-Rāzi in medicine, for example; or ibn-al-Haytham in optics; or Omar Khayyám in mathematics. Indeed, not a few works of such geniuses seem to have vanished in the original Arabic and to survive only in medieval Latin translations that helped to lay the foundations for later Western developments. Today, around the globe, all significant science is Western in style and method, whatever the pigmentation or language of the scientists.

A second pair of facts is less well recognized because they result from quite recent historical scholarship. The leadership of the West, both in technology and in science, is far older than the so-called Scientific Revolution of the 17th century or the so-called Industrial Revolution of the 18th century. These terms are in fact outmoded and obscure the true nature of what they try to describe—significant stages in two long and separate developments. By A.D. 1000 at the latest—and perhaps, feebly, as much as 200 years earlier—the West began to apply water power to industrial processes other than milling grain. This was followed in the late 12th century by the harnessing of wind power. From simple beginnings, but with remarkable consistency of style, the West rapidly expanded its skills in the development of power machinery, labor-saving devices, and automation. Those who doubt should contemplate that most monumental achievement in the history of automation: the weight-driven mechanical clock, which appeared in two forms in the early 14th century. Not in craftsmanship but in basic technological capacity, the Latin West of the later Middle Ages far outstripped its elaborate, sophisticated, and esthetically magnificent sister cultures, Byzantium and Islam. In 1444 a great Greek ecclesiastic, Bessarion, who had gone to Italy, wrote a letter to a prince in Greece. He is amazed by the superiority of Western ships, arms, textiles, glass. But above all he is astonished by the spectacle of waterwheels sawing timbers and pumping the bellows to blast furnaces. Clearly, he had seen nothing of the sort in the Near East.

By the end of the 15th century the technological superiority of Europe was such that its small, mutually hostile nations could spill out over all the rest of the world, conquering, looting, and colonizing. The symbol of this technological superiority is the fact that Portugal, one of the weakest states of the Occident, was able to become, and to remain for a century, mistress of the East Indies. And we must remember that the technology of Vasco da Gama and Albuquerque was built by pure empiricism, drawing remarkably little support or inspiration from science.

In the present-day vernacular of understanding, modern science is supposed to have begun in 1543, when both Copernicus and Vesalius published their great works. It is no derogation of their accomplishments, however, to point out that such structures as the *Fabrica* and the *De revolutionibus* do not appear overnight. The distinctive Western tradition of science, in fact, began in the late 11th century with a massive movement of translation of Arabic and Greek scientific works into Latin. A few notable books—Theophrastus, for example—escaped the West's avid new appetite for science, but within less than 200 years, effectively the entire corpus of Greek and Muslim science was available in Latin, and was being eagerly read and criticized in the new European universities. Out of criticism arose new observation, speculation, and increasing distrust of ancient authorities. By the late 13th century Europe had seized global scientific leadership from the faltering hands of Islam. It would be as absurd to deny the profound originality of Newton, Galileo, or Copernicus as to deny that of the 14th century scholastic scientists like Buridan or Oresme on whose work they built. Before the 11th century, science scarcely existed in the Latin West, even in Roman times. From the 11th century onward, the scientific sector of Occidental culture has increased in a steady crescendo.

Since both our technological and our scientific movements got their start, acquired their character, and achieved world dominance in the Middle Ages, it would seem that we cannot understand their nature or their present impact upon ecology without examining fundamental medieval assumptions and developments.

MEDIEVAL VIEW OF MAN AND NATURE

Until recently, agriculture has been the chief occupation even in "advanced" societies; hence, any change in methods of tillage has much importance. Early plows, drawn by two oxen, did not normally turn the sod but merely scratched it. Thus, cross-plowing was needed and fields tended to be squarish. In the fairly light soils and semi-arid climates of the Near East and Mediterranean, this worked well. But such a plow was inappropriate to the wet climate and often sticky soils of northern Europe. By the latter part of the 7th century after Christ, however, following obscure beginnings, certain northern peasants were using an entirely new kind of plow, equipped with a vertical knife to cut the line of the furrow, a horizontal share to slice under the sod, and a moldboard to turn it over. The friction of this plow with the soil was so great that it normally required not two but eight oxen. It attacked the land with such violence that cross-plowing was not needed, and fields tended to be shaped in long strips.

In the days of the scratch-plow, fields were distributed generally in units capable of supporting a single family. Subsistence farming was the presupposition. But no peasant owned eight oxen: to use the new and more efficient plow, peasants pooled their oxen to form large plow-teams, originally receiving (it would appear) plowed strips in proportion to their contribution. Thus, distribution of land was based no longer on the needs of a family but, rather, on the capacity of a power machine to till the earth. Man's relation to the soil was profoundly changed. Formerly man had been part of nature; now he was the exploiter of nature. Nowhere else in the world did farmers develop any analogous agricultural implement. Is it coincidence that modern technology, with its ruthlessness toward nature, has so largely been produced by descendants of these peasants of northern Europe?

This same exploitive attitude appears slightly before A.D. 830 in Western illustrated calendars. In older calendars the months were shown as passive personifications. The new Frankish calendars, which set the style for the Middle Ages, are very different: they show men coercing the world around them—plowing, harvesting, chopping trees, butchering pigs. Man and nature are two things, and man is master.

These novelties seem to be in harmony with larger intellectual patterns. What people do about their ecology depends on what they think about themselves in relation to things around them. Human ecology is deeply conditioned by beliefs about our nature and destiny—that is, by religion. To Western eyes this is very evident in, say, India or Ceylon. It is equally true of ourselves and of our medieval ancestors.

The victory of Christianity over paganism was the greatest psychic revolution in the history of our culture. It has become fashionable today to say that, for better or worse, we live in "the post-Christian age." Certainly the forms of our thinking and language have largely ceased to be Christian, but to my eye the substance often remains amazingly akin to that of the past. Our daily habits of action, for example, are dominated by an implicit faith in perpetual progress which was unknown either to Greco-Roman antiquity or to the Orient. It is rooted in, and is indefensible apart from, Judeo-Christian teleology. The fact that Communists share it merely helps to show what can be demonstrated on many other grounds: that Marxism, like Islam, is a Judeo-Christian heresy. We continue today to live, as we have lived for about 1700 years, very largely in a context of Christian axioms.

What did Christianity tell people about their relations with the environment?

While many of the world's mythologies provide stories of creation, Greco-Roman mythology was singularly incoherent in this respect. Like Aristotle, the intellectuals of the ancient West denied that the visible world had had a beginning. Indeed, the idea of a beginning was impossible in the framework of their cyclical notion of time. In sharp contrast, Christianity inherited from Judaism not only a concept of time as nonrepetitive and linear but also a striking story of creation. By gradual stages a loving and all-powerful God had created light and darkness, the heavenly bodies, and earth and all its plants, animals, birds, and fishes. Finally, God had created Adam and, as an after thought, Eve to keep man from being lonely. Man named all the animals, thus establishing his dominance over them. God planned all of this explicitly for man's benefit and rule: no item in the physical creation had any purpose save to serve man's purposes. And, although man's body is made of clay, he is not simply part of nature: he is made in God's image.

Especially in its Western form, Christianity is the most anthropocentric religion the world has seen. As early as the 2nd century both Tertullian and St. Irenaeus of Lyons were insisting that when God shaped Adam he was foreshadowing the image of the incarnate Christ, the Second Adam. Man shares, in great measure, God's transcendence of nature. Christianity, in absolute contrast to ancient paganism and Asia's religions (except, perhaps, Zoroastrianism), not only established a dualism of man and nature but also insisted that it is God's will that man exploit nature for his proper ends.

At the level of the common people this worked out in an interesting way. In Antiquity every tree, every spring, every stream, every hill had its own *genius loci,* its guardian spirit. These spirits were accessible to men, but were very unlike men; centaurs, fauns, and mermaids show their ambivalence. Before one cut a tree, mined a mountain, or dammed a brook, it was important to placate the spirit in charge of that particular situation, and to keep it placated. By destroying pagan animism, Christianity made it possible to exploit nature in a mood of indifference to the feelings of natural objects.

It is often said that for animism the Church substituted the cult of saints. True; but the cult of saints is functionally quite different from animism. The saint is not *in* natural objects; he may have special shrines, but his citizenship is in heaven. Moreover, a saint is entirely a man; he can be approached in human terms. In addition to saints, Christianity of course also had angels and demons inherited from Judaism and perhaps, at one remove, from Zoroastrianism. But these were all as mobile as the saints themselves. The spirits *in* natural objects, which formerly had protected nature from man, evaporated. Man's effective monopoly on spirit in this world was confirmed, and the old inhibitions to the exploitation of nature crumbled.

When one speaks in such sweeping terms, a note of caution is in order. Christianity is a complex faith, and its consequences differ in differing contexts. What I have said may well apply to the medieval West, where in fact technology made spectacular advances. But the Greek East, a highly civilized realm of equal Christian devotion, seems to have produced no marked technological innovation after the late 7th century, when Greek fire was invented. The key to the contrast may perhaps be found in a difference in the tonality of piety and thought which students of comparative theology find between the Greek and the Latin Churches. The Greeks believed that sin was intellectual blindness, and that salvation was found in illumination, orthodoxy—that is, clear thinking. The Latins, on the other hand, felt that sin was moral evil, and that salvation was to be found in right conduct. Eastern theology has been intellectualist. Western theology has been voluntarist. The Greek saint contemplates; the Western saint acts. The implications of Christianity for the conquest of nature would emerge more easily in the Western atmosphere.

The Christian dogma of creation, which is found in the first clause of all the Creeds, has another meaning for our comprehension of today's ecologic crisis. By revelation, God had given man the Bible, the Book of Scripture. But since God had made nature, nature also must reveal the divine mentality. The religious study of nature for the better understanding of God was known as natural theology. In the early Church, and always in the Greek East, nature was conceived primarily as a symbolic system through which God speaks to men: the ant is a sermon to sluggards; rising flames are the symbol of the soul's aspiration. This view of nature was essentially artistic rather than scientific. While Byzantium preserved and copied great numbers of ancient Greek scientific texts, science as we conceive it could scarcely flourish in such an ambiance.

However, in the Latin West by the early 13th century natural theology was following a very different bent. It was ceasing to be the decoding of the physical symbols of God's communication with man and was becoming the effort to understand God's mind by discovering how his creation operates. The rainbow was no longer simply a symbol of hope first sent to Noah after the Deluge: Robert Grosseteste, Friar Roger Bacon, and Theodoric of Freiberg produced startlingly sophisticated work on the optics of the rainbow, but they did it as a venture in religious understanding. From the 13th century onward, up to and including Leibnitz and Newton, every major scientist, in effect, explained his motivations in religious terms. Indeed if Galileo had not been so expert an amateur theologian he would have got into far less trouble: the professionals resented his intrusion. And Newton seems to have regarded himself more as a theologian than as a scientist. It was not until the late 18th century that the hypothesis of God became unnecessary to many scientists.

It is often hard for the historian to judge, when men explain why they are doing what they want to do, whether they are offering real reasons or merely culturally acceptable reasons. The consistency with which scientists during the long formative centuries of Western science said that the task and the reward of the scientist was "to think God's thoughts after him" leads one to believe that this was their real motivation. If so, then modern Western science was cast in a matrix of Christian theology. The dynamism of religious devotion, shaped by the Judeo-Christian dogma of creation, gave it impetus.

AN ALTERNATIVE CHRISTIAN VIEW

We would seem to be headed toward conclusions unpalatable to many Christians. Since both *science* and *technology* are blessed words in our contemporary vocabulary, some may be happy at the notions, first, that, viewed historically, modern science is an extrapolation of natural theology and, second, that modern technology is at least partly to be explained as an Occidental, voluntarist realization of the Christian dogma of man's transcendence of and rightful mastery over nature. But, as we now recognize, somewhat over a century ago science and technology—hitherto quite separate activities—joined to give mankind powers which, to judge by many of the ecologic effects, are out of control. If so, Christianity bears a huge burden of guilt.

I personally doubt that disastrous ecologic backlash can be avoided simply by applying to our problems more science and more technology. Our science and technology have grown out of Christian attitudes toward man's relation to nature which are almost universally held not only by Christians and neo-Christians but also by those who fondly regard themselves as post-Christians. Despite Copernicus, all the cosmos rotates around our little globe. Despite Darwin, we are *not*, in our hearts, part of the natural process. We are superior to nature, contemptuous of it, willing to use it for our slightest whim. The newly elected Governor of California, like myself a churchman but less troubled than I, spoke for the Christian tradition when he said (as is alleged), "when you've seen one redwood tree, you've seen them all." To a Christian a tree can be no more than a physical fact. The whole concept of the sacred grove is alien to Christianity and to the ethos of the West. For nearly 2 millennia Christian missionaries have been chopping down sacred groves, which are idolatrous because they assume spirit in nature.

What we do about ecology depends on our ideas of the man–nature relationship. More science and more technology are not going to get us out of the present ecologic crisis until we find a new religion, or rethink our old one. The beatniks, who are the basic revolutionaries of our time, show a sound instinct in their affinity for Zen Buddhism, which conceives of the man–nature relationship as very nearly the mirror image of the Christian view. Zen, however, is as deeply conditioned by Asian history as Christianity is by the experience of the West, and I am dubious of its viability among us.

Possibly we should ponder the greatest radical in Christian history since Christ: St. Francis of Assisi. The prime miracle of St. Francis is the fact that he did not end at the stake, as many of his left-wing followers did. He was so clearly heretical that a General of the Franciscan Order, St. Bonaventura, a great and perceptive Christian, tried to suppress the early accounts of Franciscanism. The key to an understanding of Francis is his belief in the virtue of humility—not merely for the individual but for man as a species. Francis tried to depose man from his monarchy over creation and set up a democracy of all God's creatures. With him the ant is no longer simply a homily for the lazy, flames a sign of the thrust of the soul toward union with God; now they are Brother Ant and Sister Fire, praising the Creator in their own ways as Brother Man does in his.

Later commentators have said that Francis preached to the birds as a rebuke to men who would not listen. The records do not read so: he urged the little birds to praise God, and in spiritual ecstasy they flapped their wings and chirped rejoicing. Legends of saints, especially the Irish saints, had long told of their dealings with animals but always, I believe, to show their human dominance over creatures. With Francis it is different. The land around Gubbio in the Apennines was being ravaged by a fierce wolf. St. Francis, says the legend, talked to the wolf and persuaded him of the error of his ways. The wolf repented, died in the odor of sanctity, and was buried in consecrated ground.

What Sir Steven Runciman calls the Franciscan doctrine of the animal soul" was quickly stamped out. Quite possibly it was in part inspired, consciously or unconsciously, by the belief in reincarnation held by the Cathar heretics who at that time teemed in Italy and southern France, and who presumably had got it originally from India. It is significant that at just the same moment, about 1200, traces of metempsychosis are found also in western Judaism, in the Provençal *Cabbala*. But Francis held neither to transmigration of souls nor to pantheism. His view of nature and of man rested on a unique sort of pan-psychism of all things animate and inanimate, designed for the glorification of their transcendent Creator, who, in the ultimate gesture of cosmic humility, assumed flesh, lay helpless in a manger, and hung dying on a scaffold.

I am not suggesting that many contemporary Americans who are concerned about our ecologic crisis will be either able or willing to counsel with wolves or exhort birds. However, the present increasing disruption of the global environment is the product of a dynamic technology and science which were originating in the Western medieval world against which St. Francis was rebelling in so original a way. Their growth cannot be understood historically apart from distinctive attitudes toward nature which are deeply grounded in Christian dogma. The fact that most people do not think of these attitudes as Christian is irrelevant. No new set of basic values has been accepted in our society to displace those of Christianity. Hence we shall continue to have a worsening ecologic crisis until we reject the Christian axiom that nature has no reason for existence save to serve man.

The greatest spiritual revolutionary in Western history, St. Francis, proposed what he thought was an alternative Christian view of nature and man's relation to it: he tried to substitute the idea of the equality of all creatures, including man, for the idea of man's limitless rule of creation. He failed. Both our present science and our present technology are so tinctured with orthodox Christian arrogance toward nature that no solution for our ecologic crisis can be expected from them alone. Since the roots of our trouble are so largely religious, the remedy must also be essentially religious, whether we call it that or not. We must rethink and refeel our nature and destiny. The profoundly religious, but heretical, sense of the primitive Franciscans for the spiritual autonomy of all parts of nature may point a direction. I propose Francis as a patron saint for ecologists.

Study Questions

1. Do you agree with White's assessment that it is our Judeo-Christian dominance model that has led to our ecological crisis? Go back over Genesis 1–3 and compare it with White's analysis. Is his account a correct interpretation of the text?

2. What is the appeal of St. Francis? Here is part of St. Francis's "Canticle of Brother Sun."*

> Praised be You, my Lord, with all your creatures,
> Especially Sir Brother Sun,
> Who is the day and through whom You give us light.
> Praised be you, my Lord, through Sister Moon and the stars,
> In heaven You formed them clear and precious and beautiful.
> Praised be you, my Lord, through Brother Wind,
> And through the air, cloudy and serene, and every kind of weather
> Through which You give sustenance to Your creatures.

> Praised be You, my Lord, through Sister Water,
> Which is very useful and humble and precious and chaste.
> Praised be You, my Lord, through our Sister Mother Earth,
> Who sustains us and governs us.
> And who produces varied fruits with colored flowers and herbs.

What environmental attitude does St. Francis's poem embody? Is it helpful? Is it true? Explain your judgment.

FROM: *The Canticle of Brother Sun*, translated by R. J. Armstrong and I. Brady (New York: Paulist Press, 1982).

3

The Cultural Basis of Our Environmental Crisis

LEWIS W. MONCRIEF

Lewis W. Moncrief is a sociologist who taught for many years in the Department of Park and Recreation Resources at Michigan State University.

In this reply to Lynn White's article (Reading 2), Moncrief argues that White's analysis misses the essential point that human beings have been altering the environment from their beginning. He asks, "If our environmental crisis is a 'religious problem' why are other parts of the world experiencing the same environmental problems that we are so well acquainted with in the Western world?" A more plausible account of the causes of our crisis is complex and has to do with the nature of capitalism, technology, democratization, urbanization, and individualism.

One hundred years ago at almost any location in the United States, potable water was no farther away than the closest brook or stream. Today there are hardly any streams in the United States, except in a few high mountainous reaches, that can safely satisfy human thirst without chemical treatment. An oft-mentioned satisfaction in the lives of urbanites in an earlier era was a leisurely stroll in late afternoon to get a breath of fresh air in a neighborhood park or along a quiet street. Today in many of our major metropolitan areas it is difficult to find a quiet, peaceful place to take a leisurely stroll and sometimes impossible to get a breath of fresh air. These contrasts point up the dramatic changes that have occurred in the quality of our environment.

It is not my intent in this article, however, to document the existence of an environmental crisis but rather to discuss the cultural basis for such a crisis. Particular attention will be given to the institutional structures as expressions of our culture.

SOCIAL ORGANIZATION

In her book entitled *Social Institutions*, J. O. Hertzler classified all social institutions into nine functional categories: (i) economic and industrial, (ii) matrimonial and domestic, (iii) political, (iv) religious, (v) ethical, (vi) educational, (vii) communications, (viii) esthetic, and (ix) health. Institutions exist to carry on each of these functions in all cultures, regardless of their location or relative complexity. Thus, it is not surprising that one of the analytical criteria used by anthropologists in the study of various cultures is the comparison and contrast of the various social institutions as to form and relative importance.

A number of attempts have been made to explain attitudes and behavior that are commonly associated with one institutional function as the result of influence from a presumably independent institutional factor. The classic example of such an analysis is *The Protestant Ethic and the Spirit of Capitalism* by Max Weber. In this significant work Weber attributes much of the economic and industrial growth in Western Europe and North America to capitalism, which, he argued, was an economic form that developed as a result of the religious teachings of Calvin, particularly spiritual determinism.

This reply to Lynn White's article was published in *Science*, Vol. 170, pp. 508–512 (30 October 1970). Copyright by the American Association for the Advancement of Science. Notes deleted.

Social scientists have been particularly active in attempting to assess the influence of religious teaching and practice and of economic motivation on other institutional forms and behavior and on each other. In this connection, L. White suggested that the exploitative attitude that has prompted much of the environmental crisis in Western Europe and North America is a result of the teachings of the Judeo-Christian tradition, which conceives of man as superior to all other creation and of everything else as created for his use and enjoyment. He goes on to contend that the only way to reduce the ecologic crisis which we are now facing is to "reject the Christian axiom that nature has no reason for existence save to serve man." As with other ideas that appear to be new and novel, Professor White's observations have begun to be widely circulated and accepted in scholarly circles, as witness the article by religious writer E. B. Fiske in the *New York Times* earlier this year. In this article, note is taken of the fact that several prominent theologians and theological groups have accepted this basic premise that Judeo-Christian doctrine regarding man's relation to the rest of creation is at the root of the West's environmental crisis. I would suggest that the wide acceptance of such a simplistic explanation is at this point based more on fad than on fact.

Certainly, no fault can be found with White's statement that "Human ecology is deeply conditioned by beliefs about our nature and destiny—that is, by religion." However, to argue that it is the primary conditioner of human behavior toward the environment is much more than the data that he cites to support this proposition will bear. For example, White himself notes very early in his article that there is evidence for the idea that man has been dramatically altering his environment since antiquity. If this be true, and there is evidence that it is, then this mediates against the idea that the Judeo-Christian religion uniquely predisposes cultures within which it thrives to exploit their natural resources with indiscretion. White's own examples weaken his argument considerably. He points out that human intervention in the periodic flooding of the Nile River basin and the fire-drive method of hunting by prehistoric man have both probably wrought significant "unnatural" changes in man's environment. The absence of Judeo-Christian influence in these cases is obvious.

It seems tenable to affirm that the role played by religion in man-to-man and man-to-environment relationships is one of establishing a very broad system of allowable beliefs and behavior and of articulating and invoking a system of social and spiritual rewards for those who conform and of negative sanctions for individuals or groups who approach or cross the pale of the religiously unacceptable. In other words, it defines the ball park in which the game is played, and, by the very nature of the park, some types of games cannot be played. However, the kind of game that ultimately evolves is not itself defined by the ball park. For example, where animism is practiced, it is not likely that the believers will indiscriminately destroy objects of nature because such activity would incur the danger of spiritual and social sanctions. However, the fact that another culture does not associate spiritual beings with natural objects does not mean that such a culture will invariably ruthlessly exploit its resources. It simply means that there are fewer social and psychological constraints against such action.

In the remainder of this article, I present an alternative set of hypotheses based on cultural variables which, it seems to me, are more plausible and more defensible as an explanation of the environmental crisis that is now confronting us.

No culture has been able to completely screen out the egocentric tendencies of human beings. There also exists in all cultures a status hierarchy of positions and values, with certain groups partially or totally excluded from access to these normatively desirable goals. Historically, the differences in most cultures between the "rich" and the "poor" have been great. The many very poor have often produced the wealth of the few who controlled the means of production. There may have been no alternative where scarcity of supply and unsatiated demand were economic reality. Still, the desire for a "better life" is universal; that is, the desire for higher status positions and the achievement of culturally defined desirable goals is common to all societies.

THE EXPERIENCE IN THE WESTERN WORLD

In the West two significant revolutions that occurred in the 18th and 19th centuries completely redirected its political, social, and economic destiny. These two types of revolutions were unique to the West until very recently. The French revolution marked the beginnings of widespread democratization. In specific terms, this revolution involved a redistribution of the means of production and a reallocation of the natural and human resources that are an integral part of the production process. In effect new channels of social mobility were created, which theoretically made more wealth accessible to more people. Even though the revolution was partially perpetrated in the guise of overthrowing the control of presumably Christian institutions and of destroying the influence of God over the minds of men, still it would be superficial to argue that Christianity did not influence this revolution. After all, biblical teaching is one of the strongest of all pronouncements concerning human dignity and individual worth.

At about the same time but over a more extended period, another kind of revolution was taking place, primarily in England. As White points out very well, this phenomenon, which began with a number of technological innovations, eventually consummated a marriage with natural science and began to take on the character that it has retained until today. With this revolution the productive capacity of each worker was amplified by several times his potential prior to the revolution. It also became feasible to produce goods that were not previously producible on a commercial scale.

Later, with the integration of the democratic and technological ideals, the increased wealth began to be distributed more equitably among the population. In addition, as the capital to land ratio increased in the production process and the demand grew for labor to work in the factories, large populations from the agrarian hinterlands began to concentrate in the emerging industrial cities. The stage was set for the development of the conditions that now exist in the Western world.

With growing affluence for an increasingly large segment of the population, there generally develops an increased demand for goods and services. The usual by-product of this affluence is waste from both the production and consumption processes. The disposal of that waste is further complicated by the high concentration of heavy waste producers in urban areas. Under these conditions the maxim that "Dilution is the solution to pollution" does not withstand the test of time, because the volume of such wastes is greater than the system can absorb and purify through natural means. With increasing population, increasing production, increasing urban concentrations, and increasing real median incomes for well over a hundred years, it is not surprising that our environment has taken a terrible beating in absorbing our filth and refuse.

THE AMERICAN SITUATION

The North American colonies of England and France were quick to pick up the technical and social innovations that were taking place in their motherlands. Thus, it is not surprising that the inclination to develop an industrial and manufacturing base is observable rather early in the colonies. A strong trend toward democratization also evidenced itself very early in the struggle for nationhood. In fact, Thistlewaite notes the significance of the concept of democracy as embodied in French thought to the framers of constitutional government in the colonies.

From the time of the dissolution of the Roman Empire, resource ownership in the Western world was vested primarily with the monarchy or the Roman Catholic Church, which in turn bestowed control of the land resources on vassals who pledged fealty to the sovereign. Very slowly the concept of private ownership developed during the Middle Ages in Europe, until it finally developed into the fee simple concept.

In America, however, national policy from the outset was designed to convey ownership of the land and other natural resources into the hands of the citizenry. Thomas

Jefferson was perhaps more influential in crystallizing this philosophy in the new nation than anyone else. It was his conviction that an agrarian society made up of small landowners would furnish the most stable foundation for building the nation. This concept has received support up to the present and, against growing economic pressures in recent years, through government programs that have encouraged the conventional family farm. This point is clearly relevant to the subject of this article because it explains how the natural resources of the nation came to be controlled not by a few aristocrats but by many citizens. It explains how decisions that ultimately degrade the environment are made not only by corporation boards and city engineers but by millions of owners of our natural resources. This is democracy exemplified!

CHALLENGE OF THE FRONTIER

Perhaps the most significant interpretation of American history has been Frederick Jackson Turner's much criticized thesis that the western frontier was the prime force in shaping our societies. In his own words,

> If one would understand why we are today one nation, rather than a collection of isolated states, he must study this economic and social consolidation of the country. . . . The effect of the Indian frontier as a consolidating agent in our history is important.

He further postulated that the nation experienced a series of frontier challenges that moved across the continent in waves. These included the explorers' and traders' frontier, the Indian frontier, the cattle frontier, and three distinct agrarian frontiers. His thesis can be extended to interpret the expansionist period of our history in Panama, in Cuba, and in the Philippines as a need for a continued frontier challenge.

Turner's insights furnish a starting point for suggesting a second variable in analyzing the cultural basis of the United States' environmental crisis. As the nation began to expand westward, the settlers faced many obstacles, including a primitive transportation system, hostile Indians, and the absence of physical and social security. To many frontiersmen, particularly small farmers, many of the natural resources that are now highly valued were originally perceived more as obstacles than as assets. Forests needed to be cleared to permit farming. Marshes needed to be drained. Rivers needed to be controlled. Wildlife often represented a competitive threat in addition to being a source of food. Sod was considered a nuisance—to be burned, plowed, or otherwise destroyed to permit "desirable" use of the land.

Undoubtedly, part of this attitude was the product of perceiving these resources as inexhaustible. After all, if a section of timber was put to the torch to clear it for farming, it made little difference because there was still plenty to be had very easily. It is no coincidence that the

"First Conservation Movement" began to develop about 1890. At that point settlement of the frontier was almost complete. With the passing of the frontier era of American history, it began to dawn on people that our resources were indeed exhaustible. This realization ushered in a new philosophy of our national government toward natural resources management under the guidance of Theodore Roosevelt and Gifford Pinchot. Samuel Hays has characterized this movement as the appearance of a new "Gospel of Efficiency" in the management and utilization of our natural resources.

THE PRESENT AMERICAN SCENE

America is the archetype of what happens when democracy, technology, urbanization, capitalistic mission, and antagonism (or apathy) toward natural environment are blended together. The present situation is characterized by three dominant features that mediate against quick solution to this impending crisis: (i) an absence of personal moral direction concerning our treatment of our natural resources, (ii) an inability on the part of our social institutions to make adjustments to this stress, and (iii) an abiding faith in technology.

The first characteristic is the absence of personal moral direction. There is moral disparity when a corporation executive can receive a prison sentence for embezzlement but be congratulated for increasing profits by ignoring pollution abatement laws. That the absolute cost to society of the second act may be infinitely greater than the first is often not even considered.

The moral principle that we are to treat others as we would want to be treated seems as appropriate a guide as it ever has been. The rarity of such teaching and the even more uncommon instance of its being practiced help to explain how one municipality can, without scruple, dump its effluent into a stream even though it may do irreparable damage to the resource and add tremendously to the cost incurred by downstream municipalities that use the same water. Such attitudes are not restricted to any one culture. There appears to be an almost universal tendency to maximize self-interests and a widespread willingness to shift production costs to society to promote individual ends.

Undoubtedly, much of this behavior is the result of ignorance. If our accounting systems were more efficient in computing the cost of such irresponsibility both to the present generation and to those who will inherit the environment we are creating, steps would undoubtedly be taken to enforce compliance with measures designed to conserve resources and protect the environment. And perhaps if the total costs were known, we might optimistically speculate that more voluntary compliance would result.

A second characteristic of our current situation involves institutional inadequacies. It has been said that "what belongs to everyone belongs to no one." The maxim seems particularly appropriate to the problem we are discussing. So much of our environment is so apparently abundant that it is considered a free commodity. Air and water are particularly good examples. Great liberties have been permitted in the use and abuse of these resources for at least two reasons. First, these resources have typically been considered of less economic value than other natural resources except when conditions of extreme scarcity impose limiting factors. Second, the right of use is more difficult to establish for resources that are not associated with a fixed location.

Government, as the institution representing the corporate interests of all its citizens, has responded to date with dozens of legislative acts and numerous court decisions which give it authority to regulate the use of natural resources. However, the decisiveness to act has thus far been generally lacking. This indecisiveness cannot be understood without noting that the simplistic models that depict the conflict as that of a few powerful special interests versus "The People" are altogether inadequate. A very large proportion of the total citizenry is implicated in environmental degradation; the responsibility ranges from that of the board and executives of a utility company who might wish to thermally pollute a river with impunity to that of the average citizen who votes against a bond issue to improve the efficiency of a municipal sanitation system in order to keep his taxes from being raised. The magnitude of irresponsibility among individuals and institutions might be characterized as failing along a continuum from highly irresponsible to indirectly responsible. With such a broad base of interests being threatened with every change in resource policy direction, it is not surprising, although regrettable, that government has been so indecisive.

A third characteristic of the present American scene is an abiding faith in technology. It is very evident that the idea that technology can overcome almost any problem is widespread in Western society. This optimism exists in the face of strong evidence that much of man's technology, when misused, has produced harmful results, particularly in the long run. The reasoning goes something like this: "After all, we have gone to the moon. All we need to do is allocate enough money and brainpower and we can solve any problem."

It is both interesting and alarming that many people view technology almost as something beyond human control. Rickover put it this way:

It troubles me that we are so easily pressured by purveyors of technology into permitting so called "progress" to alter our lives without attempting to control it—as if technology were an irrepressible force of nature to which we must meekly submit.

He goes on to add:

It is important to maintain a humanistic attitude toward

technology; to recognize clearly that since it is the product of human effort, technology can have no legitimate purpose but to serve man—man in general, not merely some men: future generations, not merely those who currently wish to gain advantage for themselves: man in the totality of his humanity, encompassing all his manifold interests and needs, not merely some one particular concern of his. When viewed humanistically, technology is seen not as an end in itself but a means to an end, the end being determined by man himself in accordance with the laws prevailing in his society.

In short, it is one thing to appreciate the value of technology; it is something else entirely to view it as our environmental savior—which will save us in spite of ourselves.

CONCLUSION

The forces of democracy, technology, urbanization, increasing individual wealth, and an aggressive attitude toward nature seem to be directly related to the environmental crisis now being confronted in the Western world. The Judeo-Christian tradition has probably influenced the character of each of these forces: However, to isolate religious tradition as a cultural component and to contend that it is the "historical root of our ecological crisis" is a bold affirmation for which there is little historical or scientific support.

To assert that the primary cultural condition that has created our environmental crisis is Judeo-Christian teaching avoids several hard questions. For example: Is there less tendency for those who control the resources of non-Christian cultures to live in extravagant affluence with attendant high levels of waste and inefficient consumption? If non-Judeo Christian cultures had the same levels of economic productivity, urbanization, and high average household incomes, is there evidence to indicate that these cultures would not exploit or disregard nature as our culture does?

If our environmental crisis is a "religious problem," why are other parts of the world experiencing in various degrees the same environmental problems that we are so well acquainted with in the Western world? It is readily observable that the science and technology that developed on a large scale first in the West have been adopted elsewhere. Judeo-Christian tradition has not been adopted as a predecessor to science and technology on a comparable scale. Thus, all White can defensibly argue is that the West developed modern science and technology *first*. This says nothing about the origin or existence of a particular ethic toward our environment.

In essence, White has proposed this simple model:

I	$\rightarrow$	II	$\rightarrow$	III
Judeo-Christian tradition		Science and technology		Environmental degradation

I have suggested here that, at best, Judeo-Christian teaching has had only an indirect effect on the treatment of our environment. The model could be characterized as follows:

I	$\rightarrow$	II	$\rightarrow$	III	$\rightarrow$	IV
Judeo-Christian tradition		1. Capitalism (with the attendant development of science and technology) 2. Democratization		1. Urbanization 2. Increased wealth 3. Increased population 4. Individual resource ownership		Environmental degradation

Even here, the link between Judeo-Christian tradition and the proposed dependent variables certainly have the least empirical support. One need only look at the veritable mountain of criticism of Weber's conclusions in *The Protestant Ethic and the Spirit of Capitalism* to sense the tenuous nature of this link. The second and third phases of this model are common to many parts of the world. Phase I is not.

Jean Mayer, the eminent food scientist, gave an appropriate conclusion about the cultural basis for our environmental crisis:

> It might be bad in China with 700 million poor people but 700 million rich Chinese would wreck China in no time. . . . It is the rich who wreck the environment . . . occupy much more space, consume more of each natural resource, disturb ecology more, litter the landscape . . . and create more pollution.

Study Questions

1. What is Moncrief's view of our environmental crisis?
2. What does Moncrief think about White's position? Do you agree with his critique of White's position?
3. Can you imagine how White might reply to Moncrief?

The Judeo-Christian Stewardship Attitude to Nature

PATRICK DOBEL

Patrick Dobel is associate professor and director of the Graduate School of Public Affairs at the University of Washington in Seattle.

Dobel disagrees with White's thesis that the Christian attitude toward nature is one of arrogance and dominance ("limitless rule of creation"). He argues that the Judeo-Christian attitude is an ethics of stewardship and that humility toward God regarding nature, not arrogance, is enjoined by our religious heritage.

Browsing in a local bookstore recently, I took down several of the more general books from the "Ecology" shelf. Scanning the tables of contents and indexes of 13 books, I discovered that nine of them made reference to "Christianity," "the Bible" or the "Judeo-Christian tradition." Examining their contents more closely, I found that seven of these books blamed specific Christian or Bible-based values as significant "causes" of the ecology crisis.

Over half these books referenced an article by Lynn White, Jr., titled "The Historical Roots of Our Ecologic Crisis" (*Science*, March 10, 1967). In this short, undocumented and simplistic article White argues that the root of the entire problem lies in "the Christian maxim that nature has no reason for existence save to serve man." From the Christians' penchant for cutting down sacred Druidic groves to the development of "modern science from natural theology," Christianity, White argues, laid the foundations of Western "arrogance towards nature" and "limitless rule of creation."

Almost all similar statements are indebted to White; they even cite the same examples: grief over the destruction of the sacred groves; respect for Saint Francis of Assisi. Although few of the authors have read anything about him except that he talked to birds, they have raised poor Francis to the rank of first "ecological saint," while conveniently ignoring his myriad admonitions about asceticism and communal ownership of property.

DOMINION OVER THE EARTH

The ecological indictment of Christianity boils down to two somewhat contradictory assertions: that the postulated transcendence and domination of humanity over nature encourages thoughtless exploitation of the earth and that the otherworldly orientation of Christianity encourages contempt and disregard for the earth. In documenting the first indictment authors often cite Genesis 1:26: "Let us make man in our image, after our likeness; and let them have dominion over the fish of the sea, and over the birds of the air, and over the cattle, and over every creeping thing that creeps upon the earth." Some also quote Genesis 1:29: "Be fruitful and multiply, and fill the earth and subdue it; and have dominion over the fish of the sea and over the birds of the air and over every living thing that moves upon the earth."

These texts lead to the conclusion that the Bible emphasizes the absolute superiority of humanity over the rest of creation. And this relation must be primarily one of antagonism and alienation, for "cursed is the ground because of you; in toil you shall eat of it all the days of your life. . . . In the sweat of your face you shall eat bread" (Gen. 3: 17).

Thus Christianity separates both humanity and God from the earth and destroys the inherent sacredness of the earth. This alienation is coupled with humanity's innate superiority over nature and the divine mandate to exploit nature limitlessly for human ends—a mandate that is carried out in the context of antagonism and an expectation that the earth must be treated harshly to gain the yield of human survival. Together these notions have shaped Western culture's spoliation of the earth.

In bringing the second indictment, critics point out that Christianity's otherworldly preoccupation also contributes to human abuse of the environment. Christians are instructed to "kill everything in you that belongs only to the earthly life" and to "let your thoughts be on heavenly things, not on the things that are on the earth" (Col. 3:2–5). The emphasis is upon awaiting "a new heaven and a new earth in which righteousness dwells" (II Pet. 3:13). In some ways this stress undercuts the mandates of superiority and rule since it implies that humanity rules nothing but a fallen and contemptible orb. If the contempt, however, is tied to an antagonistic human domination and the need of people to discipline their unruly bodies through work, it can provide an ethical framework to support the thoughtless and arrogant exploitation which is part of the ecology crisis. The thesis linking Calvinism with the rise of industrialization reflects this ambivalent world-hating but smug and exploitative attitude.

The critics see modern science and technology along with notions of unbridled progress and exploitation emerging from this Judeo-Christian matrix. They conclude that Christianity must accept most of the "blame" for the unique "Western" perspectives which have led to the present state of affairs. This "blame" somehow rings false when the ecologists extend the link to the later implications of a secularized technology and a liberal view of human progress.

LOOKING FOR THE ROOTS

The attempt to discover historical roots is a dubious business at best, and in this case it borders on the ludicrous. Christianity's ecological critics consistently underestimate the economic, social and political influences on modern science and economy; their approach makes for good polemics but bad history. Their thesis lacks a careful historical analysis of the intellectual and practical attitudes toward the earth and its use in the consciously Christian Middle Ages. They disregard the earth-centered ideals of the Christian Renaissance and its concern with the delicate limitations of the Great Chain of Being, and they pay little attention to the emergence of a peculiarly non-Christian deism and theism which defined God in the 17th and 18th centuries to accommodate a newly secularized nature and new developments in science and trade. These critics neglect to mention the specifically Christian prohibitions which often made religion a detriment to economic and scientific development.

They also ignore the rise of the secularized nation-state from the decay of "Christendom"; yet these new government regimes provided much of the impetus to maximize the exploitation of resources and the discovery of new lands. Most of the operative "roots" of the present crisis are to be found in the far more secularized and non-Christian world of nationalism, science and liberalism in the 16th through the 19th centuries.

Given the unsoundness of the theory that blames Christianity for the environmental crisis, it is surprising that it has gained such remarkable currency. In light of this fact there are two distinct tasks which confront the Christian community. First, this thesis should be addressed in some detail, not only to show its flaws but to discover what ideas and practices the tradition can contribute to a concrete ecological program. Second, we must use the vast ethical and conceptual resources of the Judeo-Christian tradition to develop a God-centered ecological ethic which accounts for the sacredness of the earth without losing sight of human worth and justice. In addressing myself to this second task, I will try to develop appropriate responses to the following questions through textual exegesis of the Bible: What is the ethical status of the earth as an entity in creation? What is the proper relation of humanity to the earth and its resources?

Ecological critics have nostalgically lamented the decline of "nature worship" and have spoken wistfully of the need to import "Eastern" concepts of pantheism or quietist respect for the "equality of all life." Even some of the most secularized ecologists are calling for a rediscovery of the "sacredness" of nature.

Although it is hard to discover the enduring sacredness of anything in a totally secularized world, we must keep several points in mind about these calls. First, all cultures, regardless of religion, have abused or destroyed large areas of the world either because of economic or population pressures or from simple ignorance. Second, the ethical consequences of the new nature worship, neopantheism and the militant assertion of the equality of all creaturehood pose grave problems for establishing any prior claims of worth or inherent dignity for human beings. The more undifferentiated God and the world become, the harder it is to define individual humans as worthwhile with specific claims to social justice and care. Third, a sort of mindless ecological imperative based upon such notions is ultimately reactionary and antihuman, as well as anti-Christian. There are fundamental ethical differences between plants and animals and between animals and human beings. To resort simplistically to militantly pro-earth and antiprogress positions misses the vital Christian and humanistic point that our sojourn upon the earth is not yet completed and that we must continue to work unflaggingly toward social justice and the well-being of all people.

The unique contribution a Christian ecology can make to the earth is the assertion that we can insist on a reasonable harmony with our world without abandoning our commitment to social justice for all members of our unique and self-consciously alienated species. We can love and respect our environment without obliterating all ethical and technological distinctions, and without denying the demand that we cautiously but steadily use the earth for the benefit of all humanity.

The first question to address is the status of the earth and its resources. A different way of putting this is "Who owns the earth?" The answer of the entire Judeo-Christian tradition is clear: God. "In the beginning God created the heavens and the earth" (Gen. 1:3). In direct ethical terms God created the earth, and in distributive-justice terms it belongs to him: "The earth is the Lord's and the fullness thereof" (Ps. 24:1). As an act of pure love he created a world and he "founded the earth to endure" (Ps. 119:90–91).

What kind of world did God create? The answer has two dimensions: the physical or descriptive and the ethical. As a product of nature the world was created as a law-bound entity. The laws are derivative of God's will for all creation as "maintained by your rulings" (Ps. 119:90–91). Things coexist in intricate and regulated harmony—the basic postulate of science, mythology and reason. Although we have a world of laws, it is also a world of bounty and harmony. For it had been promised that "while the earth remains, seedtime and harvest shall not cease" (Gen. 8:22). It was arranged "in wisdom" so that in the balance of nature, "All creatures depend upon you to feed them . . . you provide the food with a generous hand." God's presence ultimately "holds all things in unity" (Col. 1:16–20) and constantly "renews" the world (Ps. 104:24–30). This world abounds in life and is held together in a seamless web maintained by God-willed laws.

In ethical terms, God saw that the world was "very good" (Gen. 1:31). In love and freedom he created the world and valued it as good. All the creatures of the world also share in this goodness (I Tim. 4:4). This does not mean that the world is "good for" some purpose or simply has utilitarian value to humanity. The world, in its bounty and multiplicity of life, is independently good and ought to be respected as such.

As an independent good, the earth possesses an autonomous status as an ethical and covenanted entity. In Genesis 9:8–17, God directly includes the earth and all the animals as participants in the covenant. He urges the animals to "be fruitful and multiply. " Earlier in Genesis 1:30, he takes care specifically to grant the plant life of the earth to the creatures who possess "breath of life." In the great covenant with Noah and all humanity, he expressly includes all other creatures and the earth.

> And God said, "This is a sign of the covenant which I make between *me and you and every living creature* that is with you, for all future generations: I set my bow in the sky, and it shall be a sign of the *covenant between* me and the earth" [emphasis added].

The prophets, Isaiah especially, constantly address the earth and describe its independent travail. Paul describes the turmoil and travail of the earth as a midwife of all creation and redemption (Rom. 8:18–22). The earth must be regarded as an autonomous ethical entity bound not just by the restraints of physical law but also by respect for its inherent goodness and the covenanted limitations placed upon our sojourn. Perhaps we must think seriously of defining a category of "sins against the earth."

The proper relation between humanity and the bountiful earth is more complex. One fact is of outstanding moral relevance: the earth does not belong to humanity; it belongs to God. Jeremiah summarizes it quite succinctly: "I by my great power and outstretched arm made the earth, land and animals that are on the earth. And I can give them to whom I please" (Jer. 27:5). For an ecological ethic this fact cannot be ignored. The resources and environment of the earth are not ours in any sovereign or unlimited sense; they belong to someone else.

A TRUST FOR FUTURE GENERATIONS

Humanity's relation to the earth is dominated by the next fact: God "bestows" the earth upon all of humanity (Ps. 115:16). This gift does not, however, grant sovereign control. The prophets constantly remind us that God is still the "king" and the ruler/owner to whom the earth reverts. No one generation of people possesses the earth. The earth was made "to endure" and was given for all future generations. Consequently the texts constantly reaffirm that the gift comes under covenanted conditions, and that the covenant is "forever." The Bible is permeated with a careful concern for preserving the "land" and the "earth" as an "allotted heritage" (Ps. 2:7–12).

This point is central to the Judeo-Christian response to the world. The world is given to all. Its heritage is something of enduring value designed to benefit all future generations. Those who receive such a gift and benefit from it are duty-bound to conserve the resources and pass them on for future generations to enjoy. An "earth of abundance" (Judg. 18:10) provides for humanity's needs and survival (Gen. 1:26–28, 9:2–5). But the injunction "obey the covenant" (I Chron. 16:14–18) accompanies the gift.

There are some fairly clear principles that direct our covenanted responsibilities toward the earth. Each generation exists only as "sojourner" or "pilgrim." We hold the resources and the earth as a "trust" for future generations. Our covenanted relations to the earth—and for that matter, to all human beings—must be predicated upon the recognition and acceptance of the limits of reality. For there is a "limit upon all perfection" (Ps. 119:96), and we must discover and respect the limits upon ourselves, our use of resources, our consumption, our treatment of others and the environment with its delicate ecosystems. Abiding by the covenant means abiding by the laws of nature, both scientific and moral. In ecological terms the balance of nature embodies God's careful plan that the earth and its bounty shall provide for the needs and survival of all humanity of all generations.

The combined emphases upon God's ownership, our trusteeship and the limits of life call for an attitude of humility and care in dealing with the world. Only "the humble shall have the land for their own to enjoy untroubled peace" (Ps. 37:11). Knowledge of limits, especially of the intricacy of the ecosystems, makes humility and care a much more natural response. The transgression of limits usually brings either unknown or clearly dangerous consequences and ought to influence all actions with a singular sense of caution. Humility and respect do not mean simple awe, or withdrawal from all attempts to use or improve the bounty we are given. At the very least, they lead to the loss of arrogant ignorance which leads us to pursue policies in contradiction to the clear limits and laws of nature and particular ecosystems.

THE STEWARDSHIP IMPERATIVE

The New Testament distills these notions and adds a strong activist imperative with its account of stewardship. This activist element is a vital alternative to some of the more extreme ethical positions in reactionary ecological ethics. The parable of the good steward in Luke 12:41–48 and the parable of the talents in Matthew 25:14–30 summarize the concept. The preservation of what is given "in trust" demands a recognition of the owner's dictates for the resources. We must know the limits and laws of the world in order to use them wisely. Our actions must be guided, in part, by concerns for future generations. Above all, we must never knowingly exhaust or ruin what has been given to us. If doing so is absolutely necessary to sustain life, then equity demands that we must leave some equally accessible and beneficial legacy to replace what has been exhausted.

But there is more involved in being a "faithful and wise steward." Even the most conservative banker is obliged to improve the stock for the benefit of the heirs. The parable of the talents makes it abundantly clear that we who are entrusted with his property will be called to account for our obligation to improve the earth. The stewardship imperative assumes that the moral and ecological constraints are respected, and it adds the obligation to distribute the benefits justly. The steward must "give them their portion of the food at the proper time." Mistreating his charges, gorging himself on the resources in excess consumption, and not caring for the resources will all cause the stewards to be "cut off." True stewardship requires both respect for the trusteeship and covenanted imperatives and an active effort to improve the land for the future and to use it in a manner to benefit others. Ethical proportionality applies to all those responsible for the earth, for "when a man has had a great deal given to him on trust, even more will be expected of him" (Luke 12:48–49).

AN INFORMED HUMILITY

The lessons are clear. Any ecological ethic which takes into account both God and humanity and does not reduce both to some extension of undifferentiated nature must begin with a rejection of the unbridled sovereignty of humanity over the earth. In this rejection is the recognition that all work upon the earth must be informed by a clear understanding of and respect for the earth as an autonomous and valuable entity and the laws of nature on which the bounty of the earth depends.

These are necessary but by no means sufficient within the Judeo-Christian tradition. For the earth, while it possesses its own moral autonomy, is not God and must not be confused as such. Our own relation to it must be predicated upon a careful understanding that earth and its resources are for any generation a restricted gift held in trust for future generations. We must never lose sight of the fact that a just and informed humility provides the framework for a working relationship with the earth.

Much more work remains to be done on the "ethics of stewardship"; I have merely suggested a few ethical considerations: the obligation not to exhaust nonrenewable resources, the imperative to provide accessible replacements, the necessity to improve our heritage modestly and carefully, the greater responsibility of the advantaged to improve that which exists and to share, and the obligation to refrain from excessive consumption and waste. "Each of you has received a special gift, so like good stewards responsible for all the different gifts of God, put yourselves at the service of others" (I Pet. 4:10–11).

Study Questions

1. Compare Dobel's account with White's critique. Which account is closer to the truth? Explain your answer.
2. If human beings do not own Earth, what is our role, according to Dobel? Do you agree? Explain your answer.
3. If one does not accept a theistic version of creation, does the stewardship model make any sense? A steward is one who manages the household affairs of another person. If there is no God, Earth is not God's household. But then whose is it? To whom are we stewards?

For Further Reading

Armstrong, Susan, and Richard Botzler, eds. *Environmental Ethics*. New York: McGraw-Hill, 1993.

Attfield, Robin. *The Ethics of Environmental Concern*. New York: Columbia University Press, 1983.

Barbour, Ian G., ed. *Western Man and Environmental Ethics*. Menlo Park, CA: Addison-Wesley, 1973.

Bratton, Susan Power. "Christian Ecotheology and the Old Testament." *Environmental Ethics* 6 (1984).

———. "The Original Desert Solitaire: Early Christian Monasticism and Wilderness." *Environmental Ethics* 10, 1988.

DesJardins, Joseph. *Environmental Ethics*. Belmont, CA: Wadsworth, 1993.

Glacken, Clarence J. *Traces on the Rhodian Shore: Nature and Culture in Western Thought from Ancient Times to the End of the Eighteenth Century*. Berkeley: University of California Press, 1967.

Gruen, Lori, and Dale Jamieson, eds. *Reflecting on Nature*. New York: Oxford University Press, 1994.

Hargrove, Eugene. *Foundations of Environmental Ethics*. Englewood Cliffs, NJ: Prentice Hall, 1989.

Nash, Roderick. *The Rights of Nature*. Madison: University of Wisconsin Press, 1989.

Passmore, John. *Man's Responsibility for Nature*. New York: Scribner, 1974.

Rolston, Holmes, III. *Philosophy Gone Wild: Essays in Environmental Ethics*. Buffalo, NY: Prometheus Press, 1986.

———. *Environmental Ethics*. Philadelphia: Temple University Press, 1988.

Shrader-Frechette, Kristin. *Environmental Ethics*. Pacific Grove, CA: Boxwood Press, 1981.

Sterba, James P., ed. *Earth Ethics*. Upper Saddle River, NJ: Prentice Hall, 1994.

Taylor, Paul. *Respect for Nature*. Princeton, NJ: Princeton University Press, 1986.

VanDeVeer, Donald, and Christine Pierce, eds. *The Environmental Ethics and Policy Book*. Belmont, CA: Wadsworth, 1993.

Wenz, Peter. *Environmental Justice*. Albany, NY: SUNY Press, 1988.

Westra, Laura. *An Environmental Proposal for Ethics: The Principle of Integrity*. Lanham, MD: Rowman & Littlefield, 1994.

Wilkerson, Loren, ed. *Earthkeeping in the '90s: Stewardship of Creation*. Grand Rapids, MI: Eerdmans, 1991.

CHAPTER TWO

Animal Rights

Gorilla at an Illinois Zoo
Rescues a 3-Year Old Boy

BROOKFIELD, Ill., Aug. 16 (AP)—A 3-year-old boy fell into an exhibit occupied by gorillas at the Brookfield Zoo this afternoon, and was rescued by a female gorilla that cradled the child and brought him to zookeepers.

The boy injured his head when he fell 18 feet onto the exhibit's concrete. He was alert when taken to a hospital, although his condition was later listed as critical.

Seven gorillas were on display in the exhibit. One of them, Binti, a 7-year old female with a baby gorilla on her back, picked up the child, cradled him in her arms and placed him near a door where zookeepers could retrieve him, said Sondra Katzen, a spokeswoman for the zoo, 10 miles west of downtown Chicago.

Carrie Stewart, a visitor who witnessed the rescue, said, "Another gorilla walked toward the boy, and she kind of turned around and walked away from the other gorillas and tried to be protective."

SOURCE: *New York Times* (August 17,1996): 7. Reprinted by permission.

In addition, zookeepers sprayed water on the exhibit to keep the other gorillas away from the boy, said a second spokeswoman, Melinda Pruett-Jones. "They controlled the animals beautifully and had an emergency medical crew working on the little boy as soon as they possibly could," Ms. Pruett-Jones said.

The child was taken to Loyola University Medical Center. His condition was listed there as critical, although Michael Maggio, a spokesman for the hospital, said he did not know the precise nature of the boy's injuries. The hospital did not disclose the boy's identity and said his parents were not available to comment.

Ms. Katzen, one of the spokeswomen at the zoo, said she believed that the boy had run ahead of his mother during their visit there but that she did not know how he had been able to get over a railing, three or four feet high, that separates the exhibit from visitors.

Ms. Katzen said this was the first time anyone had fallen into the gorilla pit since the zoo created it 14 years ago.

What sort of beings are deserving of moral regard? Only human beings or animals as well? How ought we to treat animals? Do they have moral rights? Is their suffering to be equated with human suffering? Should experimentation on animals cease? Should large-scale commercial ("factory") farms be abolished because they tend to cause animals great suffering? Do we have a moral duty to become vegetarians? What exactly is the moral status of animals?

In 1975 a book appeared, which opened with the words, "This book is about the tyranny of human over non-human animals. This tyranny has caused and today is

still causing an amount of pain and suffering that can only be compared with that which resulted from the centuries of tyranny by white humans over black humans." Thus, Peter Singer began his epoch-making *Animal Liberation*, which launched the modern animal rights movement. Today thousands of people in every state of the Union, every province of Canada, and many other places in the world are part of a committed animal rights movement.

There are two separate defenses of animal rights: the utilitarian[1] and the deontological arguments. Peter Singer is the main representative of the utilitarian. Utilitarians follow Jeremy Bentham in asserting that

HICKS: *The Peaceable Kingdom*, ca. 1848. 17⅛ x 23½". New York State Historical Association, Cooperstown.

what makes beings morally considerable is not reason but *sentience*. All sentient creatures have ability to suffer and, as such, have interests. The frustration of those interests leads to suffering. Utilitarianism seeks to maximize the satisfaction of interests whether they be those of humans or animals. In some cases, human interests will make special claims on us; for example, humans but not mice or pigs will need schools and books. But if a pig and a child are in pain and you only have one pain reliever, you may have a moral dilemma as to who should receive the pain reliever. Utilitarians will generally allow some animal experimentation; for example, if experimenting on chimpanzees promises to help us find a cure for AIDS, it's probably justified, but a utilitarian animal liberationist like Singer would also be willing to experiment on retarded children if it maximized utility.

The second type of defense of animal rights is the deontological *rights* position of which Tom Regan is the foremost proponent. The equal-rights position on animal rights contends that the same essential psychological properties—desires, memory, intelligence, and so on—link all animals and the human animal and thereby give us equal intrinsic value upon which equal rights are founded. These rights are inalienable and cannot be forfeited. Contrary to Singer, we have no right to experiment on chimpanzees in order to maximize satisfaction of interests—that's exploitation. Animals like people are "ends in themselves," persons, so that utility is not sufficient to override these rights. Regan is thus

more radical than Singer. He calls for not reform but the total dissolution of commercial animal farming, the total elimination of hunting and trapping, the total abolition of animal experiments. Just as we would condemn a scientist who took children and performed dangerous experiments on them for the good of others, so we must condemn the institutions that use coercion on animals.

Both utilitarian and deontological animal rights proponents have been attacked on their own ground. R. G. Frey, for example, has argued that utilitarianism does not justify the sweeping indictments or proposals that Singer advocates. Because of the greater complexity of the human psyche and its social system, utility will be maximized by exploiting animals. What is needed is an amelioration of existing large-scale farms and safeguards in animal experimentation to ensure against unnecessary suffering.

In our readings, Mary Anne Warren attacks Regan's deontological position for failing to see important differences between human beings and even higher animals, especially our ability to reason. Warren, who agrees that we do have duties to be kind to animals, not to kill them without good reason, and to do what we can to make their lives enjoyable, points out that Regan's notion of inherent value is obscure.

Finally, J. Baird Callicott's seminal article "Animal Liberation" challenges the traditional view that divides the ideological landscape into two groups: the anthropocentrists and the environmentalist-humane moralists (i.e., the animal liberationists). Callicott sets forth a triangular division, consisting of ethical humanists, humane moralists, and ethical holists, those like Aldo Leopold (Reading 18) who reject the atomistic assumptions of the other two groups. Callicott levels arguments against both the anthropocentrists and the animal rights advocates in order to make a case for the wider environmental ethics.

We begin our readings with Kant's view that since animals are not self-conscious rational agents capable of forming the moral law, they are not directly morally considerable.

Note

1. *Utilitarianism* is the view that the morally right act is the one that maximizes utility. It aims at producing the best overall consequences. *Deontological* ethics hold that certain features in the moral act itself have intrinsic value regardless of the consequences. It is wrong to kill innocent people even to procure good consequences.

5

Rational Beings Alone Have Moral Worth

IMMANUEL KANT

Immanuel Kant (1724–1804) was born into a deeply pietistic Lutheran family in Königsberg, Germany, and was a professor of philosophy at the University of Königsberg. He is a premier philosopher in the Western tradition, setting forth major works in metaphysics, philosophy of religion, and ethics.

Here, Kant first argues that rational beings are ends-in-themselves and must never be used as mere means. Only they have intrinsic moral worth. Animals are not persons because they are not rational, self-conscious beings capable of grasping the moral law. Since they are not part of the kingdom of moral legislators, we who are members of that "kingdom" do not owe them anything. But we should be kind to them since that will help develop good character in us and help us treat our fellow human beings with greater consideration. That is, our duties to animals are simply indirect duties to other human beings.

I. SECOND FORMULATION OF THE CATEGORICAL IMPERATIVE: HUMANITY AS AN END IN ITSELF

The will is conceived as a faculty of determining oneself to action in *accordance with the conception of certain laws*. And such a faculty can be found only in rational beings. Now that which serves the will as the objective ground of its self-determination is the *end,* and if this is assigned by reason alone, it must hold for all rational

beings. On the other hand, that which merely contains the ground of possibility of the action of which the effect is the end, this is called the *means*. The subjective ground of the desire is the *spring*, the objective ground of the volition is the *motive*; hence the distinction between subjective ends which rest on springs, and objective ends which depend on motives valid for every rational being. Practical principles are *formal* when they abstract from all subjective ends; they are *material* when they assume these, and therefore particular springs of action. The ends which a rational being proposes to himself at pleasure as *effects* of his actions (material ends) are all only relative, for it is only their relation to the particular desires of the subject that gives them their worth, which therefore cannot furnish principles universal and necessary for all rational beings and for every volition, that is to say practical laws. Hence all these relative ends can give rise only to hypothetical imperatives.

Supposing, however, that there were something *whose existence* has *in itself* an absolute worth, something which, being *an end in itself*, could be a source of definite laws, then in this and this alone would lie the source of a possible categorical imperative, *i.e.* a practical law.

Now I say: man and generally any rational being *exists* as an end in himself, *not merely as a means* to be arbitrarily used by this or that will, but in all his actions, whether they concern himself or other rational beings, must be always regarded at the same time as an end. All objects of the inclinations have only a conditional worth; for if the inclinations and the wants founded on them did not exist, then their object would be without value. But the inclinations themselves being sources of want are so far from having an absolute worth for which they should be desired, that, on the contrary, it must be the universal wish of every rational being to be wholly

The first section is from Kant's *Foundation of the Metaphysics of Morals* (1873), trans. T. K. Abbott. The second section is from Kant's *Lectures on Ethics*, trans. Louis Infield (New York: Harper & Row, 1963).

free from them. Thus the worth of any object which is *to be acquired* by our action is always conditional. Beings whose existence depends not on our will but on nature's, have nevertheless, if they are nonrational beings, only a relative value as means, and are therefore called *things*; rational beings, on the contrary, are called *persons*, because their very nature points them out as ends in themselves, that is as something which must not be used merely as means, and so far therefore restricts freedom of action (and is an object of respect). These, therefore, are not merely subjective ends whose existence has a worth *for us* as an effect of our action, but *objective ends,* that is things whose existence is an end in itself: an end moreover for which no other can be substituted, which they should subserve *merely* as means, for otherwise nothing whatever would possess *absolute worth;* but if all worth were conditioned and therefore contingent, then there would be no supreme practical principle of reason whatever.

If then there is a supreme practical principle or, in respect of the human will, a categorical imperative, it must be one which, being drawn from the conception of that which is necessarily an end for everyone because it is an *end in itself,* constitutes an *objective* principle of will, and can therefore serve as a universal practical law. The foundation of this principle is: *rational nature exists as an end in itself.* Man necessarily conceives his own existence as being so: so far then this is a *subjective* principle of human actions. But every other rational being regards its existence similarly, just on the same rational principle that holds for me: so that it is at the same time an objective principle, from which as a supreme practical law all laws of the will must be capable of being deduced. Accordingly the practical imperative will be as follows: *So act as to treat humanity, whether in thine own person or in that of any other, in every case as an end withal, never as means only.* We will now inquire whether this can be practically carried out.

II.

Baumgarten speaks of duties towards beings which are beneath us and beings which are above us. But so far as animals are concerned, we have no direct duties. Animals are not self-conscious and are there merely as a means to an end. That end is man. We can ask, "Why do animals exist?" But to ask, "Why does man exist?" is a meaningless question. *Our duties towards animals are merely indirect duties towards humanity.* Animal nature has analogies to human nature, and by doing our duties to animals in respect of manifestations of human nature, we indirectly do our duty towards humanity. Thus, if a dog has served his master long and faithfully, his service, on the analogy of human service,

deserves reward, and when the dog has grown too old to serve, his master ought to keep him until he dies. Such action helps to support us in our duties towards human beings, where they are bounden duties. If then any acts of animals are analogous to human acts and spring from the same principles, we have duties towards the animals because thus we cultivate the corresponding duties towards human beings. If a man shoots his dog because the animal is no longer capable of service, he does not fail in his duty to the dog, for the dog cannot judge, but his *act is inhuman and damages in himself that humanity which it is his duty to show towards mankind.* If he is not to stifle his human feelings, he must practise kindness towards animals, for he who is cruel to animals becomes hard also in his dealing with men. We can judge the heart of a man by his treatment of animals. Hogarth depicts this in his engravings. He shows how cruelty grows and develops. He shows the child's cruelty to animals, pinch the tail of a dog or a cat; he then depicts the grown man in his cart running over a child; and lastly, the culmination of cruelty in murder. He thus brings home to us in a terrible fashion the rewards of cruelty, and this should be an impressive lesson to children. The more we come in contact with animals and observe their behaviour, the more we love them, for we see how great is their care for their young. It is then difficult for us to be cruel in thought even to a wolf. Leibnitz used a tiny worm for purposes of observation, and then carefully replaced it with its leaf on the tree so that it should not come to harm through any act of his. He would have been sorry—a natural feeling for a humane man—to destroy such a creature for no reason. Tender feelings towards dumb animals develop humane feelings towards mankind. In England butchers and doctors do not sit on a jury because they are accustomed to the sight of death and hardened. Vivisectionists, who use living animals for their experiments, certainly act cruelly, although their aim is praiseworthy, and they can justify their cruelty, since animals must be regarded as man's instruments; but any such cruelty for sport cannot be justified. A master who turns out his ass or his dog because the animal can no longer earn its keep manifests a small mind. The Greeks' ideas in this respect were highminded, as can be seen from the fable of the ass and the bell of ingratitude. Our duties towards animals, then, are indirect duties towards mankind.

Study Questions

1. According to Kant, do animals have rights? What capacity do they lack that deprives them of rights?
2. Why should we be kind to animals? Do you agree with Kant? How would an opponent respond to Kant's arguments?

6

Sentience as the Criterion for Moral Worth

Bernard Rollin

Bernard Rollin is professor of philosophy and director of bioethical planning at Colorado State University. He is the author of Animal Rights and Human Morality *(1981).*

In this essay, in contrast to Kant's strong anthropocentrism, Rollin sets forth a sentientist theory of moral value. Because humans and animals are sentient beings who can be harmed, they have moral rights. However, natural objects and systems, such as ecosystems, have only instrumental value. Sentientism is sufficient for a rich environmental theory.

The past two decades have witnessed a major revolutionary thrust in social moral awareness, one virtually unknown in mainstream Western ethical thinking, although not unrecognized in other cultural traditions; for example, the Navajo, whose descriptive language for nature and animals is suffused with ethical nuances; the Australian Aboriginal people; and the ancient Persians. This thrust is the recognition that nonhuman entities enjoy some moral status as objects of moral concern and deliberation. Although the investigation of the moral status of nonhuman entities has sometimes been subsumed under the global rubric of environmental ethics, such a blanket term does not do adequate justice to the substantial conceptual differences of its components.

THE MORAL STATUS OF NONHUMAN THINGS

As a bare minimum, environmental ethics comprises two fundamentally divergent concerns—namely, concern with individual nonhuman animals as direct objects of moral concern and concern with species, ecosystems, environments, wilderness areas, forests, the biosphere, and other nonsentient natural or even abstract objects as direct objects of moral concern. Usually, although with a number of major exceptions, those who give primacy to animals have tended to deny the moral significance of environments and species as direct objects of moral concern, whereas those who give moral primacy to enviro-ecological concerns tend to deny or at least downplay the moral significance of

Reprinted by permission of the publisher from *Problems of International Justice* (Westview Press, 1988), ed. Steven Luper-Foy. Notes deleted.

individual animals. Significant though these differences are, they should not cloud the dramatic nature of this common attempt to break out of a moral tradition that finds loci of value only in human beings and, derivatively, in human institutions.

Because of the revolutionary nature of these attempts, they also remain somewhat undeveloped and embryonic. . . .

The most plausible strategy in attempting to revise traditional moral theory and practice is to show that the seeds of the new moral notions or extensions of old moral notions are, in fact, already implicit in the old moral machinery developed to deal with other issues. Only when such avenues are exhausted will it make sense to recommend major rebuilding of the machinery, rather than putting it to new uses. The classic examples of such extensions are obviously found in the extension of the moral/legal machinery of Western democracies to cover traditionally disenfranchised groups such as women and minorities. The relatively smooth flow of such applications owes much of its smoothness to the plausibility of a simple argument of the form:

Our extant moral principles ought to cover all humans.
Women are humans.

∴ Our extant moral principles ought to cover women.

On the other hand, conceptually radical departures from tradition do not lend themselves to such simple rational reconstruction. Thus, for example, the principle of *favoring* members of traditionally disenfranchised groups at the expense of innocent members of nondisenfranchised groups for the sake of rectifying historically based injustice is viewed as much more morally problematic and ambivalent than simply according rights to these groups. Thus, it would be difficult to conduct a simple syllogism in defense of this practice that would garner universal acquiescence with the ease of the one indicated previously.

Thus, one needs to distinguish between moral revolutionary thrusts that are ostensibly paradoxical to common sense and practice because they have been ignored in a wholesale fashion, yet are in fact logical extensions of common morality, and those revolutionary thrusts that are genuinely paradoxical to previous moral thinking and practice because they are not implicit therein. Being genuinely paradoxical does not invalidate a new moral thrust—it does, however, place upon its proponents a substantially greater burden of proof. Those philosophers, like myself, who have argued for a recognition of the moral status of individual animals and the rights and legal status that derive therefrom, have attempted to place ourselves in the first category. We recognize that a society that kills and eats billions of animals, kills millions more in research, and disposes of millions more for relatively frivolous reasons and that relies economically on animal exploitation as a mainstay of social wealth, considers talk of elevating the moral status of animals as impossible and paradoxical. But this does not mean that such an elevation does not follow unrecognized from moral principles we all hold. Indeed, the abolition of slavery or the liberation of women appeared similarly paradoxical and economically impossible, yet gradually both were perceived as morally necessary, in part because both were implicit, albeit unrecognized, in previously acknowledged assumptions.

My own argument for elevating the status of animals has been a relatively straightforward deduction of unnoticed implications of traditional morality. I have tried to show that no morally relevant grounds for excluding animals from the full application of our moral machinery will stand up to rational scrutiny. Traditional claims that rely on notions such as animals have no souls, are inferior to humans in power or intelligence or evolutionary status, are not moral agents, are not rational, are not possessed of free will, are not capable of language, are not bound by social contract to humans, and so forth, do not serve as justifiable reasons for excluding animals and their interests from the moral arena.

By the same token, morally relevant similarities exist between us and them in the case of the "higher" animals. Animals can suffer, as Jeremy Bentham said; they have interests; what we do to them matters to them; they can feel pain, fear, anxiety, loneliness, pleasure, boredom, and so on. Indeed, the simplicity and power of the argument calling attention to such morally relevant similarities has led Cartesians from Descartes to modern physiologists with a vested interest against attributing moral status to animals to declare that animals are machines with no morally relevant modes of awareness, a point often addressed today against moral claims such as mine. In fact, such claims have become a mainstay of what I have elsewhere called the "common sense of science." Thus, one who argues for an augmented moral status for animals finds it necessary to establish philosophically and scientifically what common sense takes for granted—namely, that animals *are* conscious. Most people whose common sense is intact are not Cartesians and can see that moral talk cannot be withheld from animals and our treatment of them.

In my own work, appealing again to common moral practice, I have stressed our society's quasi-moral, quasi-legal notion of rights as a reflection of our commitment to the moral primacy of the individual, rather than the state. Rights protect what are hypothesized as the fundamental interests of human beings from cavalier encroachment by the common good—such interests as speech, assembly, belief, property, privacy, freedom from torture, and so forth. But those animals who are conscious also have fundamental interests arising out of *their* biologically given natures (or *teloi*), the infringement upon which matters greatly to them, and the fulfillment of which is central to their lives. Hence, I deduce the notion of animal rights from our common moral theory and practice and attempt to show that conceptually, at least, it is a deduction from the moral framework of the status quo rather than a major revision therein. Moral concern for individual animals follows from the hitherto ignored presence of morally relevant characteristics, primarily sentience, in animals. As a result, I am comfortable in attributing what Immanuel Kant called "intrinsic value," not merely use value, to animals if we attribute it to people.

The task is far more formidable for those who attempt to make nonsentient natural objects, such as rivers and mountains, or, worse, quasi-abstract entities, such as species and ecosystems, into direct objects of moral concern. Interestingly enough, in direct opposition to the case of animals, such moves appear prima facie plausible to common morality, which has long expressed concern for the value and preservation of some natural objects, while condoning wholesale exploitation of others. In the same way, common practice often showed extreme concern for certain favored kinds of animals, while systematically exploiting others. Thus, many people in the United States strongly oppose scientific research on dogs and cats, but are totally unconcerned about such use of rodents or swine. What is superficially plausible, however, quite unlike the case of animals, turns out to be deeply paradoxical given the machinery of traditional morality.

Many leading environmental ethicists have attempted to do for nonsentient natural objects and abstract objects the same sort of thing I have tried to do for animals—namely, attempted to elevate their status to direct objects of intrinsic value, ends in themselves, which are morally valuable not only because of their relations and utility to sentient beings, but in and of themselves. To my knowledge, none of these theorists has attempted to claim, as I do for animals, that the locus of such value lies in the fact that what we do to these entities matters to them. No one has argued that we can harm rivers, species, or ecosystems in ways that matter to them.

Wherein, then, do these theorists locate the intrinsic value of these entities? This is not at all clear in the writings, but seems to come down to one of the following doubtful moves:

1. Going from the fact that environmental factors are absolutely essential to the well-being or survival of beings that are loci of intrinsic value to the conclusion that environmental factors therefore enjoy a similar or even higher moral status. Such a move is clearly falla-

cious. Just because I cannot survive without insulin, and I am an object of intrinsic value, it does not follow that insulin is, too. In fact, the insulin is a paradigmatic example of instrumental value.

2. Going from the fact that the environment "creates" all sentient creatures to the fact that its welfare is more important than theirs. This is really a variation on (1) and succumbs to the same sort of criticism, namely, that this reasoning represents a genetic fallacy. The cause of something valuable need not itself be valuable and certainly not necessarily more valuable than its effect—its value must be established independently of its result. The Holocaust may have caused the state of Israel; that does not make the Holocaust more valuable than the state of Israel.

3. Confusing aesthetic or instrumental value for sentient creatures, notably humans, with intrinsic value and underestimating aesthetic value as a category. We shall return to this shortly, for I suspect it is the root confusion in those attempting to give nonsentient nature intrinsic value.

4. Substituting rhetoric for logic at crucial points in the discussions and using a poetic rhetoric (descriptions of natural objects in terms such as "grandeur," "majesty," "novelty," "variety") as an unexplained basis for according them "intrinsic value."

5. Going from the metaphor that infringement on natural objects "matters" to them in the sense that disturbance evokes an adjustment by their self-regulating properties, to the erroneous conclusion that such self-regulation, being analogous to conscious coping in animals, entitles them to direct moral status.

In short, traditional morality and its theory do not offer a viable way to raise the moral status of nonsentient natural objects and abstract objects so that they are direct objects of moral concern on a par with or even higher than sentient creatures. Ordinary morality and moral concern take as their focus the effects of actions on beings who can be helped and harmed, in ways that matter to them, either directly or by implication. If it is immoral to wreck someone's property, it is because it is someone's; if it is immoral to promote the extinction of species, it is because such extinction causes aesthetic or practical harm to humans or to animals or because a species is, in the final analysis, a group of harmable individuals.

There is nothing, of course, to stop environmental ethicists from making a recommendation for a substantial revision of common and national morality. But such recommendations are likely to be dismissed or whittled away by a moral version of Occam's razor: Why grant animals rights and acknowledge in animals intrinsic value? Because they are conscious and what we do to them matters to them? Why grant rocks, or trees, or species, or ecosystems rights? Because these objects have great aesthetic value, or are essential to us, or are basic

for survival? But these are paradigmatic examples of *instrumental* value. A conceptual confusion for a noble purpose is still a conceptual confusion.

There is nothing to be gained by attempting to elevate the moral status of nonsentient natural objects to that of sentient ones. One can develop a rich environmental ethic by locating the value of nonsentient natural objects in their relation to sentient ones. One can argue for the preservation of habitats because their destruction harms animals; one can argue for preserving ecosystems on the grounds of unforeseen pernicious consequences resulting from their destruction, a claim for which much empirical evidence exists. One can argue for the preservation of animal species as the sum of a group of individuals who would be harmed by its extinction. One can argue for preserving mountains, snail darters, streams, and cockroaches on aesthetic grounds. Too many philosophers forget the moral power of aesthetic claims and tend to see aesthetic reasons as a weak basis for preserving natural objects. Yet the moral imperative not to destroy unique aesthetic objects and even nonunique ones is an onerous one that is well ingrained into common practice—witness the worldwide establishment of national parks, preserves, forests, and wildlife areas.

Rather than attempting to transcend all views of natural objects as instrumental by grafting onto nature a mystical intrinsic value that can be buttressed only by poetic rhetoric, it would be far better to nurture public appreciation of subtle instrumental value, especially aesthetic value. People can learn to appreciate the unique beauty of a desert, or of a fragile ecosystem, or even of a noxious creature like a tick, when they understand the complexity and history therein and can read the story each life form contains. I am reminded of a colleague in parasitology who is loath to destroy worms he has studied upon completing his research because he has aesthetically learned to value their complexity of structure, function, and evolutionary history and role.

It is important to note that the attribution of value to nonsentient objects as a relational property arising out of their significance (recognized or not) for sentient beings does not denigrate the value of natural objects. Indeed, this attribution does not even imply that the interests or desires of individual sentient beings always trump concern for nonsentient ones. Our legal system has, for example, valuable and irreplaceable property laws that forbid owners of aesthetic objects, say a collection of Vincent Van Gogh paintings, to destroy them at will, say by adding them to one's funeral pyre. To be sure, this restriction on people's right to dispose of their own property arises out of a recognition of the value of these objects to other humans, but this is surely quite sensible. How else would one justify such a restriction? Nor, as we said earlier, need one limit the value of natural objects to their relationship to humans. Philosophically, one could, for example, sensibly (and commonsensically) argue for preservation of acreage from the golf-course developer because failure to do so would mean the destruction of thousands of sentient creatures' habitats—a major infringement of their interests—while building the golf course would fulfill the rarefied and inessential interests of a few.

Thus, in my view, one would accord moral concern to natural objects in a variety of ways, depending on the sort of object being considered. Moral status for individual animals would arise from their sentience. Moral status of species and their protection from humans would arise from the fact that a species is a collection of morally relevant individuals; moral status also would arise from the fact that humans have an aesthetic concern in not letting a unique and irreplaceable aesthetic object (or group of objects) disappear forever from our *Umwelt* (environment). Concern for wilderness areas, mountains, deserts, and so on would arise from their survival value for sentient animals as well as from their aesthetic value for humans. (Some writers have suggested that this aesthetic value is so great as to be essential to human mental/physical health, a point perfectly compatible with my position.)

Nothing in what I have said as yet tells us how to weigh conflicting interests, whether between humans and other sentient creatures or between human desires and environmental protection. How does one weigh the aesthetic concern of those who oppose blasting away part of a cliff against the pragmatic concern of those who wish to build on a cliffside? But the problem of weighing is equally thorny in traditional ethics— witness lifeboat questions or questions concerning the allocation of scarce medical resources. Nor does the intrinsic value approach help in adjudicating such issues. How does one weigh the alleged intrinsic value of a cliffside against the interests of the (intrinsic-value-bearing) homebuilders?

Furthermore, the intrinsic value view can lead to results that are repugnant to common sense and ordinary moral consciousness. Thus, for example, it follows from what has been suggested by one intrinsic value theorist that if a migratory herd of plentiful elk were passing through an area containing an endangered species of moss, it would be not only permissible but obligatory to kill the elk in order to protect the moss because in one case we would lose a species, in another "merely" individuals. In my view, such a case has a less paradoxical resolution. Destruction of the moss does not matter to the moss, whereas elk presumably care about living or being injured. Therefore, one would give prima facie priority to the elk. This might presumably be trumped if, for example, the moss were a substratum from which was extracted an ingredient necessary to stop a raging, lethal epidemic in humans or animals. But such cases— and indeed most cases of conflicting interests—must be decided on the actual occasion. These cases are decided by a careful examination of the facts of the situation. Thus, our suggestion of a basis for environmental ethics does not qualitatively change the situation from that of current ethical deliberation, whereas granting intrinsic value to natural objects would leave us with a "whole new ball game"—and one where we do not know the rules.

In sum, then, the question of environmental ethics . . . must be analyzed into two discrete components. First are those questions that pertain to direct objects of moral concern—nonhuman animals whose sentience we have good reason to suspect—and that require the application of traditional moral notions to a hitherto ignored domain of moral objects. Second are those questions pertaining to natural objects or abstract natural objects. Although it is nonsensical to attribute intrinsic or direct moral value to these objects, they nonetheless must become (and are indeed becoming) central to our social moral deliberations. This centrality derives from our increasing recognition of the far-reaching and sometimes subtle instrumental value these objects have for humans and animals. Knowing that contamination of remote desert areas by pollutants can destroy unique panoplies of fragile beauty, or that dumping wastes into the ocean can destroy a potential source of antibiotics, or that building a pipeline can have undreamed-of harmful effects goes a long way toward making us think twice about these activities—a far longer way than endowing them with quasi-mystical rhetorical status subject to (and begging for) positivistic torpedoing. . . .

Study Questions

1. Do you agree with Rollin's thesis that all and only sentient creatures have intrinsic value? Critically compare his arguments with Kant's position.
2. Is sentientism sufficient for an environmental ethics? Would it be better if we regarded ecosystems and rain forests and trees as having intrinsic value?

7

A Utilitarian Defense of Animal Liberation

PETER SINGER

Peter Singer did his graduate work at Oxford University and is a member of the Philosophy Department at La Trobe University in Australia. His book Animal Liberation *(1975), from which the following selection is taken, is one of the most influential books ever written on the subject. It has converted many to the animal rights movement. Singer argues that animal liberation today is analogous to racial and gender justice in the past. Just as people once thought it incredible that women or blacks should be treated as equal to white men, so now speciesists mock the idea that all animals should be given equal consideration. Singer defines* speciesism *(a term devised by Richard Ryder) as the prejudice (unjustified bias) that favors one's own species over every other. What equalizes all sentient beings is our ability to suffer. In that, we and animals are equal and deserving equal consideration of interests. Singer's argument is a utilitarian one having as its goal the maximization of interest satisfaction.*

In recent years a number of oppressed groups have campaigned vigorously for equality. The classic instance is the Black Liberation movement, which demands an end to the prejudice and discrimination that has made blacks second-class citizens. The immediate appeal of the black liberation movement and its initial, if limited, success made it a model for other oppressed groups to follow. We became familiar with liberation movements for Spanish-Americans, gay people, and a variety of other minorities. When a majority group—women—began their campaign, some thought we had come to the end of the road. Discrimination on the basis of sex, it has been said, is the last universally accepted form of discrimination, practiced without secrecy or pretense even in those liberal circles that have long prided themselves on their freedom from prejudice against racial minorities.

One should always be wary of talking of "the last remaining form of discrimination." If we have learnt anything from the liberation movements, we should have learnt how difficult it is to be aware of latent prejudice in our attitudes to particular groups until this prejudice is forcefully pointed out.

A liberation movement demands an expansion of our moral horizons and an extension or reinterpretation of the basic moral principle of equality. Practices that were previously regarded as natural and inevitable come to be seen as the result of an unjustifiable prejudice. Who can say with confidence that all his or her attitudes and practices are beyond criticism? If we wish to avoid being numbered amongst the oppressors, we must be prepared to re-think even our most fundamental attitudes. We need to consider them from the point of view of those most disadvantaged by our attitudes, and the practices that follow from these attitudes. If we can make this unaccustomed mental switch we may discover a pattern in our attitudes and practices that consistently operates so as to benefit one group—usually the one to which we ourselves belong—at the expense of another. In this way we may come to see that there is a case for a new liberation movement. My aim is to advocate that we make this mental switch in respect of our attitudes and practices towards a very large group of beings: members of species other than our own—or, as we popularly though misleadingly call them, animals. In other words, I am urging that we extend to other species the basic principle of equality that most of us recognize should be extended to all members of our own species.

All this may sound a little far-fetched, more like a parody of other liberation movements than a serious objective. In fact, in the past the idea of "The Rights of Animals" really has been used to parody the case for women's rights. When Mary Wollstonecroft, a forerunner of later feminists, published her *Vindication of the Rights of Women* in 1792, her ideas were widely regarded as absurd, and they were satirized in an anonymous publication entitled *A Vindication of the Rights of Brutes.* The author of this satire (actually Thomas Taylor, a distinguished Cambridge philosopher) tried to refute Wollstonecroft's reasonings by showing that they could be carried one stage further. If sound when applied to women, why should the arguments not be applied to dogs, cats, and horses? They seemed to hold equally well for these "brutes"; yet to hold that brutes had rights was manifestly absurd; therefore the reasoning by which this conclusion had been reached must be unsound, and if unsound when applied to brutes, it must also be unsound when applied to women, since the very same arguments had been used in each case.

One way in which we might reply to this argument is by saying that the case for equality between men and women cannot validly be extended to nonhuman animals. Women have a right to vote, for instance, because they are just as capable of making rational decisions as men are; dogs, on the other hand, are incapable of

Reprinted from *Animal Rights and Human Obligation* (Englewood Cliffs, NJ: Prentice Hall, 1976) by permission of Peter Singer.

understanding the significance of voting, so they cannot have the right to vote. There are many other obvious ways in which men and women resemble each other closely, while humans and other animals differ greatly. So, it might be said, men and women are similar beings, and should have equal rights, while humans and nonhumans are different and should not have equal rights.

The thought behind this reply to Taylor's analogy is correct up to a point, but it does not go far enough. There *are* important differences between humans and other animals, and these differences must give rise to *some* differences in the rights that each have. Recognizing this obvious fact, however, is no barrier to the case for extending the basic principle of equality to nonhuman animals. The differences that exist between men and women are equally undeniable, and the supporters of Women's Liberation are aware that these differences may give rise to different rights. Many feminists hold that women have the right to an abortion on request. It does not follow that since these same people are campaigning for equality between men and women they must support the right of men to have abortions too. Since a man cannot have an abortion, it is meaningless to talk of his right to have one. Since a pig can't vote, it is meaningless to talk of its right to vote. There is no reason why either Women's Liberation or Animal Liberation should get involved in such nonsense. The extension of the basic principle of equality from one group to another does not imply that we must treat both groups in exactly the same way, or grant exactly the same rights to both groups. Whether we should do so will depend on the nature of the members of the two groups. The basic principle of equality, I shall argue, is equality of consideration; and equal consideration for different beings may lead to different treatment and different rights.

So there is a different way of replying to Taylor's attempt to parody Wollstonecroft's arguments, a way which does not deny the differences between humans and nonhumans, but goes more deeply into the question of equality, and concludes by finding nothing absurd in the idea that the basic principle of equality applies to so called "brutes." I believe that we reach this conclusion if we examine the basis on which our opposition to discrimination on grounds of race or sex ultimately rests. We will then see that we would be on shaky ground if we were to demand equality for blacks, women, and other groups of oppressed humans while denying equal consideration to nonhumans.

When we say that all human beings, whatever their race, creed or sex, are equal, what is it that we are asserting? Those who wish to defend a hierarchical, inegalitarian society have often pointed out that by whatever test we choose, it simply is not true that all humans are equal. Like it or not, we must face the fact that humans come in different shapes and sizes; they come with differing moral capacities, differing intellectual abilities, differing amounts of benevolent feeling and sensitivity to the needs of others, differing abilities to communicate effectively, and differing capacities to experience pleasure and pain. In short, if the demand for equality were based on the actual equality of all human beings, we would have to stop demanding equality. It would be an unjustifiable demand.

Still, one might cling to the view that the demand for equality among human beings is based on the actual equality of the different races and sexes. Although humans differ as individuals in various ways, there are no differences between the races and sexes *as such*. From the mere fact that a person is black, or a woman, we cannot infer anything else about that person. This, it may be said, is what is wrong with racism and sexism. The white racist claims that whites are superior to blacks, but this is false—although there are differences between individuals, some blacks are superior to some whites in all of the capacities and abilities that could conceivably be relevant. The opponent of sexism would say the same: a person's sex is no guide to his or her abilities, and this is why it is unjustifiable to discriminate on the basis of sex.

This is a possible line of objection to racial and sexual discrimination. It is not, however, the way that someone really concerned about equality would choose, because taking this line could, in some circumstances, force one to accept a most inegalitarian society. The fact that humans differ as individuals, rather than as races or sexes, is a valid reply to someone who defends a hierarchical society like, say, South Africa, in which all whites are superior in status to all blacks. The existence of individual variations that cut across the lines of race or sex, however, provides us with no defence at all against a more sophisticated opponent of equality, one who proposes that, say, the interests of those with I.Q. ratings above 100 be preferred to the interests of those with I.Q.s below 100. Would a hierarchical society of this sort really be so much better than one based on race or sex? I think not. But if we tie the moral principle of equality to the factual equality of the different races or sexes, taken as a whole, our opposition to racism and sexism does not provide us with any basis for objecting to this kind of inegalitarianism.

There is a second important reason why we ought not to base our opposition to racism and sexism on any kind of factual equality, even the limited kind which asserts that variations in capacities and abilities are spread evenly between the different races and sexes: we can have no absolute guarantee that these abilities and capacities really are distributed evenly, without regard to race or sex, among human beings. So far as actual abilities are concerned, there do seem to be certain measurable differences between both races and sexes. These differences do not, of course, appear in each case, but only when averages are taken. More important still, we do not yet know how much of these differences is really due to the different genetic endowments of the various races and sexes, and how much is due to environmental differences that are the result of past and continuing discrimination. Perhaps all of the important differences will eventually prove to be environmental rather than genetic. Anyone opposed to racism and sexism will certainly hope that this will be so, for it will make the task of ending discrimination a lot easier; nevertheless it would be dangerous to rest the case against racism and sexism on the belief that all significant differences are environmental in origin. The opponent of, say, racism who takes this line will be unable to avoid conceding that if differences in ability did after all prove to have some generic connection with race, racism would in some way be defensible.

It would be folly for the opponent of racism to stake his whole case on a dogmatic commitment to one particular outcome of a difficult scientific issue which is still a long way from being settled. While attempts to prove that differences in certain selected abilities between races and sexes are primarily genetic in origin have certainly not been conclusive, the same must be said of attempts to prove that these differences are largely the result of environment. At this stage of the investigation we cannot be certain which view is correct, however much we may hope it is the latter.

Fortunately, there is no need to pin the case for equality to one particular outcome of this scientific investigation. The appropriate response to those who claim to have found evidence of genetically based differences in ability between the races or sexes is not to stick to the belief that the genetic explanation must be wrong, whatever evidence to the contrary may turn up: instead we should make it quite clear that the claim to equality does not depend on intelligence, moral capacity, physical strength, or similar matters of fact. Equality is a moral ideal, not a simple assertion of fact. There is no logically compelling reason for assuming that a factual difference in ability between two people justifies any *difference in the amount of consideration we give to satisfying their needs and interests*. The principle of the equality of human beings is not a description of an alleged actual equality among humans: it is a prescription of how we should treat humans.

Jeremy Bentham incorporated the essential basis of moral equality into his utilitarian system of ethics in the formula: "Each to count for one and none for more than one." In other words, the interests of every being affected by an action are to be taken into account and given the same weight as the like interests of any other being. A later utilitarian, Henry Sidgwick, put the point in this way: "The good of any one individual is of no more importance, from the point of view (if I may say so) of the Universe, than the good of any other."[1] More recently, the leading figures in contemporary moral philosophy have shown a great deal of agreement in specifying as a fundamental presupposition of their moral theories some similar requirement which operates so as to give everyone's interests equal consideration—although they cannot agree on how this requirement is best formulated.[2]

It is an implication of this principle of equality that our concern for others ought not to depend on what they are like, or what abilities they possess—although precisely what this concern requires us to do may vary according to the characteristics of those affected by what we do. It is on this basis that the case against racism and the case against sexism must both ultimately rest; and it is in accordance with this principle that speciesism is also to be condemned. If possessing a higher degree of intelligence does not entitle one human to use another for his own ends, how can it entitle humans to exploit nonhumans?

Many philosophers have proposed the principle of equal consideration of interests, in some form or other, as a basic moral principle; but, as we shall see in more detail shortly, not many of them have recognized that this principle applies to members of other species as well as to our own. Bentham was one of the few who did realize this. In a forward-looking passage, written at a time when black slaves in British dominions were still being treated much as we now treat nonhuman animals, Bentham wrote:

> The day *may* come when the rest of the animal creation may acquire those rights which never could have been witholden from them but by the hand of tyranny. The French have already discovered that the blackness of the skin is no reason why a human being should be abandoned without redress to the caprice of a tormentor. It may one day come to be recognized that the number of the legs, the villoscity of the skin, or the termination of the *os sacrum*, are reasons equally insufficient for abandoning a sensitive being to the same fate. What else is it that should trace the insuperable line? Is it the faculty of reason, or perhaps the faculty of discourse? But a full grown horse or dog is beyond comparison a more rational, as well as a more conversable animal, than an infant of a day, or a week, or even a month, old. But suppose they were otherwise, what would it avail? The question is not, Can they reason? nor Can they *talk*? but, *Can they suffer*?[3]

In this passage Bentham points to the capacity for suffering as the vital characteristic that gives a being the *right* to equal consideration. The capacity for suffering—or more strictly, for suffering and/or enjoyment or happiness—is not just another characteristic like the capacity for language, or for higher mathematics. Bentham is not saying that those who try to mark the "insuperable line" that determines whether the interests of a being should be considered happen to have selected the wrong characteristic. The capacity for suffering and enjoying things is a pre-requisite for having interests at all, a condition that must be satisfied before we can speak of interests in any meaningful way. It would be nonsense to say that it was not in the interests of a stone to be kicked along the road by a schoolboy. A stone does not have interests because it cannot suffer. Nothing that we can do to it could possibly make any difference to its welfare. A mouse, on the other hand, does have an interest in not being tormented, because it will suffer if it is.

If a being suffers, there can be no moral justification for refusing to take that suffering into consideration. No matter what the nature of the being, the principle of equality requires that its suffering be counted equally with the like suffering—in so far as rough comparisons can be made—of any other being. If a being is not capable of suffering, or of experiencing enjoyment or happiness, there is nothing to be taken into account. This is why the limit of sentience (using the term as a convenient, if not strictly accurate, shorthand for the capacity to suffer or experience enjoyment or happiness) is the only defensible boundary of concern for the interests of others. To mark this boundary by some characteristic like intelligence or rationality would be to mark it in an arbitrary way. Why not choose some other characteristic, like skin color?

The racist violates the principle of equality by giving greater weight to the interests of members of his own race, when there is a clash between their interests and the interests of those of another race. Similarly the speciesist allows the interests of his own species to override the greater interests of members of other species.[4] The pattern is the same in each case. Most human beings are speciesists. I shall now very briefly describe some of the practices that show this.

For the great majority of human beings, especially in urban, industrialized societies, the most direct form of contact with members of other species is at meal-times: we eat them. In doing so we treat them purely as means to our ends. We regard their life and well-being as subordinate to our taste for a particular kind of dish. I say "taste" deliberately—this is purely a matter of pleasing our palate. There can be no defence of eating flesh in terms of satisfying nutritional needs, since it has been established beyond doubt that we could satisfy our need for protein and other essential nutrients far more efficiently with a diet that replaced animal flesh by soy beans, or products derived from soy beans, and other high-protein vegetable products.[5]

It is not merely the act of killing that indicates what we are ready to do to other species in order to gratify our tastes. The suffering we inflict on the animals while they are alive is perhaps an even clearer indication of our speciesism than the fact that we are prepared to kill them. In order to have meat on the table at a price that people can afford, our society tolerates methods of meat production that confine sentient animals in cramped, unsuitable conditions for the entire durations of their lives. Animals are treated like machines that convert fodder into flesh, and any innovation that results in a higher "conversion ratio" is liable to be adopted. As one authority on the subject has said, "cruelty is acknowledged only when profitability ceases."[6] . . .

Since, as I have said, none of these practices cater for anything more than our pleasures of taste, our practice of rearing and killing other animals in order to eat them is a clear instance of the sacrifice of the most important interests of other beings in order to satisfy trivial interests of our own. To avoid speciesism we must stop this practice, and each of us has a moral obligation to cease supporting the practice. Our custom is all the support that the meat-industry needs. The decision to cease giving it that support may be difficult, but it is no more difficult than it would have been for a white Southerner to go against the traditions of his society and free his slaves: if we do not change our dietary habits, how can we censure those slaveholders who would not change their own way of living?

The same form of discrimination may be observed in the widespread practice of experimenting on other species in order to see if certain substances are safe for human beings, or to test some psychological theory about the effect of severe punishment on learning, or to try out various new compounds just in case something turns up. . . .

In the past, argument about vivisection has often missed this point, because it has been put in absolutist terms: Would the abolitionist be prepared to let thousands die if they could be saved by experimenting on a single animal? The way to reply to this purely hypothetical question is to pose another: *Would the experimenter be prepared to perform his experiment on an orphaned human infant, if that were the only way to save many lives?* (I say "orphan" to avoid the complication of parental feelings, although in doing so I am being overfair to the experimenter, since the nonhuman subjects of experiments are not orphans.) If the experimenter is not prepared to use an orphaned human infant, then his readiness to use nonhumans is simple discrimination, since adult apes, cats, mice and other mammals are more aware of what is happening to them, more self-directing and, so far as we can tell, at least as sensitive to pain, as any human infant. There seems to be no relevant characteristic that human infants possess that adult mammals do not have to the same or a higher degree. (Someone might try to argue that what makes it wrong to experiment on a human infant is that the infant will, in time and if left alone, develop into more than the nonhuman, but one would then, to be consistent, have to oppose abortion, since the fetus has the same potential as the infant—indeed, even contraception and abstinence might be wrong on this ground, since the egg and sperm, considered jointly, also have the same potential. In any case, this argument still gives us no reason for selecting a nonhuman, rather than a human with severe and irreversible brain damage, as the subject for our experiments.)

The experimenter, then, shows a bias in favor of his own species whenever he carries out an experiment on a nonhuman for a purpose that he would not think justified him in using a human being at an equal or lower level of sentience, awareness, ability to be self-directing, etc. No one familiar with the kind of results yielded by most experiments on animals can have the slightest doubt that if this bias were eliminated the number of experiments performed would be a minute fraction of the number performed today.

Experimenting on animals, and eating their flesh, are perhaps the two major forms of speciesism in our society. By comparison, the third and last form of speciesism is so minor as to be insignificant, but it is perhaps of some special interest to those for whom this article was written. I am referring to speciesism in contemporary philosophy.

Philosophy ought to question the basic assumptions of the age. Thinking through, critically and carefully, what most people take for granted is, I believe, the chief task of philosophy, and it is this task that makes philosophy a worthwhile activity. Regrettably, philosophy does not always live up to its historic role. Philosophers are human beings and they are subject to all the preconceptions of the society to which they belong. Sometimes they succeed in breaking free of the prevailing ideology: more often they become its most sophisticated defenders. So, in this case, philosophy as practiced in the universities today does not challenge anyone's preconceptions about our relations with other species. By their writings, those philosophers who tackle problems that touch upon the issue reveal that they make the same unquestioned assumptions as most other humans, and what they say tends to confirm the reader in his or her comfortable speciesist habits.

I could illustrate this claim by referring to the writings of philosophers in various fields—for instance, the attempts that have been made by those interested in rights to draw the boundary of the sphere of rights so that it runs parallel to the biological boundaries of the species *homo sapiens*, including infants and even mental defectives, but excluding those other beings of equal or greater capacity who are so useful to us at mealtimes and in our laboratories. I think it would be a more appropriate conclusion to this article, however, if I concentrated on the problem with which we have been centrally concerned, the problem of equality.

It is significant that the problem of *equality*, in moral and political philosophy, is invariably formulated in terms of human equality. The effect of this is that the question of the equality of other animals does not confront the philosopher, or student, as an issue itself—and this is already an indication of the failure of philosophy to challenge accepted beliefs. Still, philosophers have found it difficult to discuss the issue of human equality without raising, in a paragraph or two, the question of the status of other animals. The reason for this, which should be apparent from what I have said already, is that if humans are to be regarded as equal to one another, we need some sense of "equal" that does not require any actual, descriptive equality of capacities, talents or other qualities. If equality is to be related to any actual characteristics of humans, these characteristics

must be some lowest common denominator, pitched so low that no human lacks them—but then the philosopher comes up against the catch that any such set of characteristics which covers *all* humans will not be possessed *only by humans*. In other words, it turns out that in the only sense in which we can truly say, as an assertion of fact, that all humans are equal, at least some members of other species are also equal—equal, that is, to each other and to humans. If, on the other hand, we regard the statement "All humans are equal" in some non-factual way, perhaps as a prescription, then, as I have already argued, it is even more difficult to exclude nonhumans from the sphere of equality.

This result is not what the egalitarian philosopher originally intended to assert. Instead of accepting the radical outcome to which their own reasonings naturally point, however, most philosophers try to reconcile their beliefs in human equality and animal inequality by arguments that can only be described as devious.

As a first example, I take William Frankena's well-known article "The Concept of Social Justice." Frankena opposes the idea of basing justice on merit, because he sees that this could lead to highly inegalitarian results. Instead he proposes the principle that

> . . . all men are to be treated as equals, not because they are equal, in any respect, but *simply because they are human*. They are human because they have *emotions* and *desires*, and are able to *think*, and hence are capable of enjoying a good life in a sense in which other animals are not.[7]

But what is this capacity to enjoy the good life which all humans have, but no other animals? Other animals have emotions and desires, and appear to be capable of enjoying a good life. We may doubt that they can think—although the behavior of some apes, dolphins and even dogs suggests that some of them can—*but what is the relevance of thinking?* Frankena goes on to admit that by "the good life" he means "not so much the morally good life as the happy or satisfactory life," so thought would appear to be unnecessary for enjoying the good life; in fact to emphasize the need for thought would make difficulties for the egalitarian since only some people are capable of leading intellectually satisfying lives, or morally good lives. This makes it difficult to see what Frankena's principle of equality has to do with simply being *human*. Surely every sentient being is capable of leading a life that is happier or less miserable than some alternative life, and hence has a claim to be taken into account. In this respect the distinction between humans and nonhumans is not a sharp division, but rather a continuum along which we move gradually, and with overlaps between the species, from simple capacities for enjoyment and satisfaction, or pain and suffering, to more complex ones.

Faced with a situation in which they see a need for some basis for the moral gulf that is commonly thought to separate humans and animals, but finding no concrete difference that will do the job without undermining the equality of humans, philosophers tend to waffle. They resort to high-sounding phrases like "the intrinsic dignity of the human individual";[8] they talk of the "intrinsic worth of all men" as if men (humans?) had some worth that other beings did not,[9] or they say that humans, and only humans, are "ends in themselves," while "everything other than a person can only have value for a person."[10]

This idea of a distinctive human dignity and worth has a long history; it can be traced back directly to the Renaissance humanists, for instance to Pico della Mirandola's *Oration on the Dignity of Man*. Pico and other humanists based their estimate of human dignity on the idea that man possessed the central, pivotal position in the "Great Chain of Being" that led from the lowliest forms of matter to God himself; this view of the universe, in turn, goes back to both classical and Judeo-Christian doctrines. Contemporary philosophers have cast off these metaphysical and religious shackles and freely invoke the dignity of mankind without needing to justify the idea at all. Why should we not attribute "intrinsic dignity" or "intrinsic worth" to ourselves? Fellow-humans are unlikely to reject the accolades we so generously bestow on them, and those to whom we deny the honor are unable to object. Indeed, when one thinks only of humans, it can be very liberal, very progressive, to talk of the dignity of all human beings. In so doing, we implicitly condemn slavery, racism, and other violations of human rights. We admit that we ourselves are in some fundamental sense on a par with the poorest, most ignorant members of our own species. It is only when we think of humans as no more than a small sub-group of all the beings that inhabit our planet that we may realize that in elevating our own species we are at the same time lowering the relative status of all other species.

The truth is that the appeal to the intrinsic dignity of human beings appears to solve the egalitarian's problems only as long as it goes unchallenged. Once we ask *why* it should be that all humans—including infants, mental defectives, psychopaths, Hitler, Stalin and the rest—have some kind of dignity or worth that no elephant, pig, or chimpanzee can ever achieve, we see that this question is as difficult to answer as our original request for some relevant fact that justifies the inequality of humans and other animals. In fact, these two questions are really one: talk of intrinsic dignity or moral worth only takes the problem back one step, because any satisfactory defence of the claim that all and only humans have intrinsic dignity would need to refer to some relevant capacities or characteristics that all and only humans possess. Philosophers frequently introduce ideas of dignity, respect and worth at the point at which other reasons appear to be lacking, but this is hardly good enough. Fine phrases are the last resource of those who have run out of arguments.

In case there are those who still think it may be pos-

sible to find some relevant characteristic that distinguishes all humans from all members of other species, I shall refer again, before I conclude, to the existence of some humans who quite clearly are below the level of awareness, self-consciousness, intelligence, and sentience, of many nonhumans. I am thinking of humans with severe and irreparable brain damage, and also of infant humans. To avoid the complication of the relevance of a being's potential, however, I shall henceforth concentrate on permanently retarded humans.

Philosophers who set out to find a characteristic that will distinguish humans from other animals rarely take the course of abandoning these groups of humans by lumping them in with the other animals. It is easy to see why they do not. To take this line without re-thinking our attitudes to other animals would entail that we have the right to perform painful experiments on retarded humans for trivial reasons; similarly it would follow that we had the right to rear and kill these humans for food. To most philosophers these consequences are as unacceptable as the view that we should stop treating nonhumans in this way.

Of course, when discussing the problem of equality it is possible to ignore the problem of mental defectives, or brush it aside as if somehow insignificant.[11] This is the easiest way out. What else remains? My final example of speciesism in contemporary philosophy has been selected to show what happens when a writer is prepared to face the question of human equality and animal equality without ignoring the existence of mental defectives, and without resorting to obscurantist mumbo-jumbo. Stanley Benn's clear and honest article "Egalitarianism and Equal Consideration of Interests"[12] fits this description.

Benn, after noting the usual "evident human inequalities" argues, correctly I think, for equality of consideration as the only possible basis for egalitarianism. Yet Benn, like other writers, is thinking only of "equal consideration of human interests." Benn is quite open in his defence of this restriction of equal consideration:

> . . . not to possess human shape *is* a disqualifying condition. However faithful or intelligent a dog may be, it would be a monstrous sentimentality to attribute to him interests that could be weighed in an equal balance with those of human beings . . . if, for instance, one had to decide between feeding a hungry baby or a hungry dog, anyone who chose the dog would generally be reckoned morally defective, unable to recognize a fundamental inequality of claims.
>
> This is what distinguishes our attitude to animals from our attitude to imbeciles. It would be odd to say that we ought to respect equally the dignity or personality of the imbecile and of the rational man . . . but there is nothing odd about saying that we should respect their interests equally, that is, that we should give to the interests of each the same serious consideration as claims to considerations

necessary for some standard of well-being that we can recognize and endorse.

Benn's statement of the basis of the consideration we should have for imbeciles seems to me correct, but why should there be any fundamental inequality of claims between a dog and a human imbecile? Benn sees that if equal consideration depended on rationality, no reason could be given against using imbeciles for research purposes, as we now use dogs and guinea pigs. This will not do: "But of course we do distinguish imbeciles from animals in this regard," he says. That the common distinction is justifiable is something Benn does not question; his problem is how it is to be justified. The answer he gives is this:

> . . . we respect the interests of men and give them priority over dogs not *insofar* as they are rational, but because rationality is the human norm. We say it is *unfair* to exploit the deficiencies of the imbecile who falls short of the norm, just as it would be unfair, and not just ordinarily dishonest, to steal from a blind man. If we do not think in this way about dogs, it is because we do not see the irrationality of the dog as a deficiency or a handicap, but as normal for the species. The characteristics, therefore, that distinguish the normal man from the normal dog make it intelligible for us to talk of other men having interests and capacities, and therefore claims, of precisely the same kind as we make on our own behalf. But although these characteristics may provide the point of the distinction between men and other species, they are *not* in fact the qualifying conditions for membership, or the distinguishing criteria of the class of morally considerable persons; *and this is precisely because a man does not become a member of a different species, with its own standards of normality, by reason of not possessing these characteristics.*

The final sentence of this passage gives the argument away. An imbecile, Benn concedes, may have no characteristics superior to those of a dog; nevertheless this does not make the imbecile a member of "a different species" as the dog is. *Therefore* it would be "unfair" to use the imbecile for medical research as we use the dog. But why? That the imbecile is not rational is just the way things have worked out, and the same is true of the dog—neither is any more responsible for their mental level. If it is unfair to take advantage of an isolated defect, why is it fair to take advantage of a more general limitation? I find it hard to see anything in this argument except a defence of preferring the interests of members of our own species because they are members of our own species. To those who think there might be more to it, I suggest the following mental exercise. Assume that it has been proven that there is a difference in the average, or normal, intelligence quotient for two different races, say whites and blacks. Then substitute the term "white" for every occurrence of "men" and "black" for every occurrence of "dog" in the passage quoted; and substitute "high I.Q." for "rationality" and when Benn talks of "imbeciles" replace this term by "dumb whites"—that is, whites who fall well below the normal white I.Q. score. Finally, change "species" to "race." Now re-read the passage. It has become a defence of a rigid, no-exceptions division between whites and blacks, based on I.Q. scores, *not withstanding an admitted overlap* between whites and blacks in this respect. The revised passage is, of course, outrageous, and this is not only because we have made fictitious assumptions in our substitutions. The point is that in the original passage Benn was defending a rigid division in the amount of consideration due to members of different species, despite admitted cases of overlap. If the original did not, at first reading strike us as being as outrageous as the revised version does, this is largely because although we are not racists ourselves, most of us are speciesists. Like the other articles, Benn's stands as a warning of the ease with which the best minds can fall victim to a prevailing ideology.

Notes

1. *The Methods of Ethics* (7th Ed.), p. 382.
2. For example, R. M. Hare, *Freedom and Reason* (Oxford, 1963) and J. Rawls, *A Theory of Justice* (Harvard, 1972) a brief account of the essential agreement on this issue between these and other positions, see R. M. Hare, "Rules of War and Moral Reasoning," *Philosophy and Public Affairs*, vol. 1, no. 2 (1972).
3. *Introduction to the Principles of Morals and Legislation*, ch. XVII.
4. I owe the term "speciesism" to Richard Ryder.
5. In order to produce 1 lb. of protein in the form of beef or veal, we must feed 21 lbs. of protein to the animal. Other forms of livestock are slightly less inefficient, but the average ratio in the U.S. is still 1:8. It has been estimated that the amount of protein lost to humans in this way is equivalent to 90% of the annual world protein deficit. For a brief account, see Frances Moore Lappé, *Diet for a Small Planet* (Friends of The Earth/Ballantine, New York 1971) pp. 4–11.
6. Ruth Harrison, *Animal Machines* (Stuart, London, 1964). For an account of farming conditions, see my *Animal Liberation* (New York Review Company, 1975).
7. R. Brandt (ed.) *Social Justice* (Prentice-Hall, Englewood Cliffs, 1962), p. 19.
8. Frankena, *Op. cit*, p. 23.
9. H. A. Bedau, "Egalitarianism and the Idea of Equality" in *Nomos IX: Equality*, ed. J. R. Pennock and J. W. Chapman, New York, 1967.
10. G. Vlastos, "Justice and Equality" in Brandt, *Social Justice*, p. 48.
11. For example, Bernard Williams, "The Idea of Equality," in *Philosophy, Politics and Society* (second series), ed. P. Laslett and W. Runciman (Blackwell, Oxford, 1962), p. 118; J. Rawls, *A Theory of Justice*, pp. 509–10.

12. *Nomos IX: Equality*; the passages quoted are on p. 62ff.

Study Questions

1. According to Singer, what is the relationship between civil rights movements and the animal rights movement?

2. What is *speciesism*? Why is it bad, according to Singer? Do you agree?

3. Are all humans equal, according to Singer? In what way are all sentient beings equal?

4. How does Singer apply the notion of equal consideration of interests?

8

The Radical Egalitarian Case for Animal Rights

TOM REGAN

Professor of philosophy at North Carolina State University and a leading animal rights advocate in the United States, Tom Regan is the author of several articles and books on moral philosophy, including The Case for Animal Rights *(1983).*

Regan disagrees with Singer's utilitarian program for animal liberation, for he rejects utilitarianism as lacking a notion of intrinsic worth. Regan's position is that animals and humans all have equal intrinsic value on which their right to life and concern are based. Regan is revolutionary. He calls for not reform but the total abolition of the use of animals in science, the total dissolution of the commercial animal agriculture system, and the total elimination of commercial and sport hunting and trapping. "The fundamental wrong is the system that allows us to view animals as our resources. . . Lab animals are not our tasters; we are not their kings."

I regard myself as an advocate of animal rights—as a part of the animal rights movement. That movement, as I conceive it, is committed to a number of goals, including:

1. the total abolition of the use of animals in science
2. the total dissolution of commercial animal agriculture
3. and the total elimination of commercial and sport hunting and trapping.

There are, I know, people who profess to believe in animal rights who do not avow these goals. Factory farming they say, is wrong—violates animals' rights—but traditional animal agriculture is all right. Toxicity tests of cosmetics on animals violate their rights; but not important medical research—cancer research, for example. The clubbing of baby seals is abhorrent; but not the harvesting of adult seals. I used to think I under-

From: *In Defense of Animals*, ed. Peter Singer (Oxford: Basil Blackwell, 1985). Reprinted by permission of Blackwell Publishers.

stood this reasoning. Not any more. You don't change unjust institutions by tidying them up.

What's wrong—what's fundamentally wrong—with the way animals are treated isn't the details that vary from case to case. It's the whole system. The forlornness of the veal calf is pathetic—heart wrenching; the pulsing pain of the chimp with electrodes planted deep in her brain is repulsive; the slow, torturous death of the raccoon caught in the leg hold trap, agonizing. But what is fundamentally wrong isn't the pain, isn't the suffering, isn't the deprivation. These compound what's wrong. Sometimes—often—they make it much worse. But they are not the fundamental wrong.

The fundamental wrong is the system that allows us to view animals as our resources, here for us—to be eaten, or surgically manipulated, or put in our cross hairs for sport or money. Once we accept this view of animals—as our resources—the rest is as predictable as it is regrettable. Why worry about their loneliness, their pain, their death? Since animals exist for us, here to benefit us in one way or another, what harms them really doesn't matter—or matters only if it starts to bother us, makes us feel a trifle uneasy when we eat our veal scampi, for example. So, yes, let us get veal calves out of solitary confinement, give them more space, a little straw, a few companions. But let us keep our veal scampi.

But a little straw, more space, and a few companions don't eliminate—don't even touch—the fundamental wrong, the wrong that attaches to our viewing and treating these animals as our resources. A veal calf killed to be eaten after living in close confinement is viewed and treated in this way: but so, too, is another who is raised (as they say) "more humanely." To right the fundamental wrong of our treatment of farm animals requires more than making rearing methods "more human"—requires something quite different—requires the *total dissolution of commercial animal agriculture*.

How we do this—whether we do this, or as in the case of animals in science, whether and how we abolish their use—these are to a large extent political questions. People must change their beliefs before they change their habits. Enough people, especially those elected to public office, must believe in change—must want it—before we will have laws that protect the rights of animals. This process of change is very complicated, very demanding, very exhausting, calling for the efforts of many hands—in education, publicity, political organization and activity, down to the licking of envelopes and stamps. As a trained and practicing philosopher the sort of contribution I can make is limited, but I like to think, important. The currency of philosophy is ideas—their meaning and rational foundation—not the nuts and bolts of the legislative process say, or the mechanics of community organization. That's what I have been exploring over the past ten years or so in my essays and talks and, more recently, in my book, *The Case for Animal Rights.*[1] I believe the major conclusions I reach in that book are true because they are supported by the weight of the *best arguments.* I believe the idea of animal rights has reason, not just emotion, on its side.

In the space I have at my disposal here I can only sketch, in the barest outlines, some of the main features of the book. Its main themes—and we should not be surprised by this—involve asking and answering deep foundational moral questions, questions about what morality is, how it should be understood, what is the best moral theory all considered. I hope I can convey something of the shape I think this theory is. The attempt to do this will be—to use a word a friendly critic once used to describe my work—cerebral. In fact I was told by this person that my work is "too cerebral." But this is misleading. My feelings about how animals sometimes are treated are just as deep and just as strong as those of my more volatile compatriots. Philosophers do—to use the jargon of the day—have a right side to their brains. If it's the left side we contribute or mainly should—that's because what talents we have reside there.

How to proceed? We begin by asking how the moral status of animals has been understood by thinkers who deny that animals have rights. Then we test the mettle of their ideas by seeing how well they stand up under the heat of fair criticism. If we start our thinking in this way we soon find that some people believe that we have no duties directly to animals—that we owe nothing *to them*—that we can do nothing that *wrongs them.* Rather, we can do wrong acts that involve animals, and so we have duties regarding them, though none to them. Such views may be called indirect duty views. By way of illustration:

Suppose your neighbor kicks your dog. Then your neighbor has done something wrong. But not to your dog. The wrong that has been done is a wrong to you. After all, it is wrong to upset people, and your neighbor's kicking your dog upsets you. So you are the one who is wronged, not your dog. Or again: by kicking your dog your neighbor damages your property. And since it is wrong to damage another person's property,

your neighbor has done something wrong—to you, of course, not to your dog. Your neighbor no more wrongs your dog than your car would be wronged if the windshield were smashed. Your neighbor's duties involving your dog are indirect duties to you. More generally, all of our duties regarding animals are indirect duties to one another—to humanity.

How could someone try to justify such a view? One could say that your dog doesn't feel anything and so isn't hurt by your neighbor's kick, doesn't care about the pain since none is felt, is as unaware of anything as your windshield. Someone could say this but no rational person will since, among other considerations, such a view will commit one who holds it to the position that no human being feels pain either—that human beings also don't care about what happens to them. A second possibility is that though both humans and your dog are hurt when kicked, it is only human pain that matters. But, again, no rational person can believe this. Pain is pain wheresoever it occurs. If your neighbor's causing you pain is wrong because of the pain that is caused, we cannot rationally ignore or dismiss the moral relevance of the pain your dog feels.

Philosophers who hold indirect duty views—and many still do—have come to understand that they must avoid the two defects just noted—avoid, that is, both the view that animals don't feel anything as well as the idea that only human pain can be morally relevant. Among such thinkers the sort of view now favored is one or another form of what is called *contractarianism.*

Here, very crudely, is the root idea: morality consists of a set of rules that individuals voluntarily agree to abide by—as we do when we sign a contract (hence the name: contractarianism). Those who understand and accept the terms of the contract are covered directly—have rights created by, and recognized and protected in, the contract. And these contractors can also have protection spelled out for others who, though they lack the ability to understand morality and so cannot sign the contract themselves, are loved or cherished by those who can. Thus young children, for example, are unable to sign and lack rights. But they are protected by the contract nonetheless because of the sentimental interests of others, most notably their parents. So we have, then, duties involving these children, duties regarding them, but no duties to them. Our duties in their case are indirect duties to other human beings, usually their parents.

As for animals, since they cannot understand the contract, they obviously cannot sign; and since they cannot sign; they have no rights. Like children, however, some animals are the objects of the sentimental interest of others. You, for example, love your dog . . . or cat. So these animals—those enough people care about: companion animals, whales, baby seals, the American bald eagle—these animals, though they lack rights themselves, will be protected because of the sentimental interests of people. I have, then, according to contractarianism, no duty directly to your dog or any other animal, not even the duty not to cause them pain or suffering; my duty not to hurt them is a duty I have to those people who care about what happens to them. As for other animals, where no or little sentimental interest is present—farm animals, for example, or laboratory rats—what duties we have grow weaker and weaker, perhaps to the vanishing point. The pain and death they endure, though real, are not wrong if no one cares about them.

Contractarianism could be a hard view to refute when it comes to the moral status of animals if it was an adequate theoretical approach to the moral status of human beings. It is not adequate in this latter respect, however, which makes the question of its adequacy in the former—regarding animals—utterly moot. For consider: morality, according to the (crude) contractarian position before us, consists of rules people agree to abide by. What people? Well, enough to make a difference—enough, that is, so that collectively they have the power to enforce the rules that are drawn up in the contract. That is very well and good for the signatories—but not so good for anyone who is not asked to sign. And there is nothing in contractarianism of the sort we are discussing that guarantees or requires that everyone will have a chance to participate equitably in framing the rules of morality. The result is that this approach to ethics could sanction the most blatant forms of social, economic, moral, and political injustice, ranging from a repressive caste system to systematic racial or sexual discrimination. Might, on this theory, does make right. Let those who are the victims of injustice suffer as they will. It matters not so long as no one else—no contractor, or too few of them—cares about it. Such a theory takes one's moral breath away . . . as if, for example, there is nothing wrong with apartheid in South Africa if too few white South Africans are upset by it. A theory with so little to recommend it at the level of the ethics of our treatment of our fellow humans cannot have anything more to recommend it when it comes to the ethics of how we treat our fellow animals.

The version of contractarianism just examined is, as I have noted, a crude variety, and in fairness to those of a contractarian persuasion it must be noted that much more refined, subtle, and ingenious varieties are possible. For example, John Rawls, in his *A Theory of Justice*, sets forth a version of contractarianism that forces the contractors to ignore the accidental features of being a human being—for example, whether one is white or black, male or female, a genius or of modest intellect. Only by ignoring such features, Rawls believes, can we insure that the principles of justice contractors would agree upon are not based on bias or prejudice. Despite the improvement a view such as Rawls's shows over the cruder forms of contractarianism, it remains deficient: it systematically denies that we have direct duties to those human beings who do not have a sense of justice—young children, for instance, and many mentally retarded humans. And yet it seems reasonably certain that, were we to torture a young child or a retarded elder, we would be doing something that wrongs them, not something that is wrong if (and only if) other humans with a sense of justice are upset. And since this is true in the case of these humans, we cannot rationally deny the same in the case of animals.

Indirect duty views, then, including the best among them, fail to command our rational assent. Whatever ethical theory we rationally should accept, therefore, it must at least recognize that we have some duties directly to animals, just as we have some duties directly to each other. The next two theories I'll sketch attempt to meet this requirement.

The first I call the *cruelty-kindness view*. Simply stated, this view says that we have a direct duty to be kind to animals and a direct duty not to be cruel to them. Despite the familiar, reassuring ring of these ideas, I do not believe this view offers an adequate theory. To make this clearer, consider kindness. A kind person acts from a certain kind of motive—compassion or concern, for example. And that is a virtue. But there is no guarantee that a kind act is a right act. If I am a generous racist, for example, I will be inclined to act kindly toward members of my own own race, favoring their interests above others. My kindness would be real and, so far as it goes, good. But I trust it is too obvious to require comment that my kind acts may not be above moral reproach—may, in fact, be positively wrong because rooted in injustice. So kindness, not withstanding its status as a virtue to be encouraged, simply will not cancel the weight of a theory of right action.

Cruelty fares no better. People or their acts are cruel if they display either a lack of sympathy for or, worse, the presence of enjoyment in, seeing another suffer. Cruelty in all its guises *is* a bad thing—*is* a tragic human failing. But just as a person's being motivated by kindness does not guarantee that they do what is right, so the absence of cruelty does not assure that they avoid doing what is wrong. Many people who perform abortions, for example, are not cruel, sadistic people. But that fact about their character and motivation does not settle the terribly difficult question about the morality of abortion. The case is no different when we examine the ethics of our treatment of animals. So, yes, let us be for kindness and against cruelty. But let us not suppose that being for the one and against the other answers questions about moral right and wrong.

Some people think the theory we are looking for is *utilitarianism. A utilitarian accepts two moral principles. The first is a principle of equality: everyone's interests count, and similar interests must be counted as having similar weight or importance.* White or black, male or female, American or Iranian, human or animal: everyone's pain or frustration matter and matter equally with the like pain or frustration of anyone else. The second principle a utilitarian accepts is the principle of *utility: do that act that will bring about the best balance of satisfaction over frustration for everyone affected by the outcome.*

As a utilitarian, then, here is how I am to approach the task of deciding what I morally ought to do: I must ask who will be affected if I choose to do one thing rather than another, how much each individual will be affected, and where the best results are most likely to lie—which option, in other words, is most likely to bring about the best results, the best balance of satisfaction over frustration. That option, whatever it may be, is the one I ought to choose. That is where my moral duty lies.

The great appeal of utilitarianism rests with its uncompromising *egalitarianism*: everyone's interests count and count equally with the like interests of everyone else. The kind of odious discrimination some forms of contractarianism can justify—discrimination based on race or sex, for example—seems disallowed in principle by utilitarianism, as is speciesism—systematic discrimination based on species membership.

The sort of equality we find in utilitarianism, however, is not the sort an advocate of animal or human rights should have in mind. Utilitarianism has no room for the *equal moral rights of different individuals because it has no room for their equal inherent value or worth.* What has value for the utilitarian is the satisfaction of an individual's interests, not the individual whose interests they are. A universe in which you satisfy your desire for water, food, and warmth, is, other things being equal, better than a universe in which these desires are frustrated. And the same is true in the case of an animal with similar desires. But neither you nor the animal have any value in your own right. *Only your feelings do.*

Here is an analogy to help make the philosophical point clearer: a cup contains different liquids—sometimes sweet, sometimes bitter, sometimes a mix of the two. What has value are the liquids: the sweeter the better, the bitter the worse. The cup—the container—has no value. It's what goes into it, not what they go into, that has value. For the utilitarian, you and I are like the cup; we have no value as individuals and thus no equal value. What has value is what goes into us, what we serve as receptacles for; our feelings of satisfaction have positive value, our feelings of frustration have negative value.

Serious problems arise for utilitarianism when we remind ourselves that it enjoins us to bring about the best consequences. What does this mean? It doesn't mean the best consequences for me alone, or for my family or friends, or any other person taken individually. No, what we must do is, roughly, as follows: we must add up—somehow!—the separate satisfactions and frustrations of everyone likely to be affected by our choice, the satisfactions in one column, the frustrations in the other. We must total each column for each of the opinions before us. That is what it means to say the theory is aggregative. And then we must choose that option which is most likely to bring about the best balance of totaled satisfactions over totaled frustrations. Whatever act would lead to this outcome is the one we morally ought to perform—is where our moral duty lies. And that act quite clearly might not be the same one that would bring about the best results for me personally, or my family or friends, or a lab animal. The best aggregated consequences for everyone concerned are not necessarily the best for each individual.

That utilitarianism is an aggregative theory—that different individual's satisfactions or frustrations are added, or summed, or totaled—is the key objection to this theory. My Aunt Bea is old, inactive, a cranky, sour person, though not physically ill. She prefers to go on living. She is also rather rich. I could make a fortune if I could get my hands on her money, money she intends to give me in any event, after she dies, but which she refuses to give me now. In order to avoid a huge tax bite, I plan to donate a handsome sum of my profits to a local children's hospital. Many, many children will benefit from my generosity, and much joy will be brought to their parents, relatives, and friends. If I don't get the money rather soon, all these ambitions will come to naught. The once-in-a-lifetime-opportunity to make a real killing will be gone. Why, then, not really kill my Aunt Bea? Oh, of course I *might* get caught. But I'm no fool and, besides, her doctor can be counted on to cooperate (he has an eye for the same investment and I happen to know a good deal about his shady past). The deed can be done . . . professionally, shall we say. There is *very* little chance of getting caught. And as for my conscience being guilt ridden, I am a resourceful sort of fellow and will take more than sufficient comfort—as I lie on the beach at Acapulco—in contemplating the joy and health I have brought to so many others.

Suppose Aunt Bea is killed and the rest of the story comes out as told. Would I have done anything wrong? Anything immoral? One would have thought that I had. But not according to utilitarianism. Since what I did brought about the best balance of totaled satisfaction over frustration for all those affected by the outcome, what I did was not wrong. Indeed, in killing Aunt Bea the physician and I did what duty required.

This same kind of argument can be repeated in all sorts of cases, illustrating time after time, how the utilitarian's position leads to results that impartial people find morally callous. It is wrong to kill my Aunt Bea in the name of bringing about the best results for others. A good end does not justify an evil means. Any adequate moral theory will have to explain why this is so. Utilitarianism fails in this respect and so cannot be the theory we seek.

What to do? Where to begin anew? The place to begin, I think, is with the utilitarian's view of the value of the individual—or, rather, lack of value. In its place suppose we consider that you and I, for example, do have value as individuals—what we'll call *inherent value*. To say we have such value is to say that we are something more than, something different from, mere receptacles. Moreover, to insure that we do not pave the way for such injustices as slavery or sexual discrimination, we must believe that all who have inherent value have it equally, regardless of their sex, race, religion, birthplace, and so on. Similarly to be discarded as irrelevant are one's talents or skills, intelligence and wealth, personality or pathology, whether one is loved and admired—or despised and loathed. The genius and the retarded child, the prince and the pauper, the brain surgeon and the fruit vendor, Mother Theresa and the most unscrupulous used car salesman—all have inherent value, all possess it *equally*, and *all have an equal right to be treated with respect*, to be treated in ways that do not reduce them to the status of things, as if they exist as resources for others. My value as an individual is independent of my usefulness to you. Yours is not dependent on your usefulness to me. For either of us to treat the other in ways that fail to show respect for the other's independent value is to act immorally—is to violate the individual's rights.

Some of the rational virtues of this view—what I call the rights view—should be evident. Unlike (crude) contractarianism, for example, the rights view *in principle* denies the moral tolerability of any and all forms of racial, sexual, or social discrimination; and unlike utilitarianism, this view *in principle* denies that we can justify good results by using evil means that violate an individual's rights— denies, for example, that it could be moral to kill my Aunt Bea to harvest beneficial consequences for others. That would be to sanction the disrespectful treatment of the individual in the name of the social good, something the rights view will not—categorically will not—ever allow.

The rights view—or so I believe—is rationally the most satisfactory moral theory. It surpasses all other theories in the degree to which it illuminates and explains the foundation of our duties to one another—the domain of human morality. On this score, it has the best reasons, the best arguments, on its side. Of course, if it were possible to show that only human beings are included within its scope, then a person like myself, who believes in animal rights, would be obliged to look elsewhere than to the rights view.

But attempts to limit its scope to humans only can be shown to be rationally defective. Animals, it is true, lack many of the abilities humans possess. They can't read, do higher mathematics, build a bookcase, or make *baba ghanoush*. Neither can many human beings, however, and yet we don't say—and shouldn't say—that they (these humans) therefore have less inherent value, less of a right to be treated with respect, than do others. It is the *similarities* between those human beings who most clearly, most noncontroversially have such value—the people reading this, for example—it is our similarities, not our differences, that matter most. And the really crucial, the basic similarity is simply this: *we are each of us the experiencing subject of a life, each of us a conscious*

creature having an individual welfare that has importance to us whatever our usefulness to others*. We want and prefer things; believe and feel things; recall and expect things. And all these dimensions of our life, including our pleasure and pain, our enjoyment and suffering, our satisfaction and frustration, our continued existence or our untimely death—all make a difference to the quality of our life as lived, as experienced by us as individuals. As the same is true of those animals who concern us (those who are eaten and trapped, for example), they, too, must be viewed as the experiencing subjects of a life with inherent value of their own.

There are some who resist the idea that animals have inherent value. "Only humans have such value," they profess. How might this narrow view be defended? Shall we say that only humans have the requisite intelligence, or autonomy, or reason? But there are many, many humans who will fail to meet these standards and yet who are reasonably viewed as having value above and beyond their usefulness to others. Shall we claim that only humans belong to the right species—the species *Homo sapiens*? But this is blatant speciesism. Will it be said, then, that all—and only—humans have immortal souls? Then our opponents more than have their work cut out for them. I am myself not ill-disposed to there being immortal souls. Personally, I profoundly hope I have one. But I would not want to rest my position on a controversial, ethical issue on the even more controversial question about who or what has an immortal soul. That is to dig one's hole deeper, not climb out. Rationally, it is better to resolve moral issues without making more controversial assumptions than are needed. The question of who has inherent value is such a question, one that is more rationally resolved without the introduction of the idea of immortal souls than by its use.

Well, perhaps some will say that animals have some inherent value, only *less* than we do. Once again, however, attempts to defend this view can be shown to lack rational justification. What could be the basis of our having more inherent value than animals? Will it be their lack of reason, or autonomy, or intellect? Only if we are willing to make the same judgment in the case of humans who are similarly deficient. But it is not true that such humans—the retarded child, for example, or the mentally deranged—have less inherent value than you or I. Neither, then, can we rationally sustain the view that animals like them in being the experiencing subjects of a life have less inherent value. *All who have inherent value have it equally, whether they be human animals or not.*

Inherent value, then, belongs equally to those who are the experiencing subjects of a life. Whether it belongs to others—to rocks and rivers, trees and glaciers, for example—we do not know. And may never know. But neither do we need to know, if we are to make the case for animal rights. We do not need to know how many people, for example, are eligible to vote in the next presidential election before we can know whether I am. Similarly, we do not need to know *how many* individuals have inherent value before we can know that some do. When it comes to the case for animal rights, then what we need to know is whether the animals who, in our culture are routinely eaten, hunted, and used in our laboratories, for example, are like us in being subjects of a life. And we *do* know this. We do *know* that many—literally, billions and billions—of these animals are subjects of a life in the sense explained and so have inherent value if we do. And since, in order to have the best theory of our duties to one another, we must recognize our equal inherent value, as individuals, *reason*—not sentiment, not emotion—*reason compels us to recognize the equal inherent value of these animals*. And, with this, their equal right to be treated with respect.

That, *very* roughly, is the shape and feel of the case for animal rights. Most of the details of the supporting argument are missing. They are to be found in the book I alluded to earlier. Here, the details go begging and I must in closing, limit myself to four final points.

The first is how the theory that underlies the case for animal rights shows that the animal rights movement is a part of, not antagonistic to, the human rights movement. The theory that rationally grounds the rights of animals also grounds the rights of humans. Thus are those involved in the animal rights movement partners in the struggle to secure respect for human rights—the rights of women, for example, or minorities and workers. The animal rights movement is cut from the same moral cloth as these.

Second, having set out the broad outlines of the rights view, I can now say why its *implications for farming and science*, for example, are both clear and uncompromising. In the case of using animals in science, the rights view is categorically abolitionist. *Lab animals are not our tasters; we are not their kings.* Because these animals are treated—routinely, systematically—as if their value is reducible to their usefulness to others, they are routinely systematically treated with a lack of respect, and thus their rights routinely, systematically violated. This is just as true when they are used in trivial, duplicative, unnecessary or unwise research as it is when they are used in studies that hold out real promise of human benefits. We can't justify harming or killing a human being (my Aunt Bea, for example) just for these sorts of reasons. Neither can we do so even in the case of so lowly a creature as a laboratory rat. It is not just refinement or reduction that are called for, not just larger, cleaner cages, not just more generous use of anesthetic or the elimination of multiple surgery, not just tidying up the system. It is replacement—completely. The best we can do when it comes to using animals in science is—not to use them. That is where our duty lies, according to the rights view.

As for commercial animal agriculture, the rights view takes a similar abolitionist position. The fundamental moral wrong here is not that animals are kept in stressful close confinement, or in isolation, or that they have their pain and suffering, their needs and preferences ignored or discounted. *All* these *are* wrong, of course, but they are not the fundamental wrong. They are symptoms and effects of the deeper, systematic wrong that allows these animals to be viewed and treated as lacking independent value, as resources for us—as, indeed, a renewable resource. Giving farm animals more space, more natural environments, more companions does not right the fundamental wrong, any more than giving lab animals more anesthesia or bigger, cleaner cages would right the fundamental wrong in their case. Nothing less than the total dissolution of commercial animal agriculture will do this, just as, for similar reasons I won't develop at length here, morality requires nothing less than the total elimination of commercial and sport hunting and trapping. The rights view's implications, then, as I have said, are clear—and are uncompromising.

My last two points are about philosophy—my profession. It is most obviously, no substitute for political action. The words I have written here and in other places by themselves don't change a thing. It is what we do with the thoughts the words express—our acts, our deeds—that change things. All that philosophy can do, and all I have attempted, is to offer a vision of what our deeds could aim at. And the why. But not the how.

Finally, I am reminded of my thoughtful critic, the one I mentioned earlier, who chastised me for being "too cerebral." Well, cerebral I have been: indirect duty views, utilitarianism, contractarianism—hardly the stuff deep passions are made of. I am also reminded, however, of the image another friend once set before me— the image of the ballerina as expressive of disciplined passion. Long hours of sweat and toil, of loneliness and practice, of doubt and fatigue; that is the discipline of her craft. But the passion is there, too: the fierce drive to excel, to speak through her body, to do it right, to pierce our minds. That is the image of philosophy I would leave with you; not "too cerebral," but *disciplined passion*. Of the discipline, enough has been seen. As for the passion:

There are times, and these are not infrequent, when tears come to my eyes when I see, or read, or hear of the wretched plight of animals in the hands of humans. Their pain, their suffering, their loneliness, their innocence, their death. Anger. Rage. Pity. Sorrow. Disgust. The whole creation groans under the weight of the evil we humans visit upon these mute, powerless creatures. It *is* our heart, not just our head, that calls for an end, that demands of us that we overcome, for them, the habits and forces behind their systematic oppression. All great movements, it is written, go through three stages: ridicule, discussion, adoption. It is the realization of this third stage—adoption—that demands both our passion and our discipline, our heart and our head. *The fate of animals is in our hands. God grant we are equal to the task.*

Note

1. Tom Regan, *The Case for Animal Rights* (Berkeley: University of California Press, 1983).

Study Questions

1. How is Regan's position on animal rights different from Singer's? Explain.

2. What are Regan's reasons for granting animals equal moral rights?

3. Does Regan allow for experimentation on animals? If we have to test a dangerous AIDS vaccine, on whom should we test it?

9

A Critique of Regan's Animal Rights Theory

Mary Anne Warren

The author of several articles in moral philosophy, Mary Anne Warren teaches philosophy at San Francisco State University.

Warren reconstructs Regan's argument for animal rights and criticizes it for depending on the obscure notion of inherent value. She then argues that all rational human beings are equally part of the moral community since we can reason with each other about our behavior, whereas we cannot so reason with an animal. She puts forth a "weak animal rights theory" which asserts that we ought not to be cruel to animals or kill them without good reason.

Tom Regan has produced what is perhaps the definitive defense of the view that the basic moral rights of at least some non-human animals are in no way inferior to our own. In *The Case for Animal Rights*, he argues that all normal mammals over a year of age have the same basic moral rights.[1] Non-human mammals have essentially the same right not to be harmed or killed as we do. I shall call this "the strong animal rights position," although it is weaker than the claims made by some animal liberationists in that it ascribes rights to only some sentient animals.[2]

I will argue that Regan's case for the strong animal rights position is unpersuasive and that this position entails consequences which a reasonable person cannot accept. I do not deny that some non-human animals have moral rights; indeed, I would extend the scope of the rights claim to include all sentient animals, that is, all those capable of having experiences, including experiences of pleasure or satisfaction and pain, suffering, or frustration.[3] However, I do not think that the moral rights of most non-human animals are identical in strength to those of persons.[4] The rights of most non-human animals may be overridden in circumstances which would not justify overriding the rights of persons. There are, for instance, compelling realities which sometimes require that we kill animals for reasons which could not justify the killing of persons. I will call this view "the weak animal rights" position, even though it ascribes rights to a wider range of animals than does the strong animal rights position.

I will begin by summarizing Regan's case for the strong animal rights position and noting two problems with it. Next, I will explore some consequences of the strong animal rights position which I think are unacceptable. Finally, I will outline the case for the weak animal rights position.

REGAN'S CASE

Regan's argument moves through three stages. First, he argues that normal, mature mammals are not only sentient but have other mental capacities as well. These include the capacities for emotion, memory, belief, desire, the use of general concepts, intentional action, a sense of the future, and some degree of self-awareness. Creatures with such capacities are said to be subjects-of-a-life. They are not only alive in the biological sense but have a psychological identity over time and an existence which can go better or worse for them. Thus, they can be harmed or benefited. These are plausible claims, and well defended. One of the strongest parts of the book is the rebuttal of philosophers, such as R. G. Frey, who object to the application of such mentalistic terms to creatures that do not use a human-style language.[5] The second and third stages of the argument are more problematic.

In the second stage, Regan argues that subjects-of-a-life have inherent value. His concept of inherent value grows out of his opposition to utilitarianism. Utilitarian

Reprinted from *Between the Species*, Vol. 2, no. 4 (Fall 1987) by permission.

moral theory, he says, treats individuals as "mere receptacles" for morally significant value, in that harm to one individual may be justified by the production of a greater net benefit to other individuals. In opposition to this, he holds that subjects-of-a-life have a value independent of both the value they may place upon their lives or experiences and the value others may place upon them.

Inherent value, Regan argues, does not come in degrees. To hold that some individuals have more inherent value than others is to adopt a "perfectionist" theory, i.e., one which assigns different moral worth to individuals according to how well they are thought to exemplify some virtue(s), such as intelligence or moral autonomy. Perfectionist theories have been used, at least since the time of Aristotle, to rationalize such injustices as slavery and male domination, as well as the unrestrained exploitation of animals. Regan argues that if we reject these injustices, then we must also reject perfectionism and conclude that all subjects-of-a-life have equal inherent value. Moral agents have no more inherent value than moral patients, i.e., subjects-of-a-life who are not morally responsible for their actions.

In the third phase of the argument, Regan uses the thesis of equal inherent value to derive strong moral rights for all subjects-of-a-life. This thesis underlies the Respect Principle, which forbids us to treat beings who have inherent value as mere receptacles, i.e., mere means to the production of the greatest overall good. This principle, in turn, underlies the Harm Principle, which says that we have a direct *prima facie* duty not to harm beings who have inherent value. Together, these principles give rise to moral rights. Rights are defined as valid claims, claims to certain goods and against certain beings, i.e., moral agents. Moral rights generate duties not only to refrain from inflicting harm upon beings with inherent value but also to come to their aid when they are threatened by other moral agents. Rights are not absolute but maybe overridden in certain circumstances. Just what these circumstances are we will consider later. But first, let's look at some difficulties in the theory as thus far presented.

THE MYSTERY OF INHERENT VALUE

Inherent value is a key concept in Regan's theory. It is the bridge between the plausible claim that all normal, mature mammals—human or otherwise—are subjects-of-a-life and the more debatable claim that they all have basic moral rights of the same strength. But it is a highly obscure concept, and its obscurity makes it ill-suited to play this crucial role.

Inherent value is defined almost entirely in negative terms. It is not dependent upon the value which either the inherently valuable individual or anyone else may place upon that individual's life or experiences. It is not

(necessarily) a function of sentience or any other mental capacity, because, Regan says, some entities which are not sentient (e.g., trees, rivers, or rocks) may, nevertheless, have inherent value (p. 246). It cannot attach to anything other than an individual; species, ecosystems, and the like cannot have inherent value.

These are some of the things which inherent value is not. But what is it? Unfortunately, we are not told. Inherent value appears as a mysterious non-natural property which we must take on faith. Regan says that it is a *postulate* that subjects-of-a-life have inherent value, a postulate justified by the fact that it avoids certain absurdities which he thinks follow from a purely utilitarian theory (p. 247). But why is the postulate that *subjects-of-a-life* have inherent value? If the inherent value of a being is completely independent of the value that it or anyone else places upon its experiences, then why does the fact that it has certain sorts of experiences constitute evidence that it has inherent value? If the reason is that subjects-of-a-life have an existence which can go better or worse for them, then why isn't the appropriate conclusion that all sentient beings have inherent value, since they would all seem to meet that condition? Sentient but mentally unsophisticated beings may have a less extensive range of possible satisfactions and frustrations, but why should it follow that they have—or may have—no inherent value at all?

In the absence of a positive account of inherent value, it is also difficult to grasp the connection between being inherently valuable and having moral rights. Intuitively, it seems that value is one thing, and rights are another. It does not seem incoherent to say that some things (e.g., mountains, rivers, redwood trees) are inherently valuable and yet are not the sorts of things which can have moral rights. Nor does it seem incoherent to ascribe inherent value to some things which are not individuals, e.g., plant or animal species, though it may well be incoherent to ascribe moral rights to such things.

In short, the concept of inherent value seems to create at least as many problems as it solves. If inherent value is based on some natural property, then why not try to identify that property and explain its moral significance, without appealing to inherent value? And if it is not based on any natural property, then why should we believe in it? That it may enable us to avoid some of the problems faced by the utilitarian is not a sufficient reason, if it creates other problems which are just as serious.

IS THERE A SHARP LINE?

Perhaps the most serious problems are those that arise when we try to apply the strong animal rights position to animals other than normal, mature mammals. Regan's theory requires us to divide all living things into two categories: those which have the same inherent value and the same basic moral rights that we do, and those which have no inherent value and presumably no moral rights. But wherever we try to draw the line, such a sharp division is implausible.

It would surely be arbitrary to draw such a sharp line between normal, mature mammals and all other living things. Some birds (e.g., crows, magpies, parrots, mynahs) appear to be just as mentally sophisticated as most mammals and thus are equally strong candidates for inclusion under the subject-of-a-life criterion. Regan is not in fact advocating that we draw the line here. His claim is only that normal mature mammals are clear cases, while other cases are less clear. Yet, on his theory, there must be such a sharp line *somewhere*, since there are no degrees of inherent value. But why should we believe that there is a sharp line between creatures that are subjects-of-a-life and creatures that are not? Isn't it more likely that "subjecthood" comes in degrees, that some creatures have only a little self-awareness, and only a little capacity to anticipate the future, while some have a little more, and some a good deal more?

Should we, for instance, regard fish, amphibians, and reptiles as subjects-of-a-life? A simple yes-or-no answer seems inadequate. On the one hand, some of their behavior is difficult to explain without the assumption that they have sensations, beliefs, desires, emotions, and memories; on the other hand, they do not seem to exhibit very much self-awareness or very much conscious anticipation of future events. Do they have enough mental sophistication to count as subjects-of-a-life? Exactly how much is enough?

It is still more unclear what we should say about insects, spiders, octopi, and other invertebrate animals which have brains and sensory organs but whose minds (if they have minds) are even more alien to us than those of fish or reptiles. Such creatures are probably sentient. Some people doubt that they can feel pain, since they lack certain neurological structures which are crucial to the processing of pain impulses in vertebrate animals. But this argument is inconclusive, since their nervous systems might process pain in ways different from ours. When injured, they sometimes act as if they are in pain. On evolutionary grounds, it seems unlikely that highly mobile creatures with complex sensory systems would not have developed a capacity for pain (and pleasure), since such a capacity has obvious survival value. It must, however, be admitted that we do not *know* whether spiders can feel pain (or something very like it), let alone whether they have emotions, memories, beliefs, desires, self-awareness, or a sense of the future.

Even more mysterious are the mental capacities (if any) of mobile microfauna. The brisk and efficient way that paramecia move about in their incessant search for food *might* indicate some kind of sentience, in spite of their lack of eyes, ears, brains, and other organs associated with sentience in more complex organisms. It is conceivable—though not very probable—that they, too, are subjects-of-a-life.

The existence of a few unclear cases need not pose a serious problem for a moral theory, but in this case, the unclear cases constitute most of those with which an adequate theory of animal rights would need to deal. The subject-of-a-life criterion can provide us with little or no moral guidance in our interactions with the vast majority of animals. That might be acceptable if it could be supplemented with additional principles which would provide such guidance. However, the radical dualism of the theory precludes supplementing it in this way. We are forced to say that either a spider has the same right to life as you and I do, or it has no right to life whatever—and that only the gods know which of these alternatives is true.

Regan's suggestion for dealing with such unclear cases is to apply the "benefit of the doubt" principle. That is, when dealing with beings that may or may not be subjects-of-a-life, we should act as if they are.[6] But if we try to apply this principle to the entire range of doubtful cases, we will find ourselves with moral obligations which we cannot possibly fulfill. In many climates, it is virtually impossible to live without swatting mosquitoes and exterminating cockroaches, and not all of us can afford to hire someone to sweep the path before we walk, in order to make sure that we do not step on ants. Thus, we are still faced with the daunting task of drawing a sharp line somewhere on the continuum of life forms—this time, a line demarcating the limits of the benefit of the doubt principle.

The weak animal rights theory provides a more plausible way of dealing with this range of cases, in that it allows the rights of animals of different kinds to vary in strength. . . .

WHY ARE ANIMAL RIGHTS WEAKER THAN HUMAN RIGHTS?

How can we justify regarding the rights of persons as generally stronger than those of sentient beings which are not persons? There are a plethora of bad justifications, based on religious premises or false or unprovable claims about the differences between human and non-human nature. But there is one difference which has a clear moral relevance: people are at least sometimes capable of being moved to action or inaction by the force of reasoned argument. Rationality rests upon other mental capacities, notably those which Regan cites as criteria for being a subject-of-a-life. We share these capacities with many other animals But it is not just because we are subjects-of-a-life that we are both able and morally compelled to recognize one another as beings with equal basic moral rights. It is also because we are able to "listen to reason" in order to settle our conflicts and cooperate in shared projects. This capacity, unlike the others, may require something like a human language.

Why is rationality morally relevant? It does not make us "better" than other animals or more "perfect." It does not even automatically make us more intelligent. (Bad reasoning reduces our effective intelligence rather than increasing it.) But it is morally relevant insofar as it provides greater possibilities for cooperation and for the nonviolent resolution of problems. It also makes us more dangerous than non-rational beings can ever be. Because we are potentially more dangerous and less predictable than wolves, we need an articulated system of morality to regulate our conduct. Any human morality, to be workable in the long run, must recognize the equal moral status of all persons, whether through the postulate of equal basic moral rights or in some other way. The recognition of the moral equality of other persons is the price we must each pay for their recognition of our moral equality. Without this mutual recognition of moral equality, human society can exist only in a state of chronic and bitter conflict. The war between the sexes will persist so long as there is sexism and male domination; racial conflict will never be eliminated so long as there are racist laws and practices. But, to the extent that we achieve a mutual recognition of equality, we can hope to live together, perhaps as peacefully as wolves, achieving (in part) through explicit moral principles what they do not seem to need explicit moral principles to achieve.

Why not extend this recognition of moral equality to other creatures, even though they cannot do the same for us? The answer is that we cannot. Because we cannot reason with most non-human animals, we cannot always solve the problems which they may cause without harming them—although we are always obligated to try. We cannot negotiate a treaty with the feral cats and foxes, requiring them to stop preying on endangered native species in return for suitable concessions on our part.

> If rats invade our houses . . . we cannot reason with them, hoping to persuade them of the injustice they do us. We can only attempt to get rid of them.[7]

Aristotle was not wrong in claiming that the capacity to alter one's behavior on the basis of reasoned argument is relevant to the full moral status which he accorded to free men. Of course, he was wrong in his other premise, that women and slaves by nature cannot reason well enough to function as autonomous moral agents. Had that premise been true, so would his conclusion that women and slaves are not quite the moral equals of free men. In the case of most non-human animals, the corresponding premise is true. If, on the other hand, there are animals with whom we can learn to reason, then we are obligated to do this and to regard them as our moral equals.

Thus, to distinguish between the rights of persons and those of most other animals on the grounds that only people can alter their behavior on the basis of reasoned argument does not commit us to a perfectionist theory of the sort Aristotle endorsed. There is no excuse for refusing to recognize the moral equality of some people on the grounds that we don't regard them as quite as rational as we are, since it is perfectly clear that most people can reason well enough to determine how to act so as to respect the basic rights of others (if they choose to), and that is enough for moral equality.

But what about people who are clearly not rational? It is often argued that sophisticated mental capacities such as rationality cannot be essential for the possession of equal basic moral rights, since nearly everyone agrees that human infants and mentally incompetent persons have such rights, even though they may lack those sophisticated mental capacities. But this argument is inconclusive, because there are powerful practical and emotional reasons for protecting non-rational human beings, reasons which are absent in the case of most non-human animals. Infancy and mental incompetence are human conditions which all of us either have experienced or are likely to experience at some time. We also protect babies and mentally incompetent people because we care for them. We don't normally care for animals in the same way, and when we do—e.g., in the case of much-loved pets—we may regard them as having special rights by virtue of their relationship to us. We protect them not only for their sake but also for our own, lest we be hurt by harm done to them. Regan holds that such "side-effects" are irrelevant to moral rights, and perhaps they are. But in ordinary usage, there is no sharp line between moral rights and those moral protections which are not rights. The extension of strong moral protections to infants and the mentally impaired in no way proves that non-human animals have the same basic moral rights as people.

WHY SPEAK OF "ANIMAL RIGHTS" AT ALL?

If, as I have argued, reality precludes our treating all animals as our moral equals, then why should we still ascribe rights to them? Everyone agrees that animals are entitled to some protection against human abuse, but why speak of animal *rights* if we are not prepared to accept most animals as our moral equals? The weak animal rights position may seem an unstable compromise between the bold claim that animals have the same basic moral rights that we do and the more common view that animals have no rights at all.

It is probably impossible to either prove or disprove the thesis that animals have moral rights by producing an analysis of the concept of a moral right and checking to see if some or all animals satisfy the conditions for having rights. The concept of a moral right is complex, and it is not clear which of its strands are essential. Paradigm rights holders, i.e., mature and mentally competent persons, are *both* rational and morally autonomous beings and sentient subjects-of-a-life. Opponents of animal rights claim that rationality and moral autonomy are essential for the possession of rights, while defenders of animal rights claim that they are not. The ordinary concept of a moral right is probably not precise enough to enable us to determine who is right on purely definitional grounds.

If logical analysis will not answer the question of whether animals have moral rights, practical considerations may, nevertheless incline us to say that they do. The most plausible alternative to the view that animals have moral rights is that, while they do not have *rights*, we are, nevertheless, obligated not to be cruel to them. Regan argues persuasively that the injunction to avoid being cruel to animals is inadequate to express our obligations towards animals, because it focuses on the mental states of those who cause animal suffering, rather than on the harm done to the animals themselves (p. 158). Cruelty is inflicting pain or suffering and either taking pleasure in that pain or suffering or being more or less indifferent to it. Thus, to express the demand for the decent treatment of animals in terms of the rejection of cruelty is to invite the too easy response that those who subject animals to suffering are not being cruel because they regret the suffering they cause but sincerely believe that what they do is justified The injunction to avoid cruelty is also inadequate in that it does not preclude the killing of animals—for any reason, however trivial—so long as it is done relatively painlessly.

The inadequacy of the anti-cruelty view provides one practical reason for speaking of animal rights. Another practical reason is that this is an age in which nearly all significant moral claims tend to be expressed in terms of rights. Thus, the denial that animals have rights, however carefully qualified, is likely to be taken to mean that we may do whatever we like to them, provided that we do not violate any human rights. In such a context, speaking of the rights of animals may be the only way to persuade many people to take seriously protests against the abuse of animals.

Why not extend this line of argument and speak of the rights of trees, mountains, oceans, or anything else which we may wish to see protected from destruction? Some environmentalists have not hesitated to speak in this way, and, given the importance of protecting such elements of the natural world, they cannot be blamed for using this rhetorical device. But, I would argue that moral rights can meaningfully be ascribed only to entities which have some capacity for sentience. This is because moral rights are protections designed to protect rights holders from harms or to provide them with benefits which matter *to them*. Only beings capable of sentience can be harmed or benefited in ways which matter to them, for only such beings can like or dislike what happens to them or prefer some conditions to others. Thus, sentient animals, unlike mountains, rivers, or species, are at least logically possible candidates for moral rights. This fact together with the need to end current abuses of animals—e.g., in scientific research . . . —provides a plausible case for speaking of animal rights.

CONCLUSION

I have argued that Regan's case for ascribing strong moral rights to all normal, mature mammals is unpersuasive because (1) it rests upon the obscure concept of inherent value, which is defined only in negative terms, and (2) it seems to preclude any plausible answer to questions about the moral status of the vast majority of sentient animals. . . .

The weak animal rights theory asserts that (1) any creature whose natural mode of life includes the pursuit of certain satisfactions has the right not to be forced to exist without the opportunity to pursue those satisfactions; (2) that any creature which is capable of pain, suffering, or frustration has the right that such experiences not be deliberately inflicted upon it without some compelling reason; and (3) that no sentient being should be killed without good reason. However, moral rights are not an all-or-nothing affair. The strength of the reasons required to override the rights of a non-human organism varies, depending upon—among other things—the probability that it is sentient and (if it is clearly sentient) its probable degree of mental sophistication. . . .

Notes

1. Tom Regan, *The Case for Animal Rights* (Berkeley, University of California Press, 1983). All page references are to this edition.
2. For instance, Peter Singer, although he does nor like to speak of rights, includes all sentient beings under the protection of his basic utilitarian principle of equal respect for like interests. (*Animal Liberation* [New York: Avon Books, 1975], p. 3.)
3. The capacity for sentience like all of the mental capacities mentioned in what follows is a disposition. Dispositions do not disappear whenever they are not currently manifested. Thus, sleeping or temporarily unconscious persons or non-human animals are still sentient in the relevant sense (i.e., still capable of sentience), so long as they still have the neurological mechanisms necessary for the occurrence of experiences.
4. It is possible, perhaps probable that some non-human animals—such as cetaceans and anthropoid apes—should be regarded as persons. If so, then the weak animal rights position holds that these animals have the same basic moral rights as human persons.
5. See R. G. Frey, *Interests and Rights: The Case Against Animals* (Oxford: Oxford University Press. 1980).

6. See, for instance, p. 319, where Regan appeals to the benefit of the doubt principle when dealing with infanticide and late-term abortion.
7. Bonnie Steinbock, "Speciesism and the Idea of Equality," *Philosophy* 53 (1978):253.

Study Questions

1. Examine Warren's critique of Regan's position. What is her main criticism? How strong is her criticism?

2. What is the basis for granting human beings moral rights that we do not grant animals? Do you agree with her arguments?
3. What is the weak animal rights position? What is Warren's argument for it?

10

Animal Liberation: A Triangular Affair

J. BAIRD CALLICOTT

Baird Callicott (b. 1941) is professor of philosophy and natural resources at the University of Wisconsin, Stevens Point, and the author of several works in environmental philosophy, including In Defense of the Land Ethic *(1989).*

Callicott argues that not two but three very different ideologies inhabit the global moral terrain: the ethical humanists (or anthropocentrists), the humane moralists (or animal liberationists), and the ethical holists (or environmental ethicists). He points out that the criterion of rationality held by the humanists and the criterion of sentience each have severe problems as a single criterion for moral considerability and argues for a more holistic criterion: goodness or positive value is a function of the system which it inhabits. Environmentally, a thing is good if and only if it contributes to the "integrity, stability and beauty of the biotic community." Callicott's article is not only philosophically interesting, but it played an important historic role in separating animal rights from environmentalism. Callicott's version of Land Ethics will be studied in further detail in Reading 19.

ENVIRONMENTAL ETHICS AND ANIMAL LIBERATION

Partly because it is so new to Western philosophy (or at least heretofore only scarcely represented) *environmental ethics* has no precisely fixed conventional definition in glossaries of philosophical terminology. Aldo Leopold, however, is universally recognized as the father or founding genius of recent environmental ethics. His "land ethic" has become a modern classic and may be treated as the standard example, the paradigm case, as it were, of what an environmental ethic is. *Environmental ethics* then can be defined ostensively by using Leopold's land ethic as the exemplary type. I do not mean to suggest that all environmental ethics should necessarily conform to Leopold's paradigm, but the extent to which an ethical system resembles Leopold's land ethic might be used, for want of anything better, as a criterion to measure the extent to which it is or is not of the environmental sort.

It is Leopold's opinion, and certainly an overall review of the prevailing traditions of Western ethics, both popular and philosophical, generally confirms it, that traditional Western systems of ethics have not accorded moral standing to nonhuman beings. Animals and plants, soils and waters, which Leopold includes in his community of ethical beneficiaries, have traditionally enjoyed no moral standing, no rights, no respect, in sharp contrast to human persons whose rights and interests ideally must be fairly and equally considered if our actions are to be considered "ethical" or "moral." One fundamental and novel feature of the Leopold land ethic, therefore, is the extension of *direct* ethical considerability from people to nonhuman natural entities.

At first glance, the recent ethical movement usually labeled "animal liberation" or "animal rights" seems to be squarely and centrally a kind of environmental ethics. The more uncompromising among the animal liberationists have demanded equal moral consideration on behalf of cows, pigs, chickens, and other apparently enslaved and oppressed nonhuman animals. The theoreticians of this new

Reprinted from *Environmental Ethics*, Vol. 2.4 (Winter 1980) by permission. Notes deleted.

The author expresses his appreciation to Richard A. Watson for helpful comments on the final version of this paper.

hyperegalitarianism have coined such terms as *speciesism* (on analogy with *racism* and *sexism*) and *human chauvinism* (on analogy with *male chauvinism*), and have made animal liberation seem, perhaps not improperly, the next and most daring development of political liberalism. Aldo Leopold also draws upon metaphors of political liberalism when he tells us that his land ethic "changes the role of *Homo sapiens* from conqueror of the land community to plain member and citizen of it." For animal liberationists it is as if the ideological battles for equal rights and equal consideration for women and for racial minorities have been all but won, and the next and greatest challenge is to purchase equality, first theoretically and then practically, for all (actually only *some*) animals, regardless of species. This more rhetorically implied than fully articulated historical progression of moral rights from fewer to greater numbers of "persons" (allowing that animals may also be persons) as advocated by animal liberationists, also parallels Leopold's scenario in "The Land Ethic" of the historical extension of "ethical criteria" to more and more "fields of conduct" and to larger and larger groups of people during the past three thousand or so years. As Leopold develops it, the land ethic is a cultural "evolutionary possibility," the next "step in a sequence." For Leopold, however, the next step is much more sweeping, much more inclusive than the animal liberationists envision, since it "enlarges the boundaries of the [moral] community to include soils, waters, [and] plants . . ." as well as animals. Thus, the animal liberation movement *could* be construed as partitioning Leopold's perhaps undigestible and totally inclusive environmental ethic into a series of more assimilable stages: today animal rights, tomorrow equal rights for plants, and after that full moral standing for rocks, soil, and other earthy compounds, and perhaps sometime in the still more remote future, liberty and equality for water and other elementary bodies.

Put just this way, however, there is something jarring about such a graduated progression in the exfoliation of a more inclusive environmental ethic, something that seems absurd. A more or less reasonable case might be made for rights for some animals, but when we come to plants, soils, and waters, the frontier between plausibility and absurdity appears to have been crossed. Yet, there is no doubt that Leopold sincerely proposes that *land* (in his inclusive sense) be ethically regarded. The beech and chestnut, for example, have in his view as much "biotic right" to life as the wolf and the deer, and the effects of human actions on mountains and streams for Leopold is an ethical concern as genuine and serious as the comfort and longevity of brood hens. In fact, Leopold to all appearances never considered the treatment of brood hens on a factory farm or steers in a feed lot to be a pressing moral issue. He seems much more concerned about the integrity of the farm *wood lot* and the effects of clear-cutting steep slopes on neighboring *streams*.

Animal liberationists put their ethic into practice (and

display their devotion to it by becoming vegetarians, and the moral complexities of vegetarianism have been thoroughly debated in the recent literature as an adjunct issue to animal rights. (No one however has yet expressed, as among Butler's Erewhonians, qualms about eating plants, though such sentiments might be expected to be latently present, if the rights of plants are next to be defended.) Aldo Leopold, by contrast did not even condemn hunting animals, let alone eating them, nor did he personally abandon hunting, for which he had had an enthusiasm since boyhood, upon becoming convinced that his ethical responsibilities extended beyond the human sphere. There are several interpretations for this behavioral peculiarity. One is that Leopold did not see that his land ethic actually ought to prohibit hunting, cruelly killing, and eating animals. A corollary of this interpretation is that Leopold was so unperspicacious as deservedly to be thought stupid—a conclusion hardly comporting with the intellectual subtlety he usually evinces in most other respects. If not stupid, then perhaps Leopold was hypocritical. But if a hypocrite, we should expect him to conceal his proclivity for blood sports and flesh eating and to treat them as shameful vices to be indulged secretively. As it is, bound together between the same covers with "The Land Ethic" are his unabashed reminiscences of killing and consuming *game*. This term (like *stock*) when used of animals, moreover, appears to be morally equivalent to referring to a sexually appealing young woman as a "piece" or to a strong, young black man as a "buck"—if animal rights, that is, are to be considered as on a par with women's rights and the rights of formerly enslaved races. A third interpretation of Leopold's approbation of regulated and disciplined sport hunting (and *a fortiori* meat eating) is that it is a form of human/animal behavior not inconsistent with the land ethic as he conceived it. A corollary of this interpretation is that Leopold's land ethic and the environmental ethic of the animal liberation movement rest upon very different theoretical foundations, and that they are thus two very different forms of environmental ethics.

The urgent concern of animal liberationists for the suffering of *domestic* animals, toward which Leopold manifests an attitude which can only be described as indifference, and the urgent concern of Leopold, on the other hand, for the disappearance of *species* of plants as well as animals and for soil erosion and stream pollution, appear to be symptoms not only of very different ethical perspectives, but profoundly different cosmic visions as well. The neat similarities, noted at the beginning of this discussion, between the environmental ethic of the animal liberation movement and the classical Leopoldian land ethic appear in light of these observations to be rather superficial and to conceal substrata of thought and value which are not at all similar. The theoretical foundations of the animal liberation movement and those of the Leopoldian land ethic may even turn out not to be companionable, complementary, or mutually consistent. The animal liberationists may thus find themselves not only engaged in controversy with the many conservative philosophers upholding *apartheid* between man and "beast," but also faced with an unexpected dissent from another, very different, system of environmental ethics. Animal liberation and animal rights may well prove to be a triangular rather than, as it has so far been represented in the philosophical community, a polar controversy.

ETHICAL HUMANISM AND HUMANE MORALISM

The orthodox response of "ethical humanism" (as this philosophical perspective may be styled) to the suggestion that nonhuman animals should be accorded moral standing is that such animals are nor worthy of this high perquisite. Only human beings are rational, or capable of having interests, or possess *self*-awareness, or have linguistic abilities, or can represent the future, it is variously argued. These essential attributes taken singly or in various combinations make people somehow exclusively deserving of moral consideration. The so called "lower animals," it is insisted, lack the crucial qualification for ethical considerability and so may be treated (albeit humanely, according to some, so as not to brutalize man) as things or means, not as persons or as ends.

The theoreticians of the animal liberation movement ("humane moralists" as they may be called) typically reply as follows. Not all human beings qualify as worthy of moral regard, according to the various criteria specified. Therefore, by parity of reasoning, human persons who do not so qualify as moral patients may be treated, as animals often are, as mere things or means (e.g., used in vivisection experiments, disposed of if their existence is inconvenient, eaten, hunted, etc., etc.). But the ethical humanists would be morally outraged if irrational and inarticulate infants, for example, were used in painful or lethal medical experiments, or if severely retarded people were hunted for pleasure. Thus, the double-dealing, the hypocrisy, of ethical humanism appears to be exposed. Ethical humanism, though claiming to discriminate between worthy and unworthy ethical patients on the basis of objective criteria impartially applied, turns out after all, it seems, to be *speciesism,* a philosophically indefensible prejudice (analogous to racial prejudice) against animals. The tails side of this argument is that some animals, usually the "higher" lower animals (cetaceans, other primates, etc.), as ethological studies seem to indicate, may meet the criteria specified for moral worth, although the ethical humanists, even so, are not prepared to grant them full dignity and the rights of persons. In short, the ethical humanists' various criteria for moral standing do not include all or only human beings, humane moralists argue, although in practice ethical humanism wishes to make the class of morally considerable beings coextensive with the class of human beings.

The humane moralists, for their part, insist upon *sentience* (*sensibility* would have been a more precise word choice) as the only relevant capacity a being need possess to enjoy full moral standing. If animals, they argue, are conscious entities who, though deprived of reason, speech, forethought or even *self*-awareness (however that may be judged), are capable of suffering, then their suffering should be as much a matter of ethical concern as that of our fellow human beings, or strictly speaking, as our very own. What, after all, has rationality or any of the other allegedly uniquely human capacities to do with ethical standing? Why, in other words, should beings who reason or use speech (etc.) qualify for moral status, and those who do not fail to qualify? Isn't this just like saying that only persons with white skin should be free, or that only persons who beget and not those who bear should own property? The criterion seems utterly unrelated to the benefit for which it selects. On the other hand, the capacity to suffer is, it seems, a more relevant criterion for moral standing because—as Bentham and Mill, notable modern philosophers, and Epicurus, among the ancients, aver—pain is evil, and its opposite, pleasure and freedom from pain, good. As moral agents (and this seems axiomatic), we have a duty to behave in such a way that the effect of our actions is to promote and procure good, so far as possible, and to reduce and minimize evil. That would amount to an obligation to produce pleasure and reduce pain. Now pain is pain wherever and by whomever it is suffered. As a *moral* agent, I should not consider my pleasure and pain to be of greater consequence in determining a course of action than that of other persons. Thus, by the same token, if animals suffer pain—and among philosophers only strict Cartesians would deny that they do— then we are morally obliged to consider their suffering as much an evil to be minimized by conscientious moral agents as human suffering. Certainly actions of ours which contribute to the suffering of animals, such as hunting them, butchering and eating them, experimenting on them, etc., are on these assumptions morally reprehensible. Hence, a person who regards himself or herself as not aiming in life to live most selfishly, conveniently, or profitably, but rightly and in accord with practical principle, if convinced by these arguments, should, among other things, cease to eat the flesh of animals, to hunt them, to wear fur and leather clothing and bone ornaments and other articles made from the bodies of animals, to eat eggs and drink milk if the animal producers of these commodities are retained under inhumane circumstances, and to patronize zoos (as sources of psychological if not physical torment of animals). On the other hand, since certain very simple animals are almost certainly insensible to pleasure and pain, they may and indeed should be treated as morally inconsequential. Nor is there any *moral* reason why trees should be respected or rivers or mountains or anything which is, though living or tributary to life processes, unconscious. The humane moralists, like the moral humanists, draw a firm distinction between those beings worthy of moral consideration and those not. They simply insist upon a different but quite definite cut-off point on the spectrum of natural entities, and accompany their criterion with arguments to show that it is more ethically defensible (granting certain assumptions) and more consistently applicable than that of the moral humanists.

THE FIRST PRINCIPLE OF THE LAND ETHIC

The fundamental principle of humane moralism, as we see, is Benthamic. Good is equivalent to pleasure and, more pertinently, evil is equivalent to pain. The presently booming controversy between moral humanists and humane moralists appears, when all the learned dust has settled, to be essentially internecine; at least, the lines of battle are drawn along familiar watersheds of the conceptual terrain. A classical ethical theory, Bentham's, has been refitted and pressed into service to meet relatively new and unprecedented ethically relevant situations—the problems raised especially by factory farming and ever more exotic and frequently ill-conceived scientific research employing animal subjects. Then, those with Thomist, Kantian, Lockean, Moorean (etc.) ethical affiliation have heard the bugle and have risen to arms. It is no wonder that so many academic philosophers have been drawn into the fray. The issues have an apparent newness about them; moreover, they are socially and politically *avant garde*. But there is no serious challenge to cherished first principles. Hence, without having to undertake any creative ethical reflection or exploration, or any reexamination of historical ethical theory, a fresh debate has been stirred up. The familiar historical positions have simply been retrenched, applied, and exercised.

But what about the third (and certainly minority) party to the animal liberation debate? What sort of reasonable and coherent moral theory would at once urge that animals (and plants and soils and waters) be included in the same class with people as beings to whom ethical consideration is owed and yet not object to some of them being slaughtered (whether painlessly or not) and eaten, others hunted, trapped, and in various other ways seemingly cruelly used? Aldo Leopold provides a concise statement of what might be called the categorical imperative or principal precept of the land ethic: "A thing is right when it tends to preserve the integrity, stability, and beauty of the biotic community. It is wrong when it tends otherwise." What is especially note-worthy, and that to which attention should be directed in this proposition, is the idea that the good of the biotic *community* is the ultimate measure of the moral value, the rightness or wrongness, of actions. Thus, to hunt and kill a white-tailed deer in certain districts may not only be ethically permissible, it might actually be a moral requirement, necessary to protect the local environment, taken as a whole, from the disintegrating effects of a cervid population explosion. On the other hand, rare and endangered animals like the lynx should be especially nurtured and preserved. The lynx, cougar, and other wild feline predators, from the neo-Benthamite perspective (if consistently and evenhandedly applied) should be regarded as merciless, wanton, and incorrigible murderers of their fellow creatures, who not only kill, it should be added, but cruelly toy with their victims, thus increasing the measure of pain in the world. From the perspective of the land ethic, predators generally should be nurtured and preserved as critically important members of the biotic communities to which they are native. Certain plants, similarly, may be overwhelmingly important to the stability, integrity, and beauty of biotic communities, while some animals, such as domestic sheep (allowed perhaps by egalitarian and humane herdspersons to graze freely and to reproduce themselves without being harvested for lamb and mutton) could be a pestilential threat to the natural floral community of a given locale. Thus, the land ethic is logically coherent in demanding at once that moral consideration be given to plants as well as to animals and yet in permitting animals to be killed, trees felled, and so on. In every case the effect upon ecological systems is the decisive factor in the determination of the ethical quality of actions. . . .

THE LAND ETHIC AND THE ECOLOGICAL POINT OF VIEW

. . . Since ecology focuses upon the relationships between and among things, it inclines its students toward a more holistic vision of the world. Before the rather recent emergence of ecology as a science the landscape appeared to be, one might say, a collection of objects, some of them alive, some conscious, but all the same, an aggregate, a plurality of separate individuals. With this "atomistic" representation of things it is no wonder that moral issues might be understood as competing and mutually contradictory clashes of the "rights" of separate individuals, each separated pursuing its "interests." Ecology has made it possible to apprehend the same landscape as an articulate unity (without the least hint of mysticism or ineffability). Ordinary organic bodies have articulated and discernible parts (limbs, various organs, myriad cells); yet, because of the character of the network of relations among those parts, they form in a perfectly familiar sense a second-order whole. Ecology makes it possible to see land, similarly, as a unified system of integrally related parts, as, so to speak, a third-order organic whole.

Another analogy that has helped ecologists to convey the particular holism which their science brings to reflective attention is that land is integrated as a human community is integrated. The various parts of the "biotic community" (individual animals and plants) depend upon one another *economically* so that the system as such acquires distinct characteristics of its own. Just as it is possible to characterize and define collectively peasant societies, agrarian communities, industrial complexes, capitalist, communist, and socialist economic systems, and so on, ecology characterizes and defines various biomes as desert, savanna, wetland, tundra, woodland, etc., communities, each with its particular "professions," "roles," or "niches."

Now we may think that among the duties we as moral agents have toward ourselves is the duty of self-preservation, which may be interpreted as a duty to maintain our own organic integrity. It is not uncommon in historical moral theory, further, to find that in addition to those peculiar responsibilities we have in relation both to ourselves and to other persons severally, we also have a duty to behave in ways that do not harm the fabric of society *per se*. The land ethic, in similar fashion, calls our attention to the recently discovered integrity—in other words, the unity—of the biota and posits duties binding upon moral agents in relation to that whole. Whatever the strictly formal logical connections between the concept of a social community and moral responsibility, there appears to be a strong psychological bond between that idea and conscience. Hence, the representation of the natural environment as, in Leopold's terms, "one humming community" (or, less consistently in his discussion, a third-order organic being) brings into play, whether rationally or not, those stirrings of conscience which we feel in relation to delicately complex, functioning social and organic systems.

The neo-Benthamite humane moralists have, to be sure, digested one of the metaphysical implications of modern biology. They insist that human beings must be understood continuously with the rest of organic nature. People are (and are only) animals, and much of the rhetorical energy of the animal liberation movement is spent in fighting a rear guard action for this aspect of Darwinism against those philosophers who still cling to the dream of a special metaphysical status for people in the order of "creation." To this extent the animal liberation movement is biologically enlightened and argues from the taxonomical and evolutionary continuity of man and beast to moral standing for some nonhuman animals. Indeed, pain, in their view the very substance of evil, is something that is conspicuously common to people and other sensitive animals, something that we as people experience not in virtue of our metasimian cerebral capabilities, but because of our participation in a more generally animal, limbic-based consciousness. *If* it

is pain and suffering that is the ultimate evil besetting human life, and this not in virtue of our humanity but in virtue of our animality, then it seems only fair to promote freedom from pain for those animals who share with us in this mode of experience and to grant them rights similar to ours as a means to this end.

Recent ethological studies of other primates, cetaceans, and so on, are not infrequently cited to drive the point home, but the biological information of the animal liberation movement seems to extend no further than this—the continuity of human with other animal life forms. The more recent ecological perspective especially seems to be ignored by humane moralists. The holistic outlook of ecology and the associated value premium conferred upon the biotic community, its beauty, integrity, and stability may simply not have penetrated the thinking of the animal liberationists, or it could be that to include it would involve an intolerable contradiction with the Benthamite foundations of their ethical theory. Bentham's view of the "interests of the community" was bluntly reductive. With his characteristic bluster, Bentham wrote, "The community is a fictitious *body* composed of the individual persons who are considered as constituting as it were its *members*. The interest of the community then is, what?—the sum of the interests of the several members who compose it." Bentham's very simile—the community is like a body composed of members—gives the lie to his reduction of its interests to the sum of its parts taken severally. The interests of a person are not those of his or her cells summed up and averaged out. Our organic health and well-being, for example, require vigorous exercise and metabolic stimulation which cause stress and often pain to various parts of the body and a more rapid turnover in the life cycle of our individual cells. For the sake of the person taken as whole, some parts may be, as it were, unfairly sacrificed. On the level of social organization, the interests of society may not always coincide with the sum of the interests of its parts. Discipline, sacrifice, and individual restraint are often necessary in the social sphere to maintain social integrity as within the bodily organism. A society, indeed, is particularly vulnerable to disintegration when its members become preoccupied totally with their own particular interest, and ignore those distinct and independent interests of the community as a whole. One example, unfortunately, our own society, is altogether too close at hand to be examined with strict academic detachment. The United States seems to pursue uncritically a social policy of reductive utilitarianism, aimed at promoting the happiness of all its members severally. Each special interest accordingly clamors more loudly to be satisfied while the community as a whole becomes noticeably more and more infirm economically, environmentally, and politically.

The humane moralists, whether or not they are consciously and deliberately following Bentham on this particular, nevertheless, in point of fact, are committed to the welfare of certain kinds of animals distributively or reductively in applying their moral concern for nonhuman beings. They lament the treatment of animals, most frequently farm and laboratory animals, and plead the special interests of these beings. We might ask from the perspective of the land ethic, what the effect upon the natural environment taken as a whole would be if domestic animals were actually liberated? There is, almost certainly, very little real danger that this might actually happen, but it would be instructive to speculate on the ecological consequences.

ETHICAL HOLISM

Before we take up this question, however, some points of interest remain to be considered on the matter of a holistic versus a reductive environmental ethic. To pit the one against the other as I have done without further qualification would be mistaken. A society is constituted by its members, an organic body by its cells, and the ecosystem by the plants, animals, minerals, fluids, and gases which compose it. One cannot affect a system as a whole without affecting at least some of its components. An environmental ethic which takes as its *summum bonum* the integrity, stability, and beauty of the biotic community is not conferring moral standing on something *else* besides plants, animals, soils, and waters. Rather, the former, the good of the community as a whole, serves as a standard for the assessment of the relative value and relative ordering of its constitutive parts and therefore provides a means of adjudicating the often mutually contradictory demands of the parts considered separately for *equal* consideration. If diversity does indeed contribute to stability (a classical "law" of ecology), then *specimens* of rare and endangered species, for example, have a *prima facie* claim to preferential consideration from the perspective of the land ethic. Animals of those species, which, like the honey bee, function in ways critically important to the economy of nature, moreover, would be granted a greater claim to moral attention than psychologically more complex and sensitive ones, say, rabbits and moles, which seem to be plentiful, globally distributed, reproductively efficient, and only routinely integrated into the natural economy. Animals and plants, mountains, rivers, seas, the atmosphere are the *immediate* practical beneficiaries of the land ethic. The well-being of the biotic community, the biosphere as a whole, cannot be logically separated from their survival and welfare.

Some suspicion may arise at this point that the land ethic is ultimately grounded in *human* interests, not in those of nonhuman natural entities. Just as we might prefer a sound and attractive house to one in the opposite condition so the "goodness" of a whole, stable, and beautiful environment seems rather to be of the instru-

mental, not the autochthonous, variety. The question of ultimate value is a very sticky one for environmental as well as for all ethics and cannot be fully addressed here. It is my view that there can be no value apart from an evaluator, that all value is as it were in the eye of the beholder. The value that is attributed to the ecosystem, therefore, is humanly dependent or (allowing that other living things may take a certain delight in the well-being of the whole of things, or that the gods may) at least dependent upon some variety of morally and aesthetically sensitive consciousness. Granting this, however, there is a further, very crucial distinction to be drawn. It is possible that while things may only have value because we (or someone) values them, they may nonetheless be valued for themselves as well as for the contribution they might make to the realization of our (or someone's) interests. Children are valued for themselves by most parents. Money, on the other hand, has only an instrumental or indirect value. Which sort of value has the health of the biotic community and its members severally for Leopold and the land ethic? It is especially difficult to separate these two general sorts of value, the one of moral significance, the other merely selfish, when something that may be valued in *both ways at once* is the subject of consideration. Are pets, for example, well-treated, like children, for the sake of themselves, or, like mechanical appliances, because of the sort of services they provide their owners? Is a healthy biotic community something we value because we are so utterly and (to the biologically well-informed) so obviously dependent upon it not only for our happiness but for our very survival, or may we also perceive it disinterestedly as having an independent worth? Leopold insists upon a noninstrumental value for the biotic community and *mutatis mutandis* for its constituents. According to Leopold, collective enlightened self-interest on the part of human beings does not go far enough; the land ethic in his opinion (and no doubt this reflects his own moral intuitions) requires "love, respect, and admiration for land, and a high regard for its value." The land ethic, in Leopold's view, creates "obligations over and above self-interest." And, "obligations have no meaning without conscience, and the problem we face is the extension of the social conscience from people to land." If, in other words, any genuine ethic is possible, if it is possible to value people for the sake of themselves, then it is equally possible to value *land* in the same way.

Some indication of the genuinely biocentric value orientation of ethical environmentalism is indicated in what otherwise might appear to be gratuitous misanthropy. The biospheric perspective does not exempt *Homo sapiens* from moral evaluation in relation to the well-being of the community of nature taken as a whole. The preciousness of individual deer, as of any other specimen, is inversely proportional to the population of the species. Environmentalists, however reluctantly and painfully, do not omit to apply the same logic to their own kind. As omnivores, the population of human beings should, perhaps, be roughly twice that of bears, allowing for differences of size. A global population of more than four billion persons and showing no signs of an orderly decline presents an alarming prospect to humanists, but it is at present a global disaster (the more *per capita* prosperity, indeed, the more disastrous it appears) for the biotic community. If the land ethic were only a means of managing nature for the sake of man, misleadingly phrased in moral terminology, then man would be considered as having an ultimate value essentially different from that of his "resources." The extent of misanthropy in modern environmentalism thus may be taken as a measure of the degree to which it is biocentric. Edward Abbey in his enormously popular *Desert Solitaire* bluntly states that he would sooner shoot a man than a snake. Abbey may not be simply depraved; this is perhaps only his way of dramatically making the point that the human population has become so disproportionate from the biological point of view that if one had to choose between a specimen of *Homo sapiens* and a specimen of a rare even if unattractive species, the choice would be moot. Among academicians, Garret Hardin, a human ecologist by discipline who has written extensively on ethics, environmental and otherwise, has shocked philosophers schooled in the preciousness of human life with his "lifeboat" and "survival" ethics and his "wilderness economics." In context of the latter, Hardin recommends limiting access to wilderness by criteria of hardiness and woodcraft and would permit no emergency roads or air-borne rescue vehicles to violate the pristine purity of wilderness areas. If a wilderness adventurer should have a serious accident, Hardin recommends that he or she get out on his or her own or die in the attempt. Danger, from the strictly human-centered, psychological perspective, is part of the wilderness experience, Hardin argues, but in all probability his more important concern is to protect from mechanization the remnants of wild country that remain even if the price paid is the incidental loss of human life which, from the perspective once more of the biologist, is a commodity altogether too common in relation to wildlife and to wild landscapes. . . .

. . . Modern systems of ethics have, it must be admitted, considered the principle of the equality of persons to be inviolable. This is true, for example, of both major schools of modern ethics, the utilitarian school going back to Bentham and Mill, and the deontological, originating with Kant. The land ethic manifestly does not accord equal moral worth to each and every member of the biotic community; the moral worth of individuals (including, n.b., human individuals) is relative, to be assessed in accordance with the particular relation of each to the collective entity which Leopold called "land."

There is, however, a classical Western ethic, with the best philosophical credentials, which assumes a similar holistic posture (with respect to the social moral sphere). I have in mind Plato's moral and social philosophy. Indeed, two of the same analogies figuring in the conceptual foundations of the Leopold land ethic appear in Plato's value theory. From the ecological perspective, according to Leopold as I have pointed out, land is like an organic body or like a human society. According to Plato, body, soul, and society have similar structures and corresponding virtues. The goodness of each is a function of its structure or organization and the relative value of the parts or constituents of each is calculated according to the contribution made to the integrity, stability, and beauty of each whole. In the *Republic*, Plato, in the very name of virtue and justice, is notorious for, among other things, requiring infanticide for a child whose only offense was being born without the sanction of the state, making presents to the enemy of guardians who allow themselves to be captured alive in combat, and radically restricting the practice of medicine to the dressing of wounds and the curing of seasonal maladies on the principle that the infirm and chronically ill not only lead miserable lives but contribute nothing to the good of the polity. Plato, indeed, seems to regard individual human life and certainly human pain and suffering with complete indifference. On the other hand, he shrinks from nothing so long as it seems to him to be in the interest of the community. Among the apparently inhuman recommendations that he makes to better the community are a program of eugenics involving a phony lottery (so that those whose natural desires are frustrated, while breeding proceeds from the best stock as in a kennel or stable, will blame chance, not the design of the rulers), the destruction of the pair bond and nuclear family (in the interests of greater military and bureaucratic efficiency and group solidarity), and the utter abolition of private property.

When challenged with the complaint that he is ignoring individual human happiness (and the happiness of those belonging to the most privileged class at that), he replies that it is the well-being of the community as a whole, not that of any person or special class at which his legislation aims. This principle is readily accepted, first of all, in our attitude toward the body, he reminds us—the separate interests of the parts of which we acknowledge to be subordinate to the health and well-being of the whole—and secondly, assuming that we accept his faculty psychology, in our attitude toward the soul—whose multitude of desires must be disciplined, restrained, and, in the case of some, altogether repressed in the interest of personal virtue and a well-ordered and morally responsible life.

Given these formal similarities to Plato's moral philosophy, we may conclude that the land ethic—with its holistic good and its assignment of differential values to the several parts of the environment irrespective of their intelligence, sensibility, degree of complexity, or any other characteristic discernible in the parts considered separately—is somewhat foreign to modern systems of ethical philosophy, but perfectly familiar in the broader context of classical Western ethical philosophy. If, therefore, Plato's system of public and private justice is properly an "ethical" system, then so is the land ethic in relation to environmental virtue and excellence.

REAPPRAISING DOMESTICITY

Among the last philosophical remarks penned by Aldo Leopold before his untimely death in 1948 is the following: "Perhaps such a shift of values [as implied by the attempt to weld together the concepts of ethics and ecology] can be achieved by reappraising things unnatural, tame, and confined in terms of things natural, wild, and free." John Muir, in a similar spirit of reappraisal, had noted earlier the difference between the wild mountain sheep of the Sierra and the ubiquitous domestic variety. The latter, which Muir described as "hooved locusts," were only, in his estimation, "half alive" in comparison with their natural and autonomous counterparts. One of the more distressing aspects of the animal liberation movement is the failure of almost all its exponents to draw a sharp distinction between the very different plights (and rights) of wild and domestic animals. But this distinction lies at the very center of the land ethic. Domestic animals are creations of man. They are living artifacts, but artifacts nevertheless, and they constitute yet another mode of extension of the works of man into the ecosystem. From the perspective of the land ethic a herd of cattle, sheep, or pigs is as much or more a ruinous blight on the landscape as a fleet of four-wheel drive off-road vehicles. There is thus something profoundly incoherent (and insensitive as well) in the complaint of some animal liberationists that the "natural behavior" of chickens and bobby calves is cruelly frustrated on factory farms. It would make almost as much sense to speak of the natural behavior of tables and chairs.

Here a serious disanalogy (which no one to my knowledge has yet pointed out) becomes clearly evident between the liberation of blacks from slavery (and more recently, from civil inequality) and the liberation of animals from a similar sort of subordination and servitude. Black slaves remained, as it were, metaphysically autonomous: they were by nature if not by convention free beings quite capable of living on their own. They could not be enslaved for more than a historical interlude, for the strength of the force of their freedom was too great. They could, in other words, be retained only by a continuous counterforce, and only temporarily. This is equally true of caged wild animals. African cheetahs in American and European zoos are captive, not indentured, beings. But this is not true of cows, pigs,

sheep, and chickens. They have been bred to docility, tractability, stupidity, and dependency. It is literally meaningless to suggest that they be liberated. It is, to speak in hyperbole, a logical impossibility.

Certainly it is a practical impossibility. Imagine what would happen if the people of the world became morally persuaded that domestic animals were to be regarded as oppressed and enslaved persons and accordingly *set free*. In one scenario we might imagine that like former American black slaves they would receive the equivalent of forty acres and a mule and be turned out to survive on their own. Feral cattle and sheep would hang around farm out-buildings waiting forlornly to be sheltered and fed, or would graze aimlessly through their abandoned and deteriorating pastures. Most would starve or freeze as soon as winter settled in. Reproduction which had been assisted over many countless generations by their former owners might be altogether impossible in the feral state for some varieties, and the care of infants would be an art not so much lost as never acquired. And so in a very short time, after much suffering and agony, these species would become abruptly extinct. Or, in another scenario beginning with the same simple emancipation from human association, survivors of the first massive die-off of untended livestock might begin to recover some of their remote wild ancestral genetic traits and become smaller, leaner, heartier, and smarter versions of their former selves. An actual contemporary example is afforded by the feral mustangs ranging over parts of the American West. In time such animals as these would become (just as the mustangs are now) competitors both with their former human masters and (with perhaps more tragic consequences) indigenous wildlife for food and living space.

Foreseeing these and other untoward consequences of immediate and unplanned liberation of livestock, a human population grown morally more perfect than at present might decide that they had a duty, accumulated over thousands of years, to continue to house and feed as before their former animal slaves (whom they had rendered genetically unfit to care for themselves), but not to butcher them or make other ill use of them, including frustrating their "natural" behavior, their right to copulate freely, reproduce, and enjoy the delights of being parents. People, no longer having meat to eat, would require more vegetables, cereals, and other plant foods, but the institutionalized animal incompetents would still consume all the hay and grains (and more since they would no longer be slaughtered) than they did formerly. This would require clearing more land and bringing it into agricultural production with further loss of wildlife habitat and ecological destruction. Another possible scenario might be a decision on the part of people not literally to liberate domestic animals but simply to cease to breed and raise them. When the last livestock have been killed and eaten (or permitted to die "natural" deaths), people would become vegetarians and domestic livestock species would thus be rendered deliberately extinct (just as they had been deliberately created). But there is surely some irony in an outcome in which the beneficiaries of a humane extension of conscience are destroyed in the process of being saved.

The land ethic, it should be emphasized, as Leopold has sketched it, provides for the *rights* of nonhuman natural beings to a share in the life processes of the biotic community. The conceptual foundation of such rights, however, is less conventional than natural, based upon, as one might say, evolutionary and ecological entitlement. Wild animals and native plants have a particular place in nature, according to the land ethic, which domestic animals (because they are products of human art and represent an extended presence of human beings in the natural world) do not have. The land ethic, in sum, is as much opposed, though on different grounds, to commercial traffic in wildlife, zoos, the slaughter of whales and other marine mammals, etc., as in the humane ethic. Concern for animal (and plant) rights and well-being is as fundamental to the land ethic as to the humane ethic, but the differences between naturally evolved and humanly bred species is an essential consideration for the one, though not for the other.

The "shift of values" which results from our "reappraising things unnatural, tame, and confined in terms of things natural, wild, and free" is especially dramatic when we reflect upon the definitions of *good* and *evil* espoused by Bentham and Mill and uncritically accepted by their contemporary followers. Pain and pleasure seem to have nothing at all to do with good and evil if our appraisal is taken from the vantage point of ecological biology. Pain in particular is primarily information. In animals, it informs the central nervous system of stress, irritation, or trauma in outlying regions of the organism. A certain level of pain under optimal organic circumstances is indeed desirable as an indicator of exertion—of the degree of exertion needed to maintain fitness, to stay "in shape," and of a level of exertion beyond which it would be dangerous to go. An arctic wolf in pursuit of a caribou may experience pain in her feet or chest because of the rigors of the chase. There is nothing bad or wrong in that. Or, consider a case of injury. Suppose that a person in the course of a wilderness excursion sprains an ankle. Pain informs him or her of the injury and by its intensity the amount of further stress the ankle may endure in the course of getting to safety. Would it be better if pain were not experienced upon injury or, taking advantage of recent technology, anaesthetized? Pleasure appears to be, for the most part (unfortunately it is not always so) a reward accompanying those activities which contribute to organic maintenance, such as the pleasures associated with eating, drinking, grooming, and so on, or those which contribute to social solidarity like the pleasures of dancing, conversation, teasing, etc., or those which contribute to the continuation of the species, such as the pleasures of

sexual activity and of being parents. The doctrine that life is the happier the freer it is from pain and that the happiest life conceivable is one in which there is continuous pleasure uninterrupted by pain is biologically preposterous. A living mammal which experienced no pain would be one which had a lethal dysfunction of the nervous system. The idea that pain is evil and ought to be minimized or eliminated is as primitive a notion as that of a tyrant who puts to death messengers bearing bad news on the supposition that thus his well-being and security is improved.

More seriously still, the value commitments of the humane movement seem at bottom to betray a world-denying or rather a life-loathing philosophy. The natural world as actually constituted is one in which one being lives at the expense of others. Each organism, in Darwin's metaphor, struggles to maintain its own organic integrity. The more complex animals seem to experience (judging from our own case, and reasoning from analogy) appropriate and adaptive psychological accompaniments to organic existence. There is a palpable passion for self-preservation. There are desire, pleasure in the satisfaction of desires, acute agony attending injury, frustration, and chronic dread of death. But these experiences are the psychological substance of living. To live *is* to be anxious about life, to feel pain and pleasure in a fitting mixture, and sooner or later to die. That is the way the system works. If nature as a whole is good, then pain and death are also good. Environmental ethics in general require people to play fair in the natural system. The neo-Benthamites have in a sense taken the uncourageous approach. People have attempted to exempt themselves from the life/death reciprocities of natural processes and from ecological limitations in the name of a prophylactic ethic of maximizing rewards (pleasure) and minimizing unwelcome information (pain). To be fair, the humane moralists seem to suggest that we should attempt to project the same values into the nonhuman animal world and to widen the charmed circle—no matter that it would be biologically unrealistic to do so or biologically ruinous if, per impossible, such an environmental ethic were implemented.

There is another approach. Rather than imposing our alienation from nature and natural processes and cycles of life on other animals, we human beings could reaffirm our participation in nature by accepting life as it is given without a sugar coating. Instead of imposing artificial legalities, rights, and so on on nature, we might take the opposite course and accept and affirm natural biological laws, principles, and limitations in the human personal and social spheres. Such appears to have been the posture toward life of tribal peoples in the past. The chase was relished with its dangers, rigors, and hardships as well as its rewards: animal flesh was respectfully consumed; a tolerance for pain was cultivated; virtue and magnanimity were prized; lithic, floral, and faunal spirits were worshipped; population was routinely optimized by sexual continency, abortion, infanticide, and stylized warfare; and other life forms, although certainly appropriated, were respected as fellow players in a magnificent and awesome, if not altogether idyllic, drama of life. It is impossible today to return to the symbiotic relationship of Stone Age man to the natural environment, but the ethos of this by far the longest era of human existence could be abstracted and integrated with a future human culture seeking a viable and mutually beneficial relationship with nature. Personal, social, and environmental *health* would, accordingly, receive a premium value rather than comfort, self-indulgent pleasure, and anaesthetic insulation from pain. Sickness would be regarded as a worse evil than death. The pursuit of health or wellness at the personal, social, and environmental levels would require self-discipline in the form of simple diet, vigorous exercise, conservation, and social responsibility.

Leopold's prescription for the realization and implementation of the land ethic—the reappraisal of things unnatural, tame, and confined in terms of things natural, wild, and free—does not stop, in other words, with a reappraisal of nonhuman domestic animals in terms of their wild (or willed) counterparts; the human ones should be similarly reappraised. This means, among other things, the reappraisal of the comparatively recent values and concerns of "civilized" *Homo sapiens* in terms of those of our "savage" ancestors. Civilization has insulated and alienated us from the rigors and challenges of the natural environment. The hidden agenda of the humane ethic is the imposition of the anti-natural prophylactic ethos of comfort and soft pleasure on an even wider scale. The land ethic, on the other hand, requires a shrinkage, if at all possible, of the domestic sphere; it rejoices in a recrudescence of wilderness and a renaissance of tribal cultural experience.

The converse of those goods and evils, axiomatic to the humane ethic, may be illustrated and focused by the consideration of a single issue raised by the humane morality: a vegetarian diet. Savage people seem to have had, if the attitudes and values of surviving tribal cultures are representative, something like an intuitive grasp of ecological relationships and certainly a morally charged appreciation of eating. There is nothing more intimate than eating, more symbolic of the connectedness of life, and more mysterious. What we eat and how we eat is by no means an insignificant ethical concern.

From the ecological point of view, for human beings universally to become vegetarians is tantamount to a shift of trophic niche from omnivore with carnivorous preferences to herbivore. The shift is a downward one on the trophic pyramid, which in effect shortens those food chains terminating with man. It represents an increase in the efficiency of the conversion of solar energy from plant to human biomass, and thus, by bypassing animal intermediates, increases available food resources for human beings. The human population would probably, as past trends overwhelmingly suggest, expand in accordance with the potential thus afforded. The net result would be fewer nonhuman beings and more human beings, who, of course, have requirements of life far more elaborate than even those of domestic animals, requirements which would tax other "natural resources" (trees for shelter, minerals mined at the expense of topsoil and its vegetation, etc.) more than under present circumstances. A vegetarian human population is therefore *probably* ecologically catastrophic.

Meat eating as implied by the foregoing remarks may be more *ecologically* responsible than a wholly vegetable diet. Meat, however, purchased at the supermarket, externally packaged and internally laced with petrochemicals, fattened in feed lots, slaughtered impersonally, and, in general, mechanically processed from artificial insemination to microwave roaster, is an affront not only to physical metabolism and bodily health but to conscience as well. From the perspective of the land ethic, the immoral aspect of the factory farm has to do far less with the suffering and killing of nonhuman animals than with the monstrous transformation of living things from an organic to a mechanical mode of being. Animals, beginning with the Neolithic Revolution, have been debased through selective breeding, but they have nevertheless remained animals. With the Industrial Revolution an even more profound and terrifying transformation has overwhelmed them. They have become, in Ruth Harrison's most apt description, "animal machines." The very presence of animals, so emblematic of delicate, complex organic tissue, surrounded by machines, connected to machines, penetrated by machines in research laboratories or crowded together in space-age "production facilities" is surely the more real and visceral source of our outrage at vivisection and factory farming than the contemplation of the quantity of pain that these unfortunate beings experience. I wish to denounce as loudly as the neo-Benthamites this ghastly abuse of animal life, but also to stress that the pain and suffering of research and agribusiness animals is not greater than that endured by free-living wildlife as a consequence of predation, disease, starvation, and cold—indicating that there is something immoral about vivisection and factory farming which is not an ingredient in the natural lives and deaths of wild beings. That immoral something is the transmogrification of organic to mechanical processes.

Ethical vegetarianism to all appearances insists upon the human consumption of plants (in a paradoxical moral gesture toward those animals whose very existence is dependent upon human carnivorousness), even when the tomatoes are grown hydroponically, the lettuce generously coated with chlorinated hydrocarbons, the potatoes pumped up with chemical fertilizers, and the cereals stored with the help of chemical preservatives. The land ethic takes as much exception to the transmogrification of plants by mechanicochemical

66

means as to that of animals. The important thing, I would think, is not to eat vegetables as opposed to animal flesh, but to resist factory farming in all its manifestations, including especially its liberal application of pesticides, herbicides, and chemical fertilizers to maximize the production of *vegetable* crops.

The land ethic, with its ecological perspective, helps us to recognize and affirm the organic integrity of self and the untenability of a firm distinction between self and environment. On the ethical question of what to eat, it answers, not vegetables instead of animals, but organically as opposed to mechanicochemically produced food. Purists like Leopold prefer, in his expression, to get their "meat from God," i.e., to hunt and consume wildlife and to gather wild plant foods, and thus to live within the parameters of the aboriginal human ecological niche. Second best is eating from one's own orchard, garden, henhouse, pigpen, and barnyard. Third best is buying or bartering organic foods from one's neighbors and friends.

CONCLUSION

Philosophical controversy concerning animal liberation/rights has been most frequently represented as a polar dispute between traditional moral humanists and seemingly *avant garde* humane moralists. Further, animal liberation has been assumed to be closely allied with environmental ethics, possibly because in Leopold's classical formulation moral standing and indeed rights (of some unspecified sort) is accorded nonhuman beings, among them animals. The purpose of this discussion has been to distinguish sharply environmental ethics from the animal liberation/rights movement both in theory and practical application and to suggest, thereupon, that there is an underrepresented, but very important, point of view respecting the problem of the moral status of nonhuman animals. The debate over animal liberation, in short, should be conceived as triangular, not polar, with land ethics or environmental ethics, the third and, in my judgment, the most creative, interesting, and practicable alternative. Indeed, from this third point of view moral humanism and humane moralism appear to have much more in common with one another than either have with environmental or land ethics. On reflection one might even be led to suspect that the noisy debate between these parties has served to drown out the much deeper challenge to "business-as-usual" ethical philosophy represented by Leopold and his exponents, and to keep ethical philosophy firmly anchored to familiar modern paradigms.

Moral humanism and humane moralism, to restate succinctly the most salient conclusions of this essay, are *atomistic* or distributive in their theory of moral value, while environmental ethics (again, at least, as set out in Leopold's outline) is *holistic* or collective. Modern ethical theory, in other words, has consistently located moral value in individuals and set out certain metaphysical reasons for including some individuals and excluding others. Humane moralism remains firmly within this modern convention and centers its attention on the competing criteria for moral standing and rights holding, while environmental ethics locates ultimate value in the "biotic community" and assigns differential moral value to the constitutive individuals relatively to that standard. This is perhaps the most fundamental theoretical difference between environmental ethics and the ethics of animal liberation.

Allied to this difference are many others. One of the more conspicuous is that in environmental ethics, plants are included within the parameters of the ethical theory as well as animals. Indeed, inanimate entities such as oceans and lakes, mountains, forests, and wetlands are assigned a greater value than individual animals and in a way quite different from systems which accord them moral considerability through a further multiplication of competing individual loci of value and holders of rights.

There are intractable practical differences between environmental ethics and the animal liberation movement. Very different moral obligations follow in respect, most importantly, to domestic animals, the principal beneficiaries of the humane ethic. Environmental ethics sets a very low priority on domestic animals as they very frequently contribute to the erosion of the integrity, stability, and beauty of the biotic communities into which they have been insinuated. On the other hand, animal liberation, if pursued at the practical as well as rhetorical level, would have ruinous consequences on plants, soils, and waters, consequences which could not be directly reckoned according to humane moral theory. As this last remark suggests, the animal liberation/animal rights movement is in the final analysis utterly unpracticable. An imagined society in which all animals capable of sensibility received equal consideration or held rights to equal consideration would be so ludicrous that it might be more appropriately and effectively treated in satire than in philosophical discussion. The land ethic, by contrast, even though its ethical purview is very much wider, is nevertheless eminently practicable, since, by reference to a single good, competing individual claims may be adjudicated and relative values and priorities assigned to the myriad components of the biotic community. This is not to suggest that the implementation of environmental ethics as social policy would be easy. Implementation of the land ethic would require discipline, sacrifice, retrenchment, and massive economic reform, tantamount to a virtual revolution in prevailing attitudes and life styles. Nevertheless, it provides a unified and coherent practical principle and thus a decision procedure at the practical level which a distributive or atomistic ethic may achieve only artificially and so imprecisely as to be practically indeterminate.

Study Questions

1. Explain Callicott's thesis of the triangular division in ethics. How do ethical holists differ from humane moralists?

2. Why does Callicott reject the notion of sentience (held by Rollins and Singer) as the most important criterion for moral considerability? Why isn't pain a bad thing? Do you agree with Callicott? Explain your answer.

3. Consider Callicott's argument against vegetarianism at the end of his article. Is it a sound argument? Explain your answer.

4. Callicott's views here have been labeled "misanthropic." Can you see why they would be so judged? Do you agree with that assessment?

For Further Reading

Frey, R. G. *Rights, Killing and Suffering*. Oxford: Basil Blackwell, 1983.

Rachels, James. *Created from Animals: The Moral Implications of Darwinism*. Oxford: Oxford University Press, 1990.

Regan, Tom. *The Case for Animal Rights*. Berkeley: University of California, 1983. The most comprehensive philosophical treatise in favor of animal rights.

Regan, Tom, and Peter Singer, eds. *Animal Rights and Human Obligations*. Englewood Cliffs, NJ: Prentice-Hall, 1976.

Robbins, John. *Diet for a New America: How Your Food Choices Affect Your Health, Happiness, and the Future of Life on Earth*. Walpole, NH: Stillpoint, 1987. A strong case for vegetarianism.

Rohr, Janelle. ed. *Animal Rights: Opposing Viewpoints*. San Diego: Greenhaven Press, 1989.

Singer, Peter. *Animal Liberation*, 2d ed. New York: New York Review of Books, 1990.

VanDeVeer, D., and C. Pierce, eds. *People, Penguins, and Plastic Trees*. Belmont, CA.: Wadsworth, 1990.

CHAPTER THREE

Does Nature Have Intrinsic Value? Biocentric and Ecocentric Ethics and Deep Ecology

In this chapter, we consider the wide-ranging debate around the questions: Does nature have intrinsic value, or does it take an evaluator to impute value to anything? This chapter is grouped into four parts: the question of the intrinsic value of nature (Readings 11–14), biocentric ethics (Readings 15–17), ecocentric ethics (Readings 18 and 19), and deep ecology versus anthropocentric ethics (Readings 20–25).

Traditionally, environmental ethics in the West has been split between anthropocentric ethics and sentience-based ethics, which include the higher animals in the moral domain. We saw this debate between an ethics based in rational consciousness and sentience in the last chapter. In the last forty or fifty years, however, a deeper debate has arisen—that between nature objectivists and value subjectivists. The former hold that nature has intrinsic value, and the latter maintain that all value demands an evaluator.

We begin with Holmes Rolston's defense of nature objectivism (Reading 11). Nature is good in itself or has a good, so even if there were no sentient beings, nature would have a good. Appealing to contemporary physics, especially relativity theory, he sets forth a series of considerations meant to persuade us that nature is the bearer of value. In Reading 12 Ernest Partridge argues against Rolston. He defends the traditional view that values derive from evaluators, so a world without sentient beings would be valueless. Yet Partridge explains why his position need not be taken as an anthropocentric view.

The objectivist position takes as its principal watershed the work of Albert Schweitzer. It was Schweitzer's *Civilization and Ethics* in 1923 that launched the project of extending the range of value to include all of life. He called this position "Reverence for Life." Every living thing (every "will-to-live") in nature is endowed with something sacred or intrinsically valuable and should be respected as such:

> Just as in my own will-to-live there is a yearning for more life . . . so the same obtains in all the will-to-live around me, equally whether it can express itself to my comprehension or whether it remains unvoiced.
>
> Ethics consists in this, that I experience the necessity of practicing the same reverence for life toward all will-to-live, as toward my own.

Although Reverence for Life bears a resemblance to older Eastern views, especially Hinduism and Buddhism, about the sanctity of all of life, the chief proponents of that view usually tie their doctrines to reincarnation and the transmigration of souls. No such implications are present in Schweitzer's doctrine.

Schweitzer's thought has been a point of departure for biocentric ethics (i.e., life-centered ethics), represented by his seminal work, along with Paul Taylor's and Kenneth Goodpaster's essays (Readings 16 and 17), as well as deep ecology (Readings 20–25). In Reading 16, Paul Taylor develops Schweitzer's seminal idea. Whereas Schweitzer is not always clear about whether he regards all life-forms as equal, and he sometimes writes as though the will-to-live is embodied in the idea of pleasure and its denial in the idea of pain, Taylor is clearer, self-consciously egalitarian, and separates inherent value from the idea of hedonism (pleasure and pain). For Taylor, all living beings—from amoebas to humans—are of equal inherent value. Each living individual has a goal (what the Greeks called a *telos*), and to have a goal implies a will or desire to attain it. One's goal is one's good, so all living things are inherently good. Kant's notion "end-in-itself," which he applied only to rational beings, is radically expanded by Taylor to cover all living things.

Kenneth Goodpaster (Reading 17) offers a careful, nonegalitarian argument for the claim that possessing a life makes one to be morally considerable. The Gaia hypothesis (Chapter 5) extends this individualistic view to Earth, treating Gaia as a single organism. Richard Watson's and Murray Bookchin's articles (Readings 23 and 24) consider and attack these sorts of arguments.

Let us turn to ecocentric ethics (Readings 18 and 19). Like biocentric theories, ecocentricism also imputes intrinsic value to nature, but whereas biocentric ethics is *individualistic*, ecocentric ethics is *holistic*. It views the biosphere as a totality, including species, populations, land, and ecosystems. The primary source of the modern ecocentric movement is Aldo Leopold's (1887–1948) book *Sand County Almanac* (1949), part of which makes up Reading 18. Leopold, a Wisconsin forest ranger and, later, professor of game management at the University of Wisconsin, attempted to produce a new paradigm through which to evaluate our conduct.

Rather than seeing the environment as merely a resource for human beings, we should view it as the center of value. It is primarily the biotic community that is valuable, and this should guide our moral sensitivities. "A thing is right when it tends to preserve the integrity, stability, and beauty of the biotic community. It is wrong when it tends otherwise." So humans must change their role from conqueror of the land-community to plain member and citizen of it. We must extend our social conscience from people to ecosystems, to the land.

Brilliant though he was, Leopold was not a philosopher and did not develop the implications of his position. In Reading 19, Baird Callicott, a disciple of Leopold, attempts to draw out the full picture of the land ethic. Callicott locates the historic sources of Leopold's thought in David Hume, Adam Smith, and Charles Darwin. Hume and Smith made sympathy the basis of moral action, from which altruistic feelings arise. Darwin held that the primeval moral affections centered on the tribe, rather than its individual members. Leopold, according to Callicott, simply extended this idea to the biotic community. To quote Leopold, "The land ethic simply enlarges the boundaries of the community to include soils, waters, plants, and animals, or collectively: the land . . . It implies respect for . . . fellow members and also respect for the community as such."

Callicott holds that intrinsic value is neither purely subjective nor objective but arises when beings like us, with a certain nature, respond to nature. Some philosophers, such as Tom Regan, H. J. McCloskey, and L. W. Sumner, have interpreted Leopold as being antihuman, holding that the biocentric community is the only thing that matters. Sumner calls this "dangerous nonsense" and Regan "environmental fascism." Callicott holds that a more charitable (and accurate) interpretation is to view the land ethic as an extension of our moral consciousness, not canceling out our obligations to other human beings but putting them in a wider ecological context.

Now we turn to the most radical of the main environmental theories, deep ecology, first set forth by the Norwegian philosopher Arne Naess and elaborated by Bill Devall and George Sessions (Readings 20–22). Drawing on Eastern thought, especially Vedantic Hinduism and Buddhism, deep ecology holds that all of us—humans, nonhumans, and biotic communities—are intrinsically related to one another. Underlying all is an essential unity of being so that, in some sense, no one can realize his, her, or its deepest potential without everyone realizing it. Deep ecology is egalitarian in that everyone and everything is equally valuable as part of the whole. This transpersonal ecology calls on us to go beyond class, gender, and species and find our deepest fulfillment in harmony with nature. In its eightfold path (see Devall and Sessions's article), deep ecology calls for the promotion and greater protection of biodiversity and a reduction of human population. We must also learn to live more simply. It's motto is "Simple in Means, Rich in Ends," signifying an antimaterialist perspective.

Next, Richard Watson criticizes many of the above ecophilosophies for being antianthropocentric, that is, for opposing the place of human beings at the center of things. Murray Bookchin offers a different Marxist and anarchist critique of deep ecology, opposing it to social ecology, which opposes "social ecology" to deep ecology. Finally, James Sterba attempts to reconcile anthropocentric and nonanthropocentric ethics.

We turn to our first set of readings in intrinsic value.

DOES NATURE HAVE INTRINSIC VALUE?

11

Yes, Value Is Intrinsic in Nature

HOLMES ROLSTON, III

Holmes Rolston, III, is professor of philosophy at Colorado State University at Fort Collins. He is the president of the International Society for Environmen-tal Ethics and author of several works on environmental ethics, including Philosophy Gone Wild: Essays in Environmental Ethics (1986) and Environmental Ethics: Duties to and Values in the Natural World (1988).

In this essay, Rolston examines the fact/value problem as it applies to nature. He argues that values are objective in nature. He opposes the view put forth by William James, Wilhelm Windelband, R. B. Perry, David Hume, and many others that value depends on a subjective valuer,

Reprinted from Environmental Ethics, Vol. 4 (1982) by permission of the author.

a "spectator's mind." "Rainbowlike, only more so [values] are gifts of the spectator's mind." But, argues Rolston, modern relativity theory puts this way of looking at things in doubt. He then uses ideas from contemporary physics to see the cogency of a view attributing value to nature. His thesis is that "nature is not barren of value; it is rather the bearer of value: that both constrains and ennobles the role we humans are called to play."

I   HOW SHOULD WE VALUE NATURE?

Conceive yourself, if possible, suddenly stripped of all the emotions with which your world now inspires you, and try to imagine it *as it exists*, purely by itself, without your favourable or unfavourable, hopeful or apprehensive comment. It will be almost impossible for you to realize such a condition of negativity and deadness. No one portion of the universe would then have importance beyond another; and the whole collection of its things and series of its events would be without significance, character, expression, or perspective. Whatever of value, interest or meaning our respective worlds may appear embued with are thus pure gifts of the spectator's mind.[1]

William James' stark portrayal of the utterly valueless world, suddenly transfigured as a gift of the human coming, has proved prophetic of a dominant twentieth-century attitude. Since he wrote, we have spent upwards of a century trying to conceive of ourselves as the sole entities bringing value to an otherwise sterile environment. The effort has pervaded science and technology, humanism and existentialism, ethics and economics, metaphysics and analytic philosophy.

John Laird protested, "There is beauty . . . in sky and cloud and sea, in lilies and in sunsets, in the glow of bracken in autumn and in the enticing greenness of a leafy spring. Nature, indeed, is infinitely beautiful, and she seems to wear her beauty as she wears colour or sound. Why then should her beauty belong to us rather than to her?"[2] But Wilhelm Windelband agreed with James: value "is never found in the object itself as a property. It consists in a relation to an appreciating mind, which satisfies the desires of its will or reacts in feelings of pleasure upon the stimulation of the environment. Take away will and feeling and there is no such thing as value."[3] R. B. Perry continued with what became the prevailing opinion:

The silence of the desert is without value, until some wanderer finds it lonely and terrifying; the cataract, until some human sensibility finds it sublime, or until it is harnessed to satisfy human needs. Natural substances . . . are without value until a use is found for them, whereupon their value may increase to any desired degree of preciousness according to the eagerness with which they are coveted.

Any object, whatever it be, acquires value when any interest, whatever it be, is taken in it.[4]

But with the environmental turn, so surprising and pressing in the final quarter of our century, this subjectivism in values needs review. Ecology has a way of pulling into alternative focus the exchange between the organic self and the surrounding world. This can lead us to review what we have been learning in evolutionary biology and developmental biochemistry. We here argue that in the orientation of these recent sciences the subjective account of valuing becomes grossly strained. Living, as we say, "far from nature," it is remarkable to find as one of the insistent questions of our advanced civilization: how should we value nature? An ecological crisis has forced the question upon us. Environmental and evolutionary science suggest some different answers; and yet no science is quite prepared to handle the question.

Our valuational quandary is not merely a muddle into which philosophers have gotten us, although it is perhaps the last legacy of Cartesianism. Valuational incompetence is the soft underbelly of hard science. Something gone sour at the fact/value distinction is one of the roots of the ecological crisis. Values, it is typically said, form no part of nature, but only come with the human response to the world. This seems at once objective about nature and humane towards persons, but it also yields a value structure in the scientific West more anthropocentric by several orders of magnitude than were any of the value systems of the classical, Oriental, and primitive world views which have succumbed before it. But this more sophisticated view is, we think, wise in its own conceits.

The strategy in what follows is to fight a way through how we know what we know (what philosophers call epistemological issues surrounding the terms "subjective" and "objective") in order to reach the state of affairs in the real world and to be able to defend the existence of value there (what philosophers call ontological issues surrounding subjectivity and objectivity). This I do keeping the whole discussion as close to science as I can, while demanding a full-blooded, no-nonsense account of the phenomenon of value in, and valuing of, the natural world. Earlier on, I will be admitting to some inescapable blending of the subjective and objective, but later on, after this admission, I will defend all the objectivity I can for natural value.

II   PRIMARY, SECONDARY, AND TERTIARY QUALITIES

Galileo's astronomy forced us to convert from a literal to a perspectival understanding of the claim that the sun is setting. His physics gave us the distinction, elaborated by Locke, between primary and secondary qualities. A secondary quality is observer dependent, manufactured out of the primary motions of matter. Colour is an experiential conversion of photon radiation; taste and smell are molecular operations. This account was problematic philosophically (as Berkeley quickly saw), but it nevertheless became entrenched. The colours and sounds which Laird found nature to wear seemed rather to go with the beholding of it, reducible in the world stripped of a perceiver to matter in motion. Coached by these theories, what was then to be said of value? If the sunset is not literally a setting sun, not even red, then surely it is not literally beautiful. Samuel Alexander proposed that values were tertiary qualities.[5] Humans agree about redness, owing to their having the same organs (apart from colour blindness, etc.), but value appraisals require an interpretive judgment twice removed from the qualities actually there.

By this account, we have no organs to taste, touch, see or smell value. So it must originate at a deeper mental level. We have no options in judging length or redness (although there are aberrations). Such experiences happen to us without any liberty to refuse them. The primary and secondary qualities are always there in the scope of consciousness. They perhaps fall into the background, but they never turn off during perception. Value judgments, by contrast, have to be decided. Beauty or utility are things we must attend to. When our minds turn aside to other thoughts, though still perceiving the object, such values entirely disappear from consciousness. We can use instruments—metre sticks, spectroscopes, thermometers, mass spectrometers—on primary and secondary qualities. Something there leaves records during photography, electrophoresis or chromatography, puzzle though we may about the experiential translation of 6800 Angstrom units into redness, or how the shape of the fructose molecule, interlocked with receptors on the tongue, is experienced as sweetness. Both primary and secondary qualities are in this sense empirical, or natural. But valuational qualities do not show up on any instruments or organs devised or conceivable. This leads some, who still look for properties in the object, to think of value as an objective but "non-natural," that is, "nonempirical" quality. But, finding nothing that produces consensus or proves researchable, most judges become convinced that these tertiary qualities are overlays, not really there in the natural world. Rainbowlike, only more so, they are gifts of the spectator's mind.

But now the puzzle deepens. Just as philosophers were reaching this consensus, a revolution in physics threw overboard the primary, supposedly objective, qualities as well. Einstein showed length, mass, time and motion to be observer dependent. They too are matters of perspective, although not so much of decision as of bodily relations. At the microlevel, Heisenberg's uncertainty principle forbade any precise hold on momentum and location. Quantum mechanics left a nonsubstantial nonpicture of nature as a gauzy haze of interpenetrating wave fields, where none of the commonsense qualities made much sense, and where even space and time grew vague. It was alarming to learn how much our mental constructions enter into the descriptions of physical science, how much the observer influences the natural phenomenon by instrumentation or sense modality. As we go down smaller, objectivity decreases more and more.

Summing this up, Einstein remarked that he had taken "the last remainder of physical objectivity" from the concepts of space and time.[6] John Wheeler wrote, "A much more drastic conclusion emerges: . . . *there is no such thing as spacetime in the real world of quantum physics . . .* It is an approximation idea, an extremely good approximation under most circumstances, but always only an approximation."[7] Werner Heisenberg wrote, "When we speak of a picture of nature provided us by contemporary exact science, we do not actually mean any longer a picture of nature, but rather a picture of our relation to nature. . . . Science no longer is in the position of observer of nature, but rather recognizes itself as part of the interplay between man and nature."[8] Before this heady sort of runaway relativism, lost in a great and unspeakable plasma, the question of values being objectively there hardly seems discussable. The subjectivists have won all the chips. Even physics, that bedrock science which gave great promise of "telling it like it is," has withdrawn entirely from that kind of claim. What hope is there for value theory to do anything more than to record what appears and seems? Any bolder claim is primitive naivete.

But when we regain our wits, such relativism can be kept under more logical control. Contrary to first appearances, it can even support certain objective aspects in value judgments. For all that we have yet said, there is just as little or as much reason to think that physics is objective, as that value theory is. Judgments about what *is* (mass, space, colour) have proved observer dependent and indistinguishable from judgments about what *is good* (pleasure, beauty, grandeur). Subjectivity has eaten up everything, even the fact/value distinction. But as a matter of fact, unless we are insane, we all believe that we know some nonsubjective things about the physical world. Our judgments are not free of perceptual modification of the incoming signals, but neither, *pace* Einstein, do they lack a very large "remainder of physical objectivity." At this everyday level we do stand in some picturing relation to nature. The key is provided in Wheeler's qualification of "no such thing" with "an extremely good approximation."

"There is a hawk in the spruce beside that granite boulder." This judgment fades out on subatomic scales, diffusing away if we migrate far enough from our native range. Through optical microscopy we take photographs in colour of garnet crystals from the granite. But on the shrinking scale of electron microscopy we begin to remind ourselves that the colour (despite the black and white micrograph!) is no longer relevant, while the length and shape in crystal lattices is still pictorial. Smaller still, we become aware that we have only models of the electrons and protons which compose the granite. Shape and location dissolve into cloudy wave fields. We allow too that the weight and shape of the boulder would appear differently to an observer passing at nearly the speed of light. Even the data from the other physical levels shows up objectively, though. The space-time dilations affect clocks, cameras, meters, one's body, and everything that ages. The nonspecifiable fuzziness of electron momentum and location registers in the bands on paper recording charts. These things are not entirely inventions of the mind, although they reveal our perspectival and theoretical reach to the microscopic and astronomical levels.

However, if I restrict the scope of my claims, none of this affects the fact that we know something objectively, factually, about hawks, spruce trees and boulders. We do not know entirely all that is there at every level, nor with an objectivity that is free from subjective contribution. But agnosticism and relativism about the ultimate structure of matter does not prevent objective knowing in a middle-level sense. The breakdown of a concept, claim or function when extrapolated does not prevent its being quite true in the restricted range that it well serves. Our partial knowing need not be illusory or false, although it is approximate and perspectival. Here value judgments too can be short-scope claims about what is the case in the mundane world. The clue provided by Alexander's word "tertiary" is not something about twice-compounded observer dependence. It is about participation at the middle-structural levels where we live. The ownership feature in value judgments is important, but we need to think of value judgments as genuine, involved (if limited) claims about the world. Afterwards, we can inquire how far they can be pressed away from our native range. They do not attach to bare primary or secondary levels, but to high-level constructions of matter with which we are in exchange—initially in common experience and afterwards in the sciences of natural history. Just as we are getting incoming commands from "out there" about length, colour, hawks and trees, so too we are getting some commands about value. We start with these as native-range judgments, not as absolute ones. They are phenomenal claims, not noumenal ones. This much makes them locally objective, although it leaves unresolved how deep they run.

III JUDGMENTS ABOUT TYPES, FUNCTIONS AND VALUES

A dose of candour from the biological sciences can help cure us of the effects of the dizzying revelations of physics. Notice, for instance, that before the panorama of an ecosystem, the primary, secondary, tertiary distinction cannot do much explanatory work. If someone

asks whether a thing is alive, whether it is a seed, a moss, or a microbe, whether it is edible, and tries to answer with the vocabulary of primary, secondary and tertiary qualities, however, much compounded, he can only stammer. In order to get at the richness of the natural world, we need to make many judgments for which we have directly no organs and can make no instruments, judgments to which we must attend by decision and interpretation. Here, most of our scientific judgments are third and higher order, but we nevertheless believe that through them we are accurately corresponding with the natural world. When we pass to judgments of value, we do not need to consider them radically different in kind. This erodes the dogma that factual judgments are objective while value judgments are subjective.

The *Picea* (spruce) and *Buteo* (hawk) genetic sets, for instance, are full of information. The information is long lived, reproducing itself by means of amino-acid replacement across millions of years, a kind of fire which outlasts the sticks that feed it. But is this a compounded primary, secondary, or tertiary quality? The self-maintaining know-how is there independently of our observation, unmodified by our sense perception, primary in Locke's sense. It is nonsubjective and nonsecondary. It is quite as real as atoms, if also a bit nonsubstantial and fluid. To deny reality to this information on the basis of anything learned in physics is like denying that a newspaper picture contains information, because, under the lens, it turns out to be nothing but black dots. Objectively encapsulated in informational molecules, the spruce and hawk have a technique for making a way through the terrain they inhabit, pragmatic facts for their life projects. Yet these DNA based facts are not aggregated primary, secondary or even tertiary qualities, but involve advanced, emergent compositional levels.

Meanwhile, we humans who make these judgments begin with at-hand, uncontested experience and, via science, move from our native experiential level to elaborate, often unsettled theories about structural levels and their histories. We say that the genetic information has accumulated in stages. Some of the earliest information was the code for glycolysis, which evolved three and a half billion years ago, before there was atmospheric oxygen. The citric-acid cycle came later, cashing in on eighteen times as much energy as did glycolysis. Somewhere, photosynthesis evolved so that *Picea* can capture directly the energy of sunlight, with oxidative phosphorylation subsequently arising to use the atmosphere as an electron sink, improving the efficiency of the citric-acid cycle. The spruce and the hawk evolved under the pro-life pressures of a selective system operating over genetic mutations, fitting them into an ecological community. In all this, we are making highly educated guesses describing the objective facts, estimates which will be partly revised, partly conserved as science advances. But most of us do not believe that we inevitably become less objective and more subjective, less primary and more secondary or tertiary as we do this. World building does go on in the mind of the beholder, as we shape up theories over experience. But world building also takes place out there. We find the information or energy flow only by attending with deliberate focus of mind. But the mind does not contribute these features because it must model them by careful attention and decision. To the contrary, we discover richer qualities in nature.

What happens now if we introduce some value judgments? We might speak of the value of nutrients, of food pyramids, of the information keying glycolysis and photosynthesis, of the exploratory value of mutations with the "good" ones conserved because they have survival value. We might speak objectively of the value of the hawk's protective colouration (even admitting the secondary nature of colour). The word *value* easily attaches to life functions as these are known at and theorized for the middle ranges of experience. We need not yet speak of *human* values, not even of experienced values, but some notion of pre-subjective value seems to belong to these "going concerns" called living organisms as they move through the environment. Value here attaches to a whole form of life and is not just resident in the detached parts as elementary units. It overleaps although it is instantiated in the individual. It appears in a holistic crossplay where neutral, lesser-valued and even disvalued parts may assume transformed value in a larger matrix. Value emerges in pronounced forms at advanced structural levels and may not be visible as a Lockean primary or secondary quality.

But, as a "tertiary" quality, value can be embedded with the facts, quite as real as the information organisms contain, sometimes just the same thing differently described. Some will object that biological "value" ought to be kept in scare quotes, since this is not what we mean by value as a quality in experienced life. One then has to trace descriptively each of the natural selections culminating in the central nervous system. We can rejoice that value emerges epiphenomenally at the very last in consciousness, but we must judge value to be absent from all the incubating steps. In all the precedents we should speak more carefully, using the term "biofunction" instead.

The haemoglobin molecule is structurally evolved from and much advanced over the myoglobin molecule. It is very much "better" (= more functional) at oxygen transport, having allosteric properties which make it a sort of microcomputer in its capacities to respond to the oxygen-exchange needs of the blooded organism, as with the hawk in flight. Lubert Stryer, a biochemist, says of it emphatically, "*In the step from myoglobin to hemoglobin, we see the emergence of a macromolecule capable of perceiving information from its environment.*"[9] But a cautious value theorist will warn this chemist not to attach any "importance" to this, not to say that this step is of any value. To be really hardnosed here, this "information perceiving" is subjective poetry, only a read-back from our own experience. One might allow that it was "interesting," but not that any "interests" of the life forms in which haemoglobin evolved were at stake.

But all this careful reservation of value as a gift of the spectator's mind now seems arbitrary and narrow. As soon as we have described haemoglobin evolution, we are ready to judge it a vital and valuable upstep in the advance of life. The phenomenon of things "being important" does not arise with our awareness; it is steadily there in quantized discoveries all along the way. Galileo and Locke first subverted value theory with their mechanistic reduction of secondary to primary qualities, leaving us only an objective matter in motion. It was then compoundly subverted by Einstein's relativity, by quantum mechanics, indeterminancy and nonpicturability. These sciences probe towards ultimacy with genius and sceptical rigour. They work in the substrata with simplicity, and so leave out all but the thousandth part of an historical eventfulness that we daily experience and that other sciences do teach us to appreciate. Only by the sort of gestalt switch which can be provided by sciences at the other end of the spectrum, such as evolutionary biochemistry or ecology, dealing with the richness of natural history, can we begin to get value theory recovered from its failure of nerve.

All judgments mix theory with fact. Even the simple cases close at hand involve elements of linguistic and conceptual decision about what to call what, and where to draw the lines. An Iroquois Indian might view the hawk as his totem, or the tree and boulder as the haunt of a spirit. Certainly the scientific judgments about natural kinds (granite, *Picea*, *Buteo*) are theory laden. It is admittedly difficult, as philosophers of science know, to say why we prefer science to superstition, but it has to do, at least in part, with our persuasion that the one is a better window into the way things are. The interpreter imports something of himself into the interpreted. But the fact that we use theory laden decisions about natural operations does not stand in the way of description; it rather makes it possible. To know things as they objectively are, without observer bias, is a celebrated but elusive goal of natural science, a goal impossible to fully attain, but towards which we make progress. A physicist estimates the mass of a boulder, a mineralogist knows its composition; a biologist distinguishes spruce from fir; an ecologist describes an ecosystem. All are aided, not confused by their theories. "Mass," "granite," "*Picea*" and "homeostasis" are technical terms which serve as descriptive forms. The mind answers to its object of study; with progressive reformation we more approximately understand what is there.

In this context, judgments of natural value hardly differ from judgments of natural fact. In one sense, the subjectivists are in full command again and can insist that none of our seemingly objective seeing is done without wearing cultural eyeglasses. But, as before, the objectivist can reassert the common world of experience and the impressive observational force of science. We all do believe that in our native ranges humans know something of the structural levels of nature. We believe that scientific progress gives further, if approximate, access into what these natural types and processes are like. We judge between science and folklore, between good and bad science. When we then pass to judge whether this natural kind is good, or that life process has value, we are merely continuing the effort to map reality. One has to decide whether this is a *Picea,* as one has to decide whether this is a *lovely Picea.* On occasion, the judgment about value may be easier than is the judgment about fact. One can need more theory to "see" the information and energy flow, or the phylogenetic relationships, than one does to "see" the utility or beauty. That such interpretive judgments are subject to revision does not mean that value, in distinction from other natural properties, lies only in the mental state and is not an event in the spacetime track. The constructions we see always depend upon the instructions with which we look, yet the evolving mind is also controlled by the matter it seeks to investigate. This is true alike in science and in valuation.

We can be thrilled by a hawk in the windswept sky, by the rings of Saturn, the falls of Yosemite. We can admire the internal symmetry of a garnet crystal or appreciate the complexity of the forest humus. All these experiences come mediated by our cultural education; some are made possible by science. An Iroquois Indian would have variant experiences, or none at all. But these experiences have high elements of giveness, of finding something thrown at us, of successful observation. The "work" of observation is in order to better understand. In value theory too we have as much reason to think that our appreciative apparatus is sometimes facilitating, not preventing, getting to know what is really there.

Some natural values are of the commonsense kind and nearly universal to cultures, as with the taste of an apple, the pleasant warmth of the spring sun, the striking colours of the autumn. Even though these experiences come culturally bound, some natural impact here is shared by Iroquois and Nobel prizewinner. Experience is required, but something is there which one is fitted for and fitting into; some good is transmitted and is productive of the experience. The native enjoying, just because it is relational to nature but so universal among humans, faithfully attests what is there. It is precisely our experiential position as humans-in-nature which gives us factual access to events. Other natural values are opened up to us by scientific culture, by lenses and experiments. It is precisely our advanced knowledge, setting us apart from nature in theoretical abstraction over it, which takes us deeper into nature. Sometimes the purest revelations of

science put us in a better position to evaluate these things as they objectively are.

IV NATURAL VALUING AS ECOLOGICAL-RELATIONAL

We next present an explanation sketch of valuing consistent with natural history. Our inquiry is about the kind of natural value met within unlaboured contexts, as in pure rather than applied science, in contemplative outdoor recreation rather than in industry, in ecology rather than in economics. We are not considering, for instance, how molybdenum has value as an alloy of steel, a use which it does not have in spontaneous nature. Further, we should be cautioned against thinking that nature has some few kinds of value, or no disvalue. Nature is a plural system with values unevenly distributed and counterthrusting. Like the meanings in life, values too may come piecemeal and occasionally. Still, they come regularly enough for us to wonder whether we are coping with some value tending in the system.

Consider a causal sequence (A, B, C, D) leading to the production of an event associated with natural value (E_{nv}) which produces an event of experienced value (E_{xv}), perhaps of the beauty in a waterfall or the wealth of life in a tidal zone (see figure 1). Our consciousness also responds to the waterfall or estuary, so that we need a reverse arrow ($\downarrow$) making the affair relational. One is first tempted to say that value does not lie in either polar part, but is generated in their relations. Like science or recreation, valuing before nature is an interactive affair.

However, with this, more has been reallocated to the natural world than may at first be recognized. The act of responding has been ecologically grounded. We pass from abstract, reductionist, analytic knowledge to a participant, holistic, synthetic account of humans-in-nature. The subjective self is not a polar opposite to objective nature, not in the dyadic relation suggested by the paired arrows. It is rather enclosed by its environment, so that the self does value in environmental exchange in the manner indicated in figure 1, and on countless occasions. This is more-accurately represented (by E'_{nv} E''_{nv}) , in figure 2. The self has a semipermeable membrane.

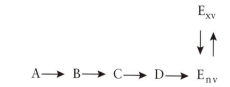

FIGURE 1

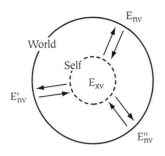

FIGURE 2

The setting is a given fact, a datum of nature, even though the subject must respond in imaginatively resourceful ways. I see things out there in the "field" which I choose to value or disvalue. But on deeper examination I find myself, a valuing agent, located within that circumscribing field. I do not have the valued object in "my field," but find myself emplaced in a concentric field for valuing. The whole possibility is among natural events, including the openness in my appraising. John Dewey remarked that "experience is *of* as well as *in* nature."[10] We say that valuing is *in* as well as *of* nature. What seems a dialectical relationship is an ecological one. We must add notice of how the whole happening, subject and its valued object, occurs in a natural ambiance (see figure 3).

When an ecologist remarks, "There goes a badger," he thinks not merely of morphology, as might a skin-in taxonomist. He has in mind a whole mosaic of functions, interconnections, food chains; a way of being embedded in a niche where the badger is what it is environmentally. When a sociologist remarks, "There goes a vicar," he is not so much identifying a human as seeing a role in the community. The being of a vicar, like that of a badger, is a contextual affair. When a philosopher says, "There goes a valuer," he should not think of a happening inside the human in such a way as to forget that this is also an ecological event. The responsibility here is a response in our natural setting.

Add the fact that the valuing subject has itself evolved out of these surroundings. All the organs and feelings mediating value—body, senses, hands, brain, will, emotion—are natural products. Nature has thrown forward the subjective experiencer quite as much as that world which is objectively experienced. On the route behind us, at least, nature has been a personifying system. We are where this track has been heading, we are perhaps its head, but we are in some sense its tail. We next sketch a further productive sequence which generates the self (S) out of ancestral precedents (O, P, Q, R), natural events in causal sequence, and here also place reverse, valuational arrows (←) indicating reactive elements which cultural and personal responses superadd to the natural basis of personality. We add an evolutionary time line to the holistic, ecological sketch (see figure 4).

Seen in broad historical scale, these lines go back to common beginnings, from which they become richer, eventually to reach the experiencing self embraced by its environment. Diverse, simple and complex forms are all maintained in and by the ecosystemic pyramid, and there are many coordinating connections which we only suggest (↘). In such a picture, even though keeping the phenomenon of human valuing central, it is increasingly difficult to see valuing as isolated or even as dialectic. Values do not exist in a natural void, but rather in a natural womb.

The sudden switch in figure 1 from horizontal, merely causal arrows (→), to a vertical, valuational arrow (↑) now seems too angular a contrast. How far experienced value is a novel emergent we need yet to inquire, but there has been the historical build up towards value, and there is presently surrounding us the invitation to value. Figure 5 gives a better representation of the first series.

The reason for the new sketch is that it is difficult to say why the arrows of valuational response should value only the immediately productive natural event and not include at least some of the precedents, with unshown coordinates as well. The last event is presently at hand, and we may have had no consciousness of value during former events. But in an evolutionary ecosystem nothing happens once and *per se*; everything is embedded in a developing process.

A critic will complain, and perhaps fiercely, that we have diagramatically sketched out single sweep lines while the real world is a much more tumultuous affair, where the valuational and constructive lines are not vectors but a near chaos of causes and happenstance, luck and struggle, serendipity and emergence, with much waste and little worth. The diagram screens off the het-

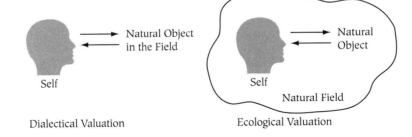

Dialectical Valuation   Ecological Valuation

FIGURE 3

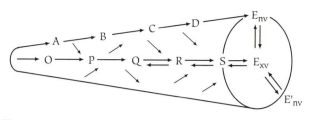

FIGURE 4

erogenous and alien character of the ingredients of value. We have straightened out strands which do not lie straight in the actual world, as though we had never heard of Darwin and his junglelike world.

There is truth in the complaint. We may wish conservatively to keep our judgments as short-scope claims. Values immediately experienced might run back to some nonvaluable base out of which they have emerged. Analogously, living organisms once emerged out of lifeless nature. A present good might have come out of historically mixed values and disvalues, as when a little good comes from much evil. Natural values might be oddly occasional, though the causal sequence is continuous. Nature is not homogenized but unevenly located, and so too with its values.

But, meanwhile, value is sometimes there before us, strikingly so, and we will sometimes be valuing contributors towards value, past or present, seen at whatever level. If ever we do extrapolate to try a systemic over-view of what is going on, the likeliest account will find some programmatic evolution towards value, and this, not because it ignores Darwin, but because it heeds his principle of natural selection, and deploys this into a selection upslope towards higher values, at least along some trends within natural operations. How do we humans come to be charged up with values, if there was and is nothing in nature charging us up so? We prefer not to believe in the special creation of values, nor in their dumbfounding epigenesis—we let them evolve. Nor is our account merely a selection from the chaotic data of nature; rather, our interpretation notices how there is a world selection of events over evolutionary time (without denying other neutral or disvalued events) which builds towards the ecological valuing in which we now participate.

We can now view primary and secondary qualities holistically from above, drawn into an ecosystem at much higher structural levels, rather than viewing the ecosystem reductionistically from below, as being merely aggregated lesser qualities. We have, so to speak, an ecology of atoms and molecules. These are not described as microparticles *per se* but as events in their neighbourhoods, valued in macroscopic waterfalls and tidal basins. Genetics and biochemistry are drawn into the drama of natural history.

Many evolutionary and ecological connections are shared between ourselves as experiencers and the natural events we appraise. These bring a new orientation towards the presence of photosynthesis, the appearance of haemoglobin, or the genetic keying of information. We discover that decomposers and predators have value objectively in the ecosystem, and then realize that our own standing as subjective valuers atop the biotic pyramid is impossible, except in consequence of decomposition and predation. An interlocking kinship suggests that values are not merely in the mind but at hand in the world. We start out valuing nature like land appraisers figuring out what it is worth to us, only to discover that we are part and parcel of this nature we appraise. The earthen landscape has upraised this landscape appraiser. We do not simply bestow value on nature; nature also conveys value to us.

V NATURAL VALUE AND CONSCIOUSNESS

If the experience of valuing is relational, what do we say of the product, value? We must clarify the connection between experience and its objective base, since, under prevailing theories, it is widely held that the phrase "unexperienced value" is a contradiction in terms, with "experienced value" a tautology. This assumption fits the existential notice that value is not received as the conclusion of an argument, or by the indifferent observation of a causal series. A value or disvalue is whatever has got some bite to it. In the case of bare knowing, the knower has an internal *representation* of what is there, perhaps calmly so. Valuing requires more an internal *excitation*. That brings emoting, and perhaps this marriage of a subject to its object gives birth to value. It enters and exits with awareness.

Of course, if natural things have values, we cannot conceivably learn this without experiences by which we are let in on them. With every such sharing there comes a caring, and this may seem to proscribe objective neutrality. But it only prescribes circumspect inquiry. All natural science is built on the experience of nature, but this does not entail that its descriptions, its "facts," only consist in those experiences. All valuing of nature is built on experience, too, but that does not entail that its descriptions, its "values,"

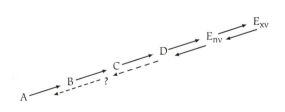

FIGURE 5

only consist in those experiences. Valuing could be a further, non-neutral way of knowing about the world. We might suppose that value is not empirical, since we have no organs and can make no instruments for it. But it could just as well be an advanced kind of experience where a more sophisticated, living instrument is required to register natural properties. Value must be lived through, *experienced,* but so as to discern the character of the surroundings one is living through. . . .

VI INTRINSIC NATURAL VALUE

Intrinsic contrasts with *instrumental; subjective* with *objective;* and we next map these terms onto each other and the natural world. *Intrinsic* value may be found in *human* experiences which are enjoyable in themselves, not needing further instrumental reference—an evening at the symphony, or one listening to loons call. Beyond this, *intrinsic natural* value recognizes value inherent in some natural occasions, without contributory human reference. The loons ought to continue to call, whether heard by humans or not. But the loon, while nonhuman, is itself a natural subject. There is something it is like to be a loon; its pains and pleasures are expressed in the call. Those who cannot conceive of nonexperienced value may allow nonhuman but not nonsubjective value. Value exists only where a subject has an object of interest.

> The being liked, or disliked of the object is its value. . . . Some sort of a subject is always requisite to there being value at all—not necessarily a *judging* subject, but a subject capable of at least motor-affective response. For the cat the cream has value, or better and more simply, the cat values the cream, or the warmth, or having her back scratched, quite regardless of her probable inability to conceive cream or to make judgments concerning warmth.[11]

Centres of experience vanish with simpler animals. In the botanical realm, we find programmes promoted, life courses generated and held to, steering cores which lock onto an individual centredness. There is a kind of "object with will," even though the feeling is gone. Every genetic set is, in that sense, a normative set; there is some "ought to be" beyond the "is," and so the plant grows, repairs itself, reproduces and defends its kind. If, after enjoying the *Trillium* in a remote woods, I step around to let it live on, I agree with this defense, and judge that here is intrinsic objective value, valued *by me,* but *for* what it is *in itself.* Value attaches to a nonsubjective form of life, but is nevertheless owned by a biological individual, a thing in itself. These things count, whether or not there is anybody to do the counting. They take account of themselves. They do what they will, which we enjoy being let in on, and which we care

to see continue when we pass on. Even a crystal is an identifiable, bounded individual, a natural kind which I may wish to protect, although it has no genetic core.

However, the "for what it is in itself" facet of "intrinsic" becomes problematic in a holistic web; it is too internal and elementary; it forgets relatedness and externality. We value the humus and brooklet because in that matrix the *Trillium* springs up. They supply nutrients and water for the lake on which the loons call. With concern about populations, species, gene pools, habitats, we need a corporate sense which can also mean "good in community." Every intrinsic value has leading and trailing "ands" pointing to values from which it comes and towards which it moves. A natural fitness and positioning make individualistic intrinsic value too system independent. Neither single subject nor single object is alone. Everything is good in a role, in a whole, although we can speak of intrinsic goodness wherever a point experience, as of the *Trillium,* is so satisfying that we pronounce it good without need to enlarge our focus. Here, while experience is indeed a value, a thing can have values that go unexperienced. Just as a human life can have meaning of which the individual is unaware (for indeed the lives of all great persons have more meaning than they know), biological individuals can play valuable genetic, ecological and evolutionary roles of which they are unaware. If the truth could be known, not only is much of value taking place in nonsentient nature, much of value is going on over our own heads as well.

For comprehensive scope, let us speak of natural *projects:* some are *subjects* (loons); some are individual organic *objects* (*Trilliums*); some are individual material *objects* (crystals); some are *communities* (the oak-hickory forest); and some are *landforms* (Mount Rainier). Every natural affair does not have value, but there are "clots" in nature, sets of affinities with projective power, systems of thrust, counterthrust and structure to which we can attach "natures" in the plural. There are achievements with beginning, endings and cycles, more or less. Some do not have wills or interests, but rather headings, trajectories, traits and successions which give them a tectonic integrity. They are projective systems, if not selective systems. This inorganic fertility produces complexes of value—a meandering river, a string of paternoster lakes—which are reworked over time. Intrinsic value need not be immutable. Anything is of value here which has a good story to it. Anything is of value which has intense harmony, or is a project of quality. There is a negentropic constructiveness in dialectic with an entropic teardown, a mode of working for which we hardly yet have an adequate scientific, much less a valuational, theory. Yet this is nature's most striking feature, one which ultimately must be valued and of value. In one sense we say that nature is indifferent to planets, mountains, rivers and *Trilliums,* but in another sense nature has bent towards making and remaking them for several billion years. These performances are worth noticing—remarkable, memorable—and they are not worth noticing just because of their tendencies to produce something else, certainly not merely because of their tendency to produce this noticing in our subjective human selves. All this gets at the root meaning of nature, its power to "generate" (Latin: *nasci, natus*).

Intrinsic natural value is a term which presides over a fading of subjective value into objective value, but also fans out from the individual to its role and matrix. Things do not have their separate natures merely in and for themselves, but they face outward and co-fit into broader natures. "Value in itself" is smeared out to become "value in togetherness." Value seeps out into the system, and we lose our capacity to identify the individual, whether subject or object, as the sole locus of value. A diagram can only suggest these diverse and complex relationships in their major zones (see figure 6). The boundaries need to be semipermeable surfaces, and there will be arrows of instrumental value (↗ ,↘) found throughout, connecting occasions of individual intrinsic value (o). Each of the upper levels includes and requires much in those below it. The upper levels do not exist independently or in isolation, but only as supported and maintained by the lower levels, though the diagram, while showing this, inadequately conveys how the higher levels are perfused with the lower ones.

The subjectivist claim might seem safer in view of the breakout problem, that of knowing what nonexperienced value is like. But it is just as bold, for it too refuses to shut value judgments off at the boundaries of experience. It asserts a descriptive, cognitive truth about the external world of nonexperience. It too is a metaphysical claim, going beyond immediate experience to judge what is not there. Science, strictly speaking, brings a null result here; a nonanswer, not a negative answer. The subjectivist claim is certainly not simple, but rather an advanced judgment made with heavy theories replacing the primary fact of experience, where we move through a world of helps and hurts always coming at us. The

logic by which one reads values out of nature is no less troublesome than the logic by which one finds values there and lets them stay.

The finding of objective value in nature is simpler and even more scientific if made with reserve. Neither native experience nor science pushes the dark back very far, but both let us in on workings which include but transcend our own existence. Immediate, middle-range experience enjoys many natural values, and one would expect this to be pragmatically competent on the local scale. When science passes to the atomic or astronomical scales, we may wish to be agnostic. But the global sciences describe an evolutionary ecosystem where, from an inchoate planet and seed of microscopic beginnings, there progressively evolves the many-splendoured panorama in which all our valuing takes place. We remain ignorant about many dynamisms and contingencies here; about what inevitability, if any, attaches to what actually did manage to happen. Nevertheless, whether rich by destiny or chance, or both, here we are, embedded in it all.

Now it does not seem simple, scientific or even safe to conceive of ourselves as subjects in metaphysical and valuational isolation from our natural launchings and underpinnings. Here, value is a powerfully penetrant notion. It slips by the emergent steps back to the generating power, away from the subject over to the web and pyramid. We certainly interpret the show, experiencing redness out of wave-lengths, beauty out of the patterned landscape. But we may be just as certain that the word known in sensory and intellectual paraphrase is structurally more complex than what comes through to register as fact and value. In that sense, in our knowing we are simplifying what is there, not enriching it, though, in another sense, the coming of humans enriches the drama, because valuers arrive in whom nature becomes conscious of itself.

In an otherwise admirable account, C. I. Lewis hedges, and grants that natural objects carry, objectively, *extrinsic* value, in effect, the standing possibility of valuation. They actually have a potential for value, even if this forever remains unexperienced or is mistakenly experienced. When an experiencer arrives, such objects do not refer us away from themselves, but we enjoy them for what they are. Nevertheless, they cannot own any intrinsic value. "*No objective existent has strictly intrinsic value; all values in objects are extrinsic only. . . . The goodness of good objects consists in the possibility of their leading to some realization of directly experienced goodness.*" Value judgments are based upon facts "obdurate and compelling" and in this sense "valuation is a form of empirical knowledge." The notion that values are only subjective is "one of the strangest aberrations ever to visit the mind of man."[12]

The word "extrinsic" suggests that, essentially still, value is a result of the human coming, whereas in ecological fact the human arrives often to trail naturally

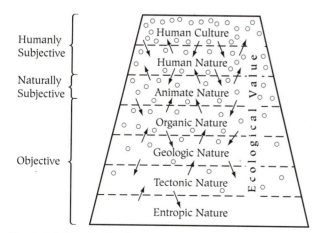

FIGURE 6 *Levels of Value in Projective Nature*

rooted values. There is nothing extraneous or accidental about the food value in a potato. When we overtake it, we recycle and amplify a natural value.[13] In evolutionary fact, there is nothing inessential or adventitious about those projective, prolife forces. They inhere in the earth itself and we latecomers inherit their work. The flow-through model of value does not find the objective side extrinsic and the subjective side intrinsic, but they are facets of one process. If, however, we revise Lewis's use of the word "extrinsic" to refer to that contributory role which natural things have, to their outward facing as this complements an inner facing, then in spontaneous nature things regularly have extrinsic as well as intrinsic value.

We can test our intuitions here by driving them to moral extremes. Let us imagine, in thought experiment, a parable of the last judgment. Suppose, a century hence, that in a tragic nuclear war each side has loosed upon the other radioactive fallout which sterilizes the genes of humans and mammals but is harmless to the flora, invertebrates, reptiles and birds. That last race of valuers, if they had conscience still, ought not to destroy the remaining biosphere. Moreover, this would not result from interest in whatever slight subjectivity might remain, for it would be better for those remaining ecosystems to continue, even if the principal valuers were taken out. That verdict would recall the Genesis parable of the first judgment in which, stage by stage, from lesser to higher forms, goodness is found at every level.

VII THE ETHIC IMPERATIVE

Future historians will find our century remarkable for its breadth of knowledge and narrowness of value judgments. Never have humans known so much about, and valued so little in, the great chain of being. As a result, the ecological crisis is not surprising. To devalue nature and inflate the human worth is to do business in a false currency. This yields a dysfunctional, monopolistic world view. We are misfits because we have misread our life-support system. We rationalize that the place we inhabit has no normative structures, and that we can do what we please. Afterwards, this view sinks down into the hinterlands of our minds, an invisible persuader which silently shapes an ethic.

One can blunder in the old, naive view that values are known in literal, uninterpreted simplicity. But there is folly also in swinging to the other extreme. In this arrogation of value to ourselves, there is what the theologians call *hubris*, overbearing pride. It is much easier to impose our wills on the world when we believe it is otherwise of no account. Nothing stays our libido; nothing demands any human-transcending concern. But ethics too, like all aspects of life, flourishes when operating in a system of checks and balances. What if, in truth, we are not only limited by the natural facts but also by natural values? What if living well is not merely a getting of what is valued, but a negotiating of values in a neighbourhood of worth? In the former belief we would forever remain juvenile. In the latter we should gain moral maturity.

There is much nobility in being self-actualizing, and nature permits us to elect some values. But such dignity is not enhanced by living as lonesome selves in a void world. There is no joy in being freaks of nature, loci of value lost in a worthless environment. The doctrine of the sterility of nature is not a boon but an evil, for it throws humans into meaninglessness, into an identity crisis. It has made much in modern life sterile. At this point, there is something encouraging about the notion of relativity. Einstein introduced us, at the levels of time, space, mass and energy, to but one form of an ecosystemic principle. Subjectivity, too, is what it is in objective circumstances. The values we own are nested in a mother matrix. To turn Bishop Butler on his head: everything is what it is in relation to other things.[14] This kind of relativity does not cause alienation and anthropocentrism; it rather cures it.

Seen in this way, it is not the objectivists but rather the thorough-going subjectivists who uphold the naturalistic fallacy. They must either derive value at a consummate stroke out of a merely factual nature, getting it, as it were, *ex nihilo*, or out of something available but to no avail without us; or they have to bring value in by skyhook from some *a priori* source. But we do not commit this fallacy because we find fact and value inseparably to coevolve. This does not deny the mystery of emerging value, but there is value in our premises as well as in our conclusion.

We humans do not play out our drama of epiphenomenal or emergent value on a valueless natural stage. The stage is the womb from whence we come, but which we really never leave. If the enduring drama has any value, that must somehow attach to the whole plot and plasma, span over from potential to persons, even though it may be diversely distributed across events. Nature is not barren of value; it is rather the bearer of value: that both constrains and ennobles the role we humans are called to play.

Notes

1. William James, *The Varieties of Religious Experience* (New York: Longmans, Green and Co., 1925), p. 150.
2. John Laird, *A Study in Realism* (Cambridge: Cambridge University Press, 1920), p. 129.
3. Wilhelm Windelband, *An Introduction to Philosophy*, trans. Joseph McCabe (London: T. Fisher Unwin Ltd., 1921), p. 215.
4. Ralph Barton Perry, *General Theory of Value* (Cambridge, Mass.: Harvard University Press, 1926), pp. 125, 115–16.

5. Samuel Alexander, *Beauty and Other Forms of Value* (New York: Thomas Y. Crowell Company, 1968), pp. 172–87.

6. Cited in Ernst Cassirer, *Substance and Function and Einstein's Theory of Relativity* (New York: Dover Publications, 1953), p. 356.

7. John Wheeler, "From Relativity to Mutability," in *The Physicist's Conception of Nature*, ed. Jagdish Mehra (Dordrecht, Holland: D. Reidel Publishing Co., 1973), p. 227.

8. Werner Heisenberg, "The Representation of Nature in Contemporary Physics," *Daedalus* 87 no. 3 (Summer 1958): 107.

9. Lubert Stryer, *Biochemistry* (San Francisco: W. H. Freeman and Co., 1975), p. 90.

10. John Dewey, *Experience and Nature* (New York: Dover Publications, 1958), p. 4a.

11. David W. Prall, *A Study in the Theory of Value* (Berkeley and Los Angeles: University of California Press, 1921), p. 227.

12. Clarence Irving Lewis, *An Analysis of Knowledge and Valuation* (La Salle, Illinois: Open Court Publishing Co., 1946), p. 387; ibid, p. 407; ibid, p. vii; ibid, p. 366.

13. The apple, Lewis would reply, cannot realize its own value. If uneaten, it rots. So its value is extrinsic; the eater's pleasure is intrinsic. But this example is misleading unless ecologically understood. The carbohydrate stored in the overwintering potato will be used, although not experienced, by the plant in the spring. Eating it overtakes energy of value to the plant. But the apple functions as a gamble in seed dispersal. Its value is realized when birds, deer or humans take the bait. The apple has been very successful; it has caught the man. While the apple takes care of the man, the man takes care of the apple. Its survival is assured as long as there are humans to care for it!

14. "Every thing is what it is, and not another thing" (Joseph Butler, preface to *Fifteen Sermons upon Human Nature* [London, 1726]).

Study Questions

1. What are Rolston's central arguments for objective values in nature? How strong are they?

2. Explain the notions of primary, secondary, and tertiary qualities. What does Rolston say about these, relevant to values in nature?

3. What does Rolston mean by "all judgments mix theory with fact" and "in this context, judgments of natural value hardly differ from judgments of natural fact"?

4. Discuss Rolston's "Natural Value as Ecological-Relational" in Part IV of this essay. What are the salient features? In what way are values "relational"?

5. How does Rolston defend his thesis that nature has intrinsic value?

12

Values in Nature: Is Anybody There?[1]

ERNEST PARTRIDGE

Ernest Partridge is the Hulings professor of humanities and environmental ethics at Northland College in Ashland, Wisconsin. His specialties include environmental ethics, policy analysis, moral philosophy, and applied ethics. He received his Ph.D. from the University of Utah and has taught philosophy at several campuses of the University of California before coming to Northland College. He has edited Responsibilities to Future Generations.

This essay deals with a troubling dilemma at the heart of environmental ethics: On the one hand, talk of "values" in nature apart from evaluators *seems incoherent. And yet, on the other hand, if values in nature imply evaluators, how are we to avoid the* anthropocentrism *that is anathema to so many ecomoralists?*

Partridge offers a compatibilist view in the opening paragraph and then goes on to critique Holmes Rolston's thesis that Nature has objective value.

I

Is extremism in the defense of the natural environment a virtue? I think not. In a reasoned defense, extremism is rarely an intellectual virtue. Yet many philosophers, in a determined attempt to refute an anthropocentric environmental ethic, have asserted an apparently extreme axiological assumption—namely, that values can exist in nature apart from and independent of a conscious reflection, or even a minimally sentient awareness, thereof. In opposition to this view and in concert with what seems to be the prevailing philosophical opinion, I will argue that the concept of "value" requires an evaluator—a being aware of the evaluated issue to whom that issue "matters." In addition, I will contend that, despite the qualms

This essay is a revision of an article that first appeared in *Philosophical Inquiry*, Vol. 8 (1986):1–2. Reprinted by permission of the author.

of many ecological moralists, this dyadic view of value does not entail anthropocentrism, or even "sentiocentrism." On the contrary, this conventional axiology leaves ample room for a nature-centered ("eco-centric") ethic. Moreover, by insisting upon the natural origin and sustenance of the subject of evaluation, and upon the natural context of evaluation, an ecological morality employing the *dyadic view* is quite capable of removing the evaluator from the central focus of environmental ethics.

There are, in fact, three basic viewpoints to be considered here: (1) "Value" is an objective quality to be discovered in natural things; I'll call this the *objective-monadic theory* (or briefly, O-M). (2) Evaluation is dyadic, but the value-bearer ("evaluator"?!) need not be conscious or sentient; e.g., something can be "good for" a plant or a rock "itself," "in its own right." I call this the *object/object-dyadism* (or O/O-D). (Because these views agree in their denial of the necessity of a subjective evaluator, they will often be treated together in this paper.) Finally, (3) the *subject/object-dyadic* view (S/O-D), which I accept, holds both that values are essentially relational and that one relatum (the "evaluator") must be at least sentient.[2] According to the S/O-D view, O-M is describing not values but properties of things that may be value components;[3] and O/O-D is describing not values but causal relationships or functions.[4]

The careful reader will notice some terminological awkwardness in the previous paragraph, which, I suspect, may be of more than semantic significance. The difficulty is that there appears to be no term that fits both the "object-relatum" and "subject-relatum" in O/O-D as well as S/O-D. In the first case (O/O-D), "value-bearer" seems the best of a number of bad choices. "Evaluator" is troublesome here, since it suggests cognition (hence *subject-object dyadism*). "Subject of values" is unacceptable for the same reason. "Beneficiary" fails on the ground that an evaluator is not necessarily a beneficiary—for example, "I (the evaluator) commend Jones for his kindness to Smith (the beneficiary)." Furthermore, to call an object (say, a rock) a "beneficiary" is to beg a point that I wish to dispute (viz., that an inanimate object can be "benefited" in "its own right"). The best solution that I can devise for O/O-D is to stipulate that the alleged "value for" is for an object that has that value (or interest), hence the term *value-bearer*. But notice that "value-bearer" will not do for S/O-D, while "evaluator" is just what is called for, since the latter term directly describes the subjective component of S/O-D. But for the same reason, it also begs the (exclusively) S/O-D position, since, as noted, the comparable relatum in O/O-D can scarcely be called an "evaluator." "Value-bearer" (adopted for O/O-D) is unacceptable for S/O-D, since it fails to convey the *spectator capacity* in S/O-D evaluation (cf. the "Jones-Smith" example, above). Is it perhaps significant that, over the ages and despite countless ethical discussions and analyses, no concept has evolved that fits both the

"value-bearer" (in O/O-D) and "evaluator" (in S/O-D) relata? Perhaps this constitutes an "ordinary-language argument" for (though not a proof of) the S/O-D view.

One of the crucial tests of the significance of philosophical dispute follows the question: "Does this make a difference?" or, more tersely, "so what?" I believe that these various views of natural evaluation do make a significant difference in our evaluations of natural things. In support of that claim, I offer these thought experiments: (a) Imagine a planet, orbiting two double stars. The planet has several moons as various in composition and appearance as the moons of Jupiter. Furthermore, this planet has a corrosive yet often transparent atmosphere. These conditions all combine to create landscapes, sunrises, lunar phases, and so forth that would be of incredible beauty were there anyone to enjoy it. But there never has been and never will be observers of these scenes, since the planet is totally and forever inhospitable to life. Are these conditions, in fact, "beautiful"? Have they any value at all if they are of value to no one? Suppose an asteroid collides with the planet, altering its physical and chemical conditions and shrouding it in an opaque atmosphere, thus obliterating all sunsets and landscapes forever. Is this collision a calamity? To whom? To no one! But if to no one, why regard it as a calamity? Or is it, in some sense, a calamity "in itself"? Did the asteroid destroy something "inherently beautiful" and "inherently valuable"? Could it be so with no one for it to be "beautiful" or "valuable" to? Is the destruction on this planet in some sense a value "loss" to the natural universe?

(b) Suppose we commit the ultimate folly of total nuclear war and, as a result, within 100 years all that remains of the biosphere is what Jonathan Schell calls "a republic of insects and grasses," no life-form more complex than a cockroach (presumably insentient).[5] Suppose too that sentient life will never again evolve on Earth (due to the subsequent expansion of the Sun) and that intelligent life-forms will never visit. Given all this, does it matter that such architectural monuments as the Taj Mahal will crumble to ruin? Suppose the government of India had erected a protective dome around the Taj Mahal so that it stood erect two hundred years after the death of the last sentient being. Other things equal, is the uninhabited planet "better" for having an intact Taj Mahal on its surface?[6]

(c) Some brief questions: Was the Grand Canyon "magnificent in itself" before it was seen by any human beings? Has the surface of Venus been "littered" and "despoiled" (made less valuable) by the spacecraft that have struck its surface? Does the sugar sit sweetly on the cupboard shelf?

These cases seem to indicate a difference in the theories. Defenders of O-M and O/O-D, believing that values can exist without sentient evaluators, will answer affirmatively to at least a few of the above questions. To all these questions, the proponent of the S/O-D position will answer "no." Those who hold that position and yet feel an intuitive tug toward assent might dispel that inclination by noting that their discomfort at the thought of the Taj Mahal in ruins, or of steel, titanium, and semiconductor rubbish strewn on Venus, results from a violation of the stipulated conditions. They "cheat" by importing themselves into the landscape through their imaginations. Unfair! The ghostly presence of the hypothetical evaluator evokes not value but "hypothetical value." The S/O-D proponent insists that we take the stipulation and challenge seriously: No sentient or intelligent beings are to observe or be affected by these events or circumstances. Do values apply? To whom? If values are alleged to "apply," but to no one, then just what might this mean? Can we make sense of this assertion?

II

A monadic response to these challenges is offered by Tom Regan who insists that "non-conscious natural objects can have value in their own right, independently of human interests." Such "inherent value," as he calls it, "is independent of any awareness, interest, or appreciation of it by any conscious being," and "the inherent value of a natural object is an objective property of that object."[7] The literalness of this interpretation is apparent as Regan applies it to specific cases:

> The inherent value of a natural object is an objective property of that object. . . . Certain stretches of the Colorado River, for example, are free, not subjectively, but objectively. The freedom expressed by (or in) the river is an objective fact. . . . The value of the river's being free is also an objective property of the river. If the river is inherently good . . . then it is a fact about the river that it is good inherently.[8]

Accordingly, natural processes may diminish the value of a river. "For example, because of various sedimentary changes, a river that is now wild and free might in time be transformed into a small, muddy creek," which may call for efforts to "improve upon" nature.[9]

The appeal to the eco-moralist of Regan's notion of "inherent natural value" is immediate and compelling, for the concept suggests a "hard," substantial, and objective status for such values—a status safely and securely founded independently of the shifts and drifts of human culture or personal taste and preference. By this account, "inherent natural values," like objective facts, are simply "out there" to be discovered (not invented), and obstinately "there" (in nature) whether or not we manage to perceive and appreciate them.[10]

Unfortunately for those finding comfort in this view, there are problems. Consider, for example, Regan's attempt to apply the notion of "inherent value" to cars:

> [It will not] do to argue that cars cannot have a good of their own because what characteristics are good making in

cars depends on what our interests are. For a car has those characteristics it has, including those that are good making, quite independently of our taking an interest in them.[11]

The second sentence simply asserts what is not in dispute—namely, that cars have properties. It does not support Regan's contention that some of these qualities are "inherently valuable." Of course, these "good-making qualities" (e.g., of cars) exist independently; but the value of these qualities are not "independent" of our taking an interest in them. He writes, "cars do not become, say, comfortable or economical by becoming the objects of our interest." Granted, but the value of being "comfortable" or "economical" is a matter that requires our attention and interest.[12] A "good" luxury car is not economical, and a "good" racing car is not comfortable. The characteristics are independent, but the "goodness" of those characteristics depends on our interest in these characteristics (better, perhaps, our "appropriate" or "reasoned" interest in them). Continuing:

> If a good car was produced by purely natural means . . . that would not make it any less a good one. It would make it an unusual one. . . . If we were to transport a good car from our world to a world inhabited by beings who did not have the interests we have, it would not cease to be a good car, though it would cease to be valued as one. A good car does not lose its goodness if we lose our interest in it.[13]

Again, it would be better to say that the car would not cease to have the qualities deemed (by us) to be good. Once again, Regan is confusing here certain properties of an object with the (subject/object-dyadic) value judgment made of those properties. Shouldn't we instead say that in this strange case that it would cease to be "a good car," even if it's properties were not altered. When he writes, above, "a good car does not lose its goodness if we lose our interest in it," all this means is that the car would keep the properties that we would prize if, contra the example, we were there to evaluate it—or, for that matter, would keep the properties that we now value from our hypothetical standpoint as hypothetical observers of this fanciful world.[14]

Next, consider Regan's attempt to apply his concept of objective "inherent" value to gardenias:

> A luxuriant gardenia, one with abundant blossoms and rich, deep, green foliage is a better gardenia than one that is so deformed and stunted that it puts forth no blossoms at all, and this is [true] quite independently of the interests other beings happen to take in them.[15]

If the flower in question is to be found in a florist shop, it is worth noting that it is an artifact—an artificial creation, by a botanist, "assembled" from natural (genetic) "media" and designed to appeal to human tastes. As such, the "better" gardenia must mean "better for us," since we (or better, "our horticulturists") selected these qualities for us. Another plant with less blossoms and foliage might produce more pollen—better for a bee. Or more seeds—better for a finch. It might be "better for" the gardenia and/or its species (whatever that means) if it were allowed to go to seed and reproduce!

And would this cultivated plant survive in the wild as well as its wild relatives? Probably not. Does that mean that it is not, after all, a "better gardenia"? Note that these alternative "evaluations" apply differing contexts to our analysis of the gardenia *per se*. Without context and a relatum, it just makes no sense to talk of something as blankly "better."

There is still worse ahead. Consider Regan's claim that the gardenia is "good," not to the florist, or the bee, or the finch, or even the ecosystem—but just "good," period. What, then, is a "bad gardenia"? A bad (or good) anything! How can we begin to answer such a question without placing an evaluator into the picture, at least hypothetically (thus deriving, presumably, a "hypothetical value")? Without an answer to such a question, or at least a decision procedure, the notion of "inherent value" is unbounded. If the concept lacks bounds, then everything is "inherently good," and "goodness" fails to qualify anything at all. "That which denotes everything, connotes nothing."

Has Regan an answer to this objection? While he asserts that "not everything in nature is inherently valuable,"[16] he offers us no means of distinguishing what is from what is not "inherently valuable." His neglect of this task could not be more explicit: "Two questions that I have not endeavored to answer are: (a) what, if anything in general, makes something inherently good, and (b) how can we know, if we can, what things are inherently good?"[17] Unfortunately for Regan's argument and his concept of "inherent value," these are precisely the questions that he must answer if we are to make any sense of what he is saying. Without answers to these questions, his theory has no meaning or justification. He has, in effect, declared conceptual bankruptcy by admitting that he is unprepared to "cash in" his concept of "inherent value" in the commerce of practical moral judgment and experience.

We turn next to the object/object-dyadic view affirming that "evaluation" implies an "evaluator" but allows that the evaluator might be nonsentient animals or plants (Kenneth Goodpaster, Paul Taylor), ecosystems and landscapes (Holmes Rolston, Christopher Stone), or even rocks (Roderick Nash).[18] O/O-D is implied by the view that nonsentient life, even things, have "goods of their own" and therefore interests and even "rights." (Again, O-M holds that "inherent" values are "in" objects; whereas O/O-D states further that these "values-in" may also be "values-for" the object.) Accordingly, the argument continues, since such entities can be harmed or benefited "in their own right," they are qualified "holders of value." Christopher Stone makes the case for plants: "The lawn tells me that it wants [or "needs"] water by a certain dryness of the blades and soil . . . the appearance of bald spots, yellowing, and a lack of springiness after being walked on."[19]

Rolston, like Goodpaster, finds value in the basic processes and functions of life itself: "Every genetic set is a propositional set, a normative set, proposing what ought to be, beyond what is, on the basis of its encoded information. So it grows, reproduces, repairs its wounds, and resists death."[20] Goodpaster finds "moral considerability" in "tendencies" of life-forms "to maintain and heal themselves."[21]

A recurrent criticism of this approach is that it is difficult to restrict "value," so conceived, to life-forms, and yet if this restriction is not successful, the concept of "value-bearer," by escaping such confinement of application, will lose significance; that is, if everything "has value," then nothing does, since "value" applied to everything would fail to qualify (distinguish) anything.[22] (This is the "denotation/connotation problem" encountered above with Regan's concept of "inherent value.") But can we draw the line at life itself? Consider the above cases. First, Stone's description of what the lawn "wants" seems much closer to the description of a car "wanting" a wash-and-wax than that of a dog or a human "wanting" a drink of water. Common to the lawn, dog, and human are some biochemical functional "needs." However, unique to the dog and the human are neural, sentient "awarenesses" of that need—in effect, an additional "need," not for water but for relief from the felt discomfort of thirst. Goodpaster's account of the "tendencies to maintain and heal themselves" applies to physical phenomena as well. For instance, a desert lake with no outlet has a "tendency to maintain and heal itself." When overfilled, it extends its area, thus increasing evaporation; when "undernourished," it retreats, decreasing evaporation. By this account, then, the Dead Sea, or the Great Salt Lake have a "need," still more an "interest," in maintaining their levels; therefore they have "goods of their own" and thus have "rights" and deserve "moral considerability." All this, I submit, constitutes a metaphorical wandering of the concepts of need, interest, and rights far beyond their appropriate "home bases."

III

At the outset, I listed two basic tasks of this paper: (a) to prove that the concept of "value" requires an evaluator (i.e., S/O-D) and (b) to indicate that S/O-D need not entail an anthropocentric environmental ethic. That second task will be facilitated by explicating a distinction within the subject/object-dyadic view.

To recapitulate: monadic and dyadic views of value are distinguished by the insistence of the defenders of the dyadic views (i.e., S/O-D and O/O-D) that values cannot stand alone but must be "values for" something—a "value-bearer" (O/O-D) or "evaluator" (S/O-D). Thus, the dyadic view insists, talk of something being "just valuable, but to nothing" is simply incoherent, like saying "its not bigger than anything in particular—just bigger" or, to use an ecological analogy, like attempting to explain "adaptation" in terms of either "organism" or "environment," but not both.[23] S/O-D parts company with O/O-D with the further insistence that the concept of value implies an evaluator that is at least sentient (in order to display "nonmoral value preferences"), if not reflective and self-conscious.[24]

Why this insistence upon sentience (at the very least)? Because, without at least minimal feeling and awareness, nothing can "matter" to a being.[25] Though commonplace in philosophical literature, the argument bears repeating: Insects, plants, "mere things" may be said to be "good" in the sense of having properties "deemed good" by others. But a "goodness of" these beings cannot be a "goodness for" them, if that "goodness" makes no difference to them. To make a difference to them that is a good (or bad) for them (for them to have "stakes" or "interests"), beings must at least have what Feinberg calls "rudimentary cognitive equipment."[26] Conversely, nothing that happens to X, matters to X, if X is irrevocably insentient and nonconscious. In short, if a being has no "stake" in events that affect it (having no "good of its own"), it has neither "standing" nor "capacity" to evaluate. It thus makes no sense to speak of such a being as an "evaluator."

S/O-D can be usefully subdivided according to the relative importance of the two relata of the dyad. "Soft S/O-D," which emphasizes the subjective component, is more likely to be associated with relativistic, subjectivistic, anthropocentric, and noncognitive theories of value and with personal preference and aesthetic taste. In contradistinction, "hard S/O-D," which emphasizes the objective component, is more likely to be associated with categorical, objectivistic, and cognitivist theories of value. It is, of course, the "hard" object-oriented S/O-D that is best equipped to claim compatibility with a nature-centered environmental ethic.

How, then, might "hard S/O-D" be conceived to be compatible with ecological morality? We might do so by comparing "evaluation" with two other types of subject/object-dyadic relations, namely, knowledge and perception. (a) In the case of knowledge according to "hard S/O-D," both "valuing" and "knowing" are dyadic ("evaluator/evaluated" and "knower/known"). Both "valuing" and "knowing" identify "hard" recalcitrant components that do not bend to our will ("facts" in knowledge and "valued objects" in evaluation). In both valuing and knowing, the objects are "discovered" and not arbitrarily and subjectively invented. In both cases, the "subject" ("knower" and "evaluator") cannot be a lifeless or insentient being. (b) In the case of perception, the exponent of "hard S/O-D" might compare "valu-

ing" to the perception of Lockean secondary qualities. In all three instances, "valuing," "knowing," and perception, the activity is directed outward, and engages the objective world (in matters of our concern, the "natural" world). As before, in all three instances, the content is "recalcitrant" to the will of the subject, and the "subject" cannot be lifeless or insentient. And, in all three cases, both relata are necessary: Without subject and object, there are no values, no knowledge, and no secondary qualities. (A "fact" is not "known" by itself; the sugar is not "sweet" unless tasted.)

With these considerations in mind, the "hard S/O-D view" is ready to accommodate the eco-moralist who wishes not to make man the "measure" of his environmental ethic. Consider some of these eco-moralistic "concerns." First, from John Laird:

> There is beauty . . . in sky and cloud and sea, in lilies and in sunsets, in the glow of bracken in autumn and in the enticing greenness of a leafy spring. Nature indeed, is infinitely beautiful, and she seems to wear her beauty as she wears color or sound. Why then should her beauty belong to us rather than to her?[27]

"Hard S/O-D" might be willing to accord to such natural values as "beauty," all the "objectivity" of "colors and sounds"—which, as secondary qualities, "exist" only when perceived and when the subject is in a position to be receptive to the natural properties and circumstances that evoke these perceptions.

Holmes Rolston rhetorically asks: "How do we humans come to be charged up with values, if there was and is nothing in nature charging us up so?"[28] The hard S/O-D view has no trouble whatever acknowledging, and even identifying, natural sources and validations of "natural values"—and likewise, our percepts, knowledge, and adaptations. Rolston also observes that we realize the wilderness "to be valuable without our will." [29] In light of the foregoing analyses and analogies, hard S/O-D can agree that wilderness may be "valuable without our will," but not, the theory insists, without our awareness—not, that is, without an evaluator. Analogously, something is "red" without our will but not without our awareness.

IV

We return at last to our opening question: Does nature, by itself, have value? Can there be "natural values" without at least a sentient, and better still a personal, evaluator? Perhaps we are now prepared to identify a naive realism, similar to that described by epistemologists, at work in both the monadic and the object/object-dyadic theories of natural value. For when someone asks: "Does nature, 'by itself,' and/or apart from persons or sentient beings, have value significance?" the next, crucial responsive question might be: "Who asks?!"

Of course, a person asks. And thus, the fact that the question of "the inherent value of nature" be asked at all means that a person is part of the landscape, if only in imagination. In a sense, then, inquiring, morally conscious persons have a "Midas touch" in that by simply inquiring about the value significance of an object or a landscape, that object or landscape gains at least potential value significance—whether the inquiry is by a potential beneficiary or simply by a disinterested "value spectator."

The "naive realism," just suggested, may thus reside in the notion that one can regard nature, or even imagine or describe it "apart from persons," and then inquire as to whether it has value "apart from persons." But in such cases, nature is *not* "apart from persons." Even to identify and describe a part of nature places that part of nature in the context of personal attention and notice—to render it, ipso facto, *not* "apart from persons." To put the matter in the "organic" and "contextual" terms preferred by eco-moralists, in the evaluation of nature, persons become necessary ingredients of the nature to be valued. However, to still the qualms about *anthropocentrism,* we might reiterate that nature too is a "necessary ingredient" of the evaluation. Thus the error of anthropocentrism may reside not in the acknowledgment that the existence of values presupposes a subject ("evaluator") but in a further insistence that the "subject" of values need be the "center," even the arbitrary "creator," of values. This inference is gratuitous. To say that a reflective (or, minimally, a sentient) being must be "in the picture" for there to be evaluations, even in imagination, does not mean that all values are to be justified in terms of their beneficial effects upon those beings, nor does it mean that all values exist directly "in behalf of" persons. Both anthropocentric and nature-centered systems of environmental ethics are defensible within the conceptual bounds of S/O-D axiology. It is the further task of the proponents of these opposing positions to defend their theories and refute their rivals, within these bounds.

To summarize: The S/O-D position claims that scrupulous and rigorous analysis will lead us to the conclusion that "permanently unperceived and unimagined nature" is valueless—"inherently, intrinsically, and instrumentally" valueless. Such a conclusion, this position insists, is forced on us by the logic of the concept of "value." But this is only half the story. The other "redeeming" half is that "permanently unperceived and unimagined nature" is, ipso facto, of no interest whatever to evaluating creatures. Is this an anthropocentric view? Not necessarily. For the attempt to "deal" with nature as if it were perceived, known, or valued without human beings is ultimately inappropriate, even incoherent. Any nature we deal with is touched, Midas-like, with value or value-potential.

Accordingly, for those concerned with environmental ethics, the question "Are there values without evaluating beings?" is an idle question. The core question of environmental ethics is "What shall we do with regard to nature?" By its very formulation, the question requires an evaluator. It makes little sense to claim, on the one hand, that we are seeking a code of conduct toward nature and then to pretend that there is any practical significance to speculation about the ontological or axiological status of entities in nature that are forever uninvolved with persons—or with any sentient beings.

If all this is not enough to reassure the eco-moralist that his environmental ethic need not be subjective, relativistic, and anthropocentric, then he might be enjoined to take his preferred "holistic" perspective and contextual methodology seriously. He should, in a word, be reminded that evaluation itself takes place in a context—a natural context. He might further reiterate his insistence that human beings, and particularly their psychological components (their "selves"), are natural entities. These selves evolve from natural sources and are sustained by natural processes. In the evaluation of nature, the subject does not "encounter" its object, spectatorlike, as much as it is "encompassed by" its object. In short, in natural evaluation, the human subject is both "within" the natural context of evaluation, and the personal and phylogenetic product of natural contexts.[30] Surely all this provides ample conceptual and theoretical resources for a nonanthropocentric environmental axiology.[31]

A Metaethical Postscript: An anonymous critic asks: [Isn't S/O-D really] "an ethical theory that provides a unified setting for (and thus an account of) various ethical notions? Other theories (other proposed organizations of concepts, e.g., Regan's) are possible, and the question is then: which is preferable?"

I reply that this essay is an attempt to display the "preferability" of S/O-D. But to respond directly to the question: By describing "value" as he does, Regan is not describing something that is coherent with normal usage of "value." Of course, he is entitled to use value in his own way, provided his unique sense of "value" (as property, or causal function, or disposition) is clearly defined and seen to be distinct from the ordinary use of "value." But it isn't. While Regan's notion of "inherent value" may have a "solid core" of acceptable meaning (akin to Rolston's "value-genes"), he attempts to attach thereto some connotations, senses, qualities, and implications of the conventional sense of "value" (as values to someone), thus "exporting" the notion of "mattering" into the objective world. That this is more than a terminological dispute is demonstrated by the "science-fiction thought experiments" early in the paper. I claim that my concept of value (S/O-D) is "preferable" in that it coheres better with (a) our general understanding of the nature of the physical world, (b) our understanding of the encounters of living organisms and nervous systems with that world, and (c) the clear, conventional and functioning usage of such "value talk" as "subjective," "objective," and, yes, "values" and "evaluation."

Notes

1. This paper has benefited from critical comments by Holmes Rolston, Dale Jamieson, and two anonymous referees for the University of Georgia conference on "Environmental Ethics: New Directions" (October 4–6, 1984) at which it was read. The author has made minor revisions for this anthology, September 1996.
2. Actually, this is something of a simplification of my view of human evaluation, which is more in tune with Peirce's triadic analysis of meaning. However, that interpretation will not be compromised by an adequate defense here of the simpler subject/object-dyadic view, on which the triadic analysis is built.
3. Holmes Rolston calls these "value-genes" in "Are Values in Nature Subjective or Objective?" *Environmental Ethics*, 4:2 (Summer 1982), p. 139.
4. S/O-D is open to a wide variety of interpretations, with ethical noncognitivists emphasizing the subjective component of the relationship and cognitivists emphasizing the objective component. I make use of this distinction in the final portion of this paper.
5. Jonathan Schell, *The Fate of the Earth* (New York: Knopf, 1982), ch. 1.
6. Dale Jamieson suggests that the answer to this question might be affirmative, due to "the preferences of the dead" (when alive) to have the Taj Mahal preserved. My disagreement with this view may be found in my "Posthumous Interest and Posthumous Respect," *Ethics,* 91:2 (January 1981), pp. 243–264.
7. Tom Regan, "The Nature and Possibility of an Environmental Ethic," *Environmental Ethics,* 3:1 (Spring 1981), pp. 19, 30–31. (Reprinted in *All That Dwell Within,* University of California Press, 1982).
8. "The Nature and Possibility of an Environmental Ethic," op. cit., 199–200.
9. Ibid., 201.
10. Holmes Rolston (who shares Regan's distrust of the S/O-D approach, but not his O-M response) forthrightly expresses the eco-moralists' suspicions of subject/object dyadism:

    Values, it is typically said, form no part of nature, but only come with the human response to the world. This seems at once objective about nature and humane toward persons, but it also yields a value structure in the scientific West more anthropocentric by several orders of magnitude than were any of the value systems of classical, Oriental, and primitive world views which have succumbed before it.

    Rolston, "Are Values in Nature Subjective or Objective?" loc. cit., 4:2 (Summer 1982), pp. 126–127.

11. "What Sorts of Beings Can Have Rights?" loc. cit., 177.
12. Because I do not necessarily wish to embrace an interest theory of value here, I would say that "attention and interest" are necessary for value, though not sufficient. Otherwise, we are perilously close to subjectivism and relativism.
13. "What Sorts of Beings Can Have Rights?" loc. cit., 177.
14. If these "good" qualities are thought of as "goods of" the car, then the concept is monadic. If "good for" the car, or "in the interest of the car," then they may be thought of as object/object-dyadic values. If this seems a quibble, the triviality of the distinction between "good of" and "good for" only serves to indicate what I already suspect; namely, that the difference between O-M and O/O-D is of little significance.
15. "What Sorts of Beings Can Have Rights?"loc. cit., 179.
16. "The Nature and Possibility of an Environmental Ethic," op. cit., 31.
17. Ibid., 33.
18. Kenneth Goodpaster, "On Being Morally Considerable," *Journal of Philosophy,* LXXV:6 (June 1978*)*; Paul Taylor, "The Ethics of Respect for Nature," *Environmental Ethics,* 3:3 (Fall 1981); Holmes Rolston (as noted here); Christopher Stone, *Should Trees Have Standing* (Los Altos, CA: Kaufmann, 1974); Roderick Nash, "Do Rocks Have Rights?" *The Center Magazine* (November-December 1978) (Nash has repeated this assertion in several different publications).
19. Stone, op. cit., 24.
20. Holmes Rolston, "Values Gone Wild," *Inquiry* 26:9 (1983): 181–120, p. 192.
21. Goodpaster, op. cit., 319.
22. Such is the criticism of W. Morton Hunt in "Are Mere Things Morally Considerable?" *Environmental Ethics,* 2:2 (Spring 1980), pp. 59–65.
23. Defenders of the monadic view ("values in"), such as Regan, are by no means excluded from accepting the dyadic interpretation ("values for") as well. The lines are drawn by the refusal of O/O-D to embrace O-M, or of S/O-D to accept either.
24. These, along with several other traits that constitute personhood, qualify the being to make "moral value judgments." I could say (and have said) much more about the significance of "personhood" to moral evaluation, and of the distinction between "moral" and nonmoral" values. However, space limitations forbid elaboration. (See my "Nature as a Moral Resource," *Environmental Ethics,* 6:2 (1984); and the "Introduction" to *Responsibilities to Future Generations* (Prometheus, 1981). For views similar to my own regarding the concept of a "person," see Mary Anne Warren's, "On the Moral and Legal Status of Abortion," *The Monist,* 57:1 (Jan. 1973), pp. 52–57. My views regarding "moral values" and "nonmoral values" are reflected in William Frankena's *Ethics,* 2d ed., (Prentice Hall, 1973), chs. I and IV.

25. This paragraph is a simple reiteration of Joel Feinberg's "interest theory of rights," which may be found in his "The Rights of Animals and Future Generations," *Philosophy and Environmental Crisis*, ed. William Blackstone (Athens: University of Georgia Press, 1974), p. 54.

26. Ibid.

27. *Study in Realism* (Cambridge, England: University Press, 1920), p. 129. (Quoted by Rolston in "Are Values in Nature . . .," loc. cit., 126.)

28. Rolston, "Are Values in Nature . . .," loc. cit., 138.

29. Rolston, "Values Gone Wild," loc. cit., 199.

30. For a splendid account of the "ecology" and the "natural history" of natural evaluation, see Rolston, "Are Values in Nature . . .," loc. cit., especially pp. 134–138.

31. These closing considerations open up a rich panorama of axiological, ethical, and other philosophical issues, which we cannot pursue this late in the presentation. I can only note, at this conclusion, that the literature on the topic of the "natural" origins and affinities of the self and of "the ecology of evaluation" is rich, extensive, suggestive, and, I believe, ultimately supportive of at least the possibility of both a subject/object-dyadic theory of value and a nature-centered environmental ethic. In my judgment, the best contemporary work in this field of "environmental axiology" is by Holmes Rolston, notwithstanding my disagreements with Rolston, explored above.

Study Questions

1. What are the two kinds of theories of objective value that Partridge opposes? Is he successful?

2. What are Partridge's two basic tasks, and how well does he succeed in achieving them?

13

Values at Stake: Does Anything Matter?
A Response to Ernest Partridge

HOLMES ROLSTON, III

A biographical sketch of Holmes Rolston III is contained in Reading 11.

In this essay, Rolston responds to Ernest Partridge's "conventional" or "normal" account that something only has value if there is a valuer to value it. He characterizes Partridge's position as a "light-in-the-refrigerator" theory. "Nothing inside is of value until I open the door and the light comes on." He asks us to consider growth and maintenance that, without any sentient awareness, still possess a good and can be benefited. He then develops his points in terms of evolutionary ecosystems.

Environmental ethics cares about nature, and this requires an account of values in nature. Ernest Partridge develops the "conventional" or "normal" account: Values are at stake if and only if something "matters" to somebody there. He worries about "environmental extremists" like myself, who have a more radical account, claiming (as I do answering the question "Are values in nature subjective or objective?") that significant natural values are already there before anybody, such as an environmentalist, comes along to evaluate these things. Though Partridge is a friend of many years and though we both care a great deal about conserving nature, I worry that his dyadic position is extremely narrow, a product of lingering Cartesian dualism, separating mind and matter, too long dominant in Western philosophy. Let's sort this out.

Certain kinds of valuing indisputably require humans, who are "subjects" in the philosophical sense, beings with subjective or experiential life. This is true with artifacts, like cars, which do not have a good of their own but only a good conferred on them by their owners, and even gardenias, if these are cultivated by florists. This is true with aesthetic experiences of nature, as of the beauty of autumn leaves. But is it true with all values in nature, for instance, in the genus *Gardenia* with its sixty wild species, evergreen shrubs in subtropical parts of China, Japan, and Africa? I will set aside astronomical and geomorphological nature, the moons of Jupiter, or rocks deep in Earth, or some lifeless canyon or river, and focus on our native range landscapes, where there is always some biotic community.

Here humans value, or evaluate, various things and events, such as whooping cranes or the hydrologic cycle; they take an interest in them. A value relationship comes into being where it did not exist before. Such valuing can be either anthropocentric (the hydrologic cycle as instrumental to our water supply) or anthropogenic, generated by humans but not centered on humans (a whooping crane valued by humans as good by itself,

This essay was written for this volume and appears here in print for the first time.

without our making any use of it). Such valuing also requires properties in nature that are objective (water recycles; the endangered cranes migrate annually); Partridge wants to be "hard" about these properties.

Are all values in nature of this kind? The answer I am defending is: No, some values are discovered, found "inherent" in nature (to use the term Partridge dislikes), and not generated in the interactive experiences of the conscious human subject. The general strategy of "Are values in nature subjective or objective?" is to lead the reader across a spectrum of values that, while remaining relational through much of the course of the argument, shifts toward less of the human contribution and more awareness of "properties" that are found in nature, until at length the reader is forced to ask whether these processes and their products might not be already valuable before humans are "in the picture."

Consider a whooping crane defending its own life, or the wild gardenias synthesizing glucose using photosynthesis, converting this to starch, and storing energy. The animals, sometimes, will be subjects of their own lives, and they too will have their preferences, simplified perhaps, but in some respects more or less like our own. So the humanistic account does have to be extended to sentient animals—and this will include the cranes. So far, Partridge will agree. But most animals (crustaceans, insects) have little or no subjective life, and all plants have only objective life, being devoid of nervous systems and felt experiences.

Such a living organism is, I maintain, a being with a good of its own. Something is of value in the biological though not the psychological sense. This claim Partridge finds extreme and incredible. "Is anybody there?" If the answer is no, if there is no conscious evaluator, no subject of experience, not even possibly, then all possibility of value lapses. When human subjects are not present, the subjectivists give a dispositional twist to value, Partridge's "hypothetical value." To say that n is valuable means that n is able to be valued, if and when a human valuer, H, comes along, but n has these properties whether or not a human arrives. Intrinsic and instrumental values in the realized sense emerge relationally with the appearance of the subject-generator.

But is nothing of any value to, or for, or in a plant? Plants, like all other organisms, are self-actualizing. A plant is not a subject, but neither is it an inanimate object, like a stone. Plants, quite alive, are unified entities of the botanical though not of the zoological kind—that is, they are not unitary organisms highly integrated with a centered neural control, but they are modular organisms with a meristem that can repeatedly and indefinitely produce new vegetative modules, additional stem nodes and leaves when there is available space and resources, as well as new reproductive modules, fruits, and seeds.

Plants make themselves; they repair injuries; they move water, nutrients, and photosynthate from cell to cell; they make tannin and other toxins and regulate their levels in defense against grazers; they make nectars and emit pheromones to influence the behavior of pollinating insects and the responses of other plants; they emit allelopathic agents to suppress invaders; they make thorns, trap insects. They can reject genetically incompatible grafts. Such capacities can be "vital," a description with values built into it.

Partridge protests: Nothing "matters" to a plant; a plant is without "minimally sentient awareness." But, though things do not matter *to* plants, a great deal matters *for* them. We ask, of a failing plant, what's the matter *with* that plant? If it is lacking sunshine and soil nutrients and we arrange for these, we say, "The tree is benefiting from them"; and *benefit* is—everywhere else we encounter it—a value word. Objectively, biologists regularly speak of the "survival value" of plant activities.

Consider, more fundamentally, the evolutionary ecosystems out of which we human valuers originated, along with myriads of other species, including those plants. Can we not view ecosystems or, more broadly, the planetary biospheric system as value-generating systems, and in a real sense value-able, able to generate value? In this connection, I use the word *projective* to move beyond *subjective* and *objective*, a wordplay intended to stimulate analysis. *Project* suggests some activity "thrown forward"; earthen nature is projective nature.[1] Nature generates the diverse marine and terrestrial environments; solar energy irradiated over matter produced, primevally, the chemical incubation of life. Over the millennia, there is natural selection for adapted fit; there appear the myriads of species filling up their habitats. There is extinction and respeciation. Forests repeatedly evolve, and so on. That is not subjective nature; but such nature is not mere object, not passive or inert until acted upon; it is "projective nature." This generativity is the most fundamental meaning of the term *nature*," to give birth." This self-organizing has been called *autopoiesis*, and there are excellent scientific analyses of this spontaneous generation of complex, living order.[2]

Partridge's mistake is to insist on the "necessity of a subjective evaluator" for all these values, "a sentient, and better still a personal, *evaluator*." I too insist on a subjective evaluator for some kinds of natural values, such as a person enjoying a sunset. But not for all kinds. "The sugar is not 'sweet' unless tasted," but the sugar is valuable to the plant whether or not we ever capture it for *our* tastes. I do hold that "'value' is [sometimes] an objective quality to be discovered in natural things" (what Partridge terms an O-M theory). I also hold that "something can be 'good for' a plant 'itself,' in its own right'" (what Partridge terms an O/O-D theory). I prefer here just to say that the plant values its own life intrinsically (or *inherently* for those who prefer that term) and makes instrumental use of the nutrients and the sunshine. (Even crystals can be harmed, and some of the earthen generativity that we value is prebiotic, but let's stay with biology for the present. That will suffice to get us out of Partridge's psychological fixation.)

Partridge insists that only sentient beings will count as evaluators or valuer bearers, and preferably those that are "reflective and self-conscious," his S/O-D theory. There must be somebody there. Value thus requires subjectivity to coagulate it in the world—the legacy of Cartesian dualism. But this confuses someone who evaluates and realizes that value is present whether or not value found to be present was previously there. In technical terms, this confuses the epistemology of value with the ontology of value. Those issues can sometimes overlap, with the kinds that do come into being as and when they are realized and known. But the two do not always overlap. Value may first be there ontologically and only later consciously, epistemologically evaluated.

In less technical terms, Partridge has a light-in-the-refrigerator theory. Nothing inside is of value until I open the door and the light comes on. Put a little differently, we humans carry the lamp that lights up value, although we require the fuel that nature provides. In Partridge's metaphor, humans have "the Midas touch";[3] nothing is worth anything until our touch turns it into gold. Actual value is an event in our consciousness, though natural items while still in the dark of value have potential intrinsic or instrumental value. Perhaps with refrigerators, what's inside is only of value because the person desires the food. Perhaps with gold, we humans have to light up a desire for it. But in nature a great deal is going on in the dark, outside of our evaluating consciousness.

Well, yes—the subjectivists may reluctantly admit—you have a point that, in a biological sense, there are functional values in nature, and natural selection is for survival value. But nevertheless the "scrupulous and rigorous philosopher will be unable to avoid the conclusion that 'permanently unperceived and unimagined nature' is valueless." The careful philosopher will put this kind of "value" in scare quotes. This is not really value at all, because there is no felt experience choosing from alternatives, no preferences being exercised, nobody there enjoying anything. Such so-called value is not of interest to philosophers because it is not a value with interest in itself. These are only "properties" in plants or in evolutionary ecosystems, not "values" located there.

But why is the organism not valuing what it is making resources of?—not consciously, but we do not want to presume that there is only conscious value or valuing. That is what we are debating, not assuming, and the scrupulous philosopher will insist on better analysis. The "no value without a valuer" account can seem persuasive, just as there are no thoughts without a thinker, no tickles without somebody there. The claim is indeed true of some kinds of value. But values are not always felt, unlike tickles; and values do not always have to be thought about. Insentient organisms are the *holders* of value, although not the *beholders* of value.

Partridge's account is too psychological, too personalist. Though his subjective evaluators are sufficient for value, a sentient valuer is not necessary for value, not in a more biological, ecological, evolutionary account. Another way is for there to be a life defended, in an individual and in a species line. Another way is for there to be a value-generating system able to generate values, such as the panorama of natural history. If you like, this introduces a revised meaning of valuer; any x is a valuer if x is value-able, able to produce or defend values.

Man is the measure of things, said Protagoras. "*Persons* become necessary *ingredients* of the nature to be valued," says Partridge, with emphasis. True, humans are the only evaluators who can reflect about what is going on on Earth and what they ought to do to conserve it. When humans do this, they must set up the scales; and in this sense humans are the measurers of things. Animals, organisms, species, and ecosystems cannot teach us how to do this evaluating. But the axiological judgments that we make do not always constitute the value, any more than the scientific scales we erect create what we thereby measure.

Humans are not so much lighting up value in a merely potentially valuable world as they are psychologically joining a planetary history, finding themselves "encompassed by" life ongoing. The valuing subject in an otherwise valueless world is an insufficient premise for the experienced conclusions of those who value such natural history. The "naive realism" is not in those environmental extremists who find values really there; it is in the humanists who think only persons are somebody enough to bring real values into the world.

Notes

1. "Projective nature" is also meant to contrast with those who take value to be a "projection" of humans onto nature, something that humans generate when they encounter an otherwise valueless nature, rather like Partridge's dyadic account.
2. Humberto R. Maturana and Francisco J. Varela, *Autopoiesis and Cognition: The Realization of the Living* (Dordrecht/Boston: Reidel, 1980); John Tyler Bonner, *The Evolution of Complexity by Means of Natural Selection* (Princeton, NJ: Princeton University Press, 1988); Stuart A. Kauffman, *The Origins of Order: Self-Organization and Selection in Evolution* (New York: Oxford University Press, 1993).
3. Perhaps not a happy metaphor, since the fable is about a person who tragically mislocates the sources of value.

Study Questions

1. Examine Rolston's arguments. Do you think they successfully defend the notion of objective or inherent value? Explain.
2. Consider Rolston's objections to Partridge. Compare their arguments. Who has made the better case?

14

Discovering a World of Values: A Response to Rolston

ERNEST PARTRIDGE

Ernest Partridge's biographical sketch is included in Reading 12.

Rarely have I felt more troubled while composing a paper than I felt while at work on "Values in Nature," for that analysis of the concept of "value" led me toward a conclusion that I dearly wished to avoid and away from positions that I cherished—positions defended and expounded by first-rate eco-philosophers such as Holmes Rolston.

And yet, how could I make any sense of a "value" without an "evaluator" that was in any significant sense different from a simple "property?" Try as I might, I could not. And so, what remained was a steadfast attempt to avoid the traps of anthropocentrism and subjectivism that seemed to be entailed by the "soft S/OD" to which my argument apparently led me. If I was to avoid those "traps," it would be by insisting that a sentient "evaluator" was not the *center* of evaluation but rather a necessary *ingredient* thereof ("hard S/OD"); in other words, that nature is indeed rich in valu-*able* things, properties, potentialities, and events ready to be discovered—all of great worth once an evaluator enters the picture, even if only hypothetically and in contemplation.

Rolston replies that this is not enough—that I remain trapped in my "extremely narrow" anthropocentrism and bewitched by Cartesian dualism. But is it not possible that our positions are in fact closer than he contends and that neither of us are "extremists"?[1] That will be my contention.

Just what is the nature of our difference? Is it factual, terminological, or in some sense deeply ontological/epistemological? Rolston sees a "deep" disagreement. I'm more inclined to see much if not most of our difference to be a matter of language and scarcely, if at all, factual.

That our differences are not factual can be recognized at once by my failure to find any dispute about the facts presented by Rolston. All that he reminds us about the properties of plants—that they "repair injuries; they move water, nutrients, and photosynthate from cell to cell" (etc.)—I grant. Similarly, I accept without qualification his description of the properties of animals and his eloquent account of evolution. How could I do otherwise and be scientifically informed?

Still more, I do not for a moment deny that "in nature a great deal is going on . . . outside of our evaluating

consciousness," and I fully endorse the naturalistic view that human life, culture, and consciousness have evolved out of, are contingent upon, and are in constant commerce with natural events and process—indeed that human life, culture, and consciousness *are* "natural processes." Thus, I find the accusation of "Cartesian dualism" to be extremely puzzling.

However, when, from my "non-Cartesian" naturalistic perspective, I encounter Rolston's description of life processes as "self-actualizing," I am put on my philosophical guard. While, in a loose, descriptive sense, I will accept that term of *self-actualizing*, I have some qualms about the Aristotelian baggage that the term carries with it. Instead, I accept the rather conventional "history of science" view that Aristotelian "final causes" (at least in the realm of natural objects and processes) proved to be much more a hindrance than an asset to scientific inquiry. The explanatory scheme, "things happen in nature because that's what they are supposed to do" has proven historically to be a thought stopper, and the development of modern science has amply demonstrated that we are well rid of it. The more modern Darwinian view, which I accept, is that variant individuals with traits conducive to self-repair and effective defense have thus survived to pass these traits on to their successors— and that these "self-actualizing vital processes" are therefore the result of prior conditions ("efficient causes") rather than a fundamental *"entelechy"* or "final cause." If it is the latter view that Rolston defends, then our differences are deep and ontological, and he posits a foundation for "objective value" that I find groundless.

Early in his rebuttal, Rolston elects to "set aside" examples of "astronomical and geomorphological nature . . . [or] some lifeless canyon or river. . ." I find this unfortunate, since these are paradigm cases for my argument. Is this "setting aside" a concession to my argument? While I would like to believe so, I will leave that for the reader to judge. For the rest, let us accept Rolston's ground rules and deal with putative "values" in the "biotic community."

That Rolston accepts at the very least an "object/object-dyadism" might be seen through a close examination of his example of the life of a tree. The "values for" that tree (note my "warning quotes") are conditions that conduce to the health and long life of the tree, including defense and repair mechanisms that will make that same tree inhospitable to invading fungi and beetles. All this is "good for" the tree but "bad for" the beetles. And if the beetles succeed in invading the tree, this is both "bad for" the tree and "good for" not only

This essay was written for this edition and appears here in print for the first time. Reprinted by permission of the author.

the beetles but also the woodpeckers, which will feast on them, and the squirrels, which will make good use of the woodpecker holes, and so on. To cite another arboreal example: *Fire* is a "disvalue for" shade-tolerant trees such as oaks and a "value for" cottonwoods and aspens. But all this is commonplace: Any good ecologist, such as Rolston, knows that in nature "you can not do just one thing," and, to state its axiological corollary, "in nature, there are no simple, unqualified 'goods' and 'bads.'" I would go further: The only "values" in the biotic community are "values-for" some organism and by implication "disvalues-for" some other. There are no detached, ownerless "values-as such." "Object-monadism" is thus rejected. (Recall that Rolston has chosen to "set aside" a consideration of abiotic nature.)

So, it seems to me that Rolston is committed to dyadism at the very least. What remains is the question of whether we have a substantive dispute regarding the alleged distinction between "subject/object" and "object/object" dyadism.

Rolston contends that there are "values-for" organisms without interests, such as plants and insects, though not for artifacts. Recall his argument:

> But, though things do not matter *to* plants, a great deal matters *for* them. We ask, of a failing plant, what's the matter *with* that plant? If it is lacking sunshine and soil nutrients and we arrange for these, we say, "The tree is benefiting from them; and *benefit* is—everywhere else we encounter it—a value word.

Unfortunately, this test of our linguistic sense accomplishes too much for Rolston, for don't we also say as much for artifacts: for example, "it is *good for* your car if you change the oil," or "it will benefit your car if you keep the ignition tuned up."

It seems, then, that "values talk" migrates from its home base of "values-to interested beings," to colonize discourse about insentient life, or even abiotic nature and lifeless artifacts. But does all this linguistic drift have much bearing on our essential question: Namely, "Is there a significant difference between "values for" sentient and contemplative beings (i.e., beings with *interests*) and "values for" insentient beings?" This difference is worth the attention of philosophers—whatever terms we might use to denote this difference.

I submit that there is. Quite simply, the former array of values *matter*—to identifiable beings with interests (which must exist, if anything is to "matter" at all). The latter set of "values," until they are (*contra*hypothesis) noticed or contemplated by sentient or reflective beings, matter not a bit to anyone or anything. It does not "matter" to a tree if it is struck down by lightning, though its vital processes end—in a manner well explicated by the science of botany. And it is of little if any concern to a beetle if it becomes woodpecker food. That these events are described as "bad for" the tree or beetle, while perfectly clear in their meaning, does nothing to erase the value distinction between, on the one hand, the rotting of a live tree on an undiscovered island, and, on the other hand, a fatal infection of a human being.

If Rolston wishes to describe the former as a "disvalue for" the tree, I am content with this—as his chosen usage of the word *value*. (Indeed, I'll say as much in my unguarded and casual conversation.) However, to retain this essential distinction, I would prefer to call such terminal circumstances in the lives of the hypothetical tree or beetle as "events" or a "set of properties" and confine the term *value* to contexts that include "evaluators." But whatever the exigencies of vocabulary, it is philosophically essential that this distinction, with the criteria of "interest" and "mattering," be maintained.

In sum, I remain convinced that the sort of "values" to which an ethicist should take special note require an *evaluator*—minimally *sentient*—but with regard to values of most concern to human beings, an evaluator that is reflective and rational. Though apparently anthropocentric and subjective, on closer inspection the "subject/object dyadism" that I defend is a generous conception that is less subjectivist, less anthropocentric, and more compatible with an "ecological point of view" than Rolston contends it to be. For while evaluators are necessary to evaluation, they are not sufficient.[2] As "ingredients" in the "evaluation transaction," evaluators do not *create* or *invent* values, they *discover* them—a point of emphatic agreement with Rolston. Our disagreement appears to be my contention that things unnoticed by and unaffecting of evaluators are, as such, without *actual* value, though they may be of great *potential* value—or of *hypothetical* value when contemplated.

In this sense, I argue, values are very much like such secondary qualities as colors, which are "in" things, are *discovered,* and yet do not exist except when perceived. (The sugar does *not* sit "sweetly" on the cupboard shelf.) Regrettably, this analogy of values with secondary qualities, crucial to my argument, is missing from Rolston's reply.

If values in nature are as I describe them, then they exist all around us, in (by definition) all the nature that we can ever encounter, think about, imagine, and cherish. What more value could we possibly need to totally involve our environmental concern, our commitment, and our love?

Notes

1. I hereby repent of the provocative opening sentence of my 1986 paper, with it's allusion to Barry Goldwater's generally forgotten 1964 acceptance speech (" . . . extremism in the defense of liberty is no sin . . ."). Perhaps my rhetorical enthusiasm got the better of me.

2. Yet note Rolston's remark: "Though [Partridge's] subjective evaluators are sufficient for value. . . ." Either he has misread my argument or I have presented it poorly. Let the reader decide.

BIOCENTRIC ETHICS

15

Reverence for Life

ALBERT SCHWEITZER

Albert Schweitzer (1875–1965) was born in Kaiserberg, Germany, and educated at Strasbourg in Alsace. He was an extraordinarily versatile genius: a concert organist, a musicologist, a New Testament scholar, a theologian, a missionary, a philosopher, and a physician who dedicated his life to the amelioration of suffering and the promotion of life. He built and served in a hospital in Lambarene in French Equatorial Africa (now Gabon). His most famous writings are The Quest for the Historical Jesus *(1906),* Out of My Life and Thought *(1933), and* Civilization and Ethics *(1923) from which the present selection is taken.*

Schweitzer describes his theory of Reverence for Life—the idea that all of life is sacred and that we must live accordingly, treating each living being as an inherently valuable "will-to-live."

Schweitzer relates how the phrase "Reverence for Life" came to him one day in 1915 while on a river journey to assist a missionary's sick wife.

> At sunset of the third day, near the village of Igendja, we moved along an island in the middle of the wide river. On a sandbank to our left, four hippopotamuses and their young plodded along in our same direction. Just then, in my great tiredness and discouragement, the phrase "Reverence for Life" struck me like a flash. As far as I knew, it was a phrase I had never heard nor ever read. l realized at once that it carried within itself the solution to the problem that had been torturing me. Now I knew a system of values which concerns itself only with our relationship to other people is incomplete and therefore lacking in power for good. Only by means of reverence for life can we establish a spiritual and humane relationship with both people and all living creatures within our reach. Only in this fashion can we avoid harming others, and, within the limits of our capacity, go to their aid whenever they need us.

The following passage is a fuller description of his views. He begins by citing the French philosopher René Descartes (1596–1650) and contrasting that theory of knowledge, which begins with an abstract, isolated self, with the deeper self-awareness that comes from our understanding that all living things ("will-to-lives") are sacred and interdependent.

Reprinted from *Civilization and Ethics*, trans. A. Naish (London: Black, 1923).

Descartes tells us that philosophizing is based on the judgment: "I think therefore I am." From this meagre and arbitrarily selected beginning it is inevitable that it should wander into the path of the abstract. It does not find the entrance to the ethical realm, and remains held fast in a dead view of the world and of life. True philosophy must commence with the most immediate and comprehensive facts of consciousness. And this may be formulated as follows: "I am life which wills to live, and I exist in the midst of life which wills to live." This is no mere excogitated subtlety. Day after day and hour after hour I proceed on my way invested in it. In every moment of reflection it forces itself on me anew. A living world- and life-view, informing all the facts of life, gushes forth from it continually, as from an eternal spring. A mystically ethical oneness with existence grows forth from it unceasingly.

Just as in my own will-to-live there is a yearning for more life, and for that mysterious exaltation of the will-to-live which is called pleasure, and terror in face of annihilation and that injury to the will-to-live which is called pain; so the same obtains in all the will-to-live around me, equally whether it can express itself to my comprehension or whether it remains unvoiced.

Ethics thus consists in this, that I experience the necessity of practising the same reverence for life toward all will-to-live, as toward my own. Therein I have already the needed fundamental principle of morality. It is *good* to maintain and cherish life; it is *evil* to destroy and to check life.

As a matter of fact, everything which in the usual ethical valuation of inter-human relations is looked upon as good can be traced back to the material and spiritual maintenance or enhancement of human life and to the effort to raise it to its highest level of value. And contrariwise everything in human relations which is considered as evil, is in the final analysis found to be material or spiritual destruction or checking of human life and slackening of the effort to raise it to its highest value. Individual concepts of good and evil which are widely divergent and apparently unconnected fit into one another like pieces which belong together, the moment they are comprehended and their essential nature is grasped in this general notion.

The fundamental principle of morality which we seek as a necessity for thought is not, however, a matter only of arranging and deepening current views of good and evil, but also of expanding and extending these. A man is really ethical only when he obeys the constraint laid on him to help all life which he is able to succour, and when he goes out of his way to avoid injuring anything living. He does not ask how far this or that life deserves sympathy as valuable in itself, nor how far it is capable of feeling. To him life as such is sacred. He shatters no ice crystal that sparkles in the sun, tears no leaf from its tree, breaks off no flower, and is careful not to crush any insect as he walks. If he works by lamplight on a summer evening, he prefers to keep the window shut and to breathe stifling air, rather than to see insect after insect fall on his table with singed and sinking wings.

If he goes out into the street after a rainstorm and sees a worm which has strayed there, he reflects that it will certainly dry up in the sunshine, if it does not quickly regain the damp soil into which it can creep, and so he helps it back from the deadly paving stones into the lush grass. Should he pass by an insect which has fallen into a pool, he spares the time to reach it a leaf or stalk on which it may clamber and save itself.

He is not afraid of being laughed at as sentimental. It is indeed the fate of every truth to be an object of ridicule when it is first acclaimed. It was once considered foolish to suppose that coloured men were really human beings and ought to be treated as such. What was once foolishness has now become a recognized truth. Today it is considered as exaggeration to proclaim constant respect for every form of life as being the serious demand of a rational ethic. But the time is coming when people will be amazed that the human race was so long before it recognized that thoughtless injury to life is incompatible with real ethics. Ethics is in its unqualified form extended responsibility with regard to everything that has life.

The general idea of ethics as a partaking of the mental atmosphere of reverence for life is not perhaps attractive. But it is the only complete notion possible. Mere sympathy is too narrow a concept to serve as the intellectual expression of the ethical element. It denotes, indeed, only a sharing of the suffering of the will-to-live. But to be ethical is to share the whole experience of all the circumstances and aspirations of the will-to-live, to live with it in its pleasures, in its yearnings, in its struggles toward perfection.

Love is a more inclusive term, since it signifies fellowship in suffering, in joy, and in effort. But it describes the ethical element only as it were by a simile, however natural and profound that simile may be. It places the solidarity created by ethics in analogy to that which nature has caused to come into being in a more or less superficial physical manner, and with a view to the fulfillment of their destiny, between two sexually attracted existences, or between these and their offspring.

Thought must strive to find a formula for the essential nature of the ethical. In so doing it is led to characterize ethics as self-devotion for the sake of life, motived by reverence for life. Although the phrase "reverence for life" may perhaps sound a trifle unreal, yet that which it denotes is something which never lets go its hold of the man in whose thought it has once found a place. Sympathy, love, and, in general, all enthusiastic feeling of real value are summed up in it. It works with restless vitality on the mental nature in which it has found a footing and flings this into the restless activity of a responsibility which never ceases and stops nowhere. Reverence for life drives a man on as the whirling thrashing screw forces a ship through the water.

The ethic of reverence for life, arising as it does out of an inward necessity, is not dependent on the question as to how far or how little it is capable of development into a satisfactory view of life. It does not need to prove that the action of ethical men, as directed to maintaining, enhancing and exalting life, has any significance for the total course of the world-process. Nor is it disturbed by the consideration that the preservation and enhancement of life which it practises are of almost no account at all beside the mighty destruction of life which takes place every moment as the result of natural forces. Determined as it is to act, it is yet able to ignore all the problems raised as to the result of its action. The fact that in the man who has become ethical a will informed by reverence for life and self-sacrifice for the sake of life exists in the world, is itself significant for the world.

The universal will-to-live experiences itself in my personal will-to-live otherwise than it does in other phenomena. For here it enters on an individualization, which, so far as I am able to gather in trying to view it from the outside, struggles only to live itself out, and not at all to become one with will-to-live external to itself. The world is indeed the grisly drama of will-to-live at variance with itself. One existence survives at the expense of another of which it yet knows nothing. But in me the will-to-live has become cognizant of the existence of other will-to-live. There is in it a yearning for unity with itself, a longing to become universal.

Why is it that the will-to-live has this experience only in myself? Is it a result of my having become capable of reflection about the totality of existence? Whither will the evolution lead which has thus begun in me?

There is no answer to these questions. It remains a painful enigma how I am to live by the rule of reverence for life in a world ruled by creative will which is at the same time destructive will, and by destructive will which is also creative.

I can do no other than hold on to the fact that the will-to-live appears in me as will-to-live which aims at becoming one with other will-to-live. This fact is the light which shines for me in the darkness. My ignorance regarding the real nature of the objective world no longer troubles me. I am set free from the world. I have been cast by my reverence for life into a state of unrest foreign to the world. By this, too, I am placed in a state of beatitude which the world cannot give. If in the happiness induced by our independence of the world I and another afford each other mutual help in understanding and in forgiveness, when otherwise will would harass other will, then the will-to-live is no longer at variance with itself. If I rescue an insect from a pool of water, then life has given itself for life, and again the self-contradiction of the will-to-live has been removed. Whenever my life has given itself out in any way for other life, my eternal will-to-live experiences union with the eternal, since all life is one. I possess a cordial which secures me from dying of thirst in the desert of life.

Therefore I recognize it as the destiny of my existence to be obedient to the higher revelation of the will-to-live which I find in myself. I choose as my activity the removal of the self-contradiction of the will-to-live, as far as the influence of my own existence extends. Knowing as I do the one thing needful, I am content to offer no opinion about the enigma of the objective world and my own being.

Thought becomes religious when it thinks itself out to the end. The ethic of reverence for life is the ethic of Jesus brought to philosophical expression, extended into cosmical form, and conceived as intellectually necessary.

The surmising and longing of all deeply religious personalities is comprehended and contained in the ethic of reverence for life. This, however, does not build up a world-view as a completed system, but resigns itself to leave the cathedral perforce incomplete. It is only able to finish the choir. Yet in this true piety celebrates a living and continuous divine service. . . .

The ethic of reverence for life also proves its own truth by the way in which it comprehends and includes the most various forms of the ethical impulse. No ethical system has yet proved capable of presenting the effort to attain self-perfection, in which man works on his own being without any action directed externally, on the one hand, and the activist ethic on the other hand, in connection and interrelation. The ethic of reverence for life accomplishes this, and in such a way that it does not merely solve an academic problem, but brings with it a real deepening of ethical insight.

Ethics is in fact reverence for the will-to-live both within and without my own personality. The immediate product of reverence for the will-to-live which I find in myself is the profound life-affirmation of resignation. I comprehend my will-to-live not only as something which lives itself out in fortunate moments of success, but also as something which is conscious of itself and its own experiences. If I do not allow this experiencing of myself to be dissipated by heedless lack of reflection, but, on the contrary, deliberately pause in it as one who feels its real value, I am rewarded by a disclosure of the secret of spiritual independence. I become a partaker in an unguessed-at freedom amid the destinies of life. At moments when I should otherwise have thought myself to be overwhelmed and crushed, I feel myself uplifted in

a state of inexpressible joy, astounding to myself, in which I am conscious of freedom from the world and experience a clarifying of my whole view of life. Resignation is the vestibule through which we pass in entering the palace of ethics. Only he who experiences inner freedom from external events in profound surrender to his own will-to-live is capable of the profound and permanent surrender of himself for the sake of other life.

As I struggle for freedom from the external occurrences of life in reverence for my own will-to-live, so also do I wrestle for freedom from myself. I practise the higher independence not only with regard to that which happens to me personally, but also in respect to the way in which I behave towards the world.

As the result of reverence for my own existence I force myself to be sincere with myself. Anything that I acquire by acting contrary to my convictions is bought too dearly. I am afraid of wounding my will-to-live with poisoned spears by disloyalty to my own personality.

That Kant places sincerity toward oneself in the very centre of his ethical system is a witness to the profundity of his own ethical perception. But he is unable to grasp the connection between self-sincerity and activist ethics because in his search for the essential nature of the ethical he never gets as far as the idea of reverence for life.

In actual practice the ethic of self-sincerity passes over unconsciously into that of self-sacrifice for others. Sincerity toward myself forces me to acts which appear so much like self-sacrifice that the current ethic derives them from this latter impulse.

Why do I forgive my fellow-man? The current ethic says that it is because I sympathize with him. It presents men as impossibly good when they forgive, and allows them to practise a kind of forgiveness which is really humiliating to the person forgiven. Thus it turns forgiveness into a sort of sweetened triumph of self-sacrifice.

The ethic of reverence for life clears away these obscure and misty notions. All forebearance and forgiveness is for it an act to which it is compelled by sincerity towards itself. I am obliged to exercise unlimited forgiveness because, if I did not forgive, I should be untrue to myself, in that I should thus act as if I were not guilty in the same way as the other has been guilty with regard to me. I must forgive the lies directed against myself, because my own life has been so many times blotted by lies; I must forgive the lovelessness, the hatred, the slander, the fraud, the arrogance which I encounter, since I myself have so often lacked love, hated, slandered, defrauded, and been arrogant. I must forgive without noise or fuss. In general I do not forgive, I do not even get as far as being merely just. And this also is no exaggeration, but a necessary extension and refinement of our usual ethic.

We have to conduct the fight against the evil element

which exists in man, not by judging others, but only by judging ourselves. The conflict with our own nature, and sincerity towards ourselves, are the instruments with which we work on others. We move silently into the midst of the struggle for that profound spiritual independence which grows from reverence for our own life. True power makes no noise. It is there, and it produces its effect. True ethic begins where the use of words stops.

The most essential element of activist ethics, even if it does appear as surrender, is thus a product of the impulse to sincerity towards oneself, and in that is contained its real value. The whole ethic of independence from the world only runs as a clear stream when it issues from this source. I am not gentle, peaceable, patient and friendly from a kindly disposition towards others, but because I thus secure the most profound independence. There is an indissoluble connection between the reverence for life with which I face my own existence, and that in which I relate myself to others in acts of self sacrifice.

It is because the current ethic possesses no fundamental principle of morality that it plunges immediately into the discussion of various conflicting opinions in the ethical realm. The ethic of reverence for life is in no hurry to do this. It takes its own time to think out its fundamental moral principle on all sites. Then, complete in itself, it takes up its own position with regard to these conflicts.

Ethics has to come to an understanding with three opponents; with lack of thought, with egoistic independence, and with the community.

Of the first of these, ethics has not usually taken sufficient account, because it never comes to any open conflict between the two. But, unnoticed, this opponent is constantly on the offensive.

Ethics can take possession of an extensive tract without encountering the troops of egoism. A man can do a great deal of good without being obliged to sacrifice his own interests or desires. Even if he does lose a little bit of his own life in so doing, it is such an insignificant fragment that he misses it no more than he would a single hair or a tiny scale of skin.

To a very large extent the attainment of inner freedom from the world, loyalty to one's own being, existence in distinction from the world, even self-sacrifice for the sake of other life, is only a matter of concentrating attention on this relation. We miss so much of it because we do not keep steadfastly to the point. We do not place ourselves directly under the pressure of the inner impulse to ethical existence. Steam spurts out in all directions from a leaky boiler. The losses of energy on every site are so great in the current ethic because it has at its command no single fundamental moral principle which can act on its thought. It cannot make its boiler steam-tight, nay, it does not even thoroughly inspect it. But reverence for life, which is always present to

thought, informs and penetrates, continually and in every direction, a man's observation, reflection and decisions. He can as little resist this process as water can hinder the dyestuff dropped into it from tinting it. The struggle with lack of thought is a conscious process and is always going on.

How does the ethic of reverence for life stand in the conflicts which arise between the inner impulse to self-sacrifice and necessary self-maintenance?

I also am subject to the variance with itself of the will-to-live. My existence is in conflict at a thousand points with that of others. The necessity is laid upon me of destroying and injuring life. If I walk along a lonely road my foot brings annihilation and pain on the tiny beings which people it. In order to maintain my own existence I am obliged to protect it from the existences which would harm it. I become a persecutor of the little mouse which inhabits my dwelling, a destroyer of the insect which desires to breed there, no less than a wholesale murderer of the bacteria which may endanger my life. I can only secure nourishment for myself by destroying animals and plants. My own good fortune is built on the injuries and hardships of my fellow-men.

How is ethics to exist at all amid the gruesome necessities to which I am a slave because the will-to-live is at variance with itself?

The current ethic seeks for a compromise. It tries to lay down rules as to how much of my own existence and of my own happiness I must give up, and how much I may continue to hold at the expense of the existence and happiness of other life. In so deciding it creates an experimental and relative ethic. That which is actually not ethical at all, but is a hotch-potch of non-ethical necessity and of real ethics, gives itself out as genuinely ethical and normative. Thus a monstrous confusion arises, and thereby a constantly increasing obscuration of the notion of the ethical element.

The ethic of reverence for life recognizes no such thing as a relative ethic. The maintenance and enhancement of life are the only things it counts as being good in themselves. All destruction of and injury to life, from whatever circumstances they may result, are reckoned by it as evil. It does not give place to ready-made accommodations of ethics and necessity which are too eager to occupy the ground. The absolute ethic of reverence makes its own agreements with the individual from moment to moment, agreements always fresh and always original and basic. It does not relieve him of the conflict, but rather forces him to decide for himself in each case how far he can remain ethical and how far he must submit himself to the necessity of destroying and harming life and thus become guilty. Man does not make ethical progress by assimilating instruction with regard to accommodations between the ethical and the necessary, but only by hearing ever more clearly the voice of the ethical element, by being ever more under the control of his own yearning to maintain and to enhance life, and by becoming ever more obstinate in his opposition to the necessity of destroying and injuring life.

In ethical conflicts it is only subjective decisions that a man has to face. No one else can determine for him where lies the utmost limit of the possibility of continuing to maintain and cherish life. He alone has to judge by allowing himself to be led by a sense of responsibility for other lives raised to the highest degree possible. We must never let this sense become dulled and blunted. In effect, however, we are doing so, if we are content to find the conflicts becoming continually more insoluble. The good conscience is an invention of the devil.

What does reverence for life teach us about the relations of man and the non-human animals?

Whenever I injure life of any kind I must be quite clear as to whether this is necessary or not. I ought never to pass the limits of the unavoidable, even in apparently insignificant cases. The countryman who has mowed down a thousand blossoms in his meadow as fodder for his cows should take care that on the way home he does not, in wanton pastime, switch off the head of a single flower growing on the edge of the road, for in so doing he injures life without being forced to do so by necessity.

Those who test operations or drugs on animals, or who inoculate them with diseases so that they may be able to help human beings by means of the results thus obtained, ought never to rest satisfied with the general idea that their dreadful doings are performed in pursuit of a worthy aim. It is their duty to ponder in every separate case whether it is really and truly necessary thus to sacrifice an animal for humanity. They ought to be filled with anxious care to alleviate as much as possible the pain which they cause. How many outrages are committed in this way in scientific institutions where narcotics are often omitted to save time and trouble! How many also when animals are made to suffer agonizing tortures, only in order to demonstrate to students scientific truths which are perfectly well known. The very fact that the animal, as a victim of research, has in his pain rendered such services to suffering men, has itself created a new and unique relation of solidarity between him and ourselves. The result is that a fresh obligation is laid on each of us to do as much good as we possibly can to all creatures in all sorts of circumstances. When I help an insect out of his troubles all that I do is to attempt to remove some of the guilt contracted through these crimes against animals.

Wherever any animal is forced into the service of man, the sufferings which it has to bear on that account are the concern of every one of us. No one ought to permit, in so far as he can prevent it, pain or suffering for which he will not take the responsibility. No one ought to rest at ease in the thought that in so doing he would mix himself up in affairs which are not his business. Let no one shirk the burden of his responsibility. When there is so much maltreatment of animals, when the cries of thirsting creatures go up unnoticed from the railway trucks, when there is so much roughness in our slaughterhouses, when in our kitchens so many animals suffer horrible deaths from unskillful hands, when animals endure unheard-of-agonies from heartless men, or are delivered to the dreadful play of children, then we are all guilty and must bear the blame.

We are afraid of shocking or offending by showing too plainly how deeply we are moved by the sufferings which man causes to the non-human creatures. We tend to reflect that others are more "rational" than we are, and would consider that which so disturbs us as customary and as a matter of course. And then, suddenly, they let fall some expression which shows us that they, too, are not really satisfied with the situation. Strangers to us hitherto, they are now quite near our own position. The masks, in which we had each concealed ourselves from the other, fall off. We now know that neither of us can cut ourselves free from the horrible necessity which plays ceaselessly around us. What a wonderful thing it is thus to get to know each other!

The ethic of reverence for life forbids any of us to deduce from the silence of our contemporaries that they, or in their case we, have ceased to feel what as thinking men we all cannot but feel. It prompts us to keep a mutual watch in this atmosphere of suffering and endurance, and to speak and act without panic according to the responsibility which we feel. It inspires us to join in a search for opportunities to afford help of some kind or other to the animals, to make up for the great amount of misery which they endure at our hands, and thus to escape for a moment from the inconceivable horrors of existence.

But the ethic of reverence for life also places us in a position of fearful responsibility with regard to our relations to other men.

We find, again, that it offers us no teaching about the bounds of legitimate self-maintenance; it calls us again to come to a separate understanding with the ethic of self-sacrifice in each individual case. According to the sense of responsibility which is my personal experience so I must decide what part of my life, my possessions, my rights, my happiness, my time or my rest, I ought to give up, and what part I ought to keep back.

Regarding the question of property, the ethic of reverence for life is outspokenly individualist in the sense that goods earned or inherited are to be placed at the disposition of the community, not according to any standards whatever laid down by society, but according to the absolutely free decision of the individual. It places all its hopes on the enhancement of the feeling of responsibility in man. It defines possessions as the property of the community, of which the individual is sovereign steward. One serves society by conducting a business from which a certain number of employees draw their means of sustenance; another, by giving away his property in order to help his fellow-men. Each one will decide on his own course somewhere between these two extreme cases according to the sense of responsibility which is determined for him by the particular circumstances of his own life. No one is to judge others. It is a question of individual responsibility; each is to value his possessions as instruments with which he is to work. It makes no difference whether the work is done by keeping and increasing, or by giving up, the property. Possessions must belong to the community in the most various ways, if they are to be used to the best advantage in its service.

Those who have very little that they can call their own are in most danger of becoming purely egoistic. A deep truth lies in the parable of Jesus, which makes the servant who had received the least the least faithful of all.

The ethic of reverence for life does not even allow me to possess my own rights absolutely. It does not allow me to rest in the thought that I, as the more capable, advance at the expense of the less capable. It presents to me as a problem what human law and opinion allow as a matter of course. It prompts me to think of others and to ponder whether I can really allow myself the intrinsic right of plucking all the fruits which my hand is physically able to reach. And then it may occur that following my regard for the existence of others, I do what

appears as foolishness to the generality of men. It may, indeed, prove itself to have been actually foolishness so far as my renunciation for the sake of others has really no useful effect. Yet all the same I was right in doing as I did. Reverence for life is the supreme motive. That which it commands has its own meaning, even if it seem foolish or useless. Indeed, we all really seek in one another for that sort of foolishness which shows that we are impelled by the higher responsibility. It is only as we become less rational in the ordinary sense of the word that the ethical disposition works out in us and solves problems previously insoluble.

Study Questions

1. What is Schweitzer's theory of reverence for life? Does it value life itself or a special feature of life?
2. Is Schweitzer an egalitarian? Are all forms of life of equal worth?
3. What does Schweitzer mean in the second paragraph of this selection where he says that the "mysterious exaltation of the will-to-live" is "called pleasure" and "injury to the will-to-live" "pain"? Is this a form of hedonism?
4. Compare Schweitzer's position with Taylor's essay, which follows, as well as with the Hindu and Buddhist views in Readings 37 and 38.

16

Biocentric Egalitarianism

PAUL TAYLOR

Paul Taylor is professor of philosophy at Brooklyn College, City University of New York, and the author of several works in ethics, including Respect for Nature *(1986), in which the ideas in the following essay are developed.*

Taylor develops Schweitzer's life-centered system of environmental ethics. He argues that each living individual has a "teleological center of life," which pursues its own good in its own way, and possesses equal inherent worth. Human beings are no more intrinsically valuable than any other living thing but should see themselves as equal members of Earth's community.

Reprinted from *Environmental Ethics*, Vol. 3 (Fall 1981) by permission.

I. HUMAN-CENTERED AND LIFE-CENTERED SYSTEMS OF ENVIRONMENTAL ETHICS

In this paper I show how the taking of a certain ultimate moral attitude toward nature, which I call "respect for nature," has a central place in the foundations of a life-centered system of environmental ethics. I hold that a set of moral norms (both standards of character and rules of conduct) governing human treatment of the natural world is a rationally grounded set if and only if, first, commitment to those norms is a practical entailment of adopting the attitude of respect for nature as an ultimate moral attitude, and second, the adopting of that attitude on the part of all rational agents can itself be justified. When the basic characteristics of the attitude of respect for nature are made clear, it will be seen that a life-centered system of environmental ethics need not be holistic or organicist in its conception of the kinds of entities that are deemed the appropriate objects of moral concern and consideration. Nor does such a system require that the concepts of ecological homeostasis, equilibrium, and integrity provide us with normative principles from which could be derived (with the addition of factual knowledge) our obligations with regard to natural ecosystems. The "balance of nature" is not itself a moral norm, however important may be the role it plays in our general outlook on the natural world that underlies the attitude of respect for nature. I argue that finally it is the good (well-being, welfare) of individual organisms, considered as entities having inherent worth, that determines our moral relations with the Earth's wild communities of life.

In designating the theory to be set forth as life-centered, I intend to contrast it with all anthropocentric views. According to the latter, human actions affecting the natural environment and its nonhuman inhabitants are right (or wrong) by either of two criteria: they have consequences which are favorable (or unfavorable) to human well-being, or they are consistent (or inconsistent) with the system of norms that protect and implement human rights. From this human-centered standpoint it is to humans and only to humans that all duties are ultimately owed. We may have responsibilities *with regard* to the natural ecosystems and biotic communities of our planet, but these responsibilities are in every case based on the contingent fact that our treatment of those ecosystems and communities of life can further the realization of human values and/or human rights. We have no obligation to promote or protect the good of nonhuman living things, independently of this contingent fact.

A life-centered system of environmental ethics is opposed to human-centered ones precisely on this point. From the perspective of a life-centered theory, we have prima facie moral obligations that are owed to wild plants and animals themselves as members of the Earth's biotic community. We are morally bound (other things being equal) to protect or promote their good for *their* sake. Our duties to respect the integrity of natural ecosystems, to preserve endangered species, and to avoid environmental pollution stem from the fact that these are ways in which we can help make it possible for wild species populations to achieve and maintain a healthy existence in a natural state. Such obligations are due those living things out of recognition of their inherent worth. They are entirely additional to and independent of the obligations we owe to our fellow humans. Although many of the actions that fulfill one set of obligations will also fulfill the other, two different grounds of obligation are involved. Their well-being, as well as human well-being, is something to be realized *as an end in itself*.

If we were to accept a life-centered theory of environmental ethics, a profound reordering of our moral universe would take place. We would begin to look at the whole of the Earth's biosphere in a new light. Our duties with respect to the "world" of nature would be seen as making prima facie claims upon us to be balanced against our duties with respect to the "world" of human civilization. We could no longer simply take the human point of view and consider the effects of our actions exclusively from the perspective of our own good.

II. THE GOOD OF A BEING AND THE CONCEPT OF INHERENT WORTH

What would justify acceptance of a life-centered system of ethical principles? In order to answer this it is first necessary to make clear the fundamental moral attitude that underlies and makes intelligible the commitment to live by such a system. It is then necessary to examine the considerations that would justify any rational agent's adopting that moral attitude.

Two concepts are essential to the taking of a moral attitude of the sort in question. A being which does not "have" these concepts, that is, which is unable to grasp their meaning and conditions of applicability, cannot be said to have the attitude as part of its moral outlook. These concepts are, first, that of the good (well-being, welfare) of a living thing, and second, the idea of an entity possessing inherent worth. I examine each concept in turn.

1. Every organism, species population, and community of life has a good of its own which moral agents can intentionally further or damage by their actions. To say that an entity has a good of its own is simply to say that, without reference to any *other* entity, it can be benefited or harmed. One can act in its overall interest or contrary to its overall interest, and environmental conditions can be good for it (advantageous to it) or bad for it (disadvantageous to it). What is good for an entity is what "does it good" in the sense of enhancing or preserving its life and well-being. What is bad for an entity is something that is detrimental to its life and well-being.[1]

We can think of the good of an individual nonhuman organism as consisting in the full development of its biological powers. Its good is realized to the extent that it is strong and healthy. It possesses whatever capacities it needs for successfully coping with its environment and so preserving its existence throughout the various stages of the normal life cycle of its species. The good of a population or community of such individuals consists in the population or community maintaining itself from generation to generation as a coherent system of genetically and ecologically related organisms whose average good is at an optimum level for the given environment. Mere *average good* means that the degree of realization of the good of *individual organisms* in the population or community is, on average, greater than would be the case under any other ecologically functioning order of interrelations among those species populations in the given ecosystem.)

The idea of a being having a good of its own, as I understand it, does not entail that the being must have interests or take an interest in what affects its life for better or for worse. We can act in a being's interest or contrary to its interest without its being interested in what we are doing to it in the sense of wanting or not wanting us to do it. It may, indeed, be wholly unaware that favorable and unfavorable events are taking place in its life. I take it that trees, for example, have no knowledge or desires or feelings. Yet it is undoubtedly the case that trees can be harmed or benefited by our actions. We can crush their roots by running a bulldozer too close to them. We can see to it that they get adequate nourishment and moisture by fertilizing and watering the soil around them. Thus we can help or hinder them in the realization of their good. It is the good of trees themselves that is thereby affected. We can similarly act so as to further the good of an entire tree population of a certain species (say, all the redwood trees in a California valley) or the good of a whole community of plant life in a given wilderness area, just as we can do harm to such a population or community.

When construed in this way, the concept of a being's good is not coextensive with sentience or the capacity for feeling pain. William Frankena has argued for a general theory of environmental ethics in which the ground of a creature's being worthy of moral consideration is its sentience. I have offered some criticisms of this view elsewhere, but the full refutation of such a position, it seems to me, finally depends on the positive reasons for accepting a life-centered theory of the kind I am defending in this essay.[2]

It should be noted further that I am leaving open the question of whether machines—in particular, those which are not only goal-directed, but also self-regulating—can properly be said to have a good of their own.[3] Since l am concerned only with human treatment of wild organisms, species populations, and communities of life as they occur in our planet's natural ecosystems, it is to those entities alone that the concept "having a good of its own" will here be applied. I am not denying that other living things, whose genetic origin and environmental conditions have been produced, controlled, and manipulated by humans for human ends, do have a good of their own in the same sense as do wild plants and animals. It is not my purpose in this essay, however, to set out or defend the principles that should guide our conduct with regard to their good. It is only insofar as their production and use by humans have good or ill effects upon natural ecosystems and their wild inhabitants that the ethics of respect for nature comes into play.

2. The second concept essential to the moral attitude of respect for nature is the idea of inherent worth. We take that attitude toward wild living things (individuals, species populations, or whole biotic communities) when and only when we regard them as entities possessing inherent worth. Indeed, it is only because they are conceived in this way that moral agents can think of themselves as having validly binding duties, obligations, and responsibilities that are *owed* to them as their *due*. I am not at this juncture arguing why they *should* be so regarded; I consider it at length below. But so regarding them is a presupposition of our taking the attitude of respect toward them and accordingly understanding ourselves as bearing certain moral relations to them. This can be shown as follows:

What does it mean to regard an entity that has a good of its own as possessing inherent worth? Two general principles are involved: the principle of moral consideration and the principle of intrinsic value.

According to the principle of moral consideration, wild living things are deserving of the concern and consideration of all moral agents simply in virtue of their being members of the Earth's community of life. From the moral point of view their good must be taken into account whenever it is affected for better or worse by the conduct of rational agents. This holds no matter what species the creature belongs to. The good of each is to be accorded some value and so acknowledged as having some weight in the deliberations of all rational agents. Of course, it may be necessary for such agents to act in ways contrary to the good of this or that particular organism or group of organisms in order to further the good of others, including the good of humans. But the principle of moral consideration prescribes that, with respect to each being an entity having its own good, every individual is deserving of consideration.

The principle of intrinsic value states that, regardless of what kind of entity it is in other respects, if it is a member of the Earth's community of life, the realization of its good is something *intrinsically* valuable. This means that its good is prima facie worthy of being preserved or promoted as an end in itself and for the sake of the entity whose good it is. Insofar as we regard any organism, species population, or life community as an entity having inherent worth, we believe that it must never be treated as if it were a mere object or thing whose entire value lies in being instrumental to the good of some other entity. The well-being of each is judged to have value in and of itself.

Combining these two principles, we can now define what it means for a living thing or group of living things to possess inherent worth. To say that it possesses inherent worth is to say that its good is deserving of the concern and consideration of all moral agents, and that the realization of its good has intrinsic value, to be pursued as an end in itself and for the sake of the entity whose good it is.

The duties owed to wild organisms, species populations, and communities of life in the Earth's natural ecosystems are grounded on their inherent worth. When rational, autonomous agents regard such entities as possessing inherent worth, they place intrinsic value on the realization of their good and so hold themselves responsible for performing actions that will have this effect and for refraining from actions having the contrary effect.

III. THE ATTITUDE OF RESPECT FOR NATURE

Why should moral agents regard wild living things in the natural world as possessing inherent worth? To answer this question we must first take into account the fact that, when rational, autonomous agents subscribe to the principles of moral consideration and intrinsic value and so conceive of wild living things as having that kind of worth, such agents are *adopting a certain ultimate moral attitude toward the natural world.* This is the attitude I call "respect for nature." It parallels the attitude of respect for persons in human ethics. When we adopt the attitude of respect for persons as the proper (fitting, appropriate) attitude to take toward all persons as persons, we consider the fulfillment of the basic interests of each individual to have intrinsic value. We thereby make a moral commitment to live a certain kind of life in relation to other persons. We place ourselves under the direction of a system of standards and rules that we consider validly binding on all moral agents as such.[4]

Similarly, when we adopt the attitude of respect for nature as an ultimate moral attitude we make a commitment to live by certain normative principles. These principles constitute the rules of conduct and standards of character that are to govern our treatment of the natural world. This is, first, an *ultimate* commitment because it is not derived from any higher norm. The attitude of respect for nature is not grounded on some other, more general, or more fundamental attitude. It sets the total framework for our responsibilities toward the natural world. It can be justified, as I show below, but its justification cannot consist in referring to a more general attitude or a more basic normative principle.

Second, the commitment is a *moral* one because it is understood to be a disinterested matter of principle. It is this feature that distinguishes the attitude of respect for nature from the set of feelings and dispositions that comprise the love of nature. The latter stems from one's personal interest in and response to the natural world. Like the affectionate feelings we have toward certain individual human beings, one's love of nature is nothing more than the particular way one feels about the natural environment and its wild inhabitants. And just as our love for an individual person differs from our respect for all persons as such (whether we happen to love them or not), so love of nature differs from respect for nature. Respect for nature is an attitude we believe all moral agents ought to have simply as moral agents, regardless of whether or not they also love nature. Indeed, we have not truly taken the attitude of respect for nature ourselves unless we believe this. To put it in a Kantian way, to adopt the attitude of respect for nature is to take a stance that one wills it to be a universal law for all rational beings. It is to hold that stance categorically, as being validly applicable to every moral agent without exception, irrespective of whatever personal feelings toward nature such an agent might have or might lack.

Although the attitude of respect for nature is in this sense a disinterested and universalizable attitude, anyone who does adopt it has certain steady, more or less permanent dispositions. These dispositions, which are themselves to be considered disinterested and universalizable, comprise three interlocking sets: dispositions to seek certain ends, dispositions to carry on one's practical reasoning and deliberation in a certain way, and dispositions to have certain feelings. We may accordingly analyze the attitude of respect for nature into the following components. (a) The disposition to aim at, and to take steps to bring about, as final and disinterested ends, the promoting and protecting of the good of organisms, species populations, and life communities in natural ecosystems. (These ends are "final" in not being pursued as means to further ends. They are "disinterested" in being independent of the self-interest of the agent.) (b) The disposition to consider actions that tend to realize those ends to be prima facie obligatory *because* they have that tendency. (c) The disposition to experience positive and negative feelings toward states of affairs in the world *because* they are favorable or unfavorable to the good of organisms, species populations, and life communities in natural ecosystems.

The logical connection between the attitude of respect for nature and the duties of a life-centered system of environmental ethics can now be made clear. Insofar as one sincerely takes that attitude and so has the three sets of dispositions, one will at the same time be disposed to comply with certain rules of duty (such as nonmaleficence and noninterference) and with standards of character (such as fairness and benevolence) that determine the obligations and virtues of moral agents with regard to the Earth's wild living things. We can say that the actions one performs and the character traits one develops in fulfilling these moral requirements are the way one *expresses* or *embodies* the attitude in one's conduct and character. In his famous essay, "Justice as Fairness," John Rawls describes the rules of the duties of human morality (such as fidelity, gratitude, honesty, and justice) as "forms of conduct in which recognition of others as persons is manifested."[5] I hold that the rules of duty governing our treatment of the natural world and its inhabitants are forms of conduct in which the attitude of respect for nature is manifested.

IV. THE JUSTIFIABILITY OF THE ATTITUDE OF RESPECT FOR NATURE

I return to the question posed earlier, which has not yet been answered: why *should* moral agents regard wild living things as possessing inherent worth? I now argue that the only way we can answer this question is by showing how adopting the attitude of respect for nature is justified for all moral agents. Let us suppose that we were able to establish that there are good reasons for adopting the attitude, reasons which are intersubjectively valid for every rational agent. If there are such reasons, they would justify anyone's having the three sets of dispositions mentioned above as constituting what it means to have the attitude. Since these include the disposition to promote or protect the good of wild living things as a disinterested and ultimate end, as well as the disposition to perform actions for the reason that they tend to realize that end, we see that such dispositions commit a person to the principles of moral consideration and intrinsic value. To be disposed to further, as an end in itself, the good of any entity in nature just because it is that kind of entity, is to be disposed to give consideration to *every* such entity and to place intrinsic value on the realization of its good. Insofar as we subscribe to these two principles we regard living things as possessing inherent worth. Subscribing to the principle is what it *means* to so regard them. To justify the attitude of respect for nature, then, is to justify commitment to these principles and thereby to justify regarding wild creatures as possessing inherent worth.

We must keep in mind that inherent worth is not some mysterious sort of objective property belonging to living things that can be discovered by empirical observation or scientific investigation. To ascribe inherent worth to an entity is not to describe it by citing some feature discernible by sense perception or inferable by inductive reasoning. Nor is there a logically necessary connection between the concept of a being having a good of its own and the concept of inherent worth. We do not contradict ourselves by asserting that an entity that has a good of its own lacks inherent worth. In order to show that such an entity "has" inherent worth we must give good reasons for ascribing that kind of value to it (placing that kind of value upon it, conceiving of it to be valuable in that way). Although it is humans (persons, valuers) who must do the valuing, for the ethics of respect for nature, the value so ascribed is not a human value. That is to say, it is not a value derived from considerations regarding human well-being or human rights. It is a value that is ascribed to nonhuman animals and plants themselves, independently of their relationship to what humans judge to be conducive to their own good.

Whatever reasons, then, justify our taking the attitude of respect for nature as defined above are also reasons that show why we *should* regard the living things of the natural world as possessing inherent worth. We saw earlier that, since the attitude is an ultimate one, it cannot be derived from a more fundamental attitude nor shown to be a special case of a more general one. On what sort of grounds, then, can it be established?

The attitude we take toward living things in the natural world depends on the way we look at them, on what kind of beings we conceive them to be, and on how we understand the relations we bear to them. Underlying and supporting our attitude is a certain *belief system* that constitutes a particular world view or outlook on nature and the place of human life in it. To give good reasons for adopting the attitude of respect for nature, then, we must first articulate the belief system which underlies and supports that attitude. If it appears that the belief system is internally coherent and well-ordered, and if, as far as we can now tell, it is consistent with all known scientific truths relevant to our knowledge of the object of the attitude (which in this case includes the whole set of the Earth's natural ecosystems and their communities of life), then there remains the task of indicating why scientifically informed and rational thinkers with a developed capacity of reality awareness can find it acceptable as a way of conceiving of the natural world and our place in it. To the extent we can do this we provide at least a reasonable argument for accepting the belief system and the ultimate moral attitude it supports.

I do not hold that such a belief system can be *proven* to be true, either inductively or deductively. As we shall see, not all of its components can be stated in the form of empirically verifiable propositions. Nor is its internal order governed by purely logical relationships. But the system as a whole, I contend, constitutes a coherent, unified, and rationally acceptable "picture" or "map" of a total world. By examining each of its main components and seeing how they fit together, we obtain a scientifically informed and well-ordered conception of nature and the place of humans in it.

This belief system underlying the attitude of respect for nature I call (for want of a better name) "the biocentric outlook on nature." Since it is not wholly analyzable into empirically confirmable assertions, it should not be thought of as simply a compendium of the biological sciences concerning our planet's ecosystems. It might best be described as a philosophical world view, to distinguish it from a scientific theory or explanatory system. However, one of its major tenets is the great lesson we have learned from the science of ecology: the interdependence of all living things in an organically unified order whose balance and stability are necessary conditions for the realization of the good of its constituent biotic communities.

Before turning to an account of the main components of the biocentric outlook, it is convenient here to set forth the overall structure of my theory of environmental ethics as it has now emerged. The ethics of respect for nature is made up of three basic elements: a belief system, an ultimate moral attitude, and a set of rules of duty and standards of character. These elements are connected with each other in the following manner. The belief system provides a certain outlook on nature which supports and makes intelligible an autonomous agent's adopting, as an ultimate moral attitude, the attitude of respect for nature. It supports and makes intelligible the attitude in the sense that, when an autonomous agent understands its moral relations to the natural world in terms of this outlook, it recognizes the attitude of respect to be the only *suitable* or *fitting* attitude to take toward all wild forms of life in the Earth's biosphere. Living things are now viewed as *the appropriate objects of the attitude of respect* and are accordingly regarded as entities possessing inherent worth. One then places intrinsic value on the promotion and protection of their good. As a consequence of this, one makes a moral commitment to abide by a set of rules of duty and to fulfill (as far as one can by one's own efforts) certain standards of good character. Given one's adoption of the attitude of respect, one makes that moral commitment because one considers those rules and standards to be validly binding on all moral agents. They are seen as embodying forms of conduct and character structures in which the attitude of respect for nature is manifested.

This three-part complex which internally orders the ethics of respect for nature is symmetrical with a theory of human ethics grounded on respect for persons. Such a theory includes, first, a conception of oneself and others as persons, that is, as centers of autonomous choice. Second, there is the attitude of respect for persons as persons. When this is adopted as an ultimate moral attitude it involves the disposition to treat every person as having inherent worth or "human dignity." Every human being, just in virtue of her or his humanity, is understood to be worthy of moral consideration, and intrinsic value is placed on the autonomy and well-being of each. This is what Kant meant by conceiving of persons as ends in themselves. Third, there is an ethical system of duties which are acknowledged to be owed by everyone to everyone. These duties are forms of conduct in which public recognition is given to each individual's inherent worth as a person.

This structural framework for a theory of human ethics is meant to leave open the issue of consequentialism (utilitarianism) versus non-consequentialism (deontology). That issue concerns the particular kind of system of rules defining the duties of moral agents toward persons. Similarly, I am leaving open in this paper the question of what particular kind of system of rules defines our duties with respect to the natural world.

V. THE BIOCENTRIC OUTLOOK ON NATURE

The biocentric outlook on nature has four main components. (1) Humans are thought of as members of the Earth's community of life, holding that membership on the same terms as apply to all the nonhuman members. (2) The Earth's natural ecosystems as a totality are seen as a complex web of interconnected elements, with the sound biological functioning of each being dependent on the sound biological functioning of the others. (This is the component referred to above as the great lesson that the science of ecology has taught us.) (3) Each individual organism is conceived of as a teleological center of life, pursuing its own good in its own way. (4) Whether we are concerned with standards of merit or with the concept of inherent worth, the claim that humans by their very nature are superior to other species is a groundless claim and, in the light of elements (1), (2), and (3) above, must be rejected as nothing more than an irrational bias in our own favor.

The conjunction of these four ideas constitutes the biocentric outlook on nature. In the remainder of this paper I give a brief account of the first three components, followed by a more detailed analysis of the fourth. I then conclude by indicating how this outlook provides a way of justifying the attitude of respect for nature.

VI. HUMANS AS MEMBERS OF THE EARTH'S COMMUNITY OF LIFE

We share with other species a common relationship to the Earth. In accepting the biocentric outlook we take the fact of our being an animal species to be a fundamental feature of our existence. We consider it an essential aspect of "the human condition." We do not deny the differences between ourselves and other species, but we keep in the forefront of our consciousness the fact that in relation to our planet's natural ecosystems we are but one species population among many. Thus we acknowledge our origin in the very same evolutionary process that gave rise to all other species and we recognize ourselves to be confronted with similar environmental challenges to those that confront them. The laws of genetics, of natural selection, and of adaptation apply equally to all of us as biological creatures. In this light we consider ourselves as one with them, not set apart from them. We, as well as they, must face certain basic conditions of existence that impose requirements on us for our survival and well-being. Each animal and plant is like us in having a good of its own. Although our human good (what is of true value in human life, including the exercise of individual autonomy in choosing our own particular value systems) is not like the good of a nonhuman animal or plant, it can no more be realized than their good can without the biological necessities for survival and physical health.

When we look at ourselves from the evolutionary point of view, we see that not only are we very recent arrivals on Earth, but that our emergence as a new species on the planet was originally an event of no particular importance to the entire scheme of things. The Earth was teeming with life long before we appeared. Putting the point metaphorically, we are relative newcomers, entering a home that has been the residence of others for hundreds of millions of years, a home that must now be shared by all of us together.

The comparative brevity of human life on Earth may be vividly depicted by imagining the geological time scale in spatial terms. Suppose we start with algae, which have been around for at least 600 million years. (The earliest protozoa actually predated this by several *billion* years.) If the time that algae have been here were represented by the length of a football field (300 feet), then the period during which sharks have been swimming in the world's oceans and spiders have been spinning their webs would occupy three quarters of the length of the field; reptiles would show up at about the center of the field; mammals would cover the last third of the field; hominids (mammals of the family *Hominidae*) the last two feet; and the species *Homo sapiens* the last six inches.

Whether this newcomer is able to survive as long as other species remains to be seen. But there is surely something presumptuous about the way humans look down on the "lower" animals, especially those that have become extinct. We consider the dinosaurs, for example, to be biological failures, though they existed on our planet for 65 million years. One writer has made the point with beautiful simplicity:

> We sometimes speak of the dinosaurs as failures; there will be time enough for that judgment when we have lasted even for one tenth as long. . . .[6]

The possibility of the extinction of the human species, a possibility which starkly confronts us in the contemporary world, makes us aware of another respect in which we should not consider ourselves privileged beings in relation to other species. This is the fact that the well-being of humans is dependent upon the ecological soundness and health of many plant and animal communities, while their soundness and health does not in the least depend upon human well-being. Indeed, from their standpoint the very existence of humans is quite unnecessary. Every last man, woman, and child would disappear from the face of the Earth without any significant detrimental consequence for the good of wild animals and plants. On the contrary, many of them would be greatly benefited. The destruction of their habitats by human "developments" would cease. The poisoning and polluting of their environment would come to an end. The Earth's land, air, and water would no longer be subject to the degradation they are now undergoing as the result of large-scale technology and uncontrolled population growth. Life communities in natural ecosystems would gradually return to their former healthy state. Tropical rain forests, for example, would again be able to make their full contribution to a life-sustaining atmosphere for the whole planet. The rivers, lakes, and oceans of the world would (perhaps) eventually become clean again. Spilled oil, plastic trash, and even radioactive waste might finally, after many centuries, cease doing their terrible work. Ecosystems would return to their proper balance, suffering only the disruptions of natural events such as volcanic eruptions and glaciation. From these the community of life could recover, as it has so often done in the past. But the ecological disasters now perpetrated on it by humans—disasters from which it might never recover—these it would no longer have to endure.

If, then, the total, final, absolute extermination of our species (by our own hands?) should take place and if we should not carry all the others with us into oblivion, not only would the Earth's community of life continue to exist, but in all probability its well-being would be enhanced. Our presence, in short, is not needed. If we were to take the standpoint of the community and give voice to its true interest, the ending of our six-inch epoch would most likely be greeted with a hearty "Good riddance!"

VII. THE NATURAL WORLD AS AN ORGANIC SYSTEM

To accept the biocentric outlook and regard ourselves and our place in the world from its perspective is to see the whole natural order of the Earth's biosphere as a complex but unified web of interconnected organisms, objects, and events. The ecological relationships between any community of living things and their environment form an organic whole of functionally interdependent parts. Each ecosystem is a small universe itself in which the interactions of its various species populations comprise an intricately woven network of cause-effect relations. Such dynamic but at the same time relatively stable structures as food chains, predator-prey relations, and plant succession in a forest are self-regulating, energy-recycling mechanisms that preserve the equilibrium of the whole.

As far as the well-being of wild animals and plants is concerned, this ecological equilibrium must not be destroyed. The same holds true of the well-being of humans. When one views the realm of nature from the perspective of the biocentric outlook, one never forgets that in the long run the integrity of the entire biosphere of our planet is essential to the realization of the good of its constituent communities of life, both human and nonhuman.

Although the importance of this idea cannot be overemphasized, it is by now so familiar and so widely acknowledged that I shall not further elaborate on it here. However, I do wish to point out that this "holistic" view of the Earth's ecological systems does not itself constitute a moral norm. It is a factual aspect of biological reality, to be understood as a set of causal connections in ordinary empirical terms. Its significance for humans is the same as its significance for nonhumans, namely, in setting basic conditions for the realization of the good of living things. Its ethical implications for our treatment of the natural environment lie entirely in the fact that our *knowledge* of these causal connections is an essential *means* to fulfilling the aims we set for ourselves in adopting the attitude of respect for nature. In addition, its theoretical implications for the ethics of respect for nature lie in the fact that it (along with the other elements of the biocentric outlook) makes the adopting of that attitude a rational and intelligible thing to do.

VIII. INDIVIDUAL ORGANISMS AS TELEOLOGICAL CENTERS OF LIFE

As our knowledge of living things increases, as we come to a deeper understanding of their life cycles, their interactions with other organisms, and the manifold ways in which they adjust to the environment, we become more fully aware of how each of them is carrying out its biological functions according to the laws of its species-specific nature. But besides this, our increasing knowledge and understanding also develop in us a sharpened awareness of the uniqueness of each individual organism. Scientists who have made careful studies of particular plants and animals, whether in the field or in laboratories, have often acquired a knowledge of their subjects as identifiable individuals. Close observation over extended periods of time has led them to an appreciation of the unique "personalities" of their subjects. Sometimes a scientist may come to take a special interest in a particular animal or plant, all the while remaining strictly objective in the gathering and recording of data. Nonscientists may likewise experience this development of interest when, as amateur naturalists, they make accurate observations over sustained periods of close acquaintance with an individual organism. As one becomes more and more familiar with the organism and its behavior, one becomes fully sensitive to the particular way it is living out its life cycle. One may become fascinated by it and even experience some involvement with its good and bad fortunes (that is, with the occurrence of environmental conditions favorable or unfavorable to the realization of its good). The organism comes to mean something to one as a unique, irreplaceable individual. The final culmination of this process is the achievement of a genuine understanding of its point of view and, with that understanding, an ability to "take" that point of view. *Conceiving of it as a center of life, one is able to look at the world from its perspective.*

This development from objective knowledge to the recognition of individuality, and from the recognition of individuality to full awareness of an organism's standpoint, is a process of heightening our consciousness of what it means to be an individual living thing. We grasp the particularity of the organism as a teleological center

of life, striving to preserve itself and to realize its own good in its own unique way.

It is to be noted that we need not be falsely anthropomorphizing when we conceive of individual plants and animals in this manner. Understanding them as teleological centers of life does not necessitate "reading into" them human characteristics. We need not, for example, consider them to have consciousness. Some of them may be aware of the world around them and others may not. Nor need we deny that different kinds and levels of awareness are exemplified when consciousness in some form is present. But conscious or not, all are equally teleological centers of life in the sense that each is a unified system of goal-oriented activities directed toward their preservation and well-being.

When considered from an ethical point of view, a teleological center of life is an entity whose "world" can be viewed from the perspective of *its* life. In looking at the world from that perspective we recognize objects and events occurring in its life as being beneficent, maleficent, or indifferent. The first are occurrences which increase its powers to preserve its existence and realize its good. The second decrease or destroy those powers. The third have neither of these effects on the entity. With regard to our human role as moral agents, we can conceive of a teleological center of life as a being whose standpoint we can take in making judgments about what events in the world are good or evil, desirable or undesirable. In making those judgments it is what promotes or protects the being's own good, not what benefits moral agents themselves, that sets the standard of evaluation. Such judgments can be made about anything that happens to the entity which is favorable or unfavorable in relation to its good. As we pointed out earlier, the entity itself need not have any (conscious) *interest* in what is happening to it for such judgments to be meaningful and true.

It is precisely judgments of this sort that we are disposed to make when we take the attitude of respect for nature. In adopting that attitude those judgments are given weight as reasons for action in our practical deliberation. They become morally relevant facts in the guidance of our conduct.

IX. THE DENIAL OF HUMAN SUPERIORITY

The fourth component of the biocentric outlook on nature is the single most important idea in establishing the justifiability of the attitude of respect for nature. Its central role is due to the special relationship it bears to the first three components of the outlook. This relationship will be brought out after the concept of human superiority is examined and analyzed.[7]

In what sense are humans alleged to be superior to other animals? We are different from them in having certain capacities that they lack. But why should these capacities be a mark of superiority? From what point of view are they judged to be signs of superiority and what sense of superiority is meant? After all, various nonhuman species have capacities that humans lack. There is the speed of a cheetah, the vision of an eagle, the agility of a monkey. Why should not these be taken as signs of *their* superiority over humans?

One answer that comes immediately to mind is that these capacities are not as *valuable* as the human capacities that are claimed to make us superior. Such uniquely human characteristics as rational thought, aesthetic creativity, autonomy and self-determination, and moral freedom, it might be held, have a higher value than the capacities found in other species. Yet we must ask: valuable to whom, and on what grounds?

The human characteristics mentioned are all valuable to humans. They are essential to the preservation and enrichment of our civilization and culture. Clearly it is from the human standpoint that they are being judged to be desirable and good. It is not difficult here to recognize a begging of the question. Humans are claiming human superiority from a strictly human point of view, that is, from a point of view in which the good of humans is taken as the standard of judgment. All we need to do is look at the capacities of nonhuman animals (or plants, for that matter) from the standpoint of *their* good to find a contrary judgment of superiority. The speed of the cheetah, for example, is a sign of its superiority to humans when considered from the standpoint of the good of its species. If it were as slow a runner as a human, it would not be able to survive. And so for all the other abilities of nonhumans which further their good but which are lacking in humans. In each case the claim to human superiority would be rejected from a nonhuman standpoint.

When superiority assertions are interpreted in this way, they are based on judgments of *merit*. To judge the merits of a person or an organism one must apply grading or ranking standards to it. (As I show below, this distinguishes judgments of merit from judgments of inherent worth.) Empirical investigation then determines whether it has the "good-making properties" (merits) in virtue of which it fulfills the standards being applied. In the case of humans, merits may be either moral or nonmoral. We can judge one person to be better than (superior to) another from the moral point of view by applying certain standards to their character and conduct. Similarly, we can appeal to nonmoral criteria in judging someone to be an excellent piano player, a fair cook, a poor tennis player, and so on. Different social purposes and roles are implicit in the making of such judgments, providing the frame of reference for the choice of standards by which the nonmoral merits of people are determined. Ultimately such purposes and roles stem from a society's way of life as a whole. Now a society's way of life may be thought of as the cultural form given to the realization of human values. Whether moral or nonmoral standards are being applied, then, all judgments of people's merits finally depend on human values. All are made from an exclusively human standpoint.

The question that naturally arises at this juncture is: why should standards that are based on human values be assumed to be the only valid criteria of merit and hence the only true signs of superiority? This question is especially pressing when humans are being judged superior in merit to nonhumans. It is true that a human being may be a better mathematician than a monkey, but the monkey may be a better tree climber than a human being. If we humans value mathematics more than tree climbing, that is because our conception of civilized life makes the development of mathematical ability more desirable than the ability to climb trees. But is it not unreasonable to judge nonhumans by the values of human civilization, rather than by values connected with what it is for a member of *that* species to live a good life? If all living things have a good of their own, it at least makes sense to judge the merits of nonhumans by standards derived from *their* good. To use only standards based on human values is already to commit oneself to holding that humans are superior to nonhumans, which is the point in question.

A further logical flaw arises in connection with the widely held conviction that humans are *morally* superior beings because they possess, while others lack, the capacities of a moral agent (free will, accountability, deliberation, judgment, practical reason). This view rests on a conceptual confusion. As far as moral standards are concerned, only beings that have the capacities of a moral agent can properly be judged to be *either* moral (morally good) *or* immoral (morally deficient). Moral standards are simply not applicable to beings that lack such capacities. Animals and plants cannot therefore be said to be morally inferior in merit to humans. Since the only beings that can have moral merits *or be deficient in such merits* are moral agents, it is conceptually incoherent to judge humans as superior to nonhumans on the ground that humans have moral capacities while nonhumans don't.

Up to this point I have been interpreting the claim that humans are superior to other living things as a grading or ranking judgment regarding their comparative merits. There is, however, another way of understanding the idea of human superiority. According to this interpretation, humans are superior to nonhumans not as regards their merits but as regards their inherent worth. Thus the claim of human superiority is to be understood as asserting that all humans, simply in virtue of their humanity, have *a greater inherent worth* than other living things.

The inherent worth of an entity does not depend on its merits.[8] To consider something as possessing inherent worth, we have seen, is to place intrinsic value on the realization of its good. This is done regardless of whatever particular merits it might have or might lack, as judged by a set of grading or ranking standards. In human affairs, we are all familiar with the principle that one's worth as a person does not vary with one's merits or lack of merits. The same can hold true of animals and plants. To regard such entities as possessing inherent worth entails disregarding their merits and deficiencies, whether they are being judged from a human standpoint or from the standpoint of their own species.

The idea of one entity having more merit than another, and so being superior to it in merit, makes perfectly good sense. Merit is a grading or ranking concept, and judgments of comparative merit are based on the different degrees to which things satisfy a given standard. But what can it mean to talk about one thing being superior to another in inherent worth? In order to get at what is being asserted in such a claim it is helpful first to look at the social origin of the concept of degrees of inherent worth.

The idea that humans can possess different degrees of inherent worth originated in societies having rigid class structures. Before the rise of modern democracies with their egalitarian outlook, one's membership in a hereditary class determined one's social status. People in the upper classes were looked up to, while those in the lower classes were looked down upon. In such a society one's social superiors and social inferiors were clearly defined and easily recognized.

Two aspects of these class-structured societies are especially relevant to the idea of degrees of inherent worth. First, those born into the upper classes were deemed more worthy of respect than those born into the lower orders. Second, the superior worth of upper class people had nothing to do with their merits nor did the inferior worth of those in the lower classes rest on their lack of merits. One's superiority or inferiority entirely derived from a social position one was born into. The modern concept of a meritocracy simply did not apply. One could not advance into a higher class by any sort of moral or nonmoral achievement. Similarly, an aristocrat held his title and all the privileges that went with it just because he was the eldest son of a titled nobleman. Unlike the bestowing of knighthood in contemporary Great Britain, one did not earn membership in the nobility by meritorious conduct.

We who live in modern democracies no longer believe in such hereditary social distinctions. Indeed, we would wholeheartedly condemn them on moral grounds as being fundamentally unjust. We have come to think of class systems as a paradigm of social injustice, it being a central principle of the democratic way of life that among humans there are no superiors and no inferiors. Thus we have rejected the whole conceptual framework in which people are judged to have different degrees of inherent worth. That idea is incompatible with our notion of human equality based on the doctrine that all humans, simply in virtue of their humanity, have the same inherent worth. (The belief in universal human rights is one form that this egalitarianism takes.)

The vast majority of people in modern democracies, however, do not maintain an egalitarian outlook when it comes to comparing human beings with other living things. Most people consider our own species to be superior to all other species and this superiority is understood to be a matter of inherent worth, not merit. There may exist thoroughly vicious and depraved humans who lack all merit. Yet because they are human they are thought to belong to a higher class of entities than any plant or animal. That one is born into the species *Homo sapiens* entitles one to have lordship over those who are one's inferiors, namely, those born into other species. The parallel with hereditary social classes is very close. Implicit in this view is a hierarchical conception of nature according to which an organism has a position of superiority or inferiority in the Earth's community of life simply on the basis of its genetic background. The "lower" orders of life are looked down upon and it is considered perfectly proper that they serve the interests of those belonging to the highest order, namely humans. The intrinsic value we place on the well-being of our fellow humans reflects our recognition of their rightful position as our equals. No such intrinsic value is to be placed on the good of other animals, unless we choose to do so out of fondness or affection for them. But their well-being imposes no moral requirement on us. In this respect there is an absolute difference in moral status between ourselves and them.

This is the structure of concepts and beliefs that people are committed to insofar as they regard humans to be superior in inherent worth to all other species. I now wish to argue that this structure of concepts and beliefs is completely groundless. If we accept the first three components of the biocentric outlook and from that perspective look at the major philosophical traditions which have supported that structure, we find it to be at bottom nothing more than the expression of an irrational bias in our own favor. The philosophical traditions themselves rest on very questionable assumptions or else simply beg the question. I briefly consider three of the main traditions to substantiate the point. These are classical Greek humanism, Cartesian dualism, and the Judeo-Christian concept of the Great Chain of Being.

The inherent superiority of humans over other species was implicit in the Greek definition of man as a rational animal. Our animal nature was identified with "brute" desires that need the order and restraint of reason to rule them (just as reason is the special virtue of those who rule in the ideal state). Rationality was then seen to be the key to our superiority over animals. It enables us to live on a higher plane and endows us with a nobility and worth that other creatures lack. This familiar way of comparing humans with other species is deeply ingrained in our Western philosophical outlook. The point to consider here is that this view does not actually provide an argument *for* human superiority but rather makes explicit the framework of thought that is implicitly used by those who think of humans as inherently superior to nonhumans. The Greeks who held that humans, in virtue of their rational capacities, have a kind of worth greater than that of any nonrational being, never looked at rationality as but one capacity of living things among many others. But when we consider rationality from the standpoint of the first three elements of the ecological outlook, we see that its value lies in its importance for *human* life. Other creatures achieve their species-specific good without the need of rationality, although they often make use of capacities that humans lack. So the humanistic outlook of classical Greek thought does not give us a neutral (nonquestion-begging) ground on which to construct a scale of degrees of inherent worth possessed by different species of living things.

The second tradition, centering on the Cartesian dualism of soul and body, also fails to justify the claim to human superiority. That superiority is supposed to derive from the fact that we have souls while animals do not. Animals are mere automata and lack the divine element that makes us spiritual beings. I won't go into the now familiar criticisms of this two-substance view. I only add the point that, even if humans are composed of an immaterial, un-extended soul and a material, extended body, this in itself is not a reason to deem them of greater worth than entities that are only bodies. Why is a soul substance a thing that adds value to its possessor? Unless some theological reasoning is offered here (which many, including myself, would find unacceptable on epistemological grounds), no logical connection is evident. An immaterial something which thinks is better than a material something which does not think only if thinking itself has value, either intrinsically or instrumentally. Now it is intrinsically valuable to humans alone, who value it as an end in itself, and it is instrumentally valuable to those who benefit from it, namely humans.

For animals that neither enjoy thinking for its own sake nor need it for living the kind of life for which they are best adapted, it has no value. Even if "thinking" is broadened to include all forms of consciousness, there are still many living things that can do without it and yet live what is for their species a good life. The anthropocentricity underlying the claim to human superiority runs throughout Cartesian dualism.

A third major source of the idea of human superiority is the Judeo-Christian concept of the Great Chain of Being. Humans are superior to animals and plants because their Creator has given them a higher place on the chain. It begins with God at the top, and then moves to the angels, who are lower than God but higher than humans, then to humans, positioned between the angels and the beasts (partaking of the nature of both), and then on down to the lower levels occupied by nonhuman animals, plants, and finally inanimate objects. Humans, being "made in God's image," are inherently superior to animals and plants by virtue of their being closer (in their essential nature) to God.

The metaphysical and epistemological difficulties with this conception of a hierarchy of entities are, in my mind, insuperable. Without entering into this matter here, I only point out that if we are unwilling to accept the metaphysics of traditional Judaism and Christianity, we are again left without good reasons for holding to the claim of inherent human superiority.

The foregoing considerations (and others like them leave us with but one ground for the assertion that a human being, regardless of merit, is a higher kind of entity than any other living thing. This is the mere fact of the genetic makeup of the species *Homo sapiens*. But this is surely irrational and arbitrary. Why should the arrangement of genes of a certain type be a mark of superior value, especially when this fact about an organism is taken by itself, unrelated to any other aspect of its life? We might just as well refer to any other genetic makeup as a ground of superior value. Clearly we are confronted here with a wholly arbitrary claim that can only be explained as an irrational bias in our own favor.

That the claim is nothing more than a deep-seated prejudice is brought home to us when we look at our relation to other species in the light of the first three elements of the biocentric outlook. Those elements taken conjointly give us a certain overall view of the natural world and of the place of humans in it. When we take this view we come to understand other living things, their environmental conditions, and their ecological relationships in such a way as to awake in us a deep sense of our kinship with them as fellow members of the Earth's community of life. Humans and nonhumans alike are viewed together as integral parts of one unified whole in which all living things are functionally interrelated. Finally, when our awareness focuses on the individual lives of plants and animals, each is seen to share with us the characteristic of being a teleological center of life striving to realize its own good in its own unique way.

As this entire belief system becomes part of the conceptual framework through which we understand and perceive the world, we come to see ourselves as bearing a certain moral relation to nonhuman forms of life. Our ethical role in nature takes on a new significance. We begin to look at other species as we look at ourselves, seeing them as beings which have a good they are striving to realize just as we have a good we are striving to realize. We accordingly develop the disposition to view the world from the standpoint of their good as well as from the standpoint of our own good. Now if the groundlessness of the claim that humans are inherently superior to other species were brought clearly before our minds, we would not remain intellectually neutral toward that claim but would reject it as being fundamentally at variance with our total world outlook. In the absence of any good reasons for holding it, the assertion of human superiority would then appear simply as the expression of an irrational and self-serving prejudice that favors one particular species over several million others.

Rejecting the notion of human superiority entails its positive counterpart: the doctrine of species impartially. One who accepts that doctrine regards all living things as possessing inherent worth—the *same* inherent worth, since no one species has been shown to be either "higher" or "lower" than any other. Now we saw earlier that, insofar as one thinks of a living thing as possessing inherent worth, one considers it to be the appropriate object of the attitude of respect and believes that attitude to be the only fitting or suitable one for all moral agents to take toward it.

Here, then, is the key to understanding how the attitude of respect is rooted in the biocentric outlook on nature. The basic connection is made through the denial of human superiority. Once we reject the claim that humans are superior either in merit or in worth to other living things, we are ready to adopt the attitude of respect. The denial of human superiority is itself the result of taking the perspective on nature built into the first three elements of the biocentric outlook.

Now the first three elements of the biocentric outlook, it seems clear, would be found acceptable to any rational and scientifically informed thinker who is fully "open" to the reality of the lives of nonhuman organisms. Without denying our distinctively human characteristics, such a thinker can acknowledge the fundamental respects in which we are members of the Earth's community of life and in which the biological conditions necessary for the realization of our human values are inextricably linked with the whole system of nature. In addition, the conception of individual living things as teleological centers of life simply articulates how a scientifically informed thinker comes to understand them as the result of increasingly careful and detailed observations. Thus, the biocentric outlook recommends itself as an acceptable system of concepts and beliefs to anyone who is clear-minded, unbiased, and factually enlightened, and who has a developed capacity of reality awareness with regard to the lives of individual organisms. This, I submit, is as good a reason for making the moral commitment involved in adopting the attitude of respect for nature as any theory of environmental ethics could possibly have.

X. MORAL RIGHTS AND THE MATTER OF COMPETING CLAIMS

I have not asserted anywhere in the foregoing account that animals or plants have moral rights. This omission was deliberate. I do not think that the reference class of the concept, bearer of moral rights, should be extended to include nonhuman living things. My reasons for taking this position, however, go beyond the scope of this paper. I believe I have been able to accomplish many of the same ends which those who ascribe rights to animals or plants wish to accomplish. There is no reason, moreover, why plants and animals, including whole species populations and life communities, cannot be accorded *legal* rights under my theory. To grant them legal protection could be interpreted as giving them legal entitlement to be protected, and this, in fact, would be a means by which a society that subscribed to the ethics of respect for nature could give public recognition to their inherent worth.

There remains the problem of competing claims, even when wild plants and animals are not thought of as bearers of moral rights. If we accept the biocentric outlook and accordingly adopt the attitude of respect for nature as our ultimate moral attitude, how do we resolve conflicts that arise from our respect for persons in the domain of human ethics and our respect for nature in the domain of environmental ethics? This is a question that cannot be adequately dealt with here. My main purpose in this paper has been to try to establish a base point from which we can start working toward a solution to the problem. I have shown why we cannot just begin with an initial presumption in favor of the interests of our own species. It is after all within our power as moral beings to place limits on human population and technology with the deliberate intention of sharing the Earth's bounty with other species. That such sharing is an ideal difficult to realize even in an approximate way does not take away its claim to our deepest moral commitment.

Notes

1. The conceptual links between an entity *having* a good, something being good *for* it, and events doing good *to* it are examined by G. H. Von Wright in *The Varieties of Goodness* (New York: Humanities Press, 1963), chaps. 3 and 5.
2. See W. K. Frankena, "Ethics and the Environment," in K. E. Goodpaster and K. M. Sayre, eds. *Ethics and Problems of the 21st Century* (Notre Dame, University of Notre Dame Press, 1979) pp. 3–20. I critically examine Frankena's views in "Frankena on Environmental Ethics," *Monist*, forthcoming.
3. In the light of considerations set forth in Daniel Dennett's *Brain Storms: Philosophical Essays on Mind and Psychology* (Montgomery, Vermont: Bradford Books, 1978), it is advisable to leave this question unsettled at this time. When machines are developed that function in the way our brains do, we may well come to deem them proper subjects of moral consideration.
4. I have analyzed the nature of this commitment of human ethics in "On Taking the Moral Point of View," *Midwest Studies in Philosophy*, vol. 3, *Studies in Ethical Theory* (1978), pp. 35–61.

5. John Rawls, "Justice as Fairness," *Philosophical Review* 67 (1958): 183.

6. Stephen R. L Clark, *The Moral Status of Animals* (Oxford: Clarendon Press, 1977), p. 112.

7. My criticisms of the dogma of human superiority gain independent support from a carefully reasoned essay by R and V. Routley showing the many logical weaknesses in arguments for human-centered theories of environmental ethics. R. and V. Routley, "Against the Inevitability of Human Chauvinism," in K. E. Goodpaster and K. M. Sayre, eds., *Ethics and Problems of the 21st Century* (Notre Dame: University of Notre Dame Press, 1979), pp. 36–59.

8. For this way of distinguishing between merit and inherent worth, I am indebted to Gregory Vlastos, "Justice and Equality," in R. Brandt, ed., *Social Justice* (Englewood Cliffs, NJ.: Prentice-Hall 1962), pp. 31–72.

Study Questions

1. Taylor leaves the matter of resolving conflicting claims between humans and nonhumans open in this article. But in his book he lists five principles: self-defense, proportionality, minimum harm, distributive justice, and restitutive justice (restoring ill-gotten gains). The basic needs of humans and nonhumans are to be decided impartially (distributive justice), but the basic needs of nonhumans should override the non basic needs of humans. Work out implications of these principles.

2. Is Taylor's biocentrism workable? How would it apply to our relationship with viruses, bacteria, ring worms, parasites, and the predatory animals? Would the basic needs of the two weeds or worms override the needs of one human?

3. Is the notion of objective intrinsic value clear? Is it true? Do we value certain things (e.g., life) because they are intrinsically good, or are they intrinsically good because we value them?

4. What does Taylor say about the relationship between *having a good* and having *inherent worth* or being good. Can something have a good, an interest, without *being* good?

17

On Being Morally Considerable

KENNETH GOODPASTER

Kenneth Goodpaster (b. 1944) has taught philosophy at the University of Notre Dame and Harvard University Business School and now teaches at the University of St. Thomas in Minneapolis, Minnesota. He is the author or editor of several works in ethics.

Beginning with an insight from the ecologist Aldo Leopold (see Reading 18) that moral rightness involves preserving the "integrity, stability, and beauty of the biotic community," Goodpaster argues for an ethic centered in life itself. He argues against both anthropocentric ethics and ethics based on sentience, pointing out that trees and plants have needs and interests. Unlike Albert Schweitzer and Paul Taylor, Goodpaster's version of biocentric ethics is not egalitarian. Possessing a life makes one morally considerable, not of equal moral worth with human beings.

A thing is right when it tends to preserve the integrity, stability and beauty of the biotic community. It is wrong when it tends otherwise.

ALDO LEOPOLD

Reprinted from "On Being Morally Considerable," *Journal of Philosophy* (1978) by permission. Slightly edited.

What follows is a preliminary inquiry into a question which needs more elaborate treatment that an essay can provide. The question can be and has been addressed in different rhetorical formats, but perhaps G. J. Warnock's formulation of it[1] is the best to start with:

> Let us consider the question to whom principles of morality apply from, so to speak, the other end—from the standpoint not of the agent, but of the "patient." What, we may ask here, is the condition of moral *relevance*? What is the condition of having a claim to be *considered*, by rational agents to whom moral principles apply? (148)

In terminology of R. M. Hare (or even Kant), the same question might be put thus: In universalizing our putative moral maxims, what is the scope of the variable over which universalization is to range? A more legalistic idiom, employed recently by Christopher D. Stone,[2] might ask: What are the requirements for "having standing" in the moral sphere? However the question gets formulated, the thrust is in the direction of necessary and sufficient conditions on X in

1. For all A, X deserves moral consideration from A where A ranges over rational moral agents and moral "consideration" is construed broadly to include the most basic forms of practical respect (and so is not restricted to "possession of rights" by X). . . .

Modern moral philosophy has taken ethical egoism as its principal foil for developing what can fairly be called a *humanistic* perspective on value and obligation. That is, both Kantian and Humean approaches to ethics tend to view the philosophical challenge as that of providing an epistemological and motivational generalization of an agent's natural self-interested concern. Because of this preoccupation with moral "take-off," however, too little critical thought has been devoted to the flight and its destination. One result might be a certain feeling of impotence in the minds of many moral philosophers when faced with the sorts of issues mentioned earlier, issues that question the breadth of the moral enterprise more than its departure point. To be sure, questions of conservation, preservation of the environment, and technology assessment *can* be approached simply as application questions, e.g., "How shall we evaluate the alternatives available to us instrumentally in relation to humanistic satisfactions?" But there is something distressingly uncritical in this way of framing such issues—distressingly uncritical in the way that deciding foreign policy solely in terms of "the national interest" is uncritical. Or at least, so I think.

It seems to me that we should not only wonder about, but actually follow "the road not taken into the wood." Neither rationality nor the capacity to experience pleasure and pain seem to me necessary (even though they may be sufficient) conditions on moral considerability. And only our hedonistic and concentric forms of ethical reflection keep us from acknowledging this fact. Nothing short of the condition of *being alive* seems to me to be a plausible and nonarbitrary criterion. What is more, this criterion, if taken seriously, could admit of application to entities and systems of entities heretofore unimagined as claimants on our moral attention (such as the biosystem itself). Some may be inclined to take such implications as a *reductio* of the move "beyond humanism." I am beginning to be persuaded, however, that such implications may provide both a meaningful ethical vision and the hope of a more adequate action guide for the long-term future. Paradigms are crucial components in knowledge—but they can conceal as much as they reveal. Our paradigms of moral considerability are individual persons and their joys and sorrows. I want to venture the belief that the universe of moral consideration is more complex that these paradigms allow.

II

My strategy, now that my cards are on the table, will be to spell out a few rules of the game (in this section) and then to examine the "hands" of several respected philosophers whose arguments seem to count against casting the moral net as widely as I am inclined to. . . .

In the concluding section . . . , I will discuss several objections and touch on further questions needing attention.

The first . . . distinctions that must be kept clear in addressing our question has already been alluded to. It is that between moral *rights* and moral *considerability*. My inclination is to construe the notion of rights as more specific than that of considerability, largely to avoid what seem to be unnecessary complications over the requirements for something's being an appropriate "bearer of rights." The concept of rights is used in wider and narrower senses, of course. Some authors (indeed, one whom we shall consider later in this paper) use it as roughly synonymous with Warnock's notion or "moral relevance." Others believe that being a bearer of rights involves the satisfaction of much more demanding requirements. The sentiments of John Passmore[3] are probably typical of this narrower view:

> The idea of "rights" is simply not applicable to what is non-human . . . It is one thing to say that it is wrong to treat animals cruelly, quite another to say that animals have rights (116/7).

I doubt whether it is so clear that the class of rights-bearers is or ought to be restricted to human beings, but I propose to suspend this question entirely by framing the discussion in terms of the notion of moral considerability (following Warnock), except in contexts where there is reason to think the widest sense of "rights" is at work. Whether beings who deserve moral consideration in themselves, not simply by reason of their utility to human beings, also possess moral *rights* in some narrow sense is a question which will, therefore, remain open here—and it is a question the answer to which need not be determined in advance.

A second distinction is that between what might be called a *criterion of moral considerability* and a *criterion of moral significance*. The former represents the central quarry here, while the latter, which might easily get confused with the former, aims at governing *comparative* judgments of moral "weight" in cases of conflict. Whether a tree, say, deserves any moral consideration is a question that must be kept separate from the question of whether trees deserve more or less consideration than dogs, or dogs than human persons. We should not expect that the criterion for having "moral standing" at all will be the same as the criterion for adjudicating competing claims to priority among beings that merit that standing. . . .

III

Let us begin with Warnock's own answer to the question, now that the question has been clarified somewhat. In setting out his answer, Warnock argues (in my view, persuasively) against two more restrictive candidates. The first, what might be called the *Kantian principle*, amounts to little more than a reflection of the requirements of moral *agency* onto those of moral considerability:

2. For *X* to deserve moral consideration from *A*, *X* must be a rational human person.

Observing that such a criterion of considerability eliminates children and mentally handicapped adults, among others, Warnock dismisses it as intolerably narrow.

The second candidate, actually a more generous variant of the first, sets the limits of moral considerability by disjoining "potentiality":

3. For all *A*, *X* deserves moral consideration from *A* if and only if *X* is a rational human person or is a potential rational human person.

Warnock's reply to this suggestion is also persuasive. Infants and imbeciles are no doubt potentially rational, but this does not appear to be the reason why we should not maltreat them. And we would not say that an imbecile reasonably judged to be incurable would thereby reasonably be taken to have no moral claims (151). In short, it seems arbitrary to draw the boundary of moral *considerability* around rational human beings (actual or potential), however plausible it might be to draw the boundary of moral *responsibility* there.

Warnock then settles upon his own solution. The basis of moral claims, he says, may be put as follows:

. . . just as liability to be judged as a moral agent follows from one's general capability of alleviating, by moral action, the ills of the predicament, and is for that reason confined to rational beings, so the condition of being a proper "beneficiary" of moral action is the capability of *suffering* the ills of the predicament—and for that reason is not confined to rational beings, nor even to potential members of that class (151).

The criterion of moral considerability then, is located in the *capacity to suffer*:

4. For all *A*, *X* deserves moral consideration from *A* if and only if *X* is capable of suffering pain (or experiencing enjoyment).

And the defense involves appeal to what Warnock considers to be (analytically) the *object* of the moral enterprise: amelioration of "the predicament."

Now two issues arise immediately in the wake of this sort of appeal. The first has to do with Warnock's own over-all strategy in the context of the quoted passage. Earlier on in his book, he insists that the appropriate analysis of the concept of morality will lead us to an "object" whose pursuit provides the framework for ethics. But the "object" seems to be more restrictive:

. . . the general object of moral evaluation must be to contribute in some respects, by way of the actions of rational beings, to the amelioration of the human predicament—that is, of the conditions in which *these*

rational beings, humans, actually find themselves (16; emphasis in the original).

It appears that, by the time moral considerability comes up later in the book, Warnock has changed his mind about the object of morality by enlarging the "predicament" to include nonhumans.

The second issue turns on the question of analysis itself. As I suggested earlier, it is difficult to keep conceptual and substantive questions apart in the present context. We can, of course, stipulatively *define* "morality" as both having an object and having the object of mitigating suffering. But, in the absence of more argument, such definition is itself in need of a warrant. Twentieth-century preoccupation with the naturalistic or definist fallacy should have taught us at least this much.

Neither of these two observations shows that Warnock's suggested criterion is wrong, of course. But they do, I think, put us in a rather more demanding mood. And the mood is aggravated when we look to two other writers on the subject who appear to hold similar views.

W. K. Frankena, in a recent paper,[4] joins forces:

Like Warnock, I believe that there are right and wrong ways to treat infants, animals, imbeciles, and idiots even if or even though (as the case may be) they are not persons or human beings—just because they are capable of pleasure and suffering, and not just because their lives happen to have some value to or for those who clearly are persons or human beings.

And Peter Singer,[5] writes:

If a being is not capable of suffering, or of experiencing enjoyment or happiness, there is nothing to be taken into account. This is why the limit of sentience (using the term as a convenient, if not strictly accurate, shorthand for the capacity to suffer or experience enjoyment or happiness) is the only defensible boundary of concern for the interests of others (154).

I say that the mood is aggravated because, although I acknowledge and even applaud the conviction expressed by these philosophers that the capacity to suffer (or perhaps better, *sentience*) is sufficient for moral considerability, I fail to understand their reasons for thinking such a criterion necessary. To be sure, there are hints at reasons in each case. Warnock implies that nonsentient beings could not be proper "beneficiaries" of moral action. Singer seems to think that beyond sentience "there is nothing to take into account." And Frankena suggests that nonsentient beings simply do not provide us with moral reasons for respecting them unless it be potentiality for sentience.[6] Yet it is so clear that there *is* something to take into account, something that is not merely "potential sentience" and which surely does qualify beings as beneficiaries and capable of harm—namely, *life*—that the hints provided seem to me to fall short of good reasons.

Biologically, it appears that sentience is an adaptive characteristic of living organisms that provides them with a better capacity to anticipate, and so avoid, threats to life. This at least suggests, though of course it does not prove, that the capacities to suffer and to enjoy are ancillary to something more important rather than tickets to considerability in their own right. In the words of one perceptive scientific observer:

> If we view pleasure as rooted in our sensory physiology, it is not difficult to see that our neurophysiological equipment must have evolved via variation and selective retention in such a way as to record a positive signal to adaptationally satisfactory conditions and a negative signal to adaptationally unsatisfactory conditions . . . The pleasure signal is only an evolutionarily derived indicator, not the goal itself. It is the applause which signals a job well done, but not the actual completion of the job.[7]

Nor is it absurd to imagine that evolution might have resulted (indeed might still result?) in beings whose capacities to maintain, protect, and advance their lives did not depend upon mechanisms of pain and pleasure at all.

So far, then, we can see that the search for a criterion of moral considerability takes one quickly and plausibly beyond humanism. But there is a tendency, exhibited in the remarks of Warnock, Frankena, and Singer, to draw up the wagons around the notion of sentience. I have suggested that there is reason to go further and not very much in the way of argument not to. But perhaps there is a stronger and more explicit case that can be made for sentience. I think there is, in a way, and I propose to discuss it in detail in the section that follows.

IV

Joel Feinberg offers (51) what may be the clearest and most explicit case for a restrictive criterion on moral considerability (restrictive with respect to life). . . .

[In] Feinberg's discussion . . . we discover the clearest line of argument in favor of something like sentience, an argument which was only hinted at in the remarks of Warnock, Frankena, and Singer.

The central thesis defended by Feinberg is that a being cannot intelligibly be said to possess moral rights (read: deserve moral consideration) unless that being satisfies the "interest principle," and that only the subclass of humans and higher animals among living beings satisfies this principle:

> . . . the sorts of beings who can have rights are precisely those who have (or can have) interests. I have come to this tentative conclusion for two reasons: (1) because a right holder must be capable of being represented and it is impossible to represent a being that has no interests, and (2) because a right holder must be capable of being a

beneficiary in his own person, and a being without interests is a being that is incapable of being harmed or benefited, having no good or "sake" of its own (51).

Implicit in this passage are the following two arguments, interpreted in terms of moral considerability:

(A1) Only beings who can be represented can deserve moral consideration.

Only beings who have (or can have) interests can be represented.

Therefore, only beings who have (or can have) interests can deserve moral consideration.

(A2) Only beings capable of being beneficiaries can deserve moral consideration.

Only beings who have (or can have) interests are capable of being beneficiaries.

Therefore, only beings who have (or can have) interests can deserve moral consideration.

I suspect that these two arguments are at work between the lines in Warnock, Frenkena, and Singer, though of course one can never be sure. In any case, I propose to consider them as the best defense of the sentience criterion in recent literature.

I am prepared to grant, with some reservations, the first premises in each of these obviously valid arguments. The second premises, though, are *both* importantly equivocal. To claim that only beings who have (or can have) interests can be represented might mean that "mere things" cannot be represented because they have nothing to represent, no "interests" as opposed to "usefulness" to defend or protect. Similarly, to claim that only beings who have (or can have) interests are capable of being beneficiaries might mean that "mere things" are incapable of being benefited or harmed—they have no "well-being" to be sought or acknowledged by rational moral agents. So construed, Feinberg seems to be right; but he also seems to be committed to allowing any *living* thing the status of moral considerability. For as he himself admits, even plants

> . . . are not "mere things"; they are vital objects with inherited biological propensities determining their natural growth. Moreover we do say that certain conditions are "good" or "bad" for plants, thereby suggesting that plants, unlike rocks, are capable of having a "good" (51).

But Feinberg pretty clearly wants to draw the nets tighter than this—and he does so by interpreting the notion of "interests" in the two second premises more narrowly. The contrast term he favors is not "mere things" but "mindless creatures." And he makes this move by insisting that "interests" logically presuppose *desires* or *wants* or *aims*, the equipment for which is not possessed by plants (nor, we might add, by many animals or even some humans?).

But why should we accept this shift in strength of the criterion? In doing so, we clearly abandon one sense in which living organisms like plants do have interests that can be represented. There is no absurdity in imagining the representation of the needs of a tree for sun and water in the face of a proposal to cut it down or pave its immediate radius for a parking lot. We might of course, on reflection, decide to go ahead and cut it down or do the paving, but there is hardly an intelligibility problem about representing the tree's interest in our deciding not to. In the face of their obvious tendencies to maintain and heal themselves, it is very difficult to reject the idea of interests on the part of trees (and plants generally) in remaining alive.[8]

Nor will it do to suggest, as Feinberg does, that the needs (interests) of living things like trees are not really their own but implicitly *ours*: "Plants may need things in order to discharge their functions, but their functions are assigned by human interests, not their own" (54). As if it were human interests that assigned to trees the tasks of growth or maintenance! The interests at stake are clearly those of the living things themselves, not simply those of the owners or users or other human persons involved. Indeed, there is a suggestion in this passage that, to be capable of being represented, an organism must *matter* to human beings somehow—a suggestion whose implications for human rights (disenfranchisement) let alone the rights of animals (inconsistently for Feinberg, I think)—are grim.

The truth seems to be that the "interests" that nonsentient beings share with sentient beings (over and against "mere things") are far more plausible as criteria of *considerability* than the "interests" that sentient beings share (over and against "mindless creatures"). This is not to say that interests construed in the latter way are morally irrelevant—for they may play a role as criteria of moral *significance*—but it is to say that psychological or hedonic capacities seem unnecessarily sophisticated when it comes to locating the minimal conditions for something's deserving to be valued for its own sake. Surprisingly, Feinberg's own reflections on "mere things" appear to support this very point:

> . . . mere things have no conative life: no conscious wishes, desires, and hopes; or urges and impulses; or unconscious drives, aims, and goals; or latent tendencies, direction of growth, and natural fulfillments. Interests must be compounded somehow out of conations; hence mere things have no interests (49).

Together with the acknowledgment, quoted earlier, that plants, for example, are not "mere things," such observations seem to undermine the interest principle in its more restrictive form. I conclude, with appropriate caution, that the interest principle either grows to fit what we might call a "life principle" or requires an

arbitrary stipulation of psychological capacities (for desires, wants, etc.) which are neither warranted by (A1) and (A2) nor independently plausible.

V

Thus far, I have examined the views of four philosophers on the necessity of sentience or interests (narrowly conceived) as a condition on moral considerability. I have maintained that these views are not plausibly supported, when they are supported at all, because of a reluctance to acknowledge in nonsentient living beings the presence of independent needs, capacities for benefit and harm, etc. I should like, briefly, to reflect on a more general level about the roots of this reluctance before proceeding to a consideration of objections against the "life" criterion which I have been defending. In the course of this reflection, we might gain some insight into the sources of our collective hesitation in viewing environmental ethics in a "nonchauvinistic" way.

When we consider the reluctance to go beyond sentience in the context of moral consideration—and look for both explanations and justifications—two thoughts come to mind. The first is that, given the connection between beneficence (or nonmaleficence) and morality, it is natural that limits on moral considerability will come directly from limits on the range of beneficiaries (or "maleficiaries"). This is implicit in Warnock and explicit in Feinberg. The second thought is that, if one's conception of the good is *hedonistic* in character, one's conception of a beneficiary will quite naturally be restricted to beings who are capable of pleasure and pain. If pleasure or satisfaction is the only ultimate gift we have to give, morally, then it is to be expected that only those equipped to receive such a gift will enter into our moral deliberation. And if pain or dissatisfaction is the only ultimate harm we can cause, then it is to be expected that only those equipped for it will deserve our consideration. There seems, therefore, to be a noncontingent connection between a hedonistic or quasi-hedonistic theory of value and a response to the moral-considerability question which favors sentience or interest possession (narrowly conceived).

One must, of course, avoid drawing too strong a conclusion about this connection. It does not follow from the fact that hedonism leads naturally to the sentience criterion either that it entails that criterion or that one who holds that criterion must be a hedonist in his theory of value. For one might be a hedonist with respect to the good and yet think that moral consideration was, on other grounds, restricted to a subclass of the beings capable of enjoyment or pain. And one might hold to the sentience criterion for considerability while denying that pleasure, for example, was the only intrinsically good thing in the life of a human (or nonhuman) being. So hedonism about value and the sentience criterion of moral considerability are not logically equivalent. Nor does either entail the other. But there is some sense, I think, in which they mutually support each other—both in terms of "rendering plausible" and in terms of "helping to explain." As Derek Parfit is fond of putting it, "there are no entailments, but then there seldom are in moral reasoning."[9]

Let me hazard the hypothesis, then, that there is a nonaccidental affinity between a person's or a society's conception of value and its conception of moral considerability. More specifically, there is an affinity between hedonism or some variation on hedonism and a predilection for the sentience criterion of considerability or some variation on it. The implications one might draw from this are many. In the context of a quest for a richer moral framework to deal with a new awareness of the environment, one might be led to expect significant resistance from a hedonistic society unless one forced one's imperatives into an instrumental form. One might also be led to an appreciation of how technology aimed at largely hedonistic goals could gradually "harden the hearts" of a civilization to the biotic community in which it lives—at least until crisis or upheaval raised some questions.

VI

Let us now turn to several objections that might be thought to render a "life principle" of moral considerability untenable quite independently of the adequacy or inadequacy of the sentience or interest principle.

(O1) A principle of moral respect or consideration for life in all its forms is mere Schweitzerian romanticism, even if it does not involve, as it probably does, the projection of mental or psychological categories beyond their responsible boundaries into the realms of plants, insects, and microbes.

(R1) This objection misses the central thrust of my discussion, which is *not* that the sentience criterion is necessary, but applicable to all life forms—rather the point is that the possession of sentience is not necessary for moral considerability. Schweitzer himself may have held the former view—and so have been "romantic"— but this is beside the point.

(O2) To suggest seriously that moral considerability is coextensive with life is to suggest that conscious, feeling beings have no more central role in the moral life than vegetables, which is downright absurd—if not perverse.

(R2) This objection misses the central thrust of my discussion as well, for a different reason. It is consistent with acknowledging the moral considerability of all life forms to go on to point out differences of moral significance among these life forms. And as far as perversion is concerned, history will perhaps be a better judge of our civilization's treatment of animals and the living environment on that score.

(O3) Consideration of life can serve as a criterion only to the degree that life itself can be given a precise definition; and it can't.

(R3) I fail to see why a criterion of moral considerability must be strictly decidable in order to be tenable. Surely rationality, potential rationality, sentience, and the capacity for or possession of interests fare no better here. Moreover, there do seem to be empirically respectable accounts of the nature of living beings available which are not intolerably vague or open-textured:

> The typifying mark of a living system . . . appears to be its persistent state of low entropy, sustained by metabolic processes for accumulating energy, and maintained in equilibrium with its environment by homeostatic feedback processes.[10]

Granting the need for certain further qualifications, a definition such as this strikes me as not only plausible in its own right, but ethically illuminating, since it suggests that the core of moral concern lies in respect for self-sustaining organization and integration in the face of pressures toward high entropy.

(O4) If life, as understood in the previous response, is really taken as the key to moral considerability, then it is possible that larger systems besides our ordinarily understood "linear" extrapolations from human beings (e.g., animals, plants, etc.) might satisfy the conditions, such as the biosystem as a whole. This surely would be a *reductio* of the life principle.

(R4) At best, it would be a *reductio* of the life principle in this form or without qualification. But it seems to be that such (perhaps surprising) implications, if true, should be taken seriously. There is some evidence that the biosystem as a whole exhibits behavior approximating to the definition sketched above,[11] and I see no reason to deny it moral considerability on that account. Why should the universe of moral considerability map neatly onto our medium-sized framework of organisms?

(O5) There are severe epistemological problems about imputing interests, benefits, harms, etc. to nonsentient beings. What is it for a tree to have needs?

(R5) I am not convinced that the epistemological problems are more severe in this context than they would be in numerous others which the objector would probably not find problematic. Christopher Stone has put this point nicely:

> I am sure I can judge with more certainty and meaningfulness whether and when my lawn wants (needs) water than the Attorney General can judge whether and when the United States wants (needs) to take an appeal from an adverse judgment by a lower court. The lawn tells me that it wants water by a certain dryness of the blades and soil—immediately obvious to the touch—the appearance of bald spots, yellowing, and a lack of springiness after being walked on; how does "the United States" communicate to the Attorney General? (24).

We make decisions in the interests of others or on behalf of others every day—"others" whose wants are far less verifiable than those of most living creatures.

(O6) Whatever the force of the previous objections, the clearest and most decisive refutation of the principle of respect for life is that one cannot *live* according to it, nor is there any indication in nature that we were intended to. We must eat, experiment to gain knowledge, protect ourselves from predation (macroscopic and microscopic), and in general deal with the overwhelming complexities of the moral life while remaining psychologically intact. To take seriously the criterion of considerability being defended, all these things must be seen as somehow morally wrong.

(R6) This objection, if it is not met by implication in (R2), can be met, I think, by recalling the distinction made earlier between regulative and operative moral consideration. It seems to me that there clearly are limits to the operational character of respect for living things. We must eat, and usually this involves killing (though not always). We must have knowledge, and sometimes this involves experimentation with living things and killing (though not always). We must protect ourselves from predation and disease, and sometimes this involves killing (though not always). The regulative character of the moral consideration due to all living things asks, as far as I can see, for sensitivity and awareness, not for suicide (psychic or otherwise). But it is not vacuous, in that it does provide a *ceteris paribus* encouragement in the direction of nutritional, scientific, and medical practices of a genuinely life-respecting sort.

As for the implicit claim, in the objection, that since nature doesn't respect life, we needn't, there are two rejoinders. The first is that the premise is not so clearly true. Gratuitous killing in nature is rare indeed. The second, and more important, response is that the issue at hand has to do with the appropriate moral demands to be made on rational moral agents, not on beings who are not rational moral agents. Besides, this objection would tell equally against *any* criterion of moral considerability so far as I can see, if the suggestion is that nature is amoral.

Notes

1. *The Object of Morality* (New York: Methuen, 1971); parenthetical page references to Warnock will be to this book.
2. *Should Trees Have Standing?* (Los Altos: William Kaufmann, 1974).
3. Passmore, *Man's Responsibility for Nature* (New York: Scribners, 1974).
4. "Ethics and the Environment" in K. Goodpaster and K. Sayre, eds., *Ethics and Problems of the 21st Century* (Notre Dame University Press, 1978).
5. "All Animals Are Equal," in Tom Regan and Peter Singer, *Animal Rights and Human Obligations* (Englewood Cliffs, NJ: Prentice Hall, 1976), p. 316.
6. "I can see no reason, from the moral point of view, why we should respect something that is alive but has no conscious sentiency and so can experience no pleasure or pain, joy or suffering, unless perhaps it is potentially a consciously sentient being, as in the case of a fetus. Why, if leaves and trees have no capacity to feel pleasure or to suffer, should I tear no leaf from a tree? Why should I respect its location any more than that of a stone in my driveway, if no benefit or harm comes to any person or sentient being by my moving it?" ("Ethics and the Environment").
7. Mark W. Lipsey, "Value Science and Developing Society," paper delivered to the Society for Religion in Higher Education, Institute on Society, Technology and Values (July 15–Aug. 4, 1973).
8. See Albert Szent-Gyorgyi, *The Living State* (New York: Academic Press, 1972), esp. ch. vi, "Vegetable Defense Systems."
9. "Later Selves and Moral Principles," in A. Montefiori, ed. *Philosophy and Personal Relations* (Boston: Routledge & Kegan Paul, 1973), p. 147.
10. K. M. Sayre, *Cybernetics and the Philosophy of Mind* (New York: Humanities, 1976), p. 91.
11. See J. Lovelock and S. Epton, "The Quest for Gaia," *The New Scientist* LXV, 935 (Feb. 6, 1975). [Reprinted in this volume as Reading 28.]

Study Questions

1. Compare Goodpaster's version of biocentric ethics with Schweitzer's and Taylor's versions. What are the similarities and differences? Which has the stronger case?
2. According to Goodpaster, what does modern moral philosophy take as its main obstacle in developing a *humanistic* perspective on value and obligation? How does this fact affect modern ethics?
3. What does Goodpaster mean by "moral considerability"?
4. What are Goodpaster's objections to those like Feinberg and Singer who would make *sentience* the necessary condition for moral considerability?
5. What is Goodpaster's definition of "interests"? Do you agree that all living things have needs and interests? Is this morally significant?

18

Ecocentrism: The Land Ethic

Aldo Leopold

Aldo Leopold (1887–1947) worked for the U.S. Forest Service before becoming the first professor of Wildlife Management at the University of Wisconsin. He is considered the father of "The Land Ethic." His main work is Sand Country Almanac (1947) *from which our selection is taken.*

Leopold, distressed at the degradation of the environment, says we must begin to realize our symbiotic relationship to Earth so that we value "the land" or biotic community for its own sake. We must come to see ourselves, not as conquerors of the land but rather as plain members and citizens of the biotic community.

When god-like Odysseus returned from the wars in Troy, he hanged all on one rope a dozen slave-girls of his household whom he suspected of misbehavior during his absence.

This hanging involved no question of propriety. The girls were property. The disposal of property was then, as now, a matter of expediency, not of right and wrong.

Concepts of right and wrong were not lacking from Odysseus' Greece: witness the fidelity of his wife through the long years before at last his black-prowed galleys clove the wine-dark seas for home. The ethical structure of that day covered wives, but had not yet been extended to human chattels. During the three thousand years which have since elapsed, ethical criteria have been extended to many fields of conduct, with corresponding shrinkages in those judged by expediency only.

THE ETHICAL SEQUENCE

This extension of ethics, so far studied only by philosophers, is actually a process in ecological evolution. Its sequences may be described in ecological as well as in philosophical terms. An ethic, ecologically, is a limitation on freedom of action in the struggle for existence. An ethic, philosophically, is a differentiation of social from anti-social conduct. These are two definitions of one thing. The thing has its origin in the tendency of interdependent individuals or groups to evolve modes of co-operation. The ecologist calls these symbioses. Politics and economics are advanced symbioses in which the original free-for-all competition has been replaced, in part, by cooperative mechanisms with an ethical content.

The complexity of cooperative mechanisms has increased with population density, and with the efficiency of tools. It was simpler, for example, to define the anti-social uses of sticks and stones in the days of the mastodons than of bullets and billboards in the age of motors.

The first ethics dealt with the relation between individuals; the Mosaic Decalogue is an example. Later accretions dealt with the relation between the individual and society. The Golden Rule tries to integrate the individual to society; democracy to integrate social organization to the individual.

There is as yet no ethic dealing with man's relation to land and to the animals and plants which grow upon it. Land, like Odysseus' slave-girls, is still property. The land-relation is still strictly economic, entailing privileges but not obligations.

The extension of ethics to this third element in human environment is, if I read the evidence correctly, an evolutionary possibility and an ecological necessity. It is the third step in a sequence. The first two have already been taken. Individual thinkers since the days of Ezekiel and Isaiah have asserted that the despoliation of land is not only inexpedient but wrong. Society, however, has not yet affirmed their belief. I regard the present conservation movement as the embryo of such an affirmation.

An ethic may be regarded as a mode of guidance for meeting ecological situations so new or intricate, or involving such deferred reactions, that the path of social expediency is not discernible to the average individual. Animal instincts are modes of guidance for the individual in meeting such situations. Ethics are possibly a kind of community instinct in-the-making.

THE COMMUNITY CONCEPT

All ethics so far evolved rest upon a single premise: that the individual is a member of a community of interdependent parts. His instincts prompt him to compete for his place in the community, but his ethics prompt him also to cooperate (perhaps in order that there may be a place to compete for).

The land ethic simply enlarges the boundaries of the

community to include soils, waters, plants, and animals, or collectively: the land.

This sounds simple: do we not already sing our love for and obligation to the land of the free and the home of the brave? Yes, but just what and whom do we love? Certainly not the soil, which we are sending helter-skelter downriver. Certainly not the waters, which we assume have no function except to turn turbines, float barges, and carry off sewage. Certainly not the plants, of which we exterminate whole communities without batting an eye. Certainly not the animals, of which we have already extirpated many of the largest and most beautiful species. A land ethic of course cannot prevent the alteration, management, and use of these "resources," but it does affirm their right to continued existence, and, at least in spots, their continued existence in a natural state.

In short, a land ethic changes the role of *Homo sapiens* from conqueror of the land-community to plain member and citizen of it. It implies respect for his fellow-members, and also respect for the community as such.

In human history, we have learned (I hope) that the conqueror role is eventually self-defeating. Why? Because it is implicit in such a role that the conqueror knows, *ex cathedra,* just what makes the community clock tick, and just what and who is valuable, and what and who is worthless, in community life. It always turns out that he knows neither, and this is why his conquests eventually defeat themselves.

In the biotic community, a parallel situation exists. Abraham knew exactly what the Land was for: it was to drip milk and honey into Abraham's mouth. At the present moment, the assurance with which we regard this assumption is inverse to the degree of our education.

The ordinary citizen today assumes that science knows what makes the community clock tick; the scientist is equally sure that he does not. He knows that the biotic mechanism is so complex that its workings may never be fully understood.

That man is, in fact, only a member of a biotic team is shown by an ecological interpretation of history. Many historical events, hitherto explained solely in terms of human enterprise, were actually biotic interactions between people and land. The characteristics of the land determined the facts quite as potently as the characteristics of the men who lived on it.

Consider, for example, the settlement of the Mississippi valley In the years following the Revolution, three groups were contending for its control: the native Indian, the French and English traders, and the American settlers. Historians wonder what would have happened if the English at Detroit had thrown a little more weight into the Indian side of those tipsy scales which decided the outcome of the colonial migration into the cane-lands of Kentucky. It is time now to ponder the fact that the cane-lands, when subjected to the particular mixture of forces represented by the cow, plow, fire, and ax of the pioneer, became bluegrass.

What if the plant succession inherent in this dark and bloody ground had, under the impact of these forces, given us some worthless sedge, shrub, or weed? Would Boone and Kenton have held out? Would there have been any overflow into Ohio, Indiana, Illinois, and Missouri? Any Louisiana Purchase? Any transcontinental union of new states? Any Civil War?

Kentucky was one sentence in the drama of history. We are commonly told what the human actors in this drama tried to do, but we are seldom told that their success, or the lack of it, hung in large degree on the reaction of particular soils to the impact of the particular forces exerted by their occupancy. In the case of Kentucky, we do not even know where the bluegrass came from— whether it is a native species, or a stowaway from Europe.

Contrast the cane-lands with what hindsight tells us about the Southwest, where the pioneers were equally brave, resourceful, and persevering. The impact of occupancy here brought no bluegrass, or other plant fitted to withstand the bumps and buffetings of hard use. This region, when grazed by livestock, reverted through a sense of more and more worthless grasses, shrubs, and weeds to a condition of unstable equilibrium. Each recession of plant types bred erosion; each increment to erosion bred a further recession of plants. The result today is a progressive and mutual deterioration, not only of plants and soils, but of the animal community subsisting thereon. The early settlers did not expect this: on the ciénegas of New Mexico some even cut ditches to hasten it. So subtle has been its progress that few residents of the region are aware of it. It is quite invisible to the tourist who finds this wrecked landscape colorful and charming (as indeed it is, but it bears scant resemblance to what it was in 1848).

This same landscape was "developed" once before, but with quite different results. The Pueblo Indians settled the Southwest in pre-Columbian times, but they happened *not* to be equipped with range livestock. Their civilization expired, but not because their land expired.

In India, regions devoid of any sod-forming grass have been settled, apparently without wrecking the land, by the simple expedient of carrying the grass to the cow, rather than vice versa. (Was this the result of some deep wisdom, or was it just good luck? I do not know.)

In short, the plant succession steered the course of history; the pioneer simply demonstrated, for good or ill, what successions inhered in the land. Is history taught in this spirit? It will be, once the concept of land as a community really penetrates our intellectual life.

THE ECOLOGICAL CONSCIENCE

Conservation is a state of harmony between men and land. Despite nearly a century of propaganda, conservation still proceeds at a snail's pace; progress still consists largely of letterhead pieties and convention oratory. On the back forty we still slip two steps backward for each forward stride.

The usual answer to this dilemma is "more conservation education." No one will debate this, but is it certain that only the *volume* of education needs stepping up? Is something lacking in the *content* as well?

It is difficult to give a fair summary of its content in brief form, but, as I understand it, the content is substantially this: obey the law, vote right, join some organizations, and practice what conservation is profitable on your own land; the government will do the rest.

Is not this formula too easy to accomplish anything worthwhile? It defines no right or wrong, assigns no obligation, calls for no sacrifice, implies no change in the current philosophy of values. In respect of land-use, it urges only enlightened self-interest. Just how far will such education take us? An example will perhaps yield a partial answer.

By 1930 it had become clear to all except the ecologically blind that southwestern Wisconsin's topsoil was slipping seaward. In 1933 the farmers were told that if they would adopt certain remedial practices for five years, the public would donate CCC labor to install them, plus the necessary machinery and materials. The offer was widely accepted, but the practices were widely forgotten when the five-year contract period was up. The farmers continued only those practices that yielded an immediate and visible economic gain for themselves.

This led to the idea that maybe farmers would learn more quickly if they themselves wrote the rules. Accordingly the Wisconsin Legislature in 1937 passed the Soil Conservation District Law. This said to farmers, in effect: *We, the public, will furnish you free technical service and loan you specialized machinery, if you will write your own rules for land-use. Each county may write its own rules, and these will have the force of law.* Nearly all the counties promptly organized to accept the proffered help, but after a decade of operation, *no county has yet written a single rule.* There has been visible progress in such practices as strip-cropping, pasture renovation, and soil liming, but none in fencing woodlots against grazing, and none in excluding plow and cow from steep slopes. The farmers, in short, have selected those remedial practices which were profitable anyhow, and ignored those which were profitable to the community, but not clearly profitable to themselves.

When one asks why no rules have been written, one is told that the community is not yet ready to support them; education must precede rules. But the education actually in progress makes no mention of obligations to land over and above those dictated by self-interest. The net result is that we have more education but less soil, fewer healthy woods, and as many floods as in 1937.

The puzzling aspect of such situations is that the existence of obligations over and above self-interest is

taken for granted in such rural community enterprises as the betterment of roads, schools, churches, and baseball teams. Their existence is not taken for granted, nor as yet seriously discussed, in bettering the behavior of the water that falls on the land, or in the preserving of the beauty or diversity of the farm landscape. Land-use ethics are still governed wholly by economic self-interest, just as social ethics were a century ago.

To sum up: we asked the farmer to do what he conveniently could to save his soil, and he has done just that, and only that. The farmer who clears the woods off a 75 per cent slope, turns his cows into the clearing, and dumps its rainfall, rocks, and soil into the community creek, is still (if otherwise decent) a respected member of society. If he puts lime on his fields and plants his crops on contour, he is still entitled to all the privileges and emoluments of his Soil Conservation District. The District is a beautiful piece of social machinery, but it is coughing along on two cylinders because we have been too timid, and too anxious for quick success, to tell the farmer the true magnitude of his obligations. Obligations have no meaning without conscience, and the problem we face is the extension of the social conscience from people to land.

No important change in ethics was ever accomplished without an internal change in our intellectual emphasis, loyalties, affections, and convictions. The proof that conservation has not yet touched these foundations of conduct lies in the fact that philosophy and religion have not yet heard of it. In our attempt to make conservation easy, we have made it trivial.

SUBSTITUTES FOR A LAND ETHIC

When the logic of history hungers for bread and we hand out a stone, we are at pains to explain how much the stone resembles bread. I now describe some of the stones which serve in lieu of a land ethic.

One basic weakness in a conservation system based wholly on economic motives is that most members of the land community have no economic value. Wildflowers and songbirds are examples. Of the 22,000 higher plants and animals native to Wisconsin, it is doubtful whether more than 5 per cent can be sold, fed, eaten, or otherwise put to economic use. Yet these creatures are members of the biotic community, and if (as I believe) its stability depends on its integrity, they are entitled to continuance.

When one of these non-economic categories is threatened, and if we happen to love it, we invent subterfuges to give it economic importance. At the beginning of the century songbirds were supposed to be disappearing. Ornithologists jumped to the rescue with some distinctly shaky evidence to the effect that insects would eat us up if birds failed to control them. The evidence had to be economic in order to be valid.

It is painful to read these circumlocutions today. We have no land ethic yet, but we have at least drawn nearer the point of admitting that birds should continue as a matter of biotic right, regardless of the presence or absence of economic advantage to us.

A parallel situation exists in respect of predatory mammals, raptorial birds, and fish-eating birds. Time was when biologists somewhat overworked the evidence that these creatures preserve the health of game by killing weaklings, or that they control rodents for the farmer, or that they prey only on "worthless" species. Here again, the evidence had to be economic in order to be valid. It is only in recent years that we hear the more honest argument that predators are members of the community, and that no special interest has the right to exterminate them for the sake of a benefit, real or fancied, to itself. Unfortunately this enlightened view is still in the talk stage. In the field the extermination of predators goes merrily on: witness the impending erasure of the timber wolf by fiat of Congress, the Conservation Bureaus, and many state legislatures.

Some species of trees have been "read out of the party" by economics-minded foresters because they grow too slowly, or have too low a sale value to pay as timber crops: white cedar, tamarack, cypress, beech, and hemlock are examples. In Europe, where forestry is ecologically more advanced, the non-commercial tree species are recognized as members of the native forest community, to be preserved as such, within reason. Moreover some (like beech) have been found to have a valuable function in building up soil fertility. The interdependence of the forest and its constituent tree species, ground flora, and fauna is taken for granted.

Lack of economic value is sometimes a character not only of species or groups, but of entire biotic communities: marshes, bogs, dunes, and "deserts" are examples. Our formula in such cases is to relegate their conservation to government as refuges, monuments, or parks. The difficulty is that these communities are usually interspersed with more valuable private lands; the government cannot possibly own or control such scattered parcels. The net effect is that we have relegated some of them to ultimate extinction over large areas. If the private owner were ecologically minded, he would be proud to be the custodian of a reasonable proportion of such areas, which add diversity and beauty to his farm and to his community.

In some instances, the assumed lack of profit in these "waste" areas has proved to be wrong, but only after most of them had been done away with. The present scramble to reflood muskrat marshes is a case in point.

There is a clear tendency in American conservation to relegate to government all necessary jobs that private landowners fail to perform. Government ownership, operation, subsidy, or regulation is now widely prevalent in forestry, range management, soil and watershed management, park and wilderness conservation, fisheries management, and migratory bird management, with more to come. Most of this growth in governmental conservation is proper and logical, some of it is inevitable. That I imply no disapproval of it is implicit in the fact that I have spent most of my life working for it. Nevertheless the question arises: What is the ultimate magnitude of the enterprise? Will the tax base carry its eventual ramifications? At what point will governmental conservation, like the mastodon, become handicapped by its own dimensions? The answer, if there is any, seems to be in a land ethic, or some other force which assigns more obligation to the private landowner.

Industrial landowners and users, especially lumbermen and stockmen, are inclined to wail long and loudly about the extension of government ownership and regulation to land, but (with notable exceptions) they show little disposition to develop the only visible alternative: the voluntary practice of conservation on their own lands.

When the private landowner is asked to perform some unprofitable act for the good of the community, he today assents only with outstretched palm. If the act costs him cash this is fair and proper, but when it costs only forethought, open-mindedness, or time, the issue is at least debatable. The overwhelming growth of land-uses subsidies in recent years must be ascribed, in large part, to the government's own agencies for conservation education: the land bureaus, the agricultural colleges, and the extension services. As far as I can detect, no ethical obligation toward land is taught in these institutions.

To sum up: a system of conservation based solely on economic self-interest is hopelessly lopsided. It tends to ignore, and thus eventually to eliminate, many elements in the land community that lack commercial value, but that are (as far as we know) essential to its healthy functioning. It assumes, falsely, I think, that the economic parts of the biotic clock will function without the uneconomic parts. It tends to relegate to government many functions eventually too large, too complex, or too widely dispersed to be performed by government.

An ethical obligation on the part of the private owner is the only visible remedy for these situations.

THE LAND PYRAMID

An ethic to supplement and guide the economic relation to land presupposes the existence of some mental image of land as a biotic mechanism. We can be ethical only in relation to something we can see, feel, understand, love, or otherwise have faith in.

The image commonly employed in conservation education is "the balance of nature." For reasons too lengthy to detail here, this figure of speech fails to describe accurately what little we know about the land mechanism. A much truer image is the one employed in ecology: the biotic pyramid. I shall first sketch the pyramid as a symbol of land, and later develop some of its implications in terms of land-use.

Plants absorb energy from the sun. This energy flows through a circuit called the biota, which may be represented by a pyramid consisting of layers. The bottom layer is the soil. A plant layer rests on the soil, an insect layer on the plants, a bird and rodent layer on the insects, and so on up through various animal groups to the apex layer, which consists of the larger carnivores.

The species of a layer are alike not in where they came from, or in what they look like, but rather in what they eat. Each successive layer depends on those below it for food and often for other services, and each in turn furnishes food and services to those above. Proceeding upward, each successive layer decreases in numerical abundance. Thus, for every carnivore there are hundreds of his prey, thousands of their prey, millions of insects, uncountable plants. The pyramidal form of the system reflects this numerical progression from apex to base. Man shares an intermediate layer with the bears, raccoons, and squirrels which eat both meat and vegetables.

The lines of dependency for food and other services are called food chains. Thus soil-oak-deer-Indian is a chain that has now been largely converted to soil-corn-cow-farmer. Each species, including ourselves, is a link in many chains . The deer eats a hundred plants other than oak, and the cow a hundred plants other than corn. Both, then, are links in a hundred chains. The pyramid is a tangle of chains so complex as to seem disorderly, yet the stability of the system proves it to be a highly organized structure. Its functioning depends on the cooperation and competition of its diverse parts.

In the beginning, the pyramid of life was low and squat; the food chains short and simple. Evolution has added layer after layer, link after link. Man is one of thousands of accretions to the height and complexity of the pyramid. Science has given us many doubts, but it has given us at least one certainty: the trend of evolution is to elaborate and diversify the biota.

Land, then, is not merely soil; it is a fountain of energy flowing through a circuit of soils, plants, and animals. Food chains are the living channels which conduct energy upward; death and decay return it to the soil. The circuit is not closed; some energy is dissipated in decay, some is added by absorption from the air, some is stored in soils, peats, and long-lived forests; but it is a sustained circuit, like a slowly augmented revolving fund of life. There is always a net loss by downhill wash, but this is normally small and offset by the decay of rocks. It is deposited in the ocean and, in the course of geological time, raised to form new lands and new pyramids.

The velocity and character of the upward flow of energy depend on the complex structure of the plant and animal community, much as the upward flow of sap in a tree depends on its complex cellular organization.

Without this complexity, normal circulation would presumably not occur. Structure means the characteristic numbers, as well as the characteristic kinds and functions, of the component species. This interdependence between the complex structure of the land and its smooth functioning as an energy unit is one of its basic attributes.

When a change occurs in one part of the circuit, many other parts must adjust themselves to it. Change does not necessarily obstruct or divert the flow of energy; evolution is a long series of self-induced changes, the net result of which has been to elaborate the flow mechanism and to lengthen the circuit. Evolutionary changes, however, are usually slow and local. Man's invention of tools has enabled him to make changes of unprecedented violence, rapidity, and scope.

One change is in the composition of floras and faunas. The larger predators are lopped off the apex of the pyramid; food chains, for the first time in history, become shorter rather than longer. Domesticated species from other lands are substituted for wild ones, and wild ones are moved to new habitats. In this world-wide pooling of faunas and floras, some species get out of bounds as pests and diseases, others are extinguished. Such effects are seldom intended or foreseen; they represent unpredicted and often untraceable readjustments in the structure. Agricultural science is largely a race between the emergence of new pests and the emergence of new techniques for their control.

Another change touches the flow of energy through plants and animals and its return to the soil. Fertility is the ability of soil to receive, store, and release energy. Agriculture, by overdrafts on the soil, or by too radical a substitution of domestic for native species in the superstructure, may derange the channels of flow or deplete storage. Soils depleted of their storage, or of the organic matter which anchors it, wash away faster than they form. This is erosion.

Waters, like soil, are part of the energy circuit. Industry, by polluting waters or obstructing them with dams, may exclude the plants and animals necessary to keep energy in circulation.

Transportation brings about another basic change: the plants or animals grown in one region are now consumed and returned to the soil in another. Transportation taps the energy stored in rocks, and in the air, and uses it elsewhere; thus we fertilize the garden with nitrogen gleaned by the guano birds from the fishes of seas on the other side of the Equator. Thus the formerly localized and self-contained circuits are pooled on a world-wide scale.

The process of altering the pyramid for human occupation releases stored energy, and this often gives rise, during the pioneering period, to a deceptive exuberance of plant and animal life, both wild and tame. These releases of biotic capital tend to becloud or postpone the penalties of violence.

This thumbnail sketch of land as an energy circuit conveys three basic ideas:

1. That land is not merely soil.
2. That the native plants and animals kept the energy circuit open; others may or may not.
3. That man-made changes are of a different order than evolutionary changes, and have effects more comprehensive than is intended or foreseen.

These ideas, collectively, raise two basic issues: Can the land adjust itself to the new order? Can the desired alterations be accomplished with less violence?

Biotas seem to differ in their capacity to sustain violent conversion. Western Europe, for example, carries a far different pyramid than Caesar found there. Some large animals are lost; swampy forests have become meadows or plowland; many new plants and animals are introduced, some of which escape as pests; the remaining natives are greatly changed in distribution and abundance. Yet the soil is still there and, with the help of imported nutrients, still fertile; and waters flow normally; the new structure seems to function and to persist. There is no visible stoppage or derangement of the circuit.

Western Europe, then, has a resistant biota. Its inner processes are tough, elastic, resistant to strain. No matter how violent the alterations, the pyramid, so far, has developed some new *modus vivendi* which preserves its habitability for man, and for most of the other natives.

Japan seems to present another instance of radical conversion without disorganization.

Most other civilized regions, and some as yet barely touched by civilization, display various stages of disorganization, varying from initial symptoms to advanced wastage. In Asia Minor and North Africa diagnosis is confused by climatic changes, which may have been either the cause or the effect of advanced wastage. In the United States the degree of disorganization varies locally; it is worst in the Southwest, the Ozarks, and parts of the South, and least in New England and the Northwest. Better land-uses may still arrest it in the less advanced regions. In parts of Mexico, South America, South Africa, and Australia a violent and accelerating wastage is in progress, but I cannot assess the prospects.

This almost world-wide display of disorganization in the land seems to be similar to disease in an animal, except that it never culminates in complete disorganization or death. The land recovers, but at some reduced level of complexity, and with a reduced carrying capacity for people, plants, and animals. Many biotas currently regarded as "lands of opportunity" are in fact already subsisting on exploitative agriculture, i.e. they have already exceeded their sustained carrying capacity. Most of South America is overpopulated in this sense.

In arid regions we attempt to offset the process of wastage by reclamation, but it is only too evident that the prospective longevity of reclamation projects is often short. In our own West, the best of them may not last a century.

The combined evidence of history and ecology seems to support one general deduction: the less violent the man-made changes, the greater the probability of successful readjustment in the pyramid. Violence, in turn, varies with human population density; a dense population requires a more violent conversion. In this respect, North America has a better chance for permanence than Europe, if she can contrive to limit her density.

This deduction runs counter to our current philosophy, which assumes that because a small increase in density enriched human life, that an indefinite increase will enrich it indefinitely. Ecology knows of no density relationship that holds for indefinitely wide limits. All gains from density are subject to a law of diminishing returns.

Whatever may be the equation for men and land, it is improbable that we as yet know all its terms. Recent discoveries in mineral and vitamin nutrition reveal unsuspected dependencies in the up-circuit: incredibly minute quantities of certain substances determine the value of soils to plants, of plants to animals. What of the down-circuit? What of the vanishing species, the preservation of which we now regard as an esthetic luxury? They helped build the soil; in what unsuspected ways may they be essential to its maintenance? Professor Weaver proposes that we use prairie flowers to refloculate the wasting soils of the dust bowl; who knows for what purpose cranes and condors, otters and grizzlies may some day be used?

LAND HEALTH AND THE A-B CLEAVAGE

A land ethic, then, reflects the existence of an ecological conscience, and this in turn reflects a conviction of individual responsibility for the health of the land. Health is the capacity of the land for self-renewal. Conservation is our effort to understand and preserve this capacity.

Conservationists are notorious for their dissensions. Superficially these seem to add up to mere confusion, but a more careful scrutiny reveals a single plane of cleavage common to many specialized fields. In each field one group (A) regards the land as soil, and its function as commodity-production; another group (B) regards the land as a biota, and its function as something broader. How much broader is admittedly in a state of doubt and confusion.

In my own field, forestry, group A is quite content to grow trees like cabbages, with cellulose as the basic forest commodity. It feels no inhibition against violence; its ideology is agronomic. Group B, on the other hand, sees forestry as fundamentally different from agronomy because it employs natural species, and manages a natural environment rather than creating an artificial one. Group B prefers natural reproduction on principle. It worries on biotic as well as economic grounds about the loss of species like chestnut, and the threatened loss of the white pines. It worries about a whole series of secondary forest functions: wildlife, recreation, watersheds, wilderness areas. To my mind, Group B feels the stirrings of an ecological conscience.

In the wildlife field, a parallel cleavage exists. For Group A the basic commodities are sport and meat; the yardsticks of production are ciphers of take in pheasants and trout. Artificial propagation is acceptable as a permanent as well as a temporary recourse—if its unit costs permit. Group B, on the other hand, worries about a whole series of biotic side-issues. What is the cost in predators of producing a game crop? Should we have further recourse to exotics? How can management restore the shrinking species, like prairie grouse, already hopeless as shootable game? How can management restore the threatened rarities, like trumpeter swan and whooping crane? Can management principles be extended to wildflowers? Here again it is clear to me that we have the same A-B cleavage as in forestry.

In the larger field of agriculture I am less competent to speak, but there seem to be somewhat parallel cleavages. Scientific agriculture was actively developing before ecology was born, hence a slower penetration of ecological concepts might be expected. Moreover the farmer, by the very nature of his techniques, must modify the biota more radically than the forester or the wildlife manager. Nevertheless, there are many discontents in agriculture which seem to add up to a new vision of "biotic farming."

Perhaps the most important of these is the new evidence that poundage or tonnage is no measure of the food-value of farm crops; the products of fertile soil may be qualitatively as well as quantitatively superior. We can bolster poundage from depleted soils by pouring on imported fertility, but we are not necessarily bolstering food-value. The possible ultimate ramifications of this idea are so immense that I must leave their exposition to abler pens.

The discontent that labels itself "organic farming," while bearing some of the earmarks of a cult, is nevertheless biotic in its direction, particularly in its insistence on the importance of soil flora and fauna.

The ecological fundamentals of agriculture are just as poorly known to the public as in other fields of land-use. For example, few educated people realize that the marvelous advances in technique made during recent decades are improvements in the pump, rather than the well. Acre for acre, they have barely sufficed to offset the sinking level of fertility.

In all of these cleavages, we see repeated the same basic paradoxes: man the conqueror *versus* man the biotic citizen; science the sharpener of his sword *versus* science the searchlight on his universe; land the slave and servant *versus* land the collective organism. Robinson's injunction to Tristram may well be applied, at this juncture, to *Homo sapiens* as a species in geological time:

> Whether you will or not
> You are a King, Tristram, for you are one
> Of the time-tested few that leave the world,
> When they are gone, not the same place it was.
> Mark what you leave.

THE OUTLOOK

It is inconceivable to me that an ethical relation to land can exist without love, respect, and admiration for land, and a high regard for its value. By value, I of course mean something far broader than mere economic value; I mean value in the philosophical sense.

Perhaps the most serious obstacle impeding the evolution of a land ethic is the fact that our educational and economic system is headed away from, rather than toward, an intense consciousness of land. Your true modern is separated from the land by many middlemen, and by innumerable physical gadgets. He has no vital relation to it; to him it is the space between cities on which crops grow. Turn him loose for a day on the land, and if the spot does not happen to be a golf links or a "scenic" area, he is bored stiff. If crops could be raised by hydroponics instead of farming, it would suit him very well. Synthetic substitutes for wood, leather, wool, and other natural land products suit him better than the originals. In short, land is something he has "outgrown."

Almost equally serious as an obstacle to a land ethic is the attitude of the farmer for whom the land is still an adversary, or a taskmaster that keeps him in slavery. Theoretically, the mechanization of farming ought to cut the farmer's chains, but whether it really does is debatable.

One of the requisites for an ecological comprehension of land is an understanding of ecology, and this is by no means co-extensive with "education"; in fact, much higher education seems deliberately to avoid ecological concepts. An understanding of ecology does not necessarily originate in courses bearing ecological labels; it is quite as likely to be labeled geography, botany, agronomy, history, or economics. This is as it should be, but whatever the label, ecological training is scarce.

The case for a land ethic would appear hopeless but for the minority which is in obvious revolt against these "modern" trends.

The "key-log" which must be moved to release the evolutionary process for an ethic is simply this: quit thinking about decent land-use as solely an economic problem. Examine each question in terms of what is ethically and esthetically right, as well as what is economically expedient. A thing is right when it tends to preserve the integrity, stability, and beauty of the biotic community. It is wrong when it tends otherwise.

It of course goes without saying that economic feasibility limits the tether of what can or cannot be done for land. It always has and it always will. The fallacy the economic determinists have tied around our collective neck, and which we now need to cast off, is the belief that economics determines *all* land-use. This is simply not true. An innumerable host of actions and attitudes, comprising perhaps the bulk of all land relations, is determined by the land-users' tastes and predilections, rather than by his purse. The bulk of all land relations hinges on investments of time, forethought, skill, and faith rather than on investments of cash. As a land-user thinketh, so is he.

I have purposely presented the land ethic as a product of social evolution because nothing so important as an ethic is ever "written." Only the most superficial student of history supposes that Moses "wrote" the Decalogue; it evolved in the minds of a thinking community, and Moses wrote a tentative summary of it for a "seminar." I say tentative because evolution never stops.

The evolution of a land ethic is an intellectual as well as emotional process. Conservation is paved with good intentions which prove to be futile, or even dangerous, because they are devoid of critical understanding either of the land, or of economic land-use. I think it is a truism that as the ethical frontier advances from the individual to the community, its intellectual content increases.

The mechanism of operation is the same for any ethic: social approbation for right actions, social disapproval for wrong actions.

By and large, our present problem is one of attitudes and implements. We are remodeling the Alhambra with a steamshovel, and we are proud of our yardage. We shall hardly relinquish the shovel, which after all has many good points, but we are in need of gentler and more objective criteria for its successful use.

Study Questions

1. Does Leopold make a case for the intrinsic value of the biotic community, or does he only assume this?
2. Analyze Leopold's view of humans and of biotic communities. How do we resolve conflicts between their claims and needs? Which are more important, ecosystems or individuals?
3. Critically discuss the strengths and weaknesses of Leopold's position.

19

The Conceptual Foundations of the Land Ethic

J. BAIRD CALLICOTT

J. Baird Callicott (b. 1941), is professor of philosophy and natural resources at the University of Wisconsin, Stevens Point, and the author of several works in environmental philosophy, including In Defense of the Land Ethic *(1989) from which this essay is taken.*

Callicott develops the philosophical implications of Leopold's land ethic. He shows how it is rooted in the eighteenth-century Scottish Sentimentalist School of David Hume and Adam Smith, who said that ethics is based in natural sympathy or sentiments. Leopold, adding a Darwinian dimension to these thoughts, extended the notion of natural sentiments to ecosystems as the locus of value. Callicott argues that Leopold is not claiming that we should sacrifice basic human needs to the environment, but rather that we should see ourselves as members of a wider ecological community.

The two great cultural advances of the past century were the Darwinian theory and the development of geology. . . .

Just as important, however, as the origin of plants, animals, and soil is the question of how they operate as a community. That task has fallen to the new science of ecology, which is daily uncovering a web of interdependencies so intricate as to amaze—were he here—even Darwin himself, who, of all men, should have least cause to tremble before the veil.

ALDO LEOPOLD, FRAGMENT 6B16, NO. 36, LEOPOLD PAPERS, UNIVERSITY OF WISCONSIN—MADISON ARCHIVES

I

As Wallace Stegner observes, *A Sand County Almanac* is considered "almost a holy book in conservation circles," and Aldo Leopold a prophet, "an American Isaiah." And as Curt Meine points out, "The Land Ethic" is the climactic essay of *Sand County*, "the upshot of 'The Upshot.'" One might, therefore, fairly say that the recommendation and justification of moral

Reprinted from *Companion to a Sand County Almanac* (Madison: WI: University of Wisconsin Press, 1987) by permission. Footnotes deleted.

obligations on the part of people to nature is what the prophetic *A Sand County Almanac* is all about.

But, with few exceptions, "The Land Ethic" has not been favorably received by contemporary academic philosophers. Most have ignored it. Of those who have not, most have been either nonplussed or hostile. Distinguished Australian philosopher John Passmore dismissed it out of hand, in the first book-length academic discussion of the new philosophical subdiscipline called "environmental ethics." In a more recent and more deliberate discussion, the equally distinguished Australian philosopher H. J. McCloskey patronized Aldo Leopold and saddled "The Land Ethic" with various far-fetched "interpretations." He concludes that "there is a real problem in attributing a coherent meaning to Leopold's statements, one that exhibits his land ethic as representing a major advance in ethics rather than a retrogression to a morality of a kind held by various primitive peoples." Echoing McCloskey, English philosopher Robin Attfield went out of his way to impugn the philosophical respectability of "The Land Ethic." And Canadian philosopher L. W. Sumner has called it "dangerous nonsense." Among those philosophers more favorably disposed, "The Land Ethic" has usually been simply quoted, as if it were little more than a noble, but naive, moral plea, altogether lacking a supporting theoretical framework—that is, foundational principles and premises which lead, by compelling argument, to ethical precepts.

The professional neglect, confusion, and (in some cases) contempt for "The Land Ethic" may, in my judgment, be attributed to three things: (1) Leopold's extremely condensed prose style in which an entire conceptual complex may be conveyed in a few sentences, or even in a phrase or two; (2) his departure from the assumptions and paradigms of contemporary philosophical ethics; and (3) the unsettling practical implications to which a land ethic appears to lead. "The Land Ethic," in short, is, from a philosophical point of view, abbreviated, unfamiliar, and radical.

Here I first examine and elaborate the compactly expressed abstract elements of the land ethic and expose the "logic" which binds them into a proper, but revolutionary, moral theory. I then discuss the controversial features of the land ethic and defend them against actual and potential criticism. I hope to show that the land ethic cannot be ignored as merely the groundless emotive exhortations of a moonstruck conservationist or dismissed as entailing wildly untoward practical consequences. It poses, rather, a serious intellectual challenge to business-as-usual moral philosophy.

II

"The Land Ethic" opens with a charming and poetic evocation of Homer's Greece, the point of which is to suggest that today land is just as routinely and remorselessly enslaved as human beings then were. A panoramic glance backward to our most distant cultural origins, Leopold suggests, reveals a slow but steady moral development over three millennia. More of our relationships and activities ("fields of conduct") have fallen under the aegis of moral principles ("ethical criteria") as civilization has grown and matured. If moral growth and development continue, as not only a synoptic review of history, but recent past experience suggest that it will, future generations will censure today's casual and universal environmental bondage as today we censure the casual and universal human bondage of three thousand years ago.

A cynically inclined critic might scoff at Leopold's sanguine portrayal of human history. Slavery survived as an institution in the "civilized" West, more particularly in the morally self-congratulatory United States, until a mere generation before Leopold's own birth. And Western history from imperial Athens and Rome to the Spanish Inquisition and the Third Reich has been a disgraceful series of wars, persecutions, tyrannies, pogroms, and other atrocities.

The history of moral practice, however, is not identical with the history of moral consciousness. Morality is not descriptive; it is prescriptive or normative. In light of this distinction, it is clear that today, despite rising rates of violent crime in the United States and institutional abuses of human rights in Iran, Chile, Ethiopia, Guatemala, South Africa, and many other places, and despite persistent organized social injustice and oppression in still others, moral consciousness is expanding more rapidly now than ever before. Civil rights, human rights, women's liberation, children's liberation, animal liberation, and so forth, all indicate, as expressions of newly emergent moral ideals, that ethical consciousness (as distinct from practice) has if anything recently accelerated—thus confirming Leopold's historical observation.

III

Leopold next points out that "this extension of ethics, so far studied only by philosophers"—and therefore, the implication is clear, not very satisfactorily studied "is actually a process in ecological evolution" (p. 202). What Leopold is saying here, simply, is that we may understand the history of ethics, fancifully alluded to by means of the Odysseus vignette, in biological as well as philosophical terms. From a biological point of view, an ethic is "a limitation on freedom of action in the struggle for existence" (p. 202). . . .

Let me put the problem in perspective. How, . . . did ethics originate and, once in existence, grow in scope and complexity?

The oldest answer in living human memory is theological. God (or the gods) imposes morality on people.

And God (or the gods) sanctions it. A most vivid and graphic example of this kind of account occurs in the Bible when Moses goes up on Mount Sinai to receive the Ten Commandments directly from God. That text also clearly illustrates the divine sanctions (plagues, pestilences, droughts, military defeats, and so forth) for moral disobedience. Ongoing revelation of the divine will, of course, as handily and as simply explains subsequent moral growth and development.

Western philosophy, on the other hand, is almost unanimous in the opinion that the origin of ethics in human experience has somehow to do with human reason. Reason figures centrally and pivotally in the "social contract theory" of the origin and nature of morals in all its ancient, modern, and contemporary expressions from Protagoras, to Hobbes, to Rawls. Reason is the wellspring of virtue, according to both Plato and Aristotle, and of categorical imperatives, according to Kant. In short, the weight of Western philosophy inclines to the view that we are moral beings because we are rational beings. The ongoing sophistication of reason and the progressive illumination it sheds upon the good and the right explain "the ethical sequence," the historical growth and development of morality, noticed by Leopold.

An evolutionary natural historian, however, cannot be satisfied with either of these general accounts of the origin and development of ethics. The idea that God gave morals to man is ruled out in principle—as any supernatural explanation of a natural phenomenon is ruled out in principle in natural science. And while morality might *in principle* be a function of human reason (as, say, mathematical calculation clearly is), to suppose that it is so *in fact* would be to put the cart before the horse. Reason appears to be a delicate, variable, and recently emerged faculty. It cannot, under any circumstances, be supposed to have evolved in the absence of complex linguistic capabilities which depend, in turn, for their evolution upon a highly developed social matrix. But we cannot have become social beings unless we assumed limitations on freedom of action in the struggle for existence. Hence we must have become ethical before we became rational.

Darwin, probably in consequence of reflections somewhat like these, turned to a minority tradition of modern philosophy for a moral psychology consistent with and useful to a general evolutionary account of ethical phenomena. A century earlier, Scottish philosophers David Hume and Adam Smith had argued that ethics rest upon feelings or "sentiments"—which, to be sure, may be both amplified and informed by reason. And since in the animal kingdom feelings or sentiments are arguably far more common or widespread than reason, they would be a far more likely starting point for an evolutionary account of the origin and growth of ethics.

Darwin's account, to which Leopold unmistakably (if elliptically) alludes in "The Land Ethic," begins with the parental and filial affections common, perhaps, to all mammals. Bonds of affection and sympathy between parents and offspring permitted the formation of small, closely knit social groups, Darwin argued. Should the parental and familial affections bonding family members chance to extend to less closely related individuals, that would permit an enlargement of the family group. And should the newly extended community more successfully defend itself and/or more efficiently provision itself, the inclusive fitness of its members severally would be increased, Darwin reasoned. Thus the more diffuse familial affections, which Darwin (echoing Hume and Smith) calls the "social sentiments" would be spread throughout a population.

Morality, properly speaking—that is, morality as opposed to mere altruistic instinct—requires, in Darwin's terms, "intellectual powers" sufficient to recall the past and imagine the future, "the power of language" sufficient to express "common opinion," and "habituation" to patterns of behavior deemed, by common opinion, to be socially acceptable and beneficial. Even so, ethics proper, in Darwin's account, remains firmly rooted in moral feelings or social sentiments which were—no less than physical faculties, he expressly avers—naturally selected, by the advantages for survival and especially for successful reproduction, afforded by society.

The protosociobiological perspective on ethical phenomena, to which Leopold as a natural historian was heir, leads him to a generalization which is remarkably explicit in his condensed and often merely resonant rendering of Darwin's more deliberate and extended paradigm: Since "the thing [ethics] has its origin in the tendency of interdependent individuals or groups to evolve modes of co-operation, . . . all ethics so far evolved rest upon a single premise: that the individual is a member of a community of interdependent parts" (p. 202–3).

Hence, we may expect to find that the scope and specific content of ethics will reflect both the perceived boundaries and actual structure or organization of a cooperative community or society. *Ethics and society or community are correlative.* This single, simple principle constitutes a powerful tool for the analysis of moral natural history, for the anticipation of future moral development (including, ultimately, the land ethic), and for systematically deriving the specific precepts, the prescriptions and proscriptions, of an emergent and culturally unprecedented ethic like a land or environmental ethic.

IV

Anthropological studies of ethics reveal that in fact the boundaries of the moral community are generally coextensive with the perceived boundaries of society. And the peculiar (and, from the urbane point of view, sometimes inverted) representation of virtue and vice in tribal society—the virtue, for example, of sharing to the point of personal destitution and the vice of privacy and private property—reflects and fosters the life way of tribal peoples. Darwin, in his leisurely, anecdotal discussion, paints a vivid picture of the intensity, peculiarity, and sharp circumscription of "savage" mores: "A savage will risk his life to save that of a member of the same community, but will be wholly indifferent about a stranger." As Darwin portrays them, tribespeople are at once paragons of virtue "within the limits of the same tribe" and enthusiastic thieves, manslaughterers, and torturers without.

For purposes of more effective defense against common enemies, or because of increased population density, or in response to innovations in subsistence methods and technologies, or for some mix of these or other forces, human societies have grown in extent or scope and changed in form or structure. Nations—like the Iroquois nation or the Sioux nation—came into being upon the merger of previously separate and mutually hostile tribes. Animals and plants were domesticated and erstwhile hunter-gatherers became herders and farmers. Permanent habitations were established. Trade, craft, and (later) industry flourished. With each change in society came corresponding and correlative changes in ethics. The moral community expanded to become co-extensive with the newly drawn boundaries of societies and the representation of virtue and vice, right and wrong, good and evil, changed to accommodate, foster, and preserve the economic and institutional organization of emergent social orders.

Today we are witnessing the painful birth of a human supercommunity, global in scope. Modern transportation and communication technologies, international economic interdependencies, international economic entities, and nuclear arms have brought into being a "global village." It has not yet become fully formed and it is at tension—a very dangerous tension—with its predecessor, the nation-state. Its eventual institutional structure, a global federalism or whatever it may turn out to be, is at this point completely unpredictable. Interestingly, however, a corresponding global human ethic—the "human rights" ethic, as it is popularly called—has been more definitely articulated.

Most educated people today pay lip service at least to the ethical precept that all members of the human species, regardless of race, creed, or national origin, are endowed with certain fundamental rights which it is wrong not to respect. According to the evolutionary scenario set out by Darwin, the contemporary moral ideal of human rights is a response to a perception—however vague and indefinite—that mankind worldwide is united into one society, one community, however indeterminate or yet institutionally unorganized. As Darwin presciently wrote:

As man advances in civilization, and small tribes are

united into larger communities, the simplest reason would tell each individual that he ought to extend his social instincts and sympathies to all the members of the same nation, though personally unknown to him. This point being once reached, there is only an artificial barrier to prevent his sympathies extending to the men of all nations and races. If, indeed, such men are separated from him by great differences of appearance or habits, experience unfortunately shows us how long it is, before we look at them as our fellow-creatures.

According to Leopold, the next step in this sequence beyond the still incomplete ethic of universal humanity, a step that is clearly discernible on the horizon, is the land ethic. The "community concept" has, so far, propelled the development of ethics from the savage clan to the family of man. "The land ethic simply enlarges the boundary of the community to include soils, water, plants, and animals, or collectively: the land" (p. 204).

As the foreword to *Sand County* makes plain, the overarching thematic principle of the book is the inculcation of the idea—through narrative description, discursive exposition, abstractive generalization, and occasional preachment—"that land is a community" (viii). The community concept is "the basic concept of ecology" (viii). Once land is popularly perceived as a biotic community—as it is professionally perceived in ecology—a correlative land ethic will emerge in the collective cultural consciousness.

V

Although anticipated as far back as the mid-eighteenth century—in the notion of an "economy of nature"—the concept of the biotic community was more fully and deliberately developed as a working model or paradigm for ecology by Charles Elton in the 1920s. The natural world is organized as an intricate corporate society in which plants and animals occupy "niches," or as Elton alternatively called them, "roles" or "professions," in the economy of nature. As in a feudal community, little or no socioeconomic mobility (upward or otherwise) exists in the biotic community. One is born to one's trade.

Human society, Leopold argues, is founded, in large part, upon mutual security and economic interdependency and preserved only by limitations on freedom of action in the struggle for existence—that is, by ethical constraints. Since the biotic community exhibits, as modern ecology reveals, an analogous structure, it too can be preserved, given the newly amplified impact of "mechanized man," only by analogous limitations on freedom of action—that is, by a land ethic (viii). A land ethic, furthermore, is not only "an ecological necessity," but an "evolutionary possibility" because a moral response to the natural environment—Darwin's social sympathies, sentiments, and instincts translated and codified into a body of principles and precepts—would be automatically triggered in human beings by ecology's social representation of nature (p. 203).

Therefore, the key to the emergence of a land ethic is, simply, universal ecological literacy.

VI

The land ethic rests upon three scientific cornerstones: (1) evolutionary and (2) ecological biology set in a background of (3) Copernican astronomy. Evolutionary theory provides the conceptual link between ethics and social organization and development. It provides a sense of "kinship with fellow-creatures" as well, "fellow-voyagers" with us in the "odyssey of evolution" (p. 109). It establishes a diachronic link between people and nonhuman nature.

Ecological theory provides a synchronic link—the community concept—a sense of social integration of human and nonhuman nature. Human beings, plants, animals, soils, and waters are "all interlocked in one humming community of cooperations and competitions, one biota." The simplest reason, to paraphrase Darwin, should, therefore, tell each individual that he or she ought to extend his or her social instincts and sympathies to all the members of the biotic community though different from him or her in appearance or habits.

And although Leopold never directly mentions it in *A Sand County Almanac*, the Copernican perspective, the perception of the earth as "a small planet" in an immense and utterly hostile universe beyond, contributes, perhaps subconsciously, but nevertheless very powerfully, to our sense of kinship, community, and interdependence with fellow denizens of the earth household. It scales the earth down to something like a cozy island paradise in a desert ocean.

Here in outline, then, are the conceptual and logical foundations of the land ethic: Its conceptual elements are a Copernican cosmology, a Darwinian protosociobiological natural history of ethics, Darwinian ties of kinship among all forms of life on earth, and an Eltonian model of the structure of biocenoses all overlaid on a Humean–Smithian moral psychology. Its logic is that natural selection has endowed human beings with an affective moral response to perceived bonds of kinship and community membership and identity; that today the natural environment, the land, is represented as a community, the biotic community; and that, therefore, an environmental or land ethic is both possible—the biopsychological and cognitive conditions are in place—and necessary, since human beings collectively have acquired the power to destroy the integrity, diversity, and stability of the environing and supporting economy of nature. In the remainder of this essay I discuss special features and problems of the land ethic germane to moral philosophy.

The most salient feature of Leopold's land ethic is its provision of what Kenneth Goodpaster has carefully called "moral considerability" for the biotic community per se, not just for fellow members of the biotic community.

> In short, a land ethic changes the role of *Homo sapiens* from conqueror of the land-community to plain member and citizen of it. It implies respect for his fellow-members, *and also respect for the community as such.* (p. 204, emphasis added)

The land ethic, thus, has a holistic as well as an individualistic cast.

Indeed, as "The Land Ethic" develops, the focus of moral concern shifts gradually away from plants, animals, soils, and waters severally to the biotic community collectively. Toward the middle, in the subsection called "Substitutes for a Land Ethic," Leopold invokes the "biotic rights" of *species*—as the context indicates—of wildflowers, songbirds, and predators. In "The Outlook," the climactic section of "The Land Ethic," nonhuman natural entities, first appearing as fellow members, then considered in profile as species, are not so much as mentioned in what might be called the "summary moral maxim" of the land ethic: "A thing is right when it tends to preserve the integrity, stability, and beauty of the biotic community. It is wrong when it tends otherwise" (p. 224–25).

By this measure of right and wrong, not only would it be wrong for a farmer, in the interest of higher profits, to clear the woods off a 75 percent slope, turn his cows into the clearing and dump its rainfall, rocks, and soil into the community creek, it would also be wrong for the federal fish and wildlife agency, in the interest of individual animal welfare, to permit populations of deer, rabbits, feral burros, or whatever to increase unchecked and thus to threaten the integrity, stability, and beauty of the biotic communities of which they are members. The land ethic not only provides moral considerability for the biotic community per se, but ethical consideration of its individual members is preempted by concern for the preservation of the integrity, stability, and beauty of the biotic community. The land ethic, thus, not only has a holistic aspect; it is holistic with a vengeance.

The holism of the land ethic, more than any other feature, sets it apart from the predominant paradigm of modern moral philosophy. It is, therefore, the feature of the land ethic which requires the most patient theoretical analysis and the most sensitive practical interpretation.

VII

As Kenneth Goodpaster pointed out, mainstream modern ethical philosophy has taken egoism as its point of departure and reached a wider circle of moral entitlement by a process of generalization: I am sure that *I*, the enveloped ego, am intrinsically or inherently valuable and thus that *my* interests ought to be considered, taken into account, by "others" when their actions may substantively affect *me*. My own claim to moral consideration, according to the conventional wisdom, ultimately rests upon a psychological capacity—rationality or sentiency were the classical candidates of Kant and Bentham, respectively—which is arguably valuable in itself and which thus qualifies *me* for moral standing. However, then I am forced grudgingly to grant the same moral consideration I demand from others, on this basis, to those others who can also claim to possess the same general psychological characteristic.

A criterion of moral value and consideration is thus identified. Goodpaster convincingly argues that mainstream moral theory is based, when all the learned dust has settled, on this simple paradigm of ethical justification and logic exemplified by the Benthamic and Kantian prototypes. If the criterion of moral values and consideration is pitched low enough—as it is in Bentham's criterion of sentiency—a wide variety of animals are admitted to moral entitlement. If the criterion of moral value and consideration is pushed lower still—as it is in Albert Schweitzer's reverence-for-life ethic—all minimally conative things (plants as well as animals) would be extended moral considerability. The contemporary animal liberation/rights, and reverence-for-life/life-principle ethics are, at bottom, simply direct applications of the modern classical paradigm of moral argument. But this standard modern model of ethical theory provides no possibility whatever for the moral consideration of wholes—of threatened population of animals and plants, or of endemic, rare, or endangered species, or of biotic communities, or most expansively, of the biosphere in its totality—since wholes per se have no psychological experience of any kind. Because mainstream modern moral theory has been "psychocentric," it has been radically and intractably individualistic or "atomistic" in its fundamental theoretical orientation.

Hume, Smith, and Darwin diverged from the prevailing theoretical model by recognizing that altruism is as fundamental and autochthonous in human nature as is egoism. According to their analysis, moral value is not identified with a natural quality objectively present in morally considerable beings—as reason and/or sentiency is objectively present in people and/or animals—it is, as it were, projected by valuing subjects.

Hume and Darwin, furthermore, recognize inborn moral sentiments which have society as such as their natural object. Hume insists that "we must renounce the theory which accounts for every moral sentiment by the principle of self-love. We must adopt a more *publick affection* and allow that the *interests of society* are not, *even on their own account,* entirely indifferent to us." And Darwin, somewhat ironically (since "Darwinian evolution" very often means natural selection operating exclusively with respect to individuals), sometimes writes as if morality had no other object than the commonweal, the welfare of the community as a corporate entity:

> We have now seen that actions are regarded by savages, and were probably so regarded by primeval man, as good or bad, solely as they obviously affect the welfare of the tribe,—not that of the species, nor that of the individual member of the tribe. This conclusion agrees well with the belief that the so called moral sense is aboriginally derived from social instincts, for both relate at first exclusively to the community.

Theoretically then, the biotic community owns what Leopold, in the lead paragraph of "The Outlook," calls "value in the philosophical sense"—that is, direct moral considerability—because it is a newly discovered proper object of a specially evolved "publick affection" or "moral sense" which all psychologically normal human beings have inherited from a long line of ancestral social primates (p. 223).

VIII

In the land ethic, as in all earlier stages of social–ethical evolution, there exists a tension between the good of the community as a whole and the "rights" of its individual members considered severally. . . .

In any case, the conceptual foundations of the land ethic provide a well-informed, self-consistent theoretical basis for including both fellow members of the biotic community and the biotic community itself (considered as a corporate entity) within the purview of morals. The preemptive emphasis, however, on the welfare of the community as a whole, in Leopold's articulation of the land ethic, while certainly consistent with its Humean–Darwinian theoretical foundations, is not determined by them alone. The overriding holism of the land ethic results, rather, more from the way our moral sensibilities are informed by ecology.

IX

Ecological thought, historically, has tended to be holistic in outlook. Ecology is the study of the relationships of organisms to one another and to the elemental environment. These relationships bind the *relata*—plants, animals, soils, and waters—into a seamless fabric. The ontological primacy of objects and the ontological subordination of relationships characteristic of classical Western science is, in fact, reversed in ecology. Ecological relationships determine the nature of organisms rather than the other way around. A species is what it is because it has adapted to a niche in the ecosystem. The whole, the system itself, thus, literally and quite straightforwardly shapes and forms its component species.

Antedating Charles Elton's community model of ecology was F. E. Clements and S. A. Forbes's organism model. Plants and animals, soils and waters, according to this paradigm, are integrated into one superorganism. Species are, as it were, its organs; specimens its cells. Although Elton's community paradigm (later modified, as we shall see, by Arthur Tansley's ecosystem idea) is the principal and morally fertile ecological concept of "The Land Ethic," the more radically holistic superorganism paradigm of Clements and Forbes resonates in "The Land Ethic" as an audible overtone. In the peroration of "Land Health and the A-B Cleavage," for example, which immediately precedes "The Outlook," Leopold insists that

> in all these cleavages, we see repeated the same basic paradoxes: man the conqueror *versus* man the biotic citizen; science the sharpener of his sword *versus* science the searchlight on his universe; land the slave and servant *versus* land the collective organism. (p. 223)

And on more than one occasion Leopold, in the latter quarter of "The Land Ethic," talks about the "health" and "disease" of the land—terms which are at once descriptive and normative and which, taken literally, characterize only organisms proper.

In an early essay, "Some Fundamentals of Conservation in the Southwest," Leopold speculatively flirted with the intensely holistic superorganism model of the environment as a paradigm pregnant with moral implications. . . .

Had Leopold retained this overall theoretical approach in "The Land Ethic," the land ethic would doubtless have enjoyed more critical attention from philosophers. The moral foundations of a land or, as he might then have called it, "earth" ethic would rest upon the hypothesis that the Earth is alive and ensouled—possessing inherent psychological characteristics, logically parallel to reason and sentiency. This notion of a conative whole earth could plausibly have served as a general criterion of intrinsic worth and moral considerability, in the familiar format of mainstream moral thought.

Part of the reason, therefore, that "The Land Ethic" emphasizes more and more the integrity, stability, and beauty of the environment as a whole, and less and less the biotic right of individual plants and animals to life, liberty, and the pursuit of happiness, is that the superorganism ecological paradigm invites one, much more than does the community paradigm, to hypostatize, to reify the whole, and to subordinate its individual members.

In any case, as we see, rereading "The Land Ethic" in light of "Some Fundamentals," the whole Earth organism image of nature is vestigially present in Leopold's later thinking. Leopold may have abandoned the "earth ethic" because ecology had abandoned the organism analogy in favor of the community analogy as a working theoretical paradigm. And the community model

was more suitably given moral implications by the social/sentimental ethical natural history of Hume and Darwin.

Meanwhile, the biotic community ecological paradigm itself had acquired, by the late thirties and forties, a more holistic cast of its own. In 1935 British ecologist Arthur Tansley pointed out that from the perspective of physics the "currency" of the "economy of nature" is energy. Tansley suggested that Elton's qualitative and descriptive food chains, food webs, trophic niches, and biosocial professions could be quantitatively expressed by means of a thermodynamic flow model. It is Tansley's state-of-the-art thermodynamic paradigm of the environment that Leopold explicitly sets out as a "mental image of land" in relation to which "we can be ethical" (p. 214). And it is the ecosystemic model of land which informs the cardinal practical precepts of the land ethic.

"The Land Pyramid" is the pivotal section of "The Land Ethic"—the section which effects a complete transition from concern for "fellow-members" to the "community as such." It is also its longest and most technical section. A description of the "ecosystem" (Tansley's deliberately nonmetaphorical term) begins with the sun. Solar energy "flows through a circuit called the biota" (p. 215). It enters the biota through the leaves of green plants and courses through plant-eating animals, and then on to omnivores and carnivores. At last the tiny fraction of solar energy converted to biomass by green plants remaining in the corpse of a predator, animal feces, plant detritus, or other dead organic material is garnered by decomposers—worms, fungi, and bacteria. They recycle the participating elements and degrade into entropic equilibrium any remaining energy. According to this paradigm

> land, then, is not merely soil; it is a fountain of energy flowing through a circuit of soils, plants, and animals. Food chains are the living channels which conduct energy upward; death and decay return it to the soil. The circuit is not closed; . . . but it is a sustained circuit, like a slowly augmented revolving fund of life. (p. 216)

In this exceedingly abstract (albeit poetically expressed) model of nature, process precedes substance and energy is more fundamental than matter. Individual plants and animals become less autonomous beings than ephemeral structures in a patterned flux of energy. According to Yale biophysicist Harold Morowitz,

> viewed from the point of view of modern [ecology], each living thing . . . is a dissipative structure, that is it does not endure in and of itself but only as a result of the continual flow of energy in the system. An example might be instructive. Consider a vortex in a stream of flowing water. The vortex is a structure made of an ever-changing group of water molecules. It does not exist as an entity in the classical Western sense; it exists only because of the

flow of water through the stream. In the same sense, the structures out of which biological entities are made are transient, unstable entities with constantly changing molecules, dependent on a constant flow of energy from food in order to maintain form and structure. . . . From this point of view the reality of individuals is problematic because they do not exist per se but only as local perturbations in this universal flow.

Though less bluntly stated and made more palatable by the unfailing charm of his prose, Leopold's proffered mental image of land is just as expansive, systemic, and distanced as Morowitz's. The maintenance of "the complex structure of the land and its smooth functioning as an energy unit" emerges in "The Land Pyramid" as the *summum bonum* of the land ethic (p. 216).

X

From this good Leopold derives several practical principles slightly less general, and therefore more substantive, than the summary moral maxim of the land ethic distilled in "The Outlook." "The trend of evolution [not its "goal," since evolution is ateleological] is to elaborate and diversify the biota" (p. 216). Hence, among our cardinal duties is the duty to preserve what species we can, especially those at the apex of the pyramid—the top carnivores. "In the beginning, the pyramid of life was low and squat; the food chains short and simple. Evolution has added layer after layer, link after link" (pp. 215–16). Human activities today, especially those like systematic deforestation in the tropics, resulting in abrupt massive extinctions of species, are in effect "devolutionary"; they flatten the biotic pyramid; they choke off some of the channels and gorge others (those which terminate in our own species).

The land ethic does not enshrine the ecological status quo and devalue the dynamic dimension of nature. Leopold explains that "evolution is a long series of self-induced changes, the net result of which has been to elaborate the flow mechanism and to lengthen the circuit. Evolutionary changes, however, are usually slow and local. Man's invention of tools has enabled him to make changes of unprecedented violence, rapidity, and scope" (pp. 216–17). "Natural" species extinction, that is, species extinction in the normal course of evolution, occurs when a species is replaced by competitive exclusion or evolves into another form. Normally speciation outpaces extinction. Mankind inherited a richer, more diverse world than had ever existed before in the 3.5 billion-year odyssey of life on Earth. What is wrong with anthropogenic species extirpation and extinction is the *rate* at which it is occurring and the *result*: biological impoverishment instead of enrichment.

Leopold goes on here to condemn, in terms of its impact on the eco-system, "the world-wide pooling of faunas and floras," that is, the indiscriminate introduction of exotic and domestic species and the dislocation of native and endemic species, mining the soil for its stored biotic energy, leading ultimately to diminished fertility and to erosion; and polluting and damming water courses (p. 217).

According to the land ethic, therefore: Thou shalt not extirpate or render species extinct; thou shalt exercise great caution in introducing exotic and domestic species into local exosystems, in exacting energy from the soil and releasing it into the biota, and in damming or polluting water courses; and thou shalt be especially solicitous of predatory birds and mammals. Here in brief are the express moral precepts of the land ethic. They are all explicitly informed—not to say derived—from the energy circuit model of the environment.

XI

The living channels—food chains—through which energy courses are composed of individual plants and animals. A central, stark fact lies at the heart of ecological processes: Energy, the currency of the economy nature, passes from one organism to another, not from hand to hand, like coined money, but, so to speak, from stomach to stomach. Eating *and being eaten*, living *and dying* are what make the biotic community hum.

The precepts of the land ethic, like those of all previous accretions, reflect and reinforce the structure of the community to which it is correlative. Trophic asymmetries constitute the kernel of the biotic community. It seems unjust, unfair. But that is how the economy of nature is organized (and has been for thousands of millions of years). The land ethic, thus, affirms as good, and strives to preserve, the very inequities in nature whose social counterparts in human communities are condemned as bad and would be eradicated by familiar social ethics, especially by the more recent Christian and secular egalitarian exemplars. A "right to life" for individual members is not consistent with the structure of the biotic community and hence is not mandated by the land ethic. This disparity between the land ethic and its more familiar social precedents contributes to the apparent devaluation of individual members of the biotic community and augments and reinforces the tendency of the land ethic, driven by the systemic vision of ecology, toward a more holistic or community-per-se orientation.

Of the few moral philosophers who have given the land ethic a moment's serious thought, most have regarded it with horror because of its emphasis on the good of the community and its deemphasis on the welfare of individual members of the community. Not only are other sentient creatures members of the biotic community and subordinate to its integrity, beauty, and stability; so are *we*. Thus, if it is not only morally permissible, from the point of view of the land ethic, but morally required, that members of certain species be abandoned to predation and other vicissitudes of wild life or even deliberately culled (as in the case of alert and sentient whitetail deer) for the sake of the integrity, stability, and beauty of the biotic community, how can we consistently exempt ourselves from a similar draconian regime? We too are only "plain members and citizens" of the biotic community. And our global population is growing unchecked. According to William Aiken, from the point of view of the land ethic, therefore, "massive human diebacks would be good. It is our duty to cause them. It is our species' duty, relative to the whole, to eliminate 90 percent of our numbers." Thus, according to Tom Regan, the land ethic is a clear case of "environmental fascism."

Of course Leopold never intended the land ethic to have either inhumane or antihumanitarian implications or consequences. But whether he intended them or not, a logically consistent deduction from the theoretical premises of the land ethic might force such untoward conclusions. And given their magnitude and monstrosity, these derivations would constitute a *reductio ad absurdum* of the whole land ethic enterprise and entrench and reinforce our current human chauvinism and moral alienation from nature. If this is what membership in the biotic community entails, then all but the most radical misanthropes would surely want to opt out.

XII

The land ethic, happily, implies neither inhumane nor inhuman consequences. That some philosophers think it must follows more from their own theoretical presuppositions than from the theoretical elements of the land ethic itself. Conventional modern ethical theory rests moral entitlement, as I earlier pointed out, on a criterion or qualification. If a candidate meets the criterion—rationality of sentiency are the most commonly posited—he, she, or it is entitled to equal moral standing with others who possess the same qualification in equal degree. Hence, reasoning in this philosophically orthodox way, and forcing Leopold's theory to conform: if human beings are, with other animals, plants, soils, and waters, equally members of the biotic community, and if community membership is the criterion of equal moral consideration, then not only do animals, plants, soils, and waters have equal (highly attenuated) "rights," but human beings are equally subject to the same subordination of individual welfare and rights in respect to the good of the community as a whole.

But the land ethic, as I have been at pains to point out, is heir to a line of moral analysis different from that institutionalized in contemporary moral philosophy. From the biosocial evolutionary analysis of ethics upon which Leopold builds the land ethic, it (the land ethic) neither replaces nor overrides previous accretions. Prior

moral sensibilities and obligations attendant upon and correlative to prior strata of social involvement remain operative and preemptive.

Being citizens of the United States, or the United Kingdom, or the Soviet Union, or Venezuela, or some other nation-state, and therefore having national obligations and patriotic duties, does not mean that we are not also members of smaller communities or social groups—cities or townships, neighborhoods, and families—or that we are relieved of the peculiar moral responsibilities attendant upon and correlative to these memberships as well. Similarly, our recognition of the biotic community and our immersion in it does not imply that we do not also remain members of the human community—the "family of man" or "global village"—or that we are relieved of the attendant and correlative moral responsibilities of that membership, among them to respect universal human rights and uphold the principles of individual human worth and dignity. The biosocial development of morality does not grow in extent like an expanding balloon, leaving no trace of its previous boundaries, so much like the circumference of a tree. Each emergent, and larger, social unit is layered over the more primitive, and intimate, ones.

Moreover, as a general rule, the duties correlative to the inner social circles to which we belong eclipse those correlative to the rings farther from the heartwood when conflicts arise. Consider our moral revulsion when zealous ideological nationalists encourage children to turn their parents in to the authorities if their parents dissent from the political or economic doctrines of the ruling party. A zealous environmentalist who advocated visiting war, famine, or pestilence on human populations (those existing somewhere else, of course) in the name of the integrity, beauty, and stability of the biotic community would be similarly perverse. Family obligations in general come before nationalistic duties and humanitarian obligations in general come before environmental duties. The land ethic, therefore, is not draconian or fascist. It does not cancel human morality. The land ethic may, however, as with any new accretion, demand choices which affect, in turn, the demands of the more interior social-ethical circles. Taxes and the military draft may conflict with family-level obligations. While the land ethic, certainly, does not cancel human morality, neither does it leave it unaffected.

Nor is the land ethic inhumane. Nonhuman fellow members of the biotic community have no "human rights," because they are not, by definition, members of the human community. As fellow members of the biotic community, however, they deserve respect.

How exactly to express or manifest respect, while at the same time abandoning our fellow members of the biotic community to their several fates or even actively consuming them for our own needs (and wants), or deliberately making them casualties of wildlife management for ecological integrity, is a difficult and delicate question.

Fortunately, American Indian and other traditional patterns of human–nature interaction provide rich and detailed models. Algonkian woodland peoples, for instance, represented animals, plants, birds, waters, and minerals as other-than-human persons engaged in reciprocal, mutually beneficial socioeconomic intercourse with human beings. Tokens of payment, together with expressions of apology, were routinely offered to the beings whom it was necessary for these Indians to exploit. Care not to waste the usable parts and care in the disposal of unusable animal and plant remains were also an aspect of the respectful, albeit necessarily consumptive, Algonkian relationship with fellow members of the land community. As I have more fully argued elsewhere, the Algonkian portrayal of human–nature relationships is, indeed, although certainly different in specifics, identical in abstract form to that recommended by Leopold in the land ethic. . . . Is the land ethic prudential or deontological? Is the land ethic, in other words, a matter of enlightened (collective, human) self-interest, or does it genuinely admit nonhuman natural entities and nature as a whole to true moral standing?

The conceptual foundations of the land ethic, as I have here set them out, and much of Leopold's hortatory rhetoric, would certainly indicate that the land ethic is deontological (or duty oriented) rather than prudential. In the section significantly titled "The Ecological Conscience," Leopold complains that the then-current conservation philosophy is inadequate because "it defines no right or wrong, assigns no obligation, calls for no sacrifice, implies no change in the current philosophy of values. In respect of land-use, it urges *only* enlightened self-interest" (pp. 207–8, emphasis added). Clearly, Leopold himself thinks that the land ethic goes beyond prudence. In this section he disparages mere "self-interest" two more times, and concludes that "obligations have no meaning without conscience, and the problem we face is the extension of the social conscience from people to land" (p. 209).

In the next section, "Substitutes for a Land Ethic," he mentions rights twice—the "biotic right" of birds to continuance and the absence of a right on the part of human special interest to exterminate predators.

Finally, the first sentences of "The Outlook" read: "It is inconceivable to me that an ethical relation to land can exist without love, respect, and admiration for land, and a high regard for its value. By value, I of course mean something far broader than mere economic value; I mean value in the philosophical sense" (p. 223). By "value in the philosophical sense," Leopold can only mean what philosophers more technically call "intrinsic value" or "inherent worth." Something that has intrinsic value or inherent worth is valuable in and of itself, not because of what it can do for us. "Obligation," "sacrifice," "a conscience," "respect," the ascription of rights, and intrinsic value—all of these are consistently opposed to self-interest and seem to indicate decisively that the land ethic is of the deontological type.

Some philosophers, however, have seen it differently. Scott Lehmann, for example, writes,

> Although Leopold claims for communities of plants and animals a "right to continued existence," his argument is homocentric, appealing to the human stake in preservation. Basically it is an argument from enlightened self-interest, where the self in question is not an individual human being but humanity—present and future—as a whole.

Lehmann's claim has some merits, even though it flies in the face of Leopold's express commitments. Leopold does frequently lapse into the language of (collective, long-range, human) self-interest. Early on, for example, he remarks, "in human history, we have learned (I hope) that the conqueror role is eventually *self*-defeating" (p. 204, emphasis added). And later, of the 95 percent of Wisconsin species which cannot be "sold, fed, eaten, or otherwise put to economic use," Leopold reminds us that "these creatures are members of the biotic community, and if (as I believe) its stability depends on its integrity, they are entitled to continuance" (p. 210). The implication is clear: the economic 5 percent cannot survive if a significant portion of the uneconomic 95 percent are extirpated; nor may *we*, it goes without saying, survive without these "resources."

Leopold, in fact, seems to be consciously aware of this moral paradox. Consistent with the biosocial foundations of his theory, he expresses it in sociobiological terms:

> An ethic may be regarded as a mode of guidance for meeting ecological situations so new or intricate, or involving such deferred reactions, that the path of social expediency is not discernible to the average individual. Animal instincts are modes of guidance for the individual in meeting such situations. Ethics are possibly a kind of community instinct in-the-making. (p. 203)

From an objective, descriptive sociobiological point of view, ethics evolve because they contribute to the inclusive fitness of their carriers (or, more reductively still, to the multiplication of their carriers' genes); they are expedient. However, the path to self-interest (or to the self-interest of the selfish gene) is not discernible to the participating individuals (nor, certainly, to their genes). Hence, ethics are grounded in instinctive feeling—love, sympathy, respect—not in self-conscious calculating intelligence. Somewhat like the paradox of hedonism—the notion that one cannot achieve happiness if one directly pursues happiness per se and not other things—one can only secure self-interest by putting the interests of others on a par with one's own (in this case long-range collective human self-interest and the interest of other forms of life and of the biotic community per se).

So, is the land ethic deontological or prudential, after

all? It is both—self-consistently both—depending upon one's point of view. From the inside, from the lived, felt point of view of the community member with evolved moral sensibilities, it is deontological. It involves an affective–cognitive posture of genuine love, respect, admiration, obligation, self-sacrifice, conscience, duty, and the ascription of intrinsic value and biotic rights. From the outside, from the objective and analytic scientific point of view, it is prudential. "There is no other way for land to survive the impact of mechanized man," nor, therefore, for mechanized man to survive his own impact upon the land (p. viii).

Study Questions

1. What are the three reasons for the professional neglect, confusion and neglect of Leopold's "land ethics," according to Callicott?

2. How is the land ethic different from classical and mainstream modern ethical philosophy, such as Kant's and Bentham's systems? Note Goodpaster's criticisms on which Callicott draws.

3. Is Callicott successful in arguing for the natural basis of value in the interaction between valuers (humans) and the environment? Can you see any problems with this view?

4. Leopold wrote "A thing is right when it tends to preserve the integrity, stability, and beauty of the biotic community. It is wrong when it tends otherwise." This passage has been interpreted by some to mean that humans should be sacrificed if they interfere with the good of the biotic community. Callicott tries to modify this statement, removing the misanthropic implications. Go over his defense. Has Callicott strengthened or weakened Leopold's land ethic by modifying it as he does?

DEEP ECOLOGY

20

The Shallow and the Deep, Long-Range Ecological Movement

ARNE NAESS

Arne Naess (b. 1912) was for many years the head of the philosophy department of the University of Oslo, Norway, and the founder of the modern theory of deep ecology.

"Deep ecology" (or "ecosophy" = ecological wisdom) is a movement calling for a deeper questioning and a deeper set of answers to our environmental concerns. Specifically, it calls into question some of the major assumptions about consumerism and materialism, challenging us to live more simply. Its motto is "Simple in Means, Rich in Ends." It seeks self-realization through oneness with all things. The following is Naess's now classic summary of his lecture at the 3rd World Future Research Conference, Bucharest, September 3, 1972. Naess included the following abstract:

Ecologically responsible policies are concerned only in part with pollution and resource depletion. There are deeper concerns which touch upon principles of diversity, complexity, autonomy, decentralization, symbiosis, egalitarianism, and classlessness.

Reprinted from *Inquiry* 16 (Spring 1973) by permission.

The emergence of ecologists from their former relative obscurity marks a turning-point in our scientific communities. But their message is twisted and misused. A shallow, but presently rather powerful movement, and a deep, but less influential movement, compete for our attention. I shall make an effort to characterize the two.

1. The Shallow Ecology movement: Fight against pollution and resource depletion. Central objective: the health and affluence of people in the developed countries.

2. The Deep Ecology movement: (1) Rejection of the man-in-environment image in favour of the *relational, total-field image*. Organisms as knots in the biospherical net or field of intrinsic relations. An intrinsic relation between two things A and B is such that the relation belongs to the definitions or basic constitutions of A and B, so that without the relation, A and B are no longer the same things. The total-field model dissolves not only the man-in-environment concept, but every compact thing-in-milieu concept—except when talking at a superficial or preliminary level of communication.

(2) *Biospherical egalitarianism*—in principle. The "in principle" clause is inserted because any realistic praxis necessitates some killing, exploitation, and suppression. The ecological field-worker acquires a deep-

seated respect, or even veneration, for ways and forms of life. He reaches an understanding from within, a kind of understanding that others reserve for fellow men and for a narrow section of ways and forms of life. To the ecological field-worker, *the equal right to live and blossom* is an intuitively clear and obvious value axiom. Its restriction to humans is an anthropocentrism with detrimental effects upon the life quality of humans themselves. This quality depends in part upon the deep pleasure and satisfaction we receive from close partnership with other forms of life. The attempt to ignore our dependence and to establish a master–slave role has contributed to the alienation of man from himself.

Ecological egalitarianism implies the reinterpretation of the future-research variable, "level of crowding," so that *general* mammalian crowding and loss of life-equality is taken seriously, not only human crowding. (Research on the high requirements of free space of certain mammals has, incidentally, suggested that theorists of human urbanism have largely underestimated human life-space requirements. Behavioural crowding symptoms [neuroses, aggressiveness, loss of traditions . . .] are largely the same among mammals.)

(3) *Principles of diversity and symbiosis.* Diversity enhances the potentialities of survival, the chances of new modes of life, the richness of forms. And the so-called struggle of life, and survival of the fittest, should be interpreted in the sense of ability to coexist and cooperate in complex relationships, rather than ability to kill, exploit, and suppress. "Live and let live" is a more powerful ecological principle than "Either you or me."

The latter tends to reduce the multiplicity of kinds of forms of life, and also to create destruction within the communities of the same species. Ecologically inspired attitudes therefore favour diversity of human ways of life, of cultures, of occupations, of economies. They support the fight against economic and cultural, as much as military, invasion and domination, and they are opposed to the annihilation of seals and whales as much as to that of human tribes or cultures.

(4) *Anti-class posture.* Diversity of human ways of life is in part due to (intended or unintended) exploitation and suppression on the part of certain groups. The exploiter lives differently from the exploited, but both are adversely affected in their potentialities of self-realization. The principle of diversity does not cover differences due merely to certain attitudes or behaviours forcibly blocked or restrained. The principles of ecological egalitarianism and of symbiosis support the same anti-class posture. The ecological attitude favours the extension of all three principles to any group conflicts, including those of today between developing and developed nations. The three principles also favour extreme caution towards any over-all plans for the future, except those consistent with wide and widening classless diversity.

(5) Fight against *pollution and resource depletion.* In this fight ecologists have found powerful supporters, but sometimes to the detriment of their total stand. This happens when attention is focused on pollution and resource depletion rather than on the other points, or when projects are implemented which reduce pollution but increase evils of the other kinds. Thus, if prices of life necessities increase because of the installation of anti-pollution devices, class differences increase too. An ethics of responsibility implies that ecologists do not serve the shallow, but the deep ecological movement. That is, not only point (5), but all seven points must be considered together.

Ecologists are irreplaceable informants in any society, whatever their political contour. If well organized, they have the power to reject jobs in which they submit themselves to institutions or to planners with limited ecological perspectives. As it is now, ecologists sometimes serve masters who deliberately ignore the wider perspectives.

(6) *Complexity, not complication.* The theory of ecosystems contains an important distinction between what is complicated without any Gestalt or unifying principles—we may think of finding our way through a chaotic city—and what is complex. A multiplicity of more or less lawful, interacting factors may operate together to form a unity, a system. We make a shoe or use a map or integrate a variety of activities into a workaday pattern. Organisms, ways of life, and interactions in the biosphere in general, exhibit complexity of such an astoundingly high level as to colour the general outlook of ecologists. Such complexity makes thinking in terms of vast systems inevitable. It also makes for a keen, steady perception of the profound *human ignorance* of biospherical relationships and therefore of the effect of disturbances.

Applied to humans, the complexity-not-complication principle favours division of labour, *not fragmentation of labour.* It favours integrated actions in which the whole person is active, not mere reactions. It favours complex economies, an integrated variety of means of living. (Combinations of industrial and agricultural activity, of intellectual and manual work, of specialized and non-specialized occupations, of urban and non-urban activity, of work in city and recreation in nature with recreation in city and work in nature . . .)

It favours soft technique and "soft future-research," less prognosis, more clarification of possibilities. More sensitivity towards continuity and live traditions, and—most importantly—towards our state of ignorance.

The implementation of ecologically responsible policies requires in this century an exponential growth of technical skill and invention—but in new directions, directions which today are not consistently and liberally supported by the research policy organs of our nation-states.

(7) *Local autonomy and decentralization.* The vulnerability of a form of life is roughly proportional to

the weight of influences from afar, from outside the local region in which that form has obtained an ecological equilibrium. This lends support to our efforts to strengthen local self-government and material and mental self-sufficiency. But these efforts presuppose an impetus towards decentralization. Pollution problems, including those of thermal pollution and recirculation of materials, also lead us in this direction, because increased local autonomy, if we are able to keep other factors constant, reduces energy consumption. (Compare an approximately self-sufficient locality with one requiring the importation of foodstuff, materials for house construction, fuel and skilled labour from other continents. The former may use only five per cent of the energy used by the latter.) Local autonomy is strengthened by a reduction in the number of links in the hierarchical chains of decision. (For example, a chain consisting of local board, municipal council, highest sub-national decision-maker, a state-wide institution in a state federation, a federal national government institution, a coalition of nations, and of institutions, e.g. E.E.C.* top levels, and a global institution, can be reduced to one made up of local board, nation-wide institution, and global institution.) Even if a decision follows majority rules at each step, many local interests may be dropped along the line, if it is too long.

Summing up, then, it should, first of all, be borne in mind that the norms and tendencies of the Deep Ecology movement are not derived from ecology by logic or induction. Ecological knowledge and the life-style of the ecological field-worker have *suggested, inspired, and fortified* the perspectives of the Deep Ecology movement. Many of the formulations in the above seven-point survey are rather vague generalizations, only tenable if made more precise in certain directions. But all over the world the inspiration from ecology has shown remarkable convergencies. The survey does not pretend to be more than one of the possible condensed codifications of these convergencies.

Secondly, it should be fully appreciated that the significant tenets of the Deep Ecology movement are clearly and forcefully *normative*. They express a value priority system only in part based on results (or lack of results, cf. point [6]) of scientific research. Today, ecologists try to influence policy-making bodies largely through threats, through predictions concerning pollutants and resource depletion, knowing that policy-makers accept at least certain minimum *norms* concerning health and just distribution. But it is clear that there is a vast number of people in all countries, and even a considerable number of people in power, who accept as

* E.E.C. stands for European Economic Community.

valid the wider norms and values characteristic of the Deep Ecology movement. There are political potentials in this movement which should not be overlooked and which have little to do with pollution and resource depletion. In plotting possible futures, the norms should be freely used and elaborated.

Thirdly, in so far as ecology movements deserve our attention, they are *ecophilosophical* rather than ecological. Ecology is *limited* science which makes *use* of scientific methods. Philosophy is the most general forum of debate on fundamentals, descriptive as well as prescriptive, and political philosophy is one of its subsections. By an *ecosophy* I mean a philosophy of ecological harmony or equilibrium. A philosophy as a kind of *sofia* wisdom, is openly normative, it contains *both* norms, rules, postulates, value priority announcements *and* hypotheses concerning the state of affairs in our universe. Wisdom is policy wisdom, prescription, not only scientific description and prediction.

The details of an ecosophy will show many variations due to significant differences concerning not only "facts" of pollution, resources, population, etc., but also value priorities. Today, however, the seven points listed provide one unified framework for ecosophical systems.

In general system theory, systems are mostly conceived in terms of causally or functionally interacting or interrelated items. An ecosophy, however, is more like a system of the kind constructed by Aristotle or Spinoza. It is expressed verbally as a set of sentences with a variety of functions, descriptive and prescriptive. The basic relation is that between subsets of premises and subsets of conclusions, that is, the relation of derivability.

The relevant notions of derivability may be classed according to rigour, with logical and mathematical deductions topping the list, but also according to how much is implicitly taken for granted. An exposition of an ecosophy must necessarily be only moderately precise considering the vast scope of relevant ecological and normative (social, political, ethical) material. At the moment, ecosophy might profitably use models of systems, rough approximations of global systematizations. It is the global character, not preciseness in detail, which distinguishes an ecosophy. It articulates and integrates the efforts of an ideal ecological team, a team comprising not only scientists from an extreme variety of disciplines, but also students of politics and active policy-makers.

Under the name of *ecologism*, various deviations from the deep movement have been championed—primarily with a one-sided stress on pollution and resource depletion, but also with a neglect of the great differences between under- and over-developed countries in favour of a vague global approach. The global approach is essential, but regional differences must largely determine policies in the coming years.

Study Questions

1. Is *deep ecology* a good name for Naess's theory? Does it incorporate positive value unwarrantedly? If not, what should it be called?
2. Are the seven principles of the deep ecology movement good ones? Examine each one, compare them with the corresponding principles of shallow ecology, and comment on their validity.
3. Compare Naess's deep ecology with biocentrism and ecocentrism.

21

Ecosophy T: Deep Versus Shallow Ecology

ARNE NAESS

In this 1985 essay, Naess develops the philosophical implications of deep ecology, which he calls "Ecosophy." He calls his version of ecosophy "Ecosophy T." Naess develops his theory of wider self-realization through identifying one's Self with individuals, species, ecosystems, and landscapes.

THE SHALLOW AND THE DEEP ECOLOGICAL MOVEMENT

In the 1960s two convergent trends made headway: a deep ecological concern, and a concern for saving deep cultural diversity. These may be put under the general heading "deep ecology" if we view human ecology as a genuine part of general ecology. For each species of living beings there is a corresponding ecology. In what follows I adopt this terminology which I introduced in 1973 (Naess 1973).

The term *deep* is supposed to suggest explication of fundamental presuppositions of valuation as well as of facts and hypotheses. Deep ecology, therefore, transcends the limit of any particular science of today, including systems theory and scientific ecology. *Deepness of normative and descriptive premises questioned* characterize the movement.

The difference between the shallow and deep ecological movement may perhaps be illustrated by contrasting typical slogans, formulated very roughly [in Figure 1].[1]

Deep ecological argumentation questions both the left-hand and the right-hand slogans. But tentative conclusions are in terms of the latter.

The shallow ecological argument carries today much heavier weight in political life than the deep. It is therefore often necessary for tactical reasons to hide our deeper attitudes and argue strictly homocentrically. This colors the indispensible publication, *World Conservation Strategy*.[2]

As an academic philosopher raised within analytic traditions it has been natural for me to pose the questions: How can departments of philosophy, our establishment of professionals, be made interested in the matter? What are the philosophical problems explicitly and implicitly raised or answered in the deep ecological movement? Can they be formulated so to be of academic interest?

My answer is that the movement is rich in philosophical implications. There has however, been only moderately eager response in philosophical institutions.

The deep ecological movement is furthered by people and groups with much in common. Roughly speaking, what they have in common concerns ways of experiencing nature and diversity of cultures. Furthermore, many share priorities of life style, such as those of "voluntary simplicity." They wish to live "lightly" in nature. There are of course differences, but until now the conflicts of philosophically relevant opinion and of recommended policies have, to a surprisingly small degree, disturbed the growth of the movement.

In what follows I introduce some sections of a philosophy inspired by the deep ecological movement. Some people in the movement feel at home with that philosophy or at least approximately such a philosophy, others feel that they, at one or more points, clearly have different value priorities, attitudes or opinions. To avoid unfruitful polemics, I call my philosophy "Ecosophy T," using the character *T* just to emphasize that other people in the movement would, if motivated to formulate their world view and general value priorities, arrive at different ecosophies: Ecosophy "A," "B," . . . , "T," . . . , "Z."

By an "ecosophy" I here mean a philosophy inspired by the deep ecological movement. The ending *-sophy* stresses that what we modestly try to realize is wisdom rather than science or information. A philosophy, as articulated wisdom, has to be a synthesis of theory and practice. It must not shun concrete policy recommenda-

Reprinted from Arne Naess, "Identification as a Source of Deep Ecological Attitudes" in Michael Tobias, ed. *Deep Ecology* (Santa Monica, CA: IMT Productions, 1985) by permission.

FIGURE 1

SHALLOW ECOLOGY	DEEP ECOLOGY
Natural diversity is valuable as a resource for us.	Natural diversity has its own (intrinsic) value.
It is nonsense to talk about value except as value for mankind.	Equating value with value for humans reveals a racial prejudice.
Plant species should be saved because of their value as generic reserves for human agriculture and medicine.	Plant species should be saved because of their intrinsic value.
Pollution should be decreased if it threatens economic growth.	Decrease of pollution has priority over economic growth.
Third World population growth threatens ecological equilibrium.	World population at the present level threatens ecosystems but the population and behavior of industrial states more than that of any others. Human population is today excessive.
"Resource" means resource for humans.	"Resource" means resource for living beings.
People will not tolerate a broad decease in their standard of living.	People should not tolerate a broad decrease in the quality of life but in the standard of living in overdeveloped countries.
Nature is cruel and necessarily so.	Man is cruel but not necessarily so.

tions but has to base them on fundamental priorities of value and basic views concerning the development of our societies.[3]

Which societies? The movement started in the richest industrial societies, and the words used by its academic supporters inevitably reflect the cultural provinciality of those societies. The way I am going to say things perhaps reflects a bias in favor of analytic philosophy intimately related to social science, including academic psychology. It shows itself in my acceptance in Ecosophy T of the theory of thinking in terms of "gestalts." But this provinciality and narrowness of training does not imply criticism of contributions in terms of trends or traditions of wisdom with which I am not at home, and it does not imply an underestimation of the immense value of what artists in many counties have contributed to the movement.

SELECTED ECOSOPHICAL TOPICS

The themes of Ecosophy T which will be introduced are the following:

The narrow self (ego) and the comprehensive Self (written with capital *S*)

Self-realization as the realization of the comprehensive Self, not the cultivation of the ego

The process of identification as the basic tool of widening the self and as a natural consequence of increased maturity

Strong identification with the whole of nature in its diversity and interdependence of parts as a source of active participation in the deep ecological movement

Identification as a source of belief in intrinsic values. The question of "objective" validity.[4]

SELF-REALIZATION, YES, BUT WHICH SELF?

When asked about *where* their self, their "I," or their ego is, some people place it in the neighborhood of the *larynx*. When thinking, we can sometimes perceive movement in that area. Others find it near their eyes. Many tend to feel that their ego, somehow, is inside their body, or identical with the whole of it, or with its functioning. Some call their ego spiritual, or immaterial and not within space. This has interesting consequences. A Bedouin in Yemen would not have an ego nearer the equator than a whale-hunting eskimo. "Nearer" implies space.

William James (1890: Chapter 10) offers an excellent introduction to the problems concerning the constitution and the limits of the self.

> The Empirical Self of each of us is all that he is tempted to call by the name of *me*. But it is clear that between what a man calls *me* and what he simply calls *mine* the line is difficult to draw. We feel and act about certain things that are ours very much as we feel and act about ourselves. Our fame, our children, the work of our hands, may be as dear to us as our bodies are, and arouse the same feelings and the same acts of reprisal if attacked. And our bodies, themselves, are they simply ours, or are they *us*?
>
> The body is the innermost part of *the material Self* in each of us; and certain parts of the body seem more intimately ours than the rest. The clothes come next. . . . Next, our immediate family is a part of ourselves. Our father and mother, our wife and babes, are bone of our bone and flesh of our flesh. When they die, a part of our very selves is gone. If they do anything wrong, it is our shame. If they are insulted, our anger flashes forth as readily as if we stood in their place . Our *home* comes next. Its scenes are part of our life; its aspects awaken the tenderest feelings of affection.

One of his conclusions is of importance to the concepts of self-realization: "We see then that we are dealing with a fluctuating material. The same object being sometimes treated as a part of me, at other times is simply mine, and then again as if I had nothing to do with it all."

If the term *self-realization* is applied, it should be kept in mind that "I," "me," "ego," and "self" have shifting denotations. Nothing is evident and indisputable. Even *that* we are is debatable if we make the question dependent upon answering *what* we are.

One of the central terms in Indian philosophy is *ātman*. Until this century it was mostly translated with "spirit," but it is now generally recognized that "self" is more appropriate. It is a term with similar connotations and ambiguities as those of "self"—analyzed by William James and other Western philosophers and psychologists. Gandhi represented a *maha-ātman*, a *mahatma*, a great (and certainly very wide) self. As a term for a kind of metaphysical maximum self we find *ātman* in *The Bhagavadgita*.

Verse 29 of Chapter 6 is characteristic of the truly great *ātman*. The Sanskrit of this verse is not overwhelmingly difficult and deserves quotation ahead of translations.

sarvabhūtastham ātmānam
sarvabhutāni cā'tmani
Itsate yogayuktātmā
sarvatra samadarśanah

Radhakrisnan: "He whose self is harmonized by yoga seeth the Self abiding in all beings and all beings in Self; everywhere he sees the same."

Eliot Deutsch: "He whose self is disciplined by yoga sees the Self abiding in all beings and all beings in the Self; he sees the same in all beings."

Juan Mascaró: "He sees himself in the heart of all beings and he sees all beings in his heart. This is the vision of the Yogi of harmony, a vision which is ever one."

Gandhi: "The man equipped with *yoga* looks on all with an impartial eye, seeing *Atman* in all beings and all beings in *Atman*."

Self-realization in its absolute maximum is, as I see it, the mature experience of oneness in diversity as depicted in the above verse. The minimum is the self-realization by more or less consistent egotism—by the narrowest experience of what constitutes one's self and a maximum of alienation. As empirical beings we dwell somewhere in between, but increased maturity involves increase of the wideness of the self.

The self-realization maximum should not necessarily be conceived as a mystical or meditational state. "By meditation some perceive the Self in the self by the self; others by the path of knowledge and still others by the path of works (*karma-yoga*)" [*Gita*: Chapter 13, verse 24]. Gandhi was a *karma-yogi*, realizing himself through social and political action.

The terms *mystical union* and *mysticism* are avoided here for three reasons: First, strong mystical traditions stress the dissolution of individual selves into a nondiversified supreme whole. Both from cultural and ecological point of view diversity and individuality are essential. Second, there is a strong terminological trend within scientific communities to associate mysticism with vagueness and confusion.[5] Third, mystics tend to agree that mystical consciousness is rarely sustained under normal, everyday conditions. But strong, wide identification *can* color experience under such conditions.

Gandhi was only marginally concerned with "nature." In his *ashram* poisonous snakes were permitted to live inside and outside human dwellings. Anti-poison medicines were frowned upon. Gandhi insisted that trust awakens trust, and that snakes have the same right to live and blossom as the humans (Naess, 1974).

THE PROCESS OF IDENTIFICATION

How do we develop a wider self? What kind of process makes it possible? One way of answering these questions: There is a process of ever-widening identification and ever-narrowing alienation which widens the self. The self is as comprehensive as the totality of our identifications. Or, more succinctly: Our Self is that with which we identify. The question then reads: How do we widen identifications?

Identification is a spontaneous, non-rational, but not irrational, process through which *the interest or interests of another being are reacted to as our own interest or interests*. The emotional tone of gratification or frustration is a consequence carried over from the other to oneself: joy elicits joy, sorrow sorrow. Intense identification obliterates the experience of a distinction between *ego* and *alter*, between me and the sufferer. But only momentarily or intermittently: If my fellow being tries to vomit, I do not, or at least not persistently, try to vomit. I recognize that we are different individuals.

The term *identification, in the sense used here*, is rather technical, but there are today scarcely any alternatives. "Solidarity"' and a corresponding adjective in German, "solidarisch," and the corresponding words in Scandinavian languages are very common and useful. But genuine and spontaneous solidarity with others already presupposes a process of identification. Without identification, no solidarity. Thus, the latter term cannot quite replace the former.

The same holds true of empathy and sympathy. It is a necessary, but not sufficient condition of empathy and sympathy that one "sees" or experiences something similar or identical with oneself.[6]

A high level of identification does not eliminate conflicts of interest: Our vital interests, if we are not plants, imply killing at least some other living beings. A culture of hunters, where identification with hunted animals reaches a remarkably high level, does not prohibit killing for food. But a great variety of ceremonies and rituals have the function to express the gravity of the alienating incident and restore the identification.

Identification with individuals, species, ecosystems and landscapes results in difficult problems of priority. What should be the relation of ecosystem ethics to other parts of general ethics?

There are no definite limits to the broadness and intensity of identification. Mammals and birds sometimes show remarkable, often rather touching, intraspecies and cross-species identification. Konrad Lorenz tells of how one of his bird friends tried to seduce him, trying to push him into its little home. This presupposes a deep identification between bird and man (but also an alarming mistake of size). In certain forms of mysticism, there is an experience of identification with every life form, using this term in a wide sense. Within the deep ecological movement, poetical and philosophical expressions of such experiences are not uncommon. In the shallow ecological movement, intense and wide identification is described and explained psychologically. In the deep movement this philosophy is at least taken seriously: reality consists of wholes which we cut down rather than of isolated items which we put together. In other words: there is not, strictly speaking, a primordial causal process of identification, but one of largely unconscious alienation which is overcome in experiences of identity. To some "environmental" philosophers such thoughts seem to be irrational, even "rubbish."[7] This is, as far as I can judge, due to a too narrow conception of irrationality.

The opposite of *identification* is *alienation*, if we use these ambiguous terms in one of their basic meanings.[8]

The alienated son does perhaps what is required of a son toward his parents, but as performance of moral duties and as a burden, not spontaneously, out of joy. If one loves and respects oneself, identification will be positive, and, in what follows, the term covers this case. Self-hatred or dislike of certain of one's traits induces hatred and dislike of the beings with which one identifies.

Identification is not limited to beings which can reciprocate: Any animal, plant, mountain, ocean may induce such processes. In poetry this is articulated most impressively, but ordinary language testifies to its power as a universal human trait.

Through identification, higher level unity is experienced: from identifying with "one's nearest," higher unities are created through circles of friends, local communities, tribes, compatriots, races, humanity, life, and, ultimately, as articulated by religious and philosophic leaders, unity with the supreme whole, the "world" in a broader and deeper sense than the usual. I prefer a terminology such that the largest units are not said to comprise life *and* "the not living." One may broaden the sense of "living" so that any natural whole, however, large, is a living whole.

This way of thinking and feeling at its maximum corresponds to that of the enlightened, or yogi, who sees "the same," the *ātman*, and who is not alienated from anything.

The process of identification is sometimes expressed in terms of loss of self and gain of Self through "self-less" action. Each new sort of identification corresponds to a widening of the self, and strengthens the urge to further widening, furthering Self-seeking. This urge is in the system of Spinoza called *conatus in suo esse perseverare*, striving to persevere in oneself or one's being (*in se, in suo esse*). It is not a mere urge to survive, but to increase the level of *acting out* (ex) *one's own nature or essence*, and is not different from the urge toward higher levels of "freedom" (*libertas*). Under favorable circumstances, this involves wide identification.

In Western social science, self-realization is the term most often used for the competitive development of a person's talents and the pursuit of an individual's specific interests (Maslow and others). A conflict is foreseen between giving self-realization high priority and cultivation of social bonds, friends, family, nation, nature. Such unfortunate notions have narrow concepts of self as a point of departure. They go together with the egoism–altruism distinction. Altruism is, according to this, a moral quality developed through suppression of selfishness, through sacrifice of one's "own" interests in favor of those of others. Thus, alienation is taken to be the normal state. Identification precludes sacrifice, but not devotion. The moral of self-sacrifice presupposes immaturity. Its relative importance is clear, in so far as we all are more or less immature.

WIDENESS AND DEPTH OF IDENTIFICATION AS A CONSEQUENCE OF INCREASED MATURITY

Against the belief in fundamental ego-alter conflict, the psychology and philosophy of the (comprehensive) Self insist that the gradual maturing of a person *inevitably* widens and deepens the self through the process of identification. There is no need for altruism toward those with whom we identify. The pursuit of self-realization conceived as actualization and development of the Self takes care of what altruism is supposed to accomplish. Thus, the distinction egoism-altruism is transcended.

The notion of maturing has to do with getting out what is latent in the nature of a being. Some learning is presupposed, but thinking of present conditions of competition in industrial, economic growth societies, specialized learning may inhibit the process of maturing. A competitive cult of talents does not favor Self-realization. As a consequence of the imperfect conditions for maturing as persons, there is much pessimism or disbelief in relation to the widening of the Self, and more stress on developing altruism and moral pressure.

The conditions under which the self is widened are experienced as positive and are basically joyful. The constant exposure to life in the poorest countries through television and other media contributes to the spread of the voluntary simplicity movement (Elgin, 1981). But people laugh: What does it help the hungry that you renounce the luxuries of your own country? But identification makes the efforts of simplicity joyful and there is not a feeling of moral compulsion. The widening of the self implies widening perspectives, deepening experiences, and reaching higher levels of activeness (in Spinoza's sense, not as just being busy). Joy and activeness make the appeal to Self-realization stronger than appeal to altruism. The state of alienation is not joyful, and is often connected with feelings of being threatened and narrowed. The "rights" of other living beings are felt to threaten our "own" interests.

The close connection between trends of alienation and putting duty and altruism as a highest value is exemplified in the philosophy of Kant. Acting morally, we should not abstain from maltreating animals because of their sufferings, but because of its bad effect on us. Animals were to Kant, essentially, so different from human beings, that he felt we should not have any moral obligations toward them. Their unnecessary sufferings are morally indifferent and norms of altruism do not apply in our relations to them. When we decide ethically to be kind to them, it should be because of the favorable effect of kindness of us—a strange doctrine.

Suffering is perhaps the most potent source of identification. Only special social conditions are able to make people inhibit their normal spontaneous reaction toward suffering. If we alleviate suffering because of a spontaneous urge to do so, Kant would be willing to call the act "beautiful," but not moral. And his greatest admiration was, as we all know, for stars and the moral imperative, not spontaneous goodness. The history of cruelty inflicted in the name of morals has convinced me that increase of identification might achieve what moralizing cannot: beautiful actions.

RELEVANCE OF THE ABOVE
FOR DEEP ECOLOGY

This perhaps rather lengthy philosophical discourse serves as a preliminary for the understanding of two things: first, the powerful indignation of Rachel Carson and others who, with great courage and stubborn determination, challenged authorities in the early 1960s, and triggered the international ecological movement. Second, the radical shift (see Sahlins, 1972) toward more positive appreciation of nonindustrial cultures and minorities—also in the 1960s, and expressing itself in efforts to "save" such cultures and in a new social anthropology.

The second movement reflects identification with threatened cultures. Both reactions were made possible by doubt that the industrial societies are as uniquely progressive as they usually had been supposed to be. Former haughtiness gave way to humility or at least willingness to look for deep changes both socially and in relation to nature.

Ecological information about the intimate dependency of humanity upon decent behavior toward the natural environment offered a much needed rational and economic justification for processes of identification which many people already had more or less completed. Their relative high degree of identification with animals, plants, landscapes, were seen to correspond to *factual relations* between themselves and nature. "Not man apart" was transformed from a romantic norm to a statement of fact. The distinction between man and environment, as applied within the shallow ecological movement, was seen to be illusory. Your Self crosses the boundaries.

When it was made known that the penguins of the Antarctic might die out because of the effects of DDT upon the toughness of their eggs, there was a widespread, *spontaneous* reaction of indignation and sorrow. People who never see penguins and who would never think of such animals as "useful" in any way, insisted that they had a right to live and flourish, and that it was our obligation not to interfere. But we must admit that even the mere appearance of penguins makes intense identification easy.

Thus, ecology helped many to know more *about themselves*. We are living beings. Penguins are too. We are all expressions of life. The fateful dependencies and interrelations which were brought to light, thanks to ecologists, made it easier for people to admit and even to cultivate their deep concern for nature, and to express their latent hostility toward the excesses of the economic growth of societies.

LIVING BEINGS HAVE INTRINSIC
VALUE AND A RIGHT TO LIVE
AND FLOURISH

How can these attitudes be talked about? What are the most helpful conceptualizations and slogans?

One important attitude might be thus expressed: "Every living being has a *right* to live." One way of answering the question is to insist upon the value in themselves, the autotelic value, of every living being.

This opposes the notion that one may be justified in treating any living being as just a means to an end. It also generalizes the rightly famous dictum of Kant "never use a person solely as a means." Identification tells me: if *I* have a right to live, *you* have the same right.

Insofar as we consider ourselves and our family and friends to have an intrinsic value, the widening identification inevitably leads to the attribution of intrinsic value to others. The metaphysical maximum will then involve the attribution of intrinsic value to all living beings. The right to live is only a different way of expressing this evaluation.

THE END OF THE WHY'S

But why has *any* living being autotelic value? Faced with the ever returning question of "why?," we have to stop somewhere. Here is a place where we well might stop. We shall admit that the value in itself is something shown in intuition. We attribute intrinsic value to ourselves and our nearest, and the validity of further identification can be contested, and *is* contested by many. The negation may, however, also be attacked through series of "whys?" Ultimately, we are in the same human predicament of having to start somewhere, at least for the moment. We must stop somewhere and treat where we then stand as a foundation.

The use of "Every living being has a value in itself" as a fundamental norm or principle does not rule out other fundamentals. On the contrary, the normal situation will be one in which several, in part conflicting, fundamental norms are relevant. And some consequences of fundamental norms *seem* compatible, but in fact are not.

The designation "fundamental" does not need to mean more than "not based on something deeper," which in practice often is indistinguishable from "not derived logically from deeper premises." It must be considered a rare case, if some body is able to stick to one and only one fundamental norm. (I have made an attempt to work with a *model* with only one, Self-realization, in Ecosophy T.)

THE RIGHT TO LIVE IS ONE AND THE SAME, BUT VITAL INTERESTS OF OUR NEAREST HAVE PRIORITY OF DEFENSE

Under symbiotic conditions, there are rules which manifest two important factors operating when interests are conflicting: vitalness and nearness. The more vital interest has priority over the less vital. The nearer has priority over the more remote—in space, time, culture, species. Nearness derives its priority from our special responsibilities, obligations and insights.

The terms used in these rules are of course vague and ambiguous. But even so, the rules point toward ways of thinking and acting which do not leave us quite helpless in the many inevitable conflicts of norms. The vast increase of consequences for life in general, which industrialization and the population explosion have brought about, necessitates new guidelines.

Examples: The use of threatened species for food or clothing (fur) may be more or less vital for certain poor, nonindustrial, human communities. For the less poor, such use is clearly ecologically irresponsible. Considering the fabulous possibilities open to the richest industrial societies, it is their responsibility to assist the poor communities in such a way that undue exploitation of threatened species, populations, and ecosystems is avoided.

It may be of vital interest to a family of poisonous snakes to remain in a small area where small children play, but it is also of vital interest to children and parents that there are no accidents. The priority rule of nearness makes it justifiable for the parents to remove the snakes. But the priority of vital interest of snakes is important when deciding where to establish the playgrounds.

The importance of nearness is, to a large degree, dependent upon vital interests of communities rather than individuals. The obligations with the family keep the family together, the obligations within a nation keep it from disintegration. But if the nonvital interests of a nation, or a species, conflict with the vital interests of another nation, or of other species, the rules give priority to the "alien nation" or "alien species."

How these conflicts may be straightened out is of course much too large a subject to be treated even cursorily in this connection. What is said only points toward the existence of rules of some help. (For further discussion, see Naess [1979].)

INTRINSIC VALUES

The term "objectivism" may have undesirable associations, but value pronouncements within the deep ecological movement imply what in philosophy is often termed "value objectivism" as opposed to value subjectivism, for instance, "the emotive theory of value. " At the time of Nietzsche there was in Europe a profound movement toward separation of value as a genuine aspect of reality on a par with scientific, "factual" descriptions. Value tended to be conceived as something projected by man into a completely value-neutral reality. The *Tractatus Philosophico-Logicus* of the early Wittgenstein expresses a well-known variant of this attitude. It represents a unique trend of *alienation of value* if we compare this attitude with those of cultures other than our technological-industrial society.

The professional philosophical debate on value objectivism, which in different senses—according to different versions, posits positive and negative values independent of value for human subjects—is of course very intricate. Here I shall only point out some kinds of statements within the deep ecological movement which imply value objectivism in the sense of intrinsic value:

Animals have value in themselves, not only as resources for humans.

Animals have a right to live even if of no use to humans.

We have no right to destroy the natural features of this planet.

Nature does not belong to man.

Nature is worth defending, whatever the fate of humans.

A wilderness area has a value independent of whether humans have access to it.

In these statements, something *A* is said to have a value independent of whether *A* has a value for something else, *B*. The value of *A* must therefore be said to have a value inherent in *A*. *A* has *intrinsic value*. This does not imply that *A* has value *for B*. Thus *A* may have, and usually does have, both intrinsic and extrinsic value.

Subjectivistic arguments tend to take for granted that a subject is somehow implied. There "must be" somebody who performs the valuation process. For this subject, something may have value.

The burden of proof lies with the subjectivists insofar as naive attitudes lack the clear-cut separation of value from reality and the conception of value as something projected by man into reality or the neutral facts by a subject.

The most promising way of defending intrinsic values today is, in my view, to take gestalt thinking seriously. "Objects" will then be defined in terms of gestalts, rather than in terms of heaps of things with external relations and dominated by forces. This undermines the subject-object dualism essential for value subjectivism.

OUTLOOK FOR THE FUTURE

What is the outlook for growth of ecological, relevant identification and of policies in harmony with a high level of identification?

A major nuclear war will involve a setback of tremendous dimensions. Words need not be wasted in support of that conclusion. But continued militarization is a threat: It means further domination of technology and centralization.

Continued population growth makes benevolent policies still more difficult to pursue than they already are. Poor people in megacities do not have the opportunity to meet nature, and shortsighted policies which favor increasing the number of poor are destructive. Even a small population growth in rich nations is scarcely less destructive.

The economic policy of growth (as conceived today in the richest nations of all times) is increasingly destructive. It does not *prevent* growth of identification but makes it politically powerless. This reminds us of the possibility of significant *growth* of identification in the near future.

The increasing destruction plus increasing information about the destruction is apt to elicit strong feelings of sorrow, despair, desperate actions and tireless efforts to save what is left. With the forecast that more than a million species will die out before the year 2000 and most cultures be done away with, identification may grow rapidly among a minority.

At the present about 10% to 15% of the populace of some European countries are in favor of strong policies in harmony with the attitudes of identification. But this percentage may increase without major changes of policies. So far as I can see, the most probable course of events is continued devastation of conditions of life on this planet, combined with a powerless upsurge of sorrow and lamentation

What actually happens is often wildly "improbable," and perhaps the strong anthropocentric arguments and wise recommendations of *World Conservation Strategy* (1980) will, after all, make a significant effect.

Notes

1. For survey of the main themes of the shallow and the deep movement, see Naess (1973); elaborated in Naess (1981). See also the essay of G. Sessions in Schultz (1981) and Devall (1979). Some of the 15 views as formulated and listed by Devall would perhaps more adequately be described as part of "Ecosophy D" (D for Devall!) than as parts of a common deep ecology platform.

2. Commissioned by The United Nations Environmental Programme (UNEP) which worked together with the World Wildlife Fund (WWF). Published 1980. Copies available through IUNC, 1196 Gland, Switzerland. In India: Department of Environment.

3. This aim implies a synthesis of views developed in the different branches of philosophy—ontology, epistemology, logic, methodology, theory of value, ethics, philosophy of history, and politics. As a philosopher the deep ecologist is a "generalist."

4. For comprehensive treatment of Ecosophy T, see Naess (1981, Chapter 7).

5. See Passmore (1980). For a reasonable, unemotional approach to "mysticism," see Stahl (1975).

6. For deeper study more distinctions have to be taken into account. See, for instance, Scheler (1954) and Mercer (1972).

7. See, for instance. the chapter "Removing the Rubbish" in Passmore (1980).

8. The diverse uses of the term *alienation (Entfremdung)* has an interesting and complicated history from the time of Rousseau. Rousseau himself offers interesting observations of how social conditions through the process of alienation make *amour de soi* change into *amour propre*. I would say: How the process of maturing is hindered and self-love hardens into egotism instead of softening and widening into Self-realization.

References

Elgin, Duane, 1981. *Voluntary Simplicity.* New York: William Morrow.

James, William. 1890. *The Principles of Psychology.* New York, Chapter 10: The Consciousness of Self.

Mercer, Philip. 1972. *Sympathy and Ethics.* Oxford: The Clarendon Press. Discusses forms of identification.

Naess, A. 1973. "The Shadow and the Deep, Long Range Ecology Movement," *Inquiry* 16: (95–100).

——. 1974. *Gandhi and Group Conflict.* 1981, Oslo: Universitetsforlaget.

——. 1981. *Ekologi, samhälle och livsstil. Utkast til en ekosofi.* Stockholm: LTs förlag.

——. 1979. "Self-realization in Mixed Communities of Humans, Bears, Sheep and Wolves, " *Inquiry,* Vol. 22, (pp. 231–241).

Passmore, John. 1980. *Man's Responsibility for Nature.* 2nd ed., London: Duckworth.

Sahlins, Marshall. 1972. *Stone Age Economics.* Chicago: Aldine.

Scheler, Max. 1954. *The Nature of Sympathy.* London: Routledge & Keegan Paul.

Study Questions

1. What does Naess mean by *Ecosophy*? What does the ending *-sophy* refer to?
2. What are the basic tenets of Ecosophy T?
3. What does Naess mean by *Self-realization*? Analyze the quotations from Radhakrishnan, Eliot Deutch, Juan Mascaró, and Gandhi. What do they tell us about Self-realization?
4. How do we develop a wider Self?
5. Explain Naess's idea of *identification*. Is it mystical? How can we identify with "individuals, species, ecosystems, and landscapes?"
6. What is Naess's saying about *value objectivism*? Critically discuss this issue.

22

Deep Ecology

BILL DEVALL AND GEORGE SESSIONS

Bill Devall teaches in the sociology department at Humboldt State University in Arcata, California, and George Sessions teaches philosophy at Sierra College in Rocklin, California. Together they have authored Deep Ecology: Living as if Nature Mattered (1985) *from which the present selection is taken.*

This essay sets forth a more recent version of deep ecology than Naess's 1972 summary version, linking it to Zen Buddhism, Taoism, Native American rituals, and Christianity. They contrast deep ecology with the dominant worldview and set forth the eight principles of deep ecology.

The term *deep ecology* was coined by Arne Naess in his 1973 article, "The Shallow and the Deep, Long-Range Ecology Movements." Naess was attempting to describe the deeper, more spiritual approach to Nature exemplified in the writings of Aldo Leopold and Rachel Carson. He thought that this deeper approach resulted from a more sensitive openness to ourselves and nonhuman life around us. The essence of deep ecology is to keep asking more searching questions about human life, society, and Nature as in the Western philosophical tradition of Socrates. As examples of this deep questioning, Naess points out "that we ask why and how, where others do not. For instance, ecology as a science does not ask what kind of a society would be the best for maintaining a particular ecosystem—that is considered a question for

Reprinted from *Deep Ecology: Living as if Nature Mattered* (Salt Lake City: Peregrine Smith Books, 1985), by permission. Footnotes deleted.

value theory, for politics, for ethics." Thus deep ecology goes beyond the so-called factual scientific level to the level of self and Earth wisdom.

Deep ecology goes beyond a limited piecemeal shallow approach to environmental problems and attempts to articulate a comprehensive religious and philosophical worldview. The foundations of deep ecology are the basic intuitions and experiencing of ourselves and Nature which comprise ecological consciousness. Certain outlooks on politics and public policy flow naturally from this consciousness. And in the context of this book, we discuss the minority tradition as the type of community most conducive both to cultivating ecological consciousness and to asking the basic questions of values and ethics addressed in these pages.

Many of these questions are perennial philosophical and religious questions faced by humans in all cultures over the ages. What does it mean to be a unique human individual? How can the individual self maintain and increase its uniqueness while also being an inseparable aspect of the whole system wherein there are no sharp breaks between self and the *other*? An ecological perspective, in this deeper sense, results in what Theodore Roszak calls "an awakening of wholes greater than the sum of their parts. In spirit, the discipline is contemplative and therapeutic."

Ecological consciousness and deep ecology are in sharp contrast with the dominant worldview of technocratic–industrial societies which regard humans as isolated and fundamentally separate from the rest of Nature, as superior to, and in charge of, the rest of creation. But the view of humans as separate and superior to the rest of Nature is only part of larger cultural patterns. For thousands of years, Western culture has become increasingly obsessed with the idea of *dominance*: with dominance of humans over nonhuman Nature, masculine over the feminine, wealthy and powerful over the poor, with the dominance of the West over non-Western cultures. Deep ecological consciousness allows us to see through these erroneous and dangerous illusions.

For deep ecology, the study of our place in the Earth household includes the study of ourselves as part of the organic whole. Going beyond a narrowly materialist scientific understanding of reality, the spiritual and the material aspects of reality fuse together. While the leading intellectuals of the dominant worldview have tended to view religion as "just superstition," and have looked upon ancient spiritual practice and enlightenment, such as found in Zen Buddhism, as essentially subjective, the search for deep ecological consciousness is the search for a more objective consciousness and state of being through an active deep questioning and meditative process and way of life.

Many people have asked these deeper questions and cultivated ecological consciousness within the context of different spiritual traditions—Christianity, Taoism, Buddhism, and Native American rituals, for example.

While differing greatly in other regards, many in these traditions agree with the basic principles of deep ecology.

Warwick Fox, an Australian philosopher, has succinctly expressed the central intuition of deep ecology: "It is the idea that we can make no firm ontological divide in the field of existence: That there is no bifurcation in reality between the human and the non-human realms . . . to the extent that we perceive boundaries, we fall short of deep ecological consciousness."

From this most basic insight or characteristic of deep ecological consciousness, Arne Naess has developed two *ultimate norms* or intuitions which are themselves not derivable from other principles or intuitions. They are arrived at by the deep questioning process and reveal the importance of moving to the philosophical and religious level of wisdom. They cannot be validated, of course, by the methodology of modern science based on its usual mechanistic assumptions and its very narrow definition of data. These ultimate norms are *self-realization* and *biocentric equality*.

I. SELF-REALIZATION

In keeping with the spiritual traditions of many of the world's religions, the deep ecology norm of self-realization goes beyond the modern Western *self* which is defined as an isolated ego striving primarily for hedonistic gratification or for a narrow sense of individual salvation in this life or the next. This socially programmed sense of the narrow self or social self dislocates us, and leaves us prey to whatever fad or fashion is prevalent in our society or social reference group. We are thus robbed of beginning the search for our unique spiritual/biological personhood. Spiritual growth, or unfolding, begins when we cease to understand or see ourselves as isolated and narrow competing egos and begin to identify with other humans from our family and friends to, eventually, our species. But the deep ecology sense of self requires a further maturity and growth, an identification which goes beyond humanity to include the nonhuman world. We must see beyond our narrow contemporary cultural assumptions and values, and the conventional wisdom of our time and place, and this is best achieved by the meditative deep questioning process. Only in this way can we hope to attain full mature personhood and uniqueness.

A nurturing nondominating society can help in the "real work" of becoming a whole person. The "real work" can be summarized symbolically as the realization of "self-in-Self" where "Self" stands for organic wholeness. This process of the full unfolding of the self can also be summarized by the phrase, "No one is saved until we are all saved," where the phrase "one" includes not only me, an individual human, but all humans, whales, grizzly bears, whole rain forest ecosystems, mountains and rivers, the tiniest microbes in the soil, and so on.

II. BIOCENTRIC EQUALITY

The intuition of biocentric equality is that all things in the biosphere have an equal right to live and blossom and to reach their own individual forms of unfolding and self-realization within the larger Self-realization. This basic intuition is that all organisms and entities in the ecosphere, as parts of the interrelated whole, are equal in intrinsic worth. Naess suggests that biocentric equality as an intuition is true in principle, although in the process of living, all species use each other as food, shelter, etc. Mutual predation is a biological fact of life, and many of the world's religions have struggled with the spiritual implications of this. Some animal liberationists who attempt to side-step this problem by advocating vegetarianism are forced to say that the entire plant kingdom including rain forests have no right to their own existence. This evasion flies in the face of the basic intuition of equality. Aldo Leopold expressed this intuition when he said humans are "plain citizens" of the biotic community, not lord and master over all other species.

Biocentric equality is intimately related to the all-inclusive Self-realization in the sense that if we harm the rest of Nature then we are harming ourselves. There are no boundaries and everything is interrelated. But insofar as we perceive things as individual organisms or entities, the insight draws us to respect all human and nonhuman individuals in their own right as parts of the whole without feeling the need to set up hierarchies of species with humans at the top.

The practical implications of this intuition or norm suggest that we should live with minimum rather than maximum impact on other species and on the Earth in general. Thus we see another aspect of our guiding principle: "simple in means, rich in ends."

A fuller discussion of the biocentric norm as it unfolds itself in practice begins with the realization that we, as individual humans, and as communities of humans, have vital needs which go beyond such basics as food, water, and shelter to include love, play, creative expression, intimate relationships with a particular landscape (or Nature taken in its entirety) as well as intimate relationships with other humans, and the vital need for spiritual growth, for becoming a mature human being.

Our vital material needs are probably more simple than many realize. In technocratic-industrial societies there is overwhelming propaganda and advertising which encourages false needs and destructive desires designed to foster increased production and consumption of goods. Most of this actually diverts us from facing reality in an objective way and from beginning the "real work" of spiritual growth and maturity.

Many people who do not see themselves as supporters of deep ecology nevertheless recognize an overriding vital human need for a healthy and high-quality natural environment for humans, if not for all life, with minimum intrusion of toxic waste, nuclear radiation from human enterprises, minimum acid rain and smog, and enough free flowing wilderness so humans can get in touch with their sources, the natural rhythms and the flow of time and place.

Drawing from the minority tradition and from the wisdom of many who have offered the insight of interconnectedness, we recognize that deep ecologists can offer suggestions for gaining maturity and encouraging the processes of harmony with Nature, but that there is no grand solution which is guaranteed to save us from ourselves.

The ultimate norms of deep ecology suggest a view of the nature of reality and our place as an individual (many in the one) in the larger scheme of things. They cannot be fully grasped intellectually but are ultimately experiential. We encourage readers to consider our further discussion of the psychological, social and ecological implications of these norms in later chapters.

As a brief summary of our position thus far, Figure 1 summarizes the contrast between the dominant worldview and deep ecology.

III. BASIC PRINCIPLES OF DEEP ECOLOGY

In April 1984, during the advent of spring and John Muir's birthday, George Sessions and Arne Naess sum-

---

FIGURE 1

DOMINANT WORLDVIEW	DEEP ECOLOGY
Dominance over Nature	Harmony with Nature
Natural environment as resource for humans	All nature has intrinsic worth/biospecies equality
Material/economic growth for growing human population	Elegantly simple material needs (material goals serving the larger goal of self-realization)
Belief in ample resource reserves	Earth "supplies" limited
High technological progress and solutions	Appropriate technology; nondominating science
Consumerism	Doing with enough/recycling
National/centralized community	Minority tradition/bioregion

marized fifteen years of thinking on the principles of deep ecology while camping in Death Valley, California. In this great and special place, they articulated these principles in a literal, somewhat neutral way, hoping that they would be understood and accepted by persons coming from different philosophical and religious positions.

Readers are encouraged to elaborate their own versions of deep ecology, clarify key concepts and think through the consequences of acting from these principles.

Basic Principles

1. The well-being and flourishing of human and non-human Life on Earth have value in themselves (synonyms: intrinsic value, inherent value). These values are independent of the usefulness of the nonhuman world for human purposes.
2. Richness and diversity of life forms contribute to the realization of these values and are also values in themselves.
3. Humans have no right to reduce this richness and diversity except to satisfy *vital* needs.
4. The flourishing of human life and cultures is compatible with a substantial decrease of the human population. The flourishing of nonhuman life requires such a decrease.
5. Present human interference with the nonhuman world is excessive, and the situation is rapidly worsening.
6. Policies must therefore be changed. These policies affect basic economic, technological, and ideological structures. The resulting state of affairs will be deeply different from the present.
7. The ideological change is mainly that of appreciating *life quality* (dwelling in situations of inherent value) rather than adhering to an increasingly higher standard of living. There will be a profound awareness of the difference between big and great.
8. Those who subscribe to the foregoing points have an obligation directly or indirectly to try to implement the necessary changes.

Naess and Sessions Provide Comments on the Basic Principles

RE (1). This formulation refers to the biosphere, or more accurately, to the ecosphere as a whole. This includes individuals, species, populations, habitat, as well as human and nonhuman cultures. From our current knowledge of all-pervasive intimate relationships, this implies a fundamental deep concern and respect. Ecological processes of the planet should, on the whole, remain intact. "The world environment should remain 'natural'" (Gary Snyder).

The term "life" is used here in a more comprehensive nontechnical way to refer also to what biologists classify as "nonliving"; rivers (watersheds), landscapes, ecosystems. For supporters of deep ecology, slogans such as "Let the river live" illustrate this broader usage so common in most cultures.

Inherent value as used in (1) is common in deep ecology literature ("The presence of inherent value in a natural object is independent of any awareness, interest, or appreciation of it by a conscious being.")

RE (2). More technically, this is a formulation concerning diversity and complexity. From an ecological standpoint, complexity and symbiosis are conditions for maximizing diversity. So-called simple, lower, or primitive species of plants and animals contribute essentially to the richness and diversity of life. They have value in themselves and are not merely steps toward the so-called higher or rational life forms. The second principle presupposes that life itself, as a process over evolutionary time, implies an increase of diversity and richness. The refusal to acknowledge that some life forms have greater or lesser intrinsic value than others (see points 1 and 2) runs counter to the formulations of some ecological philosophers and New Age writers.

Complexity, as referred to here, is different from complication. Urban life may be more complicated than life in a natural setting without being more complex in the sense of multifaceted quality.

RE (3). The term "vital need" is left deliberately vague to allow for considerable latitude in judgment. Differences in climate and related factors, together with differences in the structures of societies as they now exist, need to be considered (for some Eskimos, snowmobiles are necessary today to satisfy vital needs).

People in the materially richest countries cannot be expected to reduce their excessive interference with the nonhuman world to a moderate level overnight. The stabilization and reduction of the human population will take time. Interim strategies need to be developed. But this in no way excuses the present complacency—the extreme seriousness of our current situation must first be realized. But the longer we wait the more drastic will be the measures needed. Until deep changes are made, substantial decreases in richness and diversity are liable to occur: the rate of extinction of species will be ten to one hundred times greater than any other period of earth history.

RE (4). The United Nations Fund for Population Activities in their State of World Population Report (1984) said that high human population growth rates (over 2.0 percent annum) in many developing countries "were diminishing the quality of life for many millions of people." During the decade 1974–1984, the world population grew by nearly 800 million—more than the size of India. "And we will be adding about one Bangladesh (population 93 million) per annum between now and the year 2000."

The report noted that "The growth rate of the human population has declined for the first time in human history. But at the same time, the number of people being added to the human population is bigger than at any time in history because the population base is larger."

Most of the nations in the developing world (including India and China) have as their official government policy the goal of reducing the rate of human population increase, but there are debates over the types of measures to take (contraception, abortion, etc.) consistent with human rights and feasibility.

The report concludes that if all governments set specific population targets as public policy to help alleviate poverty and advance the quality of life, the current situation could be improved.

As many ecologists have pointed out, it is also absolutely crucial to curb population growth in the so-called developed (i.e., overdeveloped) industrial societies. Given the tremendous rate of consumption and waste production of individuals in these societies, they represent a much greater threat and impact on the biosphere per capita than individuals in Second and Third World countries.

RE (5). This formulation is mild. For a realistic assessment of the situation, see the unabbreviated version of the l.U.C.N.'s *World Conservation Strategy*. There are other works to be highly recommended, such as Gerald Barney's *Global 2000 Report to the President of the United States*.

The slogan of "noninterference" does not imply that humans should not modify some ecosystems as do other species. Humans have modified the earth and will probably continue to do so. At issue is the nature and extent of such interference.

The fight to preserve and extend areas of wilderness or near-wilderness should continue and should focus on the general ecological functions of these areas (one such function: large wilderness areas are required in the biosphere to allow for continued evolutionary speciation of animals and plants). Most present designated wilderness areas and game preserves are not large enough to allow for such speciation.

RE (6). Economic growth as conceived and implemented today by the industrial states is incompatible with (1)–(5). There is only a faint resemblance between ideal sustainable forms of economic growth and present policies of the industrial societies. And "sustainable" still means "sustainable in relation to humans."

Present ideology tends to value things because they are scarce and because they have a commodity value. There is prestige in vast consumption and waste (to mention only several relevant factors).

Whereas "self-determination," "local community," and "think globally, act locally," will remain key terms in the ecology of human societies, nevertheless the implementation of deep changes requires increasingly global action—action across borders.

Governments in Third World countries (with the exception of Costa Rica and a few others) are uninterested in deep ecological issues. When the governments of industrial societies try to promote ecological measures through Third World governments, practically nothing is accomplished (e.g., with problems of desertification). Given this situation, support for global action through nongovernmental international organizations becomes increasingly important. Many of these organizations are able to act globally "from grassroots to grassroots," thus avoiding negative governmental interference.

Cultural diversity today requires advanced technology, that is, techniques that advance the basic goals of each culture. So-called soft, intermediate, and alternative technologies are steps in this direction.

RE (7). Some economists criticize the term "quality of life" because it is supposed to be vague. But on closer inspection, what they consider to be vague is actually the nonquantitative nature of the term. One cannot quantify adequately what is important for the quality of life as discussed here, and there is no need to do so.

RE (8). There is ample room for different opinions about priorities: what should be done first, what next? What is most urgent? What is clearly necessary as opposed to what is highly desirable but not absolutely pressing?

Study Questions

1. Analyze the eight principles of deep ecology. What problems, if any, do you find with them? Do you accept the first principle that natural objects have inherent value? What things do you think have inherent value and why?
2. What are the implications of Principle 4? If people do not voluntarily curb their population, how would a deep ecologist solve this problem?
3. Is deep ecology workable? Why, or why not?

23

A Critique of Anti-Anthropocentric Ethics

RICHARD WATSON

Richard Watson is professor of philosophy at Washington University in St. Louis and the author of several works in philosophy. Here is his abstract:

Arne Naess, John Rodman, George Sessions, and others designated herein as ecosophers, propose an egalitarian anti-anthropocentric biocentrism as a basis for a new environmental ethic. I outline their "hands-off-nature" position and show it to be based on setting man apart. The ecosophic position is thus neither egalitarian nor fully biocentric. A fully egalitarian biocentric ethic would place no more restrictions on the behavior of human beings than on the behavior of any other animals. Uncontrolled human behavior might lead to the destruction of the environment and thus to the extinction of human beings. I thus conclude that human interest in survival is the best ground on which to argue for an ecological balance which is good both for human beings and for the whole biological community.

Anthropocentric is defined specifically as the position "that considers man as the central fact, or final aim, of the universe" and generally "conceiv[es] of everything in the universe in terms of human values."[1] In the literature of environmental ethics, anti-anthropocentric biocentrism is the position that human needs, goals, and desires should not be taken as privileged or overriding in considering the needs, desires, interests, and goals of all members of all biological species taken together, and in general that the Earth as a whole should not be interpreted or managed from a human standpoint. According to this position, birds, trees, and the land itself considered as the biosphere have a right to be and to live out their individual and species' potentials, and that members of the human species have no right to disturb, perturb, or destroy the ecological balance of the planet.

An often quoted statement of this right of natural objects to continue to be as they are found to be occurs in John Rodman's "The Liberation of Nature?":

> To affirm that "natural objects" have "rights" is symbolically to affirm that ALL NATURAL ENTITIES (INCLUDING HUMANS) HAVE INTRINSIC WORTH SIMPLY BY VIRTUE OF BEING AND BEING WHAT THEY ARE.[2]

In "On the Nature and Possibility of an Environmental Ethic," Tom Regan follows an implication of this view by presenting a "preservation principle":

> By the "preservation principle" I mean a principle of nondestruction, noninterference, and, generally, nonmeddling. By characterizing this in terms of a principle, moreover, I am emphasizing that preservation (letting-be) be regarded as a moral imperative.[3]

Support for this hands-off-nature approach is provided by George Sessions in his "Spinoza, Perennial Philosophy, and Deep Ecology," where, among other things, he describes how Aldo Leopold moved from a position considering humans as stewards or managers of nature to one considering humans as "plain members" of the total biotic community.[4] As Leopold himself puts it:

> A thing is right when it tends to preserve the integrity, stability, and beauty of the biotic community. It is wrong when it tends otherwise.[5]

According to Sessions, Leopold reached this position in part as a result of his dawning realization that ecological communities are internally integrated and highly complex. He saw how human activities have disrupted many ecological communities and was himself involved in some unsuccessful attempts to manage communities of animals in the wild. These failures led Leopold to conclude that "the biotic mechanism is so complex that its workings may never be fully understood."[6]

Like many other environmentalists, Sessions associates Leopold's position with Barry Commoner's first law of ecology: "Everything is connected to everything else,"[7] according to which "any major man-made change in a natural system is likely to be *detrimental* to that system." This view, which considers all environmental managers who try to alter the environment to be suffering from scientific hubris, leads to an almost biblical statement of nescience. In this connection, Sessions quotes the ecologist Frank Egler as saying that "Nature is not only more complex than we think, but it is more complex than we can ever think." The attitude of humble acquiescence to the ways of nature which follows from this view, Sessions says, is summed up in Commoner's third law, "Nature knows best."

The position is presented at length by G. Tyler Miller, in another quotation cited by Sessions:

> One of the purposes of this Book [*Replenish the Earth*] is to show the bankruptcy of the term "spaceship earth." . . . This is an upside-down view of reality and is yet another

Reprinted from *Environmental Ethics*, Vol. 5 (Fall 1983) by permission. Notes edited.

manifestation of our arrogance toward nature. . . . Our task is not to learn how to pilot spaceship earth. It is not to learn how—as Teilhard de Chardin would have it—"to seize the tiller of the world": Our task is to give up our fantasies of omnipotence. In other words, *we must stop trying to steer* [my italics]. The solution to our present dilemma does not lie in attempting to extend our technical and managerial skills into every sphere of existence. Thus, *from a human standpoint our environmental crisis is the result* of our arrogance towards nature [Miller's italics]. Somehow we must tune our senses again to the beat of existence, sensing in nature fundamental rhythms we can trust even though we may never fully understand them. We must learn anew that it is we who belong to earth and not the earth to us. Thus rediscovery of our finitude is fundamental to any genuinely human future.[8]

Sessions, at least, is not naive about some of the problems that arise from these pronouncements. He says that if an environmental ethic is to be derived from ecological principles and concepts, this raises

the old problem of attempting to derive moral principles and imperatives from supposedly empirical fact (the "is-ought problem"). The attempt to justify ecosystem ethics on conventional utilitarian or "rights and obligations" grounds presents formidable obstacles. And, so far, little headway has been made in finding other acceptable grounds for an ecosystem ethics other than a growing intuitive ecological awareness that *it is right*.[9]

The anti-anthropocentric biocentrists have sought a metaphysical foundation for a holistic environmental ethic in Spinoza. The clearest statement of this appears in Arne Naess's "Spinoza and Ecology." Naess expands from Spinoza in sixteen points, several of which are crucial to my discussion of anti-anthropocentric biocentrism:

1. The nature conceived by field ecologists is not the passive, dead, value-neutral nature of mechanistic science, but akin to the *Deus sive Natura* of Spinoza. All-inclusive, creative (as *natura naturans*), infinitely diverse, and alive in the broad sense of pan-psychism, but also manifesting a structure, the so-called laws of nature. There are always causes to be found, but extremely complex and difficult to unearth. Nature with a capital N is intuitively conceived as perfect in a sense that Spinoza and out-door ecologists have more or less in common: it is not narrowly moral, utilitarian, or aesthetic perfection. Nature is perfect "in itself."

Perfection can only mean completeness of some sort when applied in general, and not to specifically human achievements. . . .

2. . . . The two aspects of Nature, those of extension and thought (better: non-extension), are both complete aspects of one single reality, and *perfection characterizes both*. . . .

3. . . . As an *absolutely* all-embracing reality, Nature has no purpose, aim, or goal. . . .

4. There is no established moral world-order. Human justice is not a law of nature. There are, on the other hand, no natural laws limiting the endeavour to extend the realm of justice as conceived in a society of free human beings. . . .

5. Good and evil must be defined in relation to beings for which something is good or evil, useful or detrimental. The terms are meaningless when not thus related. . . .

6. Every thing is connected with every other. . . . Intimate interconnectedness in the sense of internal rather than external relations characterizes ecological ontology. . . .

9. If one insists upon using the term "rights," every being may be said to have the right to do what is in its power. It is "right" to express its own nature as clearly and extensively as natural conditions permit.

That right which they [the animals] have in relation to us, we have in relation to them (*Ethics,* Part IV, first scholium to proposition 37).

That rights are a part of a separate moral world order is fiction.

Field ecologists tend to accept a general "right to live and blossom." Humans have no special right to kill and injure, Nature does not belong to them.[10]

Spinoza has also been cited for the general position that the ultimate goal, good, and joy of human beings is understanding which amounts to contemplation of Nature. In "Spinoza and Jeffers on Man in Nature," Sessions says:

Spinoza's purpose in philosophizing, then, is to break free from the bonds of desire and ignorance which captivate and frustrate most men, thus standing in the way of what real happiness is available to them, and to attain a higher Self which is aligned with a *correct* [my italics] understanding of God/Nature.[11]

The position, however, is not restricted to Spinoza, for, as Sessions notes elsewhere, the best-known statement of this view is probably found in Aldous Huxley's *Perennial Philosophy*:

Happiness and moral progress depend, it is [mistakenly] thought [today], on bigger and better gadgets and a higher standard of living. . . . In all the historic formulations of the Perennial Philosophy it is axiomatic that the end of human life is contemplation, or the direct and intuitive awareness of God; that action is the means to that end; that a society is good to the extent that it renders contemplation possible for its members.[12]

A difficult question that arises for advocates of this position is whether or not humans can be activists. For example, near-total passivism seems to be suggested by Michael Zimmerman in his approving summation of what he takes to be Heidegger's admonition to the Western World:

Only Western man's thinking has ended up by viewing the world as a storehouse of raw material for the enhancement of man's Power. . . . [A] new kind of thinking must . . . pass beyond the subjectivistic thinking of philosophy-science-technology. . . . Heidegger indicates that the new way must "let beings be," i.e., it must let them manifest themselves in their own presence and worth, and nor merely as objects for the all-powerful Subject.[13]

On the other hand, Naess is an activist; he and others think that civil disobedience is appropriate to thwart human "misuse" of the environment. And although Naess stresses what he calls the "biospherical egalitarianism" of all biological species on earth," he says in "Environmental Ethics and Spinoza":

Animals cannot be citizens [i.e., members of a human moral community]. But animals may, as far as I can understand, be members of *life communities* on a par with babies, lunatics, and others who do not cooperate as citizens but are cared for in part for their own good.

This is consistent with Naess's Spinozistic approach, but the more general implication of the species egalitarian approach seems to be inactivism.

In summary, advocates of anti-anthropocentric biocentrism such as Sessions speak of the Judeo-Christian-Platonic-Aristotelian tradition as leading to

an extreme subjectivist anthropocentrism in which the whole of non-human nature is viewed as a resource for man. By way of a long and convoluted intellectual history, we have managed to subvert completely the organic ecological world view of the hunter and gatherer.

Sessions goes on to deplore "the demise of pantheism and the desacralization of Nature." He then makes a statement highly typical of anti-anthropomorphic biocentrists:

Part of the genius of Bacon and Descartes was to realize, contrary to the conservatism of the Church authorities, that a new science was needed to consummate the goal of Judeo-Christian-Platonic-Aristotelian domination of nature. The Enlightenment retained the Christian idea of man's perpetual progress (now defined as increasing scientific-technological control and mastery over nature), thus setting the stage for, and passing its unbridled optimism on to, its twentieth-century successors, Marxism and American pragmatism. The floodgates had been opened. The Pythagorean theory of the cosmos and the whole idea of a meaningful perennial philosophy were swept away in a deluge of secularism, the fragmentation of knowledge, pronouncements that God was dead and the universe and life of man meaningless, industrialization, the quest for material happiness, and the consequent destruction of the environment. The emphasis was no longer upon either *God* or *Nature*, but *Man*.

Sessions by no means advocates or thinks possible a simple return to pre-Socratic religion or pantheism. But what, on the basis of ecological principles and concepts, is the underlying motif or guiding ideal today for "a correct understanding of God/Nature"? According to Naess, the proper position is an *ecosophy* defined as "a philosophy of ecological harmony or equilibrium." Thus, while deploring the Greek contribution to the present desacralization of nature, these ecosophers do acknowledge the Stoic and Epicurean contributions to the philosophy of balance, harmony, and equilibrium. They present a holistic vision of the Earth circling in dynamic ecological equilibrium as the preferred and proper contemplative object of right-thinking environmental man.

In pursuing a statement of anti-anthropomorphic biocentrism, then, I have exposed five principles of the movement:

1. The needs, desires, interests, and goals of humans are not privileged.
2. The human species should not change the ecology of the planet.
3. The world ecological system is too complex for human beings ever to understand.
4. The ultimate goal, good, and joy of humankind is contemplative understanding of Nature.
5. Nature is a holistic system of parts (of which man is merely one among many equals) all of which are internally interrelated in dynamic, harmonious, ecological equilibrium.

The moral imperative derived from this "ecosophy" is that human beings do not have the right to, and should not, alter the equilibrium.

II

I do not intend to challenge the controversial naturalistic assumption that some such environmental ethic can be derived from ecological principles and concepts. Whatever the logical problems of deriving value from fact, it is not (and probably never has been) a practical problem for large numbers of people who base their moral convictions on factual premises.

Nevertheless, it must be obvious to most careful readers that the general position characterized in section 1 suffers from serious internal contradictions. I think they are so serious that the position must be abandoned. In what follows I detail the problems that arise in the system, and then offer an alternative to the call for developing a new ecosophic ethic.

To go immediately to the heart of the matter, I take anti-anthropocentrism more seriously than do any of the ecosophers I have quoted or read. If man is a part of nature, if he is a "plain citizen," if he is just one non-privileged member of a "biospherical egalitarianism," then the human species should be treated in no way different from any other species. However, the entire tone of the position outlined in section 1 is to set man apart from nature and above all other living species. Naess says that nonhuman animals should be "cared for in part for their own good." Sessions says that humans should curb their technological enthusiasms to preserve ecological equilibrium. Rodman says flatly that man should let nature be.

Now, the posing of man against nature in any way is anthropocentric. Man is a part of nature. Human ways—human culture—and human actions are as natural as are the ways in which any other species of animals behaves. But if we view the state of nature or Nature as being natural, undisturbed, and unperturbed only when human beings are *not* present, or only when human beings are curbing their natural behavior, then we are assuming that human beings are apart from, separate from, different from, removed from, or above nature. It is obvious that the ecosophy described above is based on this position of setting man apart from or above nature. (Do I mean even "sordid" and "perverted" human behavior? Yes, that is natural, too.)

To avoid this separation of man from nature, this special treatment of human beings as other than nature, we must stress that man's works (yes, including H-bombs and gas chambers) are as natural as those of bower birds and beavers.

But civilized man wreaks havoc on the environment. We disrupt the ecology of the planet, cause the extinction of myriad other species of living things, and even alter the climate of the Earth. Should we not attempt to curb our behavior to avoid these results? Indeed we should as a matter of prudence if we want to preserve our habitat and guarantee the survival of our species. But this is anthropocentric thinking.

Only if we are thinking anthropocentrically will we set the human species apart as *the* species that is to be thwarted in its natural behavior. Anti-anthropocentric biocentrists suggest that other species are to be allowed to manifest themselves naturally. They are to be allowed to live out their evolutionary potential in interaction with one another. But man is different. Man is *too* powerful, *too* destructive of the environment and other species, *too* successful in reproducing, and so on. What a phenomenon is man! Man is so wonderfully bad that he is not to be allowed to live out his evolutionary potential in egalitarian interaction with all other species.

Why not? The only reason is anthropocentric. We are not treating man as a plain member of the biotic community. We are not treating the human species as an equal among other species. We think of man as being better than other animals, or worse, as the case may be, because man is so powerful.

One reason we think this is that we think in terms of an anthropocentric moral community. All other species are viewed as morally neutral; their behavior is neither good nor bad. But we evaluate human behavior morally. And this sets man apart. If we are to treat man as a part of nature on egalitarian terms with other species, then man's behavior must be treated as morally neutral, too. It is absurd, of course, to suggest the opposite alternative, that we evaluate the behavior of nonhuman animals morally.

Bluntly, if we think there is nothing morally wrong with one species taking over the habitat of another and eventually causing the extinction of the dispossessed species—as has happened millions of times in the history of the Earth—then we should not think that there is anything morally or ecosophically wrong with the human species dispossessing and causing the extinction of other species.

Man's nature, his role, his forte, his glory and ambition has been to propagate and thrive at the expense of many other species and to the disruption—or, neutrally, to the change—of the planet's ecology. I do not want to engage in speculation about the religion of preliterate peoples, or in debates about the interpretation of documented non-Judeo-Christian-Platonic-Aristotelian religions. I am skeptical, however, of the panegyrics about pantheism and harmonious integration with sacred Nature. But these speculations do not matter. The fact is that for about 50,000 years human beings (*Homo sapiens*) have been advancing like wildfire (to use an inflammatory metaphor) to occupy more and more of the planet. A peak of low-energy technology was reached about 35,000 years ago at which time man wiped out many species of large animals. About 10,000 years ago man domesticated plants and animals and started changing the face of the Earth with grazing, farming, deforestation, and desertification. About 200 years ago man started burning fossil fuels with results that will probably change the climate of the planet (at least temporarily) and that have already resulted in the extinction of many species of living things that perhaps might otherwise have survived. In 1945 man entered an atomic age and we now have the ability to desertify large portions of the Earth and perhaps to cause the extinction of most of the higher forms of life.

Human beings do alter things. They cause the extinction of many species, and they change the Earth's ecology. This is what humans do. This is their destiny. If they destroy many other species and themselves in the process, they do no more than has been done by many another species. The human species should be allowed—if any species can be said to have a right—to live out its evolutionary potential, to its own destruction if that is the end result. It is nature's way.

This is not a popular view. But most alternative anti-anthropocentric biocentric arguments for preserving nature are self-contradictory. Man is a part of nature. The only way man will survive is if he uses his brains to save himself. One reason why we should curb human behavior that is destructive of other species and the environment is because in the end it is destructive of the human species as well.

I hope it is human nature to survive because we are smart. But those who appeal for a new ethic or religion or ecosophy based on an intuitive belief that they know what is right not only for other people, but also for the planet as a whole, exhibit the hubris that they themselves say got us in such a mess in the first place. If the ecosphere is so complicated that we may never understand its workings, how is it that so many ecosophers are so sure that they know what is right for us to do now? Beyond the issue of man's right to do whatever he can according to the power-makes-right ecosophic ethic outlined by Naess, we may simply be wrong about what is "good" for the planet. Large numbers of species have been wiped out before, e.g., at the time the dinosaurs became extinct. Perhaps wiping out and renewal is just the way things go. Of course, a lot of genetic material is lost, but presumably all the species that ever existed came out of the same primordial soup, and could again. In situations where genetic material was limited, as in the Galapagos Islands or Australia, evolutionary radiation filled the niches. Even on the basis of our present knowledge about evolution and ecology, we have little ground to worry about the proliferation of life on Earth even if man manages to wipe out most of the species now living. Such a clearing out might be just the thing to allow for variety and diversity. And why is it that we harp about genetic banks today anyway? For one thing, we are worried that disease might wipe out our domesticated grain crops. Then where would *man* be?

Another obvious anthropocentric element in ecosophic thinking is the predilection for ecological communities of great internal variety and complexity. But the barren limestone plateaus that surround the Mediterranean now are just as much in ecological balance as were the forests that grew there before man cut them down. And "dead" Lake Erie is just as much in ecological balance with the life on the land that surrounds it as it was in pre-Columbian times. The notion of a climax situation in ecology is a human invention, based on anthropocentric ideas of variety, completion, wholeness, and balance. A preference for equilibrium rather than change, for forests over deserts, for complexity and variety over simplicity and monoculture, all of these are matters of human economics and aesthetics. What *would* it be, after all, to think like a mountain as Aldo Leopold is said to have recommended? It would be anthropocentric because mountains do not think, but also because mountains are imagined to be thinking about which human interests in their preservation or development they prefer. The anthropocentrism of ecosophers is most obvious in their pronouncements about what is normal and natural. Perhaps it is not natural to remain in equilibrium, to be in ecological balance.

As far as that goes, most of the universe is apparently dead—or at least inanimate—anyway. And as far as we know, the movement of things is toward entropy. By simplifying things, man is on the side of the universe.

And as for making a mess of things, destroying things, disrupting and breaking down things, the best information we have about the origin of the universe is that it is the result of an explosion. If we are going to derive an ethic from our knowledge of nature, is it wrong to suggest that high-technology man might be doing the right thing? Naess does try to meet this objection with his tenth principle:

> 10 There is nothing in human nature or essence, according to Spinoza, which can *only* manifest or express itself through injury to others. That is, the striving for expression of one's nature does not inevitably imply an attitude of hostile domination over other beings, human or non-human. Violence, in the sense of violent activity, is not the same as violence as injury to others.[14]

But "injury" is a human moral concept. There is no injury to others in neutral nature. Naess and Spinoza are still bound by Judeo-Christian-Platonic-Aristotelian notions of human goodness. But to call for curbing man is like trying to make vegetarians of pet cats.

I have often been puzzled about why so many environmental philosophers insist on harking to Spinoza as a ground for environmental ethics. It is perfectly plain as Curley and Lloyd point out that Spinoza's moral views are humanistic. They show how difficult it is to reconcile Spinoza's sense of freedom as the recognition of necessity with any notion of autonomy of self that is required to make moral imperatives or morality itself meaningful. That is, to recognize and accept what one is determined to do—even if this recognition and acceptance were not itself determined—is not the same as choosing between two equally possible (undetermined) courses of action. Moral action depends on free choice among undetermined alternatives.

III

There are anthropocentric foundations in most environmental and ecosophical literature. In particular, most ecosophers say outright or openly imply that human individuals and the human species would be better off if we were required to live in ecological balance with nature. Few ecosophers really think that man is just one part of nature among others. Man is privileged—or cursed—at least by having a moral sensibility that as far as we can tell no other entities have. But it is pretty clear (as I argue in "Self-Consciousness and the Rights of Nonhuman Animals and Nature") that on this planet at least only human beings are (so far) full members of a moral community. We ought to be kinder to nonhuman animals, but I do not think that this is because they have any intrinsic rights. As far as that goes, human beings have no intrinsic rights either (as Naess and Spinoza agree). We have to earn our rights as cooperating citizens in a moral community.

Because, unlike many ecosophers, I do not believe that we can return to religion, or that given what we know about the world today we can believe in pantheism or panpsychism, I think it is a mistake to strive for a new environmental ethic based on religious or mystical grounds. And I trust that I have demonstrated both how difficult it is to be fully biocentric, and also how the results of anti-anthropocentric biocentrism go far beyond the limits that ecosophers have drawn. Ecosophers obviously want to avoid the direct implications of treating the human species in the egalitarian and hands-off way they say other species should be treated. It is nice that human survival is compatible with the preservation of a rich planetary ecology, but I think it is a mistake to try to cover up the fact that human survival and the good life for man is some part of what we are interested in. There is very good reason for thinking ecologically, and for encouraging human beings to act in such a way as to preserve a rich and balanced planetary ecology: human survival depends on it.

Notes

1. *Webster's New World Dictionary*, 2nd ed. (Cleveland, Ohio: William Collins and World Publishing Co., 1976), p 59.
2. John Rodman, "The Liberation of Nature?" *Inquiry* 20 (1977): 108 (quoted with emphasis in capitals by George Sessions in *Ecophilosophy III*, p. 5a).
3. Tom Regan, "The Nature and Possibility of an Environmental Ethic," *Environmental Ethics* 3 (1981): 31–32.
4. George Sessions, "Spinoza, Perennial Philosophy, and Deep Ecology," unpublished, p 15.
5. Aldo Leopold, *A Sand County Almanac* (Oxford: Oxford University Press, 1966), p. 240 (quoted by George Sessions in "Spinoza, Perennial Philosophy, and Deep Ecology," unpublished, p. 15).
6. Ibid.
7. Barry Commoner, *The Closing Circle: Nature, Man, and Technology* (New York: Alfred A. Knopf, 1971), p. 33 (quoted by George Sessions in "Panpsychism versus Modern Materialism: Some Implications for an Ecological Ethics," unpublished, p. 35).
8. G. Tyler Miller, *Replenish the Earth* (Belmont, Calif.: Wadsworth, 1972), p. 53 (quoted by George Sessions in "Shallow and Deep Ecology: A Review of the Philosophical Literature," unpublished, pp. 44–45).
9. George Sessions, "Shallow and Deep Ecology: A Review of the Philosophical Literature," unpublished, p. 16.
10. Arne Naess, "Spinoza and Ecology," in Sigfried Hessing, ed., *Speculum Spinozanum 1677–1977* (London: Routledge & Kegan Paul, 1977), pp. 419–21.
11. Sessions, George. "Spinoza and Jeffers on Man and Nature," *Inquiry* 20 (1977): 494–95.
12. Aldous Huxley, *Perennial Philosophy* (New York: Harper's, 1945), pp. 159–60 (quoted by George Sessions in "Shallow and Deep Ecology: A Review of the Philosophical Literature," unpublished, p. 47).
13. Michael Zimmerman, "Technological Change and the End of Philosophy," unpublished, no page given (quoted by George Sessions in "Spinoza and Jeffers on Man and Nature," *Inquiry* 20 (1977): 489).
14. Arne Naess, "Spinoza and Ecology," in Sigfried Hessing, ed., *Speculum Spinozanum 1677–1977* (London: Routledge & Kegan Paul, 1977, p. 421).

Study Questions

1. What is *anthropocentrism* according to Watson? How does it differ from *biocentrism*?
2. Carefully compare Watson's criticism with the articles by Taylor, Leopold, Callicott, Naess, and Sessions. Which of these writers does he attack most directly? Do any escape his critique? Are his critical objections sound?
3. Is Watson's version of environmental anthropocentrism plausible? Explain your answer.

24

Social Ecology Versus Deep Ecology

MURRAY BOOKCHIN

Murray Bookchin has been a leading anarchist and utopian political theorist, especially regarding the philosophy of nature. He is the cofounder and director emeritus of the Institute for Social Ecology. His many books include Toward an Ecological Society, The Ecology of Freedom, *and* The Philosophy of Social Ecology.

Social ecology, which Bookchin develops in this essay, is an egalitarian system that has its roots in Marxist and anarchistic thought, though he disagrees with both at crucial points. Against Marx, Bookchin rejects economic determinism and the dictatorship of the proletariat. He rejects anarchist analysis that identifies the modern nation-state as the primary cause of social domination. Bookchin's primary attack is on social domination, and he shows how it is connected to ecology. In The Ecology of Freedom, *he writes:*

> The cultural, traditional and psychological systems of obedience and command, not merely the economic and political systems to which the terms *class* and *State* most appropriately refer. Accordingly, hierarchy and domination could easily continue to exist in a "classless" or "Stateless" society. I refer to the domination of the young by the old, of women by men, of one ethnic group by another, of "masses" by bureaucrats who profess to speak of "higher social interests," of countryside by town, and in a more subtle psychological sense, of body by mind, of spirit by a shallow instrumental rationality.

Bookchin promotes an organic view of social theory, wherein the individual finds meaning only in community that he helps create and of which he is a creation. In this essay, Bookchin opposes social ecology to deep ecology.

BEYOND "ENVIRONMENTALISM"

The environmental movement has travelled a long way beyond those annual "Earth Day" festivals when millions of school kids were ritualistically mobilized to clean up streets and their parents were scolded by Arthur Godfrey, Barry Commoner, and Paul Ehrlich. The movement has gone beyond a naive belief that

FROM: *Socialist Review*, Vol. 88, no. 3 (1988): 11–29. Published by Duke University. Reprinted with permission of the publisher.

patchwork reforms and solemn vows by EPA bureaucrats will seriously arrest the insane pace at which we are tearing down the planet.

This shopworn "Earth Day" approach toward "engineering" nature so that we can ravage the Earth with minimal effects on ourselves—an approach that I called "environmentalism"—has shown signs of giving way to a more searching and radical mentality. Today, the new word in vogue is "ecology"—be it "deep ecology," "human ecology," "biocentric ecology," "anti-humanist ecology," or, to use a term uniquely rich in meaning, "*social* ecology."

Happily, the new relevance of the word "ecology" reveals a growing dissatisfaction with attempts to use our vast ecological problems for cheaply spectacular and politically manipulative ends. Our forests disappear due to mindless cutting and increasing acid rain; the ozone layer thins out from widespread use of fluorocarbons; toxic dumps multiply all over the planet; highly dangerous, often radioactive pollutants enter into our air, water, and food chains. These innumerable hazards threaten the integrity of life itself, raising far more basic issues than can be resolved by "Earth Day" cleanups and faint-hearted changes in environmental laws.

For good reason, more and more people are trying to go beyond the vapid "environmentalism" of the early 1970s and toward an *ecological* approach: one that is rooted in an ecological philosophy, ethics, sensibility, image of nature, and, ultimately, an ecological movement that will transform our domineering market society into a nonhierarchical cooperative one that will live in harmony with nature, because its members live in harmony with each other. They are beginning to sense that there is a tie-in between the way people deal with each other as social beings—men with women, old with young, rich with poor, white with people of color, first world with third, elites with "masses"—and the way they deal with nature.

The questions that now face us are: what do we really mean by an *ecological* approach? What is a *coherent* ecological philosophy, ethics, and movement? How can the answers to these questions and many others *fit together* so that they form a meaningful and creative whole? If we are not to repeat all the mistakes of the early seventies with their hoopla about "population control," their latent anti-feminism, elitism, arrogance, and ugly authoritarian tendencies, so we must honestly and seriously appraise the new tendencies that today go under the name of one or another form of "ecology."

TWO CONFLICTING TENDENCIES

Let us agree from the outset that the word "ecology" is no magic term that unlocks the real secret of our abuse of nature. It is a word that can be as easily abused, distorted, and tainted as words like "democracy" and "freedom." Nor does the word "ecology" put us all—whoever "we" may be—in the same boat against environmentalists who are simply trying to make a rotten society work by dressing it in green leaves and colorful flowers, while ignoring the deep-seated *roots* of our ecological problems.

It is time to face the fact that there are differences within the so-called "ecology movement" of the present time that are as serious as those between the "environmentalism" and "ecologism" of the early seventies. There are barely disguised racists, survivalists, macho Daniel Boones, and outright social reactionaries who use the word "ecology" to express their views, just as there are deeply concerned naturalists, communitarians, social radicals, and feminists who use the word "ecology" to express theirs.

The differences between these two tendencies in the so-called "ecology movement" consist not only in quarrels over theory, sensibility, and ethics. They have far-reaching *practical* and *political* consequences on the way we view nature, "humanity," and ecology. Most significantly, they concern how we propose to *change* society and by what *means*.

The greatest differences that are emerging within the so-called "ecology movement" of our day are between a vague, formless, often self-contradictory ideology called "deep ecology" and a socially oriented body of ideas best termed "social ecology." Deep ecology has parachuted into our midst quite recently from the Sunbelt's bizarre mix of Hollywood and Disneyland, spiced with homilies from Taoism, Buddhism, spiritualism, reborn Christianity, and, in some cases, eco-fascism. Social ecology, on the other hand, draws its inspiration from such radical decentralist thinkers as Peter Kropotkin, William Morris, and Paul Goodman, among many others who have challenged society's vast hierarchical, sexist, class-ruled, statist, and militaristic apparatus.

Bluntly speaking, deep ecology, despite all its social rhetoric, has no real sense that our ecological problems have their roots in society and in social problems. It preaches a gospel of a kind of "original sin" that accuses a vague species called "humanity"—as though people of color were equatable with whites, women with men, the third world with the first, the poor with the rich, and the exploited with their exploiters. This vague, undifferentiated humanity is seen as an ugly "anthropocentric" thing—presumably a malignant product of natural evolution—that is "overpopulating" the planet, "devouring" its resources, destroying its wildlife and the biosphere. It assumes that some vague domain called "nature" stands opposed to a constellation of non-natural things called "human beings," with their "technology," "minds," "society," and so on. Formulated largely by privileged white male academics, deep ecology has brought sincere naturalists like Paul Shepard into the same company with patently anti-humanist and macho mountain-men like David Foreman, who writes in *Earth First!*—a Tucson-based journal that styles itself as the voice of a wilderness-oriented movement of the same name—that "humanity" is a cancer in the world of life.

It is easy to forget that this same kind of crude eco-brutalism led Hitler to fashion theories of blood and soil that led to the transport of millions of people to murder camps like Auschwitz. The same eco-brutalism now reappears a half-century later among self-professed deep ecologists who believe that famines are nature's "population control" and immigration into the US should be restricted in order to preserve "our" ecological resources.

Simply Living, an Australian periodical, published this sort of eco-brutalism as part of a laudatory interview of David Foreman by Professor Bill Devall, co-author of *Deep Ecology*, the manifesto of the deep ecology movement. Foreman, who exuberantly expressed his commitment to deep ecology, frankly informs Devall that

> When I tell people how the worst thing we could do in Ethiopia is to give aid—the best thing would be to just let nature seek its own balance, to let the people there just starve—they think this is monstrous. . . . Likewise, letting the USA be an overflow valve for problems in Latin America is not solving a thing. It's just putting more pressure on the resources we have in the USA.

One could reasonably ask what it means for "nature to seek its own balance" in a part of the world where agribusiness, colonialism, and exploitation have ravaged a once culturally and ecologically stable area like East Africa. And who is this all-American "our" that owns the "resources we have in the USA"? Is it the ordinary people who are driven by sheer need to cut timber, mine ores, operate nuclear power plants? Or are they the giant corporations that are not only wrecking the good old USA, but have produced the main problems in Latin America that are sending Indian folk across the Rio Grande? As an ex-Washington lobbyist and political huckster, David Foreman need not be expected to answer these subtle questions in a radical way. But what is truly surprising is the reaction—more precisely, the *lack* of any reaction—which marked Professor Devall's behavior. Indeed, the interview was notable for his almost reverential introduction and description of Foreman.

WHAT IS "DEEP ECOLOGY"?

Deep ecology is enough of a "black hole" of half-digested and ill-formed ideas that a man like Foreman can easily express utterly vicious notions and still sound like a fiery pro-ecology radical. The very words "deep ecology" clue us into the fact that we are not dealing with a body of clear ideas, but with an ideological toxic dump. Does it make sense, for example, to counterpose "deep ecology" with "superficial ecology" as though the word "ecology" were applicable to *everything* that involves environmental issues? Does it not completely degrade the rich meaning of the word "ecology" to append words like "shallow" and "deep" to it? Arne Naess, the pontiff of deep ecology— who, together with George Sessions and Bill Devall, inflicted this vocabulary upon us—have taken a pregnant word—ecology—and stripped it of any inner meaning and integrity by designating the most pedestrian environmentalists as "ecologists," albeit "shallow" ones, in contrast to their notion of "deep."

This is not an example of mere wordplay. It tells us something about the mindset that exists among these "deep" thinkers. To parody the word "shallow" and "deep ecology" is to show not only the absurdity of this terminology but to reveal the superficiality of its inventors. In fact, this kind of absurdity tells us more than we realize about the confusion Naess-Sessions-Devall, not to mention eco-brutalists like Foreman, have introduced into the current ecology movement. Indeed, this trio relies very heavily on the ease with which people forget the history of the ecology movement, the way in which the wheel is reinvented every few years by newly arrived individuals who, well-meaning as they may be, often accept a crude version of highly developed ideas that appeared earlier in a richer context and tradition of ideas. At worst, they shatter such contexts and traditions, picking out tasty pieces that become utterly distorted in a new, utterly alien framework. No regard is paid by such "deep thinkers" to the fact that *the new context in which an idea is placed may utterly change the meaning of the idea itself.* German "National Socialism" was militantly "anti-capitalist." But its "anti-capitalism" was placed in a strongly racist, imperialist, and seemingly "naturalist" context which extolled wilderness, a crude biologism, and anti-rationalism—features one finds in latent or explicit form in Sessions' and Devall's *Deep Ecology.*[1]

Neither Naess, Sessions, nor Devall have written a single line about decentralization, a nonhierarchical society, democracy, small-scale communities, local autonomy, mutual aid, communalism, and tolerance that was not already conceived in painstaking detail and brilliant contextualization by Peter Kropotkin a century ago. But what the boys from Ecotopia do is to totally recontextualize the framework of these ideas, bringing in personalities and notions that basically change their radical libertarian thrust. *Deep Ecology* mingles Woody Guthrie, a Communist Party centralist who no more believed in decentralization than Stalin, with Paul Goodman, an anarchist who would have been mortified to be placed in the same tradition with Guthrie. In philosophy, the book also intermingles Spinoza, a Jew in spirit if not in religious commitment, with Heidegger, a former member of the Nazi party in spirit as well as ideological affiliation—all in the name of a vague word called "process philosophy." Almost opportunistic in their use of catch-words and what Orwell called "double-speak," "process philosophy" makes it possible for Sessions-Devall to add Alfred North Whitehead to their list of ideological ancestors because he called his ideas "processual."

One could go on indefinitely describing this sloppy admixture of "ancestors," philosophical traditions, social pedigrees, and religions that often have nothing in common with each other and, properly conceived, are commonly in sharp opposition with each other. Thus, a reactionary like Thomas Malthus and the tradition he spawned is celebrated with the same enthusiasm in *Deep Ecology* as Henry Thoreau, a radical libertarian who fostered a highly humanistic tradition. Eclecticism would be too mild a word for this kind of hodge-podge, one that seems shrewdly calculated to embrace everyone under the rubric of deep ecology who is prepared to reduce ecology to a religion rather than a systematic and critical body of ideas. This kind of "ecological" thinking surfaces in an appendix to the Devall-Sessions book, called *Ecosophy T,* by Arne Naess, who regales us with flow diagrams and corporate-type tables of organization that have more in common with logical positivist forms of exposition (Naess, in fact, was an acolyte of this school of thought for years) than anything that could be truly called organic philosophy.

If we look beyond the spiritual eco-babble and examine the *context* in which demands like decentralization, small-scale communities, local autonomy, mutual aid, communalism, and tolerance are placed, the blurred images that Sessions and Devall create come into clearer focus. These demands are not intrinsically ecological or emancipatory. Few societies were more decentralized than European feudalism, which was structured around small-scale communities, mutual aid, and the communal use of land. Local autonomy was highly prized, and autarchy formed the economic key to feudal communities. Yet few societies were more hierarchical. The manorial economy of the Middle Ages placed a high premium on autarchy or "self-sufficiency" and spirituality. Yet oppression was often intolerable and the great mass of people who belonged to that society lived in utter subjugation by their "betters" and the nobility.

If "nature worship," with its bouquet of wood sprites, animistic fetishes, fertility rites and other such ceremonies, paves the way to an ecological sensibility and society, then it would be hard to understand how ancient Egypt, with its animal deities and all-presiding goddesses, managed to become one of the most hierarchical and oppressive societies in the ancient world. The Nile River, which provided the "life-giving" waters of the valley, was used in a highly ecological manner. Yet the entire society was structured around the oppression of millions of serfs by opulent nobles, such that one wonders how notions of spirituality can be given priority over the need for a critical evaluation of social structures.

Even if one grants the need for a new sensibility and outlook—a point that has been made repeatedly in the literature of social ecology—one can look behind even this limited context of deep ecology to a still broader context. The love affair of deep ecology with Malthusian doctrines, a spirituality that emphasizes self-effacement, a flirtation with a *super*naturalism that stands in flat contradiction to the refreshing naturalism that ecology has introduced into social theory, a crude positivism in the spirit of Naess—all work against a truly organic dialectic so needed to understand *development*. We shall see that all the bumper-sticker demands like decentralization, small-scale communities, local autonomy, mutual aid, communalism, tolerance, and even an avowed opposition to hierarchy, go awry when we place them in the larger context of anti-humanism and "biocentrism" that mark the authentic ideological infrastructure of deep ecology.

THE ART OF EVADING SOCIETY

The seeming ideological "tolerance" and pluralism which deep ecology celebrates has a sinister function of its own. It not only reduces richly nuanced ideas and conflicting traditions to their lowest common denominator; it legitimates extremely primitivistic and reactionary notions in the company of authentically radical contexts and traditions.

Deep ecology reduces people from social beings to a simple species—to zoological entities that are interchangeable with bears, bisons, deer, or, for that matter, fruit flies and microbes. The fact that people can consciously change themselves and society, indeed enhance that natural world in a free ecological society, is dismissed as "humanism." Deep ecology essentially ignores the social nature of humanity and the social origins of the ecological crises.

This "zoologization" of human beings and of society yields sinister results. The role of capitalism with its competitive "grow or die" market economy—an economy that would devour the biosphere whether there were 10 billion people on the planet or 10 million—is simply vaporized into a vapid spiritualism. Taoist and Buddhist pieties replace the need for social and economic analysis, and self-indulgent encounter groups replace the need for political organization and action.

Above all, deep ecologists explain the destruction of human beings in terms of the same "natural laws" that are said to govern the population vicissitudes of lemmings. The fact that major reductions of populations would not diminish levels of production and the destruction of the biosphere in a capitalist economy totally eludes Devall, Sessions, and their followers.

In failing to emphasize the unique characteristics of human societies and to give full due to the self-reflective role of human consciousness, deep ecologists essentially evade the *social* roots of the ecological crisis. Deep ecology contains no history of the emergence of society out of nature, a crucial development that brings social theory into organic contact with ecological theory. It presents no explanation of— indeed, it reveals no interest in—the emergence of hierarchy out of society, of classes out of hierarchy, of the state out of classes—in short, the highly graded social as well as ideological developments which are at the roots of the ecological problem.

Instead, we not only lose sight of the social differences that fragment "humanity" into a host of human beings—men and women, ethnic groups, oppressors and oppressed—we lose sight of the individual self in an unending flow of eco-babble that preaches the "realization of self-in-Self where the 'Self' stands for organic wholeness." More of the same cosmic eco-babble appears when we are informed that the "phrase 'one' includes not only men, an individual human, but all humans, grizzly bears, whole rain forest ecosystems, mountains and rivers, the tiniest microbes in the soil, and so on."

ON SELFHOOD AND VIRUSES

Such flippant abstractions of human individuality are extremely dangerous. Historically, a "Self" that absorbs all real existential selves has been used from time immemorial to absorb individual uniqueness and freedom into a supreme "Individual" who heads the state, churches of various sorts, adoring congregations, and spellbound constituencies. The purpose is the same, no matter how much such a "Self" is dressed up in ecological, naturalistic, and "biocentric" attributes. The Paleolithic shaman, in reindeer skins and horns, is the predecessor of the Pharaoh, the Buddha, and, in more recent times, of Hitler, Stalin, and Mussolini.

That the egotistical, greedy, and soloist bourgeois "self" has always been a repellent being goes without saying, and deep ecology as put forth by Devall and Sessions makes the most of it. But is there not a free, independently minded, ecologically concerned, idealistic self with a unique personality that can think of itself as different from "whales, grizzly bears, whole rain forest ecosystems (no less!), mountains and rivers, the tiniest microbes in the soil, and so on"? Is it not indispensable, in fact, for the individual self to disengage itself from a Pharonic "Self," discover its own capacities and uniqueness, and acquire a sense of personality, of self-control and self-direction—all traits indispensable for the achievement of *freedom*? Here, one can imagine Heidegger grimacing with satisfaction at the sight of this self-effacing and passive personality so yielding that it can easily be shaped, distorted, and manipulated by a new "ecological" state machinery with a supreme "Self" at its head. And this all in the name of a "biocentric equality" that is slowly reworked as it has been so often in history, into a social hierarchy. From Shaman to Monarch, from Priest or Priestess to Dictator, our warped social development has been marked by "nature worshippers" and their ritual Supreme Ones who produced unfinished individuals at best or deindividuated the "self-in-Self" at worst, often in the name of the "Great Connected Whole" (to use *exactly* the language of the Chinese ruling classes who kept their peasantry in abject servitude, as Leon E. Stover points out in his *The Cultural Ecology of Chinese Civilization*).

What makes this eco-babble especially dangerous today is that we are already living in a period of massive de-individuation. This is not because deep ecology or Taoism is making any serious in-roads into our own cultural ecology, but because the mass media, the commodity culture, and a market society are "reconnecting" us into an increasingly depersonalized "whole" whose essence is passivity and a chronic vulnerability to economic and political manipulation. It is not an excess of "selfhood" from which we are suffering, but rather the surrender of personality to the security and control of corporations, centralized government, and the military. If "selfhood" is identified with a grasping, "anthropocentric," and devouring personality, these traits are to be found not so much among ordinary people, who basically sense they have no control over their destinies, but among the giant corporations and state leaders who are not only plundering the planet, but also robbing from women, people of color, and the underprivileged. It is not deindividuation that the oppressed of the world require, but *reindividuation* that will transform them into active agents in the task of remaking society and arresting the growing totalitarianism that threatens to homogenize us all into a Western version of the "Great Connected Whole."

We are also confronted with the delicious "and so on" that follows the "tiniest microbes in the soil" with which our deep ecologists identify the "Self." Taking their argument to its logical extreme, one might ask: why stop with the "tiniest microbes in the soil" and ignore the leprosy microbe, the viruses that give us smallpox, polio, and, more recently, AIDS? Are they, too, not part of "all organisms and entities in the ecosphere . . . of the interrelated whole . . . equal in intrinsic worth . . . ," as Devall and Sessions remind us in their effluvium of eco-babble? Naess, Devall, and Sessions

rescue themselves by introducing a number of highly debatable qualifiers:

> The slogan of "noninterference" does not imply that humans should not modify some ecosystems as do other species. Humans have modified the Earth and will probably continue to do so. At issue is the nature and extent of such interference.

One does not leave the muck of deep ecology without having mud all over one's feet. Exactly *who* is to decide the "nature" of human "interference" in nature and the "extent" to which it can be done? What are "some" of the ecosystems we can modify and which ones are not subject to human "interference"? Here, again, we encounter the key problem that deep ecology poses for serious, ecologically concerned people: the *social* bases of our ecological problems and the role of the human species in the evolutionary scheme of things.

Implicit in deep ecology is the notion that a "Humanity" exists that accurses the natural world; that individual selfhood must be transformed into a cosmic "Selfhood" that essentially transcends the person and his or her uniqueness. Even nature is not spared from a kind of static, prepositional logic that is cultivated by the logical positivists. "Nature," in deep ecology and David Foreman's interpretation of it, becomes a kind of scenic view, a spectacle to be admired around the campfire. It is not viewed as an *evolutionary* development that is cumulative and *includes* the human species.

The problems deep ecology and biocentricity raise have not gone unnoticed in the more thoughtful press in England. During a discussion of "biocentric ethics" in *The New Scientist* 69 (1976), for example, Bernard Dixon observed that no "logical line can be drawn" between the conservation of whales, gentians, and flamingoes on the one hand and the extinction of pathogenic microbes like the smallpox virus. At which point David Ehrenfeld, in his *Arrogance of Humanism*,[2]—a work that is so selective and tendentious in its use of quotations that it should validly be renamed "The Arrogance of Ignorance"—cutely observes that the smallpox virus is "an endangered species." One wonders what to do about the AIDS virus if a vaccine or therapy should threaten its "survival"? Further, given the passion for perpetuating the "ecosystem" of every species, one wonders how smallpox and AIDS viruses should be preserved? In test tubes? Laboratory cultures? Or, to be truly "ecological" in their "native habitat," the human body? In which case, idealistic acolytes of deep ecology should be invited to offer their own bloodstreams in the interests of "biocentric equality." Certainly, "if nature should be permitted to take its course"—as Foreman advises for Ethiopians and Indian peasants—plagues, famines, suffering, wars, and perhaps even lethal asteroids of the kind that exterminated the great reptiles of the Mesozoic should not be kept from defacing the purity of "first nature" by the intervention of human ingenuity and—yes!—*technology*. With so much absurdity to unscramble, one can indeed get heady, almost dizzy, with a sense of polemical intoxication.

At root, the eclecticism which turns deep ecology into a goulash of notions and moods is insufferably reformist and surprisingly environmentalist—all its condemnations of "superficial ecology" aside. Are you, perhaps, a mild-mannered liberal? Then do not fear: Devall and Sessions give a patronizing nod to "reform legislation," "coalitions," "protests," the "women's movement" (this earns all of ten lines in their "Minority Tradition and Direct Action" essay), "working in the Christian tradition" "questioning technology" (a hammering remark, if there ever was one), "working in Green politics" (which faction, the "fundies" or the "realos"?). In short, everything can be expected in so "cosmic" a philosophy. Anything seems to pass through deep ecology's donut hole: anarchism at one extreme and eco-fascism at the other. Like the fast food emporiums that make up our culture, deep ecology is the fast food of quasi-radical environmentalists.

Despite its pretense of "radicality," deep ecology is more "New Age" and "Aquarian" than the environmentalist movements it denounces under those names. Indeed, the extent to which deep ecology accommodates itself to some of the worst features of the "dominant view" it professes to reject is seen with extraordinary clarity in one of its most fundamental and repeatedly asserted demands—namely, that the world's population must be drastically reduced, according to one of its devotees, to 500 million. If deep ecologists have even the faintest knowledge of the "population theorists" Devall and Sessions invoke with admiration—notably, Thomas Malthus, William Vogt, and Paul Ehrlich—then they would be obliged to add: by measures that are virtually eco-fascist. This specter clearly looms before us in Devall's and Sessions' sinister remark: ". . . the longer we wait [for population control], the more drastic will be the measures needed."

THE "DEEP" MALTHUSIANS

Devall and Sessions often write with smug assurance on issues they know virtually nothing about. This is most notably the case in the so-called "population debate," a debate that has raged for over two hundred years and more and involves explosive political and social issues that have pitted the most reactionary elements in English and American society against authentic radicals. In fact, the eco-babble which Devall and Sessions dump on us in only two paragraphs would require a full-sized volume of careful analysis to unravel.

Devall and Sessions hail Thomas Malthus (1766–1854) as a prophet whose warning "that human popula-

tion growth would exponentially outstrip food production . . . was ignored by the rising tide of industrial/technological optimism." First of all, Thomas Malthus was not a prophet; he was an apologist for the misery that the Industrial Revolution was inflicting on the English peasantry and working classes. His utterly fallacious argument that population increases exponentially while food supplies increase arithmetically was not ignored by England's ruling classes; it was taken to heart and even incorporated into social Darwinism as an explanation of why oppression was a necessary feature of society and why the rich, the white imperialists, and the privileged were the "fittest" who were equipped to "survive"—needless to say, at the expense of the impoverished many. Written and directed in great part as an attack upon the liberatory vision of William Godwin, Malthus' mean-spirited *Essay on the Principle of Population* tried to demonstrate that hunger, poverty, disease, and premature death are *inevitable* precisely because population and food supply increase at different rates. Hence war, famines, and plagues (Malthus later added "moral restraint") were necessary to keep population down—needless to say, among the "lower orders of society," whom he singles out as the chief offenders of his inexorable population "laws."[3] Malthus, in effect, became the ideologue par excellence for the land-grabbing English nobility in its effort to dispossess the peasantry of their traditional common lands and for the English capitalists to work children, women, and men to death in the newly emergent "industrial/technological" factory system.

Malthusianism contributed in great part to that meanness of spirit that Charles Dickens captured in his famous novels, *Oliver Twist* and *Hard Times*. The doctrine, its author, and its overstuffed wealthy beneficiaries were bitterly fought by the great English anarchist, William Godwin, the pioneering socialist, Robert Owen, and the emerging Chartist movement of English workers in the early 19th century. However, Malthusianism was naively picked up by Charles Darwin to explain his theory of "natural selection." It then became the bedrock theory for the new *social* Darwinism, so very much in vogue in the late nineteenth and early twentieth centuries, which saw society as a "jungle" in which only the "fit" (usually, the rich and white) could "survive" at the expense of the "unfit" (usually, the poor and people of color). Malthus, in effect, had provided an ideology that justified class domination, racism, the degradation of women, and, ultimately, British imperialism.

Malthusianism was not only revived in Hitler's Third Reich; it also reemerged in the late 1940s, following the discoveries of antibiotics to control infectious diseases. Riding on the tide of the new Pax Americana after World War II, William F. Vogt and a whole bouquet of neo-Malthusians were to challenge the use of the new antibiotic discoveries to control disease and prevent death—as usual, mainly in Asia, Africa, and Latin America. Again, a new "population debate" erupted, with the Rockefeller interests and large corporate sharks aligning themselves with the neo-Malthusians, and caring people of every sort aligning themselves with third world theorists like Josua de Castro, who wrote damning, highly informed critiques of this new version of misanthropy.

Zero Population Growth fanatics in the early seventies literally polluted the environmental movement with demands for a government bureau to "control" population, advancing the infamous "triage" ethic, according to which various "underdeveloped" countries would be granted or refused aid on the basis of their compliance to population control measures. In *Food First*, Francis Moore Lappe and Joseph Collins have done a superb job in showing how hunger has its origins not in "natural" shortages of food or population growth, but in social and cultural dislocations. (It is notable that Devall and Sessions do *not* list this excellent book in their bibliography.) The book has to be read to understand the reactionary implications of deep ecology's demographic positions.

Demography is a highly ambiguous and ideologically charged social discipline that cannot be reduced to a mere numbers game in biological reproduction. Human beings are not fruit flies (the species which the neo-Malthusians love to cite). Their reproductive behavior is profoundly conditioned by cultural values, standards of living, social traditions, gender relations, religious beliefs, socio-political conflicts, and various socio-political expectations. Smash up a stable, precapitalist culture and throw its people off the land into city slums, and, due to demoralization, population may soar rather than decline. As Gandhi told the British, imperialism left India's wretched poor and homeless with little more in life than the immediate gratification provided by sex and an understandably numbed sense of personal, much less social, responsibility. Reduce women to mere reproductive factories and population rates will explode.

Conversely, provide people with decent lives, education, a sense of creative meaning in life, and, above all, expand the role of women in society—and population growth begins to stabilize and population rates even reverse their direction. Nothing more clearly reveals deep ecology's crude, often reactionary, and certainly superficial ideological framework—all its decentralist, antihierarchical, and "radical" rhetoric aside—than its suffocating "biological" treatment of the population issue and its inclusion of Malthus, Vogt, and Ehrlich in its firmament of prophets.

Not surprisingly, the *Earth First!* newsletter, whose editor professes to be an enthusiastic deep ecologist, carried an article titled "Population and AIDS" which advanced the obscene argument that AIDS is desirable as a means of population control. This was no spoof. It was earnestly argued and carefully reasoned in a Paleolithic sort of way. Not only will AIDS claim large numbers of lives, asserts the author (who hides under the pseudonym of "Miss Ann Thropy," a form of black humor that could also pass as an example of macho-male arrogance), but it "may cause a breakdown in technology (read: human food supply) and its export which could also decrease human population." These people feed on human disasters, suffering, and misery, preferably in third world countries where AIDS is by far a more monstrous problem than elsewhere.

We have little reason to doubt that this mentality is perfectly consistent with the "more drastic . . . measures" Devall and Sessions believe we will have to explore. Nor is it inconsistent with Malthus and Vogt that we should make no effort to find a cure for this disease which may do so much to depopulate the world. "Biocentric democracy," I assume, should call for nothing less than a "hands-off" policy on the AIDS virus and perhaps equally lethal pathogens that appear in the human species.

WHAT IS SOCIAL ECOLOGY?

Social ecology is neither "deep," "tall," "fat," nor "thick." It is *social*. It does not fall back on incantations, sutras, flow diagrams or spiritual vagaries. It is avowedly *rational*. It does not try to regale metaphorical forms of spiritual mechanism and crude biologism with Taoist, Buddhist, Christian, or shamanistic eco-babble. It is a coherent form of *naturalism* that looks to *evolution* and the *biosphere,* not to deities in the sky or under the earth for quasi-religious and supernaturalistic explanations of natural and social phenomena.

Philosophically, social ecology stems from a solid organismic tradition in Western philosophy, beginning with Heraclitus, the near-evolutionary dialectic of Aristotle and Hegel, and the critical approach of the famous Frankfurt School—particularly its devastating critique of logical positivism (which surfaces in Naess repeatedly) and the primitivistic mysticism of Heidegger (which pops up all over the place in deep ecology's literature).

Socially, it is revolutionary, not merely "radical." It critically unmasks the entire evolution of hierarchy in all its forms, including neo-Malthusian elitism, the eco-brutalism of David Foreman, the anti-humanism of David Ehrenfeld and "Miss Ann Thropy," and the latent racism, first-world arrogance, and Yuppie nihilism of postmodernistic spiritualism. It is noted in the profound eco-anarchistic analyses of Peter Kropotkin, the radical economic insights of Karl Marx, the emancipatory promise of the revolutionary Enlightenment as articulated by the great encyclopedist, Denis Diderot, the *Enrages* of the French Revolution, the revolutionary feminist ideals of Louise Michel and Emma Goldman, the communitarian visions of Paul Goodman and E. A. Gutkind, and the various eco-revolutionary manifestoes of the early 1960s.

Politically, it is *green*—radically green. It takes its stand with the left-wing tendencies in the German Greens and extra-parliamentary street movements of European cities; with the American radical ecofeminist movement; with the demands for a new politics based on citizens' initiatives, neighborhood assemblies, and New England's tradition of town-meetings; with non-aligned anti-imperialist movements at home and abroad; with the struggle by people of color for complete freedom from the domination of privileged whites and from the superpowers.

Morally, it is *humanistic* in the high Renaissance meaning of the term, not the degraded meaning of "humanism" that has been imparted to the world by David Foreman, David Ehrenfeld, and a salad of academic deep ecologists. Humanism from its inception has meant a shift in vision from the skies to the earth, from superstition to reason, from deities to people—who are no less products of natural evolution than grizzly bears and whales. Social ecology accepts neither a "biocentricity" that essentially denies or degrades the uniqueness of human beings, human subjectivity, rationality, aesthetic sensibility, and the ethical potentiality of humanity, nor an "anthropocentricity" that confers on the privileged few the right to plunder the world of life, including human life. Indeed, it opposes "centricity" of *any* kind as a new word for hierarchy and domination—be it that of nature by a mystical "Man" or the domination of people by an equally mystical "Nature." It firmly denies that nature is a static, scenic view which Mountain Men like a Foreman survey from a peak in Nevada or a picture window that spoiled yuppies view from their ticky-tacky country homes. To social ecology, nature *is* natural *evolution,* not a cosmic arrangement of beings frozen in a moment of eternity to be abjectly revered, adored, and worshipped like Gods and Goddesses in a realm of "*super*nature." Natural evolution is nature in the very real sense that it is composed of atoms, molecules that have evolved into amino acids, proteins, unicellular organisms, genetic codes, invertebrates and vertebrates, amphibia, reptiles, mammals, primates, and human beings—all, in a cumulative thrust toward ever-greater complexity, ever-greater subjectivity, and finally, an ever-greater capacity for conceptual thought, symbolic communication, and self-consciousness.

This marvel we call "Nature" has produced a marvel we call homo sapiens—"thinking man"—and, more significantly for the development of society, "thinking woman," whose primeval domestic domain provided the arena for the origins of a caring society, human empathy, love, and idealistic commitment. The human species, in effect, is no less a product of natural evolution and differentiation than blue-green algae. To degrade the human species in the name of "anti-humanism," to deny people their uniqueness as thinking beings with an unprecedented gift for conceptual thought, is to deny the rich fecundity of natural evolution itself. To separate human beings and society from nature is to dualize and truncate nature itself, to diminish the meaning and thrust of natural evolution in the name of a "biocentricity" that spends more time disporting itself with mantras, deities, and supernature than with the realities of the biosphere and the role of society in ecological problems.

Accordingly, social ecology does not try to hide its critical and reconstructive thrust in metaphors. It calls "technological/industrial" society *capitalism*—a word which places the onus for our ecological problems on the *living* sources and *social* relationships that produce them, not on a cutesy "Third Wave" abstraction which buries these sources in technics, a technical "mentality," or perhaps the technicians who work on machines. It sees the domination of women not simply as a "spiritual" problem that can be resolved by rituals, incantations, and shamannesses, important as ritual may be in solidarizing women into a unique community of people, but in the long, highly graded, and subtly nuanced development of hierarchy, which long preceded the development of classes. Nor does it ignore class, ethnic differences, imperialism, and oppression by creating a grab-bag called "Humanity" that is placed in opposition to a mystified "Nature," divested of all development.

All of which brings us as social ecologists to an issue that seems to be totally alien to the crude concerns of deep ecology: natural evolution has conferred on human beings the capacity to form a "second" or cultural nature out of "first" or primeval nature. Natural evolution has not only provided humans with the *ability,* but also the *necessity* to be purposive interveners into "first nature," to consciously *change* "first nature" by means of a highly institutionalized form of community we call "society." It is not alien to natural evolution that a species called human beings have emerged over the billions of years who are capable of thinking in a sophisticated way. Nor is it alien for human beings to develop a highly sophisticated form of symbolic communication which a new kind of community—institutionalized, guided by thought rather than by instinct alone, and ever-changing—has emerged called "society."

Taken together, all of these human traits—intellectual, communicative, and social—have not only emerged from natural evolution and are inherently human; they can also be placed at the *service* of natural evolution to consciously increase biotic diversity, diminish suffering, foster the further evolution of new and ecologically valuable life-forms, reduce the impact of disastrous accidents or the harsh effects of mere change.

Whether this species, gifted by the creativity of natural evolution, can play the role of a nature rendered self-conscious or cut against the grain of natural evolution by simplifying the biosphere, polluting it, and undermining the cumulative results of organic evolution is above all a *social* problem. The primary question ecology faces today is whether an ecologically oriented society can be created out of the present anti-ecological one.

Unless there is a resolute attempt to fully anchor ecological dislocations in social dislocations; to challenge the vested corporate and political interests we should properly call *capitalism;* to analyze, explore, and attack hierarchy as a *reality,* not only as a sensibility; to recognize the material needs of the poor and of third world people; to function politically, and not simply as a religious cult; to give the human species and mind their due in natural evolution, rather than regard them as "cancers" in the biosphere; to examine economies as well as "souls," and freedom instead of scholastic arguments about the "rights" of pathogenic viruses—unless, in short, North American Greens and the ecology movement shift their focus toward a *social ecology* and let deep ecology sink into the pit it has created for us, the ecology movement will become another ugly wart on the skin of society.

What we must do, today, is return to *nature,* conceived in all its fecundity, richness of potentialities, and subjectivity—not to *super*nature with its shamans, priests, priestesses, and fanciful deities that are merely anthropomorphic extensions and distortions of the "Human" as all-embracing divinities. And what we must "enchant" is not only an abstract image of "Nature" *that often reflects our own systems of power, hierarchy, and domination*—but rather human beings, the human mind, the human spirit.

Notes

1. Unless otherwise indicated, all future references and quotes come from Bill Devall and George Sessions, *Deep Ecology* (Layton, UT: Gibbs M. Smith, 1985), a book which has essentially become the bible of the "movement" that bears its name.

2. David Ehrenfeld, *The Arrogance of Humanism* (New York: The Modern Library, 1978) pp. 207–211.

3. Chapter five of his *Essay,* which, for all its "concern" over the misery of the "lower classes," inveighs against the poor laws and argues that the "pressures of distress on this part of the community is an evil so deeply seated that no human ingenuity can reach it." Thomas Malthus, *On Population* (New York: The Modern Library), p. 34.

Study Questions

1. Examine Bookchin's attack on deep ecology. What are his reasons for opposing it? Are his epithets "eco-brutalism," eco-babble," and so forth, justified? Does Bookchin make a good case for rejecting deep ecology? Or are his attacks incomplete, rhetorical, and ad hominem?

2. What are Bookchin's major assumptions in this essay? Are they defended? Are they defensible?

3. What is *social ecology*? What are its main features? How well does Bookchin defend it?

4. Bookchin accuses deep ecologists of being related to logical positivism. Logical positivists were European philosophers, such as Rudoph Carnap, Moritz Schlick, and A. J. Ayer, who held to the *verification principle of meaning*—the thesis that sentences obtain their meaning by being verified by sensory experience. If a sentence cannot be verified in principle, it is meaningless, nonsense. Hence, moral judgments such as "stealing is wrong" is meaningless because *wrongness* is not a sensory experience. "Stealing is wrong (or bad)" is comparable to "stealing —Boo!" since it is simply an emotive expression. Likewise, theological statements are unverifiable, hence meaningless. Bookchin points out that the founder of deep ecology, the Norwegian philosopher, Arne Naess, was once a logical positivist. Can you see any connections between deep ecology and logical positivism? Does Bookchin provide any?

25

Environmental Justice: Reconciling Anthropocentric and Nonanthropocentric Ethics

James P. Sterba

James Sterba is professor of philosophy at the University of Notre Dame and president of the North American Society for Social Philosophy. His many books include How to Make People Just, Morality in Practice, Feminist Philosophies, *and* Justice: Alternative Political Perspectives.

Sterba has offered the following abstract:

A central debate, if not the most central debate, in contemporary environmental ethics is between those who defend anthropocentric ethics, which holds that humans are superior overall to the members of other species, and

This essay was written for this edition and appears here in print for the first time.

those who defend nonanthropocentric ethics, which holds that the members of all species are equal. In this essay, I propose to go some way toward resolving this debate by showing that, when the most morally defensible versions of each of these perspectives are laid out, they do not lead to different practical requirements. In this way, I hope to show how it is possible for defenders of anthropocentric and nonanthropocentric environmental ethics, despite their theoretical disagreement concerning whether humans are superior to members of other species, to agree on a common set of principles for achieving environmental justice.

NONANTHROPOCENTRIC ENVIRONMENTAL ETHICS

Consider first the nonanthropocentric perspective. In support of this perspective, it can be argued that we have no non-question-begging grounds for regarding the members of any living species as superior to the members of any other. It allows that the members of species differ in a myriad of ways but argues that these differences do not provide grounds for thinking that the members of any one species are superior to the members of any other. In particular, it denies that the differences between species provides grounds for thinking that humans are superior to the members of other species. Of course, the nonanthropocentric perspective recognizes that humans have distinctive traits that members of other species lack, like rationality and moral agency. It just points out that the members of nonhuman species also have distinctive traits that humans lack, like the homing ability of pigeons, the speed of the cheetah, and the ruminative ability of sheep and cattle.

Nor will it do to claim that the distinctive traits that humans have are more valuable than the distinctive traits that members of other species possess because there is no non-question-begging standpoint from which to justify that claim. From a human standpoint, rationality and moral agency are more valuable than any of the distinctive traits found in nonhuman species, since, as humans, we would not be better off if we were to trade in those traits for the distinctive traits found in nonhuman species. Yet the same holds true of nonhuman species. Generally, pigeons, cheetahs, sheep, and cattle would not be better off if they were to trade in their distinctive traits for the distinctive traits of other species.

Of course, the members of some species might be better off if they could retain the distinctive traits of their species while acquiring one or another of the distinctive traits possessed by some other species. For example, we humans might be better off if we could retain our distinctive traits while acquiring the ruminative ability of sheep and cattle. But many of the distinctive traits of species cannot be even imaginatively added to the members of other species without substantially altering the original species. For example, for the cheetah to acquire the distinctive traits possessed by humans, presumably it would have to be so transformed that its paws became something like hands to accommodate its humanlike mental capabilities, thereby losing its distinctive speed and ceasing to be a cheetah. So possessing distinctively human traits would not be good for the cheetah. And with the possible exception of our nearest evolutionary relatives, the same holds true for the members of other species; they would not be better off having distinctively human traits. Only in fairy tales and in the world of Disney can the members of nonhuman species enjoy a full array of distinctively human traits. So there would appear to be no non-question-begging perspective from which to judge that distinctively human traits are more valuable than the distinctive traits possessed by other species. Judged from a non-question-begging perspective, we would seemingly have to regard the members of all species as equals.

It might be useful at this point to make my argument even more explicit. Here is one way this could be done.

1. We should not aggress against any living being unless there are either self-evident or non-question-begging reasons for doing so. (It would be difficult to reject this principle given the various analogous principles we accept, such as the principle of formal equality: Equals should be treated equally and unequals unequally.)
2. To treat humans as superior overall to other living beings is to aggress against them by sacrificing their basic needs to meet the nonbasic needs of humans. (Definition)
3. Therefore, we should not treat humans as superior overall to other living beings unless we have either self-evident or non-question-begging reasons for doing so. (From 1 and 2)
4. We do not have either self-evident or non-question-begging reasons for treating humans as superior overall to other living beings. (That we do not have any non-question-begging reasons for treating humans as superior overall to other living beings was established by the previous argument. That we do not have any self-evident reasons for doing so, I take it, is obvious.)
5. Therefore, we should not treat humans as superior overall to other living beings. (From 3 and 4)
6. Not to treat humans as superior overall to other living beings is to treat them as equal overall to other living beings. (Definition)
7. Therefore, we should treat humans as equal overall to other living beings. (From 5 and 6)

Nevertheless, I want to go on to claim that regarding the members of all species as equals still allows for human preference in the same way that regarding all humans as equals still allows for self preference. First of all, human preference can be justified on grounds of defense. Thus, we have a

Principle of human defense: Actions that defend oneself and other human beings against harmful aggression are permissible even when they necessitate killing or harming animals or plants.

This principle of human defense allows us to defend ourselves and other human beings from harmful aggression first against our persons and the persons of other humans beings that we are committed to or happen to care about and second against our justifiably held property and the justifiably held property of other human beings that we are committed to or happen to care about.

This principle is analogous to the principle of self-defense that applies in human ethics and permits actions in defense of oneself or other human beings against harmful human aggression. In the case of human aggression, however, it will sometimes be possible to effectively defend oneself and other human beings by first suffering the aggression and then securing adequate compensation later. Since in the case of nonhuman aggression this is unlikely to obtain, more harmful preventive actions such as killing a rabid dog or swatting a mosquito will be justified. There are simply more ways to effectively stop aggressive humans than there are to stop aggressive nonhumans.

Second, human preference can also be justified on grounds of preservation. Accordingly, we have a

Principle of human preservation: Actions that are necessary for meeting one's basic needs or the basic needs of other human beings are permissible even when they require aggressing against the basic needs of animals and plants.

Now needs, in general, if not satisfied, lead to lacks or deficiencies with respect to various standards. The basic needs of humans, if not satisfied, lead to lacks or deficiencies with respect to a standard of a decent life. The basic needs of animals and plants, if not satisfied, lead to lacks or deficiencies with respect to a standard of a healthy life. The means necessary for meeting the basic needs of humans can vary widely from society to society. By contrast, the means necessary for meeting the basic needs of particular species of animals and plants are more invariant.

In human ethics, there is no principle that is strictly analogous to this principle of human preservation. There is a principle of self-preservation in human ethics that permits actions that are necessary for meeting one's own basic needs or the basic needs of other people, even if this requires *failing to meet* (through an act of omission) the basic needs of still other people. For example, we can use our resources to feed ourselves and our family, even if this necessitates failing to meet the basic needs of people in third world countries. But, in general,

we don't have a principle that allows us to *aggress against* (through an act of commission) the basic needs of some people in order to meet our own basic needs or the basic needs of other people to whom we are committed or happen to care about. Actually, the closest we come to permitting aggressing against the basic needs of other people in order to meet our own basic needs or the basic needs of people to whom we are committed or happen to care about is our acceptance of the outcome of life and death struggles in lifeboat cases, where no one has an antecedent right to the available resources. For example, if you had to fight off others in order to secure the last place in a lifeboat for yourself or for a member of your family, we might say that you justifiably aggressed against the basic needs of those whom you fought to meet your own basic needs or the basic needs of the member of your family.

Nevertheless, our survival requires a principle of preservation that permits aggressing against the basic needs of at least some other living things whenever this is necessary to meet our own basic needs or the basic needs of other human beings. Here there are two possibilities. The first is a principle of preservation that allows us to aggress against the basic needs of both humans and nonhumans whenever it would serve our own basic needs or the basic needs of other human beings. The second is the principle, given above, that allows us to aggress against the basic needs of only nonhumans whenever it would serve our own basic needs or the basic needs of other human beings. The first principle does not express any general preference for the members of the human species, and thus it permits even cannibalism provided that it serves to meet our own basic needs or the basic needs of other human beings. In contrast, the second principle does express a degree of preference for the members of the human species in cases where their basic needs are at stake. Happily, this degree of preference for our own species is still compatible with the equality of all species because favoring the members of one's own species to this extent is characteristic of the members of nearly all species with which we interact and is thereby legitimated. The reason it is legitimated is that we would be required to sacrifice the basic needs of members of the human species only if the members of other species were making similar sacrifices for the sake of members of the human species. In addition, if we were to prefer consistently the basic needs of the members of other species whenever those needs conflicted with our own (or even if we do so half the time), given the characteristic behavior of the members of other species, we would soon be facing extinction, and, fortunately, we have no reason to think that we are morally required to bring about our own extinction. For these reasons, the degree of preference for our own species found in the principle of human preservation is justified, even if we were to adopt a nonanthropocentric perspective.

Nevertheless, preference for humans can go beyond

bounds, and the bounds that are compatible with a nonanthropocentric perspective are expressed by the following:

> *Principle of disproportionality*: Actions that meet nonbasic or luxury needs of humans are prohibited when they aggress against the basic needs of animals and plants.

This principle is strictly analogous to the principle in human ethics mentioned previously that prohibits meeting some people's nonbasic or luxury needs by aggressing against the basic needs of other people.

Without a doubt, the adoption of such a principle with respect to nonhuman nature would significantly change the way we live our lives. Such a principle is required, however, if there is to be any substance to the claim that the members of all species are equal. We can no more consistently claim that the members of all species are equal and yet aggress against the basic needs of some animals or plants whenever this serves our own nonbasic or luxury needs than we can consistently claim that all humans are equal and aggress against the basic needs of some other human beings whenever this serves our nonbasic or luxury needs. Consequently, if species equality is to mean anything, it must be the case that the basic needs of the members of nonhuman species are protected against aggressive actions which only serve to meet the nonbasic needs of humans, as required by the principle of disproportionality.

So while a nonanthropocentric perspective allows for a degree of preference for the members of the human species, it also significantly limits that preference.

To see why these limits on preference for the members of the human species are all that is required for recognizing the equality of species, we need to understand the equality of species by analogy with the equality of humans. We need to see that just as we claim that humans are equal but treat them differently, so too we can claim that all species are equal but treat them differently. In human ethics, there are various interpretations given to human equality that allow for different treatment of humans. In ethical egoism, everyone is *equally at liberty* to pursue his or her own interests, but this allows us to always prefer ourselves to others, who are understood to be like opponents in a competitive game. In libertarianism, everyone has an *equal right to liberty*, but although this imposes some limits on the pursuit of self-interest, it is said to allow us to refrain from helping others in severe need. In welfare liberalism, everyone has an *equal right to welfare and opportunity*, but this need not commit us to providing everyone with exactly the same resources. In socialism, everyone has an *equal right* to self-development, and although this may commit us to providing everyone with the same resources, it still sanctions some degree of self-preference. So just as there are these various ways to interpret human equality that still allow us to treat humans differently, there are vari-

ous ways that we can interpret species equality that allow us to treat species differently.

Now one might interpret species equality in a very strong sense, analogous to the interpretation of equality found in socialism. But the kind of species equality that I have defended is more akin to the equality found in welfare liberalism or in libertarianism than it is to the equality found in socialism. In brief, this form of equality requires that we not aggress against the basic needs of the members of other species for the sake of the nonbasic needs of the members of our own species (the principle of disproportionality), but it permits us to aggress against the basic needs of the members of other species for the sake of the basic needs of the members of our own species (the principle of human preservation) and also permits us to defend the basic and even the nonbasic needs of the members of our own species against harmful aggression by members of other species (the principle of human defense). In this way, I have argued that we can accept the claim of species equality, while avoiding imposing an unreasonable sacrifice on the members of our own species.

INDIVIDUALISM AND HOLISM

It might be objected here that I have not yet taken into account the conflict within a nonanthropocentric ethics between holists and individualists. According to holists, the good of a species or the good of an ecosystem or the good of the whole biotic community can trump the good of individual living things.[1] According to individualists, the good of each individual living thing must be respected.[2]

Now one might think that holists would require that we abandon my principle of human preservation. Yet consider. Assuming that people's basic needs are at stake, how could it be morally objectionable for them to try to meet those needs, even if this were to harm nonhuman individuals, or species, or whole ecosystems, or even, to some degree, the whole biotic community? Of course, we can *ask* people in such conflict cases not to meet their basic needs in order to prevent harm to nonhuman individuals or species, ecosystems or the whole biotic community. But if people's basic needs are at stake, we cannot reasonably demand that they make such a sacrifice. We could demand, of course, that people do all that they reasonably can to keep such conflicts from arising in the first place, for, just as in human ethics, many severe conflicts of interest can be avoided simply by doing what is morally required early on. Nevertheless, when people's basic needs are at stake, the individualist perspective seems incontrovertible. We cannot reasonably require people to be saints.

At the same time, when people's basic needs are not at stake, we would be justified in acting on holistic grounds to prevent serious harm to nonhuman individuals, or species, or ecosystems, or the whole biotic community. Obviously, it will be difficult to know when our interventions will have this effect, but when we can be reasonably sure that they will, such interventions (e.g., culling elk herds in wolf-free ranges or preserving the habitat of endangered species) would be morally permissible and maybe even morally required.[3] This shows that it is possible to agree with individualists when the basic needs of human beings are at stake and to agree with holists when they are not.

Yet this combination of individualism and holism appears to conflict with the equality of species by imposing greater sacrifices on the members of nonhuman species than it does on the members of the human species. Fortunately, appearances are deceiving here. Although the proposed resolution only justifies imposing holism when people's basic needs are not at stake, it does not justify imposing individualism at all. Rather it would simply permit individualism when people's basic needs *are* at stake. Of course, we could impose holism under all conditions. But given that this would, in effect, involve going to war against people who are simply striving to meet their own basic needs in the only way they can, as permitted by the principle of human preservation, intervention in such cases would not be justified. It would involve taking away the means of survival from people, even when these means are not required for one's own survival.

Nevertheless, this combination of individualism and holism may leave animal liberationists wondering about the further implications of this resolution for the treatment of animals. Obviously, a good deal of work has already been done on this topic. Initially, philosophers thought that humanism could be extended to include animal liberation and eventually environmental concern.[4] Then Baird Callicott argued that animal liberation and environmental concern were as opposed to each other as they were to humanism.[5] The resulting conflict Callicott called "a triangular affair." Agreeing with Callicott, Mark Sagoff contended that any attempt to link together animal liberation and environmental concern would lead to "a bad marriage and a quick divorce."[6] Yet more recently, such philosophers as Mary Ann Warren have tended to play down the opposition between animal liberation and environmental concern, and even Callicott now thinks he can bring the two back together again.[7] There are good reasons for thinking that such a reconciliation is possible.

Right off, it would be good for the environment if people generally, especially people in the first world, adopted a more vegetarian diet of the sort that animal liberationists are recommending. This is because a good portion of livestock production today consumes grains that could be more effectively used for direct human consumption. For example, 90% of the protein, 99% of the carbohydrate, and 100% of the fiber value of grain is wasted by cycling it through livestock, and currently 64% of the U.S. grain crop is fed to livestock.[8] So by adopting a more vegetarian diet, people generally, and especially people in the first world, could significantly reduce the amount of farmland that has to be kept in production to feed the human population. This in turn could have beneficial effects on the whole biotic community by eliminating the amount of soil erosion and environmental pollutants that result from raising livestock. For example, it has been estimated that 85% of U.S. topsoil lost from cropland, pasture, range land, and forest land is directly associated with raising livestock.[9] So, in addition to preventing animal suffering, there are these additional reasons to favor a more vegetarian diet.

But even though a more vegetarian diet seems in order, it is not clear that the interests of farm animals would be well served if all of us became complete vegetarians. Sagoff assumes that in a completely vegetarian human world people would continue to feed farm animals as before.[10] But it is not clear that we would have any obligation to do so. Moreover, in a completely vegetarian human world, we would probably need about half of the grain we now feed livestock to meet people's nutritional needs, particularly in second and third world countries. There simply would not be enough grain to go around. And then there would be the need to conserve cropland for future generations. So in a completely vegetarian human world, it seems likely that the population of farm animals would be decimated, relegating many of the farm animals that remain to zoos. On this account, it would seem to be more in the interest of farm animals generally that they be maintained under healthy conditions, and hence not in the numbers sustainable only with factory farms, but then killed relatively painlessly and eaten, rather than that they not be maintained at all. So a completely vegetarian human world would not seem to serve the interest of farm animals.

Nor, it seems, would it be in the interest of wild species who no longer have their natural predators not to be hunted by humans. Of course, where possible, it may be preferable to reintroduce natural predators. But this may not always be possible because of the proximity of farm animals and human populations, and then if action is not taken to control the populations of wild species, disaster could result for the species and their environments. For example, deer, rabbits, squirrels, quails, and ducks reproduce rapidly, and in the absence of predators can quickly exceed the carrying capacity of their environments. So it may be in the interest of certain wild species and their environments that humans intervene periodically to maintain a balance. Of course, there will be many natural environments where it is in the interest of the environment and the wild animals that inhabit it to be simply left alone. But here too animal liberation and environmental concern would not be in conflict. For these reasons, animal liberationists would have little reason to object to the proposed combination of individualism and holism within a nonanthropocentric environmental ethics.

ANTHROPOCENTRIC ENVIRONMENTAL ETHICS

Suppose, however, we were to reject the central contention of the nonanthropocentric perspective and deny that the members of all species are equal. We might claim, for example, that humans are superior because they, through culture, "realize a greater range of values" than members of nonhuman species, or we might claim that humans are superior in virtue of their "unprecedented capacity to create ethical systems that impart worth to other life-forms."[11] Or we might offer some other grounds for human superiority. Suppose, then, we adopt this anthropocentric perspective. What follows?

First, we will still need a principle of human defense. However, there is no need to adopt a different principle of human defense from the principle favored by a nonanthropocentric perspective. Whether we judge humans to be equal or superior to the members of other species, we will still want a principle that allows us to defend ourselves and other human beings from harmful aggression, even when this necessitates killing or harming animals or plants.

Second, we will also need a principle of human preservation. But here too there is no need to adopt a different principle from the principle of human preservation favored by a nonanthropocentric perspective. Whether we judge humans to be equal or superior to the members of other species, we will still want a principle that permits actions that are necessary for meeting our own basic needs or the basic needs of other human beings, even when this requires aggressing against the basic needs of animals and plants.

The crucial question is whether we will need a different principle of disproportionality. If we judge humans to be superior to the members of other species, will we still have grounds for protecting the basic needs of animals and plants against aggressive action to meet the nonbasic or luxury needs of humans?

Here it is important to distinguish between two degrees of preference that we noted earlier. First, we could prefer the basic needs of animals and plants over the nonbasic or luxury needs of humans when to do otherwise would involve *aggressing against* (by an act of commission) the basic needs of animals and plants. Second, we could prefer the basic needs of animals and plants over the nonbasic or luxury needs of humans when to do otherwise would involve simply *failing to meet* (by an act of omission) the basic needs of animals and plants.

Now in human ethics when the basic needs of some people are in conflict with the nonbasic or luxury needs of others, the distinction between failing to meet and aggressing against basic needs seems to have little moral force. In such conflict cases, both ways of not meeting basic needs are objectionable.

In environmental ethics, however, whether we adopt an anthropocentric or a nonanthropocentric perspective, we would seem to have grounds for morally distinguishing between the two cases, favoring the basic needs of animals and plants when to do otherwise would involve *aggressing against* those needs in order to meet our own nonbasic or luxury needs, but not when it would involve simply *failing to meet* those needs in order to meet our own nonbasic or luxury needs. This degree of preference for the members of the human species would be compatible with the equality of species insofar as members of nonhuman species similarly fail to meet the basic needs of members of the human species where there is a conflict of interest.

Even so, this theoretical distinction would have little practical force since most of the ways that we have of preferring our own nonbasic needs over the basic needs of animals and plants actually involve aggressing against their basic needs to meet our own nonbasic or luxury needs rather than simply failing to meet their basic needs.

Yet even if most of the ways that we have of preferring our own nonbasic or luxury needs do involve aggressing against the basic needs of animals and plants, wouldn't human superiority provide grounds for preferring ourselves or other human beings in these ways? Or put another way, shouldn't human superiority have more theoretical and practical significance than I am allowing? Not, I claim, if we are looking for the most morally defensible position to take.

For consider: The claim that humans are superior to the members of other species, if it can be justified at all, is something like the claim that a person came in first in a race where others came in second, third, fourth, and so on. It would not imply that the members of other species are without intrinsic value. In fact, it would imply just the opposite—that the members of other species are also intrinsically valuable, although not as intrinsically valuable as humans, just as the claim that a person came in first in a race implies that the persons who came in second, third, fourth, and so on are also meritorious, although not as meritorious as the person who came in first.

This line of argument draws further support once we consider the fact that many animals and plants are superior to humans in one respect or another, for example, the sense of smell of the wolf, the acuity of sight of the eagle, the survivability of the cockroach, or the photosynthetic power of plants. So any claim of human superiority must allow for the recognition of excellences in nonhuman species, even for some excellences that are superior to their corresponding human excellences. In fact, it demands that recognition.

Moreover, if the claim of human superiority is to have any moral force, it must rest on non-question-begging grounds. Accordingly, we must be able to give a non-question-begging response to the nonanthropocentric argument for the equality of species. Yet for any such argument to be successful, it would have to recognize the intrinsic value of the members of nonhuman species. Even if it could be established that human beings have greater intrinsic value, we would still have to recognize that nonhuman nature has intrinsic value as well. So the relevant question is: How are we going to recognize the presumably lesser intrinsic value of nonhuman nature?

Now if human needs, even nonbasic or luxury ones, are always preferred to even the basic needs of the members of nonhuman species, we would not be giving any recognition to the intrinsic value of nonhuman nature. But what if we allowed the nonbasic or luxury needs of humans to trump the basic needs of nonhuman nature half the time, and half the time we allowed the basic needs of nonhuman nature to trump the nonbasic or luxury needs of humans. Would that be enough? Certainly, it would be a significant advance over what we are presently doing. For what we are presently doing is meeting the basic needs of nonhuman nature, at best, only when it serves our own needs or the needs of those we are committed to or happen to care about, and that does not recognize the intrinsic value of nonhuman nature at all. A fifty-fifty arrangement would be an advance indeed. But it would not be enough.

The reason why it would not be enough is that the claim that humans are superior to nonhuman nature no more supports the practice of aggressing against the basic needs of nonhuman nature to satisfy our own nonbasic or luxury needs than the claim that a person came in first in a race would support the practice of aggressing against the basic needs of those who came in second, third, fourth, and so on to satisfy the nonbasic or luxury needs of the person who came in first. A higher degree of merit does not translate into a right of domination, and to claim a right to aggress against the basic needs of nonhuman nature in order to meet our own nonbasic or luxury needs is clearly to claim a right of domination. All that our superiority as humans would justify is not meeting the basic needs of nonhuman nature when this conflicts with our nonbasic or luxury needs. What it does not justify is aggressing against the basic needs of nonhuman nature when this conflicts with our nonbasic or luxury needs.

OBJECTIVE AND SUBJECTIVE VALUE THEORY

Now it might be objected that my argument so far presupposes an objective theory of value that regards things as valuable because of the qualities they actually have rather than a subjective theory of value that regards things as valuable simply because humans happen to value them. However, I contend that when both these theories are defensibly formulated they will lead to the same practical requirements.

For consider: Suppose we begin with a subjective theory of value that regards things as valuable simply because humans value them. Of course, some things would be valued by humans instrumentally, others intrinsically, but, according to this theory, all things would have the value they have, if they have any value at all, simply because they are valued by humans either instrumentally or intrinsically.

One problem facing such a theory is why should we think that humans alone determine the value that things have? For example, why not say that things are valuable because the members of other species value them? Why not say that grass is valuable because zebras value it, and that zebras are valuable because lions value them, and so on? Or why not say, assuming God exists, that things are valuable because God values them?

Nor would it do simply to claim that we authoritatively determine what is valuable for ourselves, that nonhuman species authoritatively determine what is valuable for themselves, and that God authoritatively determines what is valuable for the Godhead. For what others value should at least be relevant data when authoritatively determining what is valuable for ourselves.

Another problem for a subjective theory of value is that we probably would not want to say that just anything we happen to value determines what is valuable for ourselves. For surely we would want to say that at least some of the things that people value, especially people who are evil or deficient in certain ways, are not really valuable, even for them. Merely thinking that something is valuable doesn't make it so.

Suppose then we modified this subjective theory of value to deal with these problems. Let the theory claim that what is truly valuable for people is what they would value if they had all the relevant information (including, where it is relevant, the knowledge of what others would value) and reasoned correctly. Of course, there will be many occasions where we are unsure that ideal conditions have been realized, unsure, that is, that we have all the relevant information and have reasoned correctly. And even when we are sure that ideal conditions have been realized, we may not always be willing to act upon what we come to value due to weakness of will.

Nevertheless, when a subjective theory of value is formulated in this way, it will have the same practical requirements as an objective theory of value that is also defensibly formulated. For an objective theory of value holds that what is valuable is determined by the qualities things actually have. But in order for the qualities things actually have to be valuable in the sense of being capable of being valued, they must be accessible to us, at least under ideal conditions, that is, they must be the sort of qualities that we would value if we had all the relevant information and reasoned correctly. But this is just what is valuable according to our modified subjective theory of value. So once a subjective theory of value and an objective theory of value are defensibly formulated in the manner I propose, they will lead us to value the same things.

Now it is important to note here that with respect to some of the things we value intrinsically, such as animals and plants, our valuing them depends simply on our ability to discover the value that they actually have based on their qualities, whereas for other things that we value intrinsically, such as our aesthetic experiences and the objects that provided us with those experiences, the value that these things have depends significantly on the way we are constituted. So that if we were constituted differently, what we value aesthetically would be different as well. Of course, the same holds true for some of the things that we value morally. For example, we morally value not killing human beings because of the way we are constituted. Constituted as we are, killing is usually bad for any human that we would kill. But suppose we were constituted differently such that killing human beings was immensely pleasurable for those humans that we killed, following which they immediately sprang back to life asking us to kill them again. If human beings were constituted in this way, we would no longer morally value not killing. In fact, constituted in this new way, I think we would come to morally value *killing* and the relevant rule for us might be "Kill human beings as often as you can." But while such aesthetic and moral values are clearly dependent on the way we are constituted, they still are not anthropocentric in the sense that they imply human superiority. Such values can be recognized from both an anthropocentric and a nonanthropocentric perspective.

It might be objected, however, that while the intrinsic values of an environmental ethics need not be anthropocentric in the sense that they imply human superiority, these values must be anthropocentric in the sense that humans would reasonably come to hold them. This seems correct. However, appealing to this sense of anthropocentric, Eugene Hargrove has argued that not all living things would turn out to be intrinsically valuable as a nonanthropocentric environmental ethics maintains.[12] Hargrove cites as hypothetical examples of living things that would not turn out to be intrinsically valuable the creatures in the films *Alien* and *Aliens*. What is distinctive about these creatures is that they require the deaths of many other living creatures, whomever they happen upon, to reproduce and survive as a species. Newly hatched, these creatures emerge from their eggs and immediately enter host organisms, which they keep alive and feed upon while they develop. When the creatures are fully developed, they explode out of the chest of their host organisms, killing their hosts with some fanfare. Hargrove suggests that if such creatures existed, we would not intrinsically value them because it would not be reasonable for us to do so.[13]

Following Paul Taylor, Hargrove assumes that to intrinsically value a creature is to recognize a negative duty not to destroy or harm that creature and a positive duty to protect it from being destroyed or harmed by others. Since Hargrove thinks that we would be loath to recognize any such duties with respect to such alien creatures, we would not consider them to be intrinsically valuable.

Surely it seems clear that we would seek to kill such alien creatures by whatever means are available to us, but why should that preclude our recognizing them as having intrinsic value any more than our seeking to kill any person who is engaged in lethal aggression against us would preclude our recognizing that person as having intrinsic value? To recognize something as having intrinsic value does not preclude destroying it to preserve other things that also have intrinsic value when there is good reason to do so. Furthermore, recognizing a prima facie negative duty not to destroy or harm something and a prima facie positive duty to protect it from being destroyed or harmed by others is perfectly consistent with recognizing an all-things-considered duty to destroy that thing when it is engaged in lethal aggression against us. Actually, all we are doing here is simply applying our principle of human defense, and, as I have argued earlier, there is no reason to think that the application of this principle would preclude our recognizing the intrinsic value of every living being.

Still another objection that might be raised to my reconciliationist argument is that my view is too individualistic, as evidenced by the fact that my principles of environmental justice refer to individual humans, plants, and animals, but not specifically to species or ecosystems. Now, I would certainly agree with Paul Taylor that all individual living beings as well as species populations can be benefited or harmed and have a good of their own and hence qualify as moral subjects.[14] But Taylor goes on to deny that species themselves are moral subjects with a good of their own because he regards "species" as a class name, and classes, he contends, have no good of their own.[15] Yet here I would disagree with Taylor because species are unlike abstract classes in that they evolve, split, bud off new species, become endangered, go extinct, and have interests distinct from the interests of their members.[16] For example, a particular species of deer, but not individual members of that species, can have an interest in being preyed upon. Hence, species can be benefited and harmed and have a good of their own and so should qualify on Taylor's view, as well as my own, as moral subjects. So too ecosystems should qualify as moral subjects since they can be benefited and harmed and have a good of their own, having features and interests not shared by their components.[17] Following Lawrence Johnson, we can go on to characterize moral subjects as living systems in a persistent state of low entropy sustained by metabolic processes for accumulating energy whose organic unity and self-identity is maintained in equilibrium by homeostatic feedback processes.[18] Thus, modifying my view in order to take into account species and ecosystems requires the following changes in my first three principles of environmental justice:

Principle of human defense: Actions that defend oneself and other human beings against harmful aggression are permissible even when they necessitate killing or harming individual animals or plants or even destroying whole species or ecosystems.

Principle of human preservation: Actions that are necessary for meeting one's basic needs or the basic needs of other human beings are permissible even when they require aggressing against the basic needs of individual animals and plants or even of whole species or ecosystems.

Principle of disproportionality: Actions that meet nonbasic or luxury needs of humans are prohibited when they aggress against the basic needs of individual animals and plants, or of whole species or ecosystems.

But while this modification is of theoretical interest since it allows that species and ecosystems as well as individuals count morally, it actually has little or no practical effect on the application of these principles. This is because, for the most part, the positive or negative impact the application of these principles would have on species and ecosystems is correspondingly reflected in the positive or negative impact the application of these principles would have on the individual members of those species or ecosystems. As a consequence, actions that are permitted or prohibited with respect to species and ecosystems according to the modified principles are already permitted or prohibited respectively through their correspondence with actions that are permitted or prohibited according to the unmodified principles.

However, this is not always the case. In fact, considerations about what benefits nonhuman species or subspecies as opposed to individuals of those species or subspecies have already figured in my previous argument. For example, I have argued for culling elk herds in wolf-free ranges, but this is primarily for the good of herds or species of elk and certainly not for the good of the particular elk who are being culled from those herds. I also have argued that it would be for the good of farm animals generally that they be maintained under healthy conditions and then killed relatively painlessly and eaten, rather than that they not be maintained at all. But clearly this is an argument about what would be good for existing flocks or herds, or species or subspecies of farm animals. It is not an argument about what would be good for the existing individual farm animals who would be killed relatively painlessly and eaten. Nevertheless, for the most part, because of the coincidence between the welfare of species and ecosystems and the welfare of individual members of those species and

ecosystems, the two formulations of the first three principles turn out to be practically equivalent.

In sum, I have argued that whether we endorse an anthropocentric or a nonanthropocentric environmental ethics, we should favor a principle of human defense, a principle of human preservation, and a principle of disproportionality as I have interpreted them. In the past, failure to recognize the importance of a principle of human defense and a principle of human preservation has led philosophers to overestimate the amount of sacrifice required of humans.[19] By contrast, failure to recognize the importance of a principle of disproportionality has led philosophers to underestimate the amount of sacrifice required of humans.[20] I claim that taken together these three principles strike the right balance between concerns of human welfare and the welfare of nonhuman nature.

Notes

1. Aldo Leopold's view is usually interpreted as holistic in this sense. Leopold wrote "A thing is right when it tends to preserve the integrity, stability and beauty of the biotic community. It is wrong when it tends otherwise." See his *A Sand County Almanac* (Oxford, 1949).
2. For a defender of this view, see Paul Taylor, *Respect for Nature*.
3. Where it is most likely to be morally required is where our negligent actions have caused the environmental problem in the first place.
4. Peter Singer's *Animal Liberation* (New York, 1975) inspired this view.
5. Baird Callicott, "Animal Liberation: A Triangular Affair," *Environmental Ethics* (1980): 311–328.
6. Mark Sagoff, "Animal Liberation and Environmental Ethics: Bad Marriage, Quick Divorce," *Osgood Hall Law Journal* (1984): 297–307.
7. Mary Ann Warren, "The Rights of the Nonhuman World," in *Environmental Philosophy*, edited by Robert Elliot and Arran Gare (London, 1983), 109–134; and Baird Callicott, *In Defense of the Land Ethic* (Albany, 1989), Chapter 3.
8. *Realities for the 90's* (Santa Cruz, 1991), 4.
9. Ibid, 5.
10. Sagoff, op. cit., 301–305.
11. Holmes Rolston, *Environmental Ethics* (Philadelphia, 1988), 66–68; Murray Bookchin, *The Ecology of Freedom* (Montreal, 1991), xxxvi.
12. Eugene Hargrove, "Weak Anthropocentric Intrinsic Value," in *After Earth Day*, edited by Max Oelschlaeger (Denton, 1992), 147ff.
13. Ibid., 151. Notice that there are at least two ways that X might intrinsically value Y. First, X might regard Y as good in itself for X or as an end in itself for X, by contrast with valuing Y instrumentally. Second, X might regard the good of Y as constraining the way that X

can use *Y*. This second way of intrinsically valuing *Y* is the principal way we value human beings. It is the sense of value that Kantians are referring to when they claim that people should never be used as means only. Another way to put what I have been arguing is that we should extend this second way of intrinsically valuing to animals and plants.

14. Taylor, op. cit., 17, 68–71.
15. Ibid., 68–71.
16. One way to think about species are as ongoing genetic lineages sequentially embodied in different organisms. See Lawrence Johnson, *A Morally Deep World* (New York: Cambridge University Press, 1991) 156; Rolston op. cit., Chapter 4.
17. Ecosystems can be simple or complex, stable or unstable, and they can suffer total collapse.
18. *A Morally Deep World,* Chapter 6. Happily, this definition distinguishes moral subjects (living systems) from cars, refrigerators, etc. See also Lawrence Johnson, "Toward the Moral Considerability of Species and Ecosystems," *Environmental Ethics* 14 (1992).
19. For example, in "Animal Liberation: A Triangular Affair," Baird Callicott had defended Edward Abbey's assertion that he would sooner shoot a man than a snake.
20. For example, Eugene Hargrove argues that from a traditional wildlife perspective, the lives of individual specimens of quite plentiful nonhuman species count for almost nothing at all. See Chapter 4 of his *Foundations of Environmental Ethics* (Prentice Hall, 1989).

Study Questions

1. Outline Sterba's argument for reconciling anthropocentric and nonanthropocentric ethics. First, examine his description of nonanthropocentric ethics. Next, examine his description of anthropocentric ethics. Is Sterba successful? What assumptions are necessary for his project?
2. Do you agree with Sterba that regarding members of all species as equals still allows for human preferences in the same way regarding humans as equals still allows for self-preference? What is Sterba's basis of equality? Discuss his theory of equality.
3. Consider Sterba's treatment of objective and subjective value. How does he seek to reconcile them? Is he successful?
4. At the end of his article, Sterba treats species as subjects that can be harmed or benefited just as individuals can be benefited. Do you agree? Explain your view.

For Further Reading

Attfield, Robin. *The Ethics of Environmental Concern* (New York: Columbia University, 1983).

Callicott, Baird. *In Defense of the Land Ethic* (Buffalo, NY: SUNY Press, 1989).

Chase, Alston. *In a Dark Wood: The Fight over Forests and the Rising Tyranny of Ecology.* Boston: Houghton Mifflin, 1995.

___. *Playing God at Yellowstone Park.* Fort Worth, TX: 1987.

Devall, Bill. *Simple in Means, Rich in Ends: Practicing Deep Ecology.* Salt Lake City, UT: Peregrine Smith Books, 1985.

Devall, Bill, and George Sessions. *Deep Ecology: Living as if Nature Mattered.* Salt Lake City, UT: Peregrine Smith Books, 1985.

Ehrenfeld, David. *The Arrogance of Humanism.* New York: Oxford University Press: 1978.

Fox, Warwick. "Deep Ecology: A New Philosophy of Our Time." *The Ecologist* 14 (1984).

Goodpaster, Kenneth. "On Being Morally Considerable." *Journal of Philosophy* 75 (June 1978).

Johnson, Lawrence. *A Morally Deep World.* New York: Cambridge University Press, 1991.

Leopold, Aldo. *A Sand County Almanac.* New York: Oxford University Press, 1949.

Lewis, Martin. *Green Delusions: An Environmentalist Critique of Radical Environmentalism.* Durham, NC: Duke University Press, 1992.

List, Peter C., ed. *Radical Environmentalism.* Belmont, CA: Wadsworth, 1993.

Naess, Arne. *Ecology, Community and Lifestyle,* ed. and trans. David Rothenberg. Cambridge: Cambridge University Press, 1989.

Rolston, Holmes III. *Environmental Ethics: Duties to and Values in the Natural World.* Philadelphia: Temple University Press, 1987.

Sylvan, Richard. "A Critique of Deep Ecology." *Radical Philosophy* 40 (1985).

Taylor, Paul. *Respect for Nature.* Princeton, NJ: Princeton University Press, 1986.

Wenz, Peter. *Environmental Justice.* Buffalo, NY: SUNY Press, 1988.

Zimmerman, Michael, ed. *Environmental Philosophy: From Animal Rights to Radical Ecology.* Englewood Cliffs, NJ: Prentice-Hall, 1993.

CHAPTER FOUR

Ecofeminism

Ecofeminism, a term first set forth by Francoise d'Eaubonne in 1974, is the theory that sees connections between feminism and ecology. It sees the theme of *dominance* operating in the relationships of men over women and humanity over nature. Ecofeminism is revolutionary in that it promotes the overthrow of both types of dominance, for each is oppressive. Ecofeminists argue that these two kinds of oppression are inextricably connected. They must be addressed together, rather than in isolation, and to that end we must radically revise our understanding of gender and nature.

The "logic of domination" is explored in our first essay, "The Power and Promise of Ecological Feminism," by Karen J. Warren. Warren explains the dominance perspective as the unwarranted view that some characteristics are more valuable than others and so those possessing the more valuable are entitled to dominate the less valuable. Since the "male" value of rationality has typically been priced over the "female" values of nurturing and caring, men have thought they had a

right to oppress women. Likewise, human beings have valued human traits over those of nature and have thought that these differences justified them in oppressing nature.

Warren outlines the components of traditional feminism and then outlines a way in which feminists would remove inappropriate hierarchical, racial, and sexist thinking from environmental concerns. She asserts that it is impossible to take an objective point of view on these matters but that the feminine bias is a better bias because it is more inclusive.

In the second reading, Margarita Garcia Levin takes issue with Warren, arguing that the "logic of domination" does not work. Male dominance does not necessitate oppression and may have a utilitarian or biological explanation or justification. Likewise, humanity's dominance of Earth is caused by our need to survive and our desire to flourish. Furthermore, no link exists between these two types of domination.

26

The Power and the Promise of Ecological Feminism

KAREN J. WARREN

Karen Warren is associate professor of philosophy at Macalaster College and the author of several works in feminism and environmental ethics. Here is Warren's original abstract:

Ecological feminism is the position that there are important connections—historical, symbolic, theoretical—between the domination of women and the domination of nonhuman nature. I argue that because the conceptual connections between the dual dominations of women and
nature are located in an oppressive patriarchal conceptual framework characterized by a logic of domination, (1) the logic of traditional feminism requires the expansion of feminism to include ecological feminism, and (2) ecological feminism provides a framework for developing a distinct feminist environmental ethic. I conclude that any feminist theory and any environmental ethic which fails to take seriously the interconnected domination of women and nature is simply inadequate.

I argue that the promise and power of ecological feminism is that *it provides a distinctive framework both for reconceiving feminism and for developing an environmental ethic which takes seriously connections between the domination of women and the domination of*

Reprinted from *Environmental Ethics,* Vol. 12 (Summer 1990), by permission of the author and publisher. Notes edited.

nature. I do so by discussing the nature of a feminist ethic and the ways in which ecofeminism provides a feminist and environmental ethic. I conclude that any feminist theory *and* any environmental ethic which fails to take seriously the twin and interconnected dominations of women and nature is at best incomplete and at worst simply inadequate.

FEMINISM, ECOLOGICAL FEMINISM, AND CONCEPTUAL FRAMEWORKS

Whatever else it is, feminism is at least the movement to end sexist oppression. It involves the elimination of any and all factors that contribute to the continued and systematic domination or subordination of women. While feminists disagree about the nature of and solutions to the subordination of women, all feminists agree that sexist oppression exists, is wrong, and must be abolished.

A "feminist issue" is any issue that contributes in some way to understanding the oppression of women. Equal rights, comparable pay for comparable work, and food production are feminist issues wherever and whenever an understanding of them contributes to an understanding of the continued exploitation or subjugation of women. Carrying water and searching for firewood are feminist issues wherever and whenever women's primary responsibility for these tasks contributes to their lack of full participation in decision making, income producing, or high status positions engaged in by men. What counts as a feminist issue, then, depends largely on context, particularly the historical and material conditions of women's lives.

Environmental degradation and exploitation are feminist issues because an understanding of them contributes to an understanding of the oppression of women. In India, for example, both deforestation and reforestation through the introduction of a monoculture species tree (e.g., eucalyptus) intended for commercial production are feminist issues because the loss of indigenous forests and multiple species of trees has drastically affected rural Indian women's ability to maintain a subsistence household. Indigenous forests provide a variety of trees for food, fuel, fodder, household utensils, dyes, medicines, and income-generating uses, while monoculture-species forests do not.[1] Although I do not argue for this claim here, a look at the global impact of environmental degradation on women's lives suggest important respects in which environmental degradation is a feminist issue.

Feminist philosophers claim that some of the most important feminist issues are *conceptual* ones: these issues concern how one conceptualizes such mainstay philosophical notions as reason and rationality, ethics, and what it is to be human. Ecofeminists extend this feminist philosophical concern to nature. They argue that, ultimately, some of the most important connections between the domination of women and the domi-

nation of nature are conceptual. To see this, consider the nature of conceptual frameworks.

A *conceptual framework* is a set of *basic* beliefs, values, attitudes, and assumptions which shape and reflect how one views oneself and one's world. It is a socially constructed lens though which we perceive ourselves and others. It is affected by such factors as gender, race, class, age, affectional orientation, nationality, and religious background.

Some conceptual frameworks are oppressive. An *oppressive conceptual framework* is one that explains, justifies, and maintains relationships of domination and subordination. When an oppressive conceptual framework is *patriarchal,* it explains, justifies, and maintains the subordination of women by men.

I have argued elsewhere that there are three significant features of oppressive conceptual frameworks: (1) value-hierarchical thinking, i.e., "up-down" thinking which places higher value, status, or prestige on what is "up" rather than on what is "down"; (2) value dualism's, i.e., disjunctive pairs in which the disjuncts are seen as oppositional (rather than as complementary) and exclusive (rather than as inclusive), and which place higher value (status, prestige) on one disjunct rather than the other (e.g., dualisms which give higher value or status to that which has historically been identified as "mind, " "reason," and "male" than to that which has historically been identified as "body," "emotion," and "female"); and (3) logic of domination, i.e., a structure of argumentation which leads to a justification of subordination.[2]

The third feature of oppressive conceptual frameworks is the most significant. A logic of domination is not *just* a logical structure. It also involves a substantive value system, since an ethical premise is needed to permit or sanction the "just" subordination of that which is subordinate. This justification typically is given on grounds of some alleged characteristic (e.g., rationality) which the dominant (e.g., men) have and the subordinate (e.g., women) lack.

Contrary to what many feminists and ecofeminists have said or suggested, there maybe nothing *inherently* problematic about "hierarchical thinking" or even "value-hierarchical thinking" in contexts other than contexts of oppression. Hierarchical thinking is important in daily living for classifying data, comparing information, and organizing material. Taxonomies (e.g., plant taxonomies) and biological nomenclature seem to require *some* form of "hierarchical thinking." Even "value-hierarchical thinking" may be quite acceptable in certain contexts. (The same may be said of "value dualisms" in nonoppressive contexts). For example, suppose it is true that what is unique about humans is our conscious capacity to radically reshape our social environments (or "societies"), as Murray Bookchin suggests.[3] Then one could truthfully say that humans are better equipped to radically reshape their environments than are rocks or plants—a "value-hierarchical" way of speaking.

The problem is not simply *that* value-hierarchical thinking and value dualisms are used, but *the way* in which each has been used in *oppressive conceptual frameworks* to establish inferiority and to justify subordination.[4] It is the logic of domination, *coupled with* value-hierarchical thinking and value dualisms, which "justifies" subordination. What is explanatorily basic, then, about the nature of oppressive conceptual frameworks is the logic of domination.

For ecofeminism, that a logic of domination is explanatorily basic is important for at least three reasons. First, without a logic of domination, a description of similarities and differences would be just that—a description of similarities and differences. Consider the claim, "Humans are different from plants and rocks in that humans can (and plants and rocks cannot) consciously and radically reshape the communities in which they live; humans are similar to plants and rocks in that they are both members of an ecological community." Even if humans are "better" than plants and rocks with respect to the conscious ability of humans to radically transform communities, one does not *thereby* get any *morally* relevant distinction between humans and nonhumans, or an argument for the domination of plants and rocks by humans. To get *those* conclusions one needs to add at least two powerful assumptions, viz., (A2) and (A4) in argument A below:

(A1) Humans do, and plants and rocks do not, have the capacity to consciously and radically change the community in which they live.

(A2) Whatever has the capacity to consciously and radically change the community in which it lives is morally superior to whatever lacks this capacity.

(A3) Thus, humans are morally superior to plants and rocks.

(A4) For any X and Y, if X is morally superior to Y, then X is morally justified in subordinating Y.

(A5) Thus, humans are morally justified in subordinating plants and rocks.

Without the two assumptions that *humans are morally superior* to (at least some) nonhumans, (A2), and that *superiority justifies subordination*, (A4), all one has is some difference between humans and some nonhumans. This is true *even if* that difference is given in terms of superiority. Thus, it is the logic of domination, (A4), which is the bottom line in ecofeminist discussions of oppression.

Second, ecofeminists argue that, at least in Western societies, the oppressive conceptual framework which sanctions the twin dominations of women and nature is a patriarchal one characterized by all three features of an oppressive conceptual framework Many ecofeminists claim that, historically, within at least the dominant Western culture, a patriarchal conceptual framework has sanctioned the following argument B:

(B1) Women are identified with nature and the realm of the physical; men are identified with the "human" and the realm of the mental.

(B2) Whatever is identified with nature and the realm of the physical is inferior to ("below") whatever is identified with the "human" and the realm of the mental; or, conversely, the latter is superior to ("above") the former.

(B3) Thus, women are inferior to ("below") men; or, conversely, men are superior to ("above") women.

(B4) For any X and Y, if X is superior to Y, then X is justified in subordinating Y.

(B5) Thus, men are justified in subordinating women.

If sound, argument B establishes *patriarchy*, i.e., the conclusion given at (B5) that the systematic domination of women by men is justified. But according to ecofeminists, (B5) is justified by just those three features of an oppressive conceptual framework identified earlier: value-hierarchical thinking, the assumption at (B2); value dualisms, the assumed dualism of the mental and the physical at (B1) and the assumed inferiority of the physical vis-à-vis the mental at (B2); and a logic of domination, the assumption at (B4), the same as the previous premise (A4.). Hence, according to ecofeminists, insofar as an oppressive patriarchal conceptual framework has functioned historically (within at least dominant Western culture) to sanction the twin dominations of women and nature (argument B), both argument B and the patriarchal conceptual framework, from whence it comes, ought to be rejected.

Of course, the preceding does not identify which premises of B are false. What is the status of premises (B1) and (B2)? Most, if not all, feminists claim that (B1), and many ecofeminists claim that (B2), have been assumed or asserted within the dominant Western philosophical and intellectual tradition. As such, these feminists assert, as a matter of historical fact, that the dominant Western philosophical tradition has assumed the truth of (B1) and (B2). Ecofeminists, however, either deny (B2) or do not affirm (B2). Furthermore, because some ecofeminists are anxious to deny any ahistorical identification of women with nature, some ecofeminists deny (B1) when (B1) is used to support anything other than a strictly historical claim about what has been asserted or assumed to be true within patriarchal culture—e.g., when (B1) is used to assert that women properly are identified with the realm of nature and the physical. Thus, from an ecofeminist perspective, (B1) and (B2) are properly viewed as problematic though historically sanctioned claims: they are problematic precisely because of the way they have functioned historically in a patriarchal conceptual framework and culture to sanction the dominations of women and nature.

What *all* ecofeminists agree about, then, is the way in which *the logic of domination* has functioned historically within patriarchy to sustain and justify the twin dominations of women and nature. Since *all* feminists (and not just ecofeminists) oppose patriarchy, the conclusion given at (B5), all feminists (including ecofeminists) must oppose at least the logic of domination, premise (B4), on which argument B rests—whatever the truth-value status of (B1) and (B2) *outside of* a patriarchal context.

That *all* feminists must oppose the logic of domination shows the breadth and depth of the ecofeminist critique of B: it is a critique not only of the three assumptions on which this argument for the domination of women and nature rests, viz., the assumptions at (B1), (B2), and (B4); it is also a critique of patriarchal conceptual frameworks generally, i.e., of those oppressive conceptual frameworks which put men "up" and women "down," allege some way in which women are morally inferior to men, and use that alleged difference to justify the subordination of women by men. Therefore, ecofeminism is necessary to *any* feminist critique of patriarchy, and, hence, necessary to feminism (a point I discuss again later).

Third, ecofeminism clarifies why the logic of domination, and any conceptual framework which gives rise to it, must be abolished in order both to make possible a meaningful notion of difference which does not breed domination and to prevent feminism from becoming a "support" movement based primarily on shared experiences. In contemporary society, there is no one "woman's voice," no *woman* (or *human*) *simpliciter*: every woman (or human) is a woman (or human) of some race, class, age, affectional orientation, marital status, regional or national background, and so forth. Because there are no "monolithic experiences" that all women share, feminism must be a "solidarity movement" based on shared beliefs and interests rather than a "unity in sameness" movement based on shared experiences and shared victimization. In the words of Maria Lugones, "Unity—not to be confused with solidarity—is understood as conceptually tied to domination."

Ecofeminists insist that the sort of logic of domination used to justify the domination of humans by gender, racial or ethnic, or class status is also used to justify the domination of nature. Because eliminating a logic of domination is part of a feminist critique—whether a critique of patriarchy, white supremacist culture, or imperialism—ecofeminists insist that *naturism* is properly viewed as an integral part of any feminist solidarity movement to end sexist oppression and the logic of domination which conceptually grounds it.

ECOFEMINISM RECONCEIVES FEMINISM

The discussion so far has focused on some of the oppressive conceptual features of patriarchy. As I use the phrase, the "logic of traditional feminism" refers to the location of the conceptual roots of sexist oppression, at least in Western societies, in an oppressive patriarchal conceptual framework characterized by a logic of domination. Insofar as other systems of oppression (e.g., racism, classism, ageism, heterosexism) are also conceptually maintained by a logic of domination, appeal to the logic of traditional feminism ultimately locates the basic conceptual interconnections among *all* systems of oppression in the logic of domination. It thereby explains at a *conceptual* level why the eradication of sexist oppression requires the eradication of the other forms of oppression.[5] It is by clarifying this conceptual connection between systems of oppression that a movement to end sexist oppression—traditionally the special turf of feminist theory and practice—leads to a reconceiving of feminism as *a movement to end all forms of oppression*.

Suppose one agrees that the logic of traditional feminism requires the expansion of feminism to include other social systems of domination (e.g., racism and classism). What warrants the inclusion of nature in these "social systems of domination"? Why must the logic of traditional feminism include the abolition of "naturism" (i.e., the domination or oppression of nonhuman nature) among the "isms" feminism must confront? The conceptual justification for expanding feminism to include ecofeminism is twofold. One basis has already been suggested: by showing that the conceptual connections between the dual dominations of women and nature are located in an oppressive and, at least in Western societies, patriarchal conceptual framework characterized by a logic of domination, ecofeminism explains how and why feminism, conceived as a movement to end sexist oppression, must be expanded and reconceived as also a movement to end naturism. This is made explicit by the following argument C:

(C1)   Feminism is a movement to end sexism.

(C2)   But Sexism is conceptually linked with naturism (through an oppressive conceptual framework characterized by a logic of domination).

(C3)   Thus, Feminism is (also) a movement to end naturism.

Because, ultimately, these connections between sexism and naturism are conceptual—embedded in an oppressive conceptual framework—the logic of traditional feminism leads to the embracement of ecological feminism.

The other justification for reconceiving feminism to include ecofeminism has to do with the concepts of gender and nature. Just as conceptions of gender are socially constructed, so are conceptions of nature. Of course, the claim that women and nature are social constructions does not require anyone to deny that there are actual humans and actual trees, rivers, and plants. It simply implies that *how* women and nature are conceived is a matter of historical and social reality. These conceptions vary cross-culturally and by historical time period. As a result, any discussion of the "oppression or domination of nature" involves reference to historically specific forms of social domination of nonhuman nature by humans, just as discussion of the "domination of women" refers to historically specific forms of social domination of women by men.

CLIMBING FROM ECOFEMINISM TO ENVIRONMENTAL ETHICS

Many feminists and some environmental ethicists have begun to explore the use of first-person narrative as a way of raising philosophically germane issues in ethics often lost or underplayed in mainstream philosophical ethics. Why is this so? What is it about narrative which makes it a significant resource for theory and practice in feminism and environmental ethics? Even if appeal to first-person narrative is a helpful literary device for describing ineffable experience or a legitimate social science methodology for documenting personal and social history, how is first-person narrative a valuable vehicle of argumentation for ethical decision making and theory building? One fruitful way to begin answering these questions is to ask them of a particular first-person narrative.

Consider the following first-person narrative about rock climbing:

For my very first rock climbing experience, I chose a somewhat private spot, away from other climbers and on-lookers. After studying "the chimney," I focused all my energy on making it to the top. I climbed with intense determination, using whatever strength and skills I had to accomplish this challenging feat. By midway I was exhausted and anxious. I couldn't see what to do next—where to put my hands or feet. Growing increasingly more weary as I clung somewhat desperately to the rock, I made a move. It didn't work. I fell. There I was, dangling midair above the rocky ground below, frightened but terribly relieved that the belay rope had held me. I knew I was safe. I took a look up at the climb that remained. I was determined to make it to the top. With renewed confidence and concentration, I finished the climb to the top.

On my second day of climbing, I rappelled down about 200 feet from the top of the Palisades at Lake Superior to just a few feet above the water level. I could see no one—not my belayer, not the other climbers, no one. I unhooked slowly from the rappel rope and took a deep cleansing breath. I looked all around me—really looked—and listened. I heard a cacophony of voices—birds, trickles of water on the rock before me, waves lapping against the rocks below. I closed my eyes and began to feel the rock with my hands—the cracks and crannies, the raised lichen and mosses, the almost imperceptible nubs that might provide a resting place for my fingers and toes when I began to climb. At that moment I was bathed in serenity. I began to talk to the rock in an almost inaudible, child-like way, as if the rock were my friend. I felt an overwhelming sense of gratitude for what it offered me—a chance to know myself and the rock differently, to appreciate unforeseen miracles like the tiny flowers growing in the even tinier cracks in the rock's surface, and to come to know a sense of being *in relationship* with the natural environment. It felt as if the rock and I were silent conversational partners in a longstanding friendship. I realized then that I had come to care about this cliff which was so different from me, so unmovable and invincible, independent and seemingly indifferent to my presence. I wanted to be with the rock as I climbed. Gone was the determination to conquer the rock, to forcefully impose my will on it; I wanted simply to work respectfully with the rock as I climbed. And as I climbed, that is what I felt. I felt myself *caring* for this rock and feeling thankful that climbing provided the opportunity for me to know it and myself in this new way.

There are at least four reasons why use of such a first-person narrative is important to feminism and environmental ethics. First, such a narrative gives voice to a felt sensitivity often lacking in traditional analytical ethical discourse, viz., a sensitivity to conceiving of oneself as fundamentally "in relationship with" others, including the nonhuman environment. It is a modality which *takes relationships themselves seriously*. It thereby stands in contrast to a strictly reductionist modality that takes relationships seriously only or primarily because of the nature of the *relators* or parties to those relationships (e.g., relators conceived as moral agents, right holders, interest carriers, or sentient beings). In the rock-climbing narrative above, it is the climber's relationship with the rock she climbs which takes on special significance—which is itself a locus of value—in addition to whatever moral status or moral considerability she or the rock or any other parties to the relationship may also have.

Second, such a first-person narrative gives expression to a variety of ethical attitudes and behaviors often overlooked or underplayed in mainstream Western ethics, e.g., the difference in attitudes and behaviors toward a rock when one is "making it to the top" and when one thinks of oneself as "friends with" or "caring about" the rock one climbs. These different attitudes and behaviors suggest an ethically germane contrast between two different types of relationship humans or climbers may have toward a rock: an imposed conqueror-type relationship, and an emergent caring-type relationship. This contrast grows out of, and is faithful to, felt, lived experience.

The difference between conquering and caring attitudes and behaviors in relation to the natural environment provides a third reason why the use of first-person narrative is important to feminism and environmental ethics: it provides a way of conceiving of ethics and ethical meaning as *emerging out of* particular situations moral agents find themselves in, rather than as being *imposed on* those situations (e.g., as a derivation or instantiation of some predetermined abstract principle or rule). This emergent feature of narrative centralizes the importance of *voice*. When a multiplicity of cross-cultural *voices* are centralized, narrative is able to give expression to a range of attitudes, values, beliefs, and behaviors which may be overlooked or silenced by imposed ethical meaning and theory. As a reflection of and on felt, lived experiences, the use of narrative in ethics provides a stance from which ethical discourse can be held accountable to the historical, material, and social realities in which moral subjects find themselves.

Lastly, and for our purposes perhaps most importantly, the use of narrative has argumentative significance. Jim Cheney calls attention to this feature of narrative when he claims, "To contextualize ethical deliberation is, in some sense, to provide a narrative or story, from which the solution to the ethical dilemma emerges as the fitting conclusion." Narrative has argumentative force by suggesting *what counts* as an appropriate conclusion to an ethical situation. One ethical conclusion suggested by the climbing narrative is that what counts as a proper ethical attitude toward mountains and rocks is an attitude of respect and care (whatever that turns out to be or involve), not one of domination and conquest.

In an essay entitled "In and Out of Harm's Way: Arrogance and Love," feminist philosopher Marilyn Frye distinguishes between "arrogant" and "loving" perception as one way of getting at this difference in the ethical attitudes of care and conquest.[6] Frye writes:

> The loving eye is a contrary of the arrogant eye.
>
> The loving eye knows the independence of the other. It is the eye of a seer who knows that nature is indifferent. It is the eye of one who knows that to know the seen, one must consult something other than one's own will and interests and fears and imagination. One must look at the thing. One must look and listen and check and question.
>
> The loving eye is one that pays a certain sort of attention. This attention can require a discipline but *not* a self-denial. The discipline is one of self-knowledge, knowledge of the scope and boundary of the self. . . . In particular, it is a matter of being able to tell one's own interests from those of others and of knowing where one's self leaves off and another begins. . . .
>
> The loving eye does not make the object of perception into something edible, does not try to assimilate it, does not reduce it to the size of the seer's desire, fear and imagination, and hence does not have to simplify. It knows the complexity of the other as something which will forever present new things to be known. The science of the loving eye would favor The Complexity Theory of Truth [in contrast to The Simplicity Theory of Truth] and presuppose The Endless Interestingness of the Universe.

According to Frye, the loving eye is not an invasive, coercive eye which annexes others to itself, but one which "knows the complexity of the other as something which will forever present new things to be known."

When one climbs a rock as a conqueror, one climbs with an arrogant eye. When one climbs with a loving eye, one constantly "must look and listen and check and question." One recognizes the rock as something very different, something perhaps totally indifferent to one's own presence, and finds in that difference joyous occasion for celebration. One knows "the boundary of the self," where the self—the "I," the climber—leaves off and the rock begins. There is no fusion of two into one, but a complement of two entities *acknowledged* as separate, different, independent, yet *in relationship*; they are in relationship *if only* because the loving eye is perceiving it, responding to it, noticing it, attending to it.

An ecofeminist perspective about both women and nature involves this shift in attitude from "arrogant perception" to "loving perception" of the nonhuman world. Arrogant perception of nonhumans by humans presupposes and maintains *sameness* in such a way that it expands the moral community to those beings who are thought to resemble (be like, similar to, or the same as) humans in some morally significant way. Any environmental movement or ethic based on arrogant perception builds a moral hierarchy of beings and assumes some common denominator of moral considerability in virtue of which like beings deserve similar treatment or moral consideration and unlike beings do not. Such environmental ethics are or generate a "unity in sameness." In contrast, "loving perception" presupposes and maintains *difference*—a distinction between the self and other, between human and at least some nonhumans—in such a way that perception of the other as other *is* an expression of love for one who/which is recognized at the outset as independent, dissimilar, different. As Maria Lugones says, in loving perception, "Love is seen not as fusion and erasure of difference but as incompatible with them." "Unity in sameness" alone is an *erasure of difference*.

"Loving perception" of the nonhuman natural world is an attempt to understand what it means *for humans* to care about the nonhuman world, a world *acknowledged* as being independent, different, perhaps even indifferent to humans. Humans *are* different from rocks in important ways, even if they are also both members of some ecological community. A moral community based on loving perception of oneself *in relationship with* a rock, or with the natural environment as a whole, is one which acknowledges and respects difference, whatever "sameness" also exists. The limits of loving perception are determined only by the limits of one's (e.g., a person's, a community's) ability to respond lovingly (or with appropriate care, trust, or friendship)—whether it is to other humans or to the nonhuman world and elements of it.

If what I have said so far is correct, then there are very different ways to climb a mountain and *how* one climbs it and *how* one narrates the experience of climbing it matter ethically. If one climbs with "arrogant perception," with an attitude of "conquer and control," one keeps intact the very sorts of thinking that characterize a logic of domination and an oppressive conceptual framework. Since the oppressive conceptual framework which sanctions the domination of nature is a patriarchal one, one also thereby keeps intact, even if unwittingly, a patriarchal conceptual framework. Because the dismantling of patriarchal conceptual frameworks is a feminist issue, *how* one climbs a mountain and *how* one narrates—or tells the story—about the experience of climbing also are *feminist issues*. In this way, ecofeminism makes visible why, at a conceptual level, environmental ethics is a feminist issue. I turn now to a consideration of ecofeminism as a distinctively feminist and environmental ethic.

ECOFEMINISM AS A FEMINIST AND ENVIRONMENTAL ETHIC

A feminist ethic involves a twofold commitment to critique male bias in ethics wherever it occurs, and to develop ethics which are not male-biased. Sometimes this involves articulation of values (e.g., values of care, appropriate trust, kinship, friendship) often lost or underplayed in mainstream ethics. Sometimes it involves engaging in theory building by pioneering in new directions or by revamping old theories in gender sensitive ways. What makes the critiques of old theories or conceptualizations of new ones "feminist" is that they emerge out of sex-gender analyses and reflect whatever those analyses reveal about gendered experience and gendered social reality.

As I conceive feminist ethics in the pre-feminist present, it rejects attempts to conceive of ethical theory in terms of necessary and sufficient conditions, because it assumes that there is no essence (in the sense of some transhistorical, universal, absolute abstraction) of feminist ethics. While attempts to formulate joint necessary and sufficient conditions of a feminist ethic are unfruitful, nonetheless, there are some necessary conditions, what I prefer to call "boundary conditions," of a feminist ethic. These boundary conditions clarify some of the minimal conditions of a feminist ethic without suggesting that feminist ethics has some ahistorical essence. They are like the boundaries of a quilt or collage. They delimit the territory of the piece without dictating what the interior, the design, the actual pattern of the piece looks like. Because the actual design of the quilt emerges from the multiplicity of voices of women in a cross-cultural context, the design will change over time. It is not something static.

What are some of the boundary conditions of a feminist ethic? First, nothing can become part of a feminist ethic—can be part of the quilt—that promotes sexism, racism, classism, or any other "isms" of social domination. Of course, people may disagree about what counts as a sexist act, racist attitude, classist behavior. What counts as sexism, racism, or classism may vary cross-culturally. Still, because a feminist ethic aims at eliminating sexism and sexist bias, and (as I have already shown) sexism is intimately connected in conceptualization and in practice to racism, classism, and naturism, a feminist ethic must be anti-sexist, anti-racist, anti-classist, anti-naturist and opposed to any "ism" which presupposes or advances a logic of domination.

Second, a feminist ethic is a *contextualist* ethic. A contextualist ethic is one which sees ethical discourse and practice as emerging from the voices of people located in different historical circumstances. A contextualist ethic is properly viewed as a *collage* or *mosaic*, a *tapestry* of voices that emerges out of felt experiences. Like any collage or mosaic, the point is not to have *one picture* based on a unity of voices, but a *pattern* which emerges out of the very different voices of people located in different circumstances. When a contextualist ethic is *feminist*, it gives central place to the voices of women.

Third, since a feminist ethic gives central significance to the diversity of women's voices, a feminist ethic must be structurally pluralistic rather than unitary or reductionistic. It rejects the assumption that there is "one voice" in terms of which ethical values, beliefs, attitudes, and conduct can be assessed.

Fourth, a feminist ethic reconceives ethical theory as theory in process which will change over time. Like all theory, a feminist ethic is based on some generalizations. Nevertheless, the generalizations associated with it are themselves a pattern of voices within which the different voices emerging out of concrete and alternative descriptions of ethical situations have meaning. The coherence of a feminist theory so conceived is given within a historical and conceptual context, i.e., within a set of historical, socioeconomic circumstances (including circumstances of race, class, age, and affectional orientation) and within a set of basic beliefs, values, attitudes, and assumption about the world.

Fifth, because a feminist ethic is contextualist, structurally pluralistic, and "in-process," one way to evaluate the claims of a feminist ethic is in terms of their *inclusiveness*: those claims (voices, patterns of voices) are morally and epistemologically favored (preferred, better, less partial, less biased) which are more inclusive of the felt experiences and perspectives of oppressed persons. The condition of inclusiveness requires and ensures that the diverse voices of women (as oppressed persons) will be given legitimacy in ethical theory building. It thereby helps to minimize empirical bias, e.g., bias rising from faulty or false generalizations based on stereotyping, too small a sample size, or a skewed sample. It does so by ensuring that any generalizations which are made about ethics and ethical decision making include—indeed cohere with—the patterned voices of women.

Sixth, a feminist ethic makes no attempt to provide an "objective" point of view, since it assumes that in contemporary culture there really is no such point of view. As such, it does not claim to be "unbiased" in the sense of "value-neutral" or "objective." However, it does assume that whatever bias it has as an ethic centralizing the voices of oppressed persons is a *better bias*—"better" because it is more inclusive and therefore less partial—than those which exclude those voices.

Seventh, a feminist ethic provides a central place for values typically unnoticed, underplayed, or misrepresented in traditional ethics, e.g., values of care, love, friendship, and appropriate trust. Again, it need not do this at the exclusion of considerations of rights, rules, or utility. There may be many contexts in which talk of rights or of utility is useful or appropriate. For instance, in contracts or property relationships, talk of rights may be useful and appropriate. In deciding what is cost effective or advantageous to the most people, talk of utility may be useful and appropriate. In a feminist *qua* contextualist ethic, whether or not such talk is useful or appropriate depends on the context; *other values* (e.g., values of care, trust, friendship) are *not* viewed as reducible to or captured solely in terms of such talk.

Eighth, a feminist ethic also involves a reconception of what it is to be human and what it is for humans to engage in ethical decision making, since it rejects as either meaningless or currently untenable any gender-free or gender-neutral description of humans, ethics, and ethical decision making. It thereby rejects what Alison Jaggar calls "abstract individualism," i.e., the position that it is possible to identify a human essence or human nature that exists independently of any particular historical context. Humans and human moral conduct are properly understood essentially (and not merely accidentally) in terms of networks or webs of historical and concrete relationships.

All the props are now in place for seeing how ecofeminism provides the framework for a distinctively feminist and environmental ethic. It is a feminism that critiques male bias wherever it occurs in ethics (including environmental ethics) and aims at providing an ethic (including an environmental ethic) which is not male biased—and it does so in a way that satisfies the preliminary boundary conditions of a feminist ethic.

First, ecofeminism is quintessentially anti-naturist. Its anti-naturism consists in the rejection of any way of thinking about or acting toward nonhuman nature that reflects a logic, values, or attitude of domination. Its anti-naturist, anti-sexist, anti-racist, anti-classist (and so forth,

for all other "isms" of social domination) stance forms the outer boundary of the quilt: nothing gets on the quilt which is naturist, sexist, racist, classist, and so forth.

Second, ecofeminism is a contextualist ethic. It involves a shift *from* a conception of ethics as primarily a matter of rights, rules, or principles predetermined and applied in specific cases to entities viewed as competitors in the contest of moral standing, *to* a conception of ethics as growing out of what Jim Cheney calls "defining relationships," i.e., relationships conceived in some sense as defining who one is. As a contextualist ethic, it is not that rights, or rules, or principles are *not* relevant or important. Clearly they are in certain contexts and for certain purposes. It is just that what *makes* them relevant or important is that those to whom they apply are entities *in relationship with* others.

Ecofeminism also involves an ethical shift *from* granting moral consideration to nonhumans *exclusively* on the grounds of some similarity they share with humans (e.g., rationality, interests, moral agency, sentiency, rightholder status) *to* "a highly contextual account to see clearly what a human being is and what the nonhuman world might be, morally speaking, *for* human beings."[7] For an ecofeminist, *how* a moral agent is in relationship to another becomes of central significance, not simply *that* a moral agent is a moral agent or is bound by rights, duties, virtue, or utility to act in a certain way.

Third, ecofeminism is structurally pluralistic in that it presupposes and maintains difference—difference among humans as well as between humans and at least some elements of nonhuman nature. Thus, while ecofeminism denies the "nature/culture" split, it affirms that humans are both members of an ecological community (in some respects) and different from it (in other respects). Ecofeminism's attention to relationships and community is not, therefore, an erasure of difference but a respectful acknowledgment of it.

Fourth, ecofeminism reconceives theory as theory in process. It focuses on patterns of meaning which emerge, for instance, from the storytelling and first-person narratives of women (and others) who deplore the twin dominations of women and nature. The use of narrative is one way to ensure that the content of the ethic—the pattern of the quilt—may/will change over time, as the historical and material realities of women's lives change and as more is learned about women-nature connections and the destruction of the nonhuman world.

Fifth, ecofeminism is inclusivist. It emerges from the voices of women who experience the harmful domination of nature and the way that domination is tied to their domination as women. It emerges from listening to the voices of indigenous peoples such as Native Americans who have been dislocated from their land and have witnessed the attendant undermining of such values as appropriate reciprocity, sharing, and kinship that characterize traditional Indian culture. It emerges from listening to voices of those who, like Nathan Hare, critique traditional approaches to environmental ethics as white and bourgeois, and as failing to address issues of "black ecology" and the "ecology" of the inner city and urban spaces. It also emerges out of the voices of Chipko women who see the destruction of "earth, soil, and water" as intimately connected with their own inability to survive economically. With its emphasis on inclusivity and difference, ecofeminism provides a framework for recognizing that what counts as ecology and what counts as appropriate conduct toward both human and nonhuman environments is largely a matter of context.

Sixth, as a feminism, ecofeminism makes no attempt to provide an "objective" point of view. It is a social ecology. It recognizes the twin dominations of women and nature as social problems rooted both in very concrete, historical, socioeconomic circumstances and in oppressive patriarchal conceptual frameworks which maintain and sanction these circumstances.

Seventh, ecofeminism makes a central place for values of care, love, friendship, trust, and appropriate reciprocity—values that presuppose that our relationships to others are central to our understanding of who we are. It thereby gives voice to the sensitivity that in climbing a mountain, one is doing something in relationship with an "other," an "other" whom one can come to care about and treat respectfully.

Lastly, an ecofeminist ethic involves a reconception of what it means to be human, and in what human ethical behavior consists. Ecofeminism denies abstract individualism. Humans are who we are in large part by virtue of the historical and social contexts and the relationships we are in, including our relationships with nonhuman nature. Relationships are not something extrinsic to who we are, not an "add on" feature of human nature; they play an essential role in shaping what it is to be human. Relationships of humans to the nonhuman environment are, in part, constitutive of what it is to be a human.

By making visible the interconnections among the dominations of women and nature, ecofeminism shows that both are feminist issues and that explicit acknowledgment of both is vital to any responsible environmental ethic. Feminism *must* embrace ecological feminism if it is to end the domination of women because the domination of women is tied conceptually and historically to the domination of nature.

A responsible environmental ethic also *must* embrace feminism. Otherwise, even the seemingly most revolutionary, liberational, and holistic ecological ethic will fail to take seriously the interconnected dominations of nature and women that are so much a part of the historical legacy and conceptual framework that sanctions the exploitation of nonhuman nature. Failure to make visible these interconnected, twin dominations results in an inaccurate account of how it is that nature has been and continues to be dominated and exploited and produces an environmental ethic that lacks the depth necessary to be truly *inclusive* of the realities of persons who

at least in dominant Western culture have been intimately tied with that exploitation, viz., women. Whatever else can be said in favor of such holistic ethics, a failure to make visible ecofeminist insights into the common denominators of the twin oppressions of women and nature is to perpetuate, rather than overcome, the source of that oppression.

This last point deserves further attention. It may be objected that as long as the end result is "the same"—the development of an environmental ethic which does not emerge out of or reinforce an oppressive conceptual framework—it does not matter whether that ethic (or the ethic endorsed in getting there) is feminist or not. Hence, it simply is *not* the case that any adequate environmental ethic must be feminist. My argument, in contrast, has been that it *does* matter, and for three important reasons. First, there is the scholarly issue of accurately representing historical reality, and that, ecofeminists claim, requires acknowledging the historical feminization of nature and naturalization of women as part of the exploitation of nature. Second, I have shown that the conceptual connections between the domination of women and the domination of nature are located in an oppressive and, at least in Western societies, patriarchal conceptual framework characterized by a logic of domination. Thus, I have shown that failure to notice the nature of this connection leaves at best an incomplete, inaccurate, and partial account of what is required of a conceptually adequate environmental ethic. An ethic which *does not* acknowledge this is simply *not* the same as one that does, whatever else the similarities between them. Third, the claim that, in contemporary culture, one can have an adequate environmental ethic which is *not* feminist assumes that, in contemporary culture, the label *feminist* does not add anything crucial to the nature or description of environmental ethics. I have shown that at least in contemporary culture this is false, for the word *feminist* currently helps to clarify just *how* the domination of nature is conceptually linked to patriarchy and, hence, how the liberation of nature, is conceptually linked to the termination of patriarchy. Thus, because it has critical bite in contemporary culture, it serves as an important reminder that in contemporary sex-gendered, raced, classed, and naturist culture, an unlabeled position functions as a privileged and "unmarked" position. That is, without the addition of the word *feminist*, one presents environmental ethics as if it has no bias, including male-gender bias, which is just what ecofeminists deny: failure to notice the connections between the twin oppressions of women and nature *is* male-gender bias.

One of the goals of feminism is the eradication of all oppressive sex-gender (and related race, class, age, affectional preference) categories and the creation of a world in which *difference does not breed domination*—say, the world of 4001. *If* in 4001 an "adequate environmental ethic" is a "feminist environmental ethic," the word *feminist* may then be redundant and unnecessary. However, this is *not* 4001, and in terms of the current historical and conceptual reality the dominations of nature and of women are intimately connected. Failure to notice or make visible that connection in 1990 perpetuates the mistaken (and privileged) view that "environmental ethics" is *not* a feminist issue, and that *feminist* adds nothing to environmental ethics.

CONCLUSION

I have argued in this paper that ecofeminism provides a framework for a distinctively feminist and environmental ethic. Ecofeminism grows out of the felt and theorized about connections between the domination of women and the domination of nature. As a contextualist ethic, ecofeminism refocuses environmental ethics on what nature might mean, morally speaking, *for* humans, and on how the relational attitudes of humans to others—humans as well as nonhumans—sculpt both what it is to be human and the nature and ground of human responsibilities to the nonhuman environment. Part of what this refocusing does is to take seriously the voices of women and other oppressed persons in the construction of that ethic.

A Sioux elder once told me a story about his son. He sent his seven-year-old son to live with the child's grandparents on a Sioux reservation so that he could "learn the Indian ways." Part of what the grandparents taught the son was how to hunt and kill the four leggeds of the forest. As I heard the story, the boy was taught, "to shoot your four-legged brother in his hind area, slowing it down but not killing it. Then, take the four legged's head in your hands, and look into his eyes. The eyes are where all the suffering is. Look into your brother's eyes and feel his pain. Then, take your knife and cut the four-legged under his chin, here, on his neck, so that he dies quickly. And as you do, ask your brother, the four-legged, for forgiveness for what you do. Offer also a prayer of thanks to your four-legged kin for offering his body to you just now, when you need food to eat and clothing to wear. And promise the four-legged that you will put yourself back into the earth when you die, to become nourishment for the earth, and for the sister flowers, and for the bother deer. It is appropriate that you should offer this blessing for the four-legged and, in due time, reciprocate in turn with your body in this way, as the four-legged gives life to you for your survival." As I reflect upon that story, I am struck by the power of the environmental ethic that grows out of and takes seriously narrative, context, and such values and relational attitudes as care, loving percenption, and appropriate reciprocity, and doing what is appropriate in a given situation—however that notion of appropriateness eventually gets filled out. I am also struck by what one is able to see, once one begins to explore some of the historical

and conceptual connections between the dominations of women and of nature. A *re-conceiving* and *re-visioning* of both feminism and environmental ethics, is, I think, the power and promise of ecofeminism.

Notes

1. I discuss this in my paper, "Toward an Ecofeminist Ethic."
2. The account offered here is a revision of the account given earlier in my paper "Feminism and Ecology: Making Connections." I have changed the account to be about "oppressive" rather than strictly "patriarchal" conceptual frameworks in order to leave open the possibility that there may be some patriarchal conceptual frameworks (e.g., in non-Western cultures) which are *not* properly characterized as based on value dualisms.
3. Murray Bookchin, "Social Ecology versus 'Deep Ecology'," in *Green Perspectives: Newsletter of the Green Program Project*, no. 4–5 (Summer 1987): 9.
4. It may be that in contemporary Western society, which is so thoroughly structured by categories of gender, race, class, age, and affectional orientation, that there simply is no meaningful notion of "value-hierarchical thinking" which does not function in an oppressive context. For purposes of this paper, I leave that question open.
5. At an *experiential* level, some women are "women of color," poor, old, lesbian, Jewish, and physically challenged. Thus, if feminism is going to liberate these women, it also needs to end the racism, classism, heterosexism, anti-Semitism, and discrimination against the handicapped that is constitutive of their oppression as black or Latina, or poor, or older, or lesbian, or Jewish, or physically challenged women.
6. Marilyn Frye, "In and Out of Harm's Way: Arrogance and Love," *The Politics of Reality* (Trumansburg, New York: The Crossing Press, 1983), pp. 66–76.
7. Cheney, "Eco-Feminism and Deep Ecology," p. 144.

Study Questions

1. Evaluate Warren's thesis that environmental ethics and feminist theory are necessary for one another. What are her arguments for this position? How strong are these arguments?
2. Does Warren claim that all value dualisms and hierarchies are bad? If not, which are legitimate? What does the "context" have to do with such evaluations?
3. Why exactly is it wrong for humans to dominate nature? Does Warren offer cogent arguments on this point?
4. Warren's sixth point regarding a feminist ethics is that it "makes no attempt to provide an 'objective' point of view, since it assumes that in contemporary culture there really is no such point of view." Do you agree with this? If it is impossible to argue objectively or reach an objective point of view, what implications does this have for her own arguments and position in this essay?

5. In the same paragraph that Warren discusses objectivity (see Question 4 above), she says that the feminist is just as biased as his or her opponent, but that this is a "better bias." What does Warren mean by "better bias," and what is her argument for it? Why is being inclusive better than being selective? Is she right? Explain.

27

A Critique of Ecofeminism

Margarita Garcia Levin

Margarita Garcia Levin received her Ph.D. from the University of Minnesota and teaches philosophy at Yeshiva University in New York City.

Levin first identifies three theses in Karen Warren's article:

1. *The "logic of domination" is used to justify sexism, according to which men are entitled to dominate what they are superior to, and they are superior to women.*
2. *The same logic of domination accounts for naturism, the oppression of nature.*
3. *Because of the similarity in the arguments that lead to their oppression, women must make common cause with nature, so that ecofeminism is the only appropriate response to both sexism and naturism.*

Levin then criticizes each of these theses, arguing that Warren has not supported any of them with good argument and that there are better explanations for the kind of behavior we witness between the sexes and between humans and nature.

Karen J. Warren's article "The Power and the Promise of Ecological Feminism" has two goals: to explain why feminists should be *eco*feminists and to give some indication of what ecofeminism means.

The argument in support of the first goal boils down to three sentences:

1. The oppression of women—sexism—is justified by a "logic of domination," according to which men are entitled to dominate what they are superior to, and men are superior to women.
2. The oppression of nature—naturism—is justified in the same way; men are entitled to dominate nature because of their superiority to nature.
3. Because of this similarity in the arguments that lead to their oppression, women must make common cause with nature.

Ecofeminism is the only appropriate response to both sexism and naturism.[1]

This essay was commissioned for the first edition of this work.

Warren's formulation of this argument, and indeed her entire discussion is extremely vague and loose. At no point does she define "oppression." Furthermore, her definition of "feminist issue" as anything "that contributes in some way to understanding the oppression of women" is so wide-open that, under it, the demolition of NOW [National Organization of Women] headquarters by an errant meteorite would raise "feminist issues," since it would presumably have the effect of reducing the capacity of women to fight their oppression. If this construal of Warren's words seems uncharitable, consider her own example, the introduction of Eucalyptus trees, as a monoculture species tree, in rural India, said to be a feminist issue because it reduces the ability of Indian women to find food, fuel and medicine. Has Warren forgotten that Indian men have an equal need for food, fuel and medicine? But the main point is that the *purpose* of introducing the monoculture species tree was commerce, not making the lives of women more difficult, although this may have been a side-effect. A definition of oppression that ignores intent really is going to sweep in almost anything that affects women.[2]

Speaking more broadly, the lack of concrete examples that would give us an idea of what Prof. Warren considers to be oppression—is it inability to vote, inability to divorce an unwanted spouse, less pay for more work, social expectations that women will marry and rear children?—illustrates how feminists talk only to each other and make no concessions to the possibility that their readers may not accept their basic assumptions. It is simply taken as self-evident, without argument, that women are oppressed and that this oppression must be ended.

Focusing on what we call sentence 1, Warren gives no reference to any statement of the view that men are entitled to dominate women because they are superior, and in fact this view is a caricature. Some men may well think this way, but the usual justifications for male dominance have been either utilitarian or biological. The utilitarian argument runs that both women and men will be happier in the long run if men run things because men, being more objective, analytical and comfortable giving orders, are better at running things. One may dispute this position—by claiming, for instance, that women could run things as well as men if given the chance—but it clearly takes the well-being of women as seriously as that of men. Thus, when sincerely held, the utilitarian argument cannot be called "oppressive."

The biological (quasi-)justification of male dominance is somewhat similar, although it lacks a prescriptive edge. It begins from the apparently innate greater aggressiveness of men, a sex difference which manifests itself, among other ways, in a greater male desire to attain positions of power and status. The primary scientific evidence for this sex difference is a series of "natural experiments" in which females while still in the womb were accidentally exposed to male hormones, and males still in the womb went unexposed to male hormones. In the jargon of neurology, the brains of the females were "fetally virilized," while the brains of the males were not. Despite receiving conventional socialization after birth, the subjects of these experiments went on in childhood and adulthood to exhibit the "stereotyped" traits of the sex opposite. This evidence from fetal virilization has lately been supplemented by the discovery of anatomical and functional differences between male and female brains, and of course there is in addition the anthropological evidence that men have dominated the positions of power in every known society.[3] So we must conclude—the biological argument continues—that men attain positions of power and status much more frequently than women because they *want* those positions more intensely than women do. These biological facts are not cited to show that male dominance is morally *better* than other thinkable social arrangements, any more than biology can be cited to show that walking upright is a morally better way for human beings to get around than waving their arms and flying. Rather, because "ought implies can," biology shows, first, that moral criticism of male dominance has no more point than moral criticism of walking as opposed to flying. But in addition, the biological facts imply that male dominance is not "oppressive." It does not arise from power-hungry men thwarting equally-power-hungry women. Rather, men run things because they want to, and women do other things, like attend to children, form social networks, and care for their more competitive menfolk, because *they* want to. Sex roles express the preferences of men and women. Their persistence does not involve coercion.

To be sure, nobody knew about fetal hormonalization before the present century, so that knowledge could hardly have informed traditional attitudes toward men and women. However, the perception that "boys are naturally more competitive than girls" is as old as civilization, and was never questioned by anyone until Kate Millett, Simone de Beauvoir, Elizabeth Janeway and other feminists flat-out denied it (on the basis of absolutely no evidence) a few years ago. It has been equally obvious for equally long that men mostly battle *each other,* not women, for power and status. So these perceptions may certainly be supposed to have played a major role in the traditional idea that it is "natural" for men to run things.

Sentence 2 of Warren's argument, like sentence 1, also corresponds to an idea that has had some currency, but, like sentence 1, it does very much less than justice to the way people actually think ("at least in Western society," as Prof. Warren might add). Few people would claim an individual or collective right to "dominate" nature. They would claim a right to *use* nature in the interest of their survival and prosperity. And they would not base this prerogative on man's superiority, but on what Francis Bacon called "the right of necessity." We cannot live without eating animals, harvesting crops and removing minerals from the Earth. We do what we must. Furthermore, like innate sex differences, our impulse to exploit nature cannot reasonably be criticized because it is beyond our control: every human being—every living thing—has a powerful innate drive to preserve his own existence, and, in the more recently evolved animals, an even more powerful drive to preserve the existence of his offspring. This willingness to see the rest of the world as a means for preserving one's own existence and that of one's children is inevitable in any life-form that transmits its traits to its offspring. For imagine a gene that did *not* code for this drive. It would obviously be at a disadvantage when competing for resources with genes that did code for self- and offspring-preservation at all costs. It would reproduce less readily and quickly disappear. In Heaven the lion and the lamb can lie down together because the lion need not take in energy from the environment, but the human sense of what man is entitled to do was shaped by conditions on Earth, where the needs of different creatures do not necessarily harmonize.

As with sex differences in competitiveness, the scientific reasons for the drive for self-preservation were not understood until recently, but the awareness that this drive exists must certainly be as old as mankind itself. So there is nothing anachronistic in thinking that the need to survive, rather than a conviction of "superiority," has significantly shaped our feeling of entitlement to use nature.

In short, it is only by speaking in her vague and jargon-ridden way that Prof. Warren can even make it appear that "Sexism is conceptually linked with naturism through an oppressive conceptual framework characterized by a logic of domination." If women and nature are "oppressed" at all, they are so in very different ways and for entirely different reasons. It is quite true that women are sometimes said to be more "natural" than men, where this means that they are more emotional and spontaneous, and less concerned with analyzing and following rules. Prof. Warren would seem to endorse this saying, although it is usually cited as a paradigm of the sort of stereotyping she also deplores. However, women being more "natural" in this sense hardly suggests that there is some "oppressive conceptual framework" subsuming the treatment of both.

There is a final lacuna in Prof. Warren's premises worth noting. In her article about the oppression of women and nature, with asides about the oppression of blacks, homosexuals and Jewish women (see e.g. note 5), there is not one indication of who the oppressor is. Equally curiously, there are hardly any references to men. Surely these two omissions are more than coincidence, and they strongly suggest that the supposed oppressors behind patriarchal culture are, in fact, men, in particular white men. Now perhaps Prof. Warren does not explicitly identify men as the oppressors because she thinks they, too, are victims of an oppressive conceptual framework, having been duped by the men-are-superior argument into oppressing women and nature. Many feminists do say such things as, "sexism oppresses men as well as women." But surely such a position would reify conceptual schemes to an extent inconsistent with Prof. Warren's overall stress that the "twin dominations" are rooted in "concrete, historical, socioeconomic circumstances." Historicism that insistent must derive the power of propositions from the concrete, etc. circumstances in which they are used, and when propositions are used they are used by somebody. And that somebody would have to be men. So either Warren finds it too obvious to need stating that men are the oppressors, or perhaps she is so pained by the damage men have done to the social and natural world that she cannot bear to mention their name. Or perhaps some more obscure factor is at work.

But let us suppose both of Prof. Warren's premises are true. Let us agree that there is a single pattern of thought used to justify the domination of women and the domination of nature. Prof. Warren takes it to follow immediately that anyone who opposes one of these forms of domination must oppose the other—that the cause of women against their oppressors is also the cause of nature, or in the words of a slogan of the 1960s, "Same struggle, same fight." But natural as this inference may appear, it is quite wrong.

Consider first the relation of men to their weapons and their vehicles. This relationship is in fact one of domination; men do what they want to with these things, using them as tools, taking them for joyrides, and the like. In certain respects men treat their vehicles and weapons as if they were women: they refer to ships as "she," and give their guns female names ("Big Bertha"). Does it follow that women should see themselves as in some way similar to weapons, or think that their liberation is tied to the liberation of weapons, just because (as we have agreed) men dominate their women and their weapons? I take this as a *reductio ad absurdum*, but Warren might not: she might well maintain that there is a valid point here, namely that the struggle to liberate women *is* linked to the struggle to cease using weapons as weapons—that is, feminism and pacifism are as naturally allied as feminism and anti-naturism. Very well, then, consider the attitude of the Nazis to the Jews. The Nazis spoke of Jews as vermin and a disease infecting Germany. In other words, the Nazis created a conceptual link between anti-Semitism and the germ theory of disease. It hardly follows that anyone who opposed Nazism had to oppose the germ theory of disease. Another counterexample: during the era of slavery, slaves were treated like animals, and legally classified with animals and furniture as chattel property. Within broad limits, the owner of a slave and a horse could do whatever he wanted with either. Surely this does not mean that there is a "conceptual link" between human slaves and animals, and that abolishing property rights is necessary for the overthrow of slavery.

In effect, Prof. Warren is assuming that if a person or group of people A thinks B is similar to C, and for this reason treats B and C similarly, opposition to A's treatment of B requires opposition to A's treatment of C. Quite to the contrary, just because A *thinks* B resembles C, and links B and C in his own mind, that doesn't mean that there really is a connection between them. Just because slave-holders thought that slaves, animals and furniture could all be treated as property doesn't mean that slaves *are* property, or that slaves are property if and only if furniture is. In historical fact, the enslavement of human beings was abolished not by ending the ownership of both people and animals, but by legally severing the link between them. The Emancipation Proclamation freed the slaves in the American south and left furniture still owned. Perhaps, again speaking generally, A is half-right about B and C; his treatment of B is proper but his treatment of C is not.

So Prof. Warren's argument collapses. That women and nature are treated alike by some unidentified oppressor, and are grouped together by a (presumably fallacious) logic of oppression, does not imply that a change in the treatment of women requires a change in the treatment of nature. What is needed is the additional premise that the oppression of women and nature is equally wrong, and that the logic of oppression is wrong about women in precisely the way it is wrong about nature. Absent that premise, the logic of oppression might be half-right—it might be wrong for men to dominate women, for instance, but perfectly all right for men, and women, to dominate nature.

And certainly women *are* prima facie very unlike rocks and plants, the paradigms of nature mentioned in Prof. Warren's article. Women can think, feel and entertain hopes, none of which rocks can do. In fact, dare I say it, the average woman resembles the average man much more than she resembles the average rock.

Now at this point Prof. Warren's reasoning becomes extremely difficult to follow. One would have thought that traits like susceptibility to pain are what endow women (and men) with special rights, protecting them from being treated any old way, and that a moral outlook which recognizes the special status of women (and men) would be to that extent welcome. But Warren very strongly implies that, absent a "logic of domination" characteristics like reason and susceptibility to pain are irrelevant to how anything should be treated. "[W]ithout a logic of domination," she says, "a description of similarities and differences would be just that—a description of similarities and differences." It is the "logic of domination" that takes us from the premise that X thinks and feels while rocks do not, to the conclusion that X is superior to rocks (and therefore, of course, entitled to dominate rocks.) But then, on the whole, the logic of domination starts to look like *a very good thing* for women, as well as for all other entities that can think and feel. For if Prof. Warren is right, it is precisely the logic of domination that takes us from the premise that women think and feel while rocks do not, to the conclusion that certain permissible ways of treating rocks, like dropping them from a great height to see if they break, and using them as ballast in the holds of ships, are not permissible ways to treat women. Particular versions of the "logic of domination" might construe women as not endowed with quite as many rights as men, but, on Prof. Warren's showing, any logic of domination will be a Godsend.

So why is Warren so unrelievedly negative about "the logic of domination"? What is going on? Two things. The first, relatively minor factor that blinds Prof. Warren to the merits of "value-hierarchical thinking" is the belief that judging one thing to be better than another must bring domination into the picture, at least in contemporary Western society. This of course is not true. One can judge that certain descriptive differences between works of art make some works of art better than others without believing that artists whose work is better are entitled to lord it over artists whose work is inferior. It is a not terribly exciting consequence of the is/ought distinction that descriptive differences between entities carry no moral force unless supplemented by a principle to the effect that these differences are morally relevant in *some way*. Descriptive differences between people and rocks by themselves are morally inert. But there is no reason a moral principle that engages descriptive differences must prescribe domination. After all, Prof. Warren herself makes moral distinctions. She says in so many words that ecofeminism is "*better*" than sexism, which sounds awfully "value-hierarchical."[4] Does this commit her to thinking that ecofeminists ought to dominate sexists?

But the second and much deeper contributing cause of Prof. Warren's confusion is her failure to notice that, in the "oppressive" principle that "humans are superior to nature" (and therefore entitled to dominate it), "human" covers women as well as men. She is right to think that "humans" do use "value-dualisms" to give themselves privileges they deny to nature, but—we conjecture—since she conceives these privileges as a device of patriarchy, she assumes that they must serve only the interests of the patriarchs, which is to say men. This con-

jecture imputes an extraordinary degree of obtuseness to Prof. Warren, but I see no other way of explaining her failure to see that the "value-hierarchic" logic which puts humans over nature puts women over nature. To appreciate Prof. Warren's muddle, recall those Indian women using plants for fuel and medicine. Aren't these women also dominating nature, and don't they, and we, think they have a right to? If asked, wouldn't Indian men and women agree that there are crucial differences between Indian women and "plants and rocks"? The fact is that, if women come out on the losing side when dominance logic is applied to men and women, women come out on the winning side when dominance logic is applied to humans and nature. This alone would show that the relation of men to women has little to do with the relation of either men or "humans" to nature.

We have all learned from Popper and the empiricists to distrust claims which rule nothing out; claims which are true no matter what may sound meaningful, but they aren't. The same caution should be exercised toward ethical theories. However high-sounding its language, the measure of an ethical theory is its do's and don't's. We need to know what it commands and what it forbids, the difference (if any) between following and violating it. I have already remarked on the extreme vagueness of "oppression" and its cognates as used by Warren and other feminists, so particular attention must be paid to what an ecofeminist would do that a sexist or naturist ethic would not. "Ecofeminists fight sexism and the oppression of nature" is the promissory note; now we want its cash value. Would an ecofeminist cull deer herds? Would she let forest fires burn themselves out? How would she weigh the aesthetic value of a vista against the economic value of development? Would it be all right to burn some rain forest if so doing was necessary to save a herd of elephants? Should Eskimos with no other resources be permitted to hunt whales, or should they be publicly supported on a reservation (where they will drink themselves to oblivion)? Demanding a list of specifics may appear inappropriate, even rude, but grandiose promises about "the dismantling of patriarchal conceptual frameworks" invites it.

In fact, Warren's essay supplies few indications of how ecofeminism would work. We are told that the ecofeminist ethic is a "tapestry of voices [sic]" that is "inclusive" (but not too inclusive; see note 4), and gives care, love and trust "a central place." One might suppose that, along with "naturist, sexist, racist, classist and so forth" ideas, traditional masculine concern with overall utility and rights is also excluded, but that is not so. We are told, tautologically, that "In deciding what is cost-effective or advantageous to the most people, talk of utility may be useful and appropriate." We are also told, again tautologically, that rights and rules are "relevant and important, for example, in relationships involving contracts and promises. . . It is just that what *makes* them relevant or important is that those to whom they apply are entities *in relationship with* others." The italics suggest that Prof. Warren believes the reference to relationships adds something, but it does not. It is logically impossible for one parry to have made a promise or created a contract with another *without* a relationship existing between them, if only the relation of "having contracted." We had better look elsewhere for guidance.

One example of ecofeminism in action that is discussed at some length is the way of the ecofeminist rock climber. This passage defies easy summary, but its drift is that, for an ecofeminist, "The Rock Is My Friend." Instead of climbing the rock as a conqueror, one climbs it with a "loving eye." One *acknowledges* the rock, one enters into a "*relationship*" with it. "One recognizes the rock as something very different, something perhaps totally indifferent to one's own presence [perhaps?], and finds in that difference joyous occasion for celebration." Presumably the mood turns less celebratory if one finds one's hold slipping, but Prof. Warren does not explore this possibility. Actually, this possibility is crucial. The climbing narrative does *not* suggest that the proper attitude is rock-is-my-friend. Rock-is-my-friend was the narrator's attitude when on firm ground taking in the view, etc.; to really show that rock-is-my-friend is *always* the proper attitude, the narrator would have to recount climbing the rock face without adopting a task-oriented, rock-as-thing-to-be-conquered attitude. Rocks do not reciprocate friendship; if you slip they will not reach out loving ledges to catch you.

In any event, the rock-climbing narrative Prof. Warren displays is of no evidential value, because she does not indicate its source . This is most curious, for she is otherwise far from shy about dropping footnotes. If Prof. Warren herself or another feminist wrote the passage to illustrate what an ecofeminist narrative would be like, it obviously does not show that anyone could really feel the way the narrator describes herself as feeling. One could as easily "prove" that women like brutality by writing a work of fiction in which a woman is sexually aroused by being raped. If on the other hand the passage is authentic and entirely sincere, I must note that "joy" at a rock's (possible) indifference is what psychologists call "inappropriate affect," and might predict deviant scores on the Schizophrenia and Psychoticism scales of the Minnesota Multiphasic Personality Inventory.

Apparently the big difference that feminism makes is one of *feeling*:

> [H]ow one climbs a mountain and *how* one narrates— or tells the story—about the experience of climbing are also *feminist issues*. In this way, ecofeminism makes visible why, at a conceptual level, environmental ethics *is* a feminist issue.

It could equally well be argued that dental hygiene is a feminist issue. One can attack plaque, tartar and cavities with the intention of destroying all traces of them, and while affirming the hierarchy of periodontism, reinforce the oppressive conceptual framework that sanctions sexism, racism, heterosexism, ageism and classism. Or, one can approach one's mouth with a loving perception (and toothbrush) and an awareness of our relationship to our teeth and our gums that affirms our oneness with nature, presupposing and maintaining our difference from our teeth, and respecting our teeth as different from ourselves.

The alarming thought that occurs is that Warren would probably agree with and welcome this account of toothbrushing if it appeared as a narrative in a feminist journal.

Let me make it clear that I am not condemning or ridiculing the love of nature. The meteorologist who accompanied Scott to the Antarctic wrote that he had joined the expedition "to see the wonders God created," and such feelings deserve the profoundest respect. But they are quite unlike the feelings of ecofeminists. These, if Prof. Warren is to be trusted, do not lift the mind to something higher, be it God or simply man's insignificance in the scheme of things, but are, to the contrary, highly self-congratulatory. The focus of ecofeminist nature-love is not nature at all, but the nature-lover. It is, in other words, anthropocentric and not a little narcissistic.

The final example of ecofeminism at work is Warren's version of the Sioux way to hunt deer. Instead of killing the deer as quickly as possible, the idea is to wound the deer so it will suffer, and while it is suffering you are to look into his eyes, "feel his pain," thank him for "offering his body," and then kill it. I do not doubt that Indians found it necessary to hobble deer before killing them, since an animal's hindquarters present the best target to a bowman, and it is almost impossible to propel an arrow into a large animal's heart. But the rest of the procedure described by Prof. Warren will appall anyone opposed to the needless suffering of animals, and it is foolish in its own right. A hunter can see that his prey is suffering, but he does not and cannot literally feel his prey's pain. Hunting hurts the deer more than the Sioux, and it is nonsense to pretend otherwise. Nor does the animal offer his body to the hunter. He tries to get away, and would be a great deal happier if the hunter misses. Apparently, the ecofeminist ideal is to make the wounded deer suffer longer than necessary for the sake of a ritual that is difficult to distinguish from posturing. Let me be clear, once again, that I do not condemn the hunter for bringing down the deer. Predation and pain are part of the order of things, and only a Hamlet would brood about them unduly. But I do object to doubletalk.

If I am so negative about "ecofeminism," it is as

much because of an absence as it is because of the presence of the errors and confusions we have identified. Absent from Warren's essay is any real contact with the world, or with the sexes whose relations she professes to wish to rectify. There is no real effort to come to grips with men and women as part of the natural world. It is difficult to expect insight when men and women are given no other roles than filling slots in theories about oppression.

Notes

1. The reader may wonder if I have not omitted something, but the possible impression that Prof. Warren's argument contains more may be created by her repetitiveness. This repetitiveness does not consist solely of her repeating her thesis a great many times, but also in the repeated use of formulaic phrases—"logic of domination," "the twin dominations of women and nature," "oppressive conceptual frameworks"—always marching en bloc.

2. Once again these remarks may appear unfair, because Prof. Warren does observe the forms of precision. She says, to take one of many instances, "a wolf cannot have or properly be said to have or stand in a moral relation with a moose," as if seeking to distinguish these phenomena. However, there is no difference whatever between having a relation, standing in a relation, and being properly described as standing in a relation. What is unclear remains unclear, while what is clear is repeated.

3. For a survey of the evidence with references as of mid-1980s, see Michael Levin, *Feminism and Freedom* (New Brunswick, NJ: Transaction Press, 1987). A somewhat more recent survey is Anne Moir and David Jessel, *Brain Sex* (New York: Lyle Stuart, 1991). See also Doreen Kimura, "Sex Differences in the Brain," *Scientific American* (September 1992).

4. Warren's reason for endorsing ecofeminism is its "inclusiveness," its favoring "patterns of voices [expressing] the felt experiences and perspectives of oppressed person." This, she admits, is a bias. However, she says it is a "*better bias.*" Why? Because "it is more inclusive and therefore less partial—than those which exclude those voices." In other words, favoring the voices of the oppressed is better than not favoring them because it is better. An argument could not be more blatantly circular.

Her footnote 4 seems to leave open the possibility that there might be some hierarchical thinking "in contemporary Western society" which does not involve oppression, but she is clearly very dubious.

Study Questions

1. Compare Levin's critique with Warren's original article. Identify Levin's main criticisms. How cogent are they? How might Warren respond to them? Evaluate each of Levin's major objections.

2. Is Levin fair to Warren? Do they proceed from fundamentally different assumptions about the basic relationships between males and females?

3. Levin writes that "We cannot live without eating animals, harvesting crops and removing minerals from the Earth. We do what we must. Furthermore, like innate sex differences, our impulse to exploit nature cannot reasonably be criticized because it is beyond our control . . ." Is this completely correct? Do we have to eat animals? Are our impulses to exploit nature beyond our control? Discuss your views in relationship to Levin's claims.

For Further Reading

Biehl, Janet. *Rethinking Ecofeminist Politics.* Boston: South End Press, 1991.

Cheney, Jim. "Eco-Feminism and Deep Ecology." *Environmental Ethics* 9 (1987).

Griffin. *Woman and Nature: The Roaring Inside Her.* San Francisco: Harper & Row, 1978.

Levin, Michael. *Feminism and Freedom.* New Brunswick, NJ: Transaction, 1987.

Merchant, Carolyn. *The Death of Nature: Women, Ecology, and the Scientific Revolution.* San Francisco: Harper & Row, 1980.

Plant, Judith, ed. *Healing the Wounds: The Promise of Ecofeminism.* Philadelphia: New Society Publishers, 1989.

Salleh, Ariel. "Deeper than Deep Ecology: The Eco-Feminist Connection." *Environmental Ethics* 6 (1984).

Warren, Karen J. "Feminism and Ecology: Making Connections." *Environmental Ethics* 9 (1987).

Zimmerman, Michael. "Feminism, Deep Ecology and Environmental Ethics." *Environmental Ethics* 9 (1987).

CHAPTER FIVE

The Gaia Hypothesis and Biospheric Ethics

Gaia, mother of all, I sing, oldest of gods,
Firm of foundation, who feeds all creatures living on
  Earth,
As many as move on the radiant land and swim in the sea
And fly through the air—all these does she feed with her
  bounty.
Mistress, from you come our fine children and bountiful
  harvests,
Yours is the power to give mortals life and to take it
  away.[1]

Gaia is the name for the ancient Greek goddess mother Earth. She represents the theory that Earth is a holistic organism, a living being, rather than an inert planet with living systems on it. The idea is not new. Plato speaks of the World Soul in the *Timaeus*, and Lucretius believed that Earth was a mortal being, which will grow old and finally die. The Hellenistic Jew Philo speaks of Nature as a great "All-Mother," "most ancient and most fertile of mothers . . . by way of breasts, streams of rivers and springs, bestowing [food for her children], to the end that both the plants might be watered and all animals might have abundance to drink" (*On Creation*, 133).

The idea of Earth as a Great Mother goddess was rejected by the early Christians as an idolotrous myth. "Thou shalt have no other gods before me," says the God of the Hebrews and Christians, which includes the goddess Gaia. So the idea largely died out in the West. But in the late 1960s, the British atmospheric scientist James Lovelock set forth an hypothesis about Earth, which recalled the earlier Greek ideas. Lovelock, in studying Earth's atmosphere and then comparing it with those of Mars and Venus discovered that our atmosphere was in a state of disequilibrium and no way could account for it short of the hypothesis that Earth was a self-sustaining giant organism. That is, if Earth were governed simply by geochemical systems (rather than by biological systems) like Mars and Venus, its atmosphere would have been largely carbon dioxide and nitrogen, as on Mars and Venus, in which case life would have not appeared. The composition of Earth's atmosphere, which is about 20% oxygen in the presence of highly reactive gases such as hydrogen and methane, differs from her neighbors Mars and Venus, whose atmospheres are 90% carbon dioxide. Through various feedback systems our planet functions in a mutually supportive, holistic manner so as to maintain a remarkable atmospheric equilibrium of gases in which life progresses. Gaia has goals of her own and will survive without human beings, but, Lovelock muses, humanity may have been created by Gaia as the central nervous system to help protect her from catastrophe

However, humans can harm their Mother, and ultimately themselves, by overpolluting, by destroying ecosystems, and by reducing the natural variety necessary for homeostasis. Lovelock calls on us to "make peace with Gaia on her terms and return to peaceful co-existence with our fellow creatures." This new harmony with Gaia will include preservation of species diversity and a rejection of the crude technocracy that regards Nature only as a resource. It will mean a new biospheric ethics.

Here is Lovelock's assessment of the meaning of Gaia:

> Art and science seem interconnected with each other and with religion, and to be mutually enlarging. That Gaia can be both spiritual and scientific, is, for me, deeply satisfying. From letters and conversations I have learnt that a feeling for the organism, the Earth, has survived and that many feel a need to include those old faiths in their system of belief, both for themselves and because they feel that Earth of which they are a part is under threat. In no way do I see Gaia as a sentient being, a surrogate God. To me Gaia is alive and part of the ineffable Universe and I am part of her.
>
> When that great and good man Pope John Paul travels around the world, he, in an act of great humility and respect for the Mother or Father Land, bends down and kisses the airport tarmac. I sometimes imagine him walking those few steps beyond the dead concrete to kiss the living grass; part of our true Mother and of ourselves.[2]

The Gaia hypothesis is a renewal of ancient ideas dressed in the clothes of new science. The question is whether it is anything more than a new myth or suggestive metaphor. In our second reading, James Kirchner analyzes the Gaia hypothesis, showing that there are five different Gaia hypotheses. He argues that the weak versions are not new and the strong versions are not testable. "At best, such theories do not explain observable phenomena, they just give them new names. At worst, they give one a very idiosyncratic view, which nobody else can verify or falsify, of personal experience."

Notes

1. J. Donald Hughes, *Gaia: An Ancient View of Our Planet* quoted in James Lovelock, *The Ages of Gaia* (New York: Norton, 1988).
2. Ibid.

28

In Quest for Gaia

JAMES LOVELOCK AND SIDNEY EPTON

James Lovelock is a British atmospheric chemist, who worked on the unmanned Martian lander project for NASA and the author of numerous works on the Gaia hypothesis, which he set forth in the late 1960s. Sidney Epton is a scientist at Shell's Thronton Research Center, also in England.

Lovelock and Epton ask us to consider whether Earth's living matter, air, oceans and land surface form part of a giant system, a single biological organism. They present the scientific case for such a holistic hypothesis. Then they ask, "Could man's activities reduce such a system's options so that it is no longer able to exert sufficient control to stay viable?" They answer that the answer is very likely "yes." To that end, we must adopt a new Gaian ethic.

Do the Earth's living matter, air, oceans and land surface form part of a giant system which could be seen as a single organism? Could man's activities reduce such a system's options so that it is no longer able to exert sufficient control to stay viable? Consider the following propositions:

1. Life exists only because material conditions on Earth happen to be just right for its existence:
2. Life defines the material conditions needed for its survival and makes sure that they stay there.

The first of these is the conventional wisdom. It implies that life has stood poised like a needle on its point for over 3500 million years. If the temperature or humidity or salinity or acidity or any one of a number of other variables had strayed outside a narrow range of values for any length of time, life would have been annihilated.

Proposition 2 is an unconventional view. It implies that living matter is not passive in the face of threats to its existence. It has found means, as it were, of driving the point of the needle into the table, of forcing conditions to stay within the permissible range. This article supports and develops this view.

The Sun, being a typical star of the main sequence, has evolved according to a standard and well-established pattern. A consequence of this is that during the Earth's existence the Sun's output of energy has increased substantially. The Earth now receives between 1.4 and 3.3 times more energy than it did just after its formation 4000 million years ago. The Earth's surface temperature at the time when life began has been calculated. These calculations take into account the solar input, the radiative properties of the surface and the composition of the atmosphere. At that time, the atmosphere probably contained ammonia and other complex molecules which acted like the glass in a greenhouse, that is, by reducing the radiation of heat and long-wave infra-red radiation from Earth. The calculations show that the surface temperature could indeed have been within the range we now know to be needed to start life off.

Once life began, it fed on the atmospheric blanket. Unless some means had existed for restoring to it heat-retaining gases such as ammonia, or of altering the Earth's surface to make it more heat-retentive, the planet would surely have become uniformly icebound and lifeless. The rate of increase of solar energy would have been too small to compensate. Yet the fossil record and the continuity of life gives no support to this conclusion. At the time of supposed emergence from glaciation, that is, when the radiation from the more active Sun had made up for the radiation loss due to loss of the heat-retaining gases, and when only the feeble beginnings of a new life should have been possible, complex multi-celled organisms had already evolved. Life must have found a way of keeping the temperature of the Earth's surface within the critical range of 15–30°C for hundreds of millions of years in spite of drastic changes of atmospheric composition and a large increase in the mean solar flux. The calculations were wrong because they left out the effect of the defence mechanism that life uses to protect itself.

Extinction through glaciation was not the only dan-

Reprinted from *New Scientist* (Feb. 1975).

ger. Overproduction of ammonia and other heat-retaining gases could have resulted in the opposite effect, known as the "runaway greenhouse," that is to a rapidly increasing surface temperature that would have scorched the Earth and left it permanently lifeless, as is the planet Venus now. The evidence that this did nor happen is plain—we would not have written these words nor would you be reading them (Figure 1).

Has life been able to control other conditions of existence besides the surface temperature of the Earth? A most significant fact about the Earth is the composition of its atmosphere. Almost everything about its composition seems to violate the laws of chemistry. If chemical thermodynamics alone mattered, almost all the oxygen and most of the nitrogen in the atmosphere ought to have ended up in the sea combined as nitrate ion. The air we breathe cannot be a very fortunate once-off emanation from the rocks; it can only be an artefact maintained in a steady state far from chemical equilibrium by biological processes.

The significance of this was first realised some years ago when one of us, in association with Dian Hitchcock, took up the problem of deciding whether it would be possible to detect life on Mars by the use only of spectroscopic observations on its atmosphere. Our suggestion was to look for any combination of constituents that was far from chemical equilibrium; if such was found life might exist there. (So far no such combination has been detected on either Mars or Venus.)

GAIA

It appeared to us that the Earth's biosphere was able to control at least the temperature of the Earth's surface

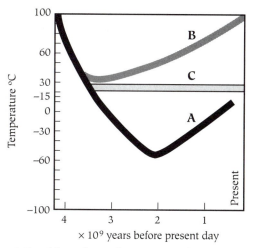

FIGURE 1 *Possible and actual temperature history of the Earth's surface. A, Possible history if living matter had not produced enough heat-retaining gases, etc.; B, possible history if living matter had over-produced heat-retaining gases (runaway greenhouse); C, actual temperature history.*

and the composition of the atmosphere. Prima facie, the atmosphere looked like a contrivance put together co-operatively by the totality of living systems to carry out certain necessary control functions. This led us to the formulation of the proposition that living matter, the air, the oceans, the land surface were parts of a giant system which was able to control temperature, the composition of the air and sea, the pH of the soil and so on so as to be optimum for survival of the biosphere The system seemed to exhibit the behaviour of a single organism, even a living creature. One having such formidable powers deserved a name to match it; William Golding, the novelist, suggested Gaia—the name given by the ancient Greeks to their Earth goddess.

The past three years have been spent in exploring and elaborating the Gaia hypothesis (in collaboration with Lynn Margulis) and checking its implications against fact. It has proved to be fruitful. It has led us along many paths and by-paths, and valuable insights have been gained especially about the consequences of Man's interaction with the biosphere. The following is a selection of some of the interesting things we have found on the way.

ATMOSPHERIC CONSTITUENTS

If Gaia is a living entity we have the right to ask questions such as "what purpose does constituent X serve in the atmosphere?" As an example, the biosphere produces about 1000 million tons of ammonia a year. Why?

As already pointed out, in early times, when the Sun was cooler than it is now, ammonia served to keep the Earth warm. At the present time, the need for ammonia is different and just as important, because we believe that ammonia keeps the soil near to pH 8 which is an optimum value for living processes. It is needed because a consequence of having nitrogen and sulphur-containing substances in the air in the presence of a vast excess of oxygen is their tendency to combine to produce strongly acid materials—thunderstorms produce tons of nitric acid and if there were no regulator such as ammonia the soil would become sour and hostile to most organisms.

Another of our beliefs is that one of the purposes of the small but definite amount of methane in the atmosphere is to regulate the oxygen content. Methane is a product of anaerobic fermentation in soil and sea. Some of the methane rises into the stratosphere where it oxidises to carbon dioxide and water, so becoming the principal source of water vapour in the upper air. The water rises further into the ionosphere and is photolysed to oxygen and hydrogen. Oxygen descends and hydrogen escapes into space. In effect, methane production is a way of transporting hydrogen from the Earth's surface to the stratosphere in sufficient quantity to maintain oxygen concentration in the lower atmosphere.

We have also found interesting and unexpected trace gases in the atmosphere, such as dimethyl sulphide, methyl iodide and carbon tetrachloride. There is no doubt that the first two are biological emissions and they may well serve to transport the essential elements, sulphur and iodine, from the sea to the land. Carbon tetrachloride does not seem to have a biological source but its uniform distribution in the atmosphere, showing no difference between the Northern and Southern hemispheres, and other evidence suggest that it is not a man-made pollutant either. Its origins are an intriguing puzzle as is the question of its function, if any (Figure 2).

For more than 3500 million years in the face of a big increase of solar output, the mean temperature of the Earth's surface must have remained within the range of 15–30°C. How did Gaia do this? She must have used several ways to keep surface temperatures so constant. Before there was a significant amount of oxygen in the air, the emission and absorption of ammonia by simple organisms may have been the control process, so making use of its heat absorbing and retaining properties. Variations of the concentration of ammonia in the air would therefore be a means of temperature control.

There must have been other ways as well, for the failure of only one year's crop of ammonia would have led to a self-accelerating temperature decline and extinction of life. One can envisage advantage being taken of the ability of certain algae to change colour from light to dark, thereby influencing the emissivity and the albedo of the surface. Later, when photosynthesising and respiring organisms existed and oxygen became a major constituent of the air, the control of the concentration of carbon dioxide, which is also a heat absorbing and retaining gas, may have been used to play a role in stabilising temperature.

GAIA AND MAN

Gaia is still a hypothesis. The facts and speculations in this article and others that we have assembled corroborate but do not prove her existence but, like all useful theories right or wrong, Gaia suggests new questions which may throw light on old ones. Let us ask another. What bearing has she on pollution, population and man's role in the living world?

Gaia has survived the most appalling of all atmospheric pollutants, namely oxygen, which was put into the atmosphere in substantial quantity about 2000 million years ago when the photosynthesisers had completed their task of oxidising the surface and the atmosphere. Whole ranges of species must have been killed off or driven into dark, oxygen-free prisons from which they have never been released; the appearance of the whole planetary surface and its chemistry were completely changed. To appreciate the impact of oxygen, think of what would happen to us if a marine organism began to photosynthesise chlorine and was successful enough to replace oxygen in the air with chlorine. This is science fiction, but oxygen was as poisonous to the primitive ferments as chlorine would be to us today.

Man's present activity as a polluter is trivial by comparison and he cannot thereby seriously change the present state of Gaia let alone hazard her existence. But there is an aspect of man's activities more disturbing than pollution. If one showed a control engineer the graph of the Earth's mean temperature against time over the past million years, he would no doubt remark that it represented the behaviour of a system in which serious instabilities could develop but which had never gone out of control. One of the laws of system control is that if a system is to maintain stability it must possess adequate variety of response, that is, have at least as many ways of countering outside disturbances as there are outside disturbances to act on it. What is to be feared is that man-the-farmer and man-the-engineer are reducing the total variety of response open to Gaia.

The growing human population of the Earth is leading us to use drastic measures to supply this population with resources, of which food has prime importance. Natural distribution of plants and animals is being changed, ecological systems destroyed and whole species altered or deleted. But any species or group of species in an ecological association may contribute just that response to an external threat that is needed to maintain the stability of Gaia. We therefore disturb and eliminate at our peril; long before the world population has grown so large that we consume the entire output from photosynthesisers, instabilities generated by lack of variety of response could intervene to put this level out of reach.

PUZZLING CLIMATE

Are there any signs that we might have triggered something off already? There is at least one such possibility—the present puzzling climate. Unprecedented temperature decreases have occurred in northern regions, such as Iceland, along with many other

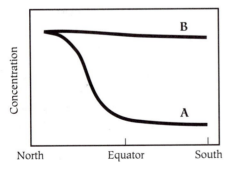

FIGURE 2 A, *Expected change of concentration with latitude of man-made atmospheric pollutant generated in northern hemisphere (eg NW Europe). B, Actual distribution of carbon tetrachloride in the atmosphere.*

unfamiliar manifestations, such as modified wind systems and rainfall distributions.

Many explanations of these climate trends have been put forward. Some mechanism that either reduces the amount of the Sun's radiation reaching the Earth or increases the amount radiated is required. Ecologists, not unexpectedly, place the blame on the products of man's activities. Increasing dustiness of the atmosphere, nuclear explosions, supersonic aircraft have all been proposed and considered, but within our admittedly limited theoretical understanding of what goes on, none has stood up well to criticism.

Another possibility which we are exploring is that one of the trace gas emissions such as that of nitrous oxide serves as a biological climate regulator. Nitrous oxide is produced naturally by soil micro-organisms at a rate of hundreds of millions of tons annually. The output varies however, as a result of agriculture, particularly from the use of nitrogenous fertilisers. We do not know how nitrous oxide could modify the climate, but the evidence suggests that it has been increasing in concentration and it is known to penetrate the stratosphere where its decomposition products could affect the ozone layer.

This climatic trend may be "just another fluctuation" of the kind which has occurred before and which will cure itself. This tends to be the meteorologists' view but the uncomfortable thought remains that none of the earlier occurrences has been explained. Perhaps some unidentified activity of man has been the common factor and nowadays there are a good deal more men about, active in many more ways. The consequences this time could well be much more serious and prolonged. We await developments somewhat uneasily.

Finally, a brief prospective look at the relation between man and Gaia, which also sums up the implications of this article. Socially organised man has the ability possessed by no other species to collect, store and process information and then to use it to manipulate the environment in a purposeful and anticipatory fashion. When our forebears became farmers they set themselves on a path, which we are still beating out, that must have had an impact on the rest of Gaia almost as revolutionary as that of the evolution of photosynthetic organisms millennia before. The area of the outside world that we, as a species, are capable of regulating to our short-term advantage has gradually expanded from the immediate locality of a settlement to vast geographical regions. This path could take us finally to the point at which the area of manipulation becomes the whole world. What happens then?

Nineteenth-century technocracy would say that we would then have won the final victory in the battle against nature. The Earth would be our spaceship, we the passengers and crew, the rest of nature, living and dead, our life-support system. But the price of victory might well be that we should have immobilised Gaia's control systems which she had established to keep the conditions on our planet at the level necessary for her and therefore our survival. The responsibility for the task of maintaining system stability would pass to us alone and it would be dauntingly difficult. As well as carrying technical burdens, we should also have to make agonising social and moral decisions, such as, how many passengers the spaceship could afford to carry and whom to throw overboard to make room.

A NEED TO SURVIVE

The easier path is to rid ourselves of 19th century technocratic thinking, to reject the idea that human existence is necessarily a battle against nature. Let us make peace with Gaia on her terms and return to peaceful co-existence with our fellow creatures. Thirty thousand years ago some of our ancestors did something like this. They abandoned primitive hunting and took up what has been called the transhumane way of life. Men lived and migrated with the animal herds, defended them against other predators and systematically culled them for food. This ensured them a more plentiful and regular supply of animal products than the random hunting mode which it superseded. But our first priority as a species is to choose from the numerous technically feasible means of limiting our own population those which are socially acceptable in social and moral terms.

Now for one more speculation. We are sure that man needs Gaia but could Gaia do without man? In man, Gaia has the equivalent of a central nervous system and an awareness of herself and the rest of the Universe. Through man, she has a rudimentary capacity, capable of development, to anticipate and guard against threats to her existence. For example, man can command just about enough capacity to ward off a collision with a planetoid the size of Icarus. Can it then be that in the course of man's evolution within Gaia he has been acquiring the knowledge and skills necessary to ensure her survival?

Study Questions

1. Explain how the Gaian hypothesis differs from the ordinary way of looking at life on Earth.
2. What is the evidence for Gaia? Are there simpler answers to these anomalies which do not posit a single life, such as the Gaia hypothesis does? Can you think of some criticisms of this hypothesis?
3. Lovelock and Epton see life on Earth best explained by a biological unity within Earth's being. How does this compare with the theistic idea that God created the world and causes these atmospheric anomalies to function in the cooperative interactive pattern in which they do? Is the Gaia hypothesis simply an attempt to substitute an internal set of reasons for God's handiwork?

29

The Gaia Hypotheses: Are They Testable? Are They Useful?

JAMES W. KIRCHNER

In March of 1988, James Kirchner, now an assistant professor of geology and geophysics, then a graduate student of the Energy and Resources Group of the University of California at Berkeley, read the following paper at the American Geophysical Union Chapman Conference in San Diego. The paper points out that there are at least five different Gaia hypotheses rather than simply one, which find expression in the work of Lovelock or his associates. The more plausible "weak" forms are not new, but the more ambitious "strong" forms seem to be untestable or "ugly." One of the leading climatologists in the world, Stephen H. Schneider, called this essay the "most serious critique to date . . . a stunning challenge to the Gaia hypothesis."

The reader may wonder why, in my title, I refer to the Gaia hypotheses in the plural. I do it because I think that many logically different theories have been put forth under the single banner of "the Gaia hypothesis." Perhaps the Gaia hypothesis is all things to all people, but the differences between these theories are both subtle and crucial. I suspect that a lot of debate has resulted from a simple misunderstanding of which of the multiple hypotheses is on the table at any one time. In the interests of clarity and precision, I propose the following taxonomy of the Gaia hypotheses:

A TAXONOMY OF THE GAIA HYPOTHESES

Influential Gaia. The weakest of the hypotheses (here I use "weak" and "strong" in reference to the extremity, not the plausibility, of the hypotheses), the influential Gaia theory asserts simply that the biota has a substantial influence over certain aspects of the abiotic world, such as the temperature and composition of the atmosphere.

Reprinted from *Scientists on Gaia*, ed. Stephen H. Schneider and P. J. Boston (Cambridge: MIT Press, 1992).

(Author's note: A substantially refined and expanded version of this contribution appeared in the May 1989 *Reviews of Geophysics* (Kirchner, 1989). That paper makes some points more carefully and precisely than this one and addresses geophysiology, Daisyworld, and Lovelock's newest book. which was in press at the time of the conference. The version presented here, by contrast, has the advantage of saying things more plainly and better revealing one practicing scientist's difficulties with Gaia.)

The Gaia hypothesis . . states that the temperature and composition of the Earth's atmosphere are actively regulated by the sum of life on the planet (Sagan and Mar gulis, 1983).

Coevolutionary Gaia. The coevolutionary Gaia hypothesis asserts that the biota influences the abiotic environment, and that the environment in turn influences the evolution of the biota by Darwinian processes.

The biota have effected profound changes on the environment of the surface of the earth. At the same time, that environment has imposed constraints on the biota, so that life and the environment may be considered as two parts of a coupled system (Watson and Lovelock, 1983).

Homeostatic Gaia. The homeostatic Gaia hypothesis asserts that the biota influences the abiotic world, and does so in a way that is stabilizing. In the language of systems analysis, the major linkages between the biota and the abiotic world are negative feedback loops.

The notion of the biosphere as an active adaptive control system able to maintain the earth in homeostasis we are calling the "Gaia" hypothesis (Lovelock and Margulis, 1974a).

Teleological Gaia. The teleological Gaia hypothesis holds that the atmosphere is kept in homeostasis, not just by the biosphere, but by and for (in some sense) the biosphere.

. . . the Earth's atmosphere is more than merely anomalous; it appears to be a contrivance specifically constituted for a set of purposes (Lovelock and Margulis 1974a).

Optimizing Gaia. The optimizing Gaia hypothesis holds that the biota manipulates its physical environment for the purpose of creating biologically favorable, or even optimal, conditions for itself.

We argue that it is unlikely that chance alone accounts for the fact that temperature, pH and the presence of compounds of nutrient elements have been, for immense periods of time, just those optimal for surface life. Rather we present the "Gaia hypothesis," the idea that energy is expended by the biota to actively maintain these optima (Lovelock and Margulis, 1974b).

This is just one taxonomy of the Gaia hypotheses. One can take issue with my way of classifying them. It can be done many other ways, but I think most will agree that it must be done somehow, because (as the examples above make clear) different people mean different things when they use the same words. Sometimes even the *same* people appear to mean different things when they use the same words. Some of these claims are relatively weak (as in the influential or coevolutionary Gaia theories, which seem to state just that the biota and the physical environment have something to do with one another), and others are, of course, quite strong stuff. If we all talk about "the Gaia hypothesis, " without specifying *which* Gaia hypothesis, we can create a lot of confusion.

This confusion can appear in different guises. One of the most serious lies in claiming that evidence for one of the weaker versions of the hypothesis somehow proves the much stronger versions of the hypothesis as well. Some believe, as I do, that the biota affects the physical environment. Some also think, as I do, that the physical environment shapes biotic evolution. Those holding these views are in good company, because scientists have thought these things for over a hundred years. So if I were asked whether I believed in the Gaia hypothesis, referring to *that* Gaia hypothesis, I would say that I do. But does that mean that I believe that the biota is part of a global cybernetic control system, the purpose of which is to create biologically optimal conditions—that is another matter entirely.

WEAK GAIA IS NOT NEW

Some might be surprised at my statement that scientists have believed in Gaia—believed in "weak" Gaia, believed that life shapes the physical environment—for over a hundred years. We have all become accustomed to reading that the Gaia hypothesis is a radical departure from the earlier view that the biota simply responds to a fixed physical environment. If that is a radical departure, then some people have been radically departing for a very long time. Consider T. H. Huxley. In 1877 he wrote what could be considered to be the very first textbook in physical geography. In it he wrote, "Since the atmosphere is constantly receiving vast volumes of carbonic acid from various sources, it might not unnaturally be assumed that this gas would unduly accumulate, and at length vitiate the entire bulk of the atmosphere. Such accumulation is, however, prevented by the action of living plants" (Huxley, 1877).

So a century ago Huxley thought the biota was responsible for the chemical disequilibrium of the atmosphere. He not only thought this, but he also thought it was elementary enough, and obvious enough, to put it into a textbook.

Thirty years earlier, Huxley's compatriot Herbert Spencer wrote about the same phenomenon. He not only thought that the biota had shaped the earth's atmosphere; he also thought that changes in the atmo-

sphere had charted the course of evolution (which Spencer called "progressive development," Darwin's *Origin of Species* being still in the future). Spencer called his theory

> . . . an entirely new and very beautiful explanation of the proximate causes of progressive development . . . not only do the organisms of the vegetable kingdom decompose the carbonic acid which has been thrown into the atmosphere by animals, but they likewise serve for the removal of those extraneous supplies of the same gas that are continually poured into it through volcanos, calcareous springs, fissures, and other such channels . . . Assuming then that the present theory, supported as it is by the fact that the constituents of the atmosphere are not in atomic proportions, and borne out likewise by the foregoing arguments, is correct, let us mark the inferences that may be drawn respecting the effects produced upon the organic creation. . . .
>
> If rapid oxidation of the blood is accompanied by a higher heat and a more perfect mental and bodily development, and if in consequence of an alteration in the composition of the air greater facilities for such oxidation are afforded, it may be reasonably inferred that there has been a corresponding advancement in the temperature and organization of the world's inhabitants (Spencer, 1844).

In other words, Spencer held that the emergence of green plants produced our present abundance of oxygen, and that oxygen made the evolution of higher animals possible. The biota, in other words, shaped the physical world in a way that seems fortuitous for the course of evolution.

My contention is not that Spencer was correct (his view is simultaneously grandiose and simplistic), but that he was, in a sense, *Gaian*. His theory has the key elements: the biota alters the physical environment, which in turn shapes biotic evolution. Indeed, his theory sounds surprisingly similar to contemporary Gaian treatments that portray the creation of earth's oxidizing atmosphere as a cathartic event, necessary for the further progress of evolution.

I certainly do not claim familiarity with the whole history of the evolution of such ideas. The fact that I could find these two "Gaian" references in an afternoon of library browsing, however, suggests to me that such passages may be relatively common. Indeed, the whole field of biogeochemistry, although more cautious in its speculations, is centrally concerned with the same biotic interactions that Gaia alludes to.

So the first two statements of the Gaia hypothesis—what I have labeled *influential* and *coevolutionary* Gaia, respectively—have a long history. This weak hypothesis has such a long history, indeed, and seems so intuitively plausible, that it seems odd to call it a hypothesis at all. Rather than a theory, it seems to be simply an observation that the physical and biotic worlds have something to do with one another. We can, of course, argue about the relative importance of these interactions.

Thus those who believe in the weak forms of the Gaia hypothesis are carrying on a long and honorable scientific tradition, but one so long, and so honorable, that it may deprive them of the pleasure of being part of a revolution in scientific thought. But what about the stronger versions of the hypothesis? Are they testable, and are they useful? Before I address that question, I must briefly review a bit of basic epistemology.

CRITERIA FOR TESTABILITY

Much of the debate surrounding any scientific theory, including the Gaia theories, consists of finding and weighing the evidence, for and against. This is the day-today-business of scientists, and of scientific conferences like the San Diego meeting. We call it testing a theory.

But not every theory can be tested. Now, as a matter of strict logic, a theory that is untestable is far worse than one that is merely false. A false theory, once known to be false, at least helps restrict the sphere of possibilities. It teaches us something, namely that the truth lies elsewhere. Testing an untestable theory, on the other hand, is simply a waste of time. So true, false, and untestable theories are, respectively, "the good, the bad, and the ugly." What must a theory be, to be testable?

First, it must be well defined. Its meaning must be clear and its terms must be unambiguous. Second, it must be intelligible in terms of observable phenomena of the real world. Finally, it must not be tautological. That is, it must not be true simply by definition. Equivalently, it must not encompass all logical possibilities. It must be logically possible for the theory to be false, and there must be some conceivable fact that, if it were in fact the case, would prove the theory false. This is what separates empirical hypotheses from pure logical deductions.

A tautology is a theory that is true no matter what the facts are. A theory should be logically consistent, but it should not be completely airtight; it has to let a little empirical truth in at some point.

METAPHORS

Metaphors constitute a whole class of untestable theories. If Shakespeare tells you that "all the world's a stage," could you test his hypothesis? I doubt it. What would you measure or observe to tell whether the world is a stage? What would a world that is *not* a stage look like? If you could complain to Shakespeare about the ambiguity of his metaphor, he might reply, "OK. The entire world is made of wooden flooring, and at the edge of the earth you'll find a few footlights." Now you have a hypothesis. You can now go out and very quickly verify that the world is not a stage, at least in that sense. But of course, in some more poetic sense, the world is indeed a stage. That is what makes metaphors so inviting; at the same time that they are literally false, they are figuratively true.

A metaphor makes a poor hypothesis because it does not specify *in what sense* the metaphor is true. Showing that the world is a stage in one sense does not prove it is a stage in any other sense. Now, "All the world's a stage" sounds a lot like "All the world is a global organism," and some have indeed claimed that the Gaia hypothesis is just a metaphor. My point is not that metaphors are useless—they inspire fruitful speculation—but that they are untestable. Treating a metaphor as a scientific proposition that is factually true or false is simply a waste of time.

Now, some may think that I'm being a terrible spoil sport, that I am far too serious about what should be considered just a metaphor, and that I take the whole Gaia hypothesis far too literally. Perhaps I do. But if Gaia is just a metaphor, why do we keep referring to the Gaia *hypothesis*? Why do we keep talking about *evidence for* or *proof of* the Gaia hypothesis? If it is a metaphor, why do we talk about it as if it were a scientific proposition, as if it were either true or false?

CRITERIA OF USEFULNESS

Besides testability, another fundamental issue to consider is usefulness. Some theories, although coherent and perhaps even true, are simply not useful in furthering scientific progress. Theories are useful to the degree that they are distinct from related theories. If a hypothesis simply restates other tried-and-true theories, or can be logically derived from them, why bother testing it?

The second major criterion of usefulness is predictive or explanatory power. Theories are useful in proportion to the phenomena they can predict or explain, and—perhaps more importantly—in inverse proportion to what they force you to assume. This is simply Ockham's Razor: *all else equal*, choose the theory that burdens you with the least baggage of unverifiable assumptions. If two theories explain the same data, reject the one that forces you to assume the most. Note that Ockham's Razor does not say that all simple theories are better than all complex ones. It simply says that one should not invoke extraordinary assumptions to explain phenomena that can be understood more straightforwardly.

If I have any quibble with weak Gaia, it is on these grounds. It is not clear that Influential Gaia or Coevolutionary Gaia say anything that was not already said by Huxley, Darwin, and others of their age. Does Gaia say anything new? If not, is there any advantage to restating tried-and-true theories in Gaian language?

The same point can be raised with respect to the strong versions of the Gaia hypotheses, to the extent that they claim to explain why the physical environment and the biota are well matched. Darwin said a long time ago that the biota fits the physical environment well. Gaia reverses the statement, and says that the physical environment suits the biota well. Is there any advantage in standing poor old Darwin on his head? And is that advantage great enough to justify the assumptions we have to make? Natural selection—without any of the embellishments that Gaia offers—explains why the environment and the biota are well matched. Organisms suited to a different environment, having been wiped out long ago, are no longer part of the biota, to which the current environment seems so well suited. Why invoke a global cybernetic control system to explain the good fit of biota to environment, if you can invoke simple natural selection instead?

HOMEOSTATIC GAIA

I shall now turn for a moment to homeostatic Gaia, which claims, in essence, that the biota is vital in maintaining the long-term stability of the physical environment. What is stability? Does it mean resistance to change, resilience under change, or bounds on the magnitude of change? The experience of ecologists in the debate over complexity and stability shows that it is hard enough to pin down the meaning of stability or homeostasis in the case of a neatly bounded ecosystem; it is harder still when the bounds are the entire biosphere. One could precisely define homeostasis, but it has never been done. So the first problem is one of definition.

There are many interrelationships between the biota and the physical environment (that is, many feedback loops). Given that any feedback loop must be either stabilizing or destabilizing, it should come as no surprise that some of them are stabilizing. The Gaia hypothesis has prompted a lot of efforts to look for biological mechanisms of homeostasis, and there are some outwardly plausible candidates.

But we should not just look for confirmatory evidence. We should be cautious in characterizing the putative stability of a paleoclimatic record that is sketchy and ambiguous, one whose error bounds could hide quite a bit of instability. More to the point, without knowing what destabilizing biological mechanisms may also be at work to undermine homeostasis—and there is every reason to believe that there are some, and that some are potent—it is impossible to make a balanced assessment of the role of the biota.

Even the most passionate advocates of Gaia will admit that the biota was once one of the most destabilizing forces on earth. The biota was responsible for the drastic shift in the earth's redox potential in the Precambrian period (a shift that made most of the earth uninhabitable for the anaerobic organisms that precipitated it). Indeed, some accounts claim that this event is evidence of the power of the biotic world and the resilience of Gaia.

But there is a fundamental problem here. If the most destabilizing period in earth's history can be cited as evidence for Gaia, and the apparent stability since can also be cited as evidence for Gaia, I'm left wondering what conceivable events could not be used as evidence for Gaia. If Gaia stabilizes, and Gaia destabilizes—those are the only two possibilities—then is there any possible behavior that is not Gaian? Is Gaia, then, simply a theory so flexible (and, by implication, free of specific empirical content) that it can be wrapped around any conceivable paleoclimatic record?

Anyone attempting a Gaian interpretation of earth's history must think hard about this. And it won't do to say that the Precambrian blue-green algae were not Gaian because they were so violently destabilizing. Such a statement is blatantly tautological. It defines Gaia as stabilizing interactions and then asserts that Gaia has a stabilizing effect. Anything defined to be homeostatic has to be stabilizing . . . there would be no other possibility, so there would be no testable hypothesis.

TELEOLOGICAL GAIA

Teleological Gaia asserts that the biota controls the environment, and does so for a purpose. There is a definitional problem here; the purpose of the putative biological control mechanism has never been defined.

A claim that the atmosphere is a "contrivance specifically constituted for a set of purposes" (Lovelock and Margulis, 1974a) is ill defined without a statement of what the purposes are. This criticism may seem silly, and the purposes may seem perfectly obvious. Clearly, the atmosphere has a number of biologically important functions. Surely the function of the atmosphere is the purpose it was contrived for.

There is a subtle, but serious, error in such a line of reasoning. It is this: if all you know is that the atmosphere functions in some way, how can you say it was contrived? How do you know what its intended purpose was? If you say its intended purpose is the function it serves, then how would you ever know if anything was *not* contrived? Everything has some function, after all. Purpose and function coincide only in contrivances that work well; whether the atmosphere works well, or is contrived at all, is precisely the question at hand. Without an independently defined purpose, teleological Gaia simply says that the atmosphere serves the purpose of doing whatever the atmosphere does.

OPTIMIZING GAIA

The theory I have termed "optimizing Gaia" tries to solve the problem of definition by stating what Gaia's purpose is: Gaia's purpose is maintaining a biologically optimal physical environment. In solving that definitional problem, it creates another. What is optimal for the whole biosphere? We can define an optimal environment for an individual organism in many ways, but what would be optimal for a blue-green anaerobe, a chimpanzee, a pine tree, and a penguin, taken together? Nor does dismissing the notion of optimality, and simply claiming that Gaia creates biologically favorable conditions, solve the problem. What would be favorable, let alone optimal, for the biota, a vast collection of diverse organisms with different, and even conflicting, requirements?

Would it be "better" for the whole biosphere to have more species, more biomas, or more productivity? No matter what the answer, the next question is unanswerable: Why should that be better?

One might respond that what we have now is optimal. But if what is optimal is simply defined by what exists, what content is left in the idea of optimality? The theory boils down to "Gaia created and maintains the world we have now, which is, of course, optimal." (Nor does the simple fact of life's persistence on Earth—great extinctions and all—prove that Gaia maintains biologically favorable conditions. Gaia must mean not just that life did persist, but that it could not fail to persist. Would the environment of a nongaian earth have been "unfavorable" enough to sterilize the planet?)

Thus it is hard to define what we mean by optimality. But we must define it, for as long as the criterion of optimality remains unspecified, optimizing Gaia is clearly a tautological theory, in the rigorous sense that it includes all logical possibilities and does not exclude any possible data. It is a basic theorem of operations research that for any behavior of a system, there is some objective function which that behavior optimizes. For any given behavior, I can write a function that the behavior maximizes. Every conceivable environment is optimal for something, as long as one has complete freedom to specify what the "something" is.

So the concept of Gaian optimization needs a lot of work to save it from tautology. But there is another serious problem. Gaian optimization is internally contradictory. Stability and optimality (for the agent supplying the regulatory mechanism) are mutually exclusive. If an organism is keeping a system stable, the stable point cannot be optimal for the organism. We can see why by looking at the Daisyworld model, in which plants regulate the temperature of a theoretical planet by changing its reflectance.

Consider a world with only white daisies. The daisies keep the temperature stable because if the temerature or solar flux rises above the stable point, more daisies grow, the surface becomes whiter, and the albedo increases. But that means that at a higher temperature, there would be more daisies. A higher temperature would be "better" for white daisies, and the daisies' response *prevents* a temperature increase that would be favorable for them. At the temperature that is optimal for the daisies, there is no stability. At the optimal point, any change in temperature decreases the number of daisies. So if the temperature increases, daisies die, and the temperature increases still further. More daisies die, and the temperature increases still further. And so on. The optimum will be reached only in an unstable transition between the stable suboptimum and total extinction.

What I have described is true of both colors of daisies, and indeed is not specific to the Daisyworld model. You can demonstrate it as a purely mathematical proposition. It is completely general. It is a straightforward theorem of systems analysis that no homeostatic system can be stable at a point that is optimal for the component supplying the homeostasis. If the biota regulates the atmosphere, the atmosphere cannot be optimal for the biota.

Besides, what do we gain by assuming that Gaia has a purpose, or that Gaia optimizes? What more can we predict or explain? If we make such extreme assumptions, but do not gain explanatory power, Ockham's Razor will slice us to ribbons.

SUMMARY

Some maybe either baffled or irritated by the discussion I have presented. Some may be thinking, "Oh come on. I'm just interested in exploring the connections between the biotic and abiotic worlds, and there's nothing wrong with that. My hypothesis is just that the organisms of the biota influence their local environments, that the sum of these influences can be globally significant, and that organisms evolve by chance and are selected by Darwinian processes, in terms of where they survive, whether they survive, and what their characteristics are."

I think that is a great starting point for illuminating research. It probably explains all that the more extreme Gaia hypotheses do, without invoking global entities, imputing teleological intentionality, or assuming optimal control. It is testable at many scales, from the laboratory to the globe. And in its basic outline it is almost certainly correct. Those holding that view are in good company, and are carrying on an honorable scientific tradition that is at least a century old.

On the other hand, those who think that the idea of a global organism is an intellectually appealing metaphor, but not a rigorous scientific theory, will only distract their colleagues by talking about it as if it were a hypothesis that could be tested or proved.

Some think that Gaia is the stabilizing interaction of the biotic and abiotic worlds. That is an interesting possibility. Given that stabilizing and destabilizing interactions are the only two choices, in any particular case there is at least a 50% chance that this theory is correct. Indeed, if Gaia were violently destabilizing throughout the earth's history, we probably would not be here to carry on this debate. In any event, we should explore all the links between the bionic and abiotic worlds . . . not just those that agree with a particular theory. The destabilizing feedbacks are important too.

Does Gaia have a purpose? Does Gaia maintain optimal conditions for life? I do not think these theories are testable. Nobody will be able to test such theories until Gaia's purpose is defined and the meaning of optimality is specified. And nobody will be able to test such theories until it is clearly stated what conceivable result of an experiment could possibly prove them false.

ADDENDA AND ERRATA

After presenting this paper, I received a number of thought-provoking questions that have made it clear that some issues I addressed needed to be discussed further, and more precisely.

MY CENTRAL CONCERN WITH GAIA

A number of people suggested that I was expecting far too much, that the nature of the hypothesis and the system itself make it unrealistic to expect that the question be answered after only a decade of work. I am not complaining that the question has not been answered, but that it has not yet been asked in a scientifically meaningful way. The central problem is not a lack of information (though good data are by no means abundant here) but a lack of something to do with the information. Until we can frame a scientifically coherent and significant question, we will not know what the answer means, or even whether we have found it.

WHY UNTESTABLE HYPOTHESES ARE UGLY

Steve Schneider asked why untestable hypotheses are "ugly." He suggested that the nuclear winter theory, although not testable, was useful in molding our approach to international security.

There are two types of untestability. Theories about nuclear winter are untestable in practice; "ugly" theories are untestable in principle (In fact, the nuclear winter theory is eminently testable. We are all at risk of becoming involuntary participants in a full-scale, uncontrolled, irreproducible experiment . . .)

Hypotheses that are untestable in principle are those for which every conceivable experiment can be shown, on logic alone, to have only one possible result. Consider the hypothesis, "Once perturbed out of steady state, the system will exhibit transient behavior until it again settles down into steady state." That will always be true of any behavior of any system. Showing that it is true in a particular case, in a particular system, cannot give you any information about the object of study.

"Always true?" one might ask. Yes indeed. The system is only perturbed out of steady state if it begins some sort of transient behavior (if there were no transient behavior, it would still, by definition, be in steady state). Similarly, when transient behavior ends, the steady state begins, by definition. Note that the hypothesis does not say a new steady state must be reached, but only that if it is, it will occur at the end of transience.

What is "ugly" about that hypothesis is that it claims to be revealing aspects of the system under study, when in fact it is just defining the words *steady state* and *transient*. Because the result of the experiment was obvious strictly as a matter of logic, the experiment and the hypothesis have no empirical content. What is truly "ugly" about these sorts of hypotheses is that they are misleading, and in the minds of the unwary they are entrancing; one believes one understands the system very, very well, because one's predictions are always confirmed.

Other "ugly" theories violate the criterion of intelligibility. Most of the pseudoscientific blather currently clogging the media is untestable because the proponents will never say exactly what they mean in terms of empirically observable things (I speak here with the prejudices of a practicing scientist). One hears a lot about "essences" and "vital forces," but never anything independently detectable. At best, such theories do not explain observable phenomena, they just give them new names. At worst, they give one a very idiosyncratic view, which nobody else can verify or falsify, of personal experience. They let us paper over our ignorance by explaining away puzzling phenomena with unobservable spirits and vapors that are assumed, but cannot be proven, to be responsible for the otherwise inexplicable facts. (It is precisely on this point that science and religion part company, in deference to their fundamentally different precepts and purposes.)

WHY NEWTON'S LAWS AND NATURAL SELECTION ARE NOT TAUTOLOGIES

I received many comments such as, "All of science is built on tautologies. Newton's law, $F = ma$, is a tautology. Survival of the fittest is a tautology. You're holding Lovelock to a standard that you wouldn't apply to Newton or Darwin." The common wisdom behind this objection is so pervasive, so persuasive, and so subtly (but seriously) fallacious, that I must spill a little ink here to straighten things out.

All definitions and purely logical deductions are tautologically true. Science is built on a system of definitions and deductions, so science is built on tautologies, but science has to consist of more than tautologies if it is to say anything about the real world, instead of about our words and how we define them. Mathematics is a very structured, elegant, and powerful system of definitions and deductions, and it is the workhorse of modern science, largely because it helps us to deduce consequences (e.g., experimental predictions) from assumptions without error. But even the best mathematics, all by itself, will tell you absolutely nothing about the real world. We also need a set of assertions about what the mathematics means in real-world terms. Mathematics is the language of science, but we still must have something to say.

Newton's $F = ma$ is just a definition. The left hand side could be called "gzork" rather than "force" and it would make no difference. With only $F = ma$, Newton can only play the engrossing game of restatement. "You give me a measurement of mass and acceleration, and I tell you what the 'force' is." $F = ma$ is—according to some of our educators—what Newton is famous for. But if Newton had stopped at $F = ma$ he would have been just as forgettable as all the non-Newtons in scientific history. What made Newton famous is that he came up with an independent measure of force. He not only asserted $F = ma$; he simultaneously asserted $F = Gm_1m_2/r^2$, and then (here was the brilliant part) he asserted that G is a universal constant, the two forces are equal, and mass is an intrinsic property of matter that means the same thing in both equations.

Those latter assertions are not definitions; they are a statement about what Newton believed to be true about the real world. They should have been warranted for three centuries or twelve orders of magnitude, whichever comes first. (Scale, not time, caught up with Newton, but that's another story).

With only definitions, Newton could only have pinned new labels on old facts. But because he understood both what force was (that which accelerates mass), and what controlled the gravitational force between planetary bodies (mass and separation), Newton could make a new statement about how the world works (the motion of planets is controlled, in a very specific way, by their relative positions and masses). And so he could explain Kepler's descriptions of planetary orbits, and the rest is history.

(As an aside, consider the difference between Newton's approach and the heuristic reasoning of the ancients about things consisting of "earth" "wanting" to return to their "proper" home. This bit of teleology can be restated in non-teleological fashion as things acting *as if* they wanted to return to their proper home, but

note how much farther Newton was able to go by not thinking teleologically at all. Newton, having what can only be termed a considerable capacity for generalization, saw that if apples fell out of trees, the moon must be "falling" too (despite the obvious difference in their apparent trajectories) and the earth must be "falling" the opposite way to meet them (despite the complete lack of apparent motion on its part). The success of ignoring teleology and appearances entirely makes me skeptical of the usefulness of simply trying to recast Gaia as the biotic world acting *as if* it wanted to create a nice home for itself . . . but perhaps this says more about my background in physics than about Gaia or the methods of science.)

The point is that science contains definitions—but not *only* definitions. Equivalently, the definitions must be reciprocal.

Which brings me to natural selection. Is "the survival of the fittest" a tautology? First of all, natural selection concerns dominance of the next generation's gene pool by the fittest, rather than merely survival of the fittest, but the tautology could exist in either case, so I will indulge in the man-on-the-street parlance. One often hears the claim that "the survival of the fittest means just the survival of those who survive." But evolutionary biology does not have to be done that way, and that is not the way competent scientists do it nor the way Darwin meant it to be done.

If one seeks to prove that the fittest survive, but assumes that the fittest survive in defining or measuring fitness (in terms of who survived), a tautology is created, one that an unwary scientist could find very seductive. Some evolutionary biologists do measure so called fitness coefficients by measuring chances of survival. They must assume that natural selection works, and so cannot—and do not—use those measurements to prove that natural selection works. (Measuring fitness coefficients or selection coefficients is really an attempt to pin down what contributes to fitness; thus these researchers assume that Darwin got the basic scheme right—but those who forgot that they were assuming this could get themselves into trouble.) To prove (without tautology) that natural selection works, an independent definition of fitness is necessary.

For example, the survival advantages of black moths on sooty trees are intuitively obvious, so one can predict (without needing the results of the experiment itself to define fitness) that blacker moths will dominate the gene pool when trees become sootier, as happened in Britain as industrialization spread. When blacker moths do in fact become dominant (remember, it did not have to come out this way; if Darwin were wrong, bright yellow moths could have become common instead), one has begun to collect evidence that natural selection (in admittedly unnatural conditions) really works.

WHY MODELS CANNOT PROVE THE GAIA HYPOTHESIS

Some think that Gaia can be proven with models (e.g., Lovelock 1983).

A model, like any other statement in mathematical language, can only derive conclusions from assumptions. It cannot show that either the assumptions or the conclusions are empirically realistic. Gaia is an assertion about the real world, not about models. The fact that Gaian mechanisms stabilize a model implies nothing about whether Gaian mechanisms are in fact stabilizing the real world. A model and the real world can give the same behavior for different reasons.

Now, that last statement is not quite fair; any testable prediction made from a hypothesis can be right for the wrong reason. That is why the logical positivists (who, I think, carried the whole thing way too far) stressed the importance of disconfirmatory evidence.

The point here is that in most cases the results from Gaian models are not the kind that can be tested against the behavior of the real world. Consequently, success for the theory is often measured, not by a good match between the model behavior and the real world, but by a good match between the model behavior and the behavior predicted by the theory. That kind of success is guaranteed (barring math or logic errors) because rather than comparing theory and data, this "test" instead compares a theory (in words) with itself (in math).

My point is not that models are useless (I use them all the time myself), but that we must do more than build models. Models can be used to deduce the consequences of Gaian thinking, but not to test the empirical realism of the Gaia hypothesis.

WHY I MENTION TELEOLOGICAL GAIA AND OPTIMIZING GAIA

I understand that Jim Lovelock's thinking has evolved considerably since 1974. I addressed at length the more far-out versions of strong Gaia, not because I thought he was still stuck in 1974, but because I think some of his followers and some of the media are still stuck in 1974, because I don't think we're doing a very good job of getting them unstuck from 1974, and because I think 1974 is (at least in this sense) a bad place to be stuck.

The common perception is that Gaia means that "the earth is alive" or that the biosphere is trying to make itself a nice home here. Because many people do not understand the risks of treating poetic statements as scientific propositions, the public at large thinks that scientists are busy trying to figure out whether the earth *really is* "alive." I don't think that perception helps any of us.

ACKNOWLEDGMENTS

J. Harte first introduced me to this topic, suggested that a taxonomy of Gaia hypotheses was needed, and offered many valuable comments and suggestions. I am grateful to M. E. Power, B. A. Roy, S. H. Schneider, H. D. Holland, J. E. Lovelock, and the conference participants for their comments, and I thank the University of California and the William and Flora Hewlett Foundation for financial support. I particularly want to acknowledge Jim Lovelock's gracious response to this paper at the conference. I wish that all scientific debates could be as free of acrimony.

References

Huxley, T. H. 1877. *Physiography*. London: Macmillan & Co.

Kirchner, J. W. 1989. The Gaia hypothesis: can it be tested? *Rev Geo-phys*, 27, 223–235.

Lovelock, J. E. 1983. Daisy World: A cybernetic proof of the Gaia hypothesis. *Coevolution Quart*, 38, 66–72.

Lovelock, J. E. and Margulis, L. 1974a. Atmospheric homeostasis by and for the biosphere: The gaia hypothesis. *Tellus*, 26, 2–9.

Lovelock, J. E. and Margulis, L. 1974b. Homeostatic tendencies of the Earth's atmosphere. *Orig life*, 5. 93–103.

Sagan, D., and Margulis, L. 1983. The Gaia perspective of ecology. *The Ecologist*, 13, 160–167.

Spencer, H. 1844. Remarks upon the theory of reciprocal dependence in the animal and vegetable creations, as regards its bearing upon paleontology. *The London, Edinburgh, and Dublin Philosophical Magazine and Journal of Science*, 24, 90–94. Reprinted in Cloud, P., ed. 1970. *Adventures in Earth History*. New York: W. H. Freeman.

Watson, A. J., and Lovelock, J. E. 1983. Biological homeostasis of the global environment: The parable of daisyworld. *Tellus*, 35B, 284–289.

Study Questions

1. Go over each of the hypotheses discussed by Kirchner. Based on the previous article by Lovelock and Epton, which seem central to the original Gaian project?

2. Why does Kirchner think that untestable hypotheses are "ugly" and that being "ugly" in science is worse than being bad? Do you agree?

3. In 1990 Lovelock responded to Kirchner's critique, saying it was a "spirited attempt to demolish all notions of Gaia. Like some figure of the Inquisition, he publicly burned several imaginary Gaias, and his pyrotechnic demolition of the strong Gaia stole the show. But when the sparks faded, the real system Gaia was still hidden only by the smoke. The flux of papers inspired by

Gaia, and now appearing in the journals, are the real proof of the value of the conference. It has not stopped peer review from censoring any mention of Gaia by name." (James E. Lovelock, "Hands Up for the Gaia Hypothesis," *Nature* 344 (1990): 100–102).

Is this an accurate description of Kirchner's paper? Of what value is the Gaia hypothesis?

For Further Reading

Burnyard, Peter, and Edward Goldsmith, eds. *Gaia, the Thesis, the Mechanisms, and the Implications*. Wadebridge, England: Wadebridge Ecological Centre, 1988.

Goldsmith, Edward. *The Way: An Ecological World-View*. Boston: Shambala, 1993.

Kirchner, J. W. "The Gaia Hypothesis: Can It Be Tested?" *Review of Geophysics* 27 (1989): 223–235.

Lovelock, J. E. *Gaia. A New Look at Life on Earth*. New York: Oxford University Press, 1981.

Lovelock, J. E., and L. Margulis. "Homeostatic Tendencies of the Earth's Atmosphere." *Origin Life* 5 (1974): 93–103.

Sagan, D., and L. Margulis. "The Gaia Perspective of Ecology." *The Ecologist* 13 (1983): 160–167.

CHAPTER SIX

Preservation of the Species, Nature, and Natural Objects

Biodiversity is our most valuable but least appreciated resource.

EDWARD O. WILSON, *THE DIVERSITY OF LIFE*

Why should we be concerned with the preservation of species? Why is biodiversity so important that we must make sacrifices to preserve and enhance it? Who cares if the snail darter, a fish of no known use to humans, perishes in the process of building a dam that will save the economy of the Tennessee Valley? Is biodiversity important in itself? Or do other species of plants and animals have only instrumental value, relative to human need? Do species have rights?

The total number of species of life is somewhere between 10 million and 30 million, of which only 1.7 million are named and only a small fraction have been studied. Yet we are destroying these species at a record rate. Many types of plants and animals, like the California condor and the blue whale, are endangered. The majority of the unnamed and unstudied species reside in tropical rain forests in poor countries and are rapidly being destroyed for economic reasons. What should be done about this destruction?

We return to the question, Do species have intrinsic value? The philosopher Nicholas Rescher says they do: "When a species vanishes from nature, the world is thereby diminished. Species do not just have an instrumental value . . . they have a value in their own right—an intrinsic value." And one of the leading proponents of the land ethic, Baird Callicott (see Reading 19), wrote, "[T]he preciousness of individual [animals] . . . is inversely proportional to the population of the species." "[T]he human population has become so disproportionate from the biological point of view that if one had to choose between a specimen of *Homo sapiens* and a specimen of a rare even if unattractive species, the choice would be moot."

Some land ethicists, like Callicott at one stage in his development, and many deep ecologists (see Chapter 3), would hold that nature has intrinsic value, so ecosystems and species should be valued in their own right. In our first reading in this section, Donella Meadows argues that three strong reasons should compel us to protect biodiversity: economic value in terms of new drugs and food products; environmental service (without the complex service of microorganisms and other species, life would stop); and genetic information (vast stores of knowledge are stored in the DNA structure of the living cells of these species). So we have two different kinds of motives: (1) self-interested concern for our survival and flourishing and (2) moral respect for something magnificent that we did not create and do not understand.

In our second reading, Lilly-Marlene Russow asks why do species matter? She argues that we normally ascribe rights to someone because he or she has interests, but species cannot suffer or have interests, since only individual objects can have interests. Since it doesn't make sense to attribute interests to species, it follows that they do not have rights, and so we cannot have obligations to them. She examines three arguments for species preservation and argues that they all fail. She concludes that individual animals can have aesthetic value, and this is the basis for our obligation to preserve animals of that sort.

In our third reading, Stephen Jay Gould rejects the stewardship model of environmentalism and argues that a simple application of the Golden Rule will justify us in treating nature kindly, even as we would want to be treated by nature.

We have looked at several arguments for the intrinsic value of Nature and the value of animals and species. Lilly-Marlene Russow's article suggested that the only value nonhuman species have is aesthetic. We want to pursue that idea with regard to natural objects in the second part of this section. Then, granting that natural objects do have some kind of value, we consider what legal standing natural objects should have.

Aesthetic Value. Some parts of nature are undomesticated by human manipulation. Vast mountain ranges or rain forests may be visited by human beings without being significantly altered. Individual objects or forests like the California Redwood trees, the Grand Canyon, or Niagara Falls may be valued for their own sake, or, at least, for aesthetic reasons. The question raised by Holmes Rolston, III (Readings 11 and 13) and Ernest Partridge (Readings 12 and 14) reemerges now: Do natural objects like Redwood trees or Niagara Falls or the Grand Canyon have intrinsic value in such a way that they cannot be replaced by artificial surrogates—for example, plastic trees, man-made waterfalls, and Disneyland gorges?

In "What's Wrong with Plastic Trees?" Martin Krieger questions the preservationist thesis that we must preserve original natural objects. He challenges us to state precisely why artificial objects may not serve us as well as natural ones. We must not worship nature but examine the cost/benefits of preserving natural objects and "wildernesses" (a human designation) in relation to other economic and social needs.

In our fifth reading, "Faking Nature," Robert Elliot considers the views of Krieger and other antipreservationists who hold the "restoration thesis." The restoration thesis argues that a restored, artificial replica of natural objects would preserve their full aesthetic value. Elliot, while granting that the restoration thesis carries some weight, argues that it leaves out too much. Comparing natural objects to art, he maintains that fakes or replicas diminish the original value. Our understanding of the origins of these objects affects our evaluation of them, so something is lost in the replication process.

In our next reading, "The Call of the Wild," Eric Katz goes even further than Elliot in rejecting the restoration thesis. He is suspicious of using *technology* to "improve" nature and argues, to the contrary, that

value inheres in nature to the extent that it avoids modification by human technology. Natural objects should not be evaluated according to their human uses but seen as possessing inherent autonomy. Furthermore, we have a duty to fight against technological incursions into nature.

Legal Standing. We usually seek to protect valuable objects that are threatened by human intervention. While our legal system covers such inanimate objects as corporations and states, it has not widely been extended to cover natural objects.

In our final reading in this section—"Should Trees Have Standing?"—Christopher Stone argues that from both anthropocentric and holistic perspectives, we should assign natural objects (rivers, oceans, trees, the atmosphere, animals) legal rights. He points out that we already grant such inanimate objects as corporations and municipalities such rights, so why not extend the rights further, using the idea of "legal guardian" to cover these objects?

Stone agrees that the idea of granting natural objects legal standing will seem "unthinkable" to many, but he notes, quoting Darwin on the expanding circle of our moral sentiments, that at one time the idea of granting equal rights to women, blacks, and children was thought to be unthinkable. He asks us to consider the arguments on their merits and appeals to anthropocentric and holistic considerations to urge us to widen our horizons toward what sorts of things are worthy of legal rights.

30

Biodiversity: The Key to Saving Life on Earth

Donella H. Meadows

Donella Meadows is an adjunct professor of environmental and policy studies at Dartmouth College and the author of several works in environmental studies, including Limits to Growth. *In this essay, Meadows sets forth three reasons for preserving biodiversity: economic, environmental, and informational. She appeals both to our enlightened self-interest and wider moral sensitivity for nature and its phenomena in calling on us to leave nature alone so that biodiversity may not be threatened by us.*

The ozone hole and the greenhouse effect have entered our public vocabulary, but we have no catchy label for

the third great environmental problem of the late 20th century. It's even more diffuse than depletion of the ozone layer or global warming, harder to grasp and summarize. The experts call it "the loss of biodiversity."

Biodiversity obviously has something to do with pandas, tigers and tropical forests. But preserving biodiversity is a much bigger job than protecting rain forests or charismatic megafauna. It's the job of protecting all life—microscopic creepy-crawlies as well as elephants and condors—and all life's habitats—tundra, prairie and swamp as well as forests.

Why care about tundra, swamp, blue beetles or little blue-stem grasses? Ecologists give three reasons, which boil down to simple self-interest on three levels of escalating importance.

• Biodiversity has both immediate and potential economic value. This is the argument most commonly put

Reprinted from *The Land Steward Letter* (Summer 1990) by permission.

forward to defend biodiversity, because it's the one our culture is most ready to hear. It cites the importance of the industries most directly dependent upon nature—fisheries, forestry, tourism, recreation and the harvesting of wild foods, medicines, dyes, rubber and chemicals.

Some ecologists are so tired of this line of reasoning that they refer wearily to the "Madagascar periwinkle argument." That obscure plant yields the drugs vincristine and vinblastine, which have revolutionized the treatment of leukemia. About a third of all modem medicines have derived from molds and plants.

The potential for future discoveries is astounding. The total number of species of life is somewhere between 10 million and 30 million, only 1.7 million of which we have named, only a fraction of which we have tested for usefulness.

The economic value of biodiversity is very real, but ecologists hate the argument because it is both arrogant and trivial. It assumes that the Earth's millions of species are here to serve the economic purposes of just one species. And even if you buy that idea, it misses the larger and more valuable ways that nature serves us.

• Biodiversity performs environmental services beyond price. How would you like the job of pollinating trillions of apple blossoms some sunny afternoon in May? It's conceivable, maybe, that you could invent a machine to do it, but inconceivable that the machine could work as elegantly and cheaply as the honeybee, much less make honey on the side.

Suppose you were assigned to turn every bit of dead organic matter, from fallen leaves to urban garbage, into nutrients that feed new life. Even if you knew how, what would it cost? A host of bacteria, molds, mites and worms do it for free. If they ever stopped, all life would stop. We would not last long if green plants stopped turning our exhaled carbon dioxide back into oxygen. Plants would not last long if a few genera of soil bacteria stopped turning nitrogen from the air into nitrate fertilizer.

Human reckoning cannot put a value on the services performed by the ecosystems of Earth. These services include the cleansing of air and water, flood control, drought prevention, pest control, temperature regulation and maintenance of the world's most valuable library—the genes of all living orgasms.

• Biodiversity contains the accumulated wisdom of nature and the key to its future. If you ever wanted to destroy a society, you would burn its libraries and kill its intellectuals. You would destroy its knowledge. Nature's knowledge is contained in the DNA within living cells. The variety of that genetic information is the driving engine of evolution, the immune system for life, the source of adaptability—not just the variety of species but also the variety of individuals within each species.

Individuals are never quite alike. Each is genetically unique mostly in subterranean ways that will only appear in future generations. We recognize that is true

of human beings. Plant and animal breeders recognize it in dogs, cattle, wheat, roses, apples. The only reason they can bring forth bigger fruits or sweeter smells or disease resistance is that those traits are already present in the genes carried by some individuals.

The amount of information in a single cell is hard to comprehend. A simple one-celled bacterium can carry genes for 1,000 traits, a flowering plant for 400,000. Biologist E. O. Wilson says the information in the genes of an ordinary house mouse, if translated into printed letters, would fill all the 15 editions of the Encyclopedia Britannica that have been published since 1768.

The wealth of generic information has been selected over billions of years to fit the ever-changing necessities of the planet. As Earth's atmosphere filled with oxygen, as land masses drifted apart, as humans invented agriculture and altered the land, there were lurking within individuals pieces of genetic code that allowed them to defend against or take advantage of the changes. These individuals were more fit for the new environment. They bred more successfully. The population began to take on their characteristics. New species came into being.

Biodiversity is the accumulation of all life's past adaptations, and it is the basis for all further adaptations (even those mediated by human gene-splicers).

That's why ecologists value biodiversity as one of Earth's great resources. It's why they take seriously the loss of even the most insignificant species; why they defend not only the preservation of species but the preservation of populations within species, and why they regard the rate of human-induced extinctions as an unparalleled catastrophe.

We don't know how many species we are eliminating, because we don't know how many species there are. It's a fair guess that, at the rate we're destroying habitat, we're pushing to extinction about one species every hour. That doesn't count the species whose populations are being reduced so greatly that diversity within the population is essentially gone. Earth has not seen a spasm of extinctions like this for 65 million years.

Biologists estimate that human beings usurp, directly or indirectly, about 40 percent of each year's total biological production. There is hardly a place on Earth where people do not log, pave, spray, drain, flood, graze, fish, plow, burn, drill, spill or dump. There is no life zone, with the possible exception of the deep ocean, that we are not degrading.

Besides "loss of diversity," biologists have another name for this problem—"biotic impoverishment." What is impoverished is not just biodiversity, it is also the human economy and human spirit.

Ecologist Paul Ehrlich describes biotic impoverishment this way: "Unless current trends are reversed, Americans will gradually be living in a nation that has fewer warblers and ducks and more starlings and herring gulls, fewer native wildflowers and more noxious weeds, fewer swallowtail butterflies and more cockroaches, smaller herds of elk and bigger herds of rats, less edible seafood, less productive croplands, less dependable supplies of pure fresh water, more desert wastes and dust storms, more frequent floods and more uncomfortable weather."

Biodiversity cannot be maintained by protecting a few species in a zoo, nor by preserving greenbelts or even national parks. To function properly nature needs more room than that. It can maintain itself, however, without human expense, without zookeepers, park rangers, foresters or gene banks. All it needs is to be left alone.

To provide their priceless pollination service, the honeybees ask only that we stop saturating the landscape with poisons, stop paving the meadows where bee-food grows and leave them enough honey to get through the winter.

To maintain our planet, our lives and our future potential, the other species have similar requests, all of which add up to: Control yourselves. Control your numbers. Control your greed. See yourselves as what you are, part of an interdependent biological community— the most intelligent part, though you don't often act that way.

So act that way, either out of a moral respect for something magnificent that you didn't create and do not understand, or out of a practical interest in your own survival.

Study Questions

1. What are Meadows's main reasons for protecting biodiversity? Do her conclusions follow from her specific reasons? Explain.
2. Why can't we simply preserve species in zoos and national parks?
3. Some species are quite harmful to humans, like the smallpox virus. Shouldn't we destroy these altogether?
4. The U.S. Endangered Species Act of 1973 protects hundreds of species, preventing activities that might further threaten these species. In December 1992, the Bush administration yielded to pressures from environmental groups and agreed to add 400 species to its list of endangered (and protected) species over the next four years, bringing the total to 750 protected species. Business groups complain that such acts hurt business and threaten jobs. Should species be protected if such protection causes unemployment and is bad for the economy?

31

Why Do Species Matter?

LILLY-MARLENE RUSSOW

Lilly-Marlene Russow teaches philosophy at Purdue University and is the author of several works in philosophy. In this essay, she first examines various test cases to show some of the complexities involved in any attempt to describe obligations to species. Next she analyzes three arguments for obligations to protect endangered species and concludes that not only do they fail but that there is a conceptual confusion in any attempt to ascribe value to a species. Whatever duty we do have in this regard must rest on the "value—often aesthetic—of individual members of certain species."

I. INTRODUCTION

Consider the following extension of the standard sort of objection to treating animals differently just because they are not humans: the fact that a being is or is not a member of species *S* is not a morally relevant fact, and

Reprinted from *Environmental Ethics*, Vol. 3 (1981) by permission.

does not justify treating that being differently from members of other species. If so, we cannot treat a bird differently *just* because it is a California condor rather than a turkey vulture The problem, then, becomes one of determining what special obligations, if any, a person might have toward California condors, and what might account for those obligations in a way that is generally consistent with the condemnation of speciesism. Since it will turn out that the solution I offer does not admit of a direct and tidy proof, what follows comprises three sections which approach this issue from different directions. The resulting triangulation should serve as justification and motivation for the conclusion sketched in the final section.

II. SPECIES AND INDIVIDUALS

Much of the discussion in the general area of ethics and animals has dealt with the rights of animals, or obligations and duties toward individual animals. The first thing to note is that some, but not all, of the actions normally thought of as obligatory with respect to the protection of vanishing species can be recast as possible duties to individual members of that species. Thus, if it could be shown that we have a *prima facie duty* not to kill a sentient being, it would follow that it would be wrong, other things being equal, to kill a blue whale or a California condor. But it would be wrong for the same reason, and to the same degree, that it would be wrong to kill a turkey vulture or a pilot whale. Similarly, if it is wrong (something which I do not think can be shown) to deprive an individual animal of its natural habitat, it would be wrong, for the same reasons and to the same degree, to do that to a member of an endangered species. And so on. Thus, an appeal to our duties toward individual animals may provide some protection, but they do not justify the claim that we should treat members of a vanishing species with *more* care than members of other species.

More importantly, duties toward individual beings (or the rights of those individuals) will not always account for all the actions that people feel obligated to do for endangered species—e.g., bring into the world as many individuals of that species as possible, protect them from natural predation, or establish separate breeding colonies. In fact, the protection of a species might involve actions that are demonstrably contrary to the interests of some or all of the individual animals: this seems true in cases when we remove all the animals we can from their natural environment and raise them in zoos, or where we severely restrict the range of a species by hunting all those outside a certain area, as is done in Minnesota to protect the timber wolf. If such efforts are morally correct, our duties to preserve a species cannot be grounded in obligations that we have toward individual animals.

Nor will it be fruitful to treat our obligations to a species as duties toward, or as arising out of the rights of, a species thought of as some special superentity. It is simply not clear that we can make sense of talk about the interests of a species in the absence of beliefs, desires, purposeful action, etc. Since having interests is generally accepted as at least a necessary condition for having rights, and since many of the duties we have toward animals arise directly out of the animals' interests, arguments which show that animals have rights, or that we have duties towards them, will not apply to species. Since arguments which proceed from interests to rights or from interests to obligations make up a majority of the literature on ethics and animals, it is unlikely that these arguments will serve as a key to possible obligations toward species.

Having eliminated the possibility that our obligations toward species are somehow parallel to, or similar to, our obligation not to cause unwarranted pain to an animal, there seem to be only a few possibilities left. We may find that our duties toward species arise not out of the interests of the species, but are rooted in the general obligation to preserve things of value. Alternatively, our obligations to species may in fact be obligations to individuals (either members of the species or other individuals), but obligations that differ from the ones just discussed in that they are not determined simply by the interests of the individual.

III. SOME TEST CASES

If we are to find some intuitively acceptable foundation for claims about our obligations to protect species, we must start afresh. In order to get clear about what, precisely, we are looking for in this context, what obligations we might think we have toward species, what moral claims we are seeking a foundation for, I turn now to a description of some test cases. An examination of these cases illustrates why the object of our search is not something as straightforward as "Do whatever is possible or necessary to preserve the existence of the species"; a consideration of some of the differences between cases will guide our search for the nature of our obligations and the underlying reasons for those obligations.

Case 1. The snail darter is known to exist only in one part of one river. This stretch of river would be destroyed by the building of the Tellico dam. Defenders of the dam have successfully argued that the dam is nonetheless necessary for the economic development and well-being of the area's population. To my knowledge, no serious or large scale attempt has been made to breed large numbers of snail darters in captivity (for any reason other than research).

Case 2. The Pére David deer was first discovered by a Western naturalist in 1865, when Pére Armand David found herds of the deer in the Imperial Gardens in Peking: even at that time, they were only known to exist in captivity. Pére David brought several animals back to Europe, where they bred readily enough so that now there are healthy populations in several major zoos. There is no reasonable hope of reintroducing the Pére David deer to its natural habitat; indeed, it is not even definitely known what its natural habitat was.

Case 3. The red wolf (*Canis rufus*) formerly ranged over the southeastern and south-central United States. As with most wolves, they were threatened, and their range curtailed, by trapping, hunting, and the destruction of habitat. However, a more immediate threat to the continued existence of the red wolf is that these changes extended the range of the more adaptable coyote, with whom the red wolf interbreeds very readily; as a result, there are very few "pure" red wolves left. An attempt has been made to capture some pure breeding stock and raise wolves on preserves.

Case 4. The Baltimore oriole and the Bullock's oriole were long recognized and classified as two separate species of birds. As a result of extensive interbreeding between the two species in areas where their ranges overlapped, the American Ornithologists' Union recently declared that there were no longer two separate species; both ex-species are now called "northern orioles."

Case 5. The Appaloosa is a breed of horse with a distinctively spotted coat; the Lewis and Clark expedition discovered that the breed was associated with the Nez Percé Indians. When the Nez Percé tribe was defeated by the U.S. Cavalry in 1877 and forced to move, their horses were scattered and interbred with other horses. The distinctive coat pattern was almost lost; not until the middle of the twentieth century was a concerted effort made to gather together the few remaining specimens and reestablish the breed.

Case 6. Many strains of laboratory rats are bred specifically for a certain type of research. Once the need for a particular variety ceases—once the type of research is completed—the rats are usually killed, with the result that the variety becomes extinct.

Case 7. It is commonly known that several diseases such as sleeping sickness, malaria, and human encephalitis are caused by one variety of mosquito but not by others. Much of the disease control in these cases is aimed at exterminating the disease carrying insect; most people do not find it morally wrong to wipe out the whole species.

Case 8. Suppose that zebras were threatened solely because they were hunted for their distinctive striped coats. Suppose, too, that we could remove this threat by selectively breeding zebras that are not striped, that look exactly like mules, although they are still pure zebras. Have we preserved all that we ought to have preserved?

What does an examination of these test cases reveal? First, that our concept of what a species *is* is not at all unambiguous; at least in part, what counts as a species is a matter of current fashions in taxonomy. Furthermore, it seems that it is not the sheer diversity or number of species that matters: if that were what is valued, moral preference would be given to taxonomic schemes that separated individuals into a larger number of species, a suggestion which seems absurd. The case of the orioles suggests that the decision as to whether to call these things one species or two is not a moral issue at all. Since we are not evidently concerned with the existence or diversity of species in *this* sense, there must be something more at issue than the simple question of whether we have today the same number of species represented as we had yesterday. Confusion sets in, however, when we try to specify another sense in which it is possible to speak of the "existence" of a species. This only serves to emphasize the basic murkiness of our intuitions about what the object of our concern really is.

This murkiness is further revealed by the fact that it is not at all obvious what we are trying to preserve in some of the test cases. Sometimes, as in the case of the Appaloosa or attempts to save a subspecies like the Arctic wolf or the Mexican wolf, it is not a whole species that is in question. But not all genetic subgroups are of interest—witness the case of the laboratory rat—and sometimes the preservation of the species at the cost of one of its externally obvious features (the stripes on a zebra) is not our only concern. This is not a minor puzzle which can be resolved by changing our question from "why do species matter?" to "why do species and/or subspecies matter?" It is rather a serious issue of what makes a group of animals "special" enough or "unique" enough to warrant concern. And of course, the test cases reveal that our intuitions are not always consistent: although the cases of the red wolf and the northern oriole are parallel in important respects, we are more uneasy about simply reclassifying the red wolf and allowing things to continue along their present path.

The final point to be established is that whatever moral weight is finally attached to the preservation of a species (or subspecies), it can be overridden. We apparently have no compunction about wiping out a species of mosquito if the benefits gained by such action are sufficiently important, although many people were unconvinced by similar arguments in favor of the Tellico dam.

The lesson to be drawn from this section can be stated in a somewhat simplistic form: it is not simply the case that we can solve our problems by arguing that there is some value attached to the mere existence of a species. Our final analysis must take account of various features or properties of certain kinds or groups of animals, and it has to recognize that our concern is with the continued existence of individuals that may or may not have some distinctive characteristics.

IV. SOME TRADITIONAL ANSWERS

There are, of course, some standard replies to the question "Why do species matter?" or, more particularly, to the question "Why do we have at least a *prima facie* duty not to cause a species to become extinct, and in some cases, a duty to try actively to preserve species?" With some tolerance for borderline cases, these replies generally fall into three groups: (1) those that appeal to our role as "stewards" or "caretakers," (2) those that claim that species have some extrinsic value (I include in this group those that argue that the species is valuable as part of the ecosystem or as a link in the evolutionary scheme of things), and (3) those that appeal to some intrinsic or inherent value that is supposed to make a species worth preserving. In this section, with the help of the test cases just discussed, I indicate some serious flaws with each of these responses.

The first type of view has been put forward in the philosophical literature by Joel Feinberg, who states that our duty to preserve whole species may be more important than any rights had by individual animals. He argues, first, that this duty does not arise from a right or claim that can properly be attributed to the species as a whole (his reasons are much the same as the ones I cited in section 2 of this paper), and second, while we have some duty to unborn generations that directs us to preserve species, that duty is much weaker than the actual duty we have to preserve species. The fact that our actual duty extends beyond our duties to future generations is explained by the claim that we have duties of "stewardship" with respect to the world as a whole. Thus, Feinberg notes that his "inclination is to seek an explanation in terms of the requirements of our unique station as rational custodians of the planet we temporarily occupy."

The main objection to this appeal to our role as stewards or caretakers is that it begs the question. The job of a custodian is to protect that which is deserving of protection, that which has some value or worth. But the issue before us now is precisely *whether* species have value, and why. If we justify our obligations of stewardship by reference to the value of that which is cared for, we cannot also explain the value by pointing to the duties of stewardship.

The second type of argument is the one which establishes the value of a species by locating it in the "larger scheme of things." That is, one might try to argue that species matter because they contribute to, or form an essential part of, some other good. This line of defense has several variations.

The first version is completely anthropocentric: it is claimed that vanishing species are of concern to us because their difficulties serve as a warning that we have polluted or altered the environment in a way that is potentially dangerous or undesirable for us. Thus, the California condor whose eggshells are weakened due to the absorption of DDT indicates that something is wrong: presumably we are being affected in subtle ways by the absorption of DDT, and that is bad for us. Alternatively, diminishing numbers of game animals may signal overhunting which, if left unchecked, would leave the sportsman with fewer things to hunt. And, as we become more aware of the benefits that might be obtained from rare varieties of plants and animals (drugs, substitutes for other natural resources, tools for research), we may become reluctant to risk the disappearance of a species that might be of practical use to us in the future.

This line of argument does not carry us very far. In the case of a subspecies, most benefits could be derived from other varieties of the same species. More important, when faced with the loss of a unique variety or species, we may simply decide that, even taking into account the possibility of error, there is not enough reason to think that the species will ever be of use; we may take a calculated risk and decide that it is not worth it. Finally, the use of a species as a danger signal may apply to species whose decline is due to some subtle and unforeseen change in the environment, but will not justify concern for a species threatened by a known and forseen event like the building of a dam.

Other attempts to ascribe extrinsic value to a species do not limit themselves to potential human and practical goods. Thus, it is often argued that each species occupies a unique niche in a rich and complex, but delicately balanced, ecosystem. By destroying a single species, we upset the balance of the whole system. On the assumption that the system as a whole should be preserved, the value of a species is determined, at least in part, by its contribution to the whole.

In assessing this argument, it is important to realize that such a justification (a) may lead to odd conclusions about some of the test cases, and (b) allows for changes which do not affect the system, or which result in the substitution of a richer, more complex system for one that is more primitive or less evolved. With regard to the first of these points, species that exist only in zoos would seem to have no special value. In terms of our test cases, the David deer does not exist as part of a system, but only in isolation. Similarly, the Appaloosa horse, a domesticated variety which is neither better suited nor worse than any other sort of horse, would not have any special value. In contrast, the whole cycle of mosquitoes, disease organisms adapted to these hosts, and other beings susceptible to those diseases is quite a complex and marvelous bit of systematic adaptation. Thus, it would seem to be wrong to wipe out the encephalitis-bearing mosquito.

With regard to the second point, we might consider changes effected by white settlers in previously isolated areas such as New Zealand and Australia. The introduction of new species has resulted in a whole new ecosystem, with many of the former indigenous species being replaced by introduced varieties. As long as the new system works, there seems to be no grounds for objections.

The third version of an appeal to extrinsic value is sometimes presented in Darwinian terms: species are important as links in the evolutionary chain. This will get us nowhere, however, because the extinction of one species, the replacement of one by another, is as much a part of evolution as is the development of a new species.

One should also consider a more general concern about all those versions of the argument which focus on the species' role in the natural order of things: all of these arguments presuppose that "the natural order of things" is, in itself, good. As William Blackstone pointed out, this is by no means obvious: "Unless one adheres dogmatically to a position of a 'reverence for all life,' the extinction of some species or forms of life may be seen as quite desirable. (This is parallel to the point often made by philosophers that not all 'customary' or 'natural' behavior is necessarily good)." Unless we have some other way of ascribing value to a system, and to the animals which actually fulfill a certain function in that system (as opposed to possible replacements), the argument will not get off the ground.

Finally, then, the process of elimination leads us to the set of arguments which point to some *intrinsic value* that a species is supposed to have. The notion that species have an intrinsic value, if established, would allow us to defend much stronger claims about human obligations toward threatened species. Thus, if a species is intrinsically valuable, we should try to preserve it even when it no longer has a place in the natural ecosystem, or when it could be replaced by another species that would occupy the same niche. Most important, we should not ignore a species just because it serves no useful purpose.

Unsurprisingly, the stumbling block is what this intrinsic value might be grounded in. Without an explanation of that, we have no nonarbitrary way of deciding whether subspecies as well as species have intrinsic value or how much intrinsic value a species might have. The last question is meant to bring out issues that will arise in cases of conflict of interests: is the intrinsic value of a species of mosquito sufficient to outweigh the benefits to be gained by eradicating the means of spreading a disease like encephalitis? Is the intrinsic value of the snail darter sufficient to outweigh the economic hardship that might be alleviated by the construction of a dam? In short, to say that something has intrinsic value does not tell us *how much* value it has, nor does it allow us to make the sorts of judgments that are often called for in considering the fate of an endangered species.

The attempt to sidestep the difficulties raised by subspecies by broadening the ascription of value to include subspecies opens a whole Pandora's box. It would follow that any genetic variation within a species that results in distinctive characteristics would need separate protection. In the case of forms developed through selective breeding, it is not clear whether we have a situation analogous to natural subspecies, or whether no special value is attached to different breeds.

In order to speak to either of these issues, and in order to lend plausibility to the whole enterprise, it would seem necessary to consider first the justification for ascribing value to whichever groups have such value. If intrinsic value does not spring from anything, if it becomes merely another way of saying that we should protect species, we are going around in circles, without explaining anything. Some further explanation is needed.

Some appeals to intrinsic value are grounded in the intuition that diversity itself is a virtue. If so, it would seem incumbent upon us to create new species wherever possible, even bizarre ones that would have no purpose other than to be different. Something other than diversity must therefore be valued.

The comparison that is often made between species and natural wonders, spectacular landscapes, or even works of art, suggest that species might have some aesthetic value. This seems to accord well with our naive intuitions, provided that *aesthetic value* is interpreted rather loosely; most of us believe that the world would be a poorer place for the loss of bald eagles in the same way that it would be poorer for the loss of the Grand Canyon or a great work of art. In all cases, the experience of seeing these things is an inherently worthwhile experience. And since diversity in some cases is a component in aesthetic appreciation, part of the previous intuition would be preserved. There is also room for degrees of selectivity and concern with superficial changes: the variety of rat that is allowed to become extinct may have no special aesthetic value, and a bird is neither more nor less aesthetically pleasing when we change its name.

There are some drawbacks to this line of argument: there are some species which, by no stretch of the imagination, are aesthetically significant. But aesthetic value can cover a surprising range of things: a tiger may be simply beautiful; a blue whale is awe-inspiring; a bird might be decorative; an Appaloosa is of interest because of its historical significance; and even a drab little plant may inspire admiration for the marvelous way it has been adapted to a special environment. Even so, there may be species such as the snail darter that simply have no aesthetic value. In these cases, lacking any alternative, we may be forced to the conclusion that such species are not worth preserving.

Seen from other angles, once again the appeal to the aesthetic value of species is illuminating. Things that have an aesthetic value compared and ranked in some cases, and commitment of resources may be made accordingly. We believe that diminishing the aesthetic value of a thing for mere economic benefits is immoral, but that aesthetic value is not absolute—that the fact that something has aesthetic value may be overridden by the fact that harming that thing, or destroying it, may result in some greater good. That is, someone who agrees to destroy a piece of Greek statuary for personal gain would be condemned as having done something immoral, but someone who is faced with a choice between saving his children and saving a "priceless" painting would be said to have skewed values if he chose to save the painting. Applying these observations to species, we can see that an appeal to aesthetic value would justify putting more effort into the preservation of one species than the preservation of another; indeed, just as we think that the doodling of a would-be artist may have no merit at all, we may think that the accidental and unfortunate mutation of a species is not worth preserving. Following the analogy, allowing a species to become extinct for *mere* economic gain might be seen as immoral, while the possibility remains open that other (human?) good might outweigh the goods achieved by the preservation of a species.

Although the appeal to aesthetic values has much to recommend it—even when we have taken account of the fact that it does not guarantee that all species matter—there seems to be a fundamental confusion that still affects the cogency of the whole argument and its application to the question of special obligations to endangered species, for if the value of a species is based on its aesthetic value, it is impossible to explain why an endangered species should be more valuable, or more worthy of preservation, than an unendangered species. The appeal to "rarity" will not help, if what we are talking about is species: each species is unique, no more or less rare than any other species: there is in each case one and only one species that we are talking about.

This problem of application seems to arise because the object of aesthetic appreciation, and hence of aesthetic value, has been misidentified, for it is not the case that we perceive, admire, and appreciate a *species*—species construed either as a group or set of similar animals or as a name that we attach to certain kinds of animals in virtue of some classification scheme. What we value is the existence of individuals with certain characteristics. If this is correct, then the whole attempt to explain why species matter by arguing that *they* have aesthetic value needs to be redirected. This is what I try to do in the final section of this paper.

V. VALUING THE INDIVIDUAL

What I propose is that the intuition behind the argument from aesthetic value is correct, but misdirected. The reasons that were given for the value of a species are, in fact, reasons for saying that an individual has value. We do not admire the grace and beauty of the species *Panthera tigris*; rather, we admire the grace and beauty of the individual Bengal tigers that we may encounter. What we value then is the existence of that individual and the existence (present or future) of individuals like that. The ways in which other individuals should be "like that" will depend on why we value that particular sort of individual: the stripes on a zebra do not matter if we value zebras primarily for the way they are adapted to a certain environment, their unique fitness for a certain sort of life. If, on the other hand, we value zebras because their stripes are aesthetically pleasing, the stripes do matter. Since our attitudes toward zebras probably include both of these features, it is not

surprising to find that my hypothetical test case produces conflicting intuitions.

The shift of emphasis from species to individuals allows us to make sense of the stronger feelings we have about endangered species in two ways. First, the fact that there are very few members of a species—the fact that we rarely encounter one—itself increases the value of those encounters. I can see turkey vultures almost every day, and I can eat apples almost every day, but seeing a bald eagle or eating wild strawberries are experiences that are much less common, more delightful just for their rarity and unexpectedness. Even snail darters, which, if we encountered them every day would be drab and uninteresting, become more interesting just because we don't—or may not—see them everyday. Second, part of our interest in an individual carries over to a desire that there be future opportunities to see these things again (just as when, upon finding a new and beautiful work of art, I will wish to go back and see it again). In the case of animals, unlike works of art, I know that this animal will not live forever, but that other animals like this one will have similar aesthetic value. Thus, because I value possible future encounters, I will also want to do what is needed to ensure the possibility of such encounters—i.e., make sure that enough presently existing individuals of this type will be able to reproduce and survive. This is rather like the duty that we have to support and contribute to museums, or to other efforts to preserve works of art.

To sum up, then: individual animals can have, to a greater or lesser degree, aesthetic value: they are valued for their simple beauty, for their awesomeness, for their intriguing adaptations, for their rarity, and for many other reasons. We have moral obligations to protect things of aesthetic value, and to ensure (in an odd sense) their continued existence; thus we have a duty to protect individual animals (the duty may be weaker or stronger depending on the value of the individual), and to ensure that there will continue to be animals of this sort (this duty will also be weaker or stronger, depending on value).

I began this paper by suggesting that our obligations to vanishing species might appear inconsistent with a general condemnation of speciesism. My proposal is not inconsistent: we value and protect animals because of their aesthetic value, not because they are members of a given species.

Study Questions

1. Do you agree with Russow's rejection of inherent value in species?
2. Is Russow's argument for aesthetic value in individual animals of certain types just another version of anthropocentrism? We get pleasure from beholding certain animals. Does that mean that they are merely resources for our enjoyment?

3. The blue whale is an endangered species, which is valuable for its oil and meat. Supposing its immediate economic value outweighs its aesthetic value, would Russow's arguments conclude that no moral evil would be done in eliminating this species? What do you think?

4. Richard Routley asks the following question to those who see no intrinsic value in other species. Suppose human beings were about to die out. Would it be morally permissible to kill (painlessly, just in case that matters) all other life on Earth before we became extinct? Why, or why not?

32

The Golden Rule—A Proper Scale for Our Environmental Crisis

Stephen Jay Gould

Stephen Jay Gould (b. 1941) is professor of paleontology at Harvard University and one of the leading evolutionary biologists in the United States. In this essay, he rejects stewardship arguments (Reading 4) and the intrinsic value arguments (Readings 11–17) for preserving endangered species. Instead, he appeals to the Golden Rule to make a general point in regard to our treatment of nature, which includes the preservation of species.

Patience enjoys a long pedigree of favor. Chaucer pronounced it "an heigh vertu, certeyn" ("The Franklin's Tale"), while the New Testament had already made a motto of the Old Testament's most famous embodiment: "Ye have heard of the patience of Job" (James 5:11). Yet some cases seem so extended in diligence and time that another factor beyond sheer endurance must lie behind the wait. When Alberich, having lost the Ring of the Nibelungen fully three operas ago, shows up in act 2 of *Götterdämmerung* to advise his son Hagen on strategies for recovery, we can hardly suppress a flicker of admiration for this otherwise unlovable character. (I happen to adore Wagner, but I do recognize that a wait through nearly all the *Ring* cycle would be, to certain unenlightened folks, the very definition of eternity in Hades.)

Patience of this magnitude usually involves a deep understanding of a fundamental principle, central to my own profession of geology but all too rarely grasped in daily life—the effects of scale. Phenomena unfold on their own appropriate scales of space and time and may be invisible in our myopic world of dimensions assessed by comparison with human height and times metered by human life spans. So much of accumulating importance at earthly scales—the results of geological erosion, evolutionary changes in lineages—is invisible by the measuring rod of a human life. So much that matters to particles in the microscopic world of molecules—the his-

tory of a dust grain subject to Brownian motion, the fate of shrunken people in *Fantastic Voyage* or *Inner Space*—either averages out to stability at our scale or simply stands below our limits of perception.

It takes a particular kind of genius or deep understanding to transcend this most pervasive of all conceptual biases and to capture a phenomenon by grasping a proper scale beyond the measuring rods of our own world. Alberich and Wotan know that pursuit of the Ring is dynastic or generational, not personal. William of Baskerville (in Umberto Eco's *Name of the Rose*) solves his medieval mystery because he alone understands that, in the perspective of centuries, the convulsive events of his own day (the dispute between papacies of Rome and Avignon) will be forgotten, while the only surviving copy of a book by Aristotle may influence millennia. Architects of medieval cathedrals had to frame satisfaction on scales beyond their own existence, for they could not live to witness the completion of their designs.

May I indulge in a personal anecdote on the subject of scale? As a child, I loved to memorize facts but rebelled at those I deemed unimportant (baseball stats were in, popes of Rome and kings of England out). In sixth grade, I had to memorize the sequence of land acquisitions that built America. I could see the rationale for learning about the Louisiana Purchase and the Mexican Cession—since they added big chunks to our totality. But I remember balking, and publicly challenging the long-suffering Ms. Stack, at the Gadsden Purchase of 1853. Why did I have to know about a sliver of southern Arizona and New Mexico?

Now I am finally hoist by my own petard (blown up by my own noxious charge, according to the etymologies). After a lifetime of complete nonimpact by the Gadsden Purchase, I have become unwittingly embroiled in a controversy about a tiny bit of territory within this smallest of American growing points. A little bit of a little bit; so much for effects of scale and the penalties of blithe ignorance.

The case is a classic representative of a genre (environmentalists versus developers) made familiar in recent

Reprinted from *Natural History* (Sept. 1990): copyright © The American Museum of Natural History; by permission.

struggles to save endangered populations—the snail darter of a few years back, the northern spotted owl versus timber interests (decided, properly in my view, for the birds on the day that I write this essay, June 2, 1990). The University of Arizona, with the backing of an intentional consortium of astronomers, wishes to build a complex of telescopes atop Mount Graham in southeastern Arizona (part of the Gadsden Purchase). But the old-growth spruce-fir habitat on the mountaintop forms the heart of the range for *Tamiasciurus hudonicus grahamensis*, the Mount Graham red squirrel—a distinct subspecies that lives nowhere else and that forms the southernmost population of the entire species. The population has already been reduced to some 100 survivors, and destruction of several acres of spruce-fir growth (to build the telescopes) within the 700 or so remaining acres of best habitat might well administer a *coup de grâce to* this fragile population.

I cannot state an expert opinion on details of this controversy (I have already confessed my ignorance about everything involving the Gadsden Purchase and its legacy). Many questions need to be answered. Is the population already too small to survive in any case? If not, could the population, with proper management, coexist with the telescopes in the remaining habitat? (Environmentalists fear change of microclimate as much or more than loss of acreage. Reduction of forest canopy will increase wind and sun, producing a drop in humidity. The squirrels survive winter by storing unopened cones in food caches beside trees. If humidity falls, cones may dry out and open, causing loss of seeds and destruction of food.)

I do not think that, practically or morally, we can defend a policy of saving every distinct local population of organisms. I can cite a good rationale for the preservation of species—for each species is a unique and separate natural object that, once lost, can never be reconstituted. But subspecies are distinct local populations of species with broader geographical ranges. Subspecies are dynamic, interbreedable, and constantly changing; what then are we saving by declaring them all inviolate? Thus, I confess that I do not agree with all arguments advanced by defenders of the Mount Graham red squirrel. One leaflet, for example, argues: "The population has been recently shown to have a fixed, homozygous allele which is unique in Western North America." Sorry folks. I will stoutly defend species, but we cannot ask for the preservation of every distinctive gene, unless we find a way to abolish death itself (for many organisms carry unique mutations).

No, I think that for local populations of species with broader ranges, the brief for preservation must be made on a case by case basis, not a general principle of preservation (lest the environmental movement ultimately lose popular support for trying to freeze a dynamic evolutionary world in *statu quo*). On this proper basis of individual merit, I am entirely persuaded that the Mount Graham red squirrel should be protected and the astronomical observatory built elsewhere—and for two reasons.

First, the red squirrel itself: the Mount Graham red is an unusually interesting local population within important species. It is isolated from all other populations and forms the southernmost extreme of the species' range. Such peripheral populations, living in marginal habitats, are of special interest to students of evolution.

Second, the habitat: environmentalists continually face the political reality that support and funding can be won for soft, cuddly, and "attractive" animals, but not for slimy, grubby, and ugly creatures (of potentially greater evolutionary interest and practical significance) or for habitats. This situation has led to the practical concept of "umbrella" or "indicator" species—surrogates for a larger ecological entity worthy of preservation. Thus, the giant panda (really quite a boring and ornery creature despite its good looks) raises money to save the remaining bamboo forests of China (and a plethora of other endangered creatures with no political clout); the northern spotted owl has just rescued some magnificent stands of old-growth giant cedars, Douglas fir, and redwoods (and I say hosanna); and the Mount Graham red squirrel may save a rare and precious habitat of extraordinary evolutionary interest.

The Pinaleno Mountains, reaching 10,720 feet at Mount Graham, are an isolated fault-block range separated from others by alluvial and desert valleys that dip to less than 3,000 feet in elevation. The high peaks of the Pinalenos contain an important and unusual fauna for two reasons. First, they harbor a junction of two biogeographic provinces: the Nearctic, or northern, by way of the Colorado Plateau, and the Neotropical, or southern, via the Mexican Plateau. The Mount Graham red squirrel (a northern species) can live this far south because high elevations reproduce the climate and habitat found near sea level in the more congenial north. Second, and more important to evolutionists, the old-growth spruce-fir habitats on the high peaks of the Pinalenos are isolated "sky islands"—10,000 year-old remnants of a habitat more widely spread over the region of the Gadsden Purchase during the height of the last Ice Age. In evolutionary terms, these isolated pieces of habitat are true islands—patches of more northern microclimate surrounded by southern desert. They are functionally equivalent to bits of land in the ocean. Consider the role that islands (like the Galapagos) have played both in developing the concepts of evolutionary theory and in acting as cradles of origin (through isolation) or vestiges of preservation for biological novelties.

Thus, whether or not the telescopes will drive the Mount Graham red squirrel to extinction (an unsettled question well outside my area of expertise), the sky islands of the Pinalenos are precious habitats that should not be compromised. Let the Mount Graham red squirrel, so worthy of preservation in its own right, also serve as an indicator species for the unique and fragile habitat that it occupies.

But why should I, a confirmed eastern urbanite who has already disclaimed all concern for the Gadsden Purchase, choose to involve myself in the case of the Mount Graham red squirrel? The answer, unsurprisingly, is that I have been enlisted—involuntarily, unawares, and on the wrong side to boot. I am simply fighting mad, and fighting back.

The June 7, 1990, *Wall Street Journal* ran a prodevelopment, antisquirrel opinion piece by Michael D. Copeland (identified as "executive director of the Political Economy Research Center in Bozeman, Montana") under the patently absurd title: "No Red Squirrels? Mother Nature May Be Better Off." (I can at least grasp, while still rejecting, the claim that nature would be no worse off if the squirrel died, but I am utterly befuddled at how anyone could argue that the squirrels inflict a positive harm upon the mother of us all!) In any case, Copeland misunderstood my writings in formulating a supposedly scientific argument for his position.

Now, scarcely a day goes by when I do not read a misrepresentation of my views (usually by creationists, racists, or football fans, in order of frequency). My response to nearly all misquotation is the effective retort of preference: utter silence. (Honorable intellectual disagreement should always be addressed; misquotation should be ignored, when possible and politically practical.) I make an exception in this case because Copeland cited me in the service of a classic false argument—indeed, the standard, almost canonical misuse of my profession of paleontology in debates about extinction. Paleontologists have been enlisted again and again, in opposition to our actual opinions and in support of attitudes that most of us regard as anathema, to uphold arguments by developers about the irrelevance (or even, in this case, the benevolence) of modern anthropogenic extinction. This standard error is a classic example of failure to understand the importance of scale—thus I return to the premise and structure of my introductory paragraphs (did you really think that I waffled on so long about scale only so that I could talk about the Gadsden Purchase?).

Paleontologists do discuss the inevitability of extinction for all species—in the long run and on the broad scale of geological time. We are fond of saying that 99 percent or more of all species that ever lived are now extinct. (My colleague Dave Raup often opens talk on extinction with a zinging one-liner: "To a first approximation, all species are extinct.") We do therefore identify extinction as the normal fate of species. We also talk a lot—more of late since new data have made the field so exciting—about the mass extinctions that punctuate the history of life from time to time. We do discuss the issue of eventual "recovery" from these extinctions, in the sense that life does rebuild or surpass its former diversity after several million years. Finally, we do allow that mass extinctions break up stable faunas and, in this sense, permit or even foster evolutionary innovations well down the road (including the dominance of mammals and the eventual origin of humans, following the death of dinosaurs).

From this set of statements about extinction in the fullness of geological time (on scales of millions of years), some apologists for development have argued that extinction at any scale (even of local populations within years or decades) poses no biological worry but, on the contrary, must be viewed as a comfortable part of an inevitable natural order. Or so Copeland states:

> Suppose we lost a species. How devastating would that be? "Mass extinctions have been recorded since the dawn of paleontology," writes Harvard paleontologist Stephen Gould . . . the most severe of these occurred approximately 250 million years ago . . . with an estimated 96 percent extinction of species, says Mr. Gould. . . . There is general agreement among scientists that today's species represent a small proportion of all those that have ever existed—probably less than 1 percent. This means that more than 99 percent of all species ever living have become extinct.

From these facts, largely irrelevant to red squirrels on Mount Graham, Copeland makes inferences about the benevolence of extinction in general (although the argument applies only to geological scales):

> Yet, in spite of these extinctions, both Mr. Gould and University of Chicago paleontologist Jack Sepkoski say that the actual number of living species has probably increased over time. [True, but not as a result of mass extinctions, despite Copeland's next sentence.] The "niches" created by extinctions provide an opportunity for a vigorous development of new species. . . . Thus, evolutionary history appears to have been characterized by millions of species extinctions and subsequent increases in species numbers. Indeed, by attempting to preserve species living on the brink of extinction, we may be wasting time, effort and money on animals that will disappear over time, regardless of our efforts.

But all will "disappear over time, regardless of our efforts"—millions of years from now for most species if we don't interfere. The mean life span of marine invertebrate species lies between 5 and 10 million years; terrestrial vertebrate species turn over more rapidly, but still average in the millions. By contrast, *Homo sapiens* may be only 250,000 years old or so and may enjoy a considerable future if we don't self-destruct. Similarly, recovery from mass extinction takes its natural measure in millions of years—as much as 10 million or more for fully rekindled diversity after major catastrophic events.

These are the natural time scales of evolution and geology on our planet. But what can such vastness possibly mean for our legitimately parochial interest in ourselves, our ethnic groups, our nations, our cultural traditions, our bloodlines? Of what conceivable significance to us is the prospect of recovery from mass extinction 10 million years down the road if our entire species, not to mention our personal family lineage, has so little prospect of surviving that long?

Capacity for recovery at geological scales has no bearing whatever upon the meaning of extinction today. We are not protecting Mount Graham red squirrels because we fear for global stability in a distant future not likely to include us. We are trying to preserve populations and environments because the comfort and decency of our present lives, and those of fellow species that share our planet, depend upon such stability. Mass extinctions may not threaten distant futures, but they are decidedly unpleasant for species in the throes of their power (particularly if triggered by such truly catastrophic events as extraterrestrial impact). At the appropriate scale of our lives, we are just a species in the midst of such a moment. And to say that we should let the squirrels go (at our immediate scale) because all species eventually die (at geological scales) makes about as much sense as arguing that we shouldn't treat an easily curable childhood infection because all humans are ultimately and inevitably mortal. I love geological time—a wondrous and expansive notion that sets the foundation of my chosen profession, but such immensity is not the proper scale of my personal life.

The same issue of scale underlies the main contributions that my profession of paleontology might make to our larger search for an environmental ethic. This decade, a prelude to the millennium, is widely and correctly viewed as a turning point that will lead either to environmental perdition or stabilization. We have fouled local nests before and driven regional faunas to extinction, but we have never been able to unleash planetary effects before our current concern with ozone holes and putative global warming. In this context, we are searching for proper themes and language to express our environmental worries.

I don't know that paleontology has a great deal to offer, but I would advance one geological insight to combat a well-meaning, but seriously flawed (and all too common), position and to focus attention on the right issue at the proper scale. Two linked arguments are often promoted as a basis for an environmental ethic:

1. That we live on a fragile planet now subject to permanent derailment and disruption by human intervention;
2. That humans must learn to act as stewards for this threatened world.

Such views, however well intentioned, are rooted in the old sin of pride and exaggerated self-importance. We are one among millions of species, *stewards of nothing*. By what argument could we, arising just a geological microsecond ago, become responsible for the affairs of a world 4.5 billion years old, teeming with life that has been evolving and diversifying for at least three-quarters of that immense span? Nature does not exist for us, had no idea we were coming, and doesn't give a damn about us. Omar Khayyám was right in all but his crimped view of the earth as battered when he made his brilliant comparison of our world to an eastern hotel:

Think, in this battered Caravanserai
Whose Portals are alternate
Night and Day,
How Sultan after Sultan with his Pomp
Abode his destined Hour, and,
    went his way.

This assertion of ultimate impotence could be countered if we, despite our late arrival, now held power over the planet's future (argument number one above). But we don't, despite popular misperception of our might. We are virtually powerless over the earth at our planet's own geological time scale. All the megatonnage in our nuclear arsenals yield but one ten-thousandth the power of the asteroid that might have triggered the Cretaceous mass extinction. Yet the earth survived that larger shock and, in wiping out dinosaurs, paved the road for the evolution of large mammals, including humans. We fear global warming, yet even the most radical model yields an earth far cooler than many happy and prosperous times of a prehuman past. We can surely destroy ourselves, and take many other species with us, but we can barely dent bacterial diversity and will surely not remove many million species of insects and mites. On geological scales, our planet will take good care of itself and let time clear the impact of any human malfeasance. The earth need never seek a henchman to wreak Henry's vengeance upon Thomas à Becket: "Who will free me from this turbulent priest?" Our planet simply waits.

People who do not appreciate the fundamental principle of appropriate scales often misread such an argument as a claim that we may therefore cease to worry about environmental deterioration—just as Copeland argued falsely that we need not fret about extinction. But I raise the same counterargument. We cannot threaten at geological scales, but such vastness is entirely inappropriate. We have a legitimately parochial interest in our own lives, the happiness and prosperity of our children, the suffering of our fellows. The planet will recover from nuclear holocaust, but we will be killed and maimed by the billions, and our cultures will perish. The earth will prosper if polar icecaps melt under a global greenhouse, but most of our major cities, built at sea level as ports and harbors, will founder, and changing agricultural patterns will uproot our populations.

We must squarely face an unpleasant historical fact. The conservation movement was born, in large part, as an elitist attempt by wealthy social leaders to preserve wilderness as a domain for patrician leisure and contemplation (against the image, so to speak, of poor immigrants traipsing in hordes through the woods with their Sunday picnic baskets). We have never entirely shaken this legacy of environmentalism as something opposed to immediate human needs, particularly of the impoverished and unfortunate. But the Third World expands and contains most of the pristine habitat that we yearn to preserve. Environmental movements cannot prevail until they convince people that clean air and water, solar power, recycling, and reforestation are best solutions (as they are) for human needs at human scales—and not for impossible distant planetary futures.

I have a decidedly unradical suggestion to make about an appropriate environmental ethic—one rooted, with this entire essay, in the issue of appropriate human scale versus the majesty, but irrelevance, of geological time. I have never been much attracted to the Kantian categorical imperative in searching for an ethic—to moral laws that are absolute and unconditional and do not involve any ulterior motive or end. The world is too complex and sloppy for such uncompromising attitudes (and God help us if we embrace the wrong principle, and then fight wars, kill, and maim in our absolute certainty). I prefer the messier "hypothetical imperatives" that invoke desire, negotiation, and reciprocity. Of these "lesser," but altogether wiser and deeper, principles, one has stood out for its independent derivation, with different words but to the same effect, in culture after culture. I imagine that our various societies grope toward this principle because structural stability, and basic decency necessary for any tolerable life, demand such a maxim. Christians call this principle the "golden rule"; Plato, Hill, and Confucius knew the same maxim by other names. I cannot think of a better principle based on enlightened self-interest. If we all treated others as we wish to be treated ourselves, then decency and stability would have to prevail.

I suggest that we execute such a pact with our planet. She holds all the cards and has immense power over us—so such a compact, which we desperately need but she does not at her own time scale, would be a blessing for us, and an indulgence for her. We had better sign the papers while she is still willing to make a deal. If we treat her nicely, she will keep us going for a while. If we scratch her, she will bleed, kick us out, bandage up, and go about her business at her planetary scale. Poor Richard told us that "necessity never made a good bargain," but the earth is kinder than human agents in the "art of the deal." She will uphold her end; we must now go and do likewise.

Study Questions

1. Is Gould correct in rejecting the major arguments for preserving the species?
2. What is Gould's argument for preserving species (e.g., the Mount Graham red squirrel)?
3. What is Gould's position on the value of human beings in comparison with other species? Do you agree with him? Defend your position.
4. Does the Golden Rule suffice to guide our actions with regard to various species? Can you think of some counterexamples? (How about our treatment of the smallpox virus?)

33

What's Wrong with Plastic Trees?

Martin H. Krieger

Martin Krieger is a research planner in the Institute of Urban and Regional Development and a lecturer in the College of Environmental Design at the University of California, Berkeley.

In this essay, he argues that rationales for preserving rare natural environments are not independent issues but involve economic, societal, and political factors. Krieger has provided this abstract:

A tree's a tree. How many more [redwoods] do you need to look at? If you've seen one, you've seen them all. [Attributed to Ronald Reagan, then candidate for governor of California.]

A tree is a tree, and when you've seen one redwood, given your general knowledge about trees, you have a pretty good idea of the characteristics of a redwood. Yet most people believe that when you've seen one, you haven't seen them all. Why is this so? What implications does this have for public policy in a world where resources are not scarce, but do have to be manufactured; where choice is always present; and where the competition for resources is becoming clearer and keener? In this article I attempt to explore some of these issues, while trying to understand the reasons that are given, or might be given, for preserving certain natural environments.

Reprinted from "What's Wrong with Plastic Trees?" *Science*, Vol. 179 (3 February 1973) by permission. Article and notes edited.

THE ECOLOGY MOVEMENT

In the past few years, a movement concerned with the preservation and careful use of the natural environment in this country has grown substantially. This ecology movement, as I shall call it, is beginning to have genuine power in governmental decision-making and is becoming a link between certain government agencies and the publics to which they are responsible. The ecology movement should be distinguished from related movements concerned with the conservation and wise use of natural resources. The latter, ascendant in the United States during the first half of this century, were mostly concerned with making sure that natural resources and environments were used in a fashion that reflected their true worth to man. This resulted in a utilitarian conception of environments and in the adoption of means to partially preserve them—for example, cost–benefit analysis and policies of multiple use on federal lands.

The ecology movement is not necessarily committed to such policies. Noting the spoliation of the environment under the policies of the conservation movement, the ecology movement demands much greater concern about what is done to the environment, independently of how much it may cost. The ecology movement seeks to have man's environment valued in and of itself and thereby prevent its being traded off for the other benefits it offers to man.

It seems likely that the ecology movement will have to become more programmatic and responsive to compromise as it moves into more responsible and bureaucratic positions vis-à-vis governments and administrative agencies. As they now stand, the policies of the ecology movement may work against resource-conserving strategies designed to lead to the movement's desired ends in 20 or 30 years. Meier has said:

> The best hope, it seems now, is that the newly evolved ideologies will progress as social movements. A number of the major tenets of the belief system may then be expected to lose their centrality and move to the periphery of collective attention. Believers may thereupon only "satisfice" with respect to these principles; they are ready to consider compromise.

What is needed in an approach midway between the preservationist and conservationist–utilitarian policies. It is necessary to find ways of preserving the opportunity for experiences in natural environments, while having, at the same time, some flexibility in the alternatives that the ecology movement could advocate.

A new approach is needed because of the success of economic arguments in the past. We are now more concerned about social equity and about finding arguments from economics for preserving "untouched" environments. Such environments have not been manipulated very much by mankind in the recent past (hundreds or thousands of years). Traditional resource economics has been concerned not as much with preservation as with deciding which intertemporal . . . use of natural re-sources over a period of years yields a maximum return to man, essentially independent of considerations of equity. If one believes that untouched environments are unlikely to have substitutes, then this economics is not very useful. In fact, a different orientation toward preservation has developed and is beginning to be applied in ways that will provide powerful arguments for preservation. At the same time, some ideas about how man experiences the environment are becoming better understood, and they suggest that the new economic approach will be in need of some modification, even if most of its assumptions are sound.

I first examine what is usually meant by natural environments and rarity; I will then examine some of the rationales for preservation. It is important to understand the character and the weak points of the usual arguments. I also suggest how our knowledge and sophistication about environments and our differential access to them are likely to lead to levers for policy changes that will effectively preserve the possibility of experiencing nature, yet offer alternatives in the management of natural resources.

One limitation of my analysis should be made clear. I have restricted my discussion to the nation-state, particularly to the United States. If it were possible to take a global view, then environmental questions would be best phrased in terms of the world's resources. If we want undisturbed natural areas, it might be best to develop some of them in other countries. But we do not live in a politically united world, and such a proposal is imperialistic at worst, and unrealistic at best. Global questions about the environment need to be considered, but they must be considered in terms of controls that can exist. If we are concerned about preserving natural environments, it seems clear that, for the moment, we will most likely have to preserve them in our own country.

THE AMERICAN FALLS: KEEPING IT NATURAL

For the last few thousand years, Niagara Falls has been receding. Water going over the Falls insinuates itself into crevices of the rock, freezes and expands in winter, and thereby causes cracks in the formation. The formation itself is a problem in that the hard rock on the surface covers a softer substratum. This weakness results not only in small amounts of erosion or small rockfalls, but also in very substantial ones when the substratum gives way. About 350,000 cubic yards (1 cubic yard equals 0.77 cubic meter) of talus lie at the base of the American Falls.

The various hydroelectric projects that have been constructed during the years have also affected the amount of water that flows over the Falls. It is now possible to alter the flow of water over the American

Falls by a factor of 2 and, consequently, to diminish that of the Horseshoe (Canadian) Falls by about 10%.

As a result of these forces, the quality of the Falls—its grandeur, its height, its smoothness of flow—changes over the millennia and the months.

There is nothing pernicious about the changes wrought by nature; the problem is that Americans' image of the Falls does not change. Our ideal of a waterfall, an ideal formed by experiences with small, local waterfalls that seem perfect and by images created by artists and photographers, is not about to change without some effort.

When one visits the Falls today, he sees rocks and debris at the base, too much or too little water going over the edge, and imperfections in the flow of water. These sights are not likely to make anyone feel that he is seeing or experiencing the genuine Niagara Falls. The consequent effects of tourism, a multimillion-dollar-per-year industry, could be substantial.

At the instigation of local forces, the American Falls International Board has been formed under the auspices of the International Joint Commission of the United States and Canada. Some $5 to $6 million are being spent to investigate, by means of "dewatering" the Falls and building scale models, policies for intervention. That such efforts are commissioned suggests that we, as a nation, believe that it is proper and possible to do something about the future evolution of the Falls. A "Fallscape" committee, which is especially concerned with the visual quality of the Falls, has been formed. It suggests that three strategies, varying in degree of intervention, be considered.

1. The Falls can be converted into a monument. By means of strengthening the structure of the Falls, it is possible to prevent rockfalls. Also, excess rock from the base can be removed. Such a strategy might cost tens of millions of dollars, a large part of this cost being for the removal of talus.
2. The Falls could become an event. Some of the rocks at the base could be removed for convenience and esthetics, but the rockfalls themselves would not be hindered. Instead, instruments for predicting rockfalls could be installed. People might then come to the Falls at certain times, knowing that they would see an interesting and grand event, part of the cycle of nature, such as Old Faithful.
3. The Falls might be treated as a show. The "director" could control the amount of water flowing over the Falls, the size of the pool below, and the amount of debris, thereby producing a variety of spectacles. Not only could there be *son et lumiere*, but it could take place on an orchestrated physical mass.

Which of these is the most nearly natural environment? Current practice, exemplified by the National Park Service's administration of natural areas, might suggest that the second procedure be followed and that the

Falls not be "perfected." But would that be the famous Niagara Falls, the place where Marilyn Monroe met her fate in the movie *Niagara*? The answer to this question lies in the ways in which efforts at preservation are presented to the public. If the public is seeking a symbolic Falls, then the Falls has to be returned to its former state. If the public wants to see a natural phenomenon at work, then the Falls should be allowed to fall.

Paradoxically, the phenomena that the public thinks of as "natural" often require great artifice in their creation. The natural phenomenon of the Falls today has been created to a great extent by hydroelectric projects over the years. Esthetic appreciation of the Falls has been conditioned by the rather mundane considerations of routes of tourist excursions and views from hotel windows, as well as the efforts of artists.

I think that we can provide a smooth flow of water over the Falls and at the same time not be completely insensitive to natural processes if we adopt a procedure like that described in the third proposal. Niagara Falls is not a virgin territory, the skyscrapers and motels will not disappear. Therefore, an aggressive attitude toward the Falls seems appropriate. This does not imply heavy-handedness in intervention (the first proposal), but a willingness to touch the "sacred" for esthetic as well as utilitarian purposes.

The effort to analyze this fairly straightforward policy question is not trivial. Other questions concerning preservation have fuzzier boundaries, less clear costs (direct and indirect), and much more complicated political considerations. For these reasons it seems worthwhile to examine some of the concepts I use in this discussion.

NATURAL ENVIRONMENTS

What is considered a natural environment depends on the particular culture and society defining it. It might be possible to create for our culture and society a single definition that is usable (that is, the definition would mean the same thing to many people), but this, of course, says nothing about the applicability of such a definition to other cultures. However, I restrict my discussion to the development of the American idea of a natural environment.

The history of the idea of the wilderness is a good example of the development of one concept of natural environment. I follow Nash's discussion[1] in the following.

A wilderness may be viewed as a state of mind, as an attitude toward a collection of trees, other plants, animals, and the land on which they all exist. The idea that a wilderness exists as a product of an intellectual movement is important. A wilderness is not discovered in the sense that some man from a civilization looked upon a piece of territory for the first time. It is the meanings that we attach to such a piece of territory that convert it to a wilderness.

The Romantic appreciation of nature, with its associated enthusiasm for the "strange, remote, solitary and mysterious," converted territory that was a threatening wildland into a desirable area capable of producing an invigorating spirit of wilderness. The "appreciation of the wilderness in this form began in cities," for whose residents the wildland was a novelty. Because of the massive destruction of this territory for resources (primarily timber), city dwellers, whose livelihood did not depend on these resources and who were not familiar with the territory, called for the preservation of wildlands. At first, they did not try to keep the most easily accessible, and therefore most economically useful, lands from being exploited, but noted that Yellowstone and the Adirondacks were rare wonders and had no other utility. They did not think of these areas as wilderness, but as untouched lands. Eventually, a battle developed between conservationists and preservationists. The conservationists (Pinchot, for example) were concerned with the wise use of lands, with science and civilization and forestry; the preservationists (Muir, for example) based their argument on art and wilderness. This latter concept of wilderness is the significant one. The preservationists converted wildland into wilderness—a good that is indivisible and valuable in itself.

This capsule history suggests that the wilderness, as we think of it now, is the product of a political effort to give a special meaning to a biological system organized in a specific way. I suspect that this history is the appropriate model for the manner in which biological systems come to be designated as special.

But it might be said that natural environments can be defined in the way ecosystems are—in terms of complexity, energy and entropy flows, and so on. This is true, but only because of all the spadework that has gone into developing in the public a consensual picture of natural environments. What a society takes to be a natural environment is one.

Natural environments are likely to be named when there are unnatural environments and are likely to be noted only when they are outnumbered by these unnatural environments. The wildlands of the past, which were frightening, were plentiful and were not valued. The new wilderness, which is a source of revitalization, is rare and so valued that it needs to be preserved.

WHEN IS SOMETHING RARE?

Something is considered to be rare when there do not exist very many objects or events that are similar to it. It is clear that one object must be distinguishable from another in order to be declared rare, but the basis for this distinction is not clear.

One may take a realist's or an idealist's view of rarity. For the realist, an object is unique within a purview: given a certain boundary, there exists no other object like it. Certainly the Grand Canyon is unique within the United States. Perhaps Niagara Falls is also unique. But there are many other waterfalls throughout the world that are equally impressive, if not of identical dimensions.

For the idealist, a rare object is one that is archetypal: it is the most nearly typical of all the objects it represents, having the most nearly perfect form. We frequently preserve archetypal specimens in museums and botanical gardens. Natural areas often have these qualities.

A given object is not always rare. Rather, it is designated as rare at one time and may, at some other time, be considered common. How does this happen? Objects become rare when a large number of people change their attitudes toward them. This may come about in a number of ways, but it is necessary that the object in question be noticed and singled out. Perhaps one individual discovers it, or perhaps it is common to everyone's experience. Someone must convince the public that the object is something special. The publicist must develop in others the ability to differentiate one object from among a large number of others, as well as to value the characteristic that makes the particular object different. If he convinces a group of people influential in the society, people who are able to affect a much larger group's beliefs, then he will have succeeded in his task. Thus it may be important that some form of snob appeal be created for the special object.

In order to create the differentiations and the differential valuations of characteristics, information and knowledge are crucial. A physical object can be transformed into an instrument of beauty, pleasure, or pride, thereby developing sufficient characteristics to be called rare, only by means of changing the knowledge we have of it and of its relation to the rest of the world. In this sense, knowledge serves an important function in the creation of rare environments, very much as knowledge in society serves an important function in designating what should be considered natural resources.

Advertising is one means of changing states of knowledge—nor does such advertising have to be wholly sponsored by commercial interests. Picture post cards, for example, are quite effective:[2]

> . . . a large number of quiet beauty spots which in consequence of the excellence of their photographs had become tourist centres. . . .
> The essential was to "establish" a picture, e.g., the Tower [of London] with barges in the foreground. People came to look for the barges and in the end wouldn't have the Tower without barges. Much of the public was very conservative and though such things as high-rise building and general facade-washing had made them [the post card producers] rephotograph the whole of London recently, some people still insisted on the old sky-line, and grubby facades, and liked to believe certain new roads had never happened.

Similarly, the publicity given to prices paid at art auctions spurs the rise of these prices.

As a *result* of the social process of creating a rare object, the usual indicators of rarity become important. Economically, prices rise; physically, the locations of the rare objects become central, or at least highly significant spatially; and socially, rare objects and their possessors are associated with statuses that are valued and activities that are considered to be good.

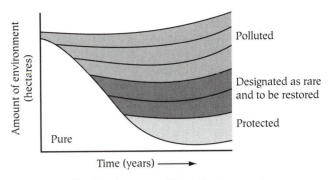

FIGURE 1 *The Development of Rare Environments*

ENVIRONMENTS CAN BE AND ARE CREATED

To recapitulate, objects are rare because men decide that they are and, through social action, convince others that they are. The rarity of an object is created through four mechanisms: designating the object as rare; differentiating it from other objects of the same species; establishing its significance; and determining its position in the context of society. The last two mechanisms are especially important, for the meaning that an environment has and its relation to other things in the society are crucial to its being considered rare. That a rare environment be irreproducible or of unchanging character is usually a necessary preliminary to our desire to preserve it. Technologies, which may involve physical processes or social organization and processes, determine how reproducible an object is, for we may make a copy of the original or we may transfer to another object the significance attached to the original. (Copying natural environments may be easier than copying artistic objects because the qualities of replicas and forgeries are not as well characterized in the case of the natural environment.) Insofar as we are incapable of doing either of these, we may desire to preserve the original environment.

In considering the clientele of rare environments, one finds that accessibility by means of transportation and communication is important. If there is no means of transportation to a rare environment then it is not likely that the public will care about that environment. An alternative to transportation is some form of communication, either verbal or pictorial, that simulates a feeling of being in the environment.

I am concerned here with the history of environments that, at first, are not considered unique. However, a similar argument could be applied to environments regarded as unique (for example, the Grand Canyon), provided they were classed with those environments most like them. Figure 1 should aid in the explanation that follows.

For example, suppose that a particular kind of environment is plentiful and that, over a period of time, frequent use causes it to become polluted. (Note that pollution need not refer just to our conventional concepts of dirtying the environment, but to a wide variety

of uncleanliness and stigma as well.) Because there is a substantial amount of that environment available, man's use of it will, at first, have little effect on his perception of its rarity. As time goes on, however, someone will notice that there used to be a great deal more of that particular environment available. Suddenly, the once vast quantities of that environment begin to look less plentiful. The environment seems more special as it becomes distinguishable from the polluted environments around it. At that point, it is likely that there will be a movement to designate some fraction of the remaining environment as rare and in need of protection. There will also be a movement to restore those parts of the environment that have already been polluted. People will intervene to convert the polluted environment to a simulation of the original one.[3]

REASONS FOR PRESERVATION

That something is rare does not imply that it must be preserved. The characteristics that distinguish it as rare must also be valued. Arguments in favor of preserving an object can be based on the fact that the object is a luxury, a necessity, or a merit.

We build temples or other monuments to our society (often by means of preservation) and believe that they represent important investments in social unity and coherence. If a forest symbolizes the frontier for a society and if that frontier is meaningful in the society's history, then there may be good reasons for preserving it. An object may also be preserved in order that it may be used in the future. Another reason, not often given but still true, for preserving things is that there is nothing else worth doing with them. For example, it may cost very little to preserve something that no one seems to have any particular reason for despoiling; therefore, we expend some small effort in trying to keep it untouched.

Natural environments are preserved for reasons of necessity also. Environments may provide ecological samples that will be useful to future generations. Recently, the long-lived bristlecone pine has helped to check radiocarbon dating and has thereby revised our knowledge of early Europe. It may be that the preservation of an environment is necessary for the preservation of an ecosystem and that our destruction of it will also destroy, as a product of a series of interactions, some highly valued aspects of our lives. Finally, it may be necessary to preserve environments in order that the economic development of the adjacent areas can proceed in a desired fashion.

Other reasons for preservation are based on merit: it may be felt by the society that it is good to preserve natural environments. It is good for people to be exposed to nature. Natural beauty is worth having, and the amenity resulting from preservation is important.

RARITY, UNIQUENESS, AND FORGERY: AN ARTISTIC INTERLUDE

The problems encountered in describing the qualities that make for "real" artistic experiences and genuine works of art are similar to those encountered in describing rare natural objects. The ideas of replica and forgery will serve to make the point.

Kubler[4] observes that, if one examines objects in a time sequence, he may decide that some are prime objects and the rest are replicas. Why should this be so? One may look at the properties of earlier objects and note that some of them serve as a source of later objects; however, since the future always has its sources in the present, any given object is a source. Therefore, one must distinguish important characteristics, perhaps arbitrarily, and say that they are seminal. Prime objects are the first to clearly and decisively exhibit important characteristics.

Why are there so few prime objects? By definition, prime objects exhibit characteristics in a clear and decisive way, and this must eliminate many other objects from the category; but why do artists not constantly create new objects, each so original that it would be prime? Not all artists are geniuses, it might be said. But this is just a restatement of the argument that most objects do not exhibit important characteristics in a clear, decisive manner. It might also be said that, if there are no followers, there will be no leaders, but this does not explain why some eras are filled with prime works and others are not.

Kubler suggests that invention, especially if too frequent, leads to chaos, which is frightening. Replication is calmer and leads only to dullness. Therefore, man would rather repair, replicate what he has done, than innovate and discard the past. We are, perhaps justifiably, afraid of what the prime objects of the future will be. We prefer natural environments to synthesized ones because we are familiar with techniques of managing the natural ones and know what the effects of such management are. Plastic trees are frightening.

What about those replicas of prime objects that are called forgeries? Something is a forgery if its provenance has been faked. Why should this bother us? If the forgery provides us with the same kind of experience we might have had with the original, except that we know it is a forgery, then we are snobbish to demand the original. But we do not like to be called snobs. Rather, we say that our opinion of the work, or the quality of our experience of it, depends on its context. History, social position, and ideology affect the way in which we experience the object. It may be concluded that our appreciation of something is only partly a product of the thing itself.

Art replicas and forgeries exist in an historical framework. So do the prime and genuine objects. And so do natural environments.

CRITERIA FOR PRESERVATION

Whatever argument one uses for preservation, there must be some criteria for deciding what to preserve. Given that something is rare and is believed to be worth preserving, rarity itself, as well as economic, ecological, or socio-historical reasons, can be used to justify preservation. I consider each of these here.

There are many economic reasons for planned intervention to achieve preservation, and I discuss two of them: one concerns the application of cost–benefit analysis to preservation; the other concerns the argument that present value should be determined by future benefits.

The work of Krutilla is an ingenious application of economics; it rescues environments from current use by arguing for their future utility.[5] The crux of the argument follows.

Nature is irreproducible compared to the materials it provides. As Barnett and Morse have shown, there have been enough substitutions of natural materials to obviate the idea of a shortage of nature resources. It also seems likely that the value of nature and of experiences in nature will increase in the future, while the supply of natural environments will remain constant. Because it is comparatively easy to produce substitutes for the materials we get from natural environments, the cost of not exploiting an environment is small, compared to the cost of producing that environment. Finally, there is an option demand for environments: that is, there will be a demand, at a certain price, for that environment in the future. If a substantial fraction of the supply of the environment is destroyed now, it will be impossible to fill the demand in the future at a reasonable price. Therefore, we are willing to pay to preserve that option. The problem is not the intertemporal use of natural environments (as it is for natural resources), but the preservation of our options to use environments in the future, or at least the reduction of uncertainty about the availability of environments in the future. . . .

Robinson has criticized Krutilla's argument from the following perspectives[6]: he suggests that the amenity valued so highly by Krutilla is not necessarily that valuable; that the experiences of nature are reproducible; that refraining from current use may be costly; and that the arguments for public intervention into such environments depend on the collective consumption aspects of these environments. That is, these environments benefit everyone, and, since people cannot be differentially charged for using them, the public must pay for these environments collectively, through government. It is well known that the users of rare environments tend to be that small fraction of the population who are better off socially and economically than the majority. How-ever, a greater difficulty than any of these may be discerned.

It seems to me that the limitations of Krutilla's argument lie in his assumptions about how quickly spoiled environments can be restored (rate of reversion) and how great the supply of environments is. Krutilla *et al.* are sensitive to the possibility that the rate of reversion may well be amenable to technological intervention:

> Perhaps more significant, however, is the need to investigate more fully the presumption of asymmetric implications of technological progress for the value of attributes of the natural environment when used as intermediate goods, compared with their retention as assets supplying final consumption services. Irreproducibility, it might be argued, is not synonymous with irreplaceability. If reasonably good substitutes can be found, by reliance on product development, the argument for the presumption of differential effects of technological progress is weakened; or if not weakened, the value which is selected [for the reversion rate]. . . would not remain unaffected.

The supply of natural environments is affected by technology in that it can manipulate both biological processes and information and significance. The advertising that created rare environments can also create plentiful substitutes. The supply of special environments can be increased dramatically by highlighting (in ways not uncommon to those of differentiating among groups of equivalent toothpastes) significant and rare parts of what are commonly thought to be uninteresting environments.

The accessibility of certain environments to population centers can be altered to create new rare environments. Also, environments that are especially rare, or are created to be especially rare, could be very far away, since people would be willing to pay more to see them. Thus it may be possible to satisfy a large variety of customers for rare environments. The following kind of situation might result.

1. Those individuals who demand "truly" natural environments could be encouraged to fly to some isolated location where a national park with such an environment is maintained; a substantial sum of money would be required of those who use such parks.

2. For those who find a rare environment in state parks or perhaps in small national parks, such parks could be made more accessible and could be developed more. In this way, a greater number of people could use them and the fee for using them would be less than the fee for using isolated areas.

3. Finally, for those who wish to have an environment that is just some trees, some woods, and some grass, there might be a very small park. Access would be very easy, and the rareness of such environments might well be enhanced beyond what is commonly thought possible by means of sophisticated methods of landscape gardening.

It seems to me that, as Krutilla suggests, the demand for rare environments is a learned one. It also seems likely that conscious public choice can manipulate this learning so that the environments which people learn to use and want reflect environments that are likely to be available at low cost. There is no lack of merit in natural environments, but this merit is not canonical.

THE VALUATION OF THE FUTURE

In any cost–benefit analysis that attempts to include future values, the rate at which the future is discounted is crucial to the analysis. (That is, a sum of money received today is worth more to us now than the same sum received in the future. To allow for this, one discounts, by a certain percent each year, these future payments.) Changes in discount rates can alter the feasibility of a given project. If different clientele's preferences for projects correspond to different discount rates at which these projects are feasible, then the choice of a particular discount rate would place the preferences of one group over another. Preservation yields benefits that come in the future. The rich have a low rate of discount compared to the poor (say, 5 percent as opposed to 10 or 20 percent) and would impute much higher present value to these future benefits than the poor would. Baumol suggests (though it is only a hunch) that:[7]

> . . . by and large, the future can be left to take care of itself. There is no need to lower artificially the social rate of discount in order to increase further the prospective wealth of future generations. . . . However, this does not mean that the future should in every respect be left at the mercy of the free market. . . . Investment in the preservation of such items then seems perfectly proper, but for this purpose the appropriate instrument would appear to be a set of selective subsidies rather than a low general discount rate that encourages indiscriminately all sorts of investment programs whether or not they are relevant.

Baumol is saying that the process of preserving environments may not always be fruitfully analyzed in terms of cost–benefit analyses; we are preserving things in very special cases, and each choice is not a utilitarian choice in any simple sense, but represents a balancing of all other costs to the society of having *no* preserved environments. Preservation often entails a gross change in policy, and utilitarian analyses cannot easily compare choices in which values may be drastically altered.

OTHER CRITERIA

We may decide to preserve things just because they are rare. In that case, we need to know which things are rarer than others. Leopold has tried to do this for a set of natural environments. He listed a large number of attributes for each environment and then weighted each attribute as follows. For any single attribute, determine how many environments share that attribute and assign each of them a value of $1/N$ units, where N is the number of environments that share an attribute. Then add all the weights for the environments; the environment with the largest weight is the rarest. It is clear that, if an environment has attributes which are unique, it will get one unit of weight for each attribute and thus its total weight will just equal the number of attributes. If all of the environments are about the same, then each of them will have roughly the same weight, which will equal the number of attributes divided by the number of environments. The procedure is sensitive to how differentiated we wish to make our attributes and to the attributes we choose. It is straightforward and usable, as Leopold has shown.

It seems to me that there are two major difficulties in this approach. The first, and more important, is that the accessibility of environments to their clientele, which Leopold treats as one of his 34 attributes, needs to be further emphasized in deciding what to preserve. An environment that is quite rare but essentially inaccessible may not be as worthy of preservation as one that is fairly common but quite accessible. The other difficulty is that probably the quantity that should be used is the amount of information possessed by each environment—rather than taking $1/N$, one should take a function of its logarithm to the base 2.

An ecological argument is that environments which contribute to our stability and survival as an ecosystem should be preserved. It is quite difficult to define what survival means, however. If it means the continued existence of man in an environment quite similar to the one he lives in now, then survival is likely to become very difficult as we use part of our environment for the maintenance of life and as new technologies come to the fore. If survival means the maintenance of a healthy and rich culture, then ecology can only partially guide us in the choices, since technology has substantially changed the risk from catastrophe in the natural world. Our complex political and social organizations may serve to develop means for survival and stability sufficient to save man from the catastrophic tricks of his own technology.

If a taxonomy of environments were established, a few environments might stand out from all the rest. But what would be the criteria involved in such a taxonomy?

Another possibility is to search for relics of cultural, historical, and social significance to the nation. Such physical artifacts are preserved because the experiences they represent affect the nature of the present society. In this sense, forests are preserved to recall a frontier, and historic homes are preserved to recall the individuals who inhabited them. Of course the problem here is that there is no simple way of ordering the importance of relics and their referents. Perhaps a survey of a large number of people might enable one to assign priorities to these relics.

Finally, it might be suggested that preservation should only be used, or could sometimes be used, to serve the interests of social justice. Rather than preserving things for what they are or for the experiences they provide, we preserve them as monuments to people who deserve commemoration or as a means of redistributing wealth (when an environment is designated as rare, local values are affected). Rather than buy forests and preserve them, perhaps we should preserve slums and suitably reward their inhabitants.

All of these criteria are problematic. Whichever ones are chosen, priorities for intervention must still be developed.

PRIORITIES FOR PRESERVING THE ENVIRONMENT

Not every problem in environmental quality is urgent, nor does every undesirable condition that exists need to be improved. We need to classify environmental problems in order that we can choose from among the possible improvements.

1. There are conditions about which we must do something soon or we will lose a special thing. These conditions pertain especially to rare environments, environments we wish to preserve for their special beauty or their uniqueness. We might allocate a fixed amount of money every year to such urgent problems. Niagara Falls might be one of these, and it might cost a fraction of a dollar per family to keep it in good repair. Wilderness and monument maintenance have direct costs of a few dollars per family per year.

2. There are situations in which conditions are poor, but fairly stable. In such situations, it might be possible to handle the problem in 10 years without too much loss. However, the losses to society resulting from the delayed improvement of these facilities need to be care-

fully computed. For example, the eutrophied Lake Erie might be such a project. There, society loses fishing and recreational facilities. It might cost $100 per family, locally, to clean up the lake. Perhaps our environmental dollar should be spent elsewhere.

3. There are also situations in which conditions are rapidly deteriorating and in which a small injection of environmental improvement and amelioration would cause dramatic changes in a trend. Smog control devices have probably raised the cost of driving by 2 or 3 percent, yet their contribution to the relative improvement of the environment in certain areas (for example, Los Angeles) has been substantial. Fifty dollars per car per year is the estimated current cost to the car owner.

4. There may be situations in which large infusions of money are needed to stop a change. These problems are especially irksome. Perhaps the best response to them would be to change the system of production sufficiently that we can avoid such costs in the future. The costs of such change, one-time costs we hope, may be much smaller than the long-term costs of the problems themselves, although this need not be the case. The development of cleaner industrial processes is a case in point.

This is not an all-inclusive or especially inventive classification of problems, but I have devised it to suggest that many of the "urgent" problems are not so urgent.

Rare environments pose special problems and may require an approach different from that required by other environments. A poor nation is unlikely to destroy very much of its special environments. It lacks the technical and economic power to do so. It may certainly perform minor miracles of destruction through a series of small decisions or in single, major projects. These latter are often done with the aid of rich countries.

The industrialized, but not wealthy, nations have wreaked havoc with their environments in their efforts to gain some degree of wealth. It is interesting that they are willing to caution the poor nations against such a course, even though it may be a very rapid way of developing. At the U.N. Conference on the Environment this year, the poor nations indicated their awareness of these problems and their desire to develop without such havoc.

The rich nations can afford to have environments that are rare and consciously preserved. These environments are comparable to the temples of old, in that these environments will be relics of *our* time, yet this is no criterion for deciding how much should be spent on "temple building." The amount of money needed is only a small proportion of a rich country's wealth (as opposed to the cost of churches in medieval times).

Politically, the situation is complicated. There are many small groups in this country for whom certain environments are highly significant. The problem for each group is to somehow get its piece of turf, preferably uncut, unrenewed, or untouched. It seems likely that the ultimate determinant of which environments are preserved will be a process of political trade-off, in which some environments are preserved for some groups and other environments for others. Natural environments are likely to be viewed in a continuum with a large number of other environments that are especially valued by some subgroup of the society. In this sense, environmental issues will become continuous with a number of other special interests and will no longer be seen as a part of a "whole earth" movement. The power of the intellectuals, in the media, and even in union bureaucracies, with their upper middle class preferences for nature, suggests that special interest groups who are advocates for the poor and working classes will have to be wary of their own staffs.

Projects might be ranked in importance on the basis of the net benefits they provide a particular group. Marglin has suggested a means by which income redistribution could be explicitly included in cost-benefit calculations for environmental programs. If one wishes to take efficiency into account, costs minus benefits could be minimized with a constraint relating to income redistribution. This is not a simple task, however, because pricing some commodities at zero dollars, seemingly the best way of attempting a redistribution of income, may not be politically desirable or feasible. As Clawson and Knetsch have pointed out, we have to be sure that in making some prices low we do not make others prohibitively high and thereby deny the persons who are to benefit access to the low-priced goods.[8] In any case, Marglin shows that the degree to which income is redistributed will depend on how the same amount of money might have been spent in alternative activities (marginal opportunity cost). This parallels Kneese and Bower's view that the level of pollution we tolerate, or is "optimal," is that at which the marginal benefits of increasing pollution are balanced by the marginal costs of abatement measures.[9]

In doing these cost–benefit calculations, one must consider the value of 10 years of clean lake (if we can clean up the lake now) versus 10 years of uneducated man (if we wait 10 years for a manpower training program). According to Freeman:[10]

> . . . [the] equity characteristics of projects *within* broad classifications . . . will be roughly similar. If this surmise is correct, then the ranking of projects within these classes is not likely to be significantly affected by equity considerations. On the other hand, we would expect more marked differences in distribution patterns among classes of projects, e.g., rural recreation vs. urban air quality.

He goes on to point out that it is unlikely that such seemingly incommensurable kinds of projects will be compared with respect to equity. I suspect that it is still possible to affect specific groups in the design of a given project; furthermore, equity can be taken into consideration more concretely at this level. Careful disaggregation, in measuring effects and benefits, will be needed to ensure that minorities are properly represented.

AN ETHICAL QUESTION

I still feel quite uncomfortable with what I have said here. I have tried to show that the utilitarian and manipulative rationality inherited from the conservationist movement and currently embodied in economic analyses and modes of argument can be helpful in deciding questions of preservation and rarity. By manipulating attitudes, we have levers for intervening into what is ordinarily considered fixed and uncontrollable. But to what end?

Our ability to manipulate preferences and values tends to lead to systems that make no sense. For example, an electrical utility encourages its customers to use more electricity, and the customers proceed to do so.As a result, there are power shortages. Similarly, if we allocate resources now in order to preserve environments for future generations, their preferences for environments may be altered by this action, and there may be larger shortages.

I also fear that my own proposals might get out of hand. My purpose in proposing interventions is not be preserve man's opportunity to experience nature, although this is important, but to promote social justice. I believe that this concern should guide our attempts to manipulate, trade off, and control environments. A summum bonum of preserving trees has no place in an ethic of social justice. If I took this ethic seriously, I could not argue the relative merits of schemes to manipulate environments. I would argue that the ecology movement is wrong and would not answer its question about what we are going to do about the earth—I would be worried about what we are going to do about men.

CONCLUSION

With some ingenuity, a transformation of our attitudes toward preservation of the environment will take place fairly soon. We will recognize the symbolic and social meanings of environments, not just their economic utility; we will emphasize their historical significance as well as the future generations that will use them.

At the same time, we must realize that there are things we may not want to trade at all, except in the sense of letting someone else have his share of the environment also. As environments become more differentiated, smaller areas will probably be given greater significance, and it may be possible for more groups to have a share.

It is likely that we shall want to apply our technology to the creation of artificial environments. It may be possible to create environments that are evocative of other environments in other times and places. It is possible that, by manipulating memory through the rewriting of history, environments will come to have new meaning. Finally, we may want to create proxy environments by means of substitution and simulation. In order to create substitutes, we must endow new objects with significance by means of advertising and by social practice. Sophistication about differentiation will become very important for appreciating the substitute environments. We may simulate the environment by means of photographs, recordings, models, and perhaps even manipulations in the brain. What we experience in natural environments may actually be more controllable than we imagine. Artificial prairies and wildernesses have been created, and there is no reason to believe that these artificial environments need be unsatisfactory for those who experience them.

Rare environments are relative, can be created, are dependent on our knowledge, and are a function of policy, not only tradition. It seems likely that economic arguments will not be sufficient to preserve environments or to suggest how we can create new ones. Rather, conscious choice about what matters, and then a financial and social investment in an effort to create significant experiences and environments, will become a policy alternative available to us.

What's wrong with plastic trees? My guess is that there is very little wrong with them. Much more can be done with plastic trees and the like[11] to give most people the feeling that they are experiencing nature. We will have to realize that the way in which we experience nature is conditioned by our society—which more and more is seen to be receptive to responsible interventions.

Bentham, the father of utilitarianism, was very concerned about the uses of the dead to the living and suggested:[12]

> If a country gentleman have rows of trees leading to his dwelling, the auto-icons [embalmed bodies in an upright position] of his family might alternate with the trees: copal varnish would protect the face from the effects of rain—caoutchouc [rubber] the habiliments.

Notes

1. R. Nash, *Wilderness and the American Mind* (Yale University Press, 1967).
2. A. Hamilton, *The Manchester Guardian*, 4 September 1971, p. 8.
3. This analysis is as useful for paintings in museums and stamps in collections as it is for trees in parks. Art museums are places where rare objects are preserved in order to enhance the quality of experience available to people. [Grana's discussions of museums makes the analogy with rare natural environments stand out. The conflict between the didactic ("New York" style) and the pure ("Boston" style) approaches to museum orga-

nization reminds one of the conflict between recreationists and preservationists. These conflicts reflect, of course, much larger issues in mass society. See C. Grana, *Transaction* 4, 20 (April 1967)]. Originally, they were developed to help artists by showing their works, thereby institutionalizing the artist's relationships with his patron-clients. Eventually, these galleries became sources of orthodoxy, thereby establishing what the acceptable forms of art were. [F. Haskell, in *International Encyclopedia of the Social Sciences*, D. Sills, Ed. (Macmillan, New York, 1968), vol. 5, p. 439.] The creation of museums and their continued development is not simply a product of the increased rareness of works of art, per se, for the rareness of a work of art is actually, in part, the result of museums. The stock of art must be viewed in terms of public and private consumption. If it is believed that the public ought to have access to art, then putting art in private collections uses it up, as far as the public is concerned. An ideology that encourages the development of means of public consumption of art—for example, building museums in order to be saved either after a life of sin (as in the case of the robber barons) or from taxes—rescues these objects from oblivion.

4. G. Kubler, *The Shape of Time* (Yale University Press, 1962).
5. J. Krutilla, *American Econ. Rev* 57, 777 (1967).
6. W. Robinson, *Land Econ.* 45, 453 (1969).
7. W. Baumol, *Amer. Econ. Rev.* 58, 788 (1968).
8. M. Clawson and J. Knetsch, *Economics of Outdoor Recreation* (Johns Hopkins Press, 1966).
9. A. Kneese and B. Bower, *Managing Water Quality: Economics, Technology and Institutions* (Johns Hopkins Press, 1972).
10. A. Freeman III, in *Environmental Quality Analysis* (Johns Hopkins Press, 1972).
11. The introduction of artificial turf and trees has not been very smooth. Adaption to the artificial product and realization of the alternatives takes some time. In the case of turf, some controversy has arisen about its being safe for football players. The rejoinders of manufacturers suggest that players and coaches have to adapt playing styles and equipment to the new surfaces (see assorted pamphlets from Monsanto, the manufacturer of Astroturf). Similarly, the introduction of plastic trees in the center meridian of Jefferson Boulevard in Los Angeles has been greeted with much criticism. As set up, there is insufficient support for living plants on the boulevard, and the only alternative is concrete.
12. J. Bentham, *Auto-Icon, or the Uses of the Dead to the Living in Dictionary of National Biography*, L. Stephen and S. Lee, eds. (Oxford University Press, 1917), vol. 2, p. 268.

Study Questions

1. What is the dispute between the conservationists (Pinchot) and preservationists (Muir), and how does Krieger try to resolve the dispute? What, if anything, does this have to do with Krieger's discussion of Niagara Falls?

2. Examine Krieger's discussion of "Natural Environments." Do you agree with him that "what a society takes to be a natural environment is one" and that "objects are rare because men decide that they are and, through social action, convince others that they are"? Explain your answer.

3. Explain the four mechanisms for creating rare objects. Does society create rarity the way it creates money or cars? Or does Krieger leave something out?—That there really are few of the items available, like photographs from the 1850s, seven-foot humans, or Condors?

4. Why are plastic trees frightening, according to Krieger? Does Krieger see anything really wrong with them? Explain your answer. Do you agree with him?

5. What does Krieger mean by proposing intervention into nature in order to promote social justice? (See especially the last paragraph before the conclusion and the conclusion itself.) Do you see any problems with his proposal for creating artificial or proxy environments? Explain your answer.

34

Faking Nature

ROBERT ELLIOT

*In this essay, Robert Elliot considers the contention by
those who would greatly alter nature that the artificial
creation of something similar would preserve whatever
aesthetic value that part of nature had in the first place.
He calls this the "restoration thesis." Elliot compares
natural areas, such as a wilderness, to works of art. He
argues that just as knowing that the Vermeer painting
you have is a replica lowers its value, so likewise knowing that the experience you are having is only a replica
of the natural original, lowers the value of that experience. "Origin is important as an integral part of the
evaluation process."*

I

Consider the following case. There is a proposal to
mine beach sands for rutile. Large areas of dune are to
be cleared of vegetation and the dunes themselves
destroyed. It is agreed, by all parties concerned, that the
dune area has value quite apart from a utilitarian one.
It is agreed, in other words, that it would be a bad thing
considered in itself for the dune area to be dramatically
altered. Acknowledging this the mining company
expresses its willingness, indeed its desire, to restore the
dune area to its original condition after the minerals
have been extracted. The company goes on to argue
that any loss of value is merely temporary and that full
value will in fact be restored. In other words they are
claiming that the destruction of what has value is compensated for by the later creation (recreation) of something of equal value. I shall call this "the restoration
thesis."

In the actual world many such proposals are made,
not because of shared conservationist principles, but as
a way of undermining the arguments of conservationists. Such proposals are in fact effective in defeating
environmentalist protest. They are also notoriously
ineffective in putting right, or indeed even seeming to
put right, the particular wrong that has been done to
the environment. The sandmining case is just one of a
number of similar cases involving such things as open-
cut mining, clear-felling of forests, river diversion, and
highway construction. Across a range of such cases
some concession is made by way of acknowledging the

FROM: *Inquiry,* Vol. 25, no. 1 (Mar. 1982), pp. 81–93. Reprinted
by permission. Footnotes deleted.

value of pieces of landscape, rivers, forests and so forth,
and a suggestion is made that this value can be restored
once the environmentally disruptive process has been
completed.

Imagine, contrary to fact, that restoration projects are
largely successful; that the environment is brought back
to its original condition and that even a close inspection
will fail to reveal that the area has been mined, clear-
felled, or whatever. If this is so then there is temptation
to think that one particular environmentalist objection is
defeated. The issue is by no means merely academic. I
have already claimed that restoration promises do in
fact carry weight against environmental arguments.
Thus Mr. Doug Anthony, the Australian Deputy Prime
Minister, saw fit to suggest that sand-mining on Fraser
Island could be resumed once "the community becomes
more informed and more enlightened as to what reclamation work is being carried out by mining companies.
. . . ." Or consider how the protests of environmentalists
might be deflected in the light of the following report of
environmental engineering in the United States.

> . . . about 2 km of creek 25 feet wide has been moved to
> accommodate a highway and in doing so engineers with
> the aid of landscape architects and biologists have rebuilt
> the creek to the same standard as before. Boulders,
> bends, irregularities and natural vegetation have all been
> designed into the new section. In addition, special log
> structures have been built to improve the habitat as part
> of a fish development program.

Not surprisingly the claim that revegetation, rehabilita-
tion, and the like restore value has been strongly contested. J. G. Mosley reports that:

> The Fraser Island Environmental Inquiry Commissioners
> did in fact face up to the question of the relevance of suc-
> cessful rehabilitation to the decision on whether to ban
> exports (of beach sand minerals) and were quite unequiv-
> ocal in saying that if the aim was to protect a natural
> area such success was irrelevant. . . . The Inquiry said:
> ". . . even if, contrary to the overwhelming weight of evi-
> dence before the Commission, successful rehabilitation of
> the flora after mining is found to be ecologically possible
> on all mined sites on the Island . . . the overall impression
> of a wild, uncultivated island refuge will be destroyed
> forever by mining."

I want to show both that there is a rational, coherent
ethical system which supports decisive objections to the

restoration thesis, and that that system is not lacking in normative appeal. The system I have in mind will make valuation depend, in part, on the presence of properties which cannot survive the disruption-restoration process. There is, however, one point that needs clarifying before discussion proceeds. Establishing that restoration projects, even if empirically successful, do not fully restore value does not by any means constitute a knockdown argument against some environmentally disruptive policy. The value that would be lost if such a policy were implemented may be just one value among many which conflict in this situation. Countervailing considerations may be decisive and the policy thereby shown to be the right one. If my argument turns out to be correct it will provide an extra, though by no means decisive, reason for adopting certain environmentalist policies. It will show that the resistance which environmentalists display in the face of restoration promises is not merely silly, or emotional, or irrational. This is important because so much of the debate assumes that settling the dispute about what is ecologically possible automatically settles the value question. The thrust of much of the discussion is that if restoration is shown to be possible, and economically feasible, then recalcitrant environmentalists are behaving irrationally, being merely obstinate or being selfish.

There are indeed familiar ethical systems which will serve to explain what is wrong with the restoration thesis in a certain range of cases. Thus preference utilitarianism will support objections to some restoration proposal if that proposal fails to maximally satisfy preferences. Likewise classical utilitarianism will lend support to a conservationist stance provided that the restoration proposal fails to maximize happiness and pleasure. However, in both cases the support offered is contingent upon the way in which the preferences and utilities line up. And it is simply not clear that they line up in such a way that the conservationist position is even usually vindicated. While appeal to utilitarian considerations might be strategically useful in certain cases they do not reflect the underlying motivation of the conservationists. The conservationists seem committed to an account of what has value which allows that restoration proposals fail to compensate for environmental destruction despite the fact that such proposals would maximize utility. What then is this distinct source of value which motivates and underpins the stance taken by, among others, the Commissioners of the Fraser Island Environmental Inquiry?

II

It is instructive to list some reasons that might be given in support of the claim that something of value would be lost if a certain bit of the environment were destroyed. It may be that the area supports a diversity of plant and animal life, it may be that it is the habitat of some endangered species, it may be that it contains striking rock formations or particularly fine specimens of mountain ash. If it is only considerations such as these that contribute to the area's value then perhaps opposition to the environmentally disruptive project would be irrational provided certain firm guarantees were available; for instance that the mining company or timber company would carry out the restoration and that it would be successful. Presumably there are steps that could be taken to ensure the continuance of species diversity and the continued existence of the endangered species. Some of the other requirements might prove harder to meet, but in some sense or other it is possible to recreate the rock formations and to plant mountain ash that will turn out to be particularly fine specimens. If value consists of the presence of objects of these various kinds, independently of what explains their presence, then the restoration thesis would seem to hold. The environmentalist needs to appeal to some feature which cannot be replicated as a source of some part of a natural area's value.

Putting the point thus, indicates the direction the environmentalist could take. He might suggest that an area is valuable, partly, because it is a natural area, one that has not been modified by human hand, one that is undeveloped, unspoilt, or even unsullied. This suggestion is in accordance with much environmentalist rhetoric, and something like it at least must be at the basis of resistance to restoration proposals. One way of teasing out the suggestion and giving it a normative basis is to take over a notion from aesthetics. Thus we might claim that what the environmental engineers are proposing is that we accept a fake or a forgery instead of the real thing. If the claim can be made good then perhaps an adequate response to restoration proposals is to point out that they merely fake nature; that they offer us something less than was taken away. Certainly there is a weight of opinion to the effect that, in art at least, fakes lack a value possessed by the real thing.

One way in which this argument might be nipped in the bud is by claiming that it is bound to exploit an ultimately unworkable distinction between what is natural and what is not. Admittedly the distinction between the natural and the non-natural requires detailed working out. This is something I do not propose doing. However, I do think the distinction can be made good in a way sufficient to the present need. For present purposes I shall take it that "natural" means something like "unmodified by human activity." Obviously some areas will be more natural than others according to the degree to which they have been shaped by human hand. Indeed most rural landscapes will, on this view, count as non-natural to a very high degree. Nor do I intend the natural/non-natural distinction to exactly parallel some dependent moral evaluations; that is, I do not want to be taken as claiming that what is natural is good and what is non-natural is not. The distinction between natural and non-natural connects with valuation in a much more subtle way than that. This is something to which I shall presently return. My claim then is that restoration policies do not always fully restore value because part of the reason that we value bits of the environment is because they are natural to a high degree. It is time to consider some counter-arguments.

An environmental engineer might urge that the exact similarity which holds between the original and the perfectly restored environment leaves no room for a value discrimination between them. He may urge that if they are *exactly* alike, down to the minutest detail (and let us imagine for the sake of argument that this is a technological possibility), then they must be *equally* valuable. The suggestion is that value-discriminations depend on there being intrinsic differences between the states of affairs evaluated. This begs the question against the environmentalist, since it simply discounts the possibility that events temporally and spatially outside the immediate landscape in question can serve as the basis of some valuation of it. It discounts the possibility that the manner of the landscape's genesis, for example, has a legitimate role in determining its value. Here are some examples which suggest that an object's origins do affect its value and our valuations of it.

Imagine that I have a piece of sculpture in my garden which is too fragile to be moved at all. For some reason it would suit the local council to lay sewerage pipes just where the sculpture happens to be. The council engineer informs me of this and explains that my sculpture will have to go. However, I need not despair because he promises to replace it with an exactly similar artifact, one which, he assures me, not even the very best experts could tell was not the original. The example may be unlikely, but it does have some point. While I may concede that the replica would be better than nothing at all (and I may not even concede that), it is utterly improbable that I would accept it as full compensation for the original. Nor is my reluctance entirely explained by the monetary value of the original work. My reluctance springs from the fact that I value the original as an aesthetic object, as an object with a specific genesis and history.

Alternatively, imagine I have been promised a Vermeer for my birthday. The day arrives and I am given a painting which looks just like a Vermeer. I am understandably pleased. However, my pleasure does not last for long. I am told that the painting I am holding is not a Vermeer but instead an exact replica of one previously destroyed. Any attempt to allay my disappointment by insisting that there just is no difference between the replica and the original misses the mark completely. There is a difference and it is one which affects my perception, and consequent valuation, of the painting. The difference of course lies in the painting's genesis.

I shall offer one last example which perhaps bears even more closely on the environmental issue. I am given a rather beautiful, delicately constructed, object. It is something I treasure and admire, something in which I find considerable aesthetic value. Everything is fine until I discover certain facts about its origin. I discover that it is carved out of the bone of someone killed especially for that purpose. This discovery affects me deeply and I cease to value the object in the way that I once did. I regard it as in some sense sullied, spoilt by the facts of its origin. The object itself has not changed but my perceptions of it have. I now know that it is not quite the kind of thing I thought it was, and that my prior valuation of it was mistaken. The discovery is like the discovery that a painting one believed to be an original is in fact a forgery. The discovery about the object's origin changes the valuation made of it, since it reveals that the object is not of the kind that I value.

What these examples suggest is that there is at least a prima facie case for partially explaining the value of objects in terms of their origins, in terms of the kinds of processes that brought them into being. It is easy to find evidence in the writings of people who have valued nature that things extrinsic to the present, immediate environment determine valuations of it. John Muir's remarks about Hetch Hetchy Valley are a case in point. Muir regarded the valley as a place where he could have direct contact with primeval nature; he valued it, not just because it was a place of great beauty, but because it was also a part of the world that had not been shaped by human hand. Muir's valuation was conditional upon certain facts about the valley's genesis; his valuation was of a, literally, natural object, of an object with a special kind of continuity with the past. The news that it was a carefully contrived elaborate *ecological* artifact would have transformed that valuation immediately and radically.

The appeal that many find in areas of wilderness, in natural forests and wild rivers depends very much on the naturalness of such places. There may be similarities between the experience one has when confronted with the multi-faceted complexity, the magnitude, the awesomeness of a very large city, and the experience one has walking through a rain forest. There may be similarities between the feeling one has listening to the roar of water over the spillway of a dam, and the feeling one has listening to a similar roar as a wild river tumbles down rapids. Despite the similarities there are also differences. We value the forest and river in part because they are representative of the world outside our dominion, because their existence is independent of us. We may value the city and the dam because of what they represent of human achievement. Pointing out the differences is not necessarily to denigrate either. However, there will be cases where we rightly judge that it is better to have the natural object than it is to have the artifact.

It is appropriate to return to a point mentioned earlier concerning the relationship between the natural and the valuable. It will not do to argue that what is natural is necessarily of value. The environmentalist can comfortably concede this point. He is not claiming that all natural phenomena have value in virtue of being natural. Sickness and disease are natural in a straightforward sense and are certainly not good. Natural phenomena such as fires, hurricanes, volcanic eruptions can totally alter landscapes and alter them for the worse. All of this can be conceded. What the environmentalist wants to claim is that, within certain constraints, the naturalness of a landscape is a reason for preserving it, a determinant of its value. Artificially transforming an utterly barren, ecologically bankrupt landscape into something richer and more subtle may be a good thing. That is a view quite compatible with the belief that replacing a rich natural environment with a rich artificial one is a bad thing. What the environmentalist insists on is that naturalness is one factor in determining the value of pieces of the environment. But that, as I have tried to suggest, is no news. The castle by the Scottish loch is a very different kind of object, valuewise, from the exact replica in the appropriately shaped environment of some Disneyland of the future. The barrenness of some Cycladic island would stand in a different, better perspective if it were not brought about by human intervention.

As I have glossed it, the environmentalist's complaint concerning restoration proposals is that nature is not replaceable without depreciation in one aspect of its value which has to do with its genesis, its history. Given this, an opponent might be tempted to argue that there is no longer any such thing as "natural" wilderness, since the preservation of those bits of it which remain is achievable only by deliberate policy. The idea is that by placing boundaries around national parks, by actively discouraging grazing, trail-biking and the like, by prohibiting sand-mining, we are turning the wilderness into an artifact, that in some negative or indirect way we are creating an environment. There is some truth in this suggestion. In fact we need to take notice of it if we do value wilderness, since positive policies *are* required to preserve it. But as an argument against my over-all claim it fails. What is significant about wilderness is its causal continuity with the past. This is something that is not destroyed by demarcating an area and declaring it a national park. There is a distinction between the "naturalness" of the wilderness itself and the means used to maintain and protect it. What remains within the park boundaries is, as it were, the real thing. The environmentalist may regret that such positive policy is required to preserve the wilderness against human, or even natural, assault. However, the regret does not follow from the belief that what remains is of depreciated value. There is a significant difference between preventing damage and repairing damage once it is done. That is the difference that leaves room for an argument in favour of a preservation policy over and above a restoration policy.

There is another important issue which needs high-

lighting. It might be thought that naturalness only matters in so far as it is perceived. In other words it might be thought that if the environmentalist engineer could perform the restoration quickly and secretly, then there would be no room for complaint. Of course, in one sense there would not be, since the knowledge which would motivate complaint would be missing. What this shows is that there can be loss of value without the loss being perceived. It allows room for valuations to be mistaken because of ignorance concerning relevant facts. Thus my Vermeer can be removed and secretly replaced with the perfect replica. I have lost something of value without knowing that I have. This is possible because it is not simply the states of mind engendered by looking at the painting, by gloatingly contemplating my possession of it, by giving myself over to aesthetic pleasure, and so on which explain why it has value. It has value because of the kind of thing that it is, and one thing that it is is a painting executed by a man with certain intentions, at a certain stage of his artistic development, living in a certain aesthetic *milieu*. Similarly, it is not just those things which make me feel the joy that wilderness makes me feel, that I value. That would be a reason for desiring such things, but that is a distinct consideration. I value the forest because it is of a specific kind, because there is a certain kind of causal history which explains its existence. Of course I can be deceived into thinking that a piece of landscape has that kind of history, has developed in the appropriate way. The success of the deception does not elevate the restored landscape to the level of the original, no more than the success of the deception in the previous example confers on the fake the value of a real Vermeer. What has value in both cases are objects which are of the kind that I value, not merely objects which I think are of that kind. This point, it should be noted, is appropriate independently of views concerning the subjectivity or objectivity of value.

An example might bring the point home. Imagine that John is someone who values wilderness. John may find himself in one of the following situations:

1. He falls into the clutches of a utilitarian-minded super-technologist. John's captor has erected a rather incredible device which he calls an experience machine. Once the electrodes are attached and the right buttons pressed one can be brought to experience anything whatsoever. John is plugged into the machine, and since his captor knows full well John's love of wilderness, given an extended experience as of hiking through a spectacular wilderness. This is environmental engineering at its most extreme. Quite assuredly John is being short-changed. John wants there to be wilderness and he wants to experience it. He wants the world to be a certain way and he wants to have experiences of a certain kind; veridical.

2. John is abducted, blindfolded and taken to a simulated, plastic wilderness area When the blindfold is removed John is thrilled by what he sees around him: the

tall gums, the wattles, the lichen on the rocks. At least that is what he thinks is there. We know better: we know that John is deceived, that he is once again being short-changed. He has been presented with an environment which he thinks is of value but isn't. If he knew that the leaves through which the artificially generated breeze now stirred were synthetic he would be profoundly disappointed, perhaps even disgusted at what at best is a cruel joke.

3. John is taken to a place which was once devastated by strip-mining. The forest which had stood there for some thousands of years had been felled and the earth torn up, and the animals either killed or driven from their habitat. Times have changed, however, and the area has been restored. Trees of the species which grew there before the devastation grow there again, and the animal species have resumed. John knows nothing of this and thinks he is in pristine forest. Once again, he has been short-changed, presented with less than what he values most.

In the same way that the plastic trees may be thought a (minimal) improvement on the experience machine, so too the real trees are an improvement on the plastic ones. In fact in the third situation there is incomparably more of value than in the second, but there could be more. The forest, though real, is not genuinely what John wants it to be. If it were not the product of contrivance he would value it more. It is a product of contrivance. Even in the situation where the devastated area regenerates rather than is restored, it is possible to understand and sympathize with John's claim that the environment does not have the fullest possible value. Admittedly in this case there is not so much room for that claim, since the environment has regenerated of its own accord. Still the regenerated environment does not have the right kind of continuity with the forest that stood there initially; that continuity has been interfered with by the earlier devastation. (In actual fact the regenerated forest is likely to be perceivably quite different to the kind of thing originally there.)

III

I have argued that the causal genesis of forests, rivers, lakes, and so on is important in establishing their value. I have also tried to give an indication of why this is. In the course of my argument I drew various analogies, implicit rather than explicit, between faking art and faking nature. This should not be taken to suggest, however, that the concepts of aesthetic evaluation and judgment are to be carried straight over to evaluations of, and judgments about, the natural environment. Indeed there is good reason to believe that this cannot be done. For one thing an apparently integral part of aesthetic evaluation depends on viewing the aesthetic object as an intentional object, as an artifact, as some-thing that is shaped by the purposes and designs of its author. Evaluating works of art involves explaining them, and judging them, in terms of their author's intentions; it involves placing them within the author's corpus of work; it involves locating them in some tradition and in some special *milieu*. Nature is not a work of art though works of art (in some suitably broad sense) may look very much like natural objects.

None of this is to deny that certain concepts which are frequently deployed in aesthetic evaluation cannot usefully and legitimately be deployed in evaluations of the environment. We admire the intricacy and delicacy of coloring in paintings as we might admire the intricate and delicate shadings in a eucalypt forest. We admire the solid grandeur of a building as we might admire the solidity and grandeur of a massive rock outcrop. And of course the ubiquitous notion of *the beautiful* has a purchase in environmental evaluations as it does in aesthetic evaluations. Even granted all this there are various arguments which might be developed to drive a wedge between the two kinds of evaluation, which would weaken the analogies between faking art and faking nature. One such argument turns on the claim that aesthetic evaluation has, as a central component, a judgmental factor, concerning the author's intentions and the like in the way that was sketched above. The idea is that nature, like works of art, may elicit any of a range of emotional responses in viewers. We may be awed by a mountain, soothed by the sound of water over rocks, excited by the power of a waterfall and so on. However, the judgmental element in aesthetic evaluation serves to differentiate it from environmental evaluation and serves to explain, or so the argument would go, exactly what it is about fakes and forgeries in art which discounts their value with respect to the original. The claim is that if there is no judgmental element in environmental evaluation, then there is no rational basis to preferring real to faked nature when the latter is a good replica. The argument can, I think, be met.

Meeting the argument does not require arguing that responses to nature count as aesthetic responses. I agree that they are not. Nevertheless there are analogies which go beyond emotional content, and which may persuade us to take more seriously the claim that faked nature is inferior. It is important to make the point that only in fanciful situations dreamt up by philosophers are there no detectable differences between fakes and originals, both in the case of artifacts and in the case of natural objects. By taking a realistic example where there are discernible, and possibly discernible, differences between the fake and the real thing, it is possible to bring out the judgmental element in responses to, and evaluations of, the environment. Right now I may not be able to tell a real Vermeer from a Van Meegaran, though I might learn to do so. By the same token I might not be able to tell apart a naturally evolved stand of mountain ash from one which has been planted, but might later acquire the ability to make the requisite judgment. Perhaps an anecdote is appropriate here. There is a particular stand of mountain ash that I had long admired. The trees were straight and tall, of uniform stature, neither densely packed nor too open-spaced. I then discovered what would have been obvious to a more expert eye, namely that the stand of mountain ash had been planted to replace original forest which had been burnt out. This explained the uniformity in size, the density and so on: it also changed my attitude to that piece of landscape. The evaluation that I make now of the landscape is to a certain extent informed, the response is not merely emotive but cognitive as well. The evaluation is informed and directed by my beliefs about the forest, the type of forest it is, its condition as a member of that kind, its causal genesis and so on. What is more, the judgmental element affects the emotive one. Knowing that the forest is not a naturally evolved forest causes me to feel differently about it: it causes me to perceive the forest differently and to assign it less value than naturally evolved forests.

Val Routley has eloquently reminded us that people who value wilderness do not do so merely because they like to soak up pretty scenery. They see much more and value much more than this. What they do see, and what they value, is very much a function of the degree to which they understand the ecological mechanisms which maintain the landscape and which determine that it appears the way it does. Similarly, knowledge of art history, of painting techniques, and the like will inform aesthetic evaluations and alter aesthetic perceptions. Knowledge of this kind is capable of transforming a hitherto uninteresting landscape into one that is compelling. Holmes Rolston has discussed at length the way in which an understanding and appreciation of ecology generates new values. He does not claim that ecology reveals values previously unnoticed, but rather that the understanding of the complexity, diversity, and integration of the natural world which ecology affords us, opens up a new area of valuation. As the facts are uncovered, the values are generated. What the remarks of Routley and Rolston highlight is the judgmental factor which is present in environmental appraisal. Understanding and evaluation do go hand in hand; and the responses individuals have to forests, wild rivers, and the like are not merely raw, emotional responses.

IV

Not all forests are alike, not all rain forests are alike. There are countless possible discriminations that the informed observer may make. Comparative judgments between areas of the natural environment are possible with regard to ecological richness, stage of development, stability, peculiar local circumstance, and the like. Judgments of this kind will very often underlie hierarchical orderings of environments in terms of their

intrinsic worth. Appeal to judgments of this kind will frequently strengthen the case for preserving some bit of the environment. . . .

One reason that a faked forest is not just as good as a naturally evolved forest is that there is always the possibility that the trained eye will tell the difference. It takes some time to discriminate areas of Alpine plain which are naturally clear of snow gums from those that have been cleared. It takes some time to discriminate regrowth forest which has been logged from forest which has not been touched. These are discriminations which it is possible to make and which are made. Moreover, they are discriminations which affect valuations. The reasons why the "faked" forest counts for less, more often than not, than the real thing are similar to the reasons why faked works of art count for less than the real thing.

Origin is important as an integral part of the evaluation process. It is important because our beliefs about it determine the valuations we make. It is also important in that the discovery that something has an origin quite different to the origin we initially believe that it has, can literally alter the way we perceive that thing. The point concerning the possibility of detecting fakes is important in that it stresses just how much detail must be written into the claim that environmental engineers can replicate nature. Even if environmental engineering could achieve such exactitude, there is, I suggest, no compelling reasons for accepting the restoration thesis. It is worth stressing though that, as a matter of strategy, environmentalists must argue the empirical inadequacy of restoration proposals. This is the strongest argument against restoration ploys, because it appeals to diverse value-frameworks, and because such proposals are promises to deliver a specific good. Showing that the good won't be delivered is thus a useful move to make.

Study Questions

1. Is Elliot correct about the analogy of nature with works of art? Is the fact that a wilderness has been replicated by human contrivance a disvaluing of the replicated product?

2. Can you imagine a situation where a natural object is replicated and where its value is greater than the original? Explain your thinking here.

3. Eugene Hargrove relates the following: Due to affects of tourism, the famous ancient cave paintings at Lascaux in France were in danger of irreparable damage. So the authorities built a full-scale model of the cave nearby (*Foundations of Environmental Ethics* [Englewood Cliffs. NJ: Prentice Hall, 1989] p. 169). Hargrove argues that, while the aesthetic experience of the replicated cave is not as valuable as the original, nevertheless, "the knowledge that the original still exists enhances the experience afforded by the representation."

Hargrove then compares this with threatened damage to natural objects. An extremely beautiful passageway in Mammoth Cave, Kentucky, called Turner Avenue, was in danger of severe damage due to tourism, so the authorities photographed it, closed it off from aesthetic experiences, and allowed only the indirect aesthetic experience that comes from beholding the pictures. Hargrove argues, analogous to the first situation, that knowledge that the original still exists enhances the experience afforded by the representation.

Do you agree with this analysis? Does such knowledge that an art work or a natural object still exists enhance the aesthetic experience? Explain.

35

The Call of the Wild: The Struggle Against Domination and the Technological Fix of Nature

Eric Katz

Eric Katz received his Ph.D from Boston University and is the director of the Science, Technology and Society Program at the New Jersey Institute of Technology in Newark. He is the author of several essays in environmental ethics, two annotated bibliographies of this field, and of Nature as Subject: Human Obligation and Natural Community. *He is currently writing a book on deep ecology.*

In this essay, I use encounters with the white-tailed deer of Fire Island to explore the "call of the wild"—the *attraction to value* that exists in a natural world outside of human control. Value exists in nature to the extent that it avoids modification by human technology. Technology "fixes" the natural world by improving it for human use or by restoring degraded ecosystems. Technology creates a "new world," an artifactual reality that is far removed from the "wildness" of nature. The technological "fix" of nature thus raises a moral issue: how is an artifact morally different from a natural and wild entity? Artifacts are human instruments; their value lies in their ability to meet human needs. Natural entities have no intrinsic functions; they were not created for any instrumental purpose. To attempt to manage natural entities is to deny their inherent autonomy: a form of domination. The moral claim of the wilderness is thus a claim against human technological domination. We have an obligation to struggle against this domination by preserving as much of the natural world as possible.

I

During the summer I live with my family on Fire Island, a barrier beach off the coast of Long Island. Most mornings, if I wake up early, I can look out my window and watch white-tailed deer munching their breakfast of flowers and leaves from the trees surrounding my house. The deer are rather tame; they have become accustomed to the transient human population that invades the island each summer. A few years ago, if they had heard me walking onto the deck, they would have jumped and run off into the thicker underbrush. Now, if they hear me, they might look up to see if I have a carrot; more likely still, they will simply ignore me and continue foraging. My experiences with these deer are the closest encounters I have with what I like to call the "wild."

Using the adjective *wild to* describe these deer is obviously a distortion of terminology. These are animals that live in and around a fairly dense human community; they consume, much to the dismay of many residents, the cultivated gardens of flowers and vegetables; they seek handouts from passing humans—my daughters often feed them breadsticks and pretzels. Yet, seeing them is different than my experience with any other animal, surely different than seeing white-tailed deer in the zoo, on a petting farm, or in a nature documentary film on television. The mornings when I find them in my yard are something special. If I walk close to one, unaware, at night, my heart beats faster. These animals are my connection to "wild nature." Despite their acceptance of the human presence, they embody something untouched and beyond humanity. They are a deep and forceful *symbol* of the wild "other." The world—my world—would be a poorer place if they were not there.

In this essay, I explore this "call of the wild"—our *attraction to value* that exists in a natural world outside of human control. To understand this value, we must understand the relationship between technology and the natural world, the ways in which humanity attempts to "fix" and mold nature to suit human purposes. Thomas

Reprinted from *Environmental Ethics* (Fall 1992) by permission. Notes edited.

Birch has described this project as the "control of otherness,"[1] a form of domination that includes the control of nature and all such outsiders of human society. Here I bring together several ideas about the philosophy of technology and the nature of artifacts, and combine them with themes raised by Birch. I argue that value exists in nature to the extent it avoids the domination of human technological practice. Technology can satisfy human wants by creating the artifactual products we desire, but it cannot supply, replace, or restore the "wild."

II

One promise of the technological enterprise is the creation of "new worlds." This optimistic view of the ability of technology to improve the human condition is based on the belief that humanity has the power to alter the physical structure of the world. Consider the words of Emmanuel Mesthene:

> We . . . have enough . . . power actually at hand to create new possibilities almost at will. By massive physical changes deliberately induced, we can literally pry new alternatives out of nature. The ancient tyranny of matter has been broken, and we know it. . . . We can change it and shape it to suit our purposes.[2]

No longer limited by the physical necessities of the "given" natural world, our technological power enables us to create a new world of our dreams and desires. Nature can be controlled; its limitations overcome; humanity can achieve its highest potential. For Mesthene, "our technical prowess literally bursts with the promise of new freedom, enhanced human dignity, and unfettered aspiration."

I admit to being mesmerized by the resonances of meaning in the concept of the "new world." The technological promise of a new dignity and freedom, a limitless opportunity, an unchained power, sounds suspiciously like the promise envisioned in the new political and social conditions of the New World of the European discovery, our homeland, the Americas. But the "new world" of the European discovery was not, in fact, a *new* world; indeed, it was a very *old* world, the world of a wild untamed nature, with a minimal human presence that was itself quite old. The freedom, dignity, and benefits of the new human population were achieved, to some degree, at the expense of the older natural world. For the new world to be useful to humanity, it had to be developed and cultivated.[3] The New World had to cease being wild.

The comparison between the taming of the American wilderness and the technological control of brute physical matter is disturbing. I do not believe that the technological control of nature is a desirable end of human activity. The control of nature is a dream, an illusion, a hallucination. It involves the replacement of the wild natural environment with a human artifactual environment. It creates a fundamental change in the value of the world. This change in value, in turn, forces a reexamination of the ethical relationship between humanity and the natural environment.

III

It is a commonplace to refer to the improvements of technology as a "technological fix." It is supposed that the advanced technology of the contemporary world can "fix" nature. The term *fix* is used here in two complementary ways: it implies either that something is broken or that it can be improved. Thus, the technological fix of nature means that natural processes can be "improved" to maximize human satisfaction and good; alternatively, damage to the environment can be repaired by the technological reconstruction of degraded ecological systems. Humans use nature to create benefits for humanity, and we can restore natural environments after they have been damaged by use. The only new aspect of this technological activity is its increased scope and power. The practical control of natural processes has increased to such an extent that we no longer acknowledge the impossibility of doing anything; nature can be improved and restored to any extent that we wish.

Both processes—the improvement-use and the restoration of nature—lead to serious questions about value and moral obligation. The idea that nature ought to be used (and improved, if necessary) for human benefit is the fundamental assumption of "resource environmentalism"—arguably the mainstream of the American conservation movement. Under this doctrine, environmental policies are designed to maximize human satisfactions or minimize human harms. The pollution of the atmosphere is a problem because of the health hazards to human beings. The extinction of a species is a problem because the extinct species may be useful to humans, or the resulting instability in the ecosystem may be harmful. The greenhouse effect is a problem because the changes in climate may have dramatic impacts on agriculture and coastal geography. With all environmental problems, the effects on humanity are the primary concern.[4]

These "human interest" resource arguments for environmental protection have been criticized by thinkers in several disciplines concerned with environmental philosophy and environmental ethics. A full inventory of the arguments against so-called "anthropocentric" environmental ethics is clearly beyond the scope of this discussion. Here I focus on one particular implication of the anthropocentric resource view, i.e., the creation of an artificial world that more adequately meets the demands of human welfare. As Martin Krieger has written:

Artificial prairies and wildernesses have been created, and there is no reason to believe that these artificial environments need be unsatisfactory for those who experience them. . . . What's wrong with plastic trees? My guess is that there is very little wrong with them. Much more can be done with plastic trees and the like to give most people the feeling that they are experiencing nature.[5]

Krieger thus argues for "responsible interventions" to manage, manipulate, and control natural environments for the promotion of human good. "A summum bonum of preserving trees has no place in an ethic of social justice." Because human social justice, the production and distribution of human goods, is the primary policy goal, the manipulation of natural processes and the creation of artificial environments is an acceptable (and probably required) human activity.

Krieger's vision of a "user-friendly" plasticized human environment is chilling; it is not a world view that has many advocates. Nevertheless, the point of his argument is that a primary concern for the human uses of the natural environment leads inevitably to a policy of human intervention and manipulation in nature, and the subsequent creation of artificial environments. If humanity is planning to "fix" the natural environment, to use it and improve it to meet human needs, wants, and interests, the conclusion of the process is a technologically created "new" world of our own design. "Wild" nature will no longer exist, merely the controlled nature that offers pleasant experiences.

The restoration of nature, the policy of repairing damaged ecosystems and habitats, leads to similar results. The central issue is the *value* of the restored environments. If a restored environment is an adequate replacement for the previously existing natural environment, then humans can use, degrade, destroy, and replace natural entities and habitats with no moral consequences whatsoever. The value in the original natural entity does not require preservation.

The value of the restored environment, however, is questionable. Robert Elliot has argued that even a technologically perfect reproduction of a natural area is not equivalent to the original.[6] Elliot uses the analogy of an art forgery, in which even a perfect copy loses the value of the original artwork. What is missing in the forgery is the causal history of the original, the fact that a particular human artist created a specific work in a specific historical period. Although the copy may be as superficially pleasing as the original, the knowledge that it is not the work created by the artist distorts and disvalues our experience. Similarly, we value a natural area because of its "special kind of continuity with the past." This history, Eugene Hargrove argues, provides the authenticity of nature. He writes: "Nature is not simply a collection of natural objects; it is a process that progressively transforms those objects. . . . When we admire nature, we also admire that his-

tory."[7] Thus, a restored nature is a fake nature; it is an artificial human creation, not the product of a historical natural process.

The technological "fix" of repairing a damaged and degraded nature is an illusion and a falsehood; elsewhere, I have called it "the big lie."[8] As with all technology, the product of nature restoration is a human artifact, not the end result of a historically based natural process. Artifacts, of course, can have positive or negative value. However, what makes the value in the artifactually restored natural environment questionable is its ostensible claim to be the original.

Both forms of technological intervention in the natural world thus lead to the same result: the establishment of an artifactual world rather than a natural one. When our policy is to use nature to our best advantage, we end up with a series of so-called "responsible interventions" that manipulate natural processes to create the most pleasant human experiences possible. When our policy is to restore and repair a degraded natural environment, we end up with an unauthentic copy of the original. The technological "fix" of nature merely produces artifacts for the satisfaction of human interests.

IV

The issue of *value* now has a sharper focus. We can ask, "What is the value of artifacts and what are the moral obligations that derive from that value?" More precisely, "How is the value of the artifacts, and the derivative moral obligations, different from the value and moral obligations concerning 'wild' nature?" Framed in this manner, the answer to the problem is clear: artifacts differ from natural entities in their anthropocentric and instrumental origins. Artifacts are products of the larger human project of the domination of the natural world.

The concepts of function and purpose are central to an understanding of artifacts. Artifacts, unlike natural objects, are created for a specific purpose. They are essentially anthropocentric instruments, tools or objects, that serve a function in human life. The existence of artifacts is centered on human life. It is impossible to imagine an artifact that is not designed to meet a human purpose, for without a foreseen use the object would not have been created.

The anthropocentric instrumentality of artifacts is completely different from the essential characteristics of natural entities, species, and ecosystems. Living natural entities and systems of entities evolve to fill ecological niches in the biosphere; they are not designed to meet human needs or interests. Andrew Brennan thus argues that natural entities have no "intrinsic functions": they are not created for a particular purpose; they have no set manner of use. We may speak as if natural individuals (e.g., predators) have roles to play in ecosystemic well-being (the maintenance of optimum population levels), but this talk is either metaphorical or fallacious. No one created or designed the mountain lion as a regulator of the deer population.[9]

From a moral point of view, the difference between purposely designed artifacts and evolving natural entities is not generally problematic. The anthropocentric instrumentality of artifacts is not a serious moral concern, for most artifacts are designed for use in human social and cultural contexts. Nevertheless, the human intervention into "wild" nature is a different process entirely. Hargrove notes how human intervention alters the aesthetic evaluation of nature: "To attempt to manipulate nature, even for aesthetic reasons, alters nature adversely from an aesthetic standpoint. Historically, manipulation of nature, even to improve it, has been considered subjugation or domination." This domination resulting from human intervention can be generalized beyond aesthetic valuations; it leads to more than just a loss of beauty. The management of nature results in the imposition of our anthropocentric purposes on areas that exist outside human society. We intervene in nature to create so-called natural objects and environments based on models of human desires, interests, and satisfactions. In doing so, we engage in the project of the human domination of nature: the reconstruction of the natural world in our own image, to suit our purposes.

Need we ask why domination is a moral issue? In the context of human social and political thought, domination is the evil that restricts, denies, or distorts individual (and social) freedom and autonomy. In the context of environmental philosophy, domination is the anthropocentric alteration of natural processes. The entities and systems that comprise nature are not permitted to be free, to pursue their own independent and unplanned course of development. Even Hargrove, who emphasizes the aesthetic value of nature, judges this loss of freedom the crucial evil of domination: it "reduces [nature's] ability to be creative." Wherever it exists, in nature or in human culture, the process of domination attacks the preeminent value of self-realization.

Is the analysis of domination appropriate here? Does it make sense to say that we can deny the autonomy, the self-realization, of natural nonhuman entities? The central assumption of this analysis is that natural entities and systems have a value in their own right, a value that transcends the instrumentality of human concerns, projects, and interests. Nature is not merely the physical matter that is the *object* of technological practice and alteration; it is also a *subject*, with its own process and history of development independent of human intervention and activity. Nature thus has a value that can be subverted and destroyed by the process of human domination. In this way, human domination, alteration, and management are issues of moral concern.

V

But does the "wild" have a moral claim on humanity? The answer to this question determines the moral status of the human domination of nature. Does the wilderness, the world of nature untouched by the technological alteration of humanity, possess a moral value worth preserving? Is the creation of a technological "new world" morally harmful? Does it destroy the value of the original New World of the European discovery of America, the untamed and "wild" wilderness? How do we discern a method for answering these questions?

It is at this point that my thoughts return to my encounters with the white-tailed deer on Fire Island. They are not truly wild, for they are no longer afraid of the human presence on the island. They seem to realize that the summer residents are not hunters. These humans come with pretzels, not rifles. Nevertheless, there are some human residents who are deeply disturbed by the existence of the deer. The deer carry ticks that are part of the life cycle of Lyme disease. They eat the flowers and vegetables of well-tended gardens. They are unpredictable, and they can knock a person down. A considerable portion of the human community thus wants the deer hunted and removed from the island.

Just the thought of losing these deer disturbs me—and until recently I did not understand why. In my lucid rational moments, I realize that they are not "wild," that they have prospered on Fire Island due to an unnatural absence of predators; their population could be decreased with no appreciable harm to the herd or the remaining natural ecosystem of the barrier beach. Nevertheless, they are the vestiges of a truly wild natural community; they are reminders that the forces of domination and subjugation do not always succeed.

Birch describes the process of wilderness preservation as "incarceration" by "the technological imperium"—i.e., by the primary social-political force of the contemporary world.[10] The entire process of creating and maintaining wilderness reservations by human law is contradictory, for the wildness is destroyed by the power of the human-technological system:

> Wilderness reservations are not meant to be voids in the fabric of domination where "anarchy" is permitted, where nature is actually liberated. Not at all. The rule of law is presupposed as supreme. Just as wilderness reservations are created by law, so too they can be abolished by law. The threat of annihilation is always maintained.

The domination of natural wildness is just one example of the system of power. "The whole point, purpose, and meaning of imperial power, and its most basic legitimation, is to give humans control over otherness."

It is here that Birch sees the contradiction in the imperial technological domination of wild nature. "The wildness is still there, and it is still wild," and it maintains its own integrity. The wildness, the otherness of nature, remains, I suggest, because the forces of the imperial power require its existence. If there is no "other" recognized as the victim of domination, then the power of the imperium is empty. There would be nothing upon which to exercise power. But maintaining the existence of the wild other, even in the diminished capacity of wilderness reservations managed by the government, lays the seeds for the subversion of the imperial domination of technology.

Birch thus recommends that we view wilderness, wherever it can be found, as a "sacred space" acting as "an implacable counterforce to the momentum of totalizing power." Wilderness appears anywhere: "old roadbeds, wild plots in suburban yards, flower boxes in urban windows, cracks in the pavement. . . ." And it appears, in my life, in the presence of the white-tailed deer of Fire Island. My commitment to the preservation of the deer in my community is part of my resistance to the total domination of the technological world.

This resistance is based on yet a deeper moral commitment: the deer themselves are members of my moral and natural community. The deer and I are partners in the continuous struggle for the preservation of autonomy, freedom, and integrity. This shared partnership creates obligations on the part of humanity for the preservation and protection of the natural world. This is the *call of the wild*—the moral claim of the natural world.

We are all impressed by the power and breadth of human technological achievements. Why is it not possible to extend this power further, until we control and dominate the entire natural universe? This insidious dream of domination can only end by respecting freedom and self-determination, wherever it exists, and by recognizing the true extent of the moral community in the natural world.

Notes

1. Thomas H. Birch, "The Incarceration of Wildness: Wilderness Areas as Prisons," *Environmental Ethics* 12 (1990): 18.
2. Emmanuel G. Mesthene, "Technology and Wisdom," in *Philosophy and Technology: Readings in the Philosophical Problems of Technology*, ed. Carl Mitcham and Robert Mackey (New York: Free Press, 1983), p. 110.
3. One of the best examples of this attitude from a historical source contemporaneous with the period of European expansion is the discussion of property by John

Locke, *Second Treatise on Government*, chap. 5, especially, secs. 40–43. Locke specifically mentions the lack of value in American land because of the absence of labor and cultivation.
4. There are sound political and motivational reasons for arguments that outline the threat to human interests caused by environmental degradation. These arguments have been the rallying cry of popular conservationists from Rachel Carson, *Silent Spring* (New York: Houghton Mifflin, 1962), to Barry Commoner, *The Closing Circle: Nature, Man, and Technology* (New York: Knopf, 1971), to Bill McKibben, *The End of Nature* (New York: Random House, 1989). My philosophical criticisms of these views do not diminish my respect for the positive social and political changes these works have inspired.
5. Martin H. Krieger, "What's Wrong with Plastic Trees?" *Science* 179 (1973): 453. [Reprinted in this volume.]
6. Robert Elliot, "Faking Nature," *Inquiry* 25 (1982): 81–93, specifically, p. 86. [Reprinted in this volume.]
7. Eugene Hargrove, *The Foundations of Environmental Ethics*, Englewood Cliffs, NJ: Prentice Hall, 1989, p. 195.
8. Eric Katz, "The Big Lie: Human Restoration of Nature," *Research in Philosophy and Technology*, 12 (1992): 231–41.
9. Andrew Brennan, "The Moral Standing of Natural Objects," *Environmental Ethics* 6 (1984): 41–44.
10. Birch, op. cit., p. 10.

Study Questions

1. What does Katz mean by a "technological fix" of nature? Is it a good thing? What does Katz think? Is he right?
2. Compare Krieger's view (previous reading) with Katz's? What does Katz think about plastic trees? What, if anything, is the difference between artificial and natural entities?
3. What is the "call of the wild"? What does Katz mean by it? Do you agree with his assessment that the natural world has a moral claim on us? That we ought to respect nature's "freedom and self-determination, wherever it exists"? Explain your answer.
4. How central to the human project (civilization) is the idea of domination? You might wish to turn to Genesis 1:28 (Reading 1 in this work) for a biblical passage on this topic.

36

Should Trees Have Standing?
Toward Legal Rights for Natural Objects

CHRISTOPHER D. STONE

Christopher Stone is professor of law at the University of Southern California, Los Angeles, and the author of several works in law and environmental ethics, including Should Trees Have Standing? *from which the present selection is taken.*

Stone argues that a strong case can be made for the "unthinkable idea" of extending legal rights to natural objects. Building on the models of inanimate objects, such as trusts, corporations, nation-states and municipalities, he proposes that we extend the notion of legal guardian for legal incompetents to cover these natural objects. Note the three main ways that natural objects are denied rights under common law and how Stone's proposal addresses these considerations.

INTRODUCTION: THE UNTHINKABLE

In *Descent of Man,* Darwin observes that the history of man's moral development has been a continual extension in the objects of his "social instincts and sympathies." Originally each man had regard only for himself and those of a very narrow circle about him; later, he came to regard more and more "not only the welfare, but the happiness of all his fellow-men"; then "his sympathies became more tender and widely diffused, extending to men of all races, to the imbecile, maimed, and other useless members of society, and finally to the lower animals. . . ."

The history of the law suggests a parallel development. Perhaps there never was a pure Hobbesian state of nature, in which no "rights" existed except in the vacant sense of each man's "right to self-defense." But it is not unlikely that so far as the earliest "families" (including extended kinship groups and clans) were concerned, everyone outside the family was suspect, alien, rightless. And even within the family, persons we presently regard as the natural holders of at least some rights had none. Take, for example, children. We know something of the early rights-status of children from the widespread practice of infanticide—especially of the deformed and female. (Senicide, as among the North American

Indians, was the corresponding rightlessness of the aged.) Maine tells us that as late as the Patria Potestas of the Romans, the father had *jus vitae necisque*—the power of life and death—over his children. A fortiori, Maine writes, he had power of "uncontrolled corporal chastisement; he can modify their personal condition at pleasure; he can give a wife to his son; he can give his daughter in marriage; he can divorce his children of either sex; he can transfer them to another family by adoption; and he can sell them." The child was less than a person: an object, a thing.

The legal rights of children have long since been recognized in principle, and are still expanding in practice. Witness, just within recent time, *In re Gault,* guaranteeing basic constitutional protections to juvenile defendants, and the Voting Rights Act of 1970. We have been making persons of children although they were not, in law, always so. And we have done the same, albeit imperfectly some would say, with prisoners, aliens, women (especially of the married variety), the insane, Blacks, foetuses, and Indians.

Nor is it only matter in human form that has come to be recognized as the possessor of rights. The world of the lawyer is peopled with inanimate right-holders: trusts, corporations, joint ventures, municipalities, Subchapter R partnerships, and nation-states, to mention just a few. Ships, still referred to by courts in the feminine gender, have long had an independent jural life, often with striking consequences. We have become so accustomed to the idea of a corporation having "its" own rights, and being a "person" and "citizen" for so many statutory and constitutional purposes, that we forget how jarring the notion was to early jurists. "That invisible, intangible and artificial being, that mere legal entity" Chief Justice Marshall wrote of the corporation in *Bank of the United States v. Deveaux*—could a suit be brought in *its* name? Ten years later, in the *Dartmouth College* case, he was still refusing to let pass unnoticed the wonder of an entity "existing only in contemplation of law." Yet, long before Marshall worried over the personifying of the modern corporation, the best medieval legal scholars had spent hundreds of years struggling with the notion of the legal nature of those great public "corporate bodies," the Church and the State. How could they exist in law, as entities transcending the living Pope and King? It was clear how a king could bind *himself*—on his honor—by a treaty. But

Reprinted from *Should Trees Have Standing? Toward Legal Rights for Natural Objects* (Los Altos: William Kaufmann, Inc., 1974), by permission. Notes deleted.

when the king died, what was it that was burdened with the obligations of, and claimed the rights under, the treaty *his* tangible hand had signed? The medieval mind saw (what we have lost our capacity to see) how *unthinkable* it was, and worked out the most elaborate conceits and fallacies to serve as anthropomorphic flesh for the Universal Church and the Universal Empire.

It is this note of the *unthinkable* that I want to dwell upon for a moment. Throughout legal history, each successive extension of rights to some new entity has been, theretofore, a bit unthinkable We are inclined to suppose the rightlessness of rightless "things" to be a decree of Nature, not a legal convention acting in support of some status quo. It is thus that we defer considering the choices involved in all their moral, social, and economic dimensions. And so the United States Supreme Court could straight-facedly tell us in *Dred Scott* that Blacks had been denied the rights of citizenship "as a subordinate and inferior class of beings, who had been subjugated by the dominant race. . . ." In the nineteenth century, the highest court in California explained that Chinese had not the right to testify against white men in criminal matters because they were "a race of people whom nature has marked as inferior, and who are incapable of progress or intellectual development beyond a certain point . . . between whom and ourselves nature has placed an impassable difference." The popular conception of the Jew in the 13th Century contributed to a law which treated them as "men *ferae naturae,* protected by a quasi-forest law. Like the roe and the deer, they form an order apart." Recall, too, that it was not so long ago that the foetus was "like the roe and the deer." In an early suit attempting to establish a wrongful death action on behalf of a negligently killed foetus (now widely accepted practice), Holmes, then on the Massachusetts Supreme Court, seems to have thought it simply inconceivable "that a man might owe a civil duty and incur a conditional prospective liability in tort to one not yet in being." The first woman in Wisconsin who thought she might have a right to practice law was told that she did not, in the following terms:

> The law of nature destines and qualifies the female sex for the bearing and nurture of the children of our race and for the custody of the homes of the world. . . . [A]ll life-long callings of women, inconsistent with these radical and sacred duties of their sex, as the profession of the law, are departures from the order of nature; and when voluntary, treason against it. . . . The peculiar qualities of womanhood, its gentle graces, its quick sensibility, its tender susceptibility, its purity, its delicacy, its emotional impulses, its subordination of hard reason to sympathetic feeling, are surely not qualifications for forensic strife. Nature has tempered woman as little for the juridical conflicts of the court room, as for the physical conflicts of the battle field. . . .

The fact is, that each time there is a movement to confer rights onto some new "entity," the proposal is bound to sound odd or frightening or laughable. This is partly because until the rightless thing receives its rights, we cannot see it as anything but a *thing* for the use of "us"—those who are holding rights at the time. In this vein, what is striking about the Wisconsin case above is that the court, for all its talk about women, so clearly was never able to see women as they are (and might become). All it could see was the popular "idealized" version of *an object it needed.* Such is the way the slave South looked upon the Black. There is something of a seamless web involved: there will be resistance to giving the thing "rights" until it can be seen and valued for itself; yet, it is hard to see it and value it for itself until we can bring ourselves to give it "rights"—which is almost inevitably going to sound inconceivable to a large group of people.

The reason for this little discourse on the unthinkable, the reader must know by now, if only from the title of the paper. I am quite seriously proposing that we give legal rights to forests, oceans, rivers and other so-called "natural objects" in the environment—indeed, to the natural environment as a whole.

As strange as such a notion may sound, it is neither fanciful nor devoid of operational content. In fact, I do not think it would be a misdescription of recent developments in the law to say that we are already on the verge of assigning some such rights, although we have not faced up to what we are doing in those particular terms. We should do so now, and begin to explore the implications such a notion would hold.

TOWARD RIGHTS FOR THE ENVIRONMENT

Now, to say that the natural environment should have rights is not to say anything as silly as that no one should be allowed to cut down a tree. We say human beings have rights, but—at least as of the time of this writing—they can be executed. Corporations have rights, but they cannot plead the fifth amendment; *In re Gault* gave 15-year-olds certain rights in juvenile proceedings, but it did not give them the right to vote. Thus, to say that the environment should have rights is not to say that it should have every right we can imagine, or even the same body of rights as human beings have. Nor is it to say that everything in the environment should have the same rights as every other thing in the environment.

What the granting of rights does involve has two sides to it. The first involves what might be called the legal-operational aspects; the second, the psychic and socio-psychic aspects. I shall deal with these aspects in turn.

THE LEGAL-OPERATIONAL ASPECTS

What It Means to Be a Holder of Legal Rights

There is, so far as I know, no generally accepted standard for how one ought to use the term "legal rights." Let me indicate how I shall be using it in this piece.

First and most obviously, if the term is to have any content at all, an entity cannot be said to hold a legal right unless and until *some public authoritative body* is prepared to give *some amount of review* to actions that are colorably inconsistent with that "right." For example, if a student can be expelled from a university and cannot get any public official, even a judge or administrative agent at the lowest level, either (i) to require the university to justify its actions (if only to the extent of filling out an affidavit alleging that the expulsion "was not wholly arbitrary and capricious") or (ii) to compel the university to accord the student some procedural safeguards (a hearing, right to counsel, right to have notice of charges), then the minimum requirements for saying that the student has a legal right to his education do not exist.

But for a thing to be *a holder of legal rights,* something more is needed than that some authoritative body will review the actions and processes of those who threaten it. As I shall use the term, "holder of legal rights," each of three additional criteria must be satisfied. All three, one will observe, go towards making a thing *count* jurally—to have a legally recognized worth and dignity in its own right, and not merely to serve as a means to benefit "us" (whoever the contemporary group of rights-holders may be). They are, first, that the thing can institute legal actions *at its behest;* second, that in determining the granting of legal relief, the court must take *injury to it* into account; and, third, that relief must run to the *benefit of it.* . . .

The Rightlessness of Natural Objects at Common Law

Consider, for example, the common law's posture toward the pollution of a stream. True, courts have always been able, in some circumstances, to issue orders that will stop the pollution. . . . But the stream itself is fundamentally rightless, with implications that deserve careful reconsideration.

The first sense in which the stream is not a rights-holder has to do with standing. The stream itself has none. So far as the common law is concerned, there is in general no way to challenge the polluter's actions save at the behest of a lower *riparian**—another human being—able to show an invasion of *his* rights. This conception of the riparian as the holder of the right to bring suit has more than theoretical interest. The lower riparians may simply not care about the pollution. They themselves may be polluting, and not wish to stir up legal waters. They may be economically dependent on their polluting neighbor. And, of course, when they discount the value of winning by the costs of bringing suit and the chances of success, the action may not seem worth undertaking. Consider, for example, that while the polluter might be injuring 100 downstream riparians $10,000 a year *in the aggregate,* each riparian separately might be suffering injury only to the extent of $100—possibly not enough for any one of them to want to press suit by himself, or even to go to the trouble and cost of securing co-plaintiffs to make it worth everyone's while. This hesitance will be especially likely when the potential plaintiffs consider the burdens the law puts in their way: proving, *e.g.,* specific damages, the "unreasonableness" of defendant's use of the water, the fact that practicable means of abatement exist, and overcoming difficulties raised by issues such as joint causality, right to pollute by prescription, and so forth. Even in states which, like California, sought to overcome these difficulties by empowering the attorney-general to sue for abatement of pollution in limited instances, the power has been sparingly invoked and, when invoked, narrowly construed by the courts.

The second sense in which the common law denies "rights" to natural objects has to do with the way in which the merits are decided in those cases in which someone is competent and willing to establish standing. At its more primitive levels, the system protected the "rights" of the property owning human with minimal weighing of any values: *Cujus est solum, ejus est usque ad coelum et ad infernos.*[†] Today we have come more and more to make balances—but only such as will adjust the economic best interests of identifiable humans. For example, continuing with the case of streams, there are commentators who speak of a "general rule" that "a riparian owner is legally entitled to have the stream flow by his land with its quality unimpaired" and observe that "an upper owner has, prima facie, no right to pollute the water." Such a doctrine, if strictly invoked, would protect the stream absolutely whenever a suit was brought; but obviously, to look around us, the law does not work that way. Almost everywhere there are doctrinal qualifications on riparian "rights" to an unpolluted stream. Although these rules vary from jurisdiction to jurisdiction, and upon whether one is suing for an equitable injunction or for damages, what they all have in common is some sort of balancing. Whether under language of "reasonable use," "reasonable methods of use," "balance of convenience" or "the public interest doctrine," what the courts are balancing, with varying degrees of directness, are the economic hardships on the upper

---

* Riparian—related to living on the bank of a natural waterway.

[†]To whosoever the soil belongs, he owns also to the sky and to the depths.

riparian (or dependent community) of abating the pollution vis-à-vis the economic hardships of continued pollution on the lower riparians. What does not weigh in the balance is the damage to the stream, its fish and turtles and "lower" life. So long as the natural environment itself is rightless, these are not matters for judicial cognizance. Thus, we find the highest court of Pennsylvania refusing to stop a coal company from discharging polluted mine water into a tributary of the Lackawana River because a plaintiff's "grievance is for a mere personal inconvenience; and . . . mere private personal inconveniences . . . must yield to the necessities of a great public industry, which although in the hands of a private corporation, subserves a great public interest." The stream itself is lost sight of in "a quantitative compromise between *two* conflicting interests."

The third way in which the common law makes natural objects rightless has to do with who is regarded as the beneficiary of a favorable judgment. Here, too, it makes a considerable difference that it is not the natural object that counts in its own right. To illustrate this point, let me begin by observing that it makes perfectly good sense to speak of, and ascertain, the legal damage to a natural object, if only in the sense of "making it whole" with respect to the most obvious factors. The costs of making a forest whole, for example, would include the costs of reseeding, repairing watersheds, restocking wildlife—the sorts of costs the Forest Service undergoes after a fire. Making a polluted stream whole would include the costs of restocking with fish, waterfowl, and other animal and vegetable life, dredging, washing out impurities, establishing natural and/or artificial aerating agents, and so forth. Now, what is important to note is that, under our present system, even if a plaintiff riparian wins a water pollution suit for damages, no money goes to the benefit of the stream itself to repair *its* damages. This omission has the further effect that, at most, the law confronts a polluter with what it takes to make the plaintiff riparians whole; this may be far less than the damages to the stream, but not so much as to force the polluter to desist. For example, it is easy to imagine a polluter whose activities damage a stream to the extent of $10,000 annually, although the aggregate damage to all the riparian plaintiffs who come into the suit is only $3000. If $3000 is less than the cost to the polluter of shutting down, or making the requisite technological changes, he might prefer to pay off the damages (*i.e.*, the legally cognizable damages) and continue to pollute the stream. Similarly, even if the jurisdiction issues an injunction at the plaintiffs' behest (rather than to order payment of damages), there is nothing to stop the plaintiffs from "selling out" the stream, *i.e.*, agreeing to dissolve or not enforce the injunction at some price (in the example above, somewhere between plaintiffs' damages—$3000—and defendant's next best economic alternative). Indeed, I take it this is exactly what Learned Hand had in mind in an opinion in which, after issuing an anti-pollution injunction, he suggests that the defendant "make its peace with the plaintiff as best it can." What is meant is a peace between *them,* and not amongst them and the river.

I ought to make clear at this point that the common law as it affects streams and rivers, which I have been using as an example so far, is not exactly the same as the law affecting other environmental objects. Indeed, one would be hard pressed to say that there was a "typical" environmental object, so far as its treatment at the hands of the law is concerned. There are some differences in the law applicable to all the various resources that are held in common: rivers, lakes, oceans, dunes, air, streams (surface and subterranean), beaches, and so forth. And there is an even greater difference as between these traditional communal resources on the one hand, and natural objects on traditionally private land, *e.g.*, the pond on the farmer's field, or the stand of trees on the suburbanite's lawn.

On the other hand, although there be these differences which would make it fatuous to generalize about a law of the natural environment, most of these differences simply underscore the points made in the instance of rivers and streams. None of the natural objects, whether held in common or situated on private land, has any of the three criteria of a rights-holder. They have no standing in their own right; their unique damages do not count in determining outcome; and they are not the beneficiaries of awards. In such fashion, these objects have traditionally been regarded by the common law, and even by all but the most recent legislation, as objects for man to conquer and master and use—in such a way as the law once looked upon "man's" relationships to African Negroes. Even where special measures have been taken to conserve them, as by seasons on game and limits on timber cutting, the dominant motive has been to conserve them *for us*—for the greatest good of the greatest number of human beings. Conservationists, so far as I am aware, are generally reluctant to maintain otherwise. As the name implies, they want to conserve and guarantee *our* consumption and *our* enjoyment of these other living things. In their own right, natural objects have counted for little, in law as in popular movements.

As I mentioned at the outset, however, the rightlessness of the natural environment can and should change; it already shows some signs of doing so.

Toward Having Standing in Its Own Right

It is not inevitable, nor is it wise, that natural objects should have no rights to seek redress in their own behalf. It is no answer to say that streams and forests cannot have standing because streams and forest cannot speak. Corporations cannot speak either; nor can states, estates. infants, incompetents, municipalities or universities. Lawyers speak for them, as they customarily do for the ordinary citizen with legal problems. One ought, I think, to handle the legal problems of natural objects as one does the problems of legal incompetents—human beings who have become vegetable. If a human being shows signs of becoming senile and has affairs that he is de jure incompetent to manage, those concerned with his well being make such a showing to the court, and someone is designated by the court with the authority to manage the incompetent's affairs. The guardian (or "conservator" or "committee"—the terminology varies) then represents the incompetent in his legal affairs. Courts make similar appointments when a corporation has become "incompetent"—they appoint a trustee in bankruptcy or reorganization to oversee its affairs and speak for it in court when that becomes necessary.

On a parity of reasoning, we should have a system in which, when a friend of a natural object perceives it to be endangered, he can apply to a court for the creation of a guardianship. Perhaps we already have the machinery to do so. California law, for example, defines an incompetent as "any person, whether insane or not, who by reason of old age, disease, weakness of mind, or other cause, is unable, unassisted, properly to manage and take care of himself or his property, and by reason thereof is likely to be deceived or imposed upon by artful or designing persons." Of course, to urge a court that an endangered river is "a person" under this provision will call for lawyers as bold and imaginative as those who convinced the Supreme Court that a railroad corporation was a "person" under the fourteenth amendment, a constitutional provision theretofore generally thought of as designed to secure the rights of freedmen. . . .

The guardianship approach, however, is apt to raise . . . [the following objection]: a committee or guardian could not judge the needs of the river or forest in its charge; indeed, the very concept of "needs," it might be said, could be used here only in the most metaphorical way. . . .

. . . Natural objects *can* communicate their wants (needs) to us, and in ways that are not terribly ambiguous. I am sure I can judge with more certainty and meaningfulness whether and when my lawn wants (needs) water, than the Attorney General can judge whether and when the United States wants (needs) to take an appeal from an adverse judgment by a lower court. The lawn tells me that it wants water by a certain dryness of the blades and soil—immediately obvious to the touch—the appearance of bald spots, yellowing, and a lack of springiness after being walked on; how does "the United States" communicate to the Attorney General? For similar reasons, the guardian-attorney for a smog endangered stand of pines could venture with more confidence that his client wants the smog stopped, than the directors of a corporation can assert that "the corporation" wants dividends declared. We make decisions on behalf of, and in the purported interests of, others every day; these "others" are often creatures whose wants are far less verifiable, and even far more metaphysical in conception, than the wants of rivers, trees, and land. . . .

The argument for "personifying" the environment, from the point of damage calculations, can best be demonstrated from the welfare economics position. Every well-working legal-economic system should be so structured as to confront each of us with the full costs that our activities are imposing on society. Ideally, a paper-mill, in deciding what to produce—and where, and by what methods—ought to be forced to take into account not only the lumber, acid and labor that its production "takes" from other uses in the society, but also what costs alternative production plans will impose on society through pollution. The legal system, through the law of contracts and the criminal law, for example, makes the mill confront the costs of the first group of demands. When, for example, the company's purchasing agent orders 1000 drums of acid from the Z Company, the Z Company can bind the mill to pay for them, and thereby reimburse the society for what the mill is removing from alternative uses.

Unfortunately, so far as the pollution costs are concerned, the allocative ideal begins to break down, because the traditional legal institutions have a more difficult time "catching" and confronting us with the full social costs of our activities. In the lakeside mill example, major riparian interests might bring an action, forcing a court to weigh *their* aggregate losses against the costs to the mill of installing the anti-pollution device. But many other interests—and I am speaking for the moment of recognized homocentric interests—are too fragmented and perhaps "too remote" causally to warrant securing representation and pressing for recovery: the people who own summer homes and motels, the man who sells fishing tackle and bait, the man who rents rowboats. There is no reason not to allow the lake to prove damages to them as the prima facie measure of damages to it. *By doing so, we in effect make the natural object, through its guardian, a jural entity competent to gather up these fragmented and otherwise unrepresented damage claims, and press them before the court even where, for legal or practical reasons, they are not going to be pressed by traditional class action plaintiffs.* Indeed, one way—the homocentric way—to view what I am proposing so far, is to view the guardian of the natural object as the guardian of unborn generations, as well as of the otherwise unrepresented, but distantly injured, contemporary humans. By making the lake itself the focus of these damages, and "incorporating" it so to speak, the legal system can effectively take proof upon, and confront the mill with, a larger and more representative measure of the damages its pollution causes.

So far, I do not suppose that my economist friends (unremittent human chauvinists, every one of them!) will have any large quarrel in principle with the concept.

Many will view it as a *trompe l'oeil* that comes down, at best, to effectuate the goals of the paragon class action, or the paragon water pollution control district. Where we are apt to part company is here—I propose going beyond gathering up the loose ends of what most people would presently recognize as economically valid damages. The guardian would urge before the court injuries not presently cognizable—the death of eagles and inedible crabs, the suffering of sea lions, the loss from the face of the earth of species of commercially valueless birds, the disappearance of a wilderness area. One might, of course, speak of the damages involved as "damages" to us humans, and indeed, the widespread growth of environmental groups shows that human beings do feel these losses. But they are not, at present, economically measurable losses: how can they have a monetary value for the guardian to prove in court?

The answer for me is simple. Wherever it carves out "property" rights, the legal system is engaged in the process of *creating* monetary worth. One's literary works would have minimal monetary value if anyone could copy them at will. Their economic value to the author is a product of the law of copyright; the person who copies a copyrighted book has to bear a cost to the copyright-holder because the law says he must. Similarly, it is through the law of torts that we have made a "right" of—and guaranteed an economically meaningful value to—privacy. (The value we place on gold—a yellow inanimate dirt—is not simply a function of supply and demand—wilderness areas are scarce and pretty too—, but results from the actions of the legal systems of the world, which have institutionalized that value; they have even done a remarkable job of stabilizing the price). I am proposing we do the same with eagles and wilderness areas as we do with copyrighted works, patented inventions, and privacy: *make* the violation of rights in them to be a cost by declaring the "pirating" of them to be the invasion of a property interest. If we do so, the net social costs the polluter would be confronted with would include not only the extended homocentric costs of his pollution (explained above) but also costs to the environment *per se*.

How, though, would these costs be calculated? When we protect an invention, we can at least speak of a fair market value for it, by reference to which damages can be computed. But the lost environmental "values" of which we are now speaking are by definition over and above those that the market is prepared to bid for: they are priceless.

One possible measure of damages, suggested earlier, would be the cost of making the environment whole, just as, when a man is injured in an automobile accident, we impose upon the responsible party the injured man's medical expenses. Comparable expenses to a polluted river would be the costs of dredging, restocking with fish, and so forth. It is on the basis of such costs as these, I assume, that we get the figure of $1 billion as the cost of saving Lake Erie. As an ideal, I think this is a good guide applicable in many environmental situations. It is by no means free from difficulties, however.

One problem with computing damages on the basis of making the environment whole is that, if understood most literally, it is tantamount to asking for a "freeze" on environmental quality, even at the costs (and there will be costs) of preserving "useless" objects. Such a "freeze" is not inconceivable to me as a general goal, especially considering that, even by the most immediately discernible homocentric interests, in so many areas we ought to be cleaning up and not merely preserving the environmental status quo. In fact, there is presently strong sentiment in the Congress for a total elimination of all river pollutants by 1985, notwithstanding that such a decision would impose quite large direct and indirect costs on us all. Here one is inclined to recall the instructions of Judge Hays, in remanding Consolidated Edison's Storm King application to the Federal Power Commission in *Scenic Hudson*:

> The Commission's renewed proceedings must include as a basic concern the preservation of natural beauty and of natural history shrines, keeping in mind that, in our affluent society, the cost of a project is only one of several factors to be considered.

Nevertheless, whatever the merits of such a goal in principle, there are many cases in which the social price tag of putting it into effect are going to seem too high to accept. Consider, for example, an oceanside nuclear generator that could produce low cost electricity for a million homes at a savings of $1 a year per home, spare us the air pollution that comes of burning fossil fuels, but which through a slight heating effect threatened to kill off a rare species of temperature-sensitive sea urchins; suppose further that technological improvements adequate to reduce the temperature to present environmental quality would expend the entire one million dollars in anticipated fuel savings. Are we prepared to tax ourselves $1,000,000 a year on behalf of the sea urchins? In comparable problems under the present law of damages, we work out practicable compromises by abandoning restoration costs and calling upon fair market value. For example, if an automobile is so severely damaged that the cost of bringing the car to its original state by repair is greater than the fair market value, we would allow the responsible tortfeasor to pay the fair market value only. Or if a human being suffers the loss of an arm (as we might conceive of the ocean having irreparably lost the sea urchins), we can fall back on the capitalization of reduced earning power (and pain and suffering) to measure the damages. But what is the fair market value of sea urchins? How can we capitalize their loss to the ocean, independent of any commercial value they may have to someone else?

One answer is that the problem can sometimes be sidestepped quite satisfactorily. In the sea urchin example, one compromise solution would be to impose on the nuclear generator the costs of making the ocean whole somewhere else, in some other way, *e.g.*, reestablishing a sea urchin colony elsewhere, or making a somehow comparable contribution. In the debate over the laying of the trans-Alaskan pipeline, the builders are apparently prepared to meet conservationists' objections halfway by re-establishing wildlife away from the pipeline, so far as is feasible.

But even if damage calculations have to be made, one ought to recognize that the measurement of damages is rarely a simple report of economic facts about "the market," whether we are valuing the loss of a foot, a foetus, or a work of fine art. Decisions of this sort are always hard, but not impossible. We have increasingly taken (human) pain and suffering into account in reckoning damages, not because we think we can ascertain them as objective "facts" about the universe, but because, even in view of all the room for disagreement, we come up with a better society by making rude estimates of them than by ignoring them. We can make such estimates in regard to environmental losses fully aware that what we are really doing is making implicit normative judgments (as with pain and suffering)—laying down rules as to what the society is going to "value" rather than reporting market evaluations. In making such normative estimates decision-makers would not go wrong if they estimated on the "high side," putting the burden of trimming the figure down on the immediate human interests present. All burdens of proof should reflect common experience; our experience in environmental matters has been a continual discovery that our acts have caused more long-range damage than we were able to appreciate at the outset.

To what extent the decision-maker should factor in costs such as the pain and suffering of animals and other sentient natural objects, I cannot say; although I am prepared to do so in principle.

THE PSYCHIC AND SOCIO-PSYCHIC ASPECTS

. . . The strongest case can be made from the perspective of human advantage for conferring rights on the environment. Scientists have been warning of the crises the earth and all humans on it face if we do not change our ways—radically—and these crises make the lost "recreational use" of rivers seem absolutely trivial. The earth's very atmosphere is threatened with frightening possibilities: absorption of sunlight, upon which the entire life cycle depends, may be diminished; the oceans may warm (increasing the "greenhouse effect" of the atmosphere), melting the polar ice caps, and destroying our great coastal cities; the portion of the atmosphere that shields us from dangerous radiation may be destroyed. Testifying before Congress, sea explorer

Jacques Cousteau predicted that the oceans (to which we dreamily look to feed our booming populations) are headed toward their own death: "The cycle of life is intricately tied up with the cycle of water . . . the water system has to remain alive if we are to remain alive on earth." We are depleting our energy and our food sources at a rate that takes little account of the needs even of humans now living.

These problems will not be solved easily; they very likely can be solved, if at all, only through a willingness to suspend the rate of increase in the standard of living (by present values) of the earth's "advanced" nations, and by stabilizing the total human population. For some of us this will involve forfeiting material comforts; for others it will involve abandoning the hope someday to obtain comforts long envied. For all of us it will involve giving up the right to have as many offspring as we might wish. Such a program is not impossible of realization, however. Many of our so called "material comforts" are not only in excess of, but are probably in opposition to, basic biological needs. Further, the "costs" to the advanced nations is not as large as would appear from Gross National Product figures. G.N.P. reflects social gain (of a sort) without discounting for the social *cost* of that gain, *e.g.*, the losses through depletion of resources, pollution, and so forth. As has well been shown, as societies become more and more "advanced," their real marginal gains become less and less for each additional dollar of G.N.P. Thus, to give up "human progress" would not be as costly as might appear on first blush.

Nonetheless, such far-reaching social changes are going to involve us in a serious reconsideration of our consciousness towards the environment. . . .

. . . A few years ago the pollution of streams was thought of only as a problem of smelly, unsightly, unpotable water, *i.e.*, to us. Now we are beginning to discover that pollution is a process that destroys wondrously subtle balances of life within the water, and as between the water and its banks. This heightened awareness enlarges our sense of the dangers to us. But it also enlarges our empathy. We are not only developing the scientific capacity, but we are cultivating the personal capacities *within us* to recognize more and more the ways in which nature—like the woman, the Black, the Indian and the Alien—is like us (and we will also become more able realistically to define, confront, live with and admire the ways in which we are all different).

The time may be on hand when these sentiments, and the early stirrings of the law, can be coalesced into a radical new theory or myth—felt as well as intellectualized—of man's relationships to the rest of nature. I do not mean "myth" in a demeaning sense of the term, but in the sense in which, at different times in history, our social "facts" and relationships have been comprehended and integrated by reference to the "myths" that we are co-signers of a social contract, that the Pope is

God's agent, and that all men are created equal. Pantheism, Shinto and Tao all have myths to offer. But they are all, each in its own fashion, quaint, primitive and archaic. What is needed is a myth that can fit our growing body of knowledge of geophysics, biology and the cosmos. In this vein, I do not think it too remote that we may come to regard the Earth, as some have suggested, as one organism, of which Mankind is a functional part—the mind, perhaps: different from the rest of nature, but different as a man's brain is from his lungs. . . .

> . . . As I see it, the Earth is only one organized "field" of activities—and so is the *human person*—but these activities take place at various levels, in different "spheres " of being and realms of consciousness. The lithosphere is not the biosphere, and the latter not the . . . ionosphere. The Earth is not *only* a material mass. Consciousness is not only "human"; it exists at animal and vegetable levels, and most likely must be latent, or operating in some form, in the molecule and the atom; and all these diverse and in a sense hierarchical modes of activity and consciousness should be seen integrated in and perhaps transcended by an all-encompassing and "eonic" planetary Consciousness.
>
> Mankind's function within the Earth-organism is to extract from the activities of all other operative systems within this organism the type of consciousness which we call "reflective" or "self"-consciousness—or, we may also say to *mentalize* and give meaning, value, and "name" to all that takes place anywhere within the Earth-field. . . .

As radical as such a consciousness may sound today, all the dominant changes we see about us point in its direction. Consider just the impact of space travel, of world-wide mass media, of increasing scientific discoveries about the interrelatedness of all life processes. Is it any wonder that the term "spaceship earth" has so captured the popular imagination? The problems we have to confront are increasingly the world-wide crises of a global organism: not pollution of a stream, but pollution of the atmosphere and of the ocean. Increasingly, the death that occupies each human's imagination is not his own, but that of the entire life cycle of the planet earth, to which each of us is as but a cell to a body.

To shift from such a lofty fancy as the planetarization of consciousness to the operation of our municipal legal system is to come down to earth hard. Before the forces that are at work, our highest court is but a frail and feeble—a distinctly human—institution. Yet, the Court may be at its best not in its work of handing down decrees, but at the very task that is called for: of summoning up from the human spirit the kindest and most generous and worthy ideas that abound there, giving them shape and reality and legitimacy. Witness the School Desegregation Cases which, more importantly than to integrate the schools (assuming they did), awakened us to moral needs which, when made visible, could not be denied. And so here, too, in the case of the environment, the Supreme Court may find itself in a position to award "rights" in a way that will contribute to a change in popular consciousness. It would be a modest move, to be sure, but one in furtherance of a large goal: the future of the planet as we know it.

How far we are from such a state of affairs, where the law treats "environmental objects" as holders of legal rights, I cannot say. But there is certainly intriguing language in one of Justice Black's last dissents, regarding the Texas Highway Department's plan to run a six-lane expressway through a San Antonio Park. Complaining of the Court's refusal to stay the plan, Black observed that "after today's decision, the people of San Antonio and the birds and animals that make their home in the park will share their quiet retreat with an ugly, smelly stream of traffic. . . . Trees, shrubs, and flowers will be mowed down." Elsewhere he speaks of the "burial of public parks," of segments of a highway which "devour parkland," and of the park's heartland. Was he, at the end of his great career, on the verge of saying—just saying—that "nature has 'rights' on its own account"? Would it be so hard to do?

Study Questions

1. Is the analogy with extending the circle of moral considerability and rights (from white male adults to women, other races, children, etc.) a good way to view our extending rights to natural objects? Or are there relevant differences? Could the Right to Life Movement use Stone's analogy-argument to institute legislation to protect fetuses?

2. Is Stone's basic argument anthropocentric? That is, underneath the concerns for granting legal standing to natural objects is there really anything more than enlightened self-interest? Or is there something further? (See Garrett Hardin's "Tragedy of the Commons" [Reading 47] for a way that would reduce Stone's arguments to an antropocentric model).

3. To which natural objects should we grant rights? If any, we'd probably choose objects traditionally valued by humans, such as the Mississippi River, the Giant Redwoods of California, the Grand Canyon and Yellowstone National Parks, but how about deer, rats, weeds, ordinary trees, bacteria, lice and termites? Would they get legal standing? Why, or why not?

4. Does the United States Endangered Species Act (1974), which as of February 1993 protects 750 endangered species, exemplify Stone's proposal? Do the Clean Air Acts do it likewise?

5. Sum up the pluses and minuses of Stone's proposal. How would granting legal rights to natural objects be a good thing, and how could it lead to bad consequences?

For Further Reading

Carlson, Alan. "Appreciation and the Natural Environment." *Journal of Aesthetics and Art* 37 (1979).

Hargrove, Eugene. *Foundations of Environmental Ethics.* Englewood Cliffs, NJ: Prentice-Hall, 1989.

Myers, Norman. *The Sinking Ark.* Oxford: Pergamon Press, 1980.

———. *The Primary Source: Tropical Forests and Our Future.* New York: Norton, 1984.

Nash, Roderick. *The Rights of Nature.* Madison: University of Wisconsin Press, 1989.

Norton, Bryan G. "Thoreau's Insect Analogies: Or Why Environmentalists Hate Mainstream Economists." *Environmental Ethics* 13:3 (1991).

———. *Why Preserve Natural Variety?* Princeton, NJ: Princeton University Press, 1987.

Shoumatoff, Alex. *The World Is Burning.* Boston: Little, Brown, 1990.

Stone, Christopher D. *Should Trees Have Standing?* Los Altos, CA: Kaufmann, 1974.

Thoreau, Henry David. "Walking." In *The Natural History Essays.* William Gibbs, 1980.

Wilson, Edward O. *The Diversity of Life.* Cambridge, MA: Harvard University Press, 1992.

———. *Biophilia.* Cambridge, MA: Harvard University Press, 1984.

Wolf, Edward. "Avoiding a Mass Extinction of Species." *State of the World 1988.* Washington, D.C.: Worldwatch Institute, 1988.

CHAPTER SEVEN

Non-Western Perspectives on Environmental Ethics

Environmental concerns are global issues. The air we breathe may have been polluted by corporations on another continent while the air we contaminate reaches Africa and Asia. The chlorofluorocarbons (CFCs) we use, which break down the ozone layer, affect everyone in the world. A nuclear disaster causes radiation fallout that spreads thousands of miles from its source. The poverty and hunger in one country may cause pressures for immigration to other countries, putting stresses on the latter's resources. Much of the oil we burn comes from the Near East, so their problems become our problems. When Iraq invaded Kuwait in 1990, our economic interests were at stake, resulting in the Gulf War. When the Iraqi army set fire to the Kuwaiti oil wells, the polluted air affected the whole world.

We need to understand each other, if for no other reason than enlightened self-interest. But a nobler motive is the quest for an international environmental ethic that takes into consideration the insights and perspectives of various cultures and points of view. Hopefully, we can learn from each other in the quest to act responsibly and lovingly toward human beings and nature. To that end a multicultural dimension is appropriate to this book.

Throughout history, religion has profoundly influenced people's attitude and behavior toward nature. Various religions look at nature, at animals, at Earth differently. Hinduism believes in an underlying sanctity of life in a way that Christianity and Judaism do not. Buddhism emphasizes passive acceptance of nature in yet a different way. Our first three readings examine non-Western religious attitudes toward nature. We begin with O. P. Dwivedi's "*Satyagraha* for Conservation: Awakening the Spirit of Hinduism," for a Hindu view of environmental philosophy. Dwivedi argues that religion can play a vital role in saving the environment. He explains the Hindu view of *satyagraha*, the persistent search of truth, with regard to the environment and shows how Hinduism has had a deep nonviolent (*ahimsa*) attitude toward animals, trees, and nature in general. He claims that non-Indian influences in India have negatively affected this philosophy, but that it is beginning to reassert itself.

In our second reading, "The Buddhist Attitude Towards Nature," Lily de Silva explains the Buddhist view of the environment. Buddhists emphasize escaping the suffering of existence, a gentle nonaggessive attitude toward nature, and sympathy toward all living things. Buddhism provides a moral and spiritual antidote to the greed and exploitation by humans of nature.

In our third reading, "Islamic Environmental Ethics, Law, and Society," Mawil Izzi Deen sets forth the Islamic view of environmental ethics as he finds it encoded in the Koran. Islam urges us to go beyond self-interest and see Earth as God's gift for satisfying our needs and for our enjoyment, not something to be exploited ruthlessly and spoiled. He offers some specific practices that aid in promoting a sustainable environmental policy.

Our last two readings consider more secular non-Western perspectives on environmental ethics. First, the Nigerian philosopher Segun Ogungbemi shows how a combination of ignorance, poverty, and poor leadership have combined with technological power to devastate much of the sub-Saharan African environment.

In our final reading, Ramachandra Guha criticizes Western movements like deep ecology as being irrelevant (and even harmful) for the third world because they fail to address two underlying causes of our global environmental crisis: overconsumption by the rich West and militarism.

You will come to see things from different perspectives in this part of our work. I hope you enjoy the experience as you interact with these different points of view.

37

Satyagraha for Conservation: Awakening the Spirit of Hinduism

O. P. DWIVEDI

O. P. Dwivedi is chair and professor, Department of Political Studies, University of Guelph, Canada, and has served as World Health Organization consultant to the Department of Environment, India. He is the co-author of Hindu Religion and the Environmental Crisis.

In this essay, Dwivedi argues that a profound environmental ethics, consisting in satyagraha *(the persistent quest for truth) permeates Hinduism. Hinduism holds to a strong version of the equal sanctity of all life and for thousands of years practiced sustainable agriculture and nonviolence* (ahimsa) *toward animals and nature. Dwivedi argues that in the last hundreds of years* satyagraha *lost much of its effectiveness, but there are signs that it is reasserting itself.*

The World Commission on Environment and Development acknowledged that to reconcile human affairs with natural laws "our cultural and spiritual heritages can reinforce our economic interests and survival imperatives." But until very recently, the role of our cultural and spiritual heritages in environmental protection and sustainable development was ignored by international bodies, national governments, policy planners, and even environmentalists. Many fear that bringing religion into the environmental movement will threaten objectivity, scientific investigation, professionalism, or democratic values. But none of these need be displaced in order to include the spiritual dimension in environmental protection. That dimension, if introduced in the process of environmental policy planning, administration, education, and law, could help create a self-consciously moral society which would put conservation and respect for God's creation first, and relegate individualism, materialism, and our modern desire to dominate nature in a subordinate place. Thus my plea for a definite role of religion in conservation and environmental protection.

From the perspective of many world religions, the abuse and exploitation of nature for immediate gain is unjust, immoral, and unethical. For example, in the ancient past, Hindus and Buddhists were careful to observe moral teachings regarding the treatment of nature. In their cultures, not only the common person

but also rulers and kings followed those ethical guidelines and tried to create an example for others. But now in the twentieth century, the materialistic orientation of the West has equally affected the cultures of the East. India, Sri Lanka, Thailand, and Japan have witnessed wanton exploitation of the environment by their own peoples, despite the strictures and injunctions inherent in their religions and cultures. Thus, no culture has remained immune from human irreverence towards nature. How can we change the attitude of human beings towards nature? Are religions the answer?

I believe that religion can evoke a kind of awareness in persons that is different from scientific or technological reasoning. Religion helps make human beings aware that there are limits to their control over the animate and inanimate world and that their arrogance and manipulative power over nature can backfire. Religion instills the recognition that human life cannot be measured by material possessions and that the ends of life go beyond conspicuous consumption.

As a matter of fact, religion can provide at least three fundamental mainstays to help human beings cope in a technological society. First, it defends the individual's existence against the depersonalizing effects of the technoindustrial process. Second, it forces the individual to recognize human fallibility and to combine realism with idealism. Third, while technology gives the individual the physical power to create or to destroy the world, religion gives the moral strength to grow in virtue by nurturing restraint, humility, and liberation from self-centredness. Directly and indirectly, religion can be a powerful source for environmental conservation and protection. Thus, we need a strategy for conservation that does not ignore the powerful influence of religions, but instead draws from all religious foundations and cultures.

World religions, each in their own way, offer a unique set of moral values and rules to guide human beings in their relationship with the environment. Religions also provide sanctions and offer stiffer penalties, such as fear of hell, for those who do not treat God's creation with respect. Although it is true that, in the recent past, religions have not been in the forefront of protecting the environment from human greed and exploitation, many are now willing to take up the challenge and help protect and conserve the environment. But their offer of help will remain purely rhetorical unless secular institutions, national governments, and international organizations are willing to acknowledge

Reprinted from *Ethics of Environment and Development*, eds. J. R. Engel and J. G. Engel (London: Bellhaven Press, 1990) by permission.

the role of religion in environmental study and education. And I believe that environmental education will remain incomplete until it includes cultural values and religious imperatives. For this, we require an ecumenical approach. While there are metaphysical, ethical, anthropological and social disagreements among world religions, a synthesis of the key concepts and precepts from each of them pertaining to conservation could become a foundation for a global environmental ethic. The world needs such an ethic.

THE RELIGION AND ENVIRONMENT DEBATE

In 1967, the historian, Lynn White, Jr., wrote an article in *Science* on the historical roots of the ecological crisis. According to White, what people do to their environment depends upon how they see themselves in relation to nature. White asserted that the exploitative view that has generated much of the environmental crisis, particularly in Europe and North America, is a result of the teachings of late medieval Latin Christianity, which conceived of humankind as superior to the rest of God's creation and everything else as created for human use and enjoyment. He suggested that the only way to address the ecological crisis was to reject the view that nature has no reason to exist except to serve humanity. White's proposition impelled scientists, theologians, and environmentalists to debate the bases of his argument that religion could be blamed for the ecological crisis.

In the course of this debate, examples from other cultures were cited to support the view that, even in countries where there is religious respect for nature, exploitation of the environment has been ruthless. Countries where Hinduism, Buddhism, Taoism and Shintoism have been practiced were cited to support the criticism of Thomas Derr, among others, that "We are simply being gullible when we take at face value the advertisement for the ecological harmony of non-Western cultures." Derr goes on to say:

> even if Christian doctrine had produced technological culture and its environmental troubles, one would be at a loss to understand the absence of the same result in equally Christian Eastern Europe. And conversely, if ecological disaster is a particularly Christian habit, how can one explain the disasters non-Christian cultures have visited upon their environments? Primitive cultures, Oriental cultures, classical cultures—all show examples of human dominance over nature which has led to ecological catastrophe. Overgrazing, deforestation and similar errors of sufficient magnitude to destroy civilizations have been committed by Egyptians, Assyrians, Romans, North Africans, Persians, Indians, Aztecs, and even Buddhists, who are foolishly supposed by some Western admirers to be immune from this sort of thing.

This chapter challenges Derr's assertion with respect to the role of the Hindu religion in the ecological crisis. We need to understand how a Hindu's attitude to nature has been shaped by his religion's view of the cosmos and creation. Such an exposition is necessary to explain the traditional values and beliefs of Hindus and hence what role Hindu religion once played with respect to human treatment of the environment. At the same time, we need to know how it is that this religion, which taught harmony with and respect for nature, and which influenced other religions such as Jainism and Buddhism, has been in recent times unable to sustain a caring attitude towards nature. What are the features of the Hindu religion which strengthen human respect for God's creation, and how were these features repressed by the modern view of the natural environment and its resources?

THE SANCTITY OF LIFE IN HINDUISM

The principle of the sanctity of life is clearly ingrained in the Hindu religion. Only God has absolute sovereignty over all creatures, thus, human beings have no dominion over their own lives or non-human life. Consequently, humanity cannot act as a viceroy of God over the planet, nor assign degrees of relative worth to other species. The idea of the Divine Being as the one underlying power of unity is beautifully expressed in the Yajurveda:

> The loving sage beholds that Being, hidden in mystery,
> wherein the universe comes to have one home;
> Therein unites and therefrom emanates the whole;
> The Omnipresent One pervades souls and matter like
>   warp and woof in created beings   (Yajurveda 32.8).

The sacredness of God's creation means no damage may be inflicted on other species without adequate justification. Therefore, all lives, human and nonhuman, are of equal value and all have the same right to existence. According to the Atharvaveda, the Earth is not for human beings alone, but for other creatures as well:

> Born of Thee, on Thee move mortal creatures;
> Thou bearest them—the biped and the quadruped;
> Thine, O Earth, are the five races of men, for whom
> Surya (Sun), as he rises spreads with his rays
>   the light that is immortal   (Atharvaveda 12.1–15).

Srsti: God's Creation

Hindus contemplate divinity as the one in many and the many in one. This conceptualization resembles both monotheism and polytheism. Monotheism is the belief in a single divine Person. In monotheistic creeds that Person is God. Polytheism, on he other hand, believes in the many; and the concept of God is not monarchical.

The Hindu concept of God resembles monotheism in that it portrays the divinity as one, and polytheism in that it contemplates the divinity as one in many. Although there are many gods, each one is the Supreme Being. This attitude we may call non-dualistic theism.

The earliest Sanskrit texts, the Veda and Upanishads, teach the non-dualism of the supreme power that existed before the creation. God as the efficient cause, and nature, *Prakrti,* as the material cause of the universe, are unconditionally accepted, as is their harmonious relationship. However, while these texts agree on the concept of non-dualistic theism, they differ in their theories regarding the creation of the universe. Why have different theories been elaborated in the Veda and the Upanishads? This is one of the most important and intriguing questions we can ask. A suitable reply is given in the Rigveda:

> He is one, but the wise call him by different names; such as Indra, Mitra, Varuna, Agni, Divya—one who pervaded all the luminous bodies, the source of light; Suparna—the protector and preserver of the universe; whose works are perfect; Matriswa—powerful like wind; Garutman—mighty by nature (Rigveda 1.164.46).

The Hindu concept of creation can be presented in four categories. First is the Vedic theory, which is followed by further elaboration in Vedanta and Sankhya philosophies; the second is Upanishadic theory; the third is known as Puranic theory; and the fourth is enunciated in the great Hindu epics *Ramayana* and *Mahabharata.* Although the Puranic theory differs from the other three, a single thought flows between them. This unifying theory is well stated in the Rigveda:

> The Vedas and the universal laws of nature which control the universe and govern the cycles of creation and dissolution were made manifest by the All-knowing One. By His great power were produced the clouds and the vapors. After the production of the vapors, there intervened a period of darkness after which the Great Lord and Controller of the universe arranged the motions which produce days, nights, and other durations of time. The Great One then produced the sun, the moon, the earth, and all other regions as He did in previous cycles of creation (Rigveda 10:190.1–3).

All the Hindu scriptures attest to the belief that the creation, maintenance, and annihilation of the cosmos is completely dependent on the Supreme will. In the *Gita,* Lord Krishna says to Arjuna: "Of all that is material and all that is spiritual in this world, know for certain that I am both its origin and dissolution" (*Gita* 7.6). And the Lord says: again "The whole cosmic order is under me. By my will it is manifested again and again and by my will, it is annihilated at the end" (*Gita* 9.8). Thus, for ancient Hindus, both God and *Prakriti* (nature) was to be one and the same. While the *Prajapati* (as mentioned in Regveda) is the creator of sky, the earth, oceans, and all other species, he is also their protector and eventual destroyer. He is the only Lord of creation. Human beings have no special privilege or authority over other creatures; on the other hand, they have more obligations and duties.

Duties to Animals and Birds

The most important aspect of Hindu theology pertaining to treatment of animal life is the belief that the Supreme Being was himself incarnated in the form of various species. The Lord says: "This form is the source and indestructible seed of multifarious incarnations within the universe, and from the particle and portion of this form, different living entities, like demigods, animals, human beings and others, are created" (*Srimad-Bhagavata* Book I, Discourse III: 5). Among the various incarnations of God (numbering from ten to twenty-four depending upon the source of the text), He first incarnated Himself in the form of a fish, then a tortoise, a boar, and a dwarf. His fifth incarnation was as a man-lion. As Rama he was closely associated with monkeys, and as Krishna he was always surrounded by the cows. Thus, other species are accorded reverence.

Further, the Hindu belief in the cycle of birth and rebirth where a person may come back as an animal or a bird gives these species not only respect, but also reverence. This provides a solid foundation for the doctrine of *ahimsa—non-violence* against animals and human beings alike. Hindus have a deep faith in the doctrine of non-violence. Almost all the Hindu scriptures place strong emphasis on the notion that God's grace can be received by not killing his creatures or harming his creation: "God, Kesava, is pleased with a person who does not harm or destroy other non-speaking creatures or animals" (Visnupurana 3.8.15). To not eat meat in Hinduism is considered both an appropriate conduct and a duty. Yajnavalkya Smriti warns of hell-fire (*Ghora Naraka*) to those who are the killers of domesticated and protected animals: "The wicked person who kills animals which are protected has to live in hell-fire for the days equal to the number of hairs on the body of that animal" (*Yajnavalkyasmriti, Acaradhyayah,* v. 180). By the end of the Vedic and Upanishadic period, Buddhism and Jainism came into existence, and the protection of animals, birds and vegetation was further strengthened by the various kings practicing these religions. These religions, which arose in part as a protest against the orthodoxy and rituals of Hindu religion, continued its precepts for environmental protection. The Buddhist emperor, Ashoka (273–236 BCE), promoted through public proclamations the planting and preservation of flora and fauna. Pillar Edicts, erected at various public places, expressed his concerns about the welfare of creatures, plants and trees and prescribed various punishments for the killing of animals, including ants, squirrels, and rats.

Flora in Hindu Religion

As early as in the time of Regveda, tree worship was quite popular and universal. The tree symbolized the various attributes of God to the Regvedic seers. Regveda regarded plants as having divine powers, with one entire hymn devoted to their praise, chiefly with reference to their healing properties. (Regveda 10.97) During the period of the great epics and Puranas, the Hindu respect for flora expanded further. Trees were considered as being animate and feeling happiness and sorrow. It is still popularly believed that every tree has a *Vriksadevata*, or "tree deity," who is worshipped with prayers and offerings of water, flowers, sweets, and encircled by sacred threads. Also, for Hindus, the planting of a tree is still a religious duty. Fifteen hundred years ago, the Matsya Purana described the proper ceremony for tree planting:

> Clean the soil first and water it. Decorate trees with garlands, burn the guggula perfume in front of them, and place one pitcher filled with water by the side of each tree. Offer prayer and oblation and then sprinkle holy water on trees. Recite hymns from the Regveda, Yajur and Sama and kindle fire. After such worship the actual plantation should be celebrated. He who plants even one tree, goes directly to Heaven and obtains Moksha (Matsya Purana 59.159).

The cutting of trees and destruction of flora were considered a sinful act. *Kautilya's Arthasastra* prescribed various punishments for destroying trees and plants:

> For cutting off the tender sprouts of fruit trees or shady trees in the parks near a city, a fine of six panas shall be imposed; for cutting of the minor branches of the same trees, twelve panas, and for cutting off the big branches, twenty four panas shall be levied. Cutting off the trunks of the same, shall be punished with the first amercement; and felling shall be punished with the middlemost amercement (*Kautilya's Arthasastra* III 19:197).

The Hindu worship of trees and plants has been based partly on utility, but mostly on religious duty and mythology. Hindu ancestors considered it their duty to save trees; and in order to do that they attached to every tree a religious sanctity.

Pradushana: Pollution and Its Prevention in Hindu Scriptures

Hindu scriptures revealed a clear conception of the ecosystem. On this basis a discipline of environmental ethics developed which formulated codes of conduct (*dharma*) and defined humanity's relationship to nature. An important part of that conduct is maintaining proper sanitation. In the past, this was considered to be the duty of everyone and any default was a punishable offence. Hindu society did not even consider it proper to throw dirt on a public path. Kautilya wrote:

> The punishment of one-eighth of a pana should be awarded to those who throw dirt on the roads. For muddy water one-fourth Pana, if both are thrown the punishment should be double. If latrine is thrown or caused near a temple, well, or pond, sacred place, or government building, then the punishment should increase gradually by one pana in each case. For urine the punishment should be only half (*Kautilya's Arthasastra* II 36:145).

Hindus considered cremation of dead bodies and maintaining the sanitation of the human habitat as essential acts. When, in about 200 BCE, Caraka wrote about *Vikrti* (pollution) and diseases, he mentioned air pollution specifically as a cause of many diseases.

> The polluted air is mixed with bad elements. The air is uncharacteristic of the season, full of moisture, stormy, hard to breathe, icy cool, hot and dry, harmful, roaring, coming at the same time from all directions, badsmelling, oily, full of dirt, sand, steam, creating diseases in the body and is considered polluted (*Caraka Samhita, Vimanastanam* III 6:1).

Similarly, about water pollution, Caraka Samhita says:

> Water is considered polluted when it is excessively smelly, unnatural in color, taste and touch, slimy, not frequented by aquatic birds, aquatic life is reduced, and the appearance is unpleasing (*Caraka Samhita, Vimanastanam* III 6:2).

Water is considered by Hindus as a powerful media of purification and also as a source of energy. Sometimes, just by the sprinkling of pure water in religious ceremonies, it is believed purity is achieved. That is why, in Regveda, prayer is offered to the deity of water: "The waters in the sky, the waters of rivers, and water in the well whose source is the ocean, may all these sacred waters protect me" (Regveda 7.49.2). The healing property and medicinal value of water has been universally accepted, provided it is pure and free from all pollution. When polluted water and pure water were the point of discussion among ancient Indian thinkers, they were aware of the reasons for the polluted water. Therefore Manu advised: "One should not cause urine, stool, cough in the water. Anything which is mixed with these unpious objects, blood and poison, should not be thrown into water" (*Manusmrti* IV: 56).

Still today, many rivers are considered sacred. Among there, the river Ganges is considered by Hindus as the most sacred and respectable. Disposal of human waste or other pollutants has been prohibited since time immemorial:

> One should not perform these 14 acts near the holy waters of the river Ganga: i.e., remove excrement, brushing and gargling, removing cerumen from body, throwing hairs, dry garlands, playing in water, taking donations,

performing sex, attachment with other sacred places, praising other holy places, washing clothes, throwing dirty clothes, thumping water and swimming (*Pravascitta Tatva* 1.535).

Persons doing such unsocial activities and engaging in acts polluting the environment were cursed: "A person, who is engaged in killing creatures, polluting wells, and ponds, and tanks and destroying gardens, certainly goes to hell" (*Padmapurana, Bhoomikhanda* 96: 7–8).

EFFECTIVENESS OF HINDUISM IN CONSERVATION

The effectiveness of any religion in protecting the environment depends upon how much faith its believers have in its precepts and injunctions. It also depends upon how those precepts are transmitted and adapted in everyday social interactions. In the case of the Hindu religion, which is practised as *dharma*—way of life— many of its precepts became ingrained in the daily life and social institutions of the people. Three specific examples are given below to illustrate this point.

The Caste System and Sustainable Development

The Hindu religion is known for its elaborate caste system which divides individuals among four main castes and several hundred sub-castes. Over the centuries, the system degenerated into a very rigid, hereditarily determined, hierarchical, and oppressive social structure, particularly for the untouchables and lower castes. But the amazing phenomenon is that it lasted for so many millennia even with centuries of domination by Islamic and Christian cultures.

One explanation by the ecologist, Madhav Gadgil, and the anthropologist, Kailash Malhotra, is that the caste system, as continued until the early decades of the twentieth century, was actually based on an ancient concept of sustainable development which disciplined the society by partitioning the use of natural resources according to specific occupations (or castes); and "created" the right social milieu in which sustainable patterns of resource use were encouraged to emerge. The caste system regulated the occupations that individuals could undertake. Thus, an "ecological space" was created in ancient Hindu society which helped to reduce competition among various people for limited natural resources. A system of "resource partitioning" emerged whereby the primary users of natural resources did not worry about encroachment from other castes. At the same time, these users also knew that if they depleted the natural resources in their own space, they would not survive economically or physically because no one would allow them to move on to other occupations.

Religious injunctions also created the psychological environment whereby each caste or sub-caste respected the occupational boundaries of the others. In a sense, the Hindu caste system can be seen as a progenitor of the concept of sustainable development.

But the system started malfunctioning during the British Raj when demands for raw materials for their fast-growing industrial economy had to be met by commercial exploitation of India's natural resources. As traditional relationships between various castes started disappearing, competition and tension grew. The trend kept on accelerating in independent India, as each caste (or sub-caste) tried to discard its traditional role and seize eagerly any opportunity to land a job. When this happened, the ancient religious injunction for doing one's prescribed duty within a caste system could no longer be maintained; this caused the disappearance of the concept of "ecological space" among Hindus. There is no doubt that the caste system also degenerated within and became a source of oppression; nevertheless, from an ecological spacing view point, the caste system played a key role in preserving India's natural riches for centuries.

Bishnois: Defenders of the Environment

The Bishnois are a small community in Rajasthan, India, who practise a religion of environmental conservation. They believe that cutting a tree or killing an animal or bird is blasphemy. Their religion, an offshoot of Hinduism, was founded by Guru Maharaj Jambaji, who was born in 1450 CE in the Marwar area. When he was young he witnessed how, during a severe drought, people cut down trees to feed animals but when the drought continued, nothing was left to feed the animals, so they died. Jambaji thought that if trees are protected, animal life would be sustained, and his community would survive. He gave 29 injunctions and principal among them being a ban on the cutting of any green tree and killing of any animal or bird. About 300 years later, when the King of Jodhpur wanted to build a new palace, he sent his soldiers to the Bishnois area where trees were in abundance. Villagers protested, and when soldiers would not pay any attention to the protest, the Bishnois, led by a woman, hugged the trees to protect them with their bodies. As soldiers kept on killing villagers, more and more of the Bishnois came forward to honour the religious injunction of their Guru Maharaj Jambaji. The massacre continued until 363 persons were killed defending trees. When the king heard about this human sacrifice, he stopped the operation, and gave the Bishnois state protection for their belief.

Today, the Bishnois community continues to protect trees and animals with the same fervour. Their community is the best example of a true Hindu-based ritual defense of the environment in India, and their sacrifices became the inspiration for the Chipko movement of 1973.

The Chipko Movement

In March 1973, in the town of Gopeshwar in Chamoli district (Uttar Pradesh, India), villagers formed a human chain and hugged the earmarked trees to keep them from being felled for a nearby factory producing sports equipment. The same situation later occurred in another village when forest contractors wanted to cut trees under licence from the Government Department of Forests. Again, in 1974, women from the village of Reni, near Joshimath in the Himalayas, confronted the loggers by hugging trees and forced contractors to leave. Since then, the *Chipko Andolan* (the movement to hug trees) has grown as a grassroots ecodevelopment movement.

The genesis of the Chipko movement is not only in the ecological or economic background, but in religious belief. Villagers have noted how industrial and commercial demands have denuded their forests, how they cannot sustain their livelihood in a deforested area, and how floods continually play havoc with their small agricultural communities. The religious basis of the movement is evident in the fact that it is inspired and guided by women. Women have not only seen how their men would not mind destroying nature in order to get money while they had to walk miles in search of firewood, fodder and other grazing materials, but, being more religious, they also are more sensitive to injunctions such as *ahimsa*. In a sense, the Chipko movement is a kind of feminist movement to protect nature from the greed of men. In the Himalayan areas, the pivot of the family is the woman. It is the woman who worries most about nature and its conservation in order that its resources are available for her family's sustenance. On the other hand, men go away to distant places in search of jobs, leaving women and old people behind. These women also believe that each tree has a *Vriksadevata* (tree god) and that the deity *Van Devi* (the Goddess of forests) will protect their family welfare. They also believe that each green tree is an abode of the Almighty God *Hari*.

The Chipko movement has caught the attention of others in India. For example, in Karnataka state, the Appiko movement began in September 1983, when 163 men, women, and children hugged the trees and forced the lumberjacks to leave. That movement swiftly spread to the adjoining districts. These people are against the kind of commercial felling of trees which clears the vegetation in its entirety. They do recognize the firewood needs of urban people (mostly poor) and therefore do not want a total ban on felling. However, they are against indiscriminate clearing and would like to see a consultative process established so that local people are able to participate in timber management.

These three examples are illustrative of the practical impact of Hinduism on conservation and sustainable development. While the effectiveness of the caste system to act as a resource partitioning system is no longer

viable, the examples of Bishnois and Chipko/Appiko are illustrative of the fact that when appeal to secular norms fails, one can draw on the cultural and religious sources for "forest *satyagraha*." ("Satyagraha" means "insistence or persistence in search of truth." In this context, the term "forest satyagraha" means "persistence in search of truth pertaining to the rights of trees."

LOSS OF RESPECT FOR NATURE

If such has been the tradition, philosophy, and ideology of Hindu religion, what then are the reasons behind the present state of environmental crisis? As we have seen, our ethical beliefs and religious values influence our behaviour towards others, including our relationship with all creatures and plant life. If, for some reason, these noble values become displaced by other beliefs which are either thrust upon the society or transplanted from another culture through invasion, then the faith of the masses in the earlier cultural tradition is shaken. As the foreign culture, language and system of administration slowly takes root and penetrates all levels of society, and as appropriate answers and leadership are not forthcoming from the religious leaders and Brahmans, it is only natural for the masses to become more inward-looking and self-centered. Under such circumstances, religious values which acted as sanctions against environmental destruction do not retain a high priority because people have to worry about their very survival and freedom; hence, respect for nature gets displaced by economic factors.

That, it seems, is what happened in India during the 700 years of foreign cultural domination. The ancient educational system which taught respect for nature and reasons for its preservation was no longer available. On the other hand, the imported culture was unable to replace the ancient Hindu religion; consequently, a conflict continued between the two value systems. The situation became more complex when, in addition to the Muslim culture, the British introduced Christianity and Western secular institutions and values. While it is too easy to blame these external forces for the change in attitudes of Hindus towards nature, nevertheless it is a fact that they greatly inhibited the religion from continuing to transmit ancient values which encourage respect and due regard for God's creation.

The Hindu religion teaches a renunciation of worldly goods, and preaches against materialism and consumerism. Such teachings could act as a great source of strength for Hindu societies in their snuggle to achieve sustainable development. I detect in countries like India and Nepal a revival of respect for ancient cultural values. Such a revival need not turn into fundamentalism; instead it could be based on the lessons learned from environmental destruction in the West, and on the relevant precepts enshrined in the Hindu scriptures. That should not cause any damage to the secularism now practised in India. As a matter of fact, this could develop into a movement whereby spiritual guidance is made available to the secular system of governance and socioeconomic interaction.

HOPE FOR OUR COMMON FUTURE

Mahatma Gandhi warned that "nature had enough for everybody's need but not for everybody's greed." Gandhi was a great believer in drawing upon the rich variety of spiritual and cultural heritages of India. His *satyagraha* movements were the perfect example of how one could confront an unjust and uncaring though extremely superior power. Similarly, the Bishnois, Chipko, and Appiko people are engaged in a kind of "forest *satyagraha*" today. Their movements could easily be turned into a common front—"satyagraha for the environment,"—to be used against the forces of big government and big business. This could include such other movements as *Mitti Bachao Abhiyan* (save the soil movement), *Van Mahotsava* (tree planting ceremony), *Chetna March* (public awareness march), *Kalpavriksha* (voluntary organization in Delhi for environmental conservation), and many others. The Hindu people are accustomed to suffering a great level of personal and physical hardships if such suffering is directed against unjust and uncaring forces. The minds of the Hindu people are slowly being awakened through the Chipko, Appiko, Bishnois, Chetna March, and other movements. *Satyagraha* for conservation could very well be a rallying point for the awakened spirit of Hinduism.

Hindu culture, in ancient and medieval times, provided a system of moral guidelines towards environmental preservation and conservation. Environmental ethics, as propounded by ancient Hindu scriptures and seers, was practised not only by common persons, but even by rulers and kings. They observed these fundamentals sometimes as religious duties, often as rules of administration or obligation for law and order, but either way these principles were properly knitted within the Hindu way of life. In Hindu culture, a human being is authorized to use natural resources, but has no divine power of control and dominion over nature and its elements. Hence, from the perspective of Hindu culture, abuse and exploitation of nature for selfish gain is unjust and sacreligious. Against the continuation of such exploitation, the only viable strategy appears to be *satyagraha* for conservation.

Study Questions

1. What are the strengths and weaknesses of the Hindu doctrine of *satyagraha* toward nature? If, as Dwivedi suggests, the teachings of the world's religions could be brought together to develop an ecumenical, global environmental ethic, what would be the unique contribution of *satyagraha*?
2. Compare the Hindu view of sanctity of life with Schweitzer's Reverence for Life (Reading 15). How are they similar and different?
3. How does Dwivedi defend the caste system in Hinduism?
4. Compare the Bishnoi and Chipko movements in India to "tree huggers" in the United States and to other Western activist movements (see the reference to the Chipko movement in Karen Warren's article, Reading 26).

38

The Buddhist Attitude Towards Nature

Lily De Silva

Lily de Silva is professor of Buddhist studies at the University of Peradeniya, Sri Lanka. In this essay, she sets forth a Buddhist perspective on environmental ethics, arguing that Buddhism emphasizes simple, nonviolent, gentle living. In its doctrine of karma and rebirth (similar to Hinduism), it recognizes that all animals and humans are spiritual entities to be treated with loving kindness.

Reprinted from *The Buddhist Attitude Towards Nature*, ed. K. Sandell (Buddhist Publication Society, Sri Lanka, 1987). Notes deleted.

Buddhism strictly limits itself to the delineation of a way of life designed to eradicate human suffering. The Buddha refused to answer questions which did not directly or indirectly bear on the central problem of human suffering and its ending. Furthermore, environmental pollution is a problem of the modern age, unheard of and unsuspected during the time of the Buddha. Therefore it is difficult to find any specific discourse which deals with the topic we are interested in here. Nevertheless, as Buddhism is a fullfledged philosophy of life reflecting all aspects of experience, it is possible to find enough material in the Pali Canon to delineate the Buddhist attitude towards nature.

The word "nature" means everything in the world which is not organised and constructed by man. The Pali equivalents which come closest to "nature" are *loka* and *yathābhūta*. The former is usually translated as "world" while the latter literally means "things as they really are." The words *dhammatā* and *niyāma* are used in the Pali Canon to mean "natural law or way."

NATURE AS DYNAMIC

According to Buddhism changeability is one of the perennial principles of nature. Everything changes in nature and nothing remains static. This concept is expressed by the Pali term *anicca*. Everything formed is in a constant process of change (*sabbe sankhārā aniccā*). The world is therefore defined as that which disintegrates (*lujjatī ti loko*); the world is so called because it is dynamic and kinetic, it is constantly in a process of undergoing change. In nature there are no static and stable "things"; there are only ever-changing, ever-moving processes. . . .

MORALITY AND NATURE

The world passes through alternating cycles of evolution and dissolution, each of which endures for a long period of time. Though change is inherent in nature, Buddhism believes that natural processes are affected by the morals of man. . . . Buddhism believes that though change is a factor inherent in nature, man's moral deterioration accelerates the process of change and brings about changes which are adverse to human well being and happiness. . . .

[S]everal suttas from the Pali Canon show that early Buddhism believes there to be a close relationship between human morality and the natural environment. This idea has been systematised in the theory of the five natural laws in the later commentaries. According to this theory, in the cosmos there are five natural laws or forces at work, namely *utuniyāma* (lit. "season-law"), *bījaniyāma* (lit. "seed-law"), *cittaniyāma*, *kammaniyāma* and *dhammaniyāma*. They can be translated as physical laws, biological laws, psychological laws, moral laws and causal laws, respectively. While the first four laws operate within their respective spheres, the last-mentioned law of causality operates *within* each of them as well as *among* them.

This means that the physical environment of any given area conditions the growth and development of its biological component, i.e., flora and fauna. These in turn influence the thought pattern of the people interacting with them. Modes of thinking determine moral standards. The opposite process of interaction is also possible. The morals of man influence not only the psychological make-up of the people but the biological and physical environment of the area as well. Thus the five laws demonstrate that man and nature are bound together in a reciprocal causal relationship with changes in one necessarily bringing about changes in the other.

The commentary on the *Cakkavattisīhanāda Sutta* goes on to explain the pattern of mutual interaction further. When mankind is demoralised through greed, famine is the natural outcome; when moral degeneration is due to ignorance, epidemic is the inevitable result; when hatred is the demoralising force, widespread violence is the ultimate outcome. If and when mankind realizes that large-scale devastation has taken place as a result of his moral degeneration, a change of heart takes place among the few surviving human beings. With gradual moral regeneration conditions improve through a long period of cause and effect and mankind again starts to enjoy gradually increasing prosperity and longer life. The world, including nature and mankind, stands or falls with the type of moral force at work. If immorality grips society, man and nature deteriorate; if morality reigns, the quality of human life and nature improves. Thus greed, hatred and delusion produce pollution within and without. Generosity, compassion and wisdom produce purity within and without. This is one reason the Buddha has pronounced that the world is led by the mind, *cittena niyata loko*. Thus man and nature, according to the ideas expressed in early Buddhism, are interdependent.

HUMAN USE OF NATURAL RESOURCES

For survival mankind has to depend on nature for his food, clothing, shelter, medicine and other requisites. For optimum benefits man has to understand nature so that he can utilise natural resources and live harmoniously with nature. By understanding the working of nature—for example, the seasonal rainfall pattern, methods of conserving water by irrigation, the soil types, the physical conditions required for growth of various food crops, etc.—man can learn to get better returns from his agricultural pursuits. But this learning has to be accompanied by moral restraint if he is to enjoy the benefits of natural resources for a long time. Man must learn to satisfy his needs and not feed his greeds. The resources of the world are not unlimited whereas man's greed knows neither limit nor satiation. Modern man in his unbridled voracious greed for pleasure and acquisition of wealth has exploited nature to the point of near impoverishment. . . .

Buddhism tirelessly advocates the virtues of non-greed, non-hatred, and non-delusion in all human pursuits. Greed breeds sorrow and unhealthy consequences. Contentment (*santuṭṭhi*) is a much praised virtue in Buddhism. The man leading a simple life with few wants easily satisfied is upheld and appreciated as an exemplary character. Miserliness and wastefulness are equally deplored in Buddhism as two degenerative extremes.

Wealth has only instrumental value; it is to be utilised for the satisfaction of man's needs. Hoarding is a senseless anti-social habit comparable to the attitude of the dog in the manger. The vast hoarding of wealth in some countries and the methodical destruction of large quantities of agricultural produce to keep the market prices from falling, while half the world is dying of hunger and starvation, is really a sad paradox of the present affluent age.

Buddhism commends frugality as a virtue in its own right. Once Ānanda explained to King Udena the thrifty economic use of robes by the monks in the following order. When new robes are received the old robes are used as coverlets, the old coverlets as mattress covers, the old mattress covers as rugs, the old rugs as dusters, and the old tattered dusters are kneaded with clay and used to repair cracked floors and walls. Thus nothing usable is wasted. Those who waste are derided as "wood-apple eaters." A man shakes the branch of a wood-apple tree and all the fruits, ripe as well as unripe, fall. The man would collect only what he wants and walk away leaving the rest to rot. Such a wasteful attitude is certainly deplored in Buddhism as not only anti-social but criminal. The excessive exploitation of nature as is done today would certainly be condemned by Buddhism in the strongest possible terms.

Buddhism advocates a gentle non-aggressive attitude towards nature. According to the *Sigālovāda Sutta* a householder should accumulate wealth as a bee collects pollen from a flower. The bee harms neither the fragrance nor the beauty of the flower, but gathers pollen to turn it into sweet honey. Similarly, man is expected to make legitimate use of nature so that he can rise above nature and realise his innate spiritual potential.

ATTITUDE TOWARDS ANIMAL AND PLANT LIFE

The well-known Five Precepts (*pañca sīla*) form the minimum code of ethics that every lay Buddhist is expected to adhere to. Its first precept involves abstention from injury to life. It is explained as the casting aside of all forms of weapons, being conscientious about depriving a living being of life. In its positive sense it means the cultivation of compassion and sympathy for all living beings. The Buddhist layman is expected to abstain from trading in meat too.

The Buddhist monk has to abide by an even stricter code of ethics than the layman. He has to abstain from practices which would involve even unintentional injury to living creatures. For instance, the Buddha promulgated the rule against going on a journey during the rainy season because of possible injury to worms and insects that come to the surface in wet weather. The same concern for non-violence prevents a monk from digging the ground. Once a monk who was a potter prior to ordination built for himself a clay hut and set it

on fire to give it a fine finish. The Buddha strongly objected to this as so many living creatures would have been burnt in the process. The hut was broken down on the Buddha's instructions to prevent it from creating a bad precedent for later generations. The scrupulous non-violent attitude towards even the smallest living creatures prevents the monks from drinking unstrained water. It is no doubt a sound hygienic habit, but what is noteworthy is the reason which prompts the practice, namely, sympathy for living creatures.

Buddhism also prescribes the practice of *mettā*, "loving-kindness" towards all creatures of all quarters without restriction. The *Karanīyamettā Sutta* enjoins the cultivation of loving-kindness towards all creatures, timid and steady, long and short, big and small, minute and great, visible and invisible, near and far, born and awaiting birth. All quarters are to be suffused with this loving attitude. Just as one's own life is precious to oneself, so is the life of the other precious to himself. Therefore a reverential attitude must be cultivated towards all forms of life. . . .

The understanding of karma and rebirth, too, prepares the Buddhist to adopt a sympathetic attitude towards animals. According to this belief it is possible for human beings to be reborn in subhuman states among animals. The *Kukkuravatika Sutta* can be cited as a canonical reference which substantiates this view. The *Jātakas* provide ample testimony to this view from commentarial literature. It is possible that our own close relatives have been reborn as animals. Therefore it is only right that we should treat animals with kindness and sympathy. The Buddhist notion of merit also engenders a gentle non-violent attitude towards living creatures. It is said that if one throws dish-washing water into a pool where there are insects and living creatures, intending that they feed on the tiny particles of food thus washed away, one accumulates merit even by such trivial generosity. According to the *Macchuddāna Jātaka* the Bodhisatta threw his leftover food into a river in order to feed the fish, and by the power of that merit he was saved from an impending disaster. Thus kindness to animals, be they big or small, is a source of merit—merit needed for human beings to improve their lot in the cycle of rebirths and to approach the final goal of Nibbāna.

Buddhism expresses a gentle non-violent attitude towards the vegetable kingdom as well. It is said that one should not even break the branch of a tree that has given one shelter. Plants are so helpful to us in providing us with all necessities of life that we are expected not to adopt a callous attitude towards them. The more strict monastic rules prevent monks from injuring plant life.

Prior to the rise of Buddhism people regarded natural phenomena such as mountains, forests, groves and trees with a sense of awe and reverence. They considered them as the abode of powerful non-human beings who could assist human beings at times of need. Though Buddhism gave man a far superior Triple Refuge (*tisaraṇa*) in the Buddha, Dhamma and Sangha, these places continued to enjoy public patronage at a popular level, as the acceptance of terrestrial non-human beings such as *devatās* and *yakkhas* did not violate the belief system of Buddhism. Therefore among the Buddhists there is a reverential attitude towards specially long-standing gigantic trees. They are called *vanaspati* in Pali, meaning "lords of the forests." As huge trees such as the ironwood, the *sāla* and the fig are also recognised as the Bodhi trees of former Buddhas, the deferential attitude towards trees is further strengthened. It is well known that the *ficus religiosa* is held as an object of great veneration in the Buddhist world today as the tree under which the Buddha attained Enlightenment.

The construction of parks and pleasure groves for public use is considered a great meritorious deed. Sakka the lord of gods is said to have reached this status as a result of social services such as the construction of parks, pleasure groves, ponds, wells and roads.

The open air, natural habitats and forest trees have a special fascination for the Eastern mind as symbols of spiritual freedom. The home life is regarded as a fetter (*sambādha*) that keeps man in bondage and misery. Renunciation is like the open air (*abbhokāsa*), nature unhampered by man's activity. . . . The Buddha's constant advice to his disciples also was to resort to natural habitats such as forest groves and glades. There, undisturbed by human activity, they could zealously engage themselves in meditation.

ATTITUDE TOWARDS POLLUTION

. . . Cleanliness was highly commended by the Buddhists both in the person and in the environment. They were much concerned about keeping water clean, be it in the river, pond or well. These sources of water were for public use and each individual had to use them with proper public-spirited caution so that others after him could use them with the same degree of cleanliness. Rules regarding the cleanliness of green grass were prompted by ethical and aesthetic considerations. Moreover, grass is food for most animals and it is man's duty to refrain from polluting it by his activities.

Noise is today recognised as a serious personal and environmental pollutant troubling everyone to some extent. . . .

The Buddha and his disciples revelled in the silent solitary natural habitats unencumbered by human activity. Even in the choice of monasteries the presence of undisturbed silence was an important quality they looked for. Silence invigorates those who are pure at heart and raises their efficiency for meditation. But silence overawes those who are impure with ignoble impulses of greed, hatred and delusion. . . .

The psychological training of the monks is so advanced that they are expected to cultivate a taste not only for external silence, but for inner silence of speech, desire and thought as well. The sub-vocal speech, the inner chatter that goes on constantly within us in our waking life, is expected to be silenced through meditation. The sage who succeeds in quelling this inner speech completely is described as a *muni*, a silent one. His inner silence is maintained even when he speaks! . . .

NATURE AS BEAUTIFUL

The Buddha and his disciples regarded natural beauty as a source of great joy and aesthetic satisfaction. The saints who purged themselves of sensuous worldly pleasures responded to natural beauty with a detached sense of appreciation. The average poet looks at nature and derives inspiration mostly by the sentiments it evokes in his own heart; he becomes emotionally involved with nature. For instance, he may compare the sun's rays passing over the mountain tops to the blush on a sensitive face, he may see a tear in a dew drop, the lips of his beloved in a rose petal, etc. But the appreciation of the saint is quite different. He appreciates nature's beauty for its own sake, and derives joy unsullied by sensuous associations and self-projected ideas. . . .

CONCLUSION

. . . In the present ecocrisis man has to look for radical solutions. "Pollution cannot be dealt with in the long term on a remedial or cosmetic basis or by tackling symptoms: all measures should deal with basic causes. These are determined largely by our values, priorities and choices." Man must reappraise his value system. The materialism that has guided his lifestyle has landed him in very severe problems. Buddhism teaches that mind is the forerunner of all things, mind is supreme. If one acts with an impure mind, i.e., a mind sullied with greed, hatred and delusion, suffering is the inevitable result. If one acts with a pure mind, i.e., with the opposite qualities of contentment, compassion and wisdom, happiness will follow like a shadow. Man has to understand that pollution in the environment has been caused because there has been psychological pollution within himself. If he wants a clean environment he has to adopt a lifestyle that springs from a moral and spiritual dimension.

Buddhism offers man a simple moderate lifestyle eschewing both extremes of self-deprivation and self-indulgence. Satisfaction of basic human necessities, reduction of wants to the minimum, frugality and contentment are its important characteristics. Each man has to order his life on moral principles, exercise self-control in the enjoyment of the senses, discharge his duties in his various social roles, and conduct himself with wisdom and self-awareness in all activities. It is only when each man adopts a simple moderate lifestyle that mankind as a whole will stop polluting the environment. This seems to be the only way of overcoming the present ecocrisis and the problem of alienation. With such a lifestyle, man will adopt a non-exploitative, non-aggressive, gentle attitude towards nature. He can then live in harmony with nature, utilising its resources for the satisfaction of his basic needs. The Buddhist admonition is to utilise nature in the same way as a bee collects pollen from the flower, neither polluting its beauty nor depleting its fragrance. Just as the bee manufactures honey out of pollen, so man should be able to find happiness and fulfilment in life without harming the natural world in which he lives.

Study Questions

1. Compare de Silva's Buddhist ethics with Dwivedi's Hindu perspective. How are they different or similar? Then compare each with Western views. Do you think we could help each other understand our responsibilities with regard to the environment?
2. How does the Buddhist concern to become liberated from suffering influence its understanding of our duties to nature?
3. Do you agree that "modes of thinking determine moral standards"?

39

Islamic Environmental Ethics, Law, and Society

MAWIL Y. IZZI DEEN (SAMARRAI)

Mawil Y. Izzi Deen (Samarrai) is assistant professor, King Abdul Aziz University, Jeddah, consultant to the Saudi Arabian Center for Science and Technology, and co-author of Islamic Principles for the Conservation of the Natural Environment. *Deen sets forth the Islamic view that the foundation of environmental protection is found in the idea that God created the world and set human beings in it to enjoy and carefully use it. Ecological balance and sustainable care of nature are promoted by Islam.*

Islamic environmental ethics, like all other forms of ethics in Islam, is based on clear-cut legal foundations which Muslims hold to be formulated by God. Thus, in Islam, an acceptance of what is legal and what is ethical has not involved the same processes as in cultures which base their laws on humanistic philosophies.

Muslim scholars have found it difficult to accept the term "Islamic Law," since "law" implies a rigidity and dryness alien to Islam. They prefer the Arabic word *Sharī'ah* (Shariah) which literally means the "source of water." The Shariah is the source of life in that it contains both legal rules and ethical principles. This is indicated by the division of the Shariah relevant to human action into the categories of: obligatory actions (*wājib*),—those which a Muslim is required to perform; devotional and ethical virtues (*mandūb*),—those actions a Muslim is

encouraged to perform, the non-observance of which, however, incurs no liability; permissible actions (*mubāh*),—those in which a Muslim is given complete freedom of choice; abominable actions (*makrūh*),—those which are morally but not legally wrong; and prohibited actions (*haram*),—all those practices forbidden by Islam.

A complete separation into the two elements, law and ethics, is thus unnecessary in Islam. For a Muslim is obliged to obey whatever God has ordered, his philosophical questions having been answered before he became a follower of the faith.

THE FOUNDATION OF ENVIRONMENTAL PROTECTION

In Islam, the conservation of the environment is based on the principle that all the individual components of the environment were created by God, and that all living things were created with different functions, functions carefully measured and meticulously balanced by the Almighty Creator. Although the various components of the natural environment serve humanity as one of their functions, this does not imply that human use is the sole reason for their creation. The comments of the medieval Muslim scholar, Ibn Tamīyah on those verses of the Holy Qur'ān which state that God created the various parts of the environment to serve humanity, are relevant here:

> In considering all these verses it must be remembered that Allah in His wisdom created these creatures for reasons

Reprinted from *Ethics of Environment and Development*, eds. J. Ronald Engel and Joan Gibb Engel (London: Bellhaven Press, 1990) by permission. Notes deleted.

other than serving man, for in these verses He only explains the benefits of these creatures [to man].

The legal and ethical reasons for protecting the environment can be summarized as follows: First, the environment is God's creation and to protect it is to preserve its values as a sign of the Creator. To assume that the environment's benefits to human beings are the sole reason for its protection may lead to environmental misuse or destruction.

Second, the component parts of nature are entities in continuous praise of their Creator. Humans may not be able to understand the form or nature of this praise, but the fact that the Qur'ān describes it is an additional reason for environmental preservation:

> The seven heavens and the earth and all that is therein praise Him, and there is not such a thing but hymneth his praise; but ye understand not their praise. Lo! He is ever Clement, Forgiving (Sūrah 17:44).

Third, all the laws of nature are laws made by the Creator and based on the concept of the absolute continuity of existence. Although God may sometimes wish otherwise, what happens, happens according to the natural law of God (sunnah), and human beings must accept this as the will of the Creator. Attempts to break the law of God must be prevented. As the Qur'an states:

> Hast thou not seen that unto Allah payeth adoration whosoever is in the heavens and whosoever is in the earth, and the sun, and the moon, and the stars, and the hills, and the trees, and the beasts, and many of mankind (Sūrah 22:18).

Fourth, the Qur'ān's acknowledgment that humankind is not the only community to live in this world— "There is not an animal in the earth, nor a flying creature flying on two wings, but they are peoples like unto you" (Sūrah 6:38)—means that while humans may currently have the upper hand over other "peoples," these other creatures are beings and, like us, are worthy of respect and protection. The Prophet Muhammad (peace be upon him) considered all living creatures worthy of protection (hurmah) and kind treatment. He was once asked whether there will be a reward from God for charity shown to animals. His reply was very explicit: "For [charity shown to] each creature which has a wet heart there is a reward." Ibn Hajar comments further upon this tradition, explaining that wetness is an indication of life (and so charity extends to all creatures), although human beings are more worthy of the charity if a choice must be made.

Fifth, Islamic environmental ethics is based on the concept that all human relationships are established on justice ('adl) and equity (ihsān): "Lo! Allah enjoineth justice and kindness" (Sūrah 16:90). The prophetic tradition limits benefits derived at the cost of animal suffering. The Prophet Muhammad instructed: "Verily Allah has prescribed equity (ihsān) in all things. Thus if you kill, kill well, and if you slaughter, slaughter well. Let each of you sharpen his blade and let him spare suffering to the animal he slaughters."

Sixth, the balance of the universe created by God must also be preserved. For "Everything with Him is measure" (Sūrah 13:8). Also, "There is not a thing but with Us are the stores thereof. And We send it not down save in appointed measure" (Sūrah 15:21).

Seventh, the environment is not in the service of the present generation alone. Rather, it is the gift of God to all ages, past, present and future. This can be understood from the general meaning of Sūrah 2:29: "He it is Who created for you all that is in the earth." The word "you" as used here refers to all persons with no limit as to time or place.

Finally, no other creature is able to perform the task of protecting the environment. God entrusted humans with the duty of viceregency, a duty so onerous and burdensome that no other creature would accept it: "Lo! We offered the trust unto the heavens and the earth and the hills, but they shrank from bearing it and were afraid of it. And man assumed it" (Sūrah 33:72).

THE COMPREHENSIVE NATURE OF ISLAMIC ETHICS

Islamic ethics is founded on two principles—human nature, and religious and legal grounds. The first principle, natural instinct (fitrah), was imprinted in the human soul by God at the time of creation (Sūrah 91:7–8). Having natural instinct, the ordinary individual can, at least to some extent, distinguish not only between good and bad, but also between these and that which is neutral, neither good nor bad. However, an ethical conscience is not a sufficient personal guide. Due to the complexities of life an ethical conscience alone cannot define the correct attitude to every problem. Moreover, a person does not live in a vacuum, but is affected by outside influences which may corrupt the ability to choose between good and evil. Outside influences include customs, personal interests, and prevailing concepts concerning one's surroundings.

The religious and legal grounds upon which Islamic ethics is founded were presented by the messengers of God. These messengers were possessed of a special nature, and since they were inspired by God, they were able to avoid the outside influences which may affect other individuals.

Legal instructions in Islam are not negative in the sense of forcing the conscience to obey. On the contrary, legal instructions have been revealed in such a way that the conscience approves and acknowledges them to be correct. Thus the law itself becomes a part of human conscience, thereby guaranteeing its application and its success.

An imported, alien law cannot work because, while it may be possible to make it legally binding, it cannot be made morally binding upon Muslims. Muslims willingly pay the poor-tax (zakāh) because they know that if they fail to do so they will be both legally and ethically responsible. Managing to avoid the legal consequences of failure to pay what is due will not help them to avoid the ethical consequences, and they are aware of this. Although a Muslim poacher may be able to shoot elephants and avoid park game wardens, if a framework based on Islamic principles for the protection of the environment has been published, he knows that he will not be able to avoid the ever-watchful divine Warden. The Muslim knows that Islamic values are all based on what God loves and wants: "And when he turns away [from thee] his effort in the land is to make mischief therein and to destroy the crops and the cattle; and Allah loveth not mischief" (Sūrah 2:205).

When the Prophet Solomon and his army were about to destroy a nest of ants, one ant warned the rest of the colony of the coming destruction. When Solomon heard this he begged God for the wisdom to do the good thing which God wanted him to do. Solomon was obviously facing an environmental problem and needed an ethical decision; he begged God for guidance:

> Till, when they reached the Valley of the Ants, an ant exclaimed: O, ants! Enter your dwellings lest Solomon and his armies crush you, unperceiving.
>
> And [Solomon] smiled, laughing at her speech, and said: My Lord, arouse me to be thankful for Thy favor wherewith Thou hast favored me and my parents, and to do good that shall be pleasing unto Thee, and include me among [the number of] Thy righteous slaves (Sūrah 27: 18–19).

Ethics in Islam is not based on a variety of separate scattered virtues, with each virtue, such as honesty or truth, standing isolated from others. Rather virtue in Islam is a part of a total, comprehensive way of life which serves to guide and control all human activity. Truthfulness is an ethical value, as are protecting life, conserving the environment, and sustaining its development within the confines of what God has ordered. When ʿĀisha, the wife of the Prophet Muhammad, was asked about his ethics she replied: "His ethics are the whole Qurʾān." The Qurʾān does not contain separate scattered ethical values. Rather it contains the instructions for a complete way of life. There are political, social and economic principles side by side with instructions for the construction and preservation of the earth.

Islamic ethical values are based not on human reasoning, as Aristotle claimed values to be, nor on what society imposes on the individual, as Durkheim thought, nor on the interests of a certain class, as Marxists maintain. In each of these claims values are affected by cir-cumstances. In Islam, ethical values are held to be based on an accurate scale which is unalterable as to time and place. Islam's values are those without which neither persons nor the natural environment can be sustained.

THE HUMAN–ENVIRONMENT RELATIONSHIP

As we have seen, within the Islamic faith, an individual's relationship with the environment is governed by certain moral precepts. These originate with God's creation of humans and the role they were given upon the Earth. Our universe, with all its diverse component elements was created by God and the human being is an essential part of His Measured and Balanced Creation. The role of humans, however, is not only to enjoy, use and benefit from their surroundings. They are expected to preserve, protect and promote their fellow creatures. The Prophet Muhammad (peace be upon him) said: "All creatures are God's dependents and the best among them is the one who is most useful to God's dependents." The Prophet of Islam looked upon himself as responsible for the trees and the animals and all natural elements. He also said: "The only reasons that God does not cause his punishment to pour over you are the elderly, the suckling babes, and the animals which graze upon your land." Muhammad prayed for rain when he was reminded that water was short, the trees suffering from drought, and animals dying. He begged for God's mercy to fall upon his creatures.

The relationship between human beings and their environment includes many features in addition to subjugation and utilization. Construction and development are primary but our relationship to nature also includes meditation, contemplation and enjoyment of its beauties. The most perfect Muslim was the Prophet Muhammad who was reported by Ibn ʿAbbās to have enjoyed gazing at greenery and running water.

When reading verses about the Earth in the Holy Qurʾān, we find strong indications that the Earth was originally a place of peace and rest for humans:

> Is not He [best] Who made the earth a fixed abode, and placed rivers in the folds thereof, and placed firm hills therein, and hath set a barrier between the two seas? Is there any God beside Allah? Nay, but most of them know not! (Sūrah 27:61)

The Earth is important to the concept of interrelation. Human beings are made from two components of the Earth—dust and water.

> And Allah hath caused you to grow as a growth from the earth, And afterward He maketh you return thereto, and He will bring you forth again, a [new] forthbringing. And Allah hath made the earth a wide expanse for you. That ye may thread the valleyways thereof (Sūrah 71:17–20).

The word "earth" (arḍ) is mentioned twice in this short quotation and in the Qur'ān the word occurs a total of 485 times, a simple measure of its importance.

The Earth is described as being subservient to humans: "He it is Who hath made the earth subservient unto you, so walk in the paths thereof and eat of His providence" (Sūrah 67:15). The Earth is also described as a receptacle: "Have we not made the earth a receptacle both for the living and the dead" (Sūrah 77: 25–26). Even more importantly, the Earth is considered by Islam to be a source of purity and a place for the worship of God. The Prophet Muhammad said: "The earth is made for me [and Muslims] as a prayer place (masjid) and as a purifier." This means that the Earth is to be used to cleanse oneself before prayer if water is unobtainable. Ibn 'Umar reported that the Prophet of Islam said: "God is beautiful and loved everything beautiful. He is generous and loves generosity and is clean and loves cleanliness."

Thus it is not surprising that the Islamic position with regard to the environment is that humans must intervene in order to protect the Earth. They may not stand back while it is destroyed. "He brought you forth from the earth and hath made you husband it" (Sūrah 11:61). For, finally, the Earth is a source of blessedness. And the Prophet Muhammad said: "Some trees are blessed as the Muslim himself, especially palm."

THE SUSTAINABLE CARE OF NATURE

Islam permits the utilization of the natural environment but this utilization should not involve unnecessary destruction. Squandering is rejected by God: "O Children of Adam! Look to your adornment at every place of worship, and eat and drink, but be not prodigal. Lo! He loveth not the prodigals" (Sūrah 7:31). In this Qur'ānic passage, eating and drinking refer to the utilization of the sources of life. Such utilization is not without controls. The component elements of life have to be protected so that their utilization may continue in a sustainable way. Yet even this preservation must be undertaken in an altruistic fashion, and not merely for its benefit to human beings. The Prophet Muhammad said: "Act in your life as though you are living forever and act for the Hereafter as if you are dying tomorrow."

These actions must not be restricted to those which will derive direct benefits. Even if doomsday were expected imminently, humans would be expected to continue their good behaviour, for Muhammad said: "When doomsday comes if someone has a palm shoot in his hand he should plant it." This hadīth encapsulates the principles of Islamic environmental ethics. Even when all hope is lost, planting should continue for planting is good in itself. The planting of the palm shoot continues the process of development and will sustain life even if one does not anticipate any benefit from it. In this, the Muslim is like the soldier who fights to the last bullet.

A theory of the sustainable utilization of the ecosystem may be deduced from Islam's assertion that life is maintained with due balance in everything: "Allah knoweth that which every female beareth and that which the wombs absorb and that which they grow. And everything with Him is measured" (Sūrah 13:8). Also: "He unto Whom belongeth the sovereignty of the heavens and the earth, He hath chosen no son nor hath He any partner in the sovereignty. He hath created everything and hath meted out for it a measure" (Sūrah 25:2).

Humans are not the owners, but the maintainers of the due balance and measure which God provided for them and for the animals that live with them.

> And after that He spread the earth,
> And produced therefrom water thereof and the
> pasture thereof,
> And He made fast the hills,
> A provision for you and for your cattle
> (Sūrah 79:30–33).

The Qur'ān goes on to say:

> But when the great disaster cometh,
> The day when man will call to mind his [whole]
> endeavor (Sūrah 79:34–35).

Humans will have a different home (ma'wā) or place of abode, different from the Earth and what it contains. The word ma'wā is the same word used in modern Arabic for "environment." One cannot help but wonder if these verses are an elaboration on the concept of sustainable development, a task that humans will undertake until their home is changed.

Sayyid Quṭb, commenting on these verses, observes that the Qur'ān, in referring to the origin of ultimate truth, used many correspondences (muwāfaqāt)—such as building the heavens, darkening the night, bringing forth human beings, spreading the earth, producing water and plants, and making the mountains fast. All these were provided for human beings and their animals as providence, and are direct signs which constitute proof as to the reality of God's measurement and calculation. Finally, Sayyid Quṭb observes that every part of God's creation was carefully made to fit into the general system, a system that testifies to the Creator's existence and the existence of a day of reward and punishment.

At this point, one must ask whether it is not a person's duty to preserve the proof of the Creator's existence while developing it. Wouldn't the wholesale destruction of the environment be the destruction of much which testifies to the greatness of God?

The concept of the sustained care of all aspects of the environment also fits into Islam's concept of charity, for charity is not only for the present generation but also for those in the future. A story is told of 'Umar ibn al-

Khattāb, the famous companion of the Prophet. He once saw that an old man, Khuzaymah ibn Thābit, had neglected his land. 'Umar asked what was preventing him from cultivating it. Khuzaymah explained that he was old and could be expected to die soon. Whereupon, Umar insisted that he should plant it. Khuzaymah's son, who narrated the story, added that his father and 'Umar planted the uncultivated land together.

This incident demonstrates how strongly Islam encourages the sustained cultivation of the land. Land should not be used and then abandoned just because the cultivator expects no personal benefit.

In Islam, law and ethics constitute the two interconnected elements of a unified world view. When considering the environment and its protection, this Islamic attitude may constitute a useful foundation for the formulation of a strategy throughout, at least, the Muslim world. Muslims who inhabit so much of the developing world may vary in local habits and customs but they are remarkably united in faith and in their attitude to life.

Islam is a religion of submission to God, master of all worlds. The Earth and all its inhabitants were created and are dominated by God. All Muslims begin their prayers five times a day with the same words from the Holy Qur'ān: "Praise be to Allah, Lord of the Worlds" (Sūrah 1:1). These opening words of the Qur'ān have become not only the most repeated but also the most loved and respected words for Muslims everywhere. Ibn Kathīr, like many other Qur'ānic commentators, considers that the word "worlds" ('ālamīn) means the different kinds of creatures that inhabit the sky, the land, and the sea. Muslims submit themselves to the Creator who made them and who made all other worlds. The same author mentions that Muslims also submit themselves to the signs of the existence of the Creator and His unity. This secondary meaning exists because "worlds" comes from the same root as signs; thus the worlds are signs of the Creator.

A Muslim, therefore, has a very special relationship with those worlds which in modern times have come to be known as the environment. Indeed, that these worlds exist and that they were made by the same Creator means that they are united and interdependent, each a part of the perfect system of creation. No conflict should exist between them; they should exist in harmony as different parts of the whole. Their coexistence could be likened to an architectural masterpiece in which every detail has been added to complete and complement the structure. Thus the details of creation serve to testify to the wisdom and perfection of the Creator.

THE PRACTICE OF ISLAMIC ENVIRONMENTAL ETHICS

Islam has always had a great influence on the formation of individual Muslim communities and the policy making of Muslim states. Environmental policy has been influenced by Islam and this influence has remained the same throughout the history of the Islamic faith.

The concept of himā (protection of certain zones) has existed since the time of the Prophet Muhammad. Himā involved the ruler or government's protection of specific unused areas. No one may build on them or develop them in any way. The Mālikī school of Islamic law described the requirements of himā to be the following. First, the need of the Muslim public for the maintenance of land in an unused state. Protection is not granted to satisfy an influential individual unless there is a public need. Second, the protected area should be limited in order to avoid inconvenience to the public. Third, the protected area should not be built on or cultivated. And fourth, the aim of protection (Zuhaylī 5:574) is the welfare of the people, for example, the protected area may be used for some restricted grazing by the animals of the poor.

The concept of himā can still be seen in many Muslim countries, such as Saudi Arabia, where it is practised by the government to protect wildlife. In a less formal way it is still practised by some bedouin tribes as a custom or tradition inherited from their ancestors.

The harīm is another ancient institution which can be traced back to the time of the Prophet Muhammad. It is an inviolable zone which may not be used or developed, save with the specific permission of the state. The harīm is usually found in association with wells, natural springs, underground water channels, rivers and trees planted on barren land or mawāt. There is careful administration of the harīm zones based on the practice of the Prophet Muhammad and the precedent of his companions as recorded in the sources of Islamic law.

At present the role of Islam in environmental protection can be seen in the formation of different Islamic organizations and the emphasis given to Islam as a motive for the protection of the environment.

Saudi Arabia has keenly sought to implement a number of projects aimed at the protection of various aspects of the environment, for example, the late King Khalid's patronage of efforts to save the Arabian ornyx from extinction.

The Meteorology and Environmental Protection Administration (MEPA) of Saudi Arabia actively promotes the principles of Islamic environmental protection. In 1983 MEPA and the International Union for the Conservation of Nature and Natural Resources commissioned a basic paper on the Islamic principles for the conservation of natural environment.

The Islamic faith has great impact on environmental issues throughout the Arab and Muslim world. The first Arab Ministerial Conference took as its theme "The Environmental Aspects of Development" and one of the topics considered was the Islamic faith and its values. The Amir of Kuwait emphasized the fundamental importance of Islam when he addressed the General

Assembly of the United Nations in 1988. He explained that Islam was the basis for justice, mercy, and cooperation between all humankind; and he called for an increase in scientific and technological assistance from the North to help conserve natural and human resources, combat pollution and support sustainable development projects.

Finally, it is imperative to acknowledge that the new morality required to conserve the environment which the World Conservation Strategy emphasizes, needs to be based on a more solid foundation. It is not only necessary to involve the public in conservation policy but also to improve its morals and alter its attitudes. In Muslim countries such changes should be brought about by identifying environmental policies with Islamic teachings. To do this, the public education system will have to supplement the scientific approach to environmental education with serious attention to Islamic belief and environmental awareness.

Study Questions

1. Compare Deen's view of the Islamic environmental ethics with the preceding views on Hinduism and Buddhism. Then compare it with Patrick Dobel's view (Reading 4) of Christian environmental ethics.
2. What insights or practices in Islam have you found that might be helpful in developing a Western environmental ethic? How would Islam contribute toward a global ecumenical environmental ethic?

40

An African Perspective on the Environmental Crisis*

Segun Ogungbemi

Segun Ogungbemi, a Yoruban from Nigeria, is associate professor at Lagos State University in Lagos, Nigeria, and the author of several works in African philosophy, ethics, and philosophy of religion.

Ogungbemi says that three principal factors contribute to the African ecological crisis: (1) ignorance and poverty, (2) science and technology, and (3) political conflict, including international economic pressures. He illustrates his thesis with regard to land, water, and air and argues that enlightened political leadership is needed in sub-Saharan Africa if environmental issues are to be satisfactorily dealt with.

One of the global problems of our time is the environmental condition of our world. Some of the environmental crises with which human beings have been grappling are of natural causes—earthquakes, volcanic eruptions, storms, droughts, diseases, and the like. Be that as it may, it is evident that man has exacerbated the situation, so that we now talk about an environmental crisis. For instance, there is air and water pollution, depletion of the ozone layers, extinction of fish and animal species, and such like. We are gripped with anxiety because of the danger of global warming. One of the questions which I think agitates our minds is, where are science, technology, and our desire for development leading us? Considering the moral, social and individual value of human existence and the threat which current environmental hazards pose to its sustainability, it seems to me that the need for immediate solutions is one of the most urgent issues which contemporary philosophy ought to address. In this paper, I have examined the nature of the environmental crisis in Africa and provided some moral and practical suggestions.

THE NATURE OF THE ENVIRONMENTAL CRISIS IN AFRICA

Broadly speaking, the nature of the environmental crisis in sub-Saharan Africa can be understood from three perspectives—one that emanates from ignorance and poverty, another from modern science and technology, and the third relative to political conflict and international economics. In other words, if we want to understand the environmental crisis in Africa, we must consider both traditional and modern societies and their contributions to the environmental hazards we now find. The majority of African peoples live in rural areas where traditional modes of living lack some basic amenities, namely, good water supplies, adequate lavatories and the like. Isaac Sindiga explains:

Clean water supplies are often unavailable and faeces disposal is a problem. Many people do not have pit latrines and help themselves in the bush. Such waste is often collected by rain water and taken to rivers where people take their livestock to water and also fetch water for domestic use.[1]

This essay was commissioned for the first edition of this volume.
*I am grateful to Professor Louis P. Pojman for sharing some of his books and articles with me. They have inspired me in writing both this article and others.

By polluting the rivers with human waste, our traditional society exposes itself to some . . . "water-borne diseases such as dysentry, typhoid and cholera."[2] This may not necessarily be due to unwillingness to change on the part of our people but it is the case that they are poor. Being poor however, does not necessarily exonerate our people from their contributions to environmental hazards which contribute to the death of many Africans.

The use of fuelwood by our traditional societies as a means of generating heat for cooking and other domestic services also contributes to the exacerbation of our environmental problems. According to Mostafa Kamal Tolba, "Fuelwood accounts for over 80% of Africa's energy use, but most is squandered on open heat fires."[3] Closely related to the issue of fuelwood as energy for domestic needs is the habit of bush burning (bush burning facilitates hunting). The excessive use of fuelwood and constant bush burning increases air pollution and also depletes forests and other natural habitats.

Having shown some of the contributions made by our traditional society to the general environmental problems of the world today, I need to say that in many ways our rural men and women have lived with nature with respect and awe. Thomas McGinn notes:

> Primitive man is capable of apologizing to mother earth when he digs up to plant crops. Contemporary man has indeed lost a sense of respect through his philosophy of exploitation.[4]

In our traditional relationship with nature, men and women recognize the importance of water, land and air management. To our traditional communities the ethics of not taking more than you need from nature is a moral code. Perhaps this may explain why earth, forests, rivers, and wind and other natural objects are traditionally believed to be both natural and divine. The philosophy behind this belief may not necessarily be religious, but a natural means by which the human environment can be preserved. The ethics of care is essential to traditional understanding of environmental protection and conservation.

One may argue that the ethics of care of traditional Africans is due largely to their inability to exploit nature for their own benefits. For instance, it is evident that Africa is the poorest area in the world. Tolba writes:

> Africa has the world's lowest life expectancy, the highest rural under-development and the severest food shortages. These are the social and economic consequences of Africa's environmental crisis, but they are rarely seen as such.[5]

The lack of development in our traditional communities may also be due to internal strife. Morag Bell explains:

> At the same time lack of progress is partly due to internal

politics which have shaken the stability necessary for effective development planning.[6]

It is important to note that whether or not there is development in our traditional communities, the ethics of not taking more than one needs from nature has its own credibility. This will be discussed later. Let us for the moment consider the contributions of modern Africa to the environmental crisis.

Today, modern Africa has benefitted from Western Civilization and industrialization even as the West has in turn benefitted from the exploitation of Africa. In contemporary Africa, however, because of the desire to develop like Europe and the United States of America, African governments and international corporations have engaged in mass destruction of our ecosystems. We all know that three basic natural resources are utilized in any development. These are land, water and air. I shall elaborate on each one of these natural resources as it is used in modern Africa.

I. LAND

If one is a physicalist, one will not hesitate to ascribe one's physical substance to the earth. If however, one is a dualist, one will argue that human life is composed fundamentally of corporeal and incorporeal substances—body and mind. This shows our natural or physical affinity to the earth. The earth, which I otherwise will refer to as land, provides most of the necessary ingredients of life for human use, namely, trees, forest, minerals, animals, vegetables, rivers, etc. Our physical developments are primarily based on land use. In modern Africa, the way in which land has been exploited goes contrary to our traditional philosophy. David Okali writes:

> Modern usage of our land by our society does not reflect a similar degree of awareness of the importance of forests and trees for the maintenance of environmental values. The drive to develop has led to wholesale abandonment of traditional practices, and values of forests land management as if development and modernization were incompatible with conservation of forest and protection of trees. The consequence of this has been a break-down in environmental stability we witness in form of severe erosion, increased turbidity and silting-up of steams, flood disasters and degradation of forest land first to grassland and then to desert. [7]

Similarly R. P. Baffour writes:

> The rapid rate of deforestation which is taking place at present in most parts of African forests, where large numbers of valuable trees are being cut down annually and shipped for lumber overseas, should give cause for grave concern to present-day Africa.[8]

There is no doubt about the rapid population growth in

Africa, and a need to feed the people requires some improvements in the traditional subsistence farming. In other words, mechanized farming has to compliment subsistence farming. The semi-arid and arid lands have been overutilized to the extent that fertilizers are needed to enrich the soils for maximum yields. Furthermore, modern Africa does not want to eat and drink only what is produced locally; it has been infected with a desire for the Western lifestyle, and to cope with this modern lifestyle it has to import goods from the industrial nations.

This importing requires increased production of export goods, namely, coffee, tea, cocoa, rubber, etc. However, the more agricultural products modern Africa has to produce the more fertilizers and other chemicals are used. The end result is that when it rains these chemicals are washed away into our rivers, lakes and oceans. The health hazards that these chemicals cause affect not only humans but also other species in our waters. With the extensive exportation of agricultural goods to Western Europe and the Americas, modern Africa has boosted the economy of the developed nations at the expense of its own. Apart from boosting the economy of the developed nations at the expense of its own, modern Africa has failed to adequately feed its own peoples. The observation of Paul Ekins is relevant to Africa. He writes:

> Paradoxically, therefore, "development" can end up giving more benefit to the rich countries which provided the initial "aid" than to the poor people in the countries which received it. . . . It is because of this sort of cycle that increasing numbers of grassroots activists in Southern countries are regarding "development" as dangerous to and exploitative of poor people in poor countries.[9]

In its bid to catch up with developed nations, modern Africa has exploited some of its essential minerals, namely, gold, copper, oil, diamonds, coal, uranium, etc., creating other ecological problems. For instance, where there are oil fields, it is a known fact that the areas are no longer good for agricultural activities. The exploitation of land minerals in modern Africa has provided jobs for many people, but the number is few when compared with the rest of the populace.

II. WATER

Africa is blessed with an abundance of water. There are lakes, streams, rivers, and of course the Atlantic and Indian oceans. Water is an essential natural resource. Apart from its aesthetic values, the food values on which Africans depend cannot be overemphasized. Baffour explains:

> The rich shoals of tuna known to exist in the Atlantic lie almost unexploited and it has been known that trawlers

as far afield as from Japan have recently been coming all the way from their home waters to fish tuna in the Atlantic and still make enormous profits. It is claimed that schools of tuna in the Atlantic can provide enough proteins for the entire world population for the next 500 years.[10]

Water is also essential to our domestic, agricultural and industrial needs. However, human activities have affected our clean waters. Charles O. Okidi writes:

> One instance was carried in newspapers as "U.S. Firms May Ship Toxic Wastes to Africa." The story was that there were U.S. industries producing wastes so highly toxic and so persistent that the U.S. laws would not permit their disposal in that country. So the companies were negotiating with some countries in Africa to allow the disposal of such wastes in their territories, in exchange for handsome foreign exchange for the national development needs of those African countries. Clearly, it must take a very gruesome sense of humor to accept that as an approach to development. But two African countries were reported to be actually involved in the negotiations.[11]

Similarly, a few years ago some Nigerian students in Italy informed the Nigerian government of a plan to dump toxic wastes on the Nigerian coast. At first the news appeared to be unfounded, but later the Nigerian government was caught up with the reality of the news. Some tons of toxic wastes were dumped at Koko in the then Bendel State of Nigeria. The drums used for transportation of the wastes were later used by local people to store water and other domestic materials. The Italian government was contacted about the incident, and the toxic wastes were cleaned up. However, some Nigerians who used the drums for water storage died. Painful as such human casualty may be, we must not lose sight of members of other species who have perished as a result of the toxic wastes dumped at Koko.

While the industrialized nations have polluted our waters, it must be noted that where African business people have developed industries, similar environmental problems have been created. Okidi writes:

> In the African context, the East African Medical Research Institute warned in 1971 that measures should be taken against pollution of Lake Victoria by industrial and municipal wastes. Up to now no actual remedial programme has been commenced. Yet more industries such as Kenya's molasses factory, breweries and cotton mills have been attracted by the water.[12]

What has happened to Lake Victoria is morally reprehensible, and it is happening to most of Africa's waters, particularly those that are in industrial locations. Water pollution is not limited to industrial areas, but is also found in our rural centres. Okidi observes:

Africa's central problems are two-fold; preventing water pollution by bacteriological agents and actual delivery of safe drinking water to rural population. It is still possible to pump water from various inland or ground sources, cheaply and with fairly inexpensive treatment to the consumers. However, careless disposal of wastes can still pollute these inland waters as well as ground waters until some unexpected pollution can be found in waters remote from industrial centres.[13]

III. AIR

Clean air is another essential resource that human beings and animal species depend on for survival. Without good air even plant life would suffer and our environment would be difficult, if not impossible, to live in. But in Africa, human activities are threatening good air. As already noted, our traditional communities depend on fuelwood for most of their energy needs, and bush burning is common. Both activities affect air quality adversely. Modern lifestyles have encouraged the abuse of good air. Industrial activities have also polluted the air, especially by the burning of industrial wastes.

With the development of modern systems of transportation, there are more cars, commercial vehicles and aeroplanes in African urban and commercial centres than ever before. It is unfortunate though that the cars and commercial vehicles imported into Africa have no emission controls. Driving on our commercial roads during the rush hours, particularly in the cities like Lagos, Ibadan, Kano, Kaduna, Accra, Dakar, Nairobi, Addis-Abbaba, etc., exposes one to a heavily polluted environment.

Further, modern African leaders have engaged themselves in what might be called a national security syndrome. The end result is the constant buildup of modern military equipment. As a matter of fact, as Tolba observes, "Of 37 countries for which data are available, only 10 spend more on agriculture than the military. This does not achieve meaningful security."[14] Since African leaders do not find any external aggressors who could be put in check militarily, they therefore turn against their own people. In other words, African countries are not presently threatened by any foreign aggressors so the leaders who want to consolidate their powers have been using military arms for their own protection. A case in point is Mobutu Seso Seko in Zaire. There are others who have engaged in oppressing their peoples simply because they want to remain in power. What is happening in Sudan, Ethiopia, Somalia, Angola, and Liberia provides other examples. The environmental pollution caused by the air raids and artillery bombardments that have taken place and which continue to take place in the above-named countries is disheartening. Apart from the pollution of the biosphere, the loss of human, animal and fish species are clear indications of leadership-madness of Africa.

POPULATION

On the population growth rate in Africa, Inga Ngel writes:

> At present, Africa's population doubles every twenty years. From 430 million during the mid-eighties, the continent will have to sustain approximately 900 million by the turn of the millenium. The prognosis for 2025 is an unbelievable 1.5 billion people. In order to preserve even the present poor standard of living, the crisis-ridden African States would have to achieve an annual economic growth rate of at least four per cent—an unattainable goal for most of them. Africa's population is growing at an unprecedented rate. Annually, an additional three per cent of people accelerate the destruction of the environment and aggravate social conflicts in the rapid growing cities. The balance between the ecosystem and man, upset for a long time already, is collapsing (Development and Cooperation No. 6/1990).

Bell (1986: 142–143) agrees that there is the problem of population growth in Africa but he is quick to note with caution:

> It has already been suggested that perhaps the most important demographic change in Africa in the recent past has been a marked increase in the population growth rate of the area. While the usual explanation for this trend is a decrease in death rates due to improvements in medical facilities, hygiene and nutrition, such an interpretation must be applied with caution. By international standards, mortality rates in Africa remain high and some investigations suggest that within parts of the continent, they are as high as ever they were. . . .While the average life expectancy at birth is about 72 years in the more developed countries, it is about 57 years in the less developed countries and a mere 47 years in Africa south of the Sahara excluding South Africa. . . . Focusing just on infant and early childhood deaths, which are the leading causes of low life expectancy, a similar pattern arises. Data on the former indicate that while the infant mortality rate is about 20 per 1000 live births in the most developed countries, many African countries have rates of over 150 and in some instances, it exceeds 200 per 1000 live births.

I do not doubt the rapid population growth in contemporary Africa. The more people we have have the more effects it has on the environment, for instance, deforestation, decimation of animal species, pollution and the like. There are, however, some issues that have to be taken into consideration when discussing population explosion in Africa, namely, disasters which have taken many lives in Africa.

Generally, reliable data on population in Africa are not available. But, for the moment, let us consider countries in Africa where conflicts and natural disasters have reduced the population in Africa, namely, Somalia,

Ethiopia, Nigeria, Kenya, Ghana, Niger, Chad, Togo, Zaire, Cameroun, Liberia, Angola, Sudan, and South Africa. What we have gained in terms of population growth rate due to improvements in medical facilities and hygiene, among others, has been lost as a result of social conflicts and natural disasters. By the time everything is settled, we may be able to have the true picture of our population. It is no wonder why Bell sounds a note of caution when we talk about population explosion in Africa.

It seems to me that it is not necessarily the case that Africa must reduce its population or watch the pendulum of population indicator. Rather, it is the case that the wealth in the world is not equitably distributed.

Oxfam, a United Kingdom based humanitarian organisation believes that poverty is the greatest scourge afflicting the human race this decade, with most countries of the South severely affected. "As the 20th Century draws to a close," the organisation says "more than a billion people in the world cannot afford the bare essentials of life." It observes that the rich countries of the North "with only 25 per cent of the world's people consume 80 per cent of the earth's resources. . . .while one in three people in the developing world does not have enough to eat" (*African Concord,* Vol. 6, No. 26, 1991).

The developed countries, particularly the U.S. and the former Soviet Union, invested heavily on the military rather than sharing the wealth of the world more equitably with poor nations.

According to Ekins, 1992:5:

The U.S. in particular still strives to improve the stealth and accuracy of its nuclear weapons, against all deterrence logic. In proceeding with the SDI (the "Star Wars" Strategic Defence Initiative), which by 1989 had cost US$17 billion . . . the US continues to signal to the USSR and the world in general that it wishes to obtain invulnerability from nuclear attack and so break the balance of deterrence in its favour.

The military aid given to African States has exacerbated the escalation of social and political and religious upheavals in Africa. The effects of wars in African States, particularly in Somalia, Liberia, Sudan, Angola, among others, have had a damaging effect both on humans and the ecosystems. If the wealth in this world had been adequately managed, there would be no need for African nations to reduce their population. One important factor which should be taken very seriously is that if we reduce our population, where are we going to get more geniuses that will contribute to the development of Africa? What Africa needs is good leadership. Many things have gone wrong under the leadership of the military in many parts of Africa, for instance, Nigeria:

It is not the best season in Nigeria. In fact, this is a season that tries man's souls, a season of vanishing happiness, arrested smiles, gloomy faces, a season when despair is now a compulsory company, a season when men and women tremble with fears about the present and the future (Bayo Onanuga: *African Concord,* Vol. 6, No. 8, 1992).

Writing in the same vein, Adebayo Williams notes:

From exhaustive research, I have come to the conclusion that if the majority of African leaders were to submit themselves to psychiatric evaluation, there may be no further need to keep innocent people in our various madhouses (*African Concord,* Vol. 6, No. 8, 1992).

One ought not to see Williams as casting aspersions on African leaders but rather, his position ought to be seen as an individual looking at the desperation of his people. For if African leaders had taker proper care of their people, there would be no need for them to go to the developed countries cap in hand begging for food, drugs and other foreign aid.

Generally, nature has a way of reducing population in the world. Recently, there was an earthquake in Egypt and many lives were lost. I believe when our population has reached an alarming situation, nature will invariably apply its brake and have a drastic reduction in our population growth rate. If our population is reduced and there happens to be a major natural disaster (e.g., volcanic eruptions, earthquakes, and others), Africa will be worse off in terms of population. The world ought to learn how to share its natural and human resources.

MILITARY SPENDING

It is observed that several African States have spent more of their income on the military rather than on social and educational development. For instance, Somalia spends about 500% of its income on the military. Ethiopia also spends over 200% of its income on the military. Today, Nigeria has spent well over N2.7 billion ($135,000.00) in Liberia while its people are wallowing in abject poverty. Mobutu Sese Seko of Zaire has plunged his country into a huge debt of about $5 billion. As a matter of fact, Mobutu Sese Seko is one of the richest leaders in Africa and his people are among the poorest.

SOME MORAL AND PRACTICAL SUGGESTIONS

In my discussion of the traditional African attitude to nature, I promised to show its credibility. The moral concept of not taking more than one needs from nature is an effort on the part of our traditional communities to, "keep a reasonable balance among the various resources constituting the ecosystem...."[15] This traditional moral wisdom has been employed for the "proper management" of our natural resources, and is what I have called the *ethics of care*. This ethics of care is not unique to traditional Africa. John Passmore writes:

> The traditional moral teaching of the West, Christian or Utilitarian, has always taught men, however, that they ought not so to act to injure their neighbours. And we have now discovered that the disposal of wastes into sea or air, the destruction of ecosystems, the procreation of large families and the depletion of resources constitute injury to our fellowmen, present and future. To that extent, conventional morality, without any supplementation whatsoever, suffices to justify our ecological concern, our demand for action against the polluter, the depleter of natural resources, the destroyer of species and wilderness.[16]

But this ethics of care of nature must not be seen as absolute even though it may have a universal appeal and application. Its universalizability can be stretched to a point, I believe, because there are many questions that have to be answered to justify its moral and epistemological warrant. Some of the questions that may be lurking in our minds are: How do we know how much we need, given the nature of human greed? Who judges whether we have been taking more or less than we need from the natural resources? If we have been taking more than we need, what are the penalties and how fair are they?

While I believe we need rapid development in Africa, the question is, can the traditional environmental wisdom be a guiding moral principle? In other words, is the environmental ethic of traditional society applicable to our contemporary situation? I believe its relevance can be seen in a reformulation of it which I term the ethics of nature-relatedness. Let me qualify this. The ethics of nature-relatedness does not imply that natural resources actually have a spiritual nature. Furthermore, it does not attribute the creation of the natural resources to a Supreme Being. That is to say, the ethics of nature-relatedness has no religious affinity. (I am aware that this position is not the traditional view.)

There are three basic elements in the ethics of nature-relatedness, namely, reason, experience and the will. The guiding force among the three elements is reason. The ethics of nature-relatedness must have reason to pilot it because morality is inseparable from reason. The ethics of nature-relatedness asserts that our natural resources do not need man for their existence and functions. As a matter of fact, if these natural resources had any rational capacity they would wonder what kind of beings humans are. The fact of the matter is that human beings cannot do without the natural resources at their disposal. By destroying our natural resources in the name of development we are invariably endangering our own existence. So the ethics of nature-relatedness can be succinctly stated as an ethics that leads human beings to seek to co-exist peacefully with nature and treat it with some reasonable concern for its worth, survival and sustainability. It is an ethics that calls for an alternative approach to our present reckless use of nature.

As we have already noted, the majority of Africans use fuelwood and engage in bush burning. Our industries pollute air and water resources, which in effect endangers our health. Is there anything we can do to reduce the danger of these human activities? Baffour provides a useful suggestion. He writes:

> Talking of sources of power, one should not ignore the possibilities of the use of solar energy which would have enormous advantages to Africa. With large areas of perennially clear and cloudless skies, the possibilities are great indeed. Already in North Africa, and to a limited degree in other parts of Africa, experiments are being conducted in the development of power from solar energy through the use of cells; but not enough work is being done in this field of study and it is commended to scientists and technologists to intensify their study of the possibilities in this field, so that even the remotest parts of Africa may be blessed with power for domestic and cottage industry.[17]

If adequate energy resources are provided for our industrial and domestic consumptions at a reasonable cost, our overdependence on fuelwood, coal, kerosene, gas and petrol would be reduced. I believe solar energy could be our safety valve in this direction.

People in several African countries have been suffering from starvation and famine. One of the causes of these problems is manmade, namely, political conflicts. Furthermore, food production for all Africans south of the Sahara is possible if we turn all the unused land areas from Senegal to Zaire into agricultural centers and use modern techniques of mechanized farming. But this cannot be done without first having all our leaders come to reason together and use their political will for our common good.

In conclusion, the environmental crisis in sub-Saharan Africa has both unique components and some it shares with other areas of the world. Poor health conditions in contemporary Africa can be attributed largely to poverty, ignorance, poor sanitation and rapid population growth. Health education, appropriate economic development, and increased literacy are all needed. There would be natural and monetary resources to address these problems if those which are currently fueling political conflicts were available. Further, plans need to be developed to reduce the amount of industrial and agricultural wastes and properly dispose of them, so that both our industrial and commercial centres and our rural areas are safe from air and water pollution. In addressing these problems, we would not only be saving ourselves from dangerous pollutants, but would be saving our ecosystems for generations to come. Our governments, industrialists, scientists, ethicists and environmentalists have more roles to play in keeping our environment safe.

Notes

1. Isaac Sindiga, *Ethnomedicine and Health Care in Kenya* (Eldoret: Moi University, Final Technical Report to the International Development Research Center for Project 1992), 6.
2. Ibid., 5.
3. Mostafa Kamal Tolba, *Sustainable Development: Constraints and Opportunities* (London: Butterworths, 1987), 207.
4. Thomas McGinn, "Ecology and Ethics" in *Philosophy for a New Generation* (ed) A. K. Bierman and James A. Gould (New York: Macmillan, 1977), 159.
5. Tolba, op. cit, 206.
6. Morag Bell, *Contemporary Africa: Development, Culture and the State* (London: Longman, 1986), 19.
7. *Nigerian Tribune* (Ibadan), 3 October 1992.
8. R. P. Baffour, "Science and Technology in Relation to Africa's Development," *The Proceedings of the First International Congress of Africanists* (London: Longmans, 1964), 303.
9. Paul Ekins, *A New World Order* (London: Routledge, 1992), 10.
10. Baffour. op. cit, 307.
11. Charles O. Okidi, "Management of Natural Resources and the Environment for Self-Reliance," *Journal of Eastern African Research and Development*, 14 (1984), 98.
12. Ibid., 98–99.
13. Ibid., 103.
14. Tolba, op. cit., 206.
15. Okidi, op. cit., 97.
16. John Passmore, "Removing the Rubbish: Reflections on the Ecological Craze," *Philosophy for a New Generation* (ed) A. K. Bierman and James A. Gould (New York: Macmillan, 1977), 175.
17. Baffour, op. cit, 304–305.

Study Questions

1. What are the greatest environmental problems in Africa, according to Ogungbemi? What causes them?
2. What sorts of things does Ogungbemi recommend as solutions?
3. Evaluate Ogungbemi's discussion on population growth. How does he view this problem? Do you agree with his assessment? Explain. (See the readings in Part 2, Chapters 9–11 for further reflection).

41

Radical Environmentalism and Wilderness Preservation:
A Third World Critique

RAMACHANDRA GUHA

Ramachandra Guha is a sociologist and historian at the Centre for Ecological Sciences, Indian Institute for Science, Bangalore, India. He has written extensively on the historical roots of ecological conflict in the East and West. The following is the original abstract he wrote for this article.

I present a Third World critique of the trend in American environmentalism known as deep ecology, analyzing each of deep ecology's central tenets: the distinction between anthropocentrism and biocentrism, the focus on wilderness preservation, the invocation of Eastern traditions, and the belief that it represents the most radical trend within environmentalism. I argue that the anthropocentrism/biocentrism distinction is of little use in understanding the dynamics of environmental degradation, that the implementation of the wilderness agenda is causing serious deprivation in the Third World, that the deep ecologist's interpretation of Eastern tradition is highly selective, and that in other cultural contexts (e.g., West Germany and India) radical environmentalism manifests itself quite differently, with a far greater emphasis on equity and the integration of ecological concerns with livelihood and work. I conclude that despite its claims to universality, deep ecology is firmly rooted in American environmental and cultural history and is inappropriate when applied to the Third World.

Even God dare not appear to the poor man except in the form of bread.

MAHATMA GANDHI

I. INTRODUCTION

The respected radical journalist Kirkpatrick Sale recently celebrated "the passion of a new and growing movement that has become disenchanted with the environmental establishment and has in recent years mounted a serious and sweeping attack on it—style, substance, systems, sensibilities and all." The vision of those whom Sale calls the "New Ecologists"—and what I refer to in this article as deep ecology—is a compelling

Reprinted from *Environmental Ethics,* Vol. 11 (Spring 1989) by permission. Notes deleted.

one. Decrying the narrowly economic goals of mainstream environmentalism, this new movement aims at nothing less than a philosophical and cultural revolution in human attitudes toward nature. In contrast to the conventional lobbying efforts of environmental professionals based in Washington, it proposes a militant defence of "Mother Earth," an unflinching opposition to human attacks on undisturbed wilderness. With their goals ranging from the spiritual to the political, the adherents of deep ecology span a wide spectrum of the American environmental movement. As Sale correctly notes, this emerging strand has in a matter of a few years made its presence felt in a number of fields: from an academic philosophy (as in the journal *Environmental Ethics*) to popular environmentalism (for example, the group Earth First!).

In this article I develop a critique of deep ecology from the perspective of a sympathetic outsider. I critique deep ecology not as a general (or even a foot soldier) in the continuing struggle between the ghosts of Gifford Pinchot and John Muir over control of the U.S. environmental movement, but as an outsider to these battles. I speak admittedly as a partisan, but of the environmental movement in India, a country with an ecological diversity comparable to the U.S., but with a radically dissimilar cultural and social history.

My treatment of deep ecology is primarily historical and sociological, rather than philosophical, in nature. Specifically, I examine the cultural rootedness of a philosophy that likes to present itself in universalistic terms. I make two main arguments: first, that deep ecology is uniquely American, and despite superficial similarities in rhetorical style, the social and political goals of radical environmentalism in other cultural contexts (e.g., West Germany and India) are quite different; second, that the social consequences of putting deep ecology into practice on a worldwide basis (what its practitioners are aiming for) are very grave indeed.

II. THE TENETS OF DEEP ECOLOGY

While I am aware that the term *deep ecology* was coined by the Norwegian philosopher Arne Naess, this article refers specifically to the American variant. Adherents of the deep ecological perspective in this country, while arguing intensely among themselves over its political and philosophical implications, share some fundamental premises about human-nature interactions. As I see it, the defining characteristics of deep ecology are fourfold:

First, deep ecology argues that the environmental movement must shift from an "anthropocentric" to a "biocentric" perspective. In many respects, an acceptance of the primacy of this distinction constitutes the litmus test of deep ecology. A considerable effort is expended by deep ecologists in showing that the dominant motif in Western philosophy has been anthropocentric—i.e., the belief that man and his works are the center of the universe—and conversely, in identifying those lonely thinkers (Leopold, Thoreau, Muir, Aldous Huxley, Santayana, etc.) who, in assigning man a more humble place in the natural order, anticipated deep ecological thinking. In the political realm, meanwhile, establishment environmentalism (shallow ecology) is chided for casting its arguments in human-centered terms. Preserving nature, the deep ecologists say, has an intrinsic worth quite apart from any benefits preservation may convey to future human generations. The anthropocentric-biocentric distinction is accepted as axiomatic by deep ecologists, it structures their discourse, and much of the present discussion remains mired within it.

The second characteristic of deep ecology is its focus on the preservation of unspoilt wilderness—and the restoration of degraded areas to a more pristine condition—to the relative (and sometimes absolute) neglect of other issues on the environmental agenda. I later identify the cultural roots and portentous consequences of this obsession with wilderness. For the moment, let me indicate three distinct sources from which it springs. Historically, it represents a playing out of the preservationist (read *radical*) and utilitarian (read *reformist*) dichotomy that has plagued American environmentalism since the turn of the century. Morally, it is an imperative that follows from the biocentric perspective; other species of plants and animals, and nature itself, have an intrinsic right to exist. And finally, the preservation of wilderness also turns on a scientific argument—viz., the value of biological diversity in stabilizing ecological regimes and in retaining a gene pool for future generations. Truly radical policy proposals have been put forward by deep ecologists on the basis of these arguments. The influential poet Gary Snyder, for example, would like to see a 90 percent reduction in human populations to allow a restoration of pristine environments, while others have argued forcefully that a large portion of the globe must be immediately cordoned off from human beings.

Third, there is a widespread invocation of Eastern spiritual traditions as forerunners of deep ecology. Deep ecology, it is suggested, was practiced both by major religious traditions and at a more popular level by "primal" peoples in non-Western settings. This comple- ments the search for an authentic lineage in Western thought. At one level, the task is to recover those dissenting voices within the Judeo-Christian tradition; at another, to suggest that religious traditions in other cultures are, in contrast, dominantly if not exclusively "biocentric" in their orientation. This coupling of (ancient) Eastern and (modern) ecological wisdom seemingly helps consolidate the claim that deep ecology is a philosophy of universal significance.

Fourth, deep ecologists, whatever their internal differences, share the belief that they are the "leading edge" of the environmental movement. As the polarity of the shallow/deep and anthropocentric/biocentric distinctions makes clear, they see themselves as the spiritual, philosophical, and political vanguard of American and world environmentalism.

III. TOWARD A CRITIQUE

Although I analyze each of these tenets independently, it is important to recognize, as deep ecologists are fond of remarking in reference to nature, the interconnectedness and unity of these individual themes.

(1) Insofar as it has begun to act as a check on man's arrogance and ecological hubris, the transition from an anthropocentric (human-centered) to a biocentric (humans as only one element in the ecosystem) view in both religious and scientific traditions is only to be welcomed. What is unacceptable are the radical conclusions drawn by deep ecology, in particular, that intervention in nature should be guided primarily by the need to preserve biotic integrity rather than by the needs of humans. The latter for deep ecologists is anthropocentric, the former biocentric. This dichotomy is, however, of very little use in understanding the dynamics of environmental degradation. The two fundamental ecological problems facing the globe are (i) overconsumption by the industrialized world and by urban elites in the Third World and (ii) growing militarization, both in a short-term sense (i.e., ongoing regional wars) and in a long-term sense (i.e., the arms race and the prospect of nuclear annihilation). Neither of these problems has any tangible connection to the anthropocentric-biocentric distinction. Indeed, the agents of these processes would barely comprehend this philosophical dichotomy. The proximate causes of the ecologically wasteful characteristics of industrial society and of militarization are far more mundane: at an aggregate level, the dialectic of economic and political structures, and at a micro-level, the life style choices of individuals. These causes cannot be reduced, whatever the level of analysis, to a deeper anthropocentric attitude toward nature; on the contrary, by constituting a grave threat to human survival, the ecological degradation they cause does not even serve the best interests of human beings! If my identification of the major dangers to the integrity of the natural world

is correct, invoking the bogy of anthropocentrism is at best irrelevant and at worst a dangerous obfuscation.

(2) If the above dichotomy is irrelevant, the emphasis on wilderness is positively harmful when applied to the Third World. If in the U.S. the preservationist/utilitarian division is seen as mirroring the conflict between "people" and "interests," in countries such as India the situation is very nearly the reverse. Because India is a long settled and densely populated country in which agrarian populations have a finely balanced relationship with nature, the setting aside of wilderness areas has resulted in a direct transfer of resources from the poor to the rich. Thus, Project Tiger, a network of parks hailed by the international conservation community as an outstanding success, sharply posits the interests of the tiger against those of poor peasants living in and around the reserve. The designation of tiger reserves was made possible only by the physical displacement of existing villages and their inhabitants; their management requires the continuing exclusion of peasants and livestock. The initial impetus for setting up parks for the tiger and other large mammals such as the rhinoceros and elephant came from two social groups, first, a class of ex-hunters turned conservationists belonging mostly to the declining Indian feudal elite and second, representatives of international agencies, such as the World Wildlife Fund (WWF) and the International Union for the Conservation of Nature and Natural Resources (IUCN), seeking to transplant the American system of national parks onto Indian soil. In no case have the needs of the local population been taken into account, and as in many parts of Africa, the designated wildlands are managed primarily for the benefit of rich tourists. Until very recently, wildlands preservation has been identified with environmentalism by the state and the conservation elite; in consequence, environmental problems that impinge far more directly on the lives of the poor—e.g, fuel, fodder, water shortages, soil erosion, and air and water pollution—have not been adequately addressed.

Deep ecology provides, perhaps unwittingly, a justification for the continuation of such narrow and inequitable conservation practices under a newly acquired radical guise. Increasingly, the international conservation elite is using the philosophical, moral, and scientific arguments used by deep ecologists in advancing their wilderness crusade. A striking but by no means atypical example is the recent plea by a prominent American biologist for the takeover of large portions of the globe by the author and his scientific colleagues. Writing in a prestigious scientific forum, the *Annual Review of Ecology and Systematics,* Daniel Janzen argues that only biologists have the competence to decide how the tropical landscape should be used. As "the representatives of the natural world," biologists are "in charge of the future of tropical ecology," and only they have the expertise and mandate to "determine whether the tropical agroscape is to be populated only

by humans, their mutualists, commensals, and parasites, or whether it will also contain some islands of the greater nature—the nature that spawned humans, yet has been vanquished by them." Janzen exhorts his colleagues to advance their territorial claims on the tropical world more forcefully, warning that the very existence of these areas is at stake: "if biologists want a tropics in which to biologize, they are going to have to buy it with care, energy, effort, strategy, tactics, time, and cash."

This frankly imperialist manifesto highlights the multiple dangers of the preoccupation with wilderness preservation that is characteristic of deep ecology. As I have suggested, it seriously compounds the neglect by the American movement of far more pressing environmental problems within the Third World. But perhaps more importantly, and in a more insidious fashion, it also provides an impetus to the imperialist yearning of Western biologists and their financial sponsors, organizations such as the WWF and the IUCN. The wholesale transfer of a movement culturally rooted in American conservation history can only result in the social uprooting of human populations in other parts of the globe.

(3) I come now to the persistent invocation of Eastern philosophies as antecedent in point of time but convergent in their structure with deep ecology. Complex and internally differentiated religious traditions—Hinduism, Buddhism, and Taoism—are lumped together as holding a view of nature believed to be quintessentially biocentric. Individual philosophers such as the Taoist Lao Tzu are identified as being forerunners of deep ecology. Even an intensely political, pragmatic, and Christian influenced thinker such as Gandhi has been accorded a wholly undeserved place in the deep ecological pantheon. Thus the Zen teacher Robert Aitken Roshi makes the strange claim that Gandhi's thought was not human-centered and that he practiced an embryonic form of deep ecology which is "traditionally Eastern and is found with differing emphasis in Hinduism, Taoism and in Theravada and Mahayana Buddhism." Moving away from the realm of high philosophy and scriptural religion, deep ecologists make the further claim that at the level of material and spiritual practice "primal" peoples subordinated themselves to the integrity of the biotic universe they inhabited.

I have indicated that this appropriation of Eastern traditions is in part dictated by the need to construct an authentic lineage and in part a desire to present deep ecology as a universalistic philosophy. Indeed, in his substantial and quixotic biography of John Muir, Michael Cohen goes so far as to suggest that Muir was the "Taoist of the [American] West." This reading of Eastern traditions is selective and does not bother to differentiate between alternate (and changing) religious and cultural traditions; as it stands, it does considerable violence to the historical record. Throughout most recorded history the characteristic form of human activity in the "East" has been a finely tuned but nonetheless conscious and dynamic manipulation of nature. Although mystics such as Lao Tzu did reflect on the spiritual essence of human relations with nature, it must be recognized that such ascetics and their reflections were supported by a society of cultivators whose relationship with nature was a far more *active* one. Many agricultural communities do have a sophisticated knowledge of the natural environment that may equal (and sometimes surpass) codified "scientific" knowledge; yet, the elaboration of such traditional ecological knowledge (in both material and spiritual contexts) can hardly be said to rest on a mystical affinity with nature of a deep ecological kind. Nor is such knowledge infallible; as the archaeological record powerfully suggests, modern Western man has no monopoly on ecological disasters.

In a brilliant article, the Chicago historian Ronald Inden points out that this romantic and essentially positive view of the East is a mirror image of the scientific and essentially pejorative view normally upheld by Western scholars of the Orient. In either case, the East constitutes the Other, a body wholly separate and alien from the West; it is defined by a uniquely spiritual and nonrational "essence," even if this essence is valorized quite differently by the two schools. Eastern man exhibits a spiritual dependence with respect to nature— on the one hand, this is symptomatic of his prescientific and backward self, on the other, of his ecological wisdom and deep ecological consciousness. Both views are monolithic, simplistic, and have the characteristic effect—intended in one case, perhaps unintended in the other—of denying agency and reason to the East and making it the privileged orbit of Western thinkers.

The two apparently opposed perspectives have then a common underlying structure of discourse in which the East merely serves as a vehicle for Western projections. Varying images of the East are raw material for political and cultural battles being played out in the West; they tell us far more about the Western commentator and his desires than about the "East." Inden's remarks apply not merely to Western scholarship on India, but to Orientalist constructions of China and Japan as well:

> Although these two views appear to be strongly opposed, they often combine together. Both have a similar interest in sustaining the Otherness of India. The holders of the dominant view, best exemplified in the past in imperial administrative discourse (and today probably by that of "development economics"), would place a traditional, superstition-ridden India in a position of perpetual tutelage to a modern, rational West. The adherents of the romantic view, best exemplified academically in the discourses of Christian liberalism and analytic psychology, concede the realm of the public and impersonal to the positivist. Taking their succour not from governments and big business, but from a plethora of religious foundations and self-help institutes, and from allies in the "consciousness industry," not to mention the important

industry of tourism, the romantics insist that India embodies a private realm of the imagination and the religious which modern, western man lacks but needs. They, therefore, like the positivists, but for just one opposite reason, have a vested interest in seeing that the Orientalist view of India as "spiritual," "mysterious," and "exotic" is perpetuated.

(4) How radical, finally, are the deep ecologists? Notwithstanding their self-image and strident rhetoric (in which the label "shallow ecology" has an opprobrium similar to that reserved for "social democratic" by Marxist-Leninists), even within the American context their radicalism is limited and it manifests itself quite differently elsewhere.

To my mind, deep ecology is best viewed as a radical trend within the wilderness preservation movement. Although advancing philosophical rather than aesthetic arguments and encouraging political militancy rather than negotiation, its practical emphasis—viz., preservation of unspoilt nature—is virtually identical. For the mainstream movement, the function of wilderness is to provide a temporary antidote to modern civilization. As a special institution within an industrialized society, the national park "provides an opportunity for respite, contrast, contemplation, and affirmation of values for those who live most of their lives in the workaday world." Indeed, the rapid increase in visitations to the national parks in postwar America is a direct consequence of economic expansion. The emergence of a popular interest in wilderness sites, the historian Samuel Hays points out, was "not a throwback to the primitive, but an integral part of the modern standard of living as people sought to add new 'amenity' and 'aesthetic' goals and desires to their earlier preoccupation with necessities and conveniences."

Here, the enjoyment of nature is an integral part of the consumer society. The private automobile (and the life style it has spawned) is in many respects the ultimate ecological villain, and an untouched wilderness the prototype of ecological harmony; yet, for most Americans it is perfectly consistent to drive a thousand miles to spend a holiday in a national park. They possess a vast, beautiful, and sparsely populated continent and are also able to draw upon the natural resources of large portions of the globe by virtue of their economic and political dominance. In consequence, America can simultaneously enjoy the material benefits of an expanding economy and the aesthetic benefits of unspoilt nature. The two poles of "wilderness" and "civilization" mutually coexist in an internally coherent whole, and philosophers of both poles are assigned a prominent place in this culture. Paradoxically as it may seem, it is no accident that Star Wars technology and deep ecology both find their fullest expression in that leading sector of Western civilization, California.

Deep ecology runs parallel to the consumer society

without seriously questioning its ecological and sociopolitical basis. In its celebration of American wilderness, it also displays an uncomfortable convergence with the prevailing climate of nationalism in the American wilderness movement. For spokesmen such as the historian Roderick Nash, the national park system is America's distinctive cultural contribution to the world, reflective not merely of its economic but of its philosophical and ecological maturity as well. In what Walter Lippman called the American century, the "American invention of national parks" must be exported worldwide. Betraying an economic determinism that would make even a Marxist shudder, Nash believes that environmental preservation is a "full stomach" phenomenon that is confined to the rich, urban, and sophisticated. Nonetheless, he hopes that "the less developed nations may eventually evolve economically and intellectually to the point where nature preservation is more than a business."

The error which Nash makes (and which deep ecology in some respects encourages) is to equate environmental protection with the protection of the wilderness. This is a distinctively American notion, born out of a unique social and environmental history. The archetypal concerns of radical environmentalists in other cultural contexts are in fact quite different. The German Greens, for example, have elaborated a devastating critique of industrial society which turns on the acceptance of environmental limits to growth. Pointing to the intimate links between industrialization, militarization, and conquest, the Greens argue that economic growth in the West has historically rested on the economic and ecological exploitation of the Third World. Rudolf Bahro is characteristically blunt:

> The working class here [in the West] is the richest lower class in the world. And if I look at the problem from the point of view of the whole of humanity, not just from that of Europe, then I must say that the metropolitan working class is the worst exploiting class in history. . . . What made poverty bearable in eighteenth or nineteenth-century Europe was the prospect of escaping it through exploitation of the periphery. But this is no longer a possibility, and continued industrialism in the Third World will mean poverty for whole generations and hunger for millions.

Here the roots of global ecological problems lie in the disproportionate share of resources consumed by the industrialized countries as a whole *and* the urban elite within the Third World. Since it is impossible to reproduce an industrial monoculture worldwide, the ecological movement in the West must begin by cleaning up its own act. The Greens advocate the creation of a "no growth" economy, to be achieved by scaling down current (and clearly unsustainable) consumption levels. This radical shift in consumption and production patterns requires the creation of alternate economic and political structures—smaller in scale and more amenable

to social participation—but it rests equally on a shift in cultural values. The expansionist character of modern Western man will have to give way to an ethic of renunciation and self-limitation, in which spiritual and communal values play an increasing role in sustaining social life. This revolution in cultural values, however, has as its point of departure an understanding of environmental processes quite different from deep ecology.

Many elements of the Green program find a strong resonance in countries such as India, where a history of Western colonialism and industrial development has benefited only a tiny elite while exacting tremendous social and environmental costs. The ecological battles presently being fought in India have as their epicenter the conflict over nature between the subsistence and largely rural sector and the vastly more powerful commercial-industrial sector. Perhaps the most celebrated of these battles concerns the Chipko (Hug the Tree) movement, a peasant movement against deforestation in the Himalayan foothills. Chipko is only one of several movements that have sharply questioned the nonsustainable demand being placed on the land and vegetative base by urban centers and industry. These include opposition to large dams by displaced peasants, the conflict between small artisan fishing and large-scale trawler fishing for export, the countrywide movements against commercial forest operations, and opposition to industrial pollution among downstream agricultural and fishing communities.

Two features distinguish these environmental movements from their Western counterparts. First, for the sections of society most critically affected by environmental degradation—poor and landless peasants, women, and tribals—it is a question of sheer survival, not of enhancing the quality of life. Second, and as a consequence, the environmental solutions they articulate deeply involve questions of equity as well as economic and political redistribution. Highlighting these differences, a leading Indian environmentalist stresses that "environmental protection per se is of least concern to most of these groups. Their main concern is about the use of the environment and who should benefit from it." They seek to wrest control of nature away from the state and the industrial sector and place it in the hands of rural communities who live within that environment but are increasingly denied access to it. These communities have far more basic needs, their demands on the environment are far less intense, and they can draw upon a reservoir of cooperative social institutions and local ecological knowledge in managing the "commons"—forest, grasslands, and the waters—on a sustainable basis. If colonial and capitalist expansion has both accentuated social inequalities and signaled a precipitous fall in ecological wisdom, an alternate ecology must rest on an alternate society and polity as well.

This brief overview of German and Indian environmentalism has some major implications for deep ecology.

Both German and Indian environmental traditions allow for a greater integration of ecological concerns with livelihood and work. They also place a greater emphasis on equity and social justice (both within individual countries and on a global scale) on the grounds that in the absence of social regeneration environmental regeneration has very little chance of succeeding. Finally, and perhaps most significantly, they have escaped the preoccupation with wilderness preservation so characteristic of American cultural and environmental history.

IV. A HOMILY

In 1958, the economist J. K Galbraith referred to over-consumption as the unasked question of the American conservation movement. There is a marked selectivity, he wrote, "in the conservationist's approach to materials consumption. If we are concerned about our great appetite for materials, it is plausible to seek to increase the supply, to decrease waste, to make better use of the stocks available, and to develop substitutes. But what of the appetite itself? Surely this is the ultimate source of the problem. If it continues its geometric course, will it not one day have to be restrained? Yet in the literature of the resource problem this is the forbidden question. Over it hangs a nearly total silence."

The consumer economy and society have expanded tremendously in the three decades since Galbraith penned these words; yet his criticisms are nearly as valid today. I have said "nearly," for there are some hopeful signs. Within the environmental movement several dispersed groups are working to develop ecologically benign technologies and to encourage less wasteful life styles. Moreover, outside the self-defined boundaries of American environmentalism, opposition to the permanent war economy is being carried on by a peace movement that has a distinguished history and impeccable moral and political credentials.

It is precisely these (to my mind, most hopeful) components of the American social scene that are missing from deep ecology. In their widely noticed book, Bill Devall and George Sessions make no mention of militarization or the movements for peace, while activists whose practical focus is on developing ecologically responsible life styles (e.g., Wendell Berry) are derided as "falling short of deep ecological awareness." A truly radical ecology in the American context ought to work toward a synthesis of the appropriate technology, alternate life style, and peace movements. By making the (largely spurious) anthropocentric-biocentric distinction central to the debate, deep ecologists may have appropriated the moral high ground, but they are at the same time doing a serious disservice to American and global environmentalism.

Study Questions

1. Is Guha's critique of deep ecology sound? How would a full application of deep ecology affect the third world? Explain.
2. How might deep ecologists like Naess, Devall, or Sessions (Readings 20–22) respond to Guha's criticisms?
3. How might Western environmentalists justify quality of life versus sheer survival?
4. Is J. K. Galbraith right that our "appetite for materials" needs to be curbed (or cured)? If so, can you convince your friends?

For Further Reading

Dwivedi, O. P., and B. N. Tiwari. *Environmental Crisis and Hindu Religion.* New Delhi, India: Gitanjali Publishing House, 1987.

Engel, J. R., and J. G. Engel, eds. *Ethics of Environmental Response.* Tucson: University of Arizona Press, 1990.

Hargrove, Eugene, ed. *Religion and Environmental Crisis.* Athens: University of Georgia Press, 1985.

Johns, David. "Relevance of Deep Ecology to the Third World." *Environmental Ethics* 12 (1990): 233–252.

CHAPTER 8

Obligations to Future Generations

What are our moral obligations to future generations? Unless a catastrophe occurs people will be alive on earth 500 or 1000 years from today. What claims do they have on us today, if any? Are they morally considerable? Would it be an evil thing if they never come to exist? Who are the "they" we are talking about? If "they" don't exist, how can we be said to have duties to "them"?

The problem of obligations to future generations is perplexing for a couple of reasons. First, "future people" do not exist, so there are no specific, flesh and blood individuals to whom we have duties. How can we have obligations to nonexistent persons? Second, even if we solve this problem with the notion of hypothetical persons or probable persons, how do we know what they will be like and what their needs and values will be? Third, even if we believe that we have some idea of their needs values, how can their needs and values compare with those of present living beings, especially our family, friends, and community? Fourth, there is the question of why should we care about future people anymore than we care about people on distant planets. From a self-interested perspective, why should I make sacrifices for people who will live in the distant future. Why should I care about posterity? What has posterity ever done for me?

It is this last question that Robert Heilbroner takes us in our first reading. Heilbroner, an economist, is perplexed and outraged by the casual way his fellow economists dismiss the question of duties to future generations, as though it's no concern of ours—since the economic model they develop cannot make it rational to save for such a long, distant future. Heilbroner believes we do have such duties, and the strength of his essay is in his insightful analysis of the problem. In our second

selection, Garrett Hardin picks up on Heilbroner's theme and develops it, arguing that while both philosophy and economics fail to give us a satisfying answer to the problem of duties to future generations, it is nonetheless one of our highest values, and legitimately so. Through fascinating illustrations of people sacrificing for future generations, he reveals an underlying paradox in our attitudes toward posterity. Hardin then outlines a plan of action, having to do with promoting special interests and education of the young.

In our third reading, Martin Golding sets forth the necessary conditions for having moral duties to others—specifically, they must be recognized as part of our moral community and their good must be recognized as good by our value system so that they can have claims against us. Golding argues that we don't know what kind of people the future will produce, and since we have reason to believe that they will be very different from us, it follows that we probably don't have any obligations to them—except duties of not leaving Earth a cesspool of pollution. Otherwise, the argument from ignorance enjoins us to embrace a hands-off policy.

In our final reading, Derek Parfit rejects Golding's argument from ignorance as well as Heilbroner's and Hardin's claims that reason doesn't guide us with regard to making provisions for posterity. Parfit examines various justification for intergenerational duties. The traditional view is that one can only commit crimes if one has an identifiable victim. Policy choices regarding energy, however, do not identity specific victims. Parfit argues that these views are wrong. Polices are bad "if those who live are worse off than those who might have lived." We are responsible for environmental policies since we could make a difference in the quality of future lives.

42

What Has Posterity Ever Done for Me?

ROBERT HEILBRONER

Robert Heilbroner was for many years professor of economics at the New School for Social Research in New York. He is the author of several books including The Worldly Philosophers *and* Marxism: For and Against.

Heilbroner asks why we should care about future people or whether humanity survives into the distant future. Citing fellow economists who argue that we have no reason to sacrifice for the unknown future,

Heilbroner expresses outrage at this callous disregard for future people. Admitting that he cannot give a rational argument for this view, he appeals to Adam Smith's principle of sentiment or inner conscience, which urges us to work for the long range survival of humanity.

Will mankind survive? Who knows? The question I want to put is more searching: Who cares? It is clear that most of us today do not care—or at least do not care enough. How many of us would be willing to give up some minor convenience—say, the use of aerosols—in the hope that this might extend the life of man on earth by a hundred years? Suppose we also knew with a high degree of certainty that humankind could not survive a thousand years unless we gave up our wasteful diet of meat, abandoned all pleasure driving, cut back on every use of energy that was not essential to the maintenance of a bare minimum. Would we care enough for posterity to pay the price of its survival?

I doubt it. A thousand years is unimaginably distant. Even a century far exceeds our powers of empathetic imagination. By the year 2075, I shall probably have been dead for three quarters of a century. My children will also likely be dead, and my grandchildren, if I have any, will be in their dotage. What does it matter to me, then, what life will be like in 2075, much less 3075? Why should I lift a finger to affect events that will have no more meaning for me seventy-five years after my death than those that happened seventy-five years before I was born?

There is no rational answer to that terrible question. No argument based on reason will lead me to care for posterity or to lift a finger in its behalf. Indeed, by every rational consideration, precisely the opposite answer is thrust upon us with irresistible force. As a Distinguished Professor of political economy at the University of London has written in the current winter issue of *Business and Society Review*:

> Suppose that, as a result of using up all the world's resources, human life did come to an end. So what? What is so desirable about an indefinite continuation of the human species, religious convictions apart? It may well be that nearly everybody who is already here on earth would be reluctant to die, and that everybody has an instinctive fear of death. But one must not confuse this with the notion that, in any meaningful sense, generations who are yet unborn can be said to be better off if they are born than if they are not.

Thus speaks the voice of rationality. It is echoed in the book *The Economic Growth Controversy* by a Distinguished Younger Economist from the Massachusetts Institute of Technology:

> . . . Geological time [has been] made comprehensible to our finite human minds by the statement that the 4.5 billion years of the earth's history [are] equivalent to once

around the world in an SST. . . . Man got on eight miles before the end, and industrial man got on six feet before the end. . . . Today we are having a debate about the extent to which man ought to maximize the length of time that he is on the airplane.

> According to what the scientists think, the sun is gradually expanding and 12 billion years from now the earth will be swallowed up by the sun. This means that our airplane has time to go round three more times. Do we want man to be on it for all three times around the world? Are we interested in man being on for another eight miles? Are we interested in man being on for another six feet? Or are we only interested in man for a fraction of a millimeter—our lifetimes?

> That led me to think: Do I care what happens a thousand years from now? . . . Do I care when man gets off the airplane? I think I basically [have come] to the conclusion that I don't care whether man is on the airplane for another eight feet, or if man is on the airplane another three times around the world.

Is it an outrageous position? I must confess it outrages me. But this is not because the economists' arguments are "wrong"—indeed, within their rational framework they are indisputably right. It is because their position reveals the limitations—worse, the suicidal dangers—of what we call "rational argument" when we confront questions that can only be decided by an appeal to an entirely different faculty from that of cool reason. More than that, I suspect that if there is cause to fear for man's survival it is because the calculus of logic and reason will be applied to problems where they have as little validity, even as little bearing, as the calculus of feeling or sentiment applied to the solution of a problem in Euclidean geometry.

If reason cannot give us a compelling argument to care for posterity—and to care desperately and totally—what can? For an answer, I turn to another distinguished economist whose fame originated in his profound examination of moral conduct. In 1759, Adam Smith published "The Theory of Moral Sentiments," in which he posed a question very much like ours, but to which he gave an answer very different from that of his latter-day descendants.

Suppose, asked Smith, that "a man of humanity" in Europe were to learn of a fearful earthquake in China—an earthquake that swallowed up its millions of inhabitants. How would that man react? He would, Smith mused, "make many melancholy reflections upon the precariousness of human life, and the vanity of all the labors of man, which could thus be annihilated in a moment. He would, too, perhaps, if he was a man of speculation, enter into many reasonings concerning the effects which this disaster might produce upon the commerce of Europe, and the trade and business of the world in general." Yet, when this fine philosophizing was over, would our "man of humanity" care much about the catastrophe in distant China? He would not. As Smith tells us, he would "pursue his business or his pleasure, take his respose for his diversion, with the same ease and tranquillity as if nothing had happened."

But now suppose, Smith says, that our man were told he was to lose his little finger on the morrow. A very different reaction would attend the contemplation of this "frivolous disaster." Our man of humanity would be reduced to a tormented state, tossing all night with fear and dread—whereas "provided he never saw them, he will snore with the most profound security over the ruin of a hundred millions of his brethren."

Next, Smith puts the critical question: Since the hurt to his finger bulks so large and the catastrophe in China so small, does this mean that a man of humanity, given the choice, would prefer the extinction of a hundred million Chinese in order to save his little finger? Smith is unequivocal in his answer. "Human nature startles at the thought," he cries, "and the world in its greatest depravity and corruption never produced such a villain as would be capable of entertaining it."

But what stays our hand? Since we are all such creatures of self-interest (and is not Smith the very patron saint of the motive of self-interest?), what moves us to give precedence to the rights of humanity over those of our own immediate well-being? The answer, says Smith, is the presence within us all of a "man within the beast," an inner creature of conscience whose insistent voice brooks no disobedience: "It is the love of what is honorable and noble, of the grandeur and dignity, and superiority of our own characters."

It does not matter whether Smith's eighteenth-century view of human nature in general or morality in particular appeals to the modern temper. What matters is that he has put the question that tests us to the quick. For it is one thing to appraise matters of life and death by the principles of rational self-interest and quite another *to take responsibility for our choice.* I cannot imagine the Distinguished Professor from the University of London personally consigning humanity to oblivion with the same equanimity with which he writes off its demise. I am certain that if the Distinguished Younger Economist from M.I.T. were made responsible for determining the precise length of stay of humanity on the SST, he would agonize over the problem and end up by exacting every last possible inch for mankind's journey.

Of course, there are moral dilemmas to be faced even if one takes one's stand on the "survivalist" principle. Mankind cannot expect to continue on earth indefinitely if we do not curb population growth, thereby consigning billions or tens of billions to the oblivion of non-birth. Yet, in this case, we sacrifice some portion of life-to-come in order that life itself may be preserved. This essential commitment to life's continuance gives us the moral authority to take measures, perhaps very harsh measures, whose justification cannot be found in the precepts of rationality, but must be sought in the unbearable anguish we feel if we imagine ourselves as the executioners of mankind.

This anguish may well be those "religious convictions," to use the phrase our London economist so casually tosses away. Perhaps to our secular cast of mind, the anguish can be more easily accepted as the furious power of the biogenetic force we see expressed in every living organism. Whatever its source, when we ask if mankind "should" survive, it is only here that we can find a rationale that gives us the affirmation we seek.

This is not to say we will discover a religious affirmation naturally welling up within us as we careen toward Armageddon. We know very little about how to convince men by recourse to reason and nothing about how to convert them to religion. A hundred faiths contend for believers today, a few perhaps capable of generating that sense of caring for human salvation on earth. But, in truth, we do not know if "religion" will win out. An appreciation of the magnitude of the sacrifices required to perpetuate life may well tempt us to opt for "rationality"—to enjoy life while it is still to be enjoyed on relatively easy terms, to write mankind a shorter ticket on the SST so that some of us may enjoy the next millimeter of the trip in first-class seats.

Yet I am hopeful that in the end a survivalist ethic will come to the fore—not from the reading of a few books or the passing twinge of a pious lecture, but from an experience that will bring home to us, as Adam Smith brought home to his "man of humanity," the personal responsibility that defies all the homicidal promptings of reasonable calculation. Moreover, I believe that the coming generations, in their encounters with famine, war, and the threatened life-carrying capacity of the globe, may be given just such an experience. It is a glimpse into the void of a universe without man. I must rest my ultimate faith on the discovery by these future generations, as the ax of the executioner passes into their hands, of the transcendent importance of posterity for them.

Study Questions

1. Why should we care about future generations? How would you answer Heilbroner's question, "Why should I lift a finger to affect events that will have no more meaning for me seventy-five years after my death than those that happened seventy-five years before I was born?"

2. Do you agree with Heilbroner that there is "no rational answer to that terrible question?" Defend your answer.

3. Do you think "religious convictions" or simply well-thought-out humanistic concerns (Adam Smith's "man of humanity") should have more weight than logic and rational argument when considering issues such as obligations to posterity? How do you decide?

43

Who Cares for Posterity?

GARRETT HARDIN

Garrett Hardin is emeritus professor of biology at the University of California, Santa Barbara, and the author of several works in biology and ethics, including The Limits of Altruism *and* Exploring New Ethics for Survival.

Hardin argues that contemporary philosophy is centered on personal relations, "I-Thou" and "Here-Now" relations, which are not applicable to future generations. He proposes that we incorporate an economic cost–benefit model in order to overcome the undue self-interest of people so that future generations may have their needs met. One method of ensuring prosperity for posterity is to allow limited special interests or privilege to the guardians of our resources so that future people will have an inheritance. He also advocates the inculcation of an ecological conscience in the young (sometimes called "ecolacy").

I

Two centuries ago the American poet John Trumbull (1750–1831) posed a question that has ever since disturbed those who want to put a wholly rational foundation under conservation policy. Why, Trumbull asked, should people act

> . . . as though there were a tie
> And obligation to posterity.
> We get them, bear them, breed, and nurse:
> What has posterity done for us?

The question is surely an ethical one. One would think that philosophers who have been dealing with ethics for more than two thousand years would by this time have developed a rather impressive intellectual apparatus for dealing with the needs of posterity; but they have not. In a thought-provoking essay on "Technology and Responsibility," Hans Jonas points out that ethical literature is almost wholly individualistic: it is addressed to private conduct rather than to public policy. Martin Buber epitomized this spirit well when he oriented his ethics around the *I-Thou* dyad. That sounds fine until a close reading reveals that the author means no more than *I-Thou, Here and Now*. The standard ethical dialogue is between people who stand face to face

with each other, seeking a reasonable basis for reciprocal altruism. Posterity has no chance to show its face in the here and now.

Except for Jonas's valuable comments, contemporary philosophy still evades the hard problem of caring for posterity's interests. Probably no recent work is well known or spoken of with such awe as John Rawls's *A Theory of Justice*, so we should see what this book has to say about "the problem of justice between generations," as Rawls puts the problem. In §44 the author candidly admits that in his hopefully comprehensive system of analysis the problem "seems to admit of no definite answer." One might suppose that he would then drop the matter but he somehow manages to talk about it for another fourteen pages without adding anything more positive than statements such as "men have a natural duty to uphold and to further just institutions." This pronouncement is less than revolutionary; it is hardly operational. Perhaps we have expected too much from philosophers. Can economists throw any more light on the problem of posterity?

Time is of the essence. In cost–benefit analysis we attempt to list and evaluate all the costs (negative benefits); similarly with all the (positive) benefits; then we strike a balance for the whole, on which action can be based. If the balance is plus, we go ahead; if minus, we stop. The decision is simple if costs and benefits are encountered at practically the same moment. But what if they are separated by a considerable gap in time? What if the benefits come now and the costs do not turn up for a generation? Contrariwise, what if costs have to be paid now for benefits that come later? How do we balance costs against benefits when time is interposed between the two?

To begin with let us take up the benefits-first problem, which throws an interesting light on human nature. When the High Aswan Dam was proposed for the Nile only its expected benefits were publicized: the additional electricity it would generate and the additional land that could be irrigated with the impounded water. The huge financial cost of the dam was acknowledged, but the world was told that it would be well worth it. It would bring the blessings of "development" to the poor people of Egypt.

People were not told certain other costs that were well known to some agricultural experts. Agriculture in the Nile below Aswan had always depended on a yearly flooding of the flat fields. This flooding accomplished two things: it leached out the salts accumulated from the

Reprinted from *The Limits of Altruism* (Indiana University Press, 1977) by permission. Notes deleted.

preceding year's evaporation of irrigation water, and it left behind one millimeter of silt, which served as fertilizer for the next year's crops. This system of agriculture had been successful for six thousand years—a unique record of long-term success. Now technologists proposed to put an end to it.

Had there been any national or international debate on the subject the debaters should have wrestled with this question: Do today's short-term benefits of more electricity and more agricultural land in the upper reaches of the river outweigh tomorrow's losses in the lower valley resulting from salination and loss of fertility? The gains are necessarily short term: all dam-lakes eventually silt up and become useless as generators of electricity and sources of abundant water. The process usually takes only a century or two, and often much less. No economically feasible method has ever been found for reclaiming a silted-up dam-lake. The loss from salination of irrigated land is also virtually permanent; treatment requires periodic flooding, but that is what the High Aswan Dam was designed to prevent. The Tigris-Euphrates valley, in which irrigation was practiced for centuries, was ruined by salination two thousand years ago—and it is still ruined.

How a cost–benefit balance would have been struck had these facts been known to the decision makers we do not know. Probably their reaction would have been that of Mr. Micawber in *David Copperfield*: "Something will turn up." Such is the faith of the technological optimists. "Eat, drink, and be merry—for tomorrow will find a solution to today's problems. We will learn how to dredge out dam-ponds—economically. We will learn how to desalinate farmland—economically. Don't wait until we've solved these problems. Plunge ahead! Science will find an answer in time."

Curiously, economists have more confidence in science and technology than scientists do. Could it be that too much knowledge is a bad thing? Should conservatism in ecological matters be labeled a vice rather than a virtue? So say the technological optimists.

Well, the High Aswan Dam has been built now, and the returns are coming in. They are worse than expected. There has not been time for appreciable salination or significant loss of soil fertility—which no one expected this soon anyway—but other disadvantages we had not foreseen have turned up. Water behind the dam is rising more slowly than had been hoped, because of unexpected leakage into surrounding rock strata and greater than expected evaporation from the surface of the lake. The present steady flow of water in irrigation channels (instead of the former intermittent flow) favors snails that carry parasitic worms. As a result, the painful and debilitating disease of schistosomiasis is more widespread among Egyptians now. There are medical measures that can be taken against the disease and sanitary measures to combat the snails, but both cost money, which is what the Egyptians are short of. In addition, the

reduction of the flow of the Nile has opened the delta to erosion by the currents of the Mediterranean; as a result, precious delta farmland is now being swept into the sea. And the stoppage of the annual fertilization of the eastern Mediterranean by flood-borne silt has destroyed 95 percent of the local sardine fisheries. The dam is proving a disaster, and sooner than anyone had thought.

Mr. Micawber, where are you now?

We come now to the opposite problem, that of weighing present costs against future benefits. For this question there is a rational economic theory. Let us see if it is adequate.

Suppose I offer to sell you something that will be worth $100 ten years from now: how much should you be willing to pay for it? If you are the standard "economic man," equipped with a hand calculator, you will say something like this: "Well, let me see: assuming the interest rate of money stays at 6 percent, I cannot afford to pay you more than $55.84 for this opportunity. So if you want to close the deal you'll have to accept $55.84 or a bit less to get me to opt for $100 ten years from now."

The reasoning is as follows. A person with some money to spare can either put it in the bank at 6 percent interest or invest it in this enterprise. Put in the bank, $55.84 (at compound interest) will amount to $100 ten years later: the proposed investment should be able to do that well. If the investor thinks the proposal is speculative he will make a lower bid (i.e., expect a higher rate of interest). If he is worried about inflation (and thinks he knows another investment that is inflation-proof) he will demand a still lower price.

In economic terms, we "discount" the future value at a discount rate (rate of interest), calling the discounted value the "present value." The present value of $100 ten years from now at a discount rate of 6 percent is $55.84; if the discount rate is 10 percent the present value is only $38.55. The formula for these calculations is:

$$\text{Present value} = \text{Future value} \div e^{bt}$$
where: e = base of natural logarithms (ln)
$b = \ln(1 + \text{interest rate})$
and t = time

The economic theory of discounting is a completely rational theory. For short periods of time it gives answers that seem intuitively right. For longer periods, we are not so sure.

A number of years ago I decided to plant a redwood tree in my backyard. As I did so I mused, "What would my economist friends say to this? Would they approve? Or would they say I was an economic fool?"

The seedling cost me $1.00. When mature the tree would (at the then current prices) have $14,000 worth of lumber in it—but it would take two thousand years to reach that value. Calculation showed that the investment of so large a sum of money as $1.00 to secure so distant a gain would be justified only if the going rate of interest was no more than 0.479 percent per year. So low a rate of interest has never been known. Plainly I was being a rather stupid "economic man" in planting that tree. *But I planted it.*

The theory of discounting scratches only the surface of the problem. What about the quid pro quo? The quid ($1.00) is mine to pay; but who gets the quo, two thousand years from now? Not I, certainly. And it is most unlikely that any of my direct descendants will get it either, history being what it is. The most I can hope for is that an anonymous posterity will benefit by my act. Almost the only benefit I get is the thought that posterity will benefit—a curious sort of quo indeed. Why bother?

I am beginning to suspect that rationality—as we now conceive it—may be insufficient to secure the end we desire, namely, taking care of the interests of posterity. (At least, some of us desire that.) I can illustrate my point with a true story, which I shall embellish with a plausible historical explanation.

During the Second World War certain fragments of information, and fragments of wood, coming out of China led the California botanist Ralph Chaney to believe that the dawn redwood, which had been thought to be extinct for hundreds of thousands of years, was still in existence. Fortunately Chaney was a person of initiative and independent means, and he promptly set out for China to look for the tree. Getting to the interior of this war-torn country was no small accomplishment, but he did it. He found the tree. It was in an area that had suffered severe deforestation for several thousand years, and there were fewer than a thousand dawn redwoods left. They were still being cut down for fuel and cabinetmaking. Most of the living specimens were in temple courtyards—and thereby hangs our tale.

What is so special about being in a temple courtyard? Just this: it makes the object sacred. The word *sacred* is not easy to define, but whatever we mean by it we mean something that stands outside the bounds of rationality, as ordinarily understood. Let me illustrate this by a fictional conversation between a priest and a peasant in a Chinese temple a thousand years ago. Knowing almost nothing of Chinese social history I cannot make the conversation idiomatically correct, but I think the sense of it will be right.

A peasant from the deforested countryside, desperate for fuel to cook his rice, has slipped into a temple courtyard and is breaking twigs off the dawn redwood when he is apprehended by the priest.

"Here, here! You can't do that!"

"But, honorable sir, I have to. See, I have a little rice in this bowl, but it is uncooked. I can't eat it that way. I'm starving. If you'll only let me have a few twigs I can cook my rice and live another day."

"I'm sorry," says the priest, "but it is forbidden. This tree is sacred. No one is allowed to harm it."

"But if I don't get this fuel I will die."

"That's too bad: the tree is sacred. If everybody did what you are trying to do there soon wouldn't be any tree left."

The peasant thinks a few moments and then gets very angry: "Do you mean to tell me that the life of a mere tree is more valuable than the life of a human being?"

Now this is a very Westernized, twentieth-century question; I doubt that an ancient Chinese would have asked it. But if he had, how would the priest have replied? He might have repeated his assertion that the tree was sacred; or he might have tried to frighten the peasant by saying that touching it would bring bad luck to him in the future. That which is sacred or taboo is generally protected by legends that tend to make the taboo operational: bad luck, the evil eye, the displeasure of the gods. Are such stories consciously concocted because the idea of posterity is too remote to he effective? Or is it just a coincidence that objects so protected do survive for posterity's enjoyment? Whatever the case, being treated as sacred can protect an object against destruction by impoverished people who might otherwise discount the future in a simplistically rational way.

Once the peasant realized that the tree was sacred (or that its destruction would bring him bad luck) he would probably have slunk out of the courtyard. But suppose we continue to endow him with twentieth-century sentiments and see what happens.

"Sir," says the peasant, "your position is a self-serving one if I ever heard such. It's all well and good for you to be so thoughtful of posterity, for you get your three square meals a day no matter what. But what about me? Why do I have to serve posterity while you stuff your belly? Where's your sense of justice?"

"You're right," admits the priest. "I *am* the beneficiary of special privilege. There's only one thing to do," he says, as he takes off his clothes, "and that is to trade positions. Take your clothes off and trade with me! From now on you are the priest and I am the peasant."

That is a noble gesture—but surely the point is obvious? The gesture solves nothing. The next day, when the priest-turned-peasant comes begging for wood, the peasant-turned-priest must refuse him. If he doesn't the tree will soon be destroyed.

But the dawn redwood did survive. The conversation was fictional but the event—saving the trees by labeling some of them sacred—is true. The ginkgo tree was also saved in this way: it was known only in temple courtyards when Western men first found it in China. Special privilege preserved the trees in the face of vital demands made by an impoverished people.

Are we in the West capable of such severity? I know of only two stories of this sort, both from the USSR. The first dates from 1921, a time of famine there. An American journalist visited a refugee camp on the Volga where almost half the people had already died of starvation. Noticing sacks of grain stacked in great mounds in an adjacent field, he asked the patriarch of the refugee community why the people did not simply overpower the lone soldier guarding the grain and help themselves. The patriarch explained that the sacks contained seed for planting the next season. "We do not steal from the future," he said.

Much the same thing happened again in the Second World War. The siege of Leningrad by the Germans lasted 900 days, killing about a quarter of the population of three million. The cold and starving inhabitants had to eat dogs, cats, rats, and dried glue from furniture joints and wallpaper. All this time truckloads of edible seeds in containers were in storage in the All-Union Institute of Plant Industry. The seeds were a precious repository of genetic variety for Russian agriculture in the future. The seeds were never touched, though hundreds of thousands of people died.

Do these stories show that starving people are just naturally noble and take the long view? No. The behavior of people in prison camps shows that the opposite is the case. Altruism evaporates as egoism takes over. It is egoism of the crudest sort: people will sacrifice every promise of tomorrow for the merest scrap of food today. It is as though the interest rate for discounting the future approached infinity.

Under severe survival conditions morality disappears, as became evident in an experiment carried out by American physiologists during the Second World War. Foreseeing the need to treat starving victims of European concentration camps after the Germans were driven back, and recognizing that there was too little sound physiological knowledge, American scientists called for volunteers to take part in starvation experiments. Some conscientious objectors, members of the Church of the Brethren, volunteered. They were extremely idealistic young men, but as their ribs started to show, their ideals evaporated. They stole food from any place they could get it, including from one another. Many people do not like to face this sort of reality about human nature, but thoughtful religious men have known it for centuries. Thomas Aquinas summarized the situation very well when he said, "Necessity knows no law."

It is futile to ask starving people to act against their own self-interest as they see it, which is an exclusively short-term self-interest. In a desperate community long-term interests can be protected only by institutional means: soldiers and policemen. These agents will be reliable only if they are fed up to some minimum level, higher than the average of the starving population. In discounting the future a man's personal discount rate is directly related to the emptiness of his stomach. Those who are the guardians of the future stores must be put in a favored position to keep their personal discount rates low—that is, to make it possible for them to believe in, and protect, the future.

In a prosperous society the interests of posterity may often be served by the actions of a multitude of people. These actions are (or at least seem to be) altruistic. That cannot happen in a desperately needy society. When necessity is in the saddle we dare not expect altruism from "the people." Only institutions can then take actions that would be called altruistic were individuals to perform them. "An institution," as George Berg has pointed out, "can be considered as an anticipating device designed to pay off its members now for behavior which will benefit and stabilize society later." An army, a police force, and a priesthood are institutions that *can* serve the needs of posterity—which they may or may not do.

Moralists try to achieve desired ends by exhorting people to be moral. They seldom succeed; and the poorer the society (other things being equal) the less their success. Institutionalists try to achieve desired ends by the proper design of institutions, allowing for the inescapable moral imperfection of the people on whose services institutions must depend. The Cardinal Rule is not violated: institution-designers count on people acting egoistically.

If there is complete equality of position and power in a needy society the interests of posterity are unlikely to be taken care of. Seeds for the future will be used for food today by a hungry people acting egoistically. To serve the future a few individuals must be put in the special position of being egoistically rewarded for protecting the seeds against the mass of people not enjoying special privilege. Well-fed soldiers acting egoistically (to preserve their institutional right to be well fed) can protect posterity's interests against the egoistic demands of today's hungry people. It is not superior morality that is most likely to serve posterity but an institutional design that makes wise use of special privilege.

I am not pleading for more special privilege in our own country. So far as posterity's interests are concerned the richer the country the less need it has for special privilege. We are rich. But I do plead for tolerance and understanding of special privilege in other countries, in poor countries. Political arrangements can never be wholly independent of the circumstances of life. We have long given lip service to this principle, recognizing that illiteracy, poverty, and certain traditions make democracy difficult. If we wish to protect posterity's interests in poor countries we must understand that distributional justice is a luxury that cannot be afforded by a country in which population overwhelms the resource base.

In a poor country, if all people are equally poor—if there is no special privilege—the future will be universally discounted at so high a rate that it will practically vanish. Posterity will be cheated; and being cheated it will, in its turn, be still poorer and will discount the future at an even higher rate. Thus a vicious cycle is established. Only special privilege can break this cycle in a poor country. We need not positively approve of special privilege; but we can only do harm if, like the missionaries of old, we seek to prevent it.

Special privilege does not insure that the interests of posterity will be taken care of in a poor country; it merely makes it possible. Those enjoying special privilege may find it in their hearts to safeguard the interests of posterity against the necessarily—and forgivably—short-sighted egoism of the desperately poor who are under the natural necessity of discounting the future at a ruinous rate. We will serve posterity's interests better if we give up the goal of diminishing special privilege in poor countries. We should seek instead to persuade the privileged to create altruistic institutions that can make things better for posterity, thus diminishing the need for special privilege in the future.

Special privilege may be *pro tempore,* as it is for drafted or enlisted soldiers (in the stories told of the USSR); or it may extend over generations by virtue of hereditary privilege. The privileged always seek to make privilege hereditary. There is much to be said against hereditary privilege, from both biological and political points of view; but it has a peculiar psychological merit from the point of view of posterity, a merit pointed out by Edmund Burke (1729–1797) when he said: "People will not look forward to posterity who never look backward to their ancestors." The image evoked by this old-fashioned voice of conservatism is one of landed gentry or nobility, reared in baronial halls lined with the pictures of ancestors, looking out over comfortable estates, which they are determined to keep intact against the demands of the less fortunate, so that their children may enjoy what they enjoy. In some psychological sense posterity and ancestors fuse together in the service of an abstraction called "family."

If Burke's psychology is right (and I think it is), he points to several ways in which posterity may be served despite the strictures of hardheaded economics. A society in which prosperity is less than universal may institutionalize special privilege. (The desired result is not guaranteed: when ill used, special privilege can have the opposite effect, of course.) Where wealth is sufficiently great and more equitably distributed, a society that held Burke's assertion to be true would be expected to modify its institutions in a number of ways. Obviously it would see to it that the teaching of history played a large role in education.

Less obviously, a society interested in posterity might decide that the policy of encouraging a high degree of mobility in the labor force should be reversed. There is considerable anecdotal evidence to show that a person's identification with the past is significantly strengthened by exposure during childhood to the sight of enduring artifacts: family portraits, a stable dwelling place, even unique trees. It is harder for a mobile family to achieve this unconscious identification with the past. It is the conventional wisdom of economics that labor mobility improves the productivity of a nation. In the short run

that may be true; but if the Burkean argument presented here is sound it means that short-term economic efficiency is purchased at the expense of long-term failure to conserve resources.

One further and rather curious point needs to be made about this argument. If I believe it to be true that location stability encourages the identification of the past with the future, that belief may have little direct effect on my own actions because my childhood is now beyond reach. Such a "belief" would be a conscious one, and it seems that only unconscious beliefs have much power to cause actions that run contrary to the dictates of simple rationality. I cannot wilfully create within myself the psychological identification whose praises I sing. The most I can do (if I am powerful and clever enough) is modify the environment of other people—of children now growing up—so that they will unconsciously come to give preference to the interests of posterity.

Here is a curious question: if, because of my own childhood I myself lack a strong feeling for place and ancestry (and hence for posterity), what would lead me to try to inculcate it in others by working to modify their childhood experiences? Isn't this process a sort of lifting one's self by one's bootstraps, a sort of second-order altruism? The problem of posterity is rich in puzzles!

Whatever the answer may be to questions like these, this much should be clear: once a society loses a keen concern for posterity, regaining such a sense will be the work not of a few years but of a generation or more. If civilization should collapse worldwide, the second tragedy would be the loss of the will to rebuild. Under the inescapable condition of dire poverty, augmented no doubt by a rejection of the past that had caused the collapse, effective concern for posterity would virtually disappear—not forever, perhaps, but until historical developments we cannot possibly foresee rekindled a concern for social continuity.

In the light of this conclusion questions of another sort should be raised. Do we yet have the knowledge needed to insure the indefinite survival of any political unit? Do we yet know how to prevent the collapse that overtook all previous civilizations? If we do, then it is safe to create One World (if we can); but if we do not, it is not advisable even to try. If collapse is still an inescapable part of the life cycle of political units then posterity would be poorly served by a fusing of all present states into one. We should instead preserve enough of the economic and social barriers between groupings of humanity so that the cancer of collapse can be localized.

If knowledge of local wretchedness in distant states should lead us altruistically to create a resource commons we would thereby become a party to the ultimate metastasis of collapse. If our understanding of the physiology and pathology of political organizations is less than total, an overriding concern for the needs of the present generation can lead to a total sacrifice of the interests of posterity. I submit that our knowledge of the laws of political behavior is less than total.

Study Questions

1. What is Hardin's critique of rationality, especially economic rationality?
2. What is the significance of Hardin's story about the peasant, desperate for fuel to cook his rice, who wants to use the dawn redwood branches for firewood?
3. Do you agree with Hardin that we should allow special privileges in some countries to certain people so long as they preserve our resources for future use? Why doesn't Hardin apply this principle to our country?
4. How does Hardin link a concern for ancestry with concerns for posterity? Is he correct?
5. Consider your situation. Is your family among the prosperous in the United States or Canada? How about in the world? How much austerity or severity can you imagine experiencing for the sake of future generations?
6. Does Hardin advocate the tearing down of barriers between nations? Why, or why not?

44

Limited Obligations to Future Generations

MARTIN GOLDING

Martin Golding is professor of philosophy at Duke University and the author of several works in philosophy of law, including Philosophy of Law.

Golding's essay divides into two parts. In the first part, he seeks to answer three questions: (1) Who are the individuals in whose regard it is maintained that we have such obligations? (2) What do these obligations oblige us to do? and (3) What kind of obligations are they? In answering these questions, Golding argues that we have obligations to those outside our immediate moral community if and only if we can recognize their good as part of our understanding of the good. In the second part of this essay, he asks whether we have reason to believe that future generations will be sufficiently like us (have our values) for us to be able to recognize such a good. Here he is skeptical.

Golding thinks that our only clear obligation to future people is to leave them alone, not to make plans for them. So while he favors pollution control and stewardship of Earth's resources, he is against the population-limiting policies. That is a problem for each generation to deal with, not one for us to impose on other generations.

PRELIMINARY QUESTIONS

Before I turn to the question of the basis of obligations [to future generations]—the necessity of the plural is actually doubtful—there are three general points to be considered: (1) Who are the individuals in whose regard it is maintained that we have such obligations, to whom do we owe such obligations? (2) What, essentially, do obligations to future generations oblige us to do, what are they aimed at? and (3), To what class of obligation do such obligations belong, what kind of obligation are they? Needless to say, in examining a notion of this sort, which is used in everyday discussion and polemic, one must be mindful of the danger of taking it—or making it out—to be more precise than it is in reality.

1. This cautionary remark seems especially appropriate in connection with the first of the above points. But the determination of the purview of obligations to future generations is both ethically and practically significant. It seems clear, at least, who does not come within their purview. Obligations to future generations are distinct from the obligations we have to our presently living fellows, who are therefore excluded from the purview of the former, although it might well be the case that *what* we owe to future generations is identical with (or overlaps) what we owe to the present generation. However, I think we may go further than this and also exclude our most immediate descendants, our children, grandchildren and great-grandchildren, perhaps. What is distinctive about the notion of obligations to future generations is, I think, that it refers to generations with which the possessors of the obligations cannot expect in a literal sense to share a common life. (Of course, if we have obligations to future generations, understood in this way, we *a fortiori* have obligations to immediate posterity.) This, at any rate, is how I shall construe the reference of such obligations; neither our present fellows nor our immediate posterity come within their purview. What can be the basis of our obligations toward individuals with whom we can-

Reprinted from *The Monist* 56 (January 1972), with permission of the author and publisher. Notes deleted.

not expect to share a common life is a question I shall consider shortly.

But if their inner boundary be drawn in this way, what can we say about their outer limits? Is there a cut-off point for the individuals in whose regard we have such obligations? Here, it seems, there are two alternatives. First, we can flatly say that there are no outer limits to their purview: all future generations come within their province. A second and more modest answer would be that we do not have such obligations towards any assignable future generation. In either case the referent is a broad and unspecified community of the future, and I think it can be shown that we run into difficulties unless certain qualifications are taken into account.

2. Our second point concerns the question of what it is that obligations to future generations oblige us to do. The short answer is that they oblige us to do many things. But an intervening step is required here, for obligations to future generations are distinct from general duties to perform acts which are in themselves intrinsically right, although such obligations give rise to duties to perform specific acts. Obligations to future generations are essentially an obligation to produce—or to attempt to produce—a desirable state of affairs *for* the community of the future, to promote conditions of good living for future generations. The many things that we are obliged to do are founded upon this obligation (which is why I earlier questioned the necessity of the plural). If we think we have an obligation to transmit our cultural heritage to future generations it is because we think that our cultural heritage promotes, or perhaps even embodies, good living. In so doing we would hardly wish to falsify the records of our civilization, for future generations must also have, as a condition of good living, the opportunity to learn from the mistakes of the past. If, in addition, we believe lying to be intrinsically wrong we would also refrain from falsifying the records; but this would not be because we think we have any special duty to tell the truth to future generations.

To come closer to contemporary discussion, consider, for example, population control, which is often grounded upon an obligation to future generations. It is not maintained that population control is intrinsically right—although the rhetoric frequently seems to approach such a claim—but rather that it will contribute towards a better life for future generations, and perhaps immediate posterity as well. (If population control were intrinsically anything, I would incline to thinking it intrinsically wrong.) On the other hand, consider the elimination of water and air pollution. Here it might be maintained that we have a definite duty to cease polluting the environment on the grounds that such pollution is intrinsically bad or that it violates a Divine command. Given the current mood of neopaganism, even secularists speak of the despoilment of the environment as a

sacrilege of sorts. When the building of a new dam upsets the ecological balance and puts the wildlife under a threat, we react negatively and feel that something bad has resulted. And this is not because we necessarily believe that our own interests or those of future generations have been undermined. Both views, but especially the latter (Divine command), represent men as holding sovereignty over nature only as trustees to whom not everything is permitted. Nevertheless, these ways of grounding the duty to care for the environment are distinguishable from a grounding of the duty upon an obligation to future generations, although one who acknowledges such an obligation will also properly regard himself as a trustee to whom not everything is permitted. Caring for the environment is presumably among the many things that the obligation to future generations obliges us to do because we thereby presumably promote conditions of good living for the community of the future.

The obligation—dropping the plural again for a moment—to future generations, then, is not an immediate catalogue of specific duties. It is in this respect rather like the responsibility that a parent has to see to the welfare of his child. Discharging one's parental responsibility requires concern, seeking, and active effort to promote the good *of* the child, which is the central obli-gation of the parent and out of which grows the specific parental obligations and duties. The use of the term "responsibility" to characterize the parent's obligation connotes, in part, the element of discretion and flexibility which is requisite to the discharging of the obligation in a variety of antecedently unforseeable situations. Determination of the specific duty is often quite problematic even—and sometimes especially—for the conscientious parent who is anxious to do what is good for his child. And, anticipating my later discussion, this also holds for obligations to future generations. There are, of course, differences, too. Parental responsibility is enriched and reinforced by love, which can hardly obtain between us and future generations. (Still, the very fact that the responsibility to promote the child's good is an obligation means that it is expected to operate even in the absence of love.) Secondly, the parental obligation is always towards assignable individuals, which is not the case with obligations to future generations. There is, however, an additional feature of likeness between the two obligations which I shall mention shortly.

3. The third point about obligations to future generations—to what class of obligation do they belong?—is that they are *owed*, albeit owed to an unspecified, and perhaps unspecifiable, community of the future. Obligations to future generations, therefore, are distinct from a general duty, when presented with alternatives for action, to choose the act which produces the greatest good. Such a duty is not owed to anyone, and the beneficiaries of my fulfilling a duty to promote the greatest

good are not necessarily individuals to whom I stand in the moral relation of having an obligation that is owed. But when I owe it to someone to promote his good, he is never, to this extent, merely an incidental beneficiary of my effort to fulfill the obligation. He has a presumptive *right* to it and can assert a claim against me for it. Obligations to future generations are of this kind. There is something which is due to the community of the future from us. The moral relation between us and future generations is one in which they have a claim against us to promote their good. Future generations are, thus, possessors of presumptive rights.

How Can Those Not Yet Born *Now* Have Claims On Us?

This conclusion is surely odd. How can future generations—the not-yet-born—*now* have claims against us? This question serves to turn us finally to consider the basis of our obligations to future generations. I think it useful to begin by discussing and removing one source of the oddity.

It should first be noticed that there is no oddity in investing present effort in order to promote a future state of affairs or in having an owed obligation to do so. The oddity arises only on a theory of obligations and claims (and, hence, of rights) that virtually identifies them with acts of willing, with the exercise of sovereignty of one over another, with the pressing of demands—in a word, with *making* claims. But, clearly, future generations are not now engaged in acts of willing, are not now exercising sovereignty over us, and are not now pressing their demands. Future generations are not now making claims against us, nor will it be *possible* for them to do so. (Our immediate posterity are in this last respect in a different case.) However, the identification of claims with making claims, demanding, is plausible within the field of rights and obligations because the content of a system of rights is historically conditioned by the making of claims. Individuals and groups put forward their claims to the goods of life, demand them as their right; and in this way the content is increasingly expanded towards the inclusion of more of these goods.

Nevertheless, as suggestive a clue as this fact is for the development of a theory of rights, there is a distinction to be drawn between *having* claims and *making* claims. The mere fact that someone claims something from me is not sufficient to establish it as his right, or that he has a claim relative to me. On the other hand, someone may have a claim relative to me whether or not he makes the claim, demands, or is even able to make a claim. (This is not to deny that claiming plays a role in the theory of rights.) Two points require attention here. First, some claims are frivolous. What is demanded cannot really be claimed as a matter of right. The crucial factor in determining this is the *social ideal,* which we may provision-

ally define as a conception of the good life for man. It serves as the yardstick by which demands, current and potential, are measured. Secondly, whether someone's claim confers an entitlement upon him to receive what is claimed *from me* depends upon my moral relation to him, on whether he is a member of my *moral community*. It is these factors, rather than any actual demanding, which establish whether someone has a claim relative to me.

Who Are the Members of My Moral Community?

Who are the members of my moral community? (Who is my neighbor?) The fact is that I am a member of more than one moral community, for I belong to a variety of groups whose members owe obligations to one another. And many of the particular obligations that are owed vary from group to group. As a result my obligations are often in conflict and I experience a fragmentation of energy and responsibility in attempting to meet my obligations. What I ought to desire for the members of one of these groups is frequently in opposition to what I ought to desire for the members of another of these groups. Moral communities are constituted, or generated, in a number of ways, one of which is especially relevant to our problem. Yet these ways are not mutually exclusive, and they can be mutually reinforcing. This is a large topic and I cannot go into its details here. It is sufficient for our purpose to take brief notice of two possible ways of generating a moral community so as to set in relief the particular kind of moral community that is requisite for obligations to future generations.

A moral community may be constituted by an explicit contract between its members. In this case the particular obligations which the members have towards each other are fixed by the terms of their bargain. Secondly, a moral community may be generated out of a social arrangement in which each member derives benefits from the efforts of other members. As a result a member acquires an obligation to share the burden of sustaining the social arrangement. Both of these are communities in which entrance and participation are fundamentally a matter of self-interest, and only rarely will there be an obligation of the sort that was discussed earlier, that is, a responsibility to secure the good of the members. In general the obligations will be of more specialized kinds. It is also apparent that obligations acquired in these ways can easily come into conflict with other obligations that one may have. Clearly, a moral community comprised of present and future generations cannot arise from either of these sources. We cannot enter into an explicit contract with the community of the future. And although future generations might derive benefits from us, these benefits cannot be reciprocated. Our immediate posterity, who will share a common life with us, are in a better position in this respect; so that obligations towards our children, born and unborn, conceivably *could* be generated from participation in a mutually beneficial social arrangement. This, however, would be misleading.

It seems, then, that communities in which entrance and participation are fundamentally matters of self-interest, do not fit our specifications. As an alternative let us consider communities based upon altruistic impulses and fellow-feeling. This, too, is in itself a large topic, and I refer to it only in order to develop a single point.

The question I began with was: Who are the members of my moral community? Now it is true that there are at least a few people towards whom I have the sentiments that are identified with altruism and sympathetic concern. But are these sentiments enough to establish for me the moral relationship of owing them an obligation? Are these enough to generate a moral community? The answer, I think, must be in the negative so long as these affections towards others remain at the level of animal feeling. The ancient distinction between mere affection, mere liking, and conscious desire is fundamental here. Genuine concern and interest in the well-being of another must be conscious concern. My desire for another's good must in this event be more than impulsive, and presupposes, rather, that I have a *conception* of his good. This conception, which cannot be a bare concept of what is incidentally a good but which is rather a conception of the good *for* him, further involves that he not be a mere blank to me but that he is characterized or described in some way in my consciousness. It is perhaps unnecessary to add that there is never any absolute guarantee that such a conceived good is not, in some sense, false or fragmentary. Nevertheless, an altruism that is literally mindless—if it can be called "altruism" at all—cannot be the basis of moral community.

But even if it be granted that I have a conception of another's good, I have not yet reached the stage of obligation towards him. We are all familiar with the kind of "taking an interest in the welfare of another" that is gracious and gift-like, a matter of *noblesse oblige*. It is not so much that this type of interest-taking tends to be casual, fleeting and fragmentary and stands in contrast to interest-taking that is constant, penetrating and concerned with the other's total good. It is, rather, a form of interest-taking, however "conceptual," that is a manifestation of an unreadiness or even an unwillingness to recognize the other's claim (as distinct, of course, from his claiming), the other's entitlement, to receive his good from me. An additional step is, therefore, required, and I think it consists in this: that I acknowledge this good as a good, that his good is good-to-me. Once I have made this step, I cannot in conscience deny the pertinence of his demand, if he makes one, although whether I should now act so as to promote his good is of course dependent on a host of factors. (Among these factors are moral considerations that determine the permissibility of various courses of action and priorities of duties.) The basis of the obligation is nevertheless secured. . . .

The structure of the situation is highlighted when a stranger puts forward his demand. The question immediately arises, shall his claim be recognized as a matter of right? Initially I have no affection for him. But is this crucial in determining whether he ought to count as a member of my moral community? The determination depends, rather, on what he is like and what are the conditions of his life. One's obligations to a stranger are never immediately clear. If a visitor from Mars or Venus were to appear, I would not know what to desire for him. I would not know whether my conception of the good life is relevant to him and to his conditions of life. The good that I acknowledge might not be good for him. Humans, of course, are in a better case than Martians or Venusians. Still, since the stranger appears as strange, different, what I maintain in my attempt to exclude him is that my conception of the good is not relevant to him, that "his kind" do not count. He, on the other hand, is in effect saying to me: Given your social ideal, you must acknowledge my claim, for it *is* relevant to me given what I am; your good is my good, also. If I should finally come to concede this, the full force of my obligation to him will be manifest to me quite independently of any fellow-feeling that might or might not be aroused. The *involuntary* character of the obligation will be clear to me, as it probably never is in the case of individuals who command one's sympathy. And once I admit him as a member of my moral community, I will also acknowledge my responsibility to secure this good for him even in the absence of any future claiming on his part.

With this we have completed the account of the constitution of the type of moral community that is required for obligations to future generations. I shall not recapitulate its elements. The step that incorporates future generations into our moral community is small and obvious. Future generations are members of our moral community because, and insofar as, our social ideal is relevant to them, given what they are and their conditions of life. I believe that this account applies also to obligations towards our immediate posterity. However, the responsibility that one has to see to the welfare of his children is in addition buttressed and qualified by social understandings concerning the division of moral labor and by natural affection. The basis of the obligations is nevertheless the same in both instances. Underlying this account is the important fact that such obligations fall into the area of the moral life which is independent of considerations of explicit contract and personal advantage. Moral duty and virtue also fall into this area. But I should like to emphasize again that I do not wish to be understood as putting this account forward as an analysis of moral virtue and duty in general.

The Inter-Generational Partnership

As we turn at long last specifically to our obligations to future generations, it is worth noticing that the term "contract" has been used to cover the kind of moral community that I have been discussing. It occurs in a famous passage in Burke's *Reflections on the Revolution in France*:

> Society is indeed a contract. Subordinate contracts for objects of mere occasional interest may be dissolved at pleasure—but the state ought not to be considered as nothing better than a partnership agreement in a trade of pepper and coffee, calico or tobacco, or some other such low concern, to be taken up for a little temporary interest, and to be dissolved by the fancy of the parties. It is to be looked upon with other reverence; because it is not a partnership in things subservient only to the gross animal existence of a temporary and perishable nature.
>
> It is a partnership in all science; a partnership in all art; a partnership in every virtue, and in all perfection. As the ends of such a partnership cannot be obtained in many generations, it becomes a partnership not only between those who are living, but between those who are living, those who are dead and those who are to be born.
>
> Each contract of each particular state is but a clause in the great primaeval contract of eternal society, linking the lower with the higher natures, connecting the visible and invisible world, according to a fixed compact sanctioned by the inviolable oath which holds all physical and all moral natures, each in their appointed place.

The contract Burke has in mind is hardly an explicit contract, for it is "between those who are living, those who are dead and those who are to be born." He implicitly affirms, I think, obligations to future generations. In speaking of the "ends of such a partnership," Burke intends a conception of the good life for man—a social ideal. And, if I do not misinterpret him, I think it also plain that Burke assumes that it is relatively the same conception of the good life whose realization is the object of the efforts of the living, the dead, and the unborn. They all revere the same social ideal. Moreover, he seems to assume that the conditions of life and of the three groups are more or less the same. And, finally, he seems to assume that the same general characterization is true of these groups ("all physical and moral natures, each in their appointed place").

Now I think that Burke is correct in making assumptions of these sorts if we are to have obligations to future generations. However, it is precisely with such assumptions that the notion of obligation to future generations begins to run into difficulties. My discussion, until this point, has proceeded on the view that we *have* obligations to future generations. But do we? I am not sure that the question can be answered in the affirmative with any certainty. I shall conclude this note with a very brief discussion of some of the difficulties. They may be summed up in the question: Is our conception—"conceptions" might be a more accurate word—of the good life for man relevant to future generations?

It will be recalled that I began by stressing the importance of fixing the purview of obligations to future generations. They comprise the community of the future, a community with which we cannot expect to share a common life. It appears to me that the more *remote* the members of this community are, the more problematic our obligations to them become. That they are members of our moral community is highly doubtful, for we probably do not know what to desire for them.

Let us consider a concrete example, namely, that of the maintenance of genetic quality. Sir Julian Huxley has stated:

> [I]f we don't do something about controlling our genetic inheritance, we are going to degenerate. Without selection, bad mutations inevitably tend to accumulate; *in the long run, perhaps 5,000 to 10,000 years from now,* we [*sic*] shall certainly have to do something about it. . . . Most mutations are deleterious, but we now keep many of them going that would otherwise have died out. If this continues indefinitely . . . then the whole genetic capacity of man will be much weakened.

This statement, and others like it, raise many issues. As I have elsewhere discussed the problems connected with eugenic programs, positive and negative, I shall not go into details here. The point I would make is this: given that we do not know the conditions of life of the very distant future generations, we do not know what we ought to desire for them even on such matters as genic constitution. The chromosome is "deleterious" or "advantageous" only relative to given circumstances. And the same argument applies against those who would promote certain social traits by means of genetic engineering (assuming that social traits are heritable). Even such a trait as intelligence does not escape immune. (There are also problems in eugenic programs having nothing to do with remoteness.) One might go so far as to say that if we have an obligation to distant future generations it is an obligation not to plan for them. Not only do we not know their conditions of life, we also do not know whether they will maintain the same (or a similar) conception of the good life for man as we do. Can we even be fairly sure that the same general characterization is true both of them and us?

The moral to be drawn from this rather extreme example is that the more distant the generation we focus upon, the less likely it is that we have an obligation to promote its good. We would be both ethically and practically well-advised to set our sights on more immediate generations and, perhaps, solely upon our immediate posterity. After all, even if we do have obligations to future generations, our obligations to immediate posterity are undoubtedly much clearer. The nearer the generations are to us, the more likely it is that our conception of the good life is relevant to them. There is certainly enough work for us to do in discharging our responsibility to promote a good life for them. But it would be unwise, both from an ethical and a practical perspective, to seek to promote the good of the very distant.

And it could also be *wrong*, if it be granted—as I think it must—that our obligations towards (and hence the rights relative to us of) near future generations and especially our immediate posterity are clearer than those of more distant generations. By "more distant" I do not necessarily mean "very distant." We shall have to be highly scrupulous in regard to anything we do for any future generation that also could adversely affect the rights of an intervening generation. Anything else would be "gambling in futures." We should, therefore, be hesitant to act on the dire predictions of certain extreme "crisis ecologists" and on the proposals of those who would have us plan for mere survival. In the main, we would be ethically well-advised to confine ourselves to removing the obstacles that stand in the way of immediate posterity's realizing the social ideal. This involves not only the active task of cleaning up the environment and making our cities more habitable, but also implies restraints upon us. Obviously, the specific obligations that we have cannot be determined in the abstract. This article is not the place for an evaluation of concrete proposals that have been made. I would only add that population limitation schemes seem rather dubious to me. I find it inherently paradoxical that we should have an obligation to future generations (near and distant) to determine in effect the very membership of those generations.

A final point. If certain trends now apparent in our biological technology continue, it is doubtful that we should regard ourselves as being under an obligation to future generations. It seems likely that the man—humanoid(?)—of the future will be Programmed Man, fabricated to order, with his finger constantly on the Delgado button that stimulates the pleasure centers of the brain. I, for one, cannot see myself as regarding the good for Programmed Man as a good-to-me. That we should do so, however, is a necessary condition of his membership in our moral community, as I have argued above. The course of these trends may very well be determined by whether we believe that we are, in the words of Burke, "but a clause in the great primaeval contract of eternal society, linking the lower with the higher natures, connecting the visible and invisible world, according to a fixed compact sanctioned by the inviolable oath which holds all physical and all moral natures, each in their appointed place." We cannot yet pretend to know the outcome of these trends. It appears that whether we have obligations to future generations in part depends on what we do for the present.

Study Questions

1. Carefully analyze Golding's argument. Why must we identify future people's concept of the good with our notion of the good before we have obligations to them? How do you understand this?
2. Look carefully at Golding's use of Burke's idea of an implicit compact (contract or partnership) "between those who are living, those who are dead and those who are to be born." How does Golding interpret this? Is his interpretation too narrow or exactly right? Explain.
3. Golding says, "Population limitation schemes seem rather dubious to me," but he admits that it "will contribute towards a better life for future generations." Is population limitation advocated only as a duty to future generations, or is it also advocated to improve the quality of life and provide adequate food and resources for those already living?

45

Energy Policy and the Further Future: The Identity Problem

Derek Parfit

Derek Parfit is a fellow in philosophy at Oxford University. He has made outstanding contributions to ethical theory and the philosophy of mind. His major work is Reasons and Persons *(1984).*

Here Parfit examines traditional ways of justifying intergenerational rights and duties. On the standard view, we hold that a crime or policy has to have a definite victim before we can call it a crime or a bad policy.

Reprinted from *Energy and the Future,* eds. Douglas MacLean and Peter G. Brown (Totawa, NJ: Rowman & Littlefield, 1983.)

But the policy choices we make regarding energy and resource use will determine who is born so that, as long as future people live worthwhile lives, on the standard view, they cannot blame us for our bad and wasteful policies. Parfit argues (or more accurately, urges us to judge) that the standard view is wrong. The principle he offers (A) is: "It is bad if those who live are worse off than those who might have lived." In this case, it doesn't matter whether different people live. We are responsible for environmental policies since we could have caused human lives to have been better off.

I have assumed that our acts may have good or bad effects in the further future.[1] Let us now examine this assumption. Consider first

The Nuclear Technician: Some technician lazily chooses not to check some tank in which nuclear wastes are buried. As a result there is a catastrophe two centuries later. Leaked radiation kills and injures thousands of people.

We can plausibly assume that, whether or not this technician checks this tank, the same particular people would be born during the next two centuries. If he had chosen to check the tank, these same people would have later lived, and escaped the catastrophe.

Is it morally relevant that the people whom this technician harms do not yet exist when he makes his choice? I have assumed here that it is not. If we know that some choice either may or will harm future people, this is an objection to this choice even if the people harmed do not yet exist. (I am to blame if I leave a man-trap on my land, which ten years later maims a five-year-old child.)

Consider next

The Risky Policy: Suppose that, as a community, we have a choice between two energy policies. Both would be completely safe for at least two centuries, but one would have certain risks for the further future. If we choose the Risky Policy, the standard of living would be somewhat higher over the next two centuries. We do choose this policy. As a result there is a similar catastrophe two centuries later, which kills and injures thousands of people.

Unlike the Nuclear Technician's choice, our choice between these policies affects who will be later born. This is not obvious, but is on reflection clear.

Our identity in fact depends partly on when we are conceived. This is so on both the main views about this subject. Consider some particular person, such as yourself. You are the nth child of your mother, and you were conceived at time t. According to one view, you could not have grown from a different pair of cells. If your mother had conceived her nth child some months earlier or later, that child would *in fact* have grown from a different pair of cells, and so would not have been you.

According to the other main view, you could have grown from different cells, or even had different parents. This would have happened if your actual parents had not conceived a child when they in fact conceived you, and some other couple had conceived an extra child who was sufficiently *like* you, or whose life turned out to be sufficiently like yours. On this other view, that child would have been you. (Suppose that Plato's actual parents never had children, and that some other ancient Greek couple had a child who wrote *The Republic*, *The Last Days of Socrates*, and so on. On this other view, this child would have been Plato.) Those who take this other view, while believing that you could have grown from a different pair of cells, would admit that this would not *in fact* have happened. On both views, it is in fact true that, if your mother had conceived her nth child in a different month, that child would not have been you, and *you* would never have existed.

It may help to shift to this example. A fourteen-year-old girl decides to have a child. We try to change her mind. We first try to persuade her that, if she has a child now, that will be worse for her. She says that, even if it will be, that is her affair. We then claim that, if she has a child now, that will be worse for her child. If she waits until she is grown up, she will be a better mother, and will be able to give her child a better start in life.

Suppose that this fourteen-year-old rejects our advice. She has a child now, and gives him a poor start in life. Was our claim correct? Would it have been better for him if she had taken our advice? If she had, *he* would never have been born. So her decision was worse for him only if it is against his interests to have been born. Even if this makes sense, it would be true only if his life was so wretched as to be worse than nothing. Assume that this is not so. We must then admit that our claim was false. We may still believe that this girl should have waited. That would have been better for her, and the different child she would have had later would have received a better start in life. But we cannot claim that, in having *this* child, what she did was worse for *him*.

Return now to the choice between our two energy policies. If we choose the Risky Policy, the standard of living will be slightly higher over the next two centuries. This effect implies another. It is not true that, whichever policy we choose, the same particular people will exist two centuries later. Given the effects of two such policies on the details of our lives, it would increasingly over time be true that people married different people. More simply, even in the same marriages, the children would increasingly be conceived at different times. (Thus the British Miners' Strike of 1974, which caused television to close down an hour early, thereby affected the timing of thousands of conceptions.) As we have seen, children conceived at different times would in fact be different children. So the proportion of those later born who would owe their existence to our choice would, like ripples in a pool, steadily grow. We can plausibly assume that, after two centuries, there would no one living who would have been born whichever policy we chose. (It may help to think of this example: how many of us could truly claim, "Even if railways had never been invented, I would still have been born?")

In my imagined case, we choose the Risky Policy. As a result, two centuries later, thousands of people are killed and injured. But if we had chosen the alternative Safe Policy, these particular people would never have existed. Different people would have existed in their place. Is our choice of the Risky Policy worse for anyone?

We can first ask, "Could a life be so bad—so diseased and deprived—that it would not be worth living? Could a life be even worse than this? Could it be worse than nothing, or as we might say 'worth not living'?" We need not answer this question. We can suppose that, whether or not lives could be worth not living, this would not be true of the lives of the people killed in the catastrophe. These people's lives would be well worth living. And we can suppose the same of those who mourn for those killed, and those whom the catastrophe disables. (Perhaps, for some of those who suffer most, the rest of their lives would be worth not living. But this would not be true of their lives as a whole.)

We can next ask: "If we cause someone to exist, who will have a life worth living, do we thereby benefit this person?" This is a difficult question. Call it the question whether *causing to exist can benefit*. Since the question is so difficult, I shall discuss the implications of both answers.

Because we chose the Risky Policy, thousands of people are later killed or injured or bereaved. But if we had chosen the Safe Policy these particular people would never have existed. Suppose we do *not* believe that causing to exist can benefit. We should ask, "If particular people live lives that are on the whole well worth living, even though they are struck by some catastrophe, is this worse for these people than if they had never existed?" Our answer must be "no." If we believe that causing to exist *can* benefit, we can say more. Since the people struck by the catastrophe live lives that are well worth living and would never have existed if we had chosen the Safe Policy, our choice of the Risky Policy is not only not worse for these people, it *benefits* them.

Let us now compare our two examples. The Nuclear Technician chooses not to check some tank. We choose the Risky Policy. Both these choices predictably cause catastrophes, which harm thousands of people. These predictable effects both seem bad, providing at least some moral objection to these choices. In the case of the technician, the objection is obvious. His choice is worse for the people who are later harmed. But this is not true of our choice of the Risky Policy. Moreover, when we understand this case, we know that this is not true. We know that, even though our choice may cause such a catastrophe, it will not be worse for anyone who ever lives.

Does this make a moral difference? There are three views. It might make all the difference, or some difference, or no difference. There might be no objection to our choice, or some objection, or the objection may be just as strong.

Some claim

Wrongs Require Victims: Our choice cannot be wrong if we know that it will be worse for no one.

This claim implies that there is no objection to our choice. We may find it hard to deny this claim, or to accept this implication.

I deny that wrongs require victims. If we know that we may cause such a catastrophe, I am sure that there is at least some moral objection to our choice. I am inclined to believe that the objection is just as strong as it would have been if, as in the case of the Nuclear Technician, our choice would be worse for future people. If this is so, it is morally irrelevant that our choice will be worse for no one. This may have important theoretical implications.

Before we pursue the question, it will help to introduce two more examples. We must continue to assume that some people can be worse off than others, in morally significant ways, and by more or less. But we need not assume that these comparisons could be even in principle precise. There may be only rough or partial comparability. By "worse off" we need not mean "less happy." We could be thinking, more narrowly, of the standard of living, or, more broadly, of the quality of life. Since it is the vaguer, I shall use the phrase "the quality of life." And I shall extend the ordinary use of the phrase "worth living." If one of two groups of people would have a lower quality of life, I shall call their lives to this extent "less worth living."

Here is another example:

Depletion: Suppose that, as a community, we must choose whether to deplete or conserve certain kinds of resources. If we choose Depletion, the quality of life over the next two centuries would be slightly higher than it would have been if we had chosen Conservation, but it may later be much lower. Life at this much lower level would, however, still be well worth living. The effects might be shown as in Figure 1.

FIGURE 1 *Effects of Choice on Future Standard of Living*

This case raises the same problem. If we choose Depletion rather than Conservation, this will lower the quality of life more than two centuries from now. But the particular people who will then be living would never have existed if instead we had chosen Conservation. So our choice of Depletion is not worse for any of these people. But our choice will cause these people to be worse off than the different people who, if we had chosen Conservation, would have later lived. This seems a bad effect, and an objection to our choice, even though it will be worse for no one.

Would the effect be worse, having greater moral weight, if it *was* worse for people? One test of our intuitions may be this. We may remember a time when we were concerned about effects on future generations, but had overlooked my point about personal identity. We may have thought that a policy like Depletion would be against the interests of future people. When we saw that this was false, did we become less concerned about effects on future generations?

I myself did not. But it may help to introduce a different example. Suppose there are two rare conditions X and Y, which cannot be detected without special tests. If a pregnant woman has condition X, this will give to the child she is carrying a certain handicap. A simple treatment would prevent this effect. If a woman has condition Y when she becomes pregnant, this will give to the child she conceives the same particular handicap. Condition Y cannot be treated, but always disappears within two months. Suppose next that we have planned two medical programs, but there are funds for only one; so one must be canceled. In the first program, millions of women would be tested during pregnancy. Those found to have condition X would be treated. In the second program, millions of women would be tested when they intend to try to become pregnant. Those found to have condition Y would be warned to postpone conception for at least two months. We are able to predict that these two programs would achieve results in as many cases. If there is Pregnancy Testing, 1,000 children a year would be born normal rather than handicapped. If there is Pre-Conception Testing, there would each year be born 1,000 normal children, rather than 1,000 different handicapped children. Would these two programs be equally worthwhile?

Let us note carefully what the difference is. As a result of either program, 1,000 couples a year would have a normal rather than a handicapped child. These would be different couples on the two programs. But since the numbers would be the same, the effects on parents and on other people would be morally equivalent. The only difference lies in the effects on the children. Note next that, in judging these effects, we need have no view about the moral status of a fetus. We can suppose that it would take a year before either kind of testing could begin. When we choose between the two programs, none of the children has yet been conceived. And all of

the children will become adults. So we are considering effects, not on present fetuses, but on future people. Assume next that the handicap in question, though it is not trivial, is not so severe as to make life doubtfully worth living. Even if it can be against our interests to have been born, this would not be true of those born with this handicap.

Since we cannot afford both programs, which should we cancel? Under one description, both would have the same effects. Suppose that conditions X and Y are the only causes of this handicap. The incidence is now 2,000 a year. Either program would halve the incidence; the rate would drop to 1,000 a year. The difference is this. If we decide to cancel Pregnancy Testing, those who are later born handicapped would be able to claim, "But for your decision, I would have been normal." Our decision will be worse for all these people. If instead we decide to cancel Pre-Conception Testing, there will later be just as many people who are born with this handicap. But none of these could truly claim, "But for your decision, I would have been normal." But for our decision, they would never have existed; their parents would have later had different children. Since their lives, though handicapped, are still worth living, our decision will not be worse for any of these people.

Does this make a moral difference? Or are the two programs equally worthwhile? Is all that matters morally how many future lives will be normal rather than handicapped? Or does it also matter whether these lives would be lived by the very same people?

I am inclined to judge these programs equally worthwhile. If Pre-Conception Testing would achieve results in a few more cases, I would judge it the better program. This matches my reactions to the questions asked above about our choice of the Risky Policy or of Depletion. There too, I think it would be bad if there would later be a catastrophe, killing and injuring thousands of people, and bad if there would later be a lower quality of life. And I think that it would not be *worse* if the people who later live would themselves have existed if we had chosen the Safe Policy or Conservation. The bad effects would not be worse if they had been, in this way, worse for any particular people.

Let us review the argument so far. If we choose the Risky Policy or Depletion, this may later cause a predictable catastrophe, or a decline in the quality of life. We naturally assume that these would be bad effects, which provide some objection to these two choices. Many think the objection is that our choices will be worse for future people. We have seen that this is false. But does this make a moral difference? There are three possible answers. It might make all the difference, or some difference, or no difference at all. When we see that our choice will be worse for no one, we may decide that there is no objection to this choice, or that there is less objection, or that the objection is just as strong.

I incline to the third answer. And I give this answer in

the case of the medical programs. But I know some people who do not share my intuitions. How can we resolve this disagreement? Is there some familiar principle to which we can appeal?

Return to the choice of the Risky Policy, which may cause a catastrophe, harming thousands of people. It may seem irrelevant here that our choice will not be worse for these future people. Can we not deserve blame for causing harm to others, even when our act is not worse for them? Suppose that I choose to drive when drunk, and in the resulting crash cause you to lose a leg. One year later, war breaks out. If you had not lost this leg, you would have been conscripted, and been killed. So my drunken driving saves your life. But I am still morally to blame.

This case reminds us that, in assigning blame, we must consider not actual but predictable effects. I knew that my drunken driving might injure others, but I could not know that it would in fact save your life. This distinction might apply to the choice between our two policies. We know that our choice of the Risky Policy may impose harm on future people. Suppose next that we have overlooked the point about personal identity. We mistakenly believe that, whichever policy we choose, the very same people will later live. We may therefore believe that, if we choose the Risky Policy, this may be worse for future people. If we believe this, our choice can be criticized. We can deserve blame for doing what we *believe* may be worse for others. This criticism stands even if our belief is false—just as I am as much to blame even if my drunken driving will in fact save your life.

Now suppose, however, that we have seen the point about personal identity. We realize that, if we choose the Risky Policy, our choice will not be worse for those people whom it later harms. Note that this is not a lucky guess. It is not like predicting that, if I cause you to lose a leg, that will later save you from death in the trenches. We know that, if we choose the Risky Policy, this may impose harms on several future people. But we also know that, if we had chosen the Safe Policy, those particular people would never have been born. Since their lives will be worth living we *know* that our choice will not be worse for them.

If we know this, we cannot be compared to a drunken driver. So how should we be criticized? Can we deserve blame for causing others to be harmed, even when we know that our act will not be worse for them? Suppose we know that the harm we cause will be fully compensated by some benefit. For us to be sure of this, the benefit must clearly outweigh the harm. Consider a surgeon who saves you from blindness, at the cost of giving you a facial scar. In scarring you, this surgeon does you harm. But he knows that his act is not worse for you. Is this enough to justify his decision? Not quite. He must not be infringing your autonomy. But this does not require that you give consent. Suppose that you are unconscious, so that he is forced to choose without consulting you. If he decides to operate, he would here deserve no blame. Though he scars your face, his act is justified. It is enough for him to know that his act will not be worse for you.

If we choose the Risky Policy, this may cause harm to many people. Since these will be future people, whom we cannot now consult, we are not infringing their autonomy. And we know that our choice will not be worse for them. Have we shown that, in the same way, the objection has been met?

The case of the surgeon shows only that the objection might be met. The choice of the Risky Policy has two special features. Why is the surgeon's act not worse for you? Because it gives you a compensating benefit. Though he scars your face, he saves you from going blind. Why is our choice of the Risky Policy not worse for those future people? Because they will owe their existence to this choice. Is this a compensating benefit? This is a difficult question. But suppose that we answer "no." Suppose we believe that to receive life, even a life worth living, is not to be benefited.[2] There is then a special reason why, if we choose the Risky Policy, this will not be worse for the people who will later live.

Here is the second special feature. If we had chosen the Safe Policy, different people would have later lived. Let us first set aside this feature. Let us consider only the people who, given our actual choice, will in fact later live. These will be the only actual people whom our choice affects. Should the objection to our choice appeal to the effects on these people? Because of our choice, they will later suffer certain harms. This seems to provide an objection. But they owe their existence to this same choice. Does this remove the objection?

Consider a second case involving a fourteen-year-old girl. If this second girl has a child now, she will give him a poor start in life. But suppose she knows that, because she has some illness, she will become sterile within the next year. Unless she has a child now, she can never have a child. Suppose that this girl chooses to have a child. Can she be criticized? She gives her child a poor start in life. But she could not have given *him* a better start in life, and his life will still be worth living. The effects on him do not seem to provide an objection. Suppose that she could also reasonably assume that, if she has this child, this would not be worse for other people. It would then seem that there is no objection to this girl's choice—not even one that is overridden by her right to have a child.

Now return to our earlier case of a fourteen-year-old girl. Like the second girl, the first girl knows that, if she has a child now, she will give him a poor start in life. But she could wait for several years and have another child, who would have a better start in life. She decides not to wait, and has a child now. If we consider the effects only on her actual child, they are just like those of the second girl's choice. But the first girl's choice surely can be criticized. The two choices differ, not in their effects on the actual children, but in the alternatives. How could the second girl avoid having a child to whom she would give a poor start in life? Only by never having a child. That is why her choice seemed not to be open to criticism. She could reasonably assume that her choice would not be worse either for her actual child or for other people. In her case, that seems all we need to know. The first girl's choice has the same effects on her actual child, and on others. But *this* girl could have waited, and given some later child a better start in life. This is the objection to her choice. Her actual child is worse off than some later child would have been.

Return now to the choice between our two social policies. Suppose that we have chosen the Risky Policy. As a result, those who later live suffer certain harms. Is this enough to make our choice open to criticism? I suggest not. Those who later live are like the actual children of the two girls. They owe their existence to our choice, so its effects are not worse for them. The objection must appeal to the alternative.

This restores the second feature that we set aside above. When we chose the Risky Policy, we imposed certain harms on our remote descendants. Were we like the second girl, whose only alternative was to have no descendants? If so, we could not be criticized. But this is not the right comparison. In choosing the Risky Policy, we were like the first girl. If we had chosen the Safe Policy, we would have had different descendants, who would not have suffered such harms.

The objection to our choice cannot appeal only to effects on those people who will later live. It must mention possible effects on the people who, if we had chosen otherwise, would have later lived. The objection must appeal to a claim like this:

(A) It is bad if those who live are worse off than those who might have lived.

We must claim that this is bad even though it will be worse for no one.

(A) is not a familiar principle. So we have not solved the problem that we reached above. Let us remember what that was. If we choose the Risky Policy, or Depletion, this may later cause a catastrophe or a decline in the quality of life. These seemed bad effects. Many writers claim that, in causing such effects, we would be acting against the interests of future people. Given the point about personal identity, this is not true. But I was inclined to think that this made no moral difference. The objection to these two choices seemed to me just as strong. Several people do not share my intuitions. Some believe that the objections must be weaker. Others believe that they disappear. On their view, our choice cannot be morally criticized if we know that it will be worse for no one. They believe that, as moral agents, we need only be concerned with the effects of our acts on all of the people who are ever actual. We need not consider people who are merely possible—those who never do live but merely might have lived. On this view, the point about identity makes a great moral difference. The effects of our two choices, the predictable catastrophe, and the decline in the quality of life, can be morally totally ignored.

We hoped to resolve this disagreement by appeal to a familiar principle. I suggest now that this cannot be done. To criticize our choice, we must appeal to a claim like (A). And we have yet to explain why (A) should have any weight. To those who reject (A), we do not yet have an adequate reply.

To explain (A), and decide its weight, we would need to go deep into moral theory. And we would need to consider cases where, in the different outcomes of our acts or policies, different numbers of people would exist. This is much too large a task to be attempted here.

I shall therefore end with a practical question. When we are discussing social policies, should we ignore the point about personal identity? Should we allow ourselves to say that a choice like that of the Risky Policy, or of Depletion, might be against the interests of people in the further future? This is not true. Should we pretend that it is? Should we let other people go on thinking that it is?

If you share my intuitions, this seems permissible. We can then use such claims as a convenient form of short-hand. Though the claims are false, we believe that this makes no moral difference. So the claims are not seriously misleading.

Suppose instead that you do not share my intuitions. You believe that, if our choice of Depletion would be worse for no one, this must make a moral difference. It would then be dishonest to conceal the point about identity. But this is what, with your intuitions, I would be tempted to do. I would not *want* people to conclude that we can be less concerned about the more remote effects of our social policies. So I would be tempted to suppress the argument for this conclusion.

Theoretical Footnote: How might the attempt to justify claim (A) take us far into moral theory? Here are some brief remarks. Consider any choice between two outcomes. Figure 2 shows that there are three kinds of choice. These can be distinguished if we ask two questions: "Would all and only the same people ever live in both outcomes?" "Would the same number of people ever live in both outcomes?"

Of these three types of choice, it is the first and third that are important. Most of our moral thinking concerns Same People Choices, where there is a given group of people whom our acts may affect. We seldom consider Different Number Choices. Those who do have found them puzzling. What this essay has discussed are the second group, Same Number Choices. These are much less puzzling than Different Number Choices. But they are not common. Once we have moved outside Same People Choices—once we are considering acts that would cause different people to exist—it is seldom

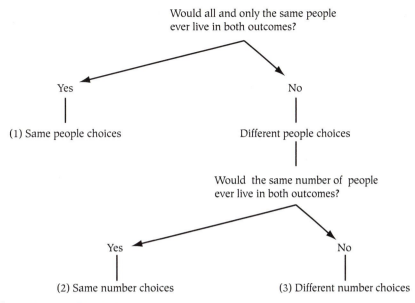

Would all and only the same people
ever live in both outcomes?

Yes   No

(1) Same people choices   Different people choices

Would the same number of people
ever live in both outcomes?

Yes   No

(2) Same number choices   (3) Different number choices

FIGURE 2 *Effects of Choice Between Two Outcomes*

true that in all of the relevant outcomes the very same numbers would exist.

According to claim (A), it is bad if those who live are worse off than those who might have lived. This claim applies straightforwardly only to Same Number Choices. Can we extend (A) to cover Different Number Choices? One extension would be the so-called "Average View." On this view, it would be worse for there to be more people if the average person would be worse off. The Average View, though popular, can be shown to be implausible.[3] But this does not cast doubt on (A). What it shows is that (A) should not be thought to cover Different Number Choices. We should restate (A) to make this explicit. But (A) *can* be made to cover Same People Choices. Our restatement might be this:

(B) If the same number of lives would be lived either way, it would be bad if people are worse off than people might have been.

The two occurrences of "people" here may refer to *different* people. That is how (B) can cover Same Number Choices. But it can also cover Same People Choices. (B) here implies that it is bad if people are worse off than *they* might have been.

Now consider a more familiar principle. This appeals to the interests of those whom our acts affect. One statement might be this:

The Person-Affecting Principle, or *PAP*: It is bad if people are affected for the worse.

What is the relation between (B) and the PAP?[4] In Same People Choices, these claims coincide. If people are worse off than they might have been, they are affected for the worse. So it will make no difference whether we appeal to (B) or to the PAP.[5]

The two claims diverge only in Same Number Choices. These are what my essay has discussed. Suppose that you share my intuitions, thinking that the point about identity makes no moral difference. You then believe that in Same Number Choices we should appeal to (B) *rather than* the PAP. If we choose Depletion, this will lower the quality of life in the further future. According to (B), this is a bad effect. When we see the point about identity, we see that this effect will be worse for no one. So it is not bad according to the PAP. If we believe that the effect is just as bad, we will here have no use for the PAP. Similar remarks apply to the choice between the two medical programs. If we believe these two programs to be equally worthwhile, we shall again appeal to (B). We shall have no use for the PAP. It draws a moral distinction where, in our view, no distinction should be drawn. It is thus like the claim that it is wrong to enslave whites.

To draw these remarks together: in Same People Choices, (B) and the PAP coincide. In Same Number Choices, we accept (B) rather than the PAP. So, wherever the claims diverge, we prefer (B).

There remain the Different Number Choices. Since we have restricted (B), we shall need some wider claim to cover these. Call this claim (X). I am not sure what (X) should be. But, if you have shared my intuitions, we can expect this. We shall have no further use for (B). It will be implied by (X).[6] So we can expect (X) to inherit (B)'s relations to the PAP. Wherever the claims diverge, we will prefer (X). In Same People Choices, (X) will imply the PAP. It will here make no difference to which we appeal. These are the cases with which most moral thinking is concerned. This explains the reputation of the PAP. This part of morality, the part concerned with human welfare is usually thought of in person-affecting terms. We appeal to the interests of those whom our acts affect. Even after we have found (X), we may continue to use the PAP in most cases. But it will be only a convenient form of short-hand. In some cases, (X) and the PAP will diverge. And we will here appeal to (X) rather than the PAP. We will here believe that, if an effect is bad according to (X), it makes no moral difference whether it is also worse for any particular people. The PAP draws a distinction where, in our view, no distinction should be drawn. We may thus conclude that this part of morality, the part concerned with human welfare, cannot be explained in person-affecting terms. Its fundamental principle will not be concerned with whether acts will be good or bad for those people whom they affect. If this is so, many moral theories need to be revised.

Notes

1. The first third of this section is adapted from my "Future Generations: Further Problems," *Philosophy & Public Affairs* 11, no. 2 (Spring 1982}.
2. Thus we might say: "We are benefited only if the alternative would not have been worse for us." "If we had never existed, this would not have been worse for us." These and similar arguments I claim not to be decisive in my "Future Generations." Even if it can be in our interests to have been conceived, most of my later claims would still stand.
3. See my "Future Generations," section IX, and Jefferson McMahan's "Problems of Population Theory" in *Ethics* (October 1981).
4. On the assumption that it cannot be in or against our interests to have been conceived. If we drop this assumption, some of the following claims need to be revised. Again, see my "Future Generations."
5. Does the equivalence go the other way? If people are affected for the worse, does this make them worse off? There is at least one exception: when they are killed. (B) should be revised to cover such exceptions. Only this ensures that, in Same People Choices, B and the PAP always coincide.

6. Consider the best-known candidates for the role of (X): the Average and Total Views. In their hedonistic forms, the Average View calls for the greatest net sum of happiness per life lived, the Total View simply calls for the greatest total net sum of happiness. When applied to population policy, these two views lie at opposite extremes. But when applied to Same Number Choices, both imply the hedonistic form of (B). This suggests that, whatever (X) should be, it, too, will imply (B). The difference between the candidates for (X) will be confined to Different Number Choices. This would be like the fact that only in Same Number Choices does (B) diverge from the PAP. I shall discuss these points more fully in my book *Reasons and Persons*, Oxford University Press, 1984.

Study Questions

1. Describe the main thesis of Parfit's essay. How does Parfit set forth the alternatives?
2. Personal identity has to do with being the same person over time. According to traditional ethics, we think that those who are harmed by our actions must be able to say that they would have been better off but for our actions. But in the case of energy or resource depletion, different people will be born than would have been had we had better policies. So, according to this view, these people cannot complain about our bad policies, since but for them, they wouldn't exist. What does Parfit say about the traditional point of view? What do you think?

For Further Reading

Feinberg, Joel. "The Rights of Animals and Unborn Generations." In his *Rights, Justice and the Bounds of Liberty*. Princeton, NJ: Princeton University Press, 1980.

Partridge, Ernest, ed. *Responsibilities to Future Generations*. Buffalo, NY: Prometheus, 1981.

Reichenbach, Bruce. "On Obligations to Future Generations." *Public Affairs Quarterly* 6.2 (April 1992).

Sikora, R. I, and Brian Barry, eds. *Obligations to Future Generations*. Philadelphia: Temple University Press, 1978.

PART TWO

Applications

INTRODUCTION

Ecological theory is vital for understanding our relation to the environment, but theory alone is not enough. While practice without theory is blind, theory without practice is sterile. Grave ecological problems face us, which call for careful ethical thinking: exponential population growth, world hunger, pollution, the use of pesticides, the greenhouse effect, energy policies (especially the issue of nuclear energy), environmentally sustainable agricultural and economic policies, as well as ways to simplify our lives so that we may live in harmony with the environment ("Live simply so that others may simply live").

All these matters are controversial. In each case, environmentalists disagree over both the nature and the extent of the problem, as well as over the solution. Ecologists like Paul Ehrlich and Garrett Hardin, who are sometimes called "Doomsdayers," warn that if we do not act immediately it may soon be too late to save our world from overpopulation and environmental degradation. Many natural resources are expected to run out (e.g., oil by 2040). The greenhouse effect, caused by man-made pollution, is expected to cause enormous damage to the environment. Ehrlich challenges us to play it safe and conserve our resources and limit population growth. To this end, he offers a version of Pascal's wager, a bet maximizing possible benefits. "If I'm right, we will save the world [by curbing population growth]. If I'm wrong, people will still be better fed, better housed, and happier, thanks to our efforts. Will anything be lost if it turns out later that we can support a much larger population than seems possible today?"[1]

On the other hand, environmental economists like Julian Simon and biologist Dixy Lee Ray, sometimes called "Cornucopians," argue that the age of scarcity is not upon us. A combination of nature's resilience and human technological innovation can cope with our environmental problems. Simon writes:

> *Natural resources.* Hold your hat—our supplies of natural resources are not finite in any economic sense. Nor does past experience give reason to expect natural resources to become more scarce. Rather, if the past is any guide, natural resources will progressively become less scarce, and less costly, and will constitute a smaller proportion of our expenses in future years. And population growth is likely to have a long-run *beneficial* impact on the natural-resource situation.[2]

In this part of our work, these issues will be discussed from various representative points of view. We begin with a debate on population. How great a problem is exponential population growth? Since the early 1950s, Earth's population has more than doubled to its present 5.8 billion, heading for more than 6 billion by the end of the century. In our readings, Garrett Hardin, Lindsey Grant, and Paul Ehrlich see population as the number one ecological issue. Others like Jacqueline Kasun, Julian Simon, and William Murdoch and Allan Oaten disagree, arguing that population itself is not a major issue and that Earth has room for many more people. How you decide on the population question will greatly influence how you respond to such questions about world hunger, economics, agriculture, pollution, and energy.

Because of its importance to the entire environmental debate, the first three chapters of Part 2 deal with population. The readings fall under three general headings: general considerations, including the use of scarce resources and the quality of life (Chapter 9); world hunger (Chapter 10); and pollution and other ecological damage (Chapter 11).

After this we turn to four chapters (12–15) on pollution, first treating the overall problem; then the problem of pesticide and herbicide use; next the greenhouse effect, the controversial issue of whether Earth is warming and whether this will have deleterious effects on the environment; and finally, toxic-waste disposal. Within these chapters the issues of air and water pollution and acid rain will also be debated.

Chapter 16 considers the difficult question of reviving nuclear power as a solution to our energy problems. Can we produce clean, safe, affordable nuclear energy? Can we solve the problem of nuclear waste? Three scientists debate the issue: John Jagger arguing for the affirmative, while Worldwatch researchers—Christopher Flavin and Nicholas Lenssen—argue for the negative.

In Chapter 17, "Economics and the Environment," we consider both whether we need to reevaluate our notions of economic success and how we should go about changing our current economic systems. In particular, should we use the economic model of risk–cost–benefit analysis with regard to environmental policy?

Finally, in Chapter 18 we examine practical ways to make the transition from a society filled with environmental problems to one in which we live off the interest rather than the principal of nature. We end with an essay by Lester Brown and his associates at Worldwatch on a vision of a sustainable society by the year 2030.

Let us turn, then, to the general question of population.

Notes

1. Paul Ehrlich, *The Population Bomb* (New York: Ballantine, 1968), p. 198.
2. Julian Simon, *The Ultimate Resource* (Princeton, NJ: Princeton University Press, 1981), p. 5.

CHAPTER NINE

Population: General Considerations

The Universal Declaration on Human Rights describes the family as the natural and fundamental unit of society. It follows that any choice and decision with regard to the size of the family must irrevocably rest with the family itself, and cannot be made by anyone else.[1]

There are too many people in the world. We are running out of space. We are running out of energy. We are running out of food. And, although too few people seem to realize it, we are running out of time.[2]

Is the world overpopulated? How serious is the increasing growth of the world's population? How does this affect the environment?

In evaluating population growth one must keep in mind that such growth increases *exponentially* rather than *linearly*. Linear growth increases by adding 1 unit to the sum: 1, 2, 3, 4, 5, and so forth. Exponential growth increases by a fixed percentage of the whole over a given time. It doubles itself: 1, 2, 4, 8, 16, 32, 64, and so forth.

Let me illustrate this with an ancient story. Once a hero defeated the enemies of his country. The emperor had the hero brought before him and promised the hero anything he wanted, large quantities of gold, wives, a high position in the kingdom, whatever. The hero produced a chess board and asked the king to put one grain of wheat on the square in the upper right-hand corner. "On the second day put two grains on the second square, and each day double the amount of the previous day on the succeeding square until all the 64 squares are filled." The emperor was astonished. "Is that all you request!" he cried, "You could have had half my kingdom, and all you ask for is a little grain?"

But the emperor soon discovered that he could not comply with the hero's request. By the time he had gotten to square 32, he found that on that square alone he owed the hero 8.6 billion grains of wheat. By the time he got to square 64, he owed 2^{64} grains of wheat, 500 times all wheat harvested in the entire world in 1993.

We calculate the doubling time of a given amount by using the *rule of 70*. If a sum increases at 1% per annum, it will double in size in 70 years. If it increases at a 2% rate per annum, it will increase fourfold in 70 years.

According to anthropologists, human beings have existed for about 3 million years. Over many millennia, their numbers slowly increased, until about 2000 years ago, at the time of Christ, 300 million people existed (a little more than the combined present population of the United States and Canada). It took 123 years for the world's population to increase from 1 billion to 2 billion, succeeding billions took 33, 14 years, and 13 years. The next billion is expected to take only 11 years and to be completed by 1998, when the world's population is expected to pass 6 billion. Today, late in 1997, Earth's population is over 5.8 billion (see Figure 1), and about 90 million will be added this year. It has more than doubled (from about 2.8 billion) since 1956. At the present rates of increase (1.8% per year), the population would double in about 39 years, reaching 11.6 billion by the year 2035. There are signs that the world's population rate is slowing slightly. The United Nations, counting on a slowdown, projects a population of between 7.9 billion and 11.9 by the year 2050.

Exponential growth is taking place in many countries. The present growth rate in Guatemala, Nigeria, Ecuador, the Philippines, Bangladesh, Ghana, Zimbabwe, and Thailand is 3.3% per annum, which means a doubling time of about 21 years. Jordan's and Syria's growth rate is 3.8%, while Kenya's is 4.2%, a doubling time of 17 years. Rwanda in East Africa has a growth rate of over 8%, which means its doubling time is less than 8.5 years. A slight increase in the world's growth rate would result in the world's population density becoming that of present-day New York City by the year 2300.

Because a disproportionate number of people in the less developed countries are under 15 years of age (averaging 39%—and in Kenya, 50%), a tremendous *demographic momentum* will cause continuing exponential population growth for a long time to come *even if* we inaugurated a zero-growth global policy tomorrow. For

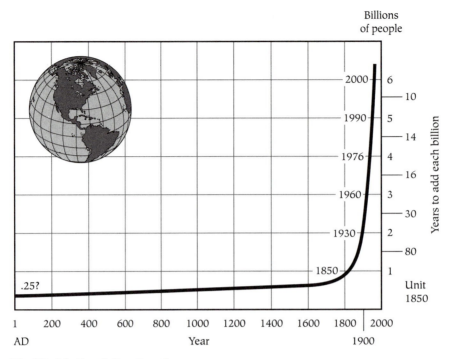

FIGURE 1 *J Curve of the World's Population Growth*

example, if over the next 33 years, the average family size of India dropped from its present 3.9 to the replacement rate of 2.2, India's present population of 870 million would still soar to about 2 billion by 2100.

How serious is this growth? The more people there are, the more food, water, and energy is needed, and the more pollution is produced. How many people can Earth reasonably sustain?

A recent United Nations report says that the problem of population growth is urgent because of "the extent of urban growth, the extent of environmental damage, the impending food crisis in many developing nations, the extent of infant and maternal mortality, and the continuing low status of women." Freshwater and topsoil are disappearing, and our cities are crammed-packed with masses of unemployed people. The recent famines and wars in Ethiopia, Angola, and Somalia have been attributed to the rapid population growth in those countries. World grain per-capita production was down in 1995 and is expected to continue to decline further, while the cost of importing grain rose. Meat production rose as more people throughout the world, especially China, demanded more meat in their diet. This is a dangerous trend since meat production involves considerable loss of nutrient energy. As more people reach middle-class lifestyles, they tend to use more resources and produce more pollution, resulting in more environmental degradation. This is sometimes referred to as *consumption overpopulation* as opposed to *people overpopulation*. Both are bad for the environment and for our long-term interests. Unless we curb our population growth, as well as simplify our lifestyles, we are doomed.

Others take exception to this picture of doom and gloom, arguing that our problems are moral and political, not demographic. We can solve our urban problems if we have the will to live together in moral equality and harmony. Technology has radically increased our energy and food resources. Enough food exists for all. The real problem is one of just distribution. Proponents of this view argue that the wealthy nations should moderate their consumptive passions, pointing out that with only 4.5% of the world's population, the United States uses 33% of its resources, 25% of its nonrenewable energy, and produces 33% of its pollution. The average American's negative impact on the environment is about forty or fifty times that of a person in the third world. In the affluent West, we must reject consumerism and simplify our lives. Those in the poorer developing nations must be allowed to improve their quality of life through education and appropriate technology.

Labels have grown up around the various positions. Those who hold that population growth is a crucial problem and who are pessimistic about our chances for survival if we do not curb population growth are called "Doomsdayers" or "Neo-Malthusians" (after the eighteenth-century clergyman Thomas Malthus). Garrett Hardin, Paul Ehrlich, Lindsey Grant, and John Holdren represent this view in our readings. On the other side, the optimists, called "Cornucopians," deny that population is a serious problem. They argue that technology and political changes can accommodate a much larger population than we presently have. Jacqueline Kasun (Reading 49), Julian Simon (Reading 60), Dixy Lee Ray and Louis Guzzo (Readings 65 and 69) represent the

Cornucopian perspective in our readings. Somewhere in the middle are those who see increasing population growth as a problem but believe that with economic and political changes (they would say, with economic and social justice), the problem can be solved without population control policies. The theory that people will voluntarily limit their procreation if they see it is in their economic and social self-interest is called the "benign demographic theory." We will examine it in relation to world hunger in Chapter 10 (William Murdoch and Allan Oaten's article) and in relation to pollution in Chapter 11 (represented by Barry Commoner, Michael Corr, and Paul Stamler). Perhaps we could call these thinkers "cautious optimists."

To get some data before us, we begin with a short editorial by Tristram Coffin (Reading 46) of *The Washington Spectator,* which succinctly sets forth a case for limiting population growth. Next we turn to Garrett Hardin's classic article (Reading 47), "The Tragedy of the Commons" in which he argues that unless strong social sanctions are enforced, self-interest will lead people to maximize personal utility, which all too often means violating the carrying capacity of the land. With regards to population, unless we have mutually coercive, mutually agreed-on restrictions on procreation, we will not survive.

Our third reading by demographer Lindsey Grant applies Hardin's theory to the American situation. He argues that population growth is a central environmental issue of our time, and because immigration is the main cause of population growth in the United States, it is a serious problem. We need to keep our immigration down to a minimum and to beget fewer children in order to stabilize—and even reduce—our total population. At the same time, Grant argues, we must simplify our lifestyles and ensure justice for all.

In our fourth reading, the Roman Catholic "Cornucopian" scholar Jacqueline Kasun takes a diametrically opposite point of view. She contends that the Doomsdayers (thinkers like Hardin and Grant), with their cries of scarcity and apocalyptic doom, are carrying on a heavy-handed policy of propaganda, filled with misinformation on the effects of a growing population. Citing an impressive array of statistics, Kasun argues that enough food and resources exist to care for a lot more people than presently inhabit Earth and that technology promises to expand resources efficiently. Population increase, rather than a liability, actually is a blessing. Such growth stimulates agricultural and economic investment, encourages governments and parents to devote greater resources to education, and inspires both more ideas and the exchange of ideas among people. Contrary to the interests of the ruling elite, we must learn to live creatively with the expanding opportunities that a growing population affords.

In the next chapters, we will examine other defenses of Neo-Malthusianism, Cornucopia, and cautious optimism. Meanwhile, the next readings deal with practical responses to population growth.

In our fifth reading, Jodi Jacobson shows how China with over 1.1 billion people, the largest population of any nation, is dealing with its population problem. After the Communist Revolution in 1948, Mao Ze-dong inaugurated a program of population expansion in order to build the economy and the army. By the mid-1960s, China's leaders concluded that the population had become too large and embarked on a reverse policy, punishing couples who had more than two children and rewarding those who had two or preferably one child.

In our last reading, Hugh LaFollette treats the ethics of propagation, which has implications wider than overpopulation. Society normally regulates potentially harmful activities, such as practicing law and medicine, selling drugs and driving vehicles, by requiring a license to do these things. But having children is as important and as potentially harmful as any of these activities. Shouldn't we require parents to qualify for having children by meeting minimal standards?

Let us turn to our readings.

Notes

1. Secretary General of the United Nations U Thant, *International Planned Parenthood News* 168 (February 1968): 3.
2. *Projectbook for the Exhibition "Population: The Problem Is Us"* (Washington, D.C.: Smithsonian Institution, circa 1970), p. 9; quoted in Jacqueline Kasun, *The War Against Population* (see Reading 49).

46

Earth, the Crowded Planet

TRISTRAM COFFIN

Tristram Coffin, who recently died, was for many years editor of The Washington Spectator, *a public concerns newsletter. In this editorial, Coffin documents the problem of exponential population growth and spells out some of its implications.*

A crucial struggle to prevent population growth from depleting the supply of food, water and fuel is being waged across the world.

A United Nations report says the problem is urgent because of "the extent of urban growth, the extent of environmental damage, the impending food crisis in many developing nations, the extent of infant and maternal mortality, and the continuing low status of women."

Planned Parenthood adds: "Rising populations strain the world's natural resources, stretch the need for food, energy, housing and jobs and increase social strife. Having 90 million more people added to the world's population every year makes every one of the world's problems more difficult to solve. Last year, world population exceeded six billion. Ninety percent of the growth will occur in developing countries of Africa, Asia and South America, many of which are already failing to adequately feed and provide social services for their present numbers."

The struggle is affected by at least three factors:

- The opposition to birth control by such powerful churches as Catholic and Muslim. Dr. R. T. Ravenholt, former director, Office of Population in AID, accuses Catholic bishops of "seeking to sabotage" birth control programs and "crippling U.S. assistance to family planning programs overseas." The *Washington Post* reports, "Estimates are that about 400,000 African Americans are Muslim."
- Parents in Third World countries who want large families in order to insure their care and security in old age.
- The awakening mood of women. The U.N. advises: "Compared with any previous generation, women are saying they want fewer children. Fertility is now falling in all regions of the developing world. The experience of the last 20 years shows that strong, well-managed family programs are highly effective.

   "By purely voluntary means, they have achieved smaller family size, healthier mothers and children, and more balanced rates of population growth in many different parts of the world and in a wide variety of social and economic settings."

One successful program, stressing the welfare and rights of women, operates in Tunisia, a largely Muslim nation: "From an average of 7.15 children per woman in the mid-1960s, Tunisia's average birth rate has fallen to just over three per woman today—about half the average for all of Africa. Tunisia has brought down its annual population growth rate to less than 1.9 percent. Thus, the accelerated economic growth of recent years has not been eaten up by new mouths to feed." (*Christian Science Monitor*)

Meanwhile, in this country, those seeking to deny women the legal right to abortion are gaining ground. More than 200 bills restricting abortion have been introduced in 45 legislatures this session.

Problems in Asia. In many areas of the world, the population crisis worsens. The recent heavy loss of life and property in Bangladesh was caused in part by "excessive population growth. . . . About 115 million people—equal to about half the U.S. population—are jammed into an area equal to one-sixty-fifth the size of the U.S. The worst lies ahead: Bangladesh will nearly double, to 199 million, by the year 2025, according to the World Bank." (*Washington Post*)

"In India's largest city, Bombay, up to five million people are living as squatters in overcrowded apartments, in condemned buildings, on pavements, along the shoulders of roads and on scraps of land." (*New York Times Magazine*)

India's population is likely to overtake China's in the next century, and "India has no effective national family planning program."

The Effect of "Too Many People"

"To say that population size or growth has no effect on economic development is incorrect. It is contradicted by every study of living standards and economic growth in the Third World. . . . The political strife and civil unrest that result from too many people contesting for the same scarce resources have contributed to one civil war after another around the world for the last half century."

George Mitchell (D-ME), Senate majority leader

A broad picture of the population problem is suggested by the following facts:

- A study by Worldwatch Institute indicates that unchecked population growth would produce "hunger-

Reprinted from *The Washington Spectator*, Vol. 17.15 (August 15, 1991), by permission of the editor.

induced rises in the death rate" and "a depletion of world food stocks." More or less chronic food scarcity and unprecedented food prices have exacerbated nutritional stress in the world's poorest countries.

"In oceanic fisheries, the growing demand for fish has led to overfishing and shrinking catches. It is also visible in land-based agriculture in densely populated poor countries, where overgrazing, deforestation and overplowing are leading to soil erosion, desert encroachment, and abandonment of cropland. . . . Population growth combined with the lesser effect of rising affluence has pushed food consumption ahead of production in recent years."

- In at least 56 countries, only 90 percent of the population has access to safe drinking water.
- In developing countries, up to half of the inhabitants live in substandard housing and only 62 percent of schoolage children are enrolled in school. Also, in these nations, 5,000 people share a doctor, in contrast to 550 per doctor in the developed world.
- Worldwatch Institute reports, "Surveys show that 500 million married women world wide want contraceptive methods but still cannot obtain them."
- Seventeen million children under the age of five die every year from malnutrition, diarrhea, low birth weight and immunizable diseases.
- People are crowding into cities in unprecedented numbers. *Development Forum* reports: "The overcrowding, the congestion, the housing shortages, the rural refugees, the pollution and waste—and all other signs and symptoms of the explosion (including crime)—intensify and grow worse. . . . Shantytowns and slums continue to expand, gobbling up green space and dehumanizing life. Megacities burst their boundaries and become bloated, sprawling hyper-cities.

"Just to keep up with today's rate of population increase, by the end of the century the developing world would have to increase by 65 percent the capacity it now has to produce and manage the urban infrastructure, services and shelter. That would mean coming up with housing, schools, hospitals, utilities, commercial structures, transportation.

"By the end of the next century, cities will be teeming with more than are alive on the entire globe today."

- The developed countries make up 21 percent of the world's population yet consume 85 percent of the world's energy—oil, coal, hydroelectric power, natural gas, and nuclear power.
- By the end of the century, the world must create 600 million new jobs to accommodate the population growth. This is based on a 2.7 percent growth rate for developing countries.
- The world will need twice as much fresh water by the year 2000. Nearly all of the available fresh water on the planet—99.9 percent—is frozen in Arctic ice caps.
- Topsoil is disappearing at the rate of 7 percent per decade. Six million hectares of land are turned into desert every year. (A hectare is the equivalent of 2.47 acres.)
- By 1980, 40 percent of the world's tropical forests had been consumed.

(The preceding data come from a variety of sources, including Worldwatch Institute, Audubon Society, Planned Parenthood and Zero Population Growth.)

The U.S. Role. In the struggle between people and resources, the U.S. plays a vital role. With only 5 percent of the world's population, we use 33 percent of the world's resources. The average American, for example, uses 54 times more resources than the average citizen of a developing country in Latin America, Asia, Africa and the Near East.

The *NPG Forum* reports: "Statistics suggest that in the U.S. we produce and consume 47 times more goods and services, per capita, than China. Because achieving and maintaining such consumption levels depend upon the availability of resources and the health of the environment that sustains them, our position is very tenuous.

"Currently, approximately 1,500 kilograms of agricultural products are produced annually to feed each American, while the Chinese make do with only 594 per capita."

This report says we are losing valuable topsoil 18 times faster than it is being replaced. In some agricultural areas in the U.S., soil productivity "has been reduced 50 percent, and in some areas [the soil] has been so severely degraded that it has been abandoned." Crop yields have been maintained or even increased by cheap fertilizer, pesticides and irrigation water.

World Food Stocks. A commentary on production compared to resources is given in a Worldwatch Institute study: "As growth in food demand has outstripped production gains, world grain reserves have been depleted and prices have climbed. As recently as 1970, grain reserves . . . amounted to 89 days of world consumption. By 1974, reserves had dropped to just over 30 days, where they have since remained.

"The decline in stocks has been accompanied by sharp price increases. The world price of wheat, which ranged between $1.58 and $1.84 per bushel between 1960 and 1971, began to climb in 1972. Since then, the price has fluctuated between $3.81 and $4.80 per bushel. The depletion of world stocks and the rise in prices have led to a degree of global food insecurity unmatched since the period of devastation and hunger immediately following World War II. . . .

"The lack of food reserves has all but wrecked the international system for responding to crop shortfalls in individual countries."

In the U.S., the heavy demand for food and the use of irrigation water have created another problem. Today, the groundwater overdraft is 25 percent higher than its replenishment rate. In addition, pollution of both surface water and groundwater raises serious concerns.

The *Forum* estimates that by 2080, population in the U.S. may increase by a third, because of high birth rates and immigration. At the same time, supplies of fossil fuels are "being rapidly depleted."

The study sees hope in solar energy, "provided that sound energy conservation and environmental policies were in effect to preserve soil, water, air and biological resources that sustain life."

Foreign Needs. Many of the materials the U.S. uses for "the good life," such as rubber, spices, inks, varnishes, paints, wood products, fabrics, pharmaceutical derivatives and oils, are imported. Thus, we have incentives to help others to conserve resources.

A *Los Angeles Times* editorial takes aim at an action by President Bush, who, "with a veto, removed American support of the U.N. Fund for Population Activities . . . in the groundless belief that some of the dollars might find their way into coercive abortion programs in China. . . . The action perpetuates canards about a successful, effective and principled U.N. program. . . .

"In the legislation vetoed by the President, $15 million of $220 million for population programs was to go to the UNFPA. Under a carefully crafted bipartisan amendment, none of the U.S. contribution would go to UNFPA's work in China."

The editorial points out that "a quarter of those now living [in the world] are hungry, and even more are malnourished. It is a situation that calls for vigorous leadership and more, not less, funds for effective world programs."

Economic columnist Hobart Rowen comments, "There is little doubt that Bush knows better. But he has willingly sublimated lifelong, on-the-record views on the desirability of strong American leadership on this issue to an effort to appease the GOP right wing. . . . The U.S. should restore itself as a world leader in the field of family planning."

"Signs of Hope." In a special report, Worldwatch Institute gives information on "World Population Trends: Signs of Hope, Signs of Stress."

"On the positive side, the growth in world population has begun to slow, reversing a longstanding trend of gradually accelerating growth that may have begun with the discovery of agriculture some 12,000 years ago."

One sign is the lowering of the birth rate in China because "it indicates what a government committed to reducing fertility can do when it attacks the problem on several fronts simultaneously." (A recent report by the *New York Times* says that, in China, the "average number of babies per woman [has dropped] from five or six in 1970 to two or three now.") Tragically, the slowdown in population growth is not due entirely to falling birth rates. In some poor countries, population growth is being periodically checked by hunger-induced death rates.

Population growth has slowed in three areas—North America, Western Europe and East Asia. It has fallen by a third in North America and East Asia and by a half in Western Europe. The latter cut its growth from 0.56 percent in 1970 to 0.32 percent in 1975.

Lester R. Brown of Worldwatch is particularly impressed by the drop in East Asia, from 1.85 percent to 1.18 percent, "influenced heavily by China's massive efforts to cut births." The Chinese program "focuses not only upon providing family planning services, including abortion, but also upon reshaping economic and social policies to encourage small families and upon an intensive public education campaign extolling the benefits of smaller families.

"East Asia's achievement is all the more noteworthy given the region's average income per person, which is quite low compared with West European and North American levels. Virtually every country in East Asia has a dynamic and highly successful family planning program. Japan, South Korea, China, Taiwan and Hong Kong rank among those countries cited as models."

In the Western Hemisphere, there is a decided difference in birth rates north and south. In the U.S. and Canada, birth rates have fallen definitively, but in Latin America, they have remained the same. "Latin America is now adding four times as many people to its population each year as is North America. Mexico alone is adding more people than are the U.S. and Canada together."

A significant reason for the drop in birth rates world wide is a growing decision by women not to have large families, and the male acceptance of this view. "The growing preference for small families [in the U.S.] was dramatically illustrated in a survey conducted in 1987 among wives aged 18 to 24, which indicated that 74 percent planned to have either one or two children. Eight years before, only 45 percent preferred one- or two-child families. . . .

"A survey of Japanese women, conducted every two years by the Population Problems Research Council, shows that for most women, the ideal number of children is dropping sharply. As recently as 1971, 33 percent wanted to have two children, but by 1975, 40 percent felt that two was the right number, and the percentage of Japanese desiring three or more decreased accordingly."

World-wide education on birth control, access to contraceptives and improvement in the status of women will help stem the world's population growth. Such a program requires money—money that can and should be taken from military budgets.

Study Questions

1. How serious a problem is global population growth? Is it a universal concern or simply a local one (which some nations like India must contend with)? Make sure you understand the idea of *exponential growth* discussed in the introduction to this chapter.

2. What are the probable consequences of exponential population growth?

3. What do you think should be done about this problem? Are voluntary solutions sufficient? (Note the different solutions in the readings that follow).

47

The Tragedy of the Commons

Garrett Hardin

Garrett Hardin argues that some social problems have no technical, *that is, scientific or technological, solution, but must be addressed by moral and political means. Exponential population growth is one such problem. Hardin calls our attention to a study of the British mathematician William Forster Lloyd (1794–1852), which demonstrates that in nonregulated areas (the "commons") individual rationality and self-interest leads to disaster. Hardin applies Lloyd's study to human population growth and argues that voluntary restriction of population by families is not adequate to deal with this problem, since many will not respond to voluntary procreation limitations. We must have "mutual coercion, mutually agreed upon by the majority of the people affected."*

A biographical sketch on Garrett Hardin is included in Reading 43.

At the end of a thoughtful article on the future of nuclear war, Wiesner and York[1] concluded that: "Both sides in the arms race are . . . confronted by the dilemma of steadily increasing military power and steadily decreasing national security. *It is our considered professional judgment that this dilemma has no technical solution.* If the great powers continue to look for solutions in the area of science and technology only, the result will be to worsen the situation."

I would like to focus your attention not on the subject of the article (national security in a nuclear world) but on the kind of conclusion they reached, namely that there is no technical solution to the problem. An implicit and almost universal assumption of discussions published in professional and semi-popular scientific journals is that the problem under discussion has a technical solution. A technical solution may be defined as one that

requires a change only in the techniques of the natural sciences, demanding little or nothing in the way of change in human values or ideas of morality.

In our day (though not in earlier times) technical solutions are always welcome. Because of previous failures in prophecy, it takes courage to assert that a desired technical solution is not possible. Wiesner and York exhibited this courage; publishing in a science journal, they insisted that the solution to the problem was not to be found in the natural sciences. They cautiously qualified their statement with the phrase, "It is our considered professional judgment. . . ." Whether they were right or not is not the concern of the present article. Rather, the concern here is with the important concept of a class of human problems which can be called "no technical solution problems," and, more specifically, with the identification and discussion of one of these.

It is easy to show that the class is not a null class. Recall the game of tick-tack-toe. Consider the problem, "How can I win the game of tick-tack-toe?" It is well known that I cannot, if I assume (in keeping with the conventions of game theory) that my opponent understands the game perfectly. Put another way, there is no "technical solution" to the problem. I can win only by giving a radical meaning to the word "win." I can hit my opponent over the head; or I can drug him; or I can falsify the records. Every way in which I "win" involves, in some sense, an abandonment of the game, as we intuitively understand it. (I can also, of course, openly abandon the game—refuse to play it. This is what most adults do.)

The class of "No technical solution problems" has members. My thesis is that the "population problem," as conventionally conceived, is a member of this class. How it is conventionally conceived needs some comment. It is fair to say that most people who anguish over the population problem are trying to find a way to avoid the evils of overpopulation without relinquishing any of the privileges they now enjoy. They think that farming the seas or developing new strains of wheat will solve the prob-

Reprinted from *Science*, Vol. 162 (December 1968) by permission of the American Association for the Advancement of Science and the author.

lem—technologically. I try to show here that the solution they seek cannot be found. The population problem cannot be solved in a technical way, any more than can the problem of winning the game of tick-tack-toe.

WHAT SHALL WE MAXIMIZE?

Population, as Malthus said, naturally tends to grow "geometrically," or, as we would now say, exponentially. In a finite world this means that the per capita share of the world's goods must steadily decrease. Is ours a finite world?

A fair defense can be put forward for the view that the world is infinite; or that we do not know that it is not. But, in terms of the practical problems that we must face in the next few generations with the foreseeable technology, it is clear that we will greatly increase human misery if we do not, during the immediate future, assume that the world available to the terrestrial human population is finite. "Space" is no escape.[2]

A finite world can support only a finite population; therefore, population growth must eventually equal zero. (The case of perpetual wide fluctuations above and below zero is a trivial variant that need not be discussed.) When this condition is met, what will be the situation of mankind? Specifically, can Bentham's goal of "the greatest good for the greatest number" be realized?

No—for two reasons, each sufficient by itself. The first is a theoretical one. It is not mathematically possible to maximize for two (or more) variables at the same time. This was clearly stated by von Neumann and Morgenstern,[3] but the principle is implicit in the theory of partial differential equations, dating back at least to D'Alembert (1717–1783).

The second reason springs directly from biological facts. To live, any organism must have a source of energy (for example, food). This energy is utilized for two purposes: mere maintenance and work. For man, maintenance of life requires about 1600 kilocalories a day ("maintenance calories"). Anything that he does over and above merely staying alive will be defined as work, and is supported by "work calories" which he takes in. Work calories are used not only for what we call work in common speech; they are also required for all forms of enjoyment, from swimming and automobile racing to playing music and writing poetry. If our goal is to maximize population it is obvious what we must do: We must make the work calories per person approach as close to zero as possible. No gourmet meals, no vacations, no sports, no music, no literature, no art. . . . I think that everyone will grant, without argument or proof, that maximizing population does not maximize goods. Bentham's goal is impossible.

In reaching this conclusion I have made the usual assumption that it is the acquisition of energy that is the problem. The appearance of atomic energy has led some to question this assumption. However, given an infinite source of energy, population growth still produces an inescapable problem. The problem of the acquisition of energy is replaced by the problem of its dissipation, as J. H. Fremlin has so wittily shown.[4] The arithmetic signs in the analysis are, as it were, reversed; but Bentham's goal is still unobtainable.

The optimum population is, then, less than the maximum. The difficulty of defining the optimum is enormous; so far as I know, no one has seriously tackled this problem. Reaching an acceptable and stable solution will surely require more than one generation of hard analytical work—and much persuasion.

We want the maximum good per person; but what is good? To one person it is wilderness, to another it is ski lodges for thousands. To one it is estuaries to nourish ducks for hunters to shoot; to another it is factory land. Comparing one good with another is, we usually say, impossible because goods are incommensurable. Incommensurables cannot be compared.

Theoretically this may be true; but in real life incommensurables *are* commensurable. Only a criterion of judgment and a system of weighting are needed. In nature the criterion is survival. Is it better for a species to be small and hideable, or large and powerful? Natural selection commensurates the incommensurables. The compromise achieved depends on a natural weighting of the values of the variables.

Man must imitate this process. There is no doubt that in fact he already does, but unconsciously. It is when the hidden decisions are made explicit that the arguments begin. The problem for the years ahead is to work out an acceptable theory of weighting. Synergistic effects, nonlinear variation, and difficulties in discounting the future make the intellectual problem difficult, but not (in principle) insoluble.

Has any cultural group solved this practical problem at the present time, even on an intuitive level? One simple fact proves that none has: there is no prosperous population in the world today that has, and has had for some time, a growth rate of zero. Any people that has intuitively identified its optimum point will soon reach it, after which its growth rate becomes and remains zero.

Of course, a positive growth rate might be taken as evidence that a population is below its optimum. However, by any reasonable standards, the most rapidly growing populations on earth today are (in general) the most miserable. This association (which need not be invariable) casts doubt on the optimistic assumption that the positive growth rate of a population is evidence that it has yet to reach its optimum.

We can make little progress in working toward optimum population size until we explicitly exorcize the spirit of Adam Smith in the field of practical demography. In economic affairs, *The Wealth of Nations* (1776) popularized the "invisible hand," the idea that an individual who "intends only his own gain," is, as it were, "led by an invisible hand to promote . . . the public interest."[5] Adam Smith did not assert that this was invariably true, and perhaps neither did any of his followers. But he contributed to a dominant tendency of thought that has ever since interfered with positive action based on rational analysis, namely, the tendency to assume that decisions reached individually will, in fact, be the best decisions for an entire society. If this assumption is correct it justifies the continuance of our present policy of laissez-faire in reproduction. If it is correct we can assume that men will control their individual fecundity so as to produce the optimum population. If the assumption is not correct, we need to reexamine our individual freedoms to see which ones are defensible.

TRAGEDY OF FREEDOM IN A COMMONS

The rebuttal to the invisible hand in population control is to be found in a scenario first sketched in a little-known pamphlet[6] in 1833 by a mathematical amateur named William Forster Lloyd (1794–1852). We may well call it "the tragedy of the commons," using the word "tragedy" as the philosopher Whitehead used it:[7] "The essence of dramatic tragedy is not unhappiness. It resides in the solemnity of the remorseless working of things." He then goes on to say, "This inevitableness of destiny can only be illustrated in terms of human life by incidents which in fact involve unhappiness. For it is only by them that the futility of escape can be made evident in the drama."

The tragedy of the commons develops in this way. Picture a pasture open to all. It is to be expected that each herdsman will try to keep as many cattle as possible on the commons. Such an arrangement may work reasonably satisfactorily for centuries because tribal wars, poaching, and disease keep the numbers of both man and beast well below the carrying capacity of the land. Finally, however, comes the day of reckoning, that is, the day when the long-desired goal of social stability becomes a reality. At this point, the inherent logic of the commons remorselessly generates tragedy.

As a rational being, each herdsman seeks to maximize his gain. Explicitly or implicitly, more or less consciously, he asks, "What is the utility *to me* of adding one more animal to my herd?" This utility has one negative and one positive component.

1. The positive component is a function of the increment of one animal. Since the herdsman receives all the proceeds from the sale of the additional animal, the positive utility is nearly + 1.
2. The negative component is a function of the additional overgrazing created by one or more animal. Since, however, the effects of overgrazing are shared by all the herdsmen, the negative utility for any particular decision-making herdsman is only a fraction of − 1.

Adding together the component partial utilities, the rational herdsman concludes that the only sensible course for him to pursue is to add another animal to his herd. And another; and another. . . . But this is the conclusion reached by each and every rational herdsman sharing a commons. Therein is the tragedy. Each man is locked into a system that compels him to increase his herd without limit—in a world that is limited. Ruin is the destination toward which all men rush, each pursuing his own best interest in a society that believes in the freedom of the commons. Freedom in a commons brings ruin to all.

Some would say that this is a platitude. Would that it were! In a sense, it was learned thousands of years ago, but natural selection favors the forces of psychological denial.[8] The individual benefits as an individual from his ability to deny the truth even though society as a whole, of which he is a part, suffers. Education can counteract the natural tendency to do the wrong thing, but the inexorable success of generations requires that the basis for this knowledge be constantly refreshed.

A simple incident that occurred a few years ago in Leominster, Massachusetts, shows how perishable the knowledge is. During the Christmas shopping season the parking meters downtown were covered with plastic bags that bore tags reading: "Do not open until after Christmas. Free parking courtesy of the mayor and city council." In other words, facing the prospect of an increased demand for already scarce space, the city fathers reinstituted the system of the commons. (Cynically, we suspect that they gained more votes than they lost by this retrogressive act.)

In an approximate way, the logic of the commons has been understood for a long time, perhaps since the discovery of agriculture or the invention of private property in real estate. But it is understood mostly only in special cases which are not sufficiently generalized. Even at this late date, cattlemen leasing national land on the western ranges demonstrate no more than an ambivalent understanding, in constantly pressuring federal authorities to increase the head count to the point where overgrazing produces erosion and weed-dominance. Likewise, the oceans of the world continue to suffer from the survival of the philosophy of the commons. Maritime nations still respond automatically to the shibboleth of the "freedom of the seas." Professing to believe in the "inexhaustible resources of the oceans," they bring species after species of fish and whales closer to extinction.[9]

The National Parks present another instance of the working out of the tragedy of the commons. At present they are open to all, without limit. The parks themselves are limited in extent—there is only one Yosemite Valley—whereas population seems to grow without limit. The values that visitors seek in the parks are steadily eroded. Plainly, we must soon cease to treat the parks as commons or they will be of no value to anyone.

What shall we do? We have several options. We might sell them off as private property. We might keep them as public property, but allocate the right to enter them. The allocation might be on the basis of wealth, by the use of an auction system. It might be on the basis of merit, as defined by some agreed-upon standards. It might be by lottery. Or it might be on a first-come, first-served basis, administered to long queues. These, I think, are all the reasonable possibilities. They are all objectionable. But we must choose—or acquiesce in the destruction of the commons that we call our National Parks.

POLLUTION

In a reverse way, the tragedy of the commons reappears in problems of pollution. Here it is not a question of taking something out of the commons, but of putting something in—sewage, or chemical, radioactive, and heat wastes into water; noxious and dangerous fumes into the air, and distracting and unpleasant advertising signs into the line of sight. The calculations of utility are much the same as before. The rational man finds that his share of the cost of the wastes he discharges into the commons is less than the cost of purifying his wastes before releasing them. Since this is true for everyone, we are locked into a system of "fouling our own nest," so long as we behave only as independent, rational, free-enterprisers.

The tragedy of the commons as a food basket is averted by private property, or something formally like it. But the air and waters surrounding us cannot readily be fenced, and so the tragedy of the commons as a cesspool must be prevented by different means, by coercive laws or taxing devices that make it cheaper for the polluter to treat his pollutants than to discharge them untreated. We have not progressed as far with the solution of this problem as we have with the first. Indeed, our particular concept of private property, which deters us from exhausting the positive resources of the earth, favors pollution. The owner of a factory on the bank of a stream—whose property extends to the middle of the stream—often has difficulty seeing why it is not his natural right to muddy the waters flowing past his door. The law, always behind the times, requires elaborate stitching and fitting to adapt it to this newly perceived aspect of the commons.

The pollution problem is a consequence of population. It did not much matter how a lonely American frontiersman disposed of his waste. "Flowing water purifies itself every 10 miles," my grandfather used to say, and the myth was near enough to the truth when he was a boy, for there were not too many people. But as population became denser, the natural chemical and biological recycling processes became overloaded, calling for a redefinition of property rights.

HOW TO LEGISLATE TEMPERANCE?

Analysis of the pollution problem as a function of population density uncovers a not generally recognized principle of morality, namely: *the morality of an act is a function of the state of the system at the time it is performed.*[10] Using the commons as a cesspool does not harm the general public under frontier conditions, because there is no public; the same behavior in a metropolis is unbearable. A hundred and fifty years ago a plainsman could kill an American bison, cut out only the tongue for his dinner, and discard the rest of the animal. He was not in any important sense being wasteful. Today, with only a few thousand bison left, we would be appalled at such behavior.

In passing, it is worth noting that the morality of an act cannot be determined from a photograph. One does not know whether a man killing an elephant or setting fire to the grassland is harming others until one knows the total system in which his act appears. "One picture is worth a thousand words" said an ancient Chinese; but it may take 10,000 words to validate it. It is as tempting to ecologists as it is to reformers in general to try to persuade others by way of the photographic shortcut. But the essence of an argument cannot be photographed: it must be presented rationally—in words.

That morality is system-sensitive escaped the attention of most codifiers of ethics in the past. "Thou shalt not . . ." is the form of traditional ethical directives which make no allowance for particular circumstances. The laws of our society follow the pattern of ancient ethics, and therefore are poorly suited to governing a complex, crowded, changeable world. Our epicyclic solution is to augment statutory law with administrative law. Since it is practically impossible to spell out all the conditions under which it is safe to burn trash in the backyard or to run an automobile without smog-control, by law we delegate the details to bureaus. The result is administrative law, which is rightly feared for an ancient reason—*Quis custodiet ipsos custodes?*—"Who shall watch the watchers themselves?" John Adams said that we must have "a government of laws and not men." Bureau administrators, trying to evaluate the morality of acts in the total system, are singularly liable to corruption, producing a government by men, not laws.

Prohibition is easy to legislate (though not necessarily to enforce); but how do we legislate temperance? Experience indicates that it can be accomplished best through the mediation of administrative law. We limit possibilities unnecessarily if we suppose that the sentiment of *Quis custodiet* denies us the use of administrative law. We should rather retain the phrase as a perpetual reminder of fearful dangers we cannot avoid.

The great challenge facing us now is to invent the corrective feedbacks that are needed to keep custodians honest. We must find ways to legitimate the needed authority of both the custodians and the corrective feedbacks.

FREEDOM TO BREED IS INTOLERABLE

The tragedy of the commons is involved in population problems in another way. In a world governed solely by the principle of "dog eat dog"—if indeed there ever was such a world—how many children a family had would not be a matter of public concern. Parents who bred too exuberantly would leave fewer descendants, not more, because they would be unable to care adequately for their children. David Lack and others have found that such a negative feedback demonstrably controls the fecundity of birds.[11] But men are not birds, and have not acted like them for millenniums, at least.

If each human family were dependent only on its own resources; *if* the children of improvident parents starved to death; *if,* thus, overbreeding brought its own "punishment" to the germ line—*then* there would be no public interest in controlling the breeding of families. But our society is deeply committed to the welfare state,[12] and hence is confronted with another aspect of the tragedy of the commons.

In a welfare state, how shall we deal with the family, the religion, the race, or the class (or indeed any distinguishable and cohesive group) that adopts overbreeding as a policy to secure its own aggrandizement?[13] To couple the concept of freedom to breed with the belief that everyone born has an equal right to the commons is to lock the world into a tragic course of action.

Unfortunately this is just the course of action that is being pursued by the United Nations. In late 1967, some 30 nations agreed to the following:[14]

> The Universal Declaration of Human Rights describes the family as the natural and fundamental unit of society. It follows that any choice and decision with regard to the size of the family must irrevocably rest with the family itself, and cannot be made by anyone else.

It is painful to have to deny categorically the validity of this right; denying it, one feels as uncomfortable as a resident of Salem, Massachusetts, who denied the reality of witches in the 17th century. At the present time, in liberal quarters, something like a taboo acts to inhibit criticism of the United Nations. There is a feeling that the United Nations is "our last and best hope," that we shouldn't find fault with it; we shouldn't play into the hands of the archconservatives. However, let us not forget what Robert Louis Stevenson said: "The truth that is suppressed by friends is the readiest weapon of the enemy." If we love the truth we must openly deny the validity of the Universal Declaration of Human Rights, even though it is promoted by the United Nations. We

should also join with Kingsley Davis[15] in attempting to get Planned Parenthood–World Population to see the error of its ways in embracing the same tragic ideal.

CONSCIENCE IS SELF-ELIMINATING

It is a mistake to think that we can control the breeding of mankind in the long run by an appeal to conscience. Charles Galton Darwin made this point when he spoke on the centennial of the publication of his grandfather's great book. The argument is straightforward and Darwinian.

People vary. Confronted with appeals to limit breeding, some people will undoubtedly respond to the plea more than others. Those who have more children will produce a larger fraction of the next generation than those with more susceptible consciences. The difference will be accentuated, generation by generation.

In C. G. Darwin's words: "It may well be that it would take hundreds of generations for the progenitive instinct to develop in this way, but if it should do so, nature would have taken her revenge, and the variety *Homo contracipiens* would become extinct and would be replaced by the variety *Homo progenitivus.*"[16]

The argument assumes that conscience or the desire for children (no matter which) is hereditary—but hereditary only in the most general formal sense. The result will be the same whether the attitude is transmitted through germ cells, or exosomatically, to use A. J. Lotka's term. (If one denies the latter possibility as well as the former, then what's the point of education?) The argument has here been stated in the context of the population problem, but it applies equally well to any instance in which society appeals to an individual exploiting a commons to restrain himself for the general good—by means of his conscience. To make such an appeal is to set up a selective system that works toward the elimination of conscience from the race.

PATHOGENIC EFFECTS OF CONSCIENCE

The long-term disadvantage of an appeal to conscience should be enough to condemn it; it has serious short-term disadvantages as well. If we ask a man who is exploiting a commons to desist "in the name of conscience," what are we saying to him? What does he hear?—not only at the moment but also in the wee small hours of the night when, half asleep, he remembers not merely the words we used but also the nonverbal communication cues we gave him unawares? Sooner or later, consciously or subconsciously, he senses that he has received two communications, and that they are contradictory: (i) (intended communication) "If you don't do as we ask, we will openly condemn you for not acting like a responsible citizen"; (ii) (the unintended communication) "If you *do* behave as we ask, we will secretly condemn you for a simpleton who can be shamed into standing aside while the rest of us exploit the commons."

Everyman then is caught in what Bateson has called a "double bind." Bateson and his co-workers have made a plausible case for viewing the double bind as an important causative factor in the genesis of schizophrenia.[17] The double bind may not always be so damaging, but it always endangers the mental health of anyone to whom it is applied. "A bad conscience," said Nietzsche, "is a kind of illness."

To conjure up a conscience in others is tempting to anyone who wishes to extend his control beyond the legal limits. Leaders at the highest level succumb to this temptation. Has any President during the past generation failed to call on labor unions to moderate voluntarily their demands for higher wages, or to steel companies to honor voluntary guidelines on prices? I can recall none. The rhetoric used on such occasions is designed to produce feelings of guilt in noncooperators.

For centuries it was assumed without proof that guilt was a valuable, perhaps even indispensable, ingredient of the civilized life. Now, in this post-Freudian world, we doubt it.

Paul Goodman speaks from the modern point of view when he says: "No good has ever come from feeling guilty, neither intelligence, policy, nor compassion. The guilty do not pay attention to the object but only to themselves, and not even to their own interests, which might make sense, but to their anxieties."[18]

One does not have to be a professional psychiatrist to see the consequences of anxiety. We in the Western world are just emerging from a dreadful two-centuries-long Dark Ages of Eros that was sustained partly by prohibition laws, but perhaps more effectively by the anxiety-generating mechanisms of education. Alex Comfort has told the story well in *The Anxiety Makers*;[19] it is not a pretty one.

Since proof is difficult, we may even concede that the results of anxiety may sometimes, from certain points of view, be desirable. The larger question we should ask is whether, as a matter of policy, we should ever encourage the use of a technique the tendency (if not the intention) of which is psychologically pathogenic. We hear much talk these days of responsible parenthood; the coupled words are incorporated into the titles of some organizations devoted to birth control. Some people have proposed massive propaganda campaigns to instill responsibility into the nation's (or the world's) breeders. But what is the meaning of the word responsibility in this context? Is it not merely a synonym for the word conscience? When we use the word responsibility in the absence of substantial sanctions are we not trying to browbeat a free man in a commons into acting against his own interest? Responsibility is a verbal counterfeit for a substantial *quid pro quo*. It is an attempt to get something for nothing.

If the word responsibility is to be used at all, I suggest that it be in the sense Charles Frankel uses it.[20] "Responsibility," says this philosopher, "is the product of definite social arrangements." Notice that Frankel calls for social arrangements—not propaganda.

MUTUAL COERCION MUTUALLY AGREED UPON

The social arrangements that produce responsibility are arrangements that create coercion, of some sort. Consider bank-robbing. The man who takes money from a bank acts as if the bank were a commons. How do we prevent such action? Certainly not by trying to control his behavior solely by a verbal appeal to his sense of responsibility. Rather than rely on propaganda we follow Frankel's lead and insist that a bank is not a commons; we seek the definite social arrangements that will keep it from becoming a commons. That we thereby infringe on the freedom of would-be robbers we neither deny nor regret.

The morality of bank-robbing is particularly easy to understand because we accept complete prohibition of this activity. We are willing to say "Thou shalt not rob banks," without providing for exceptions. But temperance also can be created by coercion. Taxing is a good coercive device. To keep downtown shoppers temperate in their use of parking space we introduce parking meters for short periods, and traffic fines for longer ones. We need not actually forbid a citizen to park as long as he wants to; we need merely make it increasingly expensive for him to do so. Not prohibition, but carefully biased options are what we offer him. A Madison Avenue man might call this persuasion; I prefer the greater candor of the word coercion.

Coercion is a dirty word to most liberals now, but it need not forever be so. As with the four-letter words, its dirtiness can be cleansed away by exposure to light, by saying it over and over without apology or embarrassment. To many, the word coercion implies arbitrary decisions of distant and irresponsible bureaucrats; but this is not a necessary part of its meaning. The only kind of coercion I recommend is mutual coercion, mutually agreed upon by the majority of the people affected.

To say that we mutually agree to coercion is not to say that we are required to enjoy it, or even to pretend we enjoy it. Who enjoys taxes? We all grumble about them. But we accept compulsory taxes because we recognize that voluntary taxes would favor the conscienceless. We institute and (grumblingly) support taxes and other coercive devices to escape the horror of the commons.

An alternative to the commons need not be perfectly just to be preferable. With real estate and other material goods, the alternative we have chosen is the institution of private property coupled with legal inheritance. Is this system perfectly just? As a genetically trained biologist I deny that it is. It seems to me that, if there are to be differences in individual inheritance, legal possession should be perfectly correlated with biological inheritance—that those who are biologically more fit to be the custodians of property and power should legally inherit more. But genetic recombination continually makes a mockery of the doctrine of "like father, like son" implicit in our laws of legal inheritance. An idiot can inherit millions, and a trust fund can keep his estate intact. We must admit that our legal system of private property plus inheritance is unjust—but we put up with it because we are not convinced, at the moment, that anyone has invented a better system. The alternative of the commons is too horrifying to contemplate. Injustice is preferable to total ruin.

It is one of the peculiarities of the warfare between reform and the status quo that it is thoughtlessly governed by a double standard. Whenever a reform measure is proposed it is often defeated when its opponents triumphantly discover a flaw in it. As Kingsley Davis has pointed out,[21] worshippers of the status quo sometimes imply that no reform is possible without unanimous agreement, an implication contrary to historical fact. As nearly as I can make out, automatic rejection of proposed reforms is based on one of two unconscious assumptions: (i) that the status quo is perfect; or (ii) that the choice we face is between reform and no action; if the proposed reform is imperfect, we presumably should take no action at all, while we wait for a perfect proposal.

But we can never do nothing. That which we have done for thousands of years is also action. It also produces evils. Once we are aware that the status quo is action, we can then compare its discoverable advantages and disadvantages with the predicted advantages and disadvantages of the proposed reform, discounting as best we can for our lack of experience. On the basis of such a comparison, we can make a rational decision which will not involve the unworkable assumption that only perfect systems are tolerable.

RECOGNITION OF NECESSITY

Perhaps the simplest summary of this analysis of man's population problems is this: the commons, if justifiable at all, is justifiable only under conditions of low-population density. As the human population has increased, the commons has had to be abandoned in one aspect after another.

First we abandoned the commons in food gathering, enclosing farm land and restricting pastures and hunting and fishing areas. These restrictions are still not complete throughout the world.

Somewhat later we saw that the commons as a place

for water disposal would also have to be abandoned. Restrictions on the disposal of domestic sewage are widely accepted in the Western world; we are still struggling to close the commons to pollution by automobiles, factories, insecticide sprayers, fertilizing operations, and atomic energy installations.

In a still more embryonic state is our recognition of the evils of the commons in matters of pleasure. There is almost no restriction on the propagation of sound waves in the public medium. The shopping public is assaulted with mindless music, without its consent. Our government is paying out billions of dollars to create supersonic transport which will disturb 50,000 people for every one person who is whisked from coast to coast 3 hours faster. Advertisers muddy the airwaves of radio and television and pollute the view of travelers. We are a long way from outlawing the commons in matters of pleasure. Is this because our Puritan inheritance makes us view pleasure as something of a sin, and pain (that is, the pollution of advertising) as the sign of virtue?

Every new enclosure of the commons involves the infringement of somebody's personal liberty. Infringements made in the distant past are accepted because no contemporary complains of a loss. It is the newly proposed infringements that we vigorously oppose; cries of "rights" and "freedom" fill the air. But what does "freedom" mean? When men mutually agreed to pass laws against robbing, mankind became more free, not less so. Individuals locked into the logic of the commons are free only to bring on universal ruin; once they see the necessity of mutual coercion, they become free to pursue other goals. I believe it was Hegel who said, "Freedom is the recognition of necessity."

The most important aspect of necessity that we must now recognize, is the necessity of abandoning the commons in breeding. No technical solution can rescue us from the misery of overpopulation. Freedom to breed will bring ruin to all. At the moment, to avoid hard decisions many of us are tempted to propagandize for conscience and responsible parenthood. The temptation must be resisted, because an appeal to independently acting consciences selects for the disappearance of all conscience in the long run, and an increase in anxiety in the short.

The only way we can preserve and nurture other and more precious freedoms is by relinquishing the freedom to breed, and that very soon. "Freedom is the recognition of necessity"—and it is the role of education to reveal to all the necessity of abandoning the freedom to breed. Only so, can we put an end to this aspect of the tragedy of the commons.

Notes

1. J. B. Wiesner and H. F. York, *Sci. Amer.* 211 (No. 44), 27 (1964).
2. G. Hardin, *J. Hered.* 50, 68 (1959); S. von Hoernor, *Science* 137, 18 (1962).

3. J. von Neumann and O. Morgenstern, *Theory of Games and Economic Behavior* (Princeton Univ. Press, Princeton, NJ: 1947), p. 11.
4. J. H. Fremlin, *New Sci.*, No. 415 (1964), p. 285.
5. A. Smith, *The Wealth of Nations* (Modern Library, New York, 1937), p. 423.
6. W. F. Lloyd, *Two Lectures on the Checks to Population* (Oxford Univ. Press, Oxford, England, 1833), reprinted (in part) in *Population, Evolution, and Birth Control*, G. Hardin, Ed. (Freeman, San Francisco, 1964), p. 37.
7. A. N. Whitehead, *Science and the Modern World* (Mentor, New York, 1948), p. 17.
8. G. Hardin, Ed., *Population, Evolution and Birth Control* (Freeman, San Francisco, 1964), p. 56.
9. S. McVay, *Sci. Amer.* 216 (No. 8), 13 (1966).
10. J. Fletcher, *Situation Ethics* (Westminster, Philadelphia, 1966).
11. D. Lack, *The Natural Regulation of Animal Numbers* (Clarendon Press, Oxford, 1954).
12. H. Girvetz, *From Wealth to Welfare* (Stanford Univ. Press, Stanford, Calif., 1950).
13. G. Hardin, *Perspec. Biol. Med.* 6, 366 (1963).
14. U Thant, *Int. Planned Parenthood News*, No. 168 (February 1968), p. 3.
15. K. Davis, *Science*, 158, 730 (1967).
16. S. Tax, Ed., *Evolution After Darwin* (Univ. of Chicago Press, Chicago, 1960), vol. 2, p. 469.
17. G. Bateson, D. D. Jackson, J. Haley, J. Weakland, *Behav. Sci.* 1, 251 (1956).
18. P. Goodman, *New York Rev. Books* 1968, 10 (8), 22 (23 May 1968).
19. A. Comfort, *The Anxiety Makers* (Nelson, London, 1967).
20. C. Frankel, *The Case for Modern Man* (Harper, New York, 1955), p. 203.
21. J. D. Roslansky, *Genetics and the Future of Man* (Appleton-Century-Crofts, New York. 1966), p. 177.

Study Questions

1. What does Hardin mean when he says that the problem of population growth has no technical solution?
2. What does Hardin mean when he says, "Freedom in a commons brings ruin to all"? How does he define true "freedom" at the end of his essay?
3. Explain the idea of the tragedy of the commons as first set forth by William Forster Lloyd. How does it work?
4. How does Hardin apply the tragedy of the commons to human population growth? Do you agree with his analysis? Explain.
5. What does Hardin mean by "conscience is self-eliminating"? What is wrong with appealing to conscience to solve environmental problems?
6. How serious is the current population growth? What do you think should be done about it?

48

The Central Immigration Issue: How Many Americans?

LINDSEY GRANT

Lindsey Grant writes on population and public policy. A retired foreign service officer, he was a China specialist and served as director of the Office of Asian Communist Affairs, a National Security Council staff member, and a Department of State Policy Planning Staff member.

As Deputy Assistant Secretary of State for Environment and Population Affairs, he was Department of State coordinator for the Global 2000 *Report to the President, chairman of the Interagency Committee on International Environmental Affairs, U.S. delegate to (and vice-chairman of) the OECD Environment Committee, and U.S. member of the U.N. ECE Committee of Experts on the Environment.*

His books include Foresight and National Decisions: The Horseman and the Bureaucrat (*University Press of* America, 1988), Elephants in the Volkswagen (*a study of optimum U.S. population, published in 1992 (Freeman),* How Many Americans? (*with Leon Bouvier, Sierra Club Books, 1994*), *and* Juggernaut: Growth on a Small Planet (*Seven Locks Press, 1996*). *Grant has written the following abstract:*

The critical issue for immigration policy is its demographic impact: What is the effect on U.S. population growth? The more frequently debated questions—welfare costs and problems of cultural assimilation—are far more manageable. The population of the United States has already passed the optimum level and is not environmentally sustainable, but if unchecked it is headed for a doubling to about 500 million in the coming century, and immigration will be the source of 90% of that growth. The "two-child" family and immigration at the levels of the 1920s–1960s would lead to an actual turnaround in

This essay was commissioned for this edition and appears here in print for the first time.

U.S. population growth. One can understand why moral people may believe we must take in high levels of immigration, but their moral fervor is misplaced. It leads them to ignore our own poor and the environment we leave to our descendants, and it will eventually diminish, not enhance, our ability to help others.

As 1996 comes to a close, Congress has passed an election year "immigration reform" bill that effectively sidetracks a determined bipartisan effort to bring illegal immigration under control and to reduce legal immigration. For those concerned about immigration, the questions are again posed: Must we try again to reform the immigration system? Why do we feel that something must be done about immigration? What are the objectives of immigration laws?[1]

THE CENTRAL ISSUE AND THE SECONDARY ISSUES

Let me state the proposition at the outset. The central purpose of any immigration policy should be demographic: to help determine how many Americans there will be. It is not simply a question of being for or against immigrants or of saving money on welfare costs.

I will argue that we should seek as small a population increase as we can decently achieve and ideally a reversal of the present population growth. Pursuit of this objective will require the limitation of immigration to annual numbers approximating the rate from the 1920s to the 1960s. It will require that we control the generous tendency to welcome immigrants, and it will require that we think as a nation, not simply as interest groups.

Immigrants are, of course, individuals and not simply numbers, and the United States is justified in choosing among them, limiting certain kinds and encouraging others. We need to keep alien terrorists out of the United States (a particularly timely issue). We have concerns about health and epidemic control and drug smuggling. We prefer to decide who will come, rather than having others such as Fidel Castro do it for us, as he did in the "Mariel boatlift" of 1980. We have legitimate concerns about the very illegality of much immigration and about the strains that concentrated immigration impose on local governments' education, medical, and welfare services.

If these were indeed the only issues, most of them could be addressed (as some have suggested) by making all immigration legal and screening out the undesirable individuals or those most likely to become public charges.

Some have advocated reduced immigration on the grounds of cultural assimilation problems, particularly the concern that massive concentration of immigration from Spanish-speaking countries could lead to a bilingual society. The fragmentation of Yugoslavia and the problems of Belgium, Cyprus, Canada, Sri Lanka, and Spain with its Basque minority come immediately to mind. This concern is legitimate and it is not necessarily racist. (American national policies can now be defended as genuinely anti-racist, and current immigration law is in fact intended to diversify the national sources of immigration.) The possibility of being simply swamped by other cultures is a legitimate subject for examination, given the population pressures in the third world and the United States' magnetic pull. However, cultural diversity is itself a source of richness and creativity, and we are right to be proud of it. The nation has been remarkably successful in the past in absorbing diverse cultural streams and profiting thereby.

Environmental, resource, and economic constraints on the growth of the country's population will require much more stringent limits on the numbers of immigrants than the cultural argument alone would justify. (For the moment, I am assuming that the United States makes the effort to assimilate the immigrants. This is by no means current national policy; I will return to that problem.)

This brings up the question: How many Americans?

THE NUMBERS

Let us look briefly at U.S. population trends. The United States is alone among the large industrial nations in its continued population growth, something that has happened by accident rather than design but has tremendous ramifications.

The nation's population more than trebled from 76 million in 1900 to nearly 270 million now. About 43% of that growth consisted of post-1900 immigrants and their descendants. It is useful to graph the numbers, starting with our first census in 1790 (Figure 1). That growth is taking place in space that no longer grows.

COMING CHANGE

A conservative projection leads to a population of 397 million in 2050 and 492 million in 2100 (Figure 2), if fertility declines.[2] About 91% of the growth after 2000 will be post-2000 immigrants and their descendants. The lower bars show where we would go without any migration after 2000. Immigration is the driving force in a remarkable and continuing population surge. A less conservative projection, assuming that fertility and immigration stay where they are, leads to a population of 440 million by 2050 and passing 1/2 a billion long before the end of the century.[3]

The Census Bureau has adopted rather similar projections. Its middle projection for 2050 is 394 million,

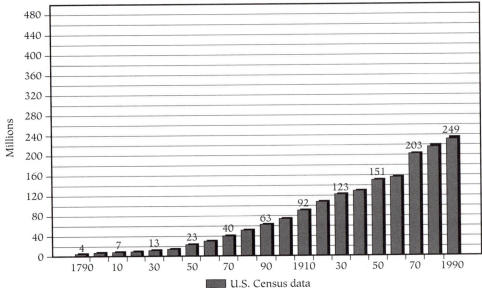

FIGURE 1

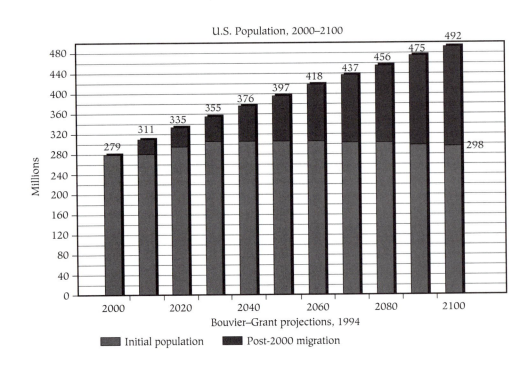

FIGURE 2

a rise of 50%. (They raised that estimate by 100 million after Congress passed the Immigration Act of 1990.) Their high projection reaches 518 million, a doubling, by 2050.

Growth will be even faster if fertility rises. Most migration is coming from societies more fertile than ours. Most projections assume that migrants' fertility will decline to the present general average, but there is at least as good reason to assume that they will raise that average, as they and their descendants come to constitute a larger fraction of the population. In other

words, those projections may be too low. There is a phenomenon the demographers call *shifting shares*. Over time, the more fertile segments of the population will become a larger proportion of the total and will thus increase total fertility and population growth. This is the human equivalent of Darwinian natural selection.[4]

The expectation of shifting shares rests on two assumptions: (1) Higher mortality does not counteract higher fertility, and (2) succeeding generations follow the patterns of their parents. Both assumptions are holding true in California, the largest state and the largest immigrant-receiving state.

These projections will probably all turn out wrong, because fertility and immigration are always changing, but they raise a note of caution: *If you are headed somewhere, you may get there.* Whichever projection you choose, it begins to put us in a league with China and India, and we would be far more destructive because of our consumption levels.

MIGRATION DATA

U.S. data on migration are remarkably bad. illegal immigration is by its nature uncounted. The Census Bureau makes heroic efforts to include illegal immigrants in the census, but people who do not want to be seen will avoid both the census and the spot surveys that are used to "validate" the original count. The Immigration and Naturalization Service (INS) stopped trying to count emigrants in 1957, and death records are not matched against immigration data, so residual totals are not available. There are literally hundreds of millions of border crossings by land each year. Most of them are not individually tabulated, and there is no way to sort out how many are permanent entrants or departures. There is no system of identification for citizens and legal residents and thus no effective way to identify who is here illegally. The INS does not count "immigration" by the number of arrivals, but rather by the number whose status is "regularized." In other words, the illegal immigrant or overstaying visitor is not counted until his/her status is legalized by such processes as an amnesty, marriage, or grant of asylum.

For what it's worth, the Census Bureau figure for annual illegal immigrants (delicately referred to as "undocumented aliens") has been around 200,000–225,000 for a decade. The INS has variously cited figures from 300,000 to 500,000, and its border patrol regularly suggests a much higher figure. Airline manifests covering arrivals and departures by air are of uncertain accuracy, but they suggest that illegal immigration by air alone (people overstaying nonimmigrant visas) may be several times as high as the official estimates of all illegal immigration.[5]

The Center for Immigration Studies undertakes to estimate the actual annual totals, using census and INS data on legal immigration and using the INS estimate of 300,000 illegal immigrants annually. As I have suggested, that may far understate the real movement. In any event, here are its results:

FY 1992: 1,183,000

FY 1993: 1,272,000

FY 1994: 1,268,000

FY 1995: 1,206,000

(Fiscal years [FY] end on September 30 rather than December 31.)[6] The INS tentatively estimates that legal immigration rose 41% in FY 1996.

We don't just need better control; we need better numbers on migration if there is to be is any serious effort to deal with population growth.

THE DEMOGRAPHIC ARGUMENT

Is there danger in continuing population growth? We live in a time of explosive technological and demographic change. In two or three generations, the human race has altered its ways of living and its relationships with Earth more profoundly than it did during the transformation from hunter-gatherer to tiller of the soil, which took millennia to accomplish. More people have been added to world population since 1950 than in all preceding time. As to the consequences, I have summarized the evidence elsewhere (see note 1). I will recount it only briefly here.

In less than 50 years, we have quadrupled the use of fossil energy (which was globally insignificant a century ago) and introduced nuclear energy. In the United States and worldwide, the use of chemical fertilizer has increased tenfold and pesticides and herbicides much more. There has been an exponential growth in the introduction of new chemicals.[7] These changes have brought prosperity to many, and society is tempted to keep playing a winning system. The problem lies in the by-products—the unintended consequences—of the new technologies. Our activities affect Earth's natural systems in ways unimaginable a century ago.

The technological revolution has been remarkably successful in producing economic goods. It has been even more successful in producing waste. When you drive your car, you use 1% or 2% of the energy in the gasoline to move you, 13% to move the vehicle, and you discard the remaining 87% as waste heat and exhaust gases, which in turn contribute to issues as diverse as human illness and world climate change.[8]

Nobody—literally nobody—understands the implications of the new reliance upon manmade chemicals. Of the chemicals important to commerce "only a few have been subjected to extensive toxicity testing and most have scarcely been tested at all."[9] That statement is about immediate, direct toxicity. Much less do we understand the processes when chemicals and heavy metals are transformed, redistributed, and released into nature.

Technological change—automation, computerization, robotics—is fundamentally altering the labor market and decreasing the need for labor. That change is intensified by population growth; third world working-age population grows about 60 million each year, and many of those people are desperate for work, anywhere.

The energy revolution is acidifying the soils and killing the forests of the northern temperate zone. The damage to conifers in New England, the southern Appalachians, and parts of California has been widely reported. Although the extent of damage is still the subject of scientific controversy, it is becoming increasingly clear that forest damage results, not simply from acidity but from the interplay of multiple stresses resulting from modern economic activity: ozone, acidic deposition, sulfur dioxide, and nitrogen oxides (in order of importance).[10]

More profound even than the loss of forests is this warning from a scientific panel convened by the White House:

> We as a committee are especially concerned about possible deleterious effects of a sustained increase in the acidity of unmanaged soils. [Their] microorganism population is particularly sensitive to a change in acidity. But it is just this bottom part of the biological cycle that is responsible for the recycling of nitrogen and carbon in the food chain. The proper functioning of the denitrifying microbes is a fundamental requirement upon which the entire biosphere depends. The evidence that increased acidity is perturbing populations of microorganisms is scanty, but the prospect of such an occurrence is grave. It may take many years of accumulation of acidity, from wet or dry deposition, before measurable consequences would be observed.
>
> Such an effect is "long-term" or "irreversible." . . .[11]

This is a remarkably serious warning couched in the understatement of science. It is perhaps the nearest thing to a doomsday warning that has resulted from any environmental problem. NAPAP (the official group charged with studying the consequences of acid precipitation) was warned by its scientific oversight board in 1991 that it had not given enough attention to exploring the effects of acid precipitation on microbes[12], and the 1992 report does not indicate that they have yet been seriously explored.

Almost as profound is the prospect of worldwide climate changes resulting from the increase in atmospheric carbon dioxide and trace gases resulting from human economic activities. The Intergovernmental Panel on Climate Change (IPCC) in December 1995 produced its Second Assessment of climate change and its probable results. It warned that human activities are changing the climate, and it predicted that among the anticipated consequences in the next century are major shifts in agriculture caused by changing rainfall patterns, plus the flooding of low-lying coasts by rising sea levels. Sea levels are already rising, and the climate is getting warmer. There is debate among scientists about the timing, speed, and specific consequences of the process, but there is very little dissent about the direction in which man-made atmospheric changes are driving climate.

The IPCC noted that carbon dioxide, methane, and nitrous oxide together cause about 80% of the anthro-

pogenic climate forcing. Most of the IPCC scenarios indicate that atmospheric concentrations (expressed in "CO_2 equivalent") will more than double in the next century. It would take "an immediate 50%–70% reduction in CO_2 emissions, and further reductions later on, to stabilize atmospheric carbon dioxide at current levels" (my emphasis). That reduction is probably impossible with a world population of even the present size; it is certainly impossible with a rising one. The United States, with its combination of a large and growing population and high emission levels, will play a critical role in determining just how bad climate warming becomes.

Even if the immediate stabilization of greenhouse gases were (miraculously) achieved, the present level of climate forcing would continue, and "global mean surface temperature would continue to rise for some centuries and sea level for many centuries."[13] But real-world emissions are rising rather than falling, driving atmospheric concentrations further upward.

Let me make clear the remarkable magnitude of what the Second Assessment is saying:

- At present levels of human activity, we are driving climate toward unknown patterns in future centuries, with serious consequences in the next century—bearing most heavily on those parts of the world least able to adjust—and uncertain consequences in centuries beyond, including perhaps a rising ocean flooding coastal plains where much of the world population lives.
- That change will accelerate in all but one of the six projections of future development.
- Even with their best efforts, the IPCC cannot imagine how we could stop the human impact; only with luck could we hold it close to its current levels.

I would propose that a realistic solution to global warming demands: (1) the enthusiastic adoption of alternative energy sources, (2) coupled with a determined effort to hold population growth down to the lowest attainable level and to reverse it as soon as possible. When the human race is changing the air it breathes and the climate it lives in, it would seem cause for more concern than is yet evident.

The world has indeed entered a new era, when economic activities may need to be changed or redirected, not because they fail to achieve the results intended but because of the unintended results. The ban on DDT the environmental legislation of the 1970s, and the current efforts throughout the industrial world to reduce the release of nitrogen and sulfur oxides into the atmosphere are just the precursors of a new process whereby economic activities must be judged, not just in terms of their direct results but in the context of the planet that supports them, if they are not to destroy us. The United States more than any other single nation will need to reduce its environmental impacts to avoid perils such as I have described.

How do population and immigration policies relate to these issues?

The point is that solutions can be envisaged for problems such as I have identified, but population is itself a central element of the equation. Population growth intensifies the socioeconomic and environmental problems the world and the nation face. It diminishes the resources available to deal with them.

THE IMMEDIATE AND THE LONG TERM

The argument concerning the effects of population growth on the United States can conveniently be separated into two time frames:

- The immediate: employment, opportunity and our obligation to American youth and minorities, "The American dream," and the social consequences when it dissolves—alienation, a nation increasingly divided between the rich and the poor, and the accompanying social turmoil.
- The long term: resources, the energy transition, environmental change, and the national patrimony.

The *immediate issues* center upon the role of immigration on the labor market. The potential immigrant labor supply is, for practical purposes, infinite. An increase in the supply of a commodity tends to drive the price of that commodity down. In this instance, the commodity is labor, and the ultimate floor price is subsistence-level wages such as prevail in much of the world today.

America's poor (and particularly its minorities) suffer from an expansion of the labor force. We are no longer a frontier. Technology is driving us. Automation makes possible enormous productivity for a few workers, if the capital is available to buy the technology. Those who cannot gain entry into the modern sector either lower their wages to compete with the machines, move into the service sector, or drop out of the labor force to become part of the floating, restless, and frequently alienated permanently unemployed.

We used to speak of the "American dream"—a decent and improving living in return for honest work, with the related ideal of a mass market of prosperous workers. We have gone the other way in the past few years and now have the widest income differentials in the industrial world. Those differentials are growing, as is the proportion of Americans below the poverty line. To acquiesce in a steadily widening income gap would be to abandon an attractive ideal and a source of national strength. It would be dangerous to assume that American workers would remain politically inert through such a process.

Proposals have been made about how to address the structural changes in the economy. The task is not easy.

There is, however, one unassailable observation: The task will be far harder if the labor supply—particularly at the skill levels at which most new American workers seek entry—is indefinitely expansible.

The need to protect the living standards of disadvantaged Americans should be one constraint on permissible levels of immigration.

The *long term issues* revolve about an inescapable moral choice: Are we willing to live by the slogan *carpe diem* and pass a poorer environment to our descendants? To people of that persuasion, there is no future, and ecological arguments are irrelevant. However, most of us would prefer not to take a downward road, and we sense an obligation to pass an undiminished patrimony on to future generations.

Any measurement of resources, seen from that viewpoint, is meaningless unless it is per capita. Let me illustrate by starting with forests. Pronatalists have used total U.S. timber resources as an argument that we need not worry about population growth. Let's look more closely. From 1952 until 1987, the figures for total standing timber rose by 24%.[14] The official estimate of standing stock in the west declined 10% in the period. The growth was in Southeastern pine plantations—a reflection of the same trend toward monoculture that has made our agriculture vulnerable—and in unmanaged northeastern hardwood forests. (Pastures that once fed workhorses before the advent of the tractor are still reverting to woodland.) So far so good. The drawback is that our total population in that period rose by 57%, so the per capita stand went down 21%—even if the official data are not cooked, which they may well be.

Overharvesting is not the only change that threatens our forests. The industrial age itself threatens them, in the form of pollution, acid rain, and the prospect of rapid global warming. At the most sanguine, the conclusion is that U.S. forests are potentially threatened by the present pattern of industrial growth and economic activity, which in turn is driven, as we have seen, by the size of the population to be served.

Problems such as these do not involve absolutes. One can always ameliorate them through substitutions—in turn raising questions as to the consequences of the substitution—or through technology. We can build with masonry or fiberglass, grow supertrees (at an environmental cost), build flimsier houses or smaller ones, or shift land from cropland or pasture to forests—all of which we have been doing. We can lessen our atmospheric and climate impacts by retreating to a primitive standard of living.

Technology, substitution, and conservation defer problems and sometimes shift them, but they do not dispose of demography. There comes a time when society must face trade-offs between halting population growth or face increasingly stringent limits on per-capita levels of pollution and resource use—and this country is into that era.

Let me continue with the example of forests. Partly to save those timber stocks from acid rain, Congress in the Acid Deposition Control Program set a target of reducing sulfur emissions (mostly by the power industry) by 10 million tons, or nearly half. There are coal-gasification technologies that could help achieve that ambitious goal, but they are expensive. It can be done more easily if total energy demand is not being pushed up by population growth.

The other principal source of acid precipitation is automobiles. We can still improve mileage per gallon, perhaps by shifting to fuel-cell engines, but technical fixes alone may not be enough. The total mileage driven may need to be constrained. The larger the population, the fewer miles per person. Per-capita consumption—your consumption—may be circumscribed by U.S. population growth, which is determined in turn by the realities of immigration.

The United States' arable acreage is somewhat larger than China's, and one periodically hears that the United States has no population problem, that it could support a population as large as China's. Fine, but what does "support" mean? At what level? Would you like to eat their diet or pull a plow, personally, as some peasants must in China? The comparison with China is presumably offered because the comparison appears so remote. That illusion fades if one thinks in terms of generations. China's population has doubled since the Communists took charge in 1949. The U.S. population is headed in the coming century to what China's was then. Population growth is not a game one can play for very long.

The easing of petroleum prices since the "oil shocks" of the 1970s should not blind us to the expectation that the petroleum era will be a short one. A few nations (the United States, Russia, and, China) have the coal to prolong the fossil-fuel era. Most industrial nations face a starker choice among nuclear energy, import dependence in a sellers' market, or a painful lowering of energy consumption. Europeans are stabilizing their populations—sometimes to the dismay of anachronistic leaders thinking of old wars—and perhaps their instinct is right.

But what if it becomes necessary to constrain the use of fossil fuels, not simply because of a diminishing supply but because of the intolerable effects upon acidity and climate?

The United States' relatively low population density per arable acre still gives us options that most countries do not have. We can make an orderly transition to a mixed system including biomass (trees and fast-growing annuals) along with solar and other sources. More crowded countries cannot.

I have focused on the related issues of air quality, climate, and forests. Part of the problem is already real; part is conjectural. Similar scenarios could be developed for agriculture, industry, or the basic issue of how much

crowding we want. In no case do I argue that population will be the *sole* determinant of national success in meeting the problems before us, but in every case it is arithmetically an element of the issue, and less population growth—or a demographic turnaround—will make the solution of other national issues less difficult. And immigration is presently the key element in demographic policy.

HOW MANY AMERICANS?

How large should this society be? How many people can the United States' area and resource base support? Should it be an object of policy to maximize the human population within such limits?

Various writers have tried to define the concept of *carrying capacity*—the number of people that can be supported by a given ecological system—but it is a tricky concept. It is easier to apply to, say, a herd of cows on unmanaged range than to humans in a complex modern society. One must make tenuous guesses about what growth can be sustained in agricultural yields within ecological constraints, what sort of diet people will eat, what techniques are or could become available to mitigate the ecological impacts of economic activity, the need for and availability of capital, the potential role of foreign trade in supplying requirements, and so on.

The Canadians years ago coined the concept of the *sustainable society*. It is an effort to describe how many people the nation can support, with what national policies, for the indefinite future without degrading the resource base. It is a useful concept to apply to carrying capacity.

By that standard, this country in some respects is already beyond its carrying capacity. I have described the degradation of the atmosphere and its potential effects. We are mining our groundwater resources and polluting them in ways that threaten drinking-water supplies. (Half the nation depends on groundwater for its drinking water.) We are eroding the topsoil off perhaps one-quarter to one-third of our farmland and degrading our rangeland. We have yet to agree how to handle our growing mountains of urban sludge and radioactive waste. New York's sewage sludge and solid wastes wash up on the beaches of Long Island and New Jersey.

It is possible to correct all this—to put our activities on a sustainable basis—but it will require both the national will and a major commitment of capital. Those capital requirements will compete with the requirements for accommodating an expanding population.

It would be foolhardy to assign a number to carrying capacity, to try to defend it, or to suggest that it is immutable. Common sense would seem to justify a simpler rule of thumb: We should try to avoid population growth until we have arrived at sustainability for the population we have. Foresight is a rolling process. Such a rule of thumb, if adopted, should be periodically reexamined at the national level to decide whether it is too strict or too lenient. A population appropriate to the fossil-fuel era may be too large for the twenty-first century.

Meanwhile, there is valuable guidance to be had from the traditional rule of the prudent: If you are uncertain of your alternatives, do not commit yourself to the irreversible one. If as a nation we should later decide that we would profit from a larger population, we can always foster immigration. If, however, it becomes apparent there are too many of us, it would take generations of continuing damage before the growth could be reversed.

And let us agree that we are not in a contest to see how many people we can cram in. The object is not to maximize human density but to provide the most congenial environment for human life—and that goal includes a respect for other plants and animals, even down to the soil microorganisms whose state of health worried the Acid Rain Peer Review Panel in 1983.

That is perhaps a good definition of *optimum population*: not the maximum potential population, or even the maximum sustainable population, but rather the size population that is most desirable. I posed the question several years ago to a number of distinguished specialists—biologists, agricultural experts, ecological economists, an energy specialist, a labor economist, a military manpower specialist, sociologists: "From the standpoint of your specialty, what would be the ideal population of the United States?" The answers ranged from 40 million to 250 million. Out of that, I selected a figure of 150 million as a reasonable compromise. It reflects, as one specialist put it, a level that could be supported at a reasonable "European" level of energy efficiency and consumption levels. It is about where the United States was at the end of World War II, when the country managed to feed its people and support extensive food exports without the current reliance on commercial fertilizers, pesticides, and monocultures, before the country cut down its agricultural shelter belts and its old-growth national forests. The nation was releasing far fewer chemicals and pollutants into the environment, and it was the principal exporter, not importer, of petroleum products.[15]

That 150 million figure might make a good target. It is not absolute; there are too many value judgments in it to permit scientific proof, but it is a start.

THE POLICY IMPLICATIONS

What kind of immigration policy is suggested by this analysis? If there were no migration, present national fertility levels would lead to the end of natural increase in about 40 years, at about 300 million, not much larger than now. This is a rather modest goal, and it might be acceptable without an acrimonious debate, which would certainly erupt if a more drastic policy were proposed. I have suggested, however, that a more ambitious goal is in order: to bring our population back down to levels of a few decades ago.

Unlike most policy fixes, a demographic policy would begin immediately to reap budgetary savings. Yet very few of our politicians and pundits even consider the idea. Proposals to address population growth find few takers because they conjure up fears of China's one-child families, of fertility controlled by forced sterilization and mandatory abortions, and of a "Fortress America" with all migration barred. The reality is much simpler and less frightening. A turnaround could be achieved with the two-child family and with immigration returned to the levels that prevailed for much of this century. On the assumption that action is held back by unwarranted fears, let me show by what relatively gentle adjustments U.S. population growth could be turned around. If the will were there, the solution would not be difficult.

STOPPING THE TREADMILL

Only two variables influence U.S. population growth: fertility and migration. Nobody wants to raise mortality. If we moved instantly to the two-child family and concurrently brought immigration under control at a level of 200,000—which was sufficient to absorb many legitimate refugees from World War II—our population in the next century would decline to the level shown in Figure 3.

If parents indeed stopped at two children, it would lead to a total fertility rate (TFR) of about 1.5 children because not all women have children and some have only one.[16] In all the debate about population growth, this simple reality is almost universally ignored. A national TFR of 1.5 in turn would make possible a gradual turnaround in the population growth that presently drives our social and environmental problems. In Figure 3, the bars labeled "planned" represent the population curve that would result if the two-child family and net annual immigration of 200,000 were to be achieved instantly. The "unplanned" bars are for comparison and show where our population is now heading.[17]

The "planned" bars are unrealistic, since things do not change instantly. They do, however, make the point that population could be brought down to 150 million and stabilized there, with fairly modest changes in behavior and policy. Perhaps even more dramatic is the TFR (total fertility rate) line (right scale). By the middle of the next century, families could be encouraged to have more children (for a TFR of 1.9), if as a society we decide that the 150 million range is a good size for the nation. Some countries have actually gone through a comparable experience. Singapore was so successful in bringing fertility down that it has changed course and encouraged somewhat larger families. Japan and Taiwan are making the same shift (perhaps prematurely). That combination offers the prospect of addressing our own future without slamming the door.

Any such planning, of course, becomes academic if illegal immigration is not brought under control. However, in most pursuits—whether law enforcement, weapons systems, or athletics—the last few percentage points of performance are usually the hardest to achieve. To eliminate 99% of illegal immigration might well require border and airport surveillance measures, internal passes, and other controls that Congress would find expensive and abhorrent. A compliance rate of 90% might be much more easily and happily achieved—but that other 10% must be factored into demographic calculations and decisions about legal quotas.

There is a "fudge factor" in my 200,000 target (which, incidentally, is the annual average level of legal immigration between the immigration acts of 1923 and 1965); I have treated it as a net figure. There is a certain amount of emigration of Americans and legal immigrants. If 200,000 is accepted again as the gross ceiling for legal immigration, that emigration may help to balance the residual illegal immigration. We simply cannot tell with precision, given the chaotic state of our migration statistics.

There are no points given for being "in favor of" stopping or reducing the growth. The question is, What do we propose to *do* about it? We need the courage to take on our demographic future. If we can so confidently urge African nations to bite the bullet and face their demographic problems, what about doing it ourselves?

Any effective program must combine several elements:

- The immigration ceiling must be a real total. Refugees would necessarily be brought back within the ceiling, as they were before 1980.
- Immediate families of American citizens would come under the quota, probably with a special priority; and we would need to end a built-in contradiction in the present migration policy. Within the present preference system, we still try to accommodate an almost limitless chain of immigrants' relatives because of the politically potent demand for "family reunification." In fact, migration necessarily implies leaving some relatives, unless entire societies are to migrate together.
- We will need much better border enforcement and monitoring of "visitors" who do not leave, but we must not rely on controlling the border alone.
- We must finally recognize that anonymity is not a constitutional right. Presently, we cannot enforce our immigration laws (or many other laws, for that matter), because we simply have no way of knowing who people are. With reliable identification, proba-

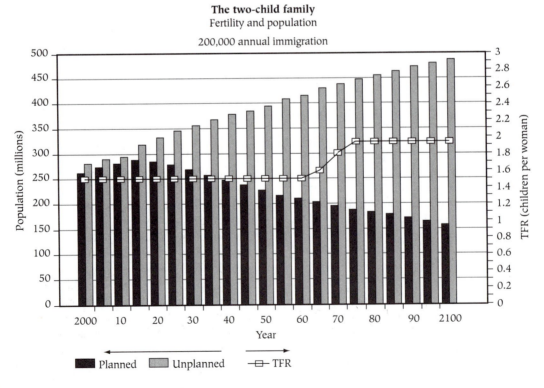

The two-child family
Fertility and population

200,000 annual immigration

FIGURE 3

bly based on Social Security numbers and a call-in system such as has been perfected by credit card companies, we could identify who is here illegally when they apply for driver's licenses or other permits, buy real estate, and the like. We would need to be willing to deport those who are not here legally; presently we deport very few, even when they are known to be here illegally. (There is an unreal quality to the entire "Proposition 187" debate. The costs of educating illegal aliens' children would not be an issue if we were enforcing our existing immigration laws.)

- Finally, we cannot influence fertility very much simply by the moralizing of a few intellectuals as to the benefits of lowering it. Couples must recognize that lower fertility is of immediate advantage to them. And that requires that our laws (taxes, housing, welfare, health services, etc.) be shaped to send the right signals.

Enough. I have gone into detail on these issues elsewhere (see note 1).

TO REBUT THE REBUTTALS

So far, I have sketched out a rationale for stabilizing the U.S. population and a set of guidelines for policies that would help to achieve it. Some readers will agree with the thrust of the argument but differ in detail. There are, however, three lines of argument that challenge the basic rationale or would make it impossible to pursue such a national policy.

1. The "competitive fertility" argument: There are pronatalists who argue (without addressing the constraints I have discussed) that more people are needed to maintain national power against growing populations in other countries.
2. The "American conscience" viewpoint: Humanitarian concern for others should take precedence over concerns about the effects of immigration upon the United States.
3. The "salad bowl" view of American policy: This attacks assimilation as colonialism by the existing establishment against minorities and argues for the preservation of linguistic and cultural separateness. In this cockpit of competing groups, factional interest takes priority over the larger social interest, and ethnic or religious leaders promote higher fertility in their own groups to enhance their political power.

Let me attempt a brief rebuttal of each of these lines of thought.

Competitive Fertility

Some articles have suggested that the industrial world (usually meaning the white world plus Japan) is getting slack about baby bearing, that it is falling behind the third world, and that it had better start breeding or encouraging immigration to avoid being submerged. Of course, the proportion is changing. The industrial world sent through a surge of population growth when death rates fell, before birth rates fell to match them. That phase seems to have ended, but the third world is now going through a population explosion more virulent than anything the West experienced. This has hardly been a cause for third world rejoicing. On the contrary, the leaders of the most populous third world countries say that they must stop the growth for their own well-being. The biggest country, China, is going through a drastic and politically dangerous effort to stop population growth out of the conviction that continued growth would lead to chaos.

The pronatalists argue that the West's moral influence will wane as its share of the globe's population diminishes. This argument assumes a correlation where none is demonstrable. Sweden with 8 million people is hardly a lesser influence in the world than Bangladesh with 120 million. Nor has their relative influence changed perceptibly in recent years as the disparity grew wider.

Here is the pronatalists' central argument:

... [I]t has been generally true that no amount of technical superiority could balance a gross population disadvantage over an extended period of time ... a large population is no guarantee of great-power status, but it is one necessary precondition. ... The advantages of a large labor force, big military establishments, and the economies of scale and production [sic] are simply too important for lasting global influence."[18]

Even more starkly: "Nations of 225 million people can afford to build submarines and aircraft carriers. Nations of 25 million cannot."[19] This is reductio ad absurdum. It is written to justify high fertility, but a tenfold reduction of the U.S. population is hardly a choice under debate. Japan in World War II, with a population of 75 million, built both, by the way—with enough energy left over for other enterprises such as the occupation of much of China.

Pronatalists worry about the supply of troops and the industrial base. The need for the former depends on what kind of war one is likely to fight, and with what weapons. Today, with our wasted assets of unemployed youth, the question is not whether we have enough potential soldiers, but rather how many we could afford to arm and to what purpose.

Concerning industrial power, we are today watching the U.S. heavy industrial base atrophy in the face of competition from such modest powers as Korea, for reasons much more complicated than raw census counts.

The pronatalists' generalization concerning power and population has not been supported by systematic reasoning or by a study of history. The idea is beguiling, but a quick mental scan of the histories of China, India, and Europe would suggest that the reverse may be true. Smaller tribes and nations have regularly bested larger ones, even before this age of technology. From classical Athens to World War II Germany and Japan, one could argue that aggressors may have failed because of hubris and the willingness to take on several major adversaries at once, but it would be very hard to argue that population has regularly been an important determinant of military success.

I would urge the pronatalists to examine the constraints I have described before taking us down their road. The third world has not accepted their suicidal proposal for a fertility race. Neither should we.

The "American Conscience"

There is something of a dichotomy apparent. Overwhelmingly, Americans say in opinion polls that they favor enforcement of our immigration laws and a scaling down of legal immigration. On the other hand, one detects both among liberals and some libertarian conservatives a resistance to the idea of tougher controls on immigration. There is natural and generous impulse to welcome the immigrant, particularly if they know him. If people are crowded elsewhere, if they are driven from their livelihood by economic or political pressures, do we not owe them the chance we have had? Most immigrants seem attractive and hard-working. Why not welcome them?

This reaction arises from a peculiarly American mindset that leads us to universalize our experience. We assume a responsibility for everything and everybody, everywhere. The United States has been a continent and a frontier more than a nation-state. We are not accustomed to thinking in terms of limits. Japan and Europe have had longer experience with limits, as their restrictive immigration policies attest.

This American world conscience comes into conflict with other moral values that should be important to us. Are we to abandon the sense of obligation to our own poor? Are we to reconcile ourselves to a society in which the rich get richer and the poor get poorer? Do we have the right to pass a progressively impoverished environment on to successive generations?

Each person must resolve this conflict for herself or himself, but I would argue that our conscience begin at home. There are good reasons both altruistic and practical to help others, but in a nation-state system our nation has neither the authority nor the obligation to save them. The president is sworn by the Constitution to "promote the general welfare, and secure the blessings of liberty to ourselves and our posterity," not the world. As other countries periodically make clear, this limitation might not be altogether unpopular abroad.

There is another level to the moral issue. As Americans, we are entitled to believe that the immigrant is happier here than he would have been at home, but it is not so certain that the movement is of benefit to the vast majority who will (one must assume) stay behind. The "brain drain" robs third world countries of talents they need; some countries such as India have bitterly resisted the drain. Similarly, migration to the United States, if it provides a safety valve by draining off the articulate and restless, may simply defer the day when their countries address their own problems. And delay intensifies the problems. By relieving some of the population pressure, it encourages high fertility rather than discouraging it.[20] And the immigrants move up the consumption scale when they come to the United States, aggravating the overall problems of world air pollution and climate change.

The third world contains about 80% of the world's population. Even by an optimistic estimate, its growth alone during this quarter-century will be more than the total population of the industrial world and more than five times that of the United States. To believe that a permissive view of immigration will significantly contribute to solving a problem of this scope is simply to engage in wishful thinking. Even if such a permissive attitude were shared throughout the industrial world (which it emphatically is not), migration could not accommodate the current surge of population. It must be dealt with, as China understands, at its origins.

We should help the third world nations address their population problem. We can help them mitigate its effects. We are, for instance, the residual grain exporter to the world, but we will be unable to continue that role if our own expanding population progressively eats up our grain surplus. We cannot solve the third world population problem by absorbing it.

To offer haven to the few who escape is to forget the many who cannot, and an expanding American population does not necessarily advance the common good. To those whose conscience stands in the way, I offer this suggestion: Your humane instincts may be sending you the wrong message.

The "Melting Pot" and the "Salad Bowl:" Where Are We Heading?

Even if the national interest demands that we limit population growth, the national interest will be politically irrelevant if we look upon ourselves not as Americans but as ethnics—if we look at fertility as a source of group power or at immigration reform as a way of "keeping out my people" rather than as a reflection of national needs.

It is something of a paradox that, at a time in our history when racism was acceptable (the Dillingham Joint Congressional Commission of 1911 is a case in point), the nation was accepting multiracial immigration and melding the immigrants into a new America. Now, at a more tolerant time when racism is an ugly charge, the pursuit of racial separateness is becoming increasingly accepted. The "salad bowl" has replaced the "melting pot." Ethnic groups are expected to retain their identity and separateness. This very separateness encourages alienation, estrangement, and competition.

As I have pointed out, it is axiomatic that (barring sufficient differences in mortality) the more fertile component of the population will become a larger proportion, which in turn will tend to drive overall fertility—and the total population—upwards. If we wish to avoid this result, national policies should encourage a melding of groups and a decline in that fertility differential.

The impulse toward "competitive fertility" exists within the United States. Spokesmen for La Raza (an Hispanic lobbying group) have boasted of the growing power associated with Hispanics' growing numbers. On the other side of the equation, American Jews are concerned that, with their low fertility, Jews may lose their identity.[21]

We may be heading for serious racial problems if the nation does not move systematically to defuse them. California is in transition from a "white" to a "multiracial" society, as those rather slippery terms are interpreted. The nation as a whole is following suit. In another two generations, whites may constitute less than one-half of the population, with very large minorities of Hispanics, Asians, and blacks, probably in that numerical order.

There is always a question about how far the ideological concerns of the articulate actually affect demographic behavior, but it would be a disaster, both demographically and socially, if the United States should become the cockpit of several competing ethnic factions who identify themselves with their factions, not with the country. If indeed we are becoming a nation of major ethnic blocs, it would behoove us to blur the differences rather than emphasizing them. Intermarriage is the most enduring solution, but that is a long process. National policies can increase or diminish the sense of ethnic separation.

Nationally and at the state level, we have already opened Pandora's box with policies that promote ethnic and linguistic separateness. A prime example is the promotion of the official use of languages other than English. It would be hard to conceive of a policy more effectively driving ethnic groups apart than encouraging them to live their lives, side-by-side, unable to talk with each other.

The wrenching debate over "reverse discrimination" is another case in point. Like our policies on language, it was born of goodwill—and it is hard to visualize how a less dramatic policy would have achieved its purposes—but it has deeply divisive consequences. Does the poor white slum youth feel less bitter toward blacks, if he is the victim of discrimination, than the black feels when the discrimination works the other way? Perhaps we must sunset the policies that constitute categorical reverse discrimination and seek to apply our laws on an individual basis. We must seek ways of ending discrimination without letting the process intensify the sense of ethnic separateness.

Color blindness is still the only enduring corrective to racial discrimination, and perhaps we had better take another look at the "melting pot" that fell into disfavor, along with nationalism, a generation ago. Both ideas require shared goals and a common identification. They justify the altruism that leads people to base their judgments on the social good rather than factional interest. The basis for good immigration policy exists only when the people agree that the shared well-being —the national interest—is a legitimate and indeed the paramount criterion for national decisions. We should balance that thought against our penchant for letting everybody do his own thing. It is legitimate to ask of any national policy, existing or proposed: Does it enhance or weaken the sense of national cohesion? Only with a sense of shared identity are we likely to be able to take the tough decisions that reason tells us are required, whether it be about economics, the environment, resources, demography, or immigration.

Notes

1. This essay updates my final chapter of *U.S. Immigration in the 1980s,* David E. Simcox, ed. (Boulder, CO: Westview Press and Washington, D.C.: Center for Immigration Studies, 1988). Revised population projections have been drawn from Leon Bouvier and Lindsey Grant, *How Many Americans?* (San Francisco: Sierra Club Books, 1994). The discussion of the two-child family draws upon my NPG FORUM paper of that name (Teaneck, NJ: Negative Population Growth, 1994). The graphs and a detailed presentation of the arguments are taken from my new book, *Juggernaut: Growth on a Finite Planet* (Santa Ana, CA: Seven Locks Press, 1996).

2. Leon F. Bouvier and Lindsey Grant, op. cit. This projection is conservative both as to immigration and fertility, using a census figure for net immigration that is substantially below present levels and assuming that immigrants' fertility drops substantially in the second generation.

3. In this projection, I have assumed constant fertility and mortality and used the Census Bureau's "high" figure of 1,370,000 of anticipated annual net immigration, which I believe is probably closer to present reality than their "medium" figure of 820,000 (1996 projection).

4. The application of natural selection to human populations is described at length in biologist Garrett Hardin's *Living Within Limits* (Oxford and New York: Oxford University Press, 1993), Chapter 16.

5. Lindsey Grant, "What We Can Learn from the Missing Airline Passengers" (Teaneck, NJ: NPG, Inc., NPG

FORUM series, November 1992). Overall, about 2 million people more arrive by air than are reported departing. Less than half the gap can be explained by official immigration figures. I suggested that, if the data are even approximately right, far more people are overstaying their visas than the official statistics suggest. If the data are wrong, it would be relatively easy to collect better data by enforcing the rules requiring departing aircraft to file manifests. The Census Bureau uses these residual figures to estimate movement to and from Puerto Rico, but not more generally, and nobody seems anxious to improve the data. It is rather foolish to spend money to collect data that you don't bother to use.

6. Center for Immigration Studies, Washington, D.C., *Immigration Statistics—1994* and *1995*. CIS Backgrounders 1–94 (May 1994) and 2–95 (July 1995).

7. Over 12 million chemicals have been listed in the American Chemical Society's Chemical Abstract Service since 1965, more than twelve times the number known to exist in 1965. (Columbus, OH: Chemical Abstract Service (CAS) *Statistical Summary 1907–1993*, January 1994; and private communication with CAS.)

8. Emmett J. Horton and W. Dale Compton, "Technological Trends in Automobiles," *Science* 225, (August 10, 1984): 587–593. The example is a Ford Escort, and I assume that passenger weight approximates 10% of GVW.

9. National Research Council report quoted in *Science*, 223. (March 16, 1984): 1154.

10. National Acid Precipitation Assessment Program (NAPAP), *1992 Report to Congress*, p. 5.

11. Executive Office of the President, *Office of Science and Technology Policy News Release*, June 28, 1983, quoting the report of the Acid Rain Peer Review Panel.

12. *Science* (April 19, 1991): 371. (NAPAP = National Acid Precipitation Assessment Program.)

13. "IPCC Second Assessment Synthesis of Scientific-Technical Information Relevant to Interpreting Article 2 of the UN Framework Convention on Climate Change, 1995" (Geneva: World Meteorological Organization, IPCC Secretariat, publication by Cambridge University Press scheduled for spring 1996). The assessment consists of an overview, plus summary reports from Working Groups I, II and III, supported by literally thousands of pages of documentation. The basis for the conclusions in the summary documents is to be found in other supporting documents, notably R. H. Williams, *Variants of a Low CO_2-Emitting Energy Supply System (LESS) for the World* (Richland, WA: Battelle Memorial Institute Pacific Northwest Laboratory, October 1995), plus the 1990 First Assessment report, IPCC, *Climate Change* (Washington D.C.: Island Press, 1991.)

14. Data are from the *Statistical Abstract of the U.S.*, 1992 and 1962.

15. Lindsey Grant et al., *Elephants in the Volkswagen* (New York: Freeman, 1992).

16. The TFR would actually be 1.495. One can make the calculation from U.S. Bureau of the Census, *Fertility of American Women: June 1992* (Publication P20-470, June 1993), Table 1. The oldest cohort (40–45 years old) has a (substantially) completed TFR of 1.999, of which 0.504 represents third-order children and above. The residual is 1.495.

17. The "unplanned" projection is from Bouvier and Grant, op. cit., Chapter 2. The "planned" projection was run by Decision Demographics, a branch of the Population Reference Bureau, at the request of Negative Population Growth, Inc., in 1992, based on the 1990 population level and assuming a TFR of 1.5 starting from that date. It is the basis for the calculations in NPG position paper "Why We Need a Smaller Population and How We Can Achieve It" (July 1992.)

18. Ben J. Wattenberg and Karl Zinsmeister, "The Birth Dearth: The Geopolitical Consequences," *Public Opinion* (December/January 1986), p. 9. Perhaps to their credit, the authors are inconsistent. Having argued the benefits of size, they then propose that industrial nations seek to bring fertility up to replacement level and that the third world bring it down to that level. This is a moderate goal, but it would vitiate the initial argument. The authors have ignored population momentum. If, miraculously, their proposal could be put in practice tomorrow, there would be something like a doubling or trebling of Third World population—if the resource base could support it—and consequently a further dramatic shrinkage of the proportion of the world's population in the industrial countries, before stability were reached.

19. Allan Carlson, "Depopulation Bomb: The Withering of the Western World," *Washington Post* (April 13, 1986): C1.

20. Virginia Abernethy has assembled substantial historical evidence that this effect is not simply conjectural. See *Population Politics* (New York: Insight Books, 1993).

21. See, for instance "Convention to Study Projected Decline in U.S. Jewish Population," *Washington Post*, (March 25, 1984): A1.

Study Questions

1. What is the central issue regarding immigration policy? How does Grant characterize the problem?

2. According to Grant, are U. S. immigration policies racist? Why, or why not?

3. What dangers does Grant identify in relation to population growth? How serious are they? Do you agree with his assessment? Explain your answer.

4. How many Americans should there be? What should we be doing to achieve this ideal figure (assuming there is one)? Discuss this question both from the point of view of Grant's analysis and Kasun's discussion (Reading 49).

5. Grant refers to "Proposition 187," the proposal passed in California that denied education to children of illegal immigrants. Should the children of illegal immigrants be educated at public expense? What does Grant say about his problem? What do you think?

49

The Unjust War Against Population

JACQUELINE KASUN

Jacqueline Kasun is professor of economics at Humboldt State University in Arcata, California. Her writings have appeared in The Wall Street Journal, The American Spectator, *and* The Christian Science Monitor. *She is the author of* The War Against Population *(1988) from which this selection is taken.*

Kasun argues that Doomsdayers like the Smithsonian Institution, Garrett Hardin (Readings 47 and 52) and Paul Ehrlich (Reading 57) are carrying out an irrational campaign against our freedom to propagate. The idea that humanity is multiplying at a horrendous rate is one of the unexamined dogmas of our time. Kasun offers evidence to the contrary and charges the Doomsdayers with bad faith and with attempting to take control of our families, churches, and other voluntary institutions around the globe.

It was a traveling exhibit for schoolchildren. Titled "Population: The Problem Is Us," it toured the country at government expense in the mid-1970s. It consisted of a set of illustrated panels with an accompanying script that stated:

> . . . there are too many people in the world. We are running out of space. We are running out of energy. We are running out of food. And, although too few people seem to realize it, we are running out of time.[1]

It told the children that "the birth rate must decrease and/or the death rate must increase" since resources were all but exhausted and mass starvation loomed. It warned that, "driven by starvation, people have been known to eat dogs, cats, bird droppings, and even their own children," and it featured a picture of a dead rat on a dinner plate as an example of future "food sources." Overpopulation, it threatened, would lead not only to starvation and cannibalism but to civil violence and nuclear war.

The exhibit was created at the Smithsonian Institution, the national museum of the U.S. government, using federal funds provided by the National Science Foundation, an agency of the U.S. government.

Concurrently, other American schoolchildren were also being treated to federally funded "population education," instructing them on "the growing pressures on global resources, food, jobs, and political stability." They read Paul Ehrlich's book, *The Population Bomb.* They were taught, falsely, that "world population is increasing at a rate of 2 percent per year whereas the food supply is increasing at a rate of 1 percent per year," and equally falsely, that "population growth and rising affluence have reduced reserves of the world's minerals." They viewed slides of the "biological catastrophes" that would result from overpopulation and held class discussions on "what responsible individuals in a 'crowded world' should or can do about population growth." They learned that the world is like a spaceship or a crowded lifeboat, to deduce the fate of mankind, which faces a "population crisis." And then, closer to home, they learned that families who have children are adding to the problems of overpopulation, and besides, children are a costly burden who "need attention. . . . 24 hours a day" and spoil marriages by making their fathers "jealous" and rendering their mothers "depleted." They were told to "say good-bye" to numerous wildlife species doomed to extinction as a result of the human population explosion.

This propaganda campaign in the public schools, which indoctrinated a generation of children, was federally funded, despite the fact that no law had committed the United States to this policy. Nor, indeed, had agreement been reached among informed groups that the problem of "overpopulation" even existed. To the contrary, during the same period the government drive against population was gaining momentum, contrary evidence was proliferating. One of the world's most prominent economic demographers, Colin Clark of Oxford University, published a book titled *Population Growth: The Advantages;* and economists Peter Bauer and Basil Yamey of the London School of Economics discovered that the population scare "relies on misleading statistics . . . misunderstands the determinants of economic progress . . . misinterprets the causalities in

Reprinted from *The War Against Population* (San Francisco: Ignatius, 1988) by permission. Notes edited.

changes in fertility and changes in income" and "envisages children exclusively as burdens." Moreover, in his major study of The *Economics of Population Growth,* Julian Simon found that population growth was economically beneficial. Other economists joined in differing from the official antinatalist position.

Commenting on this body of economic findings, Paul Ehrlich, the biologist-author of *The Population Bomb,* charged that economists "continue to whisper in the ears of politicians all kinds of nonsense." If not on the side of the angels, Ehrlich certainly found himself on the side of the U.S. government, which since the mid-1960s has become increasingly committed to a worldwide drive to reduce the growth of population. It has absorbed rapidly increasing amounts of public money, as well as the energies of a growing number of public agencies and publicly subsidized private organizations.

The spirit of the propaganda has permeated American life at all levels, from the highest reaches of the federal bureaucracy to the chronic reporting of overpopulation problems by the media and the population education being pushed in public schools. It has become so much a part of daily American life that its presuppositions and implications are scarcely examined; though volumes are regularly published on the subject, they rarely do more than restate the assumptions as a prelude to proposing even "better" methods of population planning.

But even more alarming are some neglected features inherent in the proposed needs and the probable results of population planning. The factual errors are egregious, true, and the alarmists err when they claim that world food output per person and world mineral reserves are decreasing—that, indeed, the human economic prospect has been growing worse rather than more secure and prosperous by all available objective standards. But these are not the most significant claims made by the advocates of government population planning. The most fundamental, which is often tacit rather than explicit, is that the world faces an unprecedented problem of "crisis" proportions that defies all familiar methods of solution.

Specifically, it is implied that the familiar human response to scarcity—that of economizing—is inadequate under the "new" conditions. Thus the economist's traditional reliance on the individual's ability to choose in impersonal markets is disqualified. Occasionally it is posited that the market mechanism will fail due to "externalities," but it is more often said that mankind is entering by a quantum leap into a new age in which all traditional methods and values are inapplicable. Sometimes it is implied that the uniqueness of this new age inheres in its new technology, and at other times that human nature itself is changing in fundamental respects.

Whatever the cause of this leap into an unmapped future, the widely held conclusion is that since all familiar human institutions are failing and will continue to fail in the "new" circumstances, they must be abandoned and replaced. First among these supposedly failing institutions is the market mechanism, that congeries of institutions and activities by which individuals and groups carry out production and make decisions about the allocation of resources and the distribution of income. Not only the market, but democratic political institutions as well are held to be manifestly unsuitable for the "new" circumstances. Even the traditional family is labeled for extinction because of its inability to adapt to the evolving situation. The new school family life and sex education programs, for example, stress the supposed decline of the traditional family—heterosexual marriage, blood or adoptive relationships—and its replacement by new, "optional" forms, such as communes and homosexual partnerships. Unsurprisingly, traditional moral and ethical teachings must be abandoned.

The decision to repudiate the market is of interest not only to economists but to both those capitalists and market socialists who have seen how impersonal markets can mediate the innate conflict between consumer desires and resource scarcity. The most elegant models of socialism have incorporated the market mechanism into their fundamental design. Adam Smith's "invisible hand," which leads men to serve one another and to economize in their use of resources as they pursue their own self-interest, is relied upon to a considerable extent in a number of socialist countries. John Maurice Clark called it "our main safeguard against exploitation" because it performs "the simple miracle whereby each one increases his gains by increasing his services rather than by reducing them," and Walter Eucken said it protects individuals by breaking up the great concentrations of economic power. The common element here is, of course, the realization that individual decision-making leads not to chaos but to social harmony.

This view is denied by the population planners and it is here that the debate is, or should be, joined. Why are the advocates of government population planning so sure that the market mechanism cannot handle population growth? Why are they so sure that the market will not respond as it has in the past to resource scarcities—by raising prices so as to induce consumers to economize and producers to provide substitutes? Why can individual families not be trusted to adjust the number of their children to their incomes and thus to the given availability of resources? Why do the advocates of government population control assume that human beings must "overbreed," both to their own detriment and to that of society?

It is occasionally averred that the reason for this hypothetical failure is that individuals do not bear the full costs of their childbearing decisions but transfer a large part to society and therefore tend to have "too many" children. This is a dubious claim, for it overlooks the fact that individual families do not receive all the benefits generated by their childbearing. The lifetime productivity and social contribution of children flows largely to persons other than their parents, which, it might be argued, leads families to have fewer children than would be in the best interests of society. Which of these "externalities" is the more important, or whether they balance one another, is a question that waits not merely for an answer but for a reasoned study.

Another reason commonly given for the alleged failure of personal decisions is that individuals do not know how to control the size of their families. But a deeper look makes it abundantly clear that the underlying reason is that the population planners do not believe that individuals, even if fully informed, can be relied upon to make the proper choice. The emphasis on "outreach" and the incentives that pervade the United States' domestic and foreign population efforts testify to this, as will be shown in more depth shortly.

More important than these arguments, however, is the claim that new advances in technology are not amenable to control by market forces—a traditional argument in favor of socialism. From the time of Saint Simon to that of Veblen and on to our own age, the argument has been advanced that the market forces of supply-and-demand are incapable of controlling the vast powers of modern technology. At the dawn of the nineteenth century Saint Simon called for the redesigning of human society to cope with the new forces being unleashed by science. Only planned organization and control would suffice, he claimed. "Men of business" and the market forces which they represented would have to be replaced by planning "experts." In the middle of the nineteenth century Marx created a theoretic model of the capitalist market that purported to prove that the new technological developments would burst asunder the forms of private property and capitalist markets. Three-quarters of a century later Veblen spoke for the planning mentality when he wrote in 1921:

> The material welfare of the community is unreservedly bound up with the due working of this industrial system, and therefore with its unreserved control by the engineers, who alone are competent to manage it. To do their work as it should be done these men of the industrial general staff must have a free hand, unhampered by commercial considerations . . .

In our own time, Heilbroner expresses a similar but even more profound distrust of market forces:

> . . . the external challenge of the human prospect, with its threats of runaway populations, obliterative war, and potential environmental collapse, can be seen as an extended and growing crisis induced by the advent of a command over natural processes and forces that far exceeds the reach of our present mechanisms of social control.

Heilbroner's position is uniquely modern in its pessimism. Unlike Marx and Veblen, who believed that the profit-seeking aspects of supply-and-demand unduly restricted the new technology from fulfilling its *benefi-*cent potential, Heilbroner sees the market as incapable of controlling an essentially *destructive* technology. Technology, in Heilbroner's view, brings nuclear arms, industrial pollution, and the reduction in death rates that is responsible for the population "explosion"; all of these stubbornly resist control by the market or by benign technological advance. Heilbroner has little hope that pollution-control technology, for example, will be able to offset the bad effects of industrial pollution.

An additional argument is that mankind is rapidly approaching, or has reached, the "limits to growth" or the "carrying capacity" of an earth with "finite" resources. Far from being a new position, it dates back to Thomas Malthus' *Essay on the Principle of Population* (1798),which held that the growth of population must inevitably outrun the growth of food supply. It must be one of the curiosities of our age that though Malthus' forecast has proved mistaken—that, in fact, the living standards of the average person have reached a level probably unsurpassed in history—doom is still pervasively forecast. The modern literature of "limits" is voluminous, including such works as the much-criticized *Limits to Growth* published by the Club of Rome, and the Carter administration's *Global 2000*. In common, these works predict an impending exhaustion of various world economic resources which are assumed to be absolutely fixed in quantity and for which no substitutes can be found. The world is likened to a "spaceship," as in Boulding's and Asimov's writings; or, even more pessimistically, an overloaded "lifeboat," as in Garrett Hardin's articles.

Now, in the first place, as for the common assumption in this literature that the limits are fixed and known (or, as Garrett Hardin puts it, each country's "lifeboat" carries a sign that indicates its "capacity"), no such knowledge does in fact exist—for the earth, or for any individual country, or with regard to any resource. No one knows how much petroleum exists on earth or how many people can earn their living in Illinois. What is known is that the types and quantities of economic resources are continually changing, as is the ability of given areas to support life. In the same territories in which earlier men struggled and starved, much larger populations today support themselves in comfort. The difference, of course, lies in the *knowledge* that human beings bring to the task of discovering and managing resources.

But then, secondly, the literature of limits rules out all such increasing knowledge. Indeed, in adopting the lifeboat or spaceship metaphor, the apostles of limits not only rule out all new knowledge, but the discovery of new resources, and in fact, virtually all production. Clearly, if the world is really a spaceship or a lifeboat, then both technology and resources are absolutely fixed, and beyond a low limit, population growth would be disastrous. Adherents of the view insist that that limit is either being rapidly approached or has been passed, about which more later. Important here is that even this extreme view of the human situation does not rule out the potential of market forces. Most of mankind throughout history has lived under conditions that would be regarded today as extreme, even desperate, deprivation. And over the millennia private decisions and private transactions have played an important, often a dominant, role in economic life. The historical record clearly shows that human beings can act and cooperate on their own in the best interests of survival, even under very difficult conditions. But history notwithstanding, the claims that emergencies of one kind or another require the centralized direction of economic life have been recurrent, especially during this century, which, ironically, has been the most economically prosperous. Today's advocates of coercion—the proponents of population control—posit the imminent approach of resource exhaustion, a condition wherein human beings will abandon all semblance of rational and civilized behavior.

To ward off their "emergency," the proponents of population control call for the adoption of measures that they admit would not be normally admissible. This is surely ample reason for a thoughtful and thorough examination of measures already being propagated.

Social and economic planning require an administrative bureaucracy with powers of enforcement. Modern economic analysis clearly shows that there are no impersonal, automatic mechanisms in the public sector that can simply and perfectly compensate for private market "failure." The public alternative is fraught with inequity and inefficiency, which can be substantial and exceedingly important. Although the theory of bureaucratic behavior has received less attention than that of private consumer choice, public administrators have also proved subject to greed, which hardly leads to social harmony. Government employees and contractors have the same incentives to avoid competition and form monopolies as private firms. They can increase their incomes by padding their costs and bloating their projects, and excuse it by exaggerating the need for their services and discrediting alternative solutions.

Managers of government projects have no market test to meet since they give away their products, even force them on an unwilling public, while collecting the necessary funds by force through the tax system. They can use their government grants to lobby for still more grants and to finance legal action to increase their power. They can bribe other bureaucrats and grants recipients to back their projects with the promise of reciprocal services. Through intergovernmental grants and "subventions" they can arrange their financial affairs so that apparently no one is accountable for any given decision or program. In short, the record of bureaucratic behavior confirms the statement of the great socialist scholar Oskar Lange, that "the real danger of socialism is that of a bureaucratization of economic life." The danger may well be more serious than we realize—it could be nothing less than totalitarianism.

Finally, proponents of the "population crisis" believe that not only must the *agencies* and *methods* of control be changed under the "new" circumstances but also the *criteria for choice*. Since, they argue, the technological and demographic developments of the modern age render all traditional standards of value and goodness either obsolete or questionable, these must be revised—under the leadership, of course, of those who understand the implications of the new developments.

Above all, they hold that the traditional concept of the value and dignity of the individual human being must be overhauled. The good of the *species*, as understood fully only by the advocates of the new views, must in all cases supersede the good as perceived and sought after by individuals.

Clearly, in the late twentieth century a worldview has emerged that calls into question not only the presuppositions of much of economics, but some basic political and philosophical thought as well. The history of our age may be determined by the outcome of the confrontation between these views.

It must be emphasized that the essential issue is not birth control or family planning. People have throughout history used various means to determine the size of their families, generating a great deal of discussion and debate. But the critical issue raised by recent history, especially in the United States, is whether government has the right or duty to preside over the reproductive process . . . for what reasons, to what extent?

Recent official action in the United States has proceeded as if the question had already been answered. The fact is, however, that it has been neither explicitly asked nor discussed, even as we rush toward a future shaped by its affirmative answer. It is this question that must be examined.

SCARCITY OR LIFEBOAT ECONOMICS: WHICH IS RIGHT?

The fact of scarcity is the fundamental concern of economics. As one leading textbook puts it in its opening pages, "wants exceed what is available."[2] It pertains to the rich as well as to the poor, since scarcity is not the same thing as poverty. As another text tells students, "higher production levels seem to bring in their train ever-higher consumption standards. Scarcity remains."[3]

Yet another explains,

> we are not able to produce all of everything that everyone wants free; thus we must "economize" our resources, or use them as efficiently as possible . . . human wants, if not infinite, go . . . far beyond the ability of our productive resources to satisfy them . . .[4]

That scarcity is no less real in affluent societies than in poor ones is explained in more general terms by other economists who stress the need to make *choices* whenever alternatives exist. In the words of McKenzie and Tullock,

> the individual makes *choices* from among an array of alternative options . . . in each choice situation, a person must always forgo doing one or more things when doing something else. Since *cost* is the most highly valued alternative forgone, all rational behavior involves a cost.[5]

Clearly, the affluent person or society faces a large list of highly valued alternatives, and is likely to have a difficult choice to make—to be more acutely aware of the scarcity and the need to give up one thing in order to have another. It follows that scarcity does not lessen with affluence but is more likely to increase.

Simply put, economists understand scarcity as the inescapable fact that candy bars and ice cream cannot be made out of the same milk and chocolate. A choice must be made, regardless of how much milk and chocolate there is. And the decision to produce milk and chocolate rather than cheese and coffee is another inescapable choice. And so the list continues, endlessly, constituting the core of economics. How to choose what to produce, for whom, and how, is the very stuff of economics.

It is important to notice how different these traditional economic concepts of scarcity and choice are from the notions of "lifeboat economics." In Garrett Hardin's metaphor, the lifeboat's capacity is written on its side. The doomsday literature of limits is shot through with the conceit of absolute capacity, which is alien to economics. Not the least of the differences is that in economics humanity is viewed not only as the *raison d'être* of other forms of wealth but as one of the sources of wealth; human labor and ingenuity are resources, means for creating wealth. In the lifeboat, human beings are pure burdens, straining the capacity of the boat. Which of these views is closer to reality?

Is the earth rapidly approaching or has it surpassed its capacity to support human life? But before delving into the existence and nature of limits, keep in mind that the notion of a limited carrying capacity is not the only argument for population control. The view of people, or at least of more people, as simply a curse or affliction has its adherents. Thus Kingsley Davis writes of the "population plague," and Paul Ehrlich speaks with obvious repugnance of "people, people, people, people." Other writers, both old and new, attribute, if not a negative, at least a zero value to people. Thus John D. Rockefeller III, submitting the final report of the Commission on Population Growth and the American Future, wrote:

> in the long run, no substantial benefits will result from further growth of the Nation's population, rather . . . the gradual stabilization of our population would contribute significantly to the Nation's ability to solve its problems. We have looked for, and have not found, any convincing economic argument for continued population growth. The health of our country does not depend on it, nor does the vitality of business nor the welfare of the average person.[6]

The notion embodied in this statement—that, to validate its claim to existence, a human life should justify itself by contributing to such things as the "vitality of business"—is a perfect example of the utilitarian ethic. Though economics has skirted utilitarianism at times, it was never in this sense, but rather in its belief that human beings could be rational in making choices. Economics has been content to value all things in terms of what they mean to individual human beings; it has never valued human beings in terms of supposedly higher values.

The idea that the earth is incapable of continuing to support human life suffuses United States governmental publications. The House Select Committee on Population reported in 1978 that

> the four major biological systems that humanity depends upon for food and raw materials—ocean fisheries, grasslands, forests, and croplands—are being strained by rapid population growth to the point where, in some cases, they are actually losing productive capacity.[7]

The Carter administration's *Global 2000* report, which was much criticized by research experts, predicted:

> With the persistence of human poverty and misery, the staggering growth of human population, and ever increasing human demands, the possibilities of further stress and permanent damage to the planet's resource base are very real.

Such statements have been duly broadcast by the media despite the facts, which tell a quite different story.

In the first place, world food production has increased considerably faster than population in recent decades. The increase in per capita food output between 1950 and 1977 amounted to either 28 percent or 37 percent, depending on whether United Nations or United States Department of Agriculture figures are used, as Julian Simon has shown. Clearly, this is a very substantial increase. More recent United Nations and U.S. Department of Agriculture data show that world food output has continued to match or outstrip population growth in the years since 1977. Some of the most dramatic increases have occurred in the poorest countries, those designated for "triage" by the apostles of doom. For example, rice and wheat production in India in 1983 was almost three-and-a-half times as great as in 1950. This was considerably more than twice the percentage increase in the population of India in the same period.[8]

In a recent article written at the Harvard Center for Population Studies, Nick Eberstadt calls attention to the great increases in the world food supply in recent decades. He points out that only about 2 percent of the world's population suffers from serious hunger, in contrast to the much larger estimates publicized by the

Food and Agricultural Organization of the United Nations in its applications for grants to continue its attempts to "solve" the world hunger problem. Eberstadt notes that the improving world food situation is probably reflected by the fact that "in the past thirty years, life expectancy in the less developed countries, excluding China, has risen by more than a third," and that "in the past twenty years in these same nations, death rates for one-to-four-year-olds, the age group most vulnerable to nutritional setback, have dropped by nearly half."

He points out that the much-decried increase in food imports by some less-developed countries is not a cause for alarm, but actually requires a smaller proportion of their export earnings to finance than in 1960.

In 1980, according to Eberstadt, even the poorest of the less-developed countries had to use less than 10 percent of their export earnings to pay for their food imports. The good news is underscored by the fact that these countries have been able to export their manufactured and other nonfood items so much in recent years that it is profitable—it is the efficient choice—for them to export these products in exchange for food, just as developed countries do.

The recent famine in Africa may seem to belie these optimistic findings. Africa, however, is a continent torn by war; farmers cannot cultivate and reap in battle zones, and enemy troops often seize or burn crops. Collectivist governments, also endemic in Africa, often seize crops and farm animals without regard for farmers' needs. War and socialism are two great destroyers of the food supply in Africa, as they have been in other continents.

The impressive increases in food production that have occurred in recent decades have barely scratched the surface of the available food-raising resources, according to the best authorities. Farmers use less than half of the earth's arable land and only a minute part of the water available for irrigation. Indeed, three-fourths of the world's available crop-land requires no irrigation.

How large a population could the world's agricultural resources support using presently known methods of farming? Colin Clark, former director of the Agricultural Economic Institute at Oxford University, classified world land-types by their food-raising capabilities and found that if all farmers were to use the best methods, enough food could be raised to provide an American-type diet for 35.1 billion people, more than seven times the present population. Since the American diet is a very rich one, Clark found that it would be possible to feed three times as many again, or more than twenty-two times as many as now exist, at a Japanese standard of food intake. Clark's estimate assumed that nearly half of the earth's land area would remain in conservation areas, for recreation and the preservation of wildlife.

Roger Revelle, former director of the Harvard Center for Population Studies, estimated that world agricultural resources are capable of providing an adequate diet (2,500 kilocalories per day), as well as fiber, rubber, tobacco, and beverages, for 40 billion people, or eight times the present number. This, he thought, would require the use of less than one-fourth—compared with one-ninth today—of the earth's ice-free land area. He presumed that average yields would be about one-half those presently produced in the United States Midwest. Clearly, better yields and/or the use of a larger share of the land area would support over 40 billion persons.

Revelle has estimated that the less-developed continents, those whose present food supplies are most precarious, are capable of feeding 18 billion people, or six times their present population. He has estimated that the continent of Africa alone is capable of feeding 10 billion people, which is twice the amount of the present world population and more than twenty times the 1980 population of Africa. He sees "no known physical or biological reason" why agricultural yields in Asia should not be greatly increased. In a similar vein, the Indian economist Raj Krishna has written that

> . . . the amount of land in India that can be brought under irrigation can still be doubled . . . Even in Punjab, the Indian state where agriculture is most advanced, the yield of wheat can be doubled. In other states it can be raised three to seven times. Rice yields in the monsoon season can be raised three to 13 times, rice yields in the dry season two to three-and-a-half times, jowar (Indian millet) yields two to 11 times, maize yields two to 10 times, groundnut yields three-and-a-half to five-and-a-half times and potato yields one-and-a-half to five-and-a-half times.[9]

What Mr. Krishna is, in fact, saying is that Indian agriculture is potentially capable of feeding not only the people of India but the entire population of the world!

Revelle sums up his conclusions and those of other experts by quoting Dr. David Hopper, another well-known authority on agriculture:

> The world's food problem does not arise from any physical limitation on potential output or any danger of unduly stressing the environment. The limitations on abundance are to be found in the social and political structures of nations and in the economic relations among them. The unexploited global food resource is there, between Cancer and Capricorn. The successful husbandry of that resource depends on the will and actions of men.[10]

Obviously, such great expansions of output would require large inputs of fertilizer, energy, and human labor, as Revelle puts it:

> Most of the required capital facilities can be constructed in densely populated poor countries by human labor,

with little modern machinery: in the process much rural unemployment and under-employment can be alleviated.

In other words, as Clark has noted, future generations can and will build their own farms and houses, just as in the past.

With regard to fertilizer, Clark has pointed out that the world supply of the basic ingredients, potash and sulphates, is adequate for several centuries, while the third major ingredient, nitrogen, is freely available in the atmosphere, though requiring energy for extraction. Since the world's coal supply is adequate for some 2,000 years, this should pose no great problem. Revelle states that

> in principle . . . most—perhaps all—of the energy needed in modern high-yielding agriculture could be provided by the farmers themselves. For every ton of cereal grain there are one to two tons of humanly inedible crop residues with an energy content considerably greater than the food energy in the grain.

Surprisingly, in view of the recurrent alarms about desertification, urban encroachment, and other forces supposedly reducing the amount of world agricultural land, it is actually increasing. Julian Simon has drawn attention to the data indicating this trend:

> A demographer, Joginder Kumar, found in a study at the University of California at Berkeley that there was 9 percent more total arable land in 1960 than in 1950 in 87 countries for which data were available and which constituted 73 percent of the world's total land area. And United Nations data show a 6 percent rise in the world's arable, permanent cropland from around 1963 to 1977 (the last date for which data are available).[11]

And UN data show a further increase of almost 1 percent between 1977 and 1980. Simon also notes that

> there are a total of 2.3 billion acres in the United States. Urban areas plus highways, nonagricultural roads, railroads, and airports total 61 million acres—just 2.7 percent of the total. Clearly, there is little competition between agriculture and cities and roads.

And that,

> furthermore, between 1.25 million and 1.7 million acres of cropland are being created yearly with irrigation, swamp drainage, and other reclamation techniques. This is a much larger quantity of new farmland than the amount that is converted to cities and highways each year.

Simon's point is significant: a very small share of the total land area is used for urban purposes—less than 3 percent in the United States. This is probably a high percentage by world standards since the United States has a peculiarly sprawling type of development. Doxiadis and Papaioannou have estimated that only three-tenths of 1 percent of the land surface of the earth is used for "human settlements."

Similarly, the biologist Francis P. Felice has shown that all the people in the world could be put into the state of Texas, forming one giant city with a population density less than that of many existing cities, and leaving the rest of the world empty. Each man, woman, and child in the 1984 world population could be given more than 1,500 square feet of land space in such a city (the average home in the United States ranges between 1,400 and 1,800 square feet). If one-third of the space of this city were devoted to parks and one-third to industry, each family could still occupy a single-story dwelling of average U.S. size.

In like vein, R. L. Sassone has calculated that there would be standing room for the entire population of the world within one-quarter of the area of Jacksonville, Florida.

Evidently, if the people of the world are floating in a lifeboat, it is a mammoth one quite capable of carrying many times its present passengers. An observer, in fact, would get the impression that he was looking at an empty boat, since the present occupants take up only a fraction of 1 percent of the boat's space and use less than one-ninth of its ice-free land area to raise their food and other agricultural products. The feeling of the typical air passenger that he is looking down on a mostly empty earth is correct.

On the extremely unlikely assumption that no improvements take place in technology and that population growth continues at its present rate, it will be more than a century and a quarter before world population will approach the limit of the support capacity estimated by Revelle, and almost two centuries before the limit estimated by Clark is reached. And, again on these wild surmises, what will the world be like then? At least one-half of the world's land area will still be in conservation and wildlife areas; and human settlements will occupy no more than 8 percent of the land. In a word, although by our assumptions, average living standards will no longer be able to rise, the boat will still be mostly empty.

Yet despite the optimism for human life in agriculture, and although most of the people in the less-developed world are still engaged in such work, we do live in the industrial age. Among the roughly one-third of the people who live in industrial countries, only a small proportion are farmers. In the United States, for example, one out of thirty people in the labor force is a farmer.

Even the most superficial view of the industrial economy shows how vastly it differs from the economy of agriculture. It uses a high proportion of fossil fuels and metal inputs; it is relatively independent of climate and seasons; a high proportion of its waste products are "non-biodegradable"; and it requires clustering rather than dispersal of its productive units, which encourages urbanization. While depending on agriculture for much of its resources, including its initial stock of capital, it has contributed greatly to the productivity and security of agriculture by providing energy, labor-saving machinery, and chemical fertilizers. Above all, perhaps, it has provided agriculture with cheap, fast transportation, so that local crop failures no longer mean famine.

It is generally agreed that industrialization has been important in reducing mortality and hence increasing population. And concerns regarding the limits of industry match those over the capacity of agriculture. How far can we go with the industrial process before we run out of the minerals and energy that are essential to it? How much "disruption" of nature does the industrial system create and how much can the earth and its inhabitants endure?

It is quite evident that, with few exceptions, intellectuals have never much liked the industrial process. Its noise, smoke—its obliteration of natural beauty—have never endeared it to the more genteel classes, or perhaps to anybody. But where its unattractive characteristics were once regarded as an unavoidable cost, given the benefits for human beings, now there is a growing conviction—especially among environmentalists—that these costs are unendurable and could be avoided by simply dispensing with part of the population. This is a simple choice from a set of complex alternatives, which raises much more far-reaching questions than whether we are simply "running out of everything."

First, though, the question: Are we running out of everything? If we are, the industrialization process, as well as all the benefits and problems it creates, will soon be at an end. (For those who dislike industry this should be good news indeed, though they shy away from the argument.)

On this score, the signs are clear. There is very little probability of running out of anything essential to the industrial process at any time in the foreseeable future. Over the past decades there have been recurrent predictions of the imminent exhaustion of all energy and basic metals, none of which has come about. And properly so, because it is a familiar chemical principle that nothing is ever "used up." Materials are merely changed into other forms. Some of these forms make subsequent recycling easier, others less so. It is cheaper to retrieve usable metals from the city dump than from their original ore, but once gasoline has been burned it cannot be reused as gasoline. Economists gauge the availability of basic materials by measuring their price changes over time. A material whose price has risen over time (allowing for changes in the average value of money) is becoming more scarce, while one whose price has fallen is becoming more abundant, relative to the demand for it. Two major economic studies of the availability of basic metals and fuels found no evidence of increasing scarcity over the period 1870–1972. And in 1984 a group of distinguished resource experts reported that the cost trends of nonfuel minerals for the period 1950–1980 "fail to support the increasing scarcity hypothesis."

Julian Simon has recently noted the trend of decreasing scarcity for all raw materials:

An hour's work in the United States has bought increasingly more of copper, wheat, and oil (representative and important raw materials) from 1800 to the present. And the same trend has almost surely held throughout human history. Calculations of expenditures for raw materials as a proportion of total family budgets make the same point even more strongly. These trends imply that the raw materials have been getting increasingly available and less scarce relative to the most important and most fundamental element of life, human work-time. The prices of raw materials have even been falling relative to consumer goods and the Consumer Price Index. All the items in the Consumer Price Index have been produced with increasing efficiency in terms of labor and capital over the years, but the decrease in cost of raw materials has been even greater than that of other goods, a very strong demonstration of progressively decreasing scarcity and increasing availability of raw materials.[12]

Simon also noted that the real price of electricity had fallen at the end of the 1970s to about one-third its level in the 1920s.

Even the Carter administration's gloomy *Global 2000* report admitted that "the real price of most mineral commodities has been constant or declining for many years," indicating less scarcity. Yet the report, in the face of all the evidence of a historical decline in industrial resource scarcity, trumpets an imminent reversal of the trend and an abrupt increase in the prices and scarcity of raw materials.

Other analysts disagree. As Ansley Coale points out, metals exist in tremendous quantities at lower concentrations. Geologists know that going from a concentration of 6 percent to 5 percent multiplies the available quantities by factors of ten to a thousand, depending on the metal.

Ridker and Cecelski of Resources for the Future are equally reassuring, concluding, "in the long run, most of our metal needs can be supplied by iron, aluminum, and magnesium, all of which are extractable from essentially inexhaustible sources."[13]

Even should scarcities of such materials develop, the economic impact would be small:

metals . . . are only a small fraction of the cost of finished goods. The same is true with energy. . . . In the United States, for example, non-fuel minerals account for less than one-half of one percent of the total output of goods and services, and energy costs comprise less than one percent.

In the case of fuels, the United States has currently reduced its own sources of low-cost petroleum. This can hardly be described as a "crisis," since higher-cost petroleum supplies are still available here while large reserves of low-cost petroleum remain and are being discovered in other parts of the world, though cartel influences are presently affecting prices. Extremely large deposits of coal remain in the United States and throughout the world, enough for a thousand years, possibly more than twice that, at foreseeable rates of increase in demand.

Summarizing the conclusions of a group of energy experts in 1984, Simon and Kahn wrote:

> Barring extraordinary political problems, we expect the price of oil to go down . . . there is no basis to conclude . . . that humankind will ever face a greater shortage of oil in economic terms than it does now; rather, decreasing shortage is the more likely . . .

Speaking of all kinds of energy, they concluded:

> The prospect of running out of energy is purely a bogeyman. The availability of energy has been increasing, and the meaningful cost has been decreasing, over the entire span of humankind's history. We expect this benign trend to continue at least until our sun ceases to shine in perhaps 7 billion years . . .

Furthermore, the United States has tremendous, unexploited opportunities to economize on energy. Because energy has been so cheap, Americans drive their cars more than any other people and, in some parts of the United States, heat their houses without insulation and even with open windows. A reduction in U.S. energy consumption by one-half would put us on a par with the people of western Europe, whose living standards are as high as ours.

Although history teaches that we can expect great technological changes in the future, the nature of these changes is unknown. To attempt, then, to determine the safe capacity of our lifeboat, it seems the better part of wisdom not to anticipate any miraculous rescues, such as breakthroughs in the use of solar or nuclear power. Old-fashioned as it may seem, the coal on board alone will provide us with energy for at least a millennium, to say nothing of the petroleum and natural gas—and solar and nuclear possibilities—all of which remain substantial.

The message is clear. The boat is extremely well stocked. The industrial system will not grind to a halt for lack of supplies.

But what about the disruption (an obscure term, and so all the more dreaded) supposedly created by population growth and/or industrialization? As Heilbroner puts it: "The sheer scale of our intervention into the fragile biosphere is now so great that we are forced to proceed with great caution lest we inadvertently bring about environmental damage of an intolerable sort."

Man has, of course, been intervening in the biosphere for thousands of years. Perhaps the most massive human was the invention of agriculture. It is not certain that modern industry, which is confined to much smaller areas, is having even an equal effect. Both humanity and the rest of the biosphere have apparently survived the agricultural intervention rather well; in fact, well enough so that our present anxiety is whether too many of us have survived.

"Too many for what?" springs to mind. The fact that more people are now living longer, healthier, better-fed, and more comfortable lives, and have been for many decades, rather suggests that the interventions have been the very opposite of intolerable. According to a number of authorities, the best overall index of environmental quality is life expectancy, which has been increasing throughout the world during this century. It is precisely because of this increase that population has grown even though birth rates have fallen. It is possible, of course, that what the population alarmists really mean is that there are too many *other* people for their taste, or for those who prefer solitude, which is quite another thing. . . .

These and other economists have spelled out the case against the assumptions and teachings of the population-bombers: population growth permits the easier acquisition as well as the more efficient use of the economic infrastructure—the modern transportation and communications systems, and the education, electrification, irrigation, and waste disposal systems. Population growth encourages agricultural investment—clearing and draining land, building barns and fences, improving the water supply. Population growth increases the size of the market, encouraging producers to specialize and use cost-saving methods of large-scale production. Population growth encourages governments, as well as parents, philanthropists, and taxpayers, to devote more resources to education. If wisely directed, these efforts can result in higher levels of competence in the labor force. Larger populations not only inspire more ideas but more *exchanges*, or improvements, of ideas among people, in a ratio that is necessarily more than proportional to the number of additional people. (For example, if one person joins an existing couple, the possible number of exchanges does not increase by one-third but triples.) One of the advantages of cities, as well as of large universities, is that they are mentally stimulating, that they foster creativity.

The arguments and evidence that population growth does not lead to resource exhaustion, starvation, and environmental catastrophe, fail to persuade the true believers in the population bomb. They have, after all, other rationalizations for their fears of doom. Another recurring theme of the doomsdayers is, in the words of a public affairs statement by the U.S. Department of State, that population growth increases the size of the "politically volatile age group—those 15–24 years," which contributes to political unrest. Ambassador Richard Elliot Benedick, coordinator of population affairs in the U.S. State Department, spelled out the concern for the Senate Foreign Relations Committee in 1980:

> Rapid population growth . . . creates a large proportion of youth in the population. Recent experience, in Iran and other countries, shows that this younger age group—frequently unemployed and crowded into urban slums—is particularly susceptible to extremism, terrorism, and violence as outlets for frustration.[14]

The ambassador went on to enumerate a long list of countries of economic and strategic importance to the United States where, he claimed, population growth was encouraging "political instability." The list included Turkey, Egypt, Iran, Pakistan, Indonesia, Mexico, Venezuela, Nigeria, Bolivia, Brazil, Morocco, the Philippines, Zimbabwe, and Thailand—countries of special importance to the United States because of their "strategic location, provision of military bases or support, and supply of oil or other critical raw materials." While he admitted that it is "difficult to be analytically precise in pinpointing exact causes of a given historical breakdown in domestic or international order," he nevertheless insisted that "unprecedented demographic pressures" were of great significance.

No results of scientific research support Benedick's belief; it is simply another one of those unverified *assumptions* that advocates of population control rely upon to make their case. It may be, of course, that Ambassador Benedick is right: that the young tend to be more revolutionary and that public bureaucracies who want to stay in power would be wise to encourage the aging of the population through lower birth rates. As public bureaucracies increase their power in this age of growth of government, we may see an increasing manipulation of the population so as to ensure an older and more docile citizenry. However, putting aside the ethical implications and the welfare of society, and speaking only of the self-interest of the ruling bureaucracy, the risks are obvious. Such policy could arouse a deep antagonism among those on the check list, especially if they are citizens of countries who perceive the policy as a tool of outside interference in their most intimate national affairs.

The question, then, is resolved in favor of the economic notion of scarcity rather than the lifeboat model of absolute limits being the more nearly correct. While resources are always scarce relative to the demands that human beings place upon them, there is no indication of imminent, absolute limits. The limits are so far beyond the levels of our present use of resources as to be nearly invisible, and are actually receding as new knowledge develops. Ironically, though, the perception of economic scarcity may increase along with increasing wealth and income. There is no evidence whatsoever that slower rates of population growth encourage economic growth or economic welfare; on the contrary, the developing countries with *higher* rates of population growth have had higher average rates of per-capita-output growth in the period since 1950. It may, of course, be in the interests of a ruling bureaucracy to rid itself of those people it finds troublesome, but the policy can hardly promote the general welfare, and it would prove very costly, even to the ruling elites.

Notes

1. *Projectbook for the Exhibition "Population: The Problem Is Us": A Book of Suggestions or Implementing the Exhibition in Your Own Institution* (Washington: The Smithsonian Institution, undated, circulated in late 1970s), p. 9.

2. Armen A. Alchian and William R Allen, *University Economics*, 3rd ed. (Belmont: Wadsworth Publishing Co., 1972), p. 7.

3. Paul A. Samuelson, *Economics*, 11th ed. (New York: McGraw Hill, 1980), p. 17.

4. George Leland Bach, *Economics: An Introduction to Analysis and Policy*, 10th ed. (Englewood Cliffs: Prentice-Hall, Inc., 1980), p. 3.

5. Richard B. McKenzie and Gordon Tullock, *Modern Political Economy* (New York: McGraw-Hill 1978), p. 18.

6. John D. Rockefeller III, Letter to the President and Congress, transmitting the Final Report on the Commission on Population Growth and the American Future, dated March 27, 1972.

7. Select Committee on Population, Report, "World Population: Myths and Realities," U.S. House of Representatives, 95th Congress, 2nd Session (Washington: U.S. Government Printing Office, 1978), p. 5.

8. The *Global 2000 Report to the President: Global Future: Time to Act*, prepared by the Council on Environmental Quality and the U.S. Department of State (Washington: U.S. Government Printing Office, January 1981), p. ix.

9. Raj Krishna, "The Economic Development of India," *Scientific American*, vol. 243, no. 3. September 1980, pp. 173–174.

10. Revelle, "The World Supply of Agricultural Land," op. cit., p. 184, quoting W. David Hopper, "The Development of Agriculture in Developing Countries," *Scientific American*, September 1976, pp. 197–205.

11. Julian L. Simon, "Worldwide, Land for Agriculture Is Increasing, Actually," *New York Times*, October 7, 1980, p. 23.

12. Simon, "Global Confusion," op. cit., p. 11.

13. Ronald G. Ridker and Elizabeth W. Cecelski, "Resources, Environment, and Population: The Nature of Future Limits," *Population Bulletin*, vol. 34, no. 3, August 1979, p. 29.

14. Richard Elliot Benedick, Statement before the Senate Foreign Relations Committee, April 29, 1980, reprinted in *Department of State Bulletin*, vol. 80, no. 2042, September 1980, p. 58.

Study Questions

1. How strong is Kasun's case that the "Population Control Industry" is misleading us about the dangers of our present population growth?

2. According to Kasun, what is the truth about population growth in relation to scarcity of resources?

3. Compare Kasun's arguments with Hardin's. Which has the stronger case, and why?

50

China's Baby Budget

JODI JACOBSON

Jodi Jacobson is a researcher for the Worldwatch Institute and the author of several articles on women's issues in the world. In this article, Jacobson explores China's experiment in social engineering: its attempt to reduce population growth by promoting one-child families.

Few things in China are done on a small scale. The world's most populous nation has a tradition of combining its abundant labor with intensive public education to mount immense attempts at improving living standards and meeting other social and economic goals. Although history has proven that some Chinese campaigns, such as the catastrophic Great Leap Forward of the fifties, were ill-conceived, others, such as the ones to improve health and reduce illiteracy in the sixties, catapulted China far ahead of other poor countries on basic social indicators.

In a series of "patriotic public-health campaigns" conducted in the early fifties, for example, the Chinese people successfully eradicated typhus, wiped out opium addiction, and controlled venereal diseases within a few years. Later in that decade, the government mobilized millions of its citizens to move earth, if not heaven, by manually draining and dredging waterways to destroy the snails that carry schistosomiasis.

Beginning in the mid-sixties, China forced down high rates of death and chronic illness by deploying an army of "barefoot doctors" throughout the countryside. Trained in preventive and curative medicine, and backed by county and regional clinics and hospitals, these villagers provided the grass-roots contact points to what is considered the most extensive primary health-care network in the developing world. This effort also laid the groundwork for another capstone in China's development: family planning.

China's most recent experiment in social engineering—reducing population growth by promoting one-child families—is nothing less than an unprecedented attempt to change the reproductive behavior of an entire nation. Taking to population planning with characteristic zeal, the revolutionary government has strongly encouraged couples to limit themselves to one child. However, achieving the goal of zero population growth by early in the next century is proving to be a Herculean task, even for the Chinese.

Reprinted from *The Worldwatch Reader,* ed. Lester Brown (New York: Norton, 1991) by permission.

In strictly demographic terms, China already is a family planning success story. Sharp reductions in fertility since the sixties have put the country farther down the road toward a stable population size than most other Third World nations. Today, however, due to the legacy of past growth, the share of people of reproductive age in China is large and growing. This indicates that the population will continue to expand for at least three decades. Even at its current low level of fertility, China's population will exceed 1.5 billion by 2020.

This one-child policy, without a doubt the most hotly debated family planning strategy in the world, has been criticized on a number of grounds. First, it is (at least on some levels) a compulsory program in a world where even voluntary family planning remains controversial. Second, with one-child families, the next generation of elderly will have far fewer laborers to support it; this raises questions about how China will provide old-age security. Third, the policy's immediate economic benefits to the largely rural populace remain unclear.

Although alternatives to the one-child program that might meet China's population goals and lessen the growing opposition to current policy have not been universally adopted, there is some evidence that new, more lenient approaches to population planning are being tried in a majority of provinces. Nevertheless, over the next several years China will face a choice between allowing a slightly higher rate of population growth (and, perhaps, the addition of another 100 million to its population) or resorting to more stringent and compulsory measures to restrain fertility.

HITTING A GREAT WALL

At the close of the thirteenth century, when the New World was as yet unexplored and all of Europe contained only 75 million people, Chinese subjects of the Sung Dynasty already numbered 100 million. For several hundred years, sporadic increases in cultivated land and agricultural productivity underwrote population growth; the population reached a total of about 540 million in 1949.

Soon after the half-billion benchmark was reached, China scholar John King Fairbank observed that "the Chinese people's basic problem of livelihood is readily visible from the air: the brown eroded hills, the flood plains of muddy rivers, the crowded green fields . . . all the overcrowding of too many people upon too little land, and the attendant exhaustion of the land resources and of human ingenuity and fortitude in the effort to maintain life." Now that China's population has doubled, these thoughts are an even more apt description of the conflict between population and resources.

Today, China's leaders follow the population's upward climb with the nervous air of an expectant father. Their apprehensions are justifiable. With 1.1 billion people and counting, China may already have reached its environmental limits.

The threat that population growth will unravel past gains and halt further development understandably preoccupies the Chinese. Life for the average Chinese person has improved markedly since the birth of the People's Republic in 1949, at least in terms of health, nutrition, and life expectancy. As in most developing nations, though, population pressures in China threaten to undermine hard-won advances in meeting social needs. And resources—forests, land, and water—are already stretched thin.

Judging quality of life on the basis of per-capita income alone, China appears to be at the same level of development as India, its closest demographic cousin, with a population of 835 million. In both countries, annual income per person in 1989 was about $300. A look behind these figures, though, reveals some startling facts: China far outranks India and even Brazil on basic quality-of-life measures, although per-capita income in the latter was above $2,000.

In India, the infant-mortality rate—a key indicator of development—was a relatively high 96 deaths per 1,000 births (see Table 1). China's infant mortality rate was less than half that—around 44 per 1,000. Indian life expectancy at birth was 58 years, a level close to that of the poorest countries in sub-Saharan Africa. China's life expectancy of 66 years at birth ranks the nation close to the United States and Japan, which have far greater income levels. These achievements are part of the legacy of China's commitment to primary health care.

Yet, although resources are distributed more equitably in China than in many other nations, there are still acute shortages in education, housing, and health care. Additional population growth increases the competition for available resources and reduces the little surplus available to invest in boosting living standards.

Gains in food production also are at risk. With more than one-fifth of the world's population, China has only about 7 percent of its arable land. Until the mid-seventies, grain production in China barely kept pace with population growth; a history of recurrent famine is etched hard upon the collective Chinese memory. Since 1978, though, China has made great strides in raising food output.

In 1950, grain production in China hovered around 361 pounds per person, below the 397 pounds accepted as the subsistence level (see Figure 1). Production rose slowly until 1978, the year agricultural reforms were put in place. Per-capita output since then has increased substantially, to exceed the subsistence standard by a solid margin. Between 1978 and 1984, China's per-capita grain production increased 33 percent to 667 pounds per person, although it did drop back to 600 pounds during 1988's severe drought.

Comparing China with India on this count underscores the extent of its achievement. Only four times since 1950 has India managed to reach even the subsistence level, although the country has more land devoted to grain production per person than does China. In fact, each acre of productive Chinese soil must now feed 4.5 people; this leaves little margin for error.

Not only the Chinese are concerned about the size of their population, for, as demographer Ping-ti Ho has noted, "China's population is a world problem."

The global environment is one point of contention. With the world's largest coal supplies and pressures to raise living standards, China has opted so far for an energy strategy based mostly on coal consumption. Air pollution and acid rain have emerged as serious environmental problems, since 85 percent of the country's coal is burned without controls.

TABLE 1 *Basic Indicators, 1989*

COUNTRY	INFANT MORTALITY RATE	LIFE EXPECTANCY	PER CAPITA INCOME
India	96	58	$300
China	44	66	$300
Brazil	63	65	$2,020
United States	10	75	$18,430
Japan	5	78	$15,770

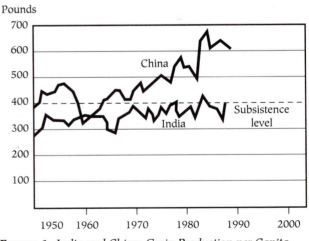

FIGURE 1 *India and China: Grain Production per Capita, 1950–89*

China is beginning to weigh in heavily as a contributor to the mounting concentration of greenhouse gases; the country is responsible for 10 percent of the carbon dioxide added to the atmosphere each year, a share that is rising quickly. Its potential contribution to ozone depletion and other global problems also raises serious concerns, not least because the Chinese government has been slow to act on international treaties, such as those limiting production and use of ozone-depleting chemicals.

Population pressures often force a choice between development strategies that bring rapid gains in the short run and those that are economically and environmentally sustainable over time. China finds itself in this bind. Rising household demands and rapid economic growth have left the country in the throes of its worst energy shortage in at least two decades. Shifting to a more sustainable energy path, one based on energy efficiency, conservation, and renewable sources, will become more difficult as population growth creates ever higher demands.

ONE IS BEST

Prior to 1970, official support for family planning was sporadic at best. In the early seventies, with the Chinese population well on its way to one billion, the government recognized the need to reduce fertility and slow growth to reduce pressure on natural resources. The state family planning agency began to promote a policy known as *wan-xi-shao*, literally "later-longer-fewer." The policy encouraged Chinese couples to marry later than the average age of 20, to lengthen the amount of time between first and subsequent births, and to have fewer children overall.

The Chinese are fond of using slogans to communicate a message, and the family planning program certainly has its share. "One is not too few, two is good, three is too many" became a national refrain under *wan-xi-shao*. The central government, recognizing the cultural and economic differences between city and farm, set separate targets for age at marriage and family size. The policy encouraged urban couples to delay marriage until ages 28 for men and 25 for women, 25 and 23 for rural couples. Originally, urban couples were limited to two children, while rural couples could have three.

In 1977, the government began to promote the two-child family universally. Although fertility had declined significantly, Chinese officials began to realize that population growth would not fall quickly to the desired rate of 1 percent per year, owing mostly to the millions of teenagers entering their childbearing years. Projections showed a baby boom ahead, a disturbing demographic echo of the period of high fertility that followed the Great Leap Forward in the early sixties.

Arguing that continued growth would defeat plans to raise living standards, the government adopted a package of economic incentives and disincentives. In 1979, a new slogan, "one is best, at most two, never a third," subtly reflected yet another change in the country's demographic goals—the shift to a policy advocating one child. To this day, couples "pledging" to have only one child receive a package of benefits from the government. The original policy neither levied sanctions on nor offered benefits to couples having two children, but promised that "those who give birth to three or more will suffer economic sanctions."

The national policy sets out the following guidelines: In urban areas, the rewards allocated to couples who sign the one-child certificate include monthly cash payments for 14 years and preference in housing allocations and job assignments; single children receive priority in free medical care and schooling, and jobs at graduation. According to the original policy, rural couples pledging to have one child were promised extra work points (the "currency" earned by farmers working communal land that determined their share of a commune's income) for 14 years, generous allocations of private land, and larger grain rations.

Couples that don't comply, and give birth to a third child, have their salaries reduced for the 14-year period, don't receive additional housing space, and have to bear the full costs of that child's birth, medical care, and schooling. Rural couples could count on reductions in workpoints, land allocations, and grain rations, in addition to paying their own health costs out of pocket. In rural areas, the mix of incentives and disincentives has changed significantly since agricultural reform got under way and communes have virtually disappeared.

BAREFOOT AND NOT PREGNANT

The Chinese exude an urgency about and a willingness to commit funds to family planning not seen in any other country. Not surprisingly, the Chinese program has been wildly successful by virtually any standard over the past two decades. This success is due to a combination of policy and strategies, including persistent efforts to develop new contraceptive technologies and disseminate them through the barefoot-doctor network. The Marriage Law of 1980, which proclaims it the responsibility of every husband and wife to practice family planning, has also been effective.

Childbearing trends, most clearly represented by total fertility rates, bear this out. Between 1960 and the mid-eighties, the total fertility rate in China fell by a remarkable 60 percent, from 6.0 to 2.4 children per woman (see Table 2). India and Indonesia, the next two largest countries in the table, reduced their total fertility rates by only 31 and 38 percent, respectively. In fact, the rate in India has not fallen at all since the late seventies.

While India's effort languishes, the Chinese have built the world's most comprehensive family planning network, one that operates on the same principle of decen-

TABLE 2 *Fertility Declines in Selected Countries, 1960–89*

COUNTRY	POPULATION 1989	TOTAL FERTILITY RATES		CHANGE
		1960	1989	
	(millions)	(average number of children per woman)		(percent)
China	1,104	6.0	2.4	–60
Mexico	87	7.2	3.8	–47
Brazil	147	6.2	3.4	–45
Indonesia	185	5.6	3.5	–38
India	835	6.2	4.3	–31

tralization that made the barefoot doctor famous the world over. At its best, the network has been the prime conduit for educating millions of Chinese on the economic, environmental, and health benefits of family planning. At its worst, it has become a tool of coercion.

One result of the Chinese commitment to family planning is that more than 73 percent of couples of reproductive age use a modern form of contraception, a rate that exceeds even the United States' at 68 percent. Moreover, the Chinese populace is highly educated about the benefits to maternal and infant health derived from lower fertility, birth-spacing, and contraceptive use.

In fact, the level of education among Chinese people about one subject—the impact of population on natural resources—probably is higher than anywhere else in the world. By decentralizing and politicizing environmental issues such as deforestation, water shortages, and soil erosion the Chinese government has succeeded, to a remarkable extent, in elevating people's awareness of the impact of their reproductive behavior on the world around them. It has attempted to change a couple's usual question of "How many children do I want?" to "How many children per family can this society afford?" These efforts notwithstanding, there are stirrings of discontent with the one-child policy. Surveys show a considerable share of Chinese couples prefer more than one child, especially if their first is a girl.

Despite the seemingly specific nature of the guidelines outlined above, the national policy has been treated only as a rough framework for a highly decentralized family planning program that places the power of enforcement in the hands of local cadres.

The national government suggests but does not dictate the actual package of incentives and disincentives; national policy is interpreted and carried out by planned-birth committees in every province, prefecture, municipality, county, and township. Among other things, these committees, made up largely of female cadres, midwives, and other family planning workers, visit households to distribute contraceptives and urge couples to comply with family planning policy.

Decentralization has had its down side, however. Because policies become increasingly more specific as they move down the chain of command, cadres have much more power than is immediately apparent. It is the mandate of local leaders to meet regional and provincial population-size and growth-rate targets. The pressure to do so has, in some provinces, resulted in incidents of coercion, including forced abortions and the mandatory insertion of an intrauterine device following a woman's first live birth, as well as criminal penalties for its removal. While the national government has reproached cadres who move from persuasion to coercion in their efforts to reach demographic targets, it is the stringency of the targets themselves and the possible ramifications of not meeting them that can lead to abuses.

RESISTANCE ON THE FARM

The one-child policy raises important questions about equity, individual choice, and human rights.

To date, many more urban than rural couples have signed on to the one-child policy; this has accentuated a difference between urban and rural fertility in China similar to that found in most developing countries. In 1983, the Chinese State Family Planning Commission estimated that 78 percent of all urban couples of childbearing age with one child had signed the certificate, as opposed to 31 percent of rural couples. Generally speaking, urban couples have lower fertility because they tend to be more highly educated and more prosperous, marry later, and hold less tightly to cultural traditions than their rural counterparts.

Apart from government policy, urban life in China offers its own built-in disincentives to big families. On average, an urban dweller has only 36 square feet of living space; often, several families live in adjoining rooms and must share kitchen and bath facilities. The high cost of clothing, education, food, and other consumer goods dissuades parents from building large families. In urban areas, either husband or wife is more likely to be working in a state-supported industry that offers social security after retirement and so obviates the need to bear sons as a hedge against poverty in old age. Perhaps more important, however, is that government control over an individual's life through the urban food rationing and employment system made gaining widespread urban adherence to the one-child policy relatively easy.

China is still a nation of farmers, however, and it's in rural areas that the battle to lower fertility is hardest to win. Cultural and economic advantages to farmers having more than one child, and at least one son, are proving difficult to counteract fully through family planning policy alone. Ironically, many of the economic reforms put in place by Deng Xiaoping, under whose leadership the one-child policy also was born, reinforce incentives for higher fertility.

In rural areas, where human labor is still the key ingredient in food production and rural industries, a family's success depends on the number of children it has to tend the fields—even more so now that agricultural reforms have largely privatized Chinese agriculture. It's in peasant homes, where sons are required to support their parents in old age, that the one-child policy faces the most resistance.

Much as they worry about fines and penalties, rural Chinese couples, like couples everywhere, are concerned about how they will fare in retirement. Unlike daughters (who generally live with and contribute to the household economy of their in-laws), Chinese sons are bound by tradition and social mores to care for their own parents. Most rural dwellers are not covered by a state-funded pension system. While rural townships are legally bound to provide the "five guarantees" (food, shelter, clothing, medical care, and burial) to elderly couples without a son, studies have shown that, even in well-off areas, this program provides minimal aid at best.

Today's current and potential Chinese parents are aware of the implications of the one-child policy on their retirement years. Demographic assessments show that the one-child family implies a sharp drop in the size of the labor force in future decades. If every family had one child, the share of the population over age 65 would reach 25 percent by 2040, as opposed to 6 percent today. Although the theoretical share is larger by an unknown quantity than what actually will bear out, since many are having more than one child, the implications for China are clear. Many developed countries with between 10 and 15 percent of their current population over age 65 already face insolvency with their social security systems. It's an open-ended question whether China will develop quickly enough to allow couples to accumulate enough of an economic surplus to care for a much larger proportion of elderly.

Interregional equity is another concern. The one-child policy has exacerbated income inequality between urban and rural areas and between advantaged and disadvantaged families within a given region, in large part because most urban and some rural areas are better able to pay incentives. In rural areas, townships must pay for benefits through the fines levied on those who have more than one child. The actual benefits disbursed range from the full menu to none at all because, in poor villages with no surplus crops, there is little if anything to redistribute from prolific couples to one child couples.

Similarly, in urban areas where amenities are better than in rural areas, though still in short supply, "preferential treatment" becomes less meaningful when nearly everyone joins the program but shortages of housing, schools, and jobs still exist. As a result, some urban couples attempt to violate their pledges because they receive no real benefits in holding to them.

SMALL HAPPINESS

In Chinese, the phrase describing a pregnant woman translates roughly into English as "she has happiness." When a woman gives birth to a son, she has "big happiness"; a daughter brings her "small happiness." Making the birth of a girl equally welcome as that of a boy is a key challenge to improving human rights and equity, not only in China, but throughout most of the world.

Raising the status of women is a goal in itself. The near-universal discrimination suffered by women in virtually every sphere of their lives has curtailed their social, economic, and personal development, severely impaired their health, and deprived them of self-esteem and fulfillment. Measured in terms of education and income levels, women's status also bears on fertility. The more opportunities women have, the fewer children they are likely to bear. On paper, China has done more than most countries to bridge the gender gap, but sexual discrimination dies hard. As demographers Fred Arnold and Liu Zhaoxiang note, "Sexual equality in the political, socioeconomic, and cultural spheres of life is guaranteed in China's constitution, but patriarchal attitudes [and practices] are still prevalent."

A distinctive preference for sons among a large section of the Chinese population remains one of the biggest roadblocks to acceptance of the one-child family. Ask a Chinese couple what sex they would like their first or only child to be and, more often than not, the answer will be "a son." No matter how many children a couple has, those with only daughters are less likely to be using contraception than those with at least one son.

Son preference varies considerably by place of residence and by parents' levels of education, but it is evident in almost every part of the country. It is strongest in towns and villages dominated by agriculture, where traditional attitudes run deepest and the perceived importance of sons as farm workers and providers of social security is ubiquitous. Interestingly, Arnold and Liu have shown that, in rural areas, son preference is substantially weaker in nonfarm villages, where women often play a vital role in operating small factories and contributing to family income.

About 60 percent of all one-child certificate holders have a son, a fact that has disturbing implications for the status of women and equity in general. At least 50 percent more boys than girls are getting preferential treatment in schooling, food rations, health care, and opportunities to compete for employment later on under the current program—all areas where girls are at a disadvantage due to traditional discrimination. In some parts of the country, where women are caught between the demands of the state to limit fertility and the demands of the husband's family to bear a son, violence against both mothers and first-born daughters has increased.

PRODUCTION VS. REPRODUCTION

The one-child policy cannot be divorced from another campaign going on in China. The "four modernizations," as the name implies, is a drive to increase per-capita production and investment in four key areas—agriculture, industry, defense, and science and technology. The Chinese government, says Qian Xinzhong, minister of public health until 1983, is worried that if population growth continues at its current pace "we will be compelled to devote a considerable amount of . . . resources to feeding the newly increased populace. That will inevitably slow down the four modernizations."

The modernization of agriculture has taken the form of the widely publicized "agricultural responsibility" system, wherein communes and work brigades have given way to the family farm. Under this system, each family is allotted a private plot and signs a contract agreeing to sell a portion of its crop to the state at a fixed price. Any surplus crops can be sold for a higher price to the state or in the market, or used by the farm household.

The spread of the responsibility system has sounded a death knell for Chinese collectives. The share of farm income derived from producing surplus crops, raising farm animals, harvesting fruit, oilseeds, and vegetables, producing handicrafts, and engaging in small-scale industrial production has risen sharply. As the share of work points in farm income has diminished, so, too, has the power of the cadres to levy fines.

Under the responsibility system, a family's success depends on its labor resources. This has created an ironic clash between agricultural and family planning policy. In some areas, plots of land are allocated according to the number of laborers a family has, a direct conflict with the disincentives to having more than one child. Many smaller families have found that they lack the humanpower needed to meet their contractual obligations to the state and still engage in additional income-earning activities. And many farmers have found that the gains derived from having an additional child, especially a son, far outweigh the costs imposed by the one-child program.

Contradictory official signals abound. In an article entitled "How a Farm Family Gets Its Income," the same Chinese press that espouses the one-child policy described how the family of Feng Maoru, a man with five sons, has prospered under agricultural reforms. Although two of his sons (and both his married daughters) live outside the village, the three remaining at home work at beekeeping, carpentry, and farming, more than tripling the family's income. The article notes that "the two sons working outside send 300 to 400 yuan a year [to their parents] for expenses, but the couple prefers to bank it." The example illustrates how in the traditional family structure, families with sons are better able to accumulate resources, take advantage of new work opportunities, and diversify their business.

These obvious incentives to have more than one child have not escaped farmers in China's poorer regions, which lead more prosperous areas in the rates of abandoning collectivization and of reproducing children.

In response, some rural family planning committees have sought to curtail the incentives to higher fertility unleashed by the responsibility system by combining agricultural production contracts with family planning contracts; in effect they have tied the couple's immediate financial well-being (the sale of its crops) to a pledge to have only one child.

IS TWO OKAY?

In China, as in every country in the process of modernization, incentives to have large families will erode. As the number of farm laborers grows, for instance, additional labor on the farm yields diminishing returns. And, when available land no longer can be subdivided among new families, those children must find alternative means of making a living. The development of cities, industries, and pension plans is accompanied by smaller families. These conditions and others, such as the spread of education and opportunities for women, will push China through a transition to lower fertility.

In the China of more than one billion people, however, this natural "demographic transition" is not occurring quickly enough to avoid seriously compromising the environment. In fact, the population may be growing more rapidly than is officially acknowledged. The introduction of economic reforms has loosened the government's grip on people, made them more mobile, more economically independent, and less subject to regulations. As a result, independent sources claim that the total fertility rate in China is actually rising; contrary to government figures, it may now exceed 2.8 children per family.

The question is, How can the Chinese significantly reduce population growth without relying on increasingly coercive measures?

China experts John Bongaarts and Susan Greenhalgh of the New York-based Population Council, a nonprofit population research institute, have proposed an alternative—patterned on *wan-xi-shao*—that involves two key elements. One is a strict "stop-at-two" rule, allowing each couple to have at most two children. The second is a set of conditions under which the stop-at-two rule would operate, including a minimum age at first birth of, say, 25. Couples could marry whenever they wanted to but must delay their first birth. Second births would have to be delayed by at least four more years.

Although at first glance this proposal seems to imply a much higher rate of growth, it is actually projected to reach the same targets as the current program. By keeping one-child family incentives in place, some people still will agree to have one child. As a result of this and the fact that a proportion of the population will experience "secondary" infertility (inability to have a second child), and others "primary" infertility, the average number of children per couple nationwide would be less than two. According to the plan, late first births and delayed second ones would space children far enough apart to affect this generation's population growth rate. Bongaarts and Greenhalgh argue that such a policy would, at least partially, resolve the conflict between the government's demographic goals and individual desires. More people would have at least one son; those who had two daughters could encourage one to assume the role of provider to her parents in old age by asking her husband to join her parents' household (a move encouraged by the government).

A form of two-child policy is starting to spread. In 1984, the national government expanded the number of situations under which people may have that many children. And recent reports from China imply that several provinces have loosened their policies in a similar fashion. Although some experts point to this trend as evidence of a liberalization of government policy, others, such as Judith Banister, a sinologist at the U.S. Census Bureau, claim that despite the apparent easing of restrictions, the policy as applied still too strongly "encourages" only one child.

HOLDING THE LINE

Recent changes notwithstanding, the future of the one-child family program may hinge on the government's willingness to address mounting concerns over social security and inequity. As events in Tiananmen Square indicate, a nascent democratic movement exists in China. A backlash to family planning in China, similar to the one that occurred in India in the mid-seventies in response to forced sterilizations, is conceivable.

For now, the Chinese government can consider several steps to bring government policy more in line with individual desires. Allowing two children is one option. Establishing a rural social security system based on need might help convince more people to have fewer children. Under such a system, the central government would extend support to the poorer and middle income rural areas that cannot sufficiently meet the "five guarantees." In China, as elsewhere, women still suffer discrimination in education, employment, and the application of legal principles in every day life. Making sure that government and private practices offer the same opportunities to women as to men would help erode gender bias and reduce fertility.

China entered the seventies with a clear choice: to bring population growth down swiftly through family planning policy or to allow nature to eventually take its course in the form of a deteriorating environment, declining living standards, and possible famine. In this way, China first reached a crossroads of demography and environment that many other countries—Bangladesh, Egypt, India, Kenya, and Nigeria, to name a few—are fast approaching.

With the one-child family, the Chinese have had to chart an unmapped course in the murky waters of human reproductive behavior. The positive aspects of their family planning efforts are evident: lower fertility, better health, and reduced pressure on natural resources and the economy. Several characteristics unique to Chinese society made these advances possible. The population is nearly homogenous, with a 93 percent Han majority. The closed nature of the political system, the Confucian tradition and the strong sense of family it fostered, and a 3,000-year history of allegiance to authority made the one-child family program succeed where it might otherwise have failed.

The Chinese approach to population and family planning subordinates the needs and desires of the individual to those of the society at large—a strategy that is unlikely to be tenable in such a form in many countries. Still, other countries can learn from and adapt some aspects of China's program. The barefoot-doctor program is one example. By decentralizing health care and family planning, providing it literally by villagers for villagers, countries can begin to combat high rates of maternal and infant mortality and provide the means and information necessary to plan families. Similarly, a widespread rural network can help to educate people about population and environmental issues. In addition, by codifying and enforcing laws, and offering women of every age educational and employment opportunities equivalent to men, countries can promote equity and lower fertility at the same time.

But the one-child policy raises a fundamental conflict, one that more and more countries are now facing: the rights of this generation to reproduce against those of future generations to an ecologically intact world.

Looking back, most Chinese officials probably wish the government had undertaken family planning efforts when their people numbered 500 million. None of today's rapidly growing countries can afford to wait as long as China did to act. Neither can the world.

Study Questions

1. Evaluate China's Baby Budget. Is China's present policy of promoting one-child families morally acceptable? Explain.

2. What can North Americans learn from the Chinese experience?

3. Do you agree with Jacobson that "None of today's rapidly growing countries can afford to wait as long as China did to act. Neither can the world."? Explain your answer.

51

Licensing Parents

HUGH LaFOLLETTE

Hugh LaFollette is professor of philosophy at Tennessee State University and the author of several works in applied ethics. In this essay, LaFollette argues that in order to reduce mistreatment of children we ought to require that prospective parents demonstrate that they are qualified to raise children. He argues against the thesis that people have a right to have children and urges us to devise a screening program analogous to our present adoption programs. Although not directly aimed at population control, LaFollette arguments are relevant to that issue.

In this essay I shall argue that the state should require all parents to be licensed. My main goal is to demonstrate that the licensing of parents is theoretically desirable, though I shall also argue that a workable and just licensing program actually could be established.

My strategy is simple. After developing the basic rationale for the licensing of parents, I shall consider several objections to the proposal and argue that these objections fail to undermine it. I shall then isolate some striking similarities between this licensing program and our present policies on the adoption of children. If we retain these adoption policies—as we surely should—then, I argue, a general licensing program should also be established. Finally, I shall briefly suggest that the reason many people object to licensing is that they think parents, particularly biological parents, own or have natural sovereignty over their children.

REGULATING POTENTIALLY HARMFUL ACTIVITIES

Our society normally regulates a certain range of activities; it is illegal to perform these activities unless one has received prior permission to do so. We require automobile operators to have licenses. We forbid people from practicing medicine, law, pharmacy, or psychiatry unless they have satisfied certain licensing requirements.

Society's decision to regulate just these activities is not ad hoc. The decision to restrict admission to certain vocations and to forbid some people from driving is based on an eminently plausible, although not often explicitly formulated, rationale. We require drivers to be licensed because driving an auto is an activity which is potentially harmful to others, safe performance of the activity requires a certain competence, and we have a moderately reliable procedure for determining that competence. The potential harm is obvious: incompetent drivers can and do maim and kill people. The best way we have of limiting this harm without sacrificing the benefits of automobile travel is to require that all drivers demonstrate at least minimal competence. We likewise license doctors, lawyers, and psychologists because they perform activities which can harm others. Obviously they must be proficient if they are to perform these activities properly, and we have moderately reliable procedures for determining proficiency.[1] Imagine a world in which everyone could legally drive a car, in which everyone could legally perform surgery, prescribe medications, dispense drugs, or offer legal advice. Such a world would hardly be desirable.

Consequently, any activity that is potentially harmful to others and requires certain demonstrated competence for its safe performance, is subject to regulation—that is, it is theoretically desirable that we regulate it. If we also have a reliable procedure for determining whether someone has the requisite competence, then the action is not only subject to regulation but ought, all things considered, to be regulated.

It is particularly significant that we license these hazardous activities, even though denying a license to someone can severely inconvenience and even harm that person. Furthermore, available competency tests are not 100 percent accurate. Denying someone a driver's license in our society, for example, would inconvenience that person acutely. In effect that person would be prohibited from working, shopping, or visiting in places reachable only by car. Similarly, people denied vocational licenses are inconvenienced, even devastated. We have all heard of individuals who had the "life-long dream" of becoming physicians or lawyers, yet were denied that dream. However, the realization that some people are disappointed or inconvenienced does not diminish our conviction that we must regulate occupations or activities that are potentially dangerous to others. Innocent people must be protected even if it means that others cannot pursue activities they deem highly desirable.

Furthermore, we maintain licensing procedures even though our competency tests are sometimes inaccurate. Some people competent to perform the licensed activity (for example, driving a car) will be unable to demon-

Reprinted from *Philosophy and Public Affairs* 9.2 (1980) by permission. Footnotes edited.

strate competence (they freeze up on the driver's test). Others may be incompetent, yet pass the test (they are lucky or certain aspects of competence—for example, the sense of responsibility—are not tested). We recognize clearly—or should recognize clearly—that no test will pick out all and only competent drivers, physicians, lawyers, and so on. Mistakes are inevitable. This does not mean we should forget that innocent people may be harmed by faulty regulatory procedures. In fact, if the procedures are sufficiently faulty, we should cease regulating that activity entirely until more reliable tests are available. I only want to emphasize here that tests need not be perfect. Where moderately reliable tests are available, licensing procedures should be used to protect innocent people from incompetents.

These general criteria for regulatory licensing can certainly be applied to parents. First, parenting is an activity potentially very harmful to children. The potential for harm is apparent: each year more than half a million children are physically abused or neglected by their parents. Many millions more are psychologically abused or neglected—not given love, respect, or a sense of self-worth. The results of this maltreatment are obvious. Abused children bear the physical and psychological scars of maltreatment throughout their lives. Far too often they turn to crime.[2] They are far more likely than others to abuse their own children. Even if these maltreated children never harm anyone, they will probably never be well-adjusted, happy adults. Therefore, parenting clearly satisfies the first criterion of activities subject to regulation.

The second criterion is also incontestably satisfied. A parent must be competent if he is to avoid harming his children; even greater competence is required if he is to do the "job" well. But not everyone has this minimal competence. Many people lack the knowledge needed to rear children adequately. Many others lack the requisite energy, temperament, or stability. Therefore, child-rearing manifestly satisfies both criteria of activities subject to regulation. In fact, I dare say that parenting is a paradigm of such activities since the potential for harm is so great (both in the extent of harm any one person can suffer and in the number of people potentially harmed) and the need for competence is so evident. Consequently, there is good reason to believe that all parents should be licensed. The only ways to avoid this conclusion are to deny the need for licensing *any* potentially harmful activity; to deny that I have identified the standard criteria of activities which should be regulated; to deny that parenting satisfies the standard criteria; to show that even though parenting satisfies the standard criteria there are special reasons why licensing parents is not theoretically desirable; or to show that there is no reliable and just procedure for implementing this program.

While developing my argument for licensing I have already identified the standard criteria for activities that should be regulated, and I have shown that they can properly be applied to parenting. One could deny the legitimacy of regulation by licensing, but in doing so one would condemn not only the regulation of parenting, but also the regulation of drivers, physicians, druggists, and doctors. Furthermore, regulation of hazardous activities appears to be a fundamental task of any stable society.

Thus only two objections remain. In the next section I shall see if there are any special reasons why licensing parents is not theoretically desirable. Then, in the following section, I shall examine several practical objections designed to demonstrate that even if licensing were theoretically desirable, it could not be justly implemented.

THEORETICAL OBJECTIONS TO LICENSING

Licensing is unacceptable, someone might say, since people have a right to have children, just as they have rights to free speech and free religious expression. They do not need a license to speak freely or to worship as they wish. Why? Because they have a right to engage in these activities. Similarly, since people have a right to have children, any attempt to license parents would be unjust.

This is an important objection since many people find it plausible, if not self-evident. However, it is not as convincing as it appears The specific rights appealed to in this analogy are not without limitations. Both slander and human sacrifice are prohibited by law; both could result from the unrestricted exercise of freedom of speech and freedom of religion. Thus, even if people have these rights, they may sometimes be limited in order to protect innocent people. Consequently, even if people had a right to have children, that right might also be limited in order to protect innocent people, in this case children. Secondly, the phrase "right to have children" is ambiguous; hence, it is important to isolate its most plausible meaning in his context. Two possible interpretations are not credible and can be dismissed summarily. It is implausible to claim either that infertile people have rights to be *given* children or that people have rights to intentionally create children biologically without incurring any subsequent responsibility to them.

A third interpretation, however, is more plausible, particularly when coupled with observations about the degree of intrusion into one's life that the licensing scheme represents. On this interpretation people have a right to rear children if they make good-faith efforts to rear procreated children the best way they see fit. One might defend this claim on the ground that licensing would require too much intrusion into the lives of sincere applicants.

Undoubtedly one should be wary of unnecessary governmental intervention into individuals' lives. In this case, though, the intrusion would not often be substantial, and when it is, it would be warranted. Those granted licenses would face merely minor intervention; only those denied licenses would encounter marked intrusion. This encroachment, however, is a necessary side-effect of licensing parents—just as it is for automobile and vocational licensing. In addition, as I shall argue in more detail later, the degree of intrusion arising from a general licensing program would be no more than, and probably less than, the present (and presumably justifiable) encroachment into the lives of people who apply to adopt children. Furthermore, since some people hold unacceptable views about what is best for children (they think children should be abused regularly), people do not automatically have rights to rear children just because they will rear them in a way they deem appropriate.

Consequently, we come to a somewhat weaker interpretation of this right claim: a person has a right to rear children if he meets certain minimal standards of child rearing. Parents must not abuse or neglect their children and must also provide for the basic needs of the children. This claim of right is certainly more credible than the previously canvassed alternatives, though some people might still reject this claim in situations where exercise of the right would lead to negative consequences, for example, to overpopulation. More to the point, though, this conditional right is compatible with licensing. On this interpretation one has a right to have children only if one is not going to abuse or neglect them. Of course the very purpose of licensing is just to determine whether people *are* going to abuse or neglect their children. If the determination is made that someone will maltreat children, then that person is subject to the limitations of the right to have children and can legitimately be denied a parenting license.

In fact, this conditional way of formulating the right to have children provides a model for formulating all alleged rights to engage in hazardous activities. Consider, for example, the right to drive a car. People do not have an unconditional right to drive, although they do have a right to drive if they are competent. Similarly, people do not have an unconditional right to practice medicine; they have a right only if they are demonstrably competent. Hence, denying a driver's or physician's license to someone who has not demonstrated the requisite competence does not deny that person's rights. Likewise, on this model, denying a parenting license to someone who is not competent does not violate that person's rights.

Of course someone might object that the right is conditional on actually being a person who will abuse or neglect children, whereas my proposal only picks out those we can reasonably predict will abuse children. Hence, this conditional right *would* be incompatible with licensing.

There are two ways to interpret this objection and it is important to distinguish these divergent formulations. First, the objection could be a way of questioning our ability to predict reasonably and accurately whether people would maltreat their own children. This is an important practical objection, but I will defer discussion of it until the next section. Second, this objection could be a way of expressing doubt about the moral propriety of the prior restraint licensing requires. A parental licensing program would deny licenses to applicants judged to be incompetent even though they had never maltreated any children. This practice would be in tension with our normal skepticism about the propriety of prior restraint.

Despite this healthy skepticism, we do sometimes use prior restraint. In extreme circumstances we may hospitalize or imprison people judged insane, even though they are not legally guilty of any crime, simply because we predict they are likely to harm others. More typically, though, prior restraint is used only if the restriction is not terribly onerous and the restricted activity is one which could lead easily to serious harm. Most types of licensing (for example, those for doctors, drivers, and druggists) fall into this latter category. They require prior restraint to prevent serious harm, and generally the restraint is minor—though it is important to remember that some individuals will find it oppressive. The same is true of parental licensing. The purpose of licensing is to prevent serious harm to children. Moreover, the prior restraint required by licensing would not be terribly onerous for many people. Certainly the restraint would be far less extensive than the presumably justifiable prior restraint of, say, insane criminals. Criminals preventively detained and mentally ill people forceably hospitalized are denied most basic liberties, while those denied parental licenses would be denied only that one specific opportunity. They could still vote, work for political candidates, speak on controversial topics, and so on. Doubtless some individuals would find the restraint onerous. But when compared to other types of restraint currently practiced, and when judged in light of the severity of harm maltreated children suffer, the restraint appears *relatively* minor.

Furthermore, we could make certain, as we do with most licensing programs, that individuals denied licenses are given the opportunity to reapply easily and repeatedly for a license. Thus, many people correctly denied licenses (because they are incompetent) would choose (perhaps it would be provided) to take counseling or therapy to improve their chances of passing the next test. On the other hand, most of those mistakenly denied licenses would probably be able to demonstrate in a later test that they would be competent parents.

Consequently, even though one needs to be wary of prior restraint, if the potential for harm is great and the restraint is minor relative to the harm we are trying to prevent—as it would be with parental licensing—then such restraint is justified. This objection, like all the theoretical objections reviewed, has failed.

PRACTICAL OBJECTIONS TO LICENSING

I shall now consider five practical objections to licensing. Each objection focuses on the problems or difficulties of implementing this proposal. According to these objections, licensing is (or may be) theoretically desirable; nevertheless, it cannot be efficiently and justly implemented.

The first objection is that there may not be, or we may not be able to discover, adequate criteria of "a good parent." We simply do not have the knowledge, and it is unlikely that we could ever obtain the knowledge, that would enable us to distinguish adequate from inadequate parents.

Clearly there is some force to this objection. It is highly improbable that we can formulate criteria that would distinguish precisely between good and less than good parents. There is too much we do not know about child development and adult psychology. My proposal, however, does not demand that we make these fine distinctions. It does not demand that we license only the best parents; rather it is designed to exclude only the very bad ones. This is not just a semantic difference, but a substantive one. Although we do not have infallible criteria for picking out good parents, we undoubtedly can identify bad ones—those who will abuse or neglect their children. Even though we could have a lively debate about the range of freedom a child should be given or the appropriateness of corporal punishment, we do not wonder if a parent who severely beats or neglects a child is adequate. We know that person isn't. Consequently, we do have reliable and usable criteria for determining who is a bad parent; we have the criteria necessary to make a licensing program work.

The second practical objection to licensing is that there is no reliable way to predict who will maltreat their children. Without an accurate predictive test, licensing would be not only unjust, but also a waste of time. Now I recognize that as a philosopher (and not a psychologist, sociologist, or social worker), I am on shaky ground if I make sweeping claims about the present or future abilities of professionals to produce such predictive tests. Nevertheless, there are some relevant observations I can offer.

Initially, we need to be certain that the demands on predictive tests are not unreasonable. For example, it would be improper to require that tests be 100 percent accurate. Procedures for licensing drivers, physicians, lawyers, druggists, etc., plainly are not 100 percent (or anywhere near 100 percent) accurate. Presumably we recognize these deficiencies yet embrace the procedures anyway. Consequently, it would be imprudent to demand considerably more exacting standards for the tests used in licensing parents.

In addition, from what I can piece together, the practical possibilities for constructing a reliable predictive test are not all that gloomy. Since my proposal does not require that we make fine line distinctions between good and less than good parents, but rather that we weed out those who are potentially very bad, we can use existing tests that claim to isolate relevant predictive characteristics—whether a person is violence-prone, easily frustrated, or unduly self-centered. In fact researchers at Nashville General Hospital have developed a brief interview questionnaire which seems to have significant predictive value. Based on their data, the researchers identified 20 percent of the interviewees as a "risk group"—those having great potential for serious problems. After one year they found "the incidence of major breakdown in parent-child interaction in the risk group was approximately four to five times as great as in the low risk group." We also know that parents who maltreat children often have certain identifiable experiences, for example, most of them were themselves maltreated as children. Consequently, if we combined our information about these parents with certain psychological test results, we would probably be able to predict with reasonable accuracy which people will maltreat their children.

However, my point is not to argue about the precise reliability of present tests. I cannot say emphatically that we now have accurate predictive tests. Nevertheless, even if such tests are not available, we could undoubtedly develop them. For example, we could begin a longitudinal study in which all potential parents would be required to take a specified battery of tests. Then these parents could be "followed" to discover which ones abused or neglected their children. By correlating test scores with information on maltreatment, a usable, accurate test could be fashioned. Therefore, I do not think that the present unavailability of such tests (if they are unavailable) would count against the legitimacy of licensing parents.

The third practical objection is that even if a reliable test for ascertaining who would be an acceptable parent were available, administrators would unintentionally misuse that test. These unintentional mistakes would clearly harm innocent individuals. Therefore, so the argument goes, this proposal ought to be scrapped. This objection can be dispensed with fairly easily unless one assumes there is some special reason to believe that more mistakes will be made in administering parenting licenses than in other regulatory activities. No matter how reliable our proceedings are, there will always be mistakes. We may license a physician who, through incompetence, would cause the death of a patient; or we may mistakenly deny a physician's license to someone who would be competent. But the fact that mistakes are made does not and should not lead us to abandon attempts to determine competence. The harm done in these cases could be far worse than the harm of mistakenly denying a person a parenting license. As far as I can tell, there is no reason to believe that more mistakes will be made here than elsewhere.

The fourth proposed practical objection claims that any testing procedure will be intentionally abused. People administering the process will disqualify people they dislike, or people who espouse views they dislike, from rearing children.

The response to this objection is parallel to the response to the previous objection, namely, that there is no reason to believe that the licensing of parents is more likely to be abused than driver's license tests or other regulatory procedures. In addition, individuals can be protected from prejudicial treatment by pursuing appeals available to them. Since the licensing test can be taken on numerous occasions, the likelihood of the applicant's working with different administrative personnel increases and therefore the likelihood decreases that intentional abuse could ultimately stop a qualified person from rearing children. Consequently, since the probability of such abuse is not more than, and may even be less than, the intentional abuse of judicial and other regulatory authority, this objection does not give us any reason to reject the licensing of parents.

The fifth objection is that we could never adequately, reasonably, and fairly enforce such a program. That is, even if we could establish a reasonable and fair way of determining which people would be inadequate parents, it would be difficult, if not impossible, to enforce the program. How would one deal with violators and what could we do with babies so conceived? There are difficult problems here, no doubt, but they are not insurmountable. We might not punish parents at all—we might just remove the children and put them up for adoption. However, even if we are presently uncertain about the precise way to establish a just and effective form of enforcement, I do not see why this should undermine my licensing proposal. If it is important enough to protect children from being maltreated by parents, then surely a reasonable enforcement procedure can be secured. At least we should assume one can be unless someone shows that it cannot.

AN ANALOGY WITH ADOPTION

So far I have argued that parents should be licensed. Undoubtedly many readers find this claim extremely radical. It is revealing to notice, however, that this program is not as radical as it seems. Our moral and legal systems already recognize that not everyone is capable of rearing children well. In fact, well-entrenched laws require adoptive parents to be investigated—in much the same ways and for much the same reasons as in the general licensing program advocated here. For example, we do not allow just anyone to adopt a child; nor do we let someone adopt without first estimating the likelihood of the person's being a good parent. In fact, the adoptive process is far more rigorous than the general licensing procedures I envision. Prior to adoption the candidates must first formally apply to adopt a child. The applicants are then subjected to an exacting home study to determine whether they really want to have children and whether they are capable of caring for and rearing them adequately. No one is allowed to adopt a child until the administrators can reasonably predict that the person will be an adequate parent. The results of these procedures are impressive. Despite the trauma children often face before they are finally adopted, they are five times less likely to be abused than children reared by their biological parents.

Nevertheless we recognize, or should recognize, that these demanding procedures exclude some people who would be adequate parents. The selection criteria may be inadequate; the testing procedures may be somewhat unreliable. We may make mistakes. Probably there is some intentional abuse of the system. Adoption procedures intrude directly in the applicants' lives. Yet we continue the present adoption policies because we think it better to mistakenly deny some people the opportunity to adopt than to let just anyone adopt.

Once these features of our adoption policies are clearly identified, it becomes quite apparent that there are striking parallels between the general licensing program I have advocated and our present adoption system. Both programs have the same aim—protecting children. Both have the same drawbacks and are subject to the same abuses. The only obvious dissimilarity is that the adoption requirements are *more* rigorous than those proposed for the general licensing program. Consequently, if we think it is so important to protect adopted children, even though people who want to adopt are less likely than biological parents to maltreat their children, then we should likewise afford the same protection to children reared by their biological parents.

I suspect, though, that many people will think the cases are not analogous. The cases are relevantly different, someone might retort, because biological parents have a natural affection for their children and the strength of this affection makes it unlikely that parents would maltreat their biologically produced children.

Even if it were generally true that parents have special natural affections for their biological offspring, that does not mean that all parents have enough affection to keep them from maltreating their children. This should be apparent given the number of children abused each year by their biological parents. Therefore, even if there is generally a bond, that does not explain why we should not have licensing procedures to protect children of parents who do not have a sufficiently strong bond. Consequently, if we continue our practice of regulating the adoption of children, and certainly we should, we are rationally compelled to establish a licensing program for all parents.

However, I am not wedded to a strict form of licensing. It may well be that there are alternative ways of regulating parents which would achieve the desired results—the protection of children—without strictly prohibiting nonlicensed people from rearing children. For example, a system of tax incentives for licensed parents, and protective services scrutiny of nonlicensed parents, might adequately protect children. If it would, I would endorse the less drastic measure. My principal concern is to protect children from maltreatment by parents. I begin by advocating the more strict form of licensing since that is the standard method of regulating hazardous activities.

I have argued that all parents should be licensed by the state. This licensing program is attractive, not because state intrusion is inherently judicious and efficacious, but simply because it seems to be the best way to prevent children from being reared by incompetent parents. Nonetheless, even after considering the previous arguments, many people will find the proposal a useless academic exercise, probably silly, and possibly even morally perverse. But why? Why do most of us find this proposal unpalatable, particularly when the arguments supporting it are good and the objections to it are philosophically flimsy?

I suspect the answer is found in a long-held, deeply ingrained attitude toward children, repeatedly affirmed in recent court decisions, and present, at least to some degree, in almost all of us. The belief is that parents own, or at least have natural sovereignty over, their children. It does not matter precisely how this belief is described, since on both views parents legitimately exercise extensive and virtually unlimited control over their children. Others can properly interfere with or criticize parental decisions only in unusual and tightly prescribed circumstances—for example, when parents severely and repeatedly abuse their children. In all other cases, the parents reign supreme.

This belief is abhorrent and needs to be supplanted with a more child-centered view. Why? Briefly put, this attitude has adverse effects on children and on the adults these children will become. Parents who hold this view may well maltreat their children. If these parents happen to treat their children well, it is only because they want to, not because they think their children deserve or have a right to good treatment. Moreover, this belief is manifestly at odds with the conviction that parents should prepare children for life as adults. Children subject to parents who perceive children in this way are likely to be adequately prepared for adulthood. Hence, to prepare children for life as adults and to protect them from maltreatment, this attitude toward children must be dislodged. As I have argued, licensing is a viable way to protect children. Furthermore, it would increase the likelihood that more children will be adequately prepared for life as adults than is now the case.

Notes

1. "When practice of a profession or calling requires special knowledge or skill and intimately affects public health, morals, order or safety, or general welfare, legislature may prescribe reasonable qualifications for persons desiring to pursue such professions or calling and require them to demonstrate possession of such qualifications by examination on subjects with which such profession or calling has to deal as a condition precedent to right to follow that profession or calling." 50 SE 2nd 735 (1949). Also see 199 US 306, 318 (1905) and 123 US 623, 661 (1887).

2. According to the National Committee for the Prevention of Child Abuse, more than 80 percent of incarcerated criminals were, as children, abused by their parents. In addition, a study in the *Journal of the American Medical Association* 168, no. 3: 1755–1758, reported that first-degree murderers from middle-class homes and who have "no history of addiction to drugs, alcoholism, organic disease of the brain, or epilepsy" were frequently found to have been subject to "remorseless physical brutality at the hands of the parents."

Study Questions

1. Go over LaFollette's arguments and show their strengths and weaknesses.
2. Do you agree with LaFollette that people do not have an unconditional right to have children? Explain.
3. What are the problems with requiring licenses to have children? Imagine the government carrying out such a program. How would it work?

For Further Reading

Bayles, Michael D., ed. *Ethics and Population.* Cambridge, MA: Schenkman, 1976.

Bouvier, Leon F. "Planet Earth 1984–2034: A Demographic Vision." *Population Bulletin* 39, no. 1 (Feb. 1984).

Dailey, Gretchen C., and Paul R. Ehrlich. "Population, Sustainability and Earth's Carrying Capacity." *BioScience* 42, no. 10 (Nov 1992).

Ehrlich, Paul, and Anne Ehrlich. *The Population Explosion.* New York: Doubleday, 1990.

Homer-Dixon, Thomas, Jeffrey Boutwell, and George Rathjen. "Environmental Change and Violent Conflict." *Scientific American* (Feb. 1993).

Kasun, Jacqueline. *The War Against Population*. San Francisco: Ignatius, 1988.

Meadows, Donella H., Dennis L Meadows, et al. *The Limits to Growth: A Report for the Club of Rome's Project on the Predicament of Mankind*. New York: Universe Books, 1972.

Mumford, Stephen D. *American Democracy & The Vatican: Population Growth & National Security*. Amherst, NY: Humanist Press, 1984.

Simon, Julian. *The Ultimate Resource*. Princeton, NJ: Princeton University Press, 1981.

———. *Population Matters: People, Resources, Environment, and Immigration*, New Brunswick, NJ: Transaction, 1989.

CHAPTER TEN

Population and World Hunger

Hunger is a child with shriveled limbs and a swollen belly
It is the grief of parents, or a person gone blind for lack
of vitamin A.[1]

The victim of starvation burns up his own body fats,
muscles and tissues for fuel. His body quite literally consumes itself and deteriorates rapidly. The kidneys, liver
and endocrine system often cease to function properly. A
shortage of carbohydrates, which play a vital role in
brain chemistry, affects the mind. Lassitude and confusion set in, so that starvation victims often seem unaware
of their plight. The body's defenses drop; disease kills
most famine victims before they have time to starve to
death. An individual begins to starve when he has lost
about a third of his normal body weight. Once this loss
exceeds 40%, death is almost inevitable.[2]

Ten thousand people starve to death every day, another
2 billion (out of a global population of over 5 billion) are
malnourished, and 460 million are permanently hungry.
Almost half of these are children. More than one-third of
the world goes to bed hungry each night. In the past 25

years, devastating famines have occurred in Bangladesh
(1974), Ethiopia (1972–74, 1984), Cambodia (1978),
Chad and Sudan (1985), and in many of the other 43
countries making up the sub-Saharan region of Africa
throughout the 1970s and 1980s, including the present
famine in Somalia. Since the 1960s conditions have deteriorated in many parts of the world.[3]

On the other hand, another third of the world lives in
affluence. Imagine ten children eating at a table. The
three healthiest eat the best food and throw much of it
away or give it to their pets. Two other children get just
enough to get by on. The other five do not get enough
food. Three of them who are weak manage to stave off
hunger pangs by eating bread and rice, but the other two
are unable to do even that and die of hunger-related diseases, such as pneumonia and dysentery. Such is the
plight of children in the world.

In the United States, enough food is thrown into the
garbage each day to feed an entire nation, more money
is spent on pet food than aid to the world's starving, and
many people are grossly overweight.

Problems of global scarcity, poverty, hunger, and famine are among the most urgent facing us. What is our duty to the hungry in our country and in other lands? What obligations do we have toward the poor abroad? What rights do the starving have against us? To what extent should hunger relief be tied to population control? These are some of the questions discussed in the readings in this chapter of our book

We begin with Garrett Hardin's famous article, "Lifeboat Ethics," in which Hardin argues that affluent societies, like lifeboats, ought to ensure their survival by preserving a safety factor of resources. Giving away its resources to needy nations or admitting needy immigrants is like taking on additional passengers who threaten to capsize the lifeboat. We help neither them nor ourselves. Aiming at perfect distributive justice ends up a perfect catastrophe. Furthermore, we have a duty to our children and grandchildren, which will be compromised if we endeavor to help the poor.

In our second reading, William Murdoch and Allan Oaten take strong issue with Hardin's assessment. They argue that Hardin's arguments rest on misleading metaphors, *lifeboat, commons,* and *ratchet,* and a fuller analysis will reveal that the situation is far more hopeful than Hardin claims. We are responsible for the plight of the poor and must take steps to alleviate their suffering.

In our third reading, Peter Singer sets forth two principles, a strong and a moderate one, which show that we have a duty to give substantial aid to those who are starving. The strong principle is: "If it is in our power to prevent something bad from happening, without thereby sacrificing anything of *comparable* moral importance, we ought, morally, to do it." The weak principle is: "If it is in our power to prevent something very bad from happening, without thereby sacrificing anything *morally significant,* we ought, morally, to do it." While Singer believes that the strong principle is correct, he is content to argue for the weaker one, which if adhered to would result in vast changes in our lifestyles. Singer means his principles to be applicable to a wide spectrum of moral theories, but they have been interpreted as founded on a utilitarian philosophy.

In our fourth reading, James Rachels argues that in the light of world hunger we have a moral duty to become vegetarians. Our last reading, an essay from the *Washington Spectator,* deals with the damage done by cattle raising.

Notes

1. Arthur Simon, *Bread for the World* (New York: Paulist Press, 1975).
2. *Time Magazine,* November 11, 1974.
3. Statistics in this introduction come from the U.N. Food and Agriculture Organization. Some of the discussion is based on Arthur Simon, op. cit.

52

Lifeboat Ethics

GARRETT HARDIN

Hardin argues that the proper metaphor that characterizes our global ecological situation is not "spaceship" but "lifeboat." The spaceship metaphor is misleading since Earth has no captain to steer it through its present and future problems. Rather, each rich nation is like a lifeboat in an ocean in which the poor of the world are swimming and in danger of drowning. Hardin argues that affluent societies, like lifeboats, ought to ensure their own survival by preserving a safety factor of resources. To give away its resources to needy nations or admitting needy immigrants is like taking on additional passengers who would threaten to cause the lifeboat to capsize. Under these conditions, it is our moral duty to refrain from aiding the poor.

A biographical sketch of Garrett Hardin is found at the beginning of Reading 43.

Reprinted from "Living on a Lifeboat," *Bioscience* 24 (1974) by permission.

No generation has viewed the problem of the survival of the human species as seriously as we have. Inevitably, we have entered this world of concern through the door of metaphor. Environmentalists have emphasized the image of the earth as a spaceship—Spaceship Earth. Kenneth Boulding . . . is the principal architect of this metaphor. It is time, he says, that we replace the wasteful "cowboy economy" of the past with the frugal "spaceship economy" required for continued survival in the limited world we now see ours to be. The metaphor is notably useful in justifying pollution control measures.

Unfortunately, the image of a spaceship is also used to promote measures that are suicidal. One of these is a generous immigration policy, which is only a particular instance of a class of policies that are in error because they lead to the tragedy of the commons. . . . These suicidal policies are attractive because they mesh with what we unthinkably take to be the ideals of "the best people." What is missing in the idealistic view is an insistence that rights and responsibilities must go together. The "generous" attitude of all too many people results in asserting inalienable rights while ignoring or denying matching responsibilities.

For the metaphor of a spaceship to be correct the aggregate of people on board would have to be under unitary sovereign control. . . . A true ship always has a captain. It is conceivable that a ship could be run by a committee. But it could not possibly survive if its course were determined by bickering tribes that claimed rights without responsibilities.

What about Spaceship Earth? It certainly has no captain, and no executive committee. The United Nations is a toothless tiger, because the signatories of its charter wanted it that way. The spaceship metaphor is used only to justify spaceship demands on common resources without acknowledging corresponding spaceship responsibilities.

An understandable fear of decisive action leads people to embrace "incrementalism"—moving toward reform by tiny stages. As we shall see, this strategy is counterproductive in the area discussed here if it means accepting rights before responsibilities. Where human survival is at stake, the acceptance of responsibilities is a precondition to the acceptance of rights, if the two cannot be introduced simultaneously.

LIFEBOAT ETHICS

Before taking up certain substantive issues let us look at an alternative metaphor, that of a lifeboat. In developing some relevant examples the following numerical values are assumed. Approximately two-thirds of the world is desperately poor, and only one-third is comparatively rich. The people in poor countries have an average per capita GNP (Gross National Product) of about $200 per year; the rich, of about $3,000. (For the United States it is nearly $5,000 per year.) Metaphorically, each rich nation amounts to a lifeboat full of comparatively rich people. The poor of the world are in other, much more crowded lifeboats. Continuously, so to speak, the poor fall out of their lifeboats and swim for a while in the water outside, hoping to be admitted to a rich lifeboat, or in some other way to benefit from the "goodies" on board. What should the passengers on a rich lifeboat do? This is the central problem of "the ethics of a lifeboat."

First we must acknowledge that each lifeboat is effectively limited in capacity. The land of every nation has a limited carrying capacity. The exact limit is a matter for argument, but the energy crunch is convincing more people every day that we have already exceeded the carrying capacity of the land. We have been living on "capital"—stored petroleum and coal—and soon we must live on income alone.

Let us look at only one lifeboat—ours. The ethical problem is the same for all, and is as follows. Here we sit, say 50 people in a lifeboat. To be generous, let us assume our boat has a capacity of 10 more, making 60. (This, however, is to violate the engineering principle of the "safety factor." A new plant disease or a bad change in the weather may decimate our population if we don't preserve some excess capacity as a safety factor.)

The 50 of us in the lifeboat see 100 others swimming in the water outside, asking for admission to the boat, or for handouts. How shall we respond to their calls? There are several possibilities.

One. We may be tempted to try to live by the Christian ideal of being "our brother's keeper," or by the Marxian ideal . . . of "from each according to his abilities, to each according to his needs." Since the needs of all are the same, we take all the needy into our boat, making a total of 150 in a boat with a capacity of 60. The boat is swamped, and everyone drowns. Complete justice, complete catastrophe.

Two. Since the boat has an unused excess capacity of 10, we admit just 10 more to it. This has the disadvantage of getting rid of the safety factor, for which action we will sooner or later pay dearly. Moreover, *which* 10 do we let in? "First come, first served?" The best 10? The neediest 10? How do we *discriminate*? And what do we say to the 90 who are excluded?

Three. Admit no more to the boat and preserve the small safety factor. Survival of the people in the lifeboat is then possible (though we shall have to be on our guard against boarding parties).

The last solution is abhorrent to many people. It is unjust, they say. Let us grant that it is.

"I feel guilty about my good luck," say some. The reply to this is simple: *Get out and yield your place to others.* Such a selfless action might satisfy the conscience of those who are addicted to guilt but it would not change the ethics of the lifeboat. The needy person to whom a guilt-addict yields his place will not himself feel guilty about his sudden good luck. (If he did he would not climb aboard.) The net result of conscience-stricken people relinquishing their unjustly held positions is the elimination of their kind of conscience from the lifeboat. The lifeboat, as it were, purifies itself of guilt. The ethics of the lifeboat persist, unchanged by such momentary aberrations.

This then is the basic metaphor within which we must work out our solutions. Let us enrich the image step by step with substantive additions from the real world.

REPRODUCTION

The harsh characteristics of lifeboat ethics are heightened by reproduction, particularly by reproductive differences. The people inside the lifeboats of the wealthy nations are doubling in numbers every 87 years; those outside are doubling every 35 years, on the average. And the relative difference in prosperity is becoming greater.

Let us, for a while, think primarily of the U.S. lifeboat. As of 1973 the United States had a population of 210 million people, who were increasing by 0.8% per year, that is, doubling in number every 87 years.

Although the citizens of rich nations are outnumbered two to one by the poor, let us imagine an equal number of poor people outside our lifeboat—a mere 210 million poor people reproducing at a quite different rate. If we imagine these to be the combined populations of Colombia, Venezuela, Ecuador, Morocco, Thailand, Pakistan, and the Philippines, the average rate of increase of the people "outside" is 3.3% per year. The doubling time of this population is 21 years.

Suppose that all these countries, and the United States, agreed to live by the Marxian ideal, "to each according to his needs," the ideal of most Christians as well. Needs, of course, are determined by population size, which is affected by reproduction. Every nation regards its rate of reproduction as a sovereign right. If our lifeboat were big enough in the beginning it might be possible to live *for a while* by Christian-Marxian ideals. *Might.*

Initially, in the model given, the ratio of non-Americans to Americans would be one to one. But consider what the ratio would be 87 years later. By this time Americans would have doubled to a population of 420 million. The other group (doubling every 21 years) would now have swollen to 3,540 million. Each American would have more than eight people to share with. How could the lifeboat possibly keep afloat?

All this involves extrapolation of current trends into the future, and is consequently suspect. Trends may change. Granted: but the change will not necessarily be favorable. If—as seems likely—the rate of population increase falls faster in the ethnic group presently inside the lifeboat than it does among those now outside, the future will turn out to be even worse than mathematics predicts, and sharing will be even more suicidal.

RUIN IN THE COMMONS

The fundamental error of the sharing ethic is that it leads to the tragedy of the commons. Under a system of private property the man (or group of men) who own property recognize their responsibility to care for it, for if they don't they will eventually suffer. A farmer, for instance, if he is intelligent, will allow no more cattle in a pasture than its carrying capacity justifies. If he overloads the pasture, weeds take over, erosion sets in, and the owner loses in the long run.

But if a pasture is run as a commons open to all, the right of each to use it is not matched by an operational responsibility to take care of it. It is no use asking independent herdsmen in a commons to act responsibly, for they dare not. The considerate herdsman who refrains from overloading the commons suffers more than a selfish one who says his needs are greater. (As Leo Durocher says, "Nice guys finish last.") Christian-Marxian idealism is counterproductive. That it *sounds* nice is no excuse. With distribution systems, as with individual morality, good intentions are no substitute for good performance.

A social system is stable only if it is insensitive to errors. To the Christian-Marxian idealist a selfish person is a sort of "error." Prosperity in the system of the commons cannot survive errors. If *everyone* would only restrain himself, all would be well; but it takes *only one less than everyone* to ruin a system of voluntary restraint. In a crowded world of less than perfect human beings—and we will never know any other—mutual ruin is inevitable in the commons. This is the core of the tragedy of the commons.

WORLD FOOD BANKS

In the international arena we have recently heard a proposal to create a new commons, namely an international depository of food reserves to which nations will contribute according to their abilities, and from which nations may draw according to their needs. Nobel laureate Norman Borlaug has lent the prestige of his name to this proposal.

A world food bank appeals powerfully to our humanitarian impulses. We remember John Donne's celebrated line, "Any man's death diminishes me." But before we rush out to see for whom the bell tolls let us recognize where the greatest political push for international granaries comes from, lest we be disillusioned later. Our experience with Public Law 480 clearly reveals the answer. This was the law that moved billions of dollars worth of U.S. grain to food-short, population-long countries during the past two decades. When P.L. 480 first came into being, a headline in the business magazine *Forbes* . . . revealed the power behind it: "Feeding the World's Hungry Millions: How It Will Mean Billions for U.S. Business."

And indeed it did. In the years 1960 and to 1970 a total of $7.9 billion was spent on the "Food for Peace" program as P.L. 480 was called. During the years 1948 to 1970 an additional $49.9 billion were extracted from American taxpayers to pay for other economic aid programs, some of which went for food and food-producing machinery. (This figure does *not* include military aid.) That P.L. 480 was a give-away program was concealed. Recipient countries went through the motions of paying for P.L. 480 food—with IOU's. In December 1973 the charade was brought to an end as far as India was concerned when the United States "forgave" India's $3.2 billion debt. . . . Public announcement of the cancellation of the debt was delayed for two months: one wonders why.

The search for a rational justification can be short-circuited by interjecting the word "emergency." Borlaug uses this word. We need to look sharply at it. What is an "emergency"? It is surely something like an accident, which is correctly defined as *an event that is certain to happen, though with a low frequency.* . . . A well-run organization prepares for everything that is certain, including accidents and emergencies. It budgets for them. It saves for them. It expects them—and mature decision-makers do not waste time complaining about accidents when they occur.

What happens if some organizations budget for emergencies and others do not? If each organization is solely responsible for its own well-being, poorly managed ones will suffer. But they should be able to learn from experience. They have a chance to mend their ways and learn to budget for infrequent but certain emergencies. The weather, for instance, always varies and periodic crop failures are certain. A wise and competent government saves out of the production of the good years in anticipation of bad years that are sure to come. This is not a new idea. The Bible tells us that Joseph taught this policy to Pharaoh in Egypt more than 2,000 years ago. Yet it is literally true that the vast majority of the governments of the world today have no such policy. They lack either the wisdom or the competence, or both. Far more difficult than the transfer of wealth from one country to another is the transfer of wisdom between sovereign powers or between generations.

"But it isn't their fault! How can we blame the poor people who are caught in an emergency? Why must we punish them?" The concepts of blame and punishment are irrelevant. The question is, what are the operational consequences of establishing a world food bank? If it is open to every country every time a need develops, slovenly rulers will not be motivated to take Joseph's advice. Why should they? Others will bail them out whenever they are in trouble.

Some countries will make deposits in the world food bank and others will withdraw from it: there will be almost no overlap. Calling such a depository-transfer unit a "bank" is stretching the metaphor of *bank* beyond its elastic limits. The proposers, of course, never call attention to the metaphorical nature of the word they use.

THE RATCHET EFFECT

An "international food bank" is really, then, not a true bank but a disguised one-way transfer device for moving wealth from rich countries to poor. In the absence of such a bank, in a world inhabited by individually responsible sovereign nations, the population of each nation would repeatedly go through a cycle of the sort shown in Figure 1. P_2 is greater than P_1, either in absolute numbers or because a deterioration of the food supply has removed the safety factor and produced a dangerously low ratio of resources to population. P_2 may be said to represent a state of overpopulation, which becomes obvious upon the appearance of an "accident," e.g., a crop failure. If the "emergency" is not met by outside help, the population drops back to the "normal" level—the "carrying capacity" of the environment—or even below. In the absence of population control by a sovereign, sooner or later the population grows to P_2 again and the cycle repeats. The long-term population curve . . . is an irregularly fluctuating one, equilibrating more or less about the carrying capacity.

A demographic cycle of this sort obviously involves great suffering in the restrictive phase, but such a cycle is normal to any independent country with inadequate population control. The third century theologian Tertullian . . . expressed what must have been the recognition of many wise men when he wrote: "The scourges of pestilence, famine, wars, and earthquakes have come to be regarded as a blessing to overcrowded nations, since they serve to prune away the luxuriant growth of the human race."

Only under a strong and farsighted sovereign—which theoretically could be the people themselves, democratically organized—can a population equilibrate at some set point below the carrying capacity, thus avoiding the pains normally caused by periodic and unavoidable disasters. For this happy state to be achieved it is necessary that those in power be able to contemplate with equanimity the "waste" of surplus food in times of bountiful

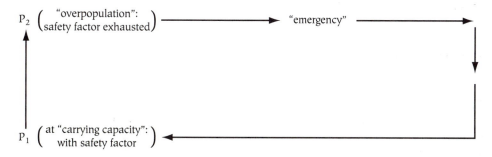

FIGURE 1 *The population cycle of a nation that has no effective, conscious population control, and which receives no aid from the outside.* P_2 *is greater then* P_1.

harvests. It is essential that those in power resist the temptation to convert extra food into extra babies. On the public relations level it is necessary that the phrase "surplus food" be replaced by "safety factor."

But wise sovereigns seem not to exist in the poor world today. The most anguishing problems are created by poor countries that are governed by rulers insufficiently wise and powerful. If such countries can draw on a world food bank in times of "emergency," the population *cycle* of Figure 1 will be replaced by the population *escalator* of Figure 2. The input of food from a food bank acts as the pawl of a ratchet, preventing the population from retracing its steps to a lower level. Reproduction pushes the population upward, inputs from the world bank prevent its moving downward. Population size escalates, as does the absolute magnitude of "accidents" and "emergencies." The process is brought to an end only by the total collapse of the whole system, producing a catastrophe of scarcely imaginable proportions.

Such are the implications of the well-meant sharing of food in a world of irresponsible reproduction.

All this is terribly obvious once we are acutely aware of the pervasiveness and danger of the commons. But many people still lack this awareness and the euphoria of the "benign demographic transition" . . . interferes with the realistic appraisal of pejoristic mechanisms. As concerns public policy, the deductions drawn from the benign demographic transition are these:

1. If the per capita GNP rises the birth rate will fall; hence, the rate of population increase will fall, ultimately producing ZPG (Zero Population Growth).
2. The long-term trend all over the world (including the poor countries) is of a rising per capita GNP (for which no limit is seen).
3. Therefore, all political interference in population matters is unnecessary; all we need to do is foster economic "development"—*note the metaphor*—and population problems will solve themselves.

Those who believe in the benign demographic transition dismiss the pejoristic mechanism of Figure 2 in the belief that each input of food from the world fosters development within a poor country thus resulting in a drop in the rate of population increase. Foreign aid has proceeded on this assumption for more than two decades. Unfortunately it has produced no indubitable instance of the asserted effect. It has, however, produced a library of excuses. The air is filled with plaintive calls for more massive foreign aid appropriations so that the hypothetical melioristic process can get started.

The doctrine of demographic laissez-faire implicit in the hypothesis of the benign demographic transition is immensely attractive. Unfortunately there is more evidence against the melioristic system than there is for it. . . . On the historical side there are many counter-examples. The rise in per capita GNP in France and Ireland during the past century has been accompanied by a rise in population growth. In the 20 years following the Second World War the same positive correlation was noted almost everywhere in the world. Never in world history before 1950 did the worldwide population growth reach 1% per annum. Now the average population growth is over 2% and shows no signs of slackening.

On the theoretical side, the denial of the pejoristic scheme of Figure 2 probably springs from the hidden acceptance of the "cowboy economy" that Boulding castigated. Those who recognize the limitations of a spaceship, if they are unable to achieve population control at a safe and comfortable level, accept the necessity of the corrective feedback of the population cycle shown in Figure 1. No one who knew in his bones that he was living on a true spaceship would countenance political support of the population escalator shown in Figure 2.

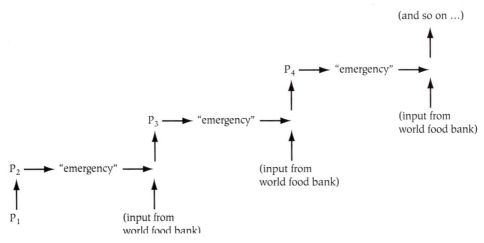

FIGURE 2 *The Population Escalator. Note that input from a world food bank acts like the pawl of a ratchet, preventing the normal population cycle shown in Figure 1 from being completed. P_{n+1} is greater than P_n and the absolute magnitude of the "emergencies" escalates. Ultimately the entire system crashes. The crash is not shown, and few can imagine it.*

ECO-DESTRUCTION VIA THE GREEN REVOLUTION

The demoralizing effect of charity on the recipient has long been known. "Give a man a fish and he will eat for a day: teach him how to fish and he will eat for the rest of his days." So runs an ancient Chinese proverb. Acting on this advice the Rockefeller and Ford Foundations have financed a multipronged program for improving agriculture in the hungry nations. The result, known as the "Green Revolution," has been quite remarkable. "Miracle wheat" and "miracle rice" are splendid technological achievements in the realm of plant genetics.

Whether or not the Green Revolution can increase food production is doubtful . . . , but in any event not particularly important. What is missing in this great and well-meaning humanitarian effort is a firm grasp of fundamentals. Considering the importance of the Rockefeller Foundation in this effort it is ironic that the late Alan Gregg, a much-respected vice president of the Foundation, strongly expressed his doubts of the wisdom of all attempts to increase food production some two decades ago. (This was before Borlaug's work—supported by Rockefeller—had resulted in the development of "miracle wheat.") Gregg . . . likened the growth and spreading of humanity over the surface of the earth to the metastasis of cancer in the human body, wryly remarking that "Cancerous growths demand food; but, as far as I know, they have never been cured by getting it. "

"Man does not live by bread alone"—the scriptural statement has a rich meaning even in the material realm. Every human being born constitutes a draft on all aspects of the environment—food, air, water, unspoiled scenery, occasional and optional solitude, beaches, contact with wild animals, fishing, hunting—the list is long and incompletely known. Food can, perhaps, be significantly increased: but what about clean beaches, unspoiled forests, and solitude? If we satisfy the need for food in a growing population we necessarily decrease the supply of other goods, and thereby increase the difficulty of equitably allocating scarce goods. . . .

The present population of India is 600 million, and it is increasing by 15 million per year. The environmental load of this population is already great. The forests of India are only a small fraction of what they were three centuries ago. Soil erosion, floods, and the psychological costs of crowding are serious. Every one of the net 15 million lives added each year stresses the Indian environment more severely. *Every life saved this year in a poor country diminishes the quality of life for subsequent generations.*

Observant critics have shown how much harm we wealthy nations have already done to poor nations through our well-intentioned but misguided attempts to help them. . . . Particularly reprehensible is our failure to carry out postaudits of these attempts. . . . Thus we have shielded our tender consciences from knowledge of the harm we have done. Must we Americans continue to fail to monitor the consequences of our external "do-gooding"? If, for instance, we thoughtlessly make it possible for the present 600 million Indians to swell to 1,200 millions by the year 2001—as their present growth rate promises—will posterity in India thank us for facilitating an even greater destruction of *their* environment? Are good intentions ever a sufficient excuse for bad consequences?

IMMIGRATION CREATES A COMMONS

I come now to the final example of a commons in action, one for which the public is least prepared for rational discussion. The topic is at present enveloped by a great silence which reminds me of a comment made by Sherlock Holmes in A. Conan Doyle's story, "Silver Blaze." Inspector Gregory had asked, "Is there any point to which you would wish to draw my attention?" To this Holmes responded:

> "To the curious incident of the dog in the night-time."
>
> "The dog did nothing in the night-time," said the Inspector.
>
> "That was the curious incident," remarked Sherlock Holmes.

By asking himself what would repress the normal barking instinct of a watchdog Holmes realized that it must be the dog's recognition of his master as the criminal trespasser. In a similar way we should ask ourselves, what repression keeps us from discussing something as important as immigration?

It cannot be that immigration is numerically of no consequence. Our government acknowledges a *net* flow of 400,000 a year. Hard data are understandably lacking on the extent of illegal entries, but a not implausible figure is 600,000 per year. . . . The natural increase of the resident population is now about 1.7 million per year. This means that the yearly gain from immigration is at least 19%, and may be 37%, of the total increase. It is quite conceivable that educational campaigns like that of Zero Population Growth, Inc., coupled with adverse social and economic factors—inflation, housing shortage, depression, and loss of confidence in national leaders—may lower the fertility of American women to a point at which all of the yearly increase in population would be accounted for by immigration. Should we not at least ask if that is what we want? How curious it is that we so seldom discuss immigration these days!

Curious, but understandable—as one finds out the moment he publicly questions the wisdom of the status quo in immigration. He who does so is promptly charged with *isolationism, bigotry, prejudice, ethnocentrism, chauvinism,* and *selfishness.* These are hard accusations to bear. It is pleasanter to talk about other matters, leaving immigration policy to wallow in the cross-currents of special interests that take no account of the good of the whole—*or of the interests of posterity.*

We Americans have a bad conscience because of things we said in the past about immigrants. Two generations ago the popular press was rife with references to *Dagos, Wops, Pollacks, Japs, Chinks,* and *Krauts*—all pejorative terms which failed to acknowledge our indebtedness to Goya, Leonardo, Copernicus, Hiroshige, Confucius, and Bach. Because the implied inferiority of foreigners was *then* the justification for keeping them out, it is *now* thoughtlessly assumed that restrictive policies can only be based on the assumption of immigrant inferiority. *This is not so.*

Existing immigration laws exclude idiots and known criminals; future laws will almost certainly continue this policy. But should we also consider the quality of the average immigrant, as compared with the quality of the average resident? Perhaps we should, perhaps we shouldn't. (What is "quality" anyway?) But the quality issue is not our concern here.

From this point on, *it will be assumed that immigrants and native-born citizens are of exactly equal quality,* however quality may be defined. The focus is only on quantity. The conclusions reached depend on nothing else, so all charges of ethnocentrism are irrelevant.

World food banks move food to the people, thus facilitating the exhaustion of the environment of the poor. By contrast, unrestricted immigration moves people to the food, thus speeding up the destruction of the environment in rich countries. Why poor people should want to make this transfer is no mystery: but why should rich hosts encourage it? This transfer, like the reverse one, is supported by both selfish interests and humanitarian impulses.

The principal selfish interests in unimpeded immigration is easy to identify; it is the interest of the employers of cheap labor, particularly that needed for degrading jobs. We have been deceived about the forces of history by the lines of Emma Lazarus inscribed on the Statue of Liberty:

> Give me your tired, your poor
> Your huddled masses yearning to breathe free,
> The wretched refuse of your teeming shore,
> Send these, the homeless, tempest-tossed, to me:
> I lift my lamp beside the golden door.

The image is one of an infinitely generous earth-mother, passively opening her arms to hordes of immigrants who come here on their own initiative. Such an image may have been adequate for the early days of colonization, but by the time these lines were written (1886) the force for immigration was largely manufactured inside our own borders by factory and mine owners who sought cheap labor not to be found among laborers already here. One group of foreigners after another was thus enticed into the United States to work at wretched jobs for wretched wages.

At present, it is largely the Mexicans who are being so exploited. It is particularly to the advantage of certain employers that there be many illegal immigrants. Illegal immigrant workers dare not complain about their working conditions for fear of being repatriated. Their presence reduces the bargaining power of all Mexican-American laborers. Cesar Chavez has repeatedly pleaded with congressional committees to close the doors to more Mexicans so that those here can negotiate effectively for higher wages and decent working conditions. Chavez understands the ethics of a lifeboat.

The interests of the employers of cheap labor are well served by the silence of the intelligentsia of the country. WASPs—White Anglo-Saxon Protestants—are particularly reluctant to call for a closing of the doors to immigration for fear of being called ethnocentric bigots. It was, therefore, an occasion of pure delight for this particular WASP to be present at a meeting when the points he would like to have made were made better by a non-WASP speaking to other non-WASPS. It was in Hawaii, and most of the people in the room were second-level Hawaiian officials of Japanese ancestry. All Hawaiians are keenly aware of the limits of their environment, and the speaker had asked how it might be practically and constitutionally possible to close the doors to more immigrants to the islands. (To Hawaiians, immigrants from the other 49 states are as much of a threat as those from other nations. There is only so much room in the islands, and the islanders know it. Sophistical arguments that imply otherwise do not impress them.)

Yet the Japanese-Americans of Hawaii have active ties with the land of their origin. This point was raised by a Japanese-American member of the audience who asked the Japanese-American speaker: "But how can we shut the doors now? We have many friends and relations in Japan that we'd like to bring to Hawaii some day so that they can enjoy this beautiful land."

The speaker smiled sympathetically and responded slowly: "Yes, but we have children now and someday we'll have grandchildren. We can bring more people here from Japan only by giving away some of the land that we hope to pass on to our grandchildren some day. What right do we have to do that?"

To be generous with one's own possessions is one thing; to be generous with posterity's is quite another. This, I think, is the point that must be gotten across to those who would, from a commendable love of distributive justice, institute a ruinous system of the commons, either in the form of a world food bank or that of unrestricted immigration. Since every speaker is a member of some ethnic group it is always possible to charge him with ethnocentrism. But even after purging an argument of ethnocentrism the rejection of the commons is still valid and necessary if we are to save at least some parts of the world from environmental ruin. Is it not desirable that at least some of the grandchildren of people now living should have a decent place in which to live?

Plainly many new problems will arise when we consciously face the immigration question and seek rational answers. No workable answers can be found if we ignore population problems. And—if the argument of this essay is correct—so long as there is no true world government to control reproduction everywhere it is impossible to survive in dignity if we are to be guided by Spaceship ethics. Without a world government that is sovereign in reproductive matters mankind lives, in fact, on a number of sovereign lifeboats. For the foreseeable future survival demands that we govern our actions by the ethics of a lifeboat. Posterity will be ill served if we do not.

Study Questions

1. What is Hardin's case against helping poor, needy countries? What is the significance of the lifeboat metaphor?
2. What is the relationship of population policies to world hunger?
3. Explain the "ratchet effect." Is Hardin right that in bringing aid to countries who do not control their population we act immorally?

53

Population and Food: A Critique of Lifeboat Ethics

WILLIAM W. MURDOCH AND ALLAN OATEN

William Murdoch is professor of biological science at the University of California at Santa Barbara and is the author of Environment: Resources, Pollution and Society *(2nd ed., 1975). Allan Oaten is also a biologist who has taught at the University of California at Santa Barbara and specializes in mathematical biology and statistics.*

Murdoch and Oaten begin by attacking Hardin's metaphors of "lifeboat," "commons," and "ratchet" as misleading. They then argue that other factors are needed to understand the population and hunger problem, including parental confidence in the future, low infant mortality rates, literacy, health care, income and employment, and an adequate diet. They claim that once the socioeconomic conditions are attended to, population size will take care of itself. Nonmilitary foreign aid to third world countries is both just and necessary if we are to prevent global disaster.

MISLEADING METAPHORS

[Hardin's] "lifeboat" article actually has two messages. The first is that our immigration policy is too generous. This will not concern us here. The second, and more important, is that by helping poor nations we will bring disaster to rich and poor alike:

Metaphorically, each rich nation amounts to a lifeboat full of comparatively rich people. The poor of the world are in other, much more crowded lifeboats. Continuously, so to speak, the poor fall out of their lifeboats and swim for a while in the water outside, hoping to be admitted to a rich lifeboat, or in some other way to benefit from the "goodies" on board. What should the passengers on a rich lifeboat do? This is the central problem of "the ethics of a lifeboat." (Hardin)

Among these so called "goodies" are food supplies and technical aid such as that which led to the Green Revolution. Hardin argues that we should withhold such resources from poor nations on the grounds that they help to maintain high rates of population increase, thereby making the problem worse. He foresees the continued supplying and increasing production of food as a process that will be "brought to an end only by the total collapse of the whole system, producing a catastrophe of scarcely imaginable proportions."

Turning to one particular mechanism for distributing these resources, Hardin claims that a world food bank is a commons—people have more motivation to draw from it than to add to it; it will have a ratchet or escalator effect on population because inputs from it will prevent population declines in over-populated countries. Thus "wealth can be steadily moved in one direction only, from the slowly-breeding rich to the rapidly-breeding poor, the process finally coming to a halt only when all countries are equally and miserably poor." Thus our help will not only bring ultimate disaster to poor countries, but it will also be suicidal for us.

As for the "benign demographic transition" to low birth rates, which some aid supporters have predicted,

Reprinted from "Population and Food: Metaphors and the Reality," *Bioscience* 25 (1975) by permission. Notes deleted.

Hardin states flatly that the weight of evidence is against this possibility.

Finally, Hardin claims that the plight of poor nations is partly their own fault: "wise sovereigns seem not to exist in the poor world today. The most anguishing problems are created by poor countries that are governed by rulers insufficiently wise and powerful." Establishing a world food bank will exacerbate this problem: "slovenly rulers" will escape the consequences of their incompetence—"Others will bail them out whenever they are in trouble"; "Far more difficult than the transfer of wealth from one country to another is the transfer of wisdom between sovereign powers or between generations."

What arguments does Hardin present in support of these opinions? Many involve metaphors: lifeboat, commons, and ratchet or escalator. These metaphors are crucial to his thesis, and it is, therefore, important for us to examine them critically.

The lifeboat is the major metaphor. It seems attractively simple, but it is in fact simplistic and obscures important issues. As soon as we try to use it to compare various policies, we find that most relevant details of the actual situation are either missing or distorted in the lifeboat metaphor. Let us list some of these details.

Most important, perhaps, Hardin's lifeboats barely interact. The rich lifeboats may drop some handouts over the side and perhaps repel a boarding party now and then, but generally they live their own lives. In the real world, nations interact a great deal, in ways that affect food supply and population size and growth, and the effect of rich nations on poor nations has been strong and not always benevolent.

First, by colonization and actual wars of commerce, and through the international marketplace, rich nations have arranged an exchange of goods that has maintained and even increased the economic imbalance between rich and poor nations. Until recently we have taken or otherwise obtained cheap raw material from poor nations and sold them expensive manufactured goods that they cannot make themselves. In the United States, the structure of tariffs and internal subsidies discriminates selectively against poor nations. In poor countries, the concentration on cash crops rather than on food crops, a legacy of colonial times, is now actively encouraged by western multinational corporations. . . . Indeed, it is claimed that in famine-stricken Sahelian Africa, multinational agribusiness has recently taken land out of food production for cash crops. . . . Although we often self-righteously take the "blame" for lowering the death rates of poor nations during the 1940s and 1950s, we are less inclined to accept responsibility for the effects of actions that help maintain poverty and hunger. Yet poverty directly contributes to the high birth rates that Hardin views with such alarm.

Second, U.S. foreign policy, including foreign aid programs, has favored "pro-Western" regimes, many of which govern in the interests of a wealthy elite and some of which are savagely repressive. Thus, it has often subsidized a gross maldistribution of income and has supported political leaders who have opposed most of the social changes that can lead to reduced birth rates. In this light, Hardin's pronouncements on the alleged wisdom gap between poor leaders and our own, and the difficulty of filling it, appear as a grim joke: our response to leaders with the power and wisdom Hardin yearns for has often been to try to replace them or their policies as soon as possible. Selective giving and withholding of both military and nonmilitary aid has been an important ingredient of our efforts to maintain political leaders we like and to remove those we do not. Brown . . . , after noting that the withholding of U.S. food aid in 1973 contributed to the downfall of the Allende government in Chile, comments that "although Americans decry the use of petroleum as a political weapon, calling it 'political blackmail,' the United States has been using food aid for political purposes for twenty years—and describing this as 'enlightened diplomacy.'"

Both the quantity and the nature of the supplies on a lifeboat are fixed. In the real world, the quantity has strict limits, but these are far from having been reached (University of California Food Task Force 1974). Nor are we forced to devote fixed proportions of our efforts and energy to automobile travel, pet food, packaging, advertising, corn-fed beef, "defense" and other diversions, many of which cost far more than foreign aid does. The fact is that enough food is now produced to feed the world's population adequately. That people are malnourished is due to distribution and to economics, not to agricultural limits (United Nations Economic and Social Council 1974).

Hardin's lifeboats are divided merely into rich and poor, and it is difficult to talk about birth rates on either. In the real world, however, there are striking differences among the birth rates of the poor countries and even among the birth rates of different parts of single countries. These differences appear to be related to social conditions (also absent from lifeboats) and may guide us to effective aid policies.

Hardin's lifeboat metaphor not only conceals facts, but misleads about the effects of his proposals. The rich lifeboat can raise the ladder and sail away. But in real life, the problem will not necessarily go away just because it is ignored. In the real world, there are armies, raw materials in poor nations, and even outraged domestic dissidents prepared to sacrifice their own and others' lives to oppose policies they regard as immoral.

No doubt there are other objections. But even this list shows the lifeboat metaphor to be dangerously inappropriate for serious policy making because it obscures far more than it reveals. Lifeboats and "lifeboat ethics" may be useful topics for those who are shipwrecked; we believe they are worthless—indeed detrimental—in discussions of food-population questions.

The ratchet metaphor is equally flawed. It, too, ignores complex interactions between birth rates and social conditions (including diets), implying as it does that more food will simply mean more babies. Also, it obscures the fact that the decrease in death rates has been caused at least as much by developments such as DDT, improved sanitation, and medical advances, as by increased food supplies, so that cutting out food aid will not necessarily lead to population declines.

The lifeboat article is strangely inadequate in other ways. For example, it shows an astonishing disregard for recent literature. The claim that we can expect no "benign demographic transition" is based on a review written more than a decade ago. . . . Yet, events and attitudes are changing rapidly in poor countries: for the first time in history, most poor people live in countries with birth control programs; with few exceptions, poor nations are somewhere on the demographic transition to lower birth rates . . . ; the population-food squeeze is now widely recognized, and governments of poor nations are aware of the relationship. Again, there is a considerable amount of evidence that birth rates can fall rapidly in poor countries given the proper social conditions (as we will discuss later); consequently, crude projections of current populations growth rates are quite inadequate for policy making.

THE TRAGEDY OF THE COMMONS

Throughout the lifeboat article, Hardin bolsters his assertions by reference to the "commons." . . . The thesis of the commons, therefore, needs critical evaluation.

Suppose several privately owned flocks, comprising 100 sheep altogether, are grazing on a public commons. They bring in an annual income of $1.00 per sheep. Fred, a herdsman, owns only one sheep. He decides to add another. But 101 is too many: the commons is overgrazed and produces less food. The sheep lose quality and income drops to 90¢ per sheep. Total income is now $90.90 instead of $100.00. Adding the sheep has brought an overall loss. But Fred has gained: *his* income is $1.80 instead of $1.00. The gain from the additional sheep, which is his alone, outweighs the loss from overgrazing, which he shares. Thus he promotes his interest at the expense of the community.

This is the problem of the commons, which seems on the way to becoming an archtype. Hardin, in particular, is not inclined to underrate its importance: "One of the major tasks of education today is to create such an awareness of the dangers of the commons that people will be able to recognize its many varieties, however disguised" . . . and "All this is terribly obvious once we are acutely aware of the pervasiveness and danger of the commons. But many people still lack this awareness. . . ."

The "commons" affords a handy way of classifying problems: the lifeboat article reveals that sharing, a generous immigration policy, world food banks, air, water, the fish populations of the ocean, and the western range lands are, or produce, a commons. It is also handy to be able to dispose of policies one does not like and "only a particular instance of a class of policies that are in error because they lead to the tragedy of the commons."

But no metaphor, even one as useful as this, should be treated with such awe. Such shorthand can be useful, but it can also mislead by discouraging and obscuring important detail. To dismiss a proposal by suggesting that "all you need to know about this proposal is that it institutes a commons and is, therefore, bad" is to assert that the proposed commons is worse than the original problem. This might be so if the problem of the commons were, indeed, a tragedy—that is, if it were insoluble. But it is not.

Hardin favors private ownership as the solution (either through private property or the selling of pollution rights). But, of course, there are solutions other than private ownership; and private ownership itself is no guarantee of carefully husbanded resources.

One alternative to private ownership of the commons is communal ownership of the sheep—or, in general, of the mechanisms and industries that exploit the resource— combined with communal planning for management. (Note, again, how the metaphor favors one solution: perhaps the "tragedy" lay not in the commons but in the sheep. "The Tragedy of the Privately Owned Sheep" lacks zing, unfortunately.) Public ownership of a commons has been tried in Peru to the benefit of the previously privately owned anchovy fishery. . . . The communally owned agriculture of China does not seem to have suffered any greater over-exploitation than that of other Asian nations.

Another alternative is cooperation combined with regulation. For example, Gulland . . . has shown that Antarctic whale stocks (perhaps the epitome of a commons since they are internationally exploited and no one owns them) are now being properly managed, and stocks are increasing. This has been achieved through cooperation in the International Whaling Commission, which has by agreement set limits to the catch of each nation.

In passing, Hardin's private ownership argument is not generally applicable to nonrenewable resources. Given discount rates, technology substitutes, and no more than an average regard for posterity, privately owned nonrenewable resources, like oil, coal and minerals, are mined at rates that produce maximum profits, rather than at those rates that preserve them for future generations. . . .

BIRTH RATES: AN ALTERNATIVE VIEW

Is the food-population spiral inevitable? A more optimistic, if less comfortable, hypothesis, presented by Rich and Brown, is increasingly tenable: contrary to the "ratchet" projection, population growth rates are affected by many complex conditions beside food supply. In particular, a set of socioeconomic conditions can be identified that motivate parents to have fewer children; under these conditions, birth rates can fall quite rapidly, sometimes even before birth control technology is available. Thus, population growth can be controlled more effectively by intelligent human intervention that sets up the appropriate conditions than by doing nothing and trusting to "natural population cycles."

These conditions are: parental confidence about the future, an improved status of women, and literacy. They require low infant mortality rates, widely available rudimentary health care, increased income and employment, and an adequate diet above subsistence levels. Expenditure on schools (especially elementary schools), appropriate health services (especially rural para-medical services), and agriculture reform (especially aid to small farmers) will be needed, and foreign aid can help here. It is essential that these improvements be spread across the population; aid can help here, too, by concentrating on the poor nations' poorest people, encouraging necessary institutional and social reforms, and making it easier for poor nations to use their own resources and initiative to help themselves. It is *not* necessary that per capita GNP be very high, certainly not as high as that of the rich countries during their gradual demographic transition. In other words, low birth rates in poor countries are achievable long before the conditions exist that were present in the rich countries in the late 19th and early 20th centuries.

Twenty or thirty years is not long to discover and assess the factors affecting birth rates, but a body of evidence is now accumulating in favor of this hypothesis. Rich and Brown show that at least 10 developing countries have managed to reduce their birth rates by an average of more than one birth per 1,000 population per year for periods of 5 to 16 years. A reduction of one birth per 1,000 per year would bring birth rates in poor countries to a rough replacement level of about 16/1,000 by the turn of the century, though age distribution effects would prevent a smooth population decline. We have listed these countries in Table 1, together with three other nations, including China, that are poor and yet have brought their birth rates down to 30 or less, presumably from rates of over 40 a decade or so ago.

These data show that rapid reduction in birth rates is possible in the developing world. No doubt it can be argued that each of these cases is in some way special. Hong Kong and Singapore are relatively rich; they, Barbados, and Mauritius are also tiny. China is able to exert great social pressure on its citizens; but China is particularly significant. It is enormous; its per capita GNP is almost as low as India's; and it started out in 1949 with a terrible health system. Also, Egypt, Chile, Taiwan, Cuba, South Korea, and Sri Lanka are quite large, and they are poor or very poor (Table 1). In fact, these examples represent an enormous range of religion, political systems, and geography and suggest that such rates of decline in the birth rate can be achieved whenever the appropriate conditions are met. "The common factor in these countries is that the *majority* of the population has shared in the economic and social benefits of significant national progress. . . . [M]aking health, education and jobs more broadly available to lower income groups in poor countries contribute[s] significantly toward the motivation for smaller families that is the prerequisite of major reduction in birth rates". . . .

The converse is also true. In Latin America, Cuba (annual per capita income $530), Chile ($720), Uruguay ($820), and Argentina ($1,160) have moderate to truly equitable distribution of goods and services and rela-

TABLE 1 *Declining Birth Rates and Per Capita Income in Selected Developing Countries. (These Are Crude Birth Rates, Uncorrected for Age Distribution.)*

		BIRTHS/1,000/YEAR		
COUNTRY	TIME SPAN	AVG. ANNUAL DECLINE IN CRUDE BIRTH RATE	CRUDE BIRTH RATE 1972	$ PER CAPITA PER YEAR 1973
Barbados	1960–69	1.5	22	570
Taiwan	1955–71	1.2	24	390
Tunisia	1966–71	1.8	35	250
Mauritius	1961–71	1.5	25	240
Hong Kong	1960–72	1.4	19	970
Singapore	1955–72	1.2	23	920
Costa Rica	1963–72	1.5	32	560
South Korea	1960–70	1.2	29	250
Egypt	1966–70	1.7	37	210
Chile	1963–70	1.2	25	720
China			30	160
Cuba			27	530
Sri Lanka			30	110

tively low birth rates (27, 26, 23, and 22, respectively). In contrast, Brazil ($420), Mexico ($670), and Venezuela ($980) have very unequal distribution of goods and services and high birth rates (38, 42, and 41, respectively). Fertility rates in poor and relatively poor nations seem unlikely to fall as long as the bulk of the population does not share in increased benefits. . . .

. . . As a disillusioning quarter-century of aid giving has shown, the obstacles of getting aid to those segments of the population most in need of it are enormous. Aid has typically benefited a small rich segment of society, partly because of the way aid programs have been designed but also because of human and institutional factors in the poor nations themselves. . . . With some notable exceptions, the distribution of income and services in poor nations is extremely skewed—much more uneven than in rich countries. Indeed, much of the population is essentially outside the economic system. Breaking this pattern will be extremely difficult. It will require not only aid that is designed specifically to benefit the rural poor, but also important institutional changes such as decentralization of decision making and the development of greater autonomy and stronger links to regional and national market for local groups and industries such as cooperative farms.

Thus, two things are being asked of rich nations and of the United States in particular: to increase nonmilitary foreign aid, including food aid, and to give it in ways, and to governments, that will deliver it to the poorest people and will improve their access to national economic institutions. These are not easy tasks, particularly the second, and there is no guarantee that birth rates will come down quickly in all countries. Still, many poor countries have, in varying degrees, begun the process of reform, and recent evidence suggests that aid and reform together can do much to solve the twin problems of high birth rates and economic underdevelopment. The tasks are far from impossible. Based on the evidence, the policies dictated by a sense of decency are also the most realistic and rational.

Study Questions

1. What are the criticisms leveled against Hardin's arguments?
2. What is Murdoch and Oaten's view on the question of population growth? What is the gradual demographic transition theory? Is their view plausible?
3. Compare Hardin's arguments with Murdochs and Oaten's response. Where does the evidence lie?

54

Famine, Affluence, and Morality

PETER SINGER

Peter Singer argues that we have a duty to provide aid to famine victims and others who are suffering from hunger and poverty. He proposes two principles, a strong and a moderate one, which show that we have a duty to give substantial aid to those who are starving. The strong principle is: "If it is in our power to prevent something bad from happening, without thereby sacrificing anything of comparable *moral importance, we ought, morally, to do it." The weak principle is: "If it is in our power to prevent something very bad from happening, without thereby sacrificing anything* morally significant, *we ought, morally, to do it."*

A biographical sketch of Peter Singer is found before Reading 7.

As I write this, in November, 1971, people are dying in East Bengal from lack of food, shelter, and medical care. The suffering and death that are occurring there now are not inevitable, not unavoidable in any fatalistic sense of the term. Constant poverty, a cyclone, and a civil war have turned at least nine million people into destitute refugees; nevertheless, it is not beyond the capacity of the richer nations to give enough assistance to reduce any further suffering to very small proportions. The decisions and actions of human beings can prevent this kind of suffering. Unfortunately, human beings have not made the necessary decisions. At the individual level, people have, with very few exceptions, not responded to the situation in any significant way. Generally speaking, people have not given large sums to relief funds; they have not written to their parliamentary representatives demanding increased government assistance; they have not demonstrated in the streets, held symbolic fasts, or done anything else directed toward providing the refugees with the means to satisfy their essential needs. At the government level, no government has given the sort of massive aid that would enable the refugees to survive for more than a few days. Britain, for instance, has given rather more than most countries. It has, to date, given £14,750,000. For comparative purposes, Britain's share of the nonrecoverable development costs of the

Reprinted from *World Hunger and Moral Obligation*, eds. William Aiken and Hugh LaFollette (Englewood Cliffs, NJ: Prentice Hall, 1977) by permission.

Anglo-French Concorde project is already in excess of £275,000,000, and on present estimates will reach £440,000,000. The implication is that the British government values a supersonic transport more than thirty times as highly as it values the lives of the nine million refugees. Australia is another country which, on a per capita basis, is well up in the "aid to Bengal" table. Australia's aid, however, amounts to less than one-twentieth of the cost of Sydney's new opera house. The total amount given, from all sources, now stands at about £65,000,000. The estimated cost of keeping the refugees alive for one year is £464,000,000. Most of the refugees have now been in the camps for more than six months. The World Bank has said that India needs a minimum of £300,000,000 in assistance from other countries before the end of the year. It seems obvious that assistance on this scale will not be forthcoming. India will be forced to choose between letting the refugees starve or diverting funds from her own development program, which will mean that more of her own people will starve in the future.[1]

These are the essential facts about the present situation in Bengal. So far as it concerns us here, there is nothing unique about this situation except its magnitude. The Bengal emergency is just the latest and most acute of a series of major emergencies in various parts of the world, arising both from natural and from man-made causes. There are also many parts of the world in which people die from malnutrition and lack of food independent of any special emergency. I take Bengal as my example only because it is the present concern, and because the size of the problem has ensured that it has been given adequate publicity. Neither individuals nor governments can claim to be unaware of what is happening there.

What are the moral implications of a situation like this? In what follows, I shall argue that the way people in relatively affluent countries react to a situation like that in Bengal cannot be justified; indeed, the whole way we look at moral issues—our moral conceptual scheme—needs to be altered, and with it, the way of life that has come to be taken for granted in our society.

In arguing for this conclusion I will not, of course, claim to be morally neutral. I shall, however, try to argue for the moral position that I take, so that anyone who accepts certain assumptions, to be made explicit, will, I hope, accept my conclusion.

I begin with the assumption that suffering and death from lack of food, shelter, and medical care are bad. I think most people will agree about this, although one may reach the same view by different routes. I shall not argue for this view. People can hold all sorts of eccentric positions, and perhaps from some of them it would not follow that death by starvation is in itself bad. It is difficult, perhaps impossible, to refute such positions, and so for brevity I will henceforth take this assumption as accepted. Those who disagree need read no further.

My next point is this: if it is in our power to prevent something bad from happening, without thereby sacrificing anything of comparable moral importance, we ought, morally, to do it. By "without sacrificing anything of comparable moral importance" I mean without causing anything else comparably bad to happen, or doing something that is wrong in itself, or failing to promote some moral good, comparable in significance to the bad thing that we can prevent. This principle seems almost as uncontroversial as the last one. It requires us only to prevent what is bad, and not to promote what is good, and it requires this of us only when we can do it without sacrificing anything that is, from the moral point of view, comparably important. I could even, as far as the application of my argument to the Bengal emergency is concerned, qualify the point so as to make it: if it is in our power to prevent something very bad from happening, without thereby sacrificing anything morally significant, we ought, morally, to do it. An application of this principle would be as follows: if I am walking past a shallow pond and see a child drowning in it, I ought to wade in and pull the child out. This will mean getting my clothes muddy, but this is insignificant, while the death of the child would presumably be a very bad thing.

The uncontroversial appearance of the principle just stated is deceptive. If it were acted upon, even in its qualified form, our lives, our society, and our world would be fundamentally changed. For the principle takes, firstly, no account of proximity or distance. It makes no moral difference whether the person I can help is a neighbor's child ten yards from me or a Bengali whose name I shall never know, ten thousand miles away. Secondly, the principle makes no distinction between cases in which I am the only person who could possibly do anything and cases in which I am just one among millions in the same position.

I do not think I need to say much in defense of the refusal to take proximity and distance into account. The fact that a person is physically near to us, so that we have personal contact with him, may make it more likely that we *shall* assist him, but this does not show that we *ought* to help him rather than another who happens to be further away. If we accept any principle of impartiality, universalizability, equality, or whatever, we cannot discriminate against someone merely because he is far away from us (or we are far away from him). Admittedly, it is possible that we are in a better position to judge what needs to be done to help a person near to us than one far away, and perhaps also to provide the assistance we judge to be necessary. If this were the case, it would be a reason for helping those near to us first. This may once have been a justification for being more concerned with the poor in one's town than with famine victims in India. Unfortunately for those who like to keep their moral responsibilities limited, instant communication and swift transportation have changed the situation. From the moral point of view, the development of the world into a "global village" has made an important, though still unrecognized, difference to our moral situation. Expert observers and supervisors, sent out by famine relief organizations or permanently stationed in famine-prone areas, can direct our aid to a refugee in Bengal almost as effectively as we could get it to someone in our own block. There would seem, therefore, to be no possible justification for discriminating on geographical grounds.

There may be a greater need to defend the second implication of my principle—that the fact that there are millions of other people in the same position, in respect to the Bengali refugees, as I am, does not make the situation significantly different from a situation in which I am the only person who can prevent something very bad from occurring. Again, of course, I admit that there is a psychological difference between the cases; one feels less guilty about doing nothing if one can point to others, similarly placed, who have also done nothing. Yet this can make no real difference to our moral obligations.[2] Should I consider that I am less obliged to pull the drowning child out of the pond if on looking around I see other people, no further away than I am, who have also noticed the child but are doing nothing? One has only to ask this question to see the absurdity of the view that numbers lessen obligation. It is a view that is an ideal excuse for inactivity; unfortunately most of the major evils—poverty, overpopulation, pollution—are problems in which everyone is almost equally involved.

The view that numbers do make a difference can be made plausible if stated in this way: if everyone in circumstances like mine gave £5 to the Bengal Relief Fund, there would be enough to provide food, shelter, and medical care for the refugees; there is no reason why I should give more than anyone else in the same circumstances as I am; therefore I have no obligation to give more than £5. Each premise in this argument is true, and the argument looks sound. It may convince us, unless we notice that it is based on a hypothetical premise, although the conclusion is not stated hypothetically. The argument would be sound if the conclusion were: if everyone in circumstances like mine were to give £5, I would have no obligation to give more than £5. If the conclusion were so stated, however, it would be obvious that the argument has no bearing on a situation in which it is not the case that everyone else gives £5. This, of course, is the actual situation. It is more or less certain that not everyone in circumstances like mine will give £5. So there will not be enough to provide the needed food, shelter, and medical care. Therefore by giving more than £5 I will prevent more suffering than I would if I gave just £5.

It might be thought that this argument has an absurd consequence. Since the situation appears to be that very few people are likely to give substantial amounts, it follows that I and everyone else in similar circumstances ought to give as much as possible, that is, at least up to the point at which by giving more one would begin to cause serious suffering for oneself and one's dependents—perhaps even beyond this point to the point of marginal utility, at which by giving more one would cause oneself and one's dependents as much suffering as one would prevent in Bengal. If everyone does this, however, there will be more than can be used for the benefit of the refugees, and some of the sacrifice will have been unnecessary. Thus, if everyone does what he ought to do, the result will not be as good as it would be if everyone did a little less than he ought to do, or if only some do all that they ought to do.

The paradox here arises only if we assume that the actions in question—sending money to the relief funds—are performed more or less simultaneously, and are also unexpected. For if it is to be expected that everyone is going to contribute something, then clearly each is not obliged to give as much as he would have been obliged to had others not been giving too. And if everyone is not acting more or less simultaneously, then those giving later will know how much more is needed, and will have no obligation to give more than is necessary to reach this amount. To say this is not to deny the principle that people in the same circumstances have the same obligations, but to point out that the fact that others have given, or may be expected to give, is a relevant circumstance: those giving after it has become known that many others are giving and those giving before are not in the same circumstances. So the seemingly absurd consequence of the principle I have put forward can occur only if people are in error about the actual circumstances—that is, if they think they are giving even when others are not, but in fact they are giving when others are. The result of everyone doing what he really ought to do cannot be worse than the result of everyone doing less than he ought to do, although the result of everyone doing what he reasonably believes he ought to do could be.

If my argument so far has been sound, neither our distance from a preventable evil nor the number of other people who, in respect to that evil, are in the same situation as we are, lessens our obligation to mitigate or prevent that evil. I shall therefore take as established the principle I asserted earlier. As I have already said, I need to assert it only in its qualified form: if it is in our power to prevent something very bad from happening, without thereby sacrificing anything else morally significant, we ought, morally, to do it.

The outcome of this argument is that our traditional moral categories are upset. The traditional distinction between duty and charity cannot be drawn, or at least, not in the place we normally draw it. Giving money to the Bengal Relief Fund is regarded as an act of charity in our society. The bodies which collect money are known as "charities." These organizations see themselves in this way—if you send them a check, you will be thanked for your "generosity." Because giving money is regarded as an act of charity, it is not thought that there is anything wrong with not giving. The charitable man may be praised, but the man who is not charitable is not condemned. People do not feel in any way ashamed or guilty about spending money on new clothes or a new car instead of giving it to famine relief. (Indeed, the alternative does not occur to them.) This way of looking at the matter cannot be justified. When we buy new clothes not to keep ourselves warm but to look "well-dressed" we are not providing for any important need. We would not be sacrificing anything significant if we were to continue to wear our old clothes, and give the money to famine relief. By doing so, we would be preventing another person from starving. It follows from what I have said earlier that we ought to give money away, rather than spend it on clothes which we do not need to keep us warm. To do so is not charitable, or generous. Nor is it the kind of act which philosophers and theologians have called "supererogatory"—an act which it would be good to do, but not wrong not to do. One the contrary, we ought to give money away, and it is wrong not to do so.

I am not maintaining that there are no acts which are charitable, or that there are no acts which it would be good to do but not wrong not to do. It may be possible to redraw the distinction between duty and charity in some other place. All I am arguing here is that the present way of drawing the distinction, which makes it an act of charity for a man living at the level of affluence which most people in the "developed nations" enjoy to give money to save someone else from starvation, cannot be supported. It is beyond the scope of my argument to consider whether the distinction should be redrawn or abolished altogether. There would be many other possible ways of drawing the distinction—for instance, one might decide that it is good to make other people as happy as possible, but not wrong not to do so.

Despite the limited nature of the revision in our moral conceptual scheme which I am proposing, the revision would, given the extent of both affluence and famine in the world today, have radical implications. These implications may lead to further objections, distinct from those I have already considered. l shall discuss two of these.

One objection to the position I have taken might be simply that it is too drastic a revision of our moral scheme. People do not ordinarily judge in the way I have suggested they should. Most people reserve their moral condemnation for those who violate some moral norm, such as the norm against taking another person's property. They do not condemn those who indulge in luxury instead of giving to famine relief. But given that I did not set out to present a morally neutral description of the way people make moral judgments, the way people do in fact judge has nothing to do with the validity of my conclusion. My conclusion follows from the principle which I advanced earlier, and unless that principle is rejected, or the arguments shown to be unsound, I think the conclusion must stand, however strange it appears.

It might, nevertheless, be interesting to consider why our society, and most other societies, do judge differently from the way I have suggested they should. In a well-known article, J. O. Urmson suggests that the imperatives of duty, which tell us what we must do, as distinct from what it would be good to do but not wrong not to do, function so as to prohibit behavior that is intolerable if men are to live together in society.[3] This may explain the origin and continued existence of the present division between acts of duty and acts of charity. Moral attitudes are shaped by the needs of society, and no doubt society needs people who will observe the rules that make social existence tolerable. From the point of view of a particular society, it is essential to prevent violations of norms against killing, stealing, and so on. It is quite inessential, however, to help people outside one's own society.

If this is an explanation of our common distinction between duty and supererogation, however, it is not a justification of it. The moral point of view requires us to look beyond the interests of our own society. Previously, as I have already mentioned, this may hardly have been feasible, but it is quite feasible now. From the moral point of view, the prevention of the starvation of millions of people outside our society must be considered at least as pressing as the upholding of property norms within our society.

It has been argued by some writers, among them Sidgwick and Urmson, that we need to have a basic moral code which is not too far beyond the capacities of the ordinary man, for otherwise there will be a general breakdown of compliance with the moral code. Crudely stated, this argument suggests that if we tell people that they ought to refrain from murder and give everything they do not really need to famine relief, they will do neither, whereas if we tell them that they ought to refrain from murder and that it is good to give to famine relief but not wrong not to do so, they will at least refrain from murder. The issue here is: Where should we draw the line between conduct that is required and conduct that is good although not required, so as to get the best possible result? This would seem to be an empirical question, although a very difficult one. One objection to the Sidgwick-Urmson line of argument is that it takes insufficient account of the effect that moral standards can have on the decisions we make. Given a society in which a wealthy man who gives 5 percent of his income to famine relief is regarded as most generous, it is not surprising that a proposal that we all ought to give away half our incomes will be thought to be absurdly unrealistic. In a society which held that no man should have more than enough while others have less than they need, such a proposal might seem narrow-minded. What it is possible for a man to do and what he is likely to do are both, l think, very greatly influenced by what people around him are doing and expecting him to do. In any case, the possibility that by spreading the idea that we ought to be doing very much more than we are to relieve famine we shall bring about a general breakdown of moral behavior seems remote. If the stakes are an end to widespread starvation, it is worth the risk. Finally, it should be emphasized that these considerations are relevant only to the issue of what we should require from others, and not to what we ourselves ought to do.

The second objection to my attack on the present distinction between duty and charity is one which has from time to time been made against utilitarianism. It follows from some forms of utilitarian theory that we all ought, morally, to be working full time to increase the balance of happiness over misery. The position I have taken here would not lead to this conclusion in all circumstances, for if there were no bad occurrences that we could prevent without sacrificing something of comparable moral importance, my argument would have no application. Given the present conditions in many parts of the world, however, it does follow from my argument that we ought, morally, to be working full time to relieve great suffering of the sort that occurs as a result of famine or other disasters. Of course, mitigating circumstances can be adduced—for instance, that if we wear ourselves out through overwork, we shall be less effective than we would otherwise have been. Nevertheless, when all considerations of this sort have been taken into account, the conclusion remains: we ought to be preventing as much suffering as we can without sacrificing something else of comparable moral importance. This conclusion is one which we may be reluctant to face. I cannot see, though, why it should be regarded as a criticism of the position for which I have argued, rather than a criticism of our ordinary standards of behavior. Since most people are self-interested to some degree, very few of us are likely to do everything that we ought to do. It would, however, hardly be honest to take this as evidence that it is not the case that we ought to do it.

It may still be thought that my conclusions are so wildly out of line with what everyone else thinks and has always thought that there must be something wrong with the argument somewhere. In order to show that my conclusions, while certainly contrary to contemporary Western moral standards, would not have seemed so extraordinary at other times and in other places, I would like to quote a passage from a writer not normally thought of as a way-out radical, Thomas Aquinas.

> Now, according to the natural order instituted by divine providence, material goods are provided for the satisfaction of human needs. Therefore the division and appropriation of property, which proceeds from human law, must not hinder the satisfaction of man's necessity from such goods. Equally, whatever a man has in superabundance is owed, of natural right, to the poor for their sustenance. So Ambrosius says, and it is also to be found in the *Decretum Gratiana*: "The bread which you withhold belongs to the hungry; the clothing you shut away, to the naked; and the money you bury in the earth is the redemption and freedom of the penniless."[4]

I now want to consider a number of points, more practical than philosophical, which are relevant to the application of the moral conclusion we have reached. These points challenge not the idea that we ought to be doing all we can to prevent starvation, but the idea that giving away a great deal of money is the best means to this end.

It is sometimes said that overseas aid should be a government responsibility, and that therefore one ought not to give to privately run charities. Giving privately, it is said, allows the government and the noncontributing members of society to escape their responsibilities.

This argument seems to assume that the more people there are who give to privately organized famine relief funds, the less likely it is that the government will take over full responsibility for such aid. This assumption is unsupported, and does not strike me as at all plausible. The opposite view—that if no one gives voluntarily, a government will assume that its citizens are uninterested in famine relief and would not wish to be forced into giving aid—seems more plausible. In any case, unless there were a definite probability that by refusing to give one would be helping to bring about massive government assistance, people who do refuse to make voluntary contributions are refusing to prevent a certain amount of suffering without being able to point to any tangible beneficial consequence of their refusal. So the onus of showing how their refusal will bring about government action is on those who refuse to give.

I do not, of course, want to dispute the contention that governments of affluent nations should be giving many times the amount of genuine, no-strings-attached aid that they are giving now. I agree, too, that giving privately is not enough, and that we ought to be campaigning actively for entirely new standards for both public and private contributions to famine relief. Indeed, I would sympathize with someone who thought that campaigning was more important than giving oneself, although I doubt whether preaching what one does not practice would be very effective. Unfortunately, for many people the idea that "it's the government's responsibility" is a reason for not giving which does not appear to entail any political action either.

Another, more serious reason for not giving to famine relief funds is that until there is effective population control, relieving famine merely postpones starvation. If we save the Bengal refugees now, others, perhaps the children of these refugees, will face starvation in a few years' time. In support of this, one may cite the now well-known facts about the population explosion and the relatively limited scope for expanded production.

This point, like the previous one, is an argument against relieving suffering that is happening now, because of a belief about what might happen in the future; it is unlike the previous point in that very good evidence can be adduced in support of this belief about the future. I will not go into the evidence here. I accept that the earth cannot support indefinitely a population rising at the present rate. This certainly poses a problem for anyone who thinks it important to prevent famine. Again, however, one could accept the argument without drawing the conclusion that it absolves one from any obligation to do anything to prevent famine. The conclusion that should be drawn is that the best means of preventing famine, in the long run, is population control. It would then follow from the position reached earlier that one ought to be doing all one can to promote population control (unless one held that all forms of population control were wrong in themselves, or would have significantly bad consequences). Since there are organizations working specifically for population control, one would then support them rather than more orthodox methods of preventing famine.

A third point raised by the conclusion reached earlier relates to the question of just how much we all ought to be giving away. One possibility, which has already been mentioned, is that we ought to give until we reach the level of marginal utility—that is, the level at which, by giving more, I would cause as much suffering to myself or my dependents as I would relieve by my gift. This would mean, of course, that one would reduce oneself to very near the material circumstances of a Bengali refugee. It will be recalled that earlier I put forward both a strong and a moderate version of the principle of preventing bad occurrences. The strong version, which required us to prevent bad things from happening unless in doing so we would be sacrificing something of comparable moral significance, does seem to require reducing ourselves to the level of marginal utility. I should also say that the strong version seems to me to be the correct one. I proposed the more moderate version—that we should prevent bad occurrences unless, to do so, we had to sacrifice something morally significant—only in order to show that even on this surely undeniable principle a great change in our way of life is required. On the more moderate principle, it may not follow that we ought to reduce ourselves to the level of marginal utility, for one might hold that to reduce oneself and one's family to this level is to cause something significantly bad to happen. Whether this is so I shall not discuss, since, as I have said, I can see no good reason for holding the moderate version of the principle rather than the strong version. Even if we accepted the principle only in its moderate form, however, it should be clear that we would have to give away enough to ensure that the consumer society, dependent as it is on people spending on trivia rather than giving to famine relief, would slow down and perhaps disappear entirely. There are several reasons why this would be desirable in itself. The value and necessity of economic growth are now being questioned not only by conservationists, but by economists as well.[5] There is no doubt, too, that the consumer society has had a distorting effect on the goals and purposes of its members. Yet looking at the matter purely from the point of view of overseas aid, there must be a limit to the extent to which we should deliberately slow down our economy; for it might be the case that if we gave away, say, 40 percent of our Gross National Product, we would slow down the economy so much that in absolute terms we would be giving less than if we gave 25 percent of the much larger GNP that we would have if we limited our contribution to this smaller percentage.

I mention this only as an indication of the sort of factor that one would have to take into account in working out

an ideal. Since Western societies generally consider one percent of the GNP an acceptable level for overseas aid, the matter is entirely academic. Nor does it affect the question of how much an individual should give in a society in which very few are giving substantial amounts.

It is sometimes said, though less often now than it used to be, that philosophers have no special role to play in public affairs, since most public issues depend primarily on an assessment of facts. On questions of fact, it is said, philosophers as such have no special expertise, and so it has been possible to engage in philosophy without committing oneself to any position on major public issues. No doubt there are some issues of social policy and foreign policy about which it can truly be said that a really expert assessment of the facts is required before taking sides or acting, but the issue of famine is surely not one of these. The facts about the existence of suffering are beyond dispute. Nor, I think, is it disputed that we can do something about it, either through orthodox methods of famine relief or through population control or both. This is therefore an issue on which philosophers are competent to take a position. The issue is one which faces everyone who has more money than he needs to support himself and his dependents, or who is in a position to take some sort of political action. These categories must include practically every teacher and student of philosophy in the universities of the Western world. If philosophy is to deal with matters that are relevant to both teachers and students, this is an issue that philosophers should discuss.

Discussion, though, is not enough. What is the point of relating philosophy to public (and personal) affairs if we do not take our conclusions seriously? In this instance, taking our conclusion seriously means acting upon it. The philosopher will not find it any easier than anyone else to alter his attitudes and way of life to the extent that, if I am right, is involved in doing everything that we ought to be doing. At the very least, though, one can make a start. The philosopher who does so will have to sacrifice some of the benefits of the consumer society, but he can find compensation in the satisfaction of a way of life in which theory and practice, if not yet in harmony, are at least coming together.

Notes

1. There was also a third possibility: that India would go to war to enable the refugees to return to their lands. Since I wrote this paper, India has taken this way out. The situation is no longer that described above, but this does not affect my argument, as the next paragraph indicates.
2. In view of the special sense philosophers often give to the term, I should say that I use "obligation" simply as the abstract noun derived from "ought," so that "I have an obligation to" means no more, and no less, than "I ought to." This usage is in accordance with the definition of

"ought" given by the *Shorter Oxford English Dictionary*: "the general verb to express duty or obligation." I do not think any issue of substance hangs on the way the term is used; sentences in which I use "obligation" could all be rewritten, although somewhat clumsily, as sentences in which a clause containing "ought" replaces the term "obligation."

3. J. O. Urmson, "Saints and Heroes," in *Essays in Moral Philosophy*, ed. Abraham L. Melden (Seattle: University of Washington Press, 1958), p. 214. For a related but significantly different view see also Henry Sidgwick, *The Methods of Ethics*, 7th ed. (London: Dover Press, 1907), pp. 220–21, 492–93.
4. *Summa Theologica*, II–II, Question 66, Article 7, in *Aquinas, Selected Political Writings*, ed. A. P. d'Entreves, trans. J. G. Dawson (Oxford: Basil Blackwell, 1948), p. 171.
5. See, for instance, John Kenneth Galbraith, The *New Industrial State* (Boston Houghton Mifflin, 1967); and E. J. Mishan, *The Costs of Economic Growth* (New York: Praeger, 1967).

Study Questions

1. Examine Singer's strong principle: "If it is in our power to prevent something bad from happening, without thereby sacrificing anything of comparable moral importance, we ought, morally, to do it." Do you agree with it? Explain.
2. What is Singer's weak principle? How does it differ from the strong principle? Do you agree with Singer about our obligations to sacrifice in order to help those in distant lands? What would happen if we took Singer's principles seriously?

55

Vegetarianism and "the Other Weight Problem"

JAMES RACHELS

James Rachels is professor of philosophy at the University of Alabama at Birmingham and the author of several articles and books in ethics, among them The End of Life *(1986) and* Created from Animals *(1990).*

Rachels argues for a moral duty to be vegetarian. Meat eating is immoral because it wastes valuable protein that could be used to feed hungry people and because it causes enormous suffering to animals.

It is now common for newspapers and magazines to carry the ultimate indictment of glutted Americans: ads for weight salons or reducing schemes next to news accounts of starvation in Africa, Latin America, or elsewhere. The pictures of big-bellied children nursing on emptied breasts tell of the other "weight problem."[1]

There are moral problems about what we eat, and about what we do with the food we control. In this essay I shall discuss some of these problems. One of my conclusions will be that it is morally wrong for us to eat meat. Many readers will find this implausible and even faintly ridiculous, as I once did. After all, meat eating is a normal, well-established part of our daily routines; people have always eaten meat; and many find it difficult even to conceive of what an alternate diet would be like. So it is not easy to take seriously the possibility

that it might be wrong. Moreover, vegetarianism is commonly associated with Eastern religions whose tenets we do not accept, and with extravagant, unfounded claims about health. A quick perusal of vegetarian literature might confirm the impression that it is all a crackpot business: tracts have titles like "Victory Through Vegetables" and promise that if one will only keep to a meatless diet one will have perfect health and be filled with wisdom. Of course we can ignore this kind of nonsense. However, there are other arguments for vegetarianism that must be taken seriously. One such argument, which has recently enjoyed wide support, has to do with the world food shortage. I will take up that argument after a few preliminaries.

I

According to the United Nations Food and Agriculture Organization, about 15,000 people die of malnutrition every day—10,000 of them are children. Millions more do not die but lead miserable lives constantly on the verge of starvation. Hunger is concentrated in poor, underdeveloped countries, out of sight of the 70 million Americans who are overweight from eating too much.

Of course, there is some malnutrition in the United States—a conservative estimate is that 40 million Americans are poor enough to qualify for assistance under the Federal Food Stamp Program, although fewer than half that number are actually helped. But it is easy to misinterpret this statistic: while many of these

Reprinted from *World Hunger and Moral Obligation*, eds. William Aiken and Hugh LaFollette (Englewood Cliffs, N.J.: Prentice Hall, 1977) by permission.

Americans don't get *enough* to eat, neither are they starving. They do not suffer the extreme deprivation that reduces one's life to nothing more than a continual desperate search for food. Moreover, even the milder degree of malnutrition is an embarrassing anomaly; we are not a poor country, especially not in food. We have an abundance of rich farmland which we use with astonishing efficiency. (Although in some important ways our use of land is very inefficient. I will come to that in a moment.) The "Foodgrain Yield" of American farms is about 3,050 pounds per acre. For comparison, we may note that only Japan does significantly better, with a yield of 4,500 pounds per acre; but in Japan 87 workers per 100 acres are needed to obtain this yield, while in the United States only *one* worker per 100 acres is required![2] If some Americans do not get enough to eat, it is not because we lack the food.

It does not require a very sophisticated argument to show that, if we have an overabundance of food while others are starving, we should not waste our surplus but make it available to those who need it. Studies indicate that the average American family throws out with the garbage about 10 percent of the food it buys.[3] Of course, it would be impractical for us to try to package up our leftover beans and potatoes at the end of each meal and send them off to the poor. But it would not be impractical for us to buy somewhat less, and contribute the leftover money to agencies that would then purchase the food we did not buy and deliver it to those in need.

The argument may be put this way: First, suppose you are about to throw out a quantity of food which you are unable to use, when someone offers to take it down the street to a child who is starving. Clearly, it would be immoral for you to refuse this offer and insist that the food go into the garbage. Second, suppose it is proposed that you *not buy* the extra food, instead give the money to provide for the child. Would it be any less immoral of you to refuse, and to continue to buy unneeded food to be discarded? The only important difference between the two cases is that by giving money, and not leftover food, better nourishment can be provided to the child more efficiently. Aside from some slight inconvenience—you would have to shop a bit more carefully—the change makes no difference to *your* interests at all. You end up with the same combination of food and money in each case. So, if it would be immoral to refuse to give the extra food to the child and insist on throwing it into the garbage, it is also immoral for us to buy and waste food when we could buy less and give the extra money for famine relief.

II

It is sometimes objected that the famine-relief efforts are futile because the problems of overpopulation and underdevelopment in some parts of the world are insol-

uble. "Feed the starving millions," it is said, "and they will survive only to produce more starving millions. When the population in those poor, overcrowded countries has doubled, and then tripled, *then* there will be famine on a scale we have hardly dreamed of. What is needed in those countries is population control and the establishment of sound agricultural systems. But, unfortunately, given the religious, political, and educational situations in those countries, and the general cultural malaise produced by generations of ignorance and grinding poverty, these objectives are impossible to attain. So we have to face the fact that transfusions of food today, no matter how massive, only postpone the inevitable starvation and probably even make it worse."

It must be conceded that, *if* the situation really were this hopeless, then we would have no obligation to provide relief for those who are starving. We are not obligated to take steps that would do no good. What is wrong with this argument is that it paints too gloomy a picture of the possibilities. We have no conclusive evidence that the situation is hopeless. On the contrary, there is good reason to think that the problems can be solved. In China starvation is no longer a serious problem. That huge population is now adequately fed, whereas thirty years ago hunger was common. Apparently, Chinese agriculture is now established on a sound basis. Of course, this has been accomplished by a social regimentation and a denial of individual freedom

The Far Side

"Lord, we thank thee."

that many of us find objectionable, and, in any case, Chinese-style regimentation cannot be expected in other countries. But this does not mean that there is no hope for other countries. In countries such as India, birth control programs can help. Contrary to what is popularly believed, such programs are not foredoomed to failure. During India's third "Five Year Plan" (1961–66) the birth rate in Bombay was reduced to only 27 per 1000 population, only a bit higher than the U.S. rate of 23 per 1000.[4] This was the best result in the country, but there were other hopeful signs as well: for example, during the same period the birth rate in a rural district of West Bengal dropped from 43 to 36 per 1000. Experts do not regard India's population problem as hopeless.

It is a disservice to the world's poor to represent the hunger problem as worse than it is; for, if the situation is made to appear hopeless, then people are liable to do nothing. Nick Eberstadt, of the Harvard Center for Population Studies, remarks that:

> Bangladesh is a case in point. The cameramen who photograph those living corpses for your evening consumption work hard to evoke a nation of unrecognizable monsters by the roadside. Unless you have been there, you would find it hard to imagine that the people of Bangladesh are friendly and energetic, and perhaps 95% of them get enough to get by. Or that Bangladesh has the richest cropland in the world, and that a well-guided aid program could help turn it from a famine center into one of the world's great breadbaskets. To most people in America the situation must look hopeless and our involvement, therefore, pointless. If the situation is so bad, why shouldn't we cut off our food and foreign aid to Bangladesh, and use it to save people who aren't going to die anyway?[5]

So, even if it is true that shipments of food *alone* will not solve the problems of famine, this does not mean that the problems cannot be solved. Short-term famine-relief efforts, together with longer-range population control programs and assistance to improve local agriculture, could greatly reduce, if not altogether eliminate, the tragedy of starvation.

III

I have already mentioned the waste of food thrown out with the garbage. That waste, as great as it is, is small in comparison to a different sort of waste which I want to describe now.

But first let me tell a little story. In this story, someone discovers a way of processing food so as to give it a radically new texture and taste. The processed food is no more nutritious than it was unprocessed, but people like the way it tastes, and it becomes very popular—so popular, in fact, that a great industry grows up and almost everyone comes to dine on it several times a week. There

is only one catch: the conversion process is extremely wasteful. Seven-eighths of the food is destroyed by the process; so that in order to produce one pound of the processed food, eight pounds of unprocessed food are needed. This means that the new kind of food is relatively expensive and only people in richer countries can afford to eat much of it. It also means that the process raises moral questions: Can it be right for some people to waste seven-eighths of their food resources, while millions of others are suffering from a lack of food? If the waste of 10 percent of one's food is objectionable, the waste of 87.5 percent is more so.

In fact, we do use a process that is just this wasteful. The process works like this: First, we use our farmland to grow an enormous quantity of grain—many times the amount that we could consume, if we consumed it as grain or grain products. But we do not consume it in this form. Instead, we feed it to animals, and then we eat the animals. The process is staggeringly inefficient: we have to feed the animals eight pounds of protein in the form of grain to get back one pound in the form of meat, for a wastage of 87.5 percent. (This is the inefficient use of farmland that I referred to earlier; farmland that could be producing eight pounds of "unprocessed" food produces only one pound "processed.")

Fully one-half of all the harvested agricultural land in the United States is planted with feed-crops. We feed 78 percent of all our grain to animals. This is the highest percentage of any country in the world; the Soviet Union, for example, uses only 28 percent of its grain in this way. The "conversion ratio" for beef cattle and veal calves is an astonishing *21 to 1*—that is, we feed these animals 21 pounds of protein in the form of grain to get back 1 pound in the form of meat. Other animals process protein more efficiently, so that the average conversion ratio is "only" 8 to 1. To see what this means for a single year, we may note that in 1968 we fed 20 million tons of protein to livestock (excluding dairy cattle), in return for which we got 2 million tons of protein in meat, for a net loss of 18 million tons. This loss, in the United States alone, was equal to 90 percent of the world's estimated protein deficit.[6]

If we did not waste grain in this manner, there would clearly be enough to feed everyone in the world quite comfortably. In 1972–1973, when the world food "shortage" was supposedly becoming acute, 632 pounds of grain was produced annually for every person on earth (500 pounds is enough for adequate nourishment). This figure is actually *rising*, in spite of population growth; the comparable figure for 1960 was under 600.[7]

What reason is there to waste this incredible amount of food? Why raise and eat animals, instead of eating a portion of the grain ourselves and using the rest to relieve hunger? The meat we eat is no more nourishing than the grain the animals are fed. The only reason for preferring to eat meat is our enjoyment of its taste; but this is hardly a sufficient reason for wasting food that is desperately needed by people who are starving. It is as if one were to say to a hungry child: "I have eight times the food I need, but I can't let you have any of it, because I am going to use it all to make myself something really tasty."

This, then, is the argument for vegetarianism that I referred to at the beginning of this essay. If, in light of the world food situation, it is wrong for us to waste enormous quantities of food, then it is wrong for us to convert grain protein into meat protein as we do. And if we were to stop doing this, then most of us would have to become vegetarians of at least a qualified sort. I say "of a qualified sort" for two reasons. First, we could still eat fish. Since we do not raise fish by feeding them food that could be consumed by humans, there is no argument against eating fish comparable to this one against eating livestock. Second, there could still be a small amount of beef, pork, etc., produced without the use of feeds suitable for human consumption, and this argument would not rule out producing and eating that meat—but this would be such a small amount that it would not be available to most of us.

This argument against meat eating will be already familiar to many readers; it has been used in numerous books and in magazine and newspaper articles.[8] I am not certain, however, that it is an absolutely conclusive argument. For one thing it may be that a mere *reduction* in the amount of meat we produce would release enough grain to feed the world's hungry. We are now wasting so much food in this way that it may not be necessary for us to stop wasting all of it, but only some of it; so we may be able to go on consuming a fair amount of meat without depriving anyone of food. If so, the argument from wasting food would not support vegetarianism, but only a simple decrease in our meat consumption, which is something entirely different. There is, however, another argument for vegetarianism which I think is conclusive. Unlike the argument from food wastage, this argument does not appeal to the interests of humans as grounds for opposition to meat eating. Instead, it appeals directly to the interests of the animals themselves. I now turn to that argument.

IV

The wrongness of cruelty to animals is often explained in terms of its effects on human beings. The idea seems to be that the animals' interests are not *themselves* morally important or worthy of protection, but, since cruelty to animals often has bad consequences for *humans*, it is wrong to make animals suffer. In legal writing, for example, cruelty to animals is included among the "victimless crimes," and the problem of justifying legal prohibitions is seen as comparable to justifying the prohibition of other behavior, such as homosexuality or the distribution of pornography, where no one (no human) is obviously hurt. Thus,

Louis Schware says that, in prohibiting the torturing of animals.

> It is not the mistreated dog who is the ultimate object of concern . . . Our concern is for the feelings of other human beings, a large proportion of whom, although accustomed to the slaughter of animals for food, readily identify themselves with a tortured dog or horse and respond with great sensitivity to its sufferings.[9]

Philosophers also adopt this attitude. Kant, for example, held that we have no direct duties to nonhuman animals. "The Categorical Imperative," the ultimate principle of morality, applies only to our dealings with humans:

> The practical imperative, therefore, is the following: Act so that you treat humanity, whether in your own person or in that of another, always as an end and never as a means only.[10]

And of other animals, Kant says:

> But so far as animals are concerned, we have no direct duties. Animals are not self-conscious, and are there merely as means to an end. That end is man.[11]

He adds that we should not be cruel to animals only because "He who is cruel to animals becomes hard also in his dealings with men."[12]

Surely this is unacceptable. Cruelty to animals ought to be opposed, not only because of the ancillary effects on humans, but because of the direct effects on the animals themselves. Animals that are tortured *suffer,* just as tortured humans suffer, and *that* is the primary reason why it is wrong. We object to torturing humans on a number of grounds, but the main one is that the victims suffer so. Insofar as nonhuman animals also suffer, we have the *same* reason to oppose torturing them, and it is indefensible to take the one suffering but not the other as grounds for objection.

Although cruelty to animals is wrong, it does not follow that we are never justified in inflicting pain on an animal. Sometimes we are justified in doing this, just as we are sometimes justified in inflicting pain on humans. It does follow, however, that there must be a *good reason* for causing the suffering, and if the suffering is great, the justifying reason must be correspondingly powerful. As an example, consider the treatment of the civet cat, a highly intelligent and sociable animal. Civet cats are trapped and placed in small cages inside darkened sheds, where the temperature is kept up to 110°F by fires.[13] They are confined in this way until they finally die. What justifies this extraordinary mistreatment? These animals have the misfortune to produce a substance that is useful in the manufacture of perfume. Musk, which is scraped from their genitals once a day for as long as they can survive, makes the scent of perfume last a bit longer after each application (The heat increases their "production" of musk.) Here Kant's rule—"Animals are merely means to an end; that end is man"—is applied with a vengeance. To promote one of the most trivial interests we have, thousands of animals are tormented for their whole lives.

It is usually easy to persuade people that this use of animals is not justified, and that we have a moral duty not to support such cruelties by consuming their products. The argument is simple: Causing suffering is not justified unless there is a good reason; the production of perfume made with musk causes considerable suffering; our enjoyment of this product is not a good enough reason to justify causing that suffering; therefore, the use of animals in this way is wrong. At least my experience has been that, once people learn the facts about musk production, they come to regard using such products as morally objectionable. They are surprised to discover, however, that an exactly analogous argument can be given in connection with the use of animals as food. Animals that are raised and slaughtered for food also suffer, and our enjoyment of the way they taste is not a sufficient justification for mistreating them.

Most people radically underestimate the amount of suffering that is caused to animals who are raised and slaughtered for food.[14] They think, in a vague way, that slaughterhouses are cruel, and perhaps even that methods of slaughter ought to be made more humane. But after all, the visit to the slaughterhouse is a relatively brief episode in the animal's life; and beyond that, people imagine that the animals are treated well enough. Nothing could be further from the truth. Today the production of meat is Big Business, and the helpless animals are treated more as machines in a factory than as living creatures.

Veal calves for example, spend their lives in pens too small to allow them to turn around or even to lie down comfortably—exercise toughens the muscles, which reduces the "quality" of the meat, and besides, allowing the animals adequate living space would be prohibitively expensive. In these pens the calves cannot perform such basic actions as grooming themselves, which they naturally desire to do, because there is not room for them to twist their heads around. It is clear that the calves miss their mothers, and like human infants they want something to suck: they can be seen trying vainly to suck the sides of their stalls. In order to keep their meat pale and tasty, they are fed a liquid diet deficient in both iron and roughage. Naturally they develop cravings for these things, because they need them. The calf's craving for iron is so strong that, if it is allowed to turn around, it will lick at its own urine, although calves normally find this repugnant. The tiny stall, which prevents the animal from turning, solves this "problem." The craving for roughage is especially strong since without it the animal cannot form a cud to chew. It cannot be given any straw for bedding, since the animal would be driven to eat it, and that would spoil the meat. For these animals the slaughterhouse is not an unpleasant end to an otherwise contented life. As terrifying as the process of slaughter is,

for them it may actually be regarded as a merciful release.

Similar stories can be told about the treatment of other animals on which we dine. In order to "produce" animals by the millions, it is necessary to keep them crowded together in small spaces. Chickens are commonly kept eight or ten to a space smaller than a newspaper page. Unable to walk around or even stretch their wings—much less build a nest—the birds become vicious and attack one another. The problem is sometimes exacerbated because the birds are so crowded that, unable to move, their feet literally grow around the wire floors of the cages, anchoring them to the spot. An "anchored" bird cannot escape attack no matter how desperate it becomes. Mutilation of the animals is an efficient solution. To minimize the damage they can do to one another, the birds' beaks are cut off. The mutilation is painful, but probably not as painful as other sorts of mutilations that are routinely practiced. Cows are castrated, not to prevent the unnatural "vices" to which overcrowded chickens are prone, but because castrated cows put on more weight, and there is less danger of meat being "tainted" by male hormones.

> In Britain an anesthetic must be used, unless the animal is very young, but in America anesthetics are not in general use. The procedure is to pin the animal down, take a knife and slit the scrotum, exposing the testicles. You then grab each testicle in turn and pull on it, breaking the cord that attaches it; on older animals it may be necessary to cut the cord.[15]

It must be emphasized that the treatment I am describing—and I have hardly scratched the surface here—is not out of the ordinary. It is typical of the way that animals raised for food are treated, now that meat production is Big Business. As Peter Singer puts it, these are the sorts of things that happened to your dinner when it was still an animal.

What accounts for such cruelties? As for the meat producers, there is no reason to think they are unusually cruel men. They simply accept the common attitude expressed by Kant: "Animals are merely means to an end; that end is man." The cruel practices are adopted not because they are cruel but because they are efficient, given that one's only concern is to produce meat (and eggs) for humans as cheaply as possible. But clearly this use of animals is immoral if anything is. Since we can nourish ourselves very well without eating them, our *only reason* for doing all this to the animals is our enjoyment of the way they taste. And this will not even come close to justifying the cruelty.

V

Does this mean that we should stop eating meat? Such a conclusion will be hard for many people to accept. It is tempting to say "What is objectionable is not *eating* the animals, but only making them suffer. Perhaps we ought to protest the way they are treated, and even work for better treatment of them. But it doesn't follow that we must stop eating them." This sounds plausible until you realize that it would be impossible to treat the animals decently and still produce meat in sufficient quantities to make it a normal part of our diets. As I have already remarked, cruel methods are used in the meat-production industry because such methods are economical; they enable the producers to market a product that people can afford. Humanely produced chicken, beef, and pork would be so expensive that only the very rich could afford them. (*Some* of the cruelties could be eliminated without too much expense—the cows could be given an anesthetic before castration, for example, even though this alone would mean a slight increase in the cost of beef. But others, such as overcrowding, could not be eliminated without really prohibitive cost.) So to work for better treatment for the animals would be to work for a situation in which most of us would *have* to adopt a vegetarian diet.

Still, there remains the interesting theoretical question: *If* meat could be produced humanely, without mistreating the animals prior to killing them painlessly, would there be anything wrong with it? The question is only of theoretical interest because the actual choice we face in the supermarket is whether to buy the remains of animals that are *not* treated humanely. Still, the question has some interest, and I want to make two comments about it.

First, it is a vexing issue whether animals have a "right to life" that is violated when we kill them for trivial purposes; but we should not simply assume until proven otherwise that they *don't* have such a right.[16] We assume that humans have a right to life—it would be wrong to murder a normal, healthy human even if it were done painlessly—and it is hard to think of any plausible rationale for granting this right to humans that does not also apply to other animals. Other animals live in communities, as do humans; they communicate with one another, and have ongoing social relationships; killing them disrupts lives that are perhaps not as complex, emotionally and intellectually, as our own, but that are nevertheless quite complicated. They suffer, and are capable of happiness as well as fear and distress, as we are. So what could be the rational basis for saying that we have a right to life, but that they don't? Or even more pointedly, what could be the rational basis for saying that a severely retarded human, who is inferior in every important respect to an intelligent animal, has a right to life but that the animal doesn't? Philosophers often treat such questions as "puzzles," assuming that there must be answers even if we are not clever enough to find them. I am suggesting that, on the contrary, there may not be any acceptable answers to these questions. If it seems, intuitively, that there *must* be some difference

between us and the other animals which confers on us, but not them, a right to life, perhaps this intuition is mistaken. At the very least, the difficulty of answering such questions should make us hesitant about asserting that it is all right to kill animals, as long as we don't make them suffer, unless we are also willing to take seriously the possibility that it is all right to kill people, so long as we don't make them suffer.

Second, it is important to see the slaughter of animals for food as part of a larger pattern that characterizes our whole relationship with the nonhuman world. Animals are wrenched from their natural homes to be made objects of our entertainment in zoos, circuses, and rodeos. They are used in laboratories not only for experiments that are themselves morally questionable,[17] but also in testing everything from shampoo to chemical weapons. They are killed so that their heads can be used as wall decorations, or their skins as ornamental clothing or rugs. Indeed, simply killing them for the fun of it is thought to be "sport." This pattern of cruel exploitation flows naturally from the Kantian attitude that animals are nothing more than things to be used for our purposes. It is this whole attitude that must be opposed, and not merely its manifestation in our willingness to hurt the animals we eat. Once one rejects this attitude and no longer regards the animals as disposable at one's whim, one ceases to think it all right to kill them, even painlessly, just for a snack.

But now let me return to the more immediate practical issue. The meat at the supermarket was not produced by humane methods. The animals whose flesh this meat was were abused in ways similar to the ones I have described. Millions of other animals are being treated in these ways now, and their flesh will soon appear in the markets. Should one support such practices by purchasing and consuming its products?

It is discouraging to realize that no animals will actually be helped simply by one person ceasing to eat meat. One consumer's behavior, by itself, cannot have a noticeable impact on an industry as vast as the meat business. However, it is important to see one's behavior in a wider context. There are already millions of vegetarians, and because they don't eat meat there is less cruelty than there otherwise would be. The question is whether one ought to side with that group, or with the carnivores whose practices cause the suffering. Compare the position of someone thinking about whether to buy slaves in the year 1820. He might reason as follows: "The whole practice of slavery is immoral, but I cannot help any of the poor slaves by keeping clear of it. If I don't buy these slaves, someone else will. One person's decision just can't by itself have any impact on such a vast business. So I may as well use slaves like everyone else." The first thing we notice is that this fellow was too pessimistic about the possibilities of a successful movement; but beyond that, there is something else wrong with his reasoning. If one really thinks that a social practice is immoral, that *in itself* is sufficient grounds for a refusal to participate. In 1848 Thoreau remarked that even if someone did not want to devote himself to the abolition movement, and actively oppose slavery, ". . . it is his duty, at least, to wash his hands of it, and, if he gives it no thought longer, not to give it practically his support." In the case of slavery, this seems clear. If it seems less clear in the case of the cruel exploitation of nonhuman animals, perhaps it is because the Kantian attitude is so deeply entrenched in us.

VI

I have considered two arguments for vegetarianism: one appealing to the interests that humans have in conserving food resources, and the other appealing directly to the interests of the animals themselves. The latter, I think, is the more compelling argument, and in an important sense it is a deeper argument. Once its force is felt, any opposition to meat eating that is based only on considerations of food wastage will seem shallow in the same way that opposition to slavery is shallow if it is based only on economic considerations. Yet the second argument does in a way reinforce the first one. In this case at least, the interests of humans and nonhumans coincide. By doing what we ought to do anyway—ceasing to exploit helpless animals—we would at the same time increase the food available for hungry people.

Notes

1. Coleman McCarthy, "Would We Sacrifice to Aid the Starving?" *Miami Herald,* 28 July 1974, page 2F.
2. These figures are based on studies conducted in 1969–1971. They are from James, Grant, "A New Development Strategy," *Foreign Policy,* 12 (1973).
3. One such study is reported in *Time,* 26 January 1976, p. 8.
4. B. L. Raina, "India," in Bernard Berelson, ed., *Family Planning and Population Programs: A Review of World Developments* (Chicago: University of Chicago Press, 1966), pp. 111–22.
5. Nick Eberstadt, "Myths of the Food Crisis," *The New York Review of Books,* 19 February 1976, p. 32. Eberstadt's article contains a good survey of the problems involved in assessing the world food situation—how bad it is, or isn't. He concludes that the situation is bad, but not at all hopeless. See also various articles in Philip H. Abelson, ed., *Food: Politics, Economics,* *Nutrition and Research* (Washington, D.C.: American Association for the Advancement of Science, 1975).
6. The figures in this paragraph are from Frances Moore Lappé, *Diet for a Small Planet* (New York: Ballantine Books, Inc., 1971), part I. This book is an excellent primer on protein.
7. Eberstadt, "Myths of the Food Crisis," p. 34.
8. For example, in Lappé's *Diet for a Small Planet,* and in several of the articles anthologized in Catherine Lerza and Michael Jacobson, eds., *Food for People Not for Profit: A Sourcebook on the Food Crisis* (New York Ballantine Books, Inc., 1975).
9. Louis B. Schwartz, "Morals Offenses and the Model Penal Code," *Columbia Law Review,* 63(1963); reprinted in Joel Feinberg and Hyman Gross, eds., *Philosophy of Law* (Encino, Calif.: Dickenson Publishing Company, Inc., 1975), p. 156.
10. Immanuel Kant, *Foundations of the Metaphysics of Morals,* trans. Lewis White Beck (Indianapolis: The Bobbs-Merrill Co., Inc., 1959), p. 47.
11. Immanuel Kant, *Lectures on Ethics,* trans. Louis Infield (New York: Harper Torchbooks, 1963), p. 239.
12. Ibid., p. 240.
13. Muriel the Lady Dowding, "Furs and Cosmetics: Too High a Price?" in Stanley and Roslind Godlovitch and John Harris, eds., *Animals, Men and Morals* (New York: Taplinger Publishing Co., Inc., 1972), p. 36.
14. By far the best account of these cruelties is to be found in Chapter 3 of Peter Singer's *Animal Liberation* (New York: New York Review Books, 1975). I have drawn on Singer's work for the factual material in the following two paragraphs. *Animal Liberation* should be consulted for a thorough treatment of matters to which I can refer here only sketchily.
15. Singer, *Animal Liberation,* p. 152.
16. It is controversial among philosophers whether animals can have any rights at all. See various essays collected in Part IV of Tom Regan and Peter Singer, eds., *Animal Rights and Human Obligations* (Englewood Cliffs, N.J.: Prentice Hall, 1976). My own defense of animal rights is given in "Do Animals Have a Right to Liberty?" pp. 205–223, and in "A Reply to VanDeVeer," pp. 230–232.
17. See Singer, *Animal Liberation,* Chap. 2.

Study Questions

1. What is the relationship between the dietary habits of Americans and world hunger?
2. What are Rachels's arguments for vegetarianism?
3. Is Rachels right that we should become vegetarians?

56

The World Food Supply:
The Damage Done by Cattle-Raising

TRISTRAM COFFIN

This article from The Washington Spectator *reports on the ecological costs of cattle-raising. For example, in California it takes 5214 gallons of water to produce one edible pound of beef, as compared to 23 gallons for the same amount of tomatoes. In addition, lowering one's meat diet is likely to result in greater health. The writers call on us to change our diet, for our own good and the good of humankind, from one heavy in meat to more grains, vegetables, and fruits.*

In this century, the number and impacts of livestock have swelled apace with human population and affluence. Since mid-century human numbers have doubled to [5.8] billion, while the number of four-legged livestock—cattle, pigs, sheep, goats, horses, buffalo and camels—has grown from 2.3 billion to 4 billion. At the same time, the fowl population multiplied from about 3 billion to nearly 11 billion. There are now three times as many domestic animals as people.[1]

A biographical sketch for Tristram Coffin preceded Reading 46.

"Currently, sufficient land, energy and water exist to feed well over twice the world's population" (*Earth Save Foundation*). But this is not the whole story. The Foundation adds, "Yet half of the world's grain harvest is fed to livestock, while millions of humans go hungry. In 1984 when thousands of Ethiopians were dying from famine, Ethiopia continued growing and shipping millions of dollars worth of livestock to the United States and other European countries."

Worldwatch Institute reports: "Rings of barren earth spread out from wells on the grasslands of Soviet Turkmenia. Heather and lilies wilt in the nature preserves of the southern Netherlands.

"Forests teeming with rare forms of plant and animal life explode in flame in Costa Rica. Water tables fall and fossil fuels are wasted in the U.S. Each of these cases of environmental decline issues from a single source: the global livestock industry."

The simple fact is that the livestock industry is a better paying customer than are hungry human beings. In turn, the industry is supported by the lusty appetite for meat of well-to-do individuals. Since 1985, North Americans have been eating 50% more beef, 280% more poultry and 33% more dairy products. In its tract "Our Food, Our World," the Foundation points out that this is a diet with one-third more fat, one-fifth less carbohydrate, and levels of protein consumption "far exceeding official recommendation.

"This increased demand for animal products has resulted in a vast reallocation of resources, has promoted the degradation of global systems, and has disrupted indigenous cultures. The impact on human health has been equally devastating."

Worldwatch advises: "Feeding the world's current population on an American style diet would require two and a half times as much grain as the world's farmers produce for all purposes. A future world of 8 to 14 billion people eating the American ration of 220 grams a day can be nothing but a flight of fancy." Why? "In the U.S., over one-third of all raw materials—including fossil fuels—consumed for all purposes are devoted to the production of livestock" [*Earth Save*].

Example: it takes 16 pounds of grain and soy to produce one pound of beef. One half the Earth's land mass is grazed for livestock, as compared to the 2% used for fruits and vegetables.

Growing cattle crops is an "extremely energy-intensive process. Farmers must pump water, plow, cultivate and fertilize the fields, then harvest and transport the crops. The number of calories of fossil fuel expended to produce one calorie of protein from beef is 78, as compared to 2 calories to produce the same one calorie of soybeans." The energy used to produce one pound of grain-fed beef is equal to one gallon of gasoline, according to Earth Save.

What about water? "Our Food, Our World" estimates that livestock production accounts for more than half of all water consumed. In California it takes 5214 gallons of water to produce one edible pound of beef, as compared to 23 gallons for the same amount of tomatoes . . . Water tables, like the Ogallala aquifer under the Great Plains states, are fast being depleted."

Marc Reisner writes in his book *California Desert,* "It offends me that we give three times more water to grow cows than we give to people in California."

The Growth of Deserts—"Our Food, Our World" contends that livestock grazing and overuse of land to grow food crops for cattle have played a major role in

Reprinted from *The Washington Spectator*, ed. Tristram Coffin, Vol. 19.2 (January 15, 1993).

the growth of deserts. "Regions most affected by desertification are all cattle-producing areas, including the western half of the U.S., Central and South America, Australia and sub-Saharan Africa. The main causes of desertification are overgrazing of livestock, overcultivation of land, improper irrigation techniques, deforestation [to clear land for cattle raising as is now occurring in the Brazilian Rain Forest].

Why? "Under persistent grazing, the bare ground becomes impermeable to rainwater, which then courses off the surface, carrying away topsoil and scouring stream beds into deep gullies. Upstream, water tables fall for lack of replenishment; downstream, flooding occurs more frequently and sediment clogs waterways, dams and estuaries. In drier climates wind sweeps away the destabilized soil."

The U.N. Environment Program estimates that 73% of the world's 3.3 billion hectares of dry rangeland is at least moderately desertified, having lost more than 25% of its carrying capacity. "There is little debate that degradation is occurring in environments where rainfall is more plentiful and regular. The perennial plants that flourish in these zones are easily disrupted by cattle; clay soils are easily compacted and rendered impervious to water; and rains often arrive in strong, sudden downpours, sluicing away soils destabilized by cattle" (Worldwatch Institute).

Philip Fradkin, writing in *Audubon* magazine, says: "The impact of countless hooves and mouths over the years has done more to alter the type of vegetarian and land forms of the West than all the water projects, strip mines, power plants, freeways, and subdivision developments combined."

A few pertinent facts: Each year, an estimated 125,000 square miles of rainforest are destroyed, together with the loss of 1,000 plant and animal species. In Central America cattle ranching has destroyed more rainforests than has any other activity. A quarter of Central American rainforests have been cleared for pasture. This creates a profitable market for cattle sold to the U.S. market.

Livestock production creates other environmental problems—the pollution of the atmosphere by carbon dioxide and methane, of water by animal wastes and pesticides. Worldwatch Institute states: "The millions of tons of animal waste that accumulate at modern production facilities can pollute rivers and groundwater if precautions are not taken. If they get into rivers or open bodies of water, nitrogen and phosphorus in manure overfertilize algae, which grow rapidly, deplete oxygen supplies, and suffocate aquatic ecosystems. From the hundreds of algae-choked Italian lakes to the murky Chesapeake Bay, and from the oxygen-starved Baltic Sea to the polluted Adriatic, animal wastes add to the nutrient loads from fertilizer runoff, human sewage and urban and industrial pollution."

In the Netherlands, the 14 million animals in feeding houses in the southern part of the nation "excrete more nitrogen- and phosphorus-rich manure than the soil can absorb . . . pushing freshwater ecosystems into decline."

And, "manure nitrogen, mixed with nitrogen from artificial fertilizers, percolates through the soil into the underground water tables as nitrates. . . . In the U.S., roughly one-fifth of the wells in livestock states, such as Iowa, Kansas and Nebraska, have nitrate levels that exceed health standards. Manure nitrogen also escapes into the air as gaseous ammonia, a pollutant that causes acid rain."

The Earth Save study looks at three problems:

- "The metabolic processes of cattle result in the emission of large quantities of methane. Each cow produces 1 pound of methane for every 2 pounds of meat it yields. The amount of methane emitted by the world's cattle annually: 100 million tons." 20% of total world methane emissions comes from cattle.
- Wastes from factory farmers, feedlots and dairies create a buildup of toxins in the land and water. The E.P.A. estimates that almost half the wells and surface streams in the U.S. are "contaminated by agricultural pollutants."
- Chemical pesticides are used so widely and in such large quantities that they "poison the environment and the human food chain. The increase in overall pesticide use since 1945, when petro-chemical based agriculture became popular, is 3,300%.

Loss of Forests—Not only rangeland, but forests, too, suffer from heavy livestock production. The Worldwatch study reports, "Forests suffer, as branches are cut for fodder or entire stands are leveled to make way for pastures. The roster of impacts from forest clearing includes the loss of watershed protection, loss of plant and animal species, and on a larger scale, substantial contributions of the greenhouse gas carbon dioxide to the atmosphere."

Examples: in Latin America, more than 20 million hectares of moist tropical forests have been cleared for cattle pasture. The U.N. Food and Agricultural Organization says that Central America has lost more than a third of its forest since the early 1960s. Nearly 70% of the deforested land in Panama and Costa Rica is now pasture.

"Eradicating tree cover sets the wheels of land degradation in motion. Shallow, acidic, and nutrient-poor, tropical soils lose critical phosphorus and other nutrients when the forest is converted to pasture. . . . Most pasture is abandoned within a decade for land newly carved from the forest . . . Forest destruction for ranching also contributes to climate change. When living plants are cut down and burned, or when they decompose, they release carbon into the atmosphere as the greenhouse gas carbon dioxide. In the atmosphere, carbon dioxide traps the heat of the sun, warming the earth. . . . The expansion of pastures into Latin

American forests has released an estimated 1.4 billion tons of carbon into the atmosphere."

Worldwatch points out that methane, a by-product of cattle-raising, is the second most important greenhouse gas.

Effect on Health—Earth Save warns, "Animal products contain large quantities of saturated fat, cholesterol and protein and no dietary fiber. The impact of this diet on human health has been devastating . . . Fortunately, by observing in a low-fat diet free of animal products, some diseases can be commonly prevented, consistently improved and sometimes cured." Some fats are associated with most of the diseases of affluence that are among the leading causes of death in industrialized countries: heart disease, stroke, breast and colon cancer. The study laments that physicians generally are taught to cure disease, but not how to prevent it. The majority "are taught little about nutrition as a preventative measure," but many are inquiring into this possibility.

"Great Protein Fiasco"—The Worldwatch study comments: "The adverse health impacts of excessive meat-eating stem in large part from what nutritionists call the *great protein fiasco*—a mistaken belief by many Westerners that they need to consume large quantities of protein. This myth, propagated as much as a century ago by health officials and governmental dietary guidelines, has resulted in Americans and other members of industrial societies ingesting twice as much protein as they need. Among the affluent, the protein myth is dangerous because of the saturated fats that accompany concentrated protein in meat and dairy products."

Low-fat diets are now recommended by the U.S. Surgeon General, the U.S. National Research Council, the American Heart Association, and the World Health Organization. They recommend lowering fat consumption to no more than 30% of calories, as compared to the U.S. norm of 37%. [Many health specialists recommend lowering the fat consumption to 10 to 15%—ed. note.]

Higher meat consumption among the well-to-do may also create a problem for the poor, "as the share of farmland devoted to feed cultivation expands, reducing production of food staples," says the Worldwatch study. It points out that in Egypt, for example, "over the past quarter-century, corn grown for animal feed has taken over cropland from wheat, rice, sorghum and millet—all staple grains fed to livestock rose from 10 to 36%."

Much the same is true in Mexico, where 30% of the grain is fed to livestock, "although 22% of the country's people suffer from malnutrition." The share of cropland growing animal food and fodder went up from 5% in 1960 to 23% in 1980. A study of agriculture in 23 third world countries showed that in 13 countries, farmers had shifted more than 10% of grain land from food crops to feed crops in the last 25 years. In nine countries, "the demand for meat among the rich was squeezing out staple production for the poor."

The picture in the U.S.: more than a million farms and ranches raise young beef, while four big companies slaughter nearly 60% of them. Since 1962, the number of huge American beef feedlots, capable of holding 16,000 head of cattle, has risen from 23 to 189. At the same time, small feedlots, holding no more than 1,000 have dropped by 117,000.

The big operations have no trouble getting government support, such as guaranteed minimum prices, government storage of surpluses, feed subsidies, import levies and product insurance. The Organization for Economic Cooperation and Development reports that in 1990 government programs in the industrial democracies gave subsidies to animal farmers and feed growers worth $120 billion.

What is the answer? The *Los Angeles Times* states: "The Seeds of Change [a group based in Santa Fe, NM] philosophy holds that adopting a plant-based diet is the best solution for improving individual health and lessening the toll of the human race on our Earth's limited resources." Seeds of Change founder Gabriel Howearth recommends:

Bush acorn squash and bush buttercup squash, both high in vitamin A and free amino acids. Jerusalem artichokes, a native North American food plant with a varied vitamin balance and useful digestive enzymes. Hopi blue starch corn grown without irrigation in the Southwest and a traditional staple of the Hopi Indians . . . Okra, containing high amounts of vitamin C and amino acids, good in vegetable soup, stew and gumbo. Amaranth, a high-protein garden grain.

Howearth's goal "is to get all kinds of people, even those who work and have limited leisure time, to grow their own food—in their backyards, on their balconies, or on their rooftops."

This is not a goal everyone can follow. What many can do is change their diet from heavy meats to more vegetables and fruits. They will be less likely to become ill, and they will help save the planet Earth.

Note

1. From *The Worldwatch Institute,* quoted in "World Food Supply: The Damage Done by Cattle-Raising." *The Washington Spectator* (Jan. 15, 1993).

Study Questions

1. Go over the figures and damage caused by cattle-raising, mentioned in this essay. Are you convinced by the article that the situation is as bad as it is made out to be? Explain your answer.
2. If the raising of cattle and other livestock is so damaging to the environment and our health, what should we be doing about it?

For Further Reading

Aiken, William, and Hugh LaFollette, eds., *World Hunger and Moral Obligation*. Englewood Cliffs, N.J.: Prentice Hall, 1977. The best collection of readings available, containing four of the readings in this chapter, plus others of great importance.

Ehrlich, Paul. *The Population Bomb.* New York: Ballantine Books, 1971. An important work, warning of the dangers of the population explosion.

Lappé, Francis, and Joseph Collins. *Food First: Beyond the Myth of Scarcity.* New York: Ballantine Books, 1978). An attack on Neo-Malthusians like Hardin in which the authors argue that we have abundant resources to solve the world's hunger problems.

O'Neill, Onora. *Faces of Hunger.* London: Allen & Unwin, 1986. A penetrating Kantian discussion of the principles and problems surrounding world hunger.

Simon, Arthur. *Bread for the World.* New York: Paulist Press, 1975. A poignant discussion of the problem of world hunger from a Christian perspective with some thoughtful solutions.

CHAPTER ELEVEN

Pollution: General Considerations

On March 24, 1989, the oil tanker *Exxon Valdez* ran aground off the Alaskan coast, spilling 1.26 million barrels of oil into Prince William Sound. It was the worst oil spill in history. The pristine beauty of the Alaskan Coast with its wealth of birds, fish, and wildlife had been degraded. Five hundred square miles of the sound were polluted. Millions of fish, birds, and wildlife had been killed, and fishermen had lost their means of livelihood. The fishing industry, which earns $100 million annually in Prince William Sound, ground to an abrupt halt. The Exxon corporation was unprepared for an accident of this magnitude. It only had 69 barrels of oil dispersant on hand in Alaska, when something like 10,000 were needed to clean up the spill. The ship's Captain Joseph Hazelwood was found guilty of negligence and operating under the influence of alcohol, and Exxon was fined $100 million. But Greenpeace put an ad in newspapers, showing Joseph Hazelwood's face, with the caption: "It wasn't his driving that caused the Alaskan oil spill. It was yours. The spill was caused by a nation drunk on oil. And a government asleep at the wheel."

Modern industrial society has provided enormous benefits, making our lives far more comfortable and freeing us from back-breaking drudgery. From electric lighting, washing machines, air conditioners, and gas-driven automobiles to medical miracles, supersonic airplanes, and microchip computers, our lives have been enriched with possibilities that a little more than a century ago existed only in dreams or in science fiction. Yet with these life-enhancing, technological wonders has come waste and pollution. This pollution in turn threatens to undo the benefits technology has brought us. How great is that threat?

Pollution may be broadly defined as any unwanted state or change in the properties of air, water, soil, or food that can have negative impact on the health, well-being, or survival of human beings or other living organisms. Most pollutants are undesirable chemicals that are produced as by-products when a resource is converted into energy or a commodity. Types of pollution include contaminated water, chemically polluted air (such as smog), toxic waste in the soil, poisoned food, high levels of radiation, and noise. They also include acid rain, cigarette smoke, alcohol, and drugs.

Three factors determine the severity of a pollutant: its chemical nature (how harmful it is to various types of living organisms), its concentration (the amount per volume of air, water, soil, or body weight), and its persistence (how long it remains in the air, water, soil, or body).

We divide a pollutant's persistence into three types: degradable, slowly degradable, and nondegradable. Degradable pollutants, such as human sewage and soil, are usually broken down completely or reduced to acceptable levels by natural chemical processes. Slowly degradable pollutants, such as DDT, plastics, aluminum cans, and chlorofluorocarbons (CFCs) often take decades to degrade to acceptable levels. Nondegradable pollutants, such as lead and mercury, are not broken down by natural processes.

We know little about the short- and long-range harmful potential of most of the more than 70,000 synthetic chemicals in commercial use on people and the environment. The Environmental Protection Agency (EPA) estimates that 80% of cancers are caused by pollution. We know that half of our air pollution is caused by the internal combustion engine of motor vehicles and that coal-burning stationary power plants produce unacceptable amounts of sulfur dioxide (SO_2). The World Health Organization (WHO) estimates that about 1 billion urban people (about one-fifth of humanity) are being exposed to health hazards from air pollution and that emphysema, an incurable lung disease, is rampant in our cities. Studies tell us that smog (a mixture of smoke and fog) is hazardous to our health and that it has caused thousands of deaths in such cities as London, New York, and Los Angeles.

In the United States, 80% of our freshwater aquifers are in danger, so a large percentage (estimates are over 30%) of our population is drinking contaminated water (see Box on p.379). By 1991 the EPA had listed 1211 hazardous waste sites for cleanup, the estimated cost of cleanup per site being $26 million. Acid rain is killing our forests and lakes.

Technology, which enhances the quality of our lives, also causes an exponential growth of dangerous pollution. Can we have both high technology and high quality of life? Or must we make radical changes in our value system, reassessing our "need" for bigger and more powerful machines?

ATLANTA—Most Americans will never encounter the parasite that contaminated Milwaukee's water. But 21 million people use water systems that aren't protected from the bug, and others swallow it when water plants improperly clean their filters, experts said Friday.

"Just a little lack of rigor can result in one of these outbreaks," said Jack Hoffbuhr of the American Water Works Association, a nonprofit foundation that tracks drinking water. "But I think most people can rest assured this is not common."

Thousands of Milwaukee residents were stricken by cryptosporidium, a protozoan about one-hundredth the size of a speck of dust. It causes severe diarrhea.

Mostly found in developing countries, it's the major cause of travelers' diarrhea. But 2 percent of the diarrhea cases in U.S. hospitals are caused by the bug, which can kill people who have weak immune systems.

"The bad news is there's no treatment for it, but the good news is it runs its course in about 14 days in healthy people," said Dr. Dennis Juranek of the U.S. Centers for Disease Control and Prevention.

Cryptosporidia lives in the intestines of animals and humans and is spread by contact with anything from diapers to water tainted by farm runoff.

Filters are the only protection from the parasite, which cannot be killed by chlorine or other chemicals, Juranek said.

DON'T DRINK THE WATER

About 21 million Americans drink unfiltered surface water. Most live in mountainous areas where people think the water's safe because it appears so clear, the Centers for Disease Control and Prevention said. A 1992 Oregon bacteria outbreak was caused by an unfiltered spring.

The earth naturally filters cryptosporidia in ground water, which is the primary source for 92 percent of the nation's water systems. But cities that draw water from rivers or lakes—such as Milwaukee—are required to chemically treat their water but not to filter it, Juranek said.

The U.S. Environmental Protection Agency is studying whether to require filtering for all water systems because of cryptosporidia, Juranek said.

People worried about the parasite shouldn't rely on home filters, Juranek and Hoffbuhr said. Most on the market won't screen out crypotosporidia, and the few that will are expensive and only produce about five gallons of water a day.

"My recommendation is boiling the water," Hoffbuhr said. "That's a fairly easy process to do and you don't have to buy those gizmos."

CDC Report to wire service, 4–10–93.

Because of its importance in the environmental debate, five chapters of Part 2 deal with pollution. We have already considered the relation of pollution to population in Chapter 10. In this chapter, we deal with general consideration of the topic: How serious is pollution on balance? and cover one form of pollution, air pollution.

In Chapter 12, we concentrate on pesticide use, which may be beneficial to agriculture but poses a threat to human and animal life. What can we say about the moral status of our present use of pesticides? In Chapter 13, we focus on one of the long-term spin-offs of pollution—the greenhouse effect, or global warming. How serious is it? In Chapter 14, we consider the problem of toxic waste and what is being done to clean it up.

We begin our readings with a sharp indictment of corporate capitalism by George Bradford. Reacting to what he perceived to be a condoning of the tragedy of Bhopal, India (where a Union Carbide factory exploded, killing 3000 people in 1984) by the *Wall Street Journal,* Bradford lashes out at the whole economic and social philosophy that permitted and is responsible for this and many other threats to humanity. In the third world, businesses cut costs by having lax safety standards.

Chemicals that are banned in the United States and Europe are produced overseas. Even in the United States and Europe, our industrial culture continues to endanger our lives. We must throw "off this Modern Way of Life," argues Bradford, for it only constitutes a "terrible burden" that threatens to crush us all.

Our second reading takes a diametrically opposite position to Bradford. Julian Simon, the consummate Cornucopian, argues that there is good evidence that pollution of air and water are actually lessening rather than increasing. Citing life expectancy as the number one indicator of environmental quality, he produces statistics to support his thesis. Compared with the past, when most people died of infectious diseases like pneumonia, gastroenteritis, or tuberculosis, today people are dying of diseases related to old age, such as cancer and heart attacks. But there is no evidence that the environment is any more carcinogenic than it was in the past. Pollution is by definition bad and we need to keep it as low as possible, but we cannot get rid of it without getting rid of the beneficial uses of resources that it accompanies. But "exaggerated warnings can be counterproductive and dangerous."

Steve Benson. *Reprinted by permission of United Features Syndicate, Inc.*

Our third reading, "People or Penguins: The Case for Optimal Pollution" by William Baxter, is essentially clarificatory in that it sets forth the relationship between resources and pollution, showing that we cannot have the good of resource use without the bad of pollution. The point is to decide on the proper balance. Those like Baxter, who take a decidedly anthropocentric point of view, argue that we ought to risk pollution that might endanger other species (as DDT does) if it promotes human advantage.

In our fourth reading, Hilary French documents the dire consequences of air pollution. Her essay provides hard data around which rational discussion can take place.

Finally, in our fifth reading, Robert N. Stavins and Bradley W. Whitehead argue for market-based incentives for environmental protection. They reject the view that the market is villainous, and urge policies that will both promote economic success and environmental progress.

57

We All Live in Bhopal

GEORGE BRADFORD

George Bradford lives in Detroit and is an editor of The Fifth Estate.

In this essay, Bradford argues that in the third world, as well as in Europe and the United States, industrial capitalism is harming hundreds of thousands of people and imposing a frightful risk on millions more by unsafe practices that pollute our air, water, soil, and food. Taking the tragic explosion of the Union Carbide insecticide plant in Bhopal, India, as his point of departure, he recounts a tale of corporate negligence and moral culpability. Calling these large corporations "corporate vampires," Bradford accuses them of turning industrial civilization into "one vast, stinking extermination camp."

George Bradford, "We All Live in Bhopal," in *Fifth Estate* (4632 Second, Detroit, MI 48201) Winter 1985: Vol. 19 No. 4 (319). Reprinted in J. Zerzan and Alice Carnes, *Questioning Technology* (Santa Cruz, CA: Freedom Press, 1988). Reprinted by permission.

Our modern way of life, dependent on dangerous industrial institutions, reeks with harmful pollution. We must rid ourselves of it before we are crushed by it.

The cinders of the funeral pyres at Bhopal are still warm, and the mass graves still fresh, but the media prostitutes of the corporations have already begun their homilies in defense of industrialism and its uncounted horrors. Some 3,000 people were slaughtered in the wake of the deadly gas cloud, and 20,000 will remain permanently disabled. The poison gas left a 25 square mile swath of dead and dying, people and animals, as it drifted southeast away from the Union Carbide factory. "We thought it was a plague," said one victim. Indeed it was: a chemical plague, an *industrial plague,*

Ashes, ashes, all fall down!

A terrible, unfortunate, "accident," we are reassured by the propaganda apparatus for Progress, for History, for "Our Modern Way of Life." A price, of course, has to be paid—since the risks are necessary to ensure a higher Standard of Living, a Better Way of Life.

The *Wall Street Journal,* tribune of the bourgeoisie, editorialized, "It is worthwhile to remember that the Union Carbide insecticide plant and the people surrounding it were where they were for compelling reasons. India's agriculture has been thriving, bringing a better life to millions of rural people, and partly because of the use of modern agricultural technology that includes applications of insect killers." The indisputable fact of life, according to this sermon, is that universal recognition that India, like everyone else, "needs technology. Calcutta-style scenes of human deprivation can be replaced as fast as the country imports the benefits of the West's industrial revolution and market economics." So, despite whatever dangers are involved, "the benefits outweigh the costs." (Dec. 13, 1984)

The *Journal* was certainly right in one regard—the reasons for the plant and the people's presence there are certainly compelling: capitalist market relations and technological invasion are as compelling as a hurricane to the small communities from which those people were uprooted. It conveniently failed to note, however, that countries like India do not import the *benefits* of industrial capitalism; those benefits are *exported* in the form of loan repayments to fill the coffers of the bankers and corporate vampires who read the *Wall Street Journal* for the latest news of their investments. The Indians only take the risks and pay the costs; in fact, for them, as for the immiserated masses of people living in the shantytowns of the Third World, there are no risks, only certain hunger and disease, only the certainty of death squad revenge for criticizing the state of things as they are.

GREEN REVOLUTION A NIGHTMARE

In fact, the Calcutta-style misery is the result of Third World industrialization and the so called industrial "Green Revolution" in agriculture. The Green Revolution, which was to revolutionize agriculture in the "backward" countries and produce greater crop yields, has only been a miracle for the banks, corporations and military dictatorships who defend them. The influx of fertilizers, technology, insecticides and bureaucratic administration exploded millennia-old rural economies based on subsistence farming, creating a class of wealthier farmers dependent upon western technologies to produce cash crops such as coffee, cotton and wheat for export, while the vast majority of farming communities were destroyed by capitalist market competition and sent like refugees into the growing cities. These victims, paralleling the destroyed peasantry of Europe's Industrial Revolution several hundred years before, joined either the permanent underclass of unemployed and underemployed slumdwellers eking out a survival on the tenuous margins of civilization, or became proletarian fodder in the Bhopals, Sao Paulos and Djakartas of an industrializing world—an industrialization process, like all industrialization in history, paid for by the pillage of nature and human beings in the countryside.

Food production goes up in some cases, of course, because the measure is only quantitative—some foods disappear while others are produced year round, even for export. *But subsistence is destroyed.* Not only does the rural landscape begin to suffer the consequences of constant crop production and use of chemicals, but the masses of people—laborers on the land and in the teeming hovels growing around the industrial plants—go hungrier in a vicious cycle of exploitation, while the wheat goes abroad to buy absurd commodities and weapons.

But subsistence is culture as well: culture is destroyed with subsistence, and people are further trapped in the technological labyrinth. The ideology of progress is there, blared louder than ever by those with something to hide, a cover-up for plunder and murder on levels never before witnessed.

INDUSTRIALIZATION OF THE THIRD WORLD

The industrialization of the Third World is a story familiar to anyone who takes even a glance at what is occurring. The colonial countries are nothing but a dumping ground and pool of cheap labor for capitalist corporations. Obsolete technology is shipped there along with the production of chemicals, medicines and other products banned in the developed world. Labor is cheap, there are few if any safety standards, and *costs are cut.* But the formula of cost-benefit still stands: the costs are simply borne by others, by the victims of Union Carbide, Dow, and Standard Oil.

Chemicals found to be dangerous and banned in the US and Europe are produced instead overseas—DDT is a well-known example of an enormous number of such products, such as the unregistered pesticide Leptophos exported by the Velsicol Corporation to Egypt which killed and injured many Egyptian farmers in the mid-1970's. Other products are simply dumped on Third World markets, like the mercury-tainted wheat which led to the deaths of as many as 5,000 Iraqis in 1972, wheat which had been imported from the US. Another example was the wanton contamination of Nicaragua's Lake Managua by a chlorine and caustic soda factory owned by Pennwalt Corporation and other investors, which caused a major outbreak of mercury poisoning in a primary source of fish for the people living in Managua.

Union Carbide's plant at Bhopal did not even meet US safety standards according to its own safety inspector, but a UN expert on international corporate behavior told the *New York Times*, "A whole list of factors is not in place to insure adequate industrial safety" throughout the Third World. "Carbide is not very different from any other chemical company in this regard." According to the *Times*, "In a Union Carbide battery plant in Jakarta, Indonesia, more than half the workers had kidney damage from mercury exposure. In an asbestos cement factory owned by the Manville Corporation 200 miles west of Bhopal, workers in 1981 were routinely covered with asbestos dust, a practice that would never be tolerated here." (12/9/84)

Some 22,500 people are killed every year by exposure to insecticides—a much higher percentage of them in the Third World than use of such chemicals would suggest. Many experts decried the lack of an "industrial culture" in the "underdeveloped" countries as a major cause of accidents and contamination. But where an "industrial culture" thrives, is the situation really much better?

INDUSTRIAL CULTURE AND INDUSTRIAL PLAGUE

In the advanced industrial nations an "industrial culture" (and little other) exists. Have such disasters been avoided as the claims of these experts would lead us to believe?

Another event of such mammoth proportions as those of Bhopal would suggest otherwise—in that case, industrial pollution killed some 4,000 people in a large population center. That was London, in 1952, when several days of "normal" pollution accumulated in stagnant air to kill and permanently injure thousands of Britons.

Then there are the disasters closer to home or to memory, for example, the Love Canal (still leaking into the Great Lakes water system), or the massive dioxin contaminations at Seveso, Italy and Times Creek, Missouri, where thousands of residents had to be permanently evacuated. And there is the Berlin and Farro

dump at Swartz Creek, Michigan, where C-56 (a pesticide by-product of Love Canal fame), hydrochloric acid and cyanide from Flint auto plants had accumulated. "They think we're not scientists and not even educated," said one enraged resident, "but anyone who's been in high school knows that cyanide and hydrochloric acid is what they mixed to kill the people in the concentration camps."

A powerful image: industrial civilization as one vast, stinking extermination camp. We all live in Bhopal, some closer to the gas chambers and to the mass graves, but all of us close enough to be victims. And Union Carbide is obviously not a fluke—the poisons are vented in the air and water, dumped in rivers, ponds and streams, fed to animals going to market, sprayed on lawns and roadways, sprayed on food crops, every day, everywhere. The result may not be as dramatic as Bhopal (which then almost comes to serve as a *diversion*, a deterrence machine to take our minds off the pervasive reality which Bhopal truly represents), but it is as deadly. When ABC News asked University of Chicago professor of public health and author of *The Politics of Cancer*, Jason Epstein, if he thought a Bhopal-style disaster could occur in the US, he replied: "I think what we're seeing in America is far more slow—not such large accidental occurrences, but a slow, gradual leakage with the result that you have excess cancers or reproductive abnormalities."

In fact, birth defects have doubled in the last 25 years. And cancer is on the rise. In an interview with the *Guardian*, Hunter College professor David Kotelchuck described the "Cancer Atlas" maps published in 1975 by the Department of Health, Education and Welfare. "Show me a red spot on these maps and I'll show you an industrial center of the US," he said. "There aren't any place names on the maps but you can easily pick out concentrations of industry. See, it's not Pennsylvania that's red it's just Philadelphia, Erie and Pittsburgh. Look at West Virginia here, there's only two red spots, the Kanawha Valley, where there are nine chemical plants including Union Carbide's, and this industrialized stretch of the Ohio River. It's the same story wherever you look."

There are 50,000 toxic waste dumps in the United States. The EPA admits that *ninety per cent* of the 90 billion pounds of toxic waste produced annually by US industry (70 per cent of it by chemical companies) is disposed of "improperly" (although we wonder what they would consider "proper" disposal). These deadly products of industrial civilization—arsenic, mercury, dioxin, cyanide, and many others—are simply dumped, "legally" and "illegally," wherever convenient to industry. Some 66,000 different compounds are used in industry. Nearly a billion tons of pesticides and herbicides comprising 225 different chemicals were produced in the US last year, and an additional 79 million pounds were imported. Some two per cent of chemical compounds have been tested for side effects. There are 15,000 chemical plants in the United States, daily manufacturing mass death.

All of the dumped chemicals are leaching into our water. Some three to four thousand wells, depending on which government agency you ask, are contaminated or closed in the US. In Michigan alone, 24 municipal water systems have been contaminated, and a thousand sites have suffered major contamination. According to the Detroit *Free Press*, "The final toll could be as many as 10,000 sites" in Michigan's "water wonderland" alone (April 15, 1984).

And the coverups go unabated here as in the Third World. One example is that of dioxin; during the proceedings around the Agent Orange investigations, it came out that Dow Chemical had lied all along about the effects of dioxin. Despite research findings that dioxin is "exceptionally toxic" with "a tremendous potential for producing chlor-acne and systemic injury," Dow's top toxicologist, V. K Rowe, wrote in 1965, "We are not in any way attempting to hide our problems under a heap of sand. But we certainly do not want to have any situations arise which will cause the regulatory agencies to become restrictive."

Now Vietnam suffers a liver cancer epidemic and a host of cancers and health problems caused by the massive use of Agent Orange there during the genocidal war waged by the US. The sufferings of the US veterans are only a drop in the bucket. And dioxin is appearing everywhere in our environment as well, in the form of recently discovered "dioxin rain."

GOING TO THE VILLAGE

When the Indian authorities and Union Carbide began to process the remaining gases in the Bhopal plant, thousands of residents fled, despite the reassurances of the authorities. The *New York Times* quoted one old man who said, "They are not believing the scientists or the state government or anybody. They only want to save their lives."

The same reporter wrote that one man had gone to the train station with his goats, "hoping that he could take them with him—anywhere, as long as it was away from Bhopal" (Dec. 14, 1984). The same old man quoted above told the reporter, "All the public has gone to the village." The reporter explained that "going to the village" is what Indians do when trouble comes.

A wise and age-old strategy for survival by which little communities always renewed themselves when bronze, iron and golden empires with clay feet fell to their ruin. But subsistence has been and is everywhere being destroyed, and with it, culture. What are we to do when there is no village to go to? When we all live in Bhopal, and Bhopal is everywhere? The comments of two women, one a refugee from Times Creek, Missouri, and another from Bhopal, come to mind. The first woman said of her former home, "This was a nice place once. Now we have to bury it." The other woman said, "Life cannot come back. Can the government pay for the lives? Can you bring those people back?"

The corporate vampires are guilty of greed, plunder, murder, slavery, extermination and devastation. And we should avoid any pang of sentimentalism when the time comes for them to pay for their crimes against humanity and the natural world. But we will have to go beyond them, to ourselves: subsistence, and with it culture, has been destroyed. We have to find our way back to the village, out of industrial civilization, out of this exterminist system.

The Union Carbides, the Warren Andersons, the "optimistic experts" and the lying propagandists all must go, but with them must go the pesticides, the herbicides, the chemical factories and the chemical way of life which is nothing but death.

Because this is Bhopal, and it is all we've got. This "once nice place" can't be simply buried for us to move on to another pristine beginning. The empire is collapsing. We must find our way back to the village, or as the North American natives said, "back to the blanket," and we must do this not by trying to save an industrial civilization which is doomed, but in that renewal of life which must take place in its ruin. By throwing off this Modern Way of Life, we won't be "giving things up" or sacrificing, but throwing off a terrible burden. Let us do so soon before we are crushed by it.

Study Questions

1. Does Bradford make his case that Western industrial society is dangerous to humanity and nature and needs to be rejected? What are the implications of Bradford's indictment? What sort of world do you think that he would want us to live in? Is Bradford a "Luddite"? (Luddites were people in England in the early nineteenth century who went around destroying machines because they believed that the Industrial Revolution was evil.)

2. Is the anger that comes through in this article justified? Is modern industrial practice really morally irresponsible? Explain your answer.

3. How might someone in the business community respond to Bradford's essay? Can our industrial practices be defended?

58

Against the Doomsdayers!

JULIAN SIMON

Julian Simon is professor of economics at the University of Maryland, College Park, and the author of several works, including The Ultimate Resource *from which this selection is taken.*

Simon argues, similarly to Jacqueline Kasun with regard to population (Reading 49), that the media and academic community are engaged in a misguided mission of doomsday propaganda aimed at convincing people that pollution is ruining our lives. He attempts to show that the contrary is actually the case. Overall his essay has four goals: (1) to clarify the economic view of pollution as a trade-off between cost and cleanliness; (2) to examine the trends of pollution as income and population have increased and show that pollution has decreased; (3) to assess pollution from the perspective of life-expectancy in order to show that things are actually getting better; and (4) to provide detailed evidence on the improvement of some facets of modern life.

According to the press and much of the academic community, the U.S. and the world are becoming increasingly polluted. A university newspaper quotes a speaker: "Man has been working to control nature for too long. Our natural resources are running out and pollution is taking its toll upon the land." The top-of-page headline of a story in the *Chicago Tribune* is, "The Pollution of Earth: 'I'm Scared,'" with the sub-headline "Air, Sea and Land—All Being Strangled":

> "I'm scared," said Joseph Sauris, 16, a sophomore at Main East Township High School, Park Ridge. . . .
>
> "I don't like the idea of leaving a dead world to my children. That might sound like a cliché, but it may be the truth someday."

And grammar-school texts fill young minds with unsupported assertions that mankind is a destroyer rather than a creator of the environment. Here are some samples from *Earth and Ecology,* a Golden Book text for children.*

> Our Dirty Air—The sea of air in which we live—our sky—is no longer sparkling clean. Once the smoke from chimneys was whisked away by winds and soon became lost in a clear sky. Then we believed that the sky could

hold all the wastes we could pour into it. By some sort of miracle, we thought, the sky kept itself clean.

> Now there are too many chimneys pouring smoke, ashes, and poisonous fumes into our sky. Where the land has been scoured of grass and forests and there are no crops planted to hold the soil, the slightest breeze whips up choking clouds of dust that spill the dirt into the air. Hour after hour, fumes from millions of automobiles' exhausts are spewed into the air. . . .

> In many large cities, there are no clear days at all now. Over portions of the earth, there is a haze, darkest where the population is greatest. Each year air pollution becomes worse as we dump greater loads into the sky.

> Yet, this is the air we must breathe to live. You can survive for days or even weeks without food, but without air, you will die in only a few minutes. Right now you are probably breathing polluted air. It is air containing poisons. Some of these poisons are kinds that do not kill immediately. They take their toll over the years, and more and more people are becoming victims of respiratory ailments. . . .

> No more Clean Waters—Once the United States was a land of pure, sparkling waters. . . . But in the few hundred years since America's discovery, its waters have been almost totally spoiled by pollution. The greatest damage has come in very recent years.

> Still, the people in many cities must drink water from these lakes and rivers. They make it drinkable by loading it with purifying chemicals. But the chemicals make the water taste bad. There is also a point at which the chemicals used to purify water become poisonous to people, too.

> Streams in the United States have indeed become open sewers carrying away wastes from industries and dwellings. The wastes are really only moved downstream to the next town or city, where more wastes are added, until the once-pure stream becomes little more than a sluggish stench.

> Now Lake Erie is dead—killed by pollution.

> Lake Michigan may be the next of the Great Lakes to be killed by man. Even sooner, a much larger body of water appears to be doomed—the giant Gulf of Mexico!

This is mostly nonsense—but dangerous nonsense, as we shall see shortly, after a bit of theory. The plan for this chapter is (1) To clarify how economics views pollution—as a trade-off between cost and cleanliness. (2) To study the trends of pollution as income and population have increased in recent decades. The finding is that, according to the most important measures, pollu-

---

Reprinted from *The Ultimate Resource* (Princeton, NJ: Princeton University Press, 1981) by permission.

*Adapted from *Golden Stamp Book of Earth and Ecology* by George S. Fichter, © 1972 by Western Publishing Company, Inc. Used by permission of the publisher.

tion has decreased, on balance. (3) To consider which is the best overall measure of pollution. Life expectancy seems to be the best, and by that measure pollution is decreasing sharply. (4) To study in a bit of detail some of the pollutions that have most worried people in recent years, such as the purity of the Great Lakes and the disposal of trash. The outlook for both examples is clearly cheerful.

THE ECONOMIC THEORY OF POLLUTION

Natural resources and pollution are the opposite sides of the same coin. For example, sooty air is undesired pollution; it may also be thought of as the absence of a desired resource, pure air. The key difference between the concepts of a natural resource and of pollution is that the goods we call "natural resources" are largely produced by private firms, which have a strong self-interest—the profit motivation—for providing consumers with what they want. A deal is made through the market, and people tend to get what they are willing to pay for. In contrast, the good we call "absence of environmental pollution" is largely produced by public agencies, in which the political mechanism that adjusts supply and demand is far less automatic and, for better or for worse, seldom uses a pricing system that would arrive at the same result as would a free market.

Another difference between natural resources and pollution is that natural-resource transactions are mostly limited in impact to the buyer and the seller, whereas one person's pollution is "external" and may touch everybody else. This difference may be more apparent than real, however. One person's demand for natural resources affects the price that all pay, at least in the short run; and conversely, the price that one person must pay for a resource depends upon the demand of all others for the resource. Much the same would be true for pollution if there were a well-adjusted system by which people had to pay for the privilege of polluting. But such a price system for regulating pollution is not easy to achieve. And hence the situations of resources and pollution do differ in how "external" they are.

The technologist views all emissions of pollutants as bad, and speculates how to get rid of them. But the economist asks about the optimal level of pollution. How much cleanliness are we willing to pay for? At some point we prefer to spend money to buy more police service or more skiing rather than more environmental cleanliness. The problem of pollution for economists is like the problem of collecting a city's garbage: Do we want to pay for daily collection, or collection every other day, or just twice a week? With environmental pollution just as with garbage, a rational answer

depends upon the cost of cleanup as well as our tastes for cleanliness. And as our society becomes richer, we can afford and are prepared to pay for more cleanliness—a trend that we shall see documented below.

TRENDS IN U.S. POLLUTION

Sound discussion of this topic requires that we think about the many forms of pollution rather than just about a single, general "pollution." And it is useful to classify pollution as (a) health-related or (b) aesthetic. Largely because it is easier to talk objectively about the former than the latter, we shall concentrate on the health-related pollutions.

Life Expectancy and Pollution

The danger of an airplane falling on your house is infinitely greater now than it was a century ago. And the danger from artificial food additives is now many times greater than it was 1,000 years ago. You may or may not worry about such dangers as these, but an alarmist can *always* find some new man-made danger that is now increasing. We must, however, resist the tendency to conclude from such evidence that our world is more polluted now than it was before airplanes or food additives or whatever danger you please.

How may we reasonably assess the trend of health-related pollutions? It would seem reasonable to go directly to health itself to measure how we are doing. The simplest and most accurate measure of health is length of life, summed up as the average life expectancy. To buttress that general measure, which includes the effects of curative medicine as well as preventive (pollution-fighting) efforts, we may look at the trends in causes of death.

In the U.S. (and the Western world as a whole) there has been a long upward climb in life expectancy for many hundreds of years. This all-important fact may be seen in Figure 1 for the twentieth century. And in the rest of the world life expectancy has been climbing steadily for decades. Surely this historical view gives no ground for alarm. Of course, history may change course tomorrow and we might be headed directly into a cataclysm. But there is no reason to believe this. And despite speculation to the contrary, life expectancy is still increasing in the U.S., and even faster than before, according to latest reports.

Next let us turn to specific causes of death. In the past, most people in the U.S. died of environmental pollution—that is, of infectious diseases such as pneumonia, tuberculosis, or gastroenteritis. Nowadays, people die of the diseases of old age, which the environment does not force upon the individual—heart disease, cancer, and strokes (Figure 2). And there seems to be no evidence that the increase in cancer is due to environmental carcinogens; rather, it is an inevitable consequence of

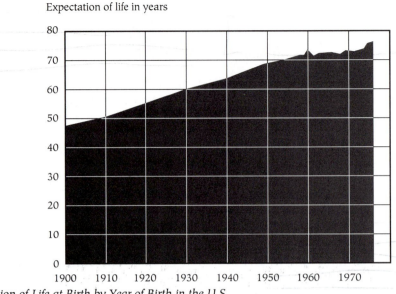

Expectation of life in years

FIGURE 1 *Expectation of Life at Birth by Year of Birth in the U.S.*

people living to older, more cancer-prone ages. The decline in accident deaths, despite increased auto use, may also be seen as an improvement in the health environment.

The worldwide picture begins to show the same characteristics. Smallpox, for example, once was a common killer; now it has been wiped out. And cholera, purely a pollution disease, is no longer an important factor in the world.

In sum: Life expectancy is the best index of the state of health-related pollution. And by this measure, pollution has been declining steadily and sharply for decades. Hence it is reasonable to say that taken together the health-affecting "pollutions" (using that term in its widest sense) have been diminishing.

AIR AND WATER POLLUTION

Pollution of the air and water are, for most people, the major environmental problems. And the popular impression is that the situation is getting worse. One reason for this impression is the widely reported Environmental Quality Index of the National Wildlife Federation. The *New York Times* headline for the 1976 report was "Environmental Quality Held Down," and the story begins, "The nation's overall environmental well-being declined slightly in 1976. . . ."

Despite the impressive name of the index, and its numerical nature, it is, according to the National Wildlife Federation, which prepares and disseminates it, "a subjective analysis [that] represent[s] [the] collective thinking of the editors of the National Wildlife Federation Staff." That is, the Environmental Quality Index represents casual observation and opinion rather than statistical facts. It includes such subjective judgments as that the trend of "living space" is "down . . . vast stretches of America are lost to development yearly." . . .

If we look at objective facts instead of "subjective analysis," we see that the quality of the environment is improving rather than worsening. The governmental Council on Environmental Quality's data on major air pollutants show sharp improvements in the last decade. Whereas the Environmental Quality Index has the quality of air declining from 1970 to 1973, the data collected from 1970 to 1974 by the official Environmental Protection Agency show a steady decline in the most important air pollutants, "particulates" and sulfur dioxide, as can be seen Figure 3.

Whereas the Environmental Quality Index says that "in cities, air quality is improving, but in the country it's getting worse," data for 1968–70 (I couldn't find a later study) show improvements in air quality in all population-classified living areas (Figure 4).

The Environmental Quality Index says "Water: Down," and their graph shows a steady deterioration from 1970 to 1977. It would be interesting to know how the National Wildlife Federation formed this impression—apparently in ignorance of the Council of Environmental Quality's 1975 report, which describes the situation as shown in Figure 5, based on U.S. Geological Survey data. The proportion of water-quality observations that had "good" drinking water rose from just over 40 percent in 1961 to about 60 percent in 1974. And the 1976 report concluded that "progress had been made in controlling municipal and industrial point sources of pollution. Major improvements in the quality of polluted streams have been documented in the preceding pages and in CEQ's previous Annual Reports."

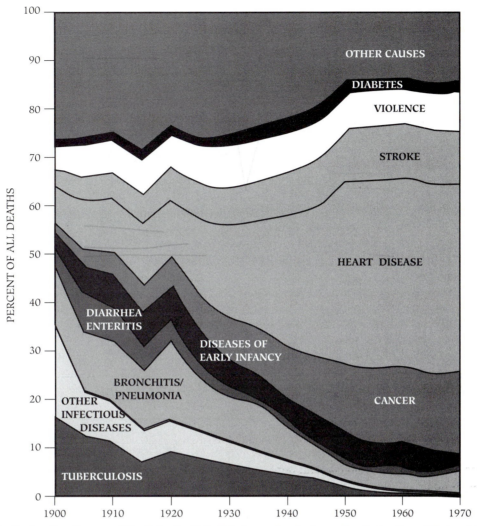

FIGURE 2 *Trends in the Leading Causes of Death in the U.S. This figure clearly shows the diminution of the most important life-destroying pollutions in the twentieth century The increase in the proportion of deaths from cancer is statistically inevitable simply because fewer people are dying at younger ages.*

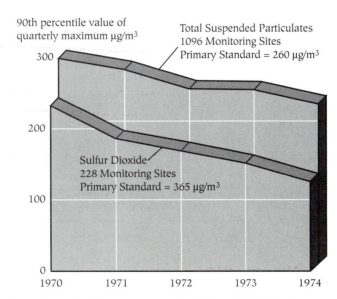

FIGURE 3a *National Pollution Trends in Sulfur Dioxide and Total Suspended Particulates*

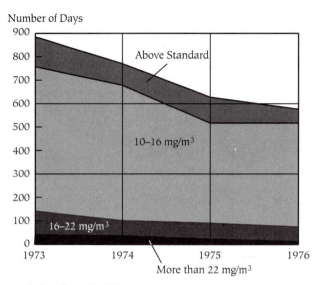

FIGURE 3b *Trends in Carbon Monoxide Levels in 13 Cities*
Note: *A darker shade represents a higher level of pollution.*

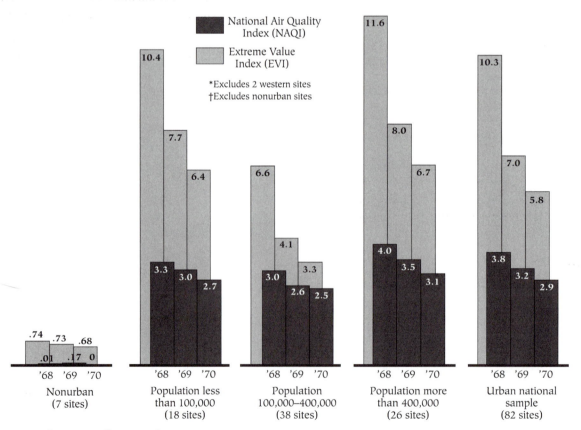

FIGURE 4 *Trends in Air Pollution in the U.S.*

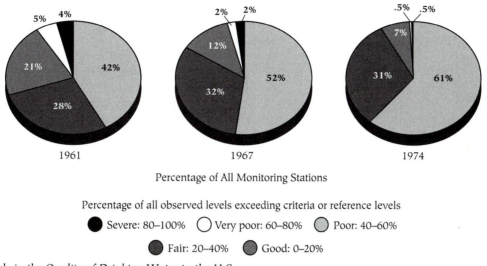

Percentage of All Monitoring Stations

Percentage of all observed levels exceeding criteria or reference levels

● Severe: 80–100% ○ Very poor: 60–80% ◐ Poor: 40–60%

◐ Fair: 20–40% ◐ Good: 0–20%

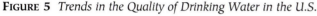

FIGURE 5 *Trends in the Quality of Drinking Water in the U.S.*

Longer-run data are hard to come by. But most students of the subject would probably agree with this assessment by Orris Herfindahl and Allen Kneese:

> Serious deterioration in some aspects of environmental quality did take place between, say, 1840 and 1940.
>
> By most measures the quality of air and water deteriorated, sometimes severely. Wild areas were brought under development, and their beauty frequently was impaired or destroyed. Game populations diminished rapidly, and in many cases ugly and congested cities were created.
>
> Since 1940, however, the quality of the environment has in some respects markedly improved. Rivers have been cleaned of their grossest floating materials; cities have substantially reduced the particulate matter in their atmosphere; some of the worse slums have been eliminated; public health, at least so far as infectious diseases are concerned, has been greatly improved; much land has been returned to a wild state, and many important varieties of wildlife have been encouraged to increase spectacularly.

In brief: Air and water are getting purer. And the public is being taken to the cleaners by such environmental groups as the National Wildlife Federation, which tell people just the opposite of the facts.

WHERE AND WHEN WAS (IS) POLLUTION LESS?

If we know the circumstances under which there will be less pollution, we can either try to change the local conditions or we can move to where there is less pollution. For the U.S., two invidious comparisons are commonly made: to socialist countries and to the past. Let us see whether the grass is greener elsewhere. (These comments are not intended as a comparison of capitalism with socialism, or of the present with the distant past; I have found no environmental data for such comparisons, and anecdotes alone are not a sound basis for them. My aim is simply to show that if one lifts one's eyes from one's own yard to others', one may see that things are not necessarily better over there.)

Socialist Countries

The Eastern European socialist countries are no paragons of environmental virtue. "Blue Only a Memory: The Danube Is Filthy," says a *New York Times* headline. "A dozen years ago we could swim in the Danube. Today the river is so dangerous it is illegal to swim in it," said the head of the Czechoslovak Research and Development Center for Environmental Pollution Control. . . . Brastislava [the capital of Slovakia] has the most polluted atmosphere and the worst environment among . . . other European cities."

The Soviet Union, too, is beset with environmental problems.

> In Russia, a huge chemical plant was built right beside a beloved tourist attraction: Yasnaya Polanya, Leo Tolstoy's gracious country estate. Unmonitored fumes are poisoning Tolstoy's forests of oak and pine, and powerless conservationists can only wince. With equal indifference, the Soviet pulp and paper industry has settled on the shores of Lake Baikal. No matter how fully the effluents are treated, they still defile the world's purest waters.
>
> The level of the Caspian Sea has dropped 872 feet since 1929, mainly because dams and irrigation projects along the Volga and Ural rivers divert incoming water. As a result, Russia's caviar output has decreased; one-third of the sturgeons' spawning grounds are high and dry. Meanwhile, most municipalities lack adequate sewage treatment plants, carbon monoxide chokes the plateau towns of Armenia, and smog shrouds the metallurgical centers of Magnitogorsk, Alma-Ata and Chelyabinsk.

Life expectancy is high and has been rising, in the socialist countries as in the U.S., of course. But perfect environmental purity has yet to be achieved there, just as in the West.

Pollution in the Past

There is a common tendency to compare the present to a hypothetical pristine past when lakes and streams were clean and when cities were free of the nuisances of modernity. But it wasn't so. Contrast a major Western metropolis today with London of 1890:

> The Strand of those days . . . was the throbbing heart of the people's essential London . . . But the mud! [a euphemism] And the noise! And the smell! All these blemishes were [the] mark of [the] horse. . . .
>
> The whole of London's crowded wheeled traffic—which in parts of the City was at times dense beyond movement—was dependent on the horse: lorry, wagon, bus, hansom and "growler," and coaches and carriages and private vehicles of all kinds, were appendages to horses . . . the characteristic aroma—for the nose recognized London with gay excitement—was of stables, which were commonly of three or four storeys with inclined ways zigzagging up the faces of them; [their] middens kept the cast-iron filigree chandeliers that glorified the reception rooms of upper- and lower-middle class homes throughout London encrusted with dead flies, and, in late summer, veiled with living clouds of them.
>
> A more assertive mark of the horse was the mud that, despite the activities of a numberous corps of red-jacketed boys who dodged among wheels and hooves with pan and brush in service to iron bins at the pavement-edge, either flooded the streets with churnings of "pea soup" that at times collected in pools over-brimming the kerbs, and at others covered the road-surface as with axle grease or bran-laden dust to the distraction of the wayfarer. In the first case, the swift-moving hansom or gig would fling sheets of such soup—where not intercepted by trousers or skirts—completely across the pavement, so that the frontages of the Strand throughout its length had an eighteen-inch plinth of mud-parge thus imposed upon it. The pea-soup condition was met by wheeled "mud carts" each attended by two ladlers clothed as for Icelandic seas in thigh boots, oilskins collared to the chin, and sou'westers sealing in the back of the neck. Splash Ho! The foot passenger now gets the mud in his eye! The axle-grease condition was met by horse-mechanized brushes and travellers in the small hours found fire-hoses washing away residues. . . .
>
> And after the mud the noise, which, again endowed by the horse, surged like a mighty heart-beat . . . and the hammering of a multitude of iron-shod hairy heels . . . , the deafening, side-drum tatoo of tyred wheels jarring from the apex of one set to the next like sticks dragging along a fence; the creaking and groaning and chirping

> and rattling of vehicles, light and heavy, thus maltreated; the jangling of chain harness and the clanging or jingling of every other conceivable thing else, augmented by the shrieking and bellowings called for from those of God's creatures who desired to impart information or proffer a request vocally—raised a din that . . . is beyond conception. It was not any such paltry thing as noise. It was an immensity of sound. . . .

There may not be overwhelming evidence for saying that in general the pollution situation has been getting better. There is (in my judgment) even less basis for saying that things have been getting worse. What is clear, however, is that there has been an increase in *concern* about pollution in the past decade. At the very same time that air and water pollution were decreasing, people were becoming progressively more worried about it, a trend that may be seen in these poll data:

Q. Compared to other parts of the country, how serious, in your opinion, do you think the problem of air/water pollution is in this area—very serious, somewhat serious, or not very serious?
A. Very Serious or Somewhat Serious:

	Air	Water
1965	28%	35%
1966	48%	49%
1967	53%	52%
1968	55%	58%
1970	69%	74%

Herfindahl and Kneese wisely note that "the present concern with environmental quality may stem as much or more from increased demands [for a clean environment] as deterioration in supply." But the cause of the concern is not fundamental to our theory; what does matter is the fact that people want a purer environment strongly enough to create it.

It is also clear that advanced economies have considerable power to purify their environments. And the key element in purification is well known. England's top anti-pollution bureaucrat, Lord Kennel, identified it precisely. "With rare and usually quickly solved exceptions, there is no contaminating factor in the environment, including noise, that defies a technical solution. All it takes is money." In other words, purification requires the will to devote the necessary part of a nation's present output and energy to do the job. Many kinds of pollution have lessened in many places—for example, filth in the streets of the U.S., buffalo dung in the streams of the Midwest, organic impurities in our foods, soot in the air, and substances that killed fish in the rivers in England.

> British rivers . . . have been polluted for a century while in America they began to grow foul only a couple of decades ago. . . . The Thames has been without fish for a century. But by 1968 some 40 different varieties had come back to the river.

Now to be seen [in London] are birds and plants long unsighted here. . . . The appearance of long-absent birds is measured by one claim that 138 species are currently identified in London, compared with less than half that number 10 years ago. . . . Gone are the killer smogs. . . . Londoners . . . are breathing air cleaner than it has been for a century . . . effect of air pollution on bronchial patients is diminishing . . . visibility is better, too . . . on an average winter day . . . about 4 miles, compared with 1.4 miles in 1958.

And here is a U.S. success story:

Long used for recreational purposes, Lake Washington [an eighteen-mile-long body of fresh water bordered by Seattle on its western shore and a number of smaller communities on its eastern shore] began to deteriorate badly soon after World War II when ten newly built waste-treatment plants began dumping some 20 million gallons of treated effluents into its water every day.

Algae thrived on the phosphorus and nitrogen in the sewage discharge, and each time more of the burgeoning aquatic plants died, so did a little bit of the lake—in the form of oxygen lost in decomposition. The lake became cloudy and malodorous, and the fish died along with the algae.

Alarmed, the state legislature in 1958 created a new authority—the Municipality of Metropolitan Seattle—and charged it with sewage disposal for the Seattle area. With the support of local residents, Metro, as the agency soon became known, built a $121 million integrated system that funnels all of the area's effluents far out into Puget Sound. In that way, the wastes are dissipated by tidal action.

Starting in 1963, the system was far enough along for the plants that had been dumping their nutritive wastes into the lake to begin, one by one, to divert their output into the new system and Puget Sound. The results were obvious in clearer, cleaner water and the return of fish populations. "When the phosphorus levels fell off, so did the algae blooms," says one zoologist, "and so did the pollution." What Lake Washington demonstrates, of course, is that pollution is not irreversible—provided the citizenry is really determined to reclaim the environment, and willing to pay for past years of neglect.

And, most astonishing of all, the Great Lakes are not dead—not even Lake Erie! Though the fish catch in Erie fell in the 1960s, it has recently increased, and in 1977 10 million pounds of fish were caught there. Ohio beaches on Lake Erie are reopening, and "trout and salmon have returned to the Detroit River, the Lake's biggest tributary." For the Great Lakes as a whole, the catch was at its lowest in history in 1965 (56 million tons), but has since rebounded to 73 million tons in 1977, not far from the average since World War I. By 1977 Lake Michigan had become an "angler's paradise . . . the finest fresh-water fishery in the world," a $350-million-a-year sport fishing industry.

What about all the other possible pollutants—PCB's, mercury, the environment warming, the environment cooling, and the rest? Because their number is as large as the environmentalist's imagination, it is not possible here or elsewhere to consider, one at a time, all the past, present, and future pollutions. The possibility of a dangerous or unaesthetic polluting effect may be raised against almost any substance we have ever produced or ever will produce. And if we act as if all *possible* dangers of a substance are also *likely* dangers, then we will become immobilized.

May I now introduce, as a surprise witness, Ralph Nader? His qualifications in the fight against pollution are almost beyond question. Here is his testimony about sodium azide, which is used in air bags for automobiles. (He is responding to a report publicized by Congressman Shuster that this chemical may cause mutations and cancer.)

Sodium azide, if you smell the gas or taste it, is very, very unsafe. So is gasoline. So are the additives in gasoline. So are battery additives. So are tire wear and tire flakes that get into the air. So are hydrocarbons. So is the nitrogen oxide, and so is carbon monoxide

It strikes me as eroding the credibility of some of these opponents who suddenly become full of such concern for these toxic substances because it happens to be in accord with what certain special industrial interests want, and so unconcerned with the massively more pervasive, massively more poisonous array of chemical substances that we too charitably call pollution.

I also spoke with Dr. Bruce Ames (chairman at the Genetics Department at the University of California–Berkeley), mentioned by Congressman Shuster. Dr. Ames was merely talking about sodium azide as it is exposed to human contact. He is not talking about sodium azide as it is solidified in pellets, and contained in sealed containers, etc. He does not have any information on that.

The point I want to make is that sodium azide, if it is exposed to acidic contact, will under certain extraordinary circumstances, given the fact that it is a solid pellet, emit a hydrozoic acid gas which is an intolerably pungent gas. If anybody has ever taken the slightest whiff of the gas, they would know it.

In all the crashes which involve air bag equipped cars on the highways, and sodium azide as the inflator, there has been no such reaction.

I don't say that by way of saying that sodium azide should be the inflator. Undoubtedly it is likely that most of the cars with air bags in the '80s will not have sodium azide.

But I do point out that the attempt to sensationalize the product in ways that are not shared by the EPA, the Department of Health, Education and Welfare, or OSHA, who know how sodium azide has been used for years in medical laboratories, for example—your attempt to sensationalize it does not receive much credibility given the source of the persons who are doing the sensationalizing.

The irony of Nader's effective defense of sodium azide is that the consumer and environmental movements in which Nader is influential have attacked many other substances and conditions in the same way that sodium azide and air bags were attacked; and now the same consumerists are suffering from irresponsible attacks on their own pet safety project, the air bag.

WASTE POLLUTION

Perhaps the silliest of pollution threats—but one that was nonetheless taken very seriously about ten years ago—was the fear of being overcome by our own wastes. We were asked to flush our toilets less frequently and to recycle all kinds of things. . . . In the course of less than a decade, however, engineers found a myriad of new ways not only to get rid of wastes but also to get value from them. "From their one-time reputation as major pollutants, garbage and sewage now seem to be acquiring the status of national resources." Within a year after Connecticut set up a Resources Recovery Authority "to manage a collection and re-use program for the entire state," the authorities could judge that "there are no technological problems with garbage any more. All that is needed is initiative."

The pollution of our living space by trash and discarded goods, especially junk cars, is a particularly interesting case. Not only can this problem be solved by the expenditure of resources for cleanup, but it also illustrates how resource scarcity is decreasing. Improved iron supplies and steel-making processes have now gotten iron and steel to the point of cheapness at which junked cars are no longer worth recycling. The old cars—if they could be stored out of sight—would be a newly created reservoir of "raw" materials for the future. In this important sense, iron is not being used up but is simply being stored in a different form for possible future use, until iron prices rise or better methods of salvage are developed. Much the same is true with many other discarded materials. But there is also an important difference from resources. The amount of junked cars and similar pollutants produced, and the price of polluting, are not automatically regulated by public demand, either by ballot vote or by dollar voting, as are market-produced-and-mediated goods. And there are strong private interests that militate against remedial actions.

The outcome of this sort of pollution, like others, will therefore depend largely on the social will and on political power.

SUMMARY

Pollution is a bad thing—by definition. There are many different sorts of pollution. Some have lessened over the years—for example, filth in the streets of our cities, and the pollutants that cause contagious diseases. Others have worsened—for example, gasoline fumes in the air, noise in many places, and atomic wastes. The long-run course of yet others, such as crime in the streets, is unknown. To summarize the direction of such a varied collection of trends is difficult, and can easily be misleading. If one has to choose a single measure of the state of pollution, the most plausible one, because the most inclusive, is life expectancy. And the expected length of a newborn's life has increased greatly in past centuries, and is still increasing.

Economists think about the reduction of pollution as a social good that can be achieved technologically, but that costs resources. This is the question before us: What is the optimal level of pollution, in light of our tastes for a cleaner environment relative to our desire for other goods?

Biologists, engineers, and environmentalists who have warned us of pollution problems and have then developed methods of abating those problems have performed a great service to mankind. And warnings about the possible dangers from coal, nuclear energy, medicines, mercury, carbon dioxide, and the like can serve a similar valuable purpose, especially in connection with ill effects that do not appear immediately but only after many years. We must keep in mind, however, that it is not possible to create a civilization that is free of such risks. The best we can do is to be alert and prudent. And exaggerated warnings can be counter-productive and dangerous.

Study Questions

1. Evaluate Simon's arguments. Does he convince you that pollution is actually receding overall? How strong is his argument that life expectancy is the best index for overall environmental quality?
2. Compare Simon's essay with the previous one by George Bradford. They say opposite things. Who is right?

59

People or Penguins:
The Case for Optimal Pollution

William F. Baxter

William Baxter is professor of law at Stanford University and the author of People or Penguins: The Case for Optimal Pollution *(1974) from which this selection is taken*

In this essay, Baxter aims at clarifying the relationship between resource use and pollution. They are the opposite sides of the same coin, the privilege and its price, the good and the bad. Baxter argues that we cannot have a pollution-free society without harming humans. If we are humanists, committed to promoting the human good above all else, as he is, we should be willing to allow pollution where it harms animals and trees if overall benefits accrue to human beings.

I start with the modest proposition that, in dealing with pollution, or indeed with any problem, it is helpful to know what one is attempting to accomplish. Agreement on how and whether to pursue a particular objective, such as pollution control, is not possible unless some more general objective has been identified and stated with reasonable precision. We talk loosely of having clean air and clean water, of preserving our wilderness areas, and so forth. But none of these is a sufficiently general objective: each is more accurately viewed as a means rather than as an end.

With regard to clean air, for example, one may ask, "how clean?" and "what does clean mean?" It is even reasonable to ask, "why have clean air?" Each of these questions is an implicit demand that a more general community goal be stated—a goal sufficiently general in its scope and enjoying sufficiently general assent among the community of actors that such "why" questions no longer seem admissible with respect to that goal.

If, for example, one states as a goal the proposition that "every person should be free to do whatever he wishes in contexts where his actions do not interfere with the interests of other human beings," the speaker is unlikely to be met with a response of "why." The goal may be criticized as uncertain in its implications or difficult to implement, but it is so basic a tenet of our civilization—it reflects a cultural value so broadly shared, at

Reprinted with permission of Columbia University Press from William F. Baxter, *People or Penguins: The Case for Optimal Pollution* (1974).

least in the abstract—that the question "why" is seen as impertinent or imponderable or both.

I do not mean to suggest that everyone would agree with the "spheres of freedom" objective just stated. Still less do I mean to suggest that a society could subscribe to four or five such general objectives that would be adequate in their coverage to serve as testing criteria by which all other disagreements might be measured. One difficulty in the attempt to construct such a list is that each new goal added will conflict, in certain applications, with each prior goal listed; and thus each goal serves as a limited qualification on prior goals.

Without any expectation of obtaining unanimous consent to them, let me set forth four goals that I generally use as ultimate testing criteria in attempting to frame solutions to problems of human organization. My position regarding pollution stems from these four criteria. If the criteria appeal to you and any part of what appears hereafter does not, our disagreement will have a helpful focus: which of us is correct, analytically, in supposing that his position on pollution would better serve these general goals. If the criteria do not seem acceptable to you, then it is to be expected that our more particular judgments will differ, and the task will then be yours to identify the basic set of criteria upon which your particular judgments rest.

My criteria are as follows:

1. The spheres of freedom criterion stated above.
2. Waste is a bad thing. The dominant feature of human existence is scarcity—our available resources, our aggregate labors, and our skill in employing both have always been, and will continue for some time to be, inadequate to yield to every man all the tangible and intangible satisfactions he would like to have. Hence, none of those resources, or labors, or skills, should be wasted—that is, employed so as to yield less than they might yield in human satisfactions.
3. Every human being should be regarded as an end rather than as a means to be used for the betterment of another. Each should be afforded dignity and regarded as having an absolute claim to an even-handed application of such rules as the community may adopt for its governance.
4. Both the incentive and the opportunity to improve his share of satisfactions should be preserved to

every individual. Preservation of incentive is dictated by the "no-waste" criterion and enjoins against the continuous, totally egalitarian redistribution of satisfactions, or wealth; but subject to that constraint, everyone should receive, by continuous redistribution if necessary, some minimal share of aggregate wealth so as to avoid a level of privation from which the opportunity to improve his situation becomes illusory.

The relationship of these highly general goals to the more specific environmental issues at hand may not be readily apparent, and I am not yet ready to demonstrate their pervasive implications. But let me give one indication of their implications. Recently scientists have informed us that use of DDT in food production is causing damage to the penguin population. For the present purposes let us accept that assertion as an indisputable scientific fact. The scientific fact is often asserted as if the correct implication—that we must stop agricultural use of DDT—followed from the mere statement of the fact of penguin damage. But plainly it does not follow if my criteria are employed.

My criteria are oriented to people, not penguins. Damage to penguins, or sugar pines, or geological marvels is, without more, simply irrelevant. One must go further, by my criteria, and say: Penguins are important because people enjoy seeing them walk about rocks; and furthermore, the well-being of people would be less impaired by halting use of DDT than by giving up penguins. In short, my observations about environmental problems will be people-oriented, as are my criteria. I have no interest in preserving penguins for their own sake.

It may be said by way of objection to this position, that it is very selfish of people to act as if each person represented one unit of importance and nothing else was of any importance. It is undeniably selfish. Nevertheless I think it is the only tenable starting place for analysis for several reasons. First, no other position corresponds to the way most people really think and act—i.e., corresponds to reality.

Second, this attitude does not portend any massive destruction of nonhuman flora and fauna, for people depend on them in many obvious ways, and they will be preserved because and to the degree that humans do depend on them.

Third, what is good for humans is, in many respects, good for penguins and pine trees—clean air for example. So that humans are, in these respects, surrogates for plant and animal life.

Fourth, I do not know how we could administer any other system. Our decisions are either private or collective. Insofar as Mr. Jones is free to act privately, he may give such preferences as he wishes to other forms of life: he may feed birds in winter and do less with himself, and he may even decline to resist an advancing polar bear on the ground that the bear's appetite is more important than those portions of himself that the bear may choose to eat. In short my basic premise does not rule out private altruism to competing life-forms. It does rule out, however, Mr. Jones' inclination to feed Mr. Smith to the bear, however hungry the bear, however despicable Mr. Smith.

Insofar as we act collectively on the other hand, only humans can be afforded an opportunity to participate in the collective decisions. Penguins cannot vote now and are unlikely subjects for the franchise—pine trees more unlikely still. Again each individual is free to cast his vote so as to benefit sugar pines if that is his inclination. But many of the more extreme assertions that one hears from some conservationists amount to tacit assertions that they are specially appointed representatives of sugar pines, and hence that their preferences should be weighted more heavily than the preferences of other humans who do not enjoy equal rapport with "nature." The simplistic assertion that agricultural use of DDT must stop at once because it is harmful to penguins is of that type.

Fifth, if polar bears or pine trees or penguins, like men, are to be regarded as ends rather than means, if they are to count in our calculus of social organization, someone must tell me how much each one counts, and someone must tell me how these life-forms are to be permitted to express their preferences, for I do not know either answer. If the answer is that certain people are to hold their proxies, then I want to know how those proxy-holders are to be selected: self-appointment does not seem workable to me.

Sixth, and by way of summary of all the foregoing, let me point out that the set of environmental issues under discussion—although they raise very complex technical questions of how to achieve any objective—ultimately raise a normative question: what *ought* we to do. Questions of *ought* are unique to the human mind and world—they are meaningless as applied to a nonhuman situation.

I reject the proposition that we *ought* to respect the "balance of nature" or to "preserve the environment" unless the reason for doing so, express or implied, is the benefit of man.

I reject the idea that there is a "right" or "morally correct" state of nature to which we should return. The word "nature" has no normative connotation. Was it "right" or "wrong" for the earth's crust to heave in contortion and create mountains and seas? Was it "right" for the first amphibian to crawl up out of the primordial ooze? Was it "wrong" for plants to reproduce themselves and alter the atmospheric composition in favor of oxygen? For animals to alter the atmosphere in favor of carbon dioxide both by breathing oxygen and eating plants? No answers can be given to these questions because they are meaningless questions.

All this may seem obvious to the point of being tedious, but much of the present controversy over environment and pollution rests on tacit normative assumptions about just such nonnormative phenomena: that it is "wrong" to impair penguins with DDT, but not to slaughter cattle for prime rib roasts. That it is wrong to kill stands of sugar pines with industrial fumes, but not to cut sugar pines and build housing for the poor. Every man is entitled to his own preferred definition of Walden Pond, but there is no definition that has any moral superiority over another, except by reference to the selfish needs of the human race.

From the fact that there is no normative definition of the natural state, it follows that there is no normative definition of clean air or pure water—hence no definition of polluted air—or of pollution—except by reference to the needs of man. The "right" composition of the atmosphere is one which has some dust in it and some lead in it and some hydrogen sulfide in it—just those amounts that attend a sensibly organized society thoughtfully and knowledgeably pursuing the greatest possible satisfaction for its human members.

The first and most fundamental step toward solution of our environmental problems is a clear recognition that our objective is not pure air or water but rather some optimal state of pollution. That step immediately suggests the question: How do we define and attain the level of pollution that will yield the maximum possible amount of human satisfaction?

Low levels of pollution contribute to human satisfaction but so do food and shelter and education and music. To attain ever lower levels of pollution, we must pay the cost of having less of these other things. I contrast that view of the cost of pollution control with the more popular statement that pollution control will "cost" very large numbers of dollars. The popular statement is true in some senses, false in others; sorting out the true and false senses is of some importance. The first step in that sorting process is to achieve a clear understanding of the difference between dollars and resources. Resources are the wealth of our nation; dollars are merely claim checks upon those resources. Resources are of vital importance; dollars are comparatively trivial.

Four categories of resources are sufficient for our purposes: At any given time a nation, or a planet if you prefer, has a stock of labor, of technological skill, of capital goods, and of natural resources (such as mineral deposits, timber, water, land, etc.). These resources can be used in various combinations to yield goods and services of all kinds—in some limited quantity. The quantity will be larger if they are combined efficiently, smaller if combined inefficiently. But in either event the resource stock is limited, the goods and services that they can be made to yield are limited; even the most efficient use of them will yield less than our population, in the aggregate, would like to have.

If one considers building a new dam, it is appropriate to say that it will be costly in the sense that it will require x hours of labor, y tons of steel and concrete, and z amount of capital goods. If these resources are devoted to the dam, then they cannot be used to build hospitals, fishing rods, schools, or electric can openers. That is the meaningful sense in which the dam is costly.

Quite apart from the very important question of how wisely we can combine our resources to produce goods and services, is the very different question of how they get distributed—who gets how many goods? Dollars constitute the claim checks which are distributed among people and which control their share of national output. Dollars are nearly valueless pieces of paper except to the extent that they do represent claim checks to some fraction of the output of goods and services. Viewed as claim checks, all the dollars outstanding during any period of time are worth, in the aggregate, the goods and services that are available to be claimed with them during that period—neither more nor less.

It is far easier to increase the supply of dollars than to increase the production of goods and services—printing dollars is easy. But printing more dollars doesn't help because each dollar then simply becomes a claim to fewer goods, i.e., becomes worth less.

The point is this: many people fall into error upon hearing the statement that the decision to build a dam, or to clean up a river, will cost $X million. It is regrettably easy to say: "It's only money. This is a wealthy country, and we have lots of money." But you cannot build a dam or clean a river with $X million—unless you also have a match, you can't even make a fire. One builds a dam or cleans a river by diverting labor and steel and trucks and factories from making one kind of goods to making another. The cost in dollars is merely a shorthand way of describing the extent of the diversion necessary. If we build a dam for $X million, then we must recognize that we will have $X million less housing and food and medical care and electric can openers as a result.

Similarly, the costs of controlling pollution are best expressed in terms of the other goods we will have to give up to do the job. This is not to say the job should not be done. Badly as we need more housing, more medical care, and more can openers, and more symphony orchestras, we could do with somewhat less of them, in my judgment at least, in exchange for somewhat cleaner air and rivers. But that is the nature of the trade-off, and analysis of the problem is advanced if that unpleasant reality is kept in mind. Once the trade-off relationship is clearly perceived, it is possible to state in a very general way what the optimal level of pollution is. I would state it as follows:

People enjoy watching penguins. They enjoy relatively clean air and smog-free vistas. Their health is improved by relatively clean water and air. Each of these benefits is a type of good or service. As a society we would be well advised to give up one washing machine if the resources that would have gone into that washing machine can yield greater human satisfaction when diverted into pollution control. We should give up one hospital if the resources thereby freed would yield more human satisfaction when devoted to elimination of noise in our cities. And so on, trade-off by trade-off, we should divert our productive capacities from the production of existing goods and services to the production of a cleaner, quieter, more pastoral nation up to—and no further than—the point at which we value more highly the next washing machine or hospital that we would have to do without than we value the next unit of environmental improvement that the diverted resources would create.

Now this proposition seems to me unassailable but so general and abstract as to be unhelpful—at least unadministerable in the form stated. It assumes we can measure in some way the incremental units of human satisfaction yielded by very different types of goods. . . . But I insist that the proposition stated describes the result for which we should be striving—and again, that it is always useful to know what your target is even if your weapons are too crude to score a bull's eye.

Study Questions

1. Evaluate the four tenets of Baxter's environmental philosophy.
   a. Which do you agree with, and which do you disagree with? Explain why.
   b. Is human benefit the only morally relevant criterion with regard to our behavior to animals and the environment?
   c. Do penguins and sugar pine trees have intrinsic value? Or is their value entirely instrumental, derived from benefits to humans?
2. Do you agree with Baxter that pollution is just the opposite side of the coin of resource use? Do you also agree that on the principle that "waste is a bad thing" we are led to use resources for human good and thus bring about some level of pollution?
3. Compare Baxter's analysis to those of Bradford and Simon. What are their similarities and differences? Does Baxter shed any light on the matter?

60

You Are What You Breathe

HILARY FRENCH

Hilary French is a staff researcher for the Worldwatch Institute.

In this essay, French provides a detailed, documented account of the devastating global effects of air pollution. Since the wind carries the polluted air from one nation to another, this problem requites international as well as national action and cooperation. If we are to solve the problem, our lifestyles will have to change.

Asked to name the world's top killers, most people wouldn't put air pollution high on their lists. A nuisance, at best, but not a terribly serious threat to health.

The facts say otherwise. In greater Athens, for example, the number of deaths rises sixfold on heavily polluted days. In Hungary, the government attributes 1 in 17 deaths to air pollution. In Bombay, breathing the air is equivalent to smoking 10 cigarettes a day. And in Beijing, air-pollution-related respiratory distress is so common that it has been dubbed the "Beijing Cough."

Air pollution is truly a global public health emergency. United Nations statistics show that more than one billion people—a fifth of humanity—live in areas where the air is not fit to breathe. Once a local phenomenon primarily affecting city dwellers and people living near factories, air pollution now reaches rural as well as urban dwellers. It's also crossing international borders.

In the United States alone, roughly 150 million people live in areas whose air is considered unhealthy by the Environmental Protection Agency (EPA). According to the American Lung Association, this leads to as many as 120,000 deaths each year.

A century ago, air pollution was caused primarily by the coal burned to fuel the industrial revolution. Since then, the problem and its causes have become more complex and widespread. In some parts of the world, including much of Eastern Europe and China, coal continues to be the main source of pollution. Elsewhere, automobiles and industries are now the primary cause.

Adding to the miasma, industries are emitting pollutants of frightening toxicity. Millions of tons of carcinogens, mutagens, and poisons pour into the air each year and damage health and habitat near their sources and, via the winds, sometimes thousands of miles away. Many regions that have enjoyed partial success combating pollution are finding their efforts overwhelmed as populations and economies grow and bring in more power plants, home furnaces, factories, and motor vehicles.

From *The Worldwatch Reader,* ed. Lester R. Brown (New York: W. W. Norton & Co., 1991) copyright © 1991 Worldwatch Institute. Reprinted by permission of The Worldwatch Institute.

Meanwhile, global warming has arisen as the preeminent environmental concern; this sometimes conveys the misleading impression that conventional air pollution is yesterday's problem. But air pollutants and greenhouse gases stem largely from fossil fuels burned in energy, transportation, and industrial systems. Having common roots, the two problems can also have common solutions. Unfortunately, policymakers persist in tackling them separately, which runs the risk of lessening one while exacerbating the other.

Air pollution has proven so intractable a phenomenon that a book could be written about the history of efforts to combat it. Law has followed law. As one problem has largely been solved, a new one has frequently emerged to take its place. Even some of the solutions have become part of the problem: The tall smokestacks built in the 1960s and 1970s to disperse emissions from huge coal-burning power plants became conduits to the upper atmosphere for the pollutants that form acid rain.

Tuning the corner on air pollution requires moving beyond patchwork, end-of-the-pipe approaches to confront pollution at its sources. This will mean reorienting energy, transportation, and industrial structures toward prevention.

TABLE 1 *Health Effects of Pollutants from Automobiles*[1]

POLLUTANT	HEALTH EFFECT
Carbon monoxide	Interferes with blood's ability to absorb oxygen; impairs perception and thinking; slows reflexes; causes drowsiness; and so can cause unconsciousness and death; if inhaled by pregnant women, may threaten growth and mental development of fetus.
Lead	Affects circulatory, reproductive, nervous, and kidney systems; suspected of causing hyperactivity and lowered learning ability in children; hazardous even after exposure ends.
Nitrogen oxides	Can increase susceptibility to viral infections such as influenza. Can also irritate the lungs and cause bronchitis and pneumonia.
Ozone	Irritates mucous membranes of respiratory system; causes coughing, choking, and impaired lung function; reduces resistance to colds and pneumonia; can aggravate chronic heart disease, asthma, bronchitis, and emphysema.
Toxic emissions	Suspected of causing cancer, reproductive problems, and birth defects. Benzene is a known carcinogen.

[1] Automobiles are a primary source, but not the only source, of these pollutants. *Sources:* National Clean Air Coalition and the U.S. Environmental Protection Agency.

CHEMICAL SOUP

Although air pollution plagues countries on all continents and at all levels of development, it comes in many different varieties. The burning of fossil fuels—predominantly coal—by power plants, industries, and home furnaces was the first pollution problem recognized as a threat to human health. The sulfur dioxide and particulate emissions associated with coal burning—either alone or in combination—can raise the incidence of respiratory diseases such as coughs and colds, asthma, bronchitis, and emphysema. Particulate matter (a general term for a complex and varying mixture of pollutants in minute solid form) can carry toxic metals deep into the lungs.

Pollution from automobiles forms a second front in the battle for clean air. One of the worst auto-related pollutants is ozone, the principal ingredient in urban smog. Formed when sunlight causes hydrocarbons (a by-product of many industrial processes and engines) to react with nitrogen oxides (produced by cars and power plants), ozone can cause serious respiratory distress. Recent U.S. research suggests that ground-level ozone causes temporary breathing difficulty and long-term lung damage at lower concentrations than previously believed.

Other dangerous pollutants spewed by automobiles include nitrogen dioxide, carbon monoxide, lead, and such toxic hydrocarbons as benzene, toluene, xylene, and ethylene dibromide (see Table 1).

At elevated levels, nitrogen dioxide can cause lung irritation, bronchitis, pneumonia, and increased susceptibility to viral infections such as influenza. Carbon monoxide can interfere with the blood's ability to absorb oxygen; this impairs perception and thinking, slow reflexes, and causes drowsiness and—in extreme cases—unconsciousness and death. If inhaled by a pregnant woman, carbon monoxide can threaten the fetus's physical and mental development.

Lead affects the circulatory, reproductive, nervous, and kidney systems. It is suspected of causing hyperactivity and lowered learning ability in children. Because it accumulates in bone and tissue, it is hazardous long after exposure ends.

Concern is growing around the world about the health threat posed by less common but extremely harmful airborne toxic chemicals such as benzene, vinyl chloride, and other volatile organic chemicals produced by automobiles and industries. These chemicals can cause a variety of illnesses, such as cancer and genetic and birth defects, yet they have received far less regulatory attention around the world than have "conventional" pollutants.

WHERE THE BREATHING ISN'T EASY

With the aid of pollution control equipment and improvements in energy efficiency, many Western industrialized countries have made significant strides in reducing emissions of sulfur dioxide and particulates. The United States, for example cut sulfur oxide emissions by

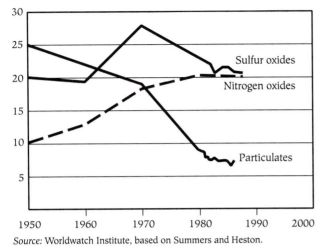

Million tons

Source: Worldwatch Institute, based on Summers and Heston.

FIGURE 1 *Emissions of Selected Pollutants in the United States, 1950–1987.*

28 percent between 1970 and 1987 and particulates by 62 percent (see Figure 1). In Japan, sulfur dioxide emissions fell by 39 percent from 1973 to 1984.

The same cannot be said for Eastern Europe and the Soviet Union, where hasty industrialization after World War II, powered by abundant high-sulfur brown coal, has led to some of the worst air pollution ever experienced. Pollution control technologies have been virtually nonexistent. And, because of heavily subsidized fuel prices and the absence of market forces governing production, these countries never made the impressive gains in energy efficiency registered in the West after the oil shocks of the 1970s.

Many developing countries also confront appalling air pollution problems. The lack of adequate pollution control technologies and regulations, plus plans to expand energy and industrial production, translates into worsening air quality in many cities. Urbanization in much of the Third World means that increasing numbers of people are exposed to polluted city air.

A 1988 report by the United Nation's Environment Program (UNEP) and the World Health Organization (WHO) gives the best picture to date of the global spread of sulfur dioxide and particulate pollution (see Table 2). Of the 54 cities with data available on sulfur dioxide pollution for 1980 to 1984, 27 were on the borderline or in violation of the WHO health standard.

High on the list were Shenyang, Tehran, and Seoul, as well as Milan, Paris, and Madrid; this indicates that sulfur dioxide problems have by no means been cured in industrial countries. Though conditions are gradually improving in most of the cities surveyed, several in the Third World reported a worsening trend.

Suspended particulate matter poses an even more pervasive threat, especially in the developing world, where the appropriate control technologies have not been installed and conditions are frequently dusty. Fully 37 of the 41 cities monitored for particulates averaged either borderline or excessive levels. Annual average concentrations were as much as five times the WHO standard in both New Delhi and Beijing.

Ozone pollution, too, has become a seemingly intractable health problem in many parts of the world. In the United States, 1988 ushered in one of the hottest and sunniest years on record, and also one of the worst for ground-level ozone in more than a decade. According to the Natural Resources Defense Council, the air in New York City violated the federal health standard on 34 days—two to three times a week, all summer long. In Los Angeles, ozone levels surged above the federal standard on 172 days. At last count 382 counties, home to more than half of all Americans, were out of compliance with the EPA ozone standard.

Ozone is becoming a problem elsewhere, too. In Mexico City, the relatively lenient government standard of a one-hour ozone peak of 0.11 parts per million not to be exceeded more than once daily is topped more than 300 days a year—nearly twice as often as Los Angeles violates its much stricter standard.

The other automobile-related pollutants also constitute a far-flung health threat. The WHO/UNEP report estimates that 15 to 20 percent of urban residents in North America and Europe are exposed to unacceptably high levels of nitrogen dioxide, 50 percent to unhealthy carbon monoxide concentrations, and a third to excessive lead levels. In a study in Mexico City, lead levels in the blood of 7 out of 10 newborns were found to exceed WHO standards. "The implication for Mexican society, that an entire generation of children will be intellectually stunted, is truly staggering," says Mexican chemist and environmental activist Manuel Guerra.

TABLE 2 *Violations of Sulfur Dioxide and Suspended Particulate Matter Standards, Selected Cities[1]*

CITY	SULFUR DIOXIDE	PARTICULATES[2]
	(number of days above WHO standard)	
New Delhi	6	294
Xian	71	273
Beijing	68	272
Shenyang	146	219
Tehran	104	174
Bangkok	0	97
Madrid	35	60
Kuala Lampur	0	37
Zagreb	30	34
Sao Paulo	12	31
Paris	46	3
New York	8	0
Milan	66	n.a.
Seoul	87	n.a.

[1] Averages of readings at a variety of monitoring sites from 1980 to 1984.
[2] For Madrid, Sao Paulo, and Paris, the reading is of smoke rather than particulates.

Source: United Nations Environment Program and World Health Organization, *Assessment of Urban Air Quality* (Nairobi: Global Environment Monitoring System, 1988).

Airborne toxic chemical emissions present no less of a danger. In the United States, the one country that has begun to tally total emissions, factories reported 1.3 million tons of hazardous emissions in 1987, including 118,000 tons of carcinogens. According to the EPA, these emissions cause about 2,000 cancer deaths a year.

These deaths fall disproportionately on certain communities. For example, in West Virginia's Kanawha Valley—home to a quarter of a million people and 13 major chemical plants—state health department records show that, between 1968 and 1977, the incidence of respiratory cancer was more than 21 percent above the national average. According to EPA statistics, a lifetime of exposure to the airborne concentrations of butadiene, chloroform, and ethylene oxide in this valley could cause cancer in 1 resident in 1,000.

Unfortunately, data are not so extensive for other countries. Wherever uncontrolled polluting industries such as chemical plants, smelters, and paper mills exist, however, emission levels are undoubtedly high. Measurements of lead and cadmium in the soil of the upper Silesian towns of Olkosz and Slawkow in Poland, for instance, are among the highest recorded anywhere in the world.

The health damage inflicted by air pollution comes at great human cost; it also carries an economic price tag. The American Lung Association estimates that air pollution costs the United States $40 billion annually in health care and lost productivity.

CLEARING THE AIR

In the Western industrial world, the last 20 years has been a period of intense political and scientific activity aimed at restoring clean air. The approaches to date, however, have tended to be technological Band-Aids rather than efforts to address the roots of the problem.

Scrubbers, nitrogen-oxides control technologies, and new cleaner-burning coal technologies can all reduce emissions dramatically, but they are not the ultimate solutions. For one, they can create environmental problems of their own, such as the need to dispose of scrubber ash, a hazardous waste. Second, they do little if anything to reduce carbon dioxide emissions, so make no significant contribution to slowing global warming.

For these reasons, technologies of this kind are best viewed as a bridge to the day when energy-efficient societies are the norm and pollution-free sources such as solar, wind, and water power provide the bulk of the world's electricity.

Improving energy efficiency is a clean air priority. Such measures as more-efficient refrigerators and lighting can markedly and cost-effectively reduce electricity consumption; this will in turn reduce emissions. Equally important, the savings that results from not building power plants because demand has been cut by efficiency

can more than offset the additional cost of installing scrubbers at existing plants.

Using conservative assumptions, the Washington, D.C.–based American Council for an Energy Efficient Economy concluded that cutting sulfur dioxide emissions steeply with a scrubbers/conservation combination could actually save consumers in the Midwest up to $8 billion.

Similar rethinking can help reduce auto emissions. To date, modifying car engines and installing catalytic converters have been the primary strategies employed to lower harmful emissions. These devices reduce hydrocarbon emissions by an average of 87 percent, carbon monoxide by an average of 85 percent, and nitrogen oxides by 62 percent over the life of a vehicle. Although catalytic converters are sorely needed in countries that don't require them, they alone are not sufficient. Expanding auto fleets are overwhelming the good they do, even in countries that have mandated their use.

Alternative fuels, such as methanol, ethanol, natural gas, hydrogen, and electricity, are being pushed by many governments as the remedy for the air pollution quagmire. Although these fuels may have some role to play eventually, they can by no means be viewed as a panacea.

Reducing air pollution in cities is likely to require a major shift away from automobiles as the cornerstone of urban transportation systems. As congestion slows traffic to a crawl in many cities, driving to work is becoming unattractive anyway. Convenient public transportation, car pooling, and measures that facilitate bicycle commuting are the cheapest, most effective ways for metropolitan areas to proceed.

Driving restrictions already exist in many of the world's cities. For example, Florence has turned its downtown into a pedestrian mall during daylight hours. Budapest bans motor traffic from all but two streets in the downtown area during particularly polluted spells. In Mexico City and Santiago, one-fifth of all vehicles are kept off the streets each weekday based on their license-plate numbers.

As with power plant and auto emissions, efforts to control airborne toxic chemicals will be most successful if they focus on minimizing waste rather than simply on controlling emissions. Such a strategy also prevents waste from being shifted from one form to another. For instance, control technologies such as scrubbers and filters produce hazardous solid wastes that must be disposed on land.

The Congressional Office of Technology Assessment has concluded it is technically and economically feasible for U.S. industries to lower production of toxic wastes and pollutants by up to 50 percent within the next few years. Similar possibilities exist in other countries.

Freedom of environmental information can also be a powerful regulatory tool. In the United States, "right-to-know" legislation requiring industries to release data on their toxic emissions has been instrumental in raising public awareness of the threat and spurring more responsible industrial behavior. The Monsanto Company, a major chemical producer, was so embarrassed by the enormous pollution figures it was required to release in 1989 that it simultaneously announced its intention to cut back emissions 90 percent by 1992.

Few European countries have released information about emissions from industrial plants, although that may change if the European Economic Community (EEC) issues a directive now in draft form on freedom of information regarding environmental matters. The recent political transformation in Eastern Europe and the Soviet Union are gradually improving the environmental data flow, although much progress in this area remains to be made.

SOLUTION FROM SMOG CITY

In most parts of the world, air pollution is now squarely on the public policy agenda. This is a promising sign. Unfortunately, the public's desire for clean air has not yet been matched with the political leadership needed to provide it. Recent developments at the national and international levels, though constituting steps forward, remain inadequate to the task.

In the United States, for example, recent major amendments to the Clean Air Act of 1970 will cut acid rain emissions in half, tighten emissions standards for automobiles significantly, and require much stricter control of toxic air pollutants.

Almost any legislation would be an improvement. Twenty years after the act became law, 487 counties still are not in compliance. But the legislation fails to address the problem at a fundamental level by not encouraging energy efficiency, waste reduction, and a revamping of transportation systems and urban designs.

Los Angeles—with the worst air quality in the United States—is one of the first regions in the world to really understand that lasting change will not come through mere tinkering. Under a bold new air-quality plan embracing the entire region, the city government will discourage automobile use, boost public transportation, and control household and industrial activities that contribute to smog.

For example, paints and solvents will have to be reformulated to produce fewer ozone-forming fumes; gasoline-powered lawn mowers and lighter fluid will be banned; carpooling will be mandated; and the number of cars per family limited. Even though the plan has been approved by all of the relevant state and federal agencies, implementing it at the local level will be a challenge.

Most of Europe, though quicker than the United States to cut back sharply on the emissions that cause acid rain, has been slower to tackle urban air quality. Non-EEC countries such as Austria, Norway, Sweden, and Switzerland have had strong auto emissions control legislation in place for several years, but until recently the EEC had been unable to agree on its own stringent standards.

This finally changed in June 1989, when the EEC Council of Environmental Ministers ended a nearly four-year debate and approved new standards for small cars. These will be as tough as those now in effect in the United States. To meet them, small cars will have to be equipped with catalytic converters. Although an important step forward, it's somewhat ironic that Europe sees its adoption of U.S. standards as a major victory at the same time the United States realizes these regulations don't go far enough.

In Eastern Europe and the Soviet Union, air pollution emerged as a pressing political issue as *glasnost* and the revolutions of 1989 opened up public debate. Air pollution in much of the region is taking a devastating toll on human health. Fledgling governments in Eastern Europe are under pressure to show some improvements.

A HELPFUL HAND

To make a dent in their pollution, Eastern Europe and the Soviet Union will need Western technologies and a dose of domestic economic and environmental reform. Given current economic conditions in these countries, money for purchasing pollution control, energy efficiency, renewable energy, and waste reduction technologies will have to come in part in the form of environmental aid from the West.

Aid of this kind can be classified as enlightened philanthropy, since stemming pollution in Eastern Europe, where even rudimentary controls are still lacking, can yield a far greater return on the investment than taking further incremental steps at home. To illustrate this point, Sweden receives 89 percent of the sulfur that contributes to the acid rain poisoning its lakes and forests from other countries. Because much of this is of Eastern European origin, anything Sweden does to combat emissions there helps at home.

Air pollution is beginning to emerge on the political agenda in the Third World as well. In Cubatão, Brazil, a notoriously polluted industrial city known as "the Valley of Death," a five-year-old government cleanup campaign is starting to make a dent in the problem. Total emissions of particulates, for instance, were cut from 521,600 pounds a day in 1984 to 156,000 in 1989.

Mexico City, too, is embarking on an ambitious cleanup. With the support of the World Bank, Japan, the United States, and West Germany, the municipal government is introducing a package of measures aimed at cutting automotive pollution dramatically over the next two to three years. As part of the plan, driving will be restricted on certain days. In March 1991, Mexican President Carlos Salinas de Gortari ordered the shutdown of a large oil refinery on the outskirts of Mexico City that has long been a major contributor to the city's pollution problem.

Industrial countries are involved in a variety of efforts to assist developing countries with air pollution problems. The International Environmental Bureau in Switzerland and the World Environment Center in New York City help facilitate transfer of pollution control information and technology to the Third World. The World Bank is exploring ways to step up its air pollution control activities. One proposed project involving the World Bank and the UN Development Program would help Asian governments confront urban air pollution, among other environmental problems.

Legislation passed by the U.S. Congress requires the Agency for International Development to encourage energy efficiency and renewable energy through its programs in the interests of slowing global warming. This step will reduce air pollution at the same time.

While the means are available to clear the air, it will be a difficult task. In the West, powerful businesses such as auto manufacturers and electric utilities will strongly resist measures that appear costly. In Eastern Europe, the Soviet Union, and the developing world, extreme economic problems coupled with shortages of hard currency mean that money for pollution prevention and control is scarce.

Overcoming these barriers will require fundamental modifications of economic systems. As long as air pollu-tion's costs remain external to economic accounting systems, utilities, industries, and individuals will have little incentive to reduce the amount of pollution they generate. Taxes, regulations, and public awareness can all be harnessed to bring the hidden costs of air pollution out into the open.

On the promising side, faced with mounting costs to human health and the environment, people on every continent are beginning to look at pollution prevention through a different economic lens. Rather than a financial burden, they're seeing that it is a sound investment. The old notion that pollution is the price of progress seems finally to be becoming a relic of the past.

Study Questions

1. What conclusions should we come to after reading French's assessment of the hazards of air pollution? What does the data signify for the future?
2. If you were to propose a plan to solve the problem of air pollution, how would you begin? What sort of measures would you take both locally and nationally? How would you deal with other nations who are polluting the atmosphere?
3. Is air pollution an area that the United Nations should be involved in? Explain your reasoning.

61

Market-Based Incentives for Environmental Protection

ROBERT N. STAVINS AND BRADLEY W. WHITEHEAD

Robert Stavins is associate professor of public policy at the Center for Science and International Affairs in the John F. Kennedy School of Government at Harvard University. Bradley Whitehead is a management consultant at McKinsey and Company, Inc., in Cleveland, Ohio.

Stavins and Whitehead argue that a new situation has arisen in the United States (but the same situation is applicable to other nations), calling for new environmental strategies. Whereas in the 1970s and early 1980s a need existed for government to intervene with strict regulations, such as the Clean Air Act, we now face a situation where budget deficits, an economic recession, and greater foreign competition call for measures that will make it worthwhile for businesses to cut pollution while still maintaining reasonable levels of

profit. They argue that a market-based approach is superior to a command-and-control regulatory approach. Command-and-control regulations set uniform standards regardless of their uneven impact. Market-based approaches provide incentives to companies to invest in pollution control.

As the United States prepares to address the environmental challenges of the 1990s, it faces an economic and political context fundamentally different from that of the 1970s, when the first environmental measures were enacted. More than a decade of large budget deficits, sluggish productivity growth, and intensified foreign competition has spurred interest in environmental approaches that lower compliance and administrative burdens for industry and government. Public restiveness over the size of government expenditures also has heightened interest in environmental approaches that require less bureaucracy and governmental intrusion into business and household decisions. These forces for change have led to a quest for innovative environmental policy instruments.

From *Environment*, Vol. 34, No. 7, September 1992, pp. 7–11, 29–42. Reprinted with permission of the Helen Dwight Reid Educational Foundation. Published by Heldref Publications, 1319 Eighteenth St., NW, Washington, DC 20036-1802.

NEW CHALLENGES FOR ENVIRONMENTAL POLICY

Many environmentalists in the 1970s and early 1980s viewed the market as villainous because it drove businesses to pursue profits without regard for environmental consequences. According to this view, the government should make decisions concerning appropriate technologies and emissions levels in light of the "externalities"—social costs created by businesses but borne by others in society—that the business world ignores. Furthermore, the government should not merely specify policy goals but also intervene in decisions about the production process itself. The explicit goal of some legislation during this period was to maximize the benefits of environmental protection regardless of the costs. Indeed, some statutes and regulations explicitly forbade the consideration of costs in setting standards. For example, when the ambient standards for criteria air pollutants are set under the Clean Air Act, the costs of meeting the standards may not, according to law, be taken into consideration.

This philosophy has driven much of the environmental progress over the last two decades, and in many places, the environment is cleaner now than it was before. But the United States and the world continue to face major environmental challenges, including such ongoing problems as urban smog, groundwater pollution, and acid rain and other, newly recognized problems, such as global climate change and indoor air pollution. Moreover, the economic and political contexts in which environmental policy is formulated have changed significantly. The challenge for policymakers today is to devise policies that harness rather than obstruct market forces.

The Need for Cost-Effectiveness

The days have ended when the United States could afford to consider environmental protection in isolation from costs. The U.S. Environmental Protection Agency (EPA) estimates that the nation now spends more than $100 billion annually to comply with federal environmental laws and regulations, and there is heightened concern over the impact of these regulations on the strength of the economy and its ability to compete in international markets. As a result, policymakers are increasingly cautious about the degree and type of regulatory burdens placed on businesses and individuals.

The existence of federal, state, and local budget deficits makes it difficult for the United States to increase environmental protection simply by spending more money on programs and policies already in place. A new sensitivity to private costs exists, as well. U.S. citizens and policymakers have not lost sight of the benefits of environmental protection, but they are giving increased attention to cost-effective environmental policies. To

some people, the concern over cost-effectiveness means getting more environmental protection for the same level of expenditures; to others, it means getting the same level of protection for less money. To both, however, it means making the most of scarce resources and maximizing returns on the resources invested—business costs, regulatory effort, political capital, and taxes—to improve the quality of the environment.

Harness Market Forces

An indicator of the presence of such concerns was the adoption of a market-based approach to the control of acid rain in the 1990 Clean Air Act Amendments—tradable "pollution reduction credits." The adoption of this approach suggests that some political leaders recognize that market forces are not only part of the problem but also a potential part of the solution. By dictating behavior and removing profit opportunities, past environmental regulation has placed unnecessary burdens on the economy and stifled the development of new, more effective environmental technologies. Furthermore, such policies have helped engender an adversarial relationship among regulators, environmentalists, and private industry. As a result, excessive economic resources often have been used for litigation and other forms of conflict among concerned parties.

Policies are needed to mobilize and harness the power of market forces for the environment and to make economic and environmental interests compatible and mutually supportive. Policymakers must begin to link the twin forces of government and industry, without extravagant investment.

POLICIES FOR ENVIRONMENTAL PROTECTION

There are two steps to formulating environmental policy: choosing the overall goal and selecting a means to achieve that goal. Market-based environmental policies that focus on the means of achieving policy goals are largely neutral with respect to the selected goals and provide cost-effective methods for reaching those goals. Before investigating market incentives, in general, and pollution charges, in particular, it is useful to review the regulatory approach most frequently used—command-and-control.

Command-and-Control Regulatory Approaches

Command-and-control regulations tend to force all businesses to adopt the same measures and practices for pollution control and thus shoulder identical shares of the pollution control burden regardless of their relative impacts. Government regulations typically set uniform standards—mostly technology- or performance-based—for all businesses. As the name suggests, technology-based standards specify the method and, sometimes, the equipment that businesses must use to comply with a regulation. Usually, regulations do not specify the technology but establish standards on the basis of a particular technology. In situations where monitoring problems are particularly severe, however, technologies are specified. For instance, all businesses in an industry are sometimes required to use the "best available technology" to control water pollution, or, in a more extreme example, electric utilities may be required to utilize a specific technology, such as electrostatic precipitators, to remove particulates. Performance standards, on the other hand, set a uniform control target for each business but allow some latitude in how to meet it. Such a standard might set the maximum allowable units of pollutant per time period but remain neutral with respect to the means by which each business reaches the goal.

Holding all businesses under the same target can be both expensive and counterproductive. Although uniform standards can sometimes be effective in limiting emissions of pollutants, they typically do so at relatively high costs to society. Specifically, uniform standards can force some businesses to use unduly expensive means of controlling pollution because the costs of controlling emissions can vary greatly between and even within businesses, and the right technology in one situation may be wrong in another. For example, in a survey of eight empirical studies of air-pollution control, the ratio of actual, aggregate costs of the conventional, command-and-control approach to the aggregate costs of least-cost benchmarks ranged from 1.07 for sulfate emissions in Los Angeles, California, to 22.0 for hydrocarbon emissions at all U.S. Du Pont plants. Indeed, the cost of controlling a given pollutant may vary by a factor of 100 or more among sources, depending upon the age and location of plants and the available technologies.

The command-and-control approach also tends to freeze the development of technologies that could provide greater levels of control. Little or no financial incentive exists for businesses to exceed their control targets, and both types of standards contain a bias against experimentation with new technologies. A business's reward for trying a new technology may be that it will subsequently be held to a higher standard of performance, without significant opportunity to benefit financially from its investment. As a result, money that could be invested in technology development is diverted to legal battles over defining acceptable technologies and standards of performance

Market-Based Policies

Unlike command-and-control policies, which seek to regulate the individual polluter, market-based policies train their sights on the overall pollution in a given area. What is important to most people, after all, is not how many particulates the local widget factory emits but the quality of the air they breathe while walking downtown or sitting in their back yards. Thus, under a market-based approach, the government establishes financial incentives so that the costs imposed on business drive an entire industry or region to reduce its aggregate level of pollution to a desired level. Then, as in any regulatory system, the government monitors and enforces compliance.

In terms of policy, a market-based approach achieves the same aggregate level of control as might be set under a command-and-control approach, but it permits the burden of pollution control to be shared more efficiently among businesses. In economic terms, market-based policies equalize the level of marginal costs of control among businesses rather than the level of control. (The marginal costs of pollution control are the additional or incremental costs of achieving an additional unit of pollution reduction.) As a result, market-based policies provide a monetary incentive for the greatest reductions in pollution by the businesses that can do so most cheaply The result is that fewer total economic resources are used to achieve the same level of pollution control, or more pollution control is obtained for the same level of resources.

Theoretically, the government could achieve such a cost-effective solution by setting different standards for each business and equating the marginal costs of control. However, such a task requires detailed information about the costs each company faces—information that the government clearly lacks and could obtain only at great cost, if at all. Market-based policies provide a way out of this impasse because they lead directly to the cost-effective allocation of the pollution control burden among businesses. By forcing businesses to factor environmental costs into their decision-making, market-based policies create powerful incentives for firms to find cleaner production technologies .

Market-based incentives also clarify the environmental debate for the general public because they focus on environmental goals rather than on the difficult technical problems of reaching those goals. One of the reasons market-based systems are not more widely used, however, is that many technical experts have sought to retain the complexity and exclude the public from such debates.

Market-based incentive systems do not represent a laissez-faire, free-market approach. Rather, the inability of a system of private markets to provide certain goods and services at the most desirable level is typically at the core of pollution problems in which the decisions of businesses and consumers do not take into account the consequences of their decisions for society. At the same time, an incentive-based policy rejects the notion that such market failures justify abandoning the market and allowing the government to dictate the behavior of businesses or consumers. Instead, market-based incentives provide freedom of choice for businesses and consumers to determine the best way to reduce pollution. By ensuring that environmental costs are factored into each company's or individual's decisionmaking process, incentive-based policies harness rather than impede market forces and channel them to achieve environmental goals at the lowest possible cost to society.

At the broadest level, market-based incentive systems fall into four categories:

- *Pollution charges.* Under this approach, polluters are charged a fee on the amount of pollution they generate. In one category of pollution charges, called deposit-refund systems, all or part of some initial charge is rebated if the individual performs certain actions.

- *Tradable permit systems.* Under this mechanism, which was used in the 1990 Clean Air Act Amendments for acid rain control, the government establishes an overall level of allowable air pollution and then allocates permits to businesses in the relevant geographic area so that each is allowed to emit some fraction of the overall total. Companies that keep their emissions below the allocated level may sell or lease their surplus permits to other firms or use them to offset excess emissions in other parts of their own facilities.

- *Removal of market barriers.* In some cases, substantial gains can be made in environmental protection by removing existing government-mandated barriers to market activity. For example, measures that facilitate the voluntary exchange of water rights can promote more efficient allocation and use of scarce water supplies while curbing the need for expensive and environmentally disruptive new water-supply projects.

- *Eliminating government subsidies.* Many existing subsidies promote economically inefficient and environmentally unsound development. For example, the U.S. Forest Service subsidizes below-cost timber sales, which recover less money than is spent on making timber available. These subsidies encourage excessive timber cutting, which leads to habitat loss and damage to watersheds.

Different mechanisms will be appropriate for different environmental problems, and no single approach is a panacea for all problems. Neither market-based policies nor conventional, command-and-control regulations hold all the answers. Furthermore, when market-based approaches are appropriate, specific circumstances will dictate which of the above categories is best.

MARKET-BASED ENVIRONMENTAL POLICIES

The use of market forces to protect the environment is not a new idea. Economists have called for market-based environmental policies for the past 25 years. Only recently, however, has the broader policy community begun to regard market instruments favorably. For instance, both U.S. President Lyndon Johnson's proposal for effluent fees and President Richard Nixon's recommendations for a tax on leaded gasoline and a fee on sulfur dioxide emissions were dismissed with little consideration.

It is important to understand what political forces have prevented broader acceptance of market-based environmental regulation over the years because these forces are likely to resist further use of such approaches beyond the new Clean Air Act Amendments. Four such forces have been most powerful. The first of these forces is the adversarial attitude that characterized the beginning of the environmental movement. Throughout much of the 1960s and 1970s, environmentalists typically characterized pollution more as a moral failing of corporate and political leaders than as a by-product of modern civilization that can be regulated and reduced but not eliminated. Although that characterization may have been necessary and successful from a political standpoint, it resulted in widespread antagonism toward corporations and a suspicion that anything supported by the business world was probably bad for the environment. Thus, for many years, market-based incentives were characterized by environmentalists not only as impractical but also as "licenses to pollute." Over time, environmental groups have frequently applied a different and more rigorous standard in measuring market-based systems against command-and-control policies, possibly because of the belief that market-based systems legitimize pollution by purporting to sell the right to pollute. This suspicion probably continues among many rank-and-file environmentalists.

A second source of resistance to market-based approaches has been the environmental bureaucracy whose work, organizational power, or even existence might be threatened by a market-based approach. Within EPA, for example, market-based policies for controlling acid rain would not require the service of agency engineers whose task in the current policy regime is to evaluate technologies for disparate sources of emissions across the country. Instead, decisions to select particular air-pollution control technologies would be left up to individual firms. In addition, there has been resistance from some staff in environmental agencies who are simply skeptical about new approaches that have not yet been applied on a large scale.

Third, resistance to market-based approaches has come from lobbyists who, having learned to influence a command-and-control regulatory system, are understandably reluctant to allow any major changes in the rules of the game. Thus, some lobbyists for both environmental organizations and the private sector, as well as some legislators, resist market-based approaches in part to protect the value of their expertise. The resistance by some industry lobbyists to putting these ideas into practice is especially notable given that the business community has long endorsed the theory of cost-effective, market-oriented approaches to environmental protection.

Finally, market-based approaches—pollution charges in particular—are problematic because they involve new taxes, which have been a controversial and often forbidden subject for much of the last decade. Although "compensating reductions" in other taxes—tax cuts that result in unchanged government revenues—can make pollution charges revenue-neutral and can improve the economic efficiency of the overall tax code, many elected officials are wary of embracing such approaches because voters and pundits might doubt that government would rebate revenues once they have been collected.

Of course, not all resistance to market-based environmental regulation stems from narrow self-interest. Some environmentalist may feel that market-based approaches will make the costs of environmental protection more salient to the public and therefore dampen popular demand for such controls. Similarly, some legislators may believe that the theories justifying pollution charges are too complex to attract broad popular support. Nevertheless, the United States has wasted many years and billions of dollars by moving so slowly to adopt market-based approaches for reasons that have more to do with narrow agendas than with the public interest. . . .

Unfortunately, a wide range of market-based initiatives has been largely ignored. In particular, the potential of pollution charge systems has received scant attention compared to other market-based instruments, possibly as a result of the same forces that for years impeded adoption of tradable permits and similar approaches, or because the concepts involved are perceived as too complex. In either case, this lack of attention should now be remedied because pollution charges have several distinct advantages over other policy instruments, especially for certain categories of environmental problems.

THE MECHANICS OF POLLUTION CHARGES

Pollution charge systems are designed to reduce polluting behavior by imposing a fee or tax on polluters. Ideally, the fee should be based on the amount of pollution generated rather than on the level of pollution-generating activities. For example, an electric utility might be charged a tax per unit of sulfur dioxide emitted rather than per unit of electricity generated. The choice of whether to tax pollution quantities, activities preceding discharge, inputs to those activities, or actual damages depends upon tradeoffs between costs of abatement, mitigation, damages, and program administration, including monitoring and enforcement. In some cases, a fee may be based on the expected or potential quantity of pollution. The Organization for Economic Cooperation and Development distinguishes five types of pollution charges: effluent charges based on the quantity of discharges; user charges, which are payments for public treatment facilities; production charges based on the potential pollution by a product; administrative charges, which are payments for such government services as registration of chemicals; and tax differentiation, which provides more favorable prices for "green" products. A true pollution charge provides incentives to businesses or consumers to reduce emissions when that action is less expensive than is continuing to pollute. Pollution charges can be applied either to producers to affect their production decisions or to consumers to affect their consumption and disposal behavior.

Although pollution poses real costs to society—for example, health effects, property damage, and aesthetic impacts—businesses typically do not have to pay for these damages and, hence, face little or no incentive to take them into account in production decisions. A business that chooses unilaterally to consider such external costs in its production decisions would be penalized by the market, through reduced cost-competitiveness. Pollution charges force businesses to pay for the external costs of pollution and to incorporate those added costs into their daily decisions.

Pollution charges also provide strong incentives for businesses to develop and adopt improved control technologies. Under a command-and-control system, businesses have no financial incentive to perform better than the regulatory standard demands. Pollution charges, however, do not specify a technology or a fixed standard. Instead, charges are incurred for each increment of pollution rather than only for pollution above a given standard. Thus, businesses are constantly motivated to improve their financial performance by developing technologies that allow them to reduce their output of pollutants.

By charging polluters a fee or tax on the amount of pollution they generate and not on their pollution-generating activities, the government gives businesses an incentive to reduce pollution up to the point at which their marginal control costs are equal to their pollution tax rates. As a result, businesses will control their pollution to different degrees, with polluters for whom control is very expensive controlling less and polluters for whom control is relatively cheap controlling more. The challenge for policymakers is to identify the desirable charge level. If the charge is too high, production may be curtailed excessively; if the charge is too low, insufficient environmental protection will result. An effective charge system thus minimizes the aggregate costs of pollution control and enables the public to pursue other environmental quality actions that might have seemed unaffordable under less efficient approaches, such as command-and-control regulations. . . .

USING POLLUTION CHARGE REVENUES

The transfer of money from polluters to the government could be substantial. For instance, the Congressional Budget Office estimates that a $100-per-ton charge on carbon dioxide emissions could result in more than $120 billion in annual revenues for the government. This situation raises the obvious question of how such revenue should be used. There are at least three possible courses of action. First, the funds could be used to reduce the federal budget deficit. This alternative has obvious appeal in times of unprecedented government borrowing.

Second, the tax revenue could finance other programs related to environmental protection, such as programs that clean up or mitigate pollution. Indeed, revenue-raising charge systems have grown from 28 percent of New Jersey's environmental protection expenditures in 1989 to 37 percent in 1991, and the level is expected to reach 55 percent by 1993. Such revenues might also be directed to assist people who are hurt economically by the change to a system of pollution charges. For instance, although pollution charges are cost-effective, cost-effectiveness should not be the only criterion policymakers use to weigh policies. Questions of fairness and equity are also important and often dominate political debate. Most environmental policies, whether command-and-control or market-based, require some tradeoff between efficiency and equity. Even when the aggregate benefits of a policy exceed its aggregate costs, usually some individuals or businesses do not benefit, such as consumers who have to pay higher prices for goods and services, employees who are laid off, or shareholders whose profits erode.

Whether and how to compensate such groups are political questions whose answers depend on the availability of resources. One of the attractions of pollution charges is that they can provide the resources necessary to buffer their own impact on specific groups. For instance, if a pollution charge was used to raise energy prices, it could impose a particular burden on low-income households. However, the revenue from the charge could be used to fund a system of "life-line rates," or free or discounted rates for the first units of energy consumed by a household. Similarly, revenues from a pollution charge that eliminated certain jobs could be used to fund job-search and job-raining programs. In addition, revenues from pollution charges might be used to compensate groups deemed to have been unfairly harmed by past environmental policies, such as residents of a neighborhood who were effectively disenfranchised by toxic wastes that were dumped nearby.

Finally, the use of pollution-charge revenues to offset reductions in other taxes may be the most attractive option. Pollution charges are "corrective" taxes that reduce market inefficiencies by discouraging undesirable activities that generate externalities. This effect contrasts sharply with that of "distortionary" taxes, which distort economic behavior by generating market inefficiencies, as in the case of corporate profit taxes, social security and other payroll taxes, and personal income taxes. The corrective nature of pollution charges provides a "double dividend": In addition to providing incentives to reduce pollution, pollution-charge revenues can finance reductions in distortionary taxes. This tradeoff is particularly important in today's political climate, in which policymakers are reluctant to consider any new taxes. A revenue-neutral tax policy change, which combines the introduction of pollution charges with the reduction or elimination of other taxes, would protect the environment by reducing harmful emissions and would reduce distortions associated with other taxes. Studies indicate that, on average, U.S. personal and corporate income taxes generate distortions or pure losses of 20 to 50 cents for every new dollar of tax revenue collected. Such a shift in tax policy would discourage socially undesirable activities such as pollution, rather than socially beneficial activities, such as labor and capital formation. . . .

POLLUTION CHARGES IN THE POLITICAL ARENA

No single policy mechanism—neither incentive-based policies in general nor pollution charges in particular—can be an environmental panacea. Pollution charges, however, promise to provide cost-effective solutions for some pressing environmental problems while spurring technological advances.

Good ideas are not self-adopting, however. Even if the new Clean Air Act provisions have signaled the beginning of a new era of environmental policy, resistance to market-based approaches has not disappeared. In addition to opposition from those who simply oppose environmental protection, pollution charges will have to overcome the same combination of self-interest and suspicion from those within the environmental protection process who have obstructed market-based approaches for decades.

Initially, it may be practical to apply pollution charges to new problems for which policy mechanisms are not already in place. Such an approach could minimize disruptions to industry and consumers, reduce the chance that regulations will work at cross purposes, and challenge the authority of fewer vested interests. If pollution charges turn out to be effective, they could serve as alternatives to environmental regulations in place today that are deemed to be ineffective or that achieve their objectives only at extremely high costs to society. Furthermore, a growing array of state and local initiatives may help pollution charges overcome public dislike for taxes, reduce the costs of environmental protection, and stimulate technological development.

In fact, pollution charges could make the process of environmental policy formulation more explicit to the U.S. population, which has always been shielded from the very real tradeoffs involved in establishing environmental goals and standards. As a result, policy discussions could move away from a narrow focus on technical specifications to a broader consideration of goals and strategies. The public could become involved in constructive debates regarding the desirable level of environmental protection and could recapture the critical decisions of environmental goal-setting from bureaucrats, technicians, and special-interest groups. As new environmental policies arise and old ones persist, the limited resources of government agencies and society at large will be stretched further and further. Pollution charges and other incentive-based instruments may eventually be the only feasible courses of action to sustain or improve environmental quality while maintaining economic well-being. With the necessary political leadership, it may be possible to begin moving in the right direction now.

Study Questions

1. According to Stavins and Whitehead, how is the environmental challenge different now than it was in the 1970s and early 1980s? Do they make a good case for their position?
2. Explain how the command-and-control regulatory approach works. What are its strengths and weaknesses?
3. Explain how market-based policies work. What are their strengths and weaknesses?
4. What is a *pollution charge?* What are the five types of pollution charges set forth by the Organization for Economic Cooperation and Development? Explain how pollution charges would provide incentives to businesses to reduce harmful emissions.

For Further Reading

Bernards, Neal, ed. *The Environmental Crisis.* San Diego, CA: Greenhaven Press, 1991.

Bogard, William. *The Bhopal Tragedy: Language, Logic and Politics in the Production of a Hazard.* Boulder, CO: Westaview, 1989.

Brown, Lester. *The Twenty Ninth Day.* New York: Norton, 1978.

———, ed. *The Worldwatch Reader.* Washington, DC: Worldwatch Institute, 1991.

Brown, Michael. *The Toxic Cloud.* New York: Harper & Row, 1987.

Gore, Albert. *Earth in Balance.* Boston: Houghton Mifflin, 1992.

Keeble, John. *Out of the Channel: The Exxon Valdez Spill.* New York: HarperCollins, 1991.

McKibbern, Bill. *The End of Nature.* New York: Random House, 1989.

Postel, Sandra. *Defusing the Toxic Threat: Controlling Pesticides and Industrial Waste.* Washington, DC: Worldwatch Institute, 1987.

Ray, Dixy Lee, and Lou Guzzo. *Trashing the Planet.* Washington, DC: Regnery Gateway, 1990.

Silver, Cheryl Pollack. *Protecting Life on Earth: Steps to Save the Ozone Layer.* Washington, DC: Worldwatch Institute, 1988.

Simon, Julian. *The Ultimate Resource.* Princeton, NJ: Princeton University Press, 1981.

Wellburn, Alan. *Air Pollution and Acid Rain.* New York: Wiley, 1988.

CHAPTER TWELVE

Pesticides

In 1962 Rachel Carson published *Silent Spring* in which she documented the effects of DDT and other pesticides on human health. She charged that these "elixers of death" were causing widespread cancer and genetic mutations, as well as wreaking havoc on birds, fish, and wildlife. Pesticides have the paradoxical consequence of producing a greater insect problem than the one they are combating because evolution selects for pesticide-resistant insects. The new "improved" insects are more lethal and in turn require more potent pesticides, which in turn lead to even more potent insects, which in turn require a still more potent pesticide . . .

A further danger of pesticides is biological magnification, the increased concentration of pollutants in living organisms. Many synthetic chemicals, such as DDT and PCB, are soluble in fat but insoluble in water and are slowly degradable by natural processes. That is, when the organism takes in DDT or PCB, the chemical becomes concentrated in the fatty tissue of the animal and is degraded very slowly. When a large fish consumes plankton or small fish with these pesticides, the chemicals become more concentrated still (Figure 1). Sufficient levels of these chemicals in an organism can harm the organism. High DDT levels in birds cause a calcium deficiency in their egg shells, so the shells are much thinner than normal. These shells break easily and so fail to protect the chicks inside the egg. Such pollution was responsible for the extinction or drastic decline of the peregrine falcon, California brown pelican, osprey, and bald eagles in the 1960s.

Carson argued that because of this inappropriate use of poisons ("biocides"), we were heading toward a time when our nation's springs would be silent with death. The book startled the nation and in 1972 led to a government ban on the use of DDT. But other pesticides, it is claimed, are still being used that are harming human beings and other species. So the message of *Silent Spring* remains relevant to our world today.

Carson's discussion is found in our first reading, which is taken from *Silent Spring*. On the other hand, Carson's doomsday message has been challenged. Michael Fumento in *Science Under Siege: Balancing Technology and the Environment* (1993) argues that most of the studies showing chemicals like Alar or dioxin to be cancer-causing were conducted under questionable circumstances. For example, in studies showing that Alar caused tumors in mice, the daily dose of Alar was over 266,000 times higher than the amount ingested every day by the children said to be at risk.[1]

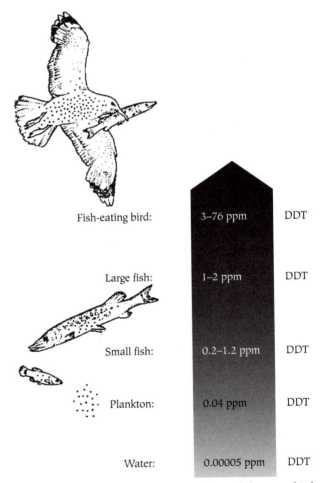

FIGURE 1 *Biological Magnification. In 1967 fish-eating birds from a Long Island salt marsh estuary contained almost a million times more DDT than could be found in the water. At each step of the food chain, DDT was concentrated, as organisms consumed and absorbed more DDT than they were able to excrete. "PPM" stands for parts per million. (Adapted from W. Keeton, Biological Science, 3rd ed. [New York: Norton, 1980].)*

Fish-eating bird: 3–76 ppm   DDT

Large fish: 1–2 ppm   DDT

Small fish: 0.2–1.2 ppm   DDT

Plankton: 0.04 ppm   DDT

Water: 0.00005 ppm   DDT

Our second reading, "The Blessings of Pesticides" by Dixy Lee Ray and Louis Guzzo, agrees with Fumento as opposed to the "doomsdayers" like Carson. Accusing Carson of "lyrical hysteria," they seek to show that the overall effects of pesticides like DDT have been beneficial. They defend the use of PCBs, dioxin, Alar, and DDT. DDT is not carcinogenic. Without these insecticides and herbicides, we would not have our present abundance of fresh fruits and vegetables.

In our next reading, Michael Fumento illustrates some of the theses in Ray and Guzzo's essay through an examination of the process that led the Environmental Protection Agency (EPA) to ban the use of Alar, a pesticide sprayed on apples, to enhance their quality and life. The decision was not only an economic tragedy for the apple growers of the state of Washington, but, Fumento argues, the process that led to the banning illustrates a dangerous antiscientific, antirational trend in which scare tactics are substituted for reason and evidence. This essay is relevant because it raises the issue of whether well-intentioned environmentalists often do more harm than good.

In our fourth reading, entomologist David Pimentel assesses the progress and problems of pesticide use since *Silent Spring* was written. On the one hand, much progress has been made so that humans and wildlife are less directly affected by the poisons in pesticides. But pesticide-resistant insects have replaced their less damaging ancestors. Furthermore, pesticides have destroyed some of the natural enemies of certain pests, so more crops are now lost to insects than when *Silent Spring* was written. But because of better overall agriculture techniques and fertilizers, the total picture is positive.

We turn now to our readings.

Note

1. Michael Fumento, *Science Under Siege: Balancing Technology and the Environment* (New York: Morrow, 1993), 46.

62

Silent Spring

RACHEL CARSON

Rachel Carson (1907–1964) was for many years a marine biologist with the U.S. Fish and Wildlife Service. She is the author of The Sea Around Us, The Edge of the Sea, *and* Silent Spring *(1962) from which the present selection is excerpted.* Silent Spring *is viewed by many as the book that launched the modern environmental movement. Her biographer, Paul Brooks, relates that Carson had noticed that pesticide and herbicide spraying had been followed by "wholesale destruction of wildlife and its habitat, and clearly endangering human life." Unable to interest others in the problem, she began to publish her findings. After several rejections,* The New Yorker *serialized parts of* Silent Spring. *The public suddenly took notice of the message that pesticides were endangering the environment as well as human beings. Her work led to the eventual government banning of DDT in 1972.*

In this excerpt from Silent Spring, *Carson describes a world ruined by chemical pollutants and argues that this is the kind of world we are heading toward with our indiscriminate use of harmful chemicals like DDT.*

1. A FABLE FOR TOMORROW

There was once a town in the heart of America where all life seemed to live in harmony with its surroundings. The town lay in the midst of a checkerboard of prosperous farms, with fields of grain and hillsides of orchards where, in spring, white clouds of bloom drifted above the green fields. In autumn, oak and maple and birch set up a blaze of color that flamed and flickered across a backdrop of pines. Then foxes barked in the hills and deer silently crossed the fields, half hidden in the mists of the fall mornings.

Along the roads, laurel, viburnum and alder, great ferns and wildflowers delighted the traveler's eye through much of the year. Even in winter the roadsides were places of beauty, where countless birds came to feed on the berries and on the seed heads of the dried weeds rising above the snow. The countryside was, in fact, famous for the abundance and variety of its bird life, and when the flood of migrants was pouring through in spring and fall people traveled from great distances to observe them. Others came to fish the streams, which flowed clear and cold out of the hills and contained shady pools where trout lay. So it had been from the days many years ago when the first settlers raised their houses, sank their wells, and built their barns.

Then a strange blight crept over the area and everything began to change. Some evil spell had settled on the community: mysterious maladies swept the flocks of chickens; the cattle and sheep sickened and died. Everywhere was a shadow of death. The farmers spoke of much illness among their families. In the town the doctors had become more and more puzzled by new kinds of sickness appearing among their patients. There had been several sudden and unexplained deaths, not only among adults but even among children, who would be stricken suddenly while at play and die within a few hours.

There was a strange stillness. The birds, for example—where had they gone? Many people spoke of them, puzzled and disturbed. The feeding stations in the backyards were deserted. The few birds seen anywhere were moribund; they trembled violently and could not fly. It was a spring without voices. On the mornings that had once throbbed with the dawn chorus of robins, catbirds, doves, jays, wrens, and scores of other bird voices there was now no sound; only silence lay over the fields and woods and marsh.

On the farms the hens brooded, but no chicks hatched. The farmers complained that they were unable to raise any pigs—the litters were small and the young survived only a few days. The apple trees were coming into bloom but no bees droned among the blossoms, so there was no pollination and there would be no fruit.

The roadsides, once so attractive, were now lined with browned and withered vegetation as though swept by fire. These, too, were silent, deserted by all living things. Even the streams were now lifeless. Anglers no longer visited them, for all the fish had died.

In the gutters under the eaves and between the shingles of the roofs, a white granular powder still showed a few patches; some weeks before it had fallen like snow upon the roofs and the lawns, the fields and streams.

No witchcraft, no enemy action had silenced the rebirth of new life in this stricken world. The people had done it themselves.

This town does not actually exist, but it might easily have a thousand counterparts in America or elsewhere in the world. I know of no community that has experienced all the misfortunes I describe. Yet every one of these disasters has actually happened somewhere, and many real communities have already suffered a substantial number of them. A grim specter has crept upon us almost unnoticed, and this imagined tragedy may easily become a stark reality we all shall know.

What has already silenced the voices of spring in countless towns in America? This book is an attempt to explain.

2. THE OBLIGATION TO ENDURE

The history of life on earth has been a history of interaction between living things and their surroundings. To a large extent, the physical form and the habits of the earth's vegetation and its animal life have been molded by the environment. Considering the whole span of earthly time, the opposite effect, in which life actually modifies its surroundings, has been relatively slight. Only within the moment of time represented by the present century has one species—man—acquired significant power to alter the nature of his world.

During the past quarter century this power has not only increased to one of disturbing magnitude but it has changed in character. The most alarming of all man's assaults upon the environment is the contamination of air, earth, rivers, and sea with dangerous and even lethal materials. This pollution is for the most part irrecoverable, the chain of evil it initiates not only in the world that must support life but in living tissues is for the most part irreversible. In this now universal contamination of the environment, chemicals are the sinister and little-recognized partners of radiation in changing the very nature of the world—the very nature of its life. Strontium 90, released through nuclear explosions into the air, comes to earth in rain or drifts down as fallout, lodges in soil, enters into the grass or corn or wheat grown there, and in time takes up its abode in the bones of a human being, there to remain until his death. Similarly, chemicals sprayed on croplands or forests or gardens lie long in soil, entering into living organisms, passing from one to another in a chain of poisoning and death. Or they pass mysteriously by underground streams until they emerge and, through the alchemy of air and sunlight, combine into new forms that kill vegetation, sicken cattle, and work unknown harm on those who drink from once pure wells. As Albert Schweitzer has said, "Man can hardly even recognize the devils of his own creation."

It took hundreds of millions of years to produce the life that now inhabits the earth—eons of time in which that developing and evolving and diversifying life reached a state of adjustment and balance with its surroundings. The environment, rigorously shaping and directing the life it supported, contained elements that were hostile as well as supporting. Certain rocks gave out dangerous radiation; even within the light of the sun, from which all life draws its energy, there were short-wave radiations with power to injure. Given time—time not in years but in millennia—life adjusts, and a balance has been reached. For time is the essential ingredient; but in the modern world there is no time.

The rapidity of change and the speed with which new situations are created follow the impetuous and heedless pace of man rather than the deliberate pace of nature. Radiation is no longer merely the background radiation of rocks, the bombardment of cosmic rays, the ultraviolet of the sun that have existed before there was any life on earth; radiation is now the unnatural creation of man's tampering with the atom. The chemicals to which life is asked to make its adjustment are no longer merely the calcium and silica and copper and all the rest of the minerals washed out of the rocks and carried in rivers to the sea; they are the synthetic creations of man's inventive mind, brewed in his laboratories, and having no counterparts in nature.

To adjust to these chemicals would require time on the scale that is nature's; it would require not merely the years of a man's life but the life of generations. And even this, were it by some miracle possible, would be futile, for the new chemicals come from our laboratories in an endless stream; almost five hundred annually find their way into actual use in the United States alone. The figure is staggering and its implications are not easily grasped—500 new chemicals to which the bodies of men and animals are required somehow to adapt each year, chemicals totally outside the limits of biologic experience.

Among them are many that are used in man's war against nature. Since the mid-1940's over 200 basic chemicals have been created for use in killing insects, weeds, rodents, and other organisms described in the modern vernacular as "pests"; and they are sold under several thousand different brand names.

These sprays, dusts, and aerosols are now applied almost universally to farms, gardens, forests, and homes—nonselective chemicals that have the power to kill every insect, the "good" and the "bad," to still the song of birds and the leaping of fish in the streams, to coat the leaves with a deadly film, and to linger on in soil—all this though the intended target may be only a few weeds or insects. Can anyone believe it is possible to lay down such a barrage of poisons on the surface of the earth without making it unfit for all life? They should not be called "insecticides," but "biocides."

The whole process of spraying seems caught up in an endless spiral. Since DDT was released for civilian use, a process of escalation has been going on in which ever more toxic materials must be found. This has happened because insects, in a triumphant vindication of Darwin's principle of the survival of the fittest, have evolved super races immune to the particular insecticide used, hence a deadlier one has always to be developed—and then a deadlier one than that. It has happened also because, for reasons to be described later, destructive insects often undergo a "flareback," or resurgence, after spraying, in numbers greater than before. Thus the chemical war is never won, and all life is caught in its violent crossfire.

Along with the possibility of the extinction of mankind by nuclear war, the central problem of our age has therefore become the contamination of man's total environment with such substances of incredible potential for harm—substances that accumulate in the tissues of plants and animals and even penetrate the germ cells to shatter or alter the very material of heredity upon which the shape of the future depends.

Some would-be architects of our future look toward a time when it will be possible to alter the human germ plasm by design. But we may easily be doing so now by inadvertence, for many chemicals, like radiation, bring about gene mutations. It is ironic to think that man

might determine his own future by something so seemingly trivial as the choice of an insect spray.

All this has been risked—for what? Future historians may well be amazed by our distorted sense of proportion. How could intelligent beings seek to control a few unwanted species by a method that contaminated the entire environment and brought the threat of disease and death even to their own kind? Yet this is precisely what we have done. We have done it, moreover, for reasons that collapse the moment we examine them. We are told that the enormous and expanding use of pesticides is necessary to maintain farm production. Yet is our real problem not one of *overproduction*? Our farms, despite measures to remove acreages from production and to pay farmers *not* to produce, have yielded such a staggering excess of crops that the American taxpayer in 1962 is paying out more than one billion dollars a year as the total carrying cost of the surplus-food storage program. And is the situation helped when one branch of the Agriculture Department tries to reduce production while another states, as it did in 1958, "It is believed generally that reduction of crop acreages under provisions of the Soil Bank will stimulate interest in use of chemicals to obtain maximum production on the land retained in crops."

All this is not to say there is no insect problem and no need of control. I am saying, rather, that control must be geared to realities, not to mythical situations, and that the methods employed must be such that they do not destroy us along with the insects.

The problem whose attempted solution has brought such a train of disaster in its wake is an accompaniment of our modern way of life. Long before the age of man, insects inhabited the earth—a group of extraordinarily varied and adaptable beings. Over the course of time since man's advent, a small percentage of the more than half a million species of insects have come into conflict with human welfare in two principal ways: as competitors for the food supply and as carriers of human disease.

Disease-carrying insects become important where human beings are crowded together, especially under conditions where sanitation is poor, as in time of natural disaster or war or in situations of extreme poverty and deprivation. Then control of some sort becomes necessary. It is a sobering fact, however, as we shall presently see, that the method of massive chemical control has had only limited success, and also threatens to worsen the very conditions it is intended to curb.

Under primitive agricultural conditions the farmer had few insect problems. These arose with the intensification of agriculture—the devotion of immense acreages to a single crop. Such a system set the stage for explosive increases in specific insect populations. Single-crop farming does not take advantage of the principles by which nature works; it is agriculture as an engineer might conceive it to be. Nature has introduced great variety into the landscape, but man has displayed a passion for simplifying it. Thus he undoes the built-in checks and balances by which nature holds the species within bounds. One important natural check is a limit on the amount of suitable habitat for each species. Obviously then, an insect that lives on wheat can build up its population to much higher levels on a farm devoted to wheat than on one in which wheat is intermingled with other crops to which the insect is not adapted.

The same thing happens in other situations. A generation or more ago, the towns of large areas of the United States lined their streets with the noble elm tree. Now the beauty they hopefully created is threatened with complete destruction as disease sweeps through the elms, carried by a beetle that would have only limited chance to build up large populations and to spread from tree to tree if the elms were only occasional trees in a richly diversified planting.

Another factor in the modern insect problem is one that must be viewed against a background of geologic and human history: the spreading of thousands of different kinds of organisms from their native homes to invade new territories. This worldwide migration has been studied and graphically described by the British ecologist Charles Elton in his recent book *The Ecology of Invasions*. During the Cretaceous Period, some hundred million years ago, flooding seas cut many land bridges between continents and living things found themselves confined in what Elton calls "colossal separate nature reserves." There, isolated from others of their kind, they developed many new species . When some of the land masses were joined again, about 15 million years ago, these species began to move out into new territories—a movement that is not only still in progress but is now receiving considerable assistance from man.

The importation of plants is the primary agent in the modern spread of species, for animals have almost invariably gone along with the plants, quarantine being a comparatively recent and not completely effective innovation. The United States Office of Plant Introduction alone has introduced almost 200,000 species and varieties of plants from all over the world. Nearly half of the 180 or so major insect enemies of plants in the United States are accidental imports from abroad, and most of them have come as hitchhikers on plants.

In new territory, out of reach of the restraining hand of the natural enemies that kept down its numbers in its native land, an invading plant or animal is able to become enormously abundant. Thus it is no accident that our most troublesome insects are introduced species.

These invasions, both the naturally occurring and those dependent on human assistance, are likely to continue indefinitely. Quarantine and massive chemical campaigns are only extremely expensive ways of buying time. We are faced, according to Dr. Elton, "with a life-and-death need not just to find new technological means of suppressing this plant or that animal"; instead we need the basic knowledge of animal populations and their relations to their surroundings that will "promote an even balance and damp down the explosive power of outbreaks and new invasions."

Much of the necessary knowledge is now available but we do not use it. We train ecologists in our universities and even employ them in our government agencies, but we seldom take their advice. We allow the chemical death rain to fall as though there were no alternative, whereas in fact there are many, and our ingenuity could soon discover many more if given opportunity.

Have we fallen into a mesmerized state that makes us accept as inevitable that which is inferior or detrimental, as though having lost the will or the vision to demand that which is good? Such thinking, in the words of the ecologist Paul Shepard, "idealizes life with only its head out of water, inches above the limits of toleration of the corruption of its own environment . . . Why should we tolerate a diet of weak poisons, a home in insipid surroundings, a circle of acquaintances who are not quite our enemies, the noise of motors with just enough relief to prevent insanity? Who would want to live in a world which is just not quite fatal?"

Yet such a world is pressed upon us. The crusade to create a chemically sterile, insect-free world seems to have engendered a fanatic zeal on the part of many specialists and most of the so-called control agencies. On every hand there is evidence that those engaged in spraying operations exercise a ruthless power. "The regulatory entomologists . . . function as prosecutor, judge and jury, tax assessor and collector and sheriff to enforce their own orders," said Connecticut entomologist Neely Turner. The most flagrant abuses go unchecked in both state and federal agencies.

It is not my contention that chemical insecticides must never be used. I do contend that we have put poisonous and biologically potent chemicals indiscriminately into the hands of persons largely or wholly ignorant of their potentials for harm. We have subjected enormous numbers of people to contact with these poisons, without their consent and often without their knowledge. If the Bill of Rights contains no guarantee that a citizen shall be secure against lethal poisons distributed either by private individuals or by public officials, it is surely only because our forefathers, despite their considerable wisdom and foresight, could conceive of no such problem.

I contend, furthermore, that we have allowed these chemicals to be used with little or no advance investigation of their effect on soil, water, wildlife, and man himself. Future generations are unlikely to condone our lack of prudent concern for the integrity of the natural world that supports all life.

There is still very limited awareness of the nature of the threat. This is an era of specialists, each of whom sees his own problem and is unaware of or intolerant of the larger frame into which it fits. It is also an era dominated by industry, in which the right to make a dollar at whatever cost is seldom challenged. When the public protests, confronted with some obvious evidence of damaging results of pesticide applications, it is fed little tranquilizing pills of half truth. We urgently need an end to these false assurances, to the sugar coating of unpalatable facts. It is the public that is being asked to assume the risks that the insect controllers calculate. The public must decide whether it wishes to continue on the present road, and it can do so only when in full possession of the facts. In the words of Jean Rostand, "The obligation to endure gives us the right to know."

Study Questions

1. What is the message of *Silent Spring*? How does Carson communicate her message?
2. Why should "insecticides" be called "biocides"? Is Carson persuasive? Has she made her case, or is she engaging in rhetoric?
3. Does Carson believe that we should ban all chemical pesticides?

63

The Blessings of Pesticides

DIXY LEE RAY AND LOUIS GUZZO

Dixy Lee Ray is a chemical biologist, and Louis Guzzo is a freelance writer.

In this article, Ray and Guzzo defend the use of chemical pesticides like DDT, Alar, PCBs, dioxins, and even asbestos. They argue that environmentalists like Rachel Carson and Paul Ehrlich are scare mongers, promoting lyrical hysteria in their ill-conceived battle against pesticides. On the whole, these pesticides are beneficial to humans and should be used discreetly, regulated, and controlled, but not banned.

No consideration of pesticides and their role in public health and agriculture would be complete without recounting the story of DDT. The events surrounding its use, overuse, and its being banned in the U.S. are dramatic. DDT was the first, best, and most remarkable of modern pesticides. Its history is a tale of triumph that ended in tragedy.

DDT, the convenient name for 1,1,1-trichloro-2,2-bis (p-chloro-phenyl) ethane, was first synthesized in 1877 and patented as an insecticide in 1939 by a Swiss chemist, Dr. Paul Muller. Its remarkable effectiveness against insects, specifically clothes moths and ectoparasites of both animals and plants, made it a welcome substitute for the toxic insecticides then in common use—arsenic, mercury, fluorine, and lead. In 1942, it was shown to kill body lice without adverse effect on humans, and it was used by all Allied troops during World War II. The result was that no Allied soldier was stricken with typhus fever (carried by lice) for the first time in the history of warfare. In World War I, by contrast, more soldiers died from typhus than from bullets.

Mosquito-borne malaria has always been man's worst disease, judged by the number of its victims. Until DDT came along, about 200 million people were stricken annually with malaria, and about two million of them died each year. Beginning in 1946, a large-scale spraying program directed against the malaria-carrying mosquito brought an immediate and dramatic decrease in these numbers. It is important to emphasize that this spraying was not indiscriminate, nor was it conducted in the natural environment. It was performed inside homes, on the interior walls. The unique behavior of the malarial mosquito—feeding at night on sleeping victims and then flying to the nearest vertical structure to rest and digest its meal—made this the ideal way to catch the largest number of adult insects.

Public health statistics from Sri Lanka testify to the effectiveness of the spraying program. In 1948, before use of DDT, there were 2.8 million cases of malaria. By 1963, there were only 17. Low levels of infection continued until the late 1960s, when the attacks on DDT in the U.S. convinced officials to suspend spraying. In 1968, there were one million cases of malaria. In 1969, the number reached 2.5 million, back to the pre-DDT levels. Moreover, by 1972, the largely unsubstantiated charges against DDT in the United States had a worldwide effect. In 1970, of two billion people living in malarial regions, 79 percent were protected and the expectation was that malaria would be eradicated. Six years after the United States banned DDT, there were 800 million cases of malaria and 8.2 million deaths per year. Even worse, because eradication programs were halted at a critical time, resistant malaria is now widespread and travelers could take it home. Much of the southern United States is favorable to the malarial mosquito. Malaria, yellow fever, and other diseases for which mosquitoes are the vector, used to be endemic in

Reprinted from *Trashing the Planet* (Washington, D.C.: Regnery Gateway, 1990), by permission. Notes deleted.

the South; mosquitoes have recently undergone an explosive population growth since their breeding grounds are now "protected" under federal law.

In 1948, Dr. Muller was awarded the Nobel Prize in medicine because of the medical importance of DDT. Dr. Samuel Simmons, chief of the technology branch of the Communicable Disease Center of the U.S. Public Health Service, said in 1959:

> The total value of DDT to mankind is inestimable. Most of the peoples of the globe have received benefit from it either directly by protection from infectious diseases and pestiferous insects or indirectly by better nutrition, cleaner food, and increased disease resistance. The discovery of DDT will always remain an historic event in the fields of public health and agriculture.

After initial success in controlling typhus and malaria, DDT was also used against yellow fever, sleeping sickness, plague, and encephalitis, all transmitted by insects and all epidemic at various times in the past in the United States.

"With the introduction of DDT to control the vectors of disease," wrote Claus and Bolander in 1977, "it seemed, for the first time in history, that man could look forward to a life of dignity, freed from the scourges of maiming disease and famine. It is no wonder, then, that its applications were greeted with general high enthusiasm."

Was the prospect of more people living better also anathema to the population-control and zero-growth organizations? There is some reason to believe so.

Plant pests also succumbed to DDT. It proved effective against spruce budworm, gypsy moth, tussock moth, pine weevil, and cotton boll weevil. So effective was DDT against such a variety of insects that it was inevitably overused. The attitude, "if a little bit is good, then more must be better," is a common human failing. Before any steps were taken to curtail and control DDT, it became ubiquitous in soil, water, and in the bodies of many living organisms. Even though no harm has ever been demonstrated to have been caused by DDT, its widespread presence in the environment was enough to give rise to alarm.

Contrary to common belief, DDT is not a persistent pesticide in the natural environment. Only in the unusual circumstances where soil is dark, dry, and devoid of microorganisms will DDT persist. Under normal environmental conditions, DDT loses its toxicity to insects in a few days, usually no more than two weeks. But its overuse did result in DDT being detected, albeit in small amounts, in soil, in water both salt and fresh, in the bodies of fish, birds, and domestic animals, and in man. This energized the opposition to its use that had first been sparked by the lyrical hysteria of Rachel Carson's book, *Silent Spring*.

The growing chorus from self-proclaimed environmentalists demanding that DDT be totally banned led to a public hearing in 1971. It should be noted that the Environmental Protection Agency, the agency responsible for regulating pesticides and for making the final decision about their use, actually took part in the hearing, testifying against DDT, along with the Environmental Defense Fund and other activist groups. The attack on DDT rested on three main allegations: that DDT caused the death of many birds and could lead to the extinction of some bird populations; that DDT was so stable that it could never be eliminated from the environment, and that DDT might cause cancer in humans. None of these charges has ever been substantiated.

It was alleged that DDT was toxic to birds that might ingest it from eating insects, earthworms, or seeds in sprayed areas. It was also charged that sub-lethal amounts of DDT in the bodies of birds caused them to lay eggs with thin shells that provided insufficient protection, resulting in the death of many chicks. These charges have been repeated so often that they are widely believed, even though they are, at best, "factoids," untrue in most instances.

Actual counts of bird populations, conducted annually by the Audubon Society at Christmastime, have shown that many bird populations were in fact increasing throughout the years of heaviest DDT spraying. For example, between 1941 and 1971, there was a 12 percent increase in robins, 21 times more cowbirds, 8 times more blackbirds, and 131 times more grackles. Gulls also increased, especially along the East Coast. Aside from robins—possibly America's most abundant bird, which some hysterical environmentalists said was "doomed" by DDT—it is the birds of prey that caught most of the anti-DDT attention, especially the osprey and the peregrine falcon. At the Hawk Mountain Sanctuary in Pennsylvania, annual surveys show 191 ospreys in 1946, compared to 600 in 1970. Each year showed some population increase. For the peregrine falcon, the numbers fluctuated from a low of 14 in 1965 to a high of 32 in 1969. Dr. Joseph Hickey, an authority on peregrines, testified at the DDT hearings that the falcon population had been declining since 1890. Its fate is more closely related to the availability of prey and nesting sites than to pesticides. For all hawks, the annual counts showed an increase from 9,291 in 1957 to 20,196 in 1967. Since it was protected by the endangered species designation, populations of the American Bald Eagle have increased significantly. Although environmentalists claim that this resurgence is due to banning DDT, there is no supportive evidence.

In the case of thin egg shells, it is a phenomenon that predates use of DDT. It has been known for decades. There are many causes: diets low in calcium or Vitamin D, fright, high nocturnal temperatures, various toxic substances, and diseases such as Newcastle's disease. Experiments designed to show a toxic effect from eating DDT failed, even though the experimenters fed their birds (pheasant and quail) from 6,000 to 20,000 times more DDT than the 0.3 parts per million residue of DDT found in food. Quail fed 200 parts per million in all their food throughout the reproductive period nevertheless hatched 80 percent of their chicks, compared with an 84 percent hatch in the control groups. No shell-thinning was reported. With pheasants handled in the same way, the DDT-treated birds hatched 80.6 percent of their eggs, compared with only 57.4 percent in the control groups.

DDT rapidly breaks down harmlessly in the natural environment. But in 1968, when DDT was still in wide use, a residue detected in food was measurable. An average daily human intake could reach 0.065 milligrams. To study the effect on humans, volunteer groups were fed up to 35 milligrams of DDT per day for periods of 21 and 27 months, with no ill effects then or in the nearly 30 years since. Most of the DDT is excreted, with some small residue, up to 12 parts per million, stored in human fat. No harm whatsoever has been detected from these trivial amounts. In sea water, which ultimately receives all the runoff from the land, more than 93 percent of all DDT is broken down in 38 days, but one part per *trillion* can be detected in inshore waters. Compare this to the irresponsible and unscientific claim by butterfly specialist and environmental guru Paul Ehrlich who charged that DDT in sea water would kill all algae (phytoplankton) and thus deprive the earth of 40 percent of its oxygen.

Finally, as for DDT being a cancer-causing agent, if one concludes that all growths, even benign tumors and lumps, are cancer, then the answer must be yes, but. . . . The "but" is important. If one accepts as "cancer" only malignant growths that can metastasize, then the answer is an unequivocal no. DDT is not a carcinogen. Laboratory studies have reported liver deformations in mice, but not in any other experimental animal (including rats). This is the basis for the charge that DDT is "cancer-causing. " The doses, given by injection, required to cause the deformation of a mouse's liver were about 100,000 times higher than any possible ingestion from DDT residues in food.

The National Cancer Institute reviewed the mouse experiment results and, in 1978, declared DDT was not a carcinogen. It is also interesting to note that deaths from liver cancer in the United States actually *decreased* by 30 percent during the years of heaviest DDT use (1944 to 1972). Moreover, millions of people were exposed to DDT during the malarial spraying programs, and those who did the spraying, 130,000 men, were exposed to high concentrations with no ill effects.

These data and much more were presented at the 1971 hearing and the recommendation, after considering 300 technical documents and the testimony of 150 scientists, was that a total ban on DDT was not desirable, based on the scientific evidence. The hearing exam-iner declared in his final decision: "There is a present need for the continued use of DDT for the essential uses defined in this case."

That was in April 1972. Nevertheless, two months later, on June 14, 1972, William Ruckelshaus, EPA administrator, banned all uses of DDT unless an essential public purpose could be proved. Why did he do it? Two years earlier, Ruckelshaus had stated his support of DDT, citing its "amazing and exemplary record of safe use." Was he trying to curry favor with the environmental activist organizations? (When he left the EPA, he signed membership solicitation letters for the Environmental Defense Fund, the organization that led the fight against DDT.) Or was he trying to demonstrate muscle and establish the power of the EPA?

Years later, Ruckelshaus admitted that "decisions by the government involving the use of toxic substances are political . . . [and] the ultimate judgment remains political. . . . [In] the case of pesticides, the power to make this judgment has been delegated to the Administrator of EPA."

The banning of DDT could not be justified on scientific grounds—regulation yes, control yes, but a total ban no. Had Ruckelshaus taken that position, instead of prohibition, back in 1972, we would still have the benefits of this important chemical today. The most important fallout from the Ruckelshaus decision on DDT was that it gave credibility to *pseudo-science*, it created an atmosphere in which scientific evidence can be pushed aside by emotion, hysteria, and political pressure. It has done inestimable damage. The technique of making unsubstantiated charges, endlessly repeated, has since been used successfully against asbestos, PCBs, dioxin, and, of course, Alar.

DDT and other insecticides, herbicides, fungicides, and rodenticides have had a tremendous effect on agriculture. So, indeed, have other chemicals, fertilizers, improved varieties of crops, and better understanding of soil treatment and crop management. All of these, in an informed, integrated program of pest management, have led to an abundance in food production undreamed of a few decades ago. Never again need there be a disaster like the famine in the 1840s in Ireland that was caused by a fungus, Fusarium, the late potato blight. That catastrophe led to the death of one third of Ireland's population from starvation, another third emigrated, and the bitterness that exists between the Irish and the English was intensified yet further. How much of the tragedy of the Emerald Isle might have been averted if a good fungicide like captan had been available?

The potato makes a good object lesson for those who think "nature knows best" and who believe manure and crop rotation are all that's needed. In the 1920s, given good soil and animal fertilizer, an exceptional yield was 75 100-pound sacks of potatoes per acre. By 1940, the best methods were producing 82 sacks per acre. Then came the introduction of modern agriculture, with its chemicals and pesticides. The results look this:

Year	100-Pound Sacks Per Acre
1950	165
1960	208
1970	247
1980s	275

The dramatic increase didn't happen without help—from technology. With the very modern problem of agricultural surpluses in this country, we forget that in the 6,000 years of known human history, such food surpluses are new and unique.

In the 1930s, soil erosion became a serious problem in the United States, dramatized by the "dust bowl" experience in the farm areas of the Midwest. Contour plowing, windbreaks, and better soil management helped, but the most important innovation involved the introduction of herbicides for weed control, thereby making extensive tillage and disturbance of the soil unnecessary.

Pesticides have reduced America's food costs 33 percent by controlling weeds, insects, mold, and rot in vegetables and fruits. They have helped to keep our food and our homes clean by controlling rats, mice, and cockroaches. Through the use of wood preservatives in pressure-treated lumber for fences, porches, decks, and homes, we have saved a forest of trees two times the size of New England.

Modern agriculture has made it possible to grow more food, poultry, dairy products, and fiber on less land. This means that more land can be returned to woodlot, forest, and recreational uses. Of the 3.6 million square miles that constitute the United States, 32 percent—or 1.13 million square miles—are forests or woodlots. Because of this, the average annual wood growth is now three and a half times more than it was in 1920. Tree-growing areas increased 18 percent from 1952 to 1977. Forests in America continue to increase in size, even while supplying a substantial portion of the world's timber needs. Better forest management, improved seedlings, and informed use of fertilizers and pesticides have made this possible. The main danger to our forests today comes from federal lands (national parks, national forests, and wilderness areas), where no management is allowed, because "nature knows best." They now serve as foci for the production and dissemination of forest pests.

The fact is, we are about 10,000 years past the point where we can consider any part of nature untouched by humans or their activities. We cannot return to that faraway time. Besides, most farms maintain uncropped areas that are important to perpetuate wildlife, and there are more than two million farm ponds in the United States where wild species thrive.

By nature, plants require many different elements to survive and grow. But nature did not distribute these elements evenly. It is up to man to supply them. For *good* plant growth, calcium, phosphorus, potassium, magnesium, and nitrogen all must be supplied. This is the function of fertilizer. The ammonia arising from cattle urine is the same as that supplied from a chemical solution. It is a myth that "man-made" or synthetic compounds are dangerous and toxic, whereas the same compounds found in nature—for example, "natural chemicals"—are safe. There is no chemical difference between them.

But ignorant opponents of all man's efforts to improve human life on this earth have continued to insist that extremely low levels of industrial chemicals can be toxic or carcinogenic and that everything "synthetic" is somehow uniquely dangerous and will cause cancer. This is not true. It is the *dose*—the size or amount of exposure—that is important. The amount of natural pesticides we eat every day is at least 10,000 times the level of pesticide residue from agricultural use of synthetics.

Arsenic, cadmium, and chromium are all officially identified as carcinogens, yet they are all naturally present in every cell in our bodies. How much arsenic do we normally have? One hundred thousand molecules per cell. How much cadmium? Two million molecules per cell. How much chromium? Seven hundred thousand per cell. To believe, as the "one molecule can cause cancer" adherents do, that one extra molecule out of several hundred thousand will disrupt the DNA molecule and cause cancer stretches credulity beyond imagination. The theory, to put it bluntly, is nonsensical scare-mongering.

People, however, are attracted to horror stories, and since the news media are primarily in the entertainment business, scientific accuracy has a very low priority. At a recent symposium sponsored by the Smithsonian Institution, Ben Bradlee, editor of *The Washington Post,* said: "To hell with the news! I'm no longer interested in news. I'm interested in causes. We don't print the truth. We don't pretend to print the truth. We print what people tell us. It's up to the public to decide what's true."

Careful studies have established that 99.99 percent of the carcinogenic materials ingested daily are either natural or produced by drinking alcohol, cooking, or smoking. The simple way to avoid any problem is to eat a balanced diet with a reasonable variety of different foods. To avoid consuming carcinogens or other toxic substances, one would have to refrain from eating carrots, radishes, onions, olives, melons, ham, shrimp, potatoes, parsley, butter rolls, broccoli, watercress, avocado, lemons, cheese, bananas, apples, oranges, tea, milk, wine, water, and much else besides.

Nitrite, nitrate, and nitrosamines can be avoided only by eliminating most vegetables, especially beets, celery, lettuce, radishes, rhubarb, mustard kale, turnips, cabbage, and. . . .

Well, it gets silly. Yet, if any of these foods were subject to tests similar to those used to screen synthetic chemicals, they would all be banned.

Study Questions

1. How strong are Ray and Guzzo's arguments? How can intelligent people and scientists so strongly disagree, as they do, over the effects of pesticides and herbicides such as DDT, Alar, PCBs, and even asbestos?

2. Do Ray and Guzzo make a convincing case that media hype and lyrical environmental hysteria have led a panic-stricken propaganda campaign against the reasonable use of pesticides?

64

Environmental Hysteria: The Alar Scare

MICHAEL FUMENTO

Michael Fumento is a researcher who lives in Los Angeles.

In this essay, Fumento examines the process that in 1989 led the Environmental Protection Agency (EPA) to ban the use of Alar, a pesticide sprayed on fruit, especially apples, to enhance their quality and life. Fumento argues that not only was the EPA decision seriously wrong but, more importantly, the process that led to the banning illustrates a dangerous antiscientific, antirational trend in which scare tactics are substituted for reason and evidence.

"The most potent cancer-causing agent in our food supply is a substance sprayed on apples to keep them on the trees longer and make them look better." Those were the first terrifying words heard by an estimated fifty million viewers of a terrifying segment of CBS's *60 Minutes,* broadcast on February 26, 1989.

And there was literally panic in the streets:

- In the Los Angeles public school district—second largest in the nation—cafeteria workers in over five hundred schools yanked apples, apple sauce, and apple pie from lunch line counters and deleted these products from their menus. Across the nation and even in Asia, stock boys and store managers pulled apple products off their shelves and packed them away, and threw out their fresh apples.
- Frenzied parents, scared for their children's lives, flooded their family physicians with calls.
- In short order the price of apples fell to their lowest point in years—around $7 for a 420-pound box, well below the $12 break-even level—and remained

Reprinted from *Science Under Siege: Balancing Technology and the Environment* (New York: William Morrow and Company, 1993). © 1993 by Michael Fumento. Reprinted by permission of the publisher. Notes deleted.

depressed for most of 1989. Industry economists have estimated immediate out-of-pocket losses for Washington State apple growers alone of $135 million for 1989. That doesn't include other expenses such as publicity campaigns to repair a damaged reputation, or costs to processors. It also doesn't include other states, although Washington is by far the largest producer of red apples. This $135 million was part of a projected revenue of $875 million, representing a 15 percent loss.

- Apple shipments from warehouses in California to Maryland declined precipitously, costing orchards a fortune and throwing produce markets into chaos. In some parts of the country, the sale of apple juice came to a virtual halt. Prices plunged—and in the months that followed, a number of orchards, most of them small and family-owned, collapsed and underwent foreclosure. "It was a real bloodbath for us this year," said Dennis Walsh, the manager of a seventy-eight-year-old apple cooperative that declared bankruptcy in 1989 after the alarm. The market was so bad that growers couldn't give their apples away, according to Walsh. "The Alar thing came after a couple of bad back-to-back years. It just killed the growers."

This was the Great Apple Scare of 1989, the result of one of the slickest, most cynical fear campaigns in recent American history. The immediate target was Alar, the trade name for daminozide, a growth regulator used to promote uniform ripening of red apples and to improve the fruit's appearance. That chemical, which had been used for twenty-one years with no observable ill effects and which had been knowingly allowed to remain on the market by the Environmental Protection Agency (EPA), was suddenly tried, convicted, and sentenced to death by the media. In fact, the larger target of those responsible for the Alar hysteria was all chemical pesticides, which many environmental extremists believe must be banned—through legislation and regulation if possible, through a smear campaign if necessary.

AN APPLE A DAY?

Alar is a chemical that was developed by the Uniroyal Chemical Company of Bethany, Connecticut, in the early 1960s to be sprayed over orchards growing varieties of red and Golden Delicious apples. It has also been used on grapes, cherries, peaches, pears, peanuts, and tomato transplants in greenhouses, and is still used on ornamental plants.

The chief advantage of Alar for the apple grower was that it allowed an entire orchard to be harvested just once instead of periodically over six weeks as individual fruits ripened. For marketers, the advantages lay in the production of more uniformly shaped and colored fruit, and in extending the usual six- to eight-month shelf life of apples up to a year. Alar can double the volume of fruit produced during the first seven years after planting, by prompting the tree to blossom one and one-half to two years earlier than otherwise. Even after that initial period, by keeping the fruit on the tree and off the ground, the chemical saved some apple growers as much as 25 percent of their crop a year. By preserving the fruit after it was picked, it allowed consumers to have fresh red apples all year long. Alar was not only the best chemical for the job, it was the only chemical with those abilities and as such was treated as a godsend when it was introduced.

Both *60 Minutes* and the Natural Resources Defense Council (NRDC), the environmentalist group that planned the anti-Alar campaign, however, downplayed the practicality and economy of Alar, treating it as though it were little more than a food dye, "improving the cosmetic appearance of crops." The media often bought into this as well. In a prealarm story, the *Los Angeles Times* ran a lengthy piece on Alar entitled "It's About Apples, and Growers' Attempt to Make Them Redder."

A FLY IN THE APPLESAUCE

After developing Alar, in 1966 Uniroyal submitted rat-feeding studies to the U.S. Department of Agriculture, then in charge of pesticide regulation. The rats had developed no tumors and the pesticide was approved, although the test would not pass today's standards since too few rats (thirty-seven) were used.

When Alar breaks down in processing for applesauce or apple juice and to some extent in the apple itself, it forms unsymmetrical 1, 1-dimethylhydrazine (UDMH), which—and this really tickled *60 Minutes* reporter Ed Bradley—is related to the chemical hydrazine that is used as a rocket fuel. Of course, you would probably need to eat a few million jars of applesauce to achieve

lift-off. In 1985, the EPA released a draft document looking at four rodent tests performed in the 1970s—three by one researcher, Dr. Bela Toth—and one in 1984, and found Alar "is a clear carcinogen in that it induces a highly significant increase in the incidence of blood-vascular tumors which are normally found at very low incidence in Swiss mice." If you received a press packet from the NRDC, as I did in January of 1990, you would have gotten this information along with a breakdown of the results of the early studies.

Scant attention (two sentences) was paid in the press packet to the findings of the Federal Insecticide, Fungicide and Rodenticide Act (FIFRA) Scientific Advisory Panel (SAP) in September 1985. In fact, after the panel finished evaluating the studies, the EPA reported: "Each of these studies, however, has been examined by the Agency and the FIFRA Scientific Advisory Panel, and has been found not to provide an adequate basis for regulatory action at this time." The EPA subsequently stated that "audits and reviews of these studies have revealed that some of the studies yielded equivocal results and that the other studies have serious flaws or shortcomings in the test methodology and documentation. These facts have led EPA to conclude that the existing studies, singly or in combination, are inadequate to serve as the basis for regulatory action against daminozide." One member of the panel, toxicologist Christopher Wilkinson, put it more succinctly. "The data were terrible," he said. A cancer researcher who was then employed by the EPA and had done a toxicological study on Alar, told me, "There were so many problems, Toth didn't even pass the laugh track."

Specifically, with the Alar studies it appears that in some cases the dose of Alar given to the animals was so large it directly killed (as opposed to giving cancer to) the animals. This is referred to as exceeding the "maximum tolerable dose," or MTD. Further, a subsequent reexamination of the slides of the test-animal tissues and organs suggested that the actual tumor incidence was less than had been reported. Further still, Toth had not used data from concurrent control animals (a control animal is one that is similar to the test animals and treated identically except that it is not given the agent being tested for carcinogenicity), but rather used control animals from an experiment conducted several years earlier. He later published the results from concurrent controls, which showed that they suffered diseases similar to those incurred in the Alar-fed animals.

There were also flaws in the UDMH studies. The UDMH was allowed to remain in the water so long that most of it probably had broken down into different chemicals. The animals used were acknowledged to have suffered, prior to entry in the study, from "severe degenerative diseases." And, again, it appears that the MTD may have been exceeded.

Given these problems, the EPA left Alar and UDMH in the question mark category, listing them as "possible carcinogens." It also lowered its estimate of potential cancers from UDMH from between 1,000 to 10,000 per million to instead 45 per million. (If something is no more than a "possible carcinogen," assigning a death rate to it is problematic, to say the least. But more on this later.)

Now here's where the scenario gets really interesting. Apparently the EPA officials had expected the SAP to rubber-stamp its decision. When it did not, Uniroyal officials were jubilant. But after the meeting, Steven Schatzow, then director of the EPA's Office of Pesticide Programs, herded SAP members into his office. The angry Schatzow demanded, "How can you do this to us?" After a heated exchange with the scientists, he concluded, "Look, I can't tell you what to do, but you might like to think about this once again." The scientists were stunned by such flagrant interference, and all refused to back down. The aforementioned former EPA researcher told me, "It was the only time I've ever seen the SAP angry. In all the years I'd been with the EPA, I never saw a directive come down like that in *that* direction." She explained that under Reagan appointee Anne Burford Gorsuch, directives had come down to give the green light to questionable chemicals, but never had she seen the EPA give the red light to a chemical no more harmful than any number of other chemicals that the EPA had not hesitated to approve. When I asked Schatzow in 1991 why he took the actions he did, he readily stated that he had already come to the conclusion that Alar or at least UDMH was a carcinogen before the SAP panel ever met. He explained that while he was not a scientist, there were scientists at the EPA who were convinced that, even though the Toth study was flawed, Alar or at least UDMH was a carcinogen, and they convinced him as well. He said he also believed the SAP panel was very "conservative" in a political sense. Of his angry reaction to the SAP panel he said, "When you've invested time in a subject you get pumped up on it."

Thus, in January 1986, the agency reluctantly delayed its proposed ban. But it ordered Uniroyal to continue testing Alar for carcinogenicity and to launch new studies to check for UDMH-induced genetic damage.

But now, in light of the regulatory setback, the NRDC, consumer activist Ralph Nader, and other anti-chemical activists sprang into action. Through threats, intimidation, and their access to media outlets, they waged war against Alar. On national television in 1987, Nader boasted of how he got supermarkets to ban Alar-treated apples:

> So I decided to go direct to the supermarkets. I called up the head of Safeway one day, in Oakland, California . . . [and] I said, "We're going to start a campaign to get Alar out of apples but why don't you save us a lot of trouble and yourself by saying that you're not going to buy any apples or apple products with Alar from your growers." A week later [he] puts out a press release saying no more Alar apple products are being bought. . . . So then we called up Grand Union, Kroger, A&P and guess what, we

said, "Safeway's not selling Alar-treated apples anymore." So they got them out.

Those stores didn't stop selling Alar-treated apples because scientific data showed the chemical to be dangerous or because they at least thought scientific data showed it to be dangerous or because consumers demanded that they stop using it. They did so because a man with a very big stick exerted brute intimidation against them. Similar pressure has been brought to bear against stores selling irradiated food. . . .

Meanwhile, the results of numerous tests came in to the EPA. Three tests to see if UDMH caused genetic damage proved negative. A fourth, initially fuzzy, was repeated and also turned out negative.

Two more animal tests on Alar also came in prior to the 1989 scare. Later a *Reader's Digest* writer reported on what happened with those tests. "The EPA phoned Ray Cardona at Uniroyal and ordered the company to *quadruple* the UDMH maximum dose levels. Cardona hung up in disbelief. The EPA was stacking the deck" (emphasis in original).

The results of a ninety-day UDMH feeding study several years earlier had indicated that the MTD for UDMH was 20 ppm per day. The EPA was ordering Uniroyal to use four times that, four times the number that could kill mice directly without necessarily causing cancer.

Uniroyal tried to appeal the EPA's demand. It went to Wilkinson, who was no longer on the SAP panel, and urged him to use his credibility with the EPA to get the agency to reconsider. Wilkinson said, "We went along to tell EPA that it was crazy to do this because you'd be exceeding the maximum tolerated dose and the animals would die." But, he added, the EPA took "not one whit of notice."

These two higher-dose tests were reported by the International Research and Development Corporation (IRDC) in August 1988. The studies involved feeding rats and mice at various dosage levels, and they demonstrated that Alar did not increase the incidence of cancer in either mice or rats when fed doses as high as 10,000 parts per million (ppm), or 1 percent of the entire diet, per day. Alar was completely off the hook. (This notwithstanding, *60 Minutes* specified that the "most potent cancer-causing agent in our food supply" was "this one chemical called *daminozide* [Alar], not UDMH" [emphasis in original]. UDMH was also negative at all doses in rats. In mice, however, while no tumors were observed at either 10 or 200 ppm/day after two years, one mouse of a group of forty-five that had been fed UDMH for one year at 40 ppm/day had a lung tumor, and blood vessel tumors (both benign and malignant). Lung tumors (benign only) were observed in eleven of fifty-two animals that had received 80 ppm of UDMH per day. As Wilkinson and Uniroyal had warned, the mice died in droves during the study.

Indeed, an amazing *80* percent of the mice had died prematurely because of extreme toxicity, strongly suggesting that the MTD had again been surpassed.

An independent review of all the studies to that date by Dr. Christine Chaisson of Technical Assessment Systems, a former EPA researcher and present consultant to the EPA, Uniroyal, and other organizations, found that "the weight of the evidence clearly favors classification of daminozide as non-carcinogenic." Although the "Chronology for Daminozide" in the NRDC's packet ends with a date in January 1989, and although the chronology appears quite comprehensive, it omitted the 1988 studies.

No study on Alar or UDMH would *ever* demonstrate a cancer risk. The next to last study was released in September 1989, several months after the Alar scare. In it, IRDC reported the results of its two-year study of rats and UDMH, stating that "it is this writer's opinion that these results do not provide conclusive evidence for a test article related oncogenic [carcinogenic] effect in this study." It is important to note that this is standard phraseology for an animal carcinogenic study. Keeping in mind that it is impossible to prove a biological negative, the studies will simply report that there is no evidence to support a positive finding.

The final UDMH study, released in February 1990, reported: "The test substance did not induce any unusual or unexpected tumors but did appear to increase the incidence rates for two common tumors of the lungs and blood vessels"; yet it further stated that indications were "the MTD was exceeded in both high and low dose animals."

But the EPA decided to ignore the possibility that the MTD had been exceeded, which makes sense since it had been the agency that ordered the MTD to be exceeded in the first place. It also decided to ignore the results of the tests on rats. It also decided to ignore the non-MTD mouse-test results. Thus, on February 1, 1989, EPA Acting Administrator John Moore issued a statement finding that "there is inescapable and direct correlation" between exposure to UDMH and "the development of life-threatening tumors" and that therefore the EPA would soon propose barring Alar. In the interim he urged farmers currently using the chemical to stop.

Amazingly, at the same time, on February 1, 1989, the EPA released a three-page statement detailing the results of laboratory animal studies on Alar and UDMH to date. The statement reported: "[1] Although biological trends were noted in the mouse study, tests at 10,000 ppm for two years with the parent compound [Alar, as opposed to UDMH] were statistically negative for cancer response. . . . [2] The cancer response in the current UDMH data is seen only in one species at a relatively high dose. . . . [and] [3] Mutagenicity data for UDMH are equivocal to negative." This refers to, among others, a test developed by University of California, Berkeley, Department of Chemistry, researcher Dr. Bruce Ames, that analyzes a chemical to determine if it causes mutations in bacterial DNA. The ability of a chemical to cause such mutations has been shown to have a fairly high correlation with chemicals that cause cancer in lab animals.

A fourth finding of the EPA in the February 1989 report was "mice in the 'high dose' study are dying early." The agency said that it believed "the death of these mice was due to the tumors, but it may nonetheless be argued that the deaths were the result of excessive toxicity, which may compromise the outcome of the study."

Thus, the EPA's own findings seemed in complete contradiction with its ruling. That made the agency at least a little uneasy, and was the explanation Moore gave for why he was not using EPA's authority to immediately suspend the use of Alar. It was not much consolation to Uniroyal or to apple growers—rather like Henry VIII's messenger telling Catherine Howard that she would soon lose her head but that she could console herself that it would be a private ceremony. Yet, this refusal to invoke an immediate ban, according to *The New York Times* report, provoked "outrage" on the part of some environmentalists.

But they needn't have worried. For help, in the form of the NRDC, Fenton Communications, the American media, and *60 Minutes* in particular, was fast on its way.

NRDC AND FENTON TO THE RESCUE

The Natural Resources Defense Council was founded in 1970 and serves as the litigation arm of the environmentalist movement though it does not normally conduct scientific studies itself. With about one hundred thousand members, it is one of the most powerful and well-funded of the nation's environmental organizations and in 1985 was rated the most influential of them by congressional and EPA staff members. As the title of a *Wall Street Journal* article indicated, NRDC's "Influence on U.S. Environmental Laws, Policies, Earns It a Reputation as a Shadow EPA." The NRDC is politically nowhere near the mainstream. Gregg Easterbrook, a regular writer for the *Atlantic, Newsweek,* and the *New Republic,* and a self-described liberal, identifies the NRDC as "hard-left; reporters rely on it for quotes expressing outrage at anything government or industry does."

In 1987, the NRDC, along with Ralph Nader and Nader's Public Citizen group, filed suit against the EPA and Uniroyal in an attempt to banish Alar, but the Alar case was one that the NRDC could not win. In late 1988, the U.S. Court of Appeals for the Ninth Circuit (Washington State) threw the case out, claiming that the NRDC lacked jurisdiction to make the challenge. So the NRDC decided to shift tactics and bypass the EPA and the courts with a study called *Intolerable Risk: Pesticides in Our Children's Food.*

Orchestrating the NRDC campaign was a public relations firm called Fenton Communications. Fenton, led by David Fenton, is an ideologically motivated organization, having earlier done work for the Marxist Sandinista government in Nicaragua, the Marxist Grenadan government of Maurice Bishop, and Soviet- and Cuban-backed Angola, which contracted to pay Fenton a minimum of $180,000 a year plus expenses to carry out an "information strategy," including contacts with "influential editors, reporters, producers, anchormen, columnists and news media executives in the United States." David Fenton was so pleased with his handling of the Alar campaign that he developed a case of what mobsters call "diarrhea of the mouth" and released a document boasting unabashedly of how he had used practically the entire American media as if they were minions.

Fenton explained that he divided the campaign into two sections in hopes that the media would treat it as separate stories, because "more repetition of NRDC's message was guaranteed." The media took the bait, along with the hook, the line, and the sinker. Story one was the NRDC's *Intolerable Risk* study. Story two, set for release one week after the release of story one, had popular actress and longtime supporter of environmental causes Meryl Streep announcing the formation of Mothers and Others for Pesticide Limits.

By agreement, CBS's *60 Minutes* was allowed to break the *Intolerable Risk* story. That agreement necessarily prevented the NRDC from submitting its report to the scientific community for "peer" review and publication in a journal of science or medicine. NRDC's decision to publish in the lay press suggested that it wished to avoid this burden. (Indeed, then-Food and Drug Administration [FDA] Commissioner Frank Young later stated, "This is one of the worst instances of where statements were made without the benefit of scientific review.") Follow-up interviews were arranged months in advance with major women's magazines like *Family Circle, Woman's Day,* and *Redbook,* usually bearing titles similar to *Redbook*'s "The Foods That Are Poisoning Your Child." Appearance dates were scheduled for *Donahue,* ABC's *Home Show,* and double appearances on NBC's *Today Show.* Mothers and Others made separate appearances on all of those shows and in many other places as well. From here the story simply snowballed, with MacNeil/Lehrer, *The New York Times* and *The Washington Post* doing follow-up stories (although the *Post* later did a critical one), as did all three evening network shows.

But dupery didn't account for all of the favorable media reaction. At a conference sponsored by the Smithsonian Institution in September 1989, titled "Global Environment: Are We Overreacting?" and cochaired by the CEOs of ABC, CBS, NBC, Turner Broadcasting System, Warner, Time, and *The Los Angeles Times* among others, Charles Alexander declared, "As the science editor of *Time* I would freely admit that on this issue

we have crossed the boundary from news reporting to advocacy." That statement received a heavy round of applause. NBC reporter Andrea Mitchell agreed, saying, "Clearly the networks have made that decision now, where you'd have to call it advocacy." Then executive-editor of *The Washington Post* Ben Bradlee did offer a cautionary note, stating, "I don't think there's any danger in what you suggest. There's a minor danger in saying it because as soon as you say, 'To hell with the news, I'm no longer interested in news, I'm interested in causes,' you've got a whole kooky constituency to respond to." To which *Wall Street Journal* editorial writer David Brooks, who appears to have been the only reporter in the country who felt the public had a right to hear about the conference, sardonically noted, "Mr. Bradlee is right. Probably a lot of 'kooks' believe in objective journalism."

At the height of the Alar alarm, the U.S. Senate called a special hearing, at which Streep and others urged that Uniroyal immediately pull Alar off the market so that consumers could be sure apples were completely safe. "What's a mother to do?" she asked. Congressman Gerry Sikorski (D-Minn.), himself vice chairman of the House Subcommittee on Health and the Environment, also testified at the Senate hearings. Sikorski admitted at the hearings, "I am not a scientist or researcher, a medical doctor or oncologist, a biologist or horticulturist. I am [only] a father." But on the first *60 Minutes* Alar installment he nonetheless felt he had the expertise to charge that the EPA "is turning American parents into the malevolent stepmother in Snow White, handing out enticingly red but fatal apples to our children." Indeed, quite ignoring the lag time between inducement of damage to DNA that eventually results in cancer and the actual appearance of the tumor, often twenty years or more, Sikorski told *60 Minutes* viewers, "Go to a cancer ward in any children's hospital in this country. See these bald, wasting away kids." Even if everything NRDC claimed about Alar were true and these kids lived on a pure applesauce and apple juice diet, they wouldn't have had *time* to have gotten their cancer from Alar. The imagery was stark. It was moving. It was false.

As is often the case during scares, industry helped cut its own throat. Those companies judged "unacceptable" by *Consumer Reports* announced immediate measures to stop using Alar-treated apples, while those that scored well on the survey sought to capitalize on it. For example, Beech-Nut Nutrition Corporation, fresh from its conviction and $2.2 million fine for having sold sugar water as apple juice, was so happy with its score on the test that it sent out two press releases alerting the media to the survey even before *Consumer Reports* released it, with one of them stating that the corporation's president would "be available for interviews about what the study findings mean for mothers of infants and for the safety of the nation's food supply generally."

Stores got in on the act too, even before the NRDC scare, by selling apples they declared to be "Alar-free."

Alas, surveys done by newspapers in several metropolitan areas revealed that luxury and health-oriented stores were not necessarily selling Alar-free apples, even when they specifically claimed they were. Those stores had the best of both worlds—profiting from the use of Alar while they profited from the fear of it. Even Safeway was implicated in such a practice, indicating that they had put one over on Ralph Nader—undoubtedly much to his chagrin.

Fenton's memo included the words, in bold type, "Usually, it takes a significant natural disaster to create this much sustained news attention for an environmental problem. We believe this experience proves there are other ways to raise public awareness for the purpose of moving the Congress and policymakers." Indeed.

Although both the EPA and the American Council on Science and Health (ACSH), an organization that frequently counters pesticide alarms, moved quickly to counter the NRDC effort, the mainstream media for the most part gave them short shrift or ignored them altogether. Thus, for example, USA Today gave no room to the opposition in its "cover story" on the NRDC report and but two sentences to the EPA in its cover story on Mothers and Others (which it quickly allowed to be refuted). The article also put in large type right below the title, " 'She [Meryl Streep] wants safe food. We all do.' $3 call to group," followed by a 900 telephone number. In effect, it provided free advertising on the front page of the newspaper to a number that would bring in money for Mothers and Others.

Indeed, while Fenton's campaign was beautifully orchestrated, it would have failed but for the eager complicity of a media reacting, as is its wont, to the pressure for sensational stories. The titles of these articles are worth the proverbial thousand words. In addition to Redbook's "Poisoning," Time proclaimed, "Watch Those Vegetables, Ma," titled another story, "Dining with Invisible Danger," and titled yet another story, "Do You Dare to Eat a Peach?" Newsweek's offering began "WARNING!" with the letters taking up one fifth of the page, and continued "Your Food, Nutritious and Delicious, May Be Hazardous to Your Health." USA Today declared, "Fear: Are We Poisoning Our Children?" People alluded to Jimmy Stewart's stone honest Mr. Smith with "Ms. Streep Goes to Washington to Stop a Bitter Harvest," and Woman's Day asked "Are Pesticides Poisoning Our Children?"

Clearly the media were convinced. Clearly they very much wanted to be. Indeed, even a representative of the NRDC later said that the media distorted and simplified the NRDC report, admitting that "most of the press reports" lacked "context or perspective." . . .

CALCULATED RISK FACTOR

All the media hype aside, just what is the risk of getting cancer from Alar? It depends on who's making the esti-

mate. Using its new data, the NRDC calculated that some 5,500 to 6,200 preschool children will eventually get cancer from exposure to Alar and seven other pesticides or metabolites (breakdown products) in just the first six years of life. For Alar specifically, they translated that into a risk of 240 cancers in a population of one million. As it happens, the NRDC's "new data" was the EPA's old data, which had been gathered before 1985 and had been rejected. But NRDC attorneys Janet Hathaway and Al Meyerhoff said it was the "best data available." Which it was, of course, for them. They simply ignored the two later tests that had appeared by then. As the EPA's John Moore commented in the May–June 1989 issue of the EPA Journal, the NRDC findings were "gravely misleading" because they were based on data "rejected in scientific peer review together with food consumption data of unproven validity." Moore said: "In the Alar case, the public was very prone to give credence to the selective and inappropriate use of data regarding consumer risks and to believe 'the worst' despite counter statements from EPA."

In addition, the NRDC built in the most conservative "safety factors" imaginable into its calculations concerning intake and effect. Wilkinson, in fact, calculated that the NRDC had overstated childhood exposure by as much as 389 times. Further, the California Department of Food and Agriculture discovered that the NRDC had arbitrarily excluded from its study food samples with no detectable pesticide residues. This alone exaggerated pesticide consumption estimates up to 500 times. Thus, while the EPA standard, if used to estimate pedestrian deaths at a street crossing, would assume the crosser to be blind, lame, and deaf, the NRDC standard would assume him to be blind, able only to crawl, deaf, and crossing the Indianapolis Speedway on Memorial Day. The EPA's new figures had calculated a risk to infants, from exposure for just eighteen months, of nine in one million, which was one-twenty-fifth times lower than the NRDC estimate.

The NRDC said that since children have lower body weights and ingest more Alar-containing products than do adults, they are at much greater risk. Indeed, said the NRDC, more than 50 percent of a person's total lifetime risk is incurred during the first five years of life. Thus, the title of the Redbook article: "The Foods That Are Poisoning Your Child" and the other titles mentioned above specifically referring to children. The NRDC's reasoning here, however, was specious. As far as the way chemicals are processed internally is concerned, there are any number of differences in the way that adults and children metabolize a given chemical; and testing on young and old animals has shown little difference in tolerance for carcinogens based on age. The best human data available, which concerns smoking and lung cancer, indicates that only a small fraction of the risk accrues during the first few years of exposure.

(Whether this applies to oral ingestion of a substance can be quite a different matter, of course.)

A joint statement of the FDA, the EPA, and the U.S. Department of Agriculture read: "Data used by NRDC which claims cancer risks from Alar are 100 times higher than the Environmental Protection Agency estimates were rejected in 1985 by an independent scientific advisory board created by Congress." It immediately went on to say that "it should also be noted that risk estimates for Alar and other pesticides based on animal testing are rough and are not precise predictions of human disease. Because of conservative assumptions used by EPA, actual risk may be lower or even zero." The statement concluded: "The FDA, EPA, and the U.S. Department of Agriculture believe there is not an imminent hazard posed to children in the consumption of apples at this time despite claims to the contrary."

Further, Moore noted in his congressional testimony that "on March 1, 1989, the National Research Council (NRC)—a part of the National Academy of Sciences—released the most comprehensive report ever assembled on the relationship between diet and health. The NRC found that there was no evidence that residues of individual pesticides in our diet contribute significantly to the overall risk of getting cancer."

WHAT DOES AN ESTIMATED RISK MEAN?

It is not widely understood what EPA or other organizations' estimates of cancer risks really mean. When such a body says "We believe that there will be as many as twelve hundred excess cancers from product X per year," most people think that really represents twelve hundred people, as if the EPA got into a time machine, went into the future, and ticked off the bodies as they entered the morgue. In fact, there are numerous recurring problems with each such estimate the EPA and other official and unofficial bodies put out. One is that they almost always extrapolate from lab animals to humans, an assumption that may not be valid. Another is that they assume that that which kills lab animals at high doses will also kill humans at the tiniest of doses. This assumption, too, may not be valid. . . .

Still another problem is that mathematical models give a range of risk estimates. When the EPA or NRDC or whoever says "as many as," they are providing an upper-bound estimate. The upper-bound estimate is the worst-case scenario. And by worst case, just that is meant. Dr. Fred Hoerger, in a paper presented at a 1985 seminar, illustrated the upper-bound estimate and its inherent distortion.

It can be said that the upper-bound estimate of rainfall for the United States is 15,000 inches per year. Since yearly rainfall in the United States averages from a few inches to perhaps 50 or 60 inches per year, this sounds outlandish. For a moment, let me justify my estimate on the basis of "prudent" predicting principles. The historical record shows the highest single-day rainfall was 43 inches in Alvin, Texas in 1979. Simply multiplying this number by the number of days in a year and extending it to the entire United States gives my estimate of 15,000 inches.

What these estimating officials don't usually tell you (unless a reporter bothers to ask them) is that the *best-case* scenario is almost always zero. But because the statement "may cause anywhere from zero to twelve hundred deaths" can (1) make it look like the estimator really has no idea, and (2) doesn't make for a good story or a good way of attracting attention to a possible problem, the bottom range of the estimate is rarely provided by the media.

THE END OF ALAR—AND THE BEGINNING OF WHAT?

On May 15, 1989, the apple industry, citing a sharp drop in sales, announced that representatives of the apple industry would stop using Alar by the fall. They said the move was purely financial and that they believed the use of the chemical posed no threat to health. Uniroyal also tossed in the towel, first halting distribution for spraying on food plants in the United States, and later doing so worldwide. This has occurred even though no other country has taken action against Alar. At this writing, Alar is still used for ornamental plants, but the EPA has moved to ban that, as well. According to Uniroyal, Alar at the time of the alarm accounted for less than 1 percent of the company's gross revenues. In addition, congressional legislation was about to be introduced to ban the chemical. Neither for the apple industry nor for Uniroyal was the fight for truth worth the losses they were taking in image and, in the case of the apple growers, in sales.

The British refused to buy into the Alar alarm of their American cousins. The Independent Advisory Committee on Pesticides in a December 1989 report stated: "When all worst case assumptions are combined . . . the intake by infants of UDMH turns out to be 150 times less than the level shown to produce no tumors in animals." The report concluded that "even for infants and children consuming the maximum quantities of apples and apple juice, subjected to the maximum treatment with daminozide, there is no risk from UDMH." The Ministry of Agriculture, Fisheries and Food accepted the advice of the Advisory Committee. Yet Uniroyal felt it would no longer even continue shipping Alar overseas, in part because some of that fruit might end up being imported back into the country, thus starting the melee all over again.

And so, Alar is gone, but its legacy lives on. "The Alar controversy served as a sparkplug for public concern," said NRDC's Janet Hathaway a year after the scare. "Now, there is activity under way to translate that concern into lasting pesticide reform. Alar was symptomatic of the problems that permeate the whole regulatory process." To be sure. But they aren't the problems that Hathaway would have us think.

In the wake of the scare, FDA Commissioner Young condemned the NRDC and its *Intolerable Risk* report, saying, "There has to be a real scientific process, and we have to be able to inform the American people where risks are real. . . . This is one of the worst instances of where statements were made without the benefit of scientific review. That's not the way to do business." Continued Young, "You cannot do risk assessment by media." An ad hoc group of fourteen prominent scientific organizations representing one hundred thousand microbiologists, toxicologists, veterinarians, and food scientists also spoke up, calling the health risks from approved agricultural chemicals "negligible or nonexistent" and stating flatly that the "public's perception of pesticide residues and their effects on the safety of the food supply differs considerably from the facts." What especially concerned them, wrote *Washington Post* business reporter Malcolm Gladwell, was that industry's decision to abandon Alar only fueled the public's misperceptions. "Lurking in the back of the minds of the scientists is a fear that the environmental movement, emboldened by its success in the Alar case, will now move on to other, more economically important agricultural chemicals." That also concerned some of Uniroyal's people. "We sold out on Alar," one told me.

GETTING PERSONAL

Uniroyal's decision to drop the domestic sale of Alar rendered congressional legislation moot. But that was not enough for some members of the lofty body. Senator Joseph Lieberman (D-Conn.), a member of the EPA oversight committee, and Senator Harry Reid (D-Nev.) attacked the EPA for its waffling on Alar, saying it was riddled with proindustry bias. They decided that the best course of action was to pursue the SAP board that had unanimously rejected the early tests indicating Alar and UDMH as carcinogens, and called for an inquiry into their alleged conflicts of interest. Lieberman stated this charge on the second *60 Minutes* Alar show. He singled out two members of the SAP board as having violated the ethics code; one of whom was Chris Wilkinson. Wilkinson's alleged violation was in having met with the EPA on Uniroyal's behalf, although he had already left the SAP by that time. The other charged member had done something similar on a different subject. After an investigation, the Department of Justice cleared both Wilkinson and the other panelist. The United States inspector general cleared the other six panelists without investigation. Whether the actions will have a chilling effect with future independent advisory boards, as was presumably the intention, remains to be seen.

It is interesting that the alleged conflicts of interest on behalf of the panelists were for having some connection to industry, even if the connection began after they had left the panel. Yet environmental activists such as Ellen Silbergeld . . . sat on the EPA's Science Advisory Board at the same time she worked for the Environmental Defense Fund, and no one seems to think anything of it. In fact, *Science* quoted Silbergeld discussing the conflict of interest problems concerning board members and industry without even hinting that she might have had one.

THE APPLE GROWERS STRIKE BACK

On November 29, 1990, a group of apple growers representing eleven Washington growers filed suit against CBS and the NRDC. It charged that the industry lost more than $100 million following the *60 Minutes* shows. Washington State grows more than 50 percent of the apples sold in the nation's supermarkets. The suit, seeking unspecified damages running to millions of dollars, alleges tortious interference with business. In other words, it is as if butcher A is suing butcher B and a newspaper because butcher B told the newspaper that butcher A was taking deliveries from the local horse farm and the newspaper printed it. Burt Chestnut, an apple grower from Wenatchee who is a plaintiff in the suit, said, "The gain is for agriculture in general nationwide, that we stop this misleading information by the media and scare tactics by environmental groups. We want the media to be responsible." But Steven Berzon, a lawyer representing the NRDC, said the lawsuit could have a chilling effect on public activism. "Beyond Alar, this suit threatened by a small group of Washington growers raises fundamental issues of free speech, and the right of citizens to petition the government on important questions of public policy," said Berzon.

But the right of free speech, whether that guaranteed in the Constitution, which pertains only to government attempts at restriction, or the more restrictive "right" against one's neighbors, has never been seen as limitless. If the head of the Washington apple growers accused Berzon of being a dues-paying member of the Aryan Nations white supremacist group and that in fact was not the case, the grower could be sued for libel and be held responsible for damage to Berzon's reputation. Does such a law have a "chilling effect" on what the apple growers may do? Certainly, but it's the kind of chill that society wants to encourage. Before you accuse someone of being a card-carrying member of a hate group, you'd better have good evidence because you can cause tremendous damage to a person if you're wrong. How strange that an organization the size and strength of the NRDC should insist that you take its word for something without waiting for all the facts to come in and then not hold it accountable for its being wrong later.

THE WAGES OF CRYING WOLF

Clearly, NRDC's media campaign was a brilliantly executed end run around the court system, the legislature, and most importantly, scientific peer review. It scored a touchdown of terror. The first to suffer were the stores; then came the apple growers, then Uniroyal. But Uniroyal and the stores will survive, as will most of the apple growers. The ultimate victims are those for whom the NRDC claims to be an advocate, the consumers.

This is especially so for consumers making a marginal living. The poorer one is, the higher is the percentage of one's income that is spent on food. Fenton boasted to *Propaganda Review* that because of the Alar scare, "lines started forming in health food stores. The sales of organic produce soared. All of which we were very happy about." It is okay for the wealthy David Fenton or the attorneys of the NRDC to pay health-food store prices for their staples. It's okay for a millionaire like Meryl Streep. But what will it do to the marginal poor who cannot qualify for food stamps or for the poor who refuse to use them? Yet the not-so-hidden agenda of the NRDC and many other environmental public interest groups is to eliminate all chemical pesticides. As the environmental writer for the *Los Angeles Times* noted: "While the NRDC has 30 lawyers and 20 scientists, it has no economist to weigh the costs of an environmental reform against its benefits." In October 1989, Janet Hathaway, in response to a Bush administration pesticide-monitoring plan, stated; "Allowing the EPA to condone continued use of a chemical whenever the benefits outweigh the risks is absolutely anathema to the environmental community." Even when the benefits *outweigh* the risks? Are those the words of an official for a group interested in applying science for the betterment of humanity, or perhaps of one that has gone over the deep end into fanaticism and utopianism?

Fanatics see everything in absolutes. Perspective means nothing to them. Indeed, perspective is deadly to the cause of the pesticide alarmists. So what if UDMH only causes cancer in mice and not rats? *Ban Alar.* So what if by the same or even stricter standards more than a score of natural chemicals have been found to be carcinogenic and have not been banned? *Ban Alar.* So what if, even assuming UDMH to be a human carcinogen; its health benefits outweigh its risks? *Ban Alar.*

One argument used by alarmists . . . is known as "erring on the side of caution." Actually, it is not an argument at all; in fact it's not even a nonargument.

Rather, it's an antiargument. It says: Instead of debating this issue, let's just assume that I'm right, because if I'm not right, no one will die, but if I am right, lives will be saved. Erring on the side of caution would dictate the banning of all products containing Alar—and many other products, as well. Radio talk show host and journalist Gary Null, in *Clearer, Cleaner, Safer, Greener,* writes:

> One of the most often used reasons for the EPA's decision not to act on a particular pesticide is that it lacks sufficient scientific data to warrant limiting or banning the pesticide. In and of itself, this reliance on scientific certainty is a case for alarm. Many critics, for instance, wonder why the government agencies, which are supposed to be protecting the public health, do not shift the burden of proof and insist that the chemical industry prove the safety of the chemical.

Simple. You can't prove a negative. You can never say a chemical is not an animal carcinogen, simply because no matter how many tests have been run, the next one may show a positive result. By this standard no chemical can ever be proven safe. One only has chemicals that have been proven unsafe, chemicals that haven't been proven unsafe, and chemicals that haven't yet been tested at all. By this standard, any time someone raises a question about a chemical, the chemical is banned. That's how "erring on the side of caution" works. Yet, as we will see, regarding virtually every major issue discussed in this book, alarmists will err on the side of caution. The reason is simple: On such a basis, they can never, ever lose. They can provide the weakest arguments in the world, but they will still prevail. What will not prevail is sanity and a proper allocation of resources. The fact is that if we always erred on the side of caution, we would bankrupt the country. Yet, when each case is considered individually, the erring proposition may lull us with its siren song.

Consider the environmental referendum California passed three years before the Alar scare in November 1986, Proposition 65, which directed the governor to list chemicals "known to the state" to cause cancer or reproductive toxic effects, followed by the posting of warnings regarding those chemicals, followed still later by a prohibition against discharge of those chemicals in significant amounts into any actual or potential source of drinking water. The terminology of the act is a nightmare to figure out, the number of chemicals to be listed has already grown from twenty-six to well over two hundred, and few of the enforcement provisions have yet gone into effect. Indeed, strictly speaking, the proposition would prohibit alcoholic drinks, since alcohol is one of the listed chemicals, being both a carcinogen and a cause of birth defects. According to Jeffrey Nedelman, vice president for public affairs for the Grocery Manufacturers of America: "In California, the birth-defect standard is ten times more stringent than anything any scientific organization in the world has endorsed." During hearings on Proposition 65, he says, "the state government brought in as witness top Ph.D.s from the academic community and people from Washington. They found toxicologists, food scientists, risk assessors, and to a man they all said this is crazy, this makes no sense. [Environmental activist Tom] Hayden was there. When his turn came he said, 'I've heard what you have to say, and my only reaction is that we in California want to be better.'"

But better than what, and at what price? Depending on who you ask in California, the state needs more money for police, more money for fire protection, more money for the homeless, more money for AIDS hospices, or simply more money left in people's pockets where it can be spent as they see fit. Should the people of California be funneling their money into a program that essentially puts a little more polish on already sparkling chrome, or should it put its money into uses where the benefit for the dollar is much earlier on the diminishing returns curve?

Alar is gone, at least for use on food-producing plants, but the conflict continues. The issue continues to be used by extremist environmentalists and others as if the threat were as real as first presented. Moreover, the removal of Alar was a successful effort on the part of environmentalist extremists who are constantly in search of an easy

new target. Quite possibly as a result of the Alar victory, their "take the pledge"-against-pesticides campaign was kicked off in September 1989, the idea being to eventually cow all grocery stores into taking part. The battle against Alar was merely a small part of the war against pesticides in general, which is a small part of the war against man-made chemicals in general, which is a small part of the war against technology in general. And make no mistake, the assailants, the besiegers of science, will settle for nothing short of total victory.

Study Questions

1. Go over Fumento's description of the process that led to the EPA's banning of Alar. If Fumento is correct about the facts in this case, what does this illustrate about dealing with environmental issues?
2. Fumento accuses the opponents of Alar of using misleading arguments, including the use of the argument that it is best to bet against the use of a pesticide because if we bet for it, someone may be harmed, but if we bet against it, no one will be harmed by it (because it won't be used). Why, according to Fumento, is this a bad argument? Do you agree? Explain.
3. Fumento blames the media for the banning of Alar. What responsibility does the media have in the debate over environmental issues?

65

Is Silent Spring Behind Us?

DAVID PIMENTEL

David Pimentel is professor of entomology at Cornell University and the author of Ecological Effects of Pesticides on Nontarget Species *(1971).*

In this selection, Pimentel assesses the progress of the pesticide problem since Rachel Carson's Silent Spring. *Assembling an array of information, he details the ways in which the situation has improved and in which it has deteriorated.*

Is *Silent Spring* behind us? Have environmental problems associated with pesticide use improved? The answer is a qualified "yes."

Rachel Carson's warning in 1962 generated widespread concern, but many years elapsed before action was taken to halt some of the environmental damage being inflicted by pesticides on our sensitive natural biota. More than 20 years later we still have not solved

all the pesticide environmental problems, although some real progress has been made.

FEWER PESTICIDE PROBLEMS DURING THE PAST TWO DECADES

Chlorinated insecticides, such as DDT, dieldrin, and toxaphene, are characterized by their spread and persistence in the environment. The widespread use of chlorinated insecticides from 1945 to 1972 significantly reduced the populations of predatory birds such as eagles, peregrine falcons, and ospreys. Trout, salmon, and other fish populations were seriously reduced, and their flesh was contaminated with pesticide residues. Snakes and other reptile populations, as well as certain insect and other invertebrate populations that were highly sensitive to the chlorinated insecticides were reduced.

Since the restriction on the use of chlorinated insecticides went into effect in 1972, the quantities of these

Reprinted from *Silent Spring Revisited*, eds. G. J. Marco, R. M. Hollingworth, W. Durham (Washington, D.C.: American Chemical Society, 1987) by permission. Notes deleted.

residues in humans and in terrestrial and aquatic ecosystems have slowly declined. From 1970 to 1974, for example, DDT residues in human adipose tissue declined by about one-half in Caucasians who were 0–14 years of age (see Table 1). The declines in other Caucasian age groups and in blacks have not been as great. In agricultural soils, DDT residues have declined by about one-half or from 0.015 parts per million (ppm) in 1968 to 0.007 ppm in 1973. The decline of DDT in soil led to a decline in the amount of DDT running into aquatic ecosystems and resulted in a significant decline in DDT residues found in various fish. For example, in lake trout caught in the Canadian waters of eastern Lake Superior, DDT residues declined from 1.04 ppm in 1971 to only 0.05 ppm in 1975. In aquatic birds that feed on fish, DDT residues also declined. For example, DDT residues in brown pelican eggs collected in South Carolina declined from 0.45 ppm in 1968 to only 0.004 ppm in 1975.

Because DDT and other organochlorine residues in terrestrial ecosystems have declined, various populations of birds, mammals, fishes, and reptiles have started to recover and increase in number. For example, peregrine falcons have been bred in the laboratory and then successfully released in the environment. Limited data do exist on the recoveries of a few animal species, but we do not know the recovery rates for those animal populations that were seriously affected by chlorinated insecticides. Those species with short generation times and high reproductive rates, like insects, have probably recovered best.

New pesticide regulations established in the early 1970s restricted the use of highly persistent pesticides, which include chlorinated insecticides. DDT, toxaphene, and dieldrin, for example, persist in the environment for 10 to 30 years. Two major problems are associated with the use of highly persistent pesticides. Annual applications of chlorinated insecticides add to the total quantity of insecticides in the environment because they degrade slowly. This persistence in the environment increases the chances for the chemicals to move out of the target area into the surrounding environment.

The amount of chlorinated insecticide residues in the environment since most of the chlorinated insecticides were banned has been declining. But because these insecticides are relatively stable, some will persist 30 years or more, and some will be present in the U.S. environment until the end of this century. Fortunately these residues are relatively low, so their effect on most organisms should be minimal.

Persistence of chlorinated insecticides in the environment is only one of the problems created by these chemicals. Their solubility in fats and oils resulted in their accumulation in the fatty tissues of animals, including humans. Thus, bioaccumulation of chlorinated insecticides is a serious environmental problem. Organisms like water fleas and fish, for example, concentrated DDT and other chlorinated insecticides from a dosage of 1 part per billion (ppb) in the environment to levels in their tissues of 100,000 times that. Bioaccumulation continues in the environment with several pesticides (e.g., parathion and 2,4-D), but restricting the use of chlorinated insecticides has reduced this environmental problem.

Movement and magnification of pesticides in the food chain also occurs, but must be carefully documented. Some organisms concentrate pesticides in their bodies 100,000-fold over levels in the ambient environment, and this condition might mistakenly be interpreted as a case of biomagnification in the food chain. Biomagnification in the food chain has been documented with birds like osprey and gulls that feed on fish and has proven to be a serious problem to these predaceous birds.

INCREASED PESTICIDE PROBLEMS DURING THE PAST TWO DECADES

Although restricted use of chlorinated insecticides has relieved some environmental problems, the escalation of pesticide use since 1970 has intensified several other environmental and social problems. Pesticide production and use has increased 2.3-fold since 1970, from around 1.0 to nearly 1.5 billion pounds annually.

Recent research has documented the fact that certain pesticide use may actually increase pest problems. For example, herbicides like 2,4-D used at recommended dosages on corn increased the susceptibility of corn to both insects and plant pathogens. Also the reproduction of certain insects can be stimulated by low dosages of certain insecticides, as occurred in the Colorado potato beetle. For example, sublethal doses of parathion increase egg production by 65%. In addition, most of the insecticides that replaced the chlorinated insecticides are more toxic per unit weight than the chlorinated insecticides.

If one pesticide is more toxic and more biologically active than another, it is not necessarily hazardous to the

TABLE 1 *Total DDT Equivalent Residues in Human Adipose Tissue from General U.S. Population by Race*

AGE (YEARS)	1970	1971	1972	1973	1974
Caucasians					
0–14	4.16	3.32	2.79	2.59	2.15
15–44	6.89	6.56	6.01	5.71	4.91
45 and above	8.01	7.50	7.00	6.63	6.55
Negroes					
0–14	5.54	7.30		4.68	3.16
15–44	10.88	13.92	11.32	9.97	9.18
45 and above	16.56	19.57	15.91	14.11	11.91

NOTE: All residues are measured in parts per million lipid weight.

environment. Risk depends on the dosage and method of application of the specific pesticide. If one pesticide's per-unit weight is more toxic than another, the more toxic chemical is usually applied at a lower dosage that will cause about a 90% kill in the pest population. Thus, a highly toxic material used at a low dosage can achieve about the same mortality as a low-toxicity material. Both high- and low-toxicity pesticides affect pests and nontarget organisms in a similar manner, but the risks to humans handling highly toxic pesticides are far greater than when handling pesticides with a low toxicity. Humans handling highly toxic pesticides like parathion are more likely to be poisoned than those handling pesticides of low toxicity like DDT. If one spills DDT and wipes the pesticide off the skin, no harm is done. However, a similar accident with parathion often leads to poisoning severe enough to require hospitalization.

Human Poisonings

Humans are exposed to pesticides by handling and applying them, by contacting them on treated vegetation, and, to a lesser extent, from their presence in food and water supplies. The number of annual human pesticide poisonings has been estimated at about 45,000; about 3000 of these are sufficiently severe to require hospitalization. The number of annual accidental deaths caused by pesticides is about 50. Accurate data on human pesticide poisonings still are not available 20 years after *Silent Spring*.

Furthermore, detecting the causes of cancer from pesticides is exceedingly difficult because of the long lag time prior to illness and the wide variety of cancer-producing factors that humans are exposed to in their daily activities. No one knows if less human cancer is caused by pesticides now than 20 years ago. Probably less than 1% of human cancers today are caused by pesticides.

We are constantly exposed to pesticides. Despite efforts to keep pesticides out of our food and water, about 50% of U.S. foods sampled by the Food and Drug Administration (FDA) contain detectable levels of pesticides. Improvements in analytical chemical procedures are helping us detect smaller and smaller quantities of pesticides in food and water. These extremely low dosages should have little or no public health effect.

Domestic Animal Poisonings

Because domestic animals are present on farms and near homes where pesticides are used, many of these animals are poisoned. Dogs and cats are most frequently affected because they often wander freely about the home and farm and have ample opportunity to come in contact with pesticides.

A major loss of livestock products (about $3 million annually) occurs when pesticide residues are found in these products. This problem will probably continue as the quantity of pesticides used continues to rise.

Bee Poisonings

Honeybees and wild bees are essential to the pollination of fruits, vegetables, forage crops, and natural plants. Pesticides kill bees, and the losses to agriculture from bee kills and the related reduction of pollination are estimated to be $135 million each year. Evidence suggests that bee poisonings are probably greater now than in 1962 for several reasons. More highly toxic insecticides are being used, and greater quantities of insecticides are being dispensed. In addition, more pesticide is being applied by aircraft, and aircraft applications are employing ultra low volume (ULV) application equipment. ULV applications require smaller droplets for coverage, and this practice tends to increase pesticide drift problems.

Crop Losses

Although pesticides are employed to protect crops from pests, some crops are damaged as a result of pesticidal treatments. Heavy pesticide use damages crops and causes declines in yields because: (1) herbicide residues that remain in the soil after use on one crop injure chemically sensitive crops planted in rotation, (2) certain desired crops cannot be planted in rotation because of knowledge of potential hazard injury, (3) excessive residues of pesticides remain on the harvested crop and result in its destruction or devaluation, (4) pesticides that are applied improperly or under unfavorable environmental conditions result in drift and other problems, and (5) pesticides drift from a treated crop to nearby crops and destroy natural enemies or the crop itself.

Although an accurate estimate of the negative impact of pesticides on crops in agriculture is extremely difficult to obtain, a conservative estimate is about $70 million annually. The problem is probably worse today than in Carson's time because 7 times more pesticide is being applied today than 20 years ago, and its use is more widespread. This statement is especially true of herbicides.

Reduced Populations of Natural Enemies

In undisturbed environments, most insect and mite populations remain at low densities because a wide array of factors, including natural enemies, control them. When insecticides or other pesticides are applied to crops to control one or more pest species, natural enemy populations are sometimes destroyed, and subsequently pest outbreaks occur.

For example, before the synthetic pesticide era (1945) the major pests of cotton in the United States were the boll weevil and cotton leafworm. When extensive insecticide use began in 1945, several other insect and mite species became serious pests. These include the cotton bollworm, tobacco budworm, looper, cotton aphid, and spider mites. In some regions where pesticides are used to control the boll weevil, as many as five additional treatments have to be made to control bollworms and budworms because their natural enemies have been destroyed. This cycle has meant more pesticide use, more natural enemies destroyed, greater pest populations, and more pesticides used.

Pesticide Resistance

In addition to destroying natural enemies, the widespread use of pesticides often causes pest populations to develop resistance and pass it on to their progeny. More than 420 species of insects and mites and several weed species have developed resistance to pesticides. Pesticide resistance in pests results in additional sprays of some pesticides or the use of alternative and often more expensive pesticides. Again the process of pest control escalates the cycle of pesticide use and the development of resistance.

An estimated $133 million worth of added sprays or more expensive pesticides has been employed to deal with the resistance problem annually. This dollar cost, of course, does not include the side effects apparent in the environment and in public health from using more pesticides and more toxic pesticides.

Fishery Losses

Pesticides in treated cropland often run off and move into aquatic ecosystems. Water-soluble pesticides are easily washed into streams and lakes, whereas other pesticides are carried with soil sediments into aquatic ecosystems. Each year several million tons of soil, and with it, pesticides, are washed into streams and lakes.

At present only a small percentage of fish kills are reported because of the procedures used in reporting fish losses. For example, 20% of the reported fish kills give no estimate of the number of dead fish because fish kills often cannot be investigated quickly enough to determine the primary cause. Also, fast-moving waters rapidly dilute all pollutants, including pesticides, and thus make the cause of the kill difficult to determine. Dead fish are washed away or sink to the bottom, so accurate counts are not possible.

Samples of water recently confirmed a steadily decreasing concentration of pesticides found in surface waters and streams from 1964 to 1978. This reduction is apparently related to the replacement of persistent pesticides with less persistent materials. Despite the reduced pesticide residues in streams, an estimated $800,000 or more in fish is lost annually (each fish was calculated to have a value of 40 cents). This estimate of

nearly $1 million probably is several times too low and does not confirm that *Silent Spring* is behind us.

Impacts on Wildlife and Microorganisms

Too little information exists to make even a conservative estimate of the populations of vertebrates, invertebrates, and microorganisms that are adversely affected by pesticides. Most invertebrates and microorganisms perform many essential functions to agriculture, forestry, and other segments of human society; such as preventing the accumulation of water, cleaning water or soil of pollutants, recycling vital chemical elements within the ecosystem, and conserving soil and water. An estimated 200,000 species of plants and animals exist in the United States and, at best, we have information on the effects of pesticides on less than 1000 species. Most of these data are based on "safe concentration" tests conducted in the laboratory. This situation confirms that little is known about pesticide effects on the natural environment. At present evaluation must be based on indicator species.

STATUS OF INTEGRATED PEST MANAGEMENT

Integrated pest management (IPM), introduced more than a decade ago, aimed to reduce pesticide use by monitoring pest populations and using pesticides only when necessary as well as augmenting pest control with alternative nonchemical strategies. What happened? IPM has not been successful, and in fact, more of all kinds of pesticides are being used in the United States and throughout the world than ever before.

The reasons for the poor performance of IPM are complex. First, IPM technology, even if it is simply monitoring pest and natural enemy populations, requires a great deal more basic information than scientists now have. This fact signals the pressing need for basic research on the ecology of pests, their natural enemies, and their environment. Also, the use of this basic information to develop control programs is much more sophisticated than routine application of pesticides. Because this technology is more sophisticated, trained manpower is needed, and often the farmer is not trained and cannot be expected to carry out effective IPM programs.

Pesticides are unquestionably simple and quick to use. They have a significant psychological advantage over IPM and especially over nonchemical controls like biological control. Biological controls gradually bring pest populations under control, but do not give the immediate satisfaction of direct kill like pesticides do. However, as research continues and greater ecological knowledge of pests and agroecosystems increases, IPM has the potential to improve pest control.

WHY ARE LOSSES DUE TO PESTS GREATER TODAY THAN 40 YEARS AGO?

Currently, an estimated 37% of all crops is lost annually to pests (13% to insects, 12% to plant pathogens, and 12% to weeds) in spite of the combined use of pesticidal and nonchemical controls. According to a survey of data collected from 1942 to the present, crop losses from weeds declined slightly from 13.8% to 12% because of a combination of improved herbicidal, mechanical, and cultural weed control practices. During the same period, losses from plant pathogens increased slightly from 10.5% to 12%.

On average, however, crop losses due to insects have increased nearly twofold (from 7% to about 13%) from the 1940s to the present in spite of a 10-fold increase in insecticide use. Thus far the impact of this loss in terms of production has been effectively offset through the use of higher yielding varieties and increased use of fertilizers.

The substantial increase in crop losses caused by insects can be accounted for by some of the major changes that have taken place in U.S. agriculture since the 1940s. These changes include

- planting of crop varieties that are increasingly susceptible to insect pests;
- destruction of natural enemies of certain pests, which in turn creates the need for additional pesticide treatments;
- increase in the development of pesticide resistance in insects;
- reduced crop rotations and crop diversity and an increase in the continuous culture of a single crop;
- reduced FDA tolerance and increased cosmetic standards of processors and retailers for fruits and vegetables;
- reduced field sanitation including less destruction of infected fruit and crop residues;
- reduced tillage, leaving more crop remains on the land surface to harbor pests for subsequent crops;
- culturing crops in climatic regions where they are more susceptible to insect attack;

- use of pesticides that alter the physiology of crop plants and make them more susceptible to insect attack.

CONCLUSION

Progress has been made on pesticide problems, but *Silent Spring* is not entirely behind us. Pesticide use continues, and the quantities of pesticides applied grow annually despite support for IPM control. In future decades, as the world population grows rapidly and agricultural production is stretched to meet food needs, we should not forget Carson's warnings.

Pesticides will continue to be effective pest controls, but the challenge now is to find ways to use them judiciously to avoid many of the environmental hazards and human poisonings that exist today. With this goal for research and development we can achieve effective, relatively safe pest control programs.

Study Questions

1. Go over Pimentel's discussion and describe the ways the pesticide problem has improved and how it has deteriorated.
2. Can you suggest ways to improve our situation still further?

For Further Reading

Bernards, Neal, ed. *The Environmental Crisis*. San Diego, CA: Greenhaven Press, 1991.

Carson, Rachel. *Silent Spring*. Boston: Houghton Mifflin, 1962.

Fumento, Michael. *Science Under Siege: Balancing Technology and the Environment*. New York: Morrow, 1993.

Graham, Frank *Since Silent Spring*. Boston: Houghton Mifflin, 1962.

Gilbert, Susan. "America Tackles the Pesticide Crisis." *The New York Times Magazine* (Oct. 8, 1989).

Marco, Gino, Robert Hollingworth, and William Durham, eds. *Silent Spring Revisited*. (Washington, D.C.: American Chemical Society, 1987.

CHAPTER THIRTEEN

Atmospheric Conditions: The Greenhouse Effect and the Ozone Layer

On July 23, 1988, Dr. James Hansen, Director of the National Aeronautics and Space Administration (NASA) Goddard Institute for Space Studies, told the U.S. Senate Committee on Energy and Natural Resources, "It's time to stop waffling so much and say that this evidence is pretty strong that the greenhouse effect is here." Occurring in Washington, D.C., during the hottest summer on record, Hansen's testimony found a receptive audience. Newspapers issued headlines announcing the greenhouse effect and gave Hansen's testimony pride of place. Many scientists agreed with Hansen's assessment, though generally were reluctant to give it the depth of conviction that Hansen expressed. Other scientists demurred, arguing that the evidence for global warming was ambiguous.

What is the greenhouse effect? It is the theory that the atmospheric gases that hover over Earth keep our planet warm in a manner analogous to the glass panes of a greenhouse. In a greenhouse, the Sun's rays (energy in the form of light) are allowed in through the glass, but the heat that is then generated is trapped by the glass. The same phenomenon occurs when you keep your car windows closed on a sunny day. The heat is trapped inside, so it is warmer in the car than outside.

Likewise, the Sun's energy reaches Earth in the form of light, infrared radiation, and small amounts of ultraviolet radiation. Earth's surface absorbs much of this solar energy, some of it being used for photosynthesis, and transforms it to heat energy, which rises back into the troposphere (the innermost layer of the atmosphere, occupying about 11 miles above sea level). But water vapor (mostly in the form of clouds), carbon dioxide (CO_2), methane, and other gases block some of the heat energy from escaping, like the panes of the greenhouse. They absorb the heat and warm Earth. Without this heat-trapping blanket, Earth's surface would cool to about 0°F (−18°C) instead of maintaining an average temperature of 57°F (14°C). Most of our planet would be frozen like Mars.

The problem, then, is not the greenhouse process but its *increased* activity. It's too much of a good thing. For the past 8000 years, Earth's average temperature has

never been warmer than 1°C, and the last time it was 2°C warmer was 125,000 years ago. Hansen and others have presented evidence that Earth has begun to get warmer and by current trends the polar ice caps will gradually melt, causing a rise in the ocean's level of anywhere from 6 to 9 feet. Millions of people living on islands and along coastlines would be displaced as their land was flooded by the oceans. While people in northern Canada, northern Russia, and Greenland might rejoice over warmer weather, most of the temperate zones would become much warmer. Air conditioner use would increase, demanding more energy and creating more pollution, which in turn would create a greater greenhouse effect. Weather patterns would change, negatively affecting agriculture and causing global starvation.

While scientists debate whether the evidence points to a significant trend in global warming, a consensus exists that prudence requires us to lower greenhouse gases (CO_2, methane, ozone, and others) wherever possible. The debate is over the seriousness of the threat. What follows are two different assessments.

Our first reading is Christopher Flavin's discussion of the greenhouse effect. Flavin argues that global warming is well under way. Though we cannot stop it in the near future, we can slow it down by changing our lifestyles. We must reduce the burning of fossil fuels and the levels of methane and ozone in the atmosphere. Otherwise, a catastrophe will occur.

In our second reading from Dixy Lee Ray and Louis Guzzo's *Trashing the Planet,* a quite different diagnosis is offered. Ray and Guzzo contend that very little evidence exists for a devastating greenhouse effect and that imponderables such as the El Niño current, volcanic activity, or solar patterns are much more significant than human pollution. They agree that reason supports significant lowerings of CO_2 and other pollutants by weaning ourselves from fossil fuels, but we shouldn't get hysterical about the sky falling or the sea rising without good evidence. Scientists ought to exercise judicious restraint in coming to their conclusions. Ray and Guzzo are also skeptical about the depletion of the ozone layer. They argue that the evidence does not support the doomsday conclusions.

66

The Heat Is On: The Greenhouse Effect

CHRISTOPHER FLAVIN

Christopher Flavin is a staff writer for the Worldwatch Institute, an institute supported by the United Nations and dedicated to environmental issues.

Flavin begins with James Hansen's fight to make our nation's leaders aware of the impending dangers of the greenhouse effect. Then he sets forth meteorologic statistics supporting the thesis that global warming will take place and that, unless we change our ways, it will lead to severe consequences for humanity.

The scene was a cool, air-conditioned U.S. Senate hearing room, but outside, temperatures were soaring through the nineties as Dr. James Hansen began his testimony. Hansen, who directs NASA's Goddard Institute for Space Studies, had a simple message: "Global warming has begun." The date was June 23, 1988, and human-induced global warming had emerged as a threat and public concern that policymakers could no longer ignore.

Only rarely are public-policy turning points so clearly marked. Scientists had accumulated empirical evidence for a phenomenon with the potential to fundamentally alter life on earth. Although much of the key data had been developed and even published in preceding months, Hansen's testimony was more definitive. A sober government scientist was publicly stating his firm conclusion that greenhouse warming is under way.

The senators and reporters present at the hearing were undoubtedly swayed in part by the fact that Washington temperatures that day were oppressively hot, and a devastating drought was searing the Midwest. The harsh summer weather that some areas of the world experienced in 1988 cannot be directly attributed to global warming, but climate scientists now believe that it was typical of the oppressive conditions likely to become commonplace as early as the nineties. In later years, conditions could grow far worse. The summer of 1988 was at minimum a mild preview and timely reminder of the costs of inaction.

From national news magazines to casual conversations, the gloomy prospect of hotter summers, recurrent droughts, more intense hurricanes, and flooded cities has edged into the public consciousness. Millions of people, many with only a vague sense of what the "greenhouse effect" is, experienced the uneasy sense of a world out of control and a human race that is irre-

vocably altering the very conditions that made modern societies possible.

Indeed, conditions that are essential to life as we know it are now at risk. By the middle of the next century, cities such as New Orleans and Venice could be flooded and abandoned. Intense heat may well cause a vast reversal of sunbelt migration as people seek out the more temperate regions of the Yukon and Siberia.

Several decades from now, Bangladesh and the Netherlands may be struggling with vast seawalls to preserve what little remains of their landscapes. The Maldives, a small, low-lying nation in the Indian Ocean, could simply cease to exist. Much of the parched American farmbelt may have been converted to meager rangeland, with ghost towns standing as the only reminder of the thriving farm economy the region once supported.

It remains to be seen whether global anxiety over climate change can be translated into effective policies to forestall the looming heat wave. Already, an impressive start has been made. By 1991, 22 nations had made commitments to limit emissions of carbon dioxide. The United States, however, not only continues to resist making a national pledge to reduce emissions, but even fails to recognize the gravity of the threat.

Only a broad international effort to slow the buildup of greenhouse gases will be sufficient to protect the climate. Encouragingly, an international conference sponsored by the government of Canada, and held just days after Hansen's testimony, reached consensus on the urgency of the problem. Negotiations for an international global warming treaty are now in progress and should culminate at the United Nations Conference on Environment and Development to be held in Brazil in 1992.

These stirrings of activity should not lull the world into complacency. Commitment to the issue could fade as quickly as the seasons change. Neither politicians nor ordinary citizens have come to grips with the profound changes in global energy and forestry trends needed to forestall global warming. By comparison, the bitterly contested clean air regulations and water pollution control legislation of the seventies were child's play.

THE GLOBAL HOTHOUSE

The earth's climate is the product of a delicate balance of energy inputs, chemical processes, and physical phenom-

Reprinted from the *Worldwatch Reader*, ed. Lester Brown (New York: Norton, 1991) by permission.

ena. On Venus, a human being's blood would boil. On Mars, a person would instantly freeze to death. This difference in temperatures is largely due to the widely varying chemical compositions of each planet's atmosphere.

All three planets receive huge quantities of solar energy, but the amount of energy that is radiated back into space in the form of heat depends on the gases in the atmosphere. Some gases such as carbon dioxide and methane tend to absorb this heat in the lower atmosphere in the same way that glass traps heat in a greenhouse and allows temperatures to build up.

The scorching temperatures of Venus are the product of an atmosphere that is composed largely of carbon dioxide, which leads to an uncontrolled greenhouse effect. Mars has too little carbon dioxide or other greenhouse gases to support above-freezing temperatures. Earth, on the other hand, has a nitrogen-based atmosphere, only 0.03 percent of which is carbon dioxide—a share that has varied only slightly over the past several million years.

The notion that human activities might disrupt this delicate balance was first proposed by the Swedish chemist Svante Arrhenius in 1896. Coal and other carbon-based fuels, such as oil and natural gas, release carbon dioxide as the basic product of their combustion. Arrhenius theorized that the rapid increase in the use of coal in Europe during the Industrial Revolution would increase carbon dioxide concentrations and cause a gradual rise in global temperatures.

The Swedish chemist's theory gathered dust for six decades; it appeared to be little more than an academic's musings. For one thing, no one was sure whether carbon dioxide concentrations were actually increasing. Then, a 1957 study by the Scripps Institute of Oceanography in California suggested that half the carbon dioxide released was being permanently trapped in the atmosphere. Humanity, stated the study, was "engaged in a great geophysical experiment."

Still, solid evidence was needed. A young graduate student by the name of Charles Keeling was given the task of setting up a carbon dioxide measuring station on the Hawaiian volcano of Mauna Loa to test the pollution-free air in the middle of the Pacific. From 315 parts per million in 1958, Keeling has measured an increase in atmospheric carbon dioxide concentration of 10 percent—to 349 parts per million. Measurements taken from air bubbles trapped in the cores of glacial ice suggest that this is substantially above the highest concentrations the earth has experienced during the past 160,000 years.

Satellite reconnaissance, improved understanding of the oceans, and more sophisticated computer models have in recent decades greatly deepened understanding of the complex forces at work in the world's climate. However, in a field in which accurate three-day weather forecasts are still elusive, it is hardly surprising that long-term climate trends defy simple analysis.

Among the most effective tools of analysis are the "global circulation models" that run on large computers and simulate the many complex phenomena that make up the global climate. By the early eighties, these models had established a fairly solid consensus about the amount of warming that could be expected if carbon dioxide buildup continues for the next 100 years—and they were surprisingly close to Arrhenius's 1896 prediction.

However, during the eighties disturbing new evidence emerged. Measuring stations reported a steady increase in other even more potent greenhouse gases, notably methane, nitrogen compounds, and chlorofluorocarbons (CFCs). Although each of these exists in the atmosphere in far smaller quantities than does carbon dioxide, their strong heat-absorbing properties mean that together their growth in the atmosphere may have as much greenhouse potential as does carbon dioxide. Further, they are complementary, because they each tend to trap different spectra of thermal radiation.

It now appears that the world is warming at twice the rate projected just five years ago. Scientists believe that by the year 2030 global average temperatures will be between 3 and 8 degrees Fahrenheit higher than they have averaged between 1950 and 1980, or warmer than the earth has been for the past two million years.

THE EVIDENCE MOUNTS

Politicians and the public have largely ignored these warnings. The reason, in essence, is the lack of an obvious record of change—that is until recently. The most compelling evidence offered by James Hansen at the 1988 hearings in Washington was a 108-year series of global average temperature figures that have been assembled by scientists in the United States and Great Britain.

These figures are based on readings taken all over the world and corrected for possible inaccuracies. Although pre-1900 figures are considered somewhat less solid, the overall trend is clear. Whereas the global average temperature in the 1890s was about 58.2 degrees, by the 1980s it had climbed to about 59.4 degrees. While temperatures had leveled off between 1940 and 1970, the accelerating rise of temperatures during the eighties has more than offset this lull (see Figure 1).

Remarkably, six of the seven warmest years since 1850 have all occurred since 1980, and 1990 was the warmest since scientists began measuring the earth's temperature. The chances against this clustering of warm years being a coincidence are overwhelming.

There is an uncanny correlation between the approximately 1 degree warming observed so far and the predictions of the climate models. Other evidence also points to greenhouse warming. The upper atmosphere is becoming cooler while the lower atmosphere warms,

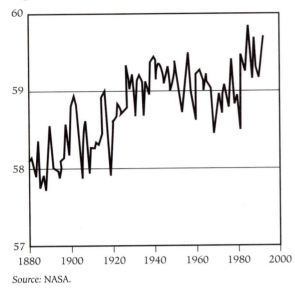

Degrees Fahrenheit

Source: NASA.

FIGURE 1 *Global Temperature, 1880–1987*

and temperatures at higher latitudes are increasing faster than they are at the equator, both in accordance with model predictions.

Although it is difficult to predict the regional effects or the extent of damage caused by climate change, most scientists agree that the build-up of carbon dioxide in the atmosphere has the potential to be devastating. The Intergovernmental Panel on Climate Change (IPCC), convened by the United Nations in 1988 to review the existing scientific evidence on global warming, confirmed in 1990 that human activities are altering the atmosphere.

The panel's report, prepared by a group of 300 scientists from more than two dozen countries, projects that by the end of the 21st century global average temperature will increase by 5.4 degrees Fahrenheit—a rate of temperature change not seen for tens of thousands of years.

WHERE ARE WE HEADED?

Some might argue that we are already experiencing climate change. Africa's Sahel has suffered extraordinary drought during much of the past decade. Western North America has had two serious droughts since the late seventies, and eastern North America has had a string of hot summers—as well as some very cold winters—during the eighties. In 1987, India experienced one of the most serious monsoon failures in recent history, and in 1988 China suffered a serious drought.

Weather is by its nature erratic, and there is no solid evidence linking these events to climate change. It is striking, however, that some of the apparent aberrations in recent weather are consistent with the greenhouse

predictions of global circulation models. These include hotter summer temperatures and more frequent droughts in central regions of China and North America and cooler conditions in Europe and other coastal areas. Climate scientists estimate that by the nineties, recurrent droughts, heat waves, and other unusual weather may have increased to the point that ordinary citizens are convinced that their climate is changing.

These changes, however, are mild compared with what is expected in later decades. Between the years 2025 and 2050, when greenhouse gas accumulation is projected to be double preindustrial levels, the global average temperature is expected to be up between 3 and 8 degrees. However, midlatitude regions, such as much of Australia, the United States, and China, may experience higher temperature rises than projected for the world as a whole—ranging as high as 8 to 10 degrees.

By then it is anticipated that Washington, D.C., will have an average of 12 days a year with temperatures over 100 degrees, compared with an average of 1 day a year recently. Ninety-degree days will go from an average of 36 per year to 87. Temperature increases in northern Africa and in the Antarctic could exceed 10 degrees. To suggest how severe the consequences of a seemingly small change can be, the coldest average temperature during the last ice age is estimated at just 10 degrees lower than today's.

If permitted to continue, global warming may soon affect economies and societies worldwide. Indeed, it can be compared to nuclear war for its potential to disrupt a wide range of human and natural systems and thus complicate the task of managing economies and coping with other problems. Water supply systems, settlement patterns, and food production could all be badly disrupted by a rapid warming.

One of the dangers of climate change is that its impacts cannot be fully anticipated. A handful of more-extreme hurricanes could kill millions of people. In much of Africa or on the Indian subcontinent, two or three drought years in a row could leave millions on the brink of starvation. Global circulation models are best at forecasting averages, but in the game of climate change, it is not the averages that kill, it is the extremes.

World agriculture, in particular, is closely tied to current weather patterns. In this decade, recurrent droughts could begin to undermine food producing systems in some areas. The long-term prospect is far gloomier. From the U.S. corn crop to China's rice harvest and Africa's subsistence crops, food production could become erratic and ultimately not sustainable at the high levels needed to support a growing population.

Forests and other forms of natural vegetation may also find it difficult to cope with climate change. Trees are adapted to a narrow range of temperature and moisture levels. A global temperature increase of several degrees could be catastrophic; it would shift climatic zones northward by hundreds of miles. If such a change occurred rapidly, there would be no opportunity for tropical forests to adequately supplant temperate ones. The resulting loss of carbon-rich trees could actually accelerate the warming—a sort of climatic death spiral.

Sea level rise is another threat. As the water in the ocean warms, it will expand. In addition, the warming at the poles will reduce the amount of water trapped in glaciers and ice caps. Studies have found that a temperature rise of 6 degrees would increase sea levels about 3 feet. This would hurt most in Asia, where rice is produced on low-lying river deltas and flood plains. Without heavy investments in dikes and seawalls to protect the rice fields from saltwater intrusion, such a rise would markedly reduce harvests. Large-areas of wetlands that nourish the world's fisheries would also be destroyed.

A rise in sea level would also affect many coastal cities. A 3-foot rise would threaten New Orleans, Cairo, and Shanghai, to cite a few. In Charleston, South Carolina, for example, it is estimated that the cost of adapting to the sea level rise projected for midcentury could reach $1.5 billion. Protecting the entire East Coast could cost as much as $100 billion. But not all countries can afford such an investment. At some point political leaders will have to decide whether to spend massive amounts of capital on dikes and other structures to prevent inundation or to abandon low-lying areas.

In an impassioned address to the UN General Assembly in October 1987, the president of the Maldives described his country as an "endangered nation." With most of its 1,196 islands barely 6 feet above sea level, little of it may be left by the end of the next century. The president poignantly noted, "We did not contribute to the impending catastrophe to our nation and alone we cannot save ourselves."

THE POLICY CHALLENGE

The world *can* save itself, but to do so will require an unprecedented mobilization of resources and a new attitude on the part of all political leaders. There is already a huge momentum behind global warming— exponential energy and population trends are forcing greenhouse gas concentrations ever upward.

Based simply on the greenhouse gases currently in the atmosphere, we are already committed to perhaps a 3-degree increase above current temperatures. But additional gases are entering the atmosphere each year, and the annual increment itself is in many cases growing. Only the highest level of commitment and far-reaching policy changes can now make a meaningful difference.

The issue is not stopping global warming; this will almost certainly not be possible within most of our lifetimes. Rather, the challenge is to slow the production of greenhouse gases immediately, so as to avoid the most sudden and catastrophic climate changes. If trends con-

tinue unabated, only radical, draconian measures would be sufficient to save the climate later on. Chlorofluorocarbons, which account for about 15 percent of the annual increment of gases responsible for global warming, are the emissions easiest to eliminate. Used as refrigerants, solvents, and blowing agents for insulation and other plastic foams, CFCs have in recent years become ubiquitous in industrial societies. In addition to warming the earth, these chemicals are destroying the protective ozone layer. For that reason, many countries are in the process of phasing them out and replacing them with substitute chemicals.

Under the Montreal Protocol of 1987, most industrial countries have agreed to phase out CFC production by 2000. This was a good start, but is not enough to protect either the climate or the ozone layer. Global CFC production has been growing at a rate of 30 percent annually, and even today's CFC levels will not be reflected fully in global temperatures for at least a decade. Additional industrial uses of chlorine are compounding the problem.

Global warming cannot be slowed unless all countries, including developing ones that do not currently produce CFCs, join in a commitment to stop production entirely by the late nineties. In addition, it is important that emissions of CFCs from existing refrigerators and air conditioners during servicing be kept to a minimum and that limits be adopted on the production of other chlorine compounds.

Of the carbon dioxide that is being added to the atmosphere, about one-fifth—equal to 10 percent of the additional greenhouse gases—is coming from deforestation in tropical countries. These figures are imprecise at best, but global warming cannot be controlled without an effective strategy to halt rampant deforestation.

In Brazil, Indonesia, and elsewhere, there are vast economic and social pressures pushing human settlements even further into the remaining forests. Broad-based development strategies combined with an infusion of international funding to protect forests and to reforest cleared areas are essential.

Large-scale planting of trees is a relatively inexpensive means of trapping carbon, and is key to protecting the climate. In addition, uncontrolled development in the tropics has to be restrained and alternative livelihoods found for the millions of desperate people who are now forced into destroying forests.

REDIRECTING ENERGY TRENDS

The most serious challenge in controlling global warming lies in reducing dependence on fossil fuels. Today's energy systems are in large measure run on carbon-based fuels that have been buried in the earth for millions of years. When oil, coal, and natural gas are burned, the carbon that makes up the fuels combines with oxygen to form carbon dioxide. Nearly 6 billion tons of carbon are liberated in this way each year, or more than a ton for each person on the planet. Carbon dioxide contributes 40 percent of the gases now warming the atmosphere, while the nitrous oxide and methane liberated from fossil fuels cause additional warming.

The World Conference on the Changing Atmosphere held in Toronto in June 1988 found a need to cut fossil fuel use by 20 percent by 2005, and national policymakers are now considering similar goals. But cuts of such a magnitude will require extraordinary efforts—probably more than politicians yet realize (see Figure 2). Indeed, without policy changes, recent trends suggest that the world is headed toward an 80 percent increase in carbon emissions in the next two decades.

The one thing that could turn this around is a commitment to improved energy efficiency. While new energy sources such as solar or nuclear power take time to develop on a large scale, efficiency can be improved right away. From 1973 to 1986, energy efficiency in the industrial countries increased at such a pace that by the mid-eighties fossil-fuel use and carbon emissions were about 25 percent lower than projected.

Today, there are a host of improved technologies available that use far less energy than those now in place. Today's cars that get just 25 miles per gallon of gasoline can be replaced by ones that get upward of 60 miles per gallon, and 60-watt light bulbs can be replaced by 13-watt bulbs that give as much light. Since much of the world's electricity is generated with coal and other fossil fuels, using electricity more efficiently is especially important.

Most official energy projections assume that worldwide energy efficiency will continue to increase by between 0.5 and 1.0 percent per year. But carbon dioxide buildup is ongoing and cumulative. Even a 1 percent rate of efficiency improvement would allow an increase in atmospheric carbon dioxide from 349 parts per million in 1988 to about 600 parts per million in 2075.

An alternative energy scenario developed by William Chandler, an energy analyst with Battelle Pacific Northwest Laboratories, demonstrates that a successful effort to improve worldwide efficiency by 2 percent annually would hold carbon dioxide concentrations to 463 parts per million in 2075 and thus substantially slow global warming.

Although many nations have implemented effective programs to improve energy efficiency in the past decade, it is generally agreed that higher energy prices were key to the vast improvements that have been made. Now that prices are down, the efficiency revolution is beginning to peter out. In the United States, for example, energy efficiency has hardly improved since 1986.

Therein lies a challenge: how to improve efficiency in a period of low energy prices. One essential step has to be higher energy taxes designed to ensure that climate change and other environmental costs of fossil-fuel use are reflected in the prices that consumers pay. This can be accomplished by excise taxes on gasoline and other fuels or across the board "carbon taxes" on all fossil fuels. Such taxes would hit coal particularly hard, since it produces more carbon per unit of energy than does either oil or natural gas. Electricity prices would rise, but so would conservation.

Large-scale programs to invest in improved efficiency in buildings are also essential. State and local governments can provide building owners with technical assistance and utility companies can be encouraged to invest in improved building efficiency rather than new plants. Also important are a combination of fuel economy standards and financial incentives to encourage the production of much more efficient automobiles. Just by using technologies available today, new cars could achieve an efficiency of at least 45 miles per gallon by the year 2000.

Even while energy efficiency is being improved, there is a clear need to continue the process of developing alternative energy sources. The outlines of a successful strategy already exist. The development of renewable energy—solar, wind, and geothermal power—has been pursued with notable success by governments and private companies since the mid-seventies. Solar collectors are a major source of hot water in Israel, wind power has taken hold in California, and geothermal energy is a major electricity source in the Philippines. However, a general takeoff in renewable energy development has yet to occur, and future advances are threatened by low energy prices and flagging government commitments.

If these energy forms are to serve as a major substitute for fossil fuels within the next decade or two, a renewed commitment to their development will have to be made almost immediately. Accelerated research and

Million tons of carbon

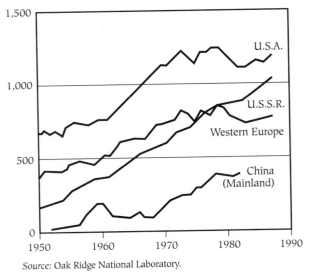

Source: Oak Ridge National Laboratory.

FIGURE 2 *Carbon Emissions from Fossil Fuels, 1950–1987*

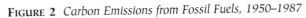

development and new programs for commercialization are particularly important.

The other alternative to fossil fuels is nuclear power. Already used to provide about 15 percent of the world's electricity, nuclear power receives strong support from many national governments, and its expansion could reduce fossil-fuel dependence. Unlike renewable energy, however, nuclear power's problems are growing. It has become increasingly expensive and accident prone in the past decade. And the critical problem of disposing of radioactive wastes remains unresolved.

Nuclear power's key obstacle is public acceptability particularly on the part of those who live near proposed plants. What is indisputable is that for nuclear power to make a real contribution to slowing global warming, hundreds of additional reactors would be needed. Unless the technology were completely revamped, that scale of expansion would be unacceptable.

REVISING NATIONAL ENERGY POLICIES

It was only a few days after Hansen's disturbing testimony that national debates over the world's energy future reopened. Policy analysts, editorial writers, and politicians were soon calling for fundamental changes in direction.

Unfortunately, advocates for everything from nuclear power to hydrogen energy have used this new threat to buttress their old arguments rather than to rethink their prejudices. Old battlelines first established when high oil prices commanded the nation's attention have in many cases been redrawn.

Nonetheless, many countries have begun to consider the possibility of lowering their dependence on fossil fuels. Australia, Austria, Denmark, Germany, and New Zealand have all agreed to meet or go beyond the Toronto goal of reducing carbon dioxide emissions 20 percent by 2005, citing improved energy efficiency and increasing reliance on renewable energy technologies as key policy tools. The European Community and other industrial nations have committed to freezing these emissions.

But the United States remains noticeably absent from the ever-growing list of industrialized countries taking actions to address global warming. In the National Energy Strategy released early in 1991, President Bush failed even to mention the need to reduce reliance on the fossil fuels responsible for carbon dioxide emissions. In fact, the policy document that is meant to guide America's energy future would actually result in an increase in carbon dioxide emissions of 26 percent between 1990 and 2010.

Other energy legislation currently before the U.S. Congress is more promising. Senator Timothy Wirth (D-CO) introduced the National Energy Efficiency and Development Act of 1991. The bill would improve the nation's energy efficiency by encouraging residential, commercial, and industrial efficiency standards, boost funding for renewable energy technologies, and provide tax incentives for efficiency investments—all measures that would tend to limit carbon emissions.

But as the Administration's energy strategy reveals, energy policymaking is often driven by self-interested industries and unions, and some—such as the oil and coal lobbies—have long pushed for policies that accelerate global warming. Key legislative committees are dominated by representatives of states and provinces that produce fossil fuels; many of the laws and tax breaks that emerge are intended to propel their growth. The tendency is simply to add global warming to a long list of considerations that go into making energy policy.

This is not enough. If the climate is to be preserved, it must become the cornerstone of national energy policymaking. Fortunately, most of the changes needed are in the longrun economical and, so, can promote national economic strength as well. But if energy policymaking continues to be the domain of short-term thinking and narrow political considerations, we should all probably begin packing for Alaska.

What would a serious commitment to slowing global warming look like? It would logically include a worldwide commitment to 50-mile-per-gallon automobile fleets, and an effort to gradually phase out coal-fired power production by improving efficiency and developing renewable energy sources. Worldwide spending on solar energy technologies could be expanded tenfold, with the goal of making it the energy source of choice for villages and suburbs by the end of the century.

A COMMON PROBLEM

In his 1970 essay "The Tragedy of the Commons," Garrett Hardin noted the enormous difficulty that people have in managing resources whose ownership is communal or poorly defined. Like the village commons that is prone to overgrazing, so today are oceans, international rivers, and the atmosphere subject to all forms of abuse. The undermining of the global climate is in some sense the ultimate tragedy of the commons. No individual nation can stop it, and we will face the tragic consequences of failing to act (see Table 1).

If climate change is to be controlled, international action may have to precede rather than follow national actions. Already, business and political leaders are arguing against stringent national policies on the grounds that by themselves they would hardly make a difference. This is particularly true for small nations that understandably perceive themselves as impotent in the face of global changes caused for the most part by the actions of their larger neighbors.

TABLE 1 *Carbon Emissions from Fossil Fuels, Selected Countries, 1987*

COUNTRY	CARBON (million tons)	CARBON PER CAPITA (tons)	CARBON PER DOLLAR GNP (grams)
U.S.A.	1,224	2.28	276
U.S.S.R	1,014	1.62	427
W. Europe	792	.94	178
China	555	.24	1,892
Japan	248	.92	154
India	150	.09	652
Canada	106	1.85	239
World	5,311	1.06	311

Source: Oak Ridge National Laboratory.

The first step in dealing with this issue globally is scientific cooperation. Already, the World Meteorological Organization and the International Council of Scientific Unions have been conducting research and coordinating international discussion on climate change for several years. Climate scientists now meet on a regular basis to assess research results and to consider policy option. At a meeting in Bellagio, Italy, in November 1987, a clear consensus was reached about the looming threat of global climate change and the need to initiate frank policy discussions.

The process of formulating an international policy response began in earnest in June 1988 at the World Conference on the Changing Atmosphere, held in Toronto and sponsored by the Canadian government. Although not a formal conference of governments, the Toronto meeting included the prime ministers of Canada and Norway and the top environmental officials of several other countries. The final statement of the conference concluded with a strong call to international action.

The conference statement went on to recommend more ambitious efforts to phase out CFCs and to reduce global carbon emissions by 20 percent by the year 2005. Half of this reduction is to be achieved via improved energy efficiency and half by the development of new energy sources.

If such goals are to be achieved, they must first be formalized in an international treaty. The Montreal Protocol on ozone protection provides a model for such an effort, as does the United Nations-sponsored Convention on Long-Range Transboundary Air Pollution, agreed to by 34 nations in Eastern and Western Europe and North America in 1979. However, for a global warming treaty to be effective, it must be far broader in scope and include additional nations.

In December 1990 a United Nations General Assembly resolution set in motion a negotiating process that could result in a global warming treaty to be signed at the 1992 United Nations Conference on Environment and Development held in Brazil. The first meeting of the Intergovernmental Negotiating Committee, set up to draft the treaty, took place near Washington, D.C., in February 1991. So far, the complex and contentious discussions involving countries of vastly different economic backgrounds have moved slowly. While European nations argue for a strong detailed treaty, the U.S. government is still playing a game of delay.

Developing countries argue that if they are going to improve efficiency vastly and reforest millions of acres, they will need funding from richer nations. One possible solution would be to create an international fund that invests in energy efficiency and reforestation, paid for by an excise tax on fossil-fuel consumption in the industrial countries.

Although the first negotiating meeting did not tackle the substantive issues of reducing greenhouse gas emissions, a treaty process is now underway. The United States, to date, has consistently opposed binding commitments to carbon reductions. But the administration must now face growing evidence that carbon reductions are economically feasible: the release in early 1991 of two studies by the National Academy of Sciences and the Congressional Office of Technology Assessment that point out the need to adopt cost-effective steps to reduce greenhouse gas emissions.

Bringing the nations of the world together to redirect their energy policies, to reforest their landscapes, and to spend millions of dollars on protecting the atmosphere may seem impossible. But there really isn't any choice. Global warming is an environmental threat on a new scale. Like the religious notion of original sin, climate change will loom as a continuing threat for humanity to consider and ultimately to manage.

Study Questions

1. Go over Flavin's article and itemize his rendition of the consequences of the global warming. If weather patterns are being radically altered, as he predicts, could this affect food production?
2. Why will the greenhouse effect cause the oceans to rise? If the oceans rise 6 to 9 feet as some have predicted, many coastlines will be flooded. What will be the effect on populations? How will nations cope with this?

67

The Greenhouse Effect: Hype and Hysteria

Dixy Lee Ray and Louis Guzzo

In this selection from their book Trashing the Planet *(1990), Ray and Guzzo argue that scientists like James Hansen are irresponsible in inferring from meager evidence that the world is doomed unless we follow a radically new course. Our authors argue that we cannot even predict a few days' weather accurately, let alone a century's. Present predictions are slippery at best, and it depends on whose computer models you're using. Vast cosmic (the Sun) and global (volcanic activity) causes probably exercise more influence on weather than human activity. At the end of this essay, Ray and Guzzo also take issue with those who believe a catastrophe will come about due to the depletion of the ozone layer.*

A biographical sketch of Ray and Guzzo is included in Reading 63.

The year 1988 ended on a high note of environmental hysteria about global warming, fueled by an unusually hot, dry summer (in the United States). Testifying at a Senate hearing, NASA's James Hansen claimed that the high temperatures presaged the onset of the long debated "greenhouse effect" caused by increased carbon dioxide (CO_2) in the atmosphere

Forgotten was the harsh winter of 1982, or of 1978, when, for example, barges carrying coal and heating oil froze in river ice and more than 200 people lost their lives in the cold weather.

Only days after *Time* magazine featured a doomed, overheated Earth as its "man of the year" for 1988, Alaska experienced the worst cold in its history. The freezing weather set in on January 12, 1989. Twenty different locations in our most northerly state recorded their lowest-ever temperatures, mainly in the range of –50 to –65 degrees Fahrenheit. At Tanana, near Fairbanks, –75 degrees Fahrenheit was reached. (The all-time low recorded anywhere in Alaska was –80 degrees in January 1971 at a Prospect Creek pipeline station.) The cold persisted; it did not moderate and begin to move south until the first week of February. Old-timers agreed that no such cold had ever been experienced before, and they expressed amazement that the temperature remained a chilly –16 degrees Fahrenheit along the coast even with an 81-knot wind blowing. This was unheard of, since usually it is coldest when the wind is quiet. In early February, the cold seeped down

from Alaska along both sides of the Rocky Mountains, bringing near-record lows both to the Pacific Northwest and throughout the Midwest south to Texas and eventually to the mid-Atlantic and New England states. Proponents of the "greenhouse-is-here-global-warming-has-begun" theory were very quiet during these weeks.

To be fair, even if the projected greenhouse warming should occur, no one would expect it to happen all at once or without intervening cold spells. So let's examine the situation more closely.

Of course, the earth, with its enveloping blanket of atmosphere, constitutes a "greenhouse." This fact has never been at issue. Indeed, were it not for the greenhouse function of air, the earth's surface might be like the moon, bitterly cold (–270 degrees Fahrenheit) at night and unbearably hot (+212 degrees Fahrenheit) during the day. Although the amount of solar energy reaching the moon is essentially the same as that reaching earth, the earth's atmosphere acts like a filter. Of the incoming solar radiation, about 20 percent is absorbed in the atmosphere, about 50 percent reaches and warms the earth's surface, and the rest is reflected back into space. As the earth's surface is warmed up, infrared radiation is emitted. It is the presence of CO_2 (and water vapor, methane, hydrocarbon, and a few other gases) in the atmosphere that absorbs the long wavelength infrared radiation, thereby producing the warming "greenhouse effect." This accounts for a net warming of the earth's atmosphere system of about 55 degrees Fahrenheit. Without this natural greenhouse, it would be difficult to sustain life on this planet.

All the important "greenhouse gases" are produced in nature, as well as by humans. For example, CO_2 comes naturally from the respiration of all living organisms and from decaying vegetation. It is also injected into the atmosphere by volcanoes and forest and grass fires. Carbon dioxide from man-made sources comes primarily from burning fossil fuels for home and building heat, for transportation, and for industrial processes. The amount of CO_2 released into the atmosphere is huge and it is commonly believed that it is divided about evenly between natural and man-made sources.

Hydrocarbons come from growing plants, especially coniferous trees, such as fir and pine, and from various industries. In the transportation arena, hydrocarbons result from incomplete oxidation of gasoline. Both hydrocarbons and methane also enter the atmosphere through the metabolism of cows and other ruminants. It is estimated that American cows produce about 50 mil-

Reprinted from *Trashing the Planet* (Washington, D.C.: Regnery Gateway, 1990) by permission. Notes deleted.

lion tons of these gases per year—and there is no control technology for such emissions. Methane seeps into the air from swamps, coal mines, and rice paddies; it is often "flared" from oil wells. The largest source of greenhouse gas may well be termites, whose digestive activities are responsible for about 50 billion tons of CO_2 and methane annually. This is 10 times more than the present world production of CO_2 from burning fossil fuel. Methane may be oxidized in the atmosphere, leading to an estimated one billion tons of carbon monoxide per year. All in all, the atmosphere is a grand mixture of gases, in a constant state of turbulence, and yet maintained in an overall state of dynamic balance.

But now this balance appears to be disturbed as CO_2 and the other major greenhouse gases are on the rise, increasing their concentration in the air at a rate of about one percent per year. CO_2 is responsible for about half of the increase. Analysis of air bubbles trapped in glacial ice and of carbon isotopes in tree rings and ocean sediment cores indicate that CO_2 levels hovered around 260 to 280 parts per million from the end of the last ice age (10,000 years ago) till the mid-nineteenth century, except for an anomalous rise 300 years ago. And these measurements also show that CO_2 concentrations have varied widely (by 20 percent) as the earth has passed through glacial and interglacial periods. While today's 25 percent increase in CO_2 can be accounted for by the burning of fossil fuels, what caused the much greater increases in the prehistoric past?

The present increase has brought the CO_2 level to 340 parts per million, up about 70 parts per million. If we add the greater amounts of methane, hydrocarbons, and so forth, there is now a total of about 407 parts per million of greenhouse gases. This is large enough so that from the greenhouse effect alone we should have experienced a global warming of about two to four degrees Fahrenheit. But this has not happened.

The observed and recorded temperature pattern since 1880 does not fit with the CO_2 greenhouse warming calculations. During the 1880s, there was a period of cooling, followed by a warming trend. The temperature rose by one degree Fahrenheit during 1900 to 1940, then fell from 1940 to 1965, and then began to rise again, increasing by about 0.3 degrees Fahrenheit since 1975. When all these fluctuations are analyzed, it appears unlikely that there has been any overall warming in the last 50 years. And if the temperature measurements taken in the northern hemisphere are corrected for the urban effect—the so called "heat island" that exists over cities due mainly to the altered albedo from removing vegetation—then it is probable that not only has there been no warming; there may have been a slight cooling. It all depends on whose computer model you choose to believe.

Clearly, there is still something that is not understood about global conditions and about the weather links between the oceans and the atmosphere. Have the experts fully taken into account the role of the sea as a sink or reservoir for CO_2, including the well known fact that much more CO dissolves in cold water than in warm? Interest in the greenhouse gases and projections of global warming has stimulated greater interest in the role that the oceans play in influencing moderately or even drastically changing global climate. The oceans hold more CO_2 than does the atmosphere, 60 times more. Complex circulation patterns that involve waters of different temperature, together with the activities of marine organisms that deposit carbonate in their skeletons, carry carbon dioxide to the depths of the ocean.

Recall that all the public furor about global warming was triggered in June 1988, when NASA scientist James Hansen testified in the U.S. Senate that the greenhouse effect is changing the climate now! He said he was 99 percent sure of it, and that "1988 would be the warmest year on record, unless there is some remarkable, improbable cooling in the remainder of the year." Well, there was. Almost while Dr. Hansen was testifying, the eastern tropical Pacific Ocean underwent a remarkable, improbable cooling—a sudden drop in temperature of seven degrees. No one knows why. But the phenomenon is not unknown; it is called La Nina to distinguish it from the more commonly occurring El Nino, or warm current, and it has happened 19 times in the last 102 years.

Dr. Hansen did not consider the possibility of La Nina, because his computer program does not take sea temperatures into account. Yet the oceans cover 73 percent of the earth's surface.

When people, including scientists, talk "global," it is hard to believe that they can ignore 73 percent of the globe, but obviously they sometimes do. It is all the more astonishing to ignore ocean-atmosphere interactions, especially in the Pacific, when it is well established that El Nino has profound and widespread effects on weather patterns and temperatures; does it not follow that La Nina may also? Indeed, some atmospheric scientists credit the severely cold winter of 1988–89 to the earlier temperature drop in the tropical Pacific.

Once again, since the greenhouse gases are increasing, what's keeping the earth from warming up? There are a number of possible explanations. Perhaps there is some countervailing phenomenon that hasn't been taken into account; perhaps the oceans exert greater lag than expected and the warming is just postponed; perhaps the sea and its carbonate-depositing inhabitants are a much greater sink than some scientists believe; perhaps the increase in CO_2 stimulates more plant growth and removal of more CO_2 than calculated; perhaps there is some other greenhouse gas, like water vapor, that is more important than CO_2; perhaps varying cloud cover provides a greater feedback and self-correcting mechanism than has been taken into account; perhaps.... The fact is, there is simply not enough good data on most of these processes to know for sure what is happening in these enormous, turbulent, interlinked, dynamic systems like atmosphere and oceanic circulation. The only thing that can be stated with certainty is that they do affect the weather. So also do forces outside the planet, and in a moment we'll look at the sun in this regard.

First, we must acknowledge that some zealots in the greenhouse issue make much of deforestation, especially in the tropical rain forests, but this topic is marked more by emotion bordering on hysteria than on solid scientific data. Good measurements on CO_2 uptake and oxygen production in tropical rain forests are lacking. Such information could be critical, because we know that in temperate climates mature trees and climax forests add little in the way of photosynthetic activity and consequent CO_2 removal from the atmosphere. Mature trees, like all living things, metabolize more slowly as they grow old. A forest of young, vigorously growing trees will remove five to seven tons more CO_2 per acre per year than old growth. There are plenty of good reasons to preserve old growth forests, but redressing the CO_2 balance is not one of them. If we are really interested (as we should be) in reducing atmospheric CO_2, we should be vigorously pursuing reforestation and the planting of trees and shrubs, including in urban areas, where local impacts on the atmosphere are greatest.

Reforestation *has* been going on through enlightened forestry practices on private lands by timber companies and as a result of changes in agriculture and land use. In the United States, the average annual wood growth is now more than three times what it was in 1920, and the growing stock has increased 18 percent from 1952 to 1977. Forests in America continue to increase in size, even while supplying a substantial fraction of the world's timber needs.

Finally, it should be kept in mind that when a tree is cut for timber, it will no longer remove CO_2 from the atmosphere, but it won't release its stored carbon either—until or unless it is burned or totally decayed. In the whole deforestation question, it would be interesting to try to determine what effect the deforestation of Europe had on temperature and climate in the nineteenth century, and, similarly, what the effect was of the earlier deforestation of the Mediterranean area and the Middle East.

If we study history, we find that there is no good or widely accepted explanation for why the earth's temperature and climate were as they were at any particular time in the past, including the recurring ice ages and the intervening warm periods. What caused the "little ice age" of the late seventeenth century and why was it preceded by 800 years of relative warmth? Is all this really due to human activity? What about natural phenomena? Recent studies of major deep sea currents in the Atlantic ocean suggest a causative relation to the onset of ice ages. Occasional unusual actions by nature can release great quantities of CO_2 and other greenhouse gases to the atmosphere.

I received my lesson in humility, my respect for the size and vast power of natural forces on May 18, 1980. For those who might not instantly recognize that date, it was a Sunday, a beautiful spring morning when at 8:31 Mount St. Helens erupted with the force of more than 500 atomic bombs. Gases and particulate matter were propelled 80,000 feet, approximately 15 miles, into the stratosphere and deposited above the ozone layer. The eruption continued for nearly 12 hours and more than four billion tons of earth were displaced.

Because Mount St. Helens is relatively accessible, there were many studies conducted and good data are available on the emissions—at least those that occurred after May 18. For the remaining seven months of 1980, Mount St. Helens released 910,000 metric tons of CO_2, 220,000 metric tons of sulfur dioxide, and unknown amounts of aerosols into the atmosphere. Many other gases, including methane, water vapor, carbon monoxide, and a variety of sulfur compounds were also released, and emissions still continue to seep from the crater and from fumaroles and crevices.

Gigantic as it was, Mount St. Helens was not a large volcanic eruption. It was dwarfed by Mount St. Augustine and Mount Redoubt in Alaska in 1976 and 1989 and El Chicon in Mexico in 1982. El Chicon was an exceptionally sulfurous eruption. The violence of its explosion sent more than 100 million tons of sulfur gases high into the stratosphere. Droplets of sulfuric acid formed; these continue to rain down onto the earth's surface. The earth, at present, appears to be in a period of active volcanism, with volcanic eruptions occurring at a rate of about 100 per year. Most of these are in remote locations, where accurate measurement of the gaseous emissions is not possible, but they must be considerable. Some estimates from large volcanic eruptions in the past suggest that all of the air polluting materials produced by man since the beginning of the industrial revolution do not begin to equal the quantities of toxic materials, aerosols, and particulates spewed into the air from just three volcanoes: Krakatoa in Indonesia in 1883, Mount Katmai in Alaska in 1912, and Hekla in Iceland in 1947. Despite these prodigious emissions, Krakatoa, for example, produced some chilly winters, spectacular sunsets, and a global temperature drop of 0.3 degrees Centigrade, but no climate change. From written records, we also know that the famous "year without a summer" that followed the eruption of Mount Tambora in 1816 meant that the summer temperature in Hartford, Connecticut, did not exceed 82 degrees Fahrenheit. No doom.

We can conclude from these volcanic events that the atmosphere is enormous and its capacity to absorb and dilute pollutants is also very great. This is no excuse, of course, to pollute the air deliberately, which would be an act of folly. But it does give us some perspective on events.

So far, we have considered only those phenomena that occur on earth that might influence global temperature, weather, and eventually the climate. "Weather" means the relatively short-term fluctuations in temperature, precipitation, winds, cloudiness, and so forth, that shift and change over periods of hours, days, or weeks. Weather patterns may be cyclic, more or less repeating themselves every few years. The "climate," on the other hand, is generally accepted to be the mean of weather changes over a period of about 30 years. Weather may change rapidly, but the climate may remain essentially the same over thousands of years, as it probably has for the last 8,000 years.

Now, what about the effects on weather of extraterrestrial phenomena? After all, it is the sun that determines the climate on earth—but the role of the sun, with its ever-shifting solar radiation, is generally ignored as being inconsequential in affecting shorter-term weather patterns. But is this really so?

Consider: the earth shifts in its position relative to the sun. Its orbit is eccentric, varying over a period of 97,000 years. The inclination of the earth's axis shifts with respect to the ecliptic over a cycle of 41,000 years, and the precession of the equinox varies over a period of 21,000 years. How do these shifts affect the amount of solar radiation reaching the earth? Some astronomers believe that at least for the last 500,000 to one million years, these phenomena are related to the initiation and dissipation of glacial and interglacial intervals.

Although it may seem to us that the sun is stable and stationary, it is in fact whirling through the Milky Way galaxy, taking its family of planets with it. Activity on the sun itself goes through periods of relative quiet and then erupts into flares and protuberances, sunspots, and gigantic upheavals that "rain" solar material out into space. One recent solar storm was measured at 43,000 miles across. This produced the largest solar flare ever recorded. Some of the increased solar radiation from such storms reaches the earth and disrupts radio communication and television transmission and increases the aurora borealis. Solar activity in the form of storms seen as sunspots has a span of roughly 11 years. It seems that the sunspots whirl clockwise for about 11 years, then reverse and go counterclockwise for another 11 years. The controlling mechanism for this reversal is unknown.

Then there is another variable. The sun "flickers"; that is, it dims and brightens slightly over a period of about 70 years. When it dims, the sunspots attain lower maxima. When the sun brightens, the sunspots have higher maxima than "normal." Although this dimming and brightening has been suspected for some time, the first actual measurement of such a "flicker" was made on April 4, 1980, when a satellite measuring solar radiation outside the earth's atmosphere recorded a 0.2 percent drop in radiation. Changes in solar radiation are now routinely measured.

Coupled with the activity of the sun, there is the moon's gravitational force, to which the earth's waters respond daily and in 28-day cycles of tides. Also, there are 20-year and 60-year tidal cycles, as well as longer ones. Moreover, the solid land also responds to the moon's gravitational force, but because we move with the ground, we do not feel it. Recently, a 556-year variation in the moon's orbit around the earth was analyzed; some meteorologists believe that the occasional confluence of all these sun-and-moon cycles may trigger dramatic changes in ocean currents and temperatures. And it is now widely acknowledged that the oceans are a major influence on the climate. There is also a 500-to-600-year cycle in volcanic activity, which appears to be near a peak at the present time.

Let's consider again. Does all this variability in solar activity really have anything to do with weather or climate? No one knows for certain. But studies are continuing, and Dr. John Eddy of the National Center for Atmospheric Research has found an interesting correlation between decades of low sunspot activity and cold periods, such as the "little ice age" of the seventeenth century, when there was a virtual absence of sunspot activity between 1645 and 1715, and decades of high sunspot activity with warm temperatures on earth.

Since the sunspot cycle is not perfectly regular and varies considerably, how do scientists determine the extent of sunspot activity that occurred decades or centuries ago? This is a neat piece of scientific detective work that merits a brief explanation. It involves another extraterrestrial phenomenon—cosmic radiation.

Cosmic rays consist of high energy particles that enter the earth's atmosphere from outer space. These energetic particles split the nuclei of atmospheric gases, giving rise to some of the background radiation to which all living organisms are exposed. Among the fission products are Potassium-40 and Carbon-14, which get into the food chain and are eaten (by animals) or absorbed (by plants), and that is one of the reasons that the bodies of all living organisms are radioactive. Of these two fission products, it is Carbon-14 that is the most interesting for tracing events in the past.

C-14, whose half-life is a relatively short 5,570 years, is being produced continuously in the atmosphere (through interaction with cosmic rays) and is continuously taken up by *living* organisms, but not by dead ones. Therefore, by measuring the amount of C-14 in dead or fossil material, one can infer the date of death. This is called carbon-dating. C-14 is a very good but not perfect clock of history, because the assumption is that the formation of C-14 is not only continuous but also that it occurs at a steady rate. But what Dr. Eddy has determined is that the rate of formation varies with the amount of cosmic radiation, which, in turn, varies with the amount of sunspot activity, because high solar activity also creates more solar wind that can compress the earth's magnetic field. This stronger field is more effective in shielding cosmic rays from the earth's atmosphere, which means that less C-14 is formed during periods of high sunspot activity. Less C-14 equates with warmer periods on earth.

Taking advantage of these phenomena, Dr. Eddy measured the C-14 radioactivity in tree rings in trees that are up to 5,000 years old. Keep in mind that the years (rings) of low C-14 equate with years of high solar activity and warm temperatures. Dr. Eddy recorded 12 prolonged periods with either unusually cold or unusually mild winters over the last 5,000 years. These correlations between solar activity and weather on earth seem good; his measurements identified the terrible winter of 1683–84, also recorded in the novel *Lorna Doone*, when trees in Somerset, England, froze and many exploded from the buildup of internal ice.

If Dr. Eddy's work and theory hold up, the mid-twentieth century was an unusually warm period, and the earth may be set soon to enter a slow return to cooler temperatures. Besides, in geologically recent times, ice ages recur about every 11,000 to 12,000 years, and it is now 11,000 years since the last one. How do all these complications interact with the greenhouse effect? Again, no one really knows. All we can say with confidence is that it is probably more complicated than many environmentalists seem to believe.

When we consider all of the complex geophysical phenomena that might affect the weather and climate on earth, from changes in ocean temperatures and currents, volcanic eruptions, solar storms, and cyclic movements of heavenly bodies, it is clear that none of these is under human control or could be influenced by human activity. Is the "greenhouse effect" and its theoretical enhancement by increases in atmospheric CO_2 from human sources more powerful or capable of overshadowing all other planetary influences? Until the supporters of the man-produced-CO_2-caused-global-warming-theory can explain warm and cold episodes in the past, we should remain skeptical. What caused the 80 parts per million increase in CO_2 during a 100-year period 300 years ago and the high peak—many times anything measured since—of 130,000 years ago?

The alteration of the chemical content of the air by *human* production of greenhouse gases, however, is something that man *can* control. And because no one knows what the ultimate consequences of heightened CO_2 might be, it is reasonable and responsible to reduce human contribution wherever possible.

Fortunately, there are ways to accomplish this. For starters, we can phase out the use of fossil fuel for making electricity and turn to the established and proven technology that has no adverse impact on the atmosphere—nuclear power. The energy of the atom now produces 20 percent of the electricity in the United States—more than the total of all electricity used in 1950. The number of nuclear power plants can be increased.

Second, we can shift to an essentially all-electric economy, utilizing electricity for direct heating of buildings and homes and extending the use of electric processes in industry. With enough electricity available, it can also be used to desalinate sea water and purify the fresh water sources that have become polluted. It can also be used to split water and obtain hydrogen, which has great potential as a clean fuel for transportation. Its "burning" produces only water vapor.

And we can turn, once again, to electric buses and trains, and eventually to electric automobiles.

None of these shifts away from fossil fuels will be easy or fast, but if we have an abundance of electricity from nuclear power plants, it can be done. That would leave fossil fuels for the important synthetics and plastic industries, and for the manufacture of medicinals, pesticides, and fertilizers.

There are also two important caveats; though steps to reduce CO_2 production may be possible for an advanced, highly technical, industrialized society with plenty of electricity, the infrastructure to make use of it, and money to spend, the story is different in the non-industrialized world. In China, for example, 936 million metric tons of coal were burned in 1987. Who is going to tell China to stop or to change? What alternative do the Chinese have? No matter what we in the Western world do, the amount of CO_2 arising from human use of fossil fuel will not be significantly reduced.

The second caveat is to remember that draconian measures intended to make rapid and large decreases in CO_2 formation won't do much good if they are so costly that they seriously impede the economy and degrade our standard of living without achieving the desired result. Certainly the level of atmospheric CO_2 is increasing, but nothing in all our knowledge of weather and climate guarantees that global warming will inevitably occur. It may, or may not; the uncertainties are legion. The computer models are too simplistic and include too many estimates and guesses and too little about the role of the hydrosphere, both water vapor and the oceans.

Notwithstanding all this, deliberate, reasoned steps can and should be taken to lower CO_2 emissions; responsible stewardship of the planet demands no less.

Finally, let's suppose that a worst case scenario does develop and that global warming does occur. If the warming caused polar ice to melt, only that on land, as in the Antarctic continent (or the glaciers of Greenland), would materially affect global sea level. When ice floats, as in the Arctic ocean, it already displaces approximately the same amount of water that would result if it were to melt. (There would be some slight thermal expansion.) Whether Arctic ice stays solid or melts would no more cause sea level to rise than ice cubes melting would cause a full glass of ice water to overflow.

Analysis of sea level data since 1900 indicates that the oceans may be rising at a rate of 10 to 25 centimeters per century (about 0.1 inch per year). The data are very sketchy and uncertain. The sea rise, if it is real, is not uniform and other phenomena, such as land subsidence or upthrust, the building and erosion of beaches by weather, and the variation of inshore currents, could all affect the few measurements that are available.

Some scientists postulate that the west Antarctic ice sheet, which is anchored on bedrock below sea level, could melt and add enough water to raise the world sea level by six or seven meters. This would be disastrous for most coastlines, but if it should happen, it would probably take several hundred years, and there is currently neither observational evidence nor scientific measurements to indicate that it is under way. In fact, new measurements show that the glaciers in Antarctica are growing, not melting.

Air temperatures in Antarctica average −40 degrees Centigrade. A five-degree rise in temperature to −35 degrees Centigrade is certainly not enough to melt ice. But somewhat warmer sea water (above one degree Centigrade) might get under the ice sheet and start it slipping into the sea; then it would float and displace an enormous volume of water, causing the sea level to rise. But this is also a very unlikely "what if?" with no evidence to support it.

Now, what about ozone in the stratosphere; how significant are the "holes" measured above Antarctica? Are we humans destroying our protective cover? Quite a few people seem to think so.

But let me start with a quotation from an analysis of the ozone problem published in the 1987–88 Annual Report of the Rand Corporation:

> The extent of ozone depletion and the severity of the consequences of projected emission levels are extremely uncertain. Projections of future depletion are based on complex simulation models that have not been reconciled with the limited available measurements. . . .
>
> Because of pervasive uncertainty about the likely extent of future ozone depletion, its relationship to the quantity of potential ozone depleters emitted, its effect on the biosphere, and the appropriate valuation of these consequences, it is not currently possible to choose the level of emission-limiting regulations that will maximize welfare by optimally balancing costs of environmental damage against those of emission control. Policymakers must act in the face of this uncertainty.

Is that all perfectly clear? What the writer is trying to say, diplomatically, I think, is that nobody knows how much ozone depletion has really taken place or what effect, if any, that ozone loss may have on the environment or on living creatures. The Rand Corporation writer emphasizes that present knowledge of ozone layer thickness is full of uncertainty and that the conclusions that have been drawn are based on incomplete computer models. There is little reliable, accurate, direct measurement. Nevertheless, he says, "policymakers must act. . . ." Why? Because some doom-predicting scientists say "irreversible damage may occur"? What is their evidence?

Given the media hoopla and hysteria surrounding the ozone issue, surely it is time to examine the whole question with some sober common sense.

We know that the earth's ozone layer is turbulent. It undergoes periodic changes in thickness. Natural fluctuations are about 15 percent and it quickly returns to equilibrium. Changes appear to be both seasonal and latitudinal. Seasonal changes above Antarctica are largest when measured at the end of winter. The changes in ozone layer thickness in Antarctica have now been measured in the Arctic, as well. (No one looked until recently.)

The best measurement data indicate that the ozone layer increased in average thickness during the 1960s and decreased during 1979–86. The decreases were comparable in magnitude to the increases of the 1960s.

The term, ozone "hole," is misleading, since it persists for only a few weeks. The Antarctic ozone "hole" grew during the early 1980s, becoming large in 1985, smaller in 1986, and reaching its greatest size in 1987. In 1988, the "hole" did not appear as expected. It was finally discovered—only 15 percent as large as predicted and displaced over the ocean.

The changes in the amount of ozone appear to be related to complex chloride chemistry and the presence of nitrous oxide. Although there is widespread belief that the necessary chloride ion comes from chlorofluorocarbon (CFC) this has not been unequivocally established. On the other hand, the eruption of Mount St. Augustine (Alaska) in 1976 injected 289 billion kilograms of hydrochloric acid directly into the stratosphere. That amount is 570 times the total world production of chlorine and fluorocarbon compounds in the year 1975. Mount Erebus, which is located just 15 kilometers upwind from McMurdo Sound, has been erupting, constantly, for the last 100 years, ejecting more than 1,000 tons of chlorine per day. Since the world production of CFC peaked at 1.1 million tons per year—equivalent to 750,000 tons of chlorine, and 300 million tons of chlorine reach the atmosphere each year through evaporation of sea water alone—we cannot be sure where the stratospheric chlorine comes from, and whether humans have any effect upon it.

So much is known. Most atmospheric scientists also agree that ozone molecules are being created and destroyed naturally by very short wavelengths of ultraviolet light from the sun. Since the same narrow band of ultraviolet light that breaks down chlorofluorocarbons (CFCs) to destroy ozone also breaks down oxygen to create ozone, the result is a balance between these two processes, a competition between CFC and O_2 for the necessary solar energy. Moreover, the result depends on the relative abundance of the two gases (CFC and O_2) in the ozone layer, and data from the National Oceanic and Atmospheric Administration (NOAA) show 60,000 ozone molecules created for every one destroyed by chlorine from a CFC molecule. It is quite possible that overall depletion of ozone is *not* occurring and indeed the NOAA data from measurements taken at the surface of the earth indicate that the total amount of ozone above the United States is actually increasing. In addition, it is known that interaction of solar wind with the earth's magnetic field, which causes the auroras, can also destroy stratospheric ozone. Solar wind comes from solar flares and these are increasing in the present period of sunspot maxama.

So is the sky falling? Still being debated among atmospheric scientists is whether the recently measured ozone changes have been occurring all along or whether they are a new phenomenon sparked by human activity or perhaps a combination of both. To quote a January 1989 summary published in *Science* (Vol. 239), "the recent losses may be natural and may result from long-term fluctuations of the general circulation of the atmosphere." Some researchers, pointing out that atmospheric dynamics can cause big changes in ozone, describe a 48-hour period at the beginning of September 1988, when the ozone decreased 10 percent over a 3 million square kilometer area. Robert T. Watson, head of NASA's upper atmospheric research program, said, "In our opinion, all provisional, we do not believe that change can be chemical [that is, caused by CFCs]. It is strong evidence that *meteorological processes alone* can effectively depress areas of ozone over the Antarctic continent." Direct evidence has yet to be produced, and Robert Watson of NASA reported that the optical diffuser plate on the Nimbus satellite had deteriorated so rapidly in space that its ozone depletion measurements are "useless garbage."

Against this background of uncertainty and the conviction of some respected scientists that natural processes may account for ozone "holes," how can public officials and governmental representatives seriously consider taking drastic action—for example, to ban CFCs—as if that would "cure" the problem, if indeed there is a problem?

Consider that in the United States economy alone, CFCs, mainly freon, are used in 100 million refrigerators, 90 million cars and trucks, 40,000 supermarket display cases, and 100,000 building air conditioners. It is estimated that banning CFCs would mean changing or replacing capital equipment valued at $135 billion. And all the proposed substitutes have problems; none is in production, most of them are toxic, and many are flammable. Of course, we could always return to using toxic ammonia and sulfur dioxide! Note that one of the biggest users of freon is refrigeration, and the most important reason for refrigeration is food preservation. If the proponents of banning CFC are so anxious to reduce its use, why aren't they out campaigning for irradiating food as a substitute for refrigeration? Food irradiation is an available technology used by all our astronauts and in hospitals for patients that require a sterile environment.

We are told that the ozone hole is important because the ozone blanket blocks much of the ultraviolet light in sunshine, which, if it penetrates to the earth's surface, could cause skin cancer, eye problems, and plant damage. This could be worrisome, except that actual records from a network of recording instruments set up in 1974 to measure ultraviolet light reaching the earth's surface have shown a continuously decreasing penetration of from 0.5 percent to 1.1 percent per year. If the theories about ozone depletion were correct, ultraviolet radiation should have been increasing, not decreasing.

Furthermore, the form of skin cancer caused by ultraviolet radiation is relatively harmless, though irritating and unsightly, and 99 percent of the cases can be cured if treated in time. On the other hand, malignant melanoma, another unrelated type of skin cancer, is generally fatal. Its appearance is not related to ultraviolet radiation; its cause is unknown. Tragically, it is increasing, by 800 percent since 1935. As for plants, most are protected by several mechanisms that function to repair damage caused by ultraviolet light. The conclusion is hard to avoid: that the claims of skin cancer due to ozone loss are simply a widely repeated scare tactic.

The historian Hans Morgenthau wrote in 1946:

> Two moods determine the attitude of our civilization to the social world: confidence in the power of reason, as represented by modern science, to solve the social problems of the age, and despair at the ever renewed failure of scientific reason to solve them.
>
> The intellectual and moral history of mankind is the story of inner insecurity, of the anticipation of impending doom, of metaphysical anxieties.

John Maddox, editor of the prestigious British journal *Nature* has said that "these days there also seems to be an underlying cataclysmic sense among people. Scientists don't seem to be immune to this."

Well, they ought to be. And we ought to remember that using our technology will go a long way toward averting those cataclysmic events and the "doom-is-almost-here" philosophy that seems to have so much appeal. Scientists owe it to society to show the way to a better life and an improved environment—through quality technology.

Study Questions

1. Compare Flavin's weather statistics for 1880–1980 with Ray and Guzzo's discussion. What conclusion do you draw?
2. Could you argue that the warming of our planet would be a good thing, for while it might displace some people on islands and coastlines, it would make places like Siberia, Northern Canada, Alaska, and Greenland more habitable?
3. Compare Flavin's arguments and evidence with Ray and Guzzo's arguments. How strong is the case for a devastating greenhouse effect?

For Further Reading

Barth, M., and J. Titus, eds. *Greenhouse Effect and Sea Level Rise: A Challenge for This Generation*. New York: Van Nostrand Reinhold, 1984.

Flavin, Christopher. "Slowing Global Warming." In *State of the World 1990*. Washington, D.C.: Worldwatch Institute, 1990.

McKibbern, Bill. *The End of Nature*. New York: Random House, 1989.

Ray, Dixy Lee, and Louis Guzzo. *Trashing the Planet*. Washington, D.C.: Regnery Gateway, 1990.

Schneider, Stephen. *Global Warming: Are We Entering the Greenhouse Century?* San Francisco: Sierra Club Books, 1989.

CHAPTER FOURTEEN

Are We Conquering Hazardous Waste?

The magnificent Niagara Falls on the New York-Canadian border is one of the scenic wonders of our nation. However, the city of Niagara is one of the most polluted cities of our nation. Water falls provide inexpensive electricity, and inexpensive electricity invites industry. Along the shorelines of the Niagara River, the spiraled pipes of distilleries issue forth effluents and fill the air with the odor of chlorine and sulfides.

Nearby is Love Canal, named after its builder, William Love. In the 1960s, a young cement technician and his wife, Tim and Karen Schroeder, bought a home along this canal and began to raise a family. They built a fiberglass swimming pool enclosed by a redwood fence. One October morning in 1964 Karen noticed that the pool had risen two feet above ground. Although perplexed by this phenomenon, they decided to wait until the next summer to pull it up and replace it with a sturdier cement pool. Summer came. But when they pulled up the pool, they beheld a large gaping hole filled with a rancid yellow and blue liquid. The chemical liquid gradually rose until it covered the entire yard. It attacked the redwood posts with such a caustic bite that after some days the fence collapsed. When the waters finally receded later that summer, the gardens and shrubs were withered and scorched.

How did these liquid chemicals get into the Schroeders' back yard? Between 1947 and 1952, Hooker Chemical Company dumped 22,000 cubic tons of chemical wastes into an old canal and covered it with dirt. In 1953 Hooker sold the canal area to the school board for $1 with the stipulation that Hooker be absolved of all future responsibility for the conditions of the land. A school and hundreds of homes were built along the canal.

Already in 1959, people began noticing a strange black sludge, which gave off malodorous fumes, leaching through their basement walls. But Niagara reeks with such odors, so the inhabitants took them for granted.

On November 21, 1968, Karen's third child (Sheri) was born with a congenital heart problem, bone blockage of the nose, partial deafness, deformed ears, and a cleft palate. She was also retarded and had an enlarged liver. When her teeth came in, they appeared in double rows.

In 1976 the City of Niagara backed Hooker when the New York State Department of Environmental Concern discovered dangerous hydrocarbons (PCBs) in basements. One part per million (1 ppm) is considered a serious environmental concern. Investigators found more than 1000 ppm in these basements. Later when Karen's parents' basement was tested, the air pollution level was 1000 times the acceptable level.

During this period, Tim had broken out in a rash, suffered fatigue, and found it difficult to stay awake during the day. The Schroeders' daughter Lauri's hair began falling out, and Karen was suffering throbbing pains in her head. They suspected that the surrounding chemical pollution was the culprit, but being people of limited means, they had nowhere to go.

Benzene was found in the soil in the area, a carcinogen, which also causes headaches, fatigue, weight loss, and dizziness.

Other families began to share their stories. It was discovered that the cancer rate around Love Canal was 35% above the national average. Thirty-one percent of the babies were born with birth defects, typically hearing loss and retardation. Between 30% and 40% of the pregnant women in any given year had miscarriages. A young boy died of unexplained kidney failure.

In 1978 New York State Public Health Authorities launched a full investigation into the matter. Over 80 dangerous chemicals, including 14 chlorinated hydrocarbons, were discovered. Later another 100 chemicals were found. PCB levels were found at 100,000 ppm. Tetradioxin, used to make Agent Orange, was identified, and Hooker finally admitted that it dumped 200 tons of it into the canal (this is 1000 times the amount used to defoliate the Vietnamese jungles). New York State spent over $250 million cleaning up the site and another $67 million relocating over 700 families from the area. It sued Hooker and Occidental Petroleum, which had bought up Hooker, for $2 billion. In 1985 Occidental Petroleum settled out of court and paid many of the families settlements of between $2000 and $400,000. The State is still seeking $250 million in punitive damages.

447

The Superfund Amendments and Reauthorization Act of 1986

The 1986 amendments of CERCLA, known as the Superfund Amendments and Reauthorization Act (SARA), authorized $8.5 billion for both the emergency response and longer term (or remedial) cleanup programs. The Superfund amendments focused on:

- **Permanent remedies.** EPA must implement permanent remedies to the maximum extent practicable. A range of treatment options will be considered whenever practicable.
- **Complying with other regulations.** Applicable or relevant and appropriate standards from other federal, state, or tribal environmental laws must be met at Superfund sites where remedial actions are taken. In addition, state standards that are more stringent than federal standards must be met in cleaning up sites.
- **Alternative treatment technologies.** Cost effective treatment and recycling must be considered as an alternative to the land disposal of wastes. Under RCRA, Congress banned land disposal of some wastes. Many Superfund site wastes, therefore, will be banned from disposal on the land; alternative treatments are under development and will be used where possible.
- **Public involvement.** Citizens living near Superfund sites have been involved in the site decisionmaking process for over five years. They will continue to be a part of this process. They also will be able to apply for technical assistance grants that may further enhance their understanding of site conditions and activities.

- **State involvement.** States and tribes are encouraged to participate actively as partners with EPA in addressing Superfund sites. They will assist in making the decisions at sites, can take responsibility in managing cleanups, and can play an important role in oversight of responsible parties.
- **Enforcement authorities.** Settlement policies already in use were strengthened through Congressional approval and inclusion in SARA. Different settlement tools, such as de minimis settlements (settlements with minor contributors), are now part of the Act.
- **Federal facility compliance.** Congress emphasized that federal facilities "are subject to, and must comply with, this Act in the same manner and to the same extent . . . as any non-government entity." Mandatory schedules have been established for federal facilities to assess their sites, and if listed on the NPL, to clean up such sites. We will be assisting and overseeing federal agencies with these new requirements.

The amendments also expand research and development, especially in the area of alternative technologies. They also provide for more training for state and federal personnel in emergency preparedness, disaster response, and hazard mitigation.

SOURCE: Environmental Protection Agency, *Environmental Progress and Challenges: EPA's Update* (Washington, D.C.: Government Printing Office, 1988), 95.

A hazardous waste is any discarded chemical that can adversely affect one's health or the environment. The Environmental Protection Agency (EPA) includes four types of waste:

1. *Ignitability or flammability* (waste oils, used organic solvents, and PCBs)
2. *Corrosive* to materials such as metals or human tissue (strong acids, strong bases)
3. *Reactivity*—unstable enough to explode or release toxic fumes (cyanide solvents)
4. *Toxicity*—toxic if handled in ways that release them into the environment (DDT, dioxins, PCBs, arsenic, mercury, and lead)

These characteristics are discussed by Jack Lewis in our first selection.

Radioactive wastes, mining wastes, oil and gas drilling wastes are not included in this list. Many environmentalists are concerned to get Congress to include these categories.

Over 275 million tons of hazardous waste are produced in the United States each year. The EPA lists 34,000 hazardous waste sites in the United States, and 1200 sites are on a National Priority List for cleanup. The General Accounting Office estimates the number of sites is between 103,000 and 425,000. The largest number of priority sites are in New Jersey, Pennsylvania, California, Michigan, and New York. It costs about $26 million to clean up a site. The total costs of cleanup could exceed $500 billion.

In 1976 Congress passed the Resource Conservation and Recovery Act (RCRA), which called on the EPA to create "cradle to grave" oversight of hazardous waste. In 1980 the Comprehensive Environmental Response, Compensation and Liability Act, known as the Superfund program, was passed by Congress. This law provided a $1.6 billion fund to be financed by the federal and state governments and by taxes on chemical and petrochemical companies, to be used to clean up hazardous-waste sites. In 1986 a new Superfund program, the Superfund Amendment and Reauthorization Act (SARA) was passed providing $9 billion to the cleanup program (see box).

The first two essays in this section examine the problems involved in the Superfund program of cleaning up hazardous-waste sites. Jack Lewis argues that the program is working. Thomas Grumbly argues that it is not yet working as it should and that the government needs to review its definition of hazardous waste, implement and enforce regulations, and improve its research into the effects of hazardous waste. In our third essay, David Sarokin of Greenpeace argues that the only solution to hazardous waste is to greatly reduce its production.

68

Superfund, RCRA, and UST: The Clean-Up Threesome

JACK LEWIS

Jack Lewis is assistant editor of the EPA Journal, *a publication of the Environmental Protection Agency.*

Lewis describes the history of the legislation regarding the inspection and cleanup of hazardous-waste sites. He argues that the problem is greater than anyone could have imagined, but three government programs—the Superfund program with its National Priorities List (NPL), the Resource Conservation and Recovery Act (RCRA), and the Underground Storage Tank program (UST)—are succeeding in cleaning up hazardous-waste sites.

LOVE CANAL LEGACY— WHERE ARE WE NOW?

As the 1970s came to a close, a series of headline stories gave Americans a look at the dangers of dumping wastes on the land. One particularly famous case was New York's Love Canal. Hazardous waste buried there over a 25-year period contaminated streams and soil and endangered the health of nearby residents. The result: evacuation of several hundred people. In Kentucky, the Valley of the Drums attracted public attention. The site of these leaking storage barrels quickly became front page news. The Chemical Control site in Elizabeth, New Jersey, contained over 40,000 barrels of hazardous wastes together with at least 100 pounds of a powerful explosive. A fire or explosion could have exposed the New York Metropolitan area population to a toxic cloud of chemicals.

In all these cases, public health and the environment were threatened; in many instances, lives were disrupted and property values depreciated. It was becoming increasingly clear that large numbers of serious hazardous waste problems were falling through the cracks of existing environmental laws. The magnitude of this problem moved Congress to enact the Comprehensive Environmental Response, Compensation, and Liability Act in 1980. CERCLA, commonly known as Superfund, was the first federal law dealing with the dangers posed by the nation's abandoned and uncontrolled hazardous waste sites.

After Discovery, the Problem Intensified

The news stories turned out to be just the beginning. Few realized the size of the problem until EPA began the process of site discovery and evaluation. Not hundreds, but thousands of potential hazardous waste sites existed, and they presented the nation with some of the most complex pollution problems it had ever faced.

In the 10 years since the Superfund program began, hazardous waste has become a major environmental concern in every part of the United States. It wasn't just the land that was contaminated by past waste-disposal practices. Chemicals in the soil were spreading into the ground water (a source of drinking water for many) and into streams, lakes, bays, and wetlands. At some sites, toxic vapors were rising into the air. Some pollutants—such as metals and solvents—had damaged vegetation, endangered wildlife, and threatened the health of people who unknowingly worked or played in contaminated soil, drank contaminated water, or ate contaminated vegetables, meat, or fish.

As site discoveries grew, cost estimates rose. Clearly, the $1.6 billion originally set aside for the fund was not enough to clean up the nation's most serious hazardous waste sites. Realizing the long-term nature of the problem and the enormous job ahead, Congress reauthorized

Reprinted from Jack Lewis, "Superfund, RCRA, and UST: The Clean-Up Threesome," *EPA Journal* (July/August 1991).

the program in 1986 for another five years, adding $8.6 billion to the fund. In 1990, Congress authorized continuing the program for another five years and added another $5.1 billion.

Priorities Had to Be Established

From the beginning of the program, Congress recognized that the federal government could not, and should not, be responsible for addressing all environmental problems stemming from past disposal practices. Therefore, EPA was directed to establish a National Priorities List (NPL) of sites to target. *The program responds to hazardous emergencies wherever they occur, but only those sites listed on the NPL qualify for long-term cleanup under Superfund.* Problems at other sites are dealt with by state and local governments, individuals, or companies. . . .

Sites on the NPL are a relatively small subset of a larger inventory of potential hazardous waste sites, but they do comprise the most complex and environmentally compelling cases. EPA has logged approximately 34,000 sites on its inventory. The Agency assesses each site within one year of its being logged. In fact, almost 32,000 sites have been assessed. Of these, 20,500 have been found to require no further federal action. Approximately 11,000 sites are awaiting further investigation.

To date, there are nearly 1,200 hazardous waste sites on the NPL; sites qualify for the NPL based on a variety of factors, including the quantity and toxicity of the wastes involved; the number of people potentially or actually exposed; the likely pathways of exposure; and the importance and vulnerability of the underlying supply of ground water. The historical rate of sites added to the NPL is approximately 100 sites per year. The Agency estimates that this rate will continue over the next several years.

For sites on the NPL, EPA is committed to taking actions that protect human health and the environment—in both the short and long-term—from unacceptable risks by eliminating, reducing, or controlling exposures to hazardous substances. As a matter of policy, to reduce the need for long-term management of the site or its waste, whenever practical the hazards posed by the contaminated material are destroyed; otherwise, the contaminated materials are to be recycled or treated to significantly reduce their toxicity, mobility, or volume. Another key goal: to return usable ground waters to their beneficial uses wherever practicable or, at a minimum, to stem further contamination and prevent exposure to the contaminated water.

At 373 NPL sites, EPA has made progress toward permanent cleanup of contamination of the land, surface water, or ground water—or a combination of these. This progress is incremental, reflecting the strategy of making sites safer by controlling acute threats immediately and of making sites cleaner by addressing the worst first.

All needed construction has been completed at 63 sites. Right now, cleanup work is underway at 310 older NPL sites, and the "pipeline" is full of sites headed for cleanup: Currently, remedies have been selected for an additional 270 sites and are either in the engineering design state, or will be shortly. And 503 sites are at the "investigation" step, where the nature of the contamination problem is thoroughly investigated and alternative remedies are evaluated. As EPA streamlines its program to address NPL sites, the Agency hopes to accelerate the pace of full site cleanup.

A site can be deleted from the NPL only if, after any cleanup has been completed, no further action is appropriate to address an actual or threatened release of a hazardous substance.

The net result of Superfund cleanup work at NPL sites has been to reduce potential risks from exposure to hazardous waste to more than 23.5 million of the 41 million people who live within four miles of these sites. This work includes the elimination of threats posed by direct contact with hazardous waste to more than 950,000 people—580,000 of whom were threatened by contact with land contamination and 411,000 of whom have had alternative drinking water supplied.

EPA estimates that the Superfund will spend approximately $27 billion on the sites currently on the NPL. And that is only part of the cost. Currently, the parties responsible for the waste perform roughly 65 percent of the work, which will account for billions more in cleanup dollars. The total average cost per site runs $26 million, and there is every reason to believe that the costs will climb as some of the more complex sites move into the clean-up phase.

Hazardous Waste Sites Are Diverse

It's virtually impossible to describe the "typical" hazardous waste site: They are extremely diverse. Many are municipal or industrial landfills. Others are manufacturing plants where operators improperly disposed of wastes. Some are large federal facilities dotted with "hot spots" of contamination from various high-tech or military activities. The chief contributors of these wastes are in our manufacturing sector.

While many sites have been abandoned, a site may still be an active operation, or it may be fully or partially closed down. Sites range dramatically in size, from a quarter-acre metal plating shop to a 250-square-mile mining area. The types of wastes they contain vary widely, too: Some of the chief constituents of wastes present in solid, liquid, and sludge forms include heavy metals—a common byproduct of many electroplating operations—and solvents or degreasing agents.

NPL sites are found in all types of settings: Slightly more are found in rural/suburban areas than in urban areas, but very few are truly remote from either homes or farms.

Yet the idea of a "site"—some kind of disposal area or dump—still doesn't portray the entire picture. Transportation spills and other industrial process or storage accidents account for some hazardous waste releases. The result can be fires, explosions, toxic vapors, and contamination of ground water used for drinking.

Since every NPL site is unique, cleanups must be tailored to the specific needs of each site and the types of wastes that contaminate it. The range of possibilities is enormous. First, the site's physical characteristics (its hydrology, geology, topography, and climate) determine how contaminants will affect the environment. Then, there is the variation in site type—landfill, manufacturing plant, military base, metal mine—the list is long. The type of waste present adds another complex dimension. Information on the health and environmental effects of hazardous wastes comes mainly from laboratory studies of pure chemicals. There still is much to learn about the nature of the complex mixtures of wastes generally found at these sites, how they affect the environment and how best to control them.

No matter how exhaustive preliminary studies may be, sampling and site observation simply cannot reveal the full extent of the problem at many sites. Uncertainties exist right up until the point where ground is broken for the clean-up work and throughout the final clean-up process. That's why there is no ready answer to the question: "How long will it take?" On average—and this includes a broad range—six to eight years will elapse between the start of the clean-up study and remedy completion.

EPA Is Developing New Site Clean-Up Technologies

While technological concepts were not fully field-tested in the early 1980s, hazardous waste clean-up efforts have begun to yield the information needed to design permanent site clean-up solutions. Since 1986, the move has been away from "containment" of hazardous wastes. Containment entails segregating the wastes in a particular place, but unfortunately many materials cannot reliably be controlled this way. This is particularly true of liquids, highly mobile substances (like solvents), and high concentrations of toxic compounds. For these wastes, treatment is the preferred approach: It reduces the toxicity, mobility, and volume of wastes.

In 1987, some type of waste treatment was being used in about 50 percent of clean-up remedies EPA selected. By 1989, that number had risen to more than 70 percent.

Hazardous Waste Poses a Variety of Threats

Hazardous waste can include products and residues from a variety of industrial, agricultural, and military activities. Some of the hazard lies in the waste itself: its con-

centration and quantity; physical or chemical nature. But much of the danger arises from improper handling, storage, and disposal practices. The result is that humans or the environment are exposed to contamination.

Wastes were poorly managed in the past because the disposers often failed to understand the potential toxic effects or realize how strictly they had to be contained. Dangerous chemicals have often migrated from uncontrolled sites. They may percolate from holding ponds and pits into underlying ground water. They may be washed over the ground into lakes, streams, and wetlands. They may evaporate, explode, or blow into the air, spreading hazardous chemicals. They may soak into soil, making land and ground water unfit for habitat or agriculture. Some hazardous chemicals build up—or bioaccumulate—when plants, animals, and people consume contaminated fool and water.

Human and Environmental Health at Risk

Determining the risks of hazardous waste to human and environmental health is a complex undertaking. Risk hinges upon how dangerous the chemical is, how people may come into contact with it, how frequently, and in combination with what other chemicals. EPA conducts risk assessments at each site, analyzing the possible ways people, animals, and plants could come into contact with contaminants.

Like the sites themselves, possible effects on human and environmental health span a broad spectrum. Adverse effects on people can range from minor physical irritation to serious health disorders. Such effects also can take the form of slowly degenerating health or of sudden serious damage. Vegetables and livestock may become contaminated and enter the food chain. A sudden poisoning event, like a hazardous waste spill or the breaching of a hazardous waste impoundment, can pose serious immediate health risks.

Health and environmental risk is complicated by the fact that, if nothing is done, people and ecosystems can suffer a gradual deterioration for years and show adverse health effects long after the fact. In addition, certain populations are sensitive: elderly people and children, endangered or threatened plants and animals. Some environments are more sensitive in the way they respond to the effects of hazardous chemicals: wetlands, coastal areas, estuaries, and many other water bodies, for example, or wild life refuges, or rare pine or shale barrens. These are fragile and valuable ecosystems that must be protected.

Industry Pays for Hazardous Waste Cleanup

Industry pays for hazardous waste cleanup through specific taxes. Over 80 percent of the fund known as "Superfund" is supported directly by excise taxes on petroleum and feedstock chemicals, some imported chemicals, and corporate environmental taxes. Financial settlements from site polluters also are returned to the fund.

Superfund dollars are used to clean up sites when those who caused the contamination can't or won't pay. Companies may be unable to pay for a variety of reasons. They may be too small—an individual or a small company without sufficient assets. Perhaps they have declared bankruptcy. In other cases, responsible owners can't be identified or found. On the other hand, many companies can and do pay for cleanup at sites they helped to contaminate.

EPA spends considerable effort tracking down the "potentially responsible parties" (PRPs)—firms and individuals who created or added to a hazardous waste problem. Indeed, the Superfund program makes it a high priority to find parties who can perform or pay for cleanup.

EPA uses a variety of enforcement tools (e.g., administrative orders, consent decrees, negotiations) to engage responsible parties in site cleanup. Every successful negotiation of a private-party cleanup means that the money in the Superfund can be directed instead to those sites that represent immediate emergencies, or that have no hope of ever being cleaned up by those responsible.

Success in making polluters pay is measurable. Participation in cleanups by PRPs increased from 40 percent in 1987 to more than 60 percent in 1989. Strictly enforcing laws that enable EPA to recover cleanup costs has saved the Superfund about $2 billion in work value since 1980. Half of that sum has been recovered since late 1986.

EPA Tackles Imminent Threats Immediately

The Superfund responds immediately to situations posing imminent threats to human health and the environment at both NPL sites and sites not on the NPL. The purpose is to make sites safe by stabilizing, preventing, or tempering the effects of a hazardous release, or the threat of one. Imminent threats might include tire fires or discarded waste drums leaking hazardous chemicals.

EPA has invested considerable resources in identifying sites that present imminent threats and in undertaking the emergency responses required. The Agency has developed teams of professionals to combat threatening situations. These emergency workers may assist in cleanup of a dangerous spill or advise state and local officials on the need for a temporary water supply, air and water monitoring, removal of contaminated soils, or relocation of residents. Either EPA or the U.S. Coast Guard has taken Superfund-financed emergency action to attack the most imminent threats of toxic exposure in more than 2,000 cases. EPA has used its enforcement authority to have responsible parties perform emergency actions in approximately 450 additional cases.

RCRA: Post-War Consumer Demand Created a Problem

Following World War II, our nation's phenomenal industrial growth was matched by a surge in consumer demand for new products. The country seized upon new "miracle" products, such as plastics, semiconductors, and coated paper goods, as soon as industry introduced them. Our appetite for material goods also created a problem: how to manage the increasing amounts of waste produced by industry and consumers alike.

In 1965, Congress passed the Solid Waste Disposal Act, the first federal law to encourage environmentally sound methods for disposal of waste. Congress amended this law in 1970 by passing the Resource Recovery Act and again in 1976 by passing the Resource Conservation and Recovery Act (RCRA).

As our knowledge about the health and environmental impacts of disposal increased, Congress revised RCRA, first in 1980 and again in 1984. The 1984 amendments were created, in large part, in response to strongly voiced citizen concerns that existing methods of hazardous waste disposal, particularly land disposal, were not safe.

Generally speaking, Superfund focuses on mistakes of the past, whereas RCRA addresses the problems of the here and now through a system of controlling hazardous waste from generation to ultimate disposal. However, RCRA does authorize EPA to require "corrective action" cleanups at RCRA-regulated hazardous waste management facilities. RCRA also regulates toxic substances and, through the UST program, petroleum products stored in underground tanks.

Hazardous Wastes Had to Be Defined

Hazardous wastes come in all shapes and forms. They may be liquids, solids, or sludges. They may be the byproducts of manufacturing processes, or simply commercial products—such as cleaning fluids or battery acid—that have been discarded.

In order to regulate hazardous wastes, EPA first had to determine which wastes would be considered hazardous under the law. The Agency spent many months talking to industry and the public to develop a definition for its regulations. As a result of this work, the regulations identify hazardous wastes based on their characteristics and also provide a list of specific wastes.

A waste is hazardous if it exhibits one or more of the following characteristics:

- *Ignitability*. Ignitable wastes can create fires under certain conditions. Examples include liquids, such as solvents that readily catch fire, and friction-sensitive substances.
- *Corrosivity*. Corrosive wastes include those that are acidic and those that are capable of corroding metal containers, such as tanks, drums, and barrels.

- *Reactivity*. Reactive wastes are unstable under normal conditions. They can create explosions and/or toxic fumes, gases, and vapors when mixed with water.
- *Toxicity*. Toxic wastes are defined as containing one or more of 39 specific compounds at levels that exceed established limits. These wastes can contaminate ground water at levels high enough to cause detrimental human health effects.

Rules for Generators of Waste

EPA designed its regulations to ensure proper management of hazardous waste from the moment the waste is generated until its ultimate disposal. The first step in the cycle is the person who actually produces the waste. Generators include large industries, small businesses, universities, and hospitals.

Under the regulations, generators must determine if their waste is hazardous and must oversee its ultimate fate. They must obtain an EPA identification number for each site at which the waste is generated.

According to EPA estimates, generators treat or dispose of about 98 percent of the nation's hazardous waste on site. On-site treatment, storage, and disposal facilities generally are found at larger businesses that can afford treatment equipment and that possess the necessary space for storage and disposal. Smaller firms, and those in crowded urban locations, are more likely to transport their waste off site where the waste is managed by a commercial firm or a publicly owned and operated facility. EPA regulations apply to both on-site and off-site facilities.

The generator must package and label waste that is to be transported off site. Proper packaging ensures that no waste leaks during transport. Labeling enables transporters and public officials, including those who respond to emergencies, to rapidly identify the waste and its hazards.

The Manifest Tracks the Waste

Although only a small percentage of the nation's hazardous waste is actually transported off site to treatment, storage, or disposal facilities, this still comprises a substantial volume: approximately 4 million tons per year. EPA requires generators to prepare a one-page form, or manifest, which identifies the type and quantity of waste, the generator, the transporter, and the facility to which the waste is being shipped.

The manifest must accompany the waste wherever it travels. Each individual handler of the waste must sign it. When the waste reaches its destination, the owner of that facility returns a copy of the manifest to the generator to confirm that the waste arrived. If the waste does not arrive as scheduled, generators must immediately notify EPA or the authorized state environmental agency.

Transporters must carry copies of the manifests and must put symbols on the vehicle to identify the waste. These symbols, like the labels on the containers, enable fire fighters, police, and other officials to immediately identify the potential hazards in case of an emergency.

Permits Ensure Safe Operation of Treatment, Storage, and Disposal Facilities (TSDFs)

The facilities that receive hazardous waste from the transporter must obtain an EPA permit to operate. *Treatment* facilities use various processes to alter the character or composition of waste. Some processes enable waste to be recovered and reused, while others reduce the volume of waste to be disposed of. *Storage* facilities hold waste until it is treated or disposed of. Historically, prior to RCRA restrictions on land disposal, most disposal facilities buried hazardous waste or piled it on the land. (See below, "Land Disposal Has Posed a Threat.")

Virtually all operating land disposal facilities and incinerators, as well as several hundred storage and treatment facilities, have now been issued RCRA permits. RCRA permits contain detailed design and operating specifications that each hazardous waste unit must comply with. Until a RCRA facility receives its permit, it is required to operate under "interim status" and comply with a more general set of management standards.

As their capacity becomes used up, and as new stringent operating requirements are imposed, many hazardous waste disposal facilities have decided to close. RCRA regulations require TSDF owners to prepare carefully for the time when their facility will close. Owners must:

- Acquire sufficient financial assurance mechanisms (such as trust funds, surety bonds, or letters of credit) to pay for completion of all operations.
- Where waste will be left on site, be prepared to pay for 30 years of groundwater monitoring, waste system maintenance, and security measures after the facility closes.
- Obtain liability insurance to cover third-party damages that may arise from accidents or waste mismanagement.

Corrective Action

The 1984 amendments added a remedial dimension to RCRA in the form of extensive "corrective action" authorities that apply to RCRA-permitted facilities and facilities operating under interim status. Under the corrective action program, if contamination is suspected at a RCRA-regulated facility, due to past or ongoing releases of hazardous waste, the owners/operators of the facility may be required to perform an investigation and follow through with remedial measures. By mandating the RCRA corrective action program, Congress supplemented EPA's existing clean-up authority under Superfund, which is meant to focus specifically on the worst abandoned or uncontrolled hazardous waste sites in the United States—namely those sites which qualify for the NPL.

EPA or an authorized state may initiate corrective action through the normal RCRA permit process or, alternatively, through an enforcement order.

Unlike Superfund, there is no federal fund to support corrective action under RCRA. Instead, facility owners and operators must provide financial assurance that they can complete corrective action as necessary. Specific corrective action requirements depend on the kind and degree of contamination identified at a facility; they may include such diverse measures as erecting a fence around a contaminated area, repairing waste unit liners, installing a pump-and-treat system to remove a plume of contamination, or excavation and treatment or removal of contaminated "hot spots."

The basic procedural steps of the corrective action process are roughly analogous to the steps followed at a Superfund NPL site. They are:

- *RCRA Facility Assessment:* Systematic identification of actual or potential releases through examination of each solid waste management unit at a facility.
- *RCRA Facility Investigation:* Characterization of the nature, extent, and rate of migration of each release.
- *Corrective Measures Study:* Identification of appropriate corrective measures; study of their likely effectiveness and feasibility.
- *Corrective Measures Implementation:* Design, construction, and implementation of corrective measures. (Appropriate *interim* measures may be taken at any point in the process.)

All steps except the initial facility assessment are conducted by the owner/operator of the RCRA facility, with oversight by EPA or a state. RCRA facility assessments are conducted directly by EPA or the state.

Land Disposal Has Posed a Threat

In the past, most hazardous waste was disposed of with only limited treatment. Improper disposal endangered public health and the environment. As a result, in the 1984 RCRA amendments Congress banned the land disposal of untreated waste unless EPA finds that there will be "no migration of hazardous constituents . . . for as long as the wastes remain hazardous."

The RCRA restrictions on land disposal have given considerable impetus to the development of waste treatment. EPA is sponsoring research on technologies to destroy, detoxify, or incinerate hazardous waste; on ways to recover and reuse it; and on methods to reduce its volume. The amendments also encourage generators to reduce the volume of waste through process changes, source separation, recycling, raw material substitution, or product substitution.

UNDERGROUND STORAGE TANKS

Leakage Problems

In the small community of Truro on Cape Cod, residents discovered their wells were contaminated with gasoline that had leaked from a nearby underground storage tank. The courts ordered the company responsible to provide residents with bottled water and to spend millions of dollars to restore the water supply. On the other side of the country, in the South Bay area of San Francisco, leaks and spills of toxic solvents from underground tanks and their pipes have severely contaminated the ground water. Thousands of other communities across the country face similar problems.

Both accidental releases and the slow seepage of petroleum products or hazardous chemicals from buried storage tanks can contaminate ground water. EPA estimates that as many as 15 to 20 percent of the approximately 1.8 million underground storage tanks in the United States covered by the federal law are either leaking now or are expected to leak. Facts such as these led Congress, in the 1984 RCRA amendments, to require EPA to regulate underground tanks containing petroleum products and hazardous chemicals. In 1986, Congress set up a $500 million trust fund, to be paid for over five years, to clean up leaks from underground petroleum storage tanks. The fund is supported by a 1/10 of a cent federal tax on certain petroleum products, primarily motor fuels. In 1990, Congress reauthorized the trust fund for an additional five years, this time with no cap on the amount of funds collected.

Owners Had to Register Their Tanks

Prior to 1984, only a few states had programs to monitor underground storage tanks (USTs). Therefore, one of the first steps EPA took was to require owners to notify and register their tanks with state or local agencies. To assist in this effort, the Agency required anyone who deposited petroleum or regulated hazardous substances in an underground storage tank—for example, the driver of a gasoline tank truck—to inform the tank owner of his or her responsibilities to fill out a notification form.

New Rules for Tank Owners

The major goal of the UST program is to protect human health and the environment from underground storage tank releases. To achieve that goal, EPA developed regulations to: ensure the use of sound, protective tank technology and management practices; require that contamination from tanks be cleaned up; require owners and operators to acquire the financial means to clean up contamination from their tanks, as mandated by the law; and establish practical and reasonable standards for the states to meet in carrying out the program.

Following are some of the specific requirements established by the UST program:

- Depending on the age of the tank, leak detection requirements for tanks and piping are being phased in over five years (by December 1993).
- Tank upgrading requirements, amounting in essence to new tank standards, for existing USTs must be met by December 1998.
- Corrective action requirements have been set whereby all suspected releases must be investigated, and for confirmed releases, specific remedial requirements must be satisfied.
- Tank owners are subject to financial responsibility requirements to assure that resources are available to pay for damage caused if leaks occur.

ACKNOWLEDGMENT

The presentation of Superfund material in this article is drawn substantially from a September 1990 EPA publication entitled Superfund: Focusing on the Nation at Large (EPA/540/8–90/009).

Study Questions

1. Describe the various ways hazardous waste harms the environment and affects human health.
2. Describe the legislation regarding hazardous-waste sites since 1976. Does this seem adequate to solve the problem of hazardous waste? What else would you suggest?
3. How does the Superfund program work? Does Lewis convince you that the three-pronged attack is succeeding? Explain your answer.
4. Who should pay for the Superfund? Taxpayers or industry? Explain your answer.

The Superfund: Significant Improvements Are Needed

THOMAS GRUMBLY

Thomas Grumbly is the president of Clean Sites, a coalition of industrialists, environmentalists, and others concerned about the problem of hazardous wastes. He is a former executive director of the Health Effects Institute.

Grumbly argues that, although the Superfund program has ameliorated the harmful effects of hazardous-waste sites, much remains to be done. He outlines and discusses five imperatives that are now lacking but necessary for success: (1) a clear definition of success in this area; (2) implementation of an equitable enforcement program; (3) remedies that involve input from people who have a stake in the land around the waste site; (4) implementation of long-term research and development; and (5) development of effective administration procedures.

Is the Superfund program, which has come under so much criticism during its 10-year history, finally succeeding? Given the quick reauthorization last year by Congress, one might be tempted to say "yes." But this enormous program still faces serious obstacles. To announce success, as EPA did in December, and not tackle the problems still facing the program, could

reverse what clearly has been an upward trend in achievements over the last three years.

This article presents a strategic analysis of the improvements needed in the program under current law. As a preliminary to the analysis, it is important to understand why Congress reauthorized the program at the end of the last session, and the lessons we should take from it. The impetus derived from a number of interests coming together at the same time:

- Congressional staff had worked long and hard on amendments to the Clean Air Act, and many still remembered the bruising nature of the previous Superfund reauthorization.
- Members of Congress and the Administration understood that hazardous waste cleanup is a "hot button" with constituents and that not enough progress had been made to warrant bringing the problem to the political forefront again.
- Environmental interests, in general, believed that the current statute favored their concerns; industrial interests were not convinced that raising their concerns would result in improvement.
- And finally, the Superfund program had made enough progress in the last two years to convince both Congress and the Administration that the program should be given a longer chance to work.

Reprinted from Thomas P. Grumbly, "Superfund: Candidly Speaking," *EPA Journal* (July/August 1991).

It is clear that the reauthorization was not intended as a message that all is well. Almost everyone believes that substantial obstacles to success remain. Many believe that the program cannot succeed as currently structured. There is, in other words, plenty of fertile ground both for debate and improvement before the next reauthorization.

THE PROBLEM: WHAT IS SUCCESS?

In December 1990, EPA published a 10-year review of Superfund in which it argued it has achieved "success on all fronts." This is an overstatement based upon a failure to understand, articulate, and analyze what real success would be. Ironically, this failure may be depriving the Agency of credit for a major victory.

There undoubtedly has been progress with respect to the volume of work being performed. The Agency has steadily increased all of what I call "inputs" over the past three years: study starts, design and construction starts, remedies selected, dollars spent, and orders issued. EPA also claims success as measured by the sheer volume of waste it has dealt with. It has moved or burned, in its own terms, more than 5,000 football fields worth of contaminated soil.

What is not clear, however, is what all these inputs mean for protecting human health and the environment. In general, EPA presents its progress in cumulative terms. Unfortunately, a close look reveals that it will not be able to maintain its current pace. It is unlikely that the input successes of 1991 will even equal the 1990 numbers. In effect, the Agency has already milked the system. Over the past few years, very few new sites have been added to the National Priorities List (NPL), and, as a result of the Agency's (and the statute's) strong focus on getting work started, the long-term clean-up pipeline is filling. Of the roughly 1,200 NPL sites, 272 have long-term cleanups underway, and remedies have been selected for 264 others. The input numbers, therefore, will tail off as the pipeline is addressed.

Another area of success cited by the Agency is its "enforcement first" strategy, which favors settling with potentially responsible parties (PRPs) over financing actions with Superfund. This strategy has dramatically increased the settlements with PRPs and the dollars obtained from the private sector. However, it has also angered the responsible party community by what they regard as a return to soaking the "deep pockets."

If EPA continues to measure success in these terms, the outlook for the program over the next few years is not promising.

In the absence of a fairly radical restructuring of how program funds are distributed, it is highly unlikely that more than 100 additional sites will have construction completed and be deleted from the NPL by the end of 1992. Since deletions are still the primary measure of success that most observers use, the least charitable assessment (the one Superfund usually receives) will show that we will have spent nearly $15 billion and eliminated only 10 percent of the country's worst hazardous waste sites.

Unfortunately, unless the program is altered, this picture doesn't change dramatically even when we look out to the end of the decade. Our best guess is that, under current rules, fewer than 500 sites will be deleted from the existing NPL by the year 2000. Considering that as many as 700 new sites are expected to be added to the NPL over the same period, we will still have 1,500 most dangerous hazardous waste sites to clean up, or 200 more than we now have. And that will be a full 20 years into the Superfund program.

In other words, the program will have declining input success, with no concomitant increase in commonly understood output success. Further, the number of cleanups underway and their cost will continue to rise. This will be the worst of all worlds. It is happening because we have not thought through what success is and what strategies have to be put in place to optimize progress at *all* the critical stages—identification, enforcement/settlement, remedy selection, construction, and site deletion.

A STRATEGIC PLAN FOR SUPERFUND

In the early years of the Superfund program, the emphasis was on private-party support and on the technologies to be applied to sites. While these issues are still important, I would argue that improving the remedy selection process and focusing on reductions in risk to human health and the environment and on the perceived competence and consistency of the government are at least as important. I would also argue that transaction costs, the great bugaboo of Superfund, would decline enormously if greater attention were paid to the managerial and scientific elements of the program.

With the program now entering maturity, the emphasis should change. EPA should cash in on its accomplishments to date and move ahead with a program that ensures cleanups are effective in the long term and adequate funds are available from the private sector to maintain momentum. This will require the combination of an elemental management approach to defining and achieving success and an analysis of the long-term scientific and technical needs of the program.

There are five imperatives to any Superfund strategic plan that are essential to success:

- Clearly define success.
- Implement an equitable enforcement program.
- Focus remedy selection around objective-setting and interaction with stakeholders.
- Invest in long-term research and development.
- Develop consistent administrative procedures.

We must do a better job of defining, measuring, and publicizing success. The critical success measure, upon which deletion from the NPL should be based, is protection of human health and the environment. In this context, it is important to note that EPA has made great strides in eradicating the worst threats that were posed by hazardous waste sites when the program began 11 years ago.

At the outset, I said that EPA may already have succeeded·in large measure. Its removal program has probably eliminated most of the *immediate* health risks posed by abandoned hazardous waste sites. We need to discover whether this is true, document it, and use the information to help EPA focus on risk reduction in its remedial efforts. To date, little credit has been given to EPA for the risk reduction these removal actions achieve.

The main reason for this lack of recognition is that the current construction-management approach to cleanup focuses on the application of technology to hazardous waste problems. It does not characterize, sufficiently, what is to be achieved from the standpoint of human health and the environment. As a result, the public and the Agency never know when the health and environmental "mark" has been achieved.

The Agency needs to think much more about the end of the game at the beginning of the process. Over the next two years, each and every NPL site needs to have its "objectives"—both qualitative and quantitative—spelled out in detail. As part of this process, explicit plans should be laid for expending the necessary resources right through deletion from the NPL. Right now, EPA has a strategy for getting a lot of balls in the air, but not for getting them down.

We need an enforcement strategy that is perceived as tough but equitable across the board. An "enforcement-first" strategy that relies too heavily on unilateral administrative orders directed at traditional deep pockets will result in a progressively declining program. A more successful strategy would demand a mix of negotiated settlements, unilateral orders, damage suits against recalcitrant parties, and a really active potentially-responsible-party search program.

This strategy would require full use of the provisions that Congress included in the 1986 Superfund amendments but which have not yet been seriously implemented, including: *de minimis* buyouts, in which PRPs with limited liability could pay cash up front to be released from future involvement in a cleanup; non-binding allocations of responsibility (NBARs) issued by EPA to assist in the organization of PRP groups; and mixed funding, in which EPA would share the initial cost of cleanup with firms that step forward to perform the work in anticipation of recovering costs at a future date from recalcitrant parties. The strategy's cornerstone, negotiating settlements with PRPs, must be based on policies governing standard consent decrees that are stringent enough to bring in sufficient clean-up dollars, but not so one-sided in character that they push companies away from seeking settlements.

We must put into place a remedy selection process that emphasizes objective-setting, clearly defined criteria, and dramatically increased communication and dialogue among all parties. Remedy selection is the linchpin of the Superfund program. It determines the level of protection for citizens living and working near sites, the level of restoration of land, and the cost to the responsible parties or to the Superfund trust fund.

Clean Sites conducted a year-long project that examined the current approach to selecting remedies. This project brought together more than 100 experts representing diverse interests. A major finding was that the current remedy selection process works backwards—EPA explores in depth all the alternative clean-up methods it plans to consider before determining the level of protection it is seeking or the potential future uses of the site. We found that no consensus exists on what constitutes "protection of health and the environment"—the law's overarching mandate for cleanup and remedies—and that levels of protection vary from site to site. We also found that definitions for other statutory criteria—permanence, long-term effectiveness, cost-effectiveness, and treatment—are ambiguous and applied inconsistently.

We issued a report recommending an alternate process in which EPA, with input from all stakeholders, would set explicit objectives for each site based on the site's expected future land and resource use. These objectives would be based on a target for an acceptable amount of residual health risk that is uniform for all sites. EPA then would explore only those clean-up methods that meet the site's objectives. Under the process we suggest, EPA would define a permanent remedy as one that will endure indefinitely and would develop at least one permanent alternative for each site. EPA would select the remedy that will endure the longest for the least cost.

This process would require that EPA give uniform definitions to statutory criteria and apply them explicitly and consistently in the process, that citizens and states be given all technical information as it becomes available, and that EPA elicit and respond to citizens', states', and responsible parties' comments *before* selecting a "preferred alternative."

We need to prompt public investment in long-term research and development in hazardous waste science and technology. We must make the investments in research and development that are necessary to improve both our fundamental understanding of the most commonly seen chemicals, as well as develop the knowledge needed for making risk assessments. While our inadequacies in exposure assessment are important to all areas of environmental policy, the economic impact of our current lack of knowledge in the area of risk assessment is most evident in the hazardous waste arena. We simply must improve the data that underpin exposure assumptions if we want EPA decision-makers to rely upon risk assessment in making decisions.

The investment is warranted. The amount of potential cleanup facing the nation is staggering. The cost of cleaning up the existing 1,200 sites on the NPL is expected to approach $40 billion. Federal facilities, ranging from those under the aegis of the Departments of Interior and Defense to the Department of Energy, could cost as much as $200 billion. And while no one yet has reliable estimates of what the costs of RCRA corrective action cleanups might be, many knowledgeable persons both in industry and in government believe that RCRA responsibilities could easily dwarf expenditures in Superfund! Beyond these federally controlled sites are an estimated 28,000 sites under the authority of state regulation, and the spending on these sites also continues to rise. In sum, it is not too much to say that we will be spending between $10 billion and $20 billion per year in hazardous waste cleanup by the year 2000 and that this will represent 10 to 20 percent of all pollution control expenditures in the United States.

This situation is a far cry from what was envisioned when congress passed Superfund in 1980. Then, hazardous waste cleanup—or at least abandoned hazardous waste site cleanup—was to be a quick mop-up of a few sites. With that emergency response scenario in mind, it is unsurprising that little thought was given to building a scientific and technical infrastructure to support the program.

Our current situation should lead us to reassess the importance of science as a critical element for successful cleanups. Not only is the problem of a magnitude to warrant major investment in making our programs more effective, but also, for better or worse, we now know that we have the time for science to play a significant role—even if it takes a decade to produce results.

A serious focus also needs to be placed on removing the impediments to improving the application of new technology. Thus far, EPA's Superfund Innovative Technology Evaluation (SITE) program has not succeeded in energizing either vendors or users in the private sector to use existing technology in new ways or to use new technology at actual sites. Perhaps the regulatory liability obstacles are key, but it seems to us that EPA could still play a role in fostering more cooperation between engineers and scientists in the private sector

and their counterparts in government. The Defense Department, and particularly the Department of Energy, also are thrashing about trying to deal with the development of remediation technologies. What is needed is a "guild" of scientists and engineers that knows no institutional bounds and has the ability to produce creative solutions to very difficult problems.

An administrative process is needed that places a premium on consistency and competent regional project managers, supported by adequate teams of program and contract personnel, and guided by teams of headquarters/regional personnel. EPA made the decision in 1988 to delegate all site-specific decisions to the 10 regions. While this decision was appropriate to speeding decision making, it has left the Agency without a central nervous system and regional personnel without sufficient direct headquarters guidance. The solution is not to redelegate back to headquarters but to build a greater level of consistency and support into the program. EPA headquarters can achieve greater consistency by ensuring adherence to uniform program guidance and uniform definitions for clean-up criteria and by building a number of highly experienced headquarters/regional teams to work intensively in specific program areas with the regions.

CONCLUSION

In the final analysis, even in the best situation, with well defined success measures, an agreed-upon relationship between risk and remedy, and a highly competent administrative force, many people would still not be happy with Superfund. Over the last four years, the Superfund program has become better managed at both the political and administrative levels. If it is to sustain public support, however, it *must* take some very hard steps or run the risk of being the White Elephant of the environment and discrediting the rest of the nation's environmental protection efforts.

Study Questions

1. Describe Grumbly's assessment of the Superfund program. How does his assessment differ from Lewis's?
2. Evaluate Grumbly's five imperatives. Are they reasonable? Is there a likelihood of achieving success in dealing with hazardous waste in the near future?

70

The Solution to Hazardous Waste: Reduce Its Production

DAVID SAROKIN

David Sarokin is an environmental consultant in New York. In this article, Sarokin argues that going to the source and reducing the production of hazardous waste is the way to eliminate the danger of toxic waste-disposal sites. This is an "upstream solution" rather than a "downstream solution," because it meets the problem at its source instead of at the end of the pipeline.

In 1986, the state's siting commission informed the citizens of New Jersey of its recommendations: 11 towns had been selected as possible sites for the construction of hazardous waste treatment or disposal facilities. The response of the people was a unanimous "NO!" At public hearings and citizen rallies the cry was the same: "Take your landfills and incinerators and put them someplace else. We don't want them here!"

Also familiar, and at first glance reasonable, was the response of the commission. In essence, it went like this: "We have hundreds of thousands of tons of hazardous wastes to dispose of—wastes that come from the creation of material we all use, materials that improve our quality of life, materials no one wants to do without. Industry has to keep manufacturing; the wastes have to go somewhere. Let's make sure they are managed safely in state-of-the-art facilities."

It is an argument repeated daily in communities around the world. The outcome of the dispute depended on the individual circumstances, but the polar stand-off between the "siters"—those that wanted to see some form of "safe" disposal—and the "NIMBYs"—those that cried "not-in-my-backyard"—was invariable.

WASTE REDUCTION

Until now. Today, there is a third variation on the old standoff, one that derives from a new way of thinking about how to solve the toxic waste crisis. Today, the response from communities around the world is more enlightened, more pointed and far more promising. Citizens are asking: Are landfills and incinerators really needed? Why do hazardous wastes have to be generated in the first place? Can't industry, with all its expertise and creativity, find a way to eliminate hazardous wastes? Let's do everything in our power to minimize hazardous wastes before we start talking about disposal facilities.

This idea is called waste reduction. It was born in the common sense realization that the generation, not the disposal, of toxic wastes is the problem. It has seized the imagination of environmentalists, industrialists, and governments around the world. It is the "upstream solution"—a way to deal with the problem at the source rather than "downstream"—at the end of the pipeline. And it has profound implications for environmentalists, industry and the world.

In the U.S., 20 states have programs in place to encourage industrial waste reduction, and the federal government is considering expanding its fledgling national program. The United Nations Economic Commission for Europe held its first conference on Non-Waste Technology in 1976 and has continued its activities since then. The governments of Austria, Denmark, France and the Netherlands, to name a few, provide funds to promote industrial waste reduction efforts.

The idea of waste reduction, at least in scientific and policy circles, is not new. More than a decade ago the U.S. Environmental Protection Agency established a preferred hierarchy of waste management practices.

The ideal option is waste reduction—not to generate toxics in the first place, wherever and whenever possible. The second alternative is recycling—for wastes that cannot be reduced, industry should find ways to reuse them. The third choice is destruction—the wastes that remain despite the best efforts to reduce or recycle should be destroyed where possible through effective treatment operations. Disposal—in pits, lagoons, deep wells and at sea—is the least desirable method of dealing with wastes.

"DOWNSTREAM" MENTALITY

Since establishing this hierarchy, the U.S. EPA is just beginning to pay attention to waste reduction. Canada also is starting to explore the reduction option. Although a number of European countries have voiced support for waste reduction, the impact of their programs is difficult to gauge. And only a handful of waste generating companies have set up waste reduction programs. Governments, industry and, to some extent, environmentalists have focused almost all their attention, time and resources on the disposal and destruction of hazardous wastes—the lowest rungs on the waste management ladder.

Reprinted from *Greenpeace* 12:1, 1988, by permission.

How one chemical company came to employ source reduction in its plant illustrates the problems with the "downstream" mentality. A chemical plant that manufactures resins—the industrial "glue" used to hold together plywood, particle board and other products—used large quantities of toxic chemicals such as phenol and formaldehyde as its major raw materials. These and other chemicals found their way into the plant's wastewater which, after on-site treatment, was discharged to the local sewage treatment plant.

That might have been the end of the story right there, had not the sewage treatment plant, because of end-of-pipeline regulations, imposed stringent restrictions on the amount of toxic chemicals it would accept in the wastewater. The company's treatment facility, an evaporation pond, was filling up with sludge faster than expected, and cost of sludge disposal was skyrocketing. Management thought of building a bigger pond, but that was too expensive as well. Besides, they were getting increasingly worried about the legal liability the company would face if groundwater beneath the pond was contaminated.

Through a variety of unique circumstances, the company was forced to consider reducing its production of toxics. For the first time in almost 30 years of resins production, the plant management took a hard look at where the wastes were coming from and what could be done to curb production.

The results were startling. Through a combination of waste reduction measures that were neither expensive nor technologically difficult, the plant reduced its generation of hazardous wastes by 93 percent and saved itself over $50,000 in sludge disposal costs. Some steps were as straightforward as flushing a chemical loading hose with water before disconnecting it to prevent toxic chemicals from dripping on the floor.

ATTITUDE ADJUSTMENT

This plant's accomplishments are encouraging, but the point of the story is this: nothing prevented the company from using the same waste reduction techniques 10, 20 or 30 years ago. The obstacles are not technological nor economic. It was simply a matter of attitude, encouraged by a flawed regulatory structure and the availability of cheap, out-of-sight disposal solutions, that determined how much attention and creativity the company focused on handling hazardous wastes.

It is only when the plants find themselves with their backs against the wall—the full on-site disposal pond, a state or government regulation, the threat of lawsuits and the growing price of the disposal option—that the upstream solution is explored.

Originally, "waste management" meant little more than finding the most convenient river or empty spot of land to dump materials. But as the use and discharge of chemicals skyrocketed (U.S. production of organic chemicals in particular grew at a rate ten times that of overall industrial production), it became clear that we are poisoning ourselves.

Now, many environmentalists are convinced that, for many toxic chemicals, no currently available disposal options are safe enough. Incinerators, sewage treatment plants and other forms of treatment produce emissions that are themselves sources of pollution. "What emerges is a paradox," says Michael Royston, author of *Pollution Prevention Pays*. "It takes resources to remove pollution; pollution generates residue. It takes more resources to dispose of this residue, and disposal of residue also produces pollution."

Solving the waste production problem involves two basic steps: first, toxic components can be replaced with non-toxic ones. For example, since PCBs [polychlorinated biphenyls] were banned as a health hazard several years ago, private industry has shifted to a variety of non-toxic alternatives. Secondly, by changing manufacturing processes, the volume of wastes produced can be significantly reduced.

The debate among source reduction advocates now is whether to use the carrot or the stick, or both. Should we institute a negative regulatory structure or establish government financing for information exchange and technical assistance? Whichever course is taken, we must insist that incentives be created to either encourage active waste reduction through financial penalties and other inducements, or require it, through new permit programs or other government mandates.

THE PRIVATE SECTOR

Opposing these measures is the long tradition of business-as-usual in the private sector. Many companies are ignoring readily available non-toxic substitutes. The very way industrial plants are staffed reflects the downstream bias: production staff, those who generate the wastes, are kept entirely independent of waste management staff, those who must find a place to put it. Successful waste reduction measures at one company are not always spread throughout the industry, partly due to a lack of dialogue on waste reduction, and partly due to industry's tendency to label everything they do a "trade secret."

Governmental regulations are unevenly enforced, riddled with loopholes (many toxics are not regulated at all) and overwhelmingly biased toward affecting what comes out of the pipeline, not the processes by which the wastes are produced. And most companies are simply not yet devoting the resources needed to identify and implement waste reduction steps.

The greatest obstacle to serious waste reduction efforts, however, is the availability of waste disposal capacity. As long as companies have landfills, deep wells, and sewage treatment plants for their wastes, there is little incentive to attempt a waste reduction strategy. This is especially true when these disposal options are cheap. It is no surprise that, in the U.S., most of the hazardous waste generated goes into the least expensive disposal route, deep well injection.

Not enough work has been done in this area to know if we can completely eliminate the need for incinerators and the like, but one thing is clear. Waste reduction can take us a long way towards minimizing the generation of hazardous wastes if only we make the effort to fulfill its potential.

Study Questions

1. What is Sarokin's assessment of the problem of cleaning up hazardous-waste sites? Is his assessment correct?
2. What is an "upstream solution" as opposed to a "downstream solution," and why does Sarokin prefer the former with regard to hazardous waste?

3. What does he think is the greatest obstacle to efforts to reduce hazardous waste?
4. Compare Sarokin's analysis with Lewis's and Grumbly's analyses. What would you recommend as the solution to the hazardous-waste problem? Explain your answer.

For Further Reading

Buchholz, Rogene A. *Principles of Environmental Management*. Englewood Cliffs, NJ: Prentice Hall, 1993, Chapters 8 and 9.

EPA Journal (July/August 1991 & May/June 1992).

Epstein, Samuel, et al. *Hazardous Wastes in America*. San Francisco: Sierra Book Club, 1982.

Gibbs, Lois. *The Love Canal Story*. Albany: State University of New York Press, 1982.

Kunreuther, Howard, and Ruth Patrick. "Managing the Risks of Hazardous Waste." *Environment* (April 1991).

Piesecki, Bruce. *Beyond Dumping: New Strategies for Controlling Toxic Contamination*. Greenwood Press, 1984.

CHAPTER FIFTEEN

Should We Revive Nuclear Power?

On April 26, 1986, one of the nuclear reactors at the Chernobyl nuclear power plant north of Kiev in the former Soviet Union experienced a steam explosion. Two blasts blew the 1000-ton roof off the reactor building, set the graphite core on fire, and flung 7000 kilograms of radioactive debris into the atmosphere. Winds carried these contaminated materials over parts of the USSR and Europe as far as 1250 miles from the plant. The accident occurred when the engineers were performing an experiment to ascertain how long a generator could continue to function after it had been disconnected from the main power supply during a power outage. A series of human errors took place in the process, which combined to cause the disaster of Chernobyl.

Thirty-one people died from the radiation poisoning, most of them firefighters and workers who tried to put out the more than 30 fires caused by the explosions. In a 20-mile radius, 125,000 people were evacuated. An estimated 24,000 evacuees received serious doses of radiation. Estimates vary widely (ranging from 1000 to 20,000) on how many cancer deaths will eventually result from the accident. No one really knows.

American proponents of nuclear power quickly pointed out that such explosions would not have occurred in U.S.–built reactors with strong containment domes (Chernobyl had no containment). But the public at large reacted in shock to Chernobyl. Opinion polls all over the United States and Europe showed an overwhelming rejection of nuclear power as a solution to our energy crisis. In the minds of many public policymakers, nuclear power was dead.

But many scientists argue that, tragic as Chernobyl was, as an industrial accident it was relatively minor. Consider the number of people who contract cancer each year due to dioxide pollution from coal-burning power stations, or the 500+ people killed shortly before Chernobyl when a Japanese airplane crashed. Viewed rationally, they argue, we must disengage ourselves from the harmful effects of fossil fuels, and nuclear power is still our best hope to provide clean, cost-effective energy.

The question we want to consider in this chapter is, Do the benefits of nuclear power outweigh the dangers of nuclear accidents and contamination from nuclear wastes?

In our first reading, John Jagger, a former Oak Ridge National Laboratory radiation biologist, explains radiation and how it works. He argues that we are all exposed to low-dose radiation, which appears to be relatively innocuous. It is doses above 50 rem, acute or chronic, that are harmful.

In our second article, Christopher Flavin argues that, though we must move away from the use of fossil fuels, nuclear power is not the answer. Accidents like Chernobyl are too dangerous, the cost of constructing safe and efficient nuclear reactors too high, and the political opposition to nuclear power too great for us to consider reviving nuclear power in the foreseeable future. We should turn our attention to renewable-energy forms, such as solar, wind, and biomass.

Jagger argues in our third reading that nuclear energy is safe and we need it. Citing an array of data, he argues that it is cleaner and safer than coal or oil. He agrees that we should use solar and wind energy wherever possible, but these will never be sufficient to supply all our energy needs. He details safe ways of disposing of nuclear waste. Jagger argues that, despite the loud protests of the antinuclear faction, no one has ever been killed in the United States from a nuclear accident and that Chernobyl, while a tragic accident, was a rare combination of mistakes in which everything went wrong that could go wrong. Judging by other accidents, such as airplane accidents, it was a minor industrial accident. The opposition against nuclear power is based mostly on ignorance and fear of the unknown.

In our final reading, "Nuclear Waste: The Problem That Won't Go Away," Nicholas Lenssen argues that (1) our ignorance of the dangers of low-level nuclear radiation, (2) our knowledge of the lethal effects of moderate doses, and (3) our inability to give a guarantee that disposed nuclear waste will not harm future generations present a strong presumption against using nuclear power. We already have a difficult problem in trying safely to dispose of the waste already produced without creating more. Lenssen's article is valuable for its global scope, reviewing the manner in which other nations are struggling with this issue.

71

The Natural World of Radiation

JOHN JAGGER

John Jagger is a radiation biologist, who holds a Ph.D. in biophysics from Yale University. He did research at the Radium Institute in Paris and the Oak Ridge National Laboratory in Tennessee, prior to spending 21 years as a professor of biology at the University of Texas at Dallas. He retired in 1986 and now writes on issues of science and public policy. In this article, he describes what radiation is, how it surrounds and permeates us, and the extent to which it may be bad for us.

Nuclear power is a controversial subject, almost solely because of fears of radiation. While economic or other factors occasionally enter the discussion, they are minor compared with the concern about radiation. Consequently, we must consider what radiation is and what it can do to us. This review will be short—further details may be found in the literature.[1]

WHAT IS RADIATION?

The radiation that is important in the nuclear power picture is what we call *ionizing radiation*. Such radiation is capable of knocking electrons out of atoms and thereby creating electrically charged atoms, or *ions*. An atom that has been thus ionized is unstable and will usually cause a chemical reaction. If the ionized atom is part of a DNA molecule—deoxyribonucleic acid, the genetic material of all living things—then it will usually damage the DNA, although in living cells most DNA damage is repaired.

Unrepaired damage in the DNA of a living cell may kill the cell, or may cause a permanent change that can be inherited by daughter cells, which we call a *mutation*. Some mutations lead to uncontrolled growth of cells. In a multicellular organism, such uncontrolled growth is called a *cancer*. If an organism is not killed outright by radiation, cancer induction is the primary long-term deleterious effect.

Ionizing radiations are therefore rather dangerous. They include X rays and gamma rays, radiations that are basically similar to light but much more energetic. Ultraviolet light, visible light, microwaves, and radio waves are relatively weak radiations—they do not ionize

atoms and are therefore relatively harmless. I say "relatively" because near-ultraviolet radiation is present in sunlight and can cause skin cancer. It is thus a natural hazard.

Besides X rays and gamma rays, *particle radiation* is also ionizing. This includes the subatomic particles called neutrons, which have no electric charge, and alpha and beta particles, which have an electric charge. These particles are emitted from the atomic nucleus (1) when that nucleus undergoes the transformation called *radioactivity*—a relatively mild process that may release alpha particles, beta particles, or gamma rays—or (2) in *nuclear fission*—a devastating process that involves actual splitting of the atomic nucleus, with the release of gamma rays and neutrons. Nuclear fission occurs in nuclear reactors and in nuclear bombs. Radioactivity occurs in nuclear reactor waste.

The alpha and beta particles are highly ionizing particles, but they penetrate only a very short distance—on the order of a millimeter—into living tissue. They are therefore dangerous only if atoms emitting them are inhaled or ingested with food or drink. Gamma rays and neutrons, on the other hand, can easily penetrate a human body and are therefore dangerous whether they are outside or inside us.

A word about radioactivity. In the process called *radioactive decay,* an atom is transformed into another, quite different, atom, with the release of radiations from its nucleus. For example, an atom of radium, a solid, decays into an atom of radon, a gas, with the emission of an alpha particle and a gamma ray. Only certain atoms are radioactive. These are called *radioisotopes.* The new atom produced by radioactive decay is called a *daughter isotope,* and it may or may not be radioactive. For example, radon gas decays into the radioactive metal polonium, but the polonium decays into stable, nonradioactive lead.

Because of this continuous decay, the radioactivity of a substance constantly decreases, making it progressively less dangerous as time goes by. The activity drops to half of its initial value in a time called the *half-life.* Half-lives vary tremendously. The half-life of iodine-131 is 8 days ("131" is the atomic weight, which characterizes the radioisotope). The half-life of uranium-238, on the other hand, is 4.5 billion years, equal to the age of Earth! *In contrast to radioactive isotopes, many chemical poisons, especially those that consist of atoms—like mercury and lead—do not decay with time and thus stay dangerous forever.*

This essay was commissioned for the first edition of this work.

We should note that all the ionizing radiations, whether gamma rays or particles, produce similar damage in biological tissues. They may produce this damage with different efficiency, but the end damage is the same, namely, ionization of atoms.

In summary, the ionizing radiations of concern with regard to nuclear power are those from (1) radioactivity: alpha particles, beta particles, and gamma rays; and (2) nuclear fission: neutrons and gamma rays. Hereafter, my use of the term *radiation* without qualification will always mean ionizing radiation.

HOW MUCH RADIATION IS AROUND US?

We have noted that we on Earth are bathed in solar radiation, which is non-ionizing but that nevertheless can induce cancer and is an environmental hazard.

But we are also bathed in ionizing radiation, called *natural background radiation*. It comes from four sources (see Figure 1):

1. *Cosmic rays*—These come from outer space and produce chiefly electrons (similar to beta particles), as they pass through the atmosphere.
2. *Terrestrial radioactivity*—Chiefly gamma rays from metals like uranium, thorium, and radium; found in rocks and soil, and in building materials like brick, stone, and sheetrock.
3. *Internal radioactivity*—Alpha, beta, and gamma rays from radioisotopes, chiefly potassium-40, which we get in our food and water, and are present throughout our bodies.
4. *Radon*—A gas that is a radioactive daughter of radium. The danger of radon is from its own daughter radioisotopes, which produce chiefly alpha particles.

Altogether, these four sources of radiation give us a radiation *dose* of about 0.30 rem per year. (A *rem* is a unit of radiation dose to biological tissue.) For a typical American, the total natural background amounts to about *21 rems in a 70-year lifetime*. This is a significant amount of radiation. Figure 1 shows that radon is the most important of these sources; it comes chiefly from the ground on which we build our houses.

In addition a typical American receives about 0.06 rem per year from medical treatments and consumer products. This means that we are exposed to a total of about 0.36 rem per year.

It is evident that most of the natural background radiation (all but cosmic and man-made; see Figure 1) comes from Earth itself. It is produced by radioactivity in the ground, which makes a lot of heat. If you go down 20 miles below the surface of Earth, the rocks are molten. Because of the high pressure, they are not as liquid as water, but they are extremely hot and they flow, rather

like molasses. All of our volcanoes, like Kilauea in Hawaii, Mount St. Helens in Washington, and Mount Pinatubo in the Philippines, are produced by the heat of this terrestrial radioactivity.

Radioactivity is a natural part of our environment, and it surrounds us all the time. Consequently, *we too are radioactive, like all living things on Earth.*

HOW BAD IS RADIATION FOR US?

Humans are killed by radiation doses of about 450 rems, provided that the exposure is to the whole body and occurs in a short time (less than a day—an acute dose). We noted above that Americans get about 21 rems in a lifetime, just from natural background radiation. Is this harmful to us or not? This is a difficult question to answer, and there is not a clear-cut conclusion. We need to consider several things.

One consideration is that living organisms have been bathed in this ionizing radiation background throughout evolution. Furthermore, because radioactive isotopes decay with time, Earth was much more radioactive in earlier ages than it is now. If this radiation were terribly harmful, there would have been no emergence and evolution of life on Earth. So we can conclude at once that this background radiation is not extremely bad for us.

But is background radiation *at all* bad for us? High doses produce all sorts of bad effects, such as cell killing, mutation, cancer, etc. But it is hard to assess low doses, because the effects are so small that it is difficult, if not impossible, to separate the radiation effect from other effects. For example, if a 70-year-old man dies of cancer, how do we know that the background radiation he accumulated in his lifetime caused his cancer, rather than the food he ate or the industrial chemicals to which he was exposed? The answer is that we don't know. So what we do is to *extrapolate* from what we do know (effects of high doses) to what we don't know (effects of low doses).

The simplest such extrapolation is a linear one. Thus, if 100 rems of radiation produce a certain level of cancer, or some other biological effect, then we can *assume* that 10 rems will produce one-tenth of that effect. This linear extrapolation is shown in Figure 2. The straight line labeled "linear" indicates that the radiation effect is proportional to the dose. This means that, no matter how low the dose, there will always be some, albeit tiny, radiation effect. Such linear extrapolation has been widely used by scientists to arrive at estimates of "safe" doses, that is, doses below which the radiation effect would be so small as to be of little concern.

Is such *linear* extrapolation valid? A U.S. National Research Council committee has recently decided that radiation induction of solid tumors appears to fit the linear hypothesis, but that induction of leukemia (a blood cancer) shows a *sublinear* effect.[2] Figure 2 shows that a sublinear effect would mean that low doses were less harmful, per unit dose, than high doses. Furthermore, studies of survivors of Hiroshima and Nagasaki have shown a *threshold* effect for induction of several tumors.[3] This means that, at sufficiently low doses, there would be *no radiation effect at all* (see Figure 2). In fact, the National Research Council committee did state that, although a linear hypothesis is recommended for solid tumors, "epidemiologic data cannot rigorously exclude the existence of a threshold" for such tumors. Such a committee, charged with establishing safety standards, must of course always err on the conservative side.

It should be recognized that all sorts of agents may show threshold dose effects. Thus, we eat salt (sodium chloride) all the time, and in fact our bodies require it. But you can kill a person with an extremely high dose of salt. The same applies to aspirin or sleeping pills or narcotics. It is not remarkable that body defenses can handle small amounts of an external agent but are overwhelmed by acute high doses.

We should also be aware that, for the same effect, some *radiations* may show thresholds while others do not. We expect that DNA repair, for example, is readily accomplished for damage by gamma rays, which produce isolated ionizations, whereas such repair may be difficult for damage by alpha particles, which are densely ionizing. Also, for one type of radiation, some *effects* may show a threshold and others not: solid tumors seem not to show a threshold for gamma-ray damage, but leukemias do.

But this is not the end of the story. Many studies[3,4] have shown a phenomenon called *radiation hormesis,* in which low doses of radiation actually produce less cancer than no dose at all—in other words, such doses actu-

ally reduce the natural background of cancer induction, implying that *a low dose of radiation may actually be beneficial.* About 10 rem per year (thirty times background) is indicated as the optimally beneficial dose.[5] This seems quite unbelievable, but many data support this conclusion.

How could this be? It is known that low-dose radiation (5–50 rem) stimulates the immune system, which then may be better able to attack natural cancers. There are other possible explanations. For example, it is well known that living cells have enzyme systems that can repair radiation damage to DNA. Some of these systems can be stimulated to action by low-dose radiation. Such a stimulated repair system might then act on cancer-inducing damages that had been produced in the DNA by things in the environment other than radiation.

This is not to say that the idea of radiation hormesis is generally accepted. It is not. Many data support the idea, and many data do not. The jury is still out.

It has recently been estimated that the chronic radiation dose (dose given at low rate over a long time) required to double the natural mutation rate in germ cells (eggs and sperm) of humans is remarkably high—about 400 rems.[6] Arthur Upton, onetime head of the National Cancer Institute, notes that "Radiation-induced heritable mutations and chromosomal abnormalities . . . have yet to be detected in humans."[7] Neither at Hiroshima and Nagasaki, nor at Chernobyl, have such mutational effects been seen, even though the doses at these places were far above background.[8] Thus, it appears that mutations that will be carried on to future generations may not occur at all at low doses.

Such genetic defects inherited by children from irradiated parents should not be confused with effects on

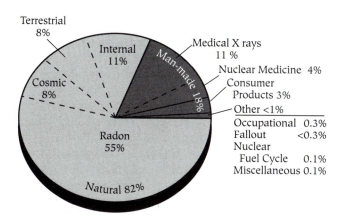

FIGURE 1 *The Percentage Contribution of Various Radiation Sources to the Total Average Effective Dose Equivalent in the U.S. Population. (From National Council on Radiation Protection and Measurements—Report #93—1987.* Ionizing Radiation Exposure of the Population of the United States. *Bethesda, MD: NCRP. Reprinted by permission of the National Council on Radiation Protection and Measurements.)*

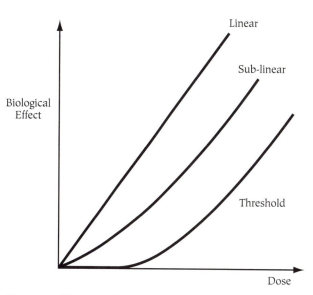

FIGURE 2 *Diagram of a Linear, a Sublinear, and a Threshold Response to Radiation. (From J. Jagger [See Note 1]. Reprinted by permission of Plenum Publishing Corp.)*

The Natural World of Radiation   465

embryos irradiated *in utero* (resulting in abnormal infants). These have been clearly shown at Hiroshima and Nagasaki, but not at Chernobyl, where the doses were much lower.[9] Damage to an embryo is essentially *somatic* damage, or damage to body cells, as opposed to heritable mutation damage, which is damage to germ cells.

Since radiation-induced cancer results from somatic mutation, it would not be surprising if background radiation did *not* produce cancer, since a lifetime background dose is 20 times less than the mutation doubling dose in germ cells. In fact, several epidemiological studies in different countries have shown a significant *negative* correlation of background radiation with cancer. Bernard Cohen, of the University of Pittsburgh, has recently reported a study covering 411 counties from all parts of the United States, that shows a negative correlation of lung cancer mortality with radon exposure.[10] In other words, for lung cancer deaths caused by radon, this study indicates at least a dose threshold and perhaps even hormesis.

Nevertheless, estimates of harmful effects of background radiation continue to be based on linear extrapolation from effects at higher doses.[11] Such extrapolation indicates that background radiation might be responsible for some 16,000 cancers per year in the U.S. population, of which about 10,000 would be due to radon (see Figure 1). Although some studies support this, the statistics are often questionable. A November 1992 survey of studies in many countries on radon and cancer concludes that positive correlations are based on an "extremely weak epidemiologic data base."[12] This implies that any real effect is probably small, since it is so difficult to demonstrate.

Finally, let us consider another type of evidence. It is known that natural background radiation varies greatly in different places. Thus, the natural background in Sweden is two times higher than in Louisiana, and in Colorado it is three times higher than in Louisiana. Yet cancer death rates actually show an opposite trend, although the differences are probably not significant— the figures are: Louisiana, 212; Sweden, 154; Colorado, 141 deaths per 100,000 people in 1989.[13] Indeed, the National Research Council BEIR V report[14] states that "no increase in the frequency of cancer has been documented in populations residing in areas of high natural background radiation."

All data to date strongly suggest that the human body has learned to cope with the low background radiation that we encounter, rendering it virtually harmless. And since background radiation is no different than other kinds of "imposed" radiation, such as from medical procedures or nuclear power activities, we may conclude that *low doses of radiation, received over a long period of time, appear to be relatively innocuous, regardless of the source of the radiation.*

Note the restriction to radiation received over a long period. Acute low doses, such as those from a nuclear accident or a nuclear bomb attack, might be more effective. Furthermore, we know that doses above about 50 rem, acute or chronic, are harmful. Workers in some areas of the nuclear industry, such as uranium miners or those involved in cleanup operations after the Chernobyl accident, may receive harmful doses. But the average citizen is harmed very little, if at all, by chronic low-dose radiation, such as that from the natural background.

Notes

1. Jagger, J. *The Nuclear Lion: What Every Citizen Should Know About Nuclear Power and Nuclear War* (New York: Plenum Press, 1991).
2. BEIR V. Committee on the Biological Effects of Ionizing Radiations, National Research Council. *Health Effects of Exposure to Low Levels of Ionizing Radiation* (Washington, D.C.: National Academy Press, 1990).
3. Kondo, S. *Health Effects of Low Level Radiation* (Osaka, Japan: Kinki University Press; and Madison, WI: Medical Physics Publishing, 1993).
4. Luckey, T. D. *Radiation Hormesis* (Boca Raton, FL: CRC Press, 1992). In contrast, the BEIR V report (Note 2), using linear extrapolation from high doses, estimates about 80 excess cancer deaths (beyond the normal 2000) per 10,000 people, following a 10-rem acute exposure.
5. Ibid.
6. Neel, J. V., et al. "The Children of Parents Exposed to Atomic Bombs: Estimates of the Genetic Doubling Dose of Radiation for Humans," *Amer. J. Human Genetics* 46 (1990): 1053–1072.
7. Upton, A. C. "The First Hundred Years of Radiation Research: What Have They Taught Us?" *Environmental Res.* 59 (1992): 36–48.
8. Jagger, J. "Nuclear Power Is Safe and We Need It," in this volume, Reading 73.
9. Ibid.
10. Cohen, B. L. "A Test of the Linear–No Threshold Theory of Radiation Carcinogenesis," *Environmental Res.* 53 (1990): 193–220.
11. BEIR V, op. cit.
12. Neuberger, J. S. "Residential Radon Exposure and Lung Cancer: An Overview of Ongoing Studies," *Health Physics* 63 (1992): 503–509.
13. Silverberg, E. and J. A. Lubera. *Cancer Statistics 1989.* Professional Education Publication (Atlanta: American Cancer Society, 1989). Also, a *negative* correlation was found between overall cancer incidence/mortality and natural background radiation exposure in a study of five cities in India (K. S. V. Nambi and S. D. Soman, *Health Physics* 52 [1987]: 653–657.
14. Beir V, op. cit.

Study Question

1. Go over Jagger's article, make sure you understand his discussion, and see if you disagree with any of his points.

Does he convince you that radiation is not the evil that it is sometimes made out to be? That we live with radiation all the time? That the few data indicating that small amounts are injurious are not statistically convincing?

72

No: The Case Against Reviving Nuclear Power

CHRISTOPHER FLAVIN

Christopher Flavin is a scientist-writer for Worldwatch Institute, an organization committed to global environmental issues and supported by the United Nations.

Flavin argues that the case against reviving nuclear power resides in the possibility of dangerous Chernobyl-like accidents, the enormous construction and maintenance costs, and the public's fear of nuclear power. He agrees with the proponents of nuclear power that we ought to move away from the burning of fossil fuels, but the answer is not nuclear power. We ought to give that up and turn to renewable energy sources such as solar, wind, and biomass, while making our cars and trucks more energy-efficient.

At 1:00 on the morning of May 26th, 1988, the Long Island Lighting Company and the State of New York reached an extraordinary settlement. The utility agreed to sell its completed but never operated nuclear plant at Shoreham to the state for one dollar, while the state promised to permanently close the $5.3 billion facility and grant the utility a series of rate increases intended to save it from imminent bankruptcy.

To one not familiar with the current status of nuclear power, the Shoreham saga has an Alice-in-Wonderland quality. How, might one wonder, could nuclear planners have sited a plant in a densely populated part of Long Island, and then pushed the project forward despite overwhelming local opposition?

How could the original construction schedule have been missed by more than a decade and the budget by more than $4 billion? How could a private company have tied its very survival to the completion of a single power plant whose cost exceeded the value of all of its other assets?

And how could the Nuclear Regulatory Commission have allowed a utility to load radioactive fuel into a plant unlikely to ever get a full operating license, an act that will add hundreds of millions of dollars to New York's expense for decommissioning Shoreham?

The Shoreham case is extreme, but it is symbolic of the problems currently facing nuclear power. It includes colossal mismanagement, cost overruns that would make the Pentagon blanch, and fierce political battles that pit citizens and local officials against government bureaucracies committed to expanding nuclear power.

Five years after the Chernobyl accident, the political and economic tide around the world is running strongly against nuclear power—pushed by many of the same forces that did in Shoreham. Nuclear power has become expensive, its growth has been mismanaged, and an increasing number of citizens are rejecting it. The daunting problems of nuclear waste disposal and nuclear materials proliferation grow ever more indomitable as governments fail to come up with solutions and the materials themselves accumulate.

Despite the lack of such solutions, some officials are now calling for a revival of nuclear power. The new impetus: global warming and other environmental threats caused by the world's reliance on fossil fuels. Once a scientific theory, human-induced climate change is now an accepted reality. The world's current energy trends are beginning to undermine the health of environmental systems crucial for humanity's survival.

As governments and international agencies look for alternatives to oil and coal, nuclear power is once again presented as a candidate. Societies are now in danger of banking on a new generation of nuclear reactors without fully understanding the enormity of the problems that ruined the last generation.

A DECADE OF SETBACKS

When disaster struck the Three Mile Island nuclear plant in March of 1979, the global nuclear industry was running at full throttle. New plants were being built at a record pace, governments were almost universally in favor of nuclear power, and public acceptance of these plans was unquestioned. Three Mile Island, however, was the first in what would be a series of setbacks for nuclear power. Now, 12 years later, the nuclear programs of nearly every country have been touched by the ripple of doubt set off by that accident and the one at Chernobyl.

At first glance, it would seem that nuclear power has continued to flourish in the past decade. Generating capacity, for example, has risen more than fourfold to

Reprinted from *The Worldwatch Reader*, ed. Lester Brown (New York: Norton 1991), by permission.

312,000 megawatts. But beneath this veneer of progress is a sick industry that is getting few new orders and in many countries is clearly winding down.

In the United States, Three Mile Island was a pivotal event. As the pioneering nuclear nation, the U.S. had by far and away the world's most ambitious nuclear program in 1979. Yet, not a single nuclear plant has been ordered in the United States since, and 108 have been canceled, including all of those ordered after 1974. The U.S. business magazine *Forbes* has called the failure of the U.S. nuclear power program "the largest managerial disaster in U.S. business history," involving perhaps $100 billion in wasted investments, cost overruns, and unnecessarily high electricity costs.

The U.S. nuclear construction industry has for the most part disappeared, and the pipeline of new projects is nearly empty, sustained only by a handful of plants that are a decade behind schedule on average. It now appears that the nuclear share of U.S. electricity production has peaked in the early nineties—at about 20 percent—and will soon begin a slow decline as older plants are retired.

It was economic more than political or technological failure that doomed nuclear power in the United States. As with the Shoreham plant, most U.S. nuclear facilities completed in the eighties are grossly uneconomical; they provide power that is five times as costly as that from plants completed a decade ago.

Hundreds of changes introduced to make nuclear power safer have added billions of dollars to costs. The industry attempted to blame regulators for requiring expensive changes, but it is clear in retrospect that the changes were needed to help avert accidents that would have caused the nuclear industry even greater damage.

EUROPE AFTER CHERNOBYL

Advocates of nuclear power often argue that the U.S. nuclear program is beset by problems of little relevance to the rest of the world. The supposed strength of nuclear power throughout Europe and much of the rest of the world is often held out as evidence that if nuclear managers and regulators would simply clean up their acts, the problems would soon be resolved.

As attractive as this argument may seem, it is belied by the declining fortunes of nuclear power across a wide spectrum of countries—from the Western democracies to the Soviet Union and the developing world. A process of gradual attrition during the early eighties has mushroomed into a massive rejection of nuclear power since Chernobyl—more for political reasons than for technological or economic ones.

In Europe, several countries have made formal commitments to shut down their nuclear programs in the wake of Chernobyl. Months after the Soviet disaster, Austria abandoned its only nuclear plant, at Zwentendorf—a plant that like the one at Shoreham had never been operated. Greece decided at about the same time to scrap plans to build its first nuclear plant.

After a protracted political debate that contributed to the collapse of two governments, Italian voters decided in March 1988 to block the expansion of the country's already stalled nuclear program. Two months later, under intense political pressure, the Italian government decided to stop work on the country's only remaining nuclear construction project, at Montalto di Castro; this leaves three completed reactors operating intermittently. Though not quite officially dead, Italy's nuclear program shows few remaining vital signs.

Early in 1988 the government of Belgium, which is already heavily nuclearized, decided to postpone expansion plans indefinitely. The Netherlands, which has no large reactors, has also canceled its plans. Switzerland, which has not completed a nuclear plant since 1980, decided in 1988 to cancel 22-year-old plans to build the country's sixth nuclear facility at Kaiseraugst.

Scandinavia's nuclear programs have also been moving in reverse. Finland, with a substantial nuclear capacity, indefinitely postponed expansion plans after Chernobyl. Sweden decided in a 1978 referendum to phase out nuclear power by 2010, despite the fact that nuclear plants supply 40 percent of the country's electricity. The Chernobyl accident forced the government to firm up these plans by scheduling the shutdown of the first two plants in 1995 and 1996. Denmark and Norway, meanwhile, have reaffirmed their vows never to develop nuclear power.

Europe's second and third largest nuclear power programs remain in a state of limbo. Nuclear opposition has flourished in West Germany since Chernobyl; this has further weakened the already remote possibility of the country's building additional nuclear plants. Several state governments and the major opposition party in the federal parliament are vehemently opposed to nuclear power, but the Christian-Democratic government continues to support it.

TABLE 1 *Public Opposition in Selected Countries to Building Additional Nuclear Power Plants[1]*

COUNTRY	BEFORE CHERNOBYL	AFTER CHERNOBYL
	(percent)	
United Kingdom	65	83
West Germany	46	83
Italy	—	79
United States	67	78
Yugoslavia	40	74
Canada	60	70
Finland	33	64
France	—	52

[1] Wording and polling techniques varied, but data are broadly comparable. Pre-Chernobyl figures are from polls taken between 1982 and 1986.

Source: Worldwatch Institute, based on Gallup and other polls.

In Great Britain, the Thatcher government got to work on a nuclear plant at Sizewell after it concluded an eight-year debate in 1987. But since then, the government has decided to forego any further construction, largely due to the objections of the country's financial community.

France, meanwhile, remains Europe's pronuclear holdout. Four more plants were completed in 1987; this gives the country a nuclear capacity second only to that of the United States. Nuclear power now supplies 75 percent of the country's electricity.

But even France's nuclear program is plagued by a growing number of technical malfunctions. In the spring of 1988, one plant at Flamanville lost its cooling capacity twice, a plant at Nogent-sur-Seine released radioactive steam, and several other plants were shut down due to radiation leaks. France has so far avoided a Three Mile Island or Chernobyl-style debacle, and it is uncertain whether the pronuclear consensus would survive such an event.

The more obvious problem in France is too much nuclear capacity. The country has been forced to sell electricity to neighboring countries at bargain prices and to run its plants at partial capacity. This gap will grow larger as more plants come on-line in the next few years. France's nuclear expansion has been slowed from one plant per year to several over the next decade, a level intended just barely to support the government-owned nuclear manufacturing industry.

The French state utility has built up an enormous debt of $37 billion, which continues to grow as high-cost nuclear electricity is subsidized so as to encourage greater consumption and justify the investment. Nuclear power has helped reduce the country's oil import bill, but it has also tended to starve other parts of the French economy of investment capital. Now, the economy is not growing nearly fast enough to support the country's large nuclear program.

SECOND THOUGHTS IN THE SOVIET UNION

Prior to Chernobyl, the Soviet nuclear program—third largest in the world—was generally thought to have avoided the morass of political problems that derailed programs in the West. The Soviet government maintained a firm commitment to nuclear power in building an industry that supplies 11 percent of the country's electricity.

Since Chernobyl, the Soviet nuclear consensus has clearly broken down. Top Soviet officials regularly contradict one another about the status of nuclear power, and local citizens groups and public officials have openly dissented from the national program.

The Chernobyl catastrophe and its aftermath have sowed seeds of doubt about nuclear power and the capacity of Soviet industry to manage it. The cleanup at Chernobyl has not gone well, and the total cost of the accident is now projected to reach $360 billion.

Meanwhile, rumors of radiation-related sickness continue to circulate in the Ukraine, and citizens report a general sense of fearfulness and unease five years after the accident. Public confidence has been further undermined by reports of subsequent mismanagement at the remaining Chernobyl reactors, breaches serious enough to require disciplinary action against key officials.

Such stories have fueled an outburst of antinuclear protests throughout the Soviet Union. Indeed, Soviet press reports indicate that all of the country's operating nuclear plants face local opposition, as do most of those being built. Even in the era of *glasnost,* such protests betray a remarkable degree of disquiet with government policy.

The most vociferous protests, not surprisingly, emanate from the Ukraine, where Chernobyl is located. Both the Ukraine Writers' Union and the Ukrainian Academy of Sciences have drafted a "manifesto" condemning the policies of the Ministry of Atomic Energy. Antinuclear petitions demanding a change of course have circulated at Moscow State University and at the Crimean Agricultural Institute.

Soviet nuclear officials have stuck to their pre-Chernobyl plans; they have agreed only to phase out production of the reactor design used at Chernobyl. Nuclear capacity in the last five-year plan was scheduled to advance by a substantial 40,000 megawatts toward the goal of supplying 21 percent of Soviet electricity by 1990. This target, however, was missed by a huge margin as Soviet nuclear capacity increased by just 6,000 megawatts since the accident.

In May 1987, it was announced that the two additional units planned at Chernobyl would not be built. This was the beginning of a long string of plants cancelled or construction halted in the face of growing public protest. Last year the Ukrainian Republic's ruling body declared it would build no new atomic power plants. This move was followed by a similar decree signed by Russian Republic President Boris Yeltsin.

It is impossible to read this litany of setbacks without suspecting that the Soviet nuclear program is in the process of coming seriously unglued. The growing cost of safety measures in the aftermath of Chernobyl will likely cast further doubt on the efficacy of nuclear investments. Portions of the Soviet scientific community now seriously question the nuclear program, and an important faction of scientists and economic planners favor an alternative approach to energy policy—in the direction of efficiency, renewable resources, and decentralized power generation.

THE SHIFTING CASE FOR NUCLEAR POWER

As nuclear power programs continue to slip into oblivion, the question remains whether countries can afford *not* to have nuclear power. Many key officials think not. Valeri Ligasov, who headed the Soviet commission that investigated the Chernobyl accident, has stated that "the future of civilization is unthinkable without the peaceful use of atomic energy."

This line is nothing new from the pronuclear camp. Although they've remained stalwart in their conviction of the necessity for atomic power, many nuclear advocates have justified it by repeatedly shifting among various arguments. In the sixties, nuclear power was pressed as an inevitable next step in the technology of energy systems. Few problems were seen as beyond the reach of scientists, and it was assumed that nuclear power would be inexpensive if not actually "too cheap to meter."

In the seventies, nuclear power was seen as an essential alternative to dwindling oil supplies, not without its own problems, but essential to stave off economic collapse. In the late eighties, with oil prices down and nuclear power programs in disarray, nuclear advocates became environmentalists, urgently arguing that only nuclear power can ease acid rain, global warming, and other threats posed by heavy use of fossil fuels.

The "technological inevitability" argument was the first to go. Since the late seventies it has become clear that the evolution of energy technology does not necessarily have to take a nuclear path. High energy prices encouraged dramatic improvements in hundreds of energy technologies, ranging from more-efficient oil refineries to less-expensive solar power.

During the past 15 years, for example, improved energy efficiency has saved far more oil than has nuclear power. Many countries now pursue the long-term development of hydroelectric and wind power, solar, energy, and biological (biomass) fuels as alternatives both to oil and nuclear power. Whatever the arguments for its development, nuclear power must now be fairly weighed against its alternatives.

Using nuclear power to fuel the economy on a large scale is possible only if it is affordable. And the best evidence available indicates that investing in nuclear power has become a risky proposition. In the United States, where financial reporting requirements are strictest, the latest generation of nuclear plants has proven to be decidedly uneconomical. These plants cost more than three times as much to build as equivalent fossil-fuel plants, and significantly more than a number of renewable energy facilities, including wind, geothermal, and biomass-fired power plants. As other power generating technologies evolve, nuclear power's financial disadvantage only widens.

Operating costs—an area in which nuclear power has traditionally enjoyed an economic advantage—are also growing malignantly. The equipment must be repaired or replaced far more frequently than was supposed. Recent surveys in the United States indicate that real operating costs have gone up almost fourfold since 1974 and that it now costs more just to operate the average nuclear plant than it does to operate a coal plant—including the cost of coal. A study by the U.S. Department of Energy suggests that some plants have become so costly to operate that it may be more economical to retire them early than to continue operations. Even writing off the $5.3 billion Shoreham plant may in the end turn out to have been a wise business decision.

At the root of these enormous cost escalations is a technology whose complexity defies human management and leads to continuing, unpredictable changes in equipment and operating procedures. Even in countries where regulatory pressures have not been as intense or public opposition as vehement, cost overruns have become endemic.

When planning a nuclear plant today, it is impossible to know how much it will cost to build, how much it will cost to operate, how long it will last, or what it will cost to decommission. This is the kind of investment that only a government or utility would make, and even they are now generally investing elsewhere.

As an alternative to oil, nuclear power's potential is also severely constrained. While nuclear power generation did substitute for oil-fired generation in Europe and Japan during the late seventies and early eighties, the power sector's use of oil is now extremely low, offering little potential for further displacement.

Throughout the world, the major claimants on the world oil supply are automobiles, trucks, buses, and industrial plants. Improved efficiency offers by far the most effective means of displacing oil in these areas.

FALSE HOPE FOR THE WORLD'S CLIMATE

The environmental argument for further nuclear expansion is at first glance more compelling than the other two. Continuing expansion of fossil fuel combustion is now causing ecological havoc around the world. Air quality in most of the world's cities continues to deteriorate, particularly in developing countries, and air pollution carried over long distances has damaged at least 22 percent of Europe's forests.

As serious as these problems are, the ultimate limit to future energy growth may lie with the earth's climate. Scientists now believe that the nearly 6 billion tons of carbon being added to the earth's atmosphere each year from the combustion of fossil fuels is contributing to irreversible climate change. Average global temperatures have already increased by about 1 degree Fahrenheit during the past century, according to a U.S. government-sponsored study published in the spring of 1988.

Global warming has begun, according to the best available scientific evidence, and climate models suggest a 9-degree rise by the middle of the next century—a faster warming than the earth has ever experienced. This would be sufficient to upset weather patterns, damage

TABLE 2 *Projections of Worldwide Nuclear Power Generating Capacity*

SOURCE AND YEAR OF PROJECTION	PROJECTION FOR		
	1980	1990	2000
	(thousand megawatts)		
International Atomic Energy Agency			
1972	315	1,300	3,500
1974	235	1,600	4,450
1976	225	1,150	2,300
1978	170	585	1,400
1980	137	458	910
1982	—	386	833
1984	—	382	605
1986	—	372	505
Worldwatch Institute			
1991	—	312	375

Sources: International Atomic Energy Agency, *Annual Reports* (Vienna: 1972–80); IAEA, *Reference Data Series No 1* (Vienna, September 1982); IAEA, *Nuclear Power Status and Trends* (Vienna: 1984–86); and Worldwatch Institute.

agricultural output, raise sea levels, and expose humanity to wrenching change. With population expanding rapidly and the world food system already stretched tight, societies would probably find it impossible to adapt to such sudden change.

New scientific evidence along with severe droughts and heat waves in several countries recently have lent a new urgency to the problem of global warming. In this light, many policymakers around the world are reassessing nuclear power. An international conference of scientists and public officials, meeting in Toronto in 1988, called for a worldwide effort to cut fossil-fuel use by 20 percent by 2005. Nuclear power was one of the energy sources the conferees suggested reevaluating for its potential to combat global warming.

Some argue that a few Chernobyls would be a small price to pay to head off global warming. Unfortunately, this is the kind of thinking that has misled nuclear planners in the past. Nuclear power is beset by problems that go well beyond its propensity for occasional accidents. Technologically, economically, and politically, nuclear power faces a series of obstacles that will prevent it from coming close to displacing enough fossil fuels to delay global warming significantly.

Analysts at the Rocky Mountain Institute, a nonprofit research organization in Colorado, have developed a nuclear scenario that reduces global warming by 20 to 30 percent by the middle of the next century through the substitution of nuclear plants for all coal-fired power plants. They found that this would require the completion of one nuclear plant every one to three days during the next 40 years. Many countries would be almost blanketed by nuclear plants, and the total cost would run to as much as $9 trillion.

A nuclear power program of this scale would require not just a reversal of a worldwide trend, but a program of nuclear construction that is ten times as large as any the world has seen. Such an effort is unthinkable, both economically and politically. Indeed, a democratic government that tried it would most likely soon be voted out of office.

Most nuclear technologists agree that a new generation of "inherently safe" reactors will have to be developed before nuclear power expands, even modestly. If governments were to throw their support into research and development programs large enough to accomplish this, it would be after the turn of the century before the first of the commercial reactors could possibly be installed.

Were such a program carried out, it would contribute virtually nothing to the 2005 goal of the Toronto conference, and would contribute only a small part of what is needed by 2050. One problem is that power generation is only part of the reason for global warming, and displacing a substantial part of even this use of fossil fuels would require an impossibly large investment in nuclear power.

TOWARD A VIABLE ENERGY STRATEGY

As the world faces the problem of global warming, it is important to come to grips with the timing of the problem. The earth now appears to be warming at a rate of about 1 degree Fahrenheit per decade, and because of time lags in the process, we are already committed to a significant increase of 3 to 4 degrees. Therefore, immediate action is needed to head off a catastrophic warming during the next several decades.

Nuclear power is clearly incapable of making a meaningful contribution during this period. The global climate would be undermined before an improved technology could even be tested—a fact that many nuclear advocates seem to be unwilling to confront.

Improved energy efficiency, however, does have the potential to reduce the projected warming in 2050 by up to half. Such a scenario requires that energy efficiency be improved by 2 percent per year beginning immediately. The technologies needed to accomplish this are at hand, and they can be economically installed. However, policy reforms are needed if we are to continue the enormous efficiency improvements made during the past decade.

In the long run, of course, societies will have to develop energy sources that replace the fossil fuels on which we rely so heavily. There are really only two alternatives: nuclear power or renewable energy sources such as solar, wind, and biomass. Since the seventies, energy policymakers and analysts have been debating the question of which path to follow. The global warming problem adds new urgency to this debate but does not make the answers any easier to come by.

Renewable energy technologies have advanced rapidly

during the past 18 years of research funding, and many are being used commercially on a fairly large scale. They have a long way to go before being ready to provide the predominant share of world energy, but it is quite possible that before improved energy efficiency begins to reach technological limits in the middle of the next century, a diverse mixture of geothermal power, wind power, biomass, and solar energy will have picked up the slack.

Nuclear advocates believe that a new generation of nuclear technologies will be ready for mass deployment as well. This is certainly an arguable point. Technological evolution is notoriously difficult to predict. However, societies are likely to find that nuclear power continues to fall short of its proponents' dreams and that it in the end faces technological, economic, and political limits that are far more intractable than those confronting renewables.

Nuclear power requires increasingly centralized energy systems and intense safety measures and security systems. Renewables are by nature diversified, decentralized, and based on relatively safe technologies. Although renewables will cost large sums to develop, they have the advantage of being more politically palatable, according to public opinion polls.

Most major governments have managed to skirt this central question by funding development of both nuclear power and renewables. The broad trend has been away from nuclear power and toward renewables, though the latter still receive a smaller share of most budgets.

The question now is whether to continue the current approach or to attempt to accelerate the development of either nuclear or renewables. There is no simple answer to this question, but if the lesson of the past decade and a half mean anything for the future, attempts to resuscitate the nuclear option will yield political friction, economic waste, and serious accidents, not a solution to the global warming problem.

Study Questions

1. Here is how Flavin sums up his position in an earlier article, "Nuclear Power's Burdened Future," *Bulletin of Atomic Scientists,* (July 1987), p. 26.

   The Faustian bargain of nuclear energy has been lost. It is high time to leave the path pursued in the use of nuclear energy in the past, to develop new alternative and clean sources of energy supply and, during the transition period, devote all efforts to ensure maximum safety. This is the price to pay to enable life to continue on this planet.

   A "Faustian bargain" refers to the legendary intellectual Faust who sold his soul to the devil for magical knowledge and power. Is this an accurate metaphor for our attraction to nuclear energy? Explain why or why not.

2. Review the major arguments against nuclear power. Which is the strongest, and which the weakest? Can you think of a response by proponents of nuclear energy?

3. After you read the next essay by John Jagger, return to Flavin's essay and compare them. Discuss the various strengths and weaknesses of these two essays.

4. Flavin seems to be saying that the post-Chernobyl public perception is the main problem in getting a viable nuclear energy program established. But if the other objections to nuclear power can be met, should this be a serious obstacle? Could education be used to affect public perception?

73

Yes: Nuclear Power Is Safe, and We Need It

For a biographical sketch, see Reading 71.

NUCLEAR POWER REACTORS

In any discussion of nuclear power, one must understand the behavior of the central player in this drama: the nuclear power reactor. This is a machine in which nuclear fission of uranium or plutonium atoms is conducted so that the energy is released in a controlled way. This energy appears in the form of heat, which may then be used to drive a steam turbine to produce electricity.

Details of the structure and operation of nuclear reactors may be found in my book.[1] Here I discuss the safety of nuclear power reactors, treating first normal operations and then various types of abnormal operation.

Normal Operations

A normally operating nuclear power plant is much safer than most people would think. But two other aspects of normal operation bother many people: transport of nuclear materials and disposal of nuclear waste. However, these are also very safe.

Radiation Emissions. What about the radiation and other toxic emissions from a nuclear power plant? In

---

This essay was commissioned for the first edition of this work.

472 Yes: Nuclear Power Is Safe, and We Need It

fact, they are almost nonexistent: neighboring populations typically receive less than 0.001 rem of radiation per year.[2] This is tiny in comparison with natural background radiation, which is 300 times higher. The highest doses permitted by the U.S. Nuclear Regulatory Commission (NRC) that may be received by a person who stayed *at the boundary fence of a nuclear power plant 24 hours a day* is only 0.010 rem per year, or 1/30 of natural background. This amount of radiation corresponds to the additional dose of cosmic rays that one receives on a round-trip jet flight from San Francisco to Tokyo. Grand Central Station in New York could not be licensed as a nuclear reactor, because the radiation from its granite blocks would violate NRC standards! The radiation emitted by nuclear power plants is therefore of no concern.

In addition, most people are not aware that coal-burning power plants emit radiation from the plant stacks, due to the presence of radium and other radioisotopes in coal. This radiation also is quite innocuous because there is so little of it, but it is worth noting that it often exceeds that of nuclear power plants. In addition, the coal-burning plant emits vast quantities of smoke, ash, and sulfur and nitrogen oxides, as well as carbon dioxide (CO_2), while the nuclear plant emits none of these. Americans are concerned with destruction of the stratospheric ozone layer by nitrogen oxides, the production of acid rain by sulfur oxides, and the greenhouse effect produced by CO_2 emissions. Burning fossil fuels for energy contributes greatly to all of these. But burning nuclear fuel contributes absolutely nothing to these dire atmospheric changes.

In summary, *a normally operating nuclear power plant emits no air pollutants and typically less radiation than a coal-burning power plant.*

Transport of Radioactive Materials. Nuclear materials must often be shipped long distances. The chief concern is with transport of "spent," or used, fuel from nuclear power plants. This fuel is highly radioactive. Yet the transport of such materials has never resulted in an accident anywhere in the world that released harmful amounts of radioactive material. There have been accidents, of course, but the nuclear material is shipped in containers designed to survive being crashed into solid walls at 80 miles per hour, hit by railroad locomotives at similar speeds, engulfed in gasoline fires for 30 minutes, and submerged in water for 8 hours. Such containers have never ruptured in an accident. To date, *the safety record on transport of radioactive materials is perfect.*

The same cannot be said for transport of other hazardous materials. Few trucks or railroad cars are involved in the transport of nuclear waste, because the quantities are so small. In contrast, gasoline truck accidents kill about 100 Americans a year, and coal-carrying trains kill some 1000 people a year.[3] Yet New York City permits trucks and trains carrying hazardous chemicals and gasoline to pass through the city. It prohibits such transport of nuclear materials. There is a name for such an attitude: paranoia.

Nuclear Waste. Disposal of nuclear waste is the major concern of those who oppose nuclear power. The problems are in fact complex and serious. But these problems have been largely solved in a technical sense—the chief barriers now to effective waste disposal are political and psychological.

As noted in the first article in this chapter ("The Natural World of Radiation"), there is a considerable amount of radioactivity in our natural environment, and this radioactivity does not appear to be particularly harmful. Therefore, if a nuclear waste–disposal site might release small amounts of radiation, this should be of little concern. In this regard, the disposal of most *low-level waste* is a minor problem. Such waste includes things like discarded clothing of nuclear workers and the tiny amounts of radioisotopes used in medical nuclear research, many of which have short half-lives. Such items can be disposed of in shallow burial sites, where they will not add significantly to the radioactivity already in the ground.

It is true that some things that are quite radioactive, such as cooling-water filters and old control rods from nuclear power plants, have been classified as low-level waste. This is undesirable and points to the need for a better classification of types of radiation waste. The criterion for low-level waste should be *waste that poses no long-term health hazard after disposal.* Such a reclassification would go a long way toward allaying citizen fears about low-level nuclear waste.

Our major concern, then, is with *high-level waste,* which by definition would include everything that is not low-level waste. Where does such waste come from? The major source is spent (used) fuel rods from reactors, which contain many highly radioactive isotopes. The danger of these isotopes for human health depends greatly on the half-life.

Radioisotopes with very long half-lives (millions of years), like uranium-235 and neptunium-237 (see Table 1), are not dangerous, because *a very long half-life means a very low level of radioactivity.* If you burn wood slowly over a long period of time, it will release heat at a low rate; but if you burn it quickly, the heat will be much more intense. The same applies to radioactive decay. For example, a miner can hold a chunk of uranium ore in his hand without being dangerously exposed to radiation (most of the radiation in a mine arises from radon gas). Thus, much of the popular concern about radioisotopes of very long half-life is a misplaced concern.

Radioisotopes with short half-lives (tens of years) are also not a great problem. They are very radioactive because of their short half-lives, but this also means that they "burn themselves out" quickly. The nuclear reac-

TABLE 1 *Half-Lives of Some Typical Radioisotopes in Spent Fuel*

RADIOISOTOPE	HALF-LIFE (YEARS)
Very long	
Uranium-235	700,000,000
Neptunium-237	2,000,000
Intermediate	
Plutonium-239	24,000
Plutonium-240	7,000
Americium-241	500
Americium-243	8,000
Short	
Strontium-90	30
Cesium-137	30
Cesium-134	2

tion that creates the energy in a nuclear plant produces *fission products,* like strontium-90 and cesium-137 and -134, with relatively short half-lives—up to 30 years. Because of their high radioactivity, they must be handled with great care, but their activity is very low after 300 years, so that very long-term disposal is not required.

Radioisotopes with intermediate half-lives (thousands of years) are the real problem. Spent fuel rods from a reactor contain some of the original uranium or plutonium, in addition to several other *transuranic elements,* such as neptunium and americium. (These elements are called *transuranic* because their atomic weight is greater than that of uranium—they do not exist in nature and are produced only by human activities.) Some transuranic elements, like neptunium-237, have very long half-lives and are therefore not a major concern. But many transuranics, like plutonium-239 and americium-243, have intermediate half-lives, of the order of thousands of years (Table 1). These isotopes are much more radioactive and, if present

in sufficient quantity, can be quite dangerous and must be sequestered for very long times.

The Nuclear Waste Policy Act of 1983 requires that untreated spent fuel, which contains high levels of transuranic isotopes with intermediate half-lives, be isolated for 10,000 years, at which time the radioactivity would have dropped to about 10 times that of uranium ore, a tolerable level since the waste would be far more isolated from humans than is natural uranium ore.

However, to dispose of such untreated spent fuel, as we plan to do in this country, is really a great waste and increases the hazard unnecessarily. If one *reprocesses* the spent fuel, over 99% of the uranium and plutonium is removed, as well as significant amounts of the other transuranic isotopes. This uranium and plutonium can then be used again in reactors, thus extending by about a factor of 100 the useful lifetime of the fuel. Equally important is a great reduction in the high-level waste volume and the time during which the waste must be sequestered.

In such reprocessed waste, the radioactivity is high to start with, after 10 years being still about 5000 times greater than that of uranium ore (Figure 1). But it drops dramatically in the first few hundred years, partly because of steady decay of the transuranics, but especially because of rapid decay of the relatively short-lived fission products. After 1000 years, the radioactivity of the waste has dropped to only 2 times that of uranium ore, and is no longer of concern (Figure 1).

To summarize, if we were to reprocess our spent nuclear fuel before we dispose of it, we would only have to sequester it for 1000 years; the longer it was held, the less dangerous it would become. One thousand years is a long time, and people have expressed concern that we would be able to keep records that long. How could we be sure that people would remember where we buried it?

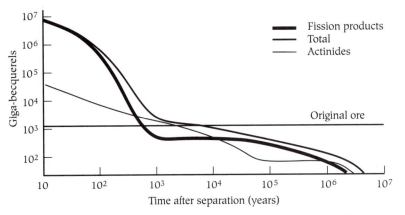

FIGURE 1 *Radioactivity per Metric Ton of Reprocessed High-Level Nuclear Waste Over Time. Both scales are logarithmic. The total radioactivity (top curve) declines rapidly for the first thousand years and more slowly thereafter. The rapid initial drop is due primarily to decay of fission products (middle heavy curve). The decay of actinides (light curve), which include uranium and the transuranics, is fairly steady with time. After 1000 (10^3) years, the total activity is down to twice the level of uranium ore. (Figure 3, from* Disposal of Radioactive Waste: Review of Safety Assessment Methods, *Nuclear Energy Agency, Organization for Economic Co-operation and Development (OECD). Paris: OECD Publications, 1991. Reprinted by permission of the OECD.)*

But this is not a real problem. We are well aware of the tombs of Egyptian pharaohs that are 5000 years old! With current techniques of preserving and duplicating information, these records would surely survive. Furthermore, deep geologic disposal of waste in rocks millions of years old would be so safe that we could almost literally forget about it!

Reprocessing is now being done in the United Kingdom, France, Russia, and India, while several countries contract with the U.K. or France for reprocessing of their fuel. The United States does not reprocess, because of a poorly conceived policy of President Carter that was aimed at limiting the worldwide spread of plutonium. We need to reprocess our spent fuel not only because it greatly reduces the waste disposal problem but also because such reprocessing would provide us with enough nuclear fuel to last tens of thousands of years. To dispose of spent fuel without reprocessing is wasteful and irrational.

Some critics of nuclear power claim that reprocessing produces more waste. This is wrong. After reprocessing, there is much waste left over, but *since virtually all the uranium and plutonium, as well as large amounts of other transuranics have been removed*, it stands to reason that the waste after reprocessing possesses far lower total radioactivity. This is mostly in the form of isotopes with relatively short half-lives. The removal of much of the transuranics, with intermediate half-lives (thousands of years), reduces the time required for storage from about 10,000 years to about 1000 years. A good deal of *chemical* waste is associated with reprocessing, but disposing of this is no more of a problem than disposal of any other chemical waste.

It should be recognized that spent nuclear fuel, fresh from a reactor, is very "hot," both in the radioactive sense and in the sense that it produces a great deal of heat. This activity drops precipitously in the early years, since much of it is in short-lived isotopes, so that waste that has been "held" for 40 years has only about 1/100 of its original radioactivity and therefore produces only 1/100 as much heat. Such fresh waste is usually held in cooling ponds of water at the reactor site. Water is an excellent absorber of both the radiation and the heat. Such "holding" of hot fuel rods is normal and safe. It greatly alleviates the later problems of sequestering the waste in a safe way.

How would we sequester the waste? There are two possibilities. We can *confine* the waste, which means sequestering it so it is safe from interference by people or by natural disasters, but it can *still be retrieved*. Retaining the possibility of retrieval is important because (1) we may very well want to use this "waste" at some future time, since radioactive isotopes are useful in a wide variety of applications, and (2) if it should be decided at some future time that the repository was not entirely safe, it would be possible to transfer the waste to another site.

The other possibility is to *isolate* the waste. This means putting it where we could never again retrieve it. This includes (1) very deep burial (perhaps 5 miles) followed by sealing off the access shafts, (2) deep-seabed disposal, or (3) disposal into outer space. The advantage of such handling is that we could forget that we had disposed of the waste and would no longer have to worry about it. The disadvantage is that we could never retrieve it.

Of the three isolation options, disposal into outer space seems least desirable. It would require great energy to blast a rocket into space with such a heavy payload and the velocity necessary to escape Earth's gravitational field. But more important, should the rocket explode in the atmosphere, the wide dissemination of so much radioactivity would be a very serious matter and could be disastrous.

Deep-seabed disposal, on the other hand, is reasonable and feasible. Environmentalists are usually appalled at such a prospect, but they may not be really thinking the problem through. Most sediments in the deep sea are hundreds of feet deep and are extremely stable. It has been estimated that plutonium-239 in such a site would not migrate more than a few meters from a *breached* canister in 100,000 years.[4] In the remote event of seepage of the waste to the surface of the sediment, the vast dilution of the oceans would quickly reduce the radioactivity per cubic meter to a tiny level. Deep-seabed disposal has been unjustly shelved because of uninformed public reaction—it deserves reexamination.

The primary option being considered is deep land burial, or *geologic disposal*. One scenario involves disposal in chambers about half a mile deep in rock that has been stable for billions of years, such as the Canadian Shield, centered in Ontario Province and extending into Minnesota and Wisconsin. Such burial could be either in a confinement mode (retrievable) or in an isolation mode.

It is proposed to treat the waste for burial by a multistep process: (1) concentration, by distillation or centrifugation, (2) immobilization, by converting the waste to a dry powder and mixing it with particles of molten glass (vitrification), which would then (3) be poured into a stainless-steel canister, which provides radiation shielding. Such canisters would be about 1 foot in diameter and 10 feet long One might think it would take millions of such canisters to hold the waste. But the volume of nuclear waste is in fact very small. *The total volume of commercial nuclear waste produced in the United States during the industry's entire history up to 1990 would fit into a small warehouse.* And this is before concentration. A year's waste from a large nuclear power plant, after reprocessing, would weigh only 15 tons and, since uranium is nineteen times as dense as water, would occupy a volume of only two cubic meters, which would fit nicely under a dining-room table.[5] Six vitrification plants are now in operation in various parts of the world—none in the United States.

Some alarm has arisen from questions about possible seepage of nuclear waste from such disposal sites over thousands of years. This alarm is misplaced. For example, a study of a model 700-foot-deep clay repository in Belgium showed that, after 100,000 years, there is less than 1 chance in 1 million of radioactive release to the air, 1 chance in 1000 of release to the land surface, and 1 chance in 100 of release to ground water. *We do not show similar concern about equally dangerous chemical wastes.* Bernard Cohen, a physicist at the University of Pittsburgh, provides an instructive comparison:

> If all the electricity now used in the United States were generated from nuclear power . . . the waste produced each year would be enough to kill over 10 billion people . . . we produce enough chlorine gas each year to kill 400 trillion people . . . enough barium to kill 100 billion, and enough arsenic trioxide to kill 10 billion. All of these numbers are calculated, as for the radioactive waste, on the assumption that *all* gets into people . . .
>
> . . . Note that the nuclear waste becomes less toxic with time, because radioactive materials decay away, leaving a harmless residue, but the chemicals listed retain their toxicity forever.[6]

One of the most promising sites under study for nuclear waste disposal is Yucca Mountain, about 90 miles northwest of Las Vegas, Nevada. This is a ridge rising 1500 feet *above* the surrounding terrain, composed of welded volcanic tuff (like cinder block but more dense). The water table is 1000 feet *below* the surrounding terrain, and the annual rainfall is only 6 inches, most of which evaporates. The area is owned and guarded by the federal government (it is 30 miles from the underground nuclear bomb testing area), and the nearest inhabitants are 15 miles away. Tests indicate that this is a very good site, although studies are still under way. Finally, Yucca Mountain is ideally configured to be a *retrievable* site. The waste could be placed in horizontal tunnels bored in from the mountainside. If the site were ever determined to be at all unsafe, the waste could be moved.

An alarm raised by Jerry Szymanski, a Department of Energy (DOE) engineering geologist, that the area might be earthquake-prone and would release groundwater into the site, evoked a scare article in *The New York Times Magazine,* called "A Mountain of Trouble" (18 Nov. 1990). This idea was unanimously rejected in April 1992 by a seventeen-member National Research Council committee,[7] on the basis of a variety of studies. Such alarms, including the title of the *Times* article, do a disservice to sincere and promising efforts to deal with nuclear waste.

It is likely that Yucca Mountain will prove to be an acceptable site for nuclear waste disposal. Yet it is being fought tooth-and-nail by the state and the people of Nevada, because of unfounded fears. The state of Nevada refused to issue permits for geologic characteri-

zation of the site, but this has now been overthrown by a federal court. To refuse even *to study* the area is short-sighted in the extreme. It would seem that these people have an obligation to answer the question: Since the waste exists and must be disposed of somewhere in the United States, where do you propose disposing of it; where is there a more suitable site?

And so our nuclear waste sits where it was produced—at the nuclear power plant sites. This is not so bad, since the longer we hold the waste, the less hazardous it becomes. Still, the water ponds in which the waste is stored are filling up, and we must face the nuclear–waste disposal problem now. It is not a matter of being for or against nuclear power. *The waste is there now,* and even if we stopped all nuclear power activity tomorrow, we would still have to dispose of it. It has been noted that:

> . . . There are some 30 *trillion* cancer doses under the surface of the United States—the deposits of uranium and its daughters. They are not sealed into glass, they are not in salt formations, they are . . . where Mother Nature decided to put them . . . and they do occasionally kill people . . . The mean number of Americans killed by ingesting uranium or its daughters from natural sources is 12 per year.
>
> . . . We take uranium ore out of the unsafe places where Nature put them, and after we extract some of its energy, we put the wastes back in a safer place than before, though we do put them back in fewer places in more concentrated form . . .[8]

Abnormal Operations

Sabotage. Sabotage, or terrorism, could involve two scenarios: either damaging the nuclear plant itself, or stealing nuclear fuel and making it into a bomb. Both of these things are very difficult to do. Without going into details, we may merely state the fact that *acts of nuclear terrorism have not so far even been attempted anywhere in the world.* This is not to say that we should not remain vigilant, but the security of the nuclear industry is in fact maintained at a very high level.

Proliferation. Some people fear that the proliferation of nuclear reactors around the world for the generation of electric power may enable more countries to build nuclear weapons. This is a debatable position.

The uranium-235 used in nuclear reactors is usually purified to about 3% of the total uranium present (the rest is uranium-238, not useful as a nuclear fuel). But a bomb requires purification to about 90%. So stealing uranium fuel from a nuclear plant is of little help in making a bomb.

The concern arises rather with the fact that most power reactors produce plutonium as a by-product of the uranium fission process. Plutonium makes a more efficient bomb than uranium. But getting weapons-grade plutonium requires use of a special "plutonium-production reactor", *followed* by separation of the plutonium in a reprocessing plant. *The reprocessing plant thus becomes the critical step in bomb production.*

The nations with lots of plutonium-production capacity are those that already have nuclear arsenals (U.S., Russia, Britain, France, and China). Japan has recently acquired such capability but shows no sign of wishing to make bombs. Undeveloped countries simply cannot develop the requisite technology. Concern therefore centers about countries of intermediate development, especially those that show signs of instability (e.g., India, Pakistan, Iraq, Iran, Libya).

Ever since 1956, the International Atomic Energy Agency (IAEA) has monitored the use of nuclear fuel throughout the world and has applied safeguards against the diversion of fuel to military uses. The Nuclear Non-Proliferation Treaty of 1970 has been signed by 144 countries. These two entities have kept nuclear materials under control in almost every country, as evidenced by the recent activities of the IAEA in Iraq, a signatory nation to the Non-Proliferation Treaty.

The best way to prevent diversion of nuclear fuel to military uses would be to have, by international agreement, only a few heavily guarded reprocessing plants in the world. These could, for example, be permitted only in the five countries that now have numerous nuclear weapons. Thus, absolute control of an essential bottleneck in weapons production could be enforced, for it is not easy to hide a nuclear-reprocessing plant. It is of interest that Japan, which could now make nuclear weapons if it so chose, has much of its reprocessing done in France.

In summary, nuclear proliferation is occurring only slowly. Smaller countries that want to make a nuclear bomb are finding it harder than they thought. Saddam Hussein is learning that. In 1964 we had five nuclear-weapons countries. In 1992 we had only seven, including Israel and Pakistan. Yet nearly 40 countries have the capability to produce nuclear weapons. Proliferation thus remains a deep concern but not a worry.

Since the United States already has nuclear weapons, proliferation is not an argument against the development of nuclear power in this country. This includes the use of breeder reactors, which produce more nuclear fuel than they consume. Development of breeder technology and reprocessing plants would provide us with a virtually infinite supply of nuclear fuel. Yet such technology is on indefinite "hold" in this country.

Accidents. Much has been made of nuclear reactor accidents, yet the fact remains that *no one has ever been killed and no civilian has even been hurt by civilian nuclear power in the United States.* The same can be said for all other countries in the world except the Soviet Union, which of course had Chernobyl.

Three Mile Island (TMI) involved a partial meltdown of the reactor core, caused by six human errors. But all the fail-safe systems worked, and no harm was done to humans. This accident represents a victory for the engineering design, not a failure, as it is usually represented. It was, of course, a failure of human operators, but one that is unlikely to happen again because of the lessons learned.

No civilian was hurt as a result of Three Mile Island. The only important radioactive release was that of 15 curies of iodine-131. This produced an average dose to people living within a 10-mile radius of the plant of 0.008 rem—equivalent to the dose of extra cosmic radiation received on a round-trip jet flight from Dallas to London. The *maximum* dose estimated to be received by any civilian after TMI was less than 0.10 rem, equivalent to 4 months of background radiation. It is significant that, since TMI, there have been no further civilian reactor meltdowns outside the Soviet Union, although the number of reactors in operation has roughly doubled.

Chernobyl was a different story, but it is a unique story. It remains the only civilian nuclear reactor accident of any biological significance in the entire history of nuclear power.

As at Three Mile Island, Chernobyl resulted from human error, but in this case of a magnitude far greater. TMI was a normal operating accident, but Chernobyl was an *experiment* that did not have to be undertaken. The experiment was to test if, in a station blackout, the "coasting-down" generators would produce enough electricity to run the cooling pumps until standby diesel generators could take over. During this test, six human errors occurred, but whereas the TMI errors mostly involved attempts by the operators to correct the problem, the errors at Chernobyl were severe violations of safety rules, probably undertaken because the operators had become quite blasé after years of operation of the plant without incident. Even the Soviets called these errors "unbelievable." Had any *one* of these errors not occurred, the accident would have been relatively minor.

There are several reasons why a Chernobyl accident would not have occurred in a Western reactor. The Chernobyl reactor permits coolant water to boil sooner, making a steam explosion (what happened at Chernobyl) more likely. The reactor is inherently unstable at low power (where it was during the accident). And the reactor had a graphite moderator (material that slows neutrons), which burned for 10 days, creating about half of the radiation release. No Western civilian reactor has any of these characteristics. In addition, the Chernobyl reactor had no containment building, which most Western reactors have.

The accident itself (disregarding for the moment the radioactive fallout) was of only medium severity, as accidents go. Thirty-one people were killed at the plant itself in the early events after the explosion, and a year later only 13 of the roughly 200 survivors at the plant were still invalids and unable to return to work. No one outside the plant was injured. Nine months earlier, a Japan Air Lines crash killed 520 people. And the accidental release of methyl isocyanate from a Union Carbide plant two years earlier in Bhopal, India, killed 3700 people outright and injured 30,000 more. In terms of outright death, Chernobyl was not a major accident.

The radioactive fallout, of course, was extensive and is the cause of most of the concern about the Chernobyl accident. In fact, the Chernobyl radiation release was about the worst one could ever have in a nuclear power plant accident: At least 50 *million* curies of radiation was released to the environment (compare the 15 curies of radioiodine released at TMI). This fallout (mostly in the form of the radioactive isotopes iodine-131 and cesium-134 and -137) was heavy in the Belarus regions (1) immediately northwest of Chernobyl itself and (2) northeast of Gomel, about 100 miles northeast of Chernobyl. What will be the consequence of this vast release of radioactivity?

As of 2 years ago, the best American estimates placed the number at 17,000 people who would develop cancer over the next 50 years.[9] This number requires some explanation. First, people who develop radiation-induced cancer *do not get cancer earlier than other people,* but when they do get the cancer, the incidence is higher than normal. This means that these people will develop their cancers late in life, like most cancer victims. Second, this estimate applies to some 600 million people in Europe and the western USSR. Over the same 50-year period, this population will experience 123 *million* cancer deaths from other causes, so those induced by the fallout of Chernobyl represent *an increase over normal cancer deaths of about 1/100 of 1%, a fraction impossible to measure.* The burning of coal in the nations of the former Soviet Union will cause as many deaths *every year* as will be caused in 50 years by the Chernobyl fallout.[10] It cannot be overemphasized that the 17,000 number is an *estimate* based on expected frequencies of cancer induction. Similar estimates could predict that people living in Denver would have a great increase of cancer deaths over people living in Dallas, because the background radiation is three times higher in Denver. In fact, however, cancer rates are the same in Dallas and Denver.

Other estimates for Chernobyl are lower. Swedish researchers predicted a total of 6000 cancer deaths over 50 years,[11] and the Academy of Medical Sciences of the USSR estimated only about 1200 excess cancer deaths over 70 years throughout the 75 million population of the central European regions of the USSR (where normal cancer deaths will number about 11 million).[12] All things considered, it appears that the fallout from Chernobyl will result in only a slightly elevated level of cancer, most of which will be in Belarus.

Are the fallout areas badly contaminated? The answer is yes for certain very spotty areas near Chernobyl and Gomel. Elsewhere, and certainly throughout Europe, the contamination was negligible. While some high radioactivity occurred in Europe immediately after the accident, these levels dropped rapidly several weeks later so that the countrywide average doses during the first year after the accident ranged from 0.076 rem in Bulgaria (the highest) to 0.001 rem in Portugal (the lowest).[13] Thus, the highest level was only about 25% of natural background radiation, which is about 0.3 rem.

Figure 2 shows how the contamination from Chernobyl compares to other sources. The data for Chernobyl are *lifetime* exposures of evacuees from the Chernobyl area, those who were most highly exposed. This is comparable to the *yearly* exposures of people to radon and other natural sources. Note that the horizontal scale is logarithmic, rising by factors of 10. Figure 2 also shows that normally operating nuclear reactors emit negligible radiation.

There is one troubling factor. In their frantic attempts to seal off the reactor core in the months after the accident, the Soviets subjected a large but currently unknown number of workers to fairly high levels of radiation, and surely some of these will experience higher cancer rates. Whether this should be considered an inescapable consequence of the accident or an unnecessary reaction on the part of the authorities remains to be decided.

One hears reports of people in Belarus and Russia having all sorts of medical problems following Chernobyl. This can be largely attributed to a paranoid fear of radiation. A 1990 study by the International Advisory Committee of the IAEA, sponsored by many organizations including the World Health Organization and the United Nations, was carried out at the request of the Soviet Union.[14] The study group consisted of some 200 scientists and medical experts from twenty-five countries and was headed by Itsuzo Shige-matsu of the Radiation Effects Research Foundation in Hiroshima. One could hardly find a more objective group! They did *not* study the people who were evacuated from the 20-mile radius of Chernobyl, nor the "cleanup crews" noted above, some of whom may have received high doses. Their mission was to examine 825,000 other people in the contaminated areas of the Soviet Union. Their conclusions were:

> There were significant non-radiation-related health disorders in the populations of both surveyed contaminated and surveyed control settlements studied under the Project, but no health disorders that could be attributed directly to radiation exposure.

It is instructive to note that, among 18,000 survivors of Hiroshima and Nagasaki who received doses above 10 rems, only 325 excess cancer deaths had occurred by 1985, 40 years later.[15]

As for genetic defects in future generations, it has been found that children conceived *after* the atomic bomb explosions, by parents exposed to radiation from the bombs, showed *no increase in genetic defects*, including untoward pregnancy outcomes, infant deaths, cancers, abnormal development, chromosomal damages, and other mutations.[16] Nor have such inherited genetic defects been observed in children born to parents exposed at Chernobyl. Such genetic defects inherited from irradiated parents must be distinguished from defects in children irradiated *in utero*. While such defects were observed after the atomic bombings, they have *not* been seen in the 1950 children who were *in utero* when their mothers were exposed at Chernobyl.

In summary, the immediate consequences of the Chernobyl accident, thirty-one early deaths, place it among typical industrial accidents. The late consequences, several thousand civilians in the former Soviet Union dying from cancer over the next 50 years, is 1/50 of the number of civilians in that area who will die from the burning of coal.

THE POWER DILEMMA

Our Appetite for Energy

The United States uses about 25% of the world's energy, about the same as that of all of the developing countries of the world put together.[17] Is this good or bad?

The wealth of the United States, like that of other highly industrialized countries, is an asset for the world, providing such things as rapid transportation, sound housing, hygiene, and modern medicine. For people everywhere, these developments have resulted in vastly enhanced personal security and the bright prospect of a fulfilled life.

But we have become so used to the idea of continual growth that we feel we are in trouble if the gross national product (GNP) does not grow every year. However, the natural resources of the world are limited; we cannot go on forever using them up. To a large extent, the welfare of individual humans has been secured, so we do not need to continue increasing our wealth without limit. Of course, poverty, starvation, and despotism are still widespread in less developed countries. But their alleviation is more a matter of allocation of resources than of further development of them.

To cap our growth in use of resources does not necessarily mean capping the GNP, which depends on efficiency and innovation as well as on use of natural resources. In the United States, we should even consider *decreasing* our use of resources.

We have in fact begun to lower the growth in use of energy. World energy use has grown more slowly than expected since 1980—less than 2% a year.[18] This downward trend must continue. The goal should be to use as little energy as we can. We could save much energy by instituting some simple practices such as building our homes half underground (where the steady temperature of the ground provides heat in winter and cooling in summer), using energy-efficient light bulbs, producing smaller newspapers, and not expecting everything we buy to come in a wrapper.

We are making progress in these areas. Our use of energy in the United States may soon level off and perhaps even decrease in the next century. If this happens, why do we need to build more nuclear plants? As with many questions, the answer is complex.

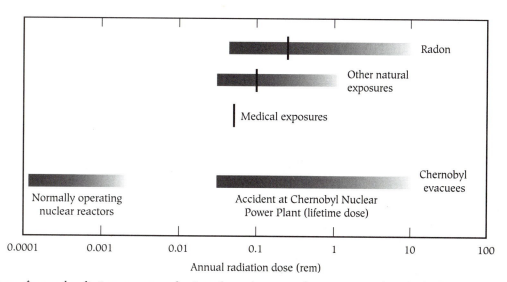

FIGURE 2 *Range of annual radiation exposures due to radon, other natural exposures, and medical radiation, compared to annual exposures due to normally operating nuclear power reactors, and the lifetime exposure of evacuees from the Chernobyl power plant accident. The horizontal scale is logarithmic. (Adapted from A. V. Nero, Jr.,* Controlling Indoor Air Pollution. *Copyright 1988 by Scientific American, Inc. All rights reserved.)*

The Toll of Coal

The fossil fuels—coal, oil, and gas—are concentrated sources of energy that are relatively easy to mine and transport. But, when burned, coal and oil are dirty, coal being the worst. A large (1000 megawatt) coal-fired power plant uses *every day* enough coal to fill a train 100 cars long, and *every day* releases to the atmosphere 50 tons of fly ash (*after* electrostatic precipitation), 500 tons of sulfur dioxide, and 100 tons of nitrogen oxides. These effluents produce acid rain and ozone depletion, to say nothing of human respiratory problems. All fossil fuels produce carbon dioxide (CO_2), a major cause of the greenhouse effect.

Some of this air pollution can be avoided by burning coal more efficiently and by "scrubbing" the coal smoke. But these measures are costly and raise the price of electric power. Nothing can be done about the CO_2.

The ground pollution of coal is also tremendous. Every year, we pile up the incredible amount of 125 million tons of ash and sludge, an amount equivalent to all the municipal junk and garbage collected in the United States annually. A power plant in Pennsylvania has used a 5-mile-long valley as a dumping site for pollutants recovered through *emission-control systems*. This valley will be filled to a depth of 400 feet in 25 years. It is instructive to compare this with the volume of nuclear waste noted earlier, namely about 2 cubic meters annually from a 1000-megawatt nuclear plant.

It should not be forgotten that coal waste contains uranium and radium. This was emphasized by Lord Marshall, chairman of the British Central Electricity Generating Board (CEGB):

> I have to inform you that yesterday the CEGB released about 300 kilograms of radioactive uranium, together with all its radioactive decay products, into the environment . . . We shall be releasing the same amount of uranium today, and we plan to do the same tomorrow. In fact, we do it every day of the year so long as we burn coal in our power stations. And we do not call that "radioactive waste," we call it coal ash.[19]

Coal contains many other poisonous metals, including mercury, lead, cadmium, gallium, and vanadium, as well as the nonmetals selenium and arsenic. These are all part of the solid waste. It is clear that cleaning up the air emissions of coal does not even begin to solve the coal-waste problem!

Table 2 summarizes the pollution produced by concentrated energy sources (fossil and nuclear) and some consequent problems. Coal produces large amounts of particles, sulfur dioxide (SO_2), nitrogen oxides (NO_x), CO_2, and ground contamination. Oil also produces these, but in some cases much less than coal; oil spills from tanker ships is a problem. Gas is relatively clean, causing little ground contamination, but still producing NO_x and CO_2. Nuclear power produces no air pollu-

TABLE 2 *Pollution and Related Problems Produced by Concentrated Energy Sources*

SOURCE	PARTICLES	SO_2	NO_x	CO_2	GROUND CONTAMINATION
Coal	X	X	X	X	X
Oil	X	X	X	X	X
Gas			X	X	
Nuclear					X
PROBLEM					
Respiratory disease	X	X	X		
Acid rain		X	X		
Ozone depletion			X		
Greenhouse effect			X	X	

tants, but nuclear waste has the potential of ground contamination by radioactivity. Nuclear power contributes to none of the problems listed.

Not only is the burning of coal dangerous to the public, but coal mining is also very hazardous for miners:

> In this century alone in the United States, more than 100,000 men lost their lives in coal mines. More than a million more were permanently disabled in mine accidents. Even more—no one knows how many—contracted pneumoconiosis (black lung disease) and spent their last years gasping for breath.[20]

Coal mining is safer than it used to be, but it is still twenty times as dangerous as the extraction and purification of uranium.

Table 3 compares estimated deaths resulting from producing all our electricity by any one technology. Included are deaths from air pollution and accidents. If we produced all our energy from coal, the hazard in terms of *deaths alone* would be twenty times that of producing all of our electricity with nuclear power. Nuclear power is no more dangerous than hydroelectric power. Gas-fired power appears to be the safest, but Table 3 does not take into account its production of CO_2, a greenhouse gas.

TABLE 3 *Estimated Annual Deaths in the U.S. if All Our Electricity Were Generated by Any One Technology[a]*

TECHNOLOGY	DEATHS
Coal	3100
Oil	1100
Gas	50
Hydroelectric	200
Nuclear	150

[a]Derived from Table 4 of Jagger (see Note 1). The estimates of deaths include air pollution and accidents. The hydroelectric figure reflects chiefly dam breakage. The nuclear figure reflects mostly cancers from one Chernobyl-type accident every 50 years.

Alternative Sources of Energy

We need energy in many forms. Some of it must be very *concentrated*, produced by a few large sources, as that used to power a large city or to power some factories, such as those that produce aluminum by electrolysis. Some energy can be *dispersed*, produced by many small sources widely scattered, like the furnaces that we use to heat our homes or the windmills used by farmers to pump water into a cattle reservoir.

The most effective sources of concentrated energy lie mostly deep within Earth: *nuclear fuels* and *fossil fuels*. They are versatile in that they can be transported over long distances.

Hydroelectric power and *geothermal power* may also be considered to represent concentrated sources. But both of these sources are limited in their geographic availability. We have already exploited most feasible sources of hydroelectric power in this country. Geothermal is limited mostly to areas west of the Rockies, Texas, and Louisiana.

Feasible sources of dispersed energy are mostly derived from the Sun: *solar power* and *wind power*. These sources occur at a very low energy density. Consequently, they will probably never be important as concentrated sources of power. It is possible to power an electric plant by using solar reflectors, but such plants are small. Both sources have limited availability, solar being not available in bad weather or at night, and wind power being geographically restricted, mostly to the Great Plains and along the northern ocean coasts.

Nevertheless, solar power has a bright future. For example, it is ideal for heating single-story schools, which have large roofs and require little heat at night. It is also feasible for heating homes and even for some small factories. But such uses are largely restricted to southern or tropical locales. It is being developed in places like India for cooking, where it replaces valuable and scarce firewood.

Much is made by opponents of nuclear power about "renewable" sources of energy, such as solar and geothermal. What is really implied is that there is an almost unlimited supply of that source. This is certainly true of solar, but it is not true for geothermal, where we are finding that such sources are easily depleted.[21] On the other hand, it is *true for nuclear*, where, with the use of breeder reactors, to say nothing of fusion reactors that would use the deuterium of the oceans, we have a virtually endless supply of energy.

Another pitch is made for "nonpolluting" sources, usually in the same breath with "renewable." Solar, wind, and the like are touted in this way. It is true that solar power is *relatively* nonpolluting, in that the power plant itself does not emit pollutants. *But the same is true of nuclear power.* Furthermore, pollutants are produced during manufacture of solar panels, and these panels must eventually be disposed of, another source of pollu-

tion. There is no free lunch. Some sources are more polluting than others, but none are totally nonpolluting. Certainly, solar is one of the least polluting, and coal one of the most polluting.

THE FUTURE OF NUCLEAR POWER

. . . The aversion people rightly feel for military applications must not spill over to the peaceful use of nuclear energy. Mankind cannot do without nuclear power.

ANDREI SAKHAROV
MEMOIRS (KNOPF, 1990)

Risk Analysis

It has been noted that nuclear power is controversial chiefly because of fears of radiation.[22] These fears are unwarranted because (1) nuclear power plants emit minuscule amounts of radiation, amounts no greater than those from coal-fired plants, (2) *the entire nuclear fuel cycle*—including mining and fabrication of fuel, operation of plants, and disposal of waste—adds only 0.1% to the natural radiation background,[23] (3) low radiation exposures, like those in our natural environment, are essentially innocuous,[24] (4) nuclear waste can be disposed of with great safety, and (5) the *only* nuclear accident to harm civilians was Chernobyl, an accident unlikely to be repeated.

Then why the fears? They stem from an unfamiliarity with radiation and a horror of its presumed effects. The graphic illustration of the ghastly power of nuclear explosions at Hiroshima and Nagasaki is transferred in the public mind to a similar revulsion against nuclear power and nuclear waste. Chernobyl is viewed with horror. The fact that it was the only accident with serious consequences in nuclear power history, and was moderate in its human consequences compared with other accidents, does little to allay such fears.

These psychological responses have led to a new area of research, that of *risk analysis*. These studies show that the *perception* of a risk rises in proportion to one's

1. *Unfamiliarity* with it.
2. *Dread* of it. This includes what is called "catastrophic potential": once-a-year airline crashes are dreaded, although they kill no more people *per year* than do automobiles *per day*.
3. *Lack of control.* I drive the car; *someone else*, whom I cannot control, flies the airplane.
4. *Lack of voluntary choice.* I decide to drive; nuclear power plants are *imposed* on me.

All these factors clearly enter into the complex of fear of nuclear technology. People fear the 31 deaths produced suddenly at Chernobyl but worry not about the roughly 50,000 deaths a year that occur on our highways. In addition, the paranoia feeds on itself.

Chernobyl is rarely called an accident; it is a "disaster." Nuclear waste is not said to be put in a repository with great care; it is "dumped." (We do dump a lot of chemical waste, with little concern.)

Much can be done about these perceptions. Among other things, people must be permitted to *make the decisions* about whether or not to have a nuclear plant and where to locate it. The same applies to waste disposal—educated citizens can face up to the problem that, regardless of the future of nuclear power, the waste is here right now and something must be done with it.

Finally, there is the concept of *risk versus benefit*. All human activities, including the production of electricity, involve some risk. One must decide if the benefit warrants the risk. We apparently have felt for many decades that the millions of American miners killed or maimed in getting coal was worth it, because electricity is so vital to our lives. Nuclear power involves far less risk.

Economics

Claims are made that nuclear power is not economically competitive with coal and oil. Such claims are incorrect. In 1985 actual costs to the consumer were 4.3 cents per kwh for nuclear power, 3.4 cents for coal, and 7.3 cents for oil.[25]

Costs are much lower in other countries. Nuclear power has been cheap in France, where 75% of electric power production is nuclear. The low costs in France are largely due to (1) government subsidies for plant construction, (2) use of a single design of nuclear power plant, making parts and operators interchangeable, and (3) the fact that they build a nuclear plant in 6 years, while we take 12 years. There have been no important safety problems with the French plants.

Much is made of the role of the federal government in subsidizing the nuclear industry. But such subsidies are often necessary to get large enterprises going. In the last century, the government made "land grants" to the railroads, giving them, free of charge, right-of-way corridors along which the new rail lines could be built. Another consideration enters when a new technology may be inherently unsafe. This was true of aviation, where the government even today provides licensing of aircraft and air traffic control, through the Federal Aviation Administration (FAA). So it was not remarkable that the government provided uranium at very low cost in the early days of nuclear power (no longer required, since we now have a glut of uranium). Furthermore, since nuclear power, like aviation, is an inherently unsafe activity, there is no question that the government should enforce safety standards, as it does through the Nuclear Regulatory Commission (NRC), and also to administer efforts to dispose of nuclear waste, as it does through the Department of Energy.

Critics of nuclear power have cited the "great expense" involved in the secure disposal of radioactive waste, as well as in the dismantling of old nuclear plants. However, disposal of spent fuel, including encasement, transport, and deep burial, as well as dismantling and disposal of old plants, will generally cost less than 10% of the initial plant cost. Since the NRC requires that nuclear plants set aside money to cover these costs, they are included in the cost of power to the consumer.

The fact of the matter is that, although it costs more to build a nuclear plant than to build a coal-fired plant, this is offset by the low operating expense of a nuclear reactor. Well-designed reactors will last for 50 years and breeder reactors for 100 years, during which time the cost of fuel is negligible; the cost of transport of fuel to the plant and of waste away from it is tiny compared to that of other power technologies. Bear in mind that a single 100-megawatt coal-fired plant uses 100 train carloads of fuel every day, much of which winds up as huge volumes of coal ash and residues from emission controls, both of which contain hazardous chemicals and radioisotopes.

The bottom line is that the marketplace will decide if nuclear power is economically feasible.

Projections

In the countries of the Organisation for Economic Cooperation and Development (OECD), which includes all of western Europe, as well as Canada, the United States, Australia, New Zealand, and Japan, about twenty new nuclear plants were built each year up to 1985. Now that initial markets have been supplied, growth is projected at a steady three plants per year from 1995 to 2010.[26] This continued growth is expected because: (1) new, safer designs, in which a meltdown is almost impossible, will help to allay public fear, however misplaced, of nuclear accidents; (2) permanent repositories for high-level waste will be under construction in the United States and other countries; (3) we shall be running out of oil; and (4) nuclear power will continue to be competitive with fossil-fueled power. Finally, (5) nuclear *fusion* is likely to become a viable energy source by 2030—fusion is not only far safer than fission power but also the waste problem is minimal and the fuel supply (nonradioactive deuterium in the oceans) virtually infinite.

The argument is sometimes made that nuclear power will not significantly decrease U.S. dependence on foreign oil because we use relatively little oil (compared to coal) for electricity production. This is true. The major use of oil in this country is to provide fuel for transport and heating oil for buildings. However, in an environmentally sound future, we should be using electric cars and light rail trains in cities. The electricity for these cars and trains could be made with nuclear power, and that indeed would make a big dent in our use of oil. Furthermore, between 1973 and 1988, our use of electricity increased by 50%, while our use of other types of energy *decreased* by 5%.[27] In other words, while our total use of power is not changing very much, there has been a great shift from other types of power to electricity, and this trend is expected to continue. This increased demand for electricity should be met by new nuclear plants, not coal or oil plants.

Such a shift to nuclear power will reduce emissions of the sulfur and nitrogen oxides and CO_2 that are so damaging to our environment. In France, in the last decade, thanks largely to nuclear power, emissions of sulfur oxides have been reduced by 70%, particulates by 60%, and CO_2 by 30%.

For heating of buildings, we should be shifting from oil to solar power and natural gas, a trend already underway. This will both decrease our dependence on foreign oil and decrease gaseous emissions. Natural gas produces little sulfur dioxide, as well as 50% less CO_2 than coal and 30% less CO_2 than oil.

A recent comprehensive study by the Electric Power Research Institute of Palo Alto, CA, projects that, by 2060, we shall have a mix of energy sources in the world.[28] Fossil fuels will be down to 54% from the present 88%, primarily due to a drop in oil production. Nuclear power and coal will be primary sources, supplying 22% and 25%, respectively. While very dirty, coal is widely and readily available, so it will continue to be used, but in advanced countries effluents will be cleaner (and more expensive). Hydropower (10%) and solar power (14%) will make significant contributions.

In the United States, use of nuclear power for production of electricity has plateaued at its present 20% and may even dip down to 15% by 2010[29] (due to decommissioning of old plants), but it is expected to rise rapidly to at least 30% of electricity production by 2060. Why these positive projections in light of the current considerable opposition to nuclear power?

Consider some trends. The Department of Energy has recently invested more than $160 million to develop a new generation of advanced reactors; GE and Westinghouse have contributed $70 million to this effort. Westinghouse and Bechtel have formed a joint venture with the Michigan utility Consumers Power to buy and operate nuclear plants. The Tennessee Valley Authority (TVA) has restarted one of its three nuclear reactors at Browns Ferry, which were shut down in 1985 to correct safety problems, and it plans to order a new reactor by the end of the decade.

Overseas, a similar picture is developing. Sweden generates 50% of its electric power with twelve reactors that are models for health and safety. In 1980, responding to public pressure, Sweden laid out a plan to phase out all of its nuclear power by 2010. Now Sweden is having second thoughts. A 1990 poll showed that a majority of Swedes opposed this phaseout as its economic and environmental consequences became clearer. Plans to shut down the first two reactors by 1996 have

now been shelved. France continues on its road to eventual 90% nuclear power from its present 75%. Japan, now making 27% of its electricity with nuclear power, is also proceeding apace, with eleven plants under construction and twenty-four more firmly committed or planned.[30]

It should be recognized that most of the problems with waste disposal in this country (Rocky Flats, Hanford, etc.) have resulted from *military* activities, incurred during our frantic haste to build an arsenal of nuclear weapons ten times larger than was needed.[31] This paranoid fear of the Soviet Union also led to use of nuclear reactors in naval vessels, a dubious practice considering the likelihood of such ships to be sunk.

This has nothing to do with *civilian* nuclear power. Nuclear waste from civilian reactors will be placed in repositories so safe that we can virtually forget that the material is there, obviating a pressing need to keep records for thousands of years. J. H. Fremlin, emeritus professor of applied radioactivity at the University of Birmingham, England, sums up the situation neatly.

> If I have encouraged some of those who have worried about the tiny effects of nuclear wastes on our far distant descendants to worry instead about the thousands of our own children who are going to die in the world's big towns from the effects of pollution by burning coal and oil, the work of writing this book will have been worth while.[32]

In this article, I have made the argument, supported by facts, that nuclear power is not only clean but also very safe. Many studies support this position. In 1989 a careful study by the Council on Scientific Affairs of the conservative American Medical Association (AMA) concluded that "generating electricity with nuclear power is acceptably safe in the United States."

But I have also argued that nuclear power is *needed*. It can vastly reduce air pollution, as the experience of France shows. It will greatly reduce the ground pollution caused by burning coal and will save many of the lives that are either lost or severely degraded by coal mining. We should in fact be *replacing* old coal-fired plants with nuclear plants. Use of light rail and electric automobiles in cities, the electric power being produced by nuclear plants, would both decrease pollution and lower our dependence upon foreign oil. Nor can nuclear/fossil power be replaced by solar power, which can certainly ease our energy requirements, but cannot serve as a concentrated source of power for large cities and heavy industry.

Finally, the notion that Americans oppose nuclear power is unwarranted. A poll of some 1500 people, conducted in 1988 (two years after Chernobyl) by Cambridge Reports, Inc., found that 20% thought nuclear power a "good choice" for the future, 49% found it a "realistic choice," and 27% a "bad choice."[33] Thus, 69% appeared to find nuclear power an acceptable future option. Virtually identical results were found in a 1989 Gallup poll.[34]

Nuclear power is clean. It is safe. And we need it.

Notes

1. Jagger, J. *The Nuclear Lion: What Every Citizen Should Know About Nuclear Power and Nuclear War* (New York: Plenum Press, 1991).
2. Ibid.
3. Cohen, B. L. *The Nuclear Energy Option: An Alternative for the 90s* (New York: Plenum Press, 1990).
4. Colley, S., and J. Thomson. "Limited Diffusion of U-Series Radionuclides at Depth in Deep-Sea Sediments," *Nature* 346 (1990):260–263.
5. Jagger, op. cit.
6. Cohen, B. L. *Before It's Too Late: A Scientist's Case FOR Nuclear Energy* (New York: Plenum Press, 1983).
7. *Ground Water at Yucca Mountain: How High Can it Rise?* Panel on Coupled Hydrologic/Tectonic/Hydrothermal Systems at Yucca Mountain; Board on Radioactive Waste Management; Commission on Geosciences, Environment, and Resources; National Research Council (Washington, D.C.: National Academy Press, 1992).
8. Beckmann, Peter. *The Health Hazards of NOT Going Nuclear* (Boulder, CO: Golem Press, 1976).
9. Jagger, op. cit.
10. Ibid.
11. Ibid.
12. Ilyin, L. A., M. I. Balanov, L. A. Buldakov, et al. "Radiocontamination Patterns and Possible Health Consequences of the Accident at the Chernobyl Nuclear Power Station," *J. Radiol. Prot.* 10, no. 1 (1990): 3–29.
13. Jagger, op. cit.
14. *The International Chernobyl Project; An Overview.* Report by an International Advisory Committee, International Atomic Energy Agency (Vienna: IAEA, 1991).
15. Jagger, op. cit.
16. Neel, J. V., et al. "The Children of Parents Exposed to Atomic Bombs: Estimates of the Genetic Doubling Dose of Radiation for Humans," *Amer. J. Human Genetics* 46 (1990): 1053–1072.
17. Flavin, C. "Energy Efficiency Falls," in *Vital Signs: 1992. The Trends That Are Shaping Our Future* (L. R. Brown, C. Flavin, and H. Hane, eds.), Worldwatch Institute (New York: Norton, 1992).
18. Ibid.
19. Fremlin, J. H. *Power Production: What Are the Risks?* 2nd ed. (New York: Adam Hilger; IOP Publishing, 1989).
20. Sheridan, D. 1977. "A Second Coal Age Promises to Slow Our Dependence on Imported Oil," *Smithsonian* 8 (August 1977): 31–36.
21. Kerr, R. A. "Geothermal Tragedy of the Commons," *Science* 253 (12 July 1991):134–135.
22. Jagger, J. "The Natural World of Radiation," in this volume, Reading 71.
23. Ibid.
24. Ibid.
25. Cohen, *Nuclear Energy Option*, op. cit.
26. *Nuclear Energy Data 1992.* Nuclear Energy Agency, Organisation for Economic Co-operation and Development (OECD) (Paris: OECD Publications 1992).
27. Cohen, *Nuclear Energy Option*, op. cit.
28. Starr, C., M. F. Searl, and S. Alpert. "Energy Sources: A Realistic Outlook," *Science* 256 (15 May 1992): 981–987.
29. *Nuclear Energy Data*, op. cit.
30. Ibid.
31. Jagger, *Nuclear Lion*, op. cit.
32. Fremlin, op. cit.
33. Nealey, S. M. *Nuclear Power Development: Prospects in the 1990s* (Columbus, OH: Battelle Press, 1990).
34. Cohen, *Nuclear Energy Option*, op. cit.

Study Questions

1. Why does Jagger think there is so much fear of nuclear power? Has he made a convincing case for the use of nuclear power?
2. Compare the statistics on the harmful effects of coal with those of nuclear power. Which would you choose for a society, and why?
3. Does Jagger convince you that Chernobyl was a unique accident that is unlikely to happen again? Explain your answer.

74

Nuclear Waste: The Problem That Won't Go Away

NICHOLAS LENSSEN

Nicholas Lenssen is a scientist who works for Worldwatch Institute, an organization dedicated to global environmental concerns and supported by the United Nations.

In his essay, Lenssen first details our knowledge of the danger of radiation. Contrary to Jagger, he claims that most scientists believe that all radiation, however small, presents a risk. Next Lenssen argues that nuclear waste has such an enormously long half-life, hundreds of thousands of years, that it is impossible to guarantee its safe disposal. He reviews the present proposals for disposal and concludes that they are all fraught with such serious problems that we should turn away from nuclear power. Still, we have to dispose of the accumulated waste. Until we meet that challenge, nuclear power proposals should be put on hold.

In December 1942, humanity's relationship with nature changed for all time. Working in a secret underground military laboratory in Chicago, an emigré Italian physicist named Enrico Fermi assembled enough uranium to cause a nuclear fission reaction. He split the atom, releasing the inherent energy that binds all matter together. Fermi's discovery almost immediately transformed warfare, eventually revolutionized medicine, and created hopes of electricity "too cheap to meter." But his experiment also generated a small packet of radioactive waste materials that will persist in a form hazardous to human health for hundreds of thousands of years.

Fifty years later, scientists have yet to find a permanent and safe way to dispose of Fermi's radioactive waste—nor of any of the 80,000-odd tons of irradiated fuel and hundreds of thousands of tons of other radioactive waste accumulated so far from the commercial generation of electricity from nuclear power. Regardless of human actions, the waste of the nuclear age that Fermi inaugurated will be among our generation's longest lasting legacies.

Only the natural decay process, which takes hundreds of thousands or even millions of years, diminishes the radioactivity of nuclear waste. No one suspected radioactivity was dangerous following its discovery in the late nineteenth century. As time passed, though, scientists found that radiation harms human health, even at low levels of exposure. And radioactive materials, carried by wind and water, can spread quickly through the environment. Burying the wastes deep in the earth, as most governments are now planning, does not guarantee they will remain sealed off from the earth's biosphere.

Though Fermi's crude experiment was aimed at building bombs, civilian nuclear reactors have created most of the radioactivity emanating from the world's nuclear wastes—nearly 95 percent of the radioactivity in wastes in the United States is from this source. And civilian waste has been growing in quantity faster than military waste: the cumulative output of irradiated fuel from nuclear electric plants around the world is now three times what it was in 1980 and 20 times what it was in 1970. Other uses of nuclear materials, especially medical ones, add little to the waste stream.

From the beginning of the nuclear age, governments neglected wastes as best they could. Working with radioactive waste was "not glamorous; there were no careers; it was messy, nobody got brownie points for caring about nuclear waste," according to Carroll Wilson, first general manager of the U.S. Atomic Energy Commission (AEC). Meanwhile, governments promised fledgling commercial nuclear industries that they would handle waste problems.

But even today, "solutions" do not seem to be close at hand. Like mirages in the desert, safe, permanent methods of isolating radioactive materials disappear under scrutiny as quickly as scientists propose them. Nor have past efforts worked as planned; old burial and storage sites have proved leaky, and the sordid condition of nuclear weapons facilities shows the potential legacy of radioactive wastes.

As the world seeks to redirect its energy future in order to reduce emissions of carbon dioxide and other greenhouse gases, efforts are being made to get stalled nuclear power construction programs on the move again. Government officials and executives in the nuclear industry believe that this will require a fast resolution of the nuclear waste problem. But just as earlier nuclear power plants were built without a full understanding of the technological and societal requirements, a rushed job to bury wastes may turn out to be an irreversible mistake.

HEALTH AND RADIATION

In 1904, just nine years after Wilhelm Röntgen's discovery of X rays, the first technicians started dying

Reprinted from *State of the World*, ed. Lester R. Brown (Washington, DC: Norton, 1992), by permission. Notes deleted.

from exposure to the mysterious beams. Although some radiologists expressed concern about their colleagues and themselves, most resisted the notion of radiation safety guidelines. Only in 1928 did the Second International Congress of Radiology succeed in setting standards to limit exposure. More than 60 years later, after tightening the standards several times, scientists are still struggling to understand just how dangerous radiation really is.

The early X-ray technicians were most concerned about radiation burns and skin ulcers. Since then, however, scientists have found that ionizing radiation can lead to cancer, leukemia, degenerative diseases (such as cataracts), mental retardation, chromosome aberrations, and genetic disorders such as neural tube defects. Radiation also weakens the immune system, allowing other diseases to run their course unchallenged. Damage from radiation occurs at the atomic level within individual cells. The energy embodied in ionizing radiation can be transferred to the affected atom, leading to damage, mutations, or even death of individual cells in the body. The cumulative effect of cellular change is what leads to health problems. Children and fetuses are particularly susceptible to radiation exposure, because their rapidly dividing cells are more sensitive to damage.

The timing and severity of health effects are closely related to the level of exposure. A single dose over 400 centisieverts usually results in painful death within a few weeks. (A centisievert measures the biological effect on the body of different types of radiation). Doses in the range of 100–400 centisieverts often lead to cancer. The health effects of lower doses, particularly those cumulatively received over a period of years, are still debated. However, most scientists believe "there is sufficient evidence that all radiation—however small—presents a risk. There is no threshold" dose of no consequence, according to Dan Benison of Argentina's Atomic Energy Agency and chairman of the International Commission on Radiological Protection (ICRP), a self-appointed body of radiological and nuclear professionals.

Human beings live in a world full of "background" radiation that comes from radon gas seeping from uranium and thorium in the earth's surface and from cosmic rays arriving from outer space. The annual average total is between 0.25 and 0.36 centisieverts. Humans and other life forms evolved over millions of years adapting to these natural levels of radiation, though scientists believe these too have an impact on human health.

Additional radiation exposure comes from human activity such as medical X rays, fallout from the testing of atomic bombs, and nuclear power and its wastes. For the average person, exposure from these sources is far lower than from background radiation, though not for some individuals working in or living near nuclear installations.

The most extensive data on radiation's health effects come from Hiroshima and Nagasaki, where scientists have been following the health of atomic bomb survivors since 1950. By comparing the causes of death of those who survived the original blasts and their estimated exposure to radiation, scientists were once confident that lower doses of radiation had an insignificant health effect. In 1986, however, a reassessment of the original doses these people received found that they had been exposed to far less radiation than previously assumed, meaning that the cancer and other health effects attributable to radiation are higher. Using these new data, a 1989 U.S. National Research Council (NRC) committee concluded that an acute dose of radiation is three times likelier to cause cancerous tumors and four times likelier to induce leukemia than was thought 10 years ago.

This information prompted the ICRP in 1990 to lower standards again for permissible levels of radiation exposure for nuclear workers. Indeed, such standards have been lowered several times since the first recommendations, from 30 centisieverts per year in 1934 to 2 centisieverts in 1990. Some scientists say the permissible level should be even lower.

A 1991 study of employees at the U.S. Oak Ridge National Laboratory in Tennessee suggested that the NRC's estimates may be too low by as much as a factor of 10. Leukemia rates were 63 percent higher for nuclear workers exposed over long periods to small doses of radiation than for non-nuclear workers. Likewise, a 1990 report on families of workers at the Sellafield nuclear reprocessing facility in England found that children are seven to eight times as likely to develop leukemia if their fathers received legal low-level doses of radiation. Perhaps the children of Japanese victims have not experienced similar increases because they were exposed to a single, larger dose rather than the chronic exposure to lower levels of radiation received by nuclear workers, hypothesizes the report's author, Dr. Martin Gardner of Britain's University of Southampton.

Other recent studies have neither confirmed nor disproved a connection between radiation from nuclear facilities and cancer. One found no radiation-induced health effects in nearby residents six years following the 1979 Three Mile Island accident. (At Oak Ridge, however, it took 26 years for the cancer rate to increase.) A U.S. National Cancer Institute report found no association between cancer and nuclear facilities. The data, however, were collected at the county level, which the authors admit could not spot radiation-induced cancer clusters.

The greatest human experiment with radiation exposure is taking place in the Ukraine and Byelorussia, where much of the 50 million curies the Soviet government says were released by the 1986 accident at Chernobyl is being felt. (A curie measures the intensity of radiation and is equal to 37 billion disintegrations per second; as a reference point, the Hiroshima and Nagasaki bombs released an estimated 1 million curies.) Chernobyl's legacy could include hundreds of thousands of additional cancer deaths, yet the Soviet government made no systematic effort to track citizens' cumulative exposure to radiation, nor to log health effects. A secret Soviet decree prohibited doctors from diagnosing illnesses as radiation-induced. Current estimates predict anything from 14,000 to 475,500 cancer deaths worldwide from Chernobyl. No one will ever know for certain.

The expanding use of radioactive materials in developing countries is particularly worrisome. In 1987, a Brazilian junk dealer opened a discarded X-ray machine and extracted a brilliant blue powder—which turned out to be radioactive cesium-137—and distributed it to his family and friends. By the time doctors determined what had happened, four people were fatally contaminated by radiation exposure and had to be buried in lead-lined coffins. An additional 44 people were hospitalized, suffering from hair loss, vomiting, and other symptoms of serious radiation sickness. Earlier mishandlings of radioactive wastes led to deaths in Algeria, Mexico, and Morocco. Third World institutions often are not well prepared to prevent accidental exposures even from the relatively small amounts of radioactive waste generated from research and medical activities that predominate in their countries.

As intentional and accidental releases have shown, radiation can quickly spread through the environment, carried by wind and water. Radioactive wastes from Soviet and U.S. weapons facilities have turned up hundreds of kilometers from their sources, contaminating wildlife, foodstuffs, and people. The fallout from atmospheric atomic bomb testing has spread around the globe and will eventually cause an estimated 2.4 million cancer deaths, according to a 1991 study commissioned by the International Physicians for the Prevention of Nuclear War.

Nuclear waste and its vast store of radioactivity presents a similar threat to future generations. A large, prolonged release of radioactive materials from nuclear wastes could affect human beings and other life over a broad area—indeed, even over much of the planet.

PERMANENT HAZARD

The term radioactive waste covers everything from piping-hot irradiated (used) fuel to mildly radioactive clothes worn by operators. Each type of waste contains its own unique blend of hundreds of distinct unstable atomic structures called radioisotopes. And each radioisotope has its own life span and potency for giving off alpha and beta particles and gamma rays, which cause harm to living tissue. Radioisotope half-lives can vary from a fraction of a second to millions of years. (The half-life is the amount of time it takes for 50 percent of the original activity to decay; after 10 half-lives, one one-thousandth of the original radioactivity would remain, an amount that can still be dangerous.) This means that the radioisotope plu-

tonium-239, for example, with a half-life of 24,400 years, is dangerous for a quarter of a million years, or 12,000 human generations. And as it decays it becomes uranium-235, its radioactive "daughter," which has a half-life of its own of 710,000 years.

Irradiated uranium fuel from commercial nuclear power plants is among the most dangerous radioactive waste. It accounts for less than 1 percent of the volume of all radioactive wastes in the United States but for 95 percent of the radioactivity. The typical commercial nuclear reactor discharges about 30 tons of irradiated fuel annually, with each ton emanating nearly 180 million curies of radioactivity and generating 1.6 megawatts of heat. Since many of the radioisotopes in irradiated fuel decay quickly, its output of radioactivity falls to 693,000 curies per ton in a year's time. After 10,000 years, just 470 curies exist in each ton. (See Table 1.)

The world's 413 commercial nuclear reactors, producing about 5 percent of the world's energy, created some 9,500 tons of irradiated fuel in 1990, bringing the world's waste accumulation of used fuel to 84,000 tons—twice as much as in 1985. (See Figure 1.) The United States is home to a quarter of this, with a radioactivity of over 20 billion curies. (See Table 2.) Within eight years, the global figure could pass 190,000 tons. Total waste generation from all the nuclear reactors now operating or under construction worldwide will exceed 450,000 tons before the plants have all closed down in the middle of the next century, projects the U.N. International Atomic Energy Agency (IAEA).

Most of the existing irradiated fuel is stored in large pools of cooling water alongside nuclear reactors. Originally designed to hold only a few years' worth of waste, space constraints have led to packing the spent fuel closer together and to the use of air-cooled vessels, including dry casks, to hold older, cooler irradiated fuel. Some countries have also opted to build large central storage facilities separate from nuclear power stations. To store older irradiated fuel, dry casks that rely on pas-

TABLE 1 *Radioactivity and Thermal Output Per Metric Ton of Irradiated Fuel from a Light-Water Reactor*

AGE	RADIOACTIVITY	THERMAL OUTPUT
(years)	(curies)	(watts)
At Discharge	177,242,000	1,595,375
1	693,000	12,509
10	405,600	1,268
100	41,960	299
1,000	1,752	55
10,000	470	14
100,000	56	1

Sources: Ronnie B. Lipschutz, *Radioactive Waste: Politics, Technology and Risk* (Cambridge, Mass.: Ballinger Publishing Company, 1980): J. O. Blomeke et al., Oak Ridge National Laboratory, "Projections of Radioactive Wastes to Be Generated by the U.S. Nuclear Power Industry," National Technical Information Service (Springfield, Va.: February 1974.)

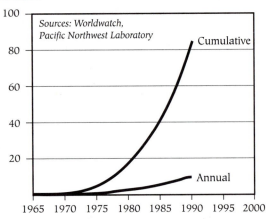

Thousands tons
irradiated fuel

FIGURE 1 *World Generation of Irradiated Fuel from Commercial Nuclear Plants, 1965–90*

sive cooling are considered safer for preventing the fuel from overheating than water-based systems, which need electric-powered pumps to circulate the water.

Some countries, such as France and the United Kingdom, reprocess their irradiated fuel. Originally developed to extract the fission by-product plutonium for atomic bomb production, reprocessing involves chemical procedures that also remove uranium not consumed in the reactor. This can then be enriched and again used as fuel. But reprocessing leaves behind radioisotopes created by splitting uranium atoms, including cesium, iodine, strontium, and technetium, which add up to 97 percent of the radioactivity of used reactor fuel. This refuse is called high-level waste. Other remainders include the products of the intense neutron bombardment of nuclear fission—elements such as americium and neptunium, known as transuranics

because they are heavier than uranium. Many of these isotopes have extremely long half-lives. Thus reprocessing's net effect is to increase the volume of radioactive wastes, including that of long-lived wastes.

Irradiated fuel is only part of the problem still piling up. Less intense though still dangerous "low-level" waste accounts for a far greater volume. Low-level waste is often portrayed as simply being radioactive materials with a half-life of 30 years or less. But debris classified as low-level can also contain longer-lived materials such as plutonium, technetium, and iodine. Technetium-99 and iodine-129, for example, have half-lives of 210,000 and 15.8 million years respectively.

More than 76,000 cubic meters of weapons-related low-level waste and 46,000 cubic meters of civilian low-level waste were buried in shallow trenches in the United States in 1989 alone. Of the latter, nearly 95 percent of the radioactivity and more than 73 percent of its volume is from the nuclear power industry, including used resins, filter sludge, and discarded equipment. Medical radioisotopes account for less than 1 percent of the radioactivity and 2 percent of the volume of civilian low-level waste. Because of the wide range of types of low-level wastes, most countries other than the United States classify the longer-lived or more intense varieties as intermediate- or medium-level.

The most voluminous though least concentrated waste comes from uranium mines and mills. Milling removes most uranium from the mined ore, but leaves about 85 percent of the radioactivity in the leftover tailings. A daughter of uranium, thorium-230, with a half-life of 77,000 years, predominates in tailings. As it decays, it turns into radium-226, and then radon-222, both potent carcinogens. In the former East Germany, just three of the Wismut uranium mines along the Czechoslovakian border have a total of more than 150 million tons of uranium tailings, with contaminated liquids contributing millions of tons more. Stabilizing these vast mountains of waste could cost as much as $23 billion. Other countries with uranium mining tailings include Australia, Canada, Czechoslovakia, France, Namibia, Niger, South Africa, the Soviet Union, and the United States.

Nuclear power reactors, along with mining and fuel facilities, also become radioactively contaminated, and like all industrial plants they eventually must close. Already, 58 generally small commercial nuclear reactors have shut worldwide, and 60 larger power plants could close by the end of this decade. Dismantling these facilities can produce a greater volume of wastes than operating them: a typical commercial reactor produces 6,200 cubic meters of low-level waste over a 40-year lifetime; demolishing it creates an additional 15,480 cubic meters of low-level waste.

The most notorious failure of governments to control nuclear wastes has occurred at U.S. and Soviet military facilities. Weapons manufacturing over the past 50 years

TABLE 2 *Accumulation of Irradiated Fuel from Commercial Nuclear Plants, 1985 and 1990, with Official Projections for 2000*

COUNTRY	1985	1990	2000
		(metric tons)	
United States	12,601	21,800	40,400
Canada[1]	9,121	17,700	33,900
Soviet Union	3,700	9,000	30,000
France[2]	2,900	7,300	20,000
Japan	3,600	7,500	18,000
Germany	1,800	3,800	8,950
Sweden	1,330	2,360	5,100
Other[2]	5,939	14,540	36,715
Total[2]	40,991	84,000	193,065

[1]Canadian total is proportionately higher due to its use of natural uranium instead of enriched uranium in its CANDU reactor technology. [2]France and United Kingdom (listed in "other" category) totals do not include 16,500 tons and 25,000 tons, respectively, produced by dual-use military and civilian reactors. Nor does the total include these additional 41,500 tons.

Source: Worldwatch Institute.

at roughly 100 U.S. military sites has led to extreme environmental pollution. According to the U.S. Office of Technology Assessment (OTA), there is "evidence that air, groundwater, surface water, sediments, and soil, as well as vegetation and wildlife, have been contaminated at most, if not all, of the Department of Energy nuclear weapons sites." Indeed, the bomb builders have contaminated everything from tumbleweeds and turtles to coyotes, frogs, and geese with radioactive wastes.

U.S. weapons plant operators often vented waste directly into the air or dumped it into the ground, where it found its way into the groundwater. Some radioactive wastes ended up in the Columbia River, contaminating shellfish hundreds of kilometers away in the Pacific Ocean. The facilities alone had some 379,000 cubic meters of liquid high-level waste from reprocessing, consisting of 1.1 billion curies of radioactivity stored in steel tanks awaiting solidification at the end of 1989. These tanks, found at the Hanford Reservation in Washington State and at the Savannah River Plant in South Carolina, have a history of leaking and an internal buildup of explosive hydrogen gas—problems the U.S. Department of Energy (DOE) has turned a blind eye to in pursuit of producing more weapons.

The situation in the Soviet Union is even worse, according to Thomas Cochran, director of the Natural Resources Defense Council's nuclear project. For the Soviet authorities, managing waste once meant dumping it in the nearest body of water. In the case of the Chelyabinsk-40 weapons facility, that was the nearby Techa River. In 1951, the Soviet government detected radioactivity in the Arctic Ocean, 1,500 kilometers from this weapons plant in the southern Ural Mountains. Weapons builders next sent waste into Lake Karachay, which Cochran now calls "the most polluted spot on the planet." Lake Karachay became so radioactive that even today standing at its shore for an hour would be lethal. In 1967, a hot, windy summer dried the lake and blew radioactive dust some 75 kilometers away, spreading contamination to 41,000 people.

By 1953, the Soviet atomic industry put into operation steel tanks for storing reprocessing wastes, although discharges into Lake Karachay did not end until the sixties. The tanks at Chelyabinsk-40 proved to be even worse than those in use in the United States. In September 1957, one overheated and exploded, spewing a radioactive cloud that contaminated thousands of hectares and required the eventual evacuation of 11,000 people.

The history of military facilities provides an example of the high costs of mishandling nuclear waste. Estimates for cleaning up the U.S. nuclear weapons plants run to more than $300 billion. But even such a vast sum may not be enough. According to OTA, "many sites may never be returned to a 'contaminant-free' condition or a condition suitable for unrestricted public access." Nuclear wastes have already created permanent sacrifice zones.

THEY CALL IT DISPOSAL

Since the beginning of the nuclear age, there has been no shortage of ideas on how to isolate radioactive waste from the biosphere. Scientists have proposed burying it under Antarctic ice sheets, injecting it into the seabed, and shooting it into outer space, allowing governments to continue to ignore the problem. But with each proposal came an array of objections. Scientists have increasingly fallen back on the idea of burying radioactive waste hundreds of meters deep in the earth's crust, arguing as does the U.S. National Research Council that geological burial is the "best, safest long-term option."

All the countries using nuclear power are pursuing geologic burial as the solution to their waste, yet by their own timelines most programs have fallen way behind schedule. In 1975, the United States planned on having a high-level waste burial site operating by 1985. The date was moved to 1989, then to 1998, 2003, and now 2010—a goal that still appears unrealistic. Likewise, Germany expected in the mid-eighties to open its deep burial facility by 1998, though the government waste agency now cites 2008 as the year of operation. Most other countries currently plan deep geologic burial no sooner than 2020, with a few aiming for even further in the future.

The nuclear industry consistently suggests that burying radioactive wastes half a kilometer underground would mark a technical solution to the problem. According to Jacques de la Ferté, head of external relations and public information at the Nuclear Energy Agency of the Organisation for Economic Cooperation and Development, the industry has "both the knowledge and the technical resources to dispose of all forms of radioactive waste in satisfactorily safe conditions."

Such blandishments not withstanding, geological disposal is nothing more than a calculated risk. Future changes in geology, land use, settlement patterns, and climate will affect the ability to isolate nuclear waste safely. As Stanford University geologist Konrad Krauskopf wrote in *Science* in 1990, "No scientist or engineer can give an absolute guarantee that radioactive waste will not someday leak in dangerous quantities from even the best of repositories."

The concept of geologic burial is fairly straightforward. Engineers would begin by mining a repository below the earth's surface; it would be made up of a broadly dispersed series of rooms from which thermally hot waste would be placed in holes drilled in the rock. Waste would be transported to the burial site in trucks, trains, or ships. Technicians would package it in specially constructed containers, made of stainless steel or other metal. Once placed in the rock, the waste containers would be surrounded by an impermeable material such as clay to retard groundwater movement. When the repository was full it would be sealed off from the surface. Finally, workers would erect some everlasting signpost to the future—in one DOE proposal, a colossal nuclear stonehenge—warning generations millennia hence of the deadly radioactive waste entombed below.

The cost of building such mausoleums is uncertain at best. In keeping with the tradition of nuclear construction projects, estimates of needed expenditures keep rising. In the United States, the expected cost of burying each ton of irradiated fuel has risen 80 percent just since 1983, with the bill for a single site holding 96,000 tons of irradiated fuel and high-level waste running upwards of $36 billion.

Knowledge about deep geology comes principally from mining, an activity that seeks to extract valuable mineral resources in a short period. With deep burial of nuclear waste, problems arise in proving that such a system can provide adequate isolation for the thousands of years necessary. "The technical problem is not of digging a hole in the ground; it's of forecasting the unknown," according to Scott Saleska, staff scientist at the Institute for Energy and Environmental Research in Maryland.

The scientific uncertainties surrounding radioactive waste burial are enormous. According to a 1990 NRC report on radioactive waste disposal, the needed long-term quantitative predictions stretch the limits of human understanding in several areas of geology and groundwater movement and chemistry. The report also notes that: "Studies done over the past two decades have led to the realization that the phenomena are more complicated than had been thought. Rather than decreasing our uncertainty, this line of research has increased the number of ways in which we know that we are uncertain."

Experience at three sites in the United States and Germany, where government scientists are assessing and preparing specific sites for housing buried nuclear waste, has so far provided more questions than answers about the nature of geologic repositories. DOE is focusing on two locations: Nevada's Yucca Mountain for high-level waste and the Waste Isolation Pilot Plant (WIPP) in southeastern New Mexico, where construction of some burial rooms has already been completed. WIPP will have become the world's first deep repository for nuclear waste in late 1991 if DOE continues with plans to place long-lived transuranic waste from the U.S. nuclear weapons program in it. Meanwhile, German nuclear planners have targeted Gorleben salt dome to house the country's high-level waste from reprocessed irradiated fuel by 2008.

The big problem with deep burial is water. In Germany, groundwater from neighboring sand and gravel layers is eroding the salt that makes up the Gorleben dome. Meanwhile, WIPP's burial rooms, more than 600 meters deep in a salt formation, are above a reservoir of brine—a saline liquid—and below a circulating groundwater system that feeds a tributary of the Rio Grande.

The salt formation at WIPP has surprised government scientists again and again. Its rooms were expected to be dry, but brine is constantly seeping through the walls. Brine and corrosive groundwater could easily eat away steel waste drums and create a radioactive slurry. Sixty percent of the transuranic waste that nuclear planners intend to bury at WIPP also contains hazardous chemicals such as flammable solvents. This "mixed waste" gives off gases, including explosive hydrogen, that could send the radioactive slurry in a plume into the aquifer above it.

Groundwater conditions at the U.S. site at Yucca Mountain, a barren, flat-topped ridge about 160 kilometers north of Las Vegas, are also raising concerns. In theory, the waste in Yucca Mountain's volcanic tuff bedrock would stay dry since the storerooms would be located more than 300 meters above the current water table, and since percolation from the surface under current climatic conditions is minimal. But critics, led by DOE geologist Jerry Szymanski, believe that an earthquake at Yucca Mountain, which is crisscrossed with more than 30 seismic faults, could dramatically raise the water table. If water came in contact with hot radioactive wastes, the resulting steam explosions could burst open the containers and rapidly spread their radioactive contents. "You flood that thing and you could blow the top off the mountain. At the very least, the radioactive material would go into the groundwater and spread to Death Valley, where there are hot springs all over the place," says University of Colorado geophysicist Charles Archambeau.

Human actions could also disrupt the planned repositories. At Yucca Mountain, there is evidence of gold and silver deposits nearby, and natural gas and potash deposits dot the area around New Mexico's WIPP. Salt domes like Gorleben are also prime targets for drillers seeking natural gas. Future efforts to tap these resources could disturb the buried nuclear waste.

Humanity's vast body of scientific knowledge pales before the challenge of isolating nuclear waste until it is harmless eons hence. In 1990, scientists discovered that a volcano 20 kilometers from Yucca Mountain erupted within the last 20,000 years—not 270,000 years ago, as they had earlier surmised. Volcanic activity could easily resume in the area before Yucca Mountain's intended lethal stockpile is inert. It is worth remembering that less than 10,000 years ago volcanoes were erupting in what is now central France, that the English Channel did not exist 7,000 years ago, and that much of the Sahara was fertile just 5,000 years ago. Only a clairvoyant could choose an inviolable, permanent hiding place for the twentieth century's nuclear legacy.

MOVING FORWARD

In the words of François Chenevier, director of the French nuclear waste agency ANDRA, "it would be irresponsible for us to benefit from nuclear power and leave it to later generations to deal with the waste." Yet that has already occurred. While nuclear reactors generate electricity for 25–40 years, their radioactive legacy will remain for hundreds of thousands of years. Compensating future generations stricken with health effects from the current stockpile of radioactive materials is impossible. Resolving the waste problem is thus a moral obligation.

Unfortunately, the problem of radioactive wastes cannot be "solved" in the normal fashion. Waste cannot be destroyed, nor can scientists prove that it will stay out of the biosphere if buried. Proof, via the scientific method, requires experimentation to confirm a hypothesis. Yet with radioactive waste, such an experiment would require gambling with people's lives over hundreds of human generations.

Sensing the inadequacy of geologic burial in 1972, nuclear pioneer Alvin Weinberg, former director of the Oak Ridge National Laboratory, suggested a startling alternative: indefinite storage in surface facilities that would be guarded and tended by a "nuclear priesthood." Such an endeavor, however, would have to overcome the fragility of human institutions. Waste will in some cases remain dangerous for far longer than the record of human history. A further weakness of above-ground storage is the potential for breaching of a storage facility, whether accidental or intentional.

Yet due to the scientific and political difficulties with burial programs, above-ground storage may be the only option well into the twenty-first century. The very frailty of this course is apparent at weapons facilities in both the Soviet Union and the United States. Governments are under pressure to stabilize swiftly both liquid waste stored in dangerous, leaky tanks and contaminated soil and groundwater to prevent their further spread into the environment.

Less of an emergency exists with irradiated fuel from civilian nuclear power plants. Both governments and independent analysts believe that technologies such as dry casks are capable of safely containing materials for more than a century, though potential problems remain regarding institutional control of the wastes and accidents. One step toward a solution, proposed by some environmentalists in Europe and the United States, is to temporarily maintain nuclear waste at the site of its generation. Retired reactors could provide a decades-long home to irradiated fuel and other wastes, thereby reducing the number of radioactive waste sites, and limiting the handling and transportation of waste. Building storage facilities away from existing reactors immediately need only be considered in those cases where reactors are located in seismically active areas or other sites where there is justification for its rapid removal.

Although most countries still expect to dismantle reactors shortly after they close, high cost estimates (from $200 million to $1 billion per reactor), technical difficulties posed by high levels of radiation found in recently closed reactors, the need to limit worker radiation exposure, and the potential lack of facilities to receive the vast volume of radioactive wastes will impede their efforts. Indeed, old reactors could soon be seen as permanent fixtures on the horizon of many countries; the United Kingdom, where commercial nuclear power first started in 1956, is the first to give up on the notion of dismantling its reactors and is now looking toward entombing them for at least 130 years. Short-term storage does not solve the problem of nuclear waste, but it could allow time for more careful consideration of longer-term options, including geologic burial, seabed burial, and longer-term storage.

But moving forward on the waste issue demands much more than scientific research and reduced technical uncertainties. It also requires a fundamental change in emphasis in current operating programs and efforts to gain the public support. Reordering priorities can only take place once the threat from different types of waste is reevaluated. In the United States, for example, the classification system for wastes requires standards based not on the source, as is done now, but on the wastes' actual radioactivity and lifetime. Likewise, reactor vessel components of the Canadian CANDU reactors will be more radioactively dangerous than irradiated fuel from the plants 130 years after they are shut down, according to Marvin Resnikoff, a physicist and director of Radioactive Waste Management Associates in New York. Despite this, Canada currently plans on shallow burial of the reactor core upon dismantling. A reclassification of waste types should address the long-term threat posed by long-lived, low-level waste.

Regaining public trust will require institutional changes, and closer scrutiny of radioactive waste programs. Credibility problems plague government nuclear agencies, including those in France, Japan, the Soviet Union, the United Kingdom, and the United States. Public distrust is rooted, in most cases, in the fact that the institutions in charge also promote nuclear power and weapons production, and have a long history of outright lies, misinformation, and secrecy associated with nuclear facilities. The same problem exists regarding the IAEA, which could play a far more constructive part in handling radioactive waste, particularly in developing countries, once it no longer had the conflicting roles of both promoter and controller of nuclear technology.

For more than a decade several reports, including those by the U.S. Office of Technology Assessment and the National Research Council's Board of Radioactive Waste Management, have called for an independent organization to take over the task of managing the country's nuclear wastes. So far, Congress has responded by requiring more oversight of the Department of Energy, while neglecting to tackle the root problem of separating the organization responsible for weapons production and nuclear power promotion from the one that manages waste. Forming autonomous and publicly accountable organizations to handle nuclear waste will go a long way in regaining public support.

In the end, the nuclear waste issue is a hostage to the overall debate on nuclear power, a debate that tears at nations. From Sweden and Germany to the Soviet Union and Italy, countries have found their political systems embroiled over the future of the atom. Due to the intense political controversy surrounding nuclear power, true progress on the waste issue may only come about once society turns away from nuclear power. Sweden, which has perhaps the broadest (though not universal) support for its nuclear waste program, made a national decision to phase out nuclear power by 2010. Without such a decision, public skepticism toward nuclear technologies and institutes only grows stronger. "If industry insists on generating more waste, there will always be confrontation. People just won't accept it," believes British environmental consultant David Lowry.

A world with six times the current number of reactors, as called for by some nuclear advocates, would require opening a new burial site every two years or so to handle the long-lived wastes generated. Yet nuclear power proponents discount or even ignore the problem of wastes when calling for vast construction programs. For example, President Bush's 1991 National Energy Strategy proposed a doubling of the number of nuclear power plants in the next 40 years, but did not discuss the need for future waste sites. As experience with nuclear power plants has demonstrated, it will not become any easier to site and construct future geologic burial facilities once the first one is opened.

Even if no more nuclear waste were created, addressing that which already exists will require attention and investments for a period that defies our usual notion of time. The challenge before human societies is to keep nuclear waste in isolation for the millennia that make up the hazardous life of these materials. In this light, no matter what becomes of nuclear power, the nuclear age will continue for a long, long time.

Study Questions

1. How would Lenssen respond to Jagger's data that people living in areas with higher background radiation actually have lower (or the same) cancer rates as those living in areas with lower levels of background radiation?

2. Compare Lenssen's arguments against nuclear energy with Jagger's. How would Jagger respond to Lenssen? I have asked him. Here is part of his response.

   1. Scientists *do* know of permanent and safe ways to dispose of nuclear waste; only political opposition, fired by an almost hysterical public reaction to the idea, prevents progress in this area.

   2. Because uranium and plutonium are 20 times as dense as water, 80,000 tons of nuclear waste [cited by Lenssen on his first page] occupies a volume equivalent to a cube 50 feet on each side. All of the high-level nuclear waste from all of the nuclear reactors in the U.S. *for all the 35 years in which we have had nuclear power,* would fill a small house. This is not the impression one gets from the bald statement of "80,000-odd tons."

   3. Solutions to the waste problem are not close at hand only because of political opposition. Furthermore, there is no harm in letting the wastes stay where they are—at the power plants themselves—for another decade or so, since their radiation is decaying *steadily* with time.

Does this help in assessing the merits of renewing a commitment to nuclear energy as the best hope in providing clean energy for our world? Go over the arguments again and explain your thoughts on this difficult and vital subject.

So we return to our original question: Do the clear benefits of nuclear energy outweigh the dangers of nuclear accidents and contamination from nuclear wastes?

For Further Reading

Fremlin, J. H. *Power Production: What are the Risks?* New York: Adam Hilger, 1989.

Jagger, John. *The Nuclear Lion.* New York: Plenum Press, 1991.

Kaku, M., and J. Trainer, eds. *Nuclear Power: Both Sides.* New York: Norton, 1983.

Lester, R. "Is Nuclear Industry Worth Saving?" *Technology Review* (Oct. 1982).

Marshall, E. "Lessons of Chernobyl," *Science* 233 (Sept. 26, 1986): 1375–76.

Routley, Richard, and Val Routley. "Nuclear Power: Some Ethical and Social Dimensions." In *And Justice for All,* eds. Tom Regan and Donald VanDeVeer. Totowa, NJ: Rowan & Allanheld, 1982.

Shrader-Frechette, K. S. *Nuclear Power and Public Policy.* Boston: Reidel, 1980.

Weinberg, Alvin. *Continuing the Nuclear Dialogue.* LaGrange, IL: American Nuclear Society, 1985.

CHAPTER SIXTEEN

Economics and the Environment

What are the implications of environmental concerns for economic thinking and sociopolitical matters? Several philosophers and environmentalists contend that taking ecology seriously entails a new understanding of economics. How do economic policies contribute to environmental degradation? Is our very way of measuring progress or economic well-being prejudicial to the environment and hence to our long-term interests? Is the GNP (gross national product), the standard measure of a nation's well-being, an adequate measure? Should we supplement or even replace it with something else? How can we do a cost–benefit analysis of the value of clean air or a wilderness or a rain forest or agricultural lifestyles?

In the past decade, the concept of a sustainable society has emerged as a dominant economic–social model. The idea is to create a society that preserves significant freedom of choice while being governed by economic and social policies wherein we live more responsibly with the environment, living off its interest instead of the principal. New paradigms are needed to design future economic policies that take into account deeper environmental values.

In this chapter, we examine two different environmentalist critiques of economic models (by William Rees and Mark Sagoff) and two defenses of the standard risk assessment and economic models (Kristin Shrader-Frechette and a joint effort by Robert Goodland and George Ledec).

In our first reading, William Rees criticizes the materialist model of economics and argues that a fundamental change in society's perceptions is a prerequisite for environmental harmony and sustainable development. He points out that the United Nations "World Commission on Environment and Development" (1987) study is flawed because it tries to put new wine in old wineskins (see Matthew 9:17). We need a new wineskin for the new wine, an innovative paradigm for economic–environmental cooperation, that treats the environment as capital.

In our second reading, Mark Sagoff examines the relevance of an economic model to environmental concerns. An economic model based on cost–benefit analysis is rooted in the utilitarian idea that all values are reducible to personal preferences and how much people would be willing to spend for a good. But sometimes we judge things to be good independent of our personal preferences. The Kantian model, which treats people as ends in themselves rather than placeholders for pleasure, conflicts with the economic model, which asserts that justice should override utilitarian–economic considerations. For example, even if keeping African Americans separate and unequal would yield a higher utility than integration with white Americans, integration is more just and should be chosen. Similarly, questions of pollution and the preservation of the wilderness may not adequately be decided on a standard economic model.

In our third reading, Kristin Shrader-Frechette defends the risk–cost–benefit analysis for environmental policy decisions against critics like Rees and Sagoff. Examining various objections to this standard, she contends that the method, though limited, is fine. Paraphrasing Shakespeare, she concludes, "The fault, dear readers, is not with the science but with ourselves, that we are underlings who use it badly."

In our fourth reading, Robert Goodland and George Ledec follow up considerations like those put forth by Shrader-Frechette and defend a version of the standard view of economics, arguing that it can meet the legitimate concerns voiced by the preceding writers. We need not throw out the cost–benefit model in advancing our environmental goals. Whether Goodland and Ledec are successful in meeting the major criticisms must be left for you to discuss and decide.

75

Sustainable Development: Economic Myths and Ecological Realities

WILLIAM E. REES

William Rees is a bioecologist who teaches the ecological basis for planning and economic development at the University of British Columbia's School of Community and Regional Planning in Canada.

Rees responds to the 1987 United Nations' "World Commission on Environment and Development" report, calling for a global view of sustainable development that is both economically sound and environmentally progressive. He points out that the problem with this report is that it accepts the standard model of economics, which is fundamentally materialist. Rees argues that a new model of economics is needed if we are to do justice to environmental values. We must realize that the environment is capital, which is nonrenewable. Then we must learn to live off the interest, not depleting the capital, but holding it in perpetuity.

INTRODUCTION

This paper develops one perspective on prospects for a sustainable future in Canada and the rest of the developed world. It is inspired by the recent publication of *Our Common Future*, the report of the United Nations' "World Commission on Environment and Development." . . . The UN study has stimulated an unprecedented level of public debate on environment and development-related matters, wherever it is available, much of which focuses on the intriguingly hopeful concept of "sustainable development."

Before addressing sustainable development directly, I would like to say a few things about Western society's perceptions of "the way things are" respecting people, development, and the environment. The following reasons for doing so also provide the premises of the paper.

1. While we think we act from factual knowledge, much individual action and government policy on development and environment is based on unconscious belief, on what Stafford Beer (1981) might call our "shared illusions";
2. This collective perception of reality is the real problem. Our culturally "shared illusions" stand in the way of sustainable development;
3. It follows that a fundamental change in society's perceptions and attitudes is a prerequisite for environmental harmony.

Reprinted from *Trumpeter* (Vol. 5.4, Fall 1988) by permission. Notes deleted.

"True, the fluorocarbon industry's threat to the ozone layer may very well be serious, but the ozone layer's threat to the fluorocarbon industry is equally serious." ©1980 by Sidney Harris—"All Ends Up," William Kaufman, Inc.

Let us be clear that by "perception," I am not referring to the garden variety beliefs and opinions that are amenable to change with the next edition of the National News or the Globe and Mail. Rather, I mean the unconscious "facts" and unquestioned assumptions out of which we more or less automatically react in the conduct of our day-to-day affairs. These culturally-transmitted perceptions shape our social relationships, our political systems, and the nature of economic enterprise. In short, I am talking about the deep-rooted beliefs and perceptions that constitute society's common philosophy and worldview. (The academically inclined may prefer the term "cultural paradigm.")

Whatever name we give it, it is this shared experience of reality that determines where we are "coming from" as a society. Since it also influences where we are going, it is worth some reflection here.

SCIENTIFIC MATERIALISM: SHALLOW SOIL FOR SUSTAINABLE DEVELOPMENT

The worldview that presently dominates is rooted in 19th century scientific materialism. . . . Building on the experimental "natural philosophy" of the previous 200 years, the late 1880's saw the deep entrenchment of scientific rationality and its companion, social utilitarianism, as the primary beacons of human progress.

Descartes had set the stage in the 17th Century with his division of reality into the separate and independent realms of mind and matter. This "Cartesian" division encouraged people to see themselves as separate and distinct from a physical reality "out there," and provided the perceptual framework for all subsequent scientific inquiry. But it was Bacon who gave modern science its raison d'etre by arguing that knowledge gained through science should be put to work. "From this perspective, knowledge is regarded not as an end but as a means, expressed and applied in technology, by which humans assume power over the material world" . . . .

The resultant flowering of science and technology made possible the industrial revolution and unprecedented levels of material production. Not surprisingly, scientific method became associated with a glowing material future, while traditional thinking and values were scorned as obsolete and reactionary. Indeed, science came to be equated with the only true knowledge. "Facts" that have no authority of science behind them, are written off "as having no epistemological status at all" . . . . The scientific worldview had succeeded in separating material knowledge from values, and asserted the primacy of the former over the latter. . . .

This materialistic rational empiricism remains the dominant paradigm of Western society. To judge from economic behavior, we see the external world, the biosphere, mainly as a warehouse to be plundered in satisfaction of the material needs and wants of humankind. Certainly, too, reductionist science remains our only acceptable analytic mode. Society's prevailing ecological myth sees "the environment" in terms of isolated, individual resources or, at best, as a mechanical construction, whose component parts are bendable to human will and purpose.

Even the organization of governments reflects this analytic perspective. Environmental management is institutionally segregated into Departments of Fisheries, Forests and Land, Water, Energy and Mines, etc., with little regard to interdependent properties of the whole. Ironically, this often leaves our federal and provincial Departments of Environment with little to do!

THE ASSUMPTIONS OF ECONOMICS

Modern economics springs from similar conceptual roots. The founders of the neoclassical school, impressed with the spectacular successes of Newtonian physics, strove to create economics as a sister science, "the mechanics of utility and self-interest" . . . . The major consequences of this mechanical analogue is a traditional view of economic process as "a self-sustaining circular flow between production and consumption within a completely closed system." By this perception, "everything . . . turns out to be just a pendulum movement. One business 'cycle' follows another . . . If events alter the supply and demand propensities, the economic world returns to its previous position as soon as these events fade out." In short, "complete reversibility is the general rule, just as in mechanics. . . ."

An important corollary of this equilibrium model is that mainstream economics essentially ignores the self-evident, continuous exchange of material resources (resources and waste disposal), and the unidirectional flow of free energy, between the economic process and the biophysical environment.

A second corollary of equilibrium theory is that continuous growth becomes theoretically possible. . . . Indeed, latter day economists seem to believe "not only in the possibility of continuous material growth, but in its axiomatic necessity" . . . . This "growmania" . . . "has given rise to an immense literature in which exponential growth is taken as the normal state of affairs." . . . Meanwhile, any damage to environmental processes caused by this explosive human activity is assumed to be inconsequential or reversible.

That growth is entrenched as the measure of progress is evident from a glance at the business pages of any daily newspaper. The annual percent increase in gross national product (GNP) is still taken as every nation's primary indicator of national health. Rates of under 3% are considered sluggish, and most politicians and economic planners do not feel at ease until real growth in GNP tops 4% per annum. While such rates may seem modest, even a 4% increase implies a doubling of economic activity in a mere 17 years!

With its fixation on growth, the new conservatism of such countries as the US, Britain, and Canada increasingly demands that people accept the rigorous discipline of the marketplace as the primary wellspring of values and social well-being. Meanwhile, businessmen and technocrats have become the heroes of the new age and prominent role models for youth. The competitive ethic provides the accepted standard for individual self worth, with success measured in terms of conspicuous consumption and the accumulation of personal property. In some circles it is fashionable to be both socially unconcerned and aggressively oblivious to environmental destruction. While individual rights are loudly proclaimed, there is telling silence over matters of social responsibility.

It is noteworthy in this context, that capitalist states depend on the increasing size of the national economic pie to ensure that the poor receive enough of the national wealth to survive. Indeed, it is not exaggerating to say that economic growth is the major instrument of social policy. By sustaining hope for improvement, it relieves the pressure for policies aimed at more equitable distribution of wealth.

THE ECOLOGICAL REALITY

There are two ecological problems with common economic expectations. First, the expanding economic system is inextricably linked to the biosphere. Every economy draws on the physical environment for non-renewable resources and on ecosystems for renewable resources, and all the products of economic activity (i.e., both the waste products of the manufacturing process and the final consumer goods) are eventually discharged back into the biosphere as waste.

The ultimate regulator of this activity, and one that modern economic theory essentially ignores, the second law of thermodynamics (the entropy law): **In any closed isolated system, available energy and matter are continuously and irrevocably degraded to the unavailable state. . . .** The effect of this law is to declare that all so-called economic "production" is really "consumption"!

Since modern economies are partially dependent on stocks of non-renewable material and energy resources, the Second Law declares that they necessarily consume and degrade the very resources which sustains them. The substitution of one depleting resource for another can only be a stopgap on the road to scarcity. Even resource recycling has a net negative impact on remaining stocks of available energy and material. In short, much economic activity contributes to a constant increase in global net entropy (disorder), through the continuous dissipation of free energy and matter. Contrary to the assumptions of neoclassical theory, there is no equilibrium of any sort in the material relationship between industrial economies and the environment.

This means that the growth of many national economies (e.g., Japan, the US) can be sustained only by continuous resource imports from elsewhere, and only in the short run. The global economy, for all practical purposes, is a closed system, a reality that is little affected by shuffling resources around (world trade). Thus, contrary to the implicit assumptions of neo-classical economics, **sustainable development based on prevailing patterns of consumptive resource use is not even theoretically conceivable.**

The second ecological difficulty with the growth-dependent economy stems from the functional dynamics of ecosystems themselves. Ecosystems, like economic systems, depend on fixed stocks of material resources. However, the material resources of ecosystems are constantly being transformed and recycled throughout the system via food-webs at the local level, and biogeochemical cycles on a global scale. In addition, evolution and succession in Nature tend toward greater order and resilience.

The material cycles and developmental trends of ecosystems thus appear at first glance to defy the thermodynamic law. **Ecosystems seem to be inherently self-sustaining and self-organizing, and therefore to contribute to a reduction in global net entropy.** This is possible only because ecosystems, unlike economic systems, are driven by an external source of free energy, the sun. Through photosynthesis, the steady stream of solar energy sustains essentially all biological activity and makes possible the diversity of life on Earth.

Material recycling, the self-renewing property of ecosystems, is therefore the source of all renewable resources used by the human economy. Moreover, since the flow of solar radiation is constant, steady, and reliable, **resource production from the ecological sector is potentially sustainable over any time scale relevant to humankind.**

But only potentially. Even ecological productivity is ultimately limited, in part, by the rate of energy input (the "solar flux") itself. Ecosystems therefore do not grow indefinitely. Unlike our present economy, which expands through intrinsic positive feedback, ecosystems are held in "steady-state" or dynamic equilibrium, regulated by limiting factors and negative feedback.

Why is this significant? First, human beings and their economies are now a dominant component of all the world's major ecosystems. Since these economies are growing and the ecosystems within which they are embedded are not, the consumption of ecological resources everywhere threatens to exceed sustainable rates of biological production. Second, overexploitation is exacerbated by pollution, which impairs the remaining productivity of ecosystems. (Recent reports that acid rain may be reducing rates of tree growth by as much as 25% in parts of eastern Canada serve as a timely example.) In short, modern industrial economies both directly undermine the potential for sustainable development through over-harvesting, and indirectly compromise future production through residuals discharge. It takes no special genius to realize that such trends are unsustainable.

The point of all this is not to argue for abandonment of scientific rationality or even the growth paradigm. Science, technology, and the human ingenuity to use them, are among the key factors required for sustainable development. However, I do want to stress that our current worldview, however successful in the past, is a dangerously shallow perception of present reality. In fact, the foregoing analysis shows many of its basic assumptions to be wrong. While this was of little consequence when the scale of human activity was limited, it is at the heart of the environment-development conundrum today. Only when we admit this possibility will the development question shift from: how to promote growth, to: how to achieve sustainability.

SUSTAINABLE DEVELOPMENT: CAN WE GET THERE FROM HERE?

According to the World Commission on Environment and Development, **sustainable development is devel-**

opment that meets the needs of the present without compromising the ability of future generations to meet their own needs. There is nothing very threatening—or substantial here. However, **Our Common Future** goes on to define needs as the "essential needs of the world's poor, to which overriding priority should be given." It also recognized the "limitations imposed by the state of technology and social organization on the environment's ability to meet those needs" . . . . These latter considerations raise painful questions for modern society.

To expand on the issues involved, let us define sustainable development as **any form of positive change which does not erode the ecological, social, or political systems upon which society is dependent.** Planning for sustainable development must therefore explicitly acknowledge ecological limits on the economy, and to be politically viable, have the full understanding, support, and involvement of the people affected. This in turn suggests the need for political and planning processes that are informed, open, and fair.

Social equity will inevitably become a central consideration. The World Commission reported that the 26% of the world's population living in developed countries consumes 80–86% of nonrenewable resources and up to 34–53% of food products. . . . Emerging ecological and social constraints suggest that reducing the present gap in standards of living between the rich and poor (between and within nations) may well require that the rich reduce both present consumption and future expectations so that the poor may enjoy a fairer share of the world's resources.

Ecologically and socially concerned citizens accept such notions as self-evident, but the more profound implications of sustainable development seem invisible to the mainstream worldview. For example, Canada was the first nation to respond with its own policy initiative to the work of the World Commission. The National Task Force on Environment and Economy was established in October 1986 to initiate dialogue and recommend action on environment-economy integration in Canada. Its subsequent report . . . is regarded by government and industry as a milestone document, but with suspicion by environmentalists and other critics.

Stepping to the right of the World Commission, the Task Force defined sustainable development as "development which ensures that the utilization of resources and the environment today does not damage prospects for their use by future generations." Its report goes on to state that at the core of the concept is the requirement "that current practices should not diminish the possibility of maintaining or improving living standards in the future." Also: "Sustainable development does not require the preservation of the current stock of natural resources or any particular mix of . . . assets." Nor does it place "artificial" limits on economic growth, provided

that such growth is "economically and environmentally sustainable" . . . .

This definition is self-contradictory and thus difficult to interpret rationally. First, as previously emphasized, the present generation cannot use any nonrenewable energy or material resource (e.g., oil, natural gas, phosphate ore) without eliminating the prospect for its use by future generations. Thus, the main part of the definition is simply invalid. Second, the Task Force is reluctant to admit the possibility that living standards for some may have to be reduced that others might live at all. It avoids this issue entirely. Third, and consistent with the foregoing, the Task Force clings to the growth ethic, implying that an expanding economy is the preferred, if not the only solution, to social inequity. Fourth, the Task Force disallows the possibility that the preservation of certain "mixes" of ecological resource systems may well be essential to sustainability.

In the final analysis, then, the Task Force definition of sustainable development could be used to defend practically any pattern of economic activity, including the status quo (which, one suspects, was the general idea).

To be fair, the Task Force does provide numerous recommendations for improved economic planning and environmental assessment; for demonstration projects in sustainable development; for more research into ecological problems; for better government-industry cooperation in the integration of environment and economy, etc. However, in failing to recognize its own epistemological assumptions, the Task Force was constrained from stretching beyond such commonplace adjustments.

One problem is that the Task Force report (and, to a lesser extent, **Our Common Future**) was written from within the materialist growth paradigm. This paradigm is the ecological equivalent of rose-coloured glasses. With our vision pleasantly impaired, we will always ask first that Nature continue to meet our growing demands; it is literally beyond imagining that we should seriously adapt to Nature's constraints.

Now do not get me wrong. There may well be a grand idea in the Task Force that is struggling to get out. But the fact there is a struggle is my central point. The idea we need cannot be born of the prevailing worldview; it is missing too many essential elements. If we are serious about sustainable development, we cannot get there from here, at least not directly. We have to start from a different paradigm.

TOWARD A NEW PARADIGM

I would like now to sketch some of the errant elements I believe are central to any ecologically sound approach to sustainable development. To promote understanding, I will use a metaphor drawn from the current paradigm and a model we all know, capital investment.

Environment as Capital

In the simplest case, if you have money to invest and manage it wisely, you expect your capital to grow. Indeed, the objective of this form of "development" is to accumulate capital (money, equipment, physical plant), to be better off after making your investment than before. Certainly no one sets out to deliberately lose his/her financial shirt.

Try now to conceive various living species and ecosystems processes as forms of capital. It is easy to think of species we harvest this way, since we all know that a given stock of fish, trees, or cattle is capable of generating variable rates of return (growth and reproduction) depending on the goals and skills of management. But we are much less aware of the valuable hidden services performed by ecosystems' processes mainly because they are performed so well. One example would be the inherent capacity of local ecosystems and the biosphere to absorb, neutralize, and recycle organic and nutrient wastes. These are free services that we might otherwise have to pay for, and as such can be considered as a return on our "investment" in the ecological capital doing the chore.

Clearly, any human activity dependent on the consumptive use of ecological resources (forestry, fisheries, agriculture, waste disposal, urban sprawl onto agricultural land) cannot be sustained indefinitely if it consumes not only the annual production from that resource (the "interest"), but also cuts into the capital base. In this simple truth lies the essence of our environmental crisis. We have not only been living off our ecological interest but also consuming the capital, and the rate at which we are doing so is increasing year by year. This is the inevitable consequence of exponential growth. Some examples:

1. Most major world fisheries peaked far short of their potential productivity in the early 1970's, and many, including B.C. salmon and Atlantic cod, are in a continuing state of decline from over-fishing and habitat destruction.
2. Historic forestry practices in B.C. have greatly reduced the last major temperate rain-forest, and our present "economic" clearcut methods leave an ecological disaster of denuded slopes and eroded soils. Meanwhile, tropical forests, habitat to half the world's species, have been reduced by 40%, and are being cut at the rate of 10–20 million hectares (ha.) (1–2%) per year;
3. The prairie soils of the North American breadbasket have lost half their organic content and natural nutrients under mechanized agriculture. Soil erosion from cultivated land typically claims 22 metric tons/ha./year, about ten times the rate of soil building . . . ;
4. Abetted by deforestation, over-grazing, and inappropriate land use, the world's deserts claim an additional 21 million ha. of previously habitable land/year;
5. Acid rain is sterilizing thousands of lakes, destroying fisheries, and threatening forest and agricultural productivity in much of the Northern hemisphere;
6. Carbon dioxide production from the burning of fossil fuels and destruction of forests has long exceeded the capacity of the oceans and terrestrial plants to absorb the excess. Atmospheric CO_2 has risen 25% in the industrial age and is expected to double from preindustrial levels in the next century, contributing significantly to the greenhouse effect and potentially disastrous global warming.

Admittedly, interpreting such trends is difficult and their ultimate significance controversial. However, viewed in the same light as rising standards of living, the decline of the biosphere provides a novel perspective on the origins of our unprecedented wealth. These intersecting curves reveal that since the beginning of the steam age, we have been busily converting ecological capital into financial and material capital.

This means that much of our wealth is illusion. We have simply drawn down one account (the biosphere) to add to another (the bank). It might even be argued that we have been collectively impoverished in the process. Much potentially renewable environmental capital has been permanently converted into machinery, plant, and possessions that will eventually wear out and have to be replaced (at the cost of additional resources—that irritating Second Law again!).

To put it another way, we have long been enjoying a free ride for which we now have to ante up. Forest products and food are undervalued in the marketplace to the extent the prices we pay do not include the costs of resource maintenance. Our paychecks and corporate profits are excessive to the extent that the resource base which produced them has been run down. That new CD player and the family's second car represent capital that was not plowed back into agriculture, soils management, and waste control. In simplest terms, the "good life" for some humans has been subsidized at the expense of all other life, and ultimately of our children and their descendants.

Living on the Interest

This suggests that for the foreseeable future, sustainable development is only possible if we are willing to live on the interest of our remaining ecological endowment. Fortunately, this is still generous enough, and with careful husbanding it should be possible to restore and even build up our capital base.

Success in this endeavor will obviously require a rewrite of the prevailing environmental myth and humankind's role in the scheme of things. To begin, the new eco-paradigm must dissolve our separateness and reunite humankind with the biosphere.

Let us be clear that while better environmental management may be an essential interim step, we are not merely talking about tougher environmental regulation or improved impact assessment. History has shown that restrictive measures to control inappropriate activities are simply inadequate. This is because regulation must be imposed to protect some social value that is perceived as secondary if not inimical to the interests of the regulatee. Corporations oriented to maximizing profits do not voluntarily incur the costs of pollution control. Moreover, if the general interests of society (or at least the politician) are more closely associated with profit than environment, regulations are not enthusiastically enforced.

True sustainable development cannot be forced. Rather, it is the natural product of a society that "comes from" a profound sense of being in, and of, the natural world. As noted at the outset, sustainable development requires a shift in fundamental social attitudes and values, a change in worldview. People must acquire in their bones a sense that violation of the biosphere is violation of self.

From this perspective, it would be psychologically and socially unconscionable for anyone to advance a development or resource management proposal whose long-term effect would be to reduce our ecological capital. Just as today, no sane person sets out purposely to go financially bankrupt, no one would dream of launching an ecologically bankrupt scheme. On the contrary, development would be planned and implemented, without force or coercion, in ways that would maintain or increase the renewable resource base. "Return on investment" would acquire a double meaning. Both ecological and financial criteria have to be satisfied in the cost/benefit calculus.

Think for the moment how different things would be today had enhancing our ecological capital been taken for granted as the guiding principle of resource development in British Columbia for the last 100 years. There would be no concerns that sawmills in the interior may run out of timber; no fight between loggers and conservationists over the last uncut valley in the southern half of the province; South Moresby would have been declared a National Park long ago; commercial and sport fishermen would not be locked in a bitter dispute over declining shares of a diminishing resource (and the costly salmon-enhancement program would not have been necessary). It might have cost more along the way, but paradoxically, we would be richer today.

To ears conditioned by the hard-nosed rhetoric of modern business and politics, this softer path to development will sound utterly ridiculous, vaguely threatening, or merely irrelevant. But remember, from within in the current paradigm, it is difficult to recognize any vision not supported by conventional values and assumptions. The orthodox mind can only deny the evidence and insist the Earth is flat.

This is a critical point. To acknowledge it is to admit the possibility of an alternative vision and future. With self-awareness, comes the realization that there is nothing fixed or sacred about our present way of being. Materialist society, its Rambo economics, and even the compulsive consumers of the "me" generation, are all creations of malleable culture, not of any physical law. **We made them up.** If they are no longer adapted to the changing reality, we can remake them ourselves, in an image that is.

While re-education will be a long and difficult process, it may have unexpected rewards. Human beings are multidimensional creatures, at once aggressively competitive and socially cooperative. But Western society plays up the former, while suppressing the latter; a perverted liberalism idolizes the individual, while Conservative economics deprives him/her of the community necessary to make him/her whole. The new paradigm may enable us to restore the balance in a rediscovery of self. At the least, our new consciousness should catalyze a shift in emphasis from the quantitative to the qualitative, from the material to the tangible, from growth to development, in the lives of people and communities.

The eco-paradigm is an inherently cooperative one. It springs from a felt responsibility to the whole planet and can only be expressed through socio-political effort at all levels of social organization. Although there must be leadership, no region, province, or nation can go it alone for long.

Sustainable development thus gives new meaning to McLuhan's "global village." The media that made it possible may finally have a message that makes it worthwhile. We are engaged in no less an enterprise than restoring the habitat for all of humankind, and this will require no less than total commitment and unity of purpose.

Listen for a collective sigh of relief, the arms race, which we never could afford, which consumes so much of our ecological capital, can only be seen as a perverse anachronism when viewed from the eco-paradigm. Giving up on war would free no less than 6% of gross world product for the sustainable redevelopment of the planet!

Now, of course, I am really staring off to ecotopia. It simply cannot happen, right? Perhaps, but if you cannot share this vision, take a long look from where you stand and ponder the alternative.

Study Questions

1. Does Rees make a good case that traditional economics is materialistic and hence unable to deal with the kinds of concerns raised by environmental consciousness?
2. How might a proponent of standard economics respond to Rees's thesis that we must treat the environment as capital?

76

At the Shrine of Our Lady of Fatima,
or Why Political Questions Are Not All Economic

MARK SAGOFF

Mark Sagoff is a research scholar at the Center for Philosophy and Public Policy, University of Maryland, College Park, and the author of several works on economic and social issues, including The Economy of the Earth: Philosophy, Law and the Environment *(1988).*

Sagoff examines and rejects the standard economic notion that the cost–benefit analysis is always *the proper method for deciding social and environmental issues. Contrasting utilitarian with Kantian views of the human situation, he argues that the Kantian perspective, which treats humans as ends in themselves, should override utilitarian cost–benefit assessments. Sometimes efficiency should be sacrificed for principle.*

Lewiston, New York, a well-to-do community near Buffalo, is the site of the Lake Ontario Ordnance Works, where the federal government, years ago, disposed of the residues of the Manhattan Project. These radioactive wastes are buried but are not forgotten by the residents, who say that when the wind is southerly radon gas blows through the town. Several parents at a recent conference I attended there described their terror on learning that cases of leukemia had been found among area children They feared for their own lives as well. At the other sides of the table, officials from New York State and from local corporations replied that these fears were ungrounded. People who smoke, they said, take greater risks than people who live close to waste disposal sites. One speaker talked in terms of "rational methodologies of decisionmaking." This aggravated the parents' rage and frustration.

The speaker suggested that the townspeople, were they to make their decision in a free market, would choose to live near the hazardous waste facility, if they knew the scientific facts. He told me later they were irrational—he said, "neurotic"—because they refused to recognize or act upon their own interests. The residents of Lewiston were unimpressed with his analysis of their "willingness to pay" to avoid this risk or that. They did not see what risk-benefit analysis had to do with the issues they raised.

If you take the Military Highway (as I did) from Buffalo to Lewiston, you will pass through a formidable wasteland. Landfills stretch in all directions, where enormous trucks—tiny in that landscape—incessantly deposit sludge which great bulldozers, like yellow ants, then push into the ground. These machines are the only signs of life, for in the miasma that hangs in the air, no birds, not even scavengers, are seen. Along colossal power lines which criss-cross this dismal land, the dynamos at Niagara send electric power south, where factories have fled, leaving their remains to decay. To drive along this road is to feel, oddly, the mystery and awe one experiences in the presence of so much power and decadence.

Henry Adams had a similar response to the dynamos on display at the Paris Exposition of 1900. To him "the dynamo became a symbol of infinity." To Adams, the dynamo functioned as the modern equivalent of the Virgin, that is, as the center and focus of power. "Before the end, one began to pray to it; inherited instinct taught the natural expression of man before silent and infinite force."

Adams asks in his essay "The Dynamo and the Virgin" how the products of modern industrial civilization will compare with those of the religious culture of the Middle Ages. If he could see the landfills and hazardous waste facilities bordering the power stations and honeymoon hotels of Niagara Falls he would know the answer. He would understand what happens when efficiency replaces infinity as the central conception of value. The dynamos at Niagara will not produce another Mont-Saint-Michel. "All the steam in the world," Adams wrote, "could not, like the Virgin, build Chartres."

At the Shrine of Our Lady of Fàtima, on a plateau north of the Military Highway, a larger than life sculpture of Mary looks into the chemical air. The original of this shrine stands in central Portugal, where in May, 1917, three children said they saw a Lady, brighter than the sun, raised on a cloud in an evergreen tree. Five months later, on a wet and chilly October day, the Lady again appeared, this time before a large crowd. Some who were skeptical did not see the miracle. Others in the crowd reported, however, that "the sun appeared and seemed to tremble, rotate violently and fall, dancing over the heads of the throng. . . ."

The Shrine was empty when I visited it. The cult of Our Lady of Fàtima, I imagine, has only a few devotees. The cult of Pareto optimality, however, has many. Where some people see only environmental devastation, its devotees perceive efficiency, utility, and maximization of wealth. They see the satisfaction of wants. They envision the good life. As l looked over the smudged and ruined terrain I tried to share that vision. I hope that Our Lady of Fàtima, worker of miracles, might serve, at least for the moment, as the Patroness of cost-benefit analysis. I thought of all the wants and needs that are satisfied in a landscape of honeymoon cottages, commercial strips, and dumps for hazardous waste. I saw the miracle of efficiency. The prospect, however, looked only darker in that light.

I

This essay concerns the economic decisions we make about the environment. It also concerns our political decisions about the environment. Some people have suggested that ideally these should be the same, that all environmental problems are problems in distribution. According to this view there is an environmental problem only when some resource is not allocated in equitable and efficient ways.

This approach to environmental policy is pitched entirely at the level of the consumer. It is his or her values that count, and the measure of these values is the individual's willingness to pay The problem of justice or fairness in society becomes, then, the problem of distributing goods and services so that more people get more of what they want to buy. A condo on the beach. A snowmobile for the mountains. A tank full of gas. A day of labor. The only values we have, on this view, are those which a market can price.

How much do you value open space, a stand of trees, an "unspoiled" landscape? Fifty dollars? A hundred? A thousand? This is one way to measure value. You could compare the amount consumers would pay for a townhouse or coal or a landfill and the amount they would pay to preserve an area in its "natural" state. If users would pay more for the land with the house, the coal mine, or the landfill, than without—less construction and other costs of development—then the efficient thing to do is to improve the land and thus increase its value. That is why we have so many tract developments. And pizza stands. And gas stations. And strip mines. And landfills. How much did you spend last year to preserve open space? How much for pizza and gas? "In principle, the ultimate measure of environmental quality," as one basic text assures us, "is the value people place on these . . . services or their *willingness to pay.*"

Willingness to pay. What is wrong with that? The rub is this: not all of us think of ourselves simply as *consumers.* Many of us regard ourselves *as citizens* as well.

We act as consumers to get what we want *for ourselves.* We act as citizens to achieve what we think is right or best *for the community.* The question arises, then, whether what we want for ourselves individually as consumers is consistent with the goals we would set for ourselves collectively as citizens. Would I vote for the sort of things I shop for? Are my preferences as a consumer consistent with my judgments as a citizen?

They are not. I am schizophrenic. Last year, I fixed a couple of tickets and was happy to do so since I saved fifty dollars. Yet, at election time, l helped to vote the corrupt judge out of office. I speed on the highway; yet I want the police to enforce laws against speeding. I used to buy mixers in returnable bottles—but who can bother to return them? I buy only disposables now, but, to soothe my conscience, I urge my state senator to outlaw one-way containers. I love my car; I hate the bus. Yet I vote for candidates who promise to tax gasoline to pay for public transportation. I send my dues to the Sierra Club to protect areas in Alaska I shall never visit. And I support the work of the American League to Abolish Capital Punishment although, personally, I have nothing to gain one way or the other. (When I hang, I will hang myself.) And of course I applaud the Endangered Species Act, although I have no earthly use for the Colorado squawfish or the Indiana bat. I support almost any political cause that I think will defeat my consumer interests. This is because I have contempt for—although I act upon—those interests. I have an "Ecology Now" sticker on a car that leaks oil everywhere it's parked.

The distinction between consumer and citizen preferences has long vexed the theory of public finance. Should the public economy serve the same goals as the household economy? May it serve, instead, goals emerging from our association as citizens? The question asks if we may collectively strive for and achieve only those items we individually compete for and consume. Should we aspire, instead, to public goals we may legislate as a nation?

The problem, insofar as it concerns public finance, is stated as follows by R. A. Musgrave, who reports a conversation he had with Gerhard Colm.

> He [Colm] holds that the individual voter dealing with political issues has a frame of reference quite distinct from that which underlies his allocation of income as a consumer. In the latter situation the voter acts as a private individual determined by self-interest and deals with his personal wants; in the former, he acts as a political being guided by his image of a good society. The two, Colm holds, are different things.

Are these two different things? Stephen Marglin suggests that they are. He writes:

> The preferences that govern one's unilateral market actions no longer govern his actions when the form of reference is shifted from the market to the political arena.

The Economic Man and the Citizen are for all intents and purposes two different individuals. It is not a question, therefore, of rejecting individual . . . preference maps; it is, rather, that market and political preference maps are inconsistent.

Marglin observes that if this is true, social choices optimal under one set of preferences will not be optimal under another. What, then, is the meaning of "optimality"? He notices that if we take a person's true preferences to be those expressed in the market, we may, then, neglect or reject the preferences that person reveals in advocating a political cause or position. "One might argue on welfare grounds," Marglin speculates, "for authoritarian rejection of individuals' politically revealed preferences in favor of their market revealed preferences!"

II

On February 19, 1981, President Reagan published Executive Order 12,291 requiring all administrative agencies and departments to support every new major regulation with a cost-benefit analysis establishing that the benefits of the regulation to society outweigh its costs. The Order directs the Office of Management and Budget (OMB) to review every such regulation on the basis of the adequacy of the cost-benefit analysis supporting it. This is a departure from tradition. Traditionally, regulations have been reviewed not by OMB but by the courts on the basis of their relation not to cost-benefit analysis but to authorizing legislation.

A month earlier, in January 1981, the Supreme Court heard lawyers for the American Textile Manufacturers Institute argue against a proposed Occupational Safety and Health Administration (OSHA) regulation which would have severely restricted the acceptable levels of cotton dust in textile plants. The lawyers for industry argued that the benefits of the regulation would not equal the costs. The lawyers for the government contended that the law required the tough standard. OSHA, acting consistently with Executive Order 12,291, asked the Court not to decide the cotton dust case, in order to give the agency time to complete the cost-benefit analysis required by the textile industry. The Court declined to accept OSHA's request and handed down its opinion on June 17, 1981.

The Supreme Court, in a 5–3 decision, found that the actions of regulatory agencies which conform to the OSHA law need not be supported by cost-benefit analysis. In addition, the Court asserted that Congress in writing a statute, rather than the agencies in applying it, has the primary responsibility for balancing benefits and costs. The Court said:

When Congress passed the Occupational Health and Safety Act in 1970, it chose to place preeminent value on

assuring employees a safe and healthful working environment, limited only by the feasibility of achieving such an environment. We must measure the validity of the Secretary's actions against the requirements of that Act.

The opinion upheld the finding of the Appeals Court that "Congress itself struck the balance between costs and benefits in the mandate to the agency."

The Appeals Court opinion in *American Textile Manufacturers* vs. *Donovan* supports the principle that legislatures are not necessarily bound to a particular conception of regulatory policy. Agencies that apply the law, therefore, may not need to justify on cost-benefit grounds the standards they set. These standards may conflict with the goal of efficiency and still express our political will as a nation. That is, they may reflect not the personal choices of self-interested individuals, but the collective judgments we make on historical, cultural, aesthetic, moral, and ideological grounds.

The appeal of the Reagan Administration to cost-benefit analysis, however, may arise more from political than economic considerations. The intention, seen in the most favorable light, may not be to replace political or ideological goals with economic ones but to make economic goals more apparent in regulation. This is not to say that Congress should function to reveal a collective willingness-to-pay just as markets reveal an individual willingness-to-pay. It is to suggest that Congress should do more to balance economic with ideological, aesthetic, and moral goals. To think that environmental or worker safety policy can be based exclusively on aspiration for a "natural" and "safe" world is as foolish as to hold that environmental law can be reduced to cost-benefit accounting. The more we move to one extreme, as I found in Lewiston, the more likely we are to hear from the other.

III

The labor unions won an important political victory when Congress passed the Occupational Safety and Health Act of 1970. That Act, among other things, severely restricts worker exposure to toxic substances. It instructs the Secretary of Labor to set "the standard which most adequately assures, to the extent feasible . . . that no employee will suffer material impairment of health or functional capacity even if such employee has regular exposure to the hazard . . . for the period of his working life."

Pursuant to this law, the Secretary of Labor, in 1977, reduced from ten to one part per million (ppm) the permissible ambient exposure level for benzene, a carcinogenic for which no safe threshold is known. The American Petroleum Institute thereupon challenged the new standard in court. It argued, with much evidence in its favor, that the benefits (to workers) of the one ppm standard did not equal the costs (to industry). The standard, therefore, did not appear to be a rational response to a market failure in that it did not strike an efficient balance between the interests of workers in safety and the interests of industry and consumers in keeping prices down.

The Secretary of Labor defended the tough safety standard on the ground that the law demanded it. An efficient standard might have required safety until it cost industry more to prevent a risk than it cost workers to accept it. Had Congress adopted this vision of public policy—one which can be found in many economic texts—it would have treated workers not as ends-in-themselves but as means for the production of overall utility. And this, as the Secretary saw it, was what Congress refused to do.

The United States Court of Appeals for the Fifth Circuit agreed with the American Petroleum Institute and invalidated the one ppm benzene standard. On July 2, 1980, the Supreme Court affirmed remanding the benzene standard back to OSHA for revision. The narrowly based Supreme Court decision was divided over the role economic considerations should play in judicial review. Justice Marshall, joined in dissent by three other justices, argued that the court had undone on the basis of its own theory of regulatory policy an act of Congress inconsistent with that theory. He concluded that the plurality decision of the Court "requires the American worker to return to the political arena to win a victory that he won before in 1970."

To reject cost-benefit analysis, as Justice Marshall would, as a basis for public policy making is not necessarily to reject cost-effectiveness analysis, which is an altogether different thing. "Cost-benefit analysis," one commentator points out, "is used by the decision maker to establish societal goals as well as the means for achieving these goals, whereas cost-effectiveness analysis only compares alternative means for achieving 'given' goals." Justice Marshall's dissent objects to those who would make efficiency the goal of public policy. It does not necessarily object to those who would accomplish as efficiently as possible the goals Congress sets.

IV

When efficiency is the criterion of public safety and health one tends to conceive of social relations on the model of a market, ignoring competing visions of what we as a society should be like. Yet it is obvious that there are competing conceptions of how we should relate to one another. There are some who believe, on principle, that worker safety and environmental quality ought to be protected only insofar as the benefits of protection balance the costs. On the other hand, people argue, also on principle, that neither worker safety nor environmental quality should be treated merely as a

commodity, to be traded at the margin for other commodities, but should be valued for its own sake. The conflict between these two principles is logical or moral, to be resolved by argument or debate. The question whether cost-benefit analysis should play a decisive role in policymaking is not to be decided by cost-benefit analysis. A contradiction between principles—between contending visions of the good society—cannot be settled by asking how much partisans are willing to pay for their beliefs.

The role of the *legislator*, the political role, may be more important to the individual than the role of *consumer*. The person, in other words, is not to be treated as merely a bundle of preferences to be juggled in cost-benefit analyses. The individual is to be respected as an advocate of ideas which are to be judged in relation to the reasons for them. If health and environmental statutes reflect a vision of society as something other than a market by requiring protections beyond what are efficient, then this may express not legislative ineptitude but legislative responsiveness to public values. To deny this vision because it is economically inefficient is simply to replace it with another vision. It is to insist that the ideas of the citizen be sacrificed to the psychology of the consumer.

We hear on all sides that government is routinized, mechanical, entrenched, and bureaucratized; the jargon alone is enough to dissuade the most mettlesome meddler. Who can make a difference? It is plain that for many of us the idea of a national political community has an abstract and suppositious quality. We have only our private conceptions of the good, if no way exists to arrive at a public one. This is only to note the continuation, in our time, of the trend Benjamin Constant described in the essay, *De La Liberte des Anciens Comparee a Celle des Modernes*. Constant observes that the modern world, as opposed to the ancient, emphasizes civil over political liberties, the rights of privacy and property over those of community and participation. "Lost in the multitude," Constant writes, "the individual rarely perceives the influence that he exercises," and, therefore, must be content with "the peaceful enjoyment of private independence." The individual asks only to be protected by laws common to all in his pursuit of his own self-interest. The citizen has been replaced by the consumer; the tradition of Rousseau has been supplanted by that of Locke and Mill.

Nowhere are the rights of the moderns, particularly the rights of privacy and property, less helpful than in the area of the natural environment. Here the values we wish to protect—cultural, historical, aesthetic, and moral—are public values; they depend not so much upon what each person wants individually as upon what he or she believes we stand for collectively. We refuse to regard worker health and safety as commodities; we regulate hazards as a matter of right. Likewise, we refuse to treat environmental resources simply as public goods in the economist's sense. Instead, we prevent significant deterioration of air quality not only as a matter of individual self-interest but also as a matter of collective self-respect. How shall we balance efficiency against moral, cultural, and aesthetic values in policy for the workplace and the environment? No better way has been devised to do this than by legislative debate ending in a vote. This is not the same thing as a cost-benefit analysis terminating in a bottom line.

V

It is the characteristic of cost-benefit analysis that it treats all value judgments other than those made on its behalf as nothing but statements of preference, attitude, or emotion, insofar as they are value judgments. The cost-benefit analyst regards as true the judgment that we should maximize efficiency or wealth. The analyst believes that this view can be backed by reasons; the analyst does not regard it as a preference or want for which he or she must be willing to pay. The cost-benefit analyst, however, tends to treat all other normative views and recommendations as if they were nothing but subjective reports of mental states. The analyst supposes in all such cases that "this is right" and "this is what we ought to do" are equivalent to "I want this" and "this is what I prefer." Value judgments are beyond criticism if, indeed, they are nothing but expressions of personal preference; they are incorrigible since every person is in the best position to know what he or she wants. All valuation, according to this approach, happens *in foro interno*; debate *in foro publico* has no point. On this approach, the reasons that people give for their views, unless these people are welfare economists, do not count; what counts is how much they are willing to pay to satisfy their wants. Those who are willing to pay the most, for all intents and purposes, have the right view; theirs is the more informed opinion, the better aesthetic judgment, and the deeper moral insight.

The assumption that valuation is subjective, that judgments of good and evil are nothing but expressions of desire and aversion, is not unique to economic theory. There are psychotherapists—Carl Rogers is an example—who likewise deny the objectivity or cognitivity of valuation. For Rogers, there is only one criterion of worth: it lies in "the subjective world of the individual. Only he knows it fully." The therapist shows his or her client that a "value system is not necessarily something imposed from without, but is something experienced." Therapy succeeds when the client "perceives himself in such a way that no self-experience can be discriminated as more or less worthy of positive self-regard than any other. . . ." The client then "tends to place the basis of standards within himself, recognizing that the 'goodness' or 'badness' of any experience or perceptual object

is not something inherent in that object, but is a value placed in it by himself."

Rogers points out that "some clients make strenuous efforts to have the therapist exercise the valuing function, so as to provide them with guides for action." The therapist, however, "consistently keeps the locus of evaluation with the client." As long as the therapist refuses to "exercise the valuing function" and as long as he or she practices an "unconditional positive regard" for all the affective states of the client, then the therapist remains neutral among the client's values or "sensory and visceral experiences." The role of the therapist is legitimate, Rogers suggests, because of this value neutrality. The therapist accepts all felt preferences as valid and imposes none on the client.

Economists likewise argue that their role as policymakers is legitimate because they are neutral among competing values in the client society. The political economist, according to James Buchanan, "is or should be ethically neutral: the indicated results are influenced by his own value scale only insofar as this reflects his membership in a larger group." The economist might be most confident of the impartiality of his or her policy recommendations if he or she could derive them formally or mathematically from individual preferences. If theoretical difficulties make such a social welfare function impossible, however, the next best thing, to preserve neutrality, is to let markets function to transform individual preference orderings into a collective ordering of social states. The analyst is able then to base policy on preferences that exist in society and are not necessarily his own.

Economists have used this impartial approach to offer solutions to many outstanding social problems, for example, the controversy over abortion. An economist argues that "there is an optimal number of abortions, just as there is an optimal level of pollution, or purity. . . . Those who oppose abortion could eliminate it entirely, if their intensity of feeling were so strong as to lead to payments that were greater at the margin than the price anyone would pay to have an abortion." Likewise economists, in order to determine whether the war in Vietnam was justified, have estimated the willingness to pay of those who demonstrated against it. Likewise it should be possible, following the same line of reasoning, to decide whether Creationism should be taught in the public schools, whether black and white people should be segregated, whether the death penalty should be enforced, and whether the square root of six is three. All of these questions depend upon how much people are willing to pay for their subjective preferences or wants—or none of them do. This is the beauty of cost-benefit analysis: no matter how relevant or irrelevant, wise or stupid, informed or uninformed, responsible or silly, defensible or indefensible wants may be, the analyst is able to derive a policy from them—a policy which is legitimate because, in theory, it treats all of these preferences as equally valid and good.

VI

Consider, by way of contrast, a Kantian conception of value. The individual, for Kant, is a judge of values, not a mere haver of wants, and the individual judges not for himself or herself merely, but as a member of a relevant community or group. The central idea in a Kantian approach to ethics is that some values are more reasonable than others and therefore have a better claim upon the assent of members of the community as such. The world of obligation, like the world of mathematics or the world of empirical fact, is intersubjective, it is public not private, so that objective standards of argument and criticism apply. Kant recognizes that values, like beliefs, are subjective states of mind, but he points out that like beliefs they have an objective content as well; therefore they are either correct or mistaken. Thus Kant discusses valuation in the context not of psychology but of cognition. He believes that a person who makes a value judgment—or a policy recommendation—claims to know what is *right* and not just what is *preferred*. A value judgment is like an empirical or theoretical judgment in that it claims to be *true*, not merely to be *felt*.

We have, then, two approaches to public policy before us. The first, the approach associated with normative versions of welfare economics, asserts that the only policy recommendation that can or need be defended on objective grounds is efficiency or wealth-maximization. Every policy decision after that depends only on the preponderance of feeling or preference, as expressed in willingness to pay. The Kantian approach, on the other hand, assumes that many policy recommendations other than that one may be justified or refuted on objective grounds. It would concede that the approach of welfare economics applies adequately to some questions, e.g., those which ordinary consumer markets typically settle. How many yo-yos should be produced as compared to how many frisbees? Shall pens have black ink or blue? Matters such as these are so trivial it is plain that markets should handle them. It does not follow, however, that we should adopt a market or quasi-market approach to every public question.

A market or quasi-market approach to arithmetic, for example, is plainly inadequate. No matter how much people are willing to pay, three will never be the square root of six. Similarly, segregation is a national curse and the fact that we are willing to pay for it does not make it better but only makes us worse. Similarly, the case for abortion must stand on the merits; it cannot be priced at the margin. Similarly, the war in Vietnam was a moral debacle and this can be determined without shadow-pricing the willingness to pay of those who demonstrated against it. Similarly, we do not decide to execute murderers by asking how much bleeding hearts are willing to pay to see a person pardoned and how much hard hearts are willing to pay to see him hanged. Our failures to make the right decisions in these matters are failures in arithmetic, failures in wisdom, failures in taste, failures in morality—but not market failures. There are no relevant markets to have failed. What separates these questions from those for which markets are appropriate is this. They involve matters of knowledge, wisdom, morality, and taste that admit of better or worse, right or wrong, true or false—and these concepts differ from that of economic optimality. Surely environmental questions—the protection of wilderness, habitats, water, land, and air as well as policy toward environmental safety and health—involve moral and aesthetic principles and not just economic ones. This is consistent, of course, with cost-effectiveness and with a sensible recognition of economic constraints.

The neutrality of the economist, like the neutrality of Rogers' therapist, is legitimate if private preferences or subjective wants are the only values in question. A person should be left free to choose the color of his or her necktie or necklace—but we cannot justify a theory of public policy or private therapy on that basis. If the patient seeks moral advice or tries to find reasons to justify a choice, the therapist, according to Rogers' model, would remind him or her to trust his visceral and sensory experiences. The result of this is to deny the individual status as a cognitive being capable of responding intelligently to reasons; it reduces him or her to a bundle of affective states. What Rogers' therapist does to the patient the cost-benefit analyst does to society as a whole. The analyst is neutral among our "values"—having first imposed a theory of what value is. This is a theory that is impartial among values and for that reason fails to treat the persons who have them with respect or concern. It does not treat them even as persons but only as locations at which wants may be found. And thus we may conclude that the neutrality of economics is not a basis for its legitimacy. We recognize it as an indifference toward value—an indifference so deep, so studied, and so assured that at first one hesitates to call it by its right name.

VII

The residents of Lewiston at the conference I attended demanded to know the truth about the dangers that confronted them and the reasons for these dangers. They wanted to be convinced that the sacrifice asked of them was legitimate even if it served interests other than their own. One official from a large chemical company dumping wastes in the area told them, in reply, that corporations were people and that people could talk to people about their feelings, interests, and needs. This sent a shiver through the audience. Like Joseph K. in *The Trial*, the residents of Lewiston asked for an explanation, justice, and truth, and they were told that their wants would be taken care of. They demanded to know the reasons for what was continually happening to them. They were given a personalized response instead.

This response, that corporations are "just people serving people" is consistent with a particular view of power. This is the view that identified power with the ability to get what one wants as an individual, that is, to satisfy one's personal preferences. When people in official positions in corporations or in the government put aside their personal interests, it would follow that they put aside their power as well. Their neutrality then justifies them in directing the resources of society in ways they determine to be best. This managerial role serves not their own interests but those of their clients. Cost-benefit analysis may be seen as a pervasive form of this paternalism. Behind this paternalism, as William Simon observes of the lawyer-client relationship, lies a theory of value that tends to personalize power. "It resists understanding power as a product of class, property, or institutions and collapses power into the personal needs and dispositions of the individuals who command and obey." Once the economist, the therapist, the lawyer, or the manager abjures his own interests and acts wholly on behalf of client individuals, he appears to have no power of his own and thus justifiably manipulates and controls everything. "From this perspective it becomes difficult to distinguish the powerful from the powerless. In every case, both the exercise of power and submission to it are portrayed as a matter of personal accommodation and adjustment."

The key to the personal interest or emotive theory of value, as one commentator has rightly said, "is the fact that emotivism entails the obliteration of any genuine distinction between manipulative and non-manipulative social relations." The reason is that once the effective self is made the source of all value, the public self cannot participate in the exercise of power. As Philip Reiff remarks, "the public world is constituted as one vast stranger who appears at inconvenient times and makes demands viewed as purely external and therefore with no power to elicit a moral response." There is no way to distinguish tyranny from the legitimate authority that public values and public law create.

"At the rate of progress since 1900, " Henry Adams speculates in his *Education*, "every American who lived into the year 2000 would know how to control unlimited power." Adams thought that the Dynamo would organize and release as much energy as the Virgin. Yet in the 1980s, the citizens of Lewiston, surrounded by dynamos, high tension lines, and nuclear wastes, are powerless. They do not know how to criticize power, resist power, or justify power—for to do so depends on making distinctions between good and evil, right and wrong, innocence and guilt, justice and injustice, truth and lies. These distinctions cannot be made out and have no significance within an emotive or psychological theory of value. To adopt this theory is to imagine society as a market in which individuals trade voluntarily and without coercion. No individual, no belief, no faith has authority over them. To have power to act as a nation, however, we must be able to act, at least at times, on a public philosophy, conviction, or faith. We cannot replace with economic analysis the moral function of public law. The antinomianism [*antinomian*—the rejection of law and morality] of cost-benefit analysis is not enough.

Study Questions

1. Do you agree with Sagoff in his distinction between the person as *consumer* and *citizen*? Should there be a radical divide ("schizophrenia") between our economic selves and our moral–political selves?
2. Sagoff seems to hold that not all values are subjective, but some are objectively true or better. What arguments can you think of for both views of values?
3. How is the psychotherapeutic model (Carl Rogers offers an example) similar to the economic model of value preferences? Do you agree with Sagoff that psychotherapists leave out something important? What?
4. Can the standard economic analysis incorporate Sagoff's criticism, arguing that the moral–legislative aspects can be taken into account in assessing the total cost-benefits? Or is there a fundamental cleavage between these two ways of viewing things?

77

A Defense of Risk–Cost–Benefit Analysis

KRISTIN SHRADER-FRECHETTE

Kristin Shrader-Frechette is professor in both the environmental sciences and policy program and the philosophy department at the University of South Florida. She is the author of numerous books and articles in environmental ethics and risk assessment, including Environmental Ethics *(1981),* Nuclear Power and Public Policy *(1983), and* Risk Analysis and Scientific Method *(1985).*

In this essay, Shrader-Frechette argues that critics of science, such as William Rees and Mark Sagoff (see the two previous readings), level unsound criticisms against using the cost–benefit model for making environmental decisions. After explaining the basic idea of risk–cost–benefit analysis (RCBA), she shows how it can be useful to environmentalists. Then she examines several criticisms of RCBA, including objections to it as a formal *method, an* economic *method, and an ethical method. Shrader-Frechette argues that they all fail to undermine its value as a tool for environmentalists.*

Environmentalists often criticize science. They frequently argue for a more romantic, sensitive, holistic, or profound view of the world than science provides. William Rees, for example, criticizes economics on the grounds that it falls victim to scientific materialism; in his article in this volume, he says we need a new paradigm, other than economics, for achieving sustainable development. Similarly, Mark Sagoff, also writing in this text, criticizes the economic model of benefit–cost analysis and argues that it is not always the proper method for making environmental decisions. In particular, he criticizes benefit–cost analysis as utilitarian.

This essay argues that environmentalists' criticisms of science often are misguided. The criticisms err mainly because they ignore the fact that good science can help environmental causes as well as hinder them. Economic methods, for example, can show that nuclear power is not cost effective,[1] that it makes little economic sense to bury long-lived hazardous wastes,[2] and that biological conservation is extraordinarily cost effective.[3] One reason some environmentalists are antiscience or antieconomics—and ignore the way science can help environmentalism—is that they misunderstand science. They attribute flaws to science when the errors are the result of how people use, interpret, or apply science, not

the result of science itself. Rees, for example, criticizes economics as guilty of scientific materialism, yet this essay will show that economics (benefit–cost analysis) can be interpreted in terms of many frameworks, not just scientific materialism. Similarly, Sagoff criticizes benefit–cost analysis as utilitarian, yet this essay will show that the technique is neither *purely* utilitarian, nor utilitarian in a flawed way, because those who use benefit–cost analysis can interpret it in terms of Kantian values, not just utilitarian ones. If this essay is right, then the ethical problems with economics are not with the science itself but with us, humans who interpret and use it in biased ways. In other words, the real problems of economics are the political and ethical biases of its users, not the science itself. To paraphrase Shakespeare: The fault, dear readers, is not with the science but with ourselves, that we are underlings who use it badly.

Consider the case of risk–cost–benefit analysis and attacks on it. Risk–cost–benefit analysis (RCBA), the target of many philosophers' and environmentalists' criticisms, is very likely the single, most used economic method, at least in the United States, for evaluating the desirability of a variety of technological actions—from building a liquefied natural gas facility to adding yellow dye number 2 to margarine. The 1969 National Environmental Policy Act requires that some form of RCBA be used to evaluate all federal environment-related projects.[4] Also, all U.S. regulatory agencies—with the exception perhaps of only the Occupational Health and Safety Administration (OSHA)—routinely use RCBA to help determine their policies.[5]

Basically, RCBA consists of three main steps. These are (1) identifying all the risks, costs, and benefits associated with a particular policy action; (2) converting those risk, cost, and benefit values into dollar figures; and (3) then adding them to determine whether benefits outweigh the risks and costs. Consider the proposed policy action of coating fresh vegetables with a waxy, carcinogenic chemical to allow them to be stored for longer periods of time. Associated with such a policy would be items such as the risk of worker carcinogenesis or the cost of labor and materials for coating the vegetables. The relevant benefits would include factors such as increased market value of the vegetables since the preservative coating would reduce spoilage and losses in storage.

Those who favor RCBA argue that this technique—for identifying, quantifying, comparing, and adding all factors relevant to an economic decision—ought to be

This essay, although including work previously published by the author, was written for this work and appears in this form for the first time.

one of the major considerations that any rational person takes into account in developing social policy. To my knowledge, no economist or policymaker ever has argued that RCBA ought to be the *sole basis* on which any social or environmental choice is made. Despite the fact that RCBA, an application of welfare economics, dominates U.S. decision making regarding environmental and technological issues, it continues to draw much criticism. Economists, industrial representatives, and governmental spokespersons tend to support use of RCBA, but philosophers, environmentalists, and consumer activists tend to criticize its employment.

This essay (1) summarizes the three main lines of criticism of RCBA, (2) outlines arguments for objections to RCBA, (3) shows that the allegedly most devastating criticisms of RCBA are at best misguided and at worst incorrect, and (4) reveals the real source of the alleged deficiencies of RCBA. Let us begin with the three main criticisms of RCBA. These are objections to RCBA (1) as a *formal* method, (2) as an *economic* method, and (3) as an *ethical* method.

OBJECTION 1: RCBA AS A FORMAL METHOD

The most strident criticisms of RCBA (as a *formal* method for making social decisions) come from phenomenologically oriented scholars, such as Hubert and Stuart Dreyfus at Berkeley. They argue that, because it is a rigid, formal method, RCBA cannot model all instances of "human situational understanding."[6] For example, say Stuart Dreyfus, Lawrence Tribe, and Robert Socolow, whenever someone makes a decision, whether about playing chess or driving an automobile, he or she uses intuition and not some analytic, economic "point count."[7] They claim that formal models like RCBA fail to capture the essence of human decision making. The models are too narrow and oversimplified in focusing on allegedly transparent rationality and scientific know-how. Rather, say Dreyfus and others, human decision making is mysterious, unformalizable, and intuitive, something close to wisdom.[8] This is because the performance of human decision making requires expertise and human skill acquisition that cannot be taught by means of any algorithm or formal method like RCBA.[9]

Moreover, say Robert Coburn, Amory Lovins, Alasdair MacIntyre, and Peter Self, humans not only do not go through any formal routine like RCBA, but they could not, even if they wanted to. Why not? Humans, they say, often can't distinguish costs from benefits. For example, generating increased amounts of electricity represents a cost for most environmentalists, but a benefit for most economists. Lovins and his colleagues also claim that people don't know either the probability of certain events, such as energy-related accidents, or the consequences likely to follow from them; they don't

know because humans are not like calculating machines; they cannot put a number on what they value.[10]

Although these criticisms of RCBA are thought provoking, they need not be evaluated in full here, in part because they are analyzed elsewhere.[11] Instead, it might be good merely to sketch the sorts of arguments that, when developed, are capable of answering these objections to the use of RCBA. There are at least six such arguments.

The first is that, since Dreyfus and others merely point to deficiencies in RCBA without arguing that there is some less deficient decision method superior to RCBA, they provide only necessary but not sufficient grounds for rejecting RCBA. A judgment about sufficient grounds for rejecting RCBA ought to be based on a relative evaluation of all methodologic alternatives because reasonable people only reject a method if they have a better alternative to it. Showing deficiencies in RCBA does not establish that a better method is available.

A second argument is that Dreyfus, Tribe, Socolow, and others have "proved too much." If human decision making is unavoidably intuitive and if benefits are indistinguishable from costs, as they say, then no rational, debatable, nonarbitrary form of technologic policymaking is possible. This is because rational policymaking presupposes at least that persons can distinguish what is undesirable from what is desirable, costs from benefits. If they cannot, then this problem does not count against only RCBA but against any method. Moreover, Dreyfus and others ignore the fact that no policymaking methods, including RCBA, are perfect. And if not, then no theory should be merely criticized separately, since such criticisms say nothing about which theory is the least desirable of all.

Another argument, especially relevant to Dreyfus's claims that RCBA is not useful for individual tasks, such as the decision making involved in driving a car, is that many of the objections to RCBA focus on a point not at issue. That RCBA is not amenable to *individual* decision making is not at issue. The real issue is how to take into account millions of individual opinions, to make *societal* decisions. This is because societal decision making presupposes some unifying perspective or method of aggregating preferences of many people, a problem not faced by the individual making choices. Of course, accomplishing RCBA is not like individual decision making, and that is precisely why social choices require some formal analytic tool like RCBA.

Criticisms of RCBA as a formal method are also questionable because Dreyfus and others provide an incomplete analysis of societal decision making in making appeals to wisdom and intuition. They fail to specify, in a political and practical context, *whose* wisdom and intuitions ought to be followed and what criteria ought to be used when the wisdom and intuitions of different persons conflict in an environmental controversy. RCBA answers these questions in a methodical way.

A final argument against criticisms of RCBA, as a formal method, is that Dreyfus and others are incomplete in using policy arguments that ignore the real-world importance of making decisions among finite alternatives and with finite resources. Wisdom may tell us that human life has an infinite value, but the scientific and economic reality is that attaining a zero-risk society is impossible and that there are not enough resources for saving all lives. In dismissing RCBA, Dreyfus and others fail to give their answers to the tough question of what criterion to use in distributing environmental health and safety.[12] If we do not use RCBA, what informal method is a bigger help? This realistic question they do not answer. If not, RCBA may be the best method among many bad methods.

OBJECTION 2: RCBA AS AN ECONOMIC METHOD

Although these six argument-sketches are too brief to be conclusive in answering objections to RCBA as a formal method, let us move on to the second type of criticism so that we can get to the main focus of this essay. Philosophers of science and those who are critical of mainstream economics, like Kenneth Boulding, most often criticize RCBA as a deficient economic method. Perhaps the most powerful methodologic attack on RCBA deficiencies focuses on its central methodologic assumption: Societal welfare can be measured as the algebraic sum of compensating variations (CVs). By analytically unpacking the concept of compensating variation, one can bring many RCBA deficiencies to light.

According to RCBA theory, each individual has a CV that measures the change in his or her welfare as a consequence of a proposed policy action. For example, suppose a university was considering raising the price of student parking permits from $200 per year to $400 per year and using the additional money to build a parking garage on campus. Suppose also that the university would decide whether this act or policy was desirable on the basis of the way it affected all the students. Raising the parking fees and building a garage would affect the welfare of each student differently, depending on her (or his) circumstances. According to economic theory, the CV of each student would measure her particular change in welfare. To find exactly how each student would measure her CV, her change in welfare because of the changed parking fees, we would ask her to estimate it. For example, suppose Susan drives to campus each day and has a part-time job off campus, so she cannot carpool or ride a bus because she needs her car to move efficiently between campus and work. Susan wants to have the parking garage, however, because she has to look nice in her part-time job. If the university builds the parking garage, she will not get wet and muddy walking to her car and will not have

to spend 20 minutes searching for a parking place. If someone asked Susan to put a monetary value on paying $200 more per year for parking in a garage, she might say this change was worth an additional $100, and that, even if the fees increased by $300, would rather have the parking garage. That is, Susan would say her CV was +$100 because she would gain from the new plan. However, suppose Sally also drives to campus each day and suppose her welfare is affected negatively by the increase in parking fees and the proposed parking garage. Because Sally lives at an inconvenient location two hours away, she must drive to campus and park her car every day. But because she lives so far away, has no part-time job, and is going to school with savings, Sally wants to pay as little as possible for parking and prefers the existing muddy, uncovered parking lots. If someone asks Sally to put a monetary value on paying $200 more per year for parking in a garage, she might say this change harmed her by $200. That is, Sally would say her CV was −$200. Economists who use RCBA believe that, in order to determine the desirability of building the parking garage and charging $200 more per year, they should add all the CVs of gainers (like Susan) and losers (like Sally) and see whether the gains of the action outweigh the losses.

Or consider the case of using CVs to measure the effects of building a dam. The CVs of some persons will be positive, and those of others will be negative. Those in the tourism industry might be affected positively, whereas those interested in wilderness experiences might be affected negatively. The theory is that the proposed dam is cost-beneficial if the sum of the CVs of the gainers can outweigh the sum of the CVs of the losers. In more technical language, according to economist Ezra Mishan, a CV is the sum of money that, if received or paid after the economic (or technologic) change in question, would make the individual no better or worse off than before the change. If, for example, the price of a bread loaf falls by 10 cents, the CV is the maximum sum a man would pay to be allowed to buy bread at this lower price. Per contra, if the loaf rises by 10 cents, the CV is the minimum sum the man must receive if he is to continue to feel as well off as he was before the rise in price.[13] Implicit in the notion of a CV are three basic presuppositions, all noted in standard texts on welfare economics and cost–benefit analysis: (1) the compensating variation is a measure of how gains can be so distributed to make everyone in the community better off[14]; (2) the criterion for whether one is better off is how well off feels subjectively[15]; and (3) one's feelings of being well off or better off are measured by a sum of money judged by the individual and calculated at the given set of prices on the market.[16]

According to the critics of RCBA, each of the three presuppositions built into the concept of a CV contains controversial assumptions.[17] The first presupposition, that CVs provide a measure of how to make everyone better off, is built on at least two questionable assumptions: Gains and losses, costs and benefits, for every individual in every situation can be computed numerically.[18] A second questionable assumption built into this presupposition is that employing an economic change to improve the community welfare is acceptable, even though distributional effects of this change are ignored. Many people have argued that the effect of this assumption is merely to make economic changes that let the rich get richer and the poor get poorer, thus reflecting the dominant ideologies of the power groups dominating society.

The second presupposition built into the notion of CV, that the criterion for whether one is better off is how one feels subjectively, as measured in quantitative terms, also embodies a number of doubtful assumptions. Some of these are that, as Kenneth Arrow admits, individual welfare is defined in terms of egoistic hedonism[19]; that the individual is the best judge of his welfare, that is, that preferences reveal welfare, despite the fact that utility is often different from morality[20]; that summed preferences of *individual* members of a group reveal *group* welfare[21]; and that wealthy and poor persons are equally able to judge their well-being. This last assumption has been widely criticized since willingness to pay is a function of the marginal utility of one's income. That is, rich people are more easily able to pay for improvements to their welfare than poor people are. As a consequence, poor persons obviously cannot afford to pay as much as rich persons in order to avoid the risks and other disamenities of technology-related environmental pollution.[22] That is why poor people are often forced to live in areas of high pollution, while wealthy people can afford to live in cleaner environments.

Continuing the analysis of CV, critics of RCBA point out that the third presupposition built into the notion of CV also involves a number of questionable assumptions. The presupposition that one's feelings of being better off are measured by money, and calculated in terms of market prices, includes at least one highly criticized assumption—that prices measure values. This assumption is controversial on a number of grounds. For one thing, it begs the difference between wants and morally good wants. It also ignores economic effects that distort prices. Some of these distorting effects include monopolies, externalities, speculative instabilities, and "free goods," such as clean air.[23]

Because methodologic criticisms such as these have been a major focus of much contemporary writing in philosophy of economics and in sociopolitical philosophy, discussion of them is extremely important. However, economists generally *admit* most of the preceding points but claim that they have no better alternative method to use than RCBA. If their claim is at least partially correct, as I suspect it is (see the previous section of this essay), then many of the preceding criticisms of RCBA are beside the point. Also, both economists and philosophers have devised ways of avoiding most of the troublesome pre-

suppositions and consequences of the assumptions built into the notion of compensating variation. Chief among these ways of improving RCBA are use of alternative weighting schemes and employment of various ways to make the controversial aspects of RCBA explicit and open to evaluation. Use of a weighting scheme for RCBA would enable one, for example, to "cost" inequitably distributed risks more than equitably distributed ones. Also, if one desired, it would be possible to employ Rawlsian weighting schemes for promoting the welfare of the least-well-off persons. One of the chief reforms, important for addressing the economic deficiencies of RCBA, would be to employ a form of adversary assessment in which alternative RCBA studies would be performed by groups sharing different ethical and methodologic presuppositions. Such adversary assessment has already been accomplished, with success, in Ann Arbor, Michigan, and in Cambridge, Massachusetts.[24] Hence, at least in theory, there are ways to avoid the major economic deficiencies inherent in RCBA.

OBJECTION 3: RCBA AS AN ETHICAL METHOD

The most potentially condemning criticisms of RCBA come from the ranks of moral philosophers. Most of those who criticize RCBA on ethical grounds, as one might suspect, are deontologists who employ standard complaints against utilitarians. Philosophers, such as Alasdair MacIntyre and Douglas MacLean, claim that some things are priceless and not amenable to risk–benefit costing. Alan Gewirth argues that certain commitments—for example, the right not to be caused to contract cancer—cannot be traded off (via RCBA) for some utilitarian benefit.[25] In sum, the claim of these ethicist critics of RCBA is that moral commitments, rights, and basic goods are inviolable and incommensurable and hence cannot be "bargained away" in a utilitarian scheme like RCBA, which is unable to take adequate account of them and of values like distributive justice.

Of course, the linchpin assumption of the arguments of Gewirth, MacLean, and others is that RCBA is indeed utilitarian. If this assumption can be proved wrong, then (whatever else is wrong with RCBA) it cannot be attacked on the grounds that it is utilitarian.

Misguided Ethical Criticism of RCBA

RCBA is not essentially utilitarian in some damaging sense for a number of reasons. First of all, let's admit that RCBA is indeed utilitarian in one crucial respect: The optimal choice is always determined by some function of the utilities attached to the consequences of all the options considered. Hence, reasoning in RCBA is unavoidably consequentialist.

Because it is unavoidably consequentialist, however, means neither that RCBA is consequentialist in some *disparaging* sense, nor that it is *only* consequentialist, both points that are generally begged by deontological critics of RCBA. Of course, RCBA is necessarily consequentialist, but so what? Anyone who follows some deontological theory and ignores consequences altogether is just as simplistic as anyone who focuses merely on consequences and ignores deontological elements. This is exactly the point recognized by Amartya Sen when he notes that Jeremy Bentham and John Rawls capture two different but equally important aspects of interpersonal welfare considerations.[26] Both provide necessary conditions for ethical judgments, but neither is sufficient.

Although RCBA is necessarily consequentialist, there are at least four reasons that it is not only consequentialist in some extremist or disparaging sense. *First*, any application of RCBA principles presupposes that we make some value judgments that cannot be justified by utilitarian standards alone.[27] For example, suppose we are considering which of a variety of possible actions (e.g., building a nuclear plant, a coal plant, or a solar facility) ought to be evaluated in terms of RCBA. A utilitarian value judgment would not suffice for reducing the set of options. It would not suffice for deciding which of many available chemicals to use in preserving foods in a given situation, for example, because we would not have performed the utility weighting yet. Usually we use deontological grounds for rejecting some option. For instance, we might reject chemical X as a food preservative because it is a powerful carcinogen and use of it would threaten consumers' rights to life.

Second, RCBA also presupposes another type of nonutilitarian value judgment by virtue of the fact that it would be impossible to know the utilities attached to an infinity of options because they are infinite. To reduce these options, one would have to make some nonutilitarian value judgments about which options not to consider. For example, suppose chemical Z (considered for preserving food) were known to cause death to persons with certain allergic sensitivities or to persons with diabetes. On grounds of preventing a violation of a legal right to equal protection, analysts using RCBA could simply exclude chemical Z from consideration, much as they exclude technically or economically infeasible options for consideration

Also, in the course of carrying out RCBA calculations—one is required to make a number of nonutilitarian value judgments. Some of these are: (1) There is a cardinal or ordinal scale in terms of which the consequences may be assigned some number, (2) a particular discount rate ought to be used, (3) or certain values ought to be assigned to certain consequences. For example, if policymakers subscribed to the deontological, evaluative judgment that future generations have rights equal to our own, then they could employ a zero discount rate. Nothing in the theory underlying RCBA

would prevent them from doing so and from recognizing this deontological value.

Third, one could weight the RCBA parameters to reflect whatever value system society wishes. As Ralph Keeney has noted, one could always assign the value of negative infinity to consequences alleged to be the result of an action that violated some deontological principle.[28] Thus, if one wanted to avoid any technology likely to result in violation of people's rights not to be caused to contract cancer, one could easily do so.

Fourth, RCBA is not necessarily utilitarian, as Patrick Suppes points out, because the theory could, in principle, be adopted (without change) to represent a "calculus of obligation and a theory of expected obligation"; in other words, RCBA is materially indifferent, a purely formal calculus with an incomplete theory of rationality.[29] This being so, one need not interpret only market parameters as costs. Indeed, economists have already shown that one can interpret RCBA to accommodate egalitarianism and intuitionism as well as utilitarianism.[30] More generally, Kenneth Boulding has eloquently demonstrated that economic supply–demand curves can be easily interpreted to fit even a benevolent or an altruistic ethical framework, not merely a utilitarian ethical framework.[31]

THE REAL SOURCE OF RCBA PROBLEMS

If these four arguments, from experts such as Suppes and Keeney, are correct, then much of the criticism of RCBA, at least for its alleged ethical deficiencies, has been misguided. It has been directed at the formal, economic, and ethical *theory* underlying RCBA, when apparently something else is the culprit. This final section will argue that there are at least two sources of the problems that have made RCBA so notorious. One is the dominant political ideology in terms of which RCBA has been interpreted, applied, and used. The second source of the difficulties associated with RCBA has been the tendency of both theorists and practitioners—economists and philosophers alike—to claim more objectivity for the conclusions of RCBA than the evidence warrants. Let's investigate both of these problem areas.

Perhaps the major reason that people often think, erroneously, that RCBA is utilitarian is that capitalist utilitarians first used the techniques. Yet, to believe that the logical and ethical presuppositions built into economic methods can be identified with the logical and ethical beliefs of those who originate or use the methods is to commit the genetic fallacy.[32] *Origins* do not necessarily determine *content*. And, if not, then RCBA has no built-in ties to utilitarianism.[33] What has happened is that, in practice, one *interpretation* of RCBA has been dominant. This interpretation, in terms of capitalist utilitarianism, is what is incompatible with nonutilitarian values. But this means that the problems associated with the dominant political ideology, in terms of which RCBA is interpreted, has been confused with RCBA problems. Were the methods interpreted according to a different ideology, it would be just as wrong to equate RCBA with that ideology.

Confusion about the real source of the problems with RCBA has arisen because of the difficulty of determining causality. The cause of the apparent utilitarian biases in RCBA is the dominant *ideology* in terms of which people interpret it. The cause is not the *method* itself. This is like the familiar point, which often needs reiteration, that humans, not computers, cause computer errors. Given this explanation, it is easy to see why C. B. MacPherson argues that there is no necessary incompatibility between maximizing utilities and maximizing some nonutilitarian value. The alleged incompatibility arises only after one interprets the nonutilitarian value. In this case, the alleged incompatibility arises only when one interprets utilities in terms of unlimited individual appropriations and market incentives.[34]

If the preceding view of RCBA is correct and if people have erroneously identified one—of many possible—interpretations of RCBA with the method, then obviously they have forgotten that RCBA is a formal calculus to be used with a variety of interpretations. But if they have forgotten that RCBA is open to many different interpretations, then they have identified one dominant political interpretation with RCBA itself, then they have forgotten that, because of this dominant interpretation, RCBA is politically loaded. And if they have forgotten that they are employing a utilitarian *interpretation* that is politically loaded, then they probably have assumed that RCBA is objective by virtue of its being part of science.

Utilitarian philosophers and welfare economists have been particularly prone to the errors of believing that utilitarian interpretations of decision making are objective and value-free. Utilitarian R. M. Hare argues in his book, for example, that moral philosophy can be done without ontology[35]; he also argues that moral philosophy can be done objectively and with certainty, that there are no irresolvable moral conflicts[36]; and that objective moral philosophy is utilitarian in character.[37] Hare even goes so far as to argue that a hypothetical–deductive method can be used to obtain moral evaluations and to test them.[38] Hare, one of the best moral philosophers of the century, equates utilitarian tenets with value-free, certain conclusions obtained by the scientific method of hypothesis-deduction. His error here means that we ought not be surprised that lesser minds also have failed to recognize the evaluative and interpretational component in utilitarianism and in the utilitarian interpretations of RCBA. Numerous well-known practitioners of RCBA have argued that the technique is objective, and they have failed to recognize its value component.[39] Milton Friedman calls economics objective,"[40] and Chauncey Starr, Chris Whipple, David

Okrent, and other practitioners of RCBA use the same terminology; they even claim that those who do not accept their value-laden interpretations of RCBA are following merely "subjective" interpretations.[41]

Given that both moral philosophers and practitioners of RCBA claim that their utilitarian analyses are objective, they create an intellectual climate in which RCBA is presumed to be more objective, value-free, and final than it really is. Hence, one of the major problems with RCBA is not that it is inherently utilitarian but that its users erroneously assume it has a finality that it does not possess. It is one of many possible techniques, and it has many interpretations. Were this recognized, then people would not oppose it so vehemently.

SUMMARY AND CONCLUSIONS

RCBA has many problems. As a formal method, it suggests that life is more exact and precise than it really is. As an economic method, it suggests that people make decisions on the basis of hedonism and egoism. As an ethical method, people have interpreted it in utilitarian ways, in ways that serve the majority of people, but not always the minority.

Despite all these criticisms, RCBA is often better than most environmentalists believe. It is better because criticisms of RCBA often miss the point in two important ways. First, the criticisms miss the point that society needs some methodical way to tally costs and benefits associated with its activities. While it is true that RCBA has problems because of its being a formal, economic method, this criticism of it misses the point. The point is that we humans need some clear, analytic way to help us with environmental decision making. Most people would not write a blank check in some area of personal life, and no one ought to write a blank check for solving societal problems. Not using some technique like RCBA means that we would be writing a blank check, making decisions and commitments without being aware of their costs, benefits, and consequences. All that RCBA asks of us is that we add up all the risks, benefits, and costs of our actions. It asks that we not make decisions without considering all the risks, costs, and benefits. The point is that RCBA does not need to be perfect to be useful in societal and environmental decision making; it needs only to be useful, helpful, and better than other available methods for making societal decisions.

Second, criticisms of RCBA miss the point because they blame RCBA for a variety of ethical problems, mainly problems associated with utilitarianism. RCBA, however, is merely a formal calculus for problem solving The users of RCBA are responsible for the capitalistic, utilitarian interpretation of it. If so, then what needs to be done is neither to abandon RCBA, nor to condemn it as utilitarian, but to give some philosophical lessons in the value ladenness of its interpretations. We need more ethical and epistemological sensitivity among those who interpret RCBA, and we need to recognize practical, political problems for what they are. The problem is with us, with our values, with our politics. The problem is not with RCBA methods that merely reflect our values and politics.

Notes

1. K. S. Shrader-Frechette, *Nuclear Power and Public Policy* (Boston: Kluwer, 1983), 54–60.
2. K. S. Shrader-Frechette, *Burying Uncertainty* (Berkeley: University of California Press, 1993), 239–241.
3. K. S. Shrader-Frechette and E. McCoy, *Method in Ecology* (New York: Cambridge University Press, 1993), 175–185.
4. See Ian G. Barbour, *Technology, Environment, and Human Values* (New York: Praeger, 1980), 163–164.
5. Luther J. Carter, "Dispute over Cancer Risk Quantification," *Science* 203, no. 4387 (1979): 1324–1325.
6. Stuart E. Dreyfus, "Formal Models vs. Human Situational Understanding: Inherent Limitations on the Modeling of Business Expertise," *Technology and People* 1 (1982): 133–165. See also S. Dreyfus, "The Risks! and Benefits? of Risk–Benefit Analysis," unpublished paper presented on March 24, 1983, in Berkeley, California, at the Western Division meeting of the American Philosophical Association. Stuart Dreyfus and his brother Hubert Dreyfus share the beliefs attributed to Stuart in these and other publications. They often co-author publications. See, for example, S. Dreyfus and H. Dreyfus, "The Scope, Limits, and Training Implications of Three Models of . . . Behavior," ORC 79–2 (Berkeley: Operations Research Center, University of California, February 1979).
7. S. Dreyfus, "Formal Models," op. cit., note 6, 161. See also Lawrence H. Tribe, "Technology Assessment and the Fourth Discontinuity," *Southern California Law Review* 46, no. 3 (June 1973): 659; and Robert Socolow, "Failures of Discourse," in D. Scherer and T. Attig, eds., *Ethics and the Environment* (Englewood Cliffs, NJ: Prentice Hall, 1983): 152–166.
8. S. Dreyfus, "Formal Models," op. cit., note 6, 161–163; and Douglas MacLean, "Understanding the Nuclear Power Controversy," in A. L. Caplan and H. Englehardt, eds., *Scientific Controversies* (Cambridge: Cambridge University Press, 1983), Part 5.
9. S. Dreyfus, "The Risks! and Benefits?" op. cit., note 6, 2.
10. Peter Self, *Econocrats and the Policy Process: The Politics and Philosophy of Cost–Benefit Analysis* (London: Macmillan, 1975), 70; Alisdair MacIntyre, "Utilitarians and Cost–Benefit Analysis," in D. Scherer and T. Attig, eds., *Ethics and the Environment*, op. cit., note 7, 143–145; and Amory Lovins, "Cost–Risk–Benefit Assessment in Energy Policy," *George Washington Law Review* 45, no. 5 (August 1977): 913–916, 925–926. See also Robert Coburn, "Technology Assessment, Human Good, and Freedom," in K. E. Goodpaster and K. M. Sayer, eds., *Ethics and Problems of the 21st Century* (Notre Dame: University of Notre Dame Press, 1979), 108; E. J. Mishan, Cost–Benefit Analysis (New York: Praeger, 1976), 160–161; Gunnar Myrdal, *The Political Element in the Development of Economic Theory*, Paul Steeten, trans. (Cambridge: Harvard University Press, 1955), 89: and A. Radomysler, "Welfare Economics and Economic Policy," in K. Arrow and T. Scitovsky, eds., *Readings in Welfare Economics* (Homewood, IL: Irwin, 1969), 89.
11. See K. S. Shrader-Frechette, *Science Policy, Ethics, and Economic Methodology* (Boston: Reidel, 1985), 38–54. See also K. S. Shrader-Frechette, *Risk and Rationality* (Berkeley: University of California Press, 1991), 169–196.
12. Shrader-Frechette, *Science Policy*, op. cit., note 11, 36–54; K. S. Shrader-Frechette, *Risk and Rationality*, op. cit., note 11, 169–183.
13. Mishan, *Cost–Benefit Analysis*, op. cit., note 10, 391.
14. Ibid., 390.
15. Ibid., 309.
16. E. J. Mishan, *Welfare Economics* (New York: Random House, 1969), 113; see also 107–113.
17. For a more complete analysis of these points, see K. S. Shrader-Frechette, "Technology Assessment as Applied Philosophy of Science," *Science, Technology, and Human Values* 6, no. 33 (Fall 1980), 33–50.
18. M. W. Jones-Lee, *The Value of Life* (Chicago: University of Chicago Press, 1976), 3; and R. Coburn, "Technology Assessment," in K. E. Goodpaster and K. M. Sayer, eds., *Ethics and Problems of the 21st Century*, op. cit., note 10, 109. See also Oskar Morgenstern, *On the Accuracy of Economic Observations* (Princeton, NJ: Princeton University Press, 1963), 100–101.
19. Cited in V. C. Walsh, "Axiomatic Choice Theory and Values," in Sidney Hook, ed., *Human Values and Economic Policy* (New York: New York University Press, 1967), 197.
20. See R. Coburn, "Technology Assessment," in K. E. Goodpaster and K. M. Sayer, eds., *Ethics and Problems of the 21st Century*, op. cit., note 10, 109–110; Gail Kennedy, "Social Choice and Policy Formation," in S. Hook, ed., *Human Values and Economic Policy*, op. cit., note 19, 142; and John Ladd, "The Use of Mechanical Models for the Solution of Ethical Problems," in S. Hook, ed., *Human Values and Economic Policy*, op. cit., 167–168. See also Mark Lutz and Kenneth Lux, *The Challenge of Humanistic Economics* (London: Benjamin/Cummings, 1979). Finally, see Richard Brandt, "Personal Values and the Justification of Institutions," in S. Hook, ed., *Human Values and Economic Policy*, op. cit., note 19, 37; and

John Ladd, "Models," in S. Hook, ed., *Human Values and Economic Policy*, op. cit., note 19, 159–168.

21. G. Kennedy, "Social Choice," S. Hook, ed., *Human Values and Economic Policy*, op. cit., note 20, 148, makes the same point.

22. Peter S. Albin, "Economic Values and the Values of Human Life," in S. Hook, ed., *Human Values and Economic Policy*, op. cit., note 19, 97; and M. W. Jones-Lee, *Value of Life*, op. cit., note 18, 20–55.

23. See J. A. Hobson, *Confessions of an Economic Heretic* (Sussex, England: Harvester Press, 1976), 39–40; and Benjamin M. Anderson, *Social Value* (New York: A. M. Kelley, 1966), 24, 26, 31, 162. See also Kenneth Boulding, "The Basis of Value Judgments in Economics," in S. Hook, ed., *Human Values and Economic Policy*, op. cit., note 19, 67–79; and O. Morgenstern, *Accuracy of Economic Observations*, op. cit., note 18, 19. Finally, see E. J. Mishan, *Cost–Benefit Analysis*, op. cit., note 10, 393–394; and E. F. Schumacher, *Small Is Beautiful* (New York: Harper, 1973), 38–49; as well as N. Georgescu-Roegen, *Energy and Economic Myths* (New York: Pergamon, 1976), x, 10–14.

24. See Shrader-Frechette, *Science Policy*, op. cit., note 11, Chapters 8–9; Shrader-Frechette, *Risk and Rationality*, op. cit., note 11; and B. A. Weisbrod, "Income Redistribution Effects and Benefit–Cost Analysis," in S. Chase, ed., *Problems in Public Expenditure Analysis* (Washington, D.C.: Brookings, 1972), 177–208. See also P. Dasgupta, S. Marglin, and A. Sen, *Guidelines of Project Evaluation* (New York: UNIDO, 1972); and A. V. Kneese, S. Ben-David, and W. Schulze, "The Ethical Foundations of Benefit–Cost Analysis," in D. MacLean and P. Brown, eds., "A Study of the Ethical Foundations of Benefit–Cost Techniques," unpublished report done with funding from the National Science Foundation, Program in Ethics and Values in Science and Technology, August 1979.

25. Lovins, "Cost–Risk–Benefit Assessment," op. cit., note 10, 929–930; Douglas MacLean, "Qualified Risk Assessment and the Quality of Life," in D. Zinberg, ed., *Uncertain Power* (New York: Pergamon, 1983), Part V; and Alan Gewirth, "Human Rights and the Prevention of Cancer," in D. Scherer and T. Attig, eds., *Ethics and the Environment*, op. cit., note 7, 177.

26. Amartya K. Sen, "Rawls Versus Bentham," in N. Daniels, ed., *Reading Rawls* (New York: Basic Books, 1981), 283–292.

27. Ronald Giere, "Technological Decision Making," in M. Bradie and K. Sayre, eds., *Reason and Decision* (Bowling Green, OH: Bowling Green State University Press, 1981), Part 3, makes a similar argument.

28. Ralph G. Keeney mentioned this to me in a private conversation at Berkeley in January 1983.

29. Patrick Suppes, "Decision Theory," in P. Edwards, ed., *Encyclopedia of Philosophy*, Vol. 1 and 2 (New York: Collier-Macmillan, 1967), 311.

30. P. S. Dasgupta and G. M. Heal, *Economic Theory and Exhaustible Resources* (Cambridge: Cambridge University Press, 1979), 269–281.

31. K. Boulding, "Value Judgments," in S. Hook, ed., *Human Values and Economic Policy*, op. cit., note 23, 67ff.

32. Alexander Rosenberg makes this point in *Macroeconomic Laws* (Pittsburgh: University of Pittsburgh Press, 1976), 203.

33. Tribe, "Technology Assessment," op. cit., note 7, 628–629; MacLean, "Qualified Risk Assessment," op. cit., note 25, Parts 5 and 6; MacIntyre, "Utilitarians and Cost–Benefit Analysis," op. cit., note 10, 139–142; Gewirth, "Human Rights," op. cit., note 25, 177; and C. B. MacPherson, "Democratic Theory: Ontology and Technology," in C. Mitcham and R. Mackey, eds., *Philosophy and Technology* (New York: Free Press, 1972), 167–168.

34. See note 33.

35. R. M. Hare, *Moral Thinking* (Oxford: Clarendon Press, 1981), 6 (see also 210–211).

36. Ibid, 26.

37. Ibid., 4.

38. Ibid., 12–14.

39. See, for example, Chauncey Starr, "Benefit–Cost Studies in Sociotechnical Systems," in Committee on Engineering Policy, *Perspectives on Benefit–Risk Decision Making* (Washington, D.C.: National Academy of Engineering, 1972), 26ff.; Chauncey Starr and Chris Whipple, "Risks of Risk Decisions," *Science* 208, no. 4448 (1980): 1116–1117; and D. Okrent and C. Whipple, *Approach to Societal Risk Acceptance Criteria and Risk Management*, Report no. PB–271264 (Washington, D.C.: Department of Commerce, 1977), 10.

40. Milton Friedman, "Value Judgments in Economics," in S. Hook, ed., *Human Values and Economic Policy*, op. cit., note 19, 85–88.

41. See also note 39; K. S. Shrader-Frechette, *Risk Analysis and Scientific Method* (Boston: Reidel, 1985), especially 176–189; and Shrader-Frechette, *Risk and Rationality*, op. cit., note 11, 169–196.

Study Questions

1. Compare Shrader-Frechette's essay with the two previous selections by William Rees and Mark Sagoff. How do they differ? Who has the stronger arguments?

2. What is the risk–cost–benefit analysis (RCBA), and how does it work? How valuable is it for environmental policy? Discuss Shrader-Frechette's assessment of this issue.

3. What are the major objections to RCBA that Shrader-Frechette considers? How does she deal with them? Discuss her arguments.

78

Neoclassical Economics and Principles of Sustainable Development

ROBERT GOODLAND AND GEORGE LEDEC

Robert Goodland and George Ledec work for the Department of Environmental and Scientific Affairs of the World Bank, Washington, D.C. They argue that the standard market-oriented capitalist economic theory can accommodate the concerns of environmentalists (see Readings 77–79). They admit that values are hard to measure but argue that economics can take this point into consideration. Furthermore, suitably interpreted, the economic cost–benefit analysis (CBA) can incorporate ecological considerations. They illustrate their thesis with projects of the World Bank.

PERSPECTIVE

. . . Economics is the study of allocating the resources available to society in a way that maximizes social well-being. If something must be foregone or sacrificed in order to achieve a social goal, the economic choices are involved. Economics attempts to tell us how we can make the trade-offs among tangible, material goods in the most efficient, or "Pareto-optimal," manner. A Pareto optimum is defined as a state of the economy in which all economic resources are allocated and used "efficiently," such that it is impossible to make anyone economically better off without making someone else economically worse off.

A major advantage of efficient markets is their ability to attain Pareto-optimal resource allocation (which is no small achievement). However, a Pareto-optimal allocation can occur at an ecologically unsustainable pattern of resource use, just as it can occur at an ethically undesirable pattern of income distribution. . . . Pareto optimality is defined independently of both income distribution and the physical scale of resource use. Public policy decision-making which relies exclusively on market criteria (and, by extension, cost-benefit analysis centered on present-value maximizations) can effectively address only short-term allocative efficiency—not many of the other important factors which determine human welfare. These factors include income distribution, intangible environmental goods, and the prospect of a safer future that can be achieved by sustainable natural resource use. . . .Therefore sustainability, like equitable income distribution, cannot be properly determined

with typical efficiency criteria, using techniques such as conventional economic cost-benefit analysis [CBA]. . . .

Despite the many deficiencies of CBA, it can still be useful for advancing environmental goals. Even unreasonably low or highly inaccurate estimates of environmental benefits and costs are better than none, because the alternative is to assume implicitly that these benefits and costs are zero. Rather than abandoning CBA, environmentalists should insist that it take environmental and other social costs explicitly into account. As is discussed in [the section on safe minimum standards], CBA is most useful from an environmental perspective when it is "constrained" by safe minimum standards.

PROBLEMS OF PHYSICAL MEASUREMENTS

Development projects have many "tangible" environmental consequences which, while very real, cannot readily be assigned a monetary value. This is due to the difficulties inherent in both physical estimation and monetary valuation of the relevant environmental effects. In terms of physical effects, it may be difficult, as an example, to predict a priori to what extent the building of a rural road through a forested area may affect soil erosion, as well as downstream sedimentation and water quality. Similarly, it may be very difficult to predict to what extent the projected use of agricultural chemicals in an irrigation project may reduce downstream fish catches, particularly in the longer term. In practice, physical estimation of the environmental effects of a proposed project usually amounts to little more than educated guesswork. This uncertainty is due in part to the relative lack of appropriate scientific data in most developing countries, as well as the site-specific nature of many environmental effects.

Difficulties in the physical estimation of relevant environmental effects are further compounded by the fact that relatively gradual changes in resource use can sometimes produce discontinuous and catastrophic effects in multi-species ecosystems. These changes may be counter-intuitive and irreversible. For example, there have already been a number of unexpected ecological collapses in economically important ocean fisheries. . . . There is a gradation of confidence in the physical measurement of environmental impacts, depending on what types of effects are being measured. . . .

Reprinted from *Ecological Modelling*, Vol. 38:19–47, 1987 by permission of Elsevier Science Publishers. Endnotes deleted.

Even when the physical environmental effects of a proposed project can be predicted with some accuracy, monetary valuation of these effects can still prove impossible or exceedingly difficult. This is particularly evident in the case of many "environmental services." Environmental services are beneficial functions performed by natural ecosystems, such as maintenance of water flow patterns, protection of soil, biodegradation of pollutants, recycling of wastes, support of fisheries and other economically important living resources, and regulation of climate. Despite their actual economic value and importance to meeting human needs, environmental services are frequently ignored or underestimated in CBA because they are usually public goods, not priced in the market-place. Some environmental services, such as soil fertility on private land in areas where land tenure is secure and efficient land markets exist, can be private goods, and may therefore be reflected in market values and captured in economic analyses. However, situations such as this are the exception, rather than the rule. This is particularly the case in many developing countries, where land markets are highly distorted and land tenure is often insecure.

A variety of different techniques have been used to estimate the shadow prices of environmental services. . . . Despite these methodologies, estimation of shadow prices* for tangible environmental goods and services remains incomplete and is rarely practiced on a systematic basis in project analysis.

PROBLEMS OF VALUING "INTANGIBLE" ENVIRONMENTAL BENEFITS

Intangible environmental values derive from the belief that many features of the natural world have a significant intrinsic value, quite apart from any "practical" or utilitarian (i.e., economic) value which they may have. Clearly, if a need to preserve a known species is perceived and sacrifices have to be made to achieve this need, then economic choices enter. However, the need to preserve "utilitarian" species is not yet adequately perceived; much less perceived is the need to preserve unknown species for their intrinsic value, or to avoid eliminating natural areas likely to harbor unknown or rare species. A significant and growing number of people believe that human beings should take care to avoid causing the extinction of other living species—even those species not yet known to have any practical value to humanity. Similarly, many people appreciate the mere existence of free-flowing rivers, or other undeveloped natural wonders, even when these people have no plans to visit or directly use them. Efforts to measure environmental values such as these, many of which have an ethical or spiritual basis, as an economic "willingness to pay" have yet to become satisfactory. . . .

There are a number of reasons why valuing "intangible" environmental benefits is so difficult. For example, people's preferences as self-interested, market-oriented consumers are often not consistent with their public policy opinions as socially-minded citizens. . . . This does not mean that people are necessarily irrational—just that human valuation is too complex to be reduced to a simple summation of subjective individual wants. People cannot be perfectly knowledgeable, nor can all their wants be satisfied through the market place. Many ethical values are not revealed by market-place activity, nor by Net Present Value (NPV) or other forms of CBA. To the extent that ethics are important contributors to human happiness, policy makers should attempt to accommodate such ethical values, whether or not they can be measured by CBA.

GROSS NATIONAL PRODUCT AND ENVIRONMENTAL ACCOUNTING

Gross National Product (GNP), a national account statistic that measures aggregate national generation of income, was never intended to be a complete measure of wealth or welfare, and few economists would argue that it is. Nonetheless, many institutions use GNP for exactly this purpose. As an example, many World Bank publications rank countries according to their per-capita GNP. The implicit message of such rankings is that rapid growth in per-capita GNP is an important goal of economic development. However, GNP (or the rather similar Gross Domestic Product, GDP) is seriously flawed as a measure of development success, for the following reasons:

1. GNP does not measure income distribution or even the material well-being of the bulk of a country's population. Some countries (such as China and Sri Lanka) have managed to meet the basic needs of the great majority of their populations at very low levels of per-capita GNP. Other countries (such as Brazil or Algeria) have attained much higher GNP levels and rapid growth rates, while comparatively failing to meet the basic needs of many of their citizens.

2. GNP measures only market transactions, not self-sufficient production. For example, households which grow their own food, without using purchased seeds, chemical fertilizers, biocides or other marketed inputs, do not have the value of their production reflected in GNP accounts. Self-sufficient production of food, clothing, and other goods still predominates in many developing countries, and may often be

---

*"Shadow prices" are economic values which are imputed to goods or services that have no market price (or for which the market price is considered "distorted," such that it does not accurately reflect actual social costs and benefits).

preferable to market-oriented production for a variety of environmental and social reasons.

3. GNP measures the aggregate level of economic activity, but often this activity does not actually reflect social well-being. For example, more rapid obsolescence of consumer products can increase GNP. To use a hypothetical illustration, assume that person A buys five stoves, each lasting only 2 years, and person B buys one stove that lasts 10 years. Both consumers will have gotten the same level of utility, i.e., 10 years' worth of cooking service. However, in all likelihood, person A will have contributed considerably more to the GNP account than person B.

4. Some of the economic activity measured by GNP is devoted to restoring, replacing, or compensating for environmental services lost through modern production systems. For example, sewage treatment plants reduce the water pollution that results from no longer recycling human waste as fertilizer; medical expenses help compensate for health damage due to asbestos or other unsafe products; and more frequent painting reduces corrosion damage from air pollution and acid rain. GNP therefore uncritically combines all market expenditures, irrespective of whether those expenditures are due to social "goods" or "bads." If everyone who owns a car suddenly has an accident with it, GNP will go up; if everyone who owns a house installs a solar heater, GNP will ultimately go down!

5. GNP measures economic "flows," rather than the standing or "asset" value of natural resource or other economic "stocks." This aspect, inherent in GNP accounting, can also short-change environmental concerns. Policy makers (who have been repeatedly told that rapid GNP growth is an important measure of successful development) may seek to "liquidate" their natural resource base (e.g., forests or minerals) in order to convert a stock asset into a measurable economic flow.

Resource-rich countries, or those with unused renewable resources,* can temporarily pursue such a policy of liquidation. But resource-poor countries, or those experiencing heavy population pressure on the natural resource base, may find that the undesirable effects of overexploitation (e.g., resource depletion, pollution) outweigh the benefits. . . .

---

*"Unused renewable resources" is preferred over the somewhat environmentally deterministic concept of carrying capacity. Carrying capacity is defined as the maximum number of a given species that can be supported indefinitely by a particular habitat, allowing for seasonal and random change, without any degradation of the natural resource base that would diminish the maximum population in the future. Carrying capacity is analogous to the sustainable rate of harvest and is in turn dependent on the size of the resource stock.

To the extent that privately held resources earn rent (e.g., a landlord's rented field), GNP accounts for resource depletion—but GNP includes such depletion as a benefit! However, national accounts statistics do not generally record depletion of natural resources incurred in generating income, even though this represents a loss to the country's natural resource wealth. Because many environmental services and resources are common property or public goods, their value is not reflected in the market place. Resources that are not accounted for are apt to be wasted or managed inefficiently. It is therefore important for governments to monitor their use, in order to make better-informed decisions. Modified accounting procedures would assist governments in improving resource management, including the management of consumption rates. To this end, the United Nations Environment Program (UNEP) and the World Bank have been collaborating through "environmental accounting" workshops held in 1983, 1984 and 1985. The purpose of these workshops has been to develop methods that internalize natural resource stocks and environmental services in national accounts. The main problem is how best to operationalize this concept and incorporate it in policy. Complete correction of national accounts to reflect natural resource depletion is not yet possible due to the lack of appropriate shadow prices.

NORTH-SOUTH LINKAGES

It is frequently argued that the world's developed nations will help the developing nations by promoting their own economic growth, thereby increasing their demand for goods from the developing world. . . . However, there is less than consensus on this point. Increasing affluence in the North appears more likely to increase the demand for services and high-technology goods, rather than for primary commodities from the south. . . . Furthermore, growth in industrialized countries consumes limited or scarce energy resources and often further encroaches upon the limited natural resource base of developing countries, thereby perhaps undermining their prospects for long-term sustainable development. For example, increased demand in the North for luxury or non-essential uses of finite resources, such as petroleum, is likely to drive up the prices that poor people in the South must pay for them to satisfy their more basic needs. Such increased prices may, for example, compel more poor people to strip available forests for fuelwood to meet their cooking needs. Thus, the alternative hypothesis, that increased resource consumption in the North actually hurts development prospects in the South, merits closer attention.

A related question concerns the wisdom of using the industrialized countries of North America, Europe, and Japan as development models for the Third World. To the extent that present-day natural resource consumption patterns in these countries are unsustainable over the long term, it seems imprudent to attempt to generalize such patterns to the rest of the world. For example, [others] . . . make the case that universal private ownership of automobiles is not a desirable (or attainable) goal throughout the world, because automobiles are such extravagant consumers of natural resources. Instead, Brown et al. suggest that modern transportation systems be promoted, which can benefit most of the world's population, rather than only an affluent elite. The idea is not for people to forego the benefits of modern technology, nor to remain impoverished. Rather, it is to promote those technologies and development strategies which can provide an adequate, if not extravagant, living standard for essentially the entire population on a sustainable basis.

IRREVERSIBILITY AND PRESERVATION OF FUTURE OPTIONS

Many of the environmental consequences of development projects or policies are either completely irreversible, or reversible only over a very long time scale (by human standards). Examples of more or less irreversible environmental effects include species extinctions, groundwater contamination, fossil fuel depletion, loss of the traditional knowledge of indigenous tribal peoples when they are rapidly acculturated, soil erosion, human-induced climatic changes, and the removal of slowly-reproducing ecosystems such as coral reefs and certain types of forests. Many of the natural resources which are being irreversibly lost could be of major, though largely incalculable, value to future generations. For example, even if no economic or other human use is currently known for the millions of as-yet-unstudied species and the associated evolutionary processes that exist in the world's remaining natural ecosystems, past experience indicates that some of them will prove very valuable indeed. . . . This concern is particularly urgent for the developing countries of the tropics, where species diversity is greatest and scientific knowledge is poorest. As noted recently by E. O. Wilson, species extinctions or other irreversible environmental losses are the ones which future generations are least likely to forgive this generation. . . .

Preventing irreversible environmental losses would preserve many of the options available to future generations, so that they might more effectively meet the challenges of an uncertain future. It is prudent for the present generation to pursue courses of action which foreclose relatively fewer options for the future. Some economists have therefore suggested that relative to the benefits of preservation, there is a point in many projects where the sacrifice of short-term gains is desirable in order to preserve reversibility (i.e., prevent the permanent elimination of future options).

CBA techniques usually treat irreversible costs (if they have even been considered and quantified) no differently from more readily reversible ones. . . . The inattention of CBA techniques to the special problems posed by irreversibility is unfortunate but not surprising, since CBA is based on the mechanistic concept of a readily reversible "market equilibrium." . . .

COMPARATIVE ADVANTAGE IN AGRICULTURE

The economic principle of comparative advantage is analogous to its ecological counterpart—division of labor or ecological specialization. Both can bring enormous advantage to the individuals of a community. However, comparative advantage is commonly invoked in international trade theory to justify the case for specialization among nations. As historically applied, comparative advantage has encouraged many developing nations to depend on a small number of agricultural export commodities, while attending less to domestic food production. The theory holds that it may be advantageous to sell the agricultural commodity (e.g., cocoa, palm oil) for foreign exchange and buy cheap foreign food (e.g., United States wheat). This pattern can help explain why more and more countries are importing grain, that former food exporting nations are now net importers, and that in some countries—particularly in Sub-Saharan Africa—per-capita food production has declined markedly over the past two decades. Relative emphasis on export crops rather than local food production is only one of several factors which can be blamed for the decline in food production growth, soil erosion and other environmental degradation, and inappropriate agricultural pricing policies. . . . Certainly, the ability to import food from climatically dissimilar areas provides a buffer to natural disasters such as droughts. This should be weighed against the local maintenance of some buffer capacity.

The extent to which countries should emphasize export crops versus domestic food production has sparked lively debate among economists and others concerned. . . .

To this widespread questioning of export crop promotion strategies, we now seek to add an environmental perspective. Agricultural commodity projects are usually sited on prime agricultural land in order to maximize the yields needed to support the investment. This can impair indigenous food production, which is often pushed to more marginal land as a result. Indigenous food production on marginal land often threatens watersheds and slopes that are better left intact in forest or other protective cover. Overgrazing is also more difficult to avoid on marginal land. Agricultural commodity projects need modern highways, with all their environmental impacts, including unplanned settlement and inappropriate land use in ecologically fragile areas. Many cash crops are often grown as large-scale monocultures, while food grown for local consumption by small farmers is more readily adapted to polyculture and agro-forestry systems. Monocultures are less desirable from an environmental standpoint because of their vulnerability to pests and diseases, their often heavy reliance on biocides and chemical fertilizers, and their suitability for using heavy machinery (which often compacts or otherwise damages the soil). From an environmental point of view, export crop promotion (unless it is unusually well-managed) appears to be a less desirable or riskier strategy than local food production. This argument is not to suggest that export crop production is never appropriate or desirable. Rather, we merely recommend that environmental concerns be adequately considered when recommendations are formulated for national agricultural policies and strategies, or when the pros and cons of export crop production are debated.

DISCOUNT RATE

The discount rate (r) is a time preference concept. If we choose to believe that the concept of a "socially optimum" discount rate actually exists, we must acknowledge that such a discount rate can never be precisely known because the preferences and circumstances of future generations remain unknown. . . . However, we know that sound environmental management often imposes minor, short-term costs in order to gain substantial benefits over the long term. Thus, discounting of future benefits (and costs) to net present value can severely undervalue many environmental functions and services. Although many organizations rely on CBA and discounting, some economists have recognized the significance of this flaw. . . .

The use of any particular discount rate r in CBA calculations operationalizes a subjective judgment of the relative importance of the present and the future. It is a normative proposition expressed in mathematical terms, rather than a neutral or objective quantitative assessment. We cannot prove that r for environmental functions (with the risk of irreversible losses) has to be equal to r for investment to produce market goods. The high discount rates currently used in project analysis, commonly 10% and more, discourage investments with long-term benefits, while promoting projects with long-term costs. High discount rates also imply excessive discounting of possible future environmental catastrophes (such as groundwater contamination by leaking radioactive wastes).

The most fundamental question involving discounting concerns the extent to which today's society should sacrifice material consumption to improve the well-being of the future. . . . Since the future is inherently highly uncertain, discounting many valuable natural resources at today's opportunity cost of capital (as per Barnett and Morse's "intergenerational invisible hand") is not a very prudent or risk-averse option from the point of view of the future.

SOME PRINCIPLES OF SUSTAINABLE DEVELOPMENT

Sustainable Development Defined

Although "sustainable development" has seldom been precisely defined, it has become a popular slogan among conservationists and even within elements of the mainstream development community. We therefore seek to provide in this paper a tentative definition of this important concept, as follows. Sustainable development is here defined as *a pattern of social and structural economic transformations (i.e., "development") which optimizes the economic and other societal benefits available in the present, without jeopardizing the likely potential for similar benefits in the future.* A primary goal of sustainable development is to achieve a reasonable (however defined) and equitably distributed level of economic well-being that can be perpetuated continually for many human generations. Sustainability implies a transition away from economic growth based on depletion of nonrenewable resource stocks and towards progress (i.e., improvement in the quality of life) based more on renewable resources over the long run.

This definition has major implications for economic development theory and practice, including the following five points:

1. Human well-being depends upon at least three categories of value: (a) economic efficiency (i.e., Pareto optimality), (b) equitable distribution of economic resources, and (c) "non-economic" values (e.g., religious and spiritual concerns, human dignity and pride, aesthetics, and civil liberties). It therefore makes sense for development plans to seek to optimize among these values, rather than to maximize any one (e.g., economic efficiency or growth in production), since some trade-offs are inevitable. Van Praag and Spit . . . use the welfare economic theory to make the case for more equitable income distribution.

2. Although it is impossible to predict with much precision the likely interests of future generations, it is prudent to assume that their need for natural resources (soil, air, water, forests, fisheries, plant and animal species, energy, and minerals) will not be markedly less than ours. Therefore, sustainable development implies using renewable natural resources in a manner which does not eliminate or degrade them, or otherwise diminish their usefulness for future generations. Sustainable development

therefore implies usually harvesting renewable resources on a sustained-yield basis, rather than "mining" them to near-extinction. Whales, tropical rain forests, and coral reefs are examples of renewables that are often mined rather than harvested sustainably. This policy need not be absolute, if the flow of natural products or environmental services to be lost can be readily replaced in a sustainable manner (e.g., by maintaining genetic stocks). However, exceptions to this rule need to be justified more carefully than has often been the case.

3. Sustainable development further implies using non-renewable (exhaustible) mineral resources in a manner which does not unnecessarily preclude easy access to them by future generations. For example, it will surely be easier in the future to make use of today's scrap metal if it is recycled, than if it is dumped as waste in a dispersed manner.

4. Sustainable development also implies depleting non-renewable energy resources at a slow enough rate so as to ensure the high probability of an orderly societal transition to renewable energy sources (including solar, wood and other biomass, wind, hydroelectric and other water-based sources) when non-renewable energy becomes substantially more costly. Sustainability implies using long-term planning (rather than merely short-term market forces) to guide the transition to renewable energy sources. The price of petroleum, arguably the world's most important non-renewable resource, has actually dropped sharply in the last five years in the United States, for example, tending to encourage more rapid depletion by consumers. In cases such as these, the market does not adequately reflect future scarcity.

5. In the context of agricultural or other biologically-based projects sustainability implies the permanent maintenance of biological productivity on the site, with the costs of imported inputs such as energy (e.g., diesel, biocides) and nutrients (e.g., fertilizer) not exceeding the commercial value of the site's production. Even when the crop pays for its inputs, production is not sustainable if the biological productivity of the site is impaired (e.g., by soil compaction or decrease in organic matter). In a wider context, the long-term availability of energy, fertilizers, and other exhaustible agricultural inputs must be addressed.

Steady State Economics and Limits to Growth

Conventional economic theory typically assumes that there are no limits to growth in the physical scale of production and consumption, or that these limits are so distant as to be irrelevant. Over the past decade, a great deal of evidence has surfaced which indicates that this is no longer the case. For example, recent data indicate that the productivity of forests, fisheries, croplands, and grasslands—the fundamental renewable resource systems—is on the decline worldwide in many countries. . . . The marginal cost of discovering and exploiting new mineral and fossil fuel deposits is increasing exponentially. Despite such evidence as this, even the theoretical possibility of limits to growth (not just their imminence) is flatly denied by many neoclassical economists. In this context, an interesting contrast appears to emerge between neoclassical microeconomic and macroeconomic theory. In microeconomics, growth in production (or consumption) is possible or is considered desirable only to the point where the marginal benefit (e.g., revenue) equals the marginal cost. In macroeconomic theory, there is usually no concept of the optimum size of an economy over the long term; rather, bigger is always better. This approach neglects the often severe environmental and other social costs associated with high and growing rates of per-capita natural resource consumption. Once these costs are taken into account, the limits to growth become visible.

The "limits to growth" debate can be clarified by distinguishing between growth in natural resource consumption (or "throughput") and in economic output per se (as measured by GNP or a related index). . . . Notwithstanding any conceivable technological advances, growth in natural resource consumption (whether due to an increase in population, per-capita consumption, or both) is ultimately constrained by the physical laws of thermodynamics and by the finite size of the planet. However, growth in economic output may not be similarly constrained, since innovation may continue to find ways to squeeze more "value added" from a natural resource bundle. Thus, governments concerned with long-term sustainability need not seek to limit growth in economic output, so long as they seek to stabilize aggregate natural resource consumption.

SAFE MINIMUM STANDARDS

"Safe minimum standard" (SMS) analysis . . . is one decision methodology which can be used to address those ecological concerns which are given little or no attention in economic CBA. A SMS is any non-economic criterion which a project must meet to be approved. SMS analysis is a time-tested, standard operating procedure that is widespread throughout engineering design, health planning, industrial worker safety, and other sectors. For example, a bridge is commonly designed with a safety factor of three or more to accommodate the unexpected and the unknown.

When used in the appraisal of development projects, SMSs constrain the economic CBA by specifying environmental, social, or other criteria which the project must meet in all cases. If a project is modified to meet

SMS criteria, any extra costs of such modification are automatically added to other project costs in the CBA. If a proposed project cannot be modified to meet SMS criteria, it is abandoned in favor of more environmentally or socially prudent investments. CBA which incorporates SMSs is therefore a type of constrained economic optimization.

Up to this time, the World Bank has publicly committed itself to the following SMSs in the projects it supports:

1. Projects depending on the harvest of renewable natural resources (such as forests, fisheries, and grazing lands) shall adhere to sustained-yield principles, to minimize the risk of overexploitation and degradation (through overcutting, overfishing, or overgrazing) (World Bank, 1984b).

2. Projects shall not clear, inundate, or otherwise convert ecologically important wildland ecosystems, including (but not limited to) officially designated protected areas, without adequate compensatory measures (World Bank, 1984b, 1986).

3. Projects shall avoid knowingly causing the extinction or endangerment of plant or animal species, unless adequate mitigatory measures are provided (World Bank, 1984b, 1986).

4. Any project based in one country shall not affect the environment or natural resource base of any neighboring countries without their full consent (World Bank, 1984b). Judgment is necessary in determining the cut-off point, particularly where data are inadequate (such as with acid rain).

5. Projects shall not contravene any international environmental agreement to which the borrowing country is party (World Bank, 1984b).

6. Any groups seriously disadvantaged by Bank-supported projects (such as vulnerable ethnic minorities or communities undergoing involuntary resettlement) shall be appropriately compensated to a degree that makes them no worse off (and may make them better off) than without the project. This is to be done even if the compensatory project components do not contribute to the stream of economic benefits (World Bank, 1982, 1984b).

7. Projects shall not compromise public health and safety to any degree which would be widely regarded as unacceptable by the affected people or by experienced, impartial third parties (World Bank, 1982, 1984b).

Study Questions

1. Review the main objections of Sagoff and Rees to standard economic cost–benefit analysis. Do Goodland and Ledec meet these criticisms? Identify each criticism made and then find Goodland and Ledec's attempt to meet it. How successful are they?

2. Do you think that our economic system reflects the ideals set forth by Goodland and Ledec? Explain your answer.

For Further Reading

Brown, Lester. *State of the World 1993*. New York: Norton, 1993.

Buchholz, Rogene. *Principles of Environmental Management: The Greening of Business*. Englewood Cliffs, NJ: Prentice Hall, 1993.

Clark, W. C. *Sustainable Development of the Biosphere*. Cambridge: Cambridge University Press, 1986.

Daly, Herman E., and John B. Cobb, Jr. *For the Common Good: Redirecting the Economy Toward Community, the Environment, and a Sustainable Future*. Boston: Beacon Press, 1989.

Dreyfus, S. E. "Formal Models vs. Human Situational Understanding: Inherent Limitations on the Modelling of Business Expertise," *Technology and People* 1 (1982).

Plumwood, Val, and Richard Routley, "World Rainforest Destruction—The Social and Economic Factors," *Ecologist* 12, no. 1 (January–February 1982).

Sagoff, Mark. *The Economy of the Earth*. Cambridge: Cambridge University Press, 1988.

Sayer, K. M., and K. E. Goodpaster, eds. *Ethics and Problems of the 21st Century*. Notre Dame, IN: University of Notre Dame Press, 1979.

Shrader-Frechette, Kristin. *Science, Policy, Ethics, and Economic Metholoy*. Boston: Reidel, 1985.

Shrader-Frechette, Kristin, and E. McCoy. *Method in Ecology*. New York: Cambridge University Press, 1993.

Scientific American. "Managing the Earth," Special Issue, 26, no. 3 (September 1989).

Timberlake, Lloyd. *Only One Earth: Living for the Future*. New York: Sterling, 1987.

Tokar, Michael. *The Green Alternative: Creating an Alternative Future*. San Pedro, CA: R & E Miles, 1988.

CHAPTER SEVENTEEN

From Dysfunctional to Sustainable Society

If we are to survive as a society, we will have to change our lifestyles. We may be forced to do this due to the depletion of scarce resources, such as fossil fuels, topsoil, and clean air, or due to changing climatic conditions and weather patterns caused by the greenhouse effect, or through severe population overcrowding. In the worst case, a nuclear war or other catastrophe would be the catalyst for drastic change. It would be better to change our lifestyles gradually through a process of making peace with our environment, by revealing the kinds of processes that are leading us toward a tragic end. In the last chapter, we looked at the economic dimension of environmentalism. In this chapter, we want to look at the environmental situation from the perspective of our lifestyles and general practices.

We begin with a selection from Vice President Al Gore's book *The Earth in Balance* (1992). Gore argues that our tradition contains the resources to solve our ecological crisis. He criticizes radical ecologists, like deep ecologists (see Chapter 3), but tries to incorporate some of their criticisms within the mainstream of American religious–philosophical tradition, correcting some alleged misinterpretations of it. Gore's essay deserves to be seriously debated, not simply because he occupies an influential position in government but because it is based on the general values of the Judeo–Christian tradition, which are the values of the majority of North and South Americans, for whom this work is primarily intended.

In our second essay, written expresslyfor this edition, Laura Westra argues that democracy, subject to the tyranny of the majority, is a detrimental force in the campaign to bring about environmental progress. Most damaging is our emphasis on individual rights, forget-ting that we also have responsibilities and a corresponding legitimate right *not* to be put at undue risk. Westra argues that this right can be defended and political leaders must go beyond democracy in enforcing it. A rational risk response may require political activity that is revolutionary. In our third reading, Eugene Hargrove responds to Westra, arguing that democracies are our best hope for environmental progress.

In Alan Thein Durning's "An Ecological Critique of Global Advertising," we have an insightful analysis of global pressures to create consumerism through subtle and skillful marketing skills. Advertising, as one of its proponents put it, is to make everyone unhappy until they buy the product in question. Is your hair too thin, your nose too short? Advertising offers you hope! "It preys on the weaknesses of its host? It creates an insatiable hunger. And it leads to debilitating overconsumption. In the biological realm, things of that nature are called parasites." Advertising is the global parasite of our time! Durning argues that this parasite threatens the life-blood of our world.

My short essay offers you the case for bicycling. Automobiles and trucks cause immense environmental stress, so less harmful modes of transportation must be adopted. Among these is that undervalued, wonder source of amazing power, the bicycle.

In the final article of the book, "Vision of a Sustainable World," Lester Brown, Christopher Flavin, and Sandra Postel of the Worldwatch Institute ask you to consider their vision of the task of building a sustainable world over the next 40 years. It should provoke discussion as well as challenge us to work harder toward a sustainable society.

79

Dysfunctional Civilization

Al Gore

Al Gore is Vice President of the United States and for many years was the senator from the State of Tennessee. A leading proponent of environmental concerns, in 1992 he published his book The Earth in Balance *from which the current selection is taken. After criticizing deep ecology for being antihumanistic, he attempts to identify our present social and environmental malaise via the metaphor of the dysfunctional family.*

At the heart of every human society is a web of stories that attempt to answer our most basic questions: Who are we, and why are we here? But as the destructive pattern of our relationship to the natural world becomes increasingly clear, we begin to wonder if our old stories still make sense and sometimes have gone so far as to devise entirely new stories about the meaning and purpose of human civilization.

One increasingly prominent group known as Deep Ecologists makes what I believe is the deep mistake of defining our relationship to the earth using the metaphor of disease. According to this story, we humans play the role of pathogens, a kind of virus giving the earth a rash and a fever, threatening the planet's vital life functions. Deep Ecologists assign our species the role of a global cancer, spreading uncontrollably, metastasizing in our cities and taking for our own nourishment and expansion the resources needed by the planet to maintain its health. Alternatively, the Deep Ecology story considers human civilization a kind of planetary HIV virus, giving the earth a "Gaian" form of AIDS, rendering it incapable of maintaining its resistance and immunity to our many insults to its health and equilibrium. Global warming is, in this metaphor, the fever that accompanies a victim's desperate effort to fight the invading virus whose waste products have begun to contaminate the normal metabolic processes of its host organism. As the virus rapidly multiplies, the sufferer's fever signals the beginning of the "body's" struggle to mobilize antigens that will attack the invading pathogens in order to destroy them and save the host.

The obvious problem with this metaphor is that it defines human beings as inherently and contagiously destructive, the deadly carriers of a plague upon the earth. And the internal logic of the metaphor points toward only one possible cure: eliminate people from the face of the earth. As Mike Roselle, one of the leaders of Earth First!, a group espousing Deep Ecology, has said, "You hear about the death of nature and it's true, but nature will be able to reconstitute itself once the top of the food chain is lopped off—meaning us."

Some of those who adopt this story as their controlling metaphor are actually advocating a kind of war on the human race as a means of protecting the planet. They assume the role of antigens, to slow the spread of the disease, give the earth time to gather its forces to fight off and, if necessary, eliminate the intruders. In the words of Dave Foreman, a cofounder of Earth First!, "It's time for a warrior society to rise up out of the earth and throw itself in front of the juggernaut of destruction, to be antibodies against the human pox that's ravaging this precious, beautiful planet." (Some Deep Ecologists, it should be added, are more thoughtful.)

Beyond its moral unacceptability, another problem with this metaphor is its inability to explain—in a way that is either accurate or believable—who we are and how we can create solutions for the crisis it describes. Ironically, just as René Descartes, Francis Bacon, and the other architects of the scientific revolution defined human beings as disembodied intellects separate from the physical world, Arne Naess, the Norwegian philosopher who coined the term Deep Ecology in 1973, and many Deep Ecologists of today seem to define human beings as an alien presence on the earth. In a modern version of the Cartesian dénouement of a philosophical divorce between human beings and the earth, Deep Ecologists idealize a condition in which there is no connection between the two, but they arrive at their conclusion by means of a story that is curiously opposite to that of Descartes. Instead of seeing people as creatures of abstract thought relating to the earth only through logic and theory, the Deep Ecologists make the opposite mistake, of defining the relationship between human beings and the earth almost solely in physical terms—as if we were nothing more than humanoid bodies genetically programmed to play out our bubonic destiny, having no intellect or free will with which to understand and change the script we are following.

The Cartesian approach to the human story allows us to believe that we are separate from the earth, entitled to view it as nothing more than an inanimate collection of resources that we can exploit however we like; and this fundamental misperception has led us to our current crisis. But if the new story of the Deep Ecologists is dangerously wrong, it does

---

Reprinted from *The Earth in Balance.* © 1992 by Senator Al Gore (Boston: Houghton Mifflin, 1992) by permission.

"He's the typical American Mouse—likes a drink before dinner, smokes a little, watches TV . . ."
©1980 by *Sidney Harris*—"All Ends Up." *William Kaufman, Inc.*

at least provoke an essential question: What new story can explain the relationship between human civilization and the earth—and how we have come to a moment of such crisis? One part of the answer is clear: our new story must describe and foster the basis for a natural and healthy relationship between human beings and the earth. The old story of God's covenant with both the earth and humankind, and its assignment to human beings of the role of good stewards and faithful servants, was—before it was misinterpreted and twisted in the service of the Cartesian world view—a powerful, noble, and just explanation of who we are in relation to God's earth. What we need today is a fresh telling of our story with the distortions removed.

But a new story cannot be told until we understand how this crisis between human beings and the earth developed and how it can be resolved. To achieve such an understanding, we must consider the full implications of the Cartesian model of the disembodied intellect.

Feelings represent the essential link between mind and body or, to put it another way, the link between our intellect and the physical world. Because modern civilization assumes a profound separation between the two, we have found it necessary to create an elaborate set of cultural rules designed to encourage the fullest expression of thought while simultaneously stifling the expression of feelings and emotions.

Many of these cultural rules are now finally being recognized as badly out of balance with what we are learning about the foundations of human nature. One such foundation is, of course, the brain, which is layered with our evolutionary heritage. Between the most basic and primitive part of our brain, responsible for bodily functions and instinct, and the last major structure within the brain to evolve, the part responsible for abstract thought and known as the neocortex, is the huge portion of our brain that governs emotion, called the limbic system. In a very real sense, the idea that human beings can function as disembodied intellects translates into the absurd notion that the functions of the neocortex are the only workings of our brains that matter.

Yet abstract thought is but one dimension of awareness. Our feelings and emotions, our sensations, our awareness of our own bodies and of nature—all these are indispensable to the way we experience life, mentally and physically. To define the essence of who we are in terms that correspond with the analytical activity of the neocortex is to create an intolerable dilemma: How can we concentrate purely on abstract thinking when the rest of our brain floods our awareness with feelings, emotions, and instincts?

Insisting on the supremacy of the neocortex exacts a high price, because the unnatural task of a disembodied mind is to somehow ignore the intense psychic pain that comes from the constant nagging awareness of what is missing: the experience of living in one's body as a fully integrated physical and mental being. Life confronts everyone with personal or circumstantial problems, of course, and there are many varieties of psychic pain from which we wish to escape. But the cleavage between mind and body, intellect and nature, has created a kind of psychic pain at the very root of the modern mind, making it harder for anyone who is suffering from other psychological wounds to be healed.

Indeed, it is not unreasonable to suppose that members of a civilization that allows or encourages this cleavage will be relatively more vulnerable to those mental disorders characterized by a skewed relationship between thinking and feeling. This notion may seem improbable, since we are not used to looking for the cause of psychological problems in the broad patterns of modern civilization. But it is quite common for epidemiologists to trace the cause of physical disorders to patterns adopted by societies that place extra stress on especially vulnerable individuals. Consider, for example, how the pattern of modern civilization almost certainly explains the epidemic level of high blood pressure in those countries—like the United States—that have a diet very high in sodium Although the precise causal relationship is still a mystery, epidemiologists conclude that the nearly ubiquitous tendency of modern civilization to add lots of salt to the food supply is responsible for a very high background level of hypertension. In the remaining pre-industrial cultures where the food supply is not processed and sodium consumption is low, hypertension is virtually unknown, and is considered normal for an elderly man's blood pressure to be the same as that of an infant. In our society, we assume that it is natural for blood pressure to increase with age.

Resolving high blood pressure is much easier than resolving deep psychological conflicts, however. Most people respond to psychic pain the way they respond to any pain: rather than confront its source, they recoil from it, looking immediately for ways to escape or ignore it. One of the most effective strategies for ignoring psychic pain is to distract oneself from it, to do something so pleasurable or intense or otherwise absorbing that the pain is forgotten. As a temporary strategy, this kind of distraction isn't necessarily destructive, but dependence on it over the long term becomes dangerous and, finally, some sort of addiction. Indeed, it can be argued that every addiction is caused by an intense and continuing need for distraction from psychic pain. Addiction is distraction.

We are used to thinking of addiction in terms of drugs or alcohol. But new studies of addiction have deepened our understanding of the problem, and now we know that people can become addicted to many different patterns of behavior—such as gambling compulsively or working obsessively or even watching television constantly—that distract them from having to experience directly whatever they are trying to avoid. Anyone who is unusually fearful of something—intimacy, failure, loneliness—is potentially vulnerable to addiction, because psychic pain causes a feverish hunger for distraction.

The cleavage in the modern world between mind and body, man and nature, has created a new kind of addiction: I believe that our civilization is, in effect, addicted to the consumption of the earth itself. This addictive relationship distracts us from the pain of what we have lost: a direct experience of our connection to the vividness, vibrancy, and aliveness of the rest of the natural world. The froth and frenzy of industrial civilization mask our deep loneliness for that communion with the world that can lift our spirits and fill our senses with the richness and immediacy of life itself.

We may pretend not to notice the emptiness we feel, but its effects may be seen in the unnatural volatility with which we react to those things we touch. I can best illustrate this point with a metaphor drawn from electrical engineering. A machine using lots of electrical energy must be grounded to the earth in order to stabilize the flow of electricity through the machine and to prevent a volatile current from jumping to whatever might touch it. A machine that is not grounded poses a serious threat; similarly, a person who is not "grounded" in body as well as mind, in feelings as well as thoughts, can pose a threat to whatever he or she touches. We tend to think of the powerful currents of creative energy circulating through every one of us as benign, but they can be volatile and dangerous if not properly grounded. This is especially true of those suffering from a serious addiction. No longer grounded to the deeper meaning of their lives, addicts are like someone who cannot release a 600-volt cable because the electric current is just too strong: they hold tightly to their addiction even as the life force courses out of their veins.

In a similar way, our civilization is holding ever more tightly to its habit of consuming larger and larger quantities every year of coal, oil, fresh air and water, trees, topsoil, and the thousand other substances we rip from the crust of the earth, transforming them into not just the sustenance and shelter we need but much more that we don't need: huge quantities of pollution, products for which we spend billions on advertising to convince ourselves we want, massive surpluses of products that depress prices while the products themselves go to waste, and diversions and distractions of every kind. We seem increasingly eager to lose ourselves in the forms of culture, society, technology, the media, and the rituals of production and consumption, but the price we pay is the loss of our spiritual lives.

Evidence of this spiritual loss abounds. Mental illness in its many forms is at epidemic levels, especially among children. The three leading causes of death among adolescents are drug- and alcohol-related accidents, suicide, and homicide. Shopping is now recognized as a recreational activity. The accumulation of material goods is at an all-time high, but so is the number of people who feel an emptiness in their lives.

Industrial civilization's great engines of distraction still seduce us with a promise of fulfillment. Our new power to work our will upon the world can bring with it a sudden rush of exhilaration, not unlike the momentary "rush" experienced by drug addicts when a drug injected into their bloodstream triggers changes in the chemistry of the brain. But that exhilaration is fleeting; it is not true fulfillment. And the metaphor of drug addiction applies in another way too. Over time, a drug user needs a progressively larger dose to produce an equivalent level of exhilaration; similarly, our civilization seems to require an ever-increasing level of consumption. But why do we assume that it's natural and normal for our per capita consumption of most natural resources to increase every year? Do we need higher levels of consumption to achieve the same distracting effect once produced by a small amount of consumption? In our public debates about efforts to acquire a new and awesome power through science, technology, or industry, are we sometimes less interested in a careful balancing of the pros and cons than in the great thrill to accompany the first use of the new enhancement of human power over the earth?

The false promise at the core of addiction is the possibility of experiencing the vividness and immediacy of real life without having to face the fear and pain that are also part of it. Our industrial civilization makes us a similar promise: the pursuit of happiness and comfort is paramount, and the consumption of an endless stream of shiny new products is encouraged as the best way to succeed in that pursuit. The glittering promise of easy fulfillment is so seductive that we become willing, even relieved, to forget what we really feel and abandon the search for authentic purpose and meaning in our lives.

But the promise is always false because the hunger for authenticity remains. In a healthy, balanced life, the noisy chatter of our discourse with the artificial world of our creation may distract us from the deeper rhythms of life, but it does not interrupt them. In the pathology of addiction, this dialogue becomes more than a noisy diversion; as their lives move further out of balance, addicts invest increasing amounts of energy in their relationship to the objects of their addiction. And once addicts focus on false communion with substitutes for life, the rhythm of their dull and deadening routine becomes increasingly incompatible, discordant, and dissonant with the natural harmony that entrains the music of life. As the dissonance grows more violent and the clashes more frequent, peaks of disharmony become manifest in successive crises, each one more destructive than the last.

The disharmony in our relationship to the earth, which stems in part from our addition to a pattern of consuming ever-larger quantities of the resources of the earth, is now manifest in successive crises, each marking a more destructive clash between our civilization and the natural world: whereas all threats to the environment used to be local and regional, several are now strategic. The loss of one and a half acres of rain forest every second, the sudden, thousandfold acceleration of the natural extinction rate for living species, the ozone hole above Antarctica and the thinning of the ozone layer at all latitudes, the possible destruction of the climate balance that makes our earth livable—all these suggest the increasingly violent collision between human civilization and the natural world.

Many people seem to be largely oblivious of this collision and the addictive nature of our unhealthy relationship to the earth. But education is a cure for those who lack knowledge; much more worrisome are those who will not acknowledge these destructive patterns. Indeed, many political, business, and intellectual leaders deny the existence of any such patterns in aggressive and dismissive tones. They serve as "enablers," removing inconvenient obstacles and helping to ensure that the addictive behavior continues.

The psychological mechanism of denial is complex, but again addiction serves as a model. Denial is the strategy used by those who wish to believe that they can continue their addicted lives with no ill effects for themselves or others. Alcoholics, for example, aggressively dismiss suggestions that their relationship to alcohol is wreaking havoc in their lives; repeated automobile crashes involving the same drunk driver are explained away in an alcoholic's mind as isolated accidents, each with a separate, unrelated cause.

Thus the essence of denial is the inner need of addicts not to allow themselves to perceive a connection between their addictive behavior and its destructive consequences. This need to deny is often very powerful. If addicts recognize their addiction, they might be forced to become aware of the feelings and thoughts from which they so desperately need distraction; abandoning their addiction altogether would threaten them with the loss of their principal shield against the fear of confronting whatever they are urgently trying to hold at bay.

Some theorists argue that what many addicts are trying to hold at bay is a profound sense of powerlessness. Addicts often display an obsessive need for absolute control over those few things that satisfy their craving. This need derives from, and is inversely proportional to, the sense of helplessness they feel toward the real world—whose spontaneity and resistance to their efforts at control are threatening beyond their capacity to endure.

It is important to recognize that this psychological drama takes place at the border of conscious awareness. Indeed, it is precisely that border which is being defended against the insistent intrusions of reality. Meanwhile, the dishonesty required to ensure that reality doesn't breach the ramparts often assumes such proportions that friends find it hard to believe that addicts don't know what they are doing to themselves and those around them. But the inauthenticity of addicts is, in one sense, easy to explain: they are so obsessed with the need to satisfy their craving that they subordinate all other values to it. Since a true understanding of their behavior might prove inhibiting, they insist they have no problem.

We are insensitive to our destructive impact on the earth for much the same reason, and we consequently have a similar and very powerful need for denial. Denial can take frightening and bizarre forms. For example, in southern California in 1991, the worsening five-year drought led some homeowners to actually spray-paint their dead lawns green, just as some undertakers apply cosmetics to make a corpse look natural to viewers who are emotionally vulnerable to the realization of death. As Joseph Conrad said in *The Heart of Darkness*, "The conquest of the earth is not a pretty thing when you look into it too much." But we are addicted to that conquest, and so we deny it is ugly and destructive. We elaborately justify what we are doing while turning a blind eye to the consequences. We are hostile to the messengers who warn us that we have to change, suspecting them of subversive intent and accusing them of harboring some hidden agenda—Marxism, or statism, or anarchism. ("Killing the messenger," in fact, is a well-established form of denial.) We see no relationship between the increasingly dangerous crises we are causing in the natural world; they are all accidents with separate, distinct causes. Those dead lawns, for example—could they be related to the fast-burning fires that made thousands homeless late in 1991? No matter; we are certain that we can adapt to whatever damage is done, even though the increasingly frequent manifestations of catastrophe are beginning to resemble what the humorist A. Whitney Brown describes as "a nature hike through the Book of Revelations."

The bulwark of denial isn't always impenetrable, however. In the advanced stages of addiction, when the destructive nature of the pattern becomes so overwhelmingly obvious that addicts find it increasingly difficult to ignore the need for change, a sense of resignation sets in. The addiction has by then so thoroughly defined the pattern of their lives that there seems to be no way out. Similarly, some people are finding it increasingly difficult to deny the destructive nature of our relationship to the earth, yet the response is not action but resignation. It's too late, we think; there's no way out.

But that way spells disaster, and recovery is possible. With addiction, an essential element in recovery is a willingness on the part of addicts to honestly confront the real pain they have sought to avoid. Rather than distracting their inner awareness through behavior, addicts must learn to face their pain—feel it, think it, absorb it, own it. Only then can they begin to deal honestly with it instead of running away.

So too our relationship to the earth may never be healed until we are willing to stop denying the destructive nature of the current pattern. Our seemingly compulsive need to control the natural world may have derived from a feeling of helplessness in the face of our deep and ancient fear of "Nature red in tooth and claw," but this compulsion has driven us to the edge of disaster, for we have become so successful at controlling nature that we have lost our connection to it. And we must also recognize that a new fear is now deepening our addiction: even as we revel in our success at controlling nature, we have become increasingly frightened of the consequences, and that fear only drives us to ride this destructive cycle harder and faster.

What I have called our addictive pattern of behavior is only part of the story, however, because it cannot explain the full complexity and ferocity of our assault on the earth. Nor does it explain how so many thinking and caring people can unwittingly cooperate in doing such enormous damage to the global environment and how they can continue to live by the same set of false assumptions about what their civilization is actually doing and why. Clearly, the problem involves more than the way each of us as an individual relates to the earth. It involves something that has gone terribly wrong in the way we collectively determine our mutual relationship to the earth.

A metaphor can be a valuable aid to understanding, and several metaphors have helped me understand what is wrong with the way we relate to the earth. One that has proved especially illuminating comes out of a relatively new theory about ailing families; a synthesis by psychologists and sociologists of research in addiction theory, family therapy, and systems analysis, this theory attempts to explain the workings of what has come to be called the dysfunctional family.

The idea of the dysfunctional family was first developed by theorists such as R. D. Laing, Virginia Satir, Gregory Bateson, Milton Erickson, Murray Bowen, Nathan Ackerman, and Alice Miller, and more recently it has been refined and brought to a popular audience by writers like John Bradshaw. The problem they have all sought to explain is how families made up of well-meaning, seemingly normal individuals can engender destructive relationships among themselves, driving individual family members as well as their family system into crisis.

According to the theory of dysfunctionality, unwritten rules governing how to raise children and purporting to determine what it means to be a human being are passed down from one generation of a family to the next. The modern version of these rules was shaped by the same philosophical world view that led to the scientific and technological revolution: it defines human beings as primarily intellectual entities detached from the physical world. And this definition led in turn to an assumption that feelings and emotions should be suppressed and subordinated to pure thought.

One consequence of this scientific view was a changed understanding of God. Once it became clear that science—instead of divine provenance—might explain many of nature's mysteries, it seemed safe to assume that the creator, having set the natural world in motion within discernible and predictable patterns, was somewhat removed and detached from the world, out there above us looking down. Perhaps as a consequence, the perception of families changed too. Families came to be seen as Ptolemaic systems, with the father as the patriarch and source of authority and all the other family members orbiting around him. This change had a dramatic effect on children. Before the scientific era, children almost certainly found it easier to locate and understand their place in the world because they could define themselves in relation both to their parents and to a God who was clearly present in nature. With these two firm points of reference, children were less likely to lose their direction in life. But with God receding from the natural world to an abstract place, the patriarchal figure in the family (almost always the father) effectively became God's viceroy, entitled to exercise godlike authority when enforcing the family's rules. As some fathers inevitably began to insist on being the sole source of authority, their children became confused about their own roles in a family system that was severely stressed by the demands of the dominant, all-powerful father.

Fathers were accorded godlike authority to enforce the rules, and, as Bradshaw and others argue, one of the most basic rules that emerged is that the rules themselves cannot be questioned. One of the ways dysfunctional families enforce adherence to the rules and foster the psychic numbness on which they depend is by teaching the separation between mind and body and suppressing the feelings and emotions that might otherwise undermine the rules. Similarly, one of the ways our civilization secures adherence to its rules is by teaching the separation of people from the natural world and suppressing the emotions that might allow us to feel the absence of our connection to the earth.

The rules of both perpetuate the separation of thought from feeling and require full acceptance of the shared, unspoken lies that all agree to live. Both encourage people that it is normal not to know their feelings and to feel helpless when it comes to any thought of challenging or attempting to change the assumptions and rules upon which the divorce from feeling is based. As a result, these rules frequently encouraged psychological dramas and role playing. Rules that are simultaneously unreasonable and immune to questioning can perpetuate disorders like addiction, child abuse, and some forms of depression. This is the paradigm of the dysfunctional family.

It is not uncommon for one member of a dysfunctional family to exhibit symptoms of a serious psychological disorder that will be found, upon scrutiny, to be the outward manifestation of a pattern of dysfunctionality that includes the entire family. In order to heal the patient, therapists concentrate not on the pathology of the individual but on the web of family relationships—and the unwritten rules and understandings that guide his approach to those relationships.

For example, it has long been known that the vast majority of child abusers were themselves abused as children. In analyzing this phenomenon, theorists have found the blueprint for an archetypal intergenerational pattern: the child who is a victim remembers the intensity of the experience with his body but suppresses the memory of the pain in his mind. In a vain effort to resolve his deep confusion about what happened, he is driven to repeat or "recapitulate" the drama in which a powerful older person abuses a powerless child, only this time he plays the abuser's role.

To take a more subtle example, discussed in Alice Miller's seminal work on dysfunctionality, *The Drama of the Gifted Child*, children in some families are deprived of the unconditional love essential for normal development and made to feel that something inside them is missing. Consequently these children develop a low opinion of themselves and begin to look constantly to others for the approval and validation they so desperately need. The new term "codependency" describes the reliance on another for validation and positive feelings about oneself. The energy fueling this insatiable search continues into adulthood, frequently causing addictive behavior and an approach to relationships that might be described, in the words of the popular song, as "looking for love in all the wrong places." Sadly but almost inevitably, when they themselves have children, they find in the emotional hunger of their own infant a source of intense and undiluted attention that they use to satisfy their still insatiable desire for validation and approval, in a pattern that emphasizes taking rather than giving love. In the process, they neglect to give their own child the unconditional love the child needs to feel emotionally whole and complete. The child therefore develops the same sense that something is missing inside and seeks it in the faces and emotions of others, often insatiably. Thus the cycle continues.

The theory of how families become dysfunctional usually does not require identifying any particular family member as bad or as someone intent upon consciously harming the others. Rather, it is usually the learned pattern of family rules that represents the real source of the pain and tragedy the family members experience in each generation. As a diagnosis, dysfunctionality offers a powerful source of hope, because it identifies the roots of the problems in relationships rather than in individuals, in a shared way of thinking based on inherited assumptions rather than a shared human nature based on inherited destiny. It is therefore subject to healing and transformation.

That's the good news. The bad news is that many dysfunctional rules internalized during infancy and early childhood are extremely difficult to displace. Human evolution, of course, is responsible for our very long period of childhood, during much of which we are almost completely dependent on our parents. As Ashley Montagu first pointed out decades ago, evolution encouraged the development of larger and larger human brains, but our origins in the primate family placed a limit on the ability of the birth canal to accommodate babies with ever-larger heads. Nature's solution was to encourage an extremely long period of dependence on the nurturing parent during infancy and childhood, allowing both mind and body to continue developing in an almost gestational way long after birth. But as a result of this long period of social and psychological development, children are extremely vulnerable to both good and bad influences, and in a dysfunctional family, that means they will absorb and integrate the dysfunctional rules and warped assumptions about life that are being transmitted by the parents. And since much of what parents transmit are the lessons learned during their own childhood, these rules can persist through many generations.

Every culture is like a huge extended family, and perhaps nothing more determines a culture's distinct character than the rules and assumptions about life. In the modern culture of the West, the assumptions about life we are taught as infants are heavily influenced by our Cartesian world view—namely, that human beings should be separate from the earth, just as the mind should be separate from the body, and that nature is to be subdued, just as feelings are to be suppressed. To a greater or lesser degree, these rules are conveyed to all of us, and they have powerful effects on our perception of who we are.

The model of the dysfunctional family has a direct bearing on our ways of thinking about the environment. But this model also helps describe how we have managed to create such a profound and dangerous crisis in our relationship to the environment, why this crisis is not due to our inherently evil or pathogenic qualities, and how we can heal this relationship. As the use of this metaphor suggests, however, the environmental crisis is now so serious that I believe our civilization must be considered in some basic way dysfunctional.

Like the rules of a dysfunctional family, the unwritten rules that govern our relationship to the environment have been passed down from one generation to the next since the time of Descartes, Bacon, and the other pioneers of the scientific revolution some 375 years ago. We have absorbed these rules and lived by them for centuries without seriously questioning them. As in a dysfunctional family, one of the rules in a dysfunctional civilization is that you don't question the rules.

There is a powerful psychological reason that the rules go unquestioned in a dysfunctional family. Infants or developing children are so completely dependent that they cannot afford even to think there is something wrong with the parent, even if the rules do not feel right or make sense. Since children cannot bear to identify the all-powerful parent as the source of dysfunctionality, they assume that the problem is within themselves. This is the crucial moment when the inner psychological wound is inflicted—and it is a self-inflicted wound, a fundamental loss of faith by the children in themselves. The pain of that wound often lasts an entire lifetime, and the emptiness and alienation that result can give rise to enormous amounts of psychological energy, expended during the critical period when the psyche is formed in an insatiable search for what, sadly, can never be found: unconditional love and acceptance.

Just as children cannot reject their parents, each new generation in our civilization now feels utterly dependent on the civilization itself. The food on the supermarket shelves, the water in the faucets in our homes, the shelter and sustenance, the clothing and purposeful work, our entertainment, even our identity—all these our civilization provides, and we dare not even think about separating ourselves from such beneficence.

To carry the metaphor further: just as children blame themselves as the cause of the family's dysfunction in their relationship with it, so we quietly internalize the blame for our civilization's failure to provide a feeling of community and a shared sense of purpose in life. Many who feel their lives have no meaning and feel an inexplicable emptiness and alienation simply assume that they themselves are to blame, and that something is wrong with them.

Ironically, it is our very separation from the physical world that creates much of this pain, and it is because we are taught to live so separately from nature that we feel so utterly dependent upon our civilization, which has seemingly taken nature's place in meeting all our needs. Just as the children in a dysfunctional family experience pain when their parent leads them to believe that something important is missing from their psyches, we surely experience a painful loss when we are led to believe that the connection to the natural world that is part of our birthright as a species is something unnatural, something to be rejected as a rite of passage into the civilized world. As a result, we internalize the pain of our lost sense of connection to the natural world, we consume the earth and its resources as a way to distract ourselves from the pain, and we search insatiably for artificial substitutes to replace the experience of communion with the world that has been taken from us.

Children in dysfunctional families who feel shame often construct a false self through which they relate to others. This false self can be quite elaborate as the children constantly refine the impression it makes on others by carefully gauging their reactions, to make the inauthentic appear authentic. Similarly, we have constructed in our civilization a false world of plastic flowers and Astro Turf, air conditioning and fluorescent lights, windows that don't open and background music that never stops, days when we don't know whether it has rained or not, nights when the sky never stops glowing, Walkman and Watchman, entertainment cocoons, frozen food for the microwave oven, sleepy hearts jumpstarted with caffeine, alcohol, drugs, and illusions.

In our frenzied destruction of the natural world and our apparent obsession with inauthentic substitutes for direct experience with real life, we are playing out a script passed on to us by our forebears. However, just as the unwritten rules in a dysfunctional family create and maintain a conspiracy of silence about the rules themselves, even as the family is driven toward successive crises, many of the unwritten rules of our dysfunctional civilization encourage silent acquiescence in our patterns of destructive behavior toward the natural world.

The idea of a dysfunctional civilization is by no means merely a theoretical construct. In this terrible century, after all, we have witnessed some especially malignant examples of dysfunctional civilization: the totalitarian societies of Nazi Germany under Hitler, fascist Italy under Mussolini, Soviet communism under Stalin and his heirs, and the Chinese communism of Mao Zedong and Deng Xaoping, as well as many less infamous versions of the same phenomenon. Indeed, only recently the world community mobilized a coalition of armies to face down the Baathist totalitarianism of Iraq under Saddam Hussein.

Each of these dysfunctional societies has lacked the internal validation that can only come from the freely expressed consent of the governed. Each has demonstrated an insatiable need to thrust itself and its political philosophy onto neighboring societies. Each has been oriented toward expansion through the forceful takeover of other countries. Moreover, each has fostered in its society a seamless web of shared assumptions that most people know are false but that no one dares to question. These societies reflect in macrocosm the pathology of dysfunctionality as it has been observed in families. A developing child in a dysfunctional family searches his parent's face for signals that he is whole and all is right with the world; when he finds no such approval, he begins to feel that something is wrong inside. And because he doubts his worth and authenticity, he begins controlling his inner experience—smothering spontaneity, masking emotion, diverting creativity into robotic routine, and distracting an awareness of all he is missing with an unconvincing replica of what he might have been. Similarly, when the leadership in a totalitarian society dares to look in the faces of its people for signals of what they really feel, it is seldom reassured that all is right with the world. On the contrary, the leadership begins to fear that something is wrong because its people do not—cannot—freely express the consent of the governed. They stare back, trancelike, their vacant sullenness suggesting the uneasiness and apprehension that is so pervasive among oppressed populations everywhere. Denied validation in the countenance of its citizens, the totalitarian leadership feels no choice but to try to expand, out of an insatiable ambition to find—by imposing itself on others—conclusive evidence of its inner value.

Typically, the totalitarian expansion begins with the takeover of a weak and relatively defenseless neighboring society. Hoping that this initial conquest will satiate the aggressor, other societies frequently mute their response, some because they fear they might be the next targets, others because they are sure they will not be. But if the totalitarian society is deeply dysfunctional, it will not be satisfied for long and will continue to feel a need to expand. Alas, this horrifying pattern is all too familiar: totalitarian expansions have directly caused the deaths of more than 100 million human beings in this century.

The phenomenon of modern totalitarianism is, of course, extremely complex and involves political, economic, and historical factors unique to each of its incarnations. But whatever its specific causes, the psychology of totalitarianism has always been characterized by a fear of disorientation within and a search for legitimacy without. The pathology of expansion so evident in modern totalitarian societies results from this dysfunctional pattern, and the sense of wholeness they seek cannot be restored as long as they refuse to confront the dishonesty, fear, and violence eating away at the heart of their national identity.

The unprecedented assault on the natural world by our global civilization is also extremely complex, and many of its causes are related specifically to the geographic and historical context of its many points of attack. But in psychological terms, our rapid and aggressive expansion into what remains of the wildness of the earth represents an effort to plunder from outside civilization what we cannot find inside. Our insatiable drive to rummage deep beneath the surface of the earth, remove all of the coal, petroleum, and other fossil fuels we can find, then burn them as quickly as they are found—in the process filling the atmosphere with carbon dioxide and other pollutants—is a willful expansion of our dysfunctional civilization into vulnerable parts of the natural world. And the destruction by industrial civilization of most of the rain forests and old-growth forests is a particularly frightening example of our aggressive expansion beyond proper boundaries, an insatiable drive to find outside solutions to problems arising from a dysfunctional pattern within.

Ironically, Ethiopia, the first victim of modern totalitarian expansion, has also been an early victim of the dysfunctional pattern that has led to our assault on the natural world. At the end of World War II, after the Italian fascists had been forced out, 40 percent of Ethiopia's land was covered with, and protected by, trees. Less than a half century later, after decades marked by the most rapid population growth in the world, a relentless search for fuelwood, overgrazing, and the export of wood to pay interest on debts, *less than 1 percent* of Ethiopia is covered by trees. First, much of the topsoil washed away; then the droughts came—and stayed. The millions who have starved to death and, in a real sense, victims of our dysfunctional civilization's expansionist tendencies.

In studying the prospects for halting our destructive expansion, one is almost awestruck by our relentless and seemingly compulsive drive to dominate every part of the earth. Always, the unmet needs of civilization fuel the engine of aggression; never can these needs be truly satisfied. The invaded area is laid waste, its natural productivity is eviscerated, its resources are looted and quickly consumed—and all this destruction merely stokes our appetite for still more.

The weakest and most helpless members of the dysfunctional family become the victims of abuse at the hands of those responsible for providing nurture. In a similar fashion, we systematically abuse the most vulnerable and least defended areas of the natural world: the wetlands, the rain forests, the oceans. We also abuse other members of the human family, especially those who cannot speak for themselves. We tolerate the theft of land from indigenous peoples, the exploitation of areas inhabited by the poorest populations, and—worst of all—the violation of the rights of those who will come after us. As we strip-mine the earth at a completely unsustainable rate, we are making it impossible for our children's children to have a standard of living even remotely similar to ours.

In philosophical terms, the future is, after all, a vulnerable and developing present, and unsustainable development is therefore what might be called a form of "future abuse." Like a parent violating the personal boundaries of a vulnerable child, we violate the temporal boundaries of our rightful place in the chain of human generations. After all, the men and women of every generation must share the same earth—the only earth we have—and so we also share a responsibility to ensure that what one generation calls the future will be able to mature safely into what another generation will call the present. We are now, in effect, corruptly imposing our own dysfunctional design and discordant rhythms on future generations, and these persistent burdens will be terribly difficult to carry.

Police officers, doctors, and psychologists who deal with the victims of child sexual abuse often wonder how any adult—especially a parent—could commit such a crime. How could anyone be deaf to the screams, blind to the grief, and numb to the pain their actions cause? The answer, we now know, is that a kind of psychic numbness, induced by the adults' own adaptation to the dysfunctional pattern in which they were themselves raised as children, serves to anesthetize their conscience and awareness in order to facilitate their compulsive repetition of the crime that was visited upon them.

Just as the members of a dysfunctional family emotionally anesthetize themselves against the pain they would otherwise feel, our dysfunctional civilization has developed a numbness that prevents us from feeling the pain of our alienation from our world. Both the dysfunctional family and our dysfunctional civilization abhor direct contact with the full and honest experience of life. Both keep individuals in a seamless web of abstract, unfeeling thought, focused always on others, what others are assumed to be experiencing and what others might say or do to provide the wholeness and validation so desperately sought.

But there is a way out. A pattern of dysfunctionality need not persist indefinitely, and the key to change is the harsh light of truth. Just as an addict can confront his addiction, just as a dysfunctional family can confront the unwritten rules that govern their lives, our civilization can change—must change—by confronting the unwritten rules that are driving us to destroy the earth. And, as Alice Miller and other experts have shown, the act of mourning the original loss while fully and consciously feeling the pain it has caused can heal the wound and free the victim from further enslavement. Likewise, if the global environment crisis is rooted in the dysfunctional pattern of our civilization's relationship to the natural world, confronting and fully understanding that pattern, and recognizing its destructive impact on the environment and on us, is the first step toward mourning what we have lost, healing the damage we have done to the earth and to our civilization, and coming to terms with the new story of what it means to be a steward of the earth.

Study Questions

1. What is Gore's main message? How does he illustrate it? Has he made his case? Explain your responses.
2. What is Gore's criticism of deep ecology (refer to "Deep Ecology" in Chapter 3)? What does he put in its place?

80

Environmental Risks, Rights, and the Failure of Liberal Democracy

LAURA WESTRA

Laura Westra is professor of philosophy at the University of Windsor and the secretary of the International Society for Environmental Ethics. She is the author of An Environmental Proposal for Ethics: The Principle of Integrity *(1994, Rowman Littlefield); co-editor of* Faces of Environmental Racism *(1995, Rowman Littlefield);* Perspectives on Ecological Integrity *(1995, Kluwer Academic Publishers);* The Greeks and the Environment *and* Technology and Values *(1997, Rowman Littlefield). She has published over sixty articles and chapters in books and journals.*

In this article, Westra argues that democracies are failing to come to grips with the environmental degradation that is befalling us. Traditional interpretations of rights, especially those of Judith Jarvis Thomson, fail to recognize the legitimate right not to be put at undue risk. Westra argues that this right can be defended and political leaders must go beyond democracy in enforcing it. A rational risk response may require political activity that is revolutionary.

> *If you only have procedural democracy in a society that's exhibiting internal environmental stress and already has cleavages, say, ethnic cleavages, then procedural democracy will tend to aggravate these problems and produce societal discord, rather than social concord.*
>
> THOMAS HOMER-DIXON, 1996

DEMOCRACY IS NOT ENOUGH

The list of environmental assaults on the physical integrity of ecosystems and, through them, on our physical integrity and capacities occurs equally in affluent countries of North American and Western Europe and in developing ones of Southeast Asia. The global distribution of the threats, from remote islands in the Pacific Ocean (Colborn, Dumanoski, and Myers 1996) to "pristine" areas in the Arctic (Colborn 1996; Nikiforuk, 1996), demonstrate that geographic and political boundaries are not capable of containing and limiting environmental degradation and disintegrity. A careful study of the "hot spots" and locations where the worst hazards persist, shows that they are equally global in distribution. We cannot separate democracies from—say—military regimes and other nondemocratic states on the basis of the spread and severity of the environmental threats to which their citizens are exposed.

The "toxic doughnut" area in Chicago is a persistent threat to the life and health of residents (Gaylord and Bell 1995), although it is located in a country that prides itself on its status as the "land of the free" and that routinely allows its leaders and politicians to praise its democratic institutions, in contrast with other undesirable forms of government the world over. Equally hazardous, Royal Dutch Shell Oil's operation in Ogoniland, Nigeria, uses the dictatorship of General Sani Abbacha and his military clique to enforce the acceptance of extreme health hazards on its citizens. Of course, those who oppose these hazardous corporate activities in Nigeria are brutally and violently repressed or murdered, while the Chicago residents are not.

The U.S. residents, primarily minorities in most large cities (Westra and Wenz 1995; Bullard 1994), are not imprisoned or executed, and the army is not sent in to restrain and eliminate their protests. In some sense, their plight is therefore "better": They only suffer the physical harms imposed upon them by others, and their life and health are slowly, insidiously attacked and diminished. They only suffer from "ecoviolence"; they are not imprisoned and executed if they protest, as they might have been in Nigeria. But, in some sense, their plight is even worse. Ostensibly possessed of civil rights, basic education, access to information, and constitutional guarantees about freedom of choice, life, and the pursuit of happiness, they are manipulated instead to contribute willingly (but unknowingly) to their own plight. Aggressive advertising and marketing techniques render the products of modern technology not only extremely desirable but also "necessary" as things everyone should have—"free choices," though their corporate sponsors and originators employ "trade secret" and other hard-won rules and regulations to protect themselves while keeping citizens in the dark about the effects and consequences of their choices.

At the same time, public relation (PR) departments work steadily so that questions about the risks and harms imposed, and whether they are and should be truly offset by the so-called benefits available, are raised as rarely as possible. Further, as David Korten shows, two other severe problems arise in connection with the pursuit of economic gain through techno-corporate activities. The first is a clear attack on democracy, as independent PR firms are hired at great cost to generate "public movements" and campaigns, with the double aim of "selling" their ideas and preparing the public to accept and actively pursue certain products and services. The second problem is that legislative modifications, regulations, or deregulations favorable to business, are also sought.

The result of these activities is that "free democratic choices" are neither truly free nor truly democratic. Korten (1995) cites Washington journalist William Greider:

> [The corporations'] . . . tremendous financial resources, the diversity of their interests, the squads of talented professionals—all these assets and some others—are now relentlessly focused on the politics of governing. This new institutional reality is the centerpiece in the breakdown of contemporary democracy. Corporations exist to pursue their own profit maximization, not the collective aspirations of the Society.

The problem is embedded in democracy in two senses:

1. Corporations are taken to be fictitious legal persons (French 1984) and are free to pursue their aims unless it can be proven (in the legal sense) that some citizen or citizens are directly harmed by their chosen activities. Further, there is no overarching conception of "the good" for all that can be contrasted with *their* perception of the good, which is economic rather than intellectual or spiritual.
2. Moreover, because there is no "good" to guide public policy, aside from aggregate choices and preferences, and because the latter can be and in fact often is routinely manipulated and underinformed, the myth of "one man/one vote" remains a vague ideal, not a reality.

The justification often proposed to counterbalance these negative impacts centers on the "economic advantages" provided by multinational corporate giants. But, as we indicated in the Chicago example, the economic advantage is not evenly distributed or fairly apportioned among rich and poor: Moreover, if we shift to the global scene, even economic advances depend on "relative" rather than on "absolute" income. The Bruntlandt commission proposed a "3% global increase in per capita income." That would translate into a first-year per-capita increase (in U.S. dollars) of $633 for the United States and, among others, $3.60 for Ethiopia. After 10 years, the respective figures would be $7,257 for the United States and $41 for Ethiopia: a vast advantage for the "haves" over the "have nots." Korten (1995) adds, "This advantage becomes a life-and-death issue in a resource-scarce world in which the rich and the poor are locked in mortal competition for a depleting resource base" (see also Homer-Dixon 1994).

Objections may be raised about such polarized

descriptions of corporate activities. For instance, David Crocker believes that "demonizing" corporations is philosophically fallacious and practically incorrect because many corporations are "good" and seek to support and implement the common good in their activities (Crocker, personal communication, 1996). This objection, however, is open to a counterobjection. The main point at issue is not that this or that corporation is "bad" and needs to be stopped, but that Western democracies and their institutions appear to have no mechanism available, at this time, to protect the public from hazards and harms, many of which are—in part—self-inflicted under conditions of public misinformation and manipulation.

In this case, to say that there is no need to institute radical changes and to implement a system of criminal charges against the corporate risk imposers is like saying that, because many of us are generally decent people who do not view physical assaults and murder as acceptable activities, there is no need for strong laws and sanctions about these crimes. Leaving the choice to either engage in harmful activities or not, within the ambit of the present loose regulative structures and unrealistic legal criteria (Brown and Lemons 1995), to corporate goodwill of individual firms is to support tacitly the status quo, thereby becoming accomplices to the crimes perpetrated.

So far, this work has addressed the operation of legitimate business, registered, licensed and—to some extent—regulated. This sort of business is global in scope, but even licenses and regulations tend to lose their force when they reach national borders. And what about business that is neither regulated, licensed, nor even *known* as such to any nation or state? The "shadow economy," as Ed Ayres (1996) terms it, represents an additional pervasive global threat. We used to think of some of those "business" activities or of their concomitant effects as "externalities" and think of others as "anomalies." Ayres says:

> These are untaxed, unregulated, unsanctioned and—often—unseen. Most of them are things we've heard about but only fleetingly; we think of them as anomalies, rather than as serious or systemic threats to our mainframe institutions. They range from black markets in illicit drugs, cheap weapons, endangered wildlife, toxic waste, or ozone-depleting chemicals, to grey markets in unlisted securities or unapproved treatment for cancer.

Activities that fall under the heading of "shadow economy" include subsistence agricultural workers and those in other "unregistered occupations"—illegal industries, but also the work of "unlocated populations" such as migrants and refugees; it also includes "nonlocated activity" such as that arising from "electronic exchanges." Ayres (1996) lists the "three largest industries in the world" as (1) the military ($800 billion), (2) illicit drugs ($500 billion), and (3) oil ($450 billion). All three have a "shadow " side (1 and 3) or are entirely illegitimate (2). All three are among the most hazardous activities in the world because, aside from the individual hazards they involve or represent, they are in *principle* beyond the control of society in various ways.

The solution Ayres proposes might be the right one for all forms of techno-corporate enterprise. Neither national nor international databases carry accurate information about the shadow economy, hence, in the face of global threats, Ayres suggests that the "old geopolitical maps" are obsolete. Because borders no longer function as they were intended to do, because they have become impotent to contain benign and hazardous activities alike, the present maps should be superimposed with a "new kind of map"—that is, with "maps illuminating the kinds of phenomena that now count most: the watersheds, bioregions, climatic zones and migratory routes that are essential to the security of all future economies" (Ayres 1996).

For both the legitimate and the shadow economy, it is necessary to understand the essential nature of ecological and climate functions and related global threats. It is equally necessary for all of us to understand the natural functions of natural systems and the relation between the products we buy and these systems.

For these reasons, I propose a reexamination of environmental risks and harms from the standpoint of the ethics of integrity (Westra 1994a). I will argue that a proliferation of individual and aggregate rights is undesirable from the environmental point of view (and this has been argued here as well, in support of limits for corporate rights). Still, the right to life, health, and personal physical integrity appear to be primary and worthy of strong support. Moreover, the latter is necessarily embedded in ecosystem integrity, as Holmes Rolston argues (Rolston 1996; Westra 1995a).

In the next section, I consider some examples of the recent literature on the topic of risks and harms, in order to place the integrity argument in context.

RISKS AND HARMS; RIGHTS AND CONSENT

In her book *The Realm of Rights,* Judith Jarvis Thomson (1990) argues that "we do not have a claim against *merely being put at risk of harm*" and that we ought to reject what she terms the "risk thesis"—that is, the thesis that "we have claims against others that they not impose risks of harm on us." In contrast, Anthony Ellis (1995) argues that the risk thesis can be defended despite Thomson's condemnation. I will argue that his position is essentially correct and that Thomson's difficulties in drawing the line between risk and harm, for instance, is no sound reason to reject the thesis, particularly in the face of diffuse global threats, which prompted the recent acceptance of a "precautionary principle" (Brown and Lemons 1995). I will also argue that, although democracy is taken to be the form of government that is the best supporter and defender of human rights, it is precisely the unquestioned acceptance of the primacy of democratic institutions that presents the major obstacle to the prevention of public harms, particularly environmentally induced risks to public health.

Hence, the problematic interface between rights, democratic institutions, and health risks needs to be reexamined because the public interest in this respect may not be best supported by democratic choices without further controls. I will propose an argument based on an analogy with biomedical ethics and the moral and legal status of "quarantines" in response to disease-engendered public health threats. If, contrary to Thomson's opinion, *we* have the right not to be "put at risk of harm," then we need to find the best way of reaching public-policy decisions that will ensure our rights will not be infringed. Notwithstanding the close links between civil rights and democracy, on both practical and theoretical grounds, democratic practices appear insufficient to protect us from endangerment caused by the reckless practices of individuals and corporate citizens. Throughout this discussion and for the purposes of this work, *liberal democracy* and *democracy* will refer to the form of democracy we can observe implemented in North America and in Western European nations. I will not enter into the debate about the various ideological variants present in the constitutions and institutions of democratic states, because my argument is concerned with the real consequences of democracy as it is practiced in North America and Western Europe.

Environmental risks and *environmental harms* in this section will be compared to such "harms" as exposure to contagious diseases. The environmental harms considered will be those that impose threats of grave physical injury to human health: They are the *indirect* counterparts of the *direct* harms arising from exposure to contagious diseases. The environmental threats considered will be those that seriously affect life-support systems that we depend on in various ways. For example, even a noncatastrophic event like the elimination of earthworms and other biomass in the soils at an agricultural location may be a contributing factor to hazardous floods, particularly in conjunction with climatic changes. The latter are also fostered and magnified by environmental degradation (e.g., ozone-layer and deforestation problems). Although at times local environmental hazards may be contained so that the functioning of the system or the human health in the area wherein they occur, may not be affected, the onus to prove that this is the case should be on the would-be polluter. In general, the repeated occurrences of seemingly small and localized threats lead to system failure and global health threats.

It may seem that precise comparison with health threats may not be possible. But one might argue that a combination of infectious diseases, malnutrition, some organ malfunction, and the lack of local hygiene, when occurring jointly to someone in a developing country, may also render the combination a lethal threat, despite the fact that each problem might be curable or open to some solution in itself. Hence, for the environmental threats that pose, singly or jointly, an indirect but severe threat to our health, the analogy with health-care issues seems an apt one from several standpoints:

1. The magnitude and gravity of the threats
2. The lack of specific intentions to harm on the part of those who endanger us
3. The lack of intention to inflict harm on specific individuals
4. The necessity to restrain individual freedoms (on the part of risk imposers), although neither "punishment" nor "retribution" may be appropriate conceptual categories to define the restraints imposed
5. The lack of precise proofs of either direct "guilt" or even of specific "harm" inflicted.

These difficulties are common to environmentally induced harms as well as health endangerments, despite the many differences between the two fields.

Finally, I will argue against the common assumption that consent to certain institutionally approved practices and corporate activities entails the consent to all possible "side effects," including consent to be put at risk of harm. Even though we might derive some individual and collective benefits from those activities, it can be argued that consent to be harmed cannot be given, on moral grounds.

Risks, Harms, and Consent

From a moral (Kantian) point of view, we can argue against consent to harm, as long as *harm* is understood in the physical sense, not simply in the sense of being wronged or not getting one's due (Simmons 1979). But the claim that somehow embracing the lifestyle existing in affluent countries entails giving "tacit consent" to the bad consequences accompanying that way of life needs to be examined from the standpoint of political theory as well. Tacit consent, in the context of one's political obligation to governmental institutions, may not be assumed simply because we are silent or because we do not protest.

A. John Simmons (1979) argues that, although "consent is called tacit when it is given by remaining silent and inactive . . . ," it must be expressed "by the failure to do certain things" when a certain response is *required* to signify disagreement. Unless this sequence characterizes it, the "tacit consent" may simply represent "(1) a failure to grasp the nature of the situation, (2) a lack of understanding of proper procedures, or (3) a misunder-

standing about how long one has to decide whether or not to dissent" (Simmons 1979).

Another possibility may be that a simple failure of communications has occurred. Thus, the conditions needed to establish the presence of tacit consent eliminate the possibility of simple, nonspecific voting in favor of some political institutions, without the particularity required for explicit consent to the hazardous practices in question. After citing the problems inherent in John Locke's position on this question, Simmons (1979) adds "calling consent 'tacit' on my account, specifies its mode of expression, not its lack of expression." Locke, Simmons argues, was confused about "acts of enjoyment" in one's country, such as enjoying public highways, police protection, and the like and "signs of consent" instead. Because of this confusion, Locke believed that one gave tacit consent to one's government simply because one used (and enjoyed) a country's amenities. If the same argument is applied here—that is, that enjoying some features of a system implies tacit consent for the system *in toto*, in all its activities including hazardous ones—then those who argue that by enjoying certain features of our modern, Western, technological lifestyle, we thereby give consent to any and all "side effects" that ensue might have a good point. However, they do not because this position is as "confused" as that of Locke's, Simmons (1979) argues.

Moreover, there are certain things to which we cannot consent in our social and political life. Enslavement is a clear example. Humans are created free and only acquire the obligation of a nation's citizen through consent (explicit). But, although consent is a powerful tool in general, its power does not extend to relinquishing one's "inalienable" rights, such as the right to life or to freedom itself: The right to self-defense cannot be abdicated. Thomas Hobbes (1958) says, "A man cannot lay down the right of resisting them that assault him by force to take away his life." Simmons (1979) says that Kant argues for a similar position as well:

> Kant holds that "no contract could put a man into the class of domestic animals which we use at will for any kind of service"; that is because "every man has inalienable rights which he cannot give up even if he would."

Kant holds human life to have infinite value, and he believes that humans cannot affect (or permit others to affect) their physical integrity for any advantage or any other consideration. Hence, it may be argued that the human rights representing and supporting these inalienable human goods—such as life, freedom, and physical integrity—cannot be transferred or set aside, even if *explicit (tacit)* consent were present. In this case, there is a solid historical and theoretical basis for the somewhat novel position I have advanced in support of criminalizing those activities that represent an attack on our physical being.

To be sure, it is permissible and not immoral to trade

off some of our freedom in exchange for wages, provided that respect for our humanity is present in the transaction, or for a great common ideal (say, the defense of our common freedom from enslavement), or to engage in warfare, that is, in a potentially lethal activity (in our country's defense). Not all cases are so clear-cut that they evidently fall either in one camp (of permissible activities) or in the other (of activities that represent an immoral trade-off) as some, or perhaps even all workplace activities normally entail at least some risk of harm. Even a philosophy professor who must drive her car, or walk to her teaching institution, exposes herself to some risk of traffic mishaps. If she were to remain at home and teach from her house, those risks would be avoided. But inactivity and a sedentary lifestyle are at least as hazardous to one's health as well.

We must keep in mind that the public-health threats considered here, whether they are directly posed by environmental conditions or indirectly caused by circumstances due to environmental disintegrity and degradation, are the sort of severe threats epidemiologists document (McMichael 1995); they are not the occasional or possible chance happenings one may encounter in the circumstances outlined in the previous paragraph. The health threats I have in mind are of three kinds:

1. Threats that seriously impair our natural capabilities (e.g., changes in our normal reproductive, intellectual, emotional, or immune systems).
2. Threats that pose an imminent danger of death to individuals or groups.
3. Threats that include long-term, delayed, and mutagenic effects: Like the reproductive effects in item 1, there are threats to *our species*, as well as to the affected individuals.

The effects named under these three headings have an undeniable negative impact on our rights, both human and legal, and we consider these further below in order to understand why the risk thesis should be rejected.

Risks, Harms, and Rights

W. N. Hohfeld (1923) described four forms of legal rights: (1) claim rights, (2) rights as privilege or liberty, (3) rights as power, and (4) rights as immunity. It is primarily the last form that concerns us, although where immunity rights are present, claim rights or liberty rights, for instance, may be present as well.

Hohfeld's discussion is primarily intended to clarify the meaning and scope of various judicial terms in common use and their relation to one another in order to understand the "deeper unity" present in the law: "In short the deeper the analysis, the greater becomes one's perception of fundamental unity and harmony in the law" (Hohfeld 1923). When we turn to his discussion of "immunities," both the cases and the examples he cites

show that the concept may not be the most appropriate for our purpose. In a section on "Immunities and Disabilities," he says:

> A right is one's affirmative claim against another, and a privilege is one's freedom from the right or claim of another. Similarly, a power is one's affirmative "control" over a given legal relation as against another, whereas an *immunity* [my italics] is one's freedom from the legal power or "control" of another, as regards some legal relation (Hohfeld 1923).

As an example of immunity, Hohfeld cites "exemption from taxation" as a better and more accurate term than "privilege." Hence, the meaning he proposes appears somewhat different from a concept used to refer to the right to the freedom from bodily harm. A better way to introduce the sort of "right" appropriate to our argument may be one of the personal rights, that is, the "rights of bodily safety and freedom." Hohfeld adds that it is "the duty of all of us not to interfere with our neighbors' lawful freedom." This is one of the primitive rights; it may also be termed "the right not to be interfered with" (Hohfeld 1923).

Thomson accepts the Hohfeldian framework, which includes the correlativity between rights and duties, but she rejects the risk thesis, as stated at the outset. She may base her rejection on the problem of "thresholds" and question the limits of both probability and gravity of harms as factors of the risk thesis (DeCew 1995). As Thomson rightly argues, it is problematic to identify *the* harm in many cases. She offers an example. A log left on a highway may well present a risk of harm to someone, but we have no certainty that a harm will happen to someone and no information about the possible gravity of such a harm. We can begin here to note the parallel between the example she offers of a log left on a highway (Thomson 1990; Ellis 1995), and that of risky environmental exposures or changes. She notes that we cannot be sure of several points, and that affects our acceptance of the risk thesis. These uncertainties are primarily (1) who is likely to be passing by and tripping over the log and (2) the precise harm such person or persons may incur, since these may range from very minor to quite grave depending on circumstances. We might envision icy road conditions and an elderly "tripper" or, at the other extreme, a clear, empty roadway and an athletic young person who would quickly get up with little or no harm.

In the case of environmental harms, we need not specify or prove that process X producing substance Y has actually harmed someone, before claiming that corporation Z (by engaging in process X) is liable, through Y, for the harm produced, if we accept the risk thesis. This represents the major current problem for those who are harmed: The required "proof" of harm is often unavailable, unclear, or delayed. The problems of environmental harm lie in (1) science's lack of predictive capacities; (2) the synergistic and cumulative effects of other contributory causes to the harm; (3) the lack of sustained research to sufficiently support item 2; (4) the accelerated introduction of substances, products, and processes, which further reduces the availability of research (as in item 3); (5) the difficulty of establishing clear thresholds, in the face of items 1–3; (6) the existence of harms, the effects of which develop and manifest themselves slowly over time (e.g., cancers). And this list, lengthy as it is, may only represent a partial list addressing only presently acknowledged problems (Shrader-Frechette 1991; T. Colborn et al. 1996).

However, both Ellis and Thomson agree on one issue: If an agreed-on threshold of harm is reached, then the risk violates a right. The difficulties listed above (1–6) show clearly how hard it is to draw a precise dividing line between a risk of harm that is plausible or probable and one that is not. Separating a minor harm from a significant one is equally difficult. It is also hard to indicate who specifically is "put at risk." In fact, from an environmental point of view, the level of harm inflicted may vary. For instance, a fetus, pregnant women, and older people may all encounter a greater risk than adult males from exposure to the same substance(s). It is equally impossible to specify who precisely may be at risk because some environmental hazards cause harms far from the location from where they occurred.

An example of the latter can be found in some of the recent cholera pandemics. Rita Colwell (1996) showed the connection between environmental degradation (engendered by such practices as deforestation, for instance), global climatic changes, ocean warming, the extraordinary growth of plankton in the oceans, and the way the latter fosters the spread of the *E. coli* bacterium from one continent to the other: "Cholera offers an excellent example of how greater understanding of environmental factors allows us to understand the disease better, not only its virulence but . . . its transmission and epidemiology." In this case, it would not be possible to point to *one* perpetrator, at *one* location, much less to designate specific persons as victims. Anthony Ellis (1995) argues one aspect of these issues, in response to Thomson:

> It is merely that it is indeterminate who is put at risk. If this simply means that it is hard, perhaps impossible, to find out who is put at risk, this is true, but irrelevant. If I illegitimately drop a bomb on a city, and it is impossible to determine whom, exactly, I killed, this does not imply that I did not violate anyone's rights; I violated the rights of all those I killed, whoever they may have been.

Other conceptual problems may include the following: (1) Too many people may have claims against those who impose risks; (2) the risk exposure may not actually cause harm (i.e., I dropped the bomb, but everyone was safe in an air shelter); (3) such a thesis may commit us to "absurd consequences"—for example, the consequence that "every time you drive your automobile you violate the rights of all those whom you put at risk, no matter how small the risk" (Ellis 1995). Finally, Ellis adds, we could reject such objections as the last one, by saying that "permission, in a democratic society, has been obtained in advance."

This, of course, is the crux of the problem, from the point of view of environmental hazards. Does living in a democracy, even in a Western industrialized country, with the lifestyle common to our society, mean giving *implicit* consent to risk exposure, or to the abandonment of our rights to security from harm? It does not mean giving tacit consent, as shown in our earlier discussion. Most arguments against tacit consent also show that some rights may not be relinquished, not to one's legitimate government (except in special cases, such as self-defense on behalf of one's own country, for instance; or perhaps to save another's life through a kidney donation). It is certainly immoral and impermissible to do so for economic advancement, even for one's own economic benefit. Implausible though such a thesis may be, Ellis raises it as a question, and it is often implicit and assumed in business ethics literature (Friedman 1993), with the common understanding of many who take for granted that "hazards" (unspecified) are the price one pays for technologic advances and, in general, for modern progress (Mesthene 1990; Winner 1977).

RISKS, RIGHTS, AND DEMOCRACY

John Rawls (1993) has argued that a "law of peoples" can be drawn from his theory of justice, and that a "social contract doctrine is universal in its reach." He also argued that both are not only compatible with but also dependent on a doctrine of human rights because these represent an integral part of a society's "common good conception of justice." The law in such societies must "at least uphold such basic rights as the right to life and security, to personal property, and elements of the rule of law . . ." (Rawls 1993). For our purpose, the most important element mentioned here is the "right to life and security." The Canadian Charter of Rights refers to this as "the right to life and the security of persons." According to Rawls, it might seem that both human and civil rights could be supported and in fact identified with the practices and the ideals of democratic institutions. Yet in Western democracies as well as in less developed countries, it does not appear that environmental hazards and risks have been controlled or eliminated on the basis of general human rights to freedom from harm.

It is important to understand why this is so, and a good place to start is by considering a situation where democracy, civil rights, and due process are invoked in order to demonstrate the "right" way to deal with the hazards of technology transfers to third world countries. After listing statistics about deaths related to a chemical industry's operation and marketing, Kristin Shrader-Frechette (1991) argues that corporations "have an obligation to guarantee equal protection from risk across national boundaries" rather than employ what she terms the "isolationist strategy." Corporations cannot restrict their moral and legal restraints to the activities they practice in the country of origin. Yet Shrader-Frechette admits that, "indeed, a rational risk response may require political activity that is nothing less than revolutionary." But at this time, both those in developing countries and those in minority communities in Western democracies are treated in ways that infringe their rights: Both are often "isolated" from moral consideration (Westra 1995a).

The problem is that there is no proof of intent to harm on the part of corporations or other institutions involved in these practices. In fact, if questioned, they may respond with several arguments in support of their activities. These are (1) the "social progress argument," (2) the "countervailing benefit argument," (3) "the consent argument," and (4) the "reasonable-possibility argument" (Shrader-Frechette 1991). But (1) only works if we accept the subordination of individual and group rights to some (unproven) consequentialist "good" such as "progress," a doubtful notion as it stands because of the gravity of its side effects. The next argument (2) is problematic as well: Even benefits ought not to be promoted at any cost. Shrader-Frechette (1991) says, "The argument is that a bloody loaf of bread is sometimes better than no loaf at all, that a dangerous job is preferable to no job, and that food riddled with pesticides banned is better than no food at all."

This argument is hard to defend even on utilitarian grounds, and it is impossible to support on Kantian grounds and from the standpoint of human rights. The "consent argument" (3) has been discussed and will be discussed in detail in the next section. For now, it is sufficient to note that the "free, informed consent" to which corporations appeal in defense of their limited responsibility is seldom, if ever, available from those who are "financially strapped and poorly educated." The final argument (4) suggests that risks and harms imposed are not preventable without "heroic" commitments that cannot in fairness be demanded of any corporation. But if there are human rights such as the right to the nonimposition of cancer (Gewirth 1983), then it is not heroism that is required but the simple adherence to morality.

So far, only physical, quantifiable harms have been discussed, without even envisaging the possibility of "social" or "group harms" (Simon 1995). The implication of this discussion? It is necessary though not sufficient to introduce democratic procedures and due process, globally, in order to attempt to prevent the unjust imposition of harms on the vulnerable and the disempowered. Rawls (1993) also argues for the extension of constructivist principles for justice as fairness, for "the basic structure of a closed and self-contained democratic society," to extend the ideal of justice and human rights through a "law of people." His starting point is the democratic, liberal society where he supports the "egalitarian features of the fair value of political liberties, of fair equality of opportunity, and of the difference principle." On the basis of this extension, he indicates the existence of respect for human rights and views it as a *condition* for admitting any country or national state to participate in the "law of nations." These are viewed as bedrock of any conception of justice, extended, as it were, from the starting point of appropriate basic principles within a self-contained democracy. I now turn to an examination of the real import of democracy when we consider risks and harms.

Democracy entails that collective decisions be based on open acceptance of certain choices and preferences over others and that these choices be reached through majority votes. But even in the countries where democratic systems are in power, it appears that the system is powerless to prevent the infringement of human rights through the imposition of harms to human life and health, at least through environmental means. Why does this happen? First, it is clear that democracy tends to further "the interests of the majority at the expense of the minority" (Gilbert 1995). Second, and even harder to address, is the fact that in the face of global hazards that affect everyone on Earth, there are still limits to the reach of democratic powers. For instance, in border issues that often give rise to violent conflicts, democracy is powerless because citizens on either side of the disputed border can only vote within the limits of their national area (Gilbert 1995; Westra 1994a). Further, the immense power of Western multinational corporations, which represent the source of many of these hazards, is not subject to democratic decision making, either in their country of origin or in the (less developed) host countries (Westra 1994b; Korten 1995; Donaldson 1993).

Hence, self-contained democracies are not sufficient to mitigate these risks, and it seems urgent to establish respect and accept a risk thesis that would serve to link more clearly the existence of hazardous products and practices and the clear duties of all not to infringe upon the rights to "life and security of persons," through a "law of peoples" (Rawls 1993). This would help not only those who belong to the same community and are part of the same democratic nation but also all those who might be affected by these risks anywhere else.

Yet it is unclear just how democratic systems, even if globally implemented, would help solve the problem. Now it may make sense to say that a minority who lost out on its *political* choice must, under a democracy's rule, learn to live with its loss since it occurred through fair means and a fair opportunity to change the situation exists for the future. But it would be much harder to say that all those whose preference was not on the winning side must be equally stoic in the face of unchosen, unconsented, and uncompensated harms, which a majority chose to impose upon them (Westra 1995a). As Gewirth (1983) would argue, the imposition of grave harms cannot be supported on moral grounds because it constitutes a gross infringement of human rights.

Hence, we can drive a wedge between democratic political systems and the absolute support of human rights through a reconsideration of the imposition of risks and harms. Rex Martin discusses the relation between democracy and rights in the *System of Rights* (1993), and he argues that civil rights should have priority status: "In sum, the priority of civil rights holds over aggregative considerations insofar as those considerations concern policies for civil rights directly, or concern such rights in relation to other social policy matters." Martin's argument is that, in a system of rights, "External checks over and beyond those afforded by the representative principle are required to keep majority rule from mischief. . . ." Martin (1993) admits, ". . . representative democracy has some tendencies to the same abuse (as 'class-interested majority rule'), and therefore needs additional controls."

The example we considered earlier—of hazardous technology transfers to impoverished, uninformed, and unconsenting third world people—showed a case where the input of moral theories, utilities rights, and justice was deemed necessary to redress the injustices perpetrated because of the lack of due process and democratic procedures in those countries (Shrader-Frechette 1991). But the question now is not whether the consideration of these moral theories is necessary but whether the input of democracy is *sufficient* to ensure the presence of those moral considerations, especially the primacy of individual and group rights. The main problems with democracy seem to arise in connection with consent to the risk of harm. Should a majority have the right to consent, through their vote, to practices and activities that might impose the risk of harm upon defeated minorities? And even if we should answer this question in the affirmative, does anybody—whether in a majority or minority position within a democracy—have the right to consent even to their own harm? Both these questions need to be discussed. Speaking of environmental justice, Wigley and Shrader-Frechette (1995) say, "The doctrine of free informed consent, an important part of the traditional American value system, likewise provides a foundation for environmental justice." In this context, they proceed to analyze the concept of informed consent in the context of biomedical ethics, noting that the concept has not been used in either environmental or technological ethics. The following four criteria are suggested to indicate the presence of informed consent: ". . . The risk imposers must disclose full information about the threat; potential victims must be competent to evaluate it; they must understand the danger; and they must voluntarily accept it" (Wigley and Shrader-Frechette 1995).

In the light of our earlier discussion of democratic choices and of the lack of precision in both scientific infor-

mation about specific harmful effects and of the possible geographic spread of risks, several other questions may be raised. One question might be: How and from whom should consent be sought? Another problem might be: Even if we could circumscribe a specific area where all inhabitants could be polled on such a question, the provided information may not be sufficient to guarantee that the four criteria are met, as Franz Ingelfinger, for instance, argues in "Informed (but Uneducated) Consent" (1991). The doctrine of informed consent in the biomedical setting is intended to be directed at the interaction between health-care provider and one patient or, at most, a group of patients. Hence, the consent criteria cannot be readily applied to great numbers of people from whom the risk imposers are separated by geographic location, language, cultural background, and the like.

But in that case, the imposition of wide-ranging environmental risks and harms does not fit the informed-consent model because it is more like experimentation on unconsenting subjects, contrary to the Nuremberg Code (1948). The problem is that often grave environmental hazards are, by their very nature, impossible to contain.

So far, I have argued that, unless we deal with such specifics as environmental justice at a certain location, for instance, the consent criteria cannot properly be applied. But even this argument assumes that, at least in theory and in principle, people can consent to harms, provided that they are free to choose, fully informed, and that they understand the full extent of the harm to which they are exposed. But this belief is not beyond critique. For instance, we *can* object on Kantian grounds to this assumption. Moral action implies universalizability and reversibility, and it precludes the use of any autonomous person as means to anyone's ends, even their own. Hence, as it would be impermissible, on Kantian grounds, to commit suicide even for our own "good" (e.g., for the cessation of terminal, excruciating pain); so too, it would be impermissible to accept trade-offs, such as consent to cancer risks, to obtain a hazardous job. Hence, it can be argued that

> The Categorical Imperative is formulated in such a way that consent can never be relevant in informing us of what our duties to others are. Thus one is precluded from even entertaining the notion that consent would be a defeasibility condition of the Categorical Imperative (Barnes 1996).

Although Kant's position that suicide is immoral is controversial, it is undoubtedly and clearly his position. Kant is somewhat closer to the present-day thought on not using any part of ourselves as means, even for a personally desired end. Kant is quite explicit on this point: We *cannot* consent to sales or trade-offs that would turn autonomous humans into slaves, for instance, or that might foster the exchange of bodily parts for money (Kant 1979). Hence, we can conclude that consent to harms is based on weak arguments both from the standpoint of political theory and from that of Kant's moral doctrine.

Moreover, it can also be claimed that, in general, utilitarian arguments should be considered only *after* human rights and justice principles. In that case, if consent to harm is not possible in principle, or if it is questionable even if obtained, then the introduction of truly democratic conditions and due process will not be sufficient to mitigate, let alone justify, the wide-ranging imposition of risks and harms on large numbers of unspecified persons, through environmental means. In sum, I have argued that we should accept, as Ellis suggests, the risk thesis Thomson rejects, as necessary because it can be argued that—although not all rights are primary—the right to life and freedom from harm is primary among them.

In contrast, the usually accepted connection between primary human rights and democracy can be shown to be less strong than it is generally thought to be. In that case, our next problem is: How are we to prevent harms, and to restrain risk imposers when even the "best," most enlightened form of governance (i.e., democracy) may not be sufficient to accomplish the goal? To attempt an answer, we will return to biomedical ethics and the moral and legal categories used to remedy the possible spread of infectious diseases.

RISK, RIGHTS AND CONSENT: A LESSON FROM THE "WHITE DEATH"

I have noted that biomedical ethics may not offer the best analogy for questions of consent arising from environmental and technological hazards. We could not ensure "full disclosure," reach everyone who might be at risk, and communicate clearly and understandably the extent and gravity of the harm; moreover, neither risk imposers nor risk assessors could predict accurately the probability and gravity of the harms. Yet uncertainties—endemic to scientific discourse involving a large range of variables, added to the impredictability about location, gravity of exposure, and other specifics—ought not to force us to reject with Thomson, the risk thesis.

And if we hold fast to both (1) the primacy of rights—especially the right to life and to freedom from harm—and (2) the risk thesis itself, then we need to seek another avenue to ensure that rights be protected, given the failure of present democratic institutions to guarantee appropriate restraints to risk imposers. The resurgence of many infectious diseases, assumed to have been conquered and eliminated (e.g., tuberculosis), for instance, may indicate a possible avenue for public policy. Tuberculosis is making a comeback in North America and in other parts of the world; it is now resistant to most antibiotics, harder than ever to control because of population density and other modern conditions, and therefore brings with it threats of the "white

death." Tuberculosis is highly contagious and requires very little contact to spread, unlike, for instance, sexually transmitted diseases like AIDS. It is sufficient to sit next to an infected person, to breathe the same air, to be infected. Tuberculosis is curable, but it requires a lengthy course of treatment. Many people who want to get well decide to abandon the treatment when the worst symptoms subside, despite the fact that they are still highly contagious (Davis 1995). If these persons are not prepared to persevere with their treatment and yet want to continue to lead a normal life, interacting with others, they are "endangering" not only their close associates but also the general public. The question is what to do when the disease, its course, treatment, and hazards are fully explained to contagious persons and they understand yet refuse to comply with either treatment or restraints. Some action must be taken in defense of the public interest and the public safety.

As in the case of contagious childhood diseases, what is necessary is the use of "quarantines" and other forms of involuntary restraints and treatment. The starting point is the realization that tuberculosis is a threat to public health "*par excellence*" (Davis 1995). As far as I know, however, only New York City has clear-cut legislation in this regard (at least at this time). The following course of action is supported by this new legislation:

> The City Department of Public Health may order a person removed to a hospital or detained for treatment there only if two conditions are met. First, the Department must have found the tuberculosis to be active and without treatment likely to be transmitted to others. . . . Second, the Department must have found the subject of the order unable or unwilling to undergo less restrictive treatment (Davis 1995).

The above requirements are based on "epidemiological or clinical evidence, X-rays or laboratory tests," and the final decision to commit rests with the courts in a way parallel to that designed to ensure commitment for mental illness (Davis 1995). Note that, in order to restrain the liberty of risk imposers in this context, it is not necessary to "prove" they have harmed someone in a court of law; it is sufficient to demonstrate that they and their activities are hazardous and potentially harmful to the public. Depending on the response of the infectious person to requests to be treated, the interests of public health may be served by "civil confinement for treatment," which in turn may be justified as preventing harm to the public through "reckless endangerment" (Davis 1995). In fact, jail could justifiably be used to stop the endangerment for anyone who might resist the suggested "civil confinement for treatment."

How can this situation help us conceptualize the problem of imposing restraints on those endangering the public through environmentally hazardous practices? First, we need to note that some public threats cannot be controlled through democratic institutions, that is, through *voluntary* public choices. One may counter that even the imposition of forced restraints is embedded in a general system of individual rights and democratic institutions. That is, of course, correct. But it is important to understand that rights to life and health are primary and should be put ahead of other choices and preferences. This perspective allows us to view environmental endangerment as something that needs to be controlled directly and even by coercive means, rather than something that is simply to be limited only by cost–benefit analyses or by a counting of heads and a weighing of preferences. To explain detention in medical cases, Davis (1995) says, "The alternative to detention is the moral equivalent of letting someone, without adequate justification, walk crowded streets with a large bomb that could go off at any moment."

In the "white death" threats, we are not sure of the gravity of the harm imposed; we cannot anticipate just who is at risk from the infected person with any certainty; we cannot be sure of precise numbers of potentially affected persons; we have information about risks and harms, but we cannot present a specific infected person or persons as "proof," to justify placing the risk imposer under criminal restraints. The reason and the only reason we can offer for imposing criminal restraints or civil restraints is reckless endangerment, without being able to point to one or many persons who might have been harmed.

In fact, it is in order *not* to have "victims" that we are justified in invoking civil and criminal restraints. Contrast this preventive approach with that of corporate bodies who expose persons in their immediate vicinity of their hazardous operations to risks of harms but who *demand* not proof of endangerment but clear proof of *actual harm* before they are even prepared to compensate, let alone to consider discontinuing their hazardous activities.

Much more could be said about this topic, and it is fair to say that there are disanalogies as well as analogies between cases in biomedical ethics, allowing justification for restraints in cases of reckless endangerment, and the imposition of environmental risks and harms. Perhaps the most problematic difference is that, while one person's "restraints" will only affect her life (and provide a much greater benefit in the process), restraints of corporate activities on a grand scale might have grave repercussions for all stakeholders, not only the corporation subject to restraints. Nevertheless, it seems that there are enough parallels to make a reasonable case for considering seriously the approach I suggest, for all others employed so far appear to have met with scant success.

THE GOOD AND THE COMMUNITY: LAWS RESTRAINING CHOICE

The argument I have proposed essentially contrasts individualism with communitarianism. But the latter is

viewed as a special case: the case of a community of life, whereby each individual's personal integrity and the ecological integrity of her habitat are so completely intertwined that no question can be raised about whether the value of integrity in each case is intrinsic or instrumental. Rolston (1996) makes this point eloquently in his philosophical analysis of "biological immunity":

> The organismic integrity protected by immunity has to fit into an ecosystemic integrity. An organism without a habitat is soon extinct. The immune system is zealously defending the self, but all the while the ecosystem in which this self lives is the fundamental unit of development and survival. There are no immune organisms, period; there are only immune organisms-in-ecosystems.

From the perspective of immunity, our strong individual rights to life and self-defense can easily be extended to our habitat, in line with Rolston's proposed definition of our organisms as "organisms-in-ecosystems." Hence, to invoke stronger, changed laws appears entirely defensible on grounds of self-defense. These laws must replace laws that place economically driven, unintended harms, slowly unfolding over time, in a separate category so that only clear, quickly evident and intended harms are deemed to be criminal. Attacks on our bodily integrity and our genetic capacities are also crimes; they might be defined as attacks on our capacities as a small *c*, embedded in the capital *C*, or the capacities of ecological integrity. In my previous work, the collaborative definition of integrity used the letter *C* to represent the undiminished capacities of an ecosystem in its unmanipulated state, following its natural evolutionary trajectory, free, as much as possible, from human interference or stress.

To better understand the sort of crime described in these "attacks," we may invoke the difference between premeditated murder and manslaughter. It seems intuitively true to say that pain and suffering aside, no one has the right to remove someone else's organs for their own purposes, no matter how "good" the perpetrators may perceive their purpose to be. It would seem equally intuitively true to add that it is equally impermissible to intrusively interfere with the natural functions of these organs. When the damage caused is more than damage to one individual but it becomes, as in the cases researched by Theo Colborn (Colborn et al. 1996), damage to reproductive capacities, to the next generations, hence to humanity in general, it becomes a case of attempted genocide, deserving even more than the punishment of the laws of the perpetrators' country: It requires that they be accountable to and punished by a world tribunal.

Surely, if there is a good that is not in doubt, it is the right we have to our own physical and intellectual capacities undiminished by others. This common good is neither based on the preferences of one culture or another, nor limited to any relative viewpoint, as it is compatible with a great variety of cultural "goods" and ideals. Hence, I propose our undiminished capacities c, as a basic good that permits with varying degrees of appropriateness a number of societal coercive actions, parallel to those needed to support the ecological integrity it requires to thrive C. This "good" may also be compatible with moral theories such as the Kantian respect for autonomously chosen ends and the Rawlsian emphasis on fairness and the difference principle. These possible connections need to be examined in some detail.

What does Rawls (1975) say about the good? His understanding may raise problems:

> That we have one conception of the good rather than another is not relevant from a moral standpoint. In acquiring it we are influenced by the same sort of contingencies that leads us to rule out a knowledge of our sex and class.

The defense of life through individual and systemic integrity may not be in conflict with a variety of conceptions of the good. But the wholesale acceptance of the possibility of any and all such "conceptions of the good" may well conflict with the spirit of the principle of integrity, in the same sense that utilitarianism also does. Michael Sandel (1982) examines the "status of the good" in Rawls. He argues:

> For Rawls, utilitarianism goes wrong not in conceiving the good as the satisfaction of arbitrarily given desires, undifferentiated as to worth—for justice as fairness shares in this, but only in being indifferent to the way these consummations are spread across individuals.

Although Rawls, in Sandel's estimation, departs from utilitarianism, the remaining connection with "the satisfaction of arbitrarily given desires" is—at best—compatible with the primacy of life, as the necessary prerequisite to the existence of "desires." But it is not compatible with the nonnegotiable status of the principle of integrity (PI). Some may argue, for instance, that the desire to accept a trade-off between diminished health, life span or genetic capacities, and economic advantage, if well understood, is legitimate for a society. Some may also argue that this is precisely what is happening in affluent democracies at this time; hence, only the *distributive* aspect of this "contract" should be scrutinized from the standpoint of morality, not its existence.

In contrast, the PI takes a strongly Kantian position in not permitting such trade-offs, whether or not they are fairly distributed across society. The basis of the principle of integrity is the value of integrity, which encompasses the infinite value of all life, of life-support systems, and of individual and systemic capacities, now and into the future. This excludes the possibility of legitimate trade-offs and places those concerns at the forefront of both morality and public policy. The primacy and the centrality of this value explains the emphasis on the need for national laws and for global regulative mechanisms to protect it as an absolute, rather than treating it as one value among many, subject to public choice or majoritarian preferences.

The holistic perspective is absolutely vital here: Life-support systems cannot be protected in piecemeal fashion. When hazards travel between continents, not only countries, clearly national policies will be insufficient. Global regulations and tight global security will also be required to prevent the present techno-hazard transfer between North American and Western European countries and Southeast Asian ones and into economically depressed minority areas in the affluent countries. An interesting parallel may be found in recent improvement in Canadian legislation directed at serial criminals of a special kind: the sexual predators.

One of the most horrible cases in Canada (1988–1994) saw Paul Bernardo and his wife Karla Homolka involved in terrible crimes over a lengthy period because of Bernardo's change of venue during his "career" as a rapist, torturer, and murderer. He was eventually found guilty of a series of viciously sadistic rapes in a Toronto suburb, which earned him the title of "Scarborough rapist." The DNA evidence that eventually implicated him, however, was neglected at one location when he moved to another, on the west side of Toronto, to St. Catharines, Ontario, about 50 kilometers away. There he met and married Homolka in a storybook wedding where the young, attractive couple, both blonde and blue-eyed, appeared to be the epitome of "nice" middle-class Canadians. But when Homolka's 15-year-old sister died under suspicious circumstances at their parents' home on Christmas Eve (with Karla and Bernardo in attendance) and two other schoolgirls 14 and 15 years old were eventually abducted, with only their remains found weeks later, it should have been clear that the Scarborough's rapist's career was not over. Because different police forces in different areas were involved in the investigations, the connection was not made in time to prevent at least the last two grisly murders.

Eventually, tapes recording the horror of the girls' sexual assaults and torture were discovered, and the wife, a full participant and assistant in the crimes and the abductions, testified against the husband (*The Globe and Mail* 1995). The similarity between the case of sexual predators, now the subject of a commissioned inquiry, and the hazardous practices described earlier in this essay is that both are cases of system failure. This can obviously occur even when the crimes committed are already in the criminal code as such; and even such cases cannot be easily stopped because of failures in coordination. We also need to take very seriously the crimes of ecoviolence that are not even properly treated as such now because they can lead to serial recurrences, with almost complete impunity to the perpetrators. According to Justice Archie Campbell, Head of the Commission reporting on serial predators, from 1988 to 1994, the name of Bernardo and a series of similar crimes kept "coming up." But lacking an investigative body capable of and charged with coordinating the findings of various jurisdictions, Bernardo was able to "throw investigations off stride by the simple act of moving from one police jurisdiction to another." Judge Campbell wrote, "When Bernardo stopped stalking, raping and killing in Toronto and started stalking, raping and killing in St. Catharines and Burlington, he might as well have moved to another country for a fresh start" (I. Ross, *The Globe and Mail* 1996).

Justice Campbell's remarks bring to mind the legal corporate practices that are taken for granted: Corporations simply close down one operation and move out to another location, often in a less developed country, which they perceive as less demanding in their environmental regulations. Perhaps the corporation has been charged and fined for repeated environmental infractions. Unfortunately for all of us, the move does not herald an increased environmental concern or a newly found respect for human life and its habitat. The move is most often followed by practices indicating the same disregard for human and ecological safety that led to the original problems.

As long as the charges are viewed as creating economic externalities only (and moving and reorganizing expenses are tax-deductible), the immorality becomes institutionalized, simply another way of doing business. Even repeated offenses, in different venues, cause little discomfort unless the public becomes aware of the infractions through some spectacular accident; and even then, there is no extradition for noncriminal cases. Like sexual predators, corporate predators can simply move and resume the activities that forced the move with little or no fear of retribution.

If even in criminal cases (short of murder, perhaps) it is far too easy to inflict great harm repeatedly on an unprotected public, then the move to criminalize hazardous practices, as a first step, appears inevitable. Like serial predators, corporations gain confidence and ability through repeated, almost routine moves. Unlike the average predator, they possess large resources that can be mobilized and utilized in defense of their goals. Hence, it is vital to recognize that good personal or corporate morality and conscience must be encouraged and supported through laws that will force those who lack such virtues to comply.

Therefore, to affirm the urgent need for strict global regulations for the protection of public life, health, and integrity is not to commit the hasty generalization of tarring all corporations, good and bad, with the same brush. It is intended to recognize the primacy of individual and ecological integrity and to attempt to coordinate

and institutionalize principles and ideals that are already, for the most part, present in global regulations and in national and international laws. In essence it is to recognize the role of a holistic perceptive in public decision making (Brown 1995).

Bibliography

Ayres, E. "The Expanding Shadow Economy," *Worldwatch,* (July/August 1996): 11–23.

Barnes, C. "Consent Theory: Can One Consent to Be Harmed?" Unpublished paper, presented at the University of Windsor, 1996.

Brown, D., and J. Lemons, eds. 1995. *Sustainable Development: Science Ethics and Public Policy.* Dordrecht, The Netherlands: Kluwer, 1995.

Bullard, R. *Dumping in Dixie.* Boulder, CO: Westview Press, 1994.

Colborn, Theo. "Plenary Address" to the International Association of Great Lakes Researchers, Erindale College, Toronto, May 27, 1996.

Colborn, Theo, Dianne Dumanoski, and John Peterson Myers. *Our Stolen Future.* New York: Dutton, 1996.

Colwell, Rita. "Global Change: Emerging Diseases and New Epidemics." President's Lecture, American Association for the Advancement of Science (AMSIE '96), February 1996.

Davis, M. "Arresting the White Death: Involuntary Patients, Public Health, and Medical Ethics." Paper presented at the central meeting of the American Philosophical Association, April 1995.

DeCew, J. "Rights and Risks." Comments on A. Ellis's "Risks and Rights." Unpublished paper. 1995.

Donaldson, Thomas. "Moral Minimums for Multinations." In *Ethical Issues in Business,* edited by T. Donaldson and P. Werhane. Englewood Cliffs, NJ: Prentice Hall, 1993, 58–75.

Ellis, Anthony. "Risks and Rights." Paper presented at the central meeting of the American Philosophical Association, April 1995.

French, P. A. *Collective and Corporate Responsibility.* New York: Columbia University Press, 1984.

Friedman, Milton. "The Social Responsibility of Business Is to Increase Its Profits." In *Ethical Issues in Business,* edited by T. Donaldson and P. Werhane. Englewood Cliffs, NJ: Prentice Hall, 1993, 249–254.

Gaylord, C., and E. Bell, "Environmental Justice: A National Priority." In *Faces of Environmental Racism,* edited by L. Westra and P. Wenz. Lanham, MD: Rowman & Littlefield, 1995.

Gewirth, A. "Human Rights and the Prevention of Cancer." In *Human Rights.* Chicago: University of Chicago Press, 1983, 181–217.

Gilbert, Paul. *Terrorism, Security and Nationality.* London: Routledge, 1995.

Hobbes, Thomas. *Leviathan.* New York: Bobbs-Merrill, 1958.

Hohfeld, W. N. *Fundamental Legal Conceptions.* New Haven, CT: Yale University Press, 1923.

Homer-Dixon, Thomas. "On the Threshold: Environmental Changes as Causes of Acute Conflict." *International Security* 16, no. 2 (Fall 1991): 76–116.

Homer-Dixon, Thomas. "Environmental Scarcity and Violent Conflict: Evidence from Cases." *International Security* 19, No. 1 (Summer 1994): 5–40.

Homer-Dixon, Thomas, in Hurst, Lyda, "The Global Guru," *The Toronto Star*, July 20, 1996, "Insight," pp C1 and C5.

Ingelfinger, Franz L. "Informed (but Uneducated) Consent." In *Biomedical Ethics*, edited by J. Zembaty and T. Mappes. eds., 1991, 220–221.

Kant, Immanuel. *The Metaphysical Elements of Justice.* New York: Bobbs-Merrill, 1965.

Kant, Immanuel. *On the Old Saw.* Philadelphia: University of Pennsylvania Press, 1974.

Kant, Immanuel. *Lectures on Ethics*, translated by Louis Infield. Indianapolis: Hackett, 1979, pp. 116–126 ("Duties to Oneself"); and pp. 157–160 ("Duties towards the Body Itself").

Korten, David. *When Corporations Rule the World.* West Hartford, CT: Kumarian Press, Berret Koehler Publishers, 1995.

Martin, Rex. *A System of Rights.* New York: Clarendon Press/Oxford University Press, 1993.

McMichael, Anthony J. *Planetary Overload.* Cambridge, UK: Cambridge University Press, 1995.

Mesthene, Emmanuel G. "The Role of Technology in Society." In *Technology and the Future*, 5th ed., edited by A. Teich. New York: St. Martin's Press, 1990, pp. 77–99.

Nikiforuk, A. "Arctic Pollution: Poisons for a Pristine Land." *The Globe and Mail* (July 20, 1996), D8.

Rawls, J. "The Law of Peoples" In *On Human Rights.* New York: Basic Books/HarperCollins, 1993, pp. 41–82.

Rawls, J. "From Fairness to Goodness." *Philosophical Review*, 1984 (1975): 536–554.

Rolston, Holmes, III. "Immunity in Natural History." In *Perspectives in Biology and Medicine* 39, no. 3 (Spring 1996): 353–372.

Sandel, Michael. *Liberalism and the Limits of Justice.* Cambridge, MA: Cambridge University Press, 1982.

Shrader-Frechette, K. *Risk and Rationality.* Berkeley, CA: University of California Press, 1991.

Simmons, A. John. *Moral Principles and Political Obligations.* Englewood Cliffs, NJ: Princeton University Press, 1979.

Simon, Thomas. "Group Harm." *Journal of Social Philosophy* 26, no. 3 (Winter 1995): 123–139.

Thomson, J. J. *The Realm of Rights.* Cambridge, MA: Harvard University Press, 1990.

Westra, L. *An Environmental Proposal for Ethics: The Principle of Integrity.* Lanham MD: Rowman & Littlefield, 1994a.

Westra, L. "Risky Business: Corporate Responsibility and Hazardous Products." *Business Ethics Quarterly* 4, no. 1, (1994b): 97–110.

Westra, L. "Ecosystem Integrity and Sustainability: The Foundational Value of the Wild." In *Perspectives on Ecological Integrity*, edited by L. Westra and J. Lemons. Dordrecht, The Netherlands: Kluwer, 1995a, pp. 12–33.

Westra, L. "Integrity, Health and Sustainability: Environmentalism Without Racism." In *The Science of the Total Environment.* Oxford, UK: Elsevier, for the World Health Organization, 1996.

Wigley, D., and Shrader-Frechette, K. "Consent, Equity and Environmental Justice: A Louisiana Case Study." In *Faces of Environmental Racism*, edited by L. Westra and P. Wenz. 1995. *The Faces of Environmental Racism: The Global Equity Issues*, Lanham, MD: Rowman & Littlefield, 1995, pp. 135–162.

Winner, Langdon. *Autonomous Technology.* Cambridge, MA: MIT Press, 1977.

Study Questions

1. Is Westra correct about the failure of democracies to deal with environmental degradation and risk?
2. Are there natural rights? What are they? Do we have a right against others that they not impose risks of harm on us, as Westra argues? Or is Thomson correct in rejecting such a right?
3. Is Westra's solution threatening to democracy itself?

81

Environmental Ethics and Democracy: A Response to Westra

Eugene Hargrove

Eugene Hargrove is professor of philosophy at the University of North Texas and the editor of Environmental Ethics. Among his many works is Foundations of Environmental Ethics *(1989).*

In this essay, Hargrove argues, contrary to Westra, that democracies, though imperfect, are the best political means we have to cope with the environmental degradation that is befalling us. He agrees with Westra that democracies can be guilty of the "tyranny of the majority" and undermine minority rights, but he argues that it is far worse to be coerced by undemocratic forces, "the tyranny of the minority," including the "tyranny of experts." In behalf of this pro-democracy thesis, he cites examples where an effective marriage of environmentalism and democracy are making a difference in protecting the environment. Hargrove also discusses the strategies of the environmentalists who call for higher ecological standards and the economists who call for better economic incentives to be good stewards of the environment.

There is a long history of concern about environmentalism as a threat to democracy. In 1977 William Ophuls, for example, wrote that "the return of scarcity portends the revival of age-old political evils, for our descendants if not for ourselves. In short, the golden age of individualism, liberty and democracy is all but over."[1] Similarly, in 1974 Robert Heilbronner wrote that democracy will be unable to handle the "mighty pressures and constraints" of the environmental crisis, requiring us to seek a new form of government. He continues:

> I must confess that I can picture only one such system. This is a social order that will blend a "religious" orientation with a "military" discipline. Such a monastic organization of society may be repugnant to us, but I suspect it offers the greatest promise for bringing about the profound and painful adaptations that the coming generations must make.[2]

In environmental ethics literature, in 1974 John Passmore echoed the same concern overtly in defense of democracy against environmentalism.[3] Passmore's worry that environmentalism will destroy democracy originates in part in his reading of Garret Hardin's essay, "The Tragedy of the Commons," from *Science* in 1968, in which Hardin calls for "mutual coercion, mutually agreed upon."[4] Although the words "mutually agreed upon" suggest to me that democracy might still be in place in Hardin's scenario, Passmore keys in on "mutual coercion" as an end to political freedom instead. He envisions a slippery slope of alternative possibilities:

1. This project is not feasible unless there is a change of government.
2. This project is not feasible without a change in certain of our political institutions.
3. This project is not feasible except in a totalitarian State.[5]

Passmore ultimately concludes that "our political experience does not suggest that a highly centralized system, communicating with the general public only at the bureaucratic level . . . is a desirable form of government."

> No doubt [such a government] can legislate firmly but it has an enormous inertia; it is highly resistant to change. To change, unless it is going to act tyrannically, it has first to secure agreement across an immense variety of conflicting interests. Experiments at the local government or at the national level can and do spread, should they be successful. But it is hard enough to get them accepted in the first place even at that level. Imagine the situation if the whole of Europe to say nothing of the rest of the world, had first to be convinced that censorship should be abolished, before it could anywhere be abolished. A small community can be tyrannical in the extreme, hostile to any form of enterprise or experiment. But at least there is some hope of escaping from it; the thought of a world government, from whose rules there is no escape, must fill anyone who cares about freedom with horror. Better a polluted world than this![6]

The threat of environmentalism to democracy has been discussed at length by Robert Paehlke in his essay "Democracy, Bureaucracy, and Environmentalism."[7] Examining in some detail the activities of the environmental movements in Canada, the United States, and Germany in particular, Paehlke concludes that, despite the fear of environmental totalitarianism, environmentalists have endlessly demonstrated support of democracy and have everywhere expanded democratic institutions, particularly, through their support of the right to know: "a reasoned and principled inclination of many environmental organizations to the open administration of environmental resource policies" in contrast to the earlier conservationists' faith "on expert administration and governmental bureaucracies."[8] This openness has emphasized public hearings and referendums in the United States, royal commissions in Canada, and a viable political party in Germany. As Holmes Rolston, III, writing in 1988, points out in *Environmental Ethics*, in his chapter on "Environmental Policy," there has been "steady enactment of environmentally oriented legislation" for more than a quarter century. To make his point, he lists four pages of legislation single-spaced beginning with the Clean Air Act in 1985 and ending with additions to the Clean Air Act in 1987.[9] Today Rolston could just as easily point to nearly a century and a half of environmental legislation beginning with the creation of Yellowstone and Yosemite as national parks in the United States.

Paehlke concludes that "democracy may well be the best political tool humankind has developed for mobilizing populations, especially educated and moderately prosperous populations,"[10] tools that environmentalists regularly use. Indeed, these democratic techniques have been so successful that they are now being mimicked at the international on behalf of the drafting and ratifying of the Earth Charter. As Steven Rockefeller puts it,

> . . . when the Charter has been drafted it will be circulated throughout the world as a people's treaty in the hope that millions of people and numerous religious organizations and NGOs will embrace and sign it. With a strong showing of popular support, it should be possible to achieve approval by the United Nations.[11]

In defense of the effective marriage of environmentalism and democracy, I would like to cite two examples: the protection of the Adirondacks in New York in the 1890s and the scuttling of a dam in Missouri in 1978. When the Adirondacks suddenly became the target for clear-cutting in the 1890s, the people of the state of New York responded by passing a law to prevent logging abuses in the area. When lawyers for the lumber companies found legal loopholes, the people responded once again with an amendment to the state constitution making the area forever wild and free. In Missouri in the 1970s, when it became clear that the building of the Merimac Dam was opposed by a large majority of the state, the governor and legislature established a referendum in which only those who would benefit from the dam economically, the local counties, and those who would presumably spend the money there, the people of the city of St. Louis, would be permitted to vote. Assuming that the referendum would pass handily, proponents of the dam got all politicians of the state to agree to abide by the results of the referendum forever. To the surprise of everyone, the referendum failed by a two to one margin overall and without a majority vote in favor in any county that would have been benefited economically.

Because there are innumerable environmental successes that can be pointed to as successes of democracy,

the suggestion that liberal democracy has failed environmentally is a bit misleading. Laura Westra writes, "Democracy entails that collective decisions be based on open acceptance of certain choices and preferences over others, and that these choices be legitimized by majority votes."[12] Essentially, Westra's claim is that democracy is the tyranny of the majority. In faulting democracy, however, Westra overlooks the many positive connections between democracy and environmentalism and the fact that alternatives to the majority-rule approach are as likely to be subject to tyranny. Increasing the number of people who must vote in favor of some issue could paralyze government by making agreement impossible. Eliminating the need for a majority vote, on the other hand, invites tyranny from a minority. As Passmore puts it, "The view that ecological problems are more likely to be solved in an authoritarian than in . . . a liberal democratic society rests on the implausible assumption that the authoritarian state would be ruled by ecologist-kings." He adds, "In practice there is more hope of action in democratic societies."[13]

To be sure, the requirement in democratic society that absolute agreement is not required for political action does open the door to the tyranny of the majority if that majority decides to take advantage of the minority. Generally, however, this circumstance is avoided by providing citizens protection in the form of rights. Westra argues, nevertheless, that "Notwithstanding the close links between civil rights and democracy, on both practical and theoretical grounds democratic practices appear insufficient to protect us from endangerment caused by reckless practices of individuals and corporate citizens."[14]

In response to Westra's claim, I examine several questions. First, is there any particular relationships between rights and democracy that is different from the relationship of rights with any other form of government? Second, are the protection of rights part of the democratic process? Third, is protecting rights an effective way to solve environmental problems?

Concerning the first, it seems to me that rights have no relationship of any kind with democracy that is any different than they have with any other form of government. The idea of political and moral rights is a confusing one, both conceptually and historically. Passmore, for example, confesses in a note in *Man's Responsibility for Nature* that he is troubled by the apparent dogmatism of his own observations.[15] As I have noted elsewhere, ancient Germanic freemen had a right to the use of land, according to which they were not "beholden to any superior."[16] Apparently, in the Late Middle Ages, these Germanic rights to land use were generalized to include other rights, which had previously been regarded as privileges. Because this change from privileges to rights occurred at a time when large nation-states were developing in Europe, it is reasonable to conclude that rights developed as a protection against big government. As such, there is and will always be a natural conflict between a rights perspective and any form of government, including democracy, since the point of political rights is to limit the power of government in general. This historical point seems to be consistent with the spirit of the UN Universal Declaration on Human Rights, which is aimed at promoting rights for human beings in all societies regardless of the forms of government in those particular societies.

Concerning whether rights are or should be part of the democratic process, it is true that rights are often created through a legislative process, possibly by legislators who are elected democratically, and enforced by an executive branch, possibly run at the highest levels by elected officials. However, because it is also possible that rights could be created and enforced in countries that are not considered democratic, the creation and enforcement of rights is technically no different in democratic and nondemocratic societies.

A more significant issue might be whether democracy has a special obligation, different than that of other forms of government, to enforce rights. Certainly, a democracy has a special obligation to enforce rights, particularly if those rights were created by that government and the laws formulating those rights specify action to be taken by that government as enforcement. In most cases, however, rights are enforced through litigation in courts, which themselves are not part of the democratic process. Courts exist in many forms of government and the form of those court systems seem to be independent of whether a country is democratic or not. Finally, when the litigation begins, the results depend on the merits of the case, the manner in which the rights are defined, and the precedents that have evolved over time. Although the former Soviet Union was a totalitarian system, it did offer its citizens free legal support for appeals up to its supreme court.

Finally, are rights an effective way to solve environmental problems? While it is possible that rights may be able to play an important role, to date they have not. Paehlke, for example, in his book on democracy, *Environmentalism and the Future of Progressive Politics,*[17] makes no reference to rights at all; and in his massive encyclopedia on conservation and environmentalism, he provides discussion only of the community right to know and the right to know in the workplace.[18] These rights are involved in Westra's concern with consent to risk, especially in the workplace, but the environmentalist concern has predominantly been a right to know as a determinant in policy formation. It could be that environmentalists should refocus their approach to deal more directly with a wide range of rights, but their failure to deal with rights up to this point is not clearly a failure of democracy.

The key issue for environmentalists, in the area that Westra is primarily concerned with, "the reckless practices of individuals and corporate citizens," has been a struggle over standards and incentives. This struggle is a battle between environmentalists and economists. As Steven Kelman has demonstrated in *What Price Incentives? Economists and the Environment*, environmentalists favor standards over incentives largely for moral reasons: they wish to stigmatize polluting behavior rather than forgive it in return for penance through the payment of fines or licenses.[19] The response of economists is that pollution can be more effectively (i.e., efficiently) reduced by providing financial incentives.[20] Environmentalists, however, have been unmoved, since they intend repeatedly to establish higher standards each time the current ones are met. Their goal is not to help industry find the level of pollution that is most financially agreeable but rather to require industry to operate at the lowest level of pollution that is technically feasible. Although industrial polluters remain perpetually guilty as new standards are put into place as the old are met, they do not always find the standards approach objectionable since it provides a level playing field in which the ability to compete in the market is determined by the ability of their engineering staff to develop the technology needed to meet the new standards. Voluntary improvements in pollution levels, in contrast, could easily put "good" companies out of business if the additional costs of new pollution controls increased the price of their products, making them uncompetitive. Under the standards approach, companies also have the option of asking for additional time when standards are inadvertently raised too quickly.

The standard/incentives debate is related to rights both directly and indirectly. The incentives approach is essentially a right or privilege to pollute that permits the polluter to choose the level of pollution most compatible with their financial situations. In this sense, environmentalists are trying to prevent the establishment of a right to pollute. Indirectly, moreover, the standards approach supports the interests of the individuals by keeping pollution at the lowest level that is technically possible and provides a mechanism, the raising of standards, when new technology becomes available. Indeed, the standards approach can force the creation of new technology by requiring industry to meet new standards within a specific time. Here the concern is not what is most efficient but what is best for society and the citizens that make up that society. I submit that this standards approach is more effective than a straightforward rights approach because there is a mechanism for raising standards, by legislation, which is more dependable than changes in rights through the judicial system. While a court might increase rights in a manner that would be comparable to the raising of standards through legislation, such a change would be an unusual event. It is very unlikely that a series of court decisions would increase environmental protection through rights comparable to that available through increases in standards through legislation.

Westra's concern about rights is primarily a concern about environmental justice. To be sure, the environmental movement has been little interested in this issue with its focus on wilderness preservation and its misanthropic inclinations. It is difficult to generate environmental concern for human minorities among environmentalists if they feel that the existence of human beings in general, including themselves, is damaging to nature.

Mark Sagoff, nevertheless, has effectively bridged this gap in many respects. His views can therefore serve as an indication of what the environmental movement needs to accomplish in the future. There is another kind of tyranny in addition to the tyranny of the majority: tyranny of the experts. There are two kinds of experts involved: economists and scientists. The first of these are intent on promoting the "free" market independent of democratic institutions. Supposedly, the end to regulation of the market by government will produce the optimal economic state. Sagoff has countered this claim in a number of ways: First with history. It is, he notes, the transactions of the free market "that lead to child labor, the sixteen-hour workday, and hideous workplace conditions."[21] Second, the hybrid system that has evolved depends on economic experts who measure the personal preferences of individuals in a state of ignorance. As Sagoff notes, economists in testing for preferences typically withhold information, preventing informed consent, because doing so would likely obscure the arbitrary feelings of test subjects, hiding them behind rational judgment.[22] The preferences of individuals are unpredictable when they are permitted to think about issues on the basis of information. Finally, according to Sagoff, the economists make a categorical mistake in adopting this approach: by confusing personal consumer preferences with public citizen preferences.[23] In short, Sagoff argues that what people want as consumers may not be what they would vote for as citizens. He therefore recommends as a partial cure "the democratic alternative."[24] Examples of the success of this alternative are the vote against the Merimac dam and the protection of the Adirondacks.

There are, however, other problems that cannot be solved so easily by votes or the collection of frivolous consumer preferences. These involve medical issues about the emission of dangerous chemicals, one of Westra's chief concerns. Although workers are frequently asked to give up years of their lives in return for work,[25] producing work for the economist who make these gruesome calculations, the main issues are not preferences but science. The work of these experts is not much more sophisticated than that of the economists. Douglas Crawford-Brown and Neil Pearce, for example, in "Sufficient Proof in the Scientific Justification of Environmental Actions," have shown that in the development of standards for radon in drinking water, EPA scientists made four value judgments in the course of their deliberations:

. . . (1) the choice of an explanatory theory of the environment and its relation to human health, (2) the choice of the formalization of that theory into a mathematical equation, (3) the choice of the past experience to use in determining the value of any parameters in the equation, and (4) the choice to consider the equation truly explanatory not only for past experience, but in predicting the risk associated with new levels of radon of regulatory interest.[26]

Any one, if changed slightly, could have produced a different conclusion that radon is very dangerous or not dangerous at all or some other point in between. It is this kind of problem that people seeking environmental justice encounter. Demonstrating that emissions of various kinds cause harm that require compensation is difficult and is a scientific question, not a political one, involving the choices that the scientists who produce the studies to determine the level of harm are willing to make.

Imagine that a paint-manufacturing company opens a factory next to a small community and soon thereafter the residents begin to note strange smells in the air when they go out in their backyards. At first they are simply repulsed by the smells, but soon they begin thinking that perhaps the chemical producing the smells may be harmful to their health and that of their children. They worry that someday they will get cancer from these chemicals. Assume that these residents have been given rights to protect them from harm by their government, democratic or not. If so, they can join together to sue the company to cease releasing the emissions. To be successful, however, they need to enlist the help of scientists to study the contaminants, the levels in the air, and the risk of cancer to the community. Perhaps there are already studies of these chemicals that can reduce the scientific effort to simply showing that the level is not permissible. If it is a new chemical, however, it may be very difficult to demonstrate harm on a timely basis. To show that cigarettes are significantly related to lung cancer took many years and the generation of statistical information spanning many decades. The number of people affected by the paint emissions may not be large enough to count as an adequate scientific sampling. Furthermore, decades may be required to demonstrate the statistical probability of harm. If they must prove their case by dying 30 years from now, immediate relief from the courts may be out of the question.

There is nevertheless a viable alternative. In Garland, Texas, for example, the city redefined pollution to include substances that inhibit the enjoyment of property, animals, or vegetation. In doing so, they eliminated the need for a scientific risk determination. The issue was no longer whether the residents would someday get cancer, but whether being in their backyards had ceased to be an enjoyable experience. To be sure, science still played a role. Scientists still determined the levels of contaminants in the air and tied those chemicals to the plant's emissions. Further, levels of contaminants were determined and shown to be related to the times residents found their backyards to have unpleasant odors. This aesthetic approach was successful. The company moved part of the process temporarily to another location, and the redesigned plant was back in operation without the unpleasant emissions 18 months later.[27]

Westra is correct that the environmental movement has not been very effective in defending environmental rights. There is, however, reason to think that it could effectively do so if it chose to try. Historically, the environmental movement has been a movement made up of politically advantaged citizens, and its focus has been on natural rather than urban areas. It has involved the powerful, for example, Theodore Roosevelt, and those with powerful connections, for example, John Muir and Gifford Pinchott. Although such people were little troubled with the issues that Westra is concerned, those involving environmental justice, it is probably a historical accident that they were not. James Nickel and Eduardo Viola have shown that a coalition of the civil rights movement and environmental movement in South America would be advantageous to both groups.[28] Troy Hartley similarly has argued that main reason such a coalition has not occurred in the United States is more a matter of style than of substance. The civil rights movement

> viewed the environmental movement with distaste. . . . The environmental movement was viewed as an establishment-sponsored concern designed to divert attention from fundamental civil rights. The civil rights movement preferred civil disobedience and economic boycotts to the willingness to negotiate with governments and the private sector embraced by the environmental movement.[29]

A coalition of the environmental and civil rights movements, both in democratic and nondemocratic countries, could go a long way toward solving the environmental justice issues with which Westra is concerned.

To sum up, the environmental movement has been very closely associated with the expansion of democratic institutions and with one right, the right to know, and has been little concerned with the urban environment and the environmental justice issues that arise there. The civil rights movement in contrast has been little concerned with democracy, since the protection of rights is generally carried out through litigation in court. Although democracy established civil rights in the United States, the courts rather than the government are the primary protectors of those rights. To charge that democratic institutions have failed to protect rights misconstrue the purpose of rights, which is protection of citizens from their government through legal recourse. To be sure, democracy could further increase the number of environmental rights, but once those rights were legislated the task of defending those rights falls primarily in the hands of the courts, as it does in nondemocratic countries.

There is no simple solution to our environmental problems. Democracy, where it exists, can and will continue to play an important role, as will the courts in both democratic and nondemocratic countries. Democracy may even play a role in the creation of new environmental rights. Nevertheless, it should be remembered that rights themselves are not necessarily a perfect solution, for rights can also be used to achieve immoral goals. Moreover, in some political arenas, it may be better to forge ahead without them. A Chinese student of mine once remarked that he did not think the Chinese people would ever *have a right* to a quality environment; however, he added, they might someday *have a duty* to maintain one.

Notes

1. William Ophuls, *Ecology and the Politics of Scarcity* (San Francisco: Freeman, 1997), 145.
2. Robert L. Heilbronner, *An Inquiry into the Human Prospect* (New York: Norton, 1974), 161.
3. John Passmore, *Man's Responsibility for Nature: Ecological Problems and Western Traditions* (New York: Scribner, 1974), esp. chap. 3.
4. Garrett Hardin, "The Tragedy of the Commons," *Science* 162 (1968): 1248.
5. Passmore, *Man's Responsibility for Nature*, op. cit., 59.
6. Ibid., 67.
7. Robert Paehlke, "Democracy, Bureaucracy, and Environmentalism," *Environmental Ethics* 10 (1988): 291–308.
8. Ibid., 295.
9. Holmes Rolston, III, *Environmental Ethics: Duties to and Values in the Natural World* (Philadelphia: Temple University Press, 1988), pp. 249–253.
10. Paehlke, "Democracy, Bureaucracy, and Environmentalism," op. cit., 306.
11. Steven C. Rockefeller, "Global Ethics, International Law, and the Earth Charter," *Earth Ethics* 7, nos. 3–4 (Spring/Summer 1996): 3.
12. Laura Westra, "Risks, Rights, and the Failure of Liberal Democracy," in *Environmental Ethics*, 2d ed., edited by L. P. Pojman (Belmont, CA: Wadsworth, 1997), Reading 80.
13. Passmore, *Man's Responsibility for Nature*, op. cit., 293.
14. Westra, "Failure of Liberal Democracy," op. cit.
15. Passmore, *Man's Responsibility for Nature*, op. cit., 116–117.
16. Eugene C. Hargrove, *Foundations of Environmental Ethics* (Denton, TX: Environmental Ethics Books, 1989), chap. 2.
17. Robert C. Paehlke, *Environmentalism and the Future of Progressive Politics* (New Haven, CT, and London: Yale University Press, 1989).

18. Robert C. Paehlke, ed., *Conservation and Environmentalism: An Encyclopedia* (New York and London: Garland, 1995), 566–568; 568–570.

19. Steven Kelman, *What Price Incentives? Economists and the Environment* (Boston: Auburn House, 1981), esp. 44–53.

20. See Allen V. Kneese's review of *What Price Incentives?* in *Environmental Ethics* 5 (1983): 271–275.

21. Mark Sagoff, *The Economy of the Earth: Philosophy, Law, and the Environment* (Cambridge: Cambridge University Press, 1988), 15.

22. Ibid., 81–88.

23. Ibid., 92–94.

24. Ibid., 95.

25. Ibid., 24.

26. Douglas Crawford-Brown and Neil E. Pearce, "Sufficient Proof in the Scientific Justification of Environmental Actions," *Environmental Ethics* 11 (1989): 156–157.

27. Personal communication, Richard Briley, Health Department, City of Garland.

28. James W. Nickel and Eduardo Viola, "Integrating Environmentalism and Human Rights," *Environmental Ethics* 16 (1994): 265–274.

29. Troy W. Hartley, "Environmental Justice: An Environmental Civil Rights Value Acceptable to All World Views," *Environmental Ethics* 17 (1995): 281–282, n. 16. Quoted from Richard P. Gale, "The Environmental Movement and the Left: Antagonists or Allies?" *Sociological Inquiry* 53 (1983): 179–199.

Study Questions

1. Compare Hargrove's article with Westra's. How do they differ regarding their assessment of the problem and the possibility of a solution? Compare their views on the importance of rights. Who has the better arguments? Explain your answer.

2. Hargrove gives examples of environmentalism and democracy working together for the common good. What lessons can we learn from these examples?

3. What is the debate between "standards and incentives" that Hargrove discusses (regarding environmentalists vs. economists)? Which is the better tool to use in promoting ecological well-being? Is a combination of both possible?

82

An Ecological Critique of Global Advertising

Alan Thein Durning

Alan Thein Durning is a senior researcher at Worldwatch Institute in Washington, D.C., and the author of How Much Is Enough? The Consumer Society and the Future of the Earth. *In this essay, he argues that advertising promotes consumerism, which creates artificial needs in such a way as to undermine a sustainable society. While Durning does not condemn the idea of advertising itself, as a means of providing useful information, he argues that today's Madison Avenue experts have gone far beyond the limits of that function and instead are promoting a dangerous false consciousness.*

Last January a single message was broadcast simultaneously in every inhabited part of the globe. The message was not "love thy neighbor" or "thou shalt not kill." It was "Drink Coke."

This first global advertisement was, on the face of it, simply a piece of technical showmanship—an inevitable one, considering the pace of change in telecommunications. On a symbolic level, however, it was something

more. It was a neat encapsulation of the main trend in human communications worldwide: commercialization.

For better or for worse, almost all of humanity's 5.5 billion individuals, divided among 6,000 distinct cultures, are now soaking in the same gentle bath of advertising. The unctuous voices of the marketplace are insinuating themselves into ever more remote quarters of the globe and ever more private realms of human life.

Advertising has become one of the world's premier cultural forces. Almost every living person knew the word "Coke," for example, long before the global ad. Two years ago, the trade journal Adweek published a two-page spread depicting Hitler, Lenin, Napoleon, and a Coke bottle. "Only one," read the caption, "launched a campaign that conquered the world. How did Coke succeed when history's most ambitious leaders failed? By choosing the right weapon. Advertising."

Aside from the arrogance of that statement, what is disturbing about it is its truth. Owing to skillful and persistent marketing, Coke is sold in virtually every place people live. Go to the end of a rural road on any Third World continent, walk a day up a donkey trail to a hardscrabble village, and ask for a Coke. Odds are you'll get one. This state of affairs—development workers call it

Reprinted from *Worldwatch*, Vol. 6.3 (May–June, 1993) by permission of the Worldwatch Institute.

"Coca-Colonization"—means that Coke's secret formula has probably reached more villages and slums than has clean drinking water or oral rehydration formula

The point here is not to single out Coca-Cola—others would have circum-advertised the globe soon if the soft drink empire hadn't—but rather to question whether advertising has outgrown its legitimate role in human affairs. Advertisers maintain that their craft, far from being too widely practiced, is just beginning to achieve its destiny: to stimulate business growth, create jobs, and to unify humanity by eroding the ancient hatreds that divide us and joining us together in the universal fellowship of a Coke.

But from the perspective of the Earth's long-term health, the advertising industry looks somewhat different. Stripped to its essentials, contemporary advertising has three salient characteristics. It preys on the weaknesses of its host. It creates an insatiable hunger. And it leads to debilitating over-consumption. In the biological realm, things of that nature are called parasites.

If that rather pointed metaphor is apt, we are left with the sticky problem doctors face in treating any parasite: finding a medicine and a dosage that will kill the worm without poisoning the patient. How can we restrain the excesses of advertising without resorting to poisonous state censorship or curtailing the flow of information in society? Actions that are too heavy-handed, for example, could bankrupt the free—but advertising-dependent—press.

THE MANUFACTURE OF NEEDS

The purpose of advertising, according to orthodox economic theory, is to provide us with information about the goods and services offered in the marketplace. Without that stream of information we consumers won't make informed choices, and Adam Smith's invisible hand will be not only invisible but also blind. We won't know when a better frozen dinner comes along, nor will we know where to get the best deal on a new car.

The contents of marketing messages themselves, however, show the simplemindedness of that explanation. Classified ads and yellow page telephone directories would suffice if advertising were only about telling people who already want something where to get it and what it costs. Rather, advertising is intended to expand the pool of desires, awakening wants that would lie dormant otherwise—or, as critics say, manufacturing wants that would not otherwise exist.

Entire industries have manufactured a need for themselves. Writes one advertising executive, ads can serve "to make [people] self-conscious about matter of course things such as enlarged nose pores [and] bad breath." Historically, advertisers have especially targeted women, playing on personal insecurities and self-doubt by projecting impossible ideals of feminine beauty.

As B. Earl Puckett, then head of the department store chain Allied Stores Corporation, put it 40 years ago, "It is our job to make women unhappy with what they have." Thus for those born with short, skinny eyelashes, the message mongers offer hope. For those whose hair is too straight, or too curly, or grows in the wrong places, for those whose skin is too dark or too light, for those whose body weight is distributed in anything but this year's fashion, advertising assures that synthetic salvation is close at hand.

Ads are stitched together from the eternal cravings of the human psyche. Their ingredients are images of sexual virility, eternal youth, social belonging, individual freedom, and existential fulfillment. Advertisers sell not artifacts but lifestyles, attitudes, and fantasies, hitching their wares to the infinite yearnings of the soul.

They also exploit the desire individuals in mass societies feel to define a distinctive identity. Peter Kim, director of research and consumer behavior for the advertising agency J. Walter Thompson, says the role of brands in consumer society is "much akin to the role of myth in traditional societies. Choosing a brand becomes a way for one group of consumers to differentiate themselves from another."

Advertisers are extraordinarily sophisticated in the pursuit of these ends. The most finely wrought ads are masterpieces—combining stunning imagery, bracing speed, and compelling language to touch our innermost fears and fancies. Prime-time television commercials in the industrial countries pack more suggestion into a minute than anything previously devised.

From an anthropological perspective, ads are among the supreme creations of this era, standing in relation to our technological, consumer culture as the pyramids did to the ancients and the Gothic cathedrals to the medievals. Those structures embodied faith in the transcendent, acted out a quest for immortality, and manifested hierarchical social rankings. Advertisements, like our age, are mercurial, hedonistic, image-laden, and fashion-driven; they glorify the individual, idealize consumption as the route to personal fulfillment, and affirm technological progress as the motive force of destiny.

ADVERTISING AND THE EARTH

Of course, advertising is not the only force to promote consumption in today's world. That point is amply evident in the recent history of Eastern Europe. There, where most advertising was illegal under the communist regimes of the past, popular desires for the Western consumer lifestyle were pervasive—indeed, they were among the forces that overthrew socialism. Communism had failed to deliver the goods.

Other forces driving the earth-threatening consumption levels of the world's affluent societies include everything from human nature's acquisitive streak to the erosion of informal, neighborhood sharing networks that has accompanied the rising mobility of our time. They include social pressures to keep up with the Joneses, the proliferation of "convenience" goods to meet the time-crunch created by rising working hours, national economic policies that favor consumption over savings and raw materials production over efficiency and recycling, and the prevailing trend in urban design—away from compact, human-scale cities toward anonymous, auto-scale mall and sprawl.

All these things—plus the weight of sheer purchasing power—define one of the world's most pressing environmental challenges: to trim resource consumption in industrial countries. Citizens of these nations typically consume 10 times as much energy as their developing country counterparts, along with 10 times the timber, 13 times the iron and steel, 14 times the paper, 18 times the synthetic chemicals, and 19 times the aluminum.

The consumer societies take the lion's share of the output of the world's mines, logging operations, petroleum refineries, metal smelters, paper mills, and other high-impact industrial plants. These enterprises, in turn, account for a disproportionate share of the resource depletion, environmental pollution, and habitat degradation that humans have caused worldwide. A world full of consumer societies is an ecological impossibility.

And even if advertising is not the sole force driving up consumption, it is an important one. It is a powerful champion of the consumer lifestyle, and is spreading its influence widely.

COMMERCIALIZING THE GLOBE

"Fifty years ago," wrote philosopher Ivan Illich in 1977, "most of the words an American heard were personally spoken to him as an individual, or to someone standing nearby." That certainly isn't true today. Most of the words an American—or a citizen of any industrial country—hears are sales pitches broadcast over the airwaves to us as members of a mass market. The text we read, the images we see, and the public places we visit are all dominated by commercial messages.

Take the example of commercial television, long the premier advertising medium. Aside from sleeping and working, watching television is the leading activity in most consumer societies, from the United States and the United Kingdom to Japan and Singapore.

Commercial TV is advancing around the world, and everywhere it has proved exceptionally effective at stimulating buying urges. As Anthony J. F. Reilly, chief executive of the food conglomerate H. J. Heinz, told *Fortune* magazine, "Once television is there, people of whatever shade, culture, or origin want roughly the same things." Harnessed as an educational tool, TV can be powerful and effective, as in India and Africa, where lessons are beamed to teacher-less villages. But the overwhelming trend in broadcasting almost everywhere is commercialization.

In 1985, the International Advertising Association rhapsodized: "The magical marketing tool of television has been bound with the chains of laws and regulations in much of the world, and it has not been free to exercise more than a tiny fraction of its potential as a conduit of the consumer information and economic stimulation provided by advertising. Those chains are at last being chiseled off."

During the 1980s, governments deregulated or privatized television programming in most of Western Europe. Public broadcasting monopolies splintered in Belgium, France, Italy, Germany, Norway, Portugal, Spain, and Switzerland—allowing advertising on a scale previously witnessed only in the United States. As the European Community became both a single market and a common broadcasting region this year, advertising time on European TV became a hot commodity, providing access to the region's 330 million consumers and $4 trillion of disposable income.

Meanwhile, commercial television is quickly spreading outside the industrial countries. In India, declares Gurcharan Das, chairman of Procter & Gamble India, "an advertiser can reach 200 million people every night" through television. India has gone from 3 million TVs in 1983 to more than 14 million today. Latin America has built or imported 60 million sets, almost one per family, since the early 1950s. All told, perhaps half the world's people have access to commercial television broadcasts.

The commercialization of television is just one part of the general expansion of advertising worldwide, an expansion that includes magazines and newspapers, billboards and displays, catalogs, and other media. The overall growth stands out starkly in historical trends.

Total global advertising expenditures multiplied nearly sevenfold from 1950 to 1990; they grew one-third faster than the world economy and three times faster than world population. They rose—in real, inflation-adjusted terms—from $39 billion in 1950 to $256 billion in 1990. (For comparison, the gross national product of India, the world's second most populous state, was just $253 billion that year.) In 1950, advertisers spent $16 for each person on the planet, in 1970 they spent $27, and in 1990, $48 (see Figure 1).

Americans are the most advertised-to people on Earth. U.S. marketers account for nearly half of the world's ad budget, according to the International Advertising Association in New York, spending $468 per American in 1991. Among the industrial countries, Japan is second in the advertising league, dedicating more than $300 per citizen to sales pitches each year. Western Europe is close behind. A typical European is the target of more than $200 worth of ads a year. The latest boom is underway in Eastern Europe, a region that John Lindquist of the Boston Consulting Group calls "an advertising executive's dream—people actually remember advertisements."

Advertising is growing fast in developing countries as well, though it remains small scale by Western standards. South Korea's advertising industry grew 35 to 40 percent annually in the late 1980s, and yearly ad billings in India jumped fivefold in the 1980s, surpassing one dollar per person for the first time.

AD-ING LIFE

The sheer magnitude of the advertising barrage in consumer societies has some ironic results. For one thing, the clamor for people's attention means relatively few advertisements stick. Typical Americans are exposed to some 3,000 commercial messages a day, according to *Business Week*. Amid such a din, who notices what any one ad says?

To lend their messages greater influence, marketers are forced to deliver ever higher quality pitches—and to seek new places to make them. They are constantly on the lookout for new routes into people's consciousness.

With the advent of the remote control, the mute button, and the video cassette recorder during the 1980s, people could easily avoid TV commercials, and advertisers had to seek out consumers elsewhere. Expanding on the traditional print and broadcast media, advertisers began piping messages into classrooms and doctors' offices, weaving them into the plots of feature films, posting them on chair-lift poles, printing them on postage stamps and board games, stitching them on Boy Scout merit badges and professional athletes' jerseys, mounting them in bathroom stalls, and playing them back between rings on public phones.

Marketers hired telephone solicitors, both human and computerized, to call people directly in their homes. They commissioned essays from well-known authors, packaged them between full-page ads fore and aft, and mailed them to opinion leaders to polish the sponsors' images. And they created ad-packed television programming for use at airports, bus stops, subway stations, exercise clubs, ski resorts, and supermarket checkout lines.

This creeping commercialization of life has a certain inevitability to it. As the novelty of each medium wears off, advertisers invent another one, relentlessly expanding the share of our collective attention span that they occupy with sales spiels.

Next, they will meet us at the mall, follow us to the dinner table, and shine down on us from the heavens. In shopping centers, they have begun erecting wall-sized video screens to heighten the frenzy of the shopping experience. Food engineers are turning the food supply into an advertising medium. The Viskase company of Chicago prints edible ad slogans on hot dogs, and Eggverts International is using a similar technique to advertise on thousands of eggs in Israel. Lighting engineers are hard at work on feather-weight ways to turn blimps into giant airborne neon signs, and, demonstrating that not even the sky is the limit, Coca-Cola convinced orbiting Soviet cosmonauts to sip their soda on camera a couple of years ago.

The main outcome of this deadening commercialization is to sell not particular products, but consumerism itself. The implicit message of all advertising is the idea that there is a product to solve each of life's problems. Every commercial teaches that existence would be satisfying and complete if only we bought the right things. As religious historian Robert Bellah put it, "That happiness is to be attained through limitless material acquisition is denied by every religion and philosophy known to humankind, but is preached incessantly by every American television set."

GET 'EM WHILE THEY'RE YOUNG

The commercialization of space and time has been accompanied by the commercialization of youth. Marketers are increasingly targeting the young. One specialist in marketing to children told the *Wall Street Journal*, "Even two-year-olds are concerned about their brand of clothes, and by the age of six are full-out consumers." American children and teenagers sit through about three hours of television commercials each week—20,000 ads a year, translating to 360,000 by the time they graduate from high school.

The children's market in the United States is so valuable—topping $75 billion in 1990—that American companies spent $500 million marketing to kids in 1990, five times more than they spent a decade earlier. They started cartoons centered around toys and began direct-mail marketing to youngsters enrolled in their company-sponsored "clubs."

Such saturation advertising has allowed some firms to stake huge claims in the children's market. Mattel vice

World advertising expenditures, per capita, 1950–90

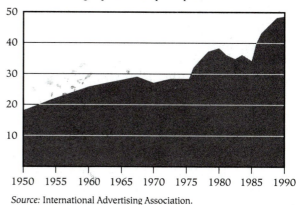

Source: International Advertising Association.

FIGURE 1

president Meryl Friedman brags, "Mattel has achieved a stunning 95 percent penetration with Barbie [dolls] among girls 3 to 11 in the United States."

Predictably, major retailers have opened Barbie departments to compete for the loyalty of doll-doting future consumers, and marketers pay premium prices to employ the dolls as an advertising medium. Barbies come equipped with Reebok shoes and Benetton clothes.

MADISON AVENUE'S PAPER TRAIL

Advertising's main ecological danger may be the consumption it inspires, but it also consumes heavily itself. Advertisers use a substantial share of the world's paper, particularly its heavily-processed high-quality paper. Paper production involves not only forest damage but also large energy inputs and pollution outputs.

Ads pack the daily mail: 14 billion glossy, difficult-to-recycle mail-order catalogs plus 38 billion other assorted ads clog the post office each year in the United States. Most of those items go straight into the trash—including 98 percent of advertising letters sent in direct-mail campaigns, according to the marketing journal *American Demographics.*

Ads fill periodicals: most American magazines reserve 60 percent of their pages for advertising, and some devote far more. *Bride's* was so proud of its February/March 1990 edition that it submitted the issue to the *Guinness Book of World Records* and boasted in *Advertising Age,* "The Biggest Magazine in History. . . . It contains 1,040 pages—including 798 advertising pages."

Newspapers are no different; in the United States, they typically contain 65 percent, up from 40 percent half a century ago. Every year, Canada cuts 42,000 acres of its primeval forests—an area the size of the District of Columbia—just to provide American dailies with newsprint on which to run advertisements.

For big and immediate paper savings, newspapers could shift classified advertising—and telephone companies their directories—onto pay-per-use electronic data bases accessible through phone lines. Still, advertising remains heavy in nonclassified sections of newspapers. Trim out all the ads and most of the text would fit in a single section.

The problem in reducing the scale of advertising in the print media is that the financial viability of newspapers and magazines is linked to the number of advertising pages they sell. In the past two years of economic recession, for example, advertising pages have been harder to sell, and many periodicals have been forced to publish fewer articles. That is not good for the flow of information in democratic societies. To get less-commercialized information sources, subscribers may have to accept higher prices, as have the readers of *Ms.,* which dropped advertising three years ago.

THE INDUSTRY OF NEEDS

The needs industry—advertising—defends itself, ultimately, by claiming that advertising, whatever its social and cultural demerits, is an indispensable component of a healthy economy. As one Madison Avenue axiom counsels, "A terrible thing happens when you don't advertise: Nothing." Advertising, in this view, isn't the trim on the industrial economy, it's the fuel. Take out the ads, and the economy sputters to a halt; put in more ads, and the economy zooms. More ads equal more wants, more wants make more spending, and more spending makes more jobs.

Some promoters even call for governments to foster more advertising. The American Advertising Federation took out a full page in *Time* magazine last March to write, "Dear Mr. President . . . We respectfully remind you of advertising's role as an engine of economic growth. It raises capital, creates jobs, and spurs production . . . It increases government revenues since jobs produce taxable income, and greater sales increase sales taxes . . . Incentives to advertise are incentives for growth."

The validity of such claims is dubious, of course, but they cut to the heart of a critical issue. Even if advertising does promote growth, the question remains as to what kind of growth. Growth in numbers of second mortgages and third cars and fourth televisions may increase the money flowing around the economy without making us one bit happier. If much advertising is an exercise in generating dissatisfaction so that people will spend more and work harder, the entire process appears morally questionable. Several generations ago, Catholic theologian John Ryan dubbed this treadmill "squirrel cage progress."

Many of the areas in which the world needs growth most desperately—environmental literacy, racial and sexual equality, and political participation, for example—are not the stuff of advertising campaigns. "Civilization, in the real sense of the term," advised Gandhi, "consists not in the multiplication, but in the deliberate and voluntary reduction of wants."

RE-CHANNELING ADVERTISING

What legitimate role is there for advertising, then? In a sustainable society, how much advertising would there be?

None! say some, as E. F. Schumacher commented in 1979: "What is the great bulk of advertising other than the stimulation of greed, envy and avarice . . . at least three of the seven deadly sins?" More succinctly, reader Charlotte Burrowes of Penacook, New Hampshire, wrote to *Worldwatch* a year ago, "There'll be a special hell for advertisers."

In fairness, though, some advertising does provide useful information about products and services. The task for democratic societies struggling to restore balance between themselves and their ecosystems is to decide how much advertising to tolerate, and while respecting the rights of individuals to speak their minds, to place appropriate limits on marketing.

The precise limits cannot yet be identified, but it may help define the issue to consider whether there are spaces that should be free of advertising. Churches? Schools? Hospitals? Funeral homes? Parks? Homes? Work places? Books? Public libraries? Public swimming pools? Public buildings? Public buses? Public streets? Mail boxes? Newspapers? Television broadcasts? What about times of day, days of the week, and times of life? Early morning? Sundays? Childhood?

Restraining the excesses of marketers and limiting commercials to their legitimate role of informing consumers would require fundamental reforms in the industry, changes that will not come about without a well-organized grassroots movement. The advertising industry is a formidable foe on the march around the world, and advertisers are masters at the slippery art of public relations. Madison Avenue can buy the best talents available to counter and circumvent reformers' campaigns, unless those campaigns are carefully focused and begin with the industry's vulnerabilities.

Advertising's Achilles heel is its willingness to push products demonstrably dangerous to human health, and this is the area where activists have been most successful and best organized. Tobacco ads are or soon will be banished from television throughout the Western democracies, and alcohol commercials are under attack as never before.

Another ready target for advertising reform activists is the assault that marketers make on children. Public sentiment runs strongly against marketing campaigns that prey on youngsters. Action for Children's Television, a citizens' group based in Boston, won a victory in late 1990 when the U.S. Congress limited television commercials aimed at children. The same year, public interest organizations in the European Com-munity pushed through standards for European television that will put strict limits on some types of ads.

The Australian Consumers' Association is attacking junk food ads, calling for a ban or tough restrictions on hawking unhealthful fare to youngsters. Of food ads aired during children's television programs, the association's research shows that 80 percent are for high-fat, high-salt, excessively packaged snacks. The American Academy of Pediatrics is similarly concerned. Noting the high proportion of advertisements for products that violate nutrition guidelines, the organization is urging Congress to ban food ads that target the young.

Alternatively, consumers could take aim at trumped-up corporate environmental claims. Since 1989, marketers have been painting their products "green" in an attempt to defuse citizen anger at corporate ecological transgressions. In 1990, for example, the oil company Texaco offered Americans "free" tree seedlings to plant for the good of the environment; to qualify, a customer had to buy eight or more gallons of gasoline. Unmentioned in the marketing literature was the fact that it takes a typical tree about four years to store as much carbon dioxide as is released in refining and burning eight gallons of fuel, and that most tree seedlings planted by amateurs promptly die.

In the United States, one fourth of all new household products introduced in 1990 advertised themselves as "ozone-friendly," "biodegradable," "recyclable," "compostable," or something similar—claims that half of all Americans recognize as "gimmickry." Environmentalists in the Netherlands and France have attempted to cut away such misinformation by introducing a 12-point environmental advertising code in their national legislatures. Ten state attorneys general are pushing for similar national standards in the United States. Meanwhile, official and unofficial organizations throughout Europe, North America, and Japan have initiated "green labeling" programs, aiming to steer consumers to environmentally preferable products.

Efforts to restrict advertising of tobacco and alcohol, to curtail advertising to children, and to regulate environmental claims of marketers are parts of a broader agenda. The nonprofit Center for the Study of Commercialism in Washington, D.C., is calling for an end to brand-name plugs in feature films, for schools to declare themselves advertising-free zones, and for revision of the tax code so that money spent on advertising is taxable.

Just as the expanding reach of advertising is not going unchallenged, small networks of citizens everywhere are beginning to confront commercial television. In Vancouver, British Columbia, English teacher Michael Maser gets secondary students to study television production so they will be able to recognize techniques used to manipulate viewers' sentiments. Millions of young people could benefit from such a course, considering how many products are pitched to them on TV. Along the same lines as Maser's teaching, the Center for Media and Values in Los Angeles has been promoting media literacy since 1989, by furnishing parents throughout North America with tips on teaching their children to watch with a critical eye.

More boldly, some attempt to fight fire with fire. The Vancouver-based Media Foundation is building a movement aimed at using the same cleverness and humor evident in much commercial advertising to promote sustainable ends. Local groups raise funds to show the group's products on commercial television and in commercial magazines. TV spots have run in California, Ontario, and a half-dozen other states and provinces. Their "Tube Head" series of ads tell viewers to shut off the set. In one magazine ad, above a photo of a dark, sleek sports car, a caption purrs, "At this price, it will surely take your breath away." And below: "$250,000." In fine print, it explains, "U.S. sticker price

:d on individual share of social costs associated with automobiles in U.S. over average car life of 10 years. Does not include . . . oil spills at sea and on land; acid rain from auto emissions . . . environmental and health costs from global warming."

The premier spot in the Media Foundation's "High on the Hog" campaign shows a gigantic animated pig frolicking on a map of North America while a narrator intones: "Five percent of the people in the world consume *one-third* of the planet's resources. . . . Those people are us." The pig belches.

Imagine a message like *that* broadcast simultaneously to every inhabited part of the globe!

Study Questions

1. Do you agree with Durning that advertising poses a dangerous threat to society? Provide illustrations from your experience to support your views on the matter.
2. How, according to Durning, is advertising like a parasite? Do you agree with him?
3. How can we ensure that advertising serves good purposes rather than environmentally bad purposes? Could the cure for advertising be worse than the parasite itself?

83

Sustainable Transportation: Pedaling Power

LOUIS P. POJMAN

I am professor of philosophy at the United States Military Academy, West Point, N.Y., and the author and editor of several works in philosophy, including Life and Death: Grappling with the Moral Dilemmas of our Time *and this volume. In this essay, I present a case for making the bicycle the main instrument for short-distance travel, arguing that it is both far more energy efficient and healthier than the automobile.*

Imagine that we invented a mighty Convenience Machine that would make our lives wonderfully more enjoyable and enable us to reach more of our goals. Unfortunately, using the machine would cost us about 50,000 lives per year, about as many casualties as 8 years of the war in Viet Nam. Would you use the machine? Should we allow it to be sold on the market?

When I have posed this question to audiences, there is virtually universal agreement that we should not use it or permit it on the open market, for no amount of comfort equals the value of a single life.

The question then becomes, why don't those who treat human life as sacred stop driving cars? The Convenience Machine in our thought experiment is the motor vehicle. Each year about 50,000 people lose their lives in automobile accidents in the United States and about 250,000 worldwide, more than those killed by the atom bombs in Hiroshima and Nagasaki in 1945. Since the introduction of the automobile in the United States 100 years ago, about 3 million people have been killed, more than in all the battlefields of all our wars.

The automobile provides us with enormous freedom and power. It makes us mobile and able to cover long distances in a short time. In moderation, the automobile could be a good thing, but we have become overdependent on it and have misused it. We have turned what could be a wonderful servant into a tyrannical idol, as the religion of Car Worship with its new urban cathedral, the multistoried parking lot, which reeks with the incense of greed, waste, and deleterious exhaust fumes. Our economy is overdependent on the motor vehicle.

Here are some facts. One out of every six dollars and one-sixth of every nonfarm job in America is related to the motor vehicle. It accounts for 20% of our GNP and an annual average of $300 to $500 billion in government subsidies, more than $1000 per person above the direct costs to car users. It accounts for 63% of our oil use ($43 billion are spent to import oil each year, one-fourth of our national trade deficit).

In the United States, the motor vehicle is the largest source of urban smog, accounting for 50% of air pollution, 13% of greenhouse gases, and 13% of chlorofluorocarbons (CFCs), thus contributing to the greenhouse effect and the breakdown of the ozone layer. Urban residents in cities throughout the world incur eye, nose, and throat irritation, asthma, headaches, heart attacks, cancer, and emphysema due to car-produced smog. Fuel emissions cause about 30,000 deaths annually in the United States.

Furthermore, cars and trucks clog up our highways and streets, causing traffic jams, which in turn greatly increase stress, contribute to hypertension, ulcers, and nervous disorders, and sometimes lead to violence and murder. These jams cause employees to arrive late at work. Governmental agencies estimate that over $100 billion are lost each year due to traffic jams. Each day 5 million vehicles crowd the Los Angeles freeways, contributing to the 100,000 hours per day that are wasted

---

This essay was written for the first edition of this work.

the country's light-rail system and fined the corporate executive officers $1 each and each company $5000. By that time, GM alone had made $25 million in additional bus and car sales.[1]

Mass transit systems need to be increased throughout the world, but for short trips, another mode of transportation is called for—the bicycle. It is an inexpensive alternative to automobile transport, thirty or forty times cheaper. When gas and maintenance is included, my two bikes, which are over 10 years old and with which I commute to work daily, each cost about $100 plus about a combined total of $500 in maintenance over a 10-year period. The material used to construct one middle-sized American car can construct 100 bicycles. In China and India, the bicycle is becoming the preferred mode of transportation; and in some cities in the Netherlands, between 40% and 50% of all trips are made by bike. In the United States, the use of bicycles as a means of transportation has increased in the past few years, from less than 1% to 2%.

The bicycle is the most efficient mode of transportation, using less energy per mile than any other mode, including walking. The energy available from an ear of corn will get you 3 1/2 miles, and there's less noise and no distilling or refining problem! The bicycle uses 35 calories per passenger mile, walking 100, rail transport 885 and the automobile 1860 (fifty-three times more than the bicycle! See Table 1).

Pedal power creates no air pollution, cuts down on stress, and provides a good source of exercise, so employees arrive at work more refreshed and healthier than those imprisoned in traffic jams. In urban areas, bicycles move at the same average speed as cars and sometimes faster. In fact, police in Seattle frequently use bikes to catch car thieves.

In addition to these environmental reasons is the aesthetic joy in feeling the wind on your face as you pump up a hill or coast downhill. You find an inner peace in being bathed in nature's breath. As your cardiovascular system goes to work, the potent analgesic properties of the brain's endorphins are released, and you get the same kind of "high" that joggers get—minus the wear

in traffic jams in that city. A total of one-third of the city's land is given over to automobile-related roads, parking lots, and gas stations (one-half of downtown Los Angeles). Estimates are that the average American commuter spends 2 years of his or her life in traffic jams. In 1907 the average speed of a horse-drawn carriage through the streets of Manhattan was 11.5 mph. Today a vehicle averaging the power of some 300 horses does the same mile at a pace of 5 mph. At present 38.4 million acres nationwide are given to roads and parking lots (that's the size of the state of Georgia).

Mass transit is both cleaner and more energy efficient. Ironically enough, in the early part of this century, the United States had an effective public transportation system in most of its cities. Trolleys and street cars were used by 20 million riders in 1920, and Los Angeles had one of the best systems in the country. In the 1940s, The National City Lines, a holding company formed by General Motors, Firestone Tire, Standard Oil, and Phillips Petroleum, bought up the privately owned streetcar systems in 100 major cities. The old systems were systematically dismantled and replaced with buses, promoting the use of cars. Gradually, the bus companies were allowed to fail in many of these cities, creating an increased demand for cars. The courts found the companies guilty of conspiracy to eliminate about 90% of

TABLE 1 *Energy Intensity of Selected Transport Modes, U.S., 1984*

MODE	CALORIES/PASSENGER MILE
Bicycling	35
Walking	100
Transit rail	885
Transit bus	920
Automobile, single occupant	1860

SOURCES: President's Council on Physical Fitness and Sports, Washington, D.C., private communication, June 23, 1988; Mary C. Holcomb et al., *Transportation Energy Data Book: Edition 9* (Oakridge, Tenn.: Oak Ridge National Laboratory, 1987).

tear on your feet and knees. Scientists reckon that the "high" released can be several times that of drugs—without the damage to your brain or pocketbook.

Of course, biking can be dangerous too, especially when using the same roads as powerful cars and trucks (90% of bicycle accidents involve collision with a car or truck). Still bikes are far safer than cars. Outnumbering cars throughout the world by two to one, only 2% of traffic fatalities involve bicycles. But the cyclist should take precautions, wearing a helmet and using a rear view mirror attached to the handle bar or helmet.

Cities like Davis and Palo Alto, both in California, have extensive bike paths, and St. Paul, Minnesota, is currently in the process of building a 17-mile bicycle freeway. The Netherlands has more than 9000 miles of bicycle paths, and Japan provides not only bicycle paths but large bicycle garages at train stations, thus combining public transportation with bicycle use. By shifting to nonmotorized transportation, countries could save millions of dollars in fuel costs. A Worldwatch researcher estimates, "If 10% of Americans who commute by car switched to bike-and-ride, more than $1.3 billion could be shaved off the U.S. oil import bill."[2] A 1983 study of American commuters showed that turning to the bicycle could save each commuter 150 gallons of gas per year.

In 1969 a group of University of Minnesota students dragged an automobile engine into downtown Minneapolis. "As a small crowd gathered, the students dropped the motor into a grave, covered it with dirt, and solemnly declared an end to the tyranny of the internal combustion engine over the lungs and lives of civilized people. As traffic rushed past on nearby streets, a young minister read the eulogy:

Ashes to ashes, dust to dust,
For the sake of mankind, iron to rust."[3]

Perhaps the university students' actions were overly dramatic and premature. The internal combustion engine is not likely to die a natural death in the near future. Hopefully, however, a less polluting, electrical car may soon be practical. But for reasons of economics, health, and land use, the bicycle, combined with increased public transportation, should replace the automobile as the preferred mode of transportation in the United States and throughout the world. As author and cyclist James McGurn writes, "The bicycle is the vehicle of a new mentality. It quietly challenges a system of values which condones dependency, wastage, inequality of mobility, and daily carnage. . . . There is every reason why cycling should be helped to enjoy another Golden Age."[4]

The time has come to dethrone the automobile as the American vehicular idol, our destructive Convenience Machine, and to replace it with ecologically sounder modes of transportation, with the person-powered two-wheeled vehicle as the centerpiece.

Notes

1. G. Tyler Miller, *Living in the Environment*, 7th ed. (Belmont, CA: Wadsworth, 1992), p. 239. This is a good source for information on this issue.
2. Marcia Lowe, "Pedaling into the Future," in *World Watch Reader*, ed. Lester Brown (Washington, D.C.: Norton, 1991).
3. Ed Ayers, "Breaking Away," *Worldwatch*, 6.1 (Jan–Feb. 1993). Ayers points our that the sprocket chain-driven bicycle and the gas-fueled combustion engine car were both invented in the same year, 1885, but the history of the two vehicles has been one wherein the bigger gadget has pushed the smaller off the road. Might makes Right—or at least, Right of Way.
4. Quoted in Marcia Lowe, "The Bicycle: Vehicle for a Small Planet" (Washington, D.C.: Worldwatch Institute, 1989), p. 46.

Study Questions

1. How feasible is the switch from automobiles to bicycles? Do you see any problems with the analysis in this article?
2. Would switching to electric cars and more efficient mass transit be more realistic ways to make progress in transportation?

84

Vision of a Sustainable World

Lester Brown, Christopher Flavin, and Sandra Postel

Lester Brown is the president of the Worldwatch Institute in Washington, D.C., an institute concerned with global environmental issues. Christopher Flavin and Sandra Postel are vice presidents for research at the Worldwatch Institute. In this essay, Brown and his associates project 40 years into the future and predict the kind of global lifestyles and economic practices that will be present in a sustainable world.

On April 22nd, 1990, millions of people around the world celebrated Earth Day. Marking the twentieth anniversary of the original Earth Day, this event came at a time when public concern about the environmental fate of the planet had soared to unprecedented heights.

Threats such as climate change and ozone depletion underscore the fact that ecological degradation has reached global proportions. Meanwhile, the increasing severity and spread of more localized problems—including soil erosion, deforestation, water scarcity, toxic contamination, and air pollution—are already beginning to slow economic and social progress in much of the world.

Governments, development agencies, and people the world over have begun to grasp the need to reverse this broad-based deterioration of the environment. But, the result so far is a flurry of fragmented activity—a new pollution law here, a larger environment staff there—that lacks any coherent sense of what, ultimately, we are trying to achieve.

Building an environmentally stable future requires some vision of what it would look like. If not coal and oil to power society, then what? If forests are no longer to be cleared to grow food, then how is a larger population to be fed? If a throwaway culture leads inevitably to pollution and resource depletion, how can we satisfy our material needs?

In sum, if the present path is so obviously unsound, what picture of the future can we use to guide our actions toward a global community that can endure?

A sustainable society is one that satisfies its needs without jeopardizing the prospects of future generations. Unfortunately, no models of sustainability exist today. Most developing nations have for the past several decades aspired to the automobile-centered, fossil-fuel-driven economies of the industrial West. From the regional problems of air pollution to the global threat of climate change, though, it is clear that these societies are far from durable; indeed, they are rapidly bringing about their own demise.

Describing the shape of a sustainable society is a risky proposition. Ideas and technologies we can't now foresee obviously will influence society's future course. Yet, just as any technology of flight must abide by the basic principles of aerodynamics, so must a lasting society satisfy some elementary criteria. With that understanding and the experience garnered in recent decades, it is possible to create a vision of a society quite different from, indeed preferable to, today's.

Time to get the world on a sustainable path is rapidly running out. We believe that if humanity achieves sustainability, it will do so within the next 40 years. If we have not succeeded by then, environmental deterioration and economic decline will be feeding on each other, pulling us down toward social decay and political upheaval. At such a point, reclaiming any hope of a sustainable future might be impossible. Our vision, therefore, looks to the year 2030, a time closer to the present than is World War II.

Whether Earth Day 2030 turns out to be a day to celebrate lasting achievements or to lament missed opportunities is largely up to each one of us as individuals, for, in the end, it is individual values that drive social change. Progress toward sustainability thus hinges on a collective deepening of our sense of responsibility to the earth and to our offspring. Without a reevaluation of our personal aspirations and motivations, we will never achieve an environmentally sound global community.

BEGIN WITH THE BASICS

In attempting to sketch the outlines of a sustainable society, we need to make some basic assumptions. First, our vision of the future assumes only existing technologies and foreseeable improvements in them. This clearly is a conservative assumption: 40 years ago, for example, some renewable energy technologies on which we base our model didn't even exist.

Second, the world economy of 2030 will not be powered by coal, oil, and natural gas. It is now well accepted that continuing heavy reliance on fossil fuels will cause catastrophic changes in climate. The most recent scientific evidence suggests that stabilizing the climate depends on eventually cutting annual global carbon emissions to some 2 billion tons per year, about one-

Reprinted from *The Worldwatch Reader*, ed. Lester R. Brown (New York: Norton, 1991), by permission.

the current level. Taking population growth into account, the world in 2030 will therefore have per-capita carbon emissions about one-eighth the level found in Western Europe today.

The choice then becomes whether to make solar or nuclear power the centerpiece of energy systems. We believe nuclear power will be rejected because of its long list of economic, social, and environmental liabilities. The nuclear industry has been in decline for over a decade. Safety concerns and the failure to develop permanent storage for nuclear waste have disenchanted many citizens.

It is possible scientists could develop new nuclear technologies that are more economical and less accident-prone. Yet, this would not solve the waste dilemma. Nor would it prevent the use of nuclear energy as a stepping stone to developing nuclear weapons. Trying to stop this in a plutonium-based economy with thousands of operating plants would require a degree of control incompatible with democratic political systems. Societies are likely to opt instead for diverse, solar-based systems.

The third major assumption is about population size. Current United Nations projections have the world headed for nearly nine billion people by 2030. This figure implies a doubling or tripling of the populations of Ethiopia, India, Nigeria, and scores of other countries where human numbers are already overtaxing natural support systems. But such growth is inconceivable. Either these societies will move quickly to encourage smaller families and bring birthrates down, or rising death rates from hunger and malnutrition will check population growth.

The humane path to sustainability by the year 2030 therefore requires a dramatic drop in birthrates. As of 1990, 13 European countries had stable or declining populations; by 2030, most countries are likely to be in that category. We assume a population 40 years from now of at most eight billion that will be either essentially stable or declining slowly toward a number the earth can comfortably support.

DAWN OF A SOLAR AGE

In many ways, the solar age today is where the coal age was when the steam engine was invented in the eighteenth century. At that time, coal was used to heat homes and smelt iron ore, but the notion of using coal-fired steam engines to power factories or transportation systems was just emerging. Only a short time later, the first railroad started running and fossil fuels began to transform the world economy.

Many technologies have been developed that allow us to harness the renewable energy of the sun effectively, but so far these devices are only in limited use. By 2030 they will be widespread and much improved. The pool of energy these technologies can tap is immense: The annual influx of accessible renewable resources in the United States is estimated at 250 times the country's current energy needs.

The mix of energy sources will reflect the climate and natural resources of particular regions. Northern Europe, for example, is likely to rely heavily on wind and hydropower. Northern Africa and the Middle East may instead use direct sunlight. Japan and the Philippines will tap their abundant geothermal energy. Southeast Asian countries will be powered largely by wood and agricultural wastes, along with sunshine. Some nations—Norway and Brazil, for example—already obtain more than half of their energy from renewables.

By 2030, solar panels will heat most residential water around the world. A typical urban landscape may have thousands of collectors sprouting from rooftops, much as television antennas do today. Electricity will come via transmission lines from solar thermal plants located in desert regions of the United States, North Africa, and central Asia. This technology uses mirrored troughs to focus sunlight onto oil-filled tubes that convey heat to a turbine and generator that then produce electricity. An 80-megawatt solar thermal plant built in the desert east of Los Angeles in 1989 converted an extraordinary 22 percent of incoming sunlight into electricity—at a third less than the cost of power from new nuclear plants.

Power will also come from photovoltaic solar cells, a semiconductor technology that converts sunlight directly into electricity. Currently, photovoltaic systems are less efficient than and four times as expensive as solar thermal power, but by 2030 their cost will be competitive. Photovoltaics will be a highly decentralized energy source found atop residential homes as well as adjacent to farms and factories.

Using this technology, homeowners throughout the world may become producers as well as consumers of electricity. Indeed, photovoltaic shingles have already been developed that turn roofing material into a power source. As costs continue to decline, many homes are apt to get their electricity from photovoltaics; in sunny regions residents will sell any surplus to the utility company.

Wind power, an indirect form of solar energy generated by the sun's differential heating of the atmosphere, is already close to being cost competitive with new coal-fired power plants. Engineers are confident they can soon unveil improved wind turbines that are economical not just in California's blustery mountain passes, where they are now commonplace, but in vast stretches of the U.S. northern plains and many other areas. Forty years from now the United States could be deriving 10 to 20 percent of its electricity from the wind.

Small-scale hydro projects are likely to be a significant source of electricity, particularly in the Third World, where the undeveloped potential is greatest. As of 1990 hydro power supplied nearly one-fifth of the

world's electricity. By 2030 that share should be much higher, although the massive dams favored by governments and international lending agencies in the late-twentieth century will represent a declining proportion of the total hydro capacity.

Living plants provide another means of capturing solar energy. Through photosynthesis, they convert sunlight into biomass that can be burned or converted to liquid fuels such as ethanol. Today, wood provides 12 percent of the world's energy, chiefly in the form of firewood and charcoal in developing countries. Its use will surely expand during the next 40 years, although resource constraints will not permit it to replace all of the vast quantities of petroleum in use today.

Geothermal energy taps the huge reservoir of heat that lies beneath the earth's surface, making it the only renewable source that does not rely on sunlight. Continuing advances will allow engineers to use previously unexploitable, lower-temperature reservoirs that are hundreds of times as abundant as those in use today. Virtually all Pacific Rim countries, as well as those along East Africa's Great Rift and the Mediterranean Sea, will draw on geothermal resources.

Nations in what now is called the Third World face the immense challenge of continuing to develop their economies without massive use of fossil fuels. One option is to rely on biomass energy in current quantities but to step up replanting efforts and to burn the biomass much more efficiently, using gasifiers and other devices. Another is to turn directly to the sun, which the Third World has in abundance. Solar ovens for cooking, solar collectors for hot water, and photovoltaics for electricity could satisfy most energy needs.

In both industrial and developing nations, energy production inevitably will be much more decentralized; this will break up the utilities and huge natural gas, coal, and oil industries that have been a dominant part of the economic scene in the late-twentieth century. Indeed, a world energy system based on the highly efficient use of renewable resources will be less vulnerable to disruption and more conducive to market economies.

EFFICIENT IN ALL SENSES

Getting total global carbon emissions down to 2 billion tons a year will require vast improvements in energy efficiency. Fortunately, many of the technologies to accomplish this feat already exist and are cost-effective. No technical breakthroughs are needed to double automobile fuel economy, triple the efficiency of lighting systems, or cut typical home heating requirements by 75 percent.

Automobiles in 2030 are apt to get at least 100 miles per gallon of fuel, four times the current average for new cars. A hint of what such vehicles may be like is seen in the Volvo LCP 2000, a prototype automobile. It is an aerodynamic four-passenger car that weighs half as much as today's models. Moreover, it has a highly efficient and clean-burning diesel engine. With the addition of a continuously variable transmission and a flywheel energy storage device, this vehicle will get 90 miles to the gallon.

Forty years from now, Thomas Edison's revolutionary incandescent light bulbs may be found only in museums—replaced by an array of new lighting systems, including halogen and sodium lights. The most important new light source may be compact fluorescent bulbs that use 18 watts rather than 75 to produce the same amount of light.

In 2030, homes are likely to be weather-tight and highly insulated; this will greatly reduce the need for g and cooling. Some superinsulated homes in the ̣adian province of Saskatchewan are already so ̣ghtly built that it doesn't pay to install a furnace. Homes of this kind use one-third as much energy as do modern Swedish homes, or one-tenth the U.S. average. Inside, people will have appliances that are on average three to four times as efficient as those in use today.

Improving energy efficiency will not noticeably change lifestyles or economic systems. A highly efficient refrigerator or light bulb provides the same service as an inefficient one—just more economically. Gains in energy efficiency alone, however, will not reduce fossil-fuel related carbon emissions by the needed amount. Additional steps to limit the use of fossil fuels are likely to reshape cities, transportation systems, and industrial patterns and foster a society that is more efficient in all senses.

By the year 2030, a much more diverse set of transportation options will exist. The typical European or Japanese city today has already taken one step toward this future. Highly developed rail and bus systems move people efficiently between home and work: In Tokyo only 15 percent of commuters drive cars to the office. The cities of 2030 are apt to be crisscrossed by inexpensive street-level light rail systems that allow people to move quickly between neighborhoods.

Automobiles will undoubtedly still be in use four decades from now, but their numbers will be fewer and their role smaller. Within cities, only electric or clean hydrogen-powered vehicles are likely to be permitted, and most of these will be highly efficient "city cars." The energy to run them may well come from solar power plants. Families might rent efficient larger vehicles for vacations.

The bicycle will also play a major role in getting people about, as it already does in much of Asia as well as in some industrial-country towns and cities—in Amsterdam and Davis, California, bike-path networks encourage widespread pedaling. There are already twice as many bikes as cars worldwide. In the bicycle-centered transport system of 2030, the ratio could easily be 10 to 1.

Forty years from now, people will live closer to their jobs, and much socializing and shopping will be done by bike rather than in a 1-ton automobile. Computerized delivery services may allow people to shop from home—consuming less time as well as less energy. Telecommunications will substitute for travel as well. In addition, a world that allows only 2 billion tons of carbon emissions cannot be trucking vast quantities of food and other items thousands of miles; this is apt to encourage more decentralization of agriculture and allow local produce suppliers to flourish.

The automobile-based modern world is now only about 40 years old, but with its damaging air pollution and traffic congestion it hardly represents the pinnacle of human social evolution. Although a world where cars play a minor role may be hard to imagine, our grandparents would have had just as hard a time visualizing today's world of traffic jams and smog-filled cities.

NOTHING TO WASTE

In the sustainable, efficient economy of 2030, waste reduction and recycling industries will have largely replaced the garbage collection and disposal companies of today. The throwaway society that emerged during the late-twentieth century uses so much energy, emits so much carbon, and generates so much air pollution, acid rain, water pollution, toxic waste, and rubbish that it is strangling itself. Rooted as it is in planned obsolescence and appeals to convenience, it will be seen by historians as an aberration.

A hierarchy of options will guide materials policy in the year 2030. The first priority, of course, will be to avoid using any nonessential item. Second will be to reuse a product directly—for example, refilling a glass beverage container. The third will be to recycle the material to form a new product. Fourth, the material can be burned to extract whatever energy it contains, as long as this can be done safely. The option of last resort will be disposal in a landfill.

In the sustainable economy of 2030, the principal source of materials for industry will be recycled goods. Most of the raw material for the aluminum mill will come from the local scrap collection center, not from the bauxite mine. The steel mills of the future will feed on worn-out automobiles, household appliances, and industrial equipment. Paper and paper products will be produced at recycling mills, in which paper will move through a series of uses, from high-quality bond to newsprint and, eventually, to cardboard boxes. Industries will turn to virgin raw materials only to replace any losses in use and recycling.

The effect on air and water quality will be obvious. For example, steel produced from scrap reduces air pollution by 85 percent, cuts water pollution by 76 percent, and eliminates mining wastes altogether. Making paper from recycled material reduces pollutants entering the air by 74 percent and the water by 35 percent. It also reduces pressures on forests in direct proportion to the amount recycled.

The economic reasons for such careful husbanding of materials will by 2030 seem quite obvious. Just 5 percent as much energy is needed to recycle aluminum as to produce it from bauxite ore. For steel produced entirely from scrap, the saving amounts to roughly two-thirds. Newsprint from recycled paper takes 25 to 60 percent less energy to make than that from wood pulp. Recycling glass saves up to a third of the energy embodied in the original product.

Societies in 2030 may also have decided to replace multi-sized and -shaped beverage containers with a set of standardized ones made of durable glass that can be reused many times. These could be used for fruit juices, beer, milk, and soda pop.

One of the cornerstones of a sustainable society will likely be its elimination of waste flows at the source. Industry will have restructured manufacturing processes to slash wastes by a third or more from 1990 levels. Food packaging, which in 1986 cost American consumers more than American farmers earned selling their crops, will have been streamlined. Food items buried in three or four layers of packaging will be a distant memory.

As recycling reaches its full potential over the next 40 years, households will begin to compost yard wastes rather than put them out for curbside pickup. A lost art in many communities now, composting will experience a revival. Garbage flows will be reduced by one-fifth or more and gardeners will have a rich source of humus.

In addition to recycling and reusing metal, glass, and paper, a sustainable society must also recycle nutrients. In nature, one organism's waste is another's sustenance. In cities, however, human sewage has become a troublesome source of water pollution. Properly treated to prevent the spread of disease and to remove contaminants, sewage will be systematically returned to the land in vegetable-growing greenbelts around cities, much as is done in Shanghai and other Asian cities today.

Other cities will probably find it more efficient to follow Calcutta's example and use treated human sewage to fertilize aquacultural operations. A steady flow of nutrients from human waste can help nourish aquatic life, which in turn is consumed by fish.

HOW TO FEED EIGHT BILLION

Imagine trying to meet the food, fuel, and timber needs of eight billion people—nearly three billion more than the current world population—with 960 billion fewer tons of topsoil (more than twice the amount on all U.S. cropland) and one billion fewer acres of trees (an area more than half the size of the continental United States).

That, in a nutshell, will be the predicament faced by society in 2030 if current rates of soil erosion and deforestation continue unaltered for the next 40 years. It is a fate that can only be avoided through major changes in land use.

Of necessity, societies in 2030 will be using the land intensively; the needs of a population more than half again as large as today's cannot be met otherwise. But, unlike the present, tomorrow's land-use patterns would be abiding by basic principles of biological stability: nutrient retention, carbon balance, soil protection, water conservation, and preservation of species diversity. Harvests will rarely exceed sustainable yields.

Meeting food needs will pose monumental challenges, as some simple numbers illustrate. By 2030, assuming cropland area expands by 5 percent between now and then and that population grows to eight bil-

lion, cropland per person will have dropped to a third less than we have in today's inadequately fed world. Virtually all of Asia, and especially China, will be struggling to feed its people from a far more meager base of per-capital cropland area.

In light of these constraints, the rural landscapes of 2030 are likely to exhibit greater diversity than they do now. Variations in soils, slope, climate, and water availability will require different patterns and strains of crops grown in different ways to maximize sustainable output. For example, farmers may adopt numerous forms of agroforestry—the combined production of crops and trees—to provide food, biomass, and fodder, while also adding nutrients to soils and controlling water runoff.

Also, successfully adapting to changed climates resulting from greenhouse warming, as well as to water scarcity and other resource constraints, may lead scientists to draw on a much broader base of crop varieties. For example, a greater area will be devoted to salt-tolerant and drought-resistant crops.

Efforts to arrest desertification, now claiming 15 million acres each year, may by 2030 have transformed the gullied highlands of Ethiopia and other degraded areas into productive terrain. Much of the sloping land rapidly losing topsoil will be terraced and protected by shrubs or nitrogen-fixing trees planted along the contour.

Halting desertification also depends on eliminating overgrazing. The global livestock herd in 2030 is likely to be much smaller than today's three billion. It seems inevitable that adequately nourishing a world population 60 percent larger than today's will preclude feeding a third of the global grain harvest to livestock and poultry, as is currently the case. As meat becomes more expensive, the diets of the affluent will move down the food chain to greater consumption of grains and vegetables; this will also prolong lifespans.

A HEALTHY RESPECT FOR FORESTS

Forests and woodlands will be valued more highly and for many more reasons in 2030 than is the case today. The planet's mantle of trees, already a third smaller than in preagricultural times and shrinking by more than 27 million acres per year now, will be stable or expanding as a result of serious efforts to slow deforestation and to replant vast areas.

Long before 2030, the clearing of most tropical forests will have ceased. Since most of the nutrients in these ecosystems are held in the leaves and biomass of the vegetation rather than in the soil, only activities that preserve the forest canopy are sustainable. While it is impossible to say how much virgin tropical forest would remain in 2030 if sustainability is achieved, certainly the rate of deforestation will have had to slow dramatically by the end of this decade. Soon thereafter it will come to a halt.

ts to identify and protect unique parcels of for-
ll probably have led to a widely dispersed network
preserves. But a large portion of tropical forests still
standing in 2030 will be exploited in a variety of benign
ways by people living in and around them. Hundreds of
"extractive reserves" will exist, areas in which local people harvest rubber, resins, nuts, fruits, medicines, and
other forest products.

Efforts to alleviate the fuel-wood crisis in developing
countries, to reduce flooding and landslides in hilly
regions, and to slow the buildup of carbon dioxide may
spur the planting of an additional 500 million acres or
so of trees. Many of these plantings will be on private
farms as part of agroforestry systems, but plantations
may also have an expanded role. Cities and villages will
turn to managed woodlands on their outskirts to contribute fuel for heating, cooking, and electricity. This
wood will substitute for some portion of coal and oil use
and, since harvested on a sustained-yield basis, will
make no net contribution of carbon dioxide to the
atmosphere.

Restoring and stabilizing the biological resource base
by 2030 depends on a pattern of land ownership and use
far more equitable than today's. Much of the degradation now occurring sterns from the heavily skewed distribution of land that, along with population growth,
pushes poor people into ever more marginal environments. Stewardship requires that people have plots large
enough to sustain their families without abusing the
land, access to means of using the land productively, and
the right to pass it on to their children.

No matter what technologies come along, the biochemical process of photosynthesis, carried out by green
plants, will remain the basis for meeting many human
needs, and its efficiency can only be marginally
improved. Given that humanity already appropriates an
estimated 40 percent of the earth's annual photosynthetic product on land, the urgency of slowing the
growth in human numbers is obvious. The sooner societies stabilize their populations, the greater will be their
opportunities for achieving equitable and stable patterns
of land use that can meet their needs indefinitely.

ECONOMIC PROGRESS IN A
NEW LIGHT

The fundamental changes that are needed in energy,
forestry, agriculture, and other physical systems cannot
occur without corresponding shifts in social, economic,
and moral character. During the transition to sustainability, political leaders and citizens alike will be forced
to reevaluate their goals and aspirations and to adjust
to a new set of principles that have at their core the welfare of future generations.

Shifts in employment will be among the most visible
as the transition gets underway. Moving from fossil
fuels to a diverse set of renewable energy sources,
extracting fewer materials from the earth and recycling
more, and revamping farming and forestry practices will
greatly expand opportunities in new areas. Job losses in
coal mining, auto production, and metals prospecting
will be offset by gains in the manufacture and sale of
photovoltaic solar cells, wind turbines, bicycles, mass-
transit equipment, and a host of technologies for recycling materials.

Since planned obsolescence will itself be obsolete in a
sustainable society, a far greater share of workers will be
employed in repair, maintenance, and recycling activities
than in the extraction of virgin materials and production
of new goods.

Wind prospectors, energy efficiency auditors, and
solar architects will be among the professions booming
from the shift to a highly efficient, renewable energy
economy. Numbering in the hundreds of thousands
today, jobs in these fields may collectively total in the
millions worldwide within a few decades. Opportunities
in forestry will expand markedly.

As the transition to a more environmentally sensitive
economy progresses, sustainability will gradually
eclipse growth as the focus of economic policymaking.
Over the next few decades, government policies will
encourage investments that promote stability and
endurance at the expense of those that simply expand
short-term production.

As a yardstick of progress, the gross national product
(GNP) will be seen as a bankrupt indicator. By measuring flows of goods and services, GNP undervalues the
qualities a sustainable society strives for, such as dura-
bility and resource protection; and overvalues planned
obsolescence and waste. The pollution caused by a coal-
burning power plant, for instance, raises GNP by requiring expenditures on lung disease treatment and the
purchase of a scrubber to control emissions. Yet society
would be far better off if power were generated in ways
that did not pollute the air in the first place.

National military budgets in a sustainable world will
be a small fraction of what they are today. Moreover,
sustainability cannot be achieved without a massive shift
of resources from military endeavors into energy efficiency, soil conservation, tree planting, family planning,
and other needed development activities. Rather than
maintaining large defense establishments, governments
may come to rely on a strengthened U.N. peacekeeping
force.

A NEW SET OF VALUES

Movement toward a lasting society cannot occur without a transformation of individual priorities and values.
Throughout the ages, philosophers and religious leaders
have denounced materialism as a path to human fulfillment. Yet societies across the ideological spectrum have

persisted in equating quality of life with increased consumption.

Because of the strain on resources it creates, materialism simply cannot survive the transition to a sustainable world. As public understanding of the need to adopt simpler and less consumptive lifestyles spreads, it will become unfashionable to own fancy new cars and clothes and the latest electronic devices. The potential benefits of unleashing the human energy now devoted to producing, advertising, buying, consuming, and discarding material goods are enormous.

As the amassing of personal and national wealth becomes less of a goal, the gap between haves and have nots will gradually close; this will eliminate many societal tensions. Ideological differences may fade as well, as nations adopt sustainability as a common cause, and as they come to recognize that achieving it requires a shared set of values that includes democratic principles, freedom to innovate, respect for human rights, and acceptance of diversity. With the cooperative tasks involved in repairing the earth so many and so large, the idea of waging war could become an anachronism.

The task of building a sustainable society is an enormous one that will take decades rather than years. Indeed, it is an undertaking that will easily absorb the energies that during the past 40 years have been devoted to the Cold War. The reward in the year 2030 could be an Earth Day with something to celebrate: the achievement of a society in balance with the resources that support it, instead of one that destroys the underpinnings of its future.

Study Questions

1. Evaluate the proposals set forth by Brown and his associates. Are they unduly optimistic about the future? Or are their predictions unrealistic? With which individual aspects do you agree or disagree? Explain your answer.
2. What do you think the world will be like in the year 2030? Set forth your vision and compare it with Brown and company.

For Further Reading

Berry, Wendell. *The Unsettling of America.* San Francisco: Sierra Club Books, 1986.

Brown, Lester. *State of the World 1993.* New York: Norton, 1993.

Clark, W. C. *Sustainable Development of the Biosphere.* Cambridge: Cambridge University Press, 1986.

Commoner, Barry. *Making Peace with the Planet.* New York: Pantheon Books, 1990.

Daly, Herman E., and John B. Cobb, Jr. *For the Common Good: Redirecting the Economy Toward Community, the Environment, and a Sustainable Future.* Boston: Beacon Press, 1989.

Dobson, Andrew, ed., *The Green Reader: Essays Toward a Sustainable Society.* San Francisco: Mercury House, 1991.

Goldsmith, Edward. *The Way: An Ecological World-View.* Boston: Sambala, 1993.

Kay, Jane Holz, *Asphalt Nation: How the Automobile Took over America and How We Can Take it Back.* NY: Crown Publishers, 1997.

Revkin, Andrew. *The Burning Season.* Boston: Houghton Mifflin, 1990.

Sagoff, Mark. *The Economy of the Earth.* Cambridge: Cambridge University Press, 1988.

Sayer, K. M., and K. E. Goodpaster, eds. *Ethics and Problems of the 21st Century.* Notre Dame, IN: University of Notre Dame Press, 1979.

Scientific American. "Managing the Earth." Special Issue, 26, no. 3 (September 1989).

Shrader-Frechette, Kristin. *Science, Policy, Ethics, and Economic Methology.* Boston: Reidel, 1985.

Timberlake, Lloyd. *Only One Earth: Living for the Future.* New York: Sterling, 1987.

Tokar, Michael. *The Green Alternative: Creating an Alternative Future.* San Pedro, CA: R & E Miles, 1988.

Westra, Laura. *The Principle of Integrity: An Environmental Proposal for Ethics.* Lanham, MD: Rowman & Littlefield, 1994.

Young, John E. *Discarding the Throwaway Society.* Washington, D.C.: Worldwatch Paper 101, 1991.

EPILOGUE

The Rio Declaration (1992)

Preamble

The United Nations Conference on Environment and Development,

Having met at Rio de Janeiro from 3 to 14 June 1992,

Reaffirming the Declaration of the United Nations Conference on the Human Environment, adopted at Stockholm on 16 June 1972, and seeking to build upon it,

With the goal of establishing a new and equitable global partnership through the creation of new levels of cooperation among States, key sectors of societies and people,

Working toward international agreements which respect the interests of all and protect the integrity of the global environmental and developmental system,

Recognizing the integral and interdependent nature of the Earth, our home,

Proclaims that:

Principle 1

Human beings are at the centre of concerns for sustainable development. They are entitled to a healthy and productive life in harmony with nature.

Principle 2

States have, in accordance with the Charter of the United Nations and the principles of international law, the sovereign right to exploit their own resources pursuant to their own environmental and developmental policies, and the responsibility to ensure that activities within their jurisdiction or control do not cause damage to the environment of other States or of areas beyond the limits of national jurisdiction.

Principle 3

The right to development must be fulfilled so as to equitably meet developmental and environmental needs of present and future generations.

The Rio Declaration, approved by the United Nations Conference on Environment and Development (Rio de Janeiro, Brazil, June 3–14, 1992) and later endorsed by the 47th session of the United Nations General Assembly on December 22, 1992.

Principle 4

In order to achieve sustainable development, environmental protection shall constitute an integral part of the development process and cannot be considered in isolation from it.

Principle 5

All States and all people shall cooperate in the essential task of eradicating poverty as an indispensable requirement for sustainable development, in order to decrease the disparities in standards of living and better meet the needs of the majority of the people of the world.

Principle 6

The special situation and needs of developing countries, particularly the least developed and those most environmentally vulnerable, shall be given special priority. International actions in the field of environment and development should also address the interests and needs of all countries.

Principle 7

States shall cooperate in a spirit of global partnership to conserve, protect and restore the health and integrity of the Earth's ecosystem. In view of the different contributions to global environmental degradation, States have common but differentiated responsibilities. The developed countries acknowledge the responsibility that they bear in the international pursuit of sustainable development in view of the pressures their societies place on the global environment and of the technologies and financial resources they command.

Principle 8

To achieve sustainable development and a higher quality of life for all people, States should reduce and eliminate unsustainable patterns of production and consumption and promote appropriate demographic policies.

Principle 9

States should cooperate to strengthen endogenous capacity-building for sustainable development by improving scientific understanding through exchanges of scientific and technological knowledge, and by enhancing the development, adaptation, diffusion and transfer of technologies, including new and innovative technologies.

Principle 10

Environmental issues are best handled with the participation of all concerned citizens, at the relevant level. At the national level, each individual shall have appropriate access to information concerning the environment that is held by public authorities, including information on hazardous materials and activities in their communities, and the opportunity to participate in decision-making processes. States shall facilitate and encourage public awareness and participation by making information widely available. Effective access to judicial and administrative proceedings, including redress and remedy, shall be provided.

Principle 11

States shall enact effective environmental legislation. Environmental standards, management objectives and priorities should reflect the environmental and developmental context to which they apply. Standards applied by some countries may be inappropriate and of unwarranted economic and social cost to other countries, in particular developing countries.

Principle 12

States should cooperate to promote a supportive and open international economic system that would lead to economic growth and sustainable development in all countries, to better address the problems of environmental degradation. Trade policy measures for environmental purposes should not constitute a means of arbitrary or unjustifiable discrimination or a disguised restriction on international trade. Unilateral action to deal with environmental challenges outside the jurisdiction of the improving country should be avoided. Environmental measures addressing transboundary or global environmental problems should, as far as possible, be based on an international consensus.

Principle 13

States shall develop national law regarding liability and compensation for the victims of pollution and other environmental damage. States shall also cooperate in an expeditious and more determined manner to develop further international law regarding liability and compensation for adverse effects of environmental damage caused by activities within their jurisdiction or control to areas beyond their jurisdiction.

Principle 14

States should effectively cooperate to discourage or prevent the relocation and transfer to other States of any activities and substances that cause severe environmental degradation or are found to be harmful to human health.

Principle 15

In order to protect the environment, the precautionary approach shall be widely applied by States according to their capabilities. Where there are threats of serious or irreversible damage, lack of full scientific certainty shall not be used as a reason for postponing cost-effective measures to prevent environmental degradation.

Principle 16

National authorities should endeavor to promote the internalization of environmental costs and the use of economic instruments, taking into account the approach that the polluter should, in principle, bear the cost of pollution, with due regard to the public interest and without distorting international trade and investment.

Principle 17

Environmental impact assessment, as a national instrument, shall be undertaken for proposed activities that are likely to have a significant adverse impact on the environment and are subject to a decision of a competent national authority.

Principle 18

States shall immediately notify other States of any natural disasters or other emergencies that are likely to produce sudden harmful effects on the environment of those States. Every effort shall be made by the international community to help States so afflicted.

Principle 19

States shall provide prior and timely notification and relevant information to potentially affected States on activities that may have a significant adverse transboundary environmental effect and shall consult with those States at an early stage and in good faith.

20

have a vital role in environmental management development. Their full participation is therefore ential to achieve sustainable development.

Principle 21

The creativity, ideals and courage of the youth of the world should be mobilized to forge a global partnership in order to achieve sustainable development and ensure a better future for all.

Principle 22

Indigenous people and their communities, and other local communities, have a vital role in environmental management and development because of their knowledge and traditional practices. States should recognize and duly support their identity, culture and interests and enable their effective participation in the achievement of sustainable development.

Principle 23

The environment and natural resources of people under oppression, domination and occupation shall be protected.

Principle 24

Warfare is inherently destructive of sustainable development. States shall therefore respect international law providing protection for the environment in times of armed conflict and cooperate in its further development, as necessary.

Principle 25

Peace, development and environmental protection are interdependent and indivisible.

Principle 26

States shall resolve all their environmental disputes peacefully and by appropriate means in accordance with the Charter of the United Nations.

Principle 27

States and people shall cooperate in good faith and in a sprint of partnership in the fulfillment of the principles embodied in this Declaration and in the further development of international law in the field of sustainable development.